ENCYCLOPEDIA OF

Victimology and Crime Prevention

Editorial Board

ENCYCLOPEDIA OF
Victimology and Crime Prevention

EDITORS

Bonnie S. Fisher
University of Cincinnati

Steven P. Lab
Bowling Green State University

1

Los Angeles | London | New Delhi
Singapore | Washington DC

For information:

 SAGE Publications, Inc.
2455 Teller Road
Thousand Oaks, California 91320
E-mail: order@sagepub.com

SAGE Publications Ltd.
1 Oliver's Yard
55 City Road
London, EC1Y 1SP
United Kingdom

SAGE Publications India Pvt. Ltd.
B 1/I 1 Mohan Cooperative Industrial Area
Mathura Road, New Delhi 110 044
India

SAGE Publications Asia-Pacific Pte. Ltd.
33 Pekin Street #02-01
Far East Square
Singapore 048763

Printed in the United States of America.

Library of Congress Cataloging-in-Publication Data

Encyclopedia of victimology and crime prevention/edited by Bonnie S. Fisher, Steven P. Lab.
    v. cm.
Includes bibliographical references and index.
ISBN 978-1-4129-6047-2 (cloth)
    1. Victims of crimes—United States—Encyclopedias. 2. Crime prevention—United States—Encyclopedias. 3. Victims of crimes—Encyclopedias. 4. Crime prevention—Encyclopedias. I. Fisher, Bonnie, 1959- II. Lab, Steven P.

HV6250.3.U5E55 2010
362.880973'03—dc22   2009031780

This book is printed on acid-free paper.

10   11   12   13   14   10 9 8 7 6 5 4 3 2 1

Publisher:	Rolf A. Janke
Assistant to the Publisher:	Michele Thompson
Acquisitions Editor:	Jim Brace-Thompson
Developmental Editor:	Carole Maurer
Reference Systems Manager:	Leticia Gutierrez
Reference Systems Coordinator:	Laura Notton
Production Editor:	Tracy Buyan
Copy Editors:	Jamie Robinson, Sheree Van Vreede
Typesetter:	C&M Digitals (P) Ltd.
Proofreaders:	Rae-Ann Goodwin, Sandy Zilka Livingston
Indexer:	Mary Fran Prottsman
Cover Designer:	Gail Buschman
Marketing Manager:	Amberlyn McKay

Contents

List of Entries

Reader's Guide

The Reader's Guide is provided to assist readers in locating articles on related topics. It classifies articles into 28 general topical categories: Business Prevention Actions; Civil Justice System; Correlates of Victimization; Courts: Alternative Remedies; Courts: Law and Justice; Crime Prevention; Crime Prevention Partnerships; Criminal Justice System; Fear of Crime; Individual Protection Actions; Interventions and Intervention Programs for Victim and Offender; Intrafamilial Offenses; Legislation and Statutes; Media and Crime Prevention; Methodology; Offenses, Special Topics; Official Crime Data; Personal Offenses; Property Offenses; Psychological, Mental, and Physical Health Issues; Residential Community Crime Prevention; School and Workplace Offenses; School-Based Crime Prevention; Services and Treatment for Victims; Theory; Victimization Scales and Surveys; Victimology; and Youth-Focused Crime Prevention. Entries may be listed under more than one topic.

Business Prevention Actions

Business Community Crime Prevention
Third-Party Policing
Workplace Violence, Prevention and Security
Workplace Violence, Training and Education

Civil Justice System

Civil Abatement
Civil Litigation
Dispute Resolution
Punitive and Compensatory Damages
Restitution
Third-Party Lawsuits

Correlates of Victimization

Age and Victimization
Correlates of Victimization
Gangs and Victimization
Guns and Victimization
Immigration and Victimization
Juvenile Offending and Victimization
Mental Illness and Victimization
Offending and Victimization

Peer Networks and Victimization
Race/Ethnicity and Victimization
Sex and Victimization
Sexual Orientation and Victimization
Substance Use and Victimization
Substance Use and Violence Against Women

Courts: Alternative Remedies

Dispute Resolution
Family Group Conferencing
Peacemaking: Alternative Court Remedies
Peacemaking/Sentencing Circles
Restitution
Restorative Justice
Victim Compensation
Victim–Offender Mediation

Courts: Law and Justice

Court Advocates
Court Appointed Special Advocates for Children
Defendants' Rights Versus Victims' Rights
Dispute Resolution
Domestic Violence/Family Violence Courts
Electronic Monitoring

Individual Protection Actions

Burglary, Prevention of
Bystander Intervention
Cybercrime, Prevention of
Rape, Protection Against
Safety Planning for Abused Children
Safety Planning for Battered Women
Violence, Protection Against

Interventions and Intervention Programs for Victim and Offender

Child Abuse, Neglect, and Maltreatment:
    Interventions for
Cognitive–Behavioral Therapy
Couples Therapy
Drug Use Forecasting/Arrestee Drug Abuse
    Monitoring
Elder Abuse, Neglect, and Maltreatment:
    Interventions for
Exploitation by Scams, Interventions for
Family Therapy
Medical and Mental Health Services
Multisystemic Therapy
Offender-Based Programs
Parents Anonymous
Pathways to Prevention
Rape Crisis Centers
Substance Abuse, Prevention of
Substance Abuse, Treatment of
Treating Rapists/Sex Offenders
Treating Violent Offenders
Women's Shelters/Help Lines
Workplace Violence and Bullying, Interventions for
Youth Violence, Interventions for

Intrafamilial Offenses

Abuse, Ritual Child
Abuse, Sibling
Abuse, Spouse
Child Abuse, Identification of
Child Abuse, Neglect, and Maltreatment
Domestic Violence
Domestic Violence, Committed by Police and
    Military Personnel
Domestic Violence, Same-Sex
Domestic Violence and Arrest Policy
Domestic Violence/Family Violence Courts

Elder Abuse, Neglect, and Maltreatment
Elder Abuse, Neglect, and Maltreatment:
    Institutional
Family Violence
Incest
Intimate Partner Violence
Male Victims of Partner Violence
Minneapolis Domestic Violence Experiment and
    Replication
Mutual Battery
Parents Anonymous
Protection/Restraining Orders
Rape
Rape, Acquaintance and Date
Rape, Marital
Repressed/Recovered Memories

Legislation and Statutes

AMBER Alert
Brady Bill
Central Registry
Child Abuse, Neglect, and Maltreatment:
    Mandatory Reporting
Child Abuse, Neglect, and Maltreatment:
    Statutory Responses
Child Protective Services
College and University Campus Legislation,
    Federal
College and University Campus
    Legislation, State
Compulsory HIV Testing
Crime and Disorder Act
Crime Victims Fund
Domestic Violence and Arrest Policy
Elder Abuse, Neglect, and Maltreatment:
    Statutory Responses
Hate and Bias Crime, Statutory Responses
Lautenberg Amendment
Law Enforcement Assistance Administration
    (LEAA)
Mandatory Reporting Statutes
Medical Examiner Response Team (MERT)
Megan's Law
President's Crime Commission Report, 1967
President's Task Force on Victims of Crime,
    1982
Rape Law Reform
Rape Shield Laws
Son of Sam Laws
Stalking Laws

Victimology

Youth-Focused Crime Prevention

About the Editors

Bonnie S. Fisher is a full professor in the School of Criminal Justice and a research fellow in the Center for Criminal Justice Research at the University of Cincinnati. Before transferring to the Division of Criminal Justice in 2000, she was an associate professor in the Department of Political Science at the University of Cincinnati. She was an assistant professor in the Department of City and Regional Planning at The Ohio State University from 1988 until 1991. Before completing her Ph.D. in political science at Northwestern University in 1988, she received her M.A. from Northwestern in 1984 and her B.A. from Illinois State University in 1981.

Fisher was an honorary visiting scholar at University of Leicester, Scarman Centre; a visiting scholar in the Department of Psychiatry, Division of Prevention and Community Research, The Consultation Center at Yale University School of Medicine; and a visiting professor in the Department of Sociology at John Jay College of Criminal Justice.

She has authored more than 150 publications and has edited or coedited four volumes that focus on victimization issues. She is coeditor of the *Security Journal,* has served as the deputy editor of *Justice Quarterly,* and is associate editor of the *Journal of Research Crime and Delinquency.*

Fisher has been the principal investigator on research examining issues concerning the victimization of college students, the sexual and stalking victimization of college women, violence against college women, and responses by colleges and universities to a report of a sexual assault. She was the principal investigator on research to examine workplace violence issues. She was the co–principal investigator on research to examine university student victimization in the East Midlands, United Kingdom. She recently completed research on the extent and nature of alcohol- and drug-enabled sexual assault of college women. Fisher was awarded a grant to address health disparity by determining vaginal and anal injury from sexual assault and performed a needs assessment concerning services provided to victimized women with disabilities and deaf women in the Cincinnati area.

She has been active in the American Society of Criminology and is now on its executive board. She is a lifetime member of the Academy of Criminal Justice Science, where she served as the chair of the Security and Crime Prevention section. She was appointed to two Governor's Task Force teams in Ohio: Campus Safety on Sexual and IPV and Stalking, and Campus Safety and Security. She also is a member of the University of Cincinnati's Sexual Offenses Response Team.

Steven P. Lab received his Ph.D. in criminology from Florida State University in 1982. He is currently a full professor of criminal justice at Bowling Green State University, where he is also director of the Criminal Justice Program and chair of the Department of Human Services. Before coming to Bowling Green in 1987, he served on the faculties of both the University of North Carolina at Charlotte and the University of Alabama–Birmingham.

Lab was a visiting professor of criminology at Keele University (England) in 1997; a visiting professor at the Jill Dando Institute of Crime Science, University College, London, in 2007; and a visiting fellow in criminology and social policy at Loughborough University (England) in 2007. He has also served as a research consultant with the Perpetuity Research Group at Leicester University

(England). In addition, he is a frequent consultant to the National Institute of Justice, U.S. Department of Justice.

Lab served as president of the Academy of Criminal Justice Sciences (ACJS) in 2004, and served on the ACJS Board for 7 years. He has also been active with the American Society of Criminology and the Environmental Criminology and Crime Analysis group.

He has been the principal investigator on National Institute of Justice (NIJ)–sponsored projects dealing with crime prevention and school safety. Lab was the principal investigator on two NIJ school crime projects that analyzed the level of victimization experienced at school by students and the actions taken by students to protect themselves. In addition, Lab led a funded project for the Ohio Office of Criminal Justice Services on domestic violence response teams.

Lab is the author of five books and 45 articles and book chapters and the editor of two books. He has made more than 80 presentations in the United States and internationally. In addition, he has been an instructor at the NIJ summer topics workshops at the University of Michigan, where he taught "Violence in Junior and Senior High Schools: Limited Knowledge and the Need for More Education." Lab also has been a consultant for the Arizona Governor's Committee on the Reformation of Juvenile Offenders.

Contributors

Charles Frederick Abel
Stephen F. Austin State University

Lynn A. Addington
American University

Eileen Ahlin
University of Maryland

Kevin M. Alligood
University of North Carolina at Charlotte

Kristin Anderson
Western Washington University

Martin A. Andresen
Simon Fraser University

Brandon K. Applegate
University of Central Florida

Catherine M. Arnold
University of Cincinnati

Elyshia D. Aseltine
University of Texas at Austin

Ron Avi Astor
University of Southern California

Joshua Lawrance Balay
Sam Houston State University

Rosemary Barberet
John Jay College of Criminal Justice

Tiffiney Y. Barfield-Cottledge
University of North Texas Dallas

Tom Barker
Eastern Kentucky University

Emmanuel Barthe
Univesity of Nevada, Reno

Katrina Baum
Bureau of Justice Statistics

Ashley Bauman
University of Cincinnati

Rami Benbenishty
Bar Ilan University, Israel

Lauren Bennett-Cattaneo
George Mason University

Beth Bjerregaard
University of North Carolina at Charlotte

Pamela G. Bond
Columbia College

Robert Bonney
YWCA of Greater Cincinnati

Leana A. Bouffard
Sam Houston State University

Noemie Bouhana
University College London

Kate Bowers
University College London

Sharon Boyd-Jackson
Kean University

Anthony A. Braga
Harvard University

Patricia L. Brantingham
Simon Fraser University

Paul J. Brantingham
Simon Fraser University

Scott A. Bresler
University of Cincinnati

Brian Bride
University of Georgia

Max L. Bromley
University of South Florida

Sandy Bromley
National Center for Victims of Crime

Jody Brook
University of Kansas

Michael E. Buerger
Bowling Green State University

Melissa W. Burek
Bowling Green State University

Carol Buschur
*University Hospital Health
Alliance*

Bryan D. Byers
Ball State University

Jacquelyn C. Campbell
Johns Hopkins University

Rebecca Campbell
Michigan State University

Alison C. Cares
*University of Massachusetts
Lowell*

Dena C. Carson
University of Missouri–St. Louis

S. Daniel Carter
Security On Campus, Inc.

Ursula Castellano
Ohio University

Courtenay E. Cavanaugh
Johns Hopkins University

Derek Chadee
University of the West Indies

Spencer Chainey
University College London

Sharon Chamard
University of Alaska Anchorage

David R. Champion
Slippery Rock University

Steven Chermak
Michigan State University

Roland Chilton
*University of Massachusetts,
Amherst*

Don Chon
Keiser University

George D. Chryssides
University of Birmingham

Ronald V. Clarke
Rutgers University

Marie Connolly
*Ministry of Social Development,
New Zealand*

Carrie L. Cook
University of Florida

AnnMarie Cordner
*Kutztown University of
Pennsylvania*

Rena Cornell
North Carolina State University

Andrew Costello
University of Sheffield

Stephen M. Cox
*Central Connecticut State
University*

Francis T. Cullen
University of Cincinnati

Leah E. Daigle
Georgia State University

Douglas J. Dallier
Florida State University

Kim Davies
Augusta State University

Stacy De Coster
North Carolina State University

Dana DeHart
University of South Carolina

Walter S. DeKeseredy
*University of Ontario Institute
of Technology*

Jeremiah Diebler
Lindsey Wilson College

Louise Dixon
University of Birmingham

William G. Doerner
Florida State University

William M. Doerner
Florida State University

Molly Dragiewicz
*University of Ontario Institute
of Technology*

Rebecca Dreke
*National Center for Victims of
Crime*

Desreen N. Dudley
*Yale University School of
Medicine*

Jessica R. Dunham
University of Cincinnati

Toni DuPont-Morales
*California State University,
Fresno*

John P. J. Dussich
*California State University,
Fresno*

John E. Eck
University of Cincinnati

Paul John Ekblom
University of the Arts London

Christine Englebrecht
University at Albany

Roger Enriquez
*University of Texas at San
Antonio*

Edna Erez
University of Illinois at Chicago

Sue Cote Escobar
*California State University,
Sacramento*

Joey Nuñez Estrada
University of Southern California

Graham Farrell
Loughborough University

David P. Farrington
University of Cambridge

Donna B. Fedus
Yale University School of Medicine

Kathleen J. Ferraro
Northern Arizona University

Charles R. Figley
Tulane University

Heather E. Finlay-Morreale
University of Cincinnati

Bonnie S. Fisher
University of Cincinnati

William F. Flack Jr.
Bucknell University

Gail Flint
West Virginia State University

Rebecca D. Foster
University of North Texas

Adrienne Freng
University of Wyoming

Michelle M. Garcia
National Center for Victims of Crime

Tammy S. Garland
University of Tennessee at Chattanooga

Meg Garvin
National Crime Victim Law Institute, Lewis & Clark Law School

Arina Gertseva
Washington State University

Jennifer C. Gibbs
University of Maryland, College Park

Chris L. Gibson
University of Florida

Wendy Perkins Gilbert
Urbana University

Martin Gill
Perpetuity Research & Consultancy International (PRCI) Ltd.

Nancy Glass
Johns Hopkins University School of Nursing

Julie L. Globokar
University of Illinois at Chicago

Denise C. Gottfredson
University of Maryland

Deshonna Collier Goubil
National Institute of Justice

Angela R. Gover
University of Colorado Denver

Nicola Graham-Kevan
University of Central Lancashire

Jack R. Greene
College of Criminal Justice

Timothy Griffin
University of Nevada, Reno

Louise Grove
Loughborough University

Paula L. Grubb
National Institute for Occupational Safety and Health

Neil Guzy
University of Pittsburgh School of Law

Karisa K. Harland
University of Iowa

Timothy C. Hart
University of Nevada, Las Vegas

Cynthia A. HartKnott
Alliance of Prison Ministry Organizations and Affiliates

Jennifer L. Hartman
University of North Carolina at Charlotte

Kristina J. Hawkins
North Carolina State University

Frederick Hawley
Western Carolina University

Dana L. Haynie
Ohio State University

Kathleen M. Heide
University of South Florida

Justin Heinonen
University of Cincinnati

James E. Hendricks
Ball State University

Billy Henson
University of Cincinnati

Eric W. Hickey
Alliant International University

Alexander Hirschfield
University of Huddersfield

Jefferson E. Holcomb
Appalachian State University

Stephen T. Holmes
University of Central Florida

Ross Homel
Griffith University

Moonki Hong
Florida State University

Tim Hope
Keele University

Amy Johnson Howton
University of Cincinnati

Jennifer L. Huck
*Indiana University of
Pennsylvania*

Patricia Paulsen Hughes
Oklahoma State University

Ronald D. Hunter
Western Carolina University

Esti Iturralde
*University of Southern
California*

Véronique Jaquier
University of Lausanne

Jana L. Jasinski
University of Central Florida

E. Lynn Jenkins
*Centers for Disease Control and
Prevention*

Holly Johnson
University of Ottawa

Shane D. Johnson
*UCL Jill Dando Institute of
Crime Science*

Helen Jones
*Manchester Metropolitan
University*

Lynn Jones
Northern Arizona University

Cheryl Lero Jonson
University of Cincinnati

Carol E. Jordan
*Center for Research on Violence
Against Women, University
of Kentucky*

Courtney Juergens
University of Central Florida

Michelle R. Kanga
University of Kansas

Richard R. E. Kania
Jacksonville State University

Heather M. Karjane
*Administrative Office of the
Trial Court, Boston*

Mark Rhys Kebbell
Griffith University

Martin Killias
University of Zurich

J. Bryan Kinney
Simon Fraser University

Lloyd Klein
*Kingsborough Community
College, City University of
New York*

Johannes Knutsson
*Norwegian Police University
College*

Spyridon Kodellas
University of Cincinnati

Mark Konty
Eastern Kentucky University

Tomislav Kovandzic
University of Texas at Dallas

Shane W. Kraus
Bowling Green State University

Joan H. Krause
*University of North Carolina at
Chapel Hill*

Betsy Wright Kreisel
University of Central Missouri

Jonathan M. Kremser
*Kutztown University of
Pennsylvania*

Karol L. Kumpfer
University of Utah

Steven P. Lab
Bowling Green State University

Jodi Lane
University of Florida

Robert H. Langworthy
University of Central Florida

Mark M. Lanier
University of Central Florida

Janet L. Lauritsen
University of Missouri–St. Louis

Richard Lawrence
St. Cloud State University

Gloria Laycock
University College London

Gavin Lee
University of California, Irvine

Justyna Lenik
Loyola University Chicago

J Robert Lilly
Northern Kentucky University

Heather Littleton
East Carolina University

Keith Gregory Logan
Kutztown University of Pennsylvania

Sharon RedHawk Love
Ball State University

Arthur J. Lurigio
Loyola University of Chicago

Kate Luther
Pacific Lutheran University

Daniel J. Lytle
University of Cincinnati

Ann MacDonald
Independent Consultant

Liz Marie Marciniak
University of Pittsburgh at Greensburg

Gayla Margolin
University of Southern California

Sandra L. Martin
University of North Carolina at Chapel Hill

Michael O. Maume
University of North Carolina Wilmington

R. I. Mawby
University of Plymouth

David C. May
Eastern Kentucky University

Pat Mayhew
Victoria University of Wellington

Paul Mazerolle
Griffith University

Richard C. McCorkle
University of Nevada at Las Vegas

William F. McDonald
Georgetown University

Danielle McGurrin
Portland State University

Samual C. McQuade III
Rochester Institute of Technology

Robert J. Meadows
California Lutheran University

Mónica Méndez
East Carolina University

Holly Ventura Miller
University of Texas, San Antonio

J. Mitchell Miller
University of Texas, San Antonio

Kristine Levan Miller
Plymouth State University

Monica K. Miller
University of Nevada, Reno

Patricia Morgan
Publix Supermarkets Inc.

Laura J. Moriarty
Virginia Commonwealth University

Mandy Morrill-Richards
University of Memphis

Brenda Elizabeth Morrison
Simon Fraser University

Kate Moss
Wolverhampton University

Lisa R. Muftic
University of North Texas

Kristina Murphy
Deakin University

Wendy J. Murphy
New England School of Law

Bernadette T. Muscat
California State University, Fresno

Elizabeth Ehrhardt Mustaine
University of Central Florida

Brad A. Myrstol
University of Arkansas

Mike Nellis
University of Strathclyde

Sami Nevala
European Monitoring Centre on Racism and Xenophobia

Graeme R. Newman
University at Albany

Rhonda Y. Ntepp
Metropolitan State College of Denver

Kevin O'Brien
National Center for Victims of Crime

Thomas J. O'Connor
Austin Peay State University

Nancy A. Orel
Bowling Green State University

Gregory P. Orvis
Dover, Delaware

M. Murat Ozer
University of Cincinnati

Amanda M. Sharp Parker
University of South Florida

Debra Patterson
Michigan State University

E. Britt Patterson
Shippensburg University

Laura A. Patterson
Shippensburg University

Brian K. Payne
Georgia State University

Ken Pease
Loughborough University

Corinne Peek-Asa
University of Iowa

Deanna M. Pérez
University of Colorado Denver

Elicka S. L. Peterson
*Appalachian State
University*

Daniel W. Phillips III
Lindsey Wilson College

Nickie Phillips
St. Francis College

Mari B. Pierce
Western Oregon University

Adriana Pilafova
George Mason University

Wm. C. Plouffe Jr.
*Kutztown University of
Pennsylvania*

Emma Poulton
Durham University

Tim Prenzler
Griffith University

Ethel Quayle
University of Edinburgh

Chitra Raghavan
*John Jay College of Criminal
Justice*

Francine C. Raguso
Montclair State University

Michael Rand
U.S. Bureau of Justice Statistics

Winifred L. Reed
National Institute of Justice

Saundra Regan
University of Cincinnati

Joan A. Reid
University of South Florida

Angela K. Reitler
University of Cincinnati

Callie Marie Rennison
University of Colorado–Denver

Danielle M. Reynald
*NSCR-Netherlands Institute for
the Study of Crime & Law
Enforcement*

Bradford W. Reyns
University of Cincinnati

Tara N. Richards
University of South Florida

Melissa L. Ricketts
Shippensburg University

Jenn Roark
*University of Colorado at
Boulder*

Matthew Robinson
Appalachian State University

John K. Roman
Urban Institute

Dennis P. Rosenbaum
*University of Illinois at
Chicago*

Lorie Rubenser
Sul Ross State

Jeffrey P. Rush
Austin Peay State University

Ghazaleh Samandari
*University of North Carolina at
Chapel Hill*

Shannon A. Santana
*University of North Carolina
Wilmington*

Jordan Satinsky
*University of Maryland
University College*

Robert Schehr
Northern Arizona University

Heidi L. Scherer
University of Cincinnati

Louis B. Schlesinger
*John Jay College of Criminal
Justice*

Andrea Schoepfer
*California State University, San
Bernardino*

Christopher J. Schreck
*Rochester Institute of
Technology*

Jennifer Schwartz
Washington State University

Martin D. Schwartz
Ohio University

Lawrence J. Schweinhart
*High/Scope Educational
Research Foundation*

Hannah Scott
*University of Ontario Institute
of Technology*

Michael S. Scott
*University of Wisconsin Law
School*

Phyllis Sharps
*Johns Hopkins University
School of Nursing*

Margaret Shaw
International Centre for the Prevention of Crime

J. Eagle Shutt
University of Louisville

John J. Sloan
University of Alabama–Birmingham

Stephen Smallbone
Griffith University

Carter F. Smith
Middle Tennessee State University

Cindy J. Smith
University of Baltimore

Hayden Smith
University of South Carolina

Martha Jane Smith
Wichita State University

Paula Smith
University of Cincinnati

Jamie A. Snyder
University of Cincinnati

Lauren A. Spies
University of Southern California

Brian H. Spitzberg
San Diego State University

William A. Stadler
University of Cincinnati

Amanda L. Stein
University of Cincinnati

Charles Stelle
Bowling Green State University

Megan C. Stewart
University of Cincinnati

Robert J. Stokes
Drexel University

Tami P. Sullivan
Yale University School of Medicine

Lucia Summers
University College London

Mike Sutton
Nottingham Trent University

Kristin Swartz
University of Cincinnati

Timothy Sweet-Holp
Albany State University

Kimberly M. Tatum
University of West Florida

Rae Taylor
University of Central Florida

Ralph B. Taylor
Temple University

Terrance J. Taylor
University of Missouri–St. Louis

Pamela B. Teaster
University of Kentucky

Richard Tewksbury
University of Louisville

Devon G. Thacker
University of Colorado Boulder

Nick Tilley
University College London

Patricia G. Tjaden
Tjaden Research Corporation

Elizabeth A. Tomsich
University of Colorado

Volkan Topalli
Georgia State University

Michael Townsley
Griffith University

Jennifer L. Truman
University of Central Florida

Abbie Tuller
John Jay College of Criminal Justice

Amanda Turner
Western Washington University

Michael Turner
University of North Carolina at Charlotte

Sarah E. Ullman
University of Illinois at Chicago

Alana Van Gundy-Yoder
Miami University

Melanie J. Vicneire
University of South Carolina

Joelle Vuille
University of Lausanne

Shelly Wagers
University South Florida

Irvin Waller
University of Ottawa

Jeffrey T. Ward
University of Florida

Tara D. Warner
Bowling Green State University

Kiesha Warren-Gordon
Ball State University

Jennifer Reid Webb
University of South Carolina

Ralph A. Weisheit
Illinois State University

Elmar G. M. Weitekamp
University of Tübingen

Brandon C. Welsh
University of Massachusetts Lowell

Jo-Anne M. Wemmers
University of Montreal

Nicola J. Weston
Universities' Police Science Institute

Per-Olof H. Wikström
University of Cambridge

Pamela Wilcox
University of Cincinnati

Marian R. Williams
Appalachian State University

Romy Winter
Tasmanian Institute of Law Enforcement Studies

Mark A. Winton
University of Central Florida

Valerie D. Wise
South Suburban College

Phillip H. Witt
Independent Scholar

Jennifer S. Wong
Simon Fraser University

Richard Wortley
Griffith University

Emily M. Wright
University of South Carolina

Kersti Yllo
Wheaton College

Introduction

The modern interest in victimology and crime prevention in the United States can be traced to the turbulence of the 1960s, when crime and social unrest were escalating across the nation. The public's interest in the needs of women, children, the poor, and victims was an orchestrated national movement that voiced their concerns and fueled the federal government's response to their demands. The work of the 1967 President's Commission on Law Enforcement and the Administration of Justice, for example, heavily emphasized both crime victims and crime prevention through the development of educational programs, local crime initiatives, and research, coupled with the provision of funds for state and local law enforcement.

The last 40 years have seen exponential growth of interest in both the needs of victims of crime and how society, including governments, businesses, schools, and individuals, can effectively prevent crime. When looking at the history of victimology and crime prevention, it is fascinating to see them emerge in importance at almost the same time and experience parallel growth in terms of both academic interest and practical application. While it would be easy to see this covariation as pure chance, it is probably more correct to acknowledge the fact that these sometimes seemingly different areas are really complements of one another. Crime prevention seeks to keep individuals and their property from ever being harmed by a criminal act in the first place. Victimology estimates the extent of those harmed by a criminal act and examines the characteristics associated with being victimized, with emphasis on identifying correlates and addressing the victims' health needs and legal rights. In essence, victimology tends to focus (although not exclusively) on harm to individuals and their well-being after the criminal incident has occurred, while crime prevention tends to focus (again, not exclusively) on preventing harm from ever occurring or recurring. The victimology–crime prevention nexus provides the foundation for a comprehensive and long-lasting approach to addressing the public's risk of being victimized as well as aiding individuals in the event they are targeted by a criminal act.

The Need for This Encyclopedia

Unfortunately, a great deal of the growth in both victimology and crime prevention has taken place under the larger rubrics of criminology, criminal justice, sociology, economics, and any number of disciplines (including public health) that have had greater name recognition in both the academic and practice realms. In a sense, victimology and crime prevention have languished as subfields within more established disciplines such as criminology or criminal justice, and they have had to fight for attention and resources and to set themselves off as separate disciplines. The literature that makes up these two areas could even be considered a "fugitive" literature looking for a place to fit in and prosper intellectually. Indeed, a search for information on victims or prevention activity often leads to journals and books that only dabble in these topics, or to government or foundation documents that receive little promotion and publication. As such, comprehensive information about the history and state of knowledge in victimology or crime prevention is often hard to find in a single publication or document.

Research on victimology appears in a wide array of venues. Much of the early work in the 1950s and 1960s found an intellectual home in sociological forums. This work generally targeted specific types of victimization, including rape and sexual assault, spouse abuse, child abuse, and abuse of the elderly. These same topics, however, appear in other outlets targeting different audiences. Indeed, the problem of child abuse was first outlined in an article in the *Journal of the American Medical Association* in 1962. Today, much information about the psychological and physical health of victims is found in the many medical, nursing, and public health forums. These publications focus on another component important to understanding the impact of victimization and how to address victims' short-term and long-term emotional and health needs. Similarly, victim issues appear in criminological journals, law reviews, economics publications, psychological forums, and many other interdisciplinary forums, including those with a feminist and/or critical perspective. It was not until the advent of *Victimology* in 1976 that there was a single peer-reviewed professional journal devoted to victims. Emilio Viano founded the journal to signify victimology's intellectual autonomy from the more established fields of criminology and criminal justice. Although *Victimology* was an important new outlet for information, few professionals were aware of the journal. It struggled for years to publish a regular schedule of victim-focused issues and eventually produced its last issue in 1985.

These early efforts contributed to the expanding number of forums for victim topics that exist today. Among these are *Child Abuse & Neglect*, *Journal of Elder Abuse and Neglect*, *Journal of Family Violence*, *Journal of Interpersonal Violence*, and *Violence and Victims*. More specialized victim journals, such as *Violence Against Women*, focusing on issues central to female victims/survivors, have been successfully launched. Some of these journals are published monthly or bimonthly, yet another indicator of the increasing interest in victims and the amount of victimology research that is being generated worldwide. With the proliferation of the victims' advocacy groups and researchers using the Internet to provide and access victimological information, schedule international Web casts to discuss and exchange information, and provide a medium to engage in comparative cross-national research, there are global victim-focused activities growing by leaps and bounds daily.

The great growth in the number and breadth of victimological forums has had two (possibly counterbalancing) consequences. On the one hand, there is a large body of scholarship and general information that is now easily accessible to those interested in a wide range of victim issues. On the other hand, the sheer volume of information and the diversity in where it is found makes it very difficult to keep updated on all the information that is available. Even texts that focus on "victimology" and not any specific area of victimology can only cover a small fraction of the widely available information, and thus any such texts are limited only by the author's efforts and interests.

Crime prevention has followed a parallel path during the past 40 years. In light of the skyrocketing crime rates and social unrest during the 1960s, the public's interest in crime gave rise to these changing times as they demanded that the federal government take actions to prevent crime. One of the first areas of focus was in designing the physical environment in such a way to prevent opportunities for crime to occur. This interest manifested itself in terms of both academic interest, as evident in the publication of Jane Jacob's *The Death and Life of Great American Cities* in 1961 and C. Ray Jeffery's *Crime Prevention Through Environmental Design* in 1971, and the funding of several community prevention programs by entities such as Westinghouse Electric and federal agencies, including the U.S. Department of Justice. Most of the reports and information generated from the projects were seen by only a limited audience, particularly within the academic community. The results of these projects led to the development of many different crime prevention efforts, among which were Neighborhood Watch, Take A Bite Out Of Crime, and citizen patrols. One of the biggest shifts toward prevention came with the introduction of "situational crime prevention" in 1983 and the launching of prevention as a key component of the work of the British Home Office. Since those efforts, crime prevention has seen a tremendous growth of interest by both academics and practitioners.

At the same time that these crime prevention efforts were taking place, research and information on crime prevention struggled to find an academic and institutional home. Unfortunately, much work was found only in government reports that were hard to access (especially in the pre-Internet days). The published work was spread throughout a wide range of disciplinary forums, including criminology/criminal justice, geography, architecture, business, sociology, and political science. However, there were no journals devoted to crime prevention until the advent of *Crime Prevention and Community Safety* in 1999. The closest outlet to an ongoing publication in the area was the Crime Prevention Studies series that began in 1993. Each book in this series focuses on a special crime prevention topic, with the primary emphasis being on situational prevention approaches. Even today, there continues to be a limited number of publication outlets specifically devoted to crime prevention issues.

Crime prevention also has found a home in organizations and agencies around the world. In the United States, the National Crime Prevention Council was founded in 1982 and has kept crime prevention in the public eye through many efforts, most notably its public service announcements about crime and prevention. The International Center for the Prevention of Crime was founded in 1994 as a nongovernmental organization offering both research and advocacy for prevention activities around the world. The European Union created the European Crime Prevention Network in 2001, and the United Nations Center for International Crime Prevention is a vital link between countries for addressing cross-national crime problems. In the academic realm, the most notable event was the establishment of the Jill Dando Institute of Crime Science at University College London in 2001. While these organizations and institutions are all leaders in crime prevention, it is notable that most are relatively young and still establishing their niche in the field.

As is clear from the above description, there is little doubt that the dispersed information on and knowledge of both victimology and crime prevention need to be brought together into a comprehensive volume. This need is even more pronounced when we consider the intersections of the two disciplines. The fact that prevention is a major goal of those who work with victims and that knowledge and study of victims and their victimization are among the keys to planning crime prevention activities means that there is a great deal to be gained by studying each area with a knowledge of the other. There is a clear synergy that exists when we bring these two apparently different disciplines together into a single publication.

This encyclopedia builds that synergy. The two-volume set moves victimology and crime prevention one step further in their development and recognition as scholarly fields whose research informs practice and whose practice informs research.

Scope and Focus of the Encyclopedia

In developing this encyclopedia, it became evident that we had to limit the topics covered to those that constitute the fields of victimology and crime prevention. Discussions of victims can include victims of natural disasters, wars, diseases, and other events that are far afield from the criminal act. While these topics are certainly worthy of discussion, they simply expand the purview of victimology beyond the word count we have available. As such, in this work, "victimology" is mainly limited to issues related to actions that fall under the criminal law. Similarly, discussion of crime prevention can include a wide range of approaches, including prenatal care, investigations of biological determinants of behavior, changing the capitalistic economic structure of countries, and guaranteeing quality education programming. All of these topics have relevance to preventing crime and thus influencing crime rates, but they are not central to most crime prevention efforts and do not hold the promise that other approaches hold for preventing individuals or their property from being harmed by a criminal act. Many of these more macro-level approaches to addressing crime rates do not dovetail with discussions of individuals' victimization risks, prevention of victimization, and meeting the needs of those who have been victimized.

How the Encyclopedia Was Created

Putting together an encyclopedia requires the efforts of a large number of people at each step of the process. It is the input of those individuals that makes this work comprehensive. The encyclopedia was developed in several stages.

Stage 1—The editors identified eight individuals who are knowledgeable in various subareas of victimology and crime prevention to serve on the editorial board. Beyond their knowledge of the field, these individuals work at different institutions in different countries and with a diversity of experiences and contacts.

Stage 2—The editorial board was presented with an initial list of roughly 100 topics, which were developed by the editors as a means of jump-starting the discussion of what could or should be included. The editors and editorial board expanded the initial list to more than 400 potential topics, which had to be cut to 350 to 375 topics to meet word count limitations. The decisions on which topics to keep and which ones to cut were discussed by the board members, but the final determination of the list of entry titles, or "headwords," was made by the editors.

Stage 3—Perhaps the most important step in developing this work was in identifying authors with the expertise to write on the topics and securing their participation. This was a daunting task, considering there are entries for 370 topics in this encyclopedia. The first step in this process was to solicit the efforts of well-respected professionals in victimology and crime prevention for the lengthy "anchor essays." We were successful in getting some of the leading scholars in the field to write these entries. The second step was to personally invite qualified contributors—academics, researchers, advocates, and service providers—from a range of disciplines to write entries for the other topics. This effort required the input of the all the editorial board members as well as other noted experts in both victimology and crime prevention.

Stage 4—Authors were given general guidance in the writing of their entries; we asked them to discuss the core concepts and issues related to the topic. Respecting their expertise and their willingness to share it worldwide, we mostly left them each to include the information they felt was most important in order to provide the reader with an educated overview of the topic and supplemental reference materials that would provide guidance for further inquiry.

Stage 5—The editors reviewed all the entries as they were submitted and suggested revisions where they appeared appropriate.

Stage 6—The editors and their editorial team helped cross-reference entries, organized the Reader's Guide, constructed the appendices, and finalized the work.

How to Use This Encyclopedia

There is no one way to use a work such as this, especially given its voluminous collection of headwords, that is meaningful within victimology and crime prevention. Readers will consult this work for a wide range of purposes, and as such how they use it will vary by their individual interests and needs. We can only give suggestions that may be helpful, and those suggestions are actually incorporated into the organization of the encyclopedia.

The Reader's Guide provides guidance to the organization of the overarching broader topical headings and subentries. We have grouped the topics into 28 substantive broad headings that the reader will find helpful in seeing the main themes in victimology and crime prevention. Many of the entries appear under more than one topical heading, which we hope will suggest new avenues for discussion and investigation by the reader.

There are two types of contributions: anchor essays and headword entries. The anchor essays, which are designated as such in the List of Entries, provide a starting point for investigating the more salient victimology and crime prevention topics among the staple concepts in the two fields. Each provides an approximately 5,000-word discussion with necessary broad strokes and illustrates the connections between several issues and topics that cannot and will not be found in most of the individual entries with fewer words. A reading of these anchor essays will give readers insight that can assist in picking other specific topical entries that are appropriate for their interests; these essays also include Further Readings for readers to use to more fully explore the topic.

The headword entries provide the reader with information that describes the essence of what researchers and practitioners know about the topic. Each 1,000- to 3,000-word discussion includes the provision of definitions and core concepts and presentation of relevant research findings and practical information. Further Readings are also provided in each entry so the reader can look into the topic in more detail.

The appendix provides a wealth of information to supplement the individual anchor essays and headword entries and to lead the reader to other sources of victimology and crime prevention information. The materials on laws, legal issues, and agencies/organizations found in the appendix offer much information that will be useful to any reader who wants to further pursue any of the topics covered in the anchor essays or headword entries.

Acknowledgments

Thank you to the entire SAGE staff, in particular, Rolf Janke, for publishing this encyclopedia. We are especially thankful to Jim Brace-Thompson and Carole Maurer for their continued encouragement and feedback throughout the development of this project. Their professionalism and sense of humor carried us from stage to stage. Our production manager, Tracy Buyan, kept us moving forward to meet deadlines. Our sincere gratitude is extended to those who edited and proofread each and every entry from the first letter to the last letter, each resource in the Appendix, and the milestones in the Chronology. Jamie Robinson, Sheree Van Vreede, Rae-Ann Goodwin, and Sandy Zilka Livingston did a superb job of making the entries consistent and accurate.

Bonnie S. Fisher and Steven P. Lab

ABUSE, RITUAL CHILD

Ritual child abuse is reoccurring sexual and/or physical abuse that follows a particular pattern. The victims of ritual child sexual and physical abuse come from every culture, and their repeated abuse can cause long-term mental health and substance abuse problems. For victims of sexual and physical abuse, the cycle of violence is extremely similar. While our society has recently begun to discuss this type of crime in a more open and educated manner, this victimization continues to occur on a regular basis.

Definitions

The criminal code of every state in the United States has a definition for child abuse. These definitions vary from state to state, but their essence is the same. Those individuals, adults or juveniles, who exert power and control over children for the purpose of sexual gratification, physical abuse, or emotional abuse are in violation of state law.

- *Sexual child abuse* is defined as any intentional touching of the victim's breasts, buttocks, anus, vagina, or the penis for sexual gratification and is illegal.
- *Physical child abuse* is defined differently by different states. Some require there to have been a substantial child abuse before convicting an individual of physical abuse. In other states, very little abuse is necessary for an individual to receive a felony conviction. This entry defines physical abuse as any abuse where a mark is left on the child victim that was not the result of an accident or corporal punishment (which is still legal in many states).
- *Ritual child abuse* has been defined by experts as abuse as a reoccurring criminal act that follows a particular pattern. Perpetrators develop a pattern of attack and rarely deviate from this style of abuse.

Victims

It is important to understand that victims of ritual child abuse come from all parts of society. This type of abuse is not found only in the poorest areas of society; these acts are perpetrated in every class, race, creed, and culture.

If asked whether they are more afraid of a stranger or a relative harming their child, most people would say a stranger. However, recent research has shown that a person known to the victim is more likely to be the perpetrator of child abuse than a stranger. Lawrence Greenfeld and his colleagues reported in 1997 that 65% of child victims were victimized by people known to them. They also noted that federal data on rapists show that 99 out of 100 are male, 6 out of 10 are White, and their average age is the early 30s.

In addition, gender is related to child abuse: Research findings have shown that 91% of victims were female. And youth is also a factor, in that 89% of those victims were 6 years old or younger when they were abused for the first time. Since male victims are less likely than female victims to report abuse, it is more difficult for researchers to accurately determine the number of male victims of such abuse. It is estimated that 16% of men have experience some form of childhood abuse. Many times males do not disclose abuse for fear the abuse may cause their peers and family members to perceive them as weak.

Indicators of Ritual Child Abuse

Sexual and emotional child abuse victims rarely show any type of outward injury to indicate that they were abused. According to Curt Bartol and Anne Bartol, recent reports of rape victims show that 70% did not receive any injuries during the attack, 24% received minor physical injuries, and 4% received serious physical injuries. Children who seem to have a sudden attitude change, become scared easily, are fearful around adults, and seem depressed may need to be assessed for possible sexual or emotional child abuse.

Physical child abuse victims are more likely to have outward signs of injuries. The suspicious person would look for bruising, burns, fractures, and lacerations. Some other indicators of all three types of abuse include failing to thrive, bed-wetting, engaging in risky sexual behavior, dressing in a provocative manner, sudden weight loss or gain, and suicidal tendencies.

Suicide

Child abuse victimization has been shown to be a cause of suicidal thoughts and acts. In 2004, Mette Ystgaard and colleagues found that 58% of patients admitted to hospitals for suicide attempts disclosed that they were victims of some form of child abuse. Furthermore, the researchers discovered that victims who were repeatedly victimized, sexually or physically, were more likely to report multiple suicide attempts.

Family Environment

Family environment is another important factor in childhood victimization. Research shows that those who resided in a home without their biological father were more likely to experience some form of victimization. For a long time it was believed that fathers who lacked careers and income were more likely to inflict abuse on their children than fathers who had stable jobs and income. One 2008 study revealed that abuse occurred regardless of the father's job status.

Phases of Ritual Child Sexual Abuse

Generally there are several stages that a victim and perpetrator traverse during ritual child abuse. For the purposes of this entry, these stages will be divided into grooming, abuse, and reflection.

The Grooming Phase

During the grooming phase the perpetrator takes the time to court the child victim. The perpetrator will normally lavish gifts and attention on the child. The perpetrator will purposefully ignore other children while in the company of the victim. The victim interprets this as a positive action and may even begin to feel a sense of love and trust for the adult. The adult will create situations that show the victim's parents that he can be trusted with the child. This cycle will continue until the perpetrator feels that both the child's parents and the victim have a high level of trust for him. At this point, the perpetrator will advance to the abuse phase.

The Abuse Phase

The perpetrator does not want to startle the child by moving too quickly into the abuse. The perpetrator has spent time, money, and patience to develop the relationship. It would be wasteful to enter into a sexual arrangement too quickly. The perpetrator may start by pretending to accidentally touch the victim in a nonsexual area. This action will be repeated on several occasions until the victim no longer hesitates at the perpetrator's touch.

The perpetrator will then progress to touching or being touched by the child in a sexual manner. Perpetrators may receive this gratification in the form of a kiss, a touch, object insertion, sodomy, fellatio, cunnilingus, or sexual intercourse. However, the perpetrator may direct the victim to perform sexual acts on him or act out sexually themed games.

The victim may be confused at first, and the perpetrator may inform the child that sexual touching between people is normal. In order to reassure the child, the perpetrator may show the victim pornographic images of children and adults. The perpetrator may further reassure the child by explaining sexual activity in graphic detail.

The Reflection Phase

In this phase the victim becomes aware that the current sexual relationship is not healthy. Most victims realize that their trust and bodies have been violated, and signs of abuse may appear. This is the time when the victim makes a decision whether or not to disclose the abuse. If a disclosure is made, the perpetrator will almost always feign ignorance of the situation at first. The perpetrator may make statements like, "You know me, I wouldn't do that," "I love the child," or "That's not me—I'm a married man."

Phases of Ritual Child Physical Abuse

Child physical abuse and sexual abuse have many similarities. The main difference is that physical child abuse produces easily noticed physical effects such as broken bones, scarring, burning, and others.

The Initial Phase

During this phase of the abuse, the child is the target of the perpetrator's rage. No matter what the child does, the perpetrator, normally a parent or guardian, lashes out at the child verbally and may strike the child. During this phase, the child will attempt to placate the perpetrator to slow the attacks. The child is attempting to avoid being hurt and will do almost anything to not progress to the next phase.

The Attack Phase

When the perpetrator progresses to this phase, he or she no longer wants to discuss the reason for this anger. The attack phase may come in the form of a blitz, where the perpetrator strikes at the child wildly, inflicting a great deal of pain and damage. The attacks can be particularly brutal if the perpetrator is under the influence of alcohol or drugs at the time of the attack.

During this phase, the victim is usually in fear of his or her life; nevertheless, because this is a parent or guardian, the victim will allow the abuse to continue. In many cases, just as with the child

sexual abuse victim, the physical abuse victim believes that this is a normal part of childhood.

The Apologetic Phase

Once the attack has ceased, the perpetrator realizes what has just transpired and provides a multitude of reasons for the abuse. The perpetrator will apologize and request that the victim not contact the authorities. Soon after this phase ends, the cycle continues again with the initial phase.

Long-Term Effects

Almost 90% of victimization occurs when the child is under the age of 6. Because abuse starts at a young age, victims require long-term treatment. Furthermore, victims are less likely to form strong social bonds and have healthy intimate relationships, may suffer from flashbacks and/or substance abuse, and may require a lifetime of mental health care.

Psychological Problems and Substance Abuse

Victims of abuse in childhood require some form of mental or physical assistance throughout their lives. A 2008 study found that women who were not abused as children spent an average of $2,413 per year on therapy, whereas sexually abused women spent approximately $2,795 per year and physically abused women spent approximately $2,915 per year. Finally, women who suffered both types of child abuse spent approximately $3,203 per year. Furthermore, those victimized as children were more likely to surround themselves with individuals who had been diagnosed with depression and suicidal tendencies.

There is a causal link between childhood victimization and substance abuse. Young adults ages 19 to 23 who had experienced some form of childhood abuse were 14.3% more likely to inject illegal substances into their bodies than were their counterparts in the general population.

Criminal Conduct

Victims of both sexual and physical abuse show an increased risk of being arrested in the future compared to children who were not victimized. A study of more than 1,000 children and young adults estimated that 30% of childhood abuse victims would later have a criminal record or be an adjudicated delinquent.

Jordan Satinsky

See also Battered-Child Syndrome; Child Abuse, Identification of; Child Abuse, Neglect, and Maltreatment; Child Abuse, Neglect, and Maltreatment: Interventions for; Child Abuse, Neglect, and Maltreatment: Statutory Responses; Child Abuse, Neglect, and Maltreatment: Theories of; Safety Planning for Abused Children

Further Readings

Bonomi, A., Anderson, M., Rivara, F., Cannon, E., Fishman, P., Carrell, D., et al. (2008, March). Health care utilization and costs associated with childhood abuse. *JGIM: Journal of General Internal Medicine, 23*(3), 294–299.

Doerner, W. G., & Lab, S. P. (2005). *Victimology* (4th ed.). Newark, NJ: Anderson.

Draper, B., Pfaff, J. J., Pirkis, J., Snowdon, J., Lautenschlager, N. T., Wilson, I., et al. (2008). Long-term effects of childhood abuse on the quality of life and health of older people: Results from the depression and early prevention of suicide in general practices project. *Journal of the American Geriatrics Society, 56*, 262–271.

Greenfeld, L. A. (1997). *Sex offenses and offenders* [Brochure]. Washington, DC: U.S. Department of Justice, Bureau of Justice Statistics.

Hay, T. (2005). *Child sexual abuse.* Retrieved November 1, 2008, from http://www.phac-aspc.gc.ca/ncfv-cnivf/family violence/html/nfntsxagrsex_e.html

Lee, S. J., Guterman, N. B., & Lee, Y. (2008). Risk factors for paternal physical child abuse. *Child Abuse & Neglect, 32*, 846–858.

Ompad, D. C., Ikeda, R. M., Shah, N., Fuller, C. M., Bailey, S., Morse, E., et al. (2005). Childhood sexual abuse and age at initiation of injection drug use. In *American Journal of Public Health, 95*, 703–709.

Thompson, M. P., Kingree, J. B., & Desai, S. (2004). Gender differences in long-term health consequences of physical abuse of child: Data from a nationally representative survey. *American Journal of Public Health, 94*, 599–604.

Widom, C., & Kuhns, J. B. (1996). Childhood victimization and subsequent risk for promiscuity, prostitution, and teenage pregnancy: A prospective study. *American Journal of Public Health, 86*, 1607–1612.

Ystgaard, M., Ingebjorg, H., Loeb, M., & Mehlum, L. (2004). Is there a specific relationship between childhood sexual and physical abuse and repeated suicidal behavior? *Child Abuse & Neglect, 28*, 863–875.

Abuse, Sibling

Although many advances have been made regarding the study of abuse over the last three decades, research related to intrafamilial violence conducted by social science researchers has largely ignored the experience of sibling abuse. The lack of attention prohibits any one definition of sibling abuse from being accepted. Sibling abuse is complex, understudied, and not always easily identifiable beyond the confines of what is considered sibling rivalry.

Three facets to consider when defining sibling abuse are *perception, intent,* and *severity.* Perception refers to how each sibling frames the interaction. For example, if one sibling involved in a sibling dyad views the behavior as abusive, regardless of his or her role as survivor or perpetrator, a dynamic beyond the scope of "normal" sibling rivalry is likely present. Intent involves what a sibling hoped to accomplish through an action or behavior. When sibling abuse is present, the intent of the perpetrating brother or sister is primarily to cause harm rather than to gain access to limited family resources such as space, time, and/or affection. Severity is related to the duration and intensity of the abusive sibling behavior. As severity increases there is greater probability that the sibling relationship is abusive. Perception, intent, and severity exist within three primary categories of sibling abuse: *psychological, physical,* and *sexual.*

Psychological sibling abuse is the category of abuse in the sibling relationship that is the most difficult to define. In large part, the difficulty exists because it is often challenging to identify where sibling rivalry ends and psychological abuse begins, contributing to the phenomenon in which parents and guardians ignore or dismiss abusive actions. Some examples of psychological sibling abuse include words and actions expressing degradation and/or contempt, such as harming pets, excessive mocking, threatening, intimidating, aggravating, and destroying a sibling's belongings. These actions have a negative impact on the sense of well-being (security, self-esteem, hopefulness, interpersonal functioning) of a sibling.

Physical abuse inflicted by a sibling is more easily defined and recognized than psychological sibling abuse. Physical sibling abuse exists when one member of a sibling dyad knowingly and intentionally causes physical harm to the other sibling. Examples of this abuse include aggressive shoving, hitting, slapping, kicking, biting, pinching, scratching, and hair pulling. As severity intensifies, the sibling perpetrator may begin to use objects and weapons such as coat hangers, hairbrushes, belts, sticks, knives, guns and rifles, broken glass, razor blades, and scissors to intensify the potential for injury.

Sexual abuse among siblings is the most veiled type of sibling abuse, yet it is likely this form of incest occurs more frequently than any other type. The accessibility of siblings to each other, combined with the complication that in most cases of sibling incest no generational boundary is being crossed, supports an environment in which sexual abuse can exist for years without being detected. Sibling sexual abuse is defined as behavior of a sexual nature that is not provoked by developmentally appropriate curiosity, not suitable based on age, and not temporary. Examples of sibling sexual abuse include inappropriate fondling, touching, sexual contact, indecent exposure, forced exposure to pornography, oral sex, anal sex, digital penetration, and intercourse.

Prevalence

In spite of the lack of empirical research to date on sibling abuse, an examination of family surveys and interviews that have been conducted over the past two decades supports the likelihood that sibling abuse occurs more often than any other form of family violence. It is possible that as many as 6 out of every 10 children in the United States have experienced some type of sibling abuse. Of these children, it can be estimated that as many as 30% of reported sibling abuse cases involve severe actions, including the use of (or threat to use) weapons such as knives and guns.

The nature of the sibling relationship lends itself to the high prevalence of sibling abuse. Siblings tend to be closer in age and interact with each other more than with their peers or other family members. Often, siblings share living spaces and spend time together without others present. In addition, wide societal acceptance that all negative interaction among siblings is normal rivalry enforces a situation in which abusive sibling interactions are easily hidden or dismissed.

Consequences

Given the duration and intensity of sibling abuse, the consequences are often lasting and uniquely severe. Developmental disruptions might occur, which may lead to difficulty with peer relationships and a distorted sense of self as the siblings enter adulthood. Both survivors and perpetrators of sibling abuse are likely to experience psychological distress, which may include anxiety, posttraumatic stress disorder, self-injury, depression, and suicidal ideation. As the majority of mental health professionals are not trained to screen for sibling abuse, the most effective treatments are often not available to this population; thus psychological distress related to the abuse could be sustained for a lifetime.

Interventions

Treating sibling abuse requires treating the entire family system. Integrating family, individual, and group methods of therapy is effective in helping the survivor understand the interaction between the abusive behavior and family life. The survivor should be given the opportunity to experience feelings related to the abuse at his or her own pace and provided an opportunity to confront the perpetrating sibling, if so desired. The perpetrator can benefit from groups that focus on taking responsibility and confronting denial. Mental health professionals can promote education about sibling abuse through the development of structured parent education programs, as well as by encouraging collaborative work with law enforcement and educators regarding the facts about abusive sibling behavior.

Mandy Morrill-Richards

See also Age and Victimization; Early Victimization Theories; Family Violence; Incest; Juvenile Offending and Victimization; Mental Illness and Victimization; Youth Violence, Interventions for

Further Readings

Cutting, A., & Dunn, J. (2006). Conversations with siblings and with friends: Links between relationship quality and social understanding. *British Journal of Developmental Psychology, 24,* 73–87.

Haskins, C. (2003). Treating sibling incest using a family systems approach. *Journal of Mental Health Counseling, 25,* 337–351.

Kiselica, M., & Morrill-Richards, M. (2007). Sibling maltreatment: The forgotten abuse. *Journal of Counseling & Development, 85,* 148–161.

Phillips-Green, M. J. (2002). Sibling incest. *Family Journal: Counseling and Therapy for Couples and Families, 10,* 195–202.

Wiehe, V. R. (2000). Sibling abuse. In H. Henderson (Ed.), *Domestic violence and child abuse resource sourcebook* (pp. 409–492). Detroit, MI: Omnigraphics.

ABUSE, SPOUSE

The term *spouse abuse* is commonly used to refer to aggressive, violent, and/or controlling behaviors that take place within an intimate relationship. Spouse abuse is a high-frequency crime resulting in victims of both genders and all social classes, races and ethnicities, and educational backgrounds. To adequately address this problem, preventive methods at societal and community levels as well as more traditional intervention approaches are required. This entry examines the definitions, terminology, and prevalence of spouse abuse. It then discusses the etiology of such abuse, focusing on gender-inclusive theory and theories about perpetrators. Finally, it describes some issues related to the treatment and prevention of the problem.

Definitions

It is almost impossible to provide a single definition of spouse abuse that would be accepted by professionals from all theoretical perspectives. Many definitions have been developed for different settings (e.g., legal, medical, welfare, educational). Most of these definitions share some reference to physical, psychological, and sexual damage to the victim, emphasizing that abuse can take more than one form. In addition to physical, sexual, and psychological aggression or abuse, controlling behaviors are also considered in some definitions. Controlling behaviors are often subtle and include acts such as sulking, withholding affection, jealous and possessive behaviors, and financial control. The term *controlling behaviors* may be preferable to *psychological aggression* when describing the perpetrator's motivation for these behaviors rather than the impact of the behaviors on the victim. Studies have shown the importance of incorporating such behaviors into research definitions. For instance, it has been demonstrated that unlike physical aggression, controlling behaviors do not diminish over time. Longitudinal research also shows that these behaviors may be a precursor to physical aggression, as controlling behaviors and physical aggression have been found to co-occur within relationships. Furthermore, some women have reported the effects of controlling behaviors to be more damaging than those resulting from physical aggression.

Terminology

In addition to using various definitions, the literature uses many terms to label this form of violence, some of which reflect the true nature of the problem better than others. The most widely used term to describe violence between intimate partners is *domestic violence*. However, this term lacks specificity, as it can be used to describe all forms of violent and/or potentially abusive behavior carried out within the family unit. In addition, feminist scholars have been successful in largely defining the term *domestic violence*, resulting in it being virtually synonymous with male assault of female partners. Many researchers following this perspective have viewed and termed acts of male physical aggression as *battering* or *woman abuse;* however, such terms have been criticized for being unnecessarily narrow, as they concern only behaviors toward female victims.

Finally, distinct terms have been suggested to coin the different severity of acts. Aggression can refer to acts that are less likely to result in injury (e.g., slapping) while violence can be used to highlight acts more likely to result in injury (e.g., choking and stabbing). However, the academic literature has largely adopted the terms *partner violence* and *intimate partner violence,* whereas the clinical literature continues to use the term *domestic violence,* therefore consensus between the two domains is currently lacking. For the purpose of consistency in terminology within this encyclopedia, the problem of violence within intimate relationships will be referred to as spouse abuse in this entry.

Many researchers following this perspective have viewed and termed acts of male physical aggression *battering* or *woman abuse.* Such terms have been criticized for not being inclusive, as they concern only behaviors toward female victims. In addition, the adjective *battering* has been criticized for its connotation of severe chronic violence, which some evidence from community samples suggests may constitute a minority of all cases.

This entry uses the term *spouse abuse* for the violence in intimate relationships, while acknowledging that the use of the term *spouse* suggests that this problem only occurs in marital relationships, whereas in actuality it also occurs in cohabiting and dating relationships in both heterosexual and same-sex couples. Further, the use of the term *abuse,* which implies that a behavioral act is both inherently unwelcome and morally unjustified, may not be as straightforward as it seems. Since all behaviors occur within a relationship context, it may not be possible to deduce the motivations, consequences, legality, or morality of actions without first exploring the contextual basis for them. Finally, terms suggested for the different severity of acts include *aggression* for acts less likely to result in injury (e.g., slapping) and *violence* for acts more likely to result in injury (e.g., choking).

Prevalence and Incidence

Prevalence and incidence rates differ markedly for women and men. However, since researchers often vary in the definitions and terminology they use to classify spouse abuse, in addition to the methodology they employ in surveys that determine rates, it is difficult to compare rates across studies, countries, and time. For example, when large-scale community studies focus on the victimization (and not perpetration) of individuals in relationships, rates of victimization are disproportionately higher for women than for men. However, some large-scale community studies that have asked men and women about their victimization and perpetration of different acts during times of conflict in their relationship have revealed approximately equal rates. While the former have been criticized for not ascertaining both sides of the story, those studies are typically criticized for not viewing perpetration in context and not considering that women are often only violent in self-defense.

Based on the findings of various large-scale self-report community studies, it seems likely that an estimate between 20% and 30% for the lifetime incidence of U.S. women experiencing any violence from a partner is a sensible approximation. Countries where women hold far less sociopolitical power than men have higher rates. The range reported for men's experiences of such violence in the United States differs widely due to differences in study methodology. Agreed-upon terms and definitions and consistency in methodological approach would allow researchers to produce comparable studies and resultant prevalence and incidence rates.

Etiology

While there is general agreement that both men and women have the potential to be victims of spouse abuse, the rates at which they are found to be victimized greatly differ, as the findings are influenced by the theoretical perspective that has informed the research methodology.

Different theoretical perspectives have been proposed to account for the etiology of spouse abuse, including feminist, sociology, psychology, and criminology theories, each of which emerged from a different methodological tradition. These perspectives are described in the entry on family and domestic violence theories. Here the focus is on feminist theory and the gender-inclusive theory that was created in response to it.

The feminist perspective has been very influential in explicating the etiology of spouse abuse and putting violence against women on the political agenda in Western societies. The central feature of this theory is that men's aggression against women is used as a form of control that stems from patriarchal attitudes and, consequently, cessation of aggression and violence rests with changing or removing these attitudes. Thus intervention programs designed from this perspective tend to focus on the societal rather than individual context of the abuse and to address the psychological and emotional problems of offenders and victims at the group level.

From the feminist perspective, women's aggression and violence is viewed as a matter of self-defense, and spouse abuse is considered a male-perpetrated crime. Therefore the ability of the feminist perspective to provide an understanding of all spouse abuse situations has been questioned by some researchers. Further, researchers following the feminist perspective have investigated spouse abuse using selected samples, interviewing women in shelters or emergency departments about their victimization by their male partners and other associated issues. This research has been criticized for not using standardized tools to measure the rates of different behavioral acts carried out by both members of a couple within large representative community samples.

Some researchers have adopted and promoted an approach to the understanding and study of spouse abuse that considers the possibility that both genders can be perpetrators and/or victims of such abuse. This gender-inclusive research has most frequently measured spouse abuse using a self-report tool named the Conflict Tactics Scale (CTS), which was developed by Murray Straus in the late 1970s, or a variant of it. The development of the CTS opened the door to large-scale data collection and quantitative analysis from which prevalence and incidence figures have been calculated in various countries. The CTS asks respondents to report on the use of a number of behaviors. The use of predetermined, clearly defined behavioral categories yields results that can be compared across people and samples. It has four subscales that enable it to distinguish between rational tactics such as reasoning, verbally and symbolically aggressive acts such as shouting, and physical force such as pushing and kicking. Without this format many less severe acts of physical aggression, such as slapping and pushing, would not be identified as aggressive. Some researchers question the value of describing less severe acts of violence that may not be used out of a need to control a partner as spouse abuse. However, other researchers, such as Straus, have repeatedly demonstrated the frequent and reciprocal use of such acts in addition to more severe acts between intimate partners and the

negative consequences they produce for those involved and society at large.

The CTS was developed for use in the U.S. National Family Violence Surveys conducted by Straus and his colleagues in 1975 and 1985. These surveys found prevalence rates of approximately 12% of men and women experiencing partner violence within a 12-month period, which was higher than previous estimates based on crime surveys. These surveys also found symmetry in the use of physical aggression by men and women against their partners—a controversial finding. However, this research does acknowledge that patriarchy plays a more significant role in spouse abuse in societies where violence against female partners is perceived as a man's right. Since 1985 many studies, including large meta-analytic reviews, have been published that measure men's and women's use of physical aggression in Western countries. This work demonstrates that on average women experience higher rates of injury than men, yet their use of aggression in intimate relationships may be comparable to that of men. Furthermore, it has been shown that while men and women do use qualitatively different aggressive acts against their partner (e.g., men are more likely to choke/strangle and women to hit with an object), they engage in acts deemed to be severe and engage in threats with or use of a knife or gun at similar rates.

In summary, the type of theoretical perspective and methodology employed in research can greatly affect our understanding of both genders' experiences of victimization and perpetration. It is therefore necessary to review the methodological quality of research studies from which conclusions have been drawn, as well as research from different perspectives. When all the research is combined, the picture is one of various types of spouse abuse, which vary by the severity, frequency, and controlling nature of violence used and experienced, in addition to its reciprocity.

Theories About Perpetrators

A common and robust finding in the literature is that men who are violent with their female partners are a heterogeneous group. Thus many researchers have attempted to develop typologies of abusive men. The majority of research to date has examined male perpetrators of spouse abuse, and little work exists that investigates female perpetrators. However, longitudinal research investigating the childhood correlates of spouse abuse in men and women suggests that women and men have similar developmental risk profiles.

In the last two decades, Amy Holtzworth-Munroe and her colleagues pioneered work on typologies of male offenders. From a review of the literature, they constructed a hypothetical typology to discriminate between subtypes of abusive men living in the community. Three types of male perpetrators were classified using three descriptive dimensions: severity of violence, generality of violence, and psychopathology/personality disorder of the perpetrator. They then provided each type with a name that reflects the nature of the violence: family only (FO), generally violent/antisocial (GVA), and dysphoric/borderline (DB). These types were each proposed to account for the percentage of these abusive men residing in the community, which were 50%, 25%, and 25%, respectively.

The FO offender is hypothesized to most closely resemble those in nonviolent comparison groups, as this offender has low levels of criminality and substance abuse and infrequently uses violence. This type therefore may be limited to family members and those whose offending is of low severity. The FO offender's violence is assumed to result from a combination of low-level risk factors, such as poor communication skills with a partner, mild impulsivity, and dependency on the partner. The GVA subtype is hypothesized to have low levels of psychological distress and depression, moderate levels of anger, and a dismissive attachment style. This offender is thought to display the highest levels of impulsivity, antisocial personality, substance abuse, and criminality, using moderate to severe levels of violence both within and outside of the family unit. The DB subtype is theorized to be the most psychologically distressed and emotionally volatile, evidencing characteristics of borderline personality and high levels of dependency on and preoccupation with an intimate partner, and reacting with anger when feeling rejected, abandoned, or slighted. This type is also most likely to display high levels of depression and anger and low to moderate levels of criminality and substance abuse. Violent acts are hypothesized to be of moderate to high severity and limited mainly to family members. Empirical tests of this typology by the authors

and other researchers have proved fruitful, demonstrating the existence of each of the three types in addition to a fourth type that falls in between the GVA and FO groups on several measures.

The potential for classification systems of perpetrators to play an integral role in the development of treatment programs remains a debated point. Some researchers have suggested that a one-type-fits-all approach is appropriate for all subgroups of perpetrators, while others have shown that the efficacy of programs increases when the intervention type is matched to the offender type.

In addition to typologies of male perpetrators, some researchers have focused on classifying the couple involved in a violent relationship, examining what the members of the couple may individually contribute to the abuse while trying not to place blame on the victim. This approach to understanding spouse abuse attempts to synthesize a vast array of research and literature into a conceptually manageable account for professionals working with victims, perpetrators, or couples whose patterns of spouse abuse can be described by these categories. Michael Johnson's work has been influential, as he classified men and women in couples based on each member's use of controlling behaviors and aggression and provided labels for the various types. "Situational couple violence" (originally called "common couple violence") refers to couples where one or both partners are physically aggressive in their relationship, but not controlling. For example, the aggression may be used as an attempt to communicate strong emotions rather than to control the other's thoughts and behavior.

In the couple where perpetrators are labeled "intimate terrorists," because they use aggression and violence in a bid to control their partner, victims use either no aggression or noncontrolling aggression and are referred to as the "violent resistant" partners. Couples are given the "mutual violence control" label when they aggress against one another in a bid for control. Other researchers are now examining the different interaction and attachment styles of partners as potential contributors to spouse abuse. It is evident from such work that the classification of one person in the couple as victim and the other as perpetrator may provide an incomplete view of some spouse abuse situations.

Family Context

Research has provided empirical support for the co-occurrence of spouse abuse and child maltreatment, with estimates varying widely depending on the nature of the sample investigated. Furthermore, as demonstrated in the spouse abuse literature, aggression by men and women in the same family is particularly common. If the safety and custody of a child is of issue, it is necessary to carry out family assessments to establish all the types of violence taking place within the family and which parent is at risk of harming the child, as well as establishing who has a positive relationship with the child. Assessments should be guided by evidence-based research rather than based on stereotypical expectations of who is likely to be violent. In addition, examining spouse abuse within the context of the family as a whole is important if cycles of aversive family interactions are to cease. Etiological, intervention, and prevention models will be improved by considering all forms of possible maltreatment in the family together rather than in isolation.

Conclusion

Growing awareness of spouse abuse over several decades has led to a number of approaches to prevention, assessment, and treatment and focused on a broad population. Thus messages to the public that attempt to prevent or intervene in spouse abuse might take a perspective that includes all genders, ages, races/ethnicities, and social groups within the target population. The controversy in the literature makes it clear that understanding the complete picture of spouse abuse and its related problems is essential to stopping such abuse.

Louise Dixon and Nicola Graham-Kevan

See also Battered Woman Syndrome; Cycle of Violence, Theory of; Dating Violence; Domestic Violence; Domestic Violence, Same-Sex; Family and Domestic Violence, Theories of; Intimate Partner Violence, Theories of; Women's Use of Aggression

Further Readings

Archer, J. (2000). Sex differences in aggression between heterosexual partners: A meta-analytic review. *Psychological Bulletin, 126,* 651–680.

Dixon, L., & Browne, K. D. (2003). Heterogeneity of spouse abuse: A review. *Aggression and Violent Behavior, 8,* 107–130.

Dutton, D. G. (2007). *Rethinking domestic violence.* Vancouver: UBC Press.

Hamel, J., & Nichols, T. L. (Eds.). (2007). *Family interventions in domestic violence: A handbook of gender-inclusive theory and treatment.* New York: Springer.

Holtzworth-Munroe, A., & Stuart, G. L. (1994). Typologies of male batterers: Three subtypes and the differences among them. *Psychological Bulletin, 116,* 476–497.

Johnson, M. P., & Ferraro, K. J. (2000). Research on domestic violence in the 1990's: Making distinctions. *Journal of Marriage and Family, 62,* 948–963.

Straus, M., & Gelles, R. (1990). *Physical violence in American families.* New Brunswick, NJ: Transaction.

Straus, M., Hamby, S. L., Boney-McCoy, S., & Sugarman, D. B. (1996). The Revised Conflict Tactic Scales (CTS2): Development and preliminary psychometric data. *Journal of Family Issues, 17,* 283–316.

ADULT PROTECTIVE SERVICES

The Adult Protective Services (APS) system is designed to investigate cases of abuse and neglect and protect the well-being of older adults, individuals with disabilities, and others who are at risk for mistreatment and neglect. APS agencies are charged with investigating cases of abuse of individuals 18 and over and are analogous to agencies responsible for the investigation of child abuse. While APS systems support the entire adult population, the majority of cases involve various forms of *elder abuse* and *abuse of individuals with disabilities.* APS staff are often the first responders to reports of suspected abuse or neglect. Adult Protective Services can be described as investigation, provision of care and services, and evaluation of interventions. However, while this provides a general picture of APS, a more complete understanding involves the examination of the policies surrounding the development and implementation of APS, the general operations of the APS system, differences among APS systems, and best practice concepts for APS.

Development and Funding of Adult Protective Services

APS is supported by a number of different policies at both the federal and state levels. Title XX of the Social Security Act in 1973 created Social Services Block Grants to provide federal funding to states with the goals of providing services to protect against abuse and promote independence for older adults and individuals with disabilities. Title II and Title XII of the Older Americans Act (OAA) designate a federal-level position within the Administration on Aging to be responsible for elder abuse and neglect programs and for the creation of the National Center on Elder Abuse to act as a clearinghouse of information and best practice interventions.

How Adult Protective Services Systems Work

APS systems work through a series of steps to investigate and respond to suspected abuse, including receiving a report of suspected abuse, investigation of reports, provision of support, and monitoring of the individual and interventions. Reports of abuse can be initiated by victims, family members, professional staff, long-term-care ombudsmen, or other concerned parties through state or local APS offices or through abuse hotline services. In the case of immediate danger and emergencies, APS staff redirect the case to law enforcement and emergency medical services. If the suspected abuse is within a covered population and the risk is not immediate, then cases enter the APS system and are assigned to staff for a timely investigation. APS staff then make contact with the victim and assess issues of competency, risk of harm, and the victim's desire for intervention. APS staff develop a comprehensive service plan based on the assessment of risk, current needs, and remaining abilities and strengths of the individuals. The coordination or provision of services by APS staff may include general medical and mental health care services, legal services including investigation or financial management issues, community-based services such as nutrition or transportation, and home-based services such as home health care or home modification programs. The final step in the APS system involves the monitoring of services, evaluation of the impact of services, and adjustment of services as needed to eliminate risk, provide protection, and enhance the well-being of at-risk adults.

Differences Within Adult Protective Services Systems

While federal policies form the foundation of APS, the operations and funding of services vary widely from state to state. The provision of services varies on issues such as eligibility, types of abuse covered, classification of abuse, and the nature of reporting and investigation. While most state APS systems provide protection to all vulnerable adults, some states provide APS coverage separately for individuals who are under or over 60 years of age or have particular types of disability. State APS programs also differ in the types of abuse or neglect that are covered and investigated by APS. APS programs also differ in reporting and investigation requirements, such as whether reporting requirements are voluntary or mandatory and at what point in the investigative process referrals to law enforcement are required.

Best Practice Concepts in Adult Protective Services

The provision of APS should be consistent with best practice guidelines such as the best interests of the individual, informed and involved decision making, the maximization of independence, and an individualized approach. The goal of safety and protection for vulnerable individuals must be balanced with the goal of supporting the individual in exercising personal agency and self-determination. Adults retain their decision-making capacity unless deemed incapable through court action. The APS system must guarantee informed consent for decision making, support the involvement of clients in decision making, capitalize on the strengths of the individual, and use the least restrictive support programs to maximize the independence of clients. Finally, the APS system and programs must recognize that services should be designed with an appreciation of the social, cultural, and historical variability among individuals. With these best practice concepts in mind, APS will continue to defend vulnerable adults from abuse and neglect and offer them respectful support.

Charles Stelle

See also Age and Victimization; Disabilities, Victimization of Individuals With; Elder Abuse, Neglect, and Maltreatment; Elder Abuse, Neglect, and Maltreatment: Interventions for; Elder Abuse, Neglect, and Maltreatment: Statutory Responses

Further Readings

Daly, J. M., Jogerst, G., Brinig, M., & Dawson, J. D. (2003). Mandatory reporting: Relationship of APS statute language on state reported elder abuse. *Journal of Elder Abuse and Neglect, 15,* 1–21.

Dauenhauer, J. A., Mayer, K. C., & Mason, A. (2007). Evaluation of adult protective services: Perspectives of community professionals. *Journal of Elder Abuse and Neglect, 19,* 41–57.

Dubble, C. (2006). A policy perspective on elder justice through APS and law enforcement collaboration. *Journal of Gerontological Social Work, 46,* 35–55.

Jogerst, G., Daly, J. M., & Ingram, J. (2001). National elder abuse questionnaire: Summary of adult protective service investigator responses. *Journal of Elder Abuse and Neglect, 13,* 59–71.

Otto, J. M. (2000). The role of adult protective services in addressing abuse. *Generations, 24,* 33–38.

Web Sites

American Bar Association Commission on Law and Aging: http://www.abanet.org/aging

National Adult Protective Services Association: http://www.apsnetwork.org

National Center on Elder Abuse: http://www.ncea.aoa.gov

AGE AND VICTIMIZATION

Victimization is not randomly distributed across age groups. Research has identified several correlates to criminal victimization, one of the strongest predictors being age. Much of what is known about the relationship between age and victimization comes from the National Crime Victimization Survey (NCVS) and the Uniform Crime Reporting (UCR) Program. Together, the data from these sources broaden our understanding of crime in the United States. Establishing differences in victimization risk by age is important, as it prompts the development and enhancement of focused policy designed to reduce victimization. This entry focuses on age and victimization in the context of homicide, nonfatal violent, and property crimes. It then concludes with a discussion of the direction of future studies of age and victimization.

Age and Homicide

A general pattern exists with respect to age and homicide. Data collected from state and local law enforcement agencies and published through the FBI's UCR Program indicate that the lowest homicide rates are of children under age 14. James Alan Fox and Marianne W. Zawitz report that from age 15, homicide risk increases as age increases for almost a decade, with the highest homicide risk being of young adults ages 18 to 24. Beginning at age 25, in general, there is an inverse relationship between age and victimization risk. That is to say, the risk of homicide declines as age increases.

Rates of homicide have changed over time across age groups. Homicide rates of teens and young adults increased significantly in the late 1980s, while homicide rates for older groups were falling. Over the past decade, there has been a precipitous decline in homicide rates of younger adults, while homicide rates of older adults (ages 35–49 and 50 and older) have remained unchanged. In 2007, the average age of homicide victims was about 32 years old.

Age and Nonfatal Violent Victimization

There is an inverse relationship between age and nonfatal violent victimization (i.e., rape, robbery, sexual assault, and assault). In general, older persons are victims of nonfatal violence at lower rates than younger persons. For example, according to Patsy Klaus and Callie Marie Rennison, those age 12 to 17 had the highest rates of nonfatal violence from 1976 through the early 2000s, and those age 50 and older had the lowest rates.

Since the early 1990s, rates of nonfatal violence involving younger victims declined more dramatically than did rates of older victims. For example, according to Michael Rand, from 1994 through

2007, the violent crime rate for victims ages 12 to 15 and 16 to 19 declined 63% and 60%, respectively; for victims ages 20 to 24, the decline in the violent crime rate was more than 65% during this time period. In contrast, the decline in the rate of violence of victims ages 50 to 64 was only about 34%.

Age and Property Victimization

As measured by the NCVS, the lowest rates of overall property crime (i.e., household burglary, motor vehicle theft, and theft) are those of persons age 65 or older. According to Klaus, from 1993 to 2002, households headed by persons age 65 or older experienced property crimes at a rate about one fourth of that for households headed by persons under 25. Nonetheless, more than 9 in 10 crimes committed against the elderly (i.e., victims 65 or older) are property crimes, compared to about 4 in 10 crimes committed against victims ages 12 to 24. This pattern is unique to property crime risk and is not evident when violent crime risk is considered. Regardless of the age considered, property crime victimization rates have declined significantly over the past several years. For example, from 1996 through 2007, the decline in the property crime rate among victims ages 50 to 64 and 65-plus was about 46% and 30%, respectively.

Future Directions

In 1986, David Farrington published findings from a limited study of the relationship between age and crime. He focused on improving our understanding of the relationship between age and offending but not age and victimization, because the study of age and victimization, according to Farrington, was fairly undeveloped. Since the release of Farrington's work, our understanding of age and victimization has received considerable attention from the scientific community. Distinct patterns associated with age and victimization have been repeatedly observed and found to have some similarities with those identified by Farrington and others who have examined age and offending. Some of the most notable examples of the relationship between age and property crime, violent crime, and homicide have been presented in this entry. And while these illustrative examples are noteworthy, they represent a small fraction of the information related to age and victimization that has been produced by the research community. Scientists continue to study the age–victimization relationship, addressing important questions related to the temporal stability of the age–victimization distribution, variation in the relationship across gender and race, and how disentangling period and cohort effects from the data enables researchers to better understand these effects as well as the relationship between age and victimization. In short, while information generated from national-level data produced from the NCVS and UCR Program has furthered our understanding of the relationship between age and victimization over the past three decades, work continues in this area aimed at further evolving our understanding the role age plays in victimization.

Timothy C. Hart

See also Correlates of Victimization; National Crime Victimization Survey (NCVS); Race/Ethnicity and Victimization; Sex and Victimization; Uniform Crime Reporting (UCR) Program

Further Readings

Farrington, D. P. (1986). Age and crime. *Crime and Justice, 7,* 189–250.

Fox, J. A., & Zawitz, M. W. (2007). *Homicide trends in the United States.* Retrieved November 19, 2008, from http://www.ojp.usdoj.gov/bjs/homicide/homtrnd.htm

Klaus, P. (2005). *Crime against persons age 65 or older, 1993–2002* (NCJ-206154). Washington, DC: U.S. Bureau of Justice Statistics.

Klaus, P., & Rennison, C. M. (2002). *Age patterns in violent victimization, 1976–2000* (NCJ-190104). Washington, DC: U.S. Bureau of Justice Statistics.

Rand, M. R. (2008). *Criminal Victimization, 2007* (NCJ # 224390). Washington, DC: U.S. Government Printing Office.

ALTERNATIVE SCHOOLS

Alternative schools are often considered school-based delinquency prevention programs because they remove disruptive students from traditional public schools and place them in a smaller and more supportive environment. Alternative education programs for poor school achievers are based on a significant amount of research demonstrating that school performance is causally linked to delinquent behavior. This entry defines alternative schools, provides a brief overview of their historical roots, and summarizes research on the effectiveness of alternative schools in reducing delinquency.

Definition

Although there is no one standard model for alternative schools for delinquents, the underlying belief is that these programs should provide a more positive learning environment than traditional schools through low student-to-teacher ratios, individualized and self-paced instruction, noncompetitive performance assessments, and less structured classrooms. The alternative school concept is largely based on the idea that a self-paced curriculum allows students to work independently, and an informal classroom structure affords staff more time for individualized instruction. In addition, alternative school students are believed to be under less pressure to perform at the same level as other students, since success is measured by individual achievements rather than by comparing individual progress to that of the entire class.

In theory, students feel more comfortable in this environment and are more motivated to attend this type of school. Students attending alternative schools are believed to have higher self-esteem, higher academic performance, and decreased delinquent behaviors than they did when attending traditional schools.

Alternative education programs are difficult to define because there are many types of alternative schools. In general, alternative schools can be described as specialized educational programs that take place outside the mainstream school system. An alternative school can be defined as any school that provides alternative learning experiences beyond those provided by the traditional schools within its community and that is available to every family at no cost. This basic definition includes three criteria.

First, for a school program to be defined as an alternative, it must have a separate administrative unit with its own personnel and not be a special class or series of classes in the traditional school. Being apart from the traditional school, the alternative school can provide a more supportive and accepting environment where students feel they have more control over their lives. Also, the students will be able to avoid the negative stigmatization that may have been placed on them in their traditional school for being disruptive or low academic achievers.

Second, it is important for alternative schools to be voluntary and available to every student in the school district. These schools should not be based on assignment or strict enrollment criteria. Allowing for choice and making attendance at the alternative schools voluntary (1) makes the school responsive to the diversity of students, (2) maintains responsiveness to the needs of minority groups, (3) enhances student interest and commitment to education, and (4) restores public confidence in the schools.

Third, community participation and responsiveness are important in the development and maintenance of the alternative school. The philosophy behind the alternative education movement lies in the establishment of unique and individual programs developed for a specific local population. The primary source of support for an alternative school should be parents and students.

Beginnings

The concept of alternative education originated in the mid-1960s and grew out of a general distaste for the oppressive nature and unresponsiveness of traditional education models. The modern concept of alternative education was developed from a belief that the traditional model of education had failed to adjust to societal changes and the diverse characteristics of students. The argument followed that public schools failed to adapt to the increasing diversity of various cultures and communities. The public school system was viewed as flawed because it designated some students to fail.

Early alternative schools recruited students who were high academic achievers; however, alternative schools attracted students who had traditionally been low academic achievers. These students generally had poor attitudes toward school, needed a greater amount of staff support, and wanted more self-paced and independent instruction. It was believed that alternative schools were more desirable to low academic achievers because the curriculum and structure allowed for more independence with increased staff support, which improved poor attitudes toward school.

The number of alternative schools was expected to grow as the alternative education movement progressed through the 1970s and 1980s. In fact, the U.S. Justice Department's Office of Juvenile Justice and Delinquency Prevention promoted these programs in the early 1980s through its Delinquency Prevention through Alternative Education Initiative. However, the expected growth did not materialize and support for these programs sharply eroded due to a series of disappointing results from early evaluations of several programs.

Research

Early evaluations of alternative schools commonly found these programs did not produce positive changes in participants. The poor findings were attributed to school officials' improper use of alternative schools. That is, alternative schools tended to be used as a way to punish problem students, were commonly viewed as a place to banish misbehaving students to get them out of traditional schools, and rarely provided appropriate academic and behavioral programming.

In addition, alternative schools for delinquent youth were thought to be "too little, too late" and were typically not given adequate resources or staff to handle youth with serious behavioral problems and deficient academic skills. Little attention was given to selecting a target population of students that might best benefit from alternative education. Many school officials appeared to be more concerned with getting difficult students out of traditional schools than with thoughtfully selecting appropriate students for alternative schools.

Evaluation research on alternative schools for delinquents is sparse, but a review of alternative school research by Stephen Cox found that some alternative schools were able to produce positive effects on school performance, school attitude, and self-esteem. However, alternative schools did not significantly change participants' delinquent behavior.

Stephen M. Cox

See also Juvenile Offending and Victimization; School-Based Theories of Delinquency; School Crimes, Elementary Through High School; Seattle Social Development Project

Further Readings

Arnove, R. F., & Strout, T. (1980). Alternative schools for disruptive youth. *Educational Forum, 44,* 453–471.

Cox, S. M., Davidson, W. S., & Bynum, T. S. (1995). A meta-analytic assessment of delinquency-related outcomes of alternative education programs. *Crime & Delinquency, 41,* 219–234.

Gold, M., & Mann, D. W. (1984). *Expelled to a friendlier place: A study of alternative schools.* Ann Arbor: University of Michigan Press.

Van Acker, R. (2007). Antisocial, aggressive, and violent behavior in children and adolescents within alternative education settings: Prevention and intervention. *Preventing School Failure, 51,* 5–12.

AMBER ALERT

The AMBER (America's Missing: Broadcast Emergency Response) Alert system is a nationwide collaborative of public agencies and media outlets created to rapidly inform and recruit the public for assistance in rescuing missing children. When a child is reported missing or abducted and is believed to be in serious danger, law enforcement officials can publicize an AMBER Alert via television, radio, the Internet, and cell phone text messages. The system has produced a number of sensational successes and has been credited with saving hundreds of children's lives owing to tips from attentive citizens or because abductors were induced to return their captives after seeing the alerts.

The system was developed in Texas in response to the abduction and murder of 9-year-old Amber Hagerman in 1996. The abduction was observed and immediately reported, and police promptly searched for her, but Amber was found brutally murdered 4 days later. The tragedy inspired the idea of a public alert system in which law enforcement officials could use media outlets to enable more rapid reaction and enlistment of citizen lookouts in future child abduction cases. The result was Plan Amber, which became a model for programs in other states that were eventually consolidated into a national network as part of the 2003 federal PROTECT Act. The system is now overseen by the U.S. Department of Justice in conjunction with the

National Center for Missing and Exploited Children.

Despite the excellent intentions behind the AMBER Alert system and the claims of extraordinary success by its advocates, the available evidence suggests a more sobering picture. Although the vast majority of the cases in which AMBER Alerts are issued end with the safe recovery of the child, this is misleading for a number of reasons. First, many AMBER Alerts are issued in cases that turn out to be misunderstandings or even hoaxes. Furthermore, even in genuine kidnappings, most of the cases end positively even if the AMBER Alert did not affect the outcome. Further still, even where an AMBER Alert did help police locate and recover the child, it turns out that the vast majority of these "successes" occur in far less menacing abduction scenarios than the one involving Amber Hagerman. Whereas Amber Hagerman's abduction and murder were premeditated by a stranger, "successful" AMBER Alerts are far more likely to involve familial abductions, such as when a noncustodial parent illegally takes the child, or even unintended abductions that are incidental to other crimes (e.g., car thefts of vehicles with children in them). Finally, the evidence shows that in the most menacing situations involving strangers intending harm—the very kind of case that inspired AMBER Alert—the odds of success are very low.

Several factors limit AMBER Alert's effectiveness. The first is response time; AMBER Alerts are only rarely issued at or near the moment of abduction, because verification that a crime has occurred and any useful details about it are not usually immediately available. But in the majority of child abduction–murder cases, the victim is dead within 3 hours of the abduction, so the AMBER Alerts are often hamstrung from the beginning. Another key limitation is the complex sequence of events required for a "success." There must be relatively swift and detailed knowledge of an abduction and a quickly issued alert, followed by an informative citizen tip that leads to law enforcement response fast enough to make a difference in the outcome of the crime. Both of these obstacles are more easily overcome in less menacing abductions where the abductor (often a parent) has no sinister intent and there is sufficient time for the components required for a successful alert to occur. However, in cases involving a motivated predator bent on a heinous crime, the window of opportunity, and thus the chance of success, is very small. A final and ironic obstacle to AMBER Alert success is the rarity of the crimes it is designed to prevent. Despite a socially constructed perception that child abduction–murder is pervasive, this crime type is fortunately quite rare, and thus there simply are not that many potential victims for AMBER Alert to save.

Even if the claims of AMBER Alert effectiveness do not withstand empirical and logical scrutiny, the system still has broad appeal as a crime control narrative in which members of society come together to rescue the most compelling victims. It has thus been called *crime control theater*, functioning not as a real solution to a pervasive crime, but as a socially constructed solution to a largely socially constructed crime. In this regard AMBER Alert could be important as an illustrative microcosm of how laws are created in response to moral panic over terrifying crimes such as child abduction–murder.

Timothy Griffin and Monica K. Miller

See also Child Abuse, Neglect, and Maltreatment: Measurement of; Fear of Crime; Juvenile Offending and Victimization; Kidnapping; Missing, Exploited, and Murdered Children; Pedophilia

Further Readings

Griffin, T., & Miller, M. K. (2008). Child abduction, AMBER Alert, and crime control theater. *Criminal Justice Review, 33*(2), 159–176.

Griffin, T., Miller, M. K., Hoppe, J., Rebideaux, A., & Hammack, R. (2007). A preliminary examination of AMBER Alert's effects. *Criminal Justice Policy Review, 18*(4), 378–394.

Hargrove, T. (2005). *False alarms endangering future of AMBER Alert system.* New York: Scripps Howard News Service.

Hotaling, G., & Finkelhor, D. (1990). Estimating the number of stranger-abduction homicides of children: A review of available evidence. *Journal of Criminal Justice, 18,* 385–399.

National Center for Missing and Exploited Children. (2007). *FAQ: AMBER Alert.* Retrieved July 11, 2007, from http://www.missingkids.com/missingkids/servlet/PageServlet?LanguageCountry=en_US&PageId=2813#3

U.S. Department of Justice. (2004). *AMBER Alert: America's missing broadcast emergency response.* Retrieved July 11, 2007, from http://www.amberalert .gov/docs/AMBERCriteria.pdf

ANTICIPATORY BENEFIT

The primary and direct benefits expected from crime-preventive initiatives are those that occur after initiative implementation and in connection with targeted areas, groups, times, crimes, and methods. Other secondary benefits have, however, also been identified and reported. One of these, termed an *anticipatory benefit,* accrues if there is a decline in crime *before* a crime-prevention initiative has been put in place. Another secondary benefit, termed *diffusion of benefits*, is a crime decline *following* the implementation of a crime-prevention measure, which occurs with nontargeted areas, groups, times, crimes, and methods. The main focus of researchers who have observed or commented on anticipatory benefits has been on the preinitiative activities associated with offender misperception, particularly those related to *publicity*. There are, however, a number of other reasons that a preinitiative crime drop can occur, as discussed below. The possible presence of anticipatory benefits is important for three main reasons. First, it may increase our understanding of the mechanisms associated with crime prevention. Second, it may indicate that another factor may be added to the main crime-prevention measures that will extend their reach to other times, places, targets, crimes, and methods of doing crime. Third, it may alert researchers and policy makers to the possibility that the research design used may not be properly assessing the effectiveness of the crime-prevention measures used. This last issue is discussed in more detail below.

Reasons that anticipatory benefits occur fall into one of four general categories: (1) those unrelated to the initiative itself, (2) those related to the selection of the site or group for the initiative, (3) those related to preparation for the initiative, and (4) those related to potential offenders' misperceptions that the initiative's measures were already in effect. First, preinitiative crime falls can be a statistical artifact of a time-series analysis or due to unrelated factors such as seasonal effects. Second, sites or groups chosen for treatment may have crime rates artificially bolstered through overrecording, or they may be experiencing high crime rates that are unusual for the area or group, with the rates declining as the conditions producing the higher rates change. In some contexts this latter effect might be referred to as *selection bias*, but here it is best considered as an example of *regression to the mean*. Third, a lower level of crime can be produced before the initiative's official start-up date—if, for example, parts of it occur sooner, activities occurring in the preinitiative stage have preventive effects, or training makes officers better at reducing crime or more motivated to do so (prior to the start-up time). Fourth, potential offenders may refrain from crime if they perceive that equipment, systems, or practices are operational when they are not, or they do not remember details mentioned in media reports or publicity campaigns relating to the time, place, or manner of implementation. Details may also have been obscured purposely as part of the planned initiative. In this latter situation, ethical considerations might arise if, for example, potential victims rely on the presence of crime-prevention measures and are put at risk of harm that is greatly disproportionate to the good to be expected from the anticipatory benefit.

Researchers who noticed a preimplementation crime fall often have noted that the decline coincided with some publicity related to the impending crime-prevention initiative. Examples of this include publicity about a bike patrol at a suburban park-and-ride facility in the Vancouver area, Princess Anne announcing an initiative targeted at nonresidential burglary in Leicester in the United Kingdom, and British legislation being proposed for mandatory testing of blood-alcohol levels of drivers in advance of its becoming law. It is possible that researchers have focused on publicity because (1) crime drops resulting from preinitiative publicity may occur more often than others, (2) it may be easier to notice and report on preinitiative publicity than other types of phenomena, or (3) publicity may be seen as being more malleable than other causal factors and, therefore, more easily added to the mix of preventive measures. Misinterpretations among potential offenders about when, or whether, crime-prevention measures have taken effect also have been attributed to other causes, however, such as preinitiative site surveys and the installation of closed-circuit television cameras.

Measuring crime levels at several periods prior to the implementation date is essential if any possible anticipatory benefits are to be identified and documented. This is also useful for determining if the measures have been effective, particularly in situations where anticipatory benefits may be fairly likely. For example, if there is only a single preinitiative measurement of crime in an area and this assessment is taken *after* preinitiative publicity that has led to a fall in crime, then the real extent of the initiative's effectiveness will not be measured. A simple experimental design (random controlled trial) will not be able to overcome this problem, unless it incorporates time-series points, since the factors leading to a preinitiative crime drop may affect both its treatment and control groups. Furthermore, a process evaluation, preferably one with a qualitative component, can help determine what triggered the preinitiative crime fall since it may uncover factors that are difficult to detect with traditional outcome evaluations.

Martha Jane Smith

See also Closed-Circuit Television; Diffusion of Benefits; Displacement; Methodological Issues in Evaluating Effectiveness of Crime Prevention; Situational Crime Prevention

Further Readings

Bowers, K., & Johnson, S. (2005). Using publicity for crime preventive purposes. In N. Tilley (Ed.), *Handbook of crime prevention and community safety* (pp. 329–354). Collumpton, Devon, UK: Willan.

Guerette, R. T., & Clarke, R. V. (2003). Product life-cycles and crime: Automated teller machines and robbery. *Security Journal, 16,* 7–18.

Smith, M. J., Clarke, R. V., & Pease, K. (2002). Anticipatory benefits in crime prevention. In N. Tilley (Ed.), *Analysis for crime prevention, Crime prevention studies* (Vol. 13, pp. 71–88). Monsey, NY, & Devon, UK: Criminal Justice Press & Willan.

Weisburd, D., Wycoff, L. A., Ready, J., Eck, J. E., Hinkle, J. C., & Gajewski, F. (2006). Does crime just move around the corner? A controlled study of spatial displacement and diffusion of crime control benefits. *Criminology, 44,* 549–591.

ARSON/FIRESETTING

Arson is first and foremost a legal term. In a public health context, the same act is referred to as *firesetting.* The FBI's Uniform Crime Reporting (UCR) Program defines arson as the willful or malicious burning (or attempted burning) of a dwelling or any other type of public or personal property. Some state jurisdictions require that the destroyed property be worth a minimum monetary value in order to be classified as arson. Others retain an element of common law and require that the damaged property belong to another, or that the real or personal property be destroyed with intent to defraud an insurer. Depending on the nature of the fire and the demonstrability of intent, willful and malicious burnings may be prosecuted under a number of state and federal statutes other than arson, including reckless endangerment, criminal damage, possession of incendiary devices, insurance fraud, Racketeer Influenced and Corrupt Organizations (RICO), and civil rights laws. Under the USA Patriot Act, arson can also be prosecuted as an act of domestic terrorism. Arson may result from recklessness as well as willful behavior. To be considered arson, the fire must have been set deliberately, but the resulting destruction need not have been intended or foreseen.

Arson is an understudied phenomenon. Numerous factors related to its reporting, investigation, and prosecution limit our knowledge of the crime and its victimology. In general, arson is characterized by the absence of clear victimological and offender profiles, reflecting the complex motivational and situational structure of the act, which is alternatively portrayed as a "victimless" property crime and as a violent interpersonal offense. Arson may be committed in service of any number of ends, including crime concealment, profit making, political activism, thrill seeking, and self-destruction. The victims of arson may be the arsonist himself or herself. While arsonists may choose where and how to set a fire, the spread and result of the initial act may be beyond their control. In this sense, arson can have unintended victims, such as the firefighters charged with putting out the blaze. For victims, arson may result in economic loss, long-term physical injury, psychological distress, trauma, and death. Prevention efforts have been twofold: targeting offenders on the one hand, and manipulating the sociophysical environment on the other.

Statistics

Despite a steady drop in the number of intentionally set fires recorded by the U.S. Fire Administration since 1997, arson is still the leading cause of fires in the United States. Between 1998 and 2007, intentionally set structure fires resulted in an average of 350 deaths per year, not including the toll of the terrorist attacks on September 11, 2001, according to the U.S. Fire Administration. In 2007, the rate of arson was 24.7 per 100,000 in the population. The average loss per offense was $17,289. These figures do not include intangible costs, such as any social and psychological impact. According to the Federal Bureau of Investigation's report, *Crime in the United States 2007*, of the 64,332 offenses for which data were available, more than 42.9% involved fires in structures and almost 28% were fires in mobile property.

Measuring Arson

A number of factors contribute to the "dark figure" of arson. The term *dark figure* refers to the difference between the number of arsons known to the police and the real number of arsons committed. Establishing the origin of a fire is sometimes an impossible task. Victimization surveys conducted in the United Kingdom suggest that almost two thirds of arsons are reported to the police, which is a relatively high figure compared to report rates of other types of crime, but victims remain dependent on investigators to establish the cause of a blaze. When individuals destroy their own property, it may be in their interest to dissimulate the criminal origins of the fire. Small fires, such as fires set by children, are likely to go unreported. Federal statistics do not include fires labeled as suspicious or of unknown origin, therefore these figures are likely an underestimate of the true scope of arson. A scoping study conducted in the United Kingdom showed that, in a single year, the police recorded only about 41% of the malicious fires classified as such by the fire service, of which about 15% were solved.

Ecological Variables

Arson rates have been associated with various socioeconomic and physical variables, such as building abandonment, vacant housing, overall physical decay of urban structures, and the economic status of the local population. Structures that display signs of decay, vacancy, age, and abandonment are often targets for arsonists, and populations in the poorer census tracts experience significantly more deliberate or suspicious fires than populations in the richer tracts.

Offenders, Victims, and Targets

Children

It is not uncommon for young children to engage in fire-play and firesetting behavior. However, the vast majority of children who experiment with fire will stop engaging in the behavior once they have learned the dangers related to fire-setting. Nevertheless, a few may become recidivists. Fires lit by children tend to occur in the home. They are often spurred by curiosity or boredom and may also be a form of attention seeking. Simple match-play can result in uncontrollable destruction and injury to the child and others. In recent years, fire-play has been reported as a major cause of death among preschoolers, leading to thousands of injuries and hundreds of deaths each year in the United States.

Juveniles

Juvenile arson is associated with occasional vandalism or more general delinquency and is frequently a group activity. In the United Kingdom, a majority of offenders cautioned or found guilty of arson are between 10 and 14 years of age. The school and its immediate surroundings are often the site of the firesetting, and half the fires occur during school hours. The majority of school fires result in little or no damage, but some incidents can result in significant harm to property and/or individuals. In the United Kingdom, an estimated 20 schools experience an arson attack each week, and around 100,000 children are deprived of schooling as a consequence. Youth may also be involved in seasonal arsons, around celebratory dates such as New Year's Eve, July 4, and Halloween in the United States and Guy Fawkes Night in England. Traditionally, these holidays involve fireworks and bonfires, as well as the consumption of alcohol, which contribute to the opportunity for malicious firesetting by lowering inhibitions and facilitating access to firesetting paraphernalia. In the United States, arson fires have been estimated to rise by nearly 10% above the national average on Halloween night and Devil's Night or Mischief Night (the night before Halloween).

The Mentally Impaired

Deliberate firesetting has been linked to mental disturbances and personality disorders, such as schizophrenia, intellectual retardation, suicidal ideation, and psychopathy. Arsonists are reportedly more likely to suffer from a mental disorder than other criminals, though the few studies available suffer from sampling problems. Pathological firesetting as a syndrome is called *pyromania*. Today there is growing doubt regarding the existence of pyromania as a distinct mental disorder. The *Diagnostic and Statistical Manual of Mental Disorders* (DSM-IV) notes that pathological firesetting seems rare. Nevertheless, pyromania is still invoked to explain the deliberate setting of wildfires or the presence of arsonists among firefighters.

Criminals

Criminals may use arson to conceal evidence of another crime. For example, thieves and joy riders may set cars alight once they have stripped them of all saleable parts or have no more use of them. Arson can also be used to destroy forensic evidence in cases of burglary or murder.

Property Owners and Developers

Arson for profit entails people's destruction of their own property or business and is a form of insurance fraud. Car owners may set their old vehicles afire as a means of disposal. In some cases, landlords have used arson to chase away unwanted tenants and tenants have used it to obtain new housing. Arson may also be used to free up land for development in both urban and rural environments. This type of arson may be linked to organized criminal activity. Though insurers are the intended target of many of these fires, arson for profit can result in significant collateral damage to lives, properties, communities, and local economies.

Political Activists

Arson can also be a means of violent political action. In 1995 and 1996, the United States experienced a rash of African American church arsons, thought to be motivated by racism. Population riots often result in the burning of property, especially cars parked on the streets. Arson and bombings have been used by radical individuals and organizations, such as antiabortionists, radical environmentalists, and animal rights activists, as well as by nationalist, separatist, anarchist, Marxist, and religious fundamentalist groups, among others. Some organizations target property with minimum threat to life, while others indiscriminately target individuals. A last form of political firesetting is self-immolation, which is a form of suicide by fire intended to attract widespread attention to a collective cause. Since its very public use by Buddhist monks in South Vietnam in the 1960s, self-immolation has entered the repertoire of political protest.

Acquaintances and Intimates

Arson can also be a form of interpersonal and intimate violence. It can be the outcome of a domestic or neighboring dispute, or a means of retaliating against a perceived grievance. Victims of revenge arsons tend to share a long history of conflict with the offender. Interpersonal firesetting may result from real or perceived sexual infidelity and lead to the destruction of the partner's personal effects or to direct injury. This type of fire is likely to be set in or around the home. Both men and women are victims of intimate arson.

Prevention

Education

Efforts to prevent the occurrence of firesetting behavior typically seek to educate children, parents, teachers, and other community actors. Educational programs are adapted to the child's developmental stage. They provide basic fire safety tips and familiarize children with the consequences of firesetting. In the United Kingdom, the Arson Prevention Bureau administers Kids Zone, an interactive resource for teachers, parents, and other educators to engage children on the subject of hoax calls, fire-play, and deliberate firesetting. Lesson plans include role playing, discussions, and thought experiments, to get children thinking about the consequences of their actions and encourage them to resist peer pressure. In the United States, the Federal Emergency Management Agency (FEMA) sponsors Arson Awareness Week to focus public attention on a different aspect of the problem each year, such as the risks presented by abandoned buildings or toy lighters.

Treatment

Treatment interventions are aimed at youth and adults who have already exhibited patterns of firesetting behavior. Cognitive behavioral therapy (CBT) is the most popular approach. Treatment is conducted with adult arsonists in psychiatric institutions and with juveniles and their families in a variety of settings. CBT allows offenders to recognize the circumstances leading to the firesetting and adopt alternative coping strategies. Other approaches involve anger management, self-esteem development, assertiveness training, and satiation and aversive techniques. Medication and confinement may be used as last resort. Today, treatment options are part of the traditional fire safety apparatus, though systematic evaluations of their effectiveness are still lacking. British fire and rescue services routinely refer young firesetters for psychological assessment and counseling.

Sociosituational Interventions

Other forms of intervention target the environment rather than the offenders by reducing opportunities for arson. The United States Fire Administration offers funding to community-based organizations to tackle arson at the local level, and many of these organizations' projects have been concerned with rehabilitating vacant buildings, keeping housing at near maximum occupancy, and ensuring that structures conform to fire safety standards. In Detroit, Halloween fires have been significantly reduced by increasing guardianship through the Angels' Night project. On the nights of October 29 through 31, 50,000 volunteers watch over Detroit's neighborhoods by turning on their porch lights, "adopting" abandoned buildings, and patrolling the city streets to deter offenders and report suspicious activity. In the United Kingdom, leaflets and toolkits published by the Arson Prevention Bureau provide schools and businesses with arson vulnerability assessment checklists and practical prevention advice, such as ways to secure premises, limit access to flammable material, and reduce the scope of any fire damage.

Though the arson problem remains underaddressed, current efforts are aimed at integrating the prevention activities of various agencies and increasing the awareness of the public. In addition, public perception that arson is often a victimless crime must be challenged.

Noemie Bouhana

See also Economic Costs of Victimization; Hate and Bias Crime; Intimate Partner Violence; Offender-Based Programs; School Crimes, Elementary Through High School; Terrorism/Terror Attack; Vandalism

Further Readings

Arson Prevention Bureau. (2001). *School arson: Education under threat.* London: Association of British Insurers.

Canter, D., & Almond, L. (2002). *The burning issue: Research and strategies for reducing arson.* London: Office of the Deputy Prime Minister.

Home Office. (1998). *Safer communities: Toward effective arson control. The report of the arson scoping study.* London: Author.

Kolko, D. J. (2001). Firesetters. In C. R. Hollin (Ed.), *Handbook of offender assessment and treatment* (pp. 391–413). New York: John Wiley.

Lowenstein, L. F. (2001). Recent research into arson (1992–2000): Incidence, causes and associated features, predictions, comparative studies, and prevention treatment. *The Police Journal, 74,* 108–119.

ASSAULT: SIMPLE AND AGGRAVATED

Violent victimizations have been decreasing in the United States since the mid-1990s; nevertheless, violent victimization continues to be prevalent in American society. Assaults are the most common violent crimes committed in America, and although incidents of assault are not necessarily lethal, the potential for them to cause irreversible harm is always present. To describe the nature of assault, this entry explores the difference between assault and battery, the characteristics of simple and aggravated assault, and what groups are most likely to be victims of simple and aggravated assault in the United States.

Assault and Battery

The terms *assault* and *battery* are consistently used in conjunction with one another. Although the terms are often used interchangeably, they are, in reality, two separate offenses. While battery is the actual use of force against another person, assault is defined as attempted battery or intentionally frightening another person into believing a battery will occur. Since a battery cannot happen without the assault, the acts are merged together to hold the individual responsible for only one crime, the battery. It should be noted that some states (i.e., New York) allow for a charge of an attempted assault; however, most recognize that an "attempt to attempt a battery" is an absurd charge.

For an assault to occur, there must be specific elements present: intent, the act, the victim, and in some instances, the ability. For an act to be labeled an assault, the intent to commit a battery or to cause fear of bodily harm must be established. The battery itself does not have to be proven, but simply one person's violation of another's personal space. In addition, an act must take place that establishes an actor's having intended and/or taken significant steps toward committing the battery. In the case of establishing fear, words alone are not enough to establish an attempted battery; physical gestures must be used in conjunction with the words to support the assumption that bodily harm is imminent. The victim does not need to be aware that the crime is about to occur for police to establish assault; however, in cases of establishing fear, the victim must be made aware of the possibility of bodily harm (i.e., a threat). Finally, the ability to a commit an assault must be proven in many states.

Simple and Aggravated Assault

Although assault is legally defined as the attempt to commit battery, criminal justice agencies often combine the terms *assault* and *battery* into a single statute. Thus, the term *assault* has come to have a range of meanings, which vary from a threat of harm to a serious violent attack. According to the Uniform Crime Reporting (UCR) Program, assault is the unlawful attack by one person on another. Assault is typically broken down into two types: simple and aggravated. Simple assault can be defined as an attack or attempted attack that causes minimal to no harm and does not include the use of a weapon. For instance, one person's spitting in another person's face may be considered assault; however, in most instances, assaults typically involve minor injuries such as bruising. Simple assaults are misdemeanor offenses. Cases that result in no bodily harm are typically classified as Class C misdemeanors, and conviction typically results in the payment of a fine. In the cases in which some form of bodily injury has occurred, simple assault is classified as a Class A or B misdemeanor for which conviction may result in jail time; however, such convictions typically result in probation and/or a payment of fines.

In contrast, the UCR Program defines aggravated assault as the unlawful attack of an individual with the intent to inflict severe or aggravated bodily injury. In most instances of aggravated assault, a weapon is used or hospitalization is required due to serious injury. Although both the UCR Program and National Crime Victimization Survey (NCVS) data characterize aggravated assault as an assault with a deadly weapon, the NCVS data only define an assault as aggravated if the act resulted in two or more days of hospitalization. Since aggravated assaults are committed with such violent intent, they are considered felonies, which may result in imprisonment upon conviction. Depending on the state and the circumstances surrounding the aggravated assault, an individual convicted of aggravated assault may receive a sentence ranging anywhere from 5 to 90 years. For instance, the guidelines established under Georgia state law allows for a sentence of 5 to 20 years in prison, depending on factors including but not limited to the intent of the assault, if there was a weapon used, and the person the act was committed against (e.g., a police officer or a teacher).

On average, assaults represent the vast majority of violent victimization reports. Of the 5.2 million violent acts committed against individuals in 2007, approximately 84% of those incidents were the result of an assault. Although aggravated assault is the more serious of the crimes, simple assaults occur at higher rates than aggravated assaults. The NCVS reports that there are approximately three times as many simple as aggravated assaults. In 2007, there was an estimated rate of 13.9 per 1,000 simple assaults, compared to 3.4 per 1,000 aggravated assaults. Although there are fewer aggravated than simple assaults, more than 800,000 aggravated assaults were reported to the police. This estimate, however, is most likely an underestimate. Although victims are more likely to report aggravated assaults than simple assaults, only about 62% of aggravated assaults are reported to the police. In reality, the NCVS estimates that more than 1.2 million individuals are victims of aggravated assault.

Although the actual number of assaults that annually occur within the United States may not be determinable, who is most likely to be a perpetrator of an assault has been established. Typically, offenders are male, between the ages of 15 and 34, and of a lower socioeconomic status.

Victims of Simple and Aggravated Assault

Simple and aggravated assaults cross all socioeconomic, cultural, and geographic boundaries; however, certain populations are disproportionately represented in simple and aggravated assault data. Hence, some groups are more vulnerable to the risk of victimization through assault than others. There are a number of factors that influence who will be a victim of assault. According to the NCVS, Blacks are more likely than Whites to be a victim of an aggravated assault. For instance, in 2007, the rate of victimization for Blacks was higher than that of Whites. However, Whites were only slightly more likely to report being a victim of a simple assault. Interestingly, the NCVS reported that individuals reporting two or more races had significantly higher rates for simple and aggravated assaults than did Whites or Blacks. When taking ethnicity into consideration, Hispanics have a higher rate of both simple and aggravated assaults compared to non-Hispanics.

The 2007 data also revealed that males are more likely than females to be the victims of both simple and aggravated assaults. In 2007, the rates of simple and aggravated assaults for males were 14.5 and 4.5 per 1,000, respectively, compared to assault rates of females of 13.2 and 2.4. Males, in general, are more likely to be assaulted by strangers, while females are more likely to be victimized by someone they know; both adolescent and elderly males are also more likely to be assaulted by someone they know. Consistent with the literature, the NCVS determined that individuals under 25 years of age are more likely to be assaulted than those who are over 25. For instance, in 2007 the rates of simple and aggravated assaults for adults between the ages of 20 and 24 were 7.5 and 21.2 per 1,000, respectively, compared to 4.8 and 15.3 per 1,000 for adults between the ages of 25 and 34. Juveniles aged 16–19 had rates of assaults similar to those of adults under 25 for aggravated assaults; however, the juvenile rate for simple assaults was much higher, 34.2 per 1,000.

Income and marital status are also factors in determining if an individual will be a victim of assault. Those living below the poverty line are more likely to experience assaults. In addition, single and divorced individuals have higher rates of assaults than those who are married or widowed.

Further, geographic location plays a role in whether an individual is likely to be victimized. For instance, individuals residing in the West are more likely to be victims of simple and aggravated assault than those residing in other areas in the United States. In addition, individuals living in urban areas are more likely to be assault victims than those living in either suburban or rural areas.

The factors listed above can contribute to risk of being a victim of simple and/or aggravated assault, especially when they intersect with one another. Nevertheless, the vulnerability to assault is not endemic to a single group. Since assaults are typically spontaneous acts that often escalate in the heat of passion, anyone can be a victim of simple or aggravated assault regardless of demographic, cultural, or geographic factors.

Tammy S. Garland

See also National Crime Victimization Survey (NCVS); National Incident-Based Reporting System (NIBRS); Uniform Crime Reporting (UCR) Program

Further Readings

Alvarez, A., & Bachman, R. (2008). *Violence: The enduring problem.* Thousand Oaks, CA: Sage.

Catalano, S. M. (2006). *Criminal victimization, 2005* (BJS Bulletin). Washington, DC: U.S. Department of Justice.

Lippman, M. (2007). *Contemporary criminal law: Concepts, cases, and controversies.* Thousand Oaks, CA: Sage.

Smallenger, F. (2004). *Criminology today: An integrative introduction.* Upper Saddle River, NJ: Pearson/ Prentice Hall.

U.S. Bureau of Justice Statistics. (2003). *Criminal victimization in the United States.* Retrieved November 24, 2008, from http://www.ojp.usdoj.gov/ bjs/pub/pdf/cvus03.pdf

B

BANK AND CASH-IN-TRANSIT ROBBERY

It is important to examine highly specific types of crime, because each type has a unique criminal opportunity structure. Thus robbery is a general category of crime that includes several distinct variants; for instance, robbery occurs on streets, at post offices, at fast-food restaurants, and near automated teller machines. Although crimes at these locations all fall under the label of robbery, each crime involves different types of offenders, victims, and techniques. Therefore, it is essential to examine particular subtypes of robbery rather than robbery in general. To that end, two specific types of robbery are explored here: bank robbery and cash-in-transit robbery. Although these crimes are relatively rare, understanding them is important because they invoke fear in the community at large and sometimes result in violence.

According to the FBI's Uniform Crime Reporting Program handbook, robbery is a theft or larceny aggravated by the threat or use of force. Accordingly, bank robbery is a theft or larceny aggravated by the threat or use of force that occurs *at bank branches operated by financial institutions with federally insured deposits.* Similarly, cash-in-transit robbery refers to a theft or larceny aggravated by the threat or use of force targeted *at armored financial couriers and their guards.* Overall, bank robbery and cash-in-transit robbery are similar crimes in some respects.

For instance, both offenses involve highly secure targets that contain large sums of money. Nevertheless, these offenses also require distinctive techniques and offer unique advantages and disadvantages to different types of offenders. For these reasons, this entry discusses the characteristics of each offense, the types of offenders involved, and crime prevention strategies.

Bank Robbery Trends and Characteristics

Roughly 2 out of every 100 robberies in the Unites States occur at a bank. Among all the different types of robbery, then, bank robbery is rare. Thus, few people will ever actually have a firsthand experience as a victim or witness of bank robbery. Nevertheless, multiple sources show that bank robbery has been a mounting problem over the last few decades. In fact, some statistics suggest that bank robbery is the fastest growing type of robbery in the United States, especially in many metropolitan areas. For instance, Chicago experienced a sharp increase in the number of bank robberies during the 1990s that prompted the development of a citywide bank robbery initiative. Despite some fluctuations in the United States for certain years, the overall pattern suggests that bank robbery counts have continually climbed through the 1990s with a current average of about 7,000 incidents each year.

Increases in bank robbery have been explained by several factors. Some argue that the expansion of bank minibranches and extension of banking hours have enhanced target access for many potential robbers. In addition, bank robbery is one of the most lucrative forms of robbery. On average, bank robbers in the United States enjoy an average payoff of about $4,000 per heist. What is more, bank robbers can expect to keep their large haul, given that 80% of the money stolen in bank robberies is not recovered. Finally, bank robbery can be completed quickly (often in less than 3 minutes) and is perpetrated against targets perceived to be low risk.

There are several reasons robbers might perceive banks as low-risk targets. First, banks have highly predictable interior designs and standard operating procedures. Therefore, robbers enter a bank with a good idea of what to expect from both the physical environment and bank staff. Second, bank robbers expect victim compliance during a robbery. With bank employees trained to ensure safety during a robbery, bank robbers usually face little or no resistance. Finally, bank robbers may believe they will not be caught. This belief, however, is not entirely confirmed. Although most bank robberies are initially successful, bank robbery has one of the highest clearance rates of all types of crime. In fact, nearly two thirds of bank robberies are solved within one month. The risk of arrest, however, declines drastically as time elapses after the incident.

Bank robbery is distinguished from other forms of crime in several respects. One of these is the reporting of the crime, as U.S. banks are *required* by the Federal Deposit Insurance Corporation (FDIC) to report robbery. This requirement likely explains why bank robbery is one of the most fully reported crimes in the United States. In addition, bank robbery has a remarkably high arrest clearance rate—about 80%, according to the FBI. In fact, a high percentage of bank robbers are caught on the same day of the robbery at or near the scene of the crime. Avoiding the threat of immediate apprehension is difficult because bank robbery is reported quickly, often occurs during daylight hours, and is observable by multiple witnesses and security cameras. Finally, bank robbery differs from other crimes because of its high conviction rate. In 1990, for instance, 93% of bank robbers tried in the United States were convicted and sentenced.

Studies show that the majority of bank robberies occur in cities. However, recent trends suggest that bank robberies in smaller towns are now on the rise. Specifically, the portion of bank robberies that occurred in nonurban settings increased from 20% in 1996 to 33% in 2002.

Bank robberies appear to follow clear temporal patterns. Friday seems to be the most popular day of the week for committing bank robbery—perhaps because many bank branches have extended hours on this day. Research also shows that bank robberies cluster around certain times. Most bank robberies occur around morning and midday hours—usually between the hours of 10 a.m. and 3 p.m. Bank robbers might favor this period because banks are often less busy during these hours, meaning fewer customers to contend with during a robbery.

The use of weapons in bank robbery has received considerable research attention. Studies from both the United States and Australia suggest that the role of weapons in bank robbery has changed over the past few decades. In the United States during the 1980s, firearms were a common "tool" used in a high percentage of bank robberies. Furthermore, bank robbers in Australia often used pistols in the early 1980s, but opted for longarms near the end of the decade. After the 1980s, however, bank robbers started using fewer weapons during heists. In the United States, some reports claim that weapon use has become uncommon and is still declining. In Australia, bank robbers have begun abandoning firearms in favor of a new weapon—intimidation through sheer numbers (i.e., gangs of bank robbers). In fact, from 1998 to 2002, roughly 62% of bank robberies perpetrated by gangs of offenders did not involve a weapon.

Because robbers expect bank staff to surrender money without hesitation, many of them may feel little need to be armed. Nevertheless, some bank robbers still use firearms or other weapons. Interestingly, research shows that bank robbers who do use weapons are not likely to inflict physical harm upon victims. One study of 281 separate bank robberies revealed that there were only 2 fatalities and 19 injuries by gunfire, even though 391 of the 500 bank robbers involved were armed. The sight of a weapon will intimidate most victims during a bank robbery; therefore, armed offenders likely do not have to resort to violence to gain compliance.

Characteristics of Bank Robbers

Bank robbery is unique in that convicted bank robbers are often subject to social and criminal background investigations from law enforcement, courts, corrections, and probation. Data from these sources can be used to create a demographic sketch of bank robbers. Bank robbers are typically young adult males. Specifically, one study found that about 96% of convicted bank robbers were male, and roughly 71% were between the ages of 16 and 30. Although bank robbers are usually young, they are often older than other types of robbers. Regarding race, 56% of the sample were Black, while 43% were White. Furthermore, most bank robbers are not well educated—many dropped out of high school, while others were not educated beyond the eighth grade. Finally, a large portion of the convicted bank robbers in this study were unemployed at the time of their crime. Therefore, it is not surprising that most robbers cite the need for cash as the primary motivation for their offending.

Bank robbers can be classified as professionals or amateurs. Overall, most bank robberies are considered the work of amateurs. Amateur bank robbers are usually unarmed, undisguised, unprepared (i.e., did little planning prior to the offense), and alone during the heist. Furthermore, although most bank robberies occur during morning or midday hours, some amateurs even pick inopportune times to offend (i.e., during peak business hours when banks are full of customers). By contrast, professional bank robbers carefully plan their heists, offend in groups at opportune times, design escape routes, use disguises, obscure surveillance cameras, and use weapons or verbal threats. These practices increase professionals' likelihood of success and netting greater monetary payoffs than their amateur counterparts. Distinguishing between bank robberies committed by amateurs and those committed by professionals could help banks assess the risks of bank robbery and identify the most appropriate crime prevention strategies.

Repeat Bank Robberies

Volumes of research show that certain people and places are prone to repeat victimization. Not surprisingly, some banks are repeatedly targeted for robbery. One study of bank robbery in the United Kingdom confirms this claim, finding that after any robbery, about 50% of robbed banks are targeted again within a 3-year period. The same study also revealed that many of these repeats occurred soon after the initial robbery—with about one third of them taking place within 2 months. In all, then, repeat bank robberies are not uncommon and the risk is fairly immediate.

Some bank robbers will target the same branch if an earlier robbery was successful. In fact, research shows that the probability of a repeat bank robbery is roughly predictable from the average sum taken from prior robberies at the same branch. A successful robbery, however, does not always ensure another lucrative "hit." Researchers claim that some repeat bank robberies are actually less successful because branches have added security upgrades and provided additional staff training in response to an earlier incident. There are several reasons, besides being labeled a known success, why some banks are repeatedly robbed while others are not: Some banks are more vulnerable to repeats due to their location, business practices, and security measures.

Responses to Bank Robbery

Banks have implemented numerous measures to reduce the risk of robbery. One of the more popular and more promising strategies is hiring uniformed security guards. For instance, a study of more than 200 banking offices across several states revealed that the presence of uniformed guards reduced the risk of bank robbery by almost one robbery per year for more robbery-prone branches. The same study, however, showed that neither bullet-proof barriers nor security cameras significantly deterred bank robbers.

In other areas, some banks have also responded to robbery by keeping less cash on the premises, installing security alarms, banning disguises, offering rewards, using dye packs that stain stolen money, and using traceable bait money. More specifically, the Chicago Police Department teamed up with the FBI to conduct security seminars with more than 250 bank employees across the city. An evaluation of this initiative showed that, together with increased law enforcement efforts, the number of bank robberies in Chicago declined substantially in the months following the seminar. Given the variety of ways to reduce bank robbery, more evaluations are needed to determine which strategies hold the greatest potential for effectiveness.

Cash-in-Transit Robbery

While some robbers target banks, others prefer robbing cash-in-transit vehicles. There are two main methods for committing cash-in-transit robbery: stopping and then attacking a mobile transit vehicle, or robbing drivers or guards during delivery or collection. One study from the United Kingdom showed that most robbers preferred the latter method due to the difficulty of stopping a moving vehicle. A drawback of robbing guards "across the pavement," however, is the uncertainty about how much money they possess.

Cash-in-transit robbery has both advantages and disadvantages compared to other types of robbery. On one hand, it is attractive because robbers can net large payoffs without facing the threat of being "trapped" inside a bank or other commercial establishment. On the other hand, it is challenging because robbers must directly confront armed guards or overtake a heavily armored vehicle. Given these added challenges, cash-in-transit robbery seems to attract more experienced and skilled offenders.

Accordingly, some researchers have examined the differences in "professionalism" of cash-in-transit robbers and other types of robbers (i.e., those who target banks, post offices, or shops). Overall, these researchers have found that cash-in-transit robbers appear more "professional" in several aspects. First, they are often more experienced than other types of robbers (i.e., older and more likely to have been in prison). Second, they are more prepared—they are more likely to spend time planning the robbery, wear disguises or special clothing, utilize "tips" from other offenders, and monitor targets prior to the heist. Finally, cash-in-transit robbers take extra steps to ensure control during the robbery, by using violence or weapons and avoiding drugs and alcohol beforehand.

Justin Heinonen

See also Bystander Intervention; Closed-Circuit Television; Crime Prevention Through Environmental Design; Guns and Victimization; Repeat Victimization, Theories of; Robbery; Situational Crime Prevention

Further Readings

Borzycki, M. (2003). Bank robbery in Australia. *Trends and Issues in Crime and Criminal Justice*, no. 253. Canberra: Australian Institute of Criminology.

Carroll, P., & Loch, R. (1997). The Chicago bank robbery initiative. *FBI Law Enforcement Bulletin, 66*, 9–18.

Felson, M., & Clarke, R. V. (1998). *Opportunity makes the thief: Practical theory for crime prevention.* Police Research Series, No. 98. London: Home Office.

Gill, M. (2001). The craft of robbers of cash-in-transit vans: Crimes facilitators and the entrepreneurial approach. *International Journal of Sociology, 29*, 277–291.

Hannan, T. (1982). Bank robberies and bank security precautions. *Journal of Legal Studies, 11*, 83–92.

Haran, J. F., & Martin, J. M. (1984). The armed urban bank robber: A profile. *Federal Probation, 48*, 47–53.

Lamm Weisel, D. (2007). *Bank robbery.* Problem Guides Series, No. 48. Washington, DC: U.S. Department of Justice, Office of Community Oriented Policing Services.

Matthews, R., Pease, C., & Pease, K. (2001). Repeated bank robbery: Theme and variations. In G. Farrell & K. Pease (Eds.), *Repeat victimization: Vol. 12. Crime prevention studies* (pp. 153–164). Monsey, NY: Criminal Justice Press.

BATTERED-CHILD SYNDROME

Battered-child syndrome was the first term used by physicians in the United States to describe an array of symptoms in children physically injured or severely neglected by their caregivers. The term *battered-child syndrome* is now seldom used; terms encompassing types of abuse, such as *child maltreatment* and *child abuse*, and up-to-date medical terms, such as *shaken baby syndrome* and *nonaccidental trauma*, are more commonly employed. In the legal sector, battered-child syndrome has had limited use as an affirmative defense for parricide. However, in a historical context, the establishment of the term remains as a significant milestone in the treatment of victimized children. This entry begins with a brief definition of battered-child syndrome, then provides the historical perspective of the term's impact on the treatment and protection of battered children, a summary of U.S. statistics of child maltreatment, and the prognosis for battered children.

Definition

Battered-child syndrome is used to denote the severe physical abuse or neglect of a child, typically by a caregiver. Common manifestations are broken bones, bruises, lacerations, burns, head trauma, radiological evidences of repetitive fractures, and signs of malnutrition. Telling indications of such abuse include the caregiver's delay in seeking medical treatment for the injured child and/or giving an account of events not matching the child's injuries, as well as the child's having cigarette burns, unexplained unconsciousness, and/or bruises shaped like a fist, hand, or belt.

Historical Perspectives

Historically, childhood has been a harsh and perilous life stage. Less than 150 years ago, children were considered property and could be treated as their parents saw fit. At best, childhood was seen as a time to break the incorrigibility of children and purge evil from their hearts.

A historic U.S. court case of child abuse involved a young girl, Mary Ellen Wilson, who was being beaten and starved. In 1874, Child Protective Services did not exist; thus, Mary Ellen Wilson was represented in court by the Society of the Prevention of Cruelty to Animals. The case created a great deal of public outrage and resulted in the founding of the Society for the Prevention of Cruelty to Children. Subsequently, due to child advocacy efforts, positive progress was begun in the treatment of children. Yet the claims by these groups regarding the problem of child abuse lacked credibility. Moreover, professional accountability, such as mandatory reporting laws to prevent further abuse of children, were not yet established, leaving the majority of abused children unprotected.

"The Battered-Child Syndrome," by C. Henry Kempe and his colleagues, was published in the *Journal of the American Medical Association* in 1962, providing the much-needed recognition of the societal ill of maltreated children. Acknowledgement by the medical profession of the prevalence of life-threatening physical abuse and neglect of children was chiefly due to advances in radiology, namely diagnostic X-rays. Physical abuse of children became detectable through the X-rays' documentation of repetitive damage to children's bones, which told stories of severe abuse and provided undeniable evidence that demanded a diagnosis.

Battered-child syndrome, as presented by Kempe and his colleagues, consisted of three major components. The first element was the clinically observed manifestations of physical abuse and neglect (e.g., broken bones, bruises, head injuries, malnourishment). The second, a key diagnostic marker of battered-child syndrome, was a clear inconsistency between the caregiver's explanation of the child's physical injury and the clinical findings. Finally, the psychiatric condition of the batterer was noted as a crucial part of the syndrome. Child batterers were described as possibly suffering from psychosis, psychopathic disorders, low intelligence, alcoholism, and/or aggressive tendencies, and as having a history of childhood victimization.

The declared purpose for providing physicians with diagnostic criteria for battered-child syndrome was to guarantee that no repetition of the abuse occurred. The sway of Kempe and his colleagues and the poignant term *battered child* provided momentum for child advocacy groups. As a result, by the end of the 1960s, laws mandating that professionals report suspected cases of child abuse had been enacted in every U.S. state. In criminal court, however, unclear legislation concerning battered-child syndrome has hindered the use of the syndrome as an affirmative defense in cases of parricide committed by victimized juveniles.

Incidence of Battering

In the United States in 2006, according to national statistics, 905,000 children were reported victims of abuse or neglect, at a rate of 12 children per 1,000. The younger the child, the greater the risk, with children from birth to 1 year abused at a rate of 24 children per 1,000—double the average rate. An estimated 1,530 children died from abuse or neglect in 2006, and 78% of those killed were younger than 4 years old. These statistics are based on child abuse cases that were reported to social services agencies, investigated, and had sufficient evidence to meet the legal definition of abuse or neglect. While the true incidence of abuse is virtually impossible to determine, the data cited above are likely underestimates, as many professionals believe that many incidents of abuse and neglect are never reported to officials.

Prognosis

The prognosis for a battered child depends on whether the child survives his or her injuries, whether the injuries are permanent, and whether the child is protected from further trauma. Services that protect children often are needed to ensure the child's safety. The willingness of the caregivers to seek psychotherapy for the child that targets the effects of abuse, as well as the caregivers' participation in child–parent psychotherapy and psychoeducational parenting interventions, enhances the child's chances for recovery and decreases the likelihood of further abusive experiences.

Joan A. Reid

See also Child Abuse, Neglect, and Maltreatment; Cycle of Violence, Theory of; Family Violence; Mandatory Reporting Statutes; Shaken Baby Syndrome

Further Readings

deMause, L. (1998). The history of child abuse. *The Journal of Psychohistory, 25*(3), 1–13.

Heide, K. M., Boots, D. P., Alldredge, G., Donerly, B., & White, J. R. (2005). Battered child syndrome: An overview of case law and legislation. *Criminal Law Review, 41*(3), 219–239.

Kempe, C. H., Silverman, F. N., Steele, B. F., Droegemueller, W., & Silver, A. K. (1962). The battered-child syndrome. *Journal of the American Medical Association, 187*, 17–24.

U.S. Department of Health and Human Services, Administration on Children, Youth and Families. (2008). *Child maltreatment 2006.* Washington, DC: U.S. Government Printing Office.

BATTERED WOMAN SYNDROME

The term *battered woman syndrome* (BWS) was coined by Lenore Walker to describe the psychological impact of intimate partner violence (IPV) on women. Today BWS is best known for its use in expert testimony for battered women standing trial for the homicide of their abusive partners. Since the inception of the concept in the late 1970s, academic and legal understandings of it have advanced and it has faced immense criticism.

As a result of these critiques, *battering and its effects* is now commonly used in place of *battered woman syndrome.* This discussion begins by defining *battered woman syndrome* and outlining its use in the legal system, then provides a critical examination of the concept, and ends with the current use and understanding of BWS.

Definition

Walker coined the term *battered woman syndrome* after conducting a study of battered women in the late 1970s. In her 1984 book, *The Battered Woman Syndrome,* she describes the syndrome as a group of "psychological sequela" that victims develop from their experiences in abusive relationships. The definition of BWS has changed since it was first formulated by Walker, and there is not one consistent definition used throughout the literature, but it appears that most definitions of the term include a combination of the cycle of violence, learned helplessness, and posttraumatic stress disorder (PTSD).

Walker's term *cycle of violence* refers to the cyclical nature of abusive relationships as they move through three key phases. The cycle of violence begins with the "tension-building" stage. At this point, tension builds in the intimate relationship, but it does not result in violence. Next, the tension develops into violence at the "acute battering" stage. Following the battering, the abuser tries to make up for his actions in the "loving-contrition" stage that is commonly referred to as the "honeymoon" stage. The honeymoon stage is thought to encourage women to stay in battering relationships because they experience a decrease in violence or have nonviolent interactions with their abusers. From this perspective, abuse occurs in a cyclical manner, but the amount of time spent in each stage varies for each individual abusive situation. While the cyclical nature of violence is important to the definition of BWS, it is necessary to mention that the cycle of violence outlined above is not universally agreed upon by scholars of IPV. In addition to the cycle of violence, *learned helplessness* is also central to the definition of BWS. Following repeated abuse, some victims of IPV experience learned helplessness. After learning that their behavior does not prevent or control the violence, victims may stop trying to help themselves in their abusive situations. Learned helplessness is commonly used as an explanation for why some victims are not able to leave their abusers. Finally, the most recent addition to the definition of BWS is its connection to *posttraumatic stress disorder*. While BWS is not listed in the American Psychological Association's 1994 *Diagnostic and Statistical Manual of Mental Disorders* (DSM-IV), Walker suggests that based on the psychological symptoms of BWS, it should be considered a category of PTSD.

The definition of BWS is also dependent upon who is using the concept. For instance, a clinical psychologist may have a different understanding of BWS than someone involved in legal proceedings for a battered woman. Overall, even with varying definitions of and perspectives on BWS, it is generally characterized by the concepts of cycle of violence, learned helplessness, and its connection to PTSD, which all shed light on the ways IPV affects battered women.

Use in the Legal System

Historically, under the recommendation of their lawyers, battered women who were accused of killing their abusers either pled guilty to the offense or claimed insanity. It was not until the late 1970s that women who committed homicide while protecting themselves and/or their children against their abusive partners began to plead self-defense. At this time, the testimonies of experts, such as Walker and Julie Blackman, were introduced in order to help juries evaluate whether a battered woman's use of lethal force against her abusive partner was done in self-defense. Advocates for the use of expert testimony on BWS believed those judging battered women in the legal system might not fully understand IPV and, consequently, how victims perceive their abusive situations. Expert testimony on BWS allowed the defense to present information on IPV to the courtroom that might illuminate how an abusive situation could have had an impact on the defendant's options, choices, and actions.

Battered woman syndrome has commonly been mistaken as a legal defense for battered women who kill their abusers. BWS, though, is not an actual legal defense. It is a form of social framework testimony that can be presented in legal proceedings to help explain the actions of victims of IPV. Battered women who have killed their abusers while defending themselves, like others who have felt the need to defend themselves in a lethal manner, are able to plead traditional self-defense. However, although victims of IPV may plead self-defense, feminist scholars have critiqued the utility of self-defense for battered women. They suggest that self-defense is based on the "reasonable man" standard, which makes it difficult for women to effectively use self-defense pleas while on trial for killing their abusive partners. Battered women's cases may not appear to be typical self-defense cases because of the nature of IPV. Homicide involving an intimate partner, someone with whom the defendant shared a life and may have had children, is very different from homicide involving strangers or acquaintances. As a result of this problem, expert testimony on BWS was introduced as a way for the defense to educate the courtroom as to how the defendant perceived her abusive situation and why she felt the need to use lethal force against her intimate partner. While BWS is important to the claim of self-defense for victims of IPV, it is not the only form of support used by the defense. Typically, BWS is one part of a larger strategy to prove the actions of the battered woman were committed in self-defense.

Critiques

While BWS was introduced into the courtroom with the intent of helping juries understand the actions of women in abusive situations, it has been greatly criticized by both legal scholars and domestic violence scholars. One of the primary critiques of BWS has focused on the use of the word *syndrome*. The term *syndrome* presents an image of someone who is defective or ill. Instead of BWS being a way to help understand the effects of battering, some claim it depicts victims of IPV as pathological. Language such as this suggests there is something wrong with the victim and her actions, which is problematic to assume if she was just trying to survive her abusive situation. In addition, the term *syndrome* focuses the attention on the victim instead of on the abuser and his actions.

Another major critique of BWS is that it stereotypes battered women. Labeling the impact of abuse on women *battered woman syndrome* suggests there is one type of victim and one way that every battered woman responds. It creates the idea that some women are "real" battered women, while other women who do not measure up to the stereotype are not "real" battered women. In reality, battered women are a diverse group. Not only are women affected by abuse in different ways, but victims respond to abuse in a variety of ways (e.g., by leaving the abuser, staying with the abuser, leaving and coming back, and in some cases, lethally defending themselves against the abuse). To suggest that there is one type of battered woman overlooks the distinct experiences of victims and ignores women's agency. Furthermore, women's experiences of battering are affected by the context in which it occurs. While abuse transcends race and ethnicity, social class, gender, sexuality, religion, and culture, not all victims have the same experiences. For instance, the way a battered woman views her victimization and the resources that are available to her are dependent upon the context in which the abuse occurs. Instead of recognizing the diversity of victims and their unique experiences and responses, some scholars argue that BWS creates a stereotype of what a battered woman is and how she should respond.

Likewise, explaining their experience of learned helplessness can present a challenge to battered women standing trial for homicide, as in many cases, they may not be seen as exhibiting this part of the syndrome. A woman's defending herself and/or her children from her abusive partner is not perceived as the act of a helpless victim. This conflict between the actions of the victim and the notion of learned helplessness can be problematic. If BWS is understood as only applying to certain women who fit the stereotypical model of BWS, then women who violate this norm may not be viewed as eligible for a defense based on BWS.

Current Understandings and Use of Battered Woman Syndrome

Due to the critiques of the term *battered woman syndrome,* two phrases, *battering and its effects* and *the effects of battering,* are now being used in its place by many scholars, lawyers, and courts. These new terms acknowledge the impact of battering and, without the pitfalls of BWS, allow expert witnesses to present information on both the psychological effects and social context of abuse. While the term *battered woman syndrome* is still used in some settings, the movement to replace it with *battering and its effects* shows a growing understanding of the experiences of battered women.

Currently, expert testimony on battering and its effects may include a discussion of the nature of IPV, how IPV affects victims, the different ways victims respond to the abuse, and the context in which the abuse occurs. This kind of testimony can be presented in a general manner (e.g., by discussing the current academic understanding of IPV and the ways it affects victims) or a specific manner (e.g., by discussing the particular case framed within academic knowledge of IPV). While the particular rules surrounding the admissibility of expert testimony on BWS or battering and its effects vary by jurisdiction, it has now been allowed in courts in all U.S. states. The acceptance of expert testimony on battering and its effects shows an increased understanding of IPV within the legal system, but this does not guarantee that a victim standing trial for the death of her abuser will face a courtroom that understands her experiences as battered woman.

The use of expert testimony on battering and its effects has now been extended beyond cases of victims accused of killing their abusive partners in self-defense. This testimony has been utilized during both the sentencing process for battered women convicted of homicide and the clemency process for incarcerated victims. Furthermore, it is now recognized that battering may play a role in a variety of crimes committed by victims of IPV. In some states, testimony on battering and its effects has been presented in the defense of battered women for non-homicide-related crimes. In addition, testimony on battering and its effects is utilized in other legal situations, including prosecuting men for IPV or the homicide of their intimate partners and child custody cases.

Kate Luther

See also Battered-Child Syndrome; Cycle of Violence, Theory of; Intimate Partner Violence; Posttraumatic Stress Disorder (PTSD); Psychological and Behavioral Consequences of Victimization

Further Readings

Downs, D. A. (1996). *More than victims: Battered woman, the syndrome society, and the law.* Chicago: University of Chicago Press.

Dutton, M. A. (1996). Critique of the "battered woman syndrome" model. Harrisburg: VAWnet, a project of the National Resource Center on Domestic Violence/ Pennsylvania Coalition Against Domestic Violence. Retrieved October 28, 2008, from http://www.vawnet.org

Ferraro, K. J. (2003). The words change, but the melody lingers: The persistence of the battered woman syndrome in criminal cases involving battered women. *Violence Against Women, 9*(1), 110–129.

Lemon, N. K. D. (2001). *Domestic violence law.* St. Paul, MN: West Group.

Osthoff, S., & Maguigan, H. (2004). Explaining without pathologizing: Testimony on battering and its effects. In D. R. Loseke, R. J. Gelles, & M. M. Cavanaugh (Eds.), *Current controversies on family violence* (pp. 225–240). Thousand Oaks, CA: Sage.

Schneider, E. M. (2000). *Battered women and feminist lawmaking.* New Haven, CT: Yale University Press.

Walker, L. E. (1979). *The battered woman.* New York: Harper & Row.

Walker, L. E. (1984). *The battered woman syndrome.* New York: Springer.

BEREAVEMENT PROCESS

Following a homicide, the victim's survivor may be in a state of crisis. This entry discusses the bereavement process in general. It then describes a typology of patterns, based on the circumstances of the homicide and the lifestyles of the victim and survivor, that complicate the bereavement process of these "homicide survivors."

Most homicides are sudden and unexpected, and thus the significant others of a homicide victim have no opportunity to prepare for such a death, as they might have if an elderly family member was terminally ill. In the latter situation, significant others have an opportunity to do anticipatory grieving. Anticipatory grieving refers to the preparatory process individuals undergo when the death of someone close to them is expected, to temper the effect of the death. The anticipation of the death allows individuals to find coping mechanisms to assist them in dealing with the death. Homicide victims do not have the luxury of anticipatory grieving, which often results in a more difficult grieving process. Research has suggested that it is easier for individuals to cope with a death that is expected than with one that is sudden and earlier in the life course.

Stages of the Grieving Process

Elisabeth Kübler-Ross has organized the grieving process into four stages: (1) shock and denial, (2) anger, (3) isolation, and (4) acceptance or recovery. The first stage, shock and denial, begins immediately after the survivor is notified of the death. In an attempt to use defense mechanisms to cope with the news of the homicide, the survivor may deny that the news of the death is true. The survivor may avoid the situation and resist any information about the death. This reaction is not long-lasting and serves as a coping mechanism for the survivor. The second stage of the grieving process is anger. During this stage, the survivor releases his or her anger and frustration on anyone or anything with which he or she comes in contact. In this stage, victims experience difficulty dealing with the anger and often do not know where to direct this emotion. This anger may be internalized, with the survivor blaming himself or herself for the homicide, or the survivor may project the anger onto the offender, onto society in general, or even onto the medical staff that was unable to save the victim. The third stage, isolation, leads the survivor to feelings of aloneness. Survivors may feel that no one could possibly understand and, therefore, that they have no one to rely on through this process. Survivors may also have difficulty knowing how to deal with others. These two sets of feelings often lead to withdrawal from friends, family, and work. After the survivor has experienced these three stages, he or she begins to return to normal routines. This is known as the acceptance or recovery stage. While the experience of the death does not completely leave the individual, the survivor recognizes that life must continue.

These stages do not follow a specific timetable for all survivors. For some, the process may occur quickly, but for others, it may take years. Some survivors may regress into previous stages before reaching acceptance. Unfortunately, the bereavement process may be slowed because of the involvement of the criminal justice system. Homicide cases and trials can take years to unfold, prolonging survivors' recovery process. Although there is not extensive research on these survivors, the research that does exist suggests that the intensity of the feelings resulting from the homicide does decrease over time and eventually survivors experience a typical recovery pattern.

Survivors' Response Patterns

L. John Key noted that survivors respond to homicides differently depending on the type of homicide. He developed a typology, based on the type of homicide and the lifestyle and social context of the victim and survivor, to describe these response patterns. The five types of homicide he identified are (1) the alcohol- or other drug-related homicide, (2) the domestic violence homicide, (3) the gang-related homicide, (4) the isolated sudden homicide, and (5) the serial murder. The special circumstances of each of these homicides determine the survivors' responses to the event, and these responses may complicate their bereavement process.

The alcohol- or other drug-related homicide survivor pattern often involves survivors who had some knowledge of the victim's substance use or involvement in trafficking. With this knowledge, survivors may have anticipated that the victim would be involved in dangerous situations, and therefore may have been somewhat prepared for the potential loss of the victim. Sometimes these survivors may even feel a sense of relief once the event has occurred.

The domestic violence homicide survivor pattern may involve survivors' feeling guilty for not intervening when the early evidence of abuse appeared. These survivors may blame themselves, believing that had they intervened, their loved one would still be alive.

The gang-related homicide survivor pattern can be characterized by survivors' awareness that this homicide was a possibility. Although the survivors may have expected this event, they do not feel as though they had any control over the event, in contrast to the domestic violence homicide survivor. Gang-related homicide survivors recognize that the victim may have been a homicide offender

in the past and that it was just a matter of time before it was their loved one's turn.

Unlike the previous three types of homicide, the isolated sudden homicide and the serial murder are both completely unexpected. In these two instances, the survivors experience the bereavement process described earlier. While Key's typologies are not exhaustive, they do provide a framework for understanding how survivors respond differently to homicide.

Support for the Survivor

A critical element of the bereavement process is providing support for the survivor. This support should be initiated at the very beginning of the bereavement process, when the survivor is notified of the homicide. A healthy support system can assist with a multitude of issues facing the survivor throughout the grieving process. Counseling and homicide support groups are excellent sources of support for the survivor, as these services address the survivor's immediate and long-term needs.

Research suggests that significant others of homicide victims eventually reach a typical bereavement process, but due to special circumstances (such as the lack of anticipatory grieving, type of homicide, and background of the victim and survivor), the process differs across survivors.

Kristin Swartz

See also Death Notification; Domestic Violence; Gangs and Victimization; Homicide, Victim Advocacy Groups; Homicide and Murder; Psychological and Behavioral Consequences of Victimization; Secondary Victims of Homicide; Victim Support Groups

Further Readings

Horne, C. (2003). Families of homicide victims: Service Utilization patterns of extra- and intrafamilial homicide survivors. *Journal of Family Violence, 18,* 75–82.

Key, L. J. (1992). A working typology of grief among homicide survivors. In R. C. Cervantes (Ed.), *Substance abuse and gang violence.* Newbury Park, CA: Sage.

Kübler-Ross, E. (1997). *On death and dying.* New York: Macmillan.

BRADY BILL

The Brady Handgun Violence Prevention Act (hereafter the Brady law), which became effective on February 28, 1994, is the most significant piece of federal firearms control legislation passed in the United States since the Gun Control Act of 1968. This entry provides a brief overview of the Brady law, discusses the manner in which the law is designed to reduce gun violence, presents statistical data on the number of persons denied handguns during the first year of the law's operation, and ends with a brief comment on the most widely publicized study examining the effects of the Brady law on adult homicide.

Overview of the Brady Law

During its first 4½ years, the Brady law imposed a waiting period of 5 business days before an individual could purchase a handgun from a federally licensed firearms dealer. The law also required federal dealers to check with law enforcement authorities to see if the prospective buyers were disqualified under federal law from buying a gun, especially whether they had been convicted of a felony. The waiting period requirement was dropped after November 29, 1998, and the law's central gun-control mechanism became an instant background check on persons seeking to purchase guns of any kind, not just handguns, from federal dealers. Initially, the Brady law exempted the 18 states that already had their own gun-purchase background checks in place before 1994, but introduced new background checks into the remaining 32 states, which included about 46% of the U.S. population. Nine states originally classified as Brady states subsequently met alternative requirements, usually by implementing a permit to purchase or instant check system, and were reclassified as "Brady alternative" states.

How the Law Is Supposed to Reduce Criminal Violence

Supporters of the Brady law maintain that the law will reduce homicide by reducing the share of violent crimes resulting in death. The most clear-cut way the Brady law is meant to accomplish this goal is by denying convicted criminals access to guns through licensed gun dealers. The required background check on prospective gun buyers provided a system by which the dealers could know whether the prospective buyer is legally prohibited from purchasing a gun under previously existing gun law. The record check would at a minimum scan computerized criminal history files and also make use of records, of varying degrees of completeness, concerning other categories of persons prohibited from acquiring guns.

During the first year of Brady's operation, about 49% of denials were for a criminal record, 39% were for administrative reasons (due to delays in accessing records), 8% were for traffic offenses, and less than 5% were for other reasons (involving ineligible categories or due to restraining orders). Excluding the presumably temporary administrative denials and erroneous traffic offense denials, 91% of denials were for criminal convictions.

Despite the large number of convicted felons denied handguns from licensed gun dealers, critics have remained skeptical about the Brady law's potential to reduce violence levels, pointing out its numerous shortcomings. First, it only restricts gun acquisitions through licensed gun dealers. The best available evidence indicates that about 73% of gun acquisitions by felons are made via routes other than purchases from retail outlets, such as theft or purchases from friends and relatives. Second, with respect to the 27% of criminals who, pre-Brady, acquired guns from retail dealers, an unknown but presumably nonnegligible share could also obtain guns from unlicensed sellers or licensees willing to ignore the law by using phony identification documents to avoid being identified as a disqualified person, or by using a "straw man" without disqualifying attributes to make the purchase on behalf of the real buyer.

Former president Bill Clinton and many lesser proponents of the Brady law have cited estimates of the number of denials as measures of the law's effectiveness. It is unclear, however, whether a large number of denials can be used as a measure of the law's success. Certainly, if the law is effective, it should lead to a large share of convicted criminals who seek to buy guns from dealers somehow being blocked. Yet a large number of denials could be seen as a failure of the law's deterrence role, since it denotes that large numbers of criminals attempted to get guns from dealers irrespective of the law. In any event, the fact that a criminal was blocked from buying a gun from a dealer does not imply that he or she was prevented from acquiring a gun from any source.

The Law's Effects on Violence

The most widely cited evaluation of the Brady law concluded that its implementation was not associated with any one-time drop in adult homicide or suicide, except for suicides with firearms of those age 55 and older.

Tomislav Kovandzic

See also Crime Prevention; Guns and Victimization; Homicide and Murder

Further Readings

Jacobs, J. B., & Potter, K. A. (1995). Keeping guns out of the "wrong" hands: The Brady law and the limits of regulation. *Journal of Criminal Law and Criminology, 86*, 93–120.

Ludwig, J., & Cook, P. J. (2000). Homicide and suicide rates associated with implementation of the Brady Handgun Violence Prevention Act. *Journal of the American Medical Association, 284*, 585–591.

U.S. Bureau of Justice Statistics. (1999). *Presale handgun checks: The Brady interim period, 1994–1998* (NCJ 175034). Washington, DC: U.S. Government Printing Office.

U.S. Congressional Research Service. (1994). *Brady Handgun Violence Prevention Act* (CRS Report for Congress, Report 94–14 GOV). Washington, DC: Library of Congress.

U.S. General Accounting Office. (1996). Gun control: Implementation of the Brady Handgun Violence Prevention Act (GAO Report GAO/GGD-96–22). Washington, DC: U.S. Government Printing Office.

BRITISH CRIME SURVEY (BCS)

The British Crime Survey (BCS) is one of the longest standing national victimization surveys, although second to the U.S. National Crime Victimization Survey (NCVS) in this respect. Like other victimization surveys, it counts crimes both reported and not reported to the police, draws on victims' accounts to provide a picture of crime, and collects information to show which social groups are most vulnerable to victimization. This entry describes some main features of the BCS, outlines some of the changes that have been made to the survey, and points to some of its most important findings.

Main Features

The BCS was first conducted in 1982. It was then repeated more or less biennially until 2001, when it went onto a continuous interviewing cycle. The name British Crime Survey is something of a misnomer, as the survey only covers England and Wales. (Scotland has had a less regular series of surveys.)

The survey is carried out by the U.K. Home Office, which is responsible for analysis and publication of results. Its findings are now part of official crime statistics, along with offenses recorded by the police. This was not the case earlier on, when BCS results and police statistics were released as separate entities, giving rise to some confusion about how the two crime measures related to each other.

The BCS sample comprises those in private households age 16 or older. One person per household is interviewed (unlike in the NCVS). The respondent reports on crimes that can be seen as affecting the household as a whole (burglary, for instance). For personal crime such as assault, respondents report only on their own experiences. The survey has a "recall period" of one year (unlike the NCVS, which measures victimization over the preceding 6 months). The survey is cross-sectional, with no panel survey element as in the NCVS. BCS fieldwork has been subcontracted to private sector companies. These have changed over time, but the changes have been less frequent in recent years. Recognition of "company effects" was one factor here. Since 2001, BMRB Social Research has been the fieldwork contractor.

The survey collects extensive social and demographic information about respondents, including aspects of their lifestyle. In addition, census information is attached to the BCS to give details of respondents' neighborhoods. There also have been ethnic booster samples in most years, to better assess the victimization experience of ethnic minorities. (Results have generally shown no effect or only a modest "ethnicity" effect on victimization, once other factors are taken into account.) The sample design is complicated, but national representativeness is maintained by weighting processes.

A distinguishing feature of the BCS, particularly in earlier years, was a flexible design that allowed adroit use of variable topic components outside the main crime-counting ones. Some topics were repeated intermittently; others were introduced to test particular research ideas—for instance, the relationship between victimization and self-reported offending. Where large numbers were not needed, the sample was often spilt to allow coverage of more topics. Early ones included drunk driving, Neighborhood Watch, and obscene telephone calls. From its inception, the BCS has measured people's fear of crime, although the way in which this has been done has varied over time (reflecting lack of academic consensus about how fear is best measured). The survey has also regularly covered police–public contacts—again with several variations in approach. A more recent theme has been confidence in the criminal justice system.

Computer-Assisted Self-Interviewing

Since 1994, the BCS has used computer-assisted personal interviewing (CAPI), in which the questionnaire is programmed into a laptop computer that the interviewer uses to enter responses. A byproduct of CAPI is the ability to allow respondents to use the computer themselves to answer questions of sensitive nature—a technique known as computer-assisted self-interviewing (CASI).

CASI had its first trial in 1994, when it was used to measure rape and sexual assault. CASI modules have been regularly included in the BCS since then. They have covered sexual victimization, domestic violence, stalking, buying stolen goods, and illicit drug misuse. CASI imposes limits on the complexity of questions that can be asked, but has nonetheless proved valuable. Levels of sexual and domestic violence revealed in CASI modules, for instance, are substantially higher than those resulting from the survey's main screening methods. The CASI modules come after the main survey, and their results are reported separately and not as part of the main crime count.

Changes to the Survey

In addition to the introduction of CAPI and CASI, the BCS has undergone a number of other changes over the years. None was as significant as the redesign of the NCVS in the early 1990s, however, which resulted in a significant change in the number of some types of victimizations counted. With the BCS, the basic approach to measuring core household and personal victimization has remained unchanged.

One of the biggest changes was that the BCS began a continuous interviewing cycle in 2001, leading to inevitable changes in the calculation of annual victimization risks. The sample size has also changed over the years from a modest 11,000 core sample in the 1980s, to about 20,000 in 2000, to more than double that now. The current sample size services some numerical performance indicators for each police force area in England and Wales—for instance, it is possible to ask about "confidence in local policing." Over time, the non-crime-counting content of the BCS questionnaire has become more routinized. The main reason for this is that the BCS now measures not only aspects of police performance but also a number of other government targets. These include fear of crime, antisocial behavior, and confidence in the criminal justice system. The use of the BCS in this way has been criticized by academics who feel that the survey has fallen afoul of administrative criminology. They see the survey as having lost touch with its earlier theory-testing role (with regard to lifestyle theory, for instance), and as having little scope for exploring more nuanced measures of public reactions to crime.

Over the past few years, the BCS has taken up issues of emerging interest. It has looked at stalking, cell phone theft, identity theft, credit card fraud, Internet fraud, computer viruses and hacking, and harassing or offensive email or cell phone messages. The number of these offenses is not added to the conventional BCS crime count.

In 2006, the BCS was subject to two independent reviews. One focused on the BCS methodology. The other—by the UK Statistics Commission—looked at relationship between the BCS and police statistics in providing national crime statistics. One of the main recommendations for the BCS was to extend coverage to those under the age of 16. As an attempt to address the victimization of younger age groups in the BCS in the early 1990s was not particularly successful, there was an extensive program of work to develop and test new questions, and to assess their impact on the existing survey. Beginning in January 2009, children ages 10 to 15 in households selected to take part in the main survey have been included.

Another recommendation was to include those living in communal establishments. This was considered but found problematic, as no good sampling frame exists. A recommendation to cover the homeless has not been ruled out, but methodological work is currently on hold. A final recommendation was for more regular surveys of crimes against commercial victims. Planning for a new survey is under way.

Main Results

The BCS is a long-standing survey that has ranged widely in the topics on which it has inquired. Exhaustive description of its results is clearly not possible here, but four features of the results are described below.

Crime Trends

A main purpose of the BCS was to provide a measure of trends in crime that was independent of police statistics, which can be subject to changes in recoding practices and possible changes in the level of reporting to the police. Both the BCS and police statistics showed increasing crime in the 1980s, although the rise was sharper in police figures, reflecting growing reporting rates (possibly driven by higher levels of household insurance). The trend then reversed in the first half of the 1990s, with police figures growing less rapidly than BCS figures. Although the evidence is largely circumstantial, this was very possibly linked to the introduction of performance targets for the police to reduce crime. Both of the crime measures' figures peaked in the mid-1990s, but both have since fallen. The number of crimes now measured by the BCS is as low as the number in the first survey.

The Dark Figure

The "dark figure" of crime is a key criminological concept, essentially referring to offenses not reported to the police. The BCS is unusual in attempting to quantify the dark figure by drawing tight comparison between police figures and BCS crime estimates—at least for "matchable" offenses. Offenses are classified according to police rules, based on detailed information on the "victim form" completed by those answering affirmatively to screener questions. Various adjustments are made to police figures to maximize comparability.

Matching BCS and police counts allows for both an estimate of the dark figure and comparisons of trends in crime according to the two measures. The matching process allows an estimate of the "recording shortfall" between the number of offenses estimated to have been reported to the police and the number recorded—a part of the dark figure. While the dark figure varies between offense categories, earlier sweeps of the BCS showed that, overall, roughly two thirds of BCS crimes were not reported to the police, and roughly one third of reported crimes were not recorded by the police. The figures have changed somewhat over time, with more offenses reported and comparatively fewer left unrecorded. The extra work involved in linking police and survey figures has increased the value of BCS information.

Victimization Risks

A principal aim of victim surveys is to show how risks of crime vary for different types of social groups. In this respect, the BCS is more inclusive than police records in the United Kingdom, which provide very little about the characteristics of victims.

The picture of risks from the BCS accords with that from a wealth of other victimization surveys. Four main aspects are important here. First, men are much more vulnerable than women to assaults and robbery, although the gender difference reverses for domestic violence. Higher risks are also evident among younger people, single people, and households with children. The BCS has also established that people's lifestyles and routine activities affect their vulnerability. Second, risk is largely concentrated among the less economically and socially well placed, who tend to live in areas of high offending. Third, variations in risk across areas differ somewhat according to offense type, with robbery, for instance, being more often an inner-city crime. Fourth, the probability of repeat victimization is particularly unevenly spread. This has been firmly established by the BCS, whereas in the NCVS the handling of "series" incidents obscured the characteristics of repeat victimization to a large degree.

Self-Reported Illicit Drug Use

The BCS is now used to monitor government targets to reduce drug use among young people. For this purpose, it started to include an additional sample of those between the ages of 16 and 24, who are asked about illicit drug misuse via CASI. The most recent survey results show that 1 in 10 16- to 59-year-olds had used an illicit drug in the preceding year (mainly cannabis), with the figure double that for 16- to 24-year-olds. Class A drug use was about a third of this level. The respondents' use of any illicit drug in the preceding year had decreased between 1996 and 2007/2008, due mainly to a decline in the use of cannabis. Usage of Class A drugs has fallen less.

Pat Mayhew

See also Calculating Extent of Victimization: Incidence, Prevalence, and Rates; Fear of Crime, Measurement of; Lifestyle Theory; Methodological Issues in Counting Victims; National Crime Victimization Survey (NCVS); Race/Ethnicity and Victimization; Repeat Victimization; Victimization Surveys

Further Readings

Hough, M., & Maxfield, M. (Eds.). (2007). *Surveying crime in the 21st century*. New York: Criminal Justice.

Kershaw, C., Nicholas, S., & Walker, A. (Eds.). (2008). *Crime in England and Wales 2007/08: Findings from the British Crime Survey and police recorded crime* (Statistical Bulletin 07/08). London: Home Office.

Mayhew, P. (2007). Researching the state of crime: National and international and local surveys. In R. King & E. Wincup (Eds.), *Doing research on crime and justice* (2nd ed.). Oxford, UK: Oxford University Press.

Web Sites

Economic and Social Data Service: http://www.esds.ac.uk

Home Office Research and Statistics: http://www.homeoffice.gov.uk/rds/

BULLYING

Bullying is a complex topic, as bullying behavior occurs in many contexts in society—from schools and playgrounds to the workplace and the home. Bullies may be children or adults, and they often have pasts that are rife with problems. The behaviors that constitute bullying are diverse and often have a specific purpose and involve planning. The victims are chosen because of specific characteristics, and the bullying they experience often exacerbates these traits, leading to a cycle of increasing social isolation and lowering of self-esteem. There also are long-lasting effects of bullying on bullies and victims, as bullies are more likely than their peers to be perpetrators of crime, and victims are more likely to be abused as adults.

Researchers have only relatively recently become interested in and concerned about the victimization involved in bullying, particularly among children and adolescents. The pioneering research on this topic was done by psychologist Daniel Olweus at the University of Bergen in Norway. He began his work in 1970, but only received support from Norwegian school officials in 1982 after three boys committed suicide after being bullied and harassed. Since then, school systems in other countries have made efforts to address the problem of bullying. In the United States, bullying began to attract attention following school shootings by young men who had apparently been harassed by their peers. Bullying is now a central concern of teachers, school administrators, and parents.

Definition

Bullying behavior can occur in several forms and situations, and the definition of bullying includes the following three components. First, bullying involves intentional and aggressive behavior designed to intimidate, harass, exclude, destroy property, or physically injure others. The verbal behavior can take the form of threats, name-calling, teasing, demands for money or services, spreading of rumors, and/or obscene gestures. Some of these behaviors result in indirect bullying, such as spreading rumors; others are direct behaviors, such as name-calling.

Physical behaviors designed to bully are direct and can include tripping, shoving, pushing, or hitting. However, bullying is more likely to take the form of verbal intimidation than physical attacks. Second, for behavior to reach the level of bullying it must occur repeatedly (albeit not necessarily in the same form) and over time. Third, the victim must perceive the bully as more powerful than himself or herself in terms of physical strength, popularity, or competence.

Demographics and Extent

Among children and adolescents, bullying is most likely to occur in school than in any other place, particularly in areas that are not well supervised. Bullying also occurs on the way to and from school, at athletic events, and on field trips, as well as online, as cyberspace increasingly offers opportunities to text message and post communications that can be designated as bullying. It is also most likely to occur among males, with most victims the same gender as the bullies. Males are more likely to be involved in physically aggressive bullying than are females. So-called relational aggression is presumed to be more common among girls. This type of bullying is designed to destroy the friendships, popularity, and reputations of the victims. The victims also tend to be girls. Verbal bullying can include insulting or invective remarks about race or ethnicity. However, there are no consistent research results as to the extent of this type of bullying or its prevalence between or among racial or ethnic groups.

Bullying seems to be most common in early adolescence and to decrease substantially during the high school years. There is some debate as to why bullying decreases as adolescents age. Older teenagers may believe they have more to lose by bullying and will be dealt with more harshly than younger children, or they may have found less obvious methods of intimidation and, correspondingly, victims may have become more skilled at avoiding or dealing with bullying. The extent of bullying is reported in the research literature in terms of bullies, victims, and bully-victims. Melissa Holt, David Finkelhor, and Glenda Kaufman Kantor published a study on bullying in which they surveyed 689 fifth graders. In that study, 14.4% of the students reported they engaged in bullying behavior, 12%

indicated they were victims, and 7.8% were delineated as bully-victims, meaning they reported that they had been bulled but had also exhibited aggressive behavior toward others. These percentages are comparable to the percentages for these three groups in other research on bullying.

Characteristics and Backgrounds of Bullies and Victims

Children and adolescents who exhibit bullying behavior tend to be aggressive in their interactions with others generally. They are often impulsive and have little patience or empathy for others. Male bullies also are likely to be physically larger than their peers. Bullies may be popular among their peers and may receive support from them, even while they are exhibiting bullying behavior, particularly if their victims are generally not well liked. They usually appear confident and think well of themselves. Bullies tend to come from families where parents use inconsistent discipline. The children tend to have few limits placed on their behavior, but they are often physically punished. The parents display little warmth or affection and are often aggressive in their relationships with each other as well as others in their environment. Bullies are more likely than their peers to commit delinquent acts and crimes as adults. They are also more likely to be aggressive toward the people they date and marry.

Victims of bullying who are categorized as submissive or passive generally exhibit a well-recognized array of behaviors and background characteristics. The typical victims of bullying are anxious, particularly around their peers. These victims also appear unhappy, are quiet and withdrawn, and often are socially isolated. Generally, they have low self-esteem and report feelings of depression and loneliness. These victims are also more likely to report somatic complaints and suicidal thoughts than are their peers. If the victims are boys, they are often physically smaller than their peers. As time goes by, they may attempt to avoid the bullying situation, which often involves avoiding school and school events. Therefore, their academic progress may suffer. There is also evidence that children and adolescents who are bullied frequently will experience more severe effects from the victimizations.

A small minority of victims are termed "provocative victims" or "bully-victims," as they contribute to their victimizations by exhibiting irritating or provocative behavior as a method of gaining attention and respond to perceived persecution through aggression. Bully-victims tend to be boys. They are viewed by their peers as hostile and volatile, and they are not well liked. Bully-victims are generally disruptive at school, whether on the playground or in the classroom. They overreact to insults and even unintentional slights and gestures such as when other children accidently bump them. Whether they are being bullied or inadvertently provoked, their retaliatory behavior will usually lead to an escalation of the situation. Bully-victims, like victims, exhibit evidence of anxiety and depression and have low self-esteem. Their social life is even more dismal than that of victims, however, as they have fewer friends and are generally shunned by their peers.

The families of bullying victims are considered influential in the establishment of characteristics that lead to and are perpetuated by the victimization. One hypothesis is that the parents of victims are often overprotective and controlling, and, therefore, the children do not have an opportunity to explore the environment or relationships with other children. Parents of these children may threaten or exhibit a withdrawal of love and support if the children attempt independent behavior. Another idea is that these children are not just victimized by bullies, but come from families where they have been abused and/or neglected by their parents. This seems especially the case with bully-victims, whose home environments appear to more closely resemble that of bullies, with a disorganized family and harsh punishment. It is assumed that these backgrounds make these children particularly vulnerable to victimization, which results in further loss of self-esteem and other social deficits. Later in life, they are more likely to be victims of dating or domestic abuse than their peers and are more likely to have children who are victims of bullying.

Responses to Bullying

Olweus developed a bullying reduction program as a result of his early research on bullying in Norway, called the Olweus Bullying Prevention Program. He reported the success of this program in reducing bullying and other antisocial behavior in several studies in the early 1990s. This program is designed to be comprehensive, and significant components of this program include training teachers and parents to understand, identify, and assess bullying behavior; a survey in the school among students as to their bullying behavior and/or victimization; a commitment to supervise children during school hours; the implementation of and adherence to rules about bullying; meetings with students and parents; and identification of bullies and victims as well as significant responses to these children. The overall goal of this schoolwide program is to change the school climate so that bullying will not be rewarded or permitted, and socially acceptable behavior will be expected. The commitment of school administrators and teachers to the program is crucial in the initial and continuing reduction of bullying behavior. Comprehensive programs should also include partnerships with community agencies, such as libraries, recreation centers, and churches.

The following specific bullying prevention activities in schools were described by Rana Sampson in a U.S. Department of Justice publication on bullying. One recommendation is for schools to encourage students to report bullying anonymously through a hotline or "bully box," where they can leave notes about bullying they have observed or experienced. Increased surveillance and supervision of students is also recommended, so that recess, lunch breaks, and areas such as restrooms are more carefully monitored. Teachers should be trained to recognize and respond effectively to bullies. Finally, schools can take an active stance in terms of not tolerating bullying through an awareness campaign of eye-catching posters and classes focusing on the subject. Along with these efforts to reduce bullying, there should also be encouragement for victims to report bullying and a supportive response when this occurs.

Children respond to victimization in different ways. Boys are more likely than girls to fight back, and girls are more likely than boys to cry. Girls are also more likely to ask for help from friends, and girls tend to be more empathetic toward victims than are boys. Older children tend to respond to bullying attempts by ignoring their harassers and walking away. Prevention programs focus mainly on the behaviors of bullies and less on victims' needs and responses. A comprehensive program should include providing effective coping responses to victims. Approaches in this regard include assertiveness training and learning how to gain friends. Also, as reported by Lisa Davidson and Michelle Demaray, social support, particularly from adults such as parents and teachers, appears to decrease the internal distress experienced by victims. Therefore, response to victims should include practical behaviors that they can practice in safe environments, and emotional support from significant people, particularly adults. Also, interventions should assess victims' family situations, including interactions between the parents and children and whether the children are being victimized in other situations. This same background information is important in determining interventions for bully-victims and bullies. Both bullies and victims may need family counseling or therapy that schools do not provide.

Schools generally have policies about bullying, and some state legislatures have provided another response to bullying by passing laws addressing this issue. Susan Limber and Mark Small have summarized the legislation of states that have passed such laws. These laws differ in terms of definitions, sanctions, and responses by school officials. However, they do have some commonalities. The legislatures not only provide legal definitions of bullying but also indicate the seriousness of this behavior; they also either require training and policy development or encourage it. Schools are also encouraged to implement bullying prevention programs and are either mandated or urged to report bullying behavior to the principal. These laws provide sanctions for bullies, including suspension and assignment to a different school. Only one state requires that schools have a plan for protecting victims from further harassment. Limber and Small concluded that states should be more consistent in the definitions they use for bullying, schools should be required to develop bullying prevention programs, and sanctions for bullies should focus on school-based program participation rather than suspension.

The answers and development of effective responses to bullying are not simple. Increasing knowledge about bullies and victims indicates that there are types of bullies, victims, and bully-victims and that the ability to effectively respond to them may be partially dependent on the victim's gender and age. Therefore, the reduction of bullying will occur as a result of the combined efforts of professionals coming from many fields and viewpoints.

Gail Flint

See also Cyber and Internet Offenses; School-Based Bullying Prevention; Workplace Bullying and Psychological Aggression; Workplace Violence and Bullying, Interventions for

Further Readings

Davidson, L. M., & Demary, M. K. (2007). Social support as a moderator between victimization and internalizing-externalizing distress from bullying. *School Psychology Review*, 36, 383–405.

Dehue, F., Bolman, C., & Völlink, T. (2007). Cyberbullying: Youngsters' experiences and parental perception. *School Psychology Review*, 36, 406–412.

Holt, M. K., Finkelhor, D., & Kaufman Kantor, G. (2007). Hidden forms of victimization in elementary students involved in bullying. *School Psychology Review*, 36, 345–360.

Juvonen, J., & Graham, S. (2001). *Peer harassment in school: The plight of the vulnerable and victimized*. New York: Guilford.

Limber, S., & Small, M. A. (2003). State laws and policies to address bullying in schools. *School Psychology Review*, 32, 445–455.

Olweus, D. (1993). *Bullying at school: What we know and what we can do*. Malden, MA: Blackwell.

Olweus, D. (2003). Prevalence estimation of school bullying with the Olweus Bully/Victim Questionnaire. *Aggressive Behavior*, 29, 239–268.

Sampson, R. (2006). *Bullying in schools*. Problem-Oriented Guides for Police, Series No. 12. Washington, DC: U.S. Department of Justice, Office of Community Oriented Policing Services.

Web Sites

Bullying Awareness Week: http://www.bullying awarenessweek.org

Bullying.org: http://www.bullying.org

Stop Bullying Now! http://www.stopbullyingnow.hrsa.gov

BURGLARY

Although precise legal classifications vary, burglary is commonly understood as a person's breaking into or otherwise without permission illegally entering another's property intending to steal. Similarly, attempted burglary refers to a person's trying but failing to gain entry to another's property. However, within this broad definition there are considerable variations: for example, the nature of the property (residential, public, or commercial premises); what (if anything) is stolen; the means of entry, that is, by force, access through an unlocked door or open window, or through trickery (known in the United Kingdom as "distraction burglary"); and whether the property is occupied at the time, and if so if the victim is aware of an intruder's presence. The latter example is relatively uncommon, because burglars tend to target empty property, thus they target homes in the daytime and commercial premises at night.

Extent and Impact

Internationally, commercial burglary is far more common than domestic burglary. For example, the second Commercial Victimisation Survey in England and Wales reported that almost a quarter of retailers and manufacturers had experienced a burglary in the previous year, whereas according to the British Crime Survey (BCS) only some 2% to 3% of households in England and Wales suffer a burglary in any one year. Despite this, most of the academic research focuses on household burglary.

In this respect, domestic burglary is one of the most common property crimes. In the United States, the National Crime Victimization Survey (NCVS) shows it outnumbers motor vehicle thefts by more than 3 to 1. Although burglary rates have declined since peaking in the 1990s, the 2007 NCVS suggests that annually some 2.7% of households experience a burglary or attempted burglary. Burglary rates also tend to vary inversely with national prosperity, and there is some indication of a rise in burglary during the current recession.

In urban areas the risk of burglary is greater. According to the International Crime Victimization Survey (ICVS), in some cities in developing societies, more than 10% of the population experience a burglary annually. But as with many other crimes, anxiety exceeds risk. The same survey found that as many as 29% of respondents worldwide thought it likely that they would be burgled in the coming year.

Burglary can also have a significant impact on its victims. The act of unlawful entry to the home is seen as an invasion of privacy, and (generally unfounded) concerns that the victim may be confronted by the burglar often evoke fear and sleeplessness. Parents may also express fear for their children's safety, and older children may be directly affected by a burglary. Research in the United States has even suggested that young victims were sometimes so affected that they subsequently chose to move back home with their parents. Moreover, while it was originally standard policy for police to reassure victims that "lightning rarely strikes twice," identification of repeat victimization shows very clearly that victims of burglary, as well as violence and vehicle crime, face an increased risk of future victimization. Burglars may be attracted to a "return visit" by both the prospect of further—or replaced—valuables and the knowledge that familiarity with a property increases ease of operation, a point also used to explain "near-repeats," where homes close to, and possibly similar to, burgled properties are targeted.

Explaining Risk

The research reveals clearly that burglary is rarely a random event. Most researchers have suggested that burglaries tend to involve at least some rudimentary planning, and few are opportunistic. Why a particular property and/or victim is targeted is thus a key question for researchers. One approach to answering it involves comparing levels of risk. Alternatively, known burglars have been interviewed about their choice of targets.

These approaches address the question of risk on at least three levels:

- *Space* is the location of the home and the nature of the area in which it is situated. On this level, the issue is whether certain *locations* have higher rates of burglary than others.
- *Structure* refers to the nature of the home's design and physical structure. On this level, the

issue is whether certain *types of residence* have higher rates of burglary than others.

- *Behavior* includes citizens' consumption patterns, interpersonal relationships, and other routine activities. On this level, the issue is whether certain *subgroups of the population* have higher rates of burglary than others.

A number of theoretical approaches have been adopted, including routine activities theory, opportunity theory, and rational choice theory. Combining these approaches, it seems that the ways in which burglars of residential property identify desirable targets can be addressed using up to three criteria:

- *Guardianship* is the extent to which the home is protected and able to be protected; for example, whether it is visible to others with the motivation to provide protection. Guardianship can be distinguished according to whether it is physical (e.g., an alarm) or social (i.e., where the source is the public police, private security, neighbors, or the potential victim).
- *Accessibility* refers to the ease with which the burglar is afforded access to a home determines the home's accessibility. Accessibility may be physical (e.g., barriers restricting access) or social (e.g., the burglar lives some distance from the potential target).
- *Rewards* is a more specific term than *target attractiveness* to refer to the extent to which the target possesses, or is perceived to possess, property that is of value to the burglar.

These criteria apply across the three levels distinguished. Thus differing guardianship can help explain differential risk on all three levels. For example, homes located in gated, patrolled communities may be better protected, as may homes with burglar alarms and those that are regularly occupied. Similarly, accessibility applies on the spatial level in terms of whether potential burglars live near or pass by specific properties, on the structural level where rear doors and gates may facilitate access to homes, and on the behavioral level in terms of whether householders leave doors or windows open or locked. The influence of rewards on risk of burglary is more ambiguous. We might expect burglars to maximize potential rewards by

targeting prosperous areas (location) and choosing more affluent-looking homes (structures) whose occupants own expensive consumables (behavior). However, in the context of space, burglars break into homes near where they live rather than more affluent homes in prestigious locations, suggesting that accessibility is more influential than rewards. It may be that "rewards" receives more weight than it warrants, and that researchers rely too much on the accounts of known burglars who exaggerate their professionalism. However, although dwellings in more deprived areas experience the most burglary, more prosperous homes *within* these areas are at the greatest risk.

Minimizing Harm and Reducing Risk

Detection rates for burglary have traditionally been relatively low. This is largely due to the nature of the offense. Burglaries are usually committed when a home is empty and in the absence of witnesses. Consequently, despite a number of innovations to policing practices, there is little evidence of any significant and long-term improvement. For this reason, among others, considerable emphasis has been directed at crime reduction through increasing guardianship and reducing accessibility to property.

For example, since the 1980s there have been a number of government-led burglary reduction initiatives in disadvantaged areas. While some such initiatives have been introduced in the United States, they have been particularly common in the United Kingdom. These began with the Kirkholt Burglary Prevention Project in the Greater Manchester area, the success of which spawned the Safer Cities program, within which burglary reduction was prioritized, the Secured by Design (SBD) initiative, the Burglary Reduction Initiative, and projects targeting older people such as Locks for Pensioners and the Distraction Burglary Initiative. Much of the emphasis in these initiatives has been on technical innovations such as locks and bolts, lighting, and alley gating. Some initiatives have incorporated social prevention, especially Neighborhood Watch–based schemes, whereas others, such as the Distraction Burglary Initiative, have prioritized educating vulnerable groups to change their behavior. While the British government has put considerable positive spin on the results of these projects, proclaiming their success, independent evaluations have not always been positive. This is particularly surprising given that the British Crime Survey (BCS) demonstrates the close association between target hardening and reduced risk, and that according to the 2003/2004 ICVS, as reported on by Jan van Dijk, John van Kesteren, and Paul Smit, such measures are primarily responsible for the near-universal reduction in property crime in the U.K. over the last 15 years.

The answer to why some initiatives succeed while others fail may be found in either design or implementation failure. Design failure implies that a project was designed in such a way that it did not address burglary reduction measures adequately. Implementation failure implies that while the initiative targeted appropriate measures, its implementation failed to meet proposed outputs. Identification of the reasons for failure is crucial if policy makers are to learn from the mistakes of failed initiatives and introduce new measures to reduce burglary. If the emphasis is on exaggerating success and hiding failure, however, it is unlikely that burglary reduction measures will be improved.

This reaffirms the importance of harm-reduction policies. Although burglary victims have been mostly positive about the service they receive from the police, the police are not generally seen as a victim-oriented group. Partially in response to this situation, specialist victim service agencies have emerged in many Western industrial societies. However, while traditionally the United Kingdom has been one of a few areas of the world where many burglary victims receive support (in contrast to the United States, where the assistance is commonly offered only to victims of violence), recent changes to victim support in England and Wales mean that the original emphasis on providing a personal, practical service to burglary victims has been diluted: Services have been centralized and direct personal contact is becoming a rarity. Elsewhere, the latest ICVS suggests that unmet need (defined as the proportion of those wanting or receiving help who did not receive it) is greater among victims of burglary than among victims of any other major crime.

Reducing the extent of burglary depends on a clear understanding of which properties are most at risk and why this is the case, and designing policies to increase guardianship and reduce accessibility of homes. Reducing the impact of burglary on victims depends on identifying those in most need of support and providing appropriate help. The evidence suggests that while governments have made some progress in the former respect, services for burglary victims are still inadequate.

R. I. Mawby

See also Burglary, Prevention of; Kirkholt Burglary Prevention Project; Property Marking/Operation Identification; Repeat Victimization

Further Readings

Cromwell, P. F., Olson, J. N., & Avary, D. W. (1991). *Breaking and entering.* Newbury Park, CA: Sage.

Felson, M., & Cohen, L. E. (1980). Human ecology and crime: A routine activity approach. *Human Ecology, 8*(4), 389–405.

Hope, T. (2004). Pretend it works: Evidence and governance in the evaluation of the Reducing Burglary Initiative. *Criminal Justice, 4*(3), 287–308.

Kershaw, C., Nicholas, S., & Walker, A. (2008) *Crime in England and Wales 2007/08.* Retrieved from http://www.homeoffice.gov.uk/rds/pdfs08/hosb0708.pdf

Lynch, J. P., & Cantor, D. (1992). Ecological and behavioral influences on property victimization at home: Implications for opportunity theory. *Journal of Research in Crime and Delinquency, 29*(3), 335–362.

Maguire, M. (2004). The Crime Reduction Programme in England and Wales: Reflections on the vision and the reality. *Criminal Justice, 4*(3), 213–237.

Mawby, R. I. (2001). *Burglary.* Cullompton, UK: Willan.

Mawby, R. I. (2007). *Burglary.* International Library of Criminology, Criminal Justice and Penology, Second Series. Aldershot, UK: Ashgate.

Rand, M. R. (2008). *Criminal victimization, 2007.* Retrieved from http://www.ojp.usdoj.gov/bjs/pub/pdf/cv07.pdf

van Dijk, J., van Kesteren, J., & Smit, P. (2008). *Criminal victimisation in international perspective: Key findings from the 2004–2005 ICVS and EU ICS.* Retrieved from http://rechten.uvt.nl/icvs/pdffiles/ICVS2004_05.pdf

BURGLARY, PREVENTION OF

Burglary is a crime that traditionally has been addressed through the use of place-based crime prevention interventions. Throughout the developed world it is acknowledged that domestic burglary is a problem. For example, in the United Kingdom, burglary continues to be a volume crime of concern to the police and other agencies. This is reflected by the fact that the Home Office currently estimates the national prevalence of burglary at 2.5% and that its reduction continues to be a part of a key performance indicator for the Police Forces of England and Wales. The International Crime Victimization Survey of 2000 demonstrated some variation across countries in terms of individual burglary risk. England and Australia had the highest reported prevalence and Finland, Spain, and Japan had the lowest levels.

There are many different types and methods of burglary. For example, distraction burglary involves creating a diversion to enable an opportunity to be exploited; hook and cane burglaries involve the offender using a tool to hook a set of keys through a mailbox or mail slot; burglary with assault involves some intimidation of the victim. Whatever the type of burglary, similar measures are proposed for combating the problem, and these measures concentrate specifically on residential (rather than commercial) burglary.

Concentration of Burglary Risk

In attempting to prevent burglary, it is important to understand that burglary risks are concentrated in certain places. The repeat victimization literature is a good illustration of this. Research shows that individuals who have been burgled once are more likely to be burgled again. In fact, the British Crime Survey shows that 13% of individual households that had been burgled once were burgled at least once more in a one-year period. Ken Pease and others have demonstrated that an important element of repeat victimization risk is that it *decays over time*. In other words, an initial event is useful in detecting vulnerability and predicting the possibility of a subsequent one for a limited time only. Thus there is no point in focusing effort on a household that had a burglary a year ago, because the risk will have returned to the background risk.

Recent research reveals a further clue about spatial patterns that can be used to extend this concept. This is that a certain element of burglary risk spreads to nearby neighbors, which is known as *near repeat victimization*. Like the spread of a cold through a population, burglary risk spreads to those in close proximity to a recently burgled property. In fact, nearby neighbors are 10 times more likely to be burgled within a week of a neighbor's burglary than they are to be burgled 2 weeks later. Those in particularly close proximity to a burgled house are at particularly high risk, again for a limited amount of time. Due to the spatial and temporal concentration of burglary, it is important to have interventions that can be installed quickly and effectively in areas of high risk.

Impact of Interventions

A range of different types of intervention have been implemented to attempt to reduce burglary. The measures implemented under the U.K.'s Reducing Burglary Initiative (RBI) reflect the wide range. They include target-specific situational prevention (e.g., target hardening to an individual household through installation of a burglar alarm), area-wide situation crime prevention (such as gates restricting the back alleys of blocks of housing to residents only), offender-based schemes (such as offender rehabilitation), stakeholder schemes (attempts to "empower" the community to take action), and property marking and enforcement (to make goods easier to trace and harder to sell).

Niall Hamilton-Smith and Andrew Kent recently undertook a review of the literature on prevention of domestic burglary. Their review particularly focused on situational methods of prevention, which work by barring opportunities for crime by increasing effort, increasing risks, reducing rewards, reducing provocation, and removing excuses for crime. They found that those measures that aimed to reduce burglary through "increasing the effort" involved in committing crime were the most effective; evidence was mixed on those approaches that removed excuses, reduced provocations, increased the risks, or reduced the rewards. This demonstrates that if too much effort is involved in a crime, burglars will generally desist from undertaking it.

Another recent review, conducted by Shane Johnson and his colleagues, examined the literature available on tactical options used in the reduction of burglary. The review was comprised of five parts: the type of intervention, a summary of the evidence of its effectiveness, its cost (financial and latency of implementation), the geographical coverage of the measures, and the partners involved in implementing the intervention. The following sections are based on the findings of that review, to which the interested reader is referred for details of the references on which it was based.

Effective Strategies

Interventions that involve target hardening individual households (e.g., strengthening doors and windows or inserting alarms) have been found to reduce the risk of revictimization, but they may not affect overall area-level crime rates. This type of intervention has the advantage of being relatively low cost and quick to implement. Increasing the visibility of policing in the area also works well at reducing crime problems such as burglary. Particularly cost-effective are single-officer patrols. Other interventions with positive impacts are alley gating (blocking off rear alleys of houses to all but residents) and the use of intelligence and targeting of known offenders. However, the financial costs of these latter two types of scheme can be high due to the associated administration.

Schemes that attempt to reduce property crime through environmental design have been proven to have a significant effect. They include measures such as street closures, which demonstrate that there is a relationship between street access and crime rates, and "secure by design"–type interventions that promote securely designed housing in well-thought-through environments, where possible at the prebuilding stage. If done in situations where little alteration to existing environments is necessary, environmental design schemes can be cost-effective, although they can take some time and effort to implement.

An antiburglary strategy that has proved particularly effective is focusing on prevention of repeat burglaries. Past victimization is an excellent predictor of future risk and therefore taking action quickly after an initial event is a useful way of preventing burglary incidents. The power of using repeat victimization strategies is evident from the demonstration project undertaken in Kirkholt. It was found that focusing on treating houses that had suffered a recent incident of burglary reduced the risk of burglary by 72% over a 3-year period in the area as a whole.

Interventions With Mixed Evidence of Effectiveness

There are other types of burglary reduction strategies on which the evidence of effectiveness is more mixed. These include Neighborhood Watch–type schemes, publicity campaigns, and property-marking schemes. Neighborhood Watch–type schemes rely on the presence and involvement of others, hence they tend to have a greater impact when residents are at home during the day. Cocoon watch schemes work in a similar way, but they concentrate on direct neighbors, who are put on "high alert" after an incident and hence can increase the likelihood that a returning offender will be caught. Although their effectiveness is unclear, these schemes are very low cost.

Publicity campaigns, such as slogans aimed at pointing out risks to victims or offenders, rarely change offender behavior on their own, although they may achieve a "drip feed" effect if continued over time (that is, the campaign has a small ongoing impact due to its consistent presentation). Interestingly, publicity associated with crime prevention tactics (e.g., publicizing the launch of an antiburglary scheme in an area, or talking to the press about the success of local measures that have recently been taken) can have a crime-reductive effect.

Property marking reduces anticipated rewards because it is hard to dispose of marked property. However, its impact is likely to be due to the publicity rather than the intervention itself. In reality, property marking does little to deter offenders from breaking into a house or stealing marked property taken from it. Recent evidence suggests that Smartwater, a spray that includes a DNA-style code linking offenders to offenses and property to owners, is particularly effective at deterring offenders.

There is mixed evidence on the effectiveness of street-lighting initiatives. These aim to reduce crime in areas by encouraging use by legitimate individuals and increasing the visibility of offenders. In a systematic review of 13 street-lighting schemes, 4 showed significant reductions in property crime and 7 showed significant reductions in crime overall. Hence, there appears to be some value in using good lighting to combat burglary.

Interventions With Little or No Evidence of Effectiveness

Closed-circuit television (CCTV) interventions are only likely to have an impact on commercial burglaries or residential houses within or near the area covered by a camera. They can increase detectability, act as a deterrent, and provide reassurance—but the associated financial cost is very high. One way of attempting to increase the flexibility of such camera systems is to use redeployable CCTV that can be moved around. However, these systems are difficult to use and sensitive to misuse, and there has been no demonstration of long-term reduction in crime levels resulting from their use.

Ringmaster is a system that alerts local residents and voluntary groups of up-to-date crime information. There are mixed reviews of the success of such schemes and the way in which information is disseminated. A further issue is that organizations often worry about increasing fear of crime and will circulate information to frontline staff only, which limits the power of the intelligence.

Forensic traps are items such as silent alarms and chemically treated mats that pick up intruders' footprints. Evidence shows that high-tech forensic devices can pose numerous practical problems when used on burglaries of retail premises; they also are unlikely to be useful in domestic situations. There is more positive evidence on the effectiveness of silent alarms, which alert the police and/or security staff to the presence of an intruder.

Crime Prevention Practitioners and Implementation Issues

It is important to consider the practicality of proposed schemes in addition to their effectiveness. Some types of scheme rely on multiagency responses. For example, alley gating requires the cooperation of the police, local authorities, local residents, and other interest groups due to the legalities associated with sealing off a public right-of-way. As a rule of thumb, the greater the number of agencies involved, the more at-risk the particular initiative is of implementation failure (i.e., never being realized in practice in its conceived form). Furthermore, schemes that are equipment centered rather than people centered, those that are fairly low tech, and those that focus on specific types of crime rather than reducing crime generally tend to be easier to implement. This means that there is a good argument for sticking to basic measures such as burglar alarms rather than more complex ones like redeployable CCTV.

Project Intensity, Cost Effectiveness, and Sustainability

It might be expected that the more expensive the crime prevention project, the greater its success at reducing burglary. In an influential piece of evaluation research, Paul Ekblom and his colleagues examined scheme intensity (i.e., expense) and how it correlates with the number of burglaries reduced. For the purpose of their analysis, they divided areas into high-, medium-, and low-action areas on the basis of the amount spent per household. When they looked at burglary trends across these three groups, it was evident that there was some prima facie evidence that the high-action areas saw a drop in the burglary rate that was not mirrored by the other areas or in control areas. Other work has confirmed this trend. The implication of this finding is that it is worth investing intensively in a defined community to get the most benefit in terms of crime reduction.

A further issue relating to intensity is the extent to which a program is cost-effective. That is, if a very high-intensity scheme appears to have reduced burglary very successfully, but the unit cost of each burglary reduced is too high (especially if it exceeds the cost of dealing with the aftermath of a burglary), then it is less of an achievement and rather impractical. Finally, it is also important to consider the sustainability of a scheme; that is, how long it is likely to go on preventing crime. For example, high-visibility policing might only reduce crime while the police patrols are increased, but alley gates might remain effective for 10 years.

Kate Bowers

See also Burglary; Crime Prevention; Kirkholt Burglary Prevention Project; Reducing Burglary Initiative; Repeat Victimization; Safer Cities Program; Situational Crime Prevention

Further Readings

Ekblom, P., Law, H., & Sutton, M. (1996). *Safer cities and domestic burglary* (Home Office Study No. 164). London: Home Office.

Hamilton-Smith, N., & Kent, A. (2005). The prevention of domestic burglary. In N. Tilley (Ed.), *Handbook of crime prevention and community safety*. Cullompton, UK: Willan.

Johnson, S. D., Birks, D., McLaughlin, L., Bowers, K. J., & Pease, K. (2007). *Prospective crime mapping in operational context: Final report* (Home Office On-line Report, 19/07). London: Home Office.

Pease, K. (1998). *Repeat victimisation: Taking stock* (Preventing and Detecting Crime Paper No. 98). London: Home Office.

BUSINESS COMMUNITY CRIME PREVENTION

The business community is generally defined as corporations, partnerships, and individual proprietors who are engaged in the conduct of commerce. This definition could be expanded so that the business community includes customers and employees as well. A definition of a specific business community might include companies that share a common commercial sector, such as hotel operators, or convenience stores; or a geographic location, such as a region, city, neighborhood, or commercial strip. This entry first examines the scope of crime in the business community, and then turns to a discussion of prevention initiatives.

Crime Against Business

Crime against business is a serious public policy problem. Crime against business can occur from the inside, such as in employee theft, embezzlement, and workplace violence, or from the outside, in offenses such as burglary, robbery, and theft. Business establishments experience a much higher crime rate than do residential dwellings. Despite

having far fewer establishments, U.S. businesses have more total robberies than do residences; they also have a disproportionate amount of burglaries compared to residences. Research in Britain has shown that while only a small percentage of households fall victim to burglary, nearly one quarter of all commercial establishments have been burglarized. Estimates of the cost of commercial crime in the United States are approaching $200 billion a year, a cost that gets passed on to consumers in the form of higher prices. In essence, U.S. consumers pay a crime tax of nearly 15% of the total costs of goods and services, as the cost of crime and its prevention gets passed along to consumers.

Businesses fall victim to crime more than do residences for many reasons. As places of commerce, they contain a wealth of goods and cash that are attractive to criminals both inside and outside the business. Moreover, due to limited hours of operation, many businesses are vacant much of the day, which leads to uneven levels of surveillance, a situation that facilitates burglary and vandalism. Not all businesses become victims to crime, however. There are certain business sectors and locations where crime perpetrated by outsiders is more likely to occur. Generally, these are businesses such as retail operations that deal in cash, as well as businesses located in communities with high levels of poverty and social disorganization.

Businesses also contribute to crime in indirect ways; that is, the very nature of the business operation can facilitate crime that is either perpetrated on-site or spills out into adjacent communities. Two examples of business types that attract crime include establishments that serve alcohol and businesses that attract teenage and young adult customers. Another example of how businesses indirectly promote crime is that of commercial operations that require large parking structures, such as suburban office parks or malls. These structures can facilitate vehicle theft and thefts from automobiles, with the level of incidence being largely dependent on the relative quality of parking lot management schemes and surveillance systems.

The Importance of Business Crime Prevention

Criminal victimization is one of the leading competitive issues facing business. As business profit margins have declined in a competitive global marketplace, the pressure to stem losses attributed to crime has become more pressing. However, much of the research on business crime identifies a dearth of systematic data. Researchers have also noted a reluctance of business operators to deal with crime victimization issues in the open.

Internal Crime Prevention Techniques in the Commercial Sector

Much of the effort of crime prevention in the business community is comprised of discrete, internal actions taken at the company or establishment level. Many firms, large and small, possess some institutional capacity for crime prevention. In most cases, the resources available for crime prevention and the level of risk of the particular business sector dictate the type and level of security pursued. A company's investment in crime prevention and security is driven by many factors; primary among these factors is the effort to prevent financial loss. Losses can be direct, such as the costs associated with replacing stolen merchandise and with replacing injured or fearful employees, or involving financial liabilities associated with a failure to properly protect business premises. Indirect costs can be associated with the loss of market share due to fearful customers, decreasing stock prices due to reduced market confidence in management abilities, or a general decline in public goodwill due to criminal incidence. A nonfinancial reason for companies to engage in crime prevention efforts is their desire to protect the life and health of their employees, suppliers, and customers.

Historically, commercial efforts at on-premises crime prevention and security have been driven by situational crime prevention. This approach was born out of a frustration by a criminology that fixated on more macro explanations for crime (e.g., poverty) and offered little in the way of everyday solutions for local actors such as governments, institutions, businesses, or citizens. Situational crime prevention is defined by a set of principles that operate on the assumption that crimes can be prevented by understanding what facilitates specific crimes and adapting the environment to make these crimes less likely, thus deterring actors from committing them. One conceptualization of the theory includes five organizing principles for crime

prevention interventions. These include developing strategies that (1) increase the effort of criminals, (2) increase the risk of detection and arrest, (3) reduce the rewards of criminal acts, (4) reduce criminal provocations, and (5) remove excuses for criminal action. By applying these principles to business crime prevention, some rather straightforward techniques for commercial operators have been developed.

Using the retail sector as an example, the first principle, increasing effort, might result in higher value merchandise being isolated and secured, thus making it harder to shoplift. The second principle, increasing risk of detection, would result in a number of strategies, including store security (and undercover security) and electronic surveillance capabilities (closed-circuit television). The third principle, reducing the rewards, could include attaching tags to merchandise that can only be removed safely with store equipment (or that contains staining dyes in the case of high-end clothing). The fourth principle, reducing criminal provocations, is most frequently applied to internal criminal threats. Here, personnel and management systems that promote workplace equity can be applied to reduce the threats posed by disgruntled employees. The fifth and last principle has to do with establishing and enforcing clear behavioral rules. A set of techniques in the retail sector would be equally salient for both internal and external crime risks. Internally, setting rules about workplace culture, or the handling of cash, would be an important step in reducing employee theft. Externally, advertising a store's policy on the handling of shoplifters, or in the case of establishments that serve alcohol, making clear the standards of decorum, can be an effective tool in preventing potentially violent crime acts.

While many businesses have incorporated methods to address crime from both inside and outside sources (often referred to as security or loss prevention), they historically have lagged in their participation in larger strategic crime prevention efforts. There are a few notable reasons for this historical reluctance. The most direct involves the costs associated with extending resources to crime prevention. Clearly business operators have an interest in the security of their own staff, site, and customers. While there may be an altruistic reason for this, more likely, businesses have adopted crime prevention and security techniques as their exposure to financial liability for failure to secure their premises from crime has grown. Moreover, the fear of promoting crime vulnerability to a broader audience might negatively impact customer perceptions of an establishment, thus hurting profits.

Social and Economic Trends Affecting Business Crime Prevention

Pressures to address larger social and economic trends have led to a larger effort to develop strategic solutions, often through the use and integration of technological advances in the area of surveillance and detection equipment. In addition, businesses have become more focused on developing problem-solving partnerships that help define solutions to specific crime issues. They also have taken efforts to build larger, more resilient coalitions with other private actors with shared concerns and with public safety agencies to address broader social issues that have an impact on business victimization trends. Increasing levels of technical specialization in the economy and a globalizing marketplace for capital, labor, and consumer markets have led to increasing input from commercial interests in developing mechanisms for regulation and crime prevention strategies. Indeed, the restructuring of the economy over the past few decades from one that is dominated by manufacturing to one that is more focused on consumption and specialized services has changed the nature of crime against business. This change has included an increase in exposure to threats such as terrorism and sabotage, and fear of crime becoming a very important negative factor for consumption-based businesses. Moreover, the growth of computer- and Internet-based commercial transactions has also affected the scope and types of crime prevention concerns of business.

Other social trends germane to business crime prevention include the incredible growth in private security and the development of what one analyst has called "mass private space" (i.e., large-scale private space such as shopping, entertainment, and recreational developments that is privately owned, managed, and secured). In a more general sense, over the past few decades there has been a continued blurring between private and public property and between financial interests and services. This

has led some to see private sector interests and activities as part of a larger security governance regime that, in partnership with public sector agencies, shapes crime prevention policies, practices, and regulation.

Business Crime Prevention Collaboratives

Chambers of Commerce and Crime Prevention

A chamber of commerce is a voluntary business membership organization, often serving a local area or primary economic region. Chambers of commerce have traditionally been the main business advocacy organization in the United States, at both the national and local levels. Their services typically involve efforts at local place promotion, technical assistance, and policy lobbying. While crime prevention efforts are not usually at the forefront of chamber efforts, there have been some notable exceptions, especially when specific areas have suffered from high crime and negative public perceptions despite public policy efforts to manage the problem. Thus, local chambers have grown more involved in developing and directing crime prevention policies and programs in the United States. Examples of chamber of commerce efforts include imparting organization and technical expertise to police departments in efforts to improve strategic planning and operations. Chambers of commerce have created and sustained working groups—including federal, state, and local law enforcement, major commercial operators, and property owners-managers—to develop problem-solving solutions to crimes affecting businesses. These groups are particularly effective at information sharing, especially in the area of stopping economic crime syndicates whose existence and tactics might not be known to local actors.

One specific chamber effort includes work done by the Greater Richmond Chamber in Richmond, Virginia, a city that has experienced surges in violent crime. When the U.S. government developed the gun enforcement program Project Exile in the late 1990s, subjecting violators to a 5-year, federal mandatory minimum sentence, the Richmond Chamber became very involved in the development of a large-scale promotional campaign to assist the prevention potential of this new law.

Chambers of commerce around the United States are also involved in creating and managing crime alert networks using either email or fax; offering crime prevention advice to businesses, including performing a security vulnerability analysis and offering security system advice; and developing specific crime prevention public information campaigns, including campaigns that focus on theft from automobiles and laptop theft, to name but a few.

Business Improvement Districts

A second type of business crime prevention collaborative is the business improvement district (BID), a policy idea that has grown tremendously, especially over the past decade. Starting with just a handful of BIDs in the 1980s, the number of BIDs is now more than a thousand. Incorporated by state or local governments, BIDs derive their funding from special tax assessments on commercial property. These special districts formulate service plans for a defined commercial area. Larger organizations, usually located in central business districts and commercial concentrations, tend to invest part of their assessment in crime prevention strategies. These strategies often include developing a capacity for strategic planning for crime prevention, including funding staff with expertise in crime mapping and trend analysis and crime prevention implementations. BIDs have also been known to extend resources to policing agencies; these have taken the form of providing substation facilities, bikes for bike patrols, and funding for extra police shifts. As part of a larger crime prevention package, larger BIDs also provide some form of common area security. BIDs are also likely to share facilities with local policing operations, in some cases sharing roll calls, lockers, and break room facilities, in line with the theory that closer relationships and information sharing will have a positive effect on problem-solving partnerships focused on crime prevention.

Larger BIDs are also likely to have a full-time crime prevention planner on staff. The type of common area security varies across organizations, and can include everything from part-time contract security to armed security. Many larger BIDs, however, subscribe to a less stringent security model and see their common area personnel as a resource for district users. In keeping with this philosophy, BIDs tend to call their street personnel street concierges, customer service representatives, or ambassadors.

While the impact of BIDs as a crime prevention tool is limited to certain geographical areas that have the capacity to fund common area security and strategic planning personnel, the success of BIDs in crime prevention can be attributed to this limited focus. As most effective crime prevention strategies are formulated around good information about causal factors and focused on nuanced environmental adaptation, the localized nature of BIDs sets the stage for successful crime prevention practice. Finding ways to extend resources dedicated to developing local crime prevention expertise, common area security, and resilient partnerships with law enforcement agencies to less capitalized business districts should be an important goal for policy makers in the future.

The Safe City Initiative

A third example of a crime prevention collaborative is Safe City—a relatively new community-based initiative that has been developed, cofunded, and promoted by the Target Corporation, a major U.S. retailer. The primary goal of this initiative is to develop crime prevention partnerships between a city's law enforcement agency, business community, property managers, and local community organizations. Through this initiative, the Target Corporation seeks to improve local crime prevention problem-solving capacity. As of early 2009, there were 25 U.S. cities that had either begun or signed on for this initiative.

In addition to its organizational goals, Safe City's program goals include developing networked electronic surveillance across private and public electronic surveillance systems for better crime prevention and detection capabilities. The logic is that by linking disconnected private systems of surveillance into an integrated web, their surveillance network capabilities will be enhanced. Other efforts include offering subsidies for alternative transportation and surveillance by way of supporting the purchase of Segways for local law enforcement. Segways are personal transportation systems that might afford greater levels of interaction with the public, as well as foster speedier enforcement efforts. Other program inputs include a series of prevention guides, developed by researchers at the Urban Institute, that focus on providing evidence-based tips to users on effective prevention techniques for a series of crime types, including shoplifting, commercial burglary, public disorder, panhandling, vandalism, and car break-ins and theft—all types of crimes that are particularly troubling to businesses and business districts.

Policy Directions

Research indicates that effective, evidence-based crime prevention is less costly to society than criminal justice approaches to crime. The cost of patrol, arrest, trial, and incarceration are staggering when compared to the cost of effective strategies employed by crime prevention practitioners. While not all crime is preventable, much of the crime that occurs in the commercial sector can be prevented through either situational or managerial efforts that have an impact on the opportunity, motivation, and economic considerations in criminal decision making. While many larger businesses already are engaged in substantial crime prevention activities in their own operating spheres, ways need to be found that afford smaller operators these advantages, while also promoting crime prevention partnerships that transcend individual concerns.

The incentive for cooperation between commercial actors, law enforcement, public policy makers, and community groups is growing. This is evidenced by the growth in the type and overall incidence of the partnerships noted above. The prospect for further growth, however, is tempered by a need for more sustainable organizational models for these efforts, as many businesses have not gotten involved in these types of partnerships. Policy makers can improve this situation by providing additional incentives for crime prevention activities, such as grant support and other financial incentives and dedication of staff and expertise for group problem-solving efforts. They could also create more disincentives for crime-generating business operations through a more efficient and effective regulatory regime, and/or through civil law action that holds businesses that create crime responsible for the costs they impose on society.

Robert J. Stokes

See also Community Policing; Situational Crime Prevention; Third-Party Policing; Workplace Violence, Training and Education

Further Readings

Chamard, S. (2006). *Partnering with businesses to address public safety problems.* Problem-Oriented Guides for Police, Problem Solving Tools Series, No. 5. Washington, DC: U.S. Department of Justice.

Felson, M., & Clark, R. (Eds.). (1997). *Business and crime prevention.* Monsey, NY: Criminal Justice Press.

Fleming J., & Wood, J. (2007). *Fighting crime together: The challenges of policing and security networks.* Sydney: UNSW.

Gill, M. (2006). *The handbook of security.* New York: Palgrave Macmillan.

Rosenbaum, D., Lurigio, A., & Davis, R. (1998). *The prevention of crime: Social and situational strategies.* Belmont, CA: Wadsworth.

BYSTANDER INTERVENTION

The death of Catherine "Kitty" Genovese in New York City in 1964 focused attention on bystanders and crime. Her stabbing death, and sexual assault, were seen and heard by at least 38 people over a period of 40 minutes. Not one of those people came to her assistance or called the police. Initial theorizing included "big city apathy" and the effect of alienation within the "megalopolis." More systematic research soon followed, enabling researchers to better understand and predict the phenomenon of bystanders' helping or failing to help those in need. The term *bystander intervention* was coined to describe the direct or indirect intervention of a person present, but not involved, for the benefit and well-being of someone in need. Research on bystander intervention has been examined through the lens of prosocial and helping behavior, as well as altruism, within the fields of social psychology, sociology, criminology, medicine, political science, economics, and biology.

There are various theories as to what variables influence bystander intervention (or nonintervention), including social-cognitive, self-perception and social identity, and biological and evolutionary perspectives. From these theories, a range of studies have examined the factors that predict bystander intervention and the effect of bystander intervention on behaviors, ranging from sexual assault to bullying in schools. Other research has examined bystander intervention in the context of criminal, harmful, and emergency behaviors as a mechanism of informal social control, the strength of which is negatively correlated with the level of crime and violence. Many research studies have shown that bystander intervention can be an effective crime prevention strategy, both directly—by intervening when a crime or harmful act is under way—and indirectly—by notifying an authority.

Theories of Bystander Intervention

Social psychologists Bibb Lantané and John Darley produced the seminal work on bystander intervention, which they began by examining police reports of the murder of Kitty Genovese. They suggested that it was the large number of witnesses that caused the nonintervention, rather than apathy or indifference. Their studies showed that a person alone is likely to intervene; in contrast, when other bystanders are present, individual bystanders are less likely to intervene. Based on the five-stage decision-making model, they argued that the presence of bystanders lessens responsibility by diffusing it; this is known as the *bystander effect*. When this psychological shift occurs, a state of pluralistic ignorance arises as individuals look to others for social cues of appropriate action.

It has been suggested that when others are present the "costs" of intervention (stress, embarrassment, shame) are greater, and thus individuals are less likely to intervene. A large number of other situational factors have been studied: ambiguity of the situation, level of victim's distress and dependence, the victim's style of request and degree of physical attractiveness, and the level of threat. These situational studies, particularly the robust finding on the inverse relationship between number of bystanders and level of helping behavior, initially raised doubts about the influence of social norms and personal characteristics in understanding bystander behavior.

Self-perception theories, however, are concerned with individuals' perceptions of other people's interpretations of their behavior, and they argue that being aware that others are observing could neutralize diffusion of responsibility and negate the bystander effect. Building on this work, researchers have argued that it is the desire to act in ways expected of us (such as by "doing the right thing" and by not overreacting) that leads to bystander intervention. In a similar vein, social identity theory and self-categorization theory (SCT) argue that it is not the number of bystanders that is of primary importance, but the social categorical relations between the individuals present. A central premise of SCT is the dynamic responsiveness of the self within a social context. A change in social context can lead to a more or less inclusive self-categorization, which then influences behavior. Individual bystanders are more likely to intervene when the others present are included in a salient self-categorization; in other words, when they share a common group membership. The categorical relationship with the victim is also important; that is, when a bystander does not share a salient group membership with the victim, the bystander is more likely to experience a perceived threat and not intervene. However, when a shared common fate with the victim is salient, bystander intervention is more likely. Further, according to SCT, strong group norms of social responsibility and action play a role in the influence of prosocial behavior patterns.

Research informed by a neurobiological perspective demonstrates that the amygdala, a small area in the limbic system, is a central regulator of the "fight or flight" response commonly experienced by victims of crime and bystanders. The amygdala's anatomical connectivity processes information from two pathways: the thalmao-amygdala and the cortico-amygdala. The faster, fight or flight, pathway processes raw partial images from the thalamus; in contrast, the longer pathway processes more complex information from the cortex. If a potential emergency is not genuine, the fight or flight response can be aborted through information received from the cortex. However, if the fight or flight message is strong enough, the information from the cortex is inhibited, and individuals physiologically "freeze" for a moment in a trancelike state. The evolutionary perspective suggests that this is an adaptive response of the fight or flight reflex. By extension, what appears to happen in bystander intervention is that the bystander freezes while the more complex situational context is accessed. If the situational cues are ambiguous, bystanders will fail to act. Researchers have found that through working with individuals experiencing this trance state, they can teach these individuals how to overcome the debilitating effects of the state and intervene effectively. This research has also been found to be effective in managing other amygdala-influenced states, such as the posttraumatic stress disorder, anxiety, and depression often experienced by victims of crime and violence.

This breadth of theoretical research has been organized into a multilevel perspective: the micro level—the study of the biological origins (e.g., neural or evolutionary) of prosocial tendencies and the etiological variation in these tendencies; the meso level—the study of helper–recipient dyads in the context of a specific situation; and the macro level—the study of prosocial actions that occur within the context of groups and large organizations. This broad perspective has grounded comprehensive and multifaceted crime prevention initiatives. Crime and violence prevention approaches are also developing breadth through bridging the study of bystander intervention with the study of community readiness, development, and education.

Areas of Application

Efforts to develop the capacity of bystanders to intervene have been made in situations ranging from sexual violence, to suicide prevention, to bullying in school. Research has found that the contextual, situational, and personal variables that influence bystander behavior are consistent in the theoretical literature and suggests that active bystander intervention in situations of violence is possible and effective. Broadly, this research base advocates that primary prevention efforts that educate and skill a broad population must ground the efforts of secondary interventions such as bystander intervention.

Sexual Violence

In the context of violent crime, particularly sexual violence, research has shown that bystanders are less likely to intervene when they believe that an abuser and a victim know each other. This is relevant to violent crime, particularly sexual violence, as 70% of victims of rape and sexual assault and 50% of all victims of violent crime know their attackers. However, this effect can be ameliorated with the appropriate training. Intervention research has shown that bystanders are empowered to act when they feel a sense of responsibility and when they know what to do. This suggests that primary prevention activities that develop knowledge and skills at a community level are an important aspect of building the capacity for effective bystander intervention and crime prevention. Bystanders need to feel that it is important to intervene and that they have the skills to intervene safely and effectively. Bystanders are also empowered to act when they witness and engage with individuals who model effective intervention. Research suggests that violence, particularly sexual and intimate partner violence, will only be curtailed when broader social norms shift and a wider audience is reached.

Youth Suicide

Research on the effectiveness of bystander intervention has also been applied to the prevention of and intervention in adolescent suicide through building an understanding of adolescents' normative views on suicide, the diffusion of responsibility that can occur, and the ambiguity that bystanders often experience. Each of these factors was predictive of whether or not a teen would tell an adult about a suicidal peer. Using this knowledge base, primary intervention programs have been developed that build awareness, knowledge, and skills that teach bystanders how to take action. Youth suicide prevention is related to prevention efforts to curb bullying behavior in schools, as victims of chronic bullying are at risk of depression, suicidal ideation, and suicide.

Bullying and Violence in School

Research into the role of bystanders has become an important aspect of bullying prevention programs, identifying factors that may account for positive and negative responses of bystanders. It shows that while most students hold attitudes that are opposed to bullying behavior and supportive of victims, students' behavior in actual bullying situations (i.e., as active participants or passive bystanders) often reinforces bullying behavior. For example, the mere presence of peer bystanders can initiate and escalate bullying behavior. Rather than preventing school bullying, peers have been shown to have definable roles in the maintenance of bullying behavior through assisting, reinforcing, or ignoring bullying behavior. Students are often reluctant to take on the role of an active bystander who censures the act of bullying. These findings suggest that bullying intervention programs should be directed toward all students in order to change participant roles in the bullying process by increasing awareness, self-reflection, and skill development.

Research into school violence more broadly has defined the bystander as an active and involved participant in the social architecture of school violence rather than as a passive witness. Bullying is better understood from a triadic (bully-victim-bystander) than dyadic (bully-victim) perspective, with teachers, administrators, and students legitimizing or ameliorating bullying through their roles and activities as bystanders within the school community.

Bystanders and Social Responsibility

A number of researchers see examining the intersection of bystander intervention and prosocial behavior as a way of widening the "lens" through which active citizenship and social responsibility are viewed; that is, instead of considering bystander intervention as the endpoint, it can be viewed as part of a range of prosocial behaviors that form an ongoing process of social responsibility and active citizenship. The personal and social benefits of these behavior patterns have been shown to increase both the mental and physical health of victims, offenders, and bystanders. Research also has examined the relationship between prosocial behavior, forgiveness, and reconciliation, an important aspect of healthy interpersonal and intergroup relationships that strengthens the foundation for common group identification and action. At the same time, too much helping behavior could erode mutual and reciprocal power and status relations between the helper and the recipient and produce stratification. Research has bridged work on procedural and restorative justice with sustaining cooperative relations within neighborhoods as a vehicle for community capacity building.

Brenda Elizabeth Morrison

See also Peer Mediation; Resolving Conflict Creatively Program; Restorative Justice

Further Readings

Banyard, V. L., Plante, E. G., & Moynihan, M. M. (2004). Bystander education: Bringing a broader community perspective to sexual violence prevention. *Journal of Community Psychology, 32*(1), 61–79.

Penner, L. A., Dovidio, J. F., Pilianvin, J. A., & Schroeder, D. A. (2005). Prosocial behavior: Multilevel perspectives. *Annual Review of Psychology, 56,* 365–392.

Rigby, K., & Johnson, B. (2005). Introduction to the International Bystander Project. *Pastoral Care in Education, 23*(2), 6–9.

Twemlow, S. T., Fonagy, P., & Sacco, F. C. (2004). The role of the bystander in the social architecture of bullying and violence in schools and communities. *Annals of the New York Academy of Sciences, 1036,* 215–232.

CALCULATING EXTENT OF VICTIMIZATION: INCIDENCE, PREVALENCE, AND RATES

Measuring the extent of victimization is an important aspect of criminal justice research, and statistics can be a valuable tool in understanding victimization issues. There are two primary sources of victimization data in the United States—the FBI's Uniform Crime Reporting (UCR) Program and the Bureau of Justice Statistics' National Crime Victimization Survey (NCVS). Each of these sources provides useful data related to victimization incidence, prevalence, and rates. However, no data source is perfect, and each has issues that call into question the accuracy of the findings.

Sources of Victimization Data

Victimization data in the United States come primarily from two sources—the UCR Program and the NCVS. The UCR Program, in its annual report published by the FBI, divides crime into two categories: Part I and Part II crimes. Part I crimes are considered more severe and are restricted to eight particular crimes: murder, forcible rape, robbery, aggravated assault, burglary, larceny, motor vehicle theft, and arson. Data on an additional 21 crimes are reported in Part II. Data for these reports are compiled from nearly all police departments in the United States at the local, county, and state levels. Each police department in the United

States voluntarily sends the FBI their information on crime in their particular jurisdiction. The FBI then compiles the final report that becomes the UCR Program's report. The report is based on only official data reported to police departments, and as such does not measure those victimizations not reported to police.

The other major source for victimization data in the United States is the NCVS. The NCVS is administered by the Bureau of Justice Statistics (BJS), and utilizes a multistage sampling design to obtain annual estimates of certain types of victimization. The BJS administers surveys to persons 12 years of age or older and asks about both personal crime (e.g., sexual assault, robbery) and property crime (e.g., household burglary, theft) victimizations experienced by members of the household, as well as information about each victimization incident (e.g., the victim–offender relationship, consequences of the victimization incident).

Incidence and Prevalence

From these two data sources it is possible to obtain victimization incidence and prevalence statistics. *Incidence* refers to the proportion of respondents who are victimized by a particular crime in one year. *Prevalence* refers to the proportion of people who have ever experienced a particular type of victimization in their lifetime. The two statistics are similar, but have subtle differences. The major difference between the two statistics is temporally based. Incidence is restricted to victimization in one year, whereas prevalence refers to victimization during an entire lifetime.

Calculating Rates

A third type of victimization statistic is a victimization rate. Generally, a *rate* refers to some raw count that has been standardized by some measure of the population (e.g., the number of robberies per 100,000 people in the population). The two primary purposes of rates are to simplify information and to allow for easy comparison of data. Rates simplify information because they make the information more manageable and understandable. For example, reporting only raw numbers can be misleading. As an illustration, if a community experiences 578,962 aggravated assaults in a year, it may seem like a large number of assaults; however, that number of assaults expressed as a rate may be 5.7 per 100,000 people. The rate transforms the raw count into a more manageable and understandable number. In addition, because a rate is standardized with regard to a specific portion of the population, rates can be accurately and directly compared across communities. For example, comparing the raw number of homicides in Rhode Island to the raw number in California is not very informative because there are so many more people in California. By standardizing by some measure of the population (e.g., per 100,000 individuals), the population size has effectively been "controlled," allowing for meaningful comparison between those two states. The UCR Program and NCVS calculate their rates differently. The UCR Program calculates rates based on 100,000 members of the population for all crimes, whereas the NCVS calculates rates based on 1,000 persons for personal crime and 1,000 households for property crime. What this means is that rates from the UCR Program and the NCVS are not directly comparable without some manipulation of the figures.

Measurement and Counting Issues

Measurement and counting issues can ultimately affect victimization estimates (i.e., rates, incidence, and prevalence). Measurement issues include topics such as how to measure repeat and series victimization and how these measurement decisions can affect victimization estimates. The hierarchy rule counting strategy, which counts only the most serious crime where more than one crime has taken place, can have the effect of underestimating the extent of certain types of victimization.

Measuring Repeat and Series Victimizations

Repeat and series victimization present measurement issues that influence victimization statistics. A *repeat victimization* has occurred when a particular individual is victimized more than once in the specified time frame. Repeat victimizations can affect victimization estimates, making how they are counted and whether they are included in estimates an important estimation issue. Series victimizations present a similar dilemma. The NCVS classifies six or more similar but separate victimization events that cannot be distinctly separated and described in detail by the respondent as *series victimizations*. Series victimizations can have a significant impact upon victimization estimates, and past iterations of the NCVS have either included these series in their entirety or totally excluded them. The BJS currently excludes series victimization from its annual NCVS estimates.

The Hierarchy Rule

The hierarchy rule stipulates that only the most severe crime is counted in a criminal event involving multiple crimes. Consider the following hypothetical scenario: A victim is first robbed, then assaulted, and finally murdered. In that instance, only the homicide would be counted because of the hierarchy rule. Homicide is the most severe crime under the UCR scheme and in the above hypothetical scenario, it would be the crime reported to the FBI for UCR purposes, even though two other crimes happened within that one event. As a result, the UCR Program has been criticized for underestimating the extent of certain types of victimization.

Daniel J. Lytle and Bradford W. Reyns

See also Methodological Issues in Counting Victims; National Crime Victimization Survey (NCVS); National Incident-Based Reporting System (NIBRS); Nonreporting/Failure to Report Victimization; Stalking, Measurement of; Uniform Crime Reporting (UCR) Program; Victimization Surveys

Further Readings

Biderman, A. D. (1981). Sources of data for victimology. *Journal of Criminal Law & Criminology, 72,* 789–817.

Cantor, D., & Lynch, J. P. (2000). Self-report surveys as measures of crime and criminal victimization. *Criminal Justice 2000.* Retrieved May 19, 2009, from http://www.ncjrs.gov/criminal_justice2000/vol_4/04c.pdf

Cohen, L. E., & Land, K. C. (1984). Discrepancies between crime reports and crime surveys: Urban and structural determinants. *Criminology, 22,* 499–530.

Fisher, B. S., & Cullen, F. T. (2000). Measuring the sexual victimization of women: Evolution, current controversies, and future research. *Criminal Justice 2000.* Retrieved May 19, 2009, from http://www.ncjrs.org/criminal_justice2000/vol_4/04g.pdf

Gove, W. R., Hughes, M., & Geerken, M. (1985). Are Uniform Crime reports a valid indicator of the Index crimes? An affirmative answer with minor qualifications. *Criminology, 23,* 451–501.

Lynch, J. P., & Addington, L. A. (2007). *Understanding crime statistics: Revisiting the divergence of the NCVS and the UCR.* Cambridge, UK: Cambridge University Press.

CAMPUS CRIME, COLLEGE AND UNIVERSITY

Campus crime—illegal behavior occurring within the confines of postsecondary institutional boundaries—involves three important contexts: the legal, the social, and the security. The legal context involves judicial and legislative efforts to address campus crime, the social context includes efforts to accurately measure the extent and nature of campus crime while also identifying its major correlates, and the security context includes efforts of campus law enforcement and security to reduce/control campus crime and address new challenges, including those posed by high-tech crimes such as intrusions of university computer networks.

Legal Context

The legal context of campus crime includes postsecondary institutional liability for on-campus criminal victimizations. When lawsuits against postsecondary institutions first came before the courts in the 1970s, the courts were forced to determine whether they had legal merit. During the 1980s, an increase in these suits occurred, as plaintiffs began winning their lawsuits and the courts seemed more willing to take seriously such litigation. Finally, during the 1990s, postsecondary institutions became more proactive in trying to prevent these lawsuits by changing their campus security policies and procedures.

The courts have generally held postsecondary institutions liable for damages arising from on-campus victimizations, provided the plaintiff proves the institution owed the victim some kind of a duty, the duty was breached, and injuries resulted from that breach. Further, although courts have offered different reasoning, they have relied on several prominent theories in determining postsecondary institutional liability that focus on the relationship between the victim (plaintiff) and the institution and resulting duties owed him or her. Some courts have ruled the relationship as "special," in the sense that members of the campus community have a reasonable expectation the institution cares about their safety/security and will take steps to ensure it. Other courts have ruled the relationship is comparable to that of business owner/invitee, while still others have ruled the relationship is analogous to that of a landlord and tenant. In all three instances, specific duties toward members of the campus community arise on the part of the institution, and failure to fulfill them may result in liability.

Legislatively, Congress and nearly one half the states passed various "campus crime" statutes during the 1990s and into this decade. Congress passed the Student Right-to-Know and Campus Security Act (20 USC 1090[f]) in 1990, which in 1998 was renamed the Jeanne Clery Disclosure of Campus Security Policy and Campus Crime Statistics Act (hereafter, Clery) in remembrance of Jeanne Clery, a student who was murdered in her dorm room at Lehigh University in 1986. Clery and its state-level counterparts were intended to force postsecondary institutions to better communicate to the public the institution's crime statistics, its security policies, and its procedures for dealing with allegations of student-involved rape/sexual assault occurring on campus.

Proponents of such legislation argue that greater public awareness of campus crime will result in reduced levels of victimization, as people will take better precautions. Critics, however, argue that Clery represents a symbolic effort to address campus crime because (1) Clery's reporting requirements are based only on incidents actually reported to campus police/security, which seriously undercounts the true volume of campus crime; (2) Clery does not require postsecondary institutions to report annual statistics for on-campus theft, which victimization surveys repeatedly show is the most commonly occurring type of campus crime; and (3) sanctions for institutional noncompliance with Clery—civil fines of up to $25,000 per violation—are minimal and have rarely been implemented.

Critics of state-level campus crime legislation argue that the statutes often are not campus *crime* legislation, but rather are *enabling* legislation that allow colleges and universities to create campus police agencies; the legislation does little more than echo some of the requirements of Clery; and the statutes universally fail to contain penalties for noncompliance.

Social Context

Social scientists attempt to understand the social context of campus crime by measuring its extent and nature and identifying its major correlates. Two key areas here involve efforts to accurately estimate the victimization of college women and to identify and explore the role that students' lifestyles play in contributing to campus crime.

During the past 15 years, several national-level surveys have gathered data on the victimization experiences of college students in general and college women in particular. While the studies showed that students had lower overall rates of victimization when compared to nonstudents of similar ages, they almost universally found that a large minority of college women experienced a continuum of sexual victimization ranging from verbal harassment to rape. These studies also found that female victims often did not report their experiences to the proper authorities, blamed themselves for what had happened, or did not even perceive themselves as victims and therefore sought no help. In addition, the studies reported strong links between alcohol/drug consumption and sexual victimization, including evidence that males often planned their assaults on females by trying to debilitate them with alcohol,

drugs, or some combination of the two. Finally, the studies found that college women experiencing sexual victimization reported higher levels of depression, anxiety, hostility, and other mental health problems than did nonvictims.

The other key area of research examined the role that students' lifestyles play in explaining campus crime, particularly the use of alcohol and drugs. Alcohol, without question, is a key factor in college students' lifestyles. Evidence compiled by Harvard's College Alcohol Study (CAS), based on four, national-level studies of college student drinking patterns, indicated that about 80% of students enrolled at 4-year colleges and universities on a full-time basis drink alcohol; about 50% of these students routinely "drink to get drunk"; some 40% binge drink (drink four or more drinks in a row at one sitting in the two weeks prior to completing the survey); and roughly 20% of students binge drink frequently—at least three times during a 2-week period.

These studies also found strong links between students' alcohol abuse and self-reported offending and victimization. A 2002 survey showed that among 68,000 students enrolled at 133 colleges and universities, while student victimization was relatively rare, a pattern was discovered in which between one third and three quarters of all victims reported they had consumed alcohol or drugs prior to being victimized.

The research regarding college students' alcohol use and their victimization risk is clear: students who drink are at greater risk; the more a student drinks, the higher his or her risk for victimization; the more a student drinks away from his or her residence and among others who have reason to see the student become intoxicated or that the student does not know well, the greater the risk.

Security Context

Finally, the security context of campus crime includes not only campus policing and security, but increasingly efforts by postsecondary institutions to address such issues as high-tech crimes like identity theft and computer network intrusions involving members of the campus community as both offenders and victims.

While the first campus police officers were actually two City of New Haven officers who patrolled campus as part of their beat in 1849, research shows campus police departments evolved out of campus maintenance departments during the 19th and early 20th centuries. The responsibilities of those in the maintenance departments slowly changed from insuring the physical safety and security of the campus to enforcing campus disciplinary policies to full-fledged law enforcement. By the 1960s, in response to the political and social unrest of the time, postsecondary administrators wanted to avoid having municipal police officers on their campuses but still have a law enforcement presence there. It was then that modern campus police agencies, whose officers had full law enforcement authority, were born.

Over the next 40 years, campus police agencies adopted many of the same characteristics of municipal police agencies, including similar levels of specialization, bureaucratization, and tactical operations. Recently, like their municipal counterparts, increasing numbers of campus law enforcement agencies have adopted community-oriented policing (COP) as their new organizational model, which involves decentralization of operations, reduced levels of specialization, closer contacts with the campus community via foot or bicycle patrol, and greater emphasis on problem solving by line officers.

As campus law enforcement agencies evolved, they not only adopted organizational characteristics similar to their municipal counterparts, but also embraced emerging security technology as routine additions to their tactical and operational activities. For example, many campus police agencies routinely use closed-circuit television (CCTV) to monitor such areas as parking decks, green space, and particular buildings seen as high-level security risks due to research or other activities occurring there. Campus police and security agencies have also begun using "hot spots" analysis to identify places on campus disproportionately responsible for calls for service and to reallocate personnel accordingly. Finally, most campus police agencies have also adopted nonlethal technology such as pepper spray for use in the field.

A new challenge relating to the security context of campus crime involves high-tech crime and victimization. Samual McQuade and his colleagues at the Rochester Institute of Technology have extensively studied this issue and identified the following as the predominant forms of what they call information technology abuse (ITA): writing and distributing malware, such as viruses; disrupting computer service capabilities; spying and network intrusions, including computer hacking; fraudulent schemes, including identity theft; illegal file sharing and downloading of copyrighted material such as music or software; academic and scientific misconduct, including purchasing papers online; and online harassment, including threats and cyber-stalking. Ironically, colleges and universities commonly offer academic programs involving computer science, information technology, and related fields, where students learn the very tools needed to perpetrate these offenses. As a result, academic departments involving these fields must help to insure students in their fields develop strong ethical standards concerning the use of this technology.

As the new millennium unfolds, campus crime will continue to pose a challenge to postsecondary administrators and members of the campus community. Liability issues continue to be present for institutions of higher learning, while at the same time new challenges are posed by increasingly high-tech capabilities to victimize large numbers of people. Drinking by students also poses a challenge to postsecondary institutions, while the victimization of college women is a pressing issue that must continue to be addressed. Finally, as campus law enforcement agencies reformulate their organizational, operational, and tactical orientations, they continue to adapt to a relatively unique situation. In each of the areas discussed—legal, social, and security—campus crime continues to create both challenges and opportunities.

John J. Sloan

See also Campus Policing and Security; College and University Campus Legislation, Federal; College and University Campus Legislation, State; National Victimization Against College Women Surveys

Further Readings

Burling, P. (2003). *Crime on campus: Analyzing and managing the increasing risk of institutional liability* (2nd ed.). Washington, DC: National Association of College and University Attorneys.

Carter, S. D., & Bath, C. (2007). The evolution and components of the Jeanne Clery Act: Implications for higher education. In B. S. Fisher and J. J. Sloan III (Eds.), *Campus crime: Legal, social, and policy perspectives* (2nd ed., pp. 27–44). Springfield, IL: Charles C Thomas.

Fisher, B. S., Cullen, F. T., & Turner, M. (2000). *The sexual victimization of college women* (NCJ 182369). Washington, DC: Bureau of Justice Statistics.

Fisher, B. S., & Sloan, J. J. (Eds.). (2007). *Campus crime: Legal, social, and policy perspectives* (2nd ed.). Springfield, IL: Charles C Thomas.

McQuade, S. C. (2006). *Understanding and managing cybercrime*. Boston: Pearson Education.

Mustaine, E. E., & Tewksbury, R. (2007). The routine activities and criminal victimization of students: Lifestyle and related factors. In B. S. Fisher & J. J. Sloan III (Eds.), *Campus crime: Legal, social, and policy perspectives* (2nd ed., pp. 147–166). Springfield, IL: Charles C Thomas.

Paoline, E., & Sloan, J. J. (2003). Variability in the organizational structure of contemporary campus law enforcement agencies: A national-level analysis. *Policing: An International Journal of Police Strategies and Management*, 26, 12–639.

Pastore, A. L., & Maguire, K. (Eds.). (2003). *Sourcebook of criminal justice statistics*. Washington, DC: Bureau of Justice Statistics.

Sloan, J. J., & Shoemaker, J. (2007). State-level Clery Act initiatives: Symbolic politics or substantive policy? In B. S. Fisher & J. J. Sloan III (Eds.), *Campus crime: Legal, social, and policy perspectives* (2nd ed., pp. 201–121). Springfield, IL: Charles C Thomas.

Wechsler, H., & Wuetrich, B. (2002). *Dying to drink: Confronting binge drinking on college campuses*. Emmaus, PA: Rodale.

Web Sites

Security On Campus, Inc.: http://www.securityoncampus.org

CAMPUS POLICING AND SECURITY

Historically, it has been a challenge for campus administrators to provide a safe and secure environment for all students, and especially to protect those students who reside on campus. American colleges have taken their security responsibilities seriously, as in the past a parental-type relationship with students was assumed by colleges and universities. Currently, campus police and security departments are primarily responsible for developing comprehensive programs to provide for the safety of college communities.

The characteristics of today's campus police organizations are directly related to the changes that have occurred in institutions of higher education over the last 150 years. Therefore, this entry examines campus policing and security by providing a historical overview of the efforts made to make American college campuses safe and secure. The entry then reviews the policing issues raised and provides a snapshot of today's campus policing.

Definitions

A "campus police" department is an organization that provides the full range of police services to its collegiate community. For example, campus police officers typically have arrest authority and carry weapons while on duty in their legally defined jurisdiction. These departments operate in similarly in many ways to local law enforcement and are usually found at state-operated larger institutions.

"Campus security" departments provide personal and property protection services for their campuses, and their officers usually have no arrest authority and do not carry weapons. These departments typically have policies that require the local police to be summoned if a crime is reported or if an arrest is to be made on campus. Campus security departments are typically found at smaller and/or private institutions.

"Campus watchman" refers to the official in the 19th and early 20th centuries whose function was to lock up campus buildings and to be alert for other potential dangers such as fire hazards.

Early American College Security

Books written on the historical development of American colleges provide examples of early efforts to serve the personnel and property security needs of U.S. campuses. In colonial America, colleges established long lists of rules and regulations in an attempt to govern student conduct, and college presidents, faculty members, and even janitors provided rudimentary security services. At some institutions in the mid-1800s, students also became involved in campus security.

In 1870, Princeton created a new position on its campus called the office of the proctor. According to Jerry Witsil, this position was established to serve a policelike role and to be directly involved in student discipline. However, it would be another Ivy League institution, Yale, that would lay claim to having the first actual police force on campus. John Powell, a pioneer in campus policing, has noted that in 1894 two New Haven police officers were stationed on Yale's campus. The services they provided proved so effective that they were hired by the college as its first police force. This unit was established following a series of violent confrontations between Yale students and local townspeople.

As the 20th century approached, dramatic changes occurred within American higher education. The passage of the federal law known as the Morrill Act of 1862 established state land grant colleges throughout the country and, as a result, made college education accessible to middle-class families. Over the next several decades many new college and universities were built, and student populations grew accordingly. Moreover, with this growth colleges slowly began to experience more security-related problems.

Campus Security From 1900 to World War II

As American institutions of higher education grew in physical size to accommodate an increasing number of students, the protection of campus property and facilities became the primary focus of campus security. Watchmen were hired for this purpose, and also to work closely with deans of students to monitor student conduct. There is little evidence that serious crimes were much of a problem on American college campuses during the first third of the 20th century. Later in the century, however, the problems experienced by society in general (such as the sale and consumption of bootleg alcohol) also appeared on college campuses. In the 1940s (and 1950s), alcohol-related incidents such as disorderly conduct and destruction of property on the part of students were problems confronted by those offices responsible for student discipline and security.

Post–World War II Campus Security

The period from the end of World War II to the mid-1960s was one of slow evolution from campus "watchmen" organizations to more professional "security" departments. It was during this time that many campuses once again experienced significant growth in the number of students. A new federal law, the GI Bill, and the number of former military personnel attending college contributed substantially to the increase in students. In an effort to improve campus security departments, many institutions hired former or retired city police as officers and security chiefs. During this time, campus officers seldom had arrest authority and little specialized training. The traditional role of supervising student conduct and the emphasis on protecting property were often reflected in campus organizational hierarchy. The campus security department was typically supervised by the dean of students or the director of physical plant during the 1950s and early 1960s.

The long-term parental-type relationship between colleges and their students was altered in 1961. That year, the legal concept *in loco parentis* was struck down by the Supreme Court's decision in *Dickson v. Alabama Board of Education*. College students of age were now given the full rights and responsibilities of adults. As a result, campus administrators were required to alter many of their long-held policies and practices with regards to students. Security departments became less concerned with rule enforcement and more concerned with assisting students in making themselves more secure. In theory, colleges were still required to provide a safe and secure campus environment, but as adults, students assumed more personal responsibility.

Securing the Campus, 1960s–1980s

During the late 1960s and through the 1970s, societal events helped to bring about changes on college campuses and further alter the role of campus security agencies. Protests against the Vietnam War and other social/civil rights issues became part of everyday life on many American campuses. Campus security departments were inadequately prepared or equipped for the increase in civil disobedience, property destruction, and sometimes violent acts occurring within college boundaries. Local, county, and state police agencies were often called to assist the campus departments, but their presence often exacerbated tensions. It was during this time that most states passed laws creating campus police departments (usually at state-supported institutions), granting them the full range of police power and authority. According to campus police researcher John Sloan, it was during the 1970s that campus police departments began to closely resemble their local counterparts in both organizational structure and role. Professionalism, training, and technology became the trademarks of many progressive campus police agencies. Their role would ultimately become more "professional law enforcer" and less "rule enforcer" or "property protector."

Securing the Campus, 1980s–1990s

Institutions of higher education continued to grow during the 1980s and 1990s. For example, the *Digest of Educational Statistics* estimated that the number of colleges and universities in the United States grew from 1,500 in 1960 to almost 3,500 in 1990, and the number of students grew to approximately 14 million. Serious on-campus crimes also increased during this period, resulting in increased demands on campus police.

It was also during the 1980s and 1990s that civil liability lawsuits brought against colleges for failure to provide an adequate level of campus security and new campus crime legislation (both state and federal) influenced the role of campus police. The economic impact of lawsuits, coupled with negative publicity, had a major impact on campus security decision makers. Thus many campuses sought to improve their overall security to be in a better position to defend against lawsuits. This would in turn bring about improvements in campus police agencies.

Numerous states passed legislation placing a variety of requirements on institutions of higher education with respect to campus crime reporting and other security policy issues. The Student Right to Know and Campus Security Act of 1990 (now called the Jeanne Clery Disclosure of Campus Security Policy and Campus Crime Statistics Act) places a variety of mandates on institutions and their campus police agencies. It can be argued that the requirements of these

pieces of legislation have established legal standards for campus police that exceed those required of municipal police agencies.

Current Campus Policing and Security

Authority and Jurisdiction

The authority and jurisdiction of campus police/security organizations are typically defined in state laws. The vast majority of states grant powers of arrest and the ability to carry weapons to campus officers. These rights are accompanied by requirements that the officers meet the same minimum standards for hiring and training mandated for local police in that state. Many state-operated colleges and universities require police experience or college credit from applicants. In addition, new officers are placed in a field training program that familiarizes them with departmental policies and procedures. Smaller, private institutions of higher education do not usually possess statutory authority to make arrests or to carry weapons. The campus security departments at these colleges protect property and facilities, monitor student conduct, and provide a minimum level of personal safety for campus community members and visitors.

Status

In 1996 a report by the Bureau of Justice Statistics provided a comprehensive picture of campus police. The report identified the many organizational, administrative, and operational characteristics of current campus police agencies, many of which mirror characteristics of municipal police agencies. Among other things, Brian Reaves has noted the following findings with respect to campus police agencies today:

- More campus law enforcement agencies are using sworn and armed officers;
- Campus law enforcement agencies have kept pace with increasing enrollments;
- Campus police forces have become more diverse in terms of their employees;
- Training requirements for campus police have increased;
- Most campus police are actively engaged in community policing;

- Campus police agencies are more likely than ever to offer special programs for safety, and crime prevention;
- Campuses have better emergency access systems.

A review of these finding suggests that campus policing has continued to evolve as a profession. As campuses become larger and more complex, so too will the challenges for campus security decision makers. Unanticipated events and external influences will also play a part in the continuing evolution of campus policing. For example, the attacks of September 11, 2001, and the mass murder at Virginia Tech in 2007 prompted campuses to conduct internal reviews of security practices and policies with respect to vulnerabilities and prevention of and response to a multitude of potential threats. The mass murder incident at Virginia Tech in 2007 also produced additional internal review by campus officials, as well as external scrutiny of campus security issues relating to the prevention of and response to such threats. For the future, campus police and security administrators will need to be aware of the various factors that impact the campus environment. Given the fact that on most college campuses innovation is encouraged, the campus policing profession should continue to progress in order to anticipate campus changes and to develop ways to adequately protect the campus communities.

Max L. Bromley

See also Campus Crime, College and University; College and University Campus Legislation, Federal; College and University Campus Legislation, State

Further Readings

Bromley, M. L. (1996). Policing our campuses: A national review of statutes. *American Journal of Police*, 15(3), 1–22.

Bromley, M. L., & Territo, L. (1990). *College crime prevention and personal safety awareness*. Springfield, IL: Charles C Thomas.

Fisher, B. S., & Sloan, J. (2007). *Campus crime: Legal, social, and policy perspectives* (2nd ed.). Springfield, IL: Charles C Thomas.

Gelber, S. (1972). *The role of campus security in the college setting*. Washington, DC: U.S. Department of Justice.

Griffaton, M. C. (1995). State-level initiatives on campus crime. In B. S. Fisher & J. J. Sloan III (Eds.), *Campus crime: Legal, social and policy perspectives* (pp. 246–263). Springfield, IL: Charles C Thomas.

Neal, R. (1980). A history of campus security: Early origins. *Campus Law Enforcement Journal*, 10(6), 28–30.

Nichols, D. (1987). *The administration of public safety in higher education*. Springfield, IL: Charles C Thomas.

Powell, J., Pander, M., & Nielson, R. (1994). *Campus security and law enforcement* (2nd ed.). Newton, MA: Butterworth Heinemann.

Reaves, B., & Goldberg, A. (1996). *Campus law enforcement agencies, 1995*. Washington, DC: Department of Justice.

Sloan, J. J. (1994). The correlates of campus crime: An analysis of reported crimes on college and university campuses. *Journal of Criminal Justice*, 22(1), 51–61.

CARJACKING

During the late 1980s and the early 1990s, carjacking was brought to the national attention. The 1992 case that triggered the national debate involved Pamela Basu of Maryland. Two men pulled Basu from her car and drove away, dragging Basu, who was caught in her seatbelt, for over a mile before she fell to road. Basu died of her injuries. Basu's child was thrown from the car but was not injured. The perpetrators were subsequently prosecuted in state court for various crimes—but not for carjacking, as there was no specific state carjacking statute in existence at that time—and sentenced to extended periods of time in prison.

Carjacking, a term apparently coined by the media in response to various other sensationalized cases, is commonly understood as the taking of an automobile from a person, while he or she is in the car, with the use of force. The act usually occurs while the car is in a parking lot, stopped in traffic, or at a traffic light, and the victim is usually approached by one or more perpetrators who are armed. The frequent presence of weapons in carjackings fueled the public reaction to the crime, given the ongoing war against violent crime.

Although carjacking was not formally defined as a crime at the federal level, the prevalence of armed carjackings and the injuries suffered by innocent motorists caused a public outcry. The United States Department of Justice estimated that there were more than 35,000 carjackings and attempted carjackings each year from 1987 to 1992. Weapons were used in 77% of the carjackings and attempted carjackings. Further, 24% of victims of completed carjackings were injured, and 18% of attempted carjacking victims were injured. The carjackings were most likely to occur at night and away from the victim's home, with 29% occurring in a parking lot or garage and 45% occurring in an open area such as on the street. In addition, 49% of the perpetrators were Black and 30% were White. Males committed 88% of carjackings.

The Law

Thus Congress enacted the Anti-Car Theft Act of 1992, codified at Title 18 U.S.C. § 2119, which made carjacking a separate offense. Title 18 U.S.C. § 2119 provided that whoever possessing a firearm, takes a motor vehicle, which had passed through interstate or foreign commerce, from a person by force or intimidation, or attempts to do so, with the intent to temporarily or permanently deprive the person, shall be punished by fifteen years in prison, twenty five years in prison of serious bodily injury results, or by death or life in prison if death results. The statute was subject to numerous constitutional challenges in court under the Due Process Clause and the Commerce Clause of the United States Constitution. Subsequently, in 1994, Congress amended the statute to include unarmed carjackings. In addition, a number of states have enacted carjacking statutes. Each state has different criminal codes and each requires different elements for a conviction.

Carjacking is considered a form of theft or robbery. Theft involves the unlawful taking of property with the intent to permanently deprive the owner of the property. Theft, generally, does not involve taking the property directly from the person. Depending upon the value of the property taken, theft can be a misdemeanor or a felony. Robbery involves the unlawful taking of property directly from the person or in their person with the intent to permanently deprive the owner of the property by the use of threats or force. Robbery is considered a serious offense and is usually classified as a felony. Higher penalties are usually imposed if a weapon is used

during a robbery. Unarmed robbery has frequently been called "strong arm" robbery. The key issue for both crimes is the intent to permanently deprive the owner of the property.

One of the basic principles of criminal law is that, to be convicted of a crime, the prosecutor must prove every element of the crime beyond a reasonable doubt. For theft and robbery, one of the elements of the crimes is the intent to permanently deprive the owner of the property, which must be proved beyond a reasonable doubt.

The legal problem presented by carjacking arose from the fact that the perpetrators frequently did not intend to keep the automobile. The perpetrators would take the automobile, use it for whatever purpose it was intended (i.e., such as for a robbery get-away vehicle or a joyride), and then abandon it. A significant proportion of the automobiles that were carjacked were returned. Thus, there was a significant problem in charging carjackers with theft or robbery, as convictions were difficult to obtain. Finally, the federal carjacking statute resolved the problem caused by whether the carjacker intended to temporarily or permanently deprive the person of the automobile, as it criminalized the taking of the automobile no matter what the intent.

Statistics

According to the National Crime Victimization Surveys, between 1992 and 1996, approximately 49,000 attempted or completed carjackings occurred in the United States each year. About half of all carjackings were completed. About 7 in 10 completed carjackings involved the use of a firearm, while about 2 in 10 attempted carjackings involved the use of a firearm. Most carjackings did not result in injuries to the victims.

According to the National Crime Victimization Surveys, from 1993 to 2002, there were about 38,000 carjackings annually. Blacks and Hispanics were more often victims of carjackings than were Whites, and 93% of all carjackings occurred in urban areas. Weapons were used in 74% of the carjackings, with 45% involving firearms. Further, 32% of victims of completed carjackings and 17% of victims of attempted carjackings were injured, and 9% of the injuries were serious. Males were responsible for 93% of the carjacking incidents. In addition, 56% of the carjackers were Black and 21% were White. Finally, 68% of the carjacking incidents occurred at night, and 42% of the night-time carjackings and 50% of the daytime carjackings were completed.

As can be seen from the data, the incidence of carjackings declined over time since the issue was raised to a significant degree in the national media. As with many crimes brought to the attention of the public, with carjacking there was a reduction in incidents after enforcement efforts were increased. Also, with the enactment of laws directly related to the prosecution of carjacking and closing the legal impediments to obtaining convictions, the argument can be made that there has been some deterrent effect.

Overall, the relative incidence of carjackings compared to other crimes is low. Indeed, carjackings represent only a small fraction of the total number of automobile thefts. Even in the period from 1987 to 1992, only 2 of every 10,000 persons were subject to a carjacking. However, carjacking has received a significant amount of attention because of the possibility of severe injuries for its victims, or even death.

The general suggestions for the prevention of carjacking concern the use of caution. The public should be warned: Do not drive through areas where there is high crime. When driving through high crime and urban areas, keep your car doors locked and windows shut. Do not open the doors or windows for strangers. Common sense and reasonable caution can prevent many carjackings.

Wm. C. Plouffe Jr.

See also Crime Prevention; Deterrence; Guns and Victimization; Larceny/Theft; Motor Vehicle Theft; Robbery

Further Readings

Klaus, P. (1994). *Costs of crime to victims.* Bureau of Justice Statistics Crime Data Brief. Washington, DC: U.S. Department of Justice.

Klaus, P. (1999). *Carjacking in the United States, 1992–96* [Special report]. Washington, DC: United States Department of Justice.

Klaus, P. (2004). *National Crime Victimization Survey: Carjacking, 1993–2002.* Washington, DC: United States Department of Justice.

Michenfelder, M. C. (1995). *The federal carjacking statute: To be or not to be? An analysis of the propriety of 18 U.S.C. 2119, 39 St. Louis U.L.J. 1009.* St. Louis, MO: St. Louis University.

Rand, M. (1994). *Carjacking: National Crime Victimization Survey.* Washington, DC: U.S. Department of Justice.

CENTRAL REGISTRY

Child abuse is typically defined as the physical, sexual, or psychological maltreatment of children. Unfortunately, children are frequent and easy targets of abuse and maltreatment because they are unable to protect or help themselves. As a result, numerous agencies and departments have continued to work to develop means of protecting children from abusers. One of the more cooperative and widespread efforts is the development of central registries, also known as child abuse and neglect registries. A central registry is an online database used to maintain and track reports of child abuse and neglect. Central registries have been created at both the state and national level. They allow social services, medical, and/or police personnel, as well as employers, to check for reported incidents of child abuse that individuals committed in other areas, cities, or states. The main purpose of central registries is twofold. First, they prevent abusive parents or guardians from escaping detection by taking their children to multiple hospitals or doctors. Second, they prevent abusive individuals from getting jobs working with children or serving as foster parents. Though there are apparent benefits of central registries, there is also a moderate amount of controversy associated with them.

Design and Purpose

A central registry is an online database that contains records of prior incidents of child abuse and maltreatment. The information contained in the records typically includes: the abused child's name and address, the name and address of the parents or guardians, the name and address of the alleged perpetrator, a description of the harmful incident, and the outcome of any investigation. Certain agencies and employers can submit requests to perform prior-abuse background checks on individuals that may come into contact with children. This process helps to protect children from potential abuse by preventing individuals who have a prior record of abuse and maltreatment from coming into contact with them. Further, central registries can be used by social services, medical, and police personnel to investigate allegations of child abuse. In many instances, abusive parents or guardians will take children to different hospitals in order to avoid the suspicion that may arise as the result of continuously bringing an injured child to the hospital or doctor. With a central registry, it becomes very difficult to hide child abuse.

State Central Registries

Numerous states have had central registries for well over 20 years. Currently, every U.S. state, the District of Columbia, the Commonwealth of Puerto Rico, and the U.S. territories of American Samoa and Guam has procedures for maintaining and tracking reports of child abuse and maltreatment. However, as of 2005, only 45 states have statewide central registries. Forty-two states developed central registries as a result of statutory authorization, and the other three developed central registries as a result of administrative policy. Each state has its own specific process and documentation used to report and track suspected incidents of abuse and maltreatment. Employers or agencies within a state can use the state central registry to track prior abusive behavior that has occurred only in that state. In order to track potential abuse and maltreatment across multiple states, the national central registry should be used.

National Central Registry

Similar to state central registries, there is also a national central registry. The national central registry was developed as a result of the National Child Protection Act of 1993 (NCP Act) and the Adam Walsh Child Protection and Safety Act of 2006 (Adam Walsh Act). Essentially, the national central registry combines the information from the state registries, in order to allow agencies and employers to search for abusive incidents committed by specific individuals in any state or city across the United States. The NCP Act, which was signed by President Bill Clinton in 1993, allows employers to perform a prior-abuse background check on any individual applying for a job involving direct contact with children, such as day care services. The Adam Walsh Act, signed by President George W. Bush in 2006, mandates that the central registry be used to perform a prior-abuse background check on any individual applying to serve as a foster or adoptive parent. Unfortunately, the information in the national central registry does have limitations. It only contains information reported by those states that have state central registries. In addition, compared to many of the state central registries, the national central registry is relatively new and still has many issues that need to be worked out.

Controversy Associated With Central Registries

Though the underlying goal of central registries— to protect children from abuse—is certainly laudable, their development and use has sparked a certain amount of controversy. In an effort to prevent child abuse and maltreatment, central registries are used to track abusers rather than the children they abuse. This method is designed to restrict the opportunity for individuals to abuse. Many argue, however, that the registries may be used improperly to investigate and prosecute abusive individuals, essentially removing the focus from protecting children to punishing offenders. Further, unlike other registries—such as sex offender registries—individuals placed in central registries are never removed. As a result, punishment and stigmatization continue even after a convicted offender has completed all the requirements of his or her sentence.

Billy Henson

See also Abuse, Ritual Child; AMBER Alert; Child Abuse, Neglect, and Maltreatment; Child Abuse, Neglect, and Maltreatment: Mandatory Reporting; Child Abuse, Neglect, and Maltreatment: Statutory Response; Child Protective Services; Megan's Law; Shaken Baby Syndrome

Further Readings

Adam Walsh Child Protection and Safety Act of 2006 (H.R. 4472 [109th]).

Child Welfare Information Gateway. (2005). *Establishment and maintenance of central registries for child abuse reports: Summary of state laws.* Retrieved November 15, 2008, from http://www .childwelfare.gov/systemwide/laws_policies/statutes/ centreg.pdf

Lab, S. P. (2007). *Crime prevention: approaches, practices and evaluations* (6th ed.). Cincinnati, OH: LexisNexis/Anderson.

National Child Protection Act of 1993 (42 U.S.C. 5119a).

Underwager, R., & Wakefield, H. (1991). Central registry: Protection or oppression. *Institute for Psychological Therapy Journal, 3*(4), 221–227.

Chicago Alternative Policing Strategy (CAPS)

The Chicago Alternative Policing Strategy, or CAPS, was one of the first attempts to implement community policing comprehensively in a major American city. Five police districts implemented the CAPS strategy and structure on an experimental basis beginning in 1993, and deployment throughout the entire Chicago Police Department (CPD) occurred over the next 2 years.

Planning and Implementation

The Chicago Police Department is organized into 25 districts with a total of 279 beats. In April 1993, the department launched CAPS in five districts—Austin, Englewood, Marquette, Morgan Park, and Rogers Park. The prototype districts constituted trial runs of the new approach, allowing weaknesses and unanticipated issues to be identified and addressed before the citywide rollout. Emerging and ongoing issues were addressed by several committees; some focused on short-term corrections, while others analyzed strategic changes that would require longer planning and more extensive engineering.

Operationally, the core of the CAPS initiative was a dedicated team of patrol officers in each of the city's beats. Those officers were charged with organizing the residents, working with them to identify and prioritize the needs of the neighborhoods, and developing effective responses and solutions. Team officers were assigned to their beats for an extended term in order to develop deeper knowledge of the area and form stable working partnerships with individuals and entities within the beat. That constituted a major change from the past practice of regularly reassigning officers to new areas, a legacy of earlier anticorruption efforts.

On a daily basis, one of the primary barriers to community problem solving had been the need to respond to calls for service. Daily call demands often overwhelmed more time-intensive community projects. The CAPS structure initially removed beat officers from the 9-1-1 response queue in order to facilitate their problem-centered efforts. Separate teams of rapid-response units handled calls for police service, but were also responsible for coordinating with the beat officers. The structure was later modified to allow Priority 1 (emergency) calls to be assigned to beat officers.

The effort was not limited to uniformed patrol officers: All CPD officers in investigative and specialty assignments are required to coordinate with and support the beat teams on a regular basis. Their participation brings vital resources and special knowledge to the problem-solving approach, and insures that "stovepipes" of restricted information do not develop.

The CAPS design embodied variants of innovations and experimental programs in other jurisdictions: the split-force concept pioneered in Wilmington, Delaware; team policing, which had been pioneered in several cities in the early 1970s, but not widely adopted; and foot beats, whose effectiveness in an age of motorized patrol had been demonstrated by the Flint, Michigan, Neighborhood Foot Patrol Experiment in the early 1980s.

The principles of problem solving and community organizing are also fundamental to CAPS organization, training, and direction. In 2000, the CPD instituted a decentralized planning and management process for identification and resolution of problems in support of CAPS. Comparable to the contemporary COMPSTAT process in New York City, it delegates strategic functions to the District level. A new 9-1-1 center was inaugurated, and the CPD Research and Planning Division was transformed through civilianization and expansion.

This change in the CPD's information-processing capacity dovetailed with the CAPS process. Better and timelier information supplements community efforts at problem solving. Drawing upon the department's upgraded information systems, the data used to inform the planning and response are also used by the administration to evaluate effectiveness.

The overall thrust of the CAPS initiative was to orient all CPD officers to the community-policing philosophy, provide them with adequate tools and institutional support, and eliminate known barriers to effective community organizing. It rests upon the belief that crime prevention and crime control are community responsibilities, not the exclusive domain of the police, and will not result from police activity alone. A concurrent goal is to establish a territorial "ownership," a personal investment in their assigned beats, among CPD officers.

A corollary of the community-oriented philosophy is that the entire organization must support the community policing initiatives. Attempting to align the department's commitment to the community within a small innovation ghetto of specialist officers is a prescription for failure. If the community-policing unit is just an innovative ghetto while the rest of an agency continues to operate on the traditional model, positive results will be limited. The CPD sought input from multiple community and social service partners, both in the planning stages and throughout the implementations. The relative proportions of input from the community members are a major element of the external evaluation.

In constructing the CAPS model, the CPD established a series of committees to plan and coordinate the implementation. Planners sought the positive and negative lessons of prior experiments and programs, synthesizing them within the unique organizational aspects of the CPD. Planning partners from outside the agency were full partners in the endeavor: Some shared a common client group with the police; others were oriented to a broader municipal development perspective. A long-term independent evaluation was conducted by the Illinois Criminal Justice Information Authority, which provided annual or biannual assessments of the process over a 10-year span.

Outcomes

CAPS has been successful in achieving many of its goals, and most of the initial difficulties were overcome during the first decade of its existence. The external evaluation focused on several implementation and outcome measures; some concentrated on the community, others on the department, and still others on the quality and effectiveness of their interaction and problem-solving efforts.

Community knowledge of CAPS is high, and as participation rates for citizens grew, so did satisfaction with the police. Chicago is a famously multiethnic city, and CAPS participation and approval ratings mirror its larger racial divides. After 10 years of CAPS, all racial/ethnic groups were more positive about the police department than they had been when CAPS was inaugurated, but the gaps between groups remained relatively constant. Caucasians and African Americans were more likely to rate the police favorably than were Latinos, whose lower approval rates were strongly influenced by a variety of immigration issues.

During the early years of CAPS, the initiatives experienced the same difficulties in eliciting resident participation and leadership that have been recorded in other locations. The 10th-year evaluation noted that the highest rates of citizen participation were found in the neighborhoods with the most serious problems. This was attributed to belief that the problem resolution projects were effective, even though a relatively low proportion of identified problems have an action component. Like community meetings elsewhere, participation rates are greatest among long-term residents, older adults, and those with higher education.

As with most fledgling community-policing initiatives, CAPS experienced difficulties in organization and leadership responsibilities, including uneven rates of participation and satisfaction among all participant groups. Leadership roles developed unevenly, particularly within the police ranks, and the clarity of purpose of each meeting was often lacking. Over time, meeting quality improved, and cooperative leadership emerged. Citizen satisfaction with the process steadily increased. Police satisfaction fluctuated more than resident satisfaction, which may have been due to turnover and the periodic loss of experienced officers to reassignment, or to different expectations of success.

The impact of CAPS on serious crime is not clear. Although felony-level crimes fell in Chicago during the first decade of the CAPS, the reductions were in accord with national declines in reported crime during that period. Though Chicago experienced some steeper declines in certain types of crime, such as armed robbery, the influence of CAPS is confounded by the effects of other prevention initiatives, including greater restrictions on firearms availability and changes in drug markets. Some of the factors credited with the lower crime rate are associated with, but not specifically linked to, the CAPS outcomes of improved neighborhood conditions and police effectiveness.

Neighborhood-specific analysis of crime trends and conditions during that period showed substantial improvements in African American neighborhoods. Those improvements paralleled gains in African American confidence in and approval of the police. A causal relationship to CAPS activities remains speculative in the first instance, but may be more strongly inferred in the second. Because the two are conceptually linked, there is reason to believe CAPS played a prominent role in the resurgence. Unfortunately, like many crime prevention initiatives, CAPS overlapped with too many simultaneous initiatives to allow its effects to be distinguished without ambiguity.

Greater confidence can be placed in the CAPS influence on neighborhood problems. Issues identified in the early stages of CAPS tended to be those of physical decay, while those in later years clustered around social behavior and disorder. Concerns about physical conditions such as derelict buildings, graffiti, and trash-strewn lots declined in African American neighborhoods but not in Latino areas. Language barriers were identified as a continuing problem in Latino areas, where personal contact was far more influential than printed or broadcast dissemination of information. Specific concerns about problems in and around schools were reduced in all areas.

Internal administrative and managerial changes within the department have evolved at an uneven pace. CAPS is generally credited with making district-level managers more effective and responsible, and for improving communications and cooperation within the CPD. The legacy of policing's command-and-control orientation has been seen as restricting upward communications to a reporting function, and the overall assessment was that management was improved by the process. Ongoing issues include limited participation in CAPS by senior commanders and integration of all partners at all levels.

Future Outlook

CAPS remains the organizational backbone of the Chicago Police Department. Periodic reversion to more traditional police responses to problems remains a concern, but CAPS has endured and grown through several different city hall and CPD administrations. The department's commitment to the change process has enhanced the police role, and the community role has grown and solidified over the years.

The enduring result of CAPS has been a solidified partnership between the CPD and the communities it serves. The institutionalization of community orientation, problem analysis, and problem-solving capacity on the scale of CAPS is unprecedented. Addressing new problems as soon as they are identified cannot always guarantee success, but is a major step forward in making crime prevention a priority of police operations. Police departments will always depend upon reactive responses to a large extent. In its CAPS structure, the CPD created a way to maintain that function without sacrificing crime prevention. Sustained consultation with citizens and continued attention to quality-of-life issues yields greater community support for the police, enhanced livability in the neighborhoods, and a more responsive, intelligence-led police force.

Michael E. Buerger

See also Community Policing

Further Readings

Chicago Community Policing Evaluation Consortium. (1995). *Community policing in Chicago: Year two. An interim report.* Chicago: Illinois Criminal Justice Information Authority.

Chicago Community Policing Evaluation Consortium. (1996). *Community policing in Chicago: Year three.*

Chicago: Illinois Criminal Justice Information Authority.

Chicago Community Policing Evaluation Consortium. (1999). *Community policing in Chicago: Years five and six. An interim report.* Chicago: Illinois Criminal Justice Information Authority.

Chicago Community Policing Evaluation Consortium. (2000). *Community policing in Chicago: Year seven.* Chicago: Illinois Criminal Justice Information Authority.

Chicago Community Policing Evaluation Consortium. (2004). *Community policing in Chicago: Year ten.* Chicago: Illinois Criminal Justice Information Authority.

Northwestern University Institute for Policy Research. (n.d.). *Community policing evaluation publications.* Retrieved from http://www.northwestern.edu/ipr/publications/policing.html

Skogan, W. G. (2006). *Police and community in Chicago: A tale of three cities.* New York: Oxford University Press.

Skogan, W. G., & Harnett, S. M. (1997). *Community policing, Chicago style.* New York: Oxford University Press.

CHILD ABUSE, IDENTIFICATION OF

The identification of child abuse is a challenging task because the child victim may be reluctant to reveal his or her victimization to others. An abuser may threaten the child victim with additional punishment if the child tells of the abuse experience. There are several sources of suspicion of child abuse. They include direct witness, the child's statements, the child's injuries, the child's behavior, the parents' description of the events, and prior abuse reports. Thus, a medical professional, a social worker, or a law enforcement officer considers the totality of all information from various sources to identify whether abuse has occurred. Criminologists, however, divide child maltreatment into four categories: physical abuse, sexual abuse, emotional/psychological abuse, and neglect. This entry explores the possible indicators for each of the four typologies of child abuse and the various sources of such information. Although these indicators can have causes other than abuse, these indicators, when evaluated within each individual context, may assist professionals in evaluating alleged or suspected child maltreatment.

Identification of Physical Abuse

Information From the Child: Physical Signs

Physical signs of abuse may include a number of unexplained burns, bite marks, bruises, broken bones, black eyes, and so on. When children fall or bang into things, they tend to injure their chins, foreheads, hands, elbows, and knees. Injuries to areas that are less commonly sites of accidental injuries, such as the thighs, upper arms, genitals, buttocks, and the back of the legs or trunk, may be signs of abuse.

Bruises

Bruises on an infant's face and buttocks may signal that the infant has been intentionally assaulted by someone. For example, two black eyes seldom come from an accident. An investigator must calculate the time of injury to see if the injuries are consistent with the explanation from the child's parent or caregiver. A professional is able to estimate the age of bruises by color. The color of bruises changes from red (swollen, tender) within 2 days of the injury, to blue or purple within 2 to 5 days, to green within 5 to 7 days, to yellow within 7 to10 days, and finally to brown within 10 to 14 days. The bruises disappear within 2 to 4 weeks after the injury occurs.

Bruises on the neck whose shapes look like fingers and/or an entire palm print may be signs that the child was choked. Similar bruises on the torso, on the shoulders, or around the elbows or knees may be the indication that the child was thrown or shaken. Thus, a medical professional must carefully take a look at the shape of bruises.

Shaken Baby Syndrome

John Caffey coined the term *shaken baby syndrome* in 1974. According to Caffey, shaken baby syndrome is the product of violent shaking of a baby's arms or shoulders. One of the important characteristics of shaken baby syndrome is that it does not result in a clear external head injury; however, violent shaking a baby may lead to serious brain damage because a baby's neck muscles are not well enough developed for the baby to support his or her own head. Simple household falls and gently tossing a baby in the air during play are not very good explanations for a baby's brain injury. In most cases of shaken baby syndrome, the baby does not show skull fractures and external signs of trauma. However, the baby may begin to show symptoms such as seizures or unconsciousness immediately after the injury occurs. In a serious case, the vibrant shaking of a child may leave permanent brain damage requiring long-term medical attention or even lead to death.

Bone Fracture

Injuries resulting from physical abuse include broken and dislocated bones. Spinal fracture and other injuries to the arm and leg bones of an infant may be signs of twisting or pulling by an adult. Infants are especially unlikely to inflict such bone injuries by themselves. The presence of rib fractures, if accompanied by pressure bruises (shaped like fingers or hands), provide a hint that an adult may have squeezed the baby with enormous force. If an infant or a child has multiple fractures with different stages of healing, it could be indicative of repetitious assaults by others.

Burns

Another common cause of abuse that results in physical injury is the cigarette burn. Some abusive adults place burning cigarettes against a child's skin. However, burn marks may come from other attacks. An abusive adult may place the child in extremely hot water or place hot irons or automobile exhaust pipes against the child's body.

Burn patterns can provide clues for a child abuse investigation. Distinctively shaped dry or "contact" burns suggest that the attacker may have used instruments such as a heated wire, an iron, a space heater, or hot plate. A well-defined line between burned and unburned body parts without splash marks may be a sign that the abuser held the child firmly and carefully lowered him or her into a hot liquid. Also, the severity of the burn is generally unchanging throughout the body when the child is placed in the hot liquid by force.

Poisoning

Some abusive parents and caretakers use chemical agents as a means of maltreatment. Those most commonly used include water, salt, alcohol, marijuana, barbiturates, psychoactive drugs, tranquilizers, and opiates. The children poisoned by such chemical agents display a variety of symptoms, including irritability, listlessness, lethargy, stupor, and coma. In addition, a child may be poisoned by cleaning fluid or some other caustic substance. In such a case, there will likely be burns in the child's mouth. Accidental poisoning is seen most often in children 2 to 3 years old, and it is uncommon in children under the age of 1 or over the age of 6. Thus, poisoning of a child less than 1 or older than 6 is likely to have been intentional.

Information From the Child: Behavioral Signs

A physically abused child is also likely to exhibit behavioral symptoms. The child may be afraid of seeing his or her abusive parent(s) or care provider(s), or may feel a constant danger of being attacked and therefore may not want to go home after school. Other behavioral symptoms of physical abuse may include aggression, such as anger and attacking other children and depression. Behavioral signs are not limited to those above, however, and may include bedwetting, refusal to speak, head banging, and many others.

Information From the Parents or Caregivers

The possibilities of physical abuse may be ascertained from the statements and behavior of parents or other care providers. There are several examples suggesting the possibilities of physical abuse. First, the parents or caregivers may fail to give reasonable explanation for the child's injury. Second, the parents or caregivers may depict the child in a negative way or as evil. Third, abusive parents may delay seeking medical assistance when the child is injured. This may be due to their fear of being detected by others. Finally, abusive parents may have shown similar abusive patterns in the past.

Identification of Sexual Abuse

Information From the Child: Physical Signs

In many cases, sexual abuse does not leave distinct physical injuries to the victim. However, sexually abused children may have some physical signs. For example, the child may have a problem with walking or sitting. The child may have unexplained injuries around genital and anal areas; for example, the vagina or anus may be torn, lacerated, infected, or bloody. Unusual vaginal irritations may be due to forced sex. A child's penis may be swollen, inflamed, infected, or show signs of internal bleeding. Additional injuries may also include bruises, redness, and bleeding around genitals. The child's underwear may be torn, may have blood stains, or may contain semen. The presence of semen in the oral, anal, or vaginal cavity also discloses that the child has had sexual contact with others. Finally, the child may be pregnant or infected with a sexually transmitted disease.

Information From the Child: Behavioral Signs

The sexually abused child may exhibit sudden behavioral changes. Thus, the child may avoid changing clothes or exercising at gym class. He or she also may have unusual knowledge of sexual behavior or interest. Further, a sexually abused child may display seductive behavior that is not appropriate for his or her age. The child may experience ongoing nightmares or bedwetting. He or she may be afraid of going to a certain place or seeing a specific adult. The sexually abused child also may state that his or her body is "dirty" or "damaged." Finally, a child's drawing and writing may include sensationalized sexual images.

Information From the Parents or Caregivers

The parent or caregiver who is sexually abusing his or her child is one of two basic types. The first type is a person who primarily has sexual relationships with adults. However, the adult has sexual relationships with his or her child due to situational factors such as stresses from divorce or unemployment. Thus, social workers or law enforcement professionals investigate unusual stressors of parents or caregivers that may lead to sexual abuse of a child. The other type is the adult who is primarily attracted to children instead of adults. In these cases, social workers or law enforcement professionals need to investigate whether the adult is a pedophile. For example, the adult may collect child pornography, which is indicative of pedophilia.

Identification of Emotional Abuse

Information From the Child: Behavioral Signs

Emotionally abused children rarely show physical signs. Thus, in many cases only behavioral signs are identifiable. An emotionally abused child may be drastic in his or her behavior. Behavioral disorders such as antisocial or destructive behavior are common consequences of emotional abuse. For example, some abused children have a habit of head banging, sucking, and/or biting. Also, an emotionally abused child may display signs of neurosis such as sleep disorders, speech disorders, and the inhibition to play. He or she may be overly passive or aggressive.

Signs of Emotionally Abusive Parents or Caregivers

The causes of emotional abuse by a parent or caregiver can be divided into several types. The first type is related to factors associated with the child. For instance, caring for a child with a special problem, such as physical disability, mental disability, or serious behavioral problem, can be taxing for the parent, and the parent may respond with emotional abuse. Another type is associated with the stressors of a parent or a caregiver, such as divorce, loss of job, unwanted pregnancy, or other personal or professional stressors. Sometimes, the adult's mental illness, such as depression, or substance abuse may be an underlying cause of the emotional abuse.

Identification of Neglect

Neglect is frequently defined as a caregiver's failure to provide his or her child with basic needs such as food, clothing, shelter, medical care, and/or supervision.

Information From the Child: Physical Signs

One of the common physical signs of neglected young children is low body weight. A young child is totally dependent upon his or her caretakers for food. If a child does not receive the proper nutrition, the child can fail to gain weight as expected for his or her age. In addition, lack of proper nutrition can result in dull and thin hair and failure to develop full motor skills, which can be seen in a child's difficulty with tasks such as grabbing, reaching, and picking up objects.

Information From the Child: Behavioral Signs

There are several behavioral signs that may indicate neglect. Children who are neglected may be absent from school frequently without a clear reason (such as a sickness). A sudden drop in children's school grades also may be a consequence of neglect. Neglected children may beg or steal food at school because their parents do not provide proper sustenance. They may appear to be constantly tired, and may fall asleep in class or even in play sessions. These children may wear the same dirty clothes for several days or more, and may have a strong body odor because their parents do not wash them regularly. Further, their parents or care providers may fail to seek medical attention for them when it is needed, indicating neglect.

Finally, normal infants or toddlers are generally curious about their surroundings and spend a significant amount of time seeing other person's faces and hearing noises. However, neglected children may be disinterested in their environment. In serious cases, neglected children may not cry for help from their caregivers. They learn that they cannot rely on others to satisfy their environmental and emotional needs.

Signs of Neglecting Parents

Some neglecting parents suffer from depression and use excessive amounts of alcohol or drugs. Thus, they are incapable of taking care of their children. Other neglecting parents may leave a young child home alone. This kind of neglect not only jeopardizes the safety of the child but also may inhibit the child from fully developing awareness for personal safety.

Don Chon

See also Child Abuse, Neglect, and Maltreatment; Child Abuse, Neglect, and Maltreatment: Interventions for; Child Abuse, Neglect, and Maltreatment: Mandatory Reporting; Child Abuse, Neglect, and Maltreatment: Measurement of; Child Abuse, Neglect, and Maltreatment: Statutory Responses; Child Abuse, Neglect, and Maltreatment: Theories of; Munchausen Syndrome by Proxy; Shaken Baby Syndrome

Further Readings

Crosson-Tower, C. (2005). *Understanding child abuse and neglect*. Boston: Pearson/Allyn & Bacon.

Joughin, V. (2003). Working together child protection in A&E. *Emergency Nurse, 11*, 30–37.

U.S. Department of Justice. (2002). *Recognizing when a child's injury or illness is caused by abuse*. Washington, DC: Author.

CHILD ABUSE, NEGLECT, AND MALTREATMENT

Victimology and crime prevention cut across many fields of study, including social services. Although the perpetrators of child maltreatment are not always prosecuted, the children who are abused and neglected are undeniably crime victims. They suffer the emotional trauma of victimization in addition to the physical effects of the abuse or neglect. In many cases, the consequences of the abuse are especially traumatic because of children's subsequent separation from their loved ones. Professionals' use of best practices in responding to and trying to prevent child maltreatment is a critical part of ensuring that all children have the opportunity to grow up in a safe, nurturing environment.

Definitions

Child abuse and neglect, also referred to collectively as *child maltreatment*, comprises the legal and social definitions of specific typologies, including physical abuse, physical neglect, emotional/psychological neglect, and sexual abuse. Legal definitions of the different types of maltreatment vary from state to state, but their source is societal standards of a safe, nurturing environment that ensures a child can grow into a fully functioning, contributing member of society. The definitions below are based on those used by the American Humane Society and other standard sources in the field.

Physical Abuse

Physical abuse is the most visible of the maltreatment typologies. It is defined as inflicted, nonaccidental physical injury, or the risk of injury, to a child by a caregiver or parent. The injury often results from inappropriate or excessive discipline. Discipline and cultural practices are part of determining what crosses the threshold for the legal definition of abuse. Most of the Western world accepts corporal punishment as a means of discipline. The question becomes how one differentiates between discipline and abuse.

Generally, physical abuse is confirmed when the injury goes beyond temporary redness and results in bruises, broken bones, burns, bite marks, internal injuries, disfigurement, impairment of health or daily functioning, or risk of death.

Neglect

Neglect, the most often reported maltreatment typology, is an act of omission by the parent or caregiver that is harmful to the child. What constitutes neglect depends on societal mores, community standards and culture, and economic and political values. It is subdivided into physical, medical, educational, and in some cases emotional neglect. (Emotional neglect will be dealt with below as a separate category.)

Physical neglect, the most prevalent and recognizable form of neglect, is the omission by a parent or caregiver to provide the child with basic necessities such as food, clothing, or shelter. Examples also include poor hygiene, inadequate supervision, and an unsafe environment such as exposed wiring or broken glass on the floor.

Medical neglect is a failure to provide needed medical treatment, placing the child at serious risk of death, disfigurement, or disability. Examples of medical neglect include not giving a child with diabetes the required medication or monitoring it and not seeking immediate medical care for a child with a severe injury.

Educational neglect includes failure to make an effort to ensure that a child attends school or has a reasonable alternative for pursuing educational requirements (e.g., homeschooling). Examples include a parent permitting a child's chronic truancy, failing to enroll a child in school, or not attending to a child's special educational needs.

Emotional Neglect

Emotional neglect has many other names, including mental injury and psychological maltreatment. It is defined as an act of omission or an overt action that is inattentive to a child's need for nurturance, affection, support, and emotional development. Examples include rejection, verbal assault, isolation, torment, exploitation, belittlement, and public humiliation. Emotional neglect is one of the most difficult types of maltreatment to document because it may not be readily observable. It is often accompanied by other forms of maltreatment, such as physical abuse or neglect.

The meaning of emotional neglect has broadened as society has become aware of the impact on children of chronic or extreme intimate partner violence in the presence of children, of parental behavior that is influenced by substance abuse or mental illness, and of parents' other destructive behaviors.

Sexual Abuse

Sexual abuse involves using a child, as defined by state laws, for the sexual gratification of an adult. Although definitions vary by state, sexual abuse generally refers to a parent, adult, or child using force, coercion, or threats to engage a child in sexual acts or activities at the perpetrator's direction or for his or her purpose. Examples include fondling a child, making a child touch adult sexual organs, penetration of the child's vagina or anus, oral sex, nontouching adult masturbation in the child's presence, exposing the child to pornographic material, or engaging or soliciting the child for prostitution.

Sexual abuse falls into one of two categories based on the identity of the perpetrator. Interfamilial abuse, or incest, is usually perpetrated by a blood relative, particularly the parent or a caregiver with responsibility for caring for the child. Extrafamilial abuse is perpetrated by someone who does not live in the home.

The definitions of the maltreatment typologies overlap, and a single act may be classified as more than one type of abuse; for example, an act may be both physical abuse and emotional neglect. Similarly, several typologies may be present in one family: A family may be reported for physical neglect, but sexual abuse is discovered during the assessment. The definitions provide legal standards for prosecution and guidelines for society. The commonality among all types of maltreatment is the damaging effects on the children.

Historical Perspective

The concept of child maltreatment has evolved throughout history. Across cultures, children used to be seen as the property of their parents, having neither rights nor privileges, and infanticide was a common practice. Children's status in life was determined by the parents, and discipline was often harsh and unrestrained by society. In the ancient world as well as the more modern Western world, children of slaves were at the mercy of their masters, who exploited them physically for work and often abused them sexually. Many children worked the land or were indentured to tradesmen, who were sometimes abusive or exploitive.

Child labor increased with the burgeoning industrial revolution of the 1800s. Unregulated working conditions were often harsh for children, and children of immigrants were especially vulnerable. Many children during this time were injured, maimed, killed, or worked to the point of exhaustion in factories and mines. Whereas close-knit communities or extended families in some societies had been known to shelter and protect children without parents, the anonymity of growing cities meant that children who were separated from their families were often left to live on the streets or were housed in facilities with mentally ill adults or adult criminals.

As the settlement house movement evolved in the late 1800s, individuals began to speak out against child labor. The first organizations to help children who had been exploited or mistreated physically were voluntary, religious, and charitable organizations such as New York's Children's Aid Society.

The New York case of Mary Ellen Wilson in 1874 prompted the founding of the first child protection organization in the United States. When a neighbor reported Mary Ellen's mistreatment by her guardians to Etta Wheeler, a church worker, Wheeler took the matter to Henry Bergh of the Society for the Prevention of Cruelty to Animals. Bergh intervened, and the public awareness raised by the ensuing trial and subsequent imprisonment of the child's guardian led to the establishment of the Society for the Prevention of Cruelty to Children (SPCC) in 1875.

A new view of the concept of childhood emerged in the early 20th century as society began to recognize that children should be protected from parents who mistreat them, and that parents should be punished accordingly. New York was the first state to pass laws to protect children, and many states followed its lead. Orphanages and boarding homes sprang up across the country, and eventually institutions specifically for African American children and Native American children were also founded. The prevailing attitude of child protection advocates focused on rescuing children rather than addressing the social conditions, stresses, or lack of resources that may lead to mistreatment. The Boston chapter of the SPCC was the first to emphasize family rehabilitation, the philosophy that child protection agencies would eventually adopt.

Three significant events marked the movement toward a more regulated governmental effort to protect children from maltreatment in the United States. The first event took place in 1909, when the first public policy was initiated on child protection issues at the White House Conference on Children. The focus of the conference was removing children from abusive families. The second event, in 1912, was the federal government's establishment of the Children's Bureau for the purpose of addressing child protection. Finally, the third event was the founding in 1913 of the Child Welfare League of America, which advocated for the rights of children and for children's protection.

A prominent turning point in the child protection movement was the involvement of the medical community. John Caffey, a pediatric radiologist, noticed in the 1940s that the X-rays of some children revealed new, healed, and healing fractures that were unexplained or that lacked medical evidence to determine the cause. In 1962, Henry Kempe and his colleagues published an article in the *Journal of the American Medical Association* titled "Battered-Child Syndrome," which discussed a condition in young children who had been victims of severe physical abuse intentionally perpetrated by parents or foster parents. The national attention raised by these and similar findings by others in the medical profession resulted in the 1974 federal Child Abuse Prevention and Treatment Act (CAPTA), which includes the following:

- Mandated reporting laws requiring professionals dealing with children to report suspected abuse and neglect;
- National standards for reporting, investigating, and intervening in cases of child maltreatment;
- Development of a registry for perpetrators and child victims; and
- Grants to states with financial incentives to respond to child abuse and neglect.

By the late 1970s, child abuse and neglect had become a formalized, structured governmental program for the purpose of protecting children of all races and ethnicities, but there was still little attention given to supporting parents. With the influx of children into the foster care system in the 1980s as a result of mandatory reporting, a philosophical shift occurred to support parents through the prevention of maltreatment and family-focused intervention.

Incidence and Prevalence

Determining the number of U.S. children who experience maltreatment is more complicated than it may seem. Defining terms is essential. Prevalence is defined as the number of people who have experienced at least one act of child abuse or neglect, while incidence is the number of child maltreatment cases reported to Child Protective Services (CPS) agencies each year.

Although CAPTA set national minimum definitions for maltreatment in 1974, the details of the definitions were left to the states, creating variation and complication in determining prevalence. Prevalence determinations have also been hindered by different policies for acceptance and investigation as well as different methods used to collect data. The refinement of abuse and neglect definitions, the education of the professional public about its mandated reporting responsibilities, and the increase in community awareness of the problem have contributed to a marked increase in the number of cases reported since the mid-1970s.

The two major sources of incidence statistics are the annually updated National Child Abuse and Neglect Data System (NCANDS) and the periodic National Incidence Study (NIS). NCANDS aggregates data from states' CPS agencies. According to NCANDS, approximately 1.2% of U.S. children were maltreated in 2005, with an estimated 3.3 million referrals of child abuse or neglect to CPS agencies. In addition to CPS reports, the NIS also includes information from community professionals who have contact with children, resulting in much higher estimates. The NIS suggests that between 2.3% and 4.2% of U.S. children are maltreated each year. Experts agree that the actual prevalence of child abuse and neglect is higher than either NCANDS or the NIS reports, because many cases remain unreported.

Factors Associated With Child Maltreatment

Since the concept of a battered-child syndrome was introduced in the 1960s, theories about the causes of maltreatment have varied, influenced by the political, social, and cultural beliefs of the time. Research, however, has consistently identified certain social conditions and characteristics of families that may create an unsafe and abusive physical, emotional, and social environment. These factors include a lack of social support for the parent–child relationship, poverty, minority race/ethnicity, substance abuse or addiction, mental illness, violence in the home, and family dynamics. The presence of these factors, however, does not necessarily indicate child maltreatment. The causes of child maltreatment must be understood within the context of family dynamics.

Lack of Social Support for the Parent–Child Relationship

Parents who create safe, nurturing environments for their children usually have a social network that helps them cope with difficult situations. These parents exhibit reasonable competence in the caregiver role by separating their personal needs from those of the child and finding a balance between meeting their own needs and meeting the child's needs. If parents have experienced disruptive and chaotic early years, had few healthy relationships with adults, or were maltreated themselves, they will be less likely to have a strong support network and more likely to seek to satisfy their own personal needs ahead of their child's needs. This creates a situation that is likely to lead to child abuse and/or neglect.

In addition to the early experiences of parents, the impact of social problems on parents and the entire family threatens parents' ability to use competent and skilled parenting behaviors. These problems rarely occur in isolation. Typically these social problems are interrelated, impeding the parents' ability to be fully engaged in developing the parent–child relationship and in providing a safe, nurturing environment.

Poverty

Poverty is the most pervasive issue found in maltreating families and is particularly associated with reports of neglect. The lack of economic resources or the inadequate allocation of resources within the family can create stress for parents and an inability to meet the basic physical needs of children. Often, families who struggle with chronic economic hardships are headed by single mothers with multiple children, few employment skills, little educational success, and few supportive adult relationships. Their extended family may experience similar economic struggles. Current research also has found that parents and single-parent households experiencing chronic poverty have a much higher probability of violence in the home.

Minority Race/Ethnicity

Parents who are members of a minority race or ethnicity, such as African Americans, Pacific Islanders, and American Indians, are reported for child maltreatment more often than are White or Hispanic parents. This does not necessarily mean that these particular groups actually abuse or neglect their children more than do others, but it does mean that these groups are disproportionately represented in the child welfare system. There are many reasons for this phenomenon. Minority groups often experience social conditions that place children at risk, such as poverty, substance abuse, and mental illness, and they may come into contact more frequently with mandated reporters. Language barriers and cultural bias may also be factors in the disproportionate number of substantiated child maltreatment cases involving minorities. In addition, parents may be reported for practices that are not intended to be harmful and that, within the context of their community, are acceptable. The value systems of other cultures often conflict with that of the mainstream culture in the United States.

Adults' Substance Abuse and Addiction

Adults' abuse of and addiction to alcohol, prescription drugs, and illegal substances such as cocaine and methamphetamine place children at risk of maltreatment. Polydrug use is common; parents may be supporting a cocaine addiction as well as battling alcoholism. Prenatal exposure to any of the aforementioned substances can cause harm to a child. Parents who are abusing drugs, and especially those who become addicted, are often physically and emotionally unavailable to their children. Single parents, especially mothers, who are prosecuted in the criminal justice system for drug possession or trafficking, are likely to be incarcerated and, therefore, separated from their children.

Parents with substance abuse problems are also likely to have few supportive adult relationships. Because of the addiction, the parent places his or her own physical and emotional needs over the needs of the children. Parents who are addicted may prostitute themselves, leave children alone and unsupervised, or become homeless to support their drug use. They may become unable to provide their child with the basics, such as food, clothing, and shelter, not to mention the nurturing, stimulating environment required for the child to achieve developmental milestones.

One barrier to successful recovery that addicted parents face is the lack of consistently available and accessible treatment options. Plus, the likelihood of relapse makes providing a stable home that meets the needs of children a difficult goal for parents who are addicted.

Adults' Mental Illness

Parents with an undiagnosed or untreated mental illness have a higher risk of child maltreatment than the general population. Depression is one of the most common forms of mental illness affecting the quality of parenting. The emotional unavailability caused by a psychiatric problem can have a very damaging effect on children, particularly as it interferes with successful attachment between the child and primary caregiver. The parent may offer inappropriate or inconsistent responses to the child, leaving the child in distress. Parent–child bonding can also be affected by frequent hospitalizations that separate the child from his or her primary caregiver for extended periods of time.

Violence in the Home

A supportive environment is important to mitigating stressful times for parents. Violence between domestic partners threatens the abused parent's ability to cope, fundamentally increasing the risk of child maltreatment. The victim of domestic violence is often reluctant to leave the perpetrator, even for the sake of the children involved. If the perpetrator has not harmed the child in the past, the victim may resist the idea that child maltreatment is linked to domestic violence. A victim may believe that staying with the perpetrator is best for both the victim and the child, especially if the perpetrator controls the household's finances.

When there is violence in the home, there are frequently other problems, such as substance abuse, mental illness, poverty, and sexual abuse. A combination of stressors can place children at a higher risk for maltreatment.

Family Dynamics

The family dynamics of maltreating families vary by types of maltreatment. In neglectful families, the child may take on the role of the adult. When a child is physically abused in a family that experiences domestic violence regularly, the child may have taken on the role of protector of the mother. The social problems already mentioned may also be factors in families in which there is sexual abuse. Research findings on the causes of sexual abuse, however, are more complex than those on other maltreatment typologies. Nevertheless, findings indicate that families in which sexual abuse occurs usually have certain characteristics. The family structure has blurred boundaries and is less cohesive than that of other families. Family members may seem disengaged and find intimacy uncomfortable. The victim tends to see herself or himself as compliant and subservient, and the perpetrator as the dominant figure in the house. The perpetrator may force, coerce, blame, or threaten the child. If confronted, the perpetrator either denies the allegations or attempts to place blame on the child, indicating that the child invited the abuse. The nonoffending parent, often the mother, may not be aware of the abuse or, when told of the abuse, may not believe the child. She may be psychologically and/or economically dependent on the offender, which influences her ability to protect the child.

Impact on Children

Child maltreatment is associated with adverse effects and trauma in children as they develop and grow into adulthood. While signs of developmental delays or other difficulties do not always indicate that a child has been maltreated, research has shown that children who are harmed often experience such problems. Immediate consequences such as antisocial behaviors, low self-esteem, and guilt are common; however, even when immediate consequences are not visible, the adverse effects of child maltreatment often surface as the child enters adulthood.

Common feelings that children experience as a result of maltreatment include guilt, shame, fear, and anger. Children may feel that they deserved the abuse, or they may feel guilty or ashamed for disclosing the abuse and possibly causing the dissolution of the family or their own separation from the family. Their fear may manifest itself in nightmares or paranoia, or their anger may translate into aggression. Victims of maltreatment often have difficulty in regulating and controlling emotional responses, and they react impulsively to stressful situations. They have little mastery of self and may feel out of control, resulting in deviant or antisocial behavior.

The interruption of the attachment process between mother and child as a result of maltreatment can have negative effects through adolescence and into adulthood. Children with impaired attachment often experience problems in trusting others and fail to develop meaningful and satisfying relationships. Maltreatment is also associated with low self-esteem, which hampers children's ability to interact with others, and depression, which is also associated with isolation from families and peers. Children who have been maltreated often take on the parental role by assuming adult responsibilities, and thus skip developmental tasks that are necessary to build competence in social relationships.

Child maltreatment also impairs cognitive development. Victims often have learning disorders and fail in academics. They also may have defective moral reasoning, and they may exhibit deviant behaviors in an effort to justify to themselves their parents' mistreatment of them. Physiologically, their symptoms can include sleeplessness, encopresis (stool or bowel movement accidents), or enuresis (involuntary passage of urine).

Impact of Physical Abuse

The obvious impact of physical abuse is the effect of the injuries on the health and physical development of the child. In addition, cognitive and academic development may be delayed, resulting in poor academic performance. Examples include difficulty with problem solving and an inability to distinguish right from wrong. Children may also internalize emotions related to the abuse, resulting in anxiety and depression, or they may externalize their emotions, displaying aggressive behaviors.

Impact of Sexual Abuse

In addition to the behaviors common to all the typologies, child victims of sexual abuse often experience psychosomatic and physiological symptoms and complaints. They may believe that the abuse physically harmed their body, they may have a distorted body image in addition to low self-esteem, or they may receive the message from society that they are "damaged goods" or unlovable. They may reenact the abuse on younger children or become promiscuous in an effort to regain control of their bodies.

In cases of incest, the role confusion that often accompanies maltreatment is compounded. For example, a young girl may be groomed by her father to feel more powerful and sexually desirable than her mother. In addition, the nonoffending parent plays a key role in the impact of incest on the child by believing or denying the child's disclosure of abuse. Children who are not believed are more likely to recant their report, compromising the investigation. The parent's disbelief confirms the child's suspicions that he or she is to blame for the incidents. Failure to believe the child also influences the parent's ability to protect the child, and it may result in the child's removal from the home. As sexually abused children grow into adulthood, they may experience depression, suicidal thoughts, eating disorders, self-mutilating behaviors, substance abuse, and additional victimizations.

Impact of Neglect

Studies suggest that children who are neglected suffer very significant adverse consequences during childhood and into adulthood. The most likely cause for this is unmet basic developmental needs. Young children and infants are dependent on their parents to meet these needs, and parents' failure to do so can cause their children to have poor self-concepts, physical deficiencies, developmental delays, and lower academic scores. These children may exhibit developmental lags in language and cognitive functioning. They may also be socially passive and withdrawn from family and peers. Their deep lack of trust is difficult to overcome.

Impact of Emotional Neglect

Since emotional neglect is difficult to define and substantiate, its impact is difficult to study. This typology often occurs along with other forms of maltreatment, and studies have found that the effects of emotional neglect are similar to the effects of other typologies, interfering with the child's overall development—cognitively, emotionally, psychologically, and socially. Children who are emotionally neglected often lag behind their peers academically, and they may exhibit self-abusive behavior and anxiety.

Impact of Exposure to Family Violence

Children who witness family violence may learn that violence is an appropriate means of resolving conflict. Studies suggest that a child's exposure to marital violence, in addition to his or her being physically or sexually abused, results in lasting effects such as posttraumatic stress disorder and anxiety. More research needs to be conducted to fully explore the connection between maltreatment and violence exposure.

Mediating Factors

The impact of maltreatment depends on a number of factors, and some children exhibit fewer adverse effects than do others. Children's reactions may depend on the type of abuse, the severity of the abuse, and the prolonged nature of the abuse. An early, secure attachment between the child and caregiver can have a lasting positive effect on the child's resilience. Other mediating factors may include the child's temperament and developmental stage and the availability of support outside the family.

Response and Prevention

Since child maltreatment involves complex, interactive factors—including parent–child interaction, environment, community standards, culture, and child characteristics—response and prevention must be multifaceted. Levels of prevention include primary, secondary, and tertiary programs.

Primary Prevention

Primary prevention is typically defined as educating the general public about recognizing and reporting child maltreatment. Although determining impact is difficult, it is generally accepted that a more informed public raises awareness and reporting of incidents of suspected abuse. Distributing culturally responsive materials in churches, schools, and medical clinics can reach parents, children, and professionals. Schools of higher education can offer courses on child maltreatment to professionals in training.

Parenting programs that educate and support new parents have proven to have positive outcomes. Successful, cost-effective programs target a specific population, require high levels of engagement from participants, include both parents and children, and focus on one-on-one interactions between parents and their children. Programs that specifically target high-risk populations can also be considered a secondary prevention strategy.

Secondary Prevention

Activities that prevent abuse from occurring in high-risk populations are often referred to as secondary prevention. Parenting programs can be successful even after a family has been reported for child maltreatment—if the programs have the elements described above. Some studies have shown that risk is most effectively reduced immediately after the parent training. Thus, continued family support through a variety of services and educational opportunities may be beneficial to families over an extended period of time.

Other beneficial results of secondary prevention programs include more child-friendly beliefs and attitudes; an increased willingness to understand and accept children's developmental capabilities, emotions, and intentions; changes in beliefs about corporal punishment; changes in the roles and relationship of parent and child; and strengthening the parent's emotional well-being. Some research suggests that home visitors have a positive impact on the successfulness of parenting programs by offering education and emotional support.

Programs that address the needs of children who witness violence can help prevent abuse. Since witnessing violence in the home and/or in the community is often associated with maltreatment, programs that provide needed services to the adult victims should also be rigorous in providing children with services. Teaching children life skills (e.g., coping with stress, dealing with a crisis, developing successful relationships, problem solving) and helping them build a positive self-image can help reduce the risk of maltreatment and ameliorate the effects of violence.

Tertiary Prevention

Tertiary prevention is the response to situations where abuse has already occurred and intervention may prevent future occurrences. Some intensive programs for families already being investigated for child maltreatment offer less punitive approaches than the criminal court system offers. Drug courts in some states try to bridge the gap between the child welfare and criminal justice systems to improve outcomes for families.

Specialized units, protocols, and responses for investigating and prosecuting child maltreatment cases can help lessen the effects of abuse. Training and protocols for social workers, law enforcement, prosecutors, medical teams, and mental health counselors can enhance how children are interviewed and lessen the trauma that can occur when a report is being investigated. Child advocacy centers are also an innovative approach to providing services to child victims. Centers are child-friendly and provide comprehensive approaches to interviewing and intervening with children and families during an investigation.

In addition to protecting children physically, services need to address children's developmental, emotional, spiritual, social, academic, and mental health needs. Interventions that help parents build protective family factors can also help build resiliency in children. Developing positive relationships with extended family and other adults and enhancing life skills can help children rebuild their self-esteem and become more resilient.

Final Thoughts

Child maltreatment is a prevalent issue in the United States that is caused by multiple interrelated social and psychological factors. The complex interplay of internal and external dynamics that affect families contributes to the abuse and/or neglect of children. Although child maltreatment is difficult to define, there is no doubt of its existence and the damage it causes children and society. Because of its intense adverse effects on children, research must continue to discover best practices in preventing and responding to child maltreatment. Raising public awareness about child maltreatment and its impact on children can help protect children. Social support for children is crucial. A significant relationship with even one person can make vast improvements in a child's life.

Pamela G. Bond and Jennifer Reid Webb

See also Abuse, Ritual Child; Central Registry; Developmental and Social Victimization; Mandatory Reporting Statutes; Safety Planning for Abused Children; Sexual Orientation and Victimization

Further Readings

American Humane Society. (2009). *Newsroom: Fact sheets.* Retrieved November 10, 2008, from http://www.americanhumane.org/about-us/newsroom/fact-sheets

Berg, I. K., & Kelly, S. (2000). *Building solutions in Child Protective Services.* New York: Norton.

Briere, J., Berliner, L., Bulkley, J. A., Jenny, C., & Reid, T. (1996). *The APSAC handbook on child maltreatment.* Thousand Oaks, CA: Sage.

Christle, C. A., Harley D., Nelson, C. M., & Jones, K. (n.d.). *Promoting resilience in children: What parents can do.* Retrieved November 10, 2008, from http://cecp.air.org/familybriefs/docs/resiliency1.pdf

Crittenden, P. M. (1996). Research on maltreating families. In J. Briere (Ed.), *The handbook on child maltreatment* (pp. 158–174). Thousand Oaks, CA: Sage.

Cross, T. (2008, March). Disproportionality in child welfare. *Child Welfare, 87*(2), 11–20.

Crosson-Tower, C. (2005). *Understanding child abuse and neglect* (6th ed.). Boston: Pearson/Allyn & Bacon.

English, D. J. (1998). The extent and consequences of child maltreatment. *The Future of Children: Protecting Children from Abuse and Neglect, 8*(1), 39–53.

Garbarino, J. (1989). The incidence and prevalence of child maltreatment. *Crime and Justice: Family Violence, 11,* 219–261.

Girvin, H., DePanfilis, D., & Daining, C. (2007). Predicting program completion among families enrolled in a child neglect preventive intervention. *Research on Social Work Practice, 17,* 674–685.

Hussey, J., Chang, J. J., & Kotch, J. (2006). Child maltreatment in the United States: Prevalence, risk factors, and adolescent health consequences. *Pediatrics, 118*(3), 933–934.

Kinard, E. (2002). Services for maltreated children: Variations by maltreatment characteristics. *Child Welfare, 81*(4), 617–645.

Lundahl, B., Nimer, J., & Parsons, B. (2005). Preventing child abuse: A meta-analysis of parent training programs. *Research on Social Work Practice, 16*(3), 251–262.

Macdonald, G. (2001). *Effective interventions for child abuse and neglect.* West Sussex, UK: John Wiley.

Righthand, S., Kerr, B., & Drach, K. (2003). *Child maltreatment risk assessments: An evaluation guide.* New York: Haworth Maltreatment and Trauma.

Taylor, C. A., & Sorenson, S. B. (2007). Intervention on behalf of children exposed to intimate partner violence: Assessment of support in a diverse community-based sample. *Child Abuse and Neglect, 31,* 1155–1168.

U.S. Department of Justice. *New directions from the field: Victims' rights and services for the 21st century.* Washington, DC: Office of Justice Programs, Office for Victims of Crime.

CHILD ABUSE, NEGLECT, AND MALTREATMENT: INTERVENTIONS FOR

Once someone reports child abuse, an investigation begins. A social worker is usually the person who initiates the investigation, and then he or she makes a decision as to how to proceed. Various treatment programs are available for both the maltreated child and the abusive parent or guardian. This entry first briefly discusses the investigation of child abuse, and then describes the intervention process for the child and abuser after evidence of child abuse is found.

Investigation and Case Management

In recent years, many schools and medical centers have developed a child protection team (CPT). For example, if teachers become suspicious of maltreatment of a student, they can report the case to the CPT. Once the members of the CPT agree that they have a case of abuse, they typically pass the information to a state's child service agency. Next, the agency's social worker interviews the parties involved in the case, such as the child victim, the parents, other family members, and the reporter of the abuse. Once the social worker has confirmed the report of child abuse or neglect, he or she decides what kind of service/treatment the child victim and the abuser should receive.

Treatment Methods for Abused Child

Play Therapy

Play therapy is a form of counseling or psychotherapy in which a therapist observes a child at unstructured play. Young children are allowed to express their emotions through play rather than encouraged to verbalize them, as these children have low levels of verbal communication skill. Playing allows the child victim to release and overcome the feelings of anxiety and anger associated with the victimization. It can also enhance a child's communication skill with others.

Cognitive–Behavioral Strategies

The goal of cognitive behavioral strategies is to identify the child's emotional and behavioral responses to victimization. Sometimes, the child blames himself or herself for the abuse. Thus, therapists focus on helping the child understand that he or she is not a guilty party, but that the adults are responsible for the abuse. Cognitive–behavioral therapists help victims restore their relationships with family members.

Group Therapy

In group therapy, the victimized child participates in sessions with a group of peers who have had similar experiences of abuse. Children in group therapy are likely to realize that the abuse problem is not related only to *their* experiences, as other children have suffered similar difficulties. In addition, group therapy provides the children with an opportunity to address problematic behaviors that may have arisen as a result of the abuse suffered. The child may gain communication skills such as listening to others and sharing feelings with others. Group therapy is especially effective for alleviating the sense of loneliness and for promoting social skills.

Foster Care

Foster care is out-of-home care for a child who has been removed from his or her parent or caretaker. The foster parents, usually a third party, care for the child in a private home setting. In most cases, the foster parents are licensed and supervised by a social service agency.

During the investigation stage, the abused victim is placed in foster care by the social worker only when his or her staying home with the abusive parent may pose an additional risk of victimization. Under certain conditions, the social worker can put the child in foster care or a group home without the parent's consent. In that case, the social worker requires authorization from the court.

Foster care allows a social worker to observe the behavior of the child without the influence of his or her parents. The social worker, with the assistance of foster parents, may then be able to pinpoint specific developmental problems of the child, including communication skill deficits. In many cases, the abusive parent regularly sees the child in foster care to maintain a constructive relationship until the family can be reunited.

Group Home

Group homes are residential care facilities that provide foster care for a limited number of children, usually between the ages of 7 and 12. Some children do not respond well to being in a family setting because of the trauma they have experienced. In that case, they may require intensive therapeutic treatment before they can be placed with another family. Such treatment may include a group home environment.

Treatment Methods for Abusive Parents

Cognitive–Behavioral Strategies

Cognitive–behavioral therapy assumes that clients have irrational beliefs that require cognitive modification. Thus, the goal of cognitive–behavioral therapy is to identify specific problematic behaviors of the abusive parent by gathering information from other family members. Behavioral therapy has been found to be effective in child management, parenting, parent training and, more recently, in shaping adult behavior.

The Child Welfare League of America emphasizes the importance of intensive family-centered services (IFPS) for children. One of the oldest IFPS programs in the country is HOMEBUILDERS, which was established in Tacoma, Washington, in 1974. IFPS programs focus on intensive skill building through techniques such as values clarification, parenting training, and problem solving. Sometimes this type of program is called a "behavior-modification program."

Family Therapy

Family therapy is designed to enhance family ties. An important element of family therapy is that an individual family member must recognize how his or her behavior influences other members of the family. Family therapy offers programs for conflict management and building communication skills. Family therapy may be most helpful after the individual family member has addressed his or her intrapersonal and developmental issues through individual or group therapy sessions.

Self-Help Groups

Parents Anonymous (PA) began as a parental group in Redondo Beach, California. A former abusive mother, Jolly K., founded PA in 1969 because she felt that the services of existing social service agencies did not satisfy her needs. PA is now the largest treatment program for the prevention of child abuse, with 267 accredited organizations and local affiliates throughout the United States.

PA is based on the Alcoholics Anonymous model. PA members are parents who have maltreated their children. Volunteers comprise 75% of the membership; however, some parents become members because of a court order. PA members provide each other with mutual support to prevent future abuse; thus a member is able to call other members when he or she faces a problem within the family.

Don Chon

See also Child Abuse, Neglect, and Maltreatment; Child Abuse, Neglect, and Maltreatment: Statutory Responses; Multisystemic Therapy; Parents Anonymous

Further Readings

Crosson-Tower, C. (2005). *Understanding child abuse and neglect.* Boston: Pearson/Allyn & Bacon.

Grodner, B. (1977). A family systems approach to child abuse: Etiology and intervention. *Journal of Clinical Child Psychology, 6*(1), 32–35.

Saunders, B. E., Berliner, L., & Hanson, R. F. (Eds.). (2004). *Child physical and sexual abuse: Guidelines for treatment.* Charleston, SC: National Crime Victims Research and Treatment Center.

Wolfe, D. A. (1999). *Child abuse: Implications for child development and psychopathology.* Thousands Oaks, CA: Sage.

CHILD ABUSE, NEGLECT, AND MALTREATMENT: MANDATORY REPORTING

Federal and state laws have been enacted mandating that certain persons, usually professionals (e.g., health care providers, child care workers, mental health professionals, law enforcement officers, and teachers), report suspected and observed cases of child abuse and neglect to appropriate Child Protective Services (CPS) and law enforcement agencies. These laws vary by state and often change. Due to the lack of standard definitions of child abuse and neglect, reporting suspected child abuse and neglect is surrounded by much confusion and ambiguity. This entry explores the reporting laws, reporting controversies and barriers, and reporting procedures.

Laws

Standard definitions of child abuse and neglect usually include physical abuse (e.g., hitting a child, throwing an object at a child, or burning a child), sexual abuse (e.g., fondling a child's genitals, exhibitionism, sexual exploitation, or intercourse), emotional and psychological abuse (e.g., constantly denigrating or threatening a child), and neglect (e.g., refusing to obtain mental or physical health care, abandonment, allowing a child to use alcohol or drugs, or failing to enroll a child in school). Additional areas of abuse or neglect may include prenatal exposure to drugs, alcohol, and tobacco; corporal punishment (e.g., spanking a child); and exposure to inappropriate Internet sites.

Challenges to Reporting

Reporting child abuse and neglect can be a challenging task, as laws vary as to what constitutes abuse, how to report abuse, and who is mandated to report. In addition, time limits for reporting suspected maltreatment to the appropriate agency vary, and there are different penalties for failing to report suspected child maltreatment.

Barriers to reporting include the following: lack of education on how to report; fear of reaction from the alleged perpetrator; confusion over the definitions of abuse and neglect; fear that CPS will create additional stress for the family; fear of being blamed for mismanaging the case; and concerns about having to testify in court.

Rules for reporting abuse or neglect are often unclear. Some questions about reporting include the following: Does one report abuse when an adult tells of experiencing abuse as a child? Does one report abuse when someone reports knowing of someone who has been a victim of child abuse? How much information does one need in order to make a report? When does one make a second report on the same case? Should one report a child who is at risk for potential abuse? Answers to these questions vary depending on whom you ask.

Mandated reporters may find themselves in dilemmas when working with a family in which partner abuse has occurred. For example, one must report child abuse if a child reports witnessing partner abuse, but there is confusion regarding reporting when there is no evidence that the child directly witnessed the partner abuse. The duty to report vs. the duty to maintain confidentiality may present some professionals with an ethical dilemma.

Corporal punishment is a controversial issue. Some state laws allow for corporal punishment as long as no harm occurs. However, it remains unclear what constitutes harm. In one case, in the 1980s, corporal punishment was used legally as a means of disciplining children at a school; however, during a paddling, a child moved and was hit on the back instead of the buttocks, resulting in an injury that required medical attention.

There are disagreements that focus on religious and cultural practices. For example, there are still debates on whether clergy are mandated to report abuse. In addition, specific parenting practices may be construed as child abuse and neglect by some cultures and viewed as appropriate parenting practices by other cultures.

Researchers have obligations to report child abuse and neglect; however, certain research designs may prevent the researcher from knowing the identity of the participants and thus make it impossible to report a specific case. There continues to be debate about the limitations of the federal Certificate of Confidentiality. It is always important for researchers to work with their institutional review board to obtain guidance regarding legal and ethical issues pertaining to their research.

Reporting Procedures

A person mandated to report child abuse and neglect should follow the reporting protocols of his or her state. Many states have a toll-free number linked to a central registry that screens calls and passes on the information to the appropriate agency. These registries are staffed by trained professionals who can determine if the report meets the requirements for acceptance and investigation. Some cases will be reported to CPS, and others to law enforcement. Various agencies may work together on cases to avoid duplication of services. Some states allow a person to fax a report or complete a report online. Consultations with attorneys, colleagues, and the state Child Protective Services representatives are often warranted in suspected cases of child abuse and neglect. While someone not mandated to report may file a report anonymously, the mandated reporter may be required to provide information such as his or her name, occupation, and work address. Mandated reporters are immune from liability as long as they make the report in good faith. Physical evidence of abuse or neglect is not needed in order to make a report; suspicion that abuse and neglect has occurred or is occurring is sufficient. In summary, one needs to become familiar with state reporting laws and report any suspicions of abuse and neglect in order to reduce one's own liability and to protect victims from further abuse.

Mark A. Winton

See also Child Abuse, Neglect, and Maltreatment: Statutory Responses; Child Protective Services; Mandatory Reporting Statutes; Nonreporting/Failure to Report Victimization

Further Readings

Barnett, O. W., Miller-Perrin, C. L., & Perrin, R. D. (2005). *Family violence across the lifespan: An introduction* (2nd ed.). Thousand Oaks, CA: Sage.

Foreman, T., & Bernet, W. (2000). A misunderstanding regarding a duty to report suspected abuse. *Child Maltreatment, 5,* 190–196.

Lewis, N. K. (2003). Balancing the dictates of law and ethical practice: Empowerment of female survivors of domestic violence in the presence of overlapping child abuse. *Ethics & Behavior, 13,* 353–366.

Winton, M. A., & Mara, B. A. (2001). *Child abuse and neglect: Multidisciplinary approaches.* Boston: Allyn & Bacon.

Web Sites

Child Welfare Information Gateway: http://www.childwelfare.gov

CHILD ABUSE, NEGLECT, AND MALTREATMENT: MEASUREMENT OF

Although prevalent in our society, child maltreatment is not easily defined, nor measured. Concerns with protecting victims, while securing justice, ensuring offender rights, and preserving families, create a unique victimology of child maltreatment. Although the words *abuse* and *maltreatment* are often used interchangeably in common nomenclature, there is no strong scholarly consensus on definitions. This entry acknowledges that *maltreatment* is a more general and neutral term than *abuse,* and it includes within the broad category of child maltreatment the subcategories of abuse and neglect, and within the subsets of abuse physical, emotional, psychological, and sexual abuse, including exploitation.

Legal and Social Service Definitions

From a legal perspective, the definitions of neglect and the various forms of abuse are a function of federal and state law in the United States. The formative federal legislation defining child abuse and neglect is the Child Abuse Prevention and Treatment Act (CAPTA; P.L. 93-247) of 1974, as last amended by the Keeping Children and Families Safe Act of 2003 (P.L. 108-36). The act states that

> the term "child abuse and neglect" means, at a minimum, any recent act or failure to act on the part of a parent or caretaker, which results in death, serious physical or emotional harm, sexual abuse or exploitation, or an act or failure to act which presents an imminent risk of serious harm (P.L. 93-247, Sec. 111. [42 U.S.C. 5106G])

The CAPTA legislation mandates reporting of child maltreatment by requiring compliance of states seeking federal funding. Although CAPTA sets minimum standards, each of the 50 states determines its own legal definitions in conjunction with its penal code, and there is variation in codes from state to state.

Medical and social service providers also have a set of definitions describing the various forms of child maltreatment. In its most basic form, child neglect is the failure of the caregiver to provide adequate food, shelter, clothing, and health and emotional support. As Denise A. Hines has noted, for many forms of maltreatment, the difficulty in defining concepts stems from the blurred line between abusive and nonabusive behavior (e.g., abuse vs. corporal punishment).

Sexual abuse is a range of actions and practices between an adult and child where the child is being used for sexual gratification. It includes activities such as fondling a child's genitals, sexual penetration, incest, rape, sodomy, and indecent exposure. Exploitation through prostitution and/or pornography is also a form of sexual abuse.

Physical abuse is any action, such as hitting (with a hand or any object), kicking, burning, or otherwise harming or injuring a child. All such acts are considered abuse regardless of intent. Emotional abuse is a pattern of behavior that impairs a child's emotional development or sense of self-worth. Since emotional abuse is often difficult to prove, authorities may not be able to intervene without direct evidence of harm to the child. Emotional abuse is almost always present with other forms of maltreatment.

Micro- and Macro-Level Measurement

At the micro level, maltreatment is measured on both sides of the victim–offender relationship. To identify offenders and potential offenders, several self-reporting instruments are used for screening purposes. Peggy Nygren has made two important observations. First, all child abuse screening instruments are designed to be administered to parents, and second, there have been no controlled studies implemented to study the impacts of child abuse assessment or intervention.

One common instrument is the Kempe Family Stress Inventory (KFSI), which is a direct parent assessment. The Child Abuse Potential (CAP) inventory is used as a screening tool for the detection of physical child abuse, while the Parenting Profile Assessment (PPA) evaluates the potential of parents to be abusive or nonabusive. The Conflict Tactics Scale (CTS) includes 80 items that explore intrafamily conflict and violence, and it includes four scales: Parent–Child (Scale 1), Partner–Child (Scale 2), Parent–Partner (Scale 3), and Partner–Parent (Scale 4). Other instruments used to measure potential risk are the Hawaii Risk Indicator Screening Tools (HRIST) and the Maternal History Inventory (MHI).

Along with self-reporting, there are behavioral indicators of maltreatment, particularly for sexual abuse offenders. These behavioral indicators include vaginal, anal, and/or oral intercourse or attempted intercourse; fondling a child's breasts or genitals; exhibitionism; showing a child pornography; and filming, photographing, or videotaping any activity involving the exhibition of a child's genitals or any sexual activity with a child.

Due to the young age of most maltreatment victims, self-reports are not a feasible methodology for measuring victimization. Physical and sexual abuse, as well as neglect, are typically observed directly by teachers, health care workers, social service providers, other professionals, and laypersons who interact with children. After maltreatment is reported, interviews are often conducted with adults familiar with the alleged victim. Maltreatment is not defined by one concrete set of indicators. Rather, maltreatment is defined functionally and within the context of each situation. Safechild.org, childabuse.com, and crisiscallcenter.org publish lists of indicators to assist in the identification of potential abuse and neglect. Some such indicators are listed below, but it is important to note that these indicators can have causes other than abuse, so professional evaluation within the context of each situation is needed.

There are numerous indicators of physical abuse, including bruises and welts, possibly in unusual shapes (similar to the instrument used); lacerations such as cuts and tears; abdominal injuries; burns, including those from cigarettes or cigars and hot liquids; skeletal injuries such as fractures; and hemorrhaging due to violent shaking, throwing, or hitting.

The physical indicators of sexual abuse include difficulty in walking or sitting, bladder or urinary tract infections, pain, swelling and redness, or itching in the genital area; presences of suspicious stains, blood, or semen on the child's body, underwear, or clothing; and painful bowel movements or retention of feces. Behavioral indicators of sexual abuse include engaging in delinquent acts or running away; poor peer relationships; low self-esteem; social isolation; displaying bizarre, sophisticated, or unusual sexual knowledge or behavior; changes in eating behaviors; regressive behavior; and aggressive, hostile acting out behaviors and play.

In terms of neglect, indicators cross a wide range of physical, social, and behavioral aspects including inadequate nutrition, clothing, or hygiene; a lack of adequate shelter or unsafe or unsanitary housing; inadequate medical, dental, or mental health care; a consistent lack of supervision, or an extended period of nonsupervision, especially when a child can engage in dangerous activities; and child abandonment.

Potential emotional neglect can be identified via several behavior indicators, including acting withdrawn and/or unable to enjoy life; exhibiting bizarre behavior; low self-esteem; acting aggressive, defiant, and/or domineering; and engaging in self-destructive behavior, both physically and socially.

Two syndromic corollaries to child maltreatment are failure to thrive syndrome and Munchausen syndrome by proxy (MSP). Failure to thrive syndrome involves children 18 months or younger and may be an indicator of maltreatment. It requires a medical diagnosis, and symptoms include height below the 5th percentile; an unusually thin body type; infantile proportions; a potbelly with dull skin, paleness, and cold and mottled limbs; rocking or head banging; being solitary and unable to play; delayed development and retarded speech and/or language; ravenous appetite; and marked growth spurts when out of the home and relapses when returned to the home environment. Munchausen syndrome by proxy is an offender disorder that manifests in victim maltreatment of many forms. In both syndromes, professional diagnosis is required to identify and/or eliminate causal alternatives.

At the macro level, the National Child Abuse and Neglect Data System (NCANDS) is a national data collection and analysis system created in 1988 in response to CAPTA. Each year, NCANDS collects micro-level data from states' Child Protective Services (CPS) agencies and produces an annual report. Prior to 1993, states provided only aggregate data. In 1993 states began to submit case-level data along with the aggregated data, and in 2000 the case-level data set became the primary source of data for the reports. Although a review of data is conducted to assess the internal validity of each state's data, since not all states share common definitions of maltreatment, states must decide which of their classifications provide the best fit with NCANDS standards.

Timothy Sweet-Holp

See also Child Abuse, Identification of; Child Abuse, Neglect, and Maltreatment; Child Abuse, Neglect, and Maltreatment: Interventions for; Child Abuse, Neglect, and Maltreatment: Mandatory Reporting; Child Abuse, Neglect, and Maltreatment: Statutory Response; Child Abuse, Neglect, and Maltreatment: Theories of

Further Readings

Child Abuse Prevention and Treatment Act, P.L. 93-247, Sec. 111 [42 U.S.C. 5106G]. Available at http://www.gpoaccess.gov/uscode

Curtis, R. W., Langworthy, R. H., Barnes, A. R., & Crum, P. (1998). *Measuring child abuse and neglect: A review of methods.* A report to the Alaska Department of Corrections. Anchorage: Justice Center, University of Alaska.

Hines, D. A., & Malley-Morrison, K. (2004). *Family violence in a cultural perspective: Defining, understanding, and combating abuse.* Thousand Oaks, CA: Sage.

Hines, D. A., & Malley-Morrison, K. (2005). *Family violence in a cultural perspective: Defining, understanding, and combating abuse.* Thousand Oaks, CA: Sage.

Nygren, P., Nelson, H. D., & Klein, J. (2004). Screening children for family violence: A review of the evidence for the U.S. Prevention Services Task Force. *Annals of Family Medicine, 2*(2), 161–169.

Web Sites

Child Welfare Information Gateway, state statutes: http://www.childwelfare.gov/systemwide/laws_policies/state

CHILD ABUSE, NEGLECT, AND MALTREATMENT: STATUTORY RESPONSES

There have been various federal and state legal responses to the problem of child abuse. They include mandatory reporting laws, sex offender registration laws, guardian ad litem, mandatory minimum sentencing laws, and the screening of child care workers. This entry discusses each of these statutory responses to child abuse.

Mandatory Reporting Law

Currently, all states in the United States have mandatory reporting laws for child abuse and neglect. The goal of the mandatory reporting law is to protect abused and neglected children. Some states have enacted laws identifying specific professionals who have an obligation to notify state authorities of any child abuse and neglect. The term *mandated reporters* refers to individuals who have professional relationships with the child and the family. The professionals usually include physicians, nurses, counselors, social workers, and school personnel. Other states have enacted "any person" statutes, whereby all suspicions of abuse or neglect must be reported. For example, Florida Statute 39.201 requires "Any person who knows, or has reasonable cause to suspect, that a child has been abused, abandoned or neglected by a parent, legal custodian, caregiver, or other person responsible for the child's welfare" to report such knowledge or suspicions. Departments of human services, child welfare agencies, and child protection agencies are usually the recipients of these reports. Some states allow the report to be provided to law enforcement agencies as well.

Sex Offender Registration Laws

Megan's Law, enacted by the U.S. Congress in 1996, is an example of a sex offender registration law. Megan Kanka, a girl from New Jersey, was murdered by a neighbor who had a history of sex offenses. Following the enactment of Megan's Law, all 50 states and the District of Columbia required that certain adjudicated sex offenders must register a current address with particular criminal justice agencies. Some law enforcement agencies may make the information on the offenders available to the public. The law is designed to protect community members from sexual predators. The act required each state to register the offenders convicted of a violent sexual offense or crime against a child. However, each state can exercise discretion whether or not to publish the information on the sex offenders.

Following the federal Megan's Law, many states have passed state-level notification statutes. Some states allow the distribution of very broad information on certain sex offenders through Web sites, newspapers, door-to-door visits, and letters to individuals or organizations. The information includes the offender's name, current address, personal descriptions, charged offenses, and so on. However, some states employ a more passive approach to notification and may provide the public with the access to adjudicated sex offender information only through a law enforcement agency or its Web site.

Another example of sex offender registration laws is the Sex Offender Registration and Notification (SORN), Ohio's version of Megan's Law that went into effect in 1997. According to the law, individuals adjudicated for committing sexual offenses are grouped into one of three categories: sexually oriented offender, habitual sexual offender, and sexual predator. Sex offender registration is mandatory for all adjudicated sex offenders in Ohio. However, notification is mandatory only for adjudicated sexual predators. At the sentencing stage the judge makes a decision on whether or not a certain habitual sexual offender is subject to the mandatory notification. In Ohio the law is not applicable to sexually oriented offenders.

Guardian Ad Litem and Other Courtroom Assistance

A guardian ad litem (GAL) is an advocate for a victimized child. The GAL provides support and advice during the criminal justice proceedings, serving to maximize the interest of the child victim in family court.

Other courtroom assistance for a victimized child is also available. To minimize the stress experienced by a child who testifies in the courtroom, the court can employ several techniques. Those techniques include adjusting questions to the child's comprehension level, clearing the courtroom, and reorganizing the courtroom furniture. The court may use alternative testifying techniques for the child victim, including the use of videotaped testimony, the removal of the defendant from the child's view, and having the child testify through the closed-circuit television or a one-way mirror. In addition, some state courts allow the use of dolls to describe physical and sexual abuse of the child. By using a doll, an attorney at a court may ask the child victim to pinpoint his or her body part where the abuser touched him or her.

Other Statutory Responses

Mandatory Minimum Sentencing

Some states have passed mandatory minimum sentencing guideline for sexual offenses, especially for sex crimes against children. For example, Oregon enacted long-term mandatory minimum sentencing for 16 designated violent sexual offenses, with sentences ranging from 70 to 300 months. In Texas, the court judge can give a 25-year imprisonment sentence or even death penalty for child rapists.

Mandatory Background Checks for Child Care Workers

Many jurisdictions require that child care workers be subject to background checks. The background check is done immediately after the initiation of employment. For example, in 2000, the State of New Jersey passed the law Background Check for Childcare Workers. According to the law, a child care center owner or sponsor is required to screen his or her staff's criminal history, including sex offenses. The screening should be done by Department of Law and Public Safety and the FBI. The failure to obey the law may result in the suspension, denial, or refusal of renewal of the license of the child care facility. A person with a certain criminal history is not to be employed at child care facilities.

Don Chon

See also Central Registry; Child Abuse, Neglect, and Maltreatment; In-Camera Proceedings; Mandatory Reporting Statutes; Megan's Law

Further Readings

Beck, V. S., & Travis, L. F. (2006). Sex offender notification: A cross-state comparison. *Police Practice and Research*, 7, 293–307.

Brooks, C. M., & Perry, N. W., & Starr, S. D., & Teply, L. L. (1994). Child abuse and neglect reporting laws: Understanding interests, understanding policy. *Behavioral Sciences and the Law*, 12, 49–64.

Crosson-Tower, C. (2005). *Understanding child abuse and neglect*. Boston: Pearson/Allyn & Bacon.

Florida Statute 39.201. Retrieved from http://www .flsenate.gov/statutes/index.cfm?App_Mode=Display_ Statute&Search_String=&URL=Ch0039/Sec201 .htm&StatuteYear=2005

Gaines, J. S. (2006). Law enforcement reactions to sex offender registration and community notification. *Police Practice and Research*, 7, 249–267.

Levenson, J. S., D'Amora, D. A., & Hern, A. L. (2007). Megan's law and its impact on community re-entry. *Behavioral Science Law*, 25, 587–602.

CHILD ABUSE, NEGLECT, AND MALTREATMENT: THEORIES OF

Efforts to prevent child maltreatment must begin with a clear and coherent explanation of the problem. Theoretical attention has been directed both to the questions of how and why maltreatment occurs and to the questions of how and why maltreatment affects developmental outcomes for victims. Because of the present concern with victimology and crime prevention, this entry focuses on the first of these questions, that is, on theoretical models developed to explain how and why maltreatment occurs.

Much of the empirical and theoretical work in the field of child maltreatment has concentrated on single risk factors such as parental psychopathology, a history of maltreatment in the perpetrator's childhood, family poverty, or children's difficult temperament. There is now a broad consensus in the field that maltreatment is too complex and multifaceted to be adequately explained by any single-level theory. Integrated theories aim to explain how multiple risk and protective factors interact to produce child maltreatment. This entry describes a number of single-level explanations concerning cultural, family, individual, and situational factors, and then outlines two prominent integrated theories: social ecology theory and ecological-transactional theory.

Single-Level Theories

Cultural Explanations

All human societies have a strong stake in ensuring the health and well-being of their children, even if the cultural methods of achieving these ends differ from group to group. Most maltreatment involves individuals or families acting outside their respective cultural norms. Nevertheless, there may be cultural factors that increase the risk for child maltreatment. For example, hitting children remains widely accepted as a valid disciplinary practice in many modern Western societies, perhaps blurring the line between legitimate aggression and physical abuse. Similarly, media images and characterizations that exploit or exaggerate children's sexuality are thought to create ambiguities relating to child sexual abuse. Feminist theories propose that patriarchal cultures promote inequalities between men and children as well as men and women, and that in such cultures men are more likely to exploit their dominant position by physically, emotionally, or sexually abusing children.

Family-Level Explanations

While families generally afford the most effective natural child protection, it is also the case that most maltreatment occurs in family settings. One explanation for this is that children are dependent on, and spend most of their time with, their family, thereby increasing opportunities for maltreatment. Feminist theories propose that children can become targets of aggression or sexual interest by fathers, stepfathers, or older male siblings because of the power differential between adults and children and between males and females. Learning theories propose that negative interactions among family members can be positively or negatively reinforced,

leading to coercive cycles in which the child and caregiver increasingly rely on coercive strategies to influence the other's behavior. Unsuccessful coercive efforts by a caregiver, for example to subdue or discipline a child, may lead to an escalation of aggression or violence in an attempt to exert control. Attachment theory focuses on the effects of early bonding between children and their caregivers. Insecure attachment is implicated in child abuse and neglect in that it weakens protective bonds.

Individual-Level Explanations

Individual-level theories focus on abuse-related vulnerabilities or dispositions of victims and perpetrators. The biological and psychological immaturity of children places them at risk of abuse by older children and adults, and certain individual characteristics (e.g., difficult temperament, physical disabilities, excessive emotional neediness) may further increase this risk. A warm, supportive family environment and individual psychological resilience have been identified as important protective factors. Social learning theory proposes that childhood exposure to violence and maltreatment can lead to later abuse-related dispositions. Attachment theory proposes that insecure early attachment can lead to poor empathy and emotional regulation and a coercive or anxious interpersonal style, thus perpetuating intergenerational abuse-related vulnerabilities.

Situational Explanations

Situational theories concentrate on the effects of immediate environments on abuse-related behavior. Rational choice theory proposes that, all other things being equal, maltreatment is more likely when a potential reward (e.g., removing an aversive stimulus, sexual gratification) outweighs the potential cost (e.g., being caught and punished). Routine activities theory proposes that any crime requires the presence of a motivated offender, the presence of a suitable target, and the absence of a capable guardian. According to this formulation the immediate environment presents or restricts opportunities to enact abuse-related motivations. More recent formulations propose that the environment can actively evoke abuse-related motivations by presenting behavioral cues, social pressures, temptations, and perceived provocations.

Integrated Theories

Social Ecology Theory

Social ecology theory proposes that individual behavior is influenced by the multiple ecological systems within which the individual is socially embedded. The theory thus locates risk and protective factors for child maltreatment within and between various (individual, peer/family, school/work, neighborhood, sociocultural) levels of the victim's and perpetrator's social ecologies. Social ecology theory asserts that the influence of these systems varies along a proximal-distal continuum such that proximal (e.g., peer or family) systems exert a more direct and therefore more powerful influence than distal (e.g., neighborhood or sociocultural) systems.

Developmental–Ecological Transactional Theories

Transactional theories build on social ecology theory and aim specifically to identify etiological mechanisms and processes involved in maltreatment. These theories focus on interactions between various ecological (e.g., individual, family, and community) systems within a developmental context. Emphasis is given to interpersonal interactions (e.g., difficult child behaviors and deficient parenting skills). Maltreatment is thought to occur when potentiating (or risk) factors outweigh compensatory (or protective) factors, usually across multiple ecological levels. Potentiating and compensatory factors are understood to be relevant both to the original causes and to the developmental outcomes of maltreatment.

Stephen Smallbone

See also Child Abuse, Neglect, and Maltreatment; Cycle of Violence, Theory of; Developmental Victimology; Pedophilia; Victimization, Theories of

Further Readings

Belsky, J. (1993). Etiology of child maltreatment: A developmental-ecological analysis. *Psychological Bulletin, 114,* 413–434.

Cicchetti, D., & Toth, S. L. (2005). Child maltreatment. *Annual Review of Clinical Psychology, 1,* 409–438.

Smallbone, S., Marshall, W. L., & Wortley, R. (2008). *Preventing child sexual abuse: Evidence, policy and practice.* Cullompton, UK: Willan.

CHILD DEATH REVIEW TEAM

A child death review team (CDRT) conducts a comprehensive, multidisciplinary review of all cases in which a child under 18 years old has died due to natural causes, accidental injury, abuse, homicide, or suicide. The CDRT was created in 1978 in Los Angeles, California. CDRT members include social service providers, victim advocates, health care practitioners and emergency medical personnel, law enforcement, prosecuting attorneys, medical examiners/coroners, and others who have an occupational interest in the case. The goal of the team is to review the cases in which a child has died with two goals in mind—preventing similar cases from recurring in the future and improving the safety, health, and well-being of all children. This entry outlines the process including the goals and objectives of the CDRT.

The CDRT Process

The composition of the CDRT differs by state and even by jurisdiction within states. Regardless of the variations, typically the team is given a case file (or files) or summary sheet to review the case. Cases are subdivided into categories based upon the type of death under review. If the case requires immediate review, the team will be convened within 48 hours after the child's death. If an immediate review is not required, the CDRT will review the case as needed with meetings planned several times per year. If a case merits a periodic review, the CDRT members will receive the case file several days or sometimes weeks before the initial review meeting. Regardless of the type of review, there are six steps that CDRTs share when they meet to review cases. The CDRT's first step is to discuss all the relevant information regarding the circumstances of the child's death. At this initial meeting, it is important for all participants to share with the other team members any pertinent information regarding the case (e.g., the child, the child's family, services received, and circumstances surrounding the death). This provides all CDRT members with a full understanding of the case and the opportunity to ask questions for clarification purposes. Given the varying rules regarding individual, organizational, and/or professional levels of confidentiality, CDRT members typically do not provide written materials to the team. Instead, a verbal presentation, including a question-and-answer period, is made by each member. If there are still questions after the completion of all presentations, the case may be revisited at the next meeting, pending the gathering of more information. Likewise, if the complexities of the case necessitate greater time for case review, the initial review may be extended to a later meeting date.

After the initial meeting, the CDRT must discuss all aspects of the investigative process, including identifying the lead investigating agency and key personnel, outlining the findings of the initial investigation, determining findings from subsequent investigations, and verifying if the investigation is complete. At this point, the CDRT determines if the investigation is adequate or if something is missing. If there is information missing, the CDRT identifies suggestions to improve protocol and to streamline the investigative process, rather than finding fault or laying blame.

The third step for the CDRT is to identify if the child and/or family were utilizing any services prior to the child's death. This includes reviewing if the services were given in a timely manner, if the delivery of other services could have prevented the child's death, and if anything was absent in the delivery of services prior to the child's death. As part of this step, the CDRT is expected to determine which services may be needed currently and/or in the future to help family, friends, or schoolmates cope with the child's death. The CDRT identifies which member/agency should take the lead to ensure that services are distributed, a follow-up is conducted with recipients, and then a report is presented to the CDRT in a timely manner. As with all other stages of the CDRT review, team members provide suggestions to improve the service-delivery process.

The next step requires the CDRT to identify a host of risk factors involved in the child's death. These risks may include, but are not limited to, the family dynamics and medical, social, environmental, behavioral, and systemic factors. Team members must challenge themselves to not look for the simple, obvious answer, but to really explore the totality of factors that had an impact on the child's death. The goal of this stage is to determine if anything could have minimized or eliminated the identified risk factors and prevented the child's death. This information may prevent the death of children in the future.

The fifth step is to identify and recommend improvements within and across systems. The CDRT works collaboratively to identify problems, barriers, and gaps in services that may have contributed to the child's death. Once problems have been identified, the team works together to investigate, inquire, and suggest improvements. If one of the CDRT members represents an agency in question, he or she will be given the opportunity to explain organizational and personnel responsibilities, protocols, and limitations that may have contributed to the identified problems. If necessary, the CDRT may serve as liaison to ensure that there is an adequate response to addressing the identified concerns. During this step, it is essential for the CDRT to provide positive feedback and realistic suggestions that take into consideration limited organizational and staff resources. This process should not put individuals or organizations on the defensive, but rather, should provide an open forum to determine informed suggestions to improve and streamline the process in the future.

The final step in the CDRT process is to outline the mechanisms to prevent similar deaths in the future. The team members work together to identify and determine appropriate avenues for adopting prevention-based policies, programs, and initiatives. The CDRT may not be responsible for implementation, but it will determine what organization or entity is capable of adopting and enforcing proposed preventive actions. Finally, the CDRT must follow up on the status of the prevention program to ensure its timely implementation and enforcement. This six-step process provides an effective means of understanding a child's death, and findings from this process can be used to prevent comparable deaths in the future.

Bernadette T. Muscat

See also Battered-Child Syndrome; Child Abuse, Identification of; Child Abuse, Neglect, and Maltreatment; Child Abuse, Neglect, and

Maltreatment: Interventions for; Child Abuse, Neglect, and Maltreatment: Mandatory Reporting; Child Abuse, Neglect, and Maltreatment: Measurement of; Child Abuse, Neglect, and Maltreatment: Statutory Responses

Further Readings

Durfee, M. J., Gellert, G. A., & Tilton-Durfee, D. (1992, March/April). Origins and clinical relevance of child death review teams. *Children Today*. Retrieved December 10, 2008, from http://findarticles.com/p/articles/mi_m1053/is_n2_v21/ai_13561144

The National Center on Child Fatality Review. (2004). *Developing and maintaining the child death review team*. Retrieved December 10, 2008, from http://ican-ncfr.org/documents/Developing_and_Maintaining.pdf

National MCH Center for Child Death Review. (2005, September). *Team meeting protocols*. Retrieved December 10, 2008, from http://www.childdeath review.org/teamprotocols.htm

CHILD PORNOGRAPHY AND SEXUAL EXPLOITATION

Child pornography is not a new form of child exploitation, and it has long been implicated in other sexually abusive practices toward children. However, with each technological advance there has also been a further democratization of the availability of images and text that objectify and sexualize children. To describe these images, the term *abusive images* is now widely used by those who advocate for children's rights in relation to sexual abuse through photography; however, *child pornography* is consistently used in the majority of laws and policy documents internationally, and attempts to change terminology are thought by some to be both confusing and to not adequately capture the complex nature of the material. As such, there seems to be a widening gap between those who are concerned with the availability of sexualized depictions of children and those who feel that such depictions may be problematic but cannot be legislated against. In relation to this, the terms *sexual abuse* and *sexual exploitation* are sometimes used synonymously.

Definitions

Article 34 of the U.N. Convention on the Rights of the Child (CRC) states that parties should undertake to protect the child from all forms of sexual exploitation and sexual abuse and take all appropriate national, bilateral, and multilateral measures to prevent the exploitative use of children in pornographic performances and materials. The first international definition of child pornography was that of the Optional Protocol to the CRC on the sale of children, child prostitution, and child pornography, which entered into force on January 18, 2002. Article 2(c) defined child pornography as "any representation, by whatever means, of a child engaged in real or simulated explicit sexual activities or any representation of the sexual parts of a child primarily for sexual purposes." This document, as well as the Council of Europe's Cybercrime Convention and the European Union's Framework Decision, defines a child as under the age of 18 and includes both real depictions and simulated material within its definition of sexual exploitation of children and child pornography. The focus of the definition is on photographs that are deemed to be obscene or indecent, and this requires the depiction of explicit sexual behavior or the genitals of a child. This poses problems in terms of how we make sense of, and possibly legislate against, the large volume of sexualized material of children available on the Internet and through other media which do not meet this definition.

While there has been an increase in legislation over the last decade, it has not been harmonized across all states. A 2006 study by the International Center for Missing and Exploited Children demonstrated that of the 184 member countries of Interpol, 95 countries have no legislation at all that specifically addresses child pornography, and of those that do, 41 countries do not criminalize possession of child pornography, regardless of intent to distribute.

One issue of concern relates to digitally altered images (or pseudo-images) and virtual child pornography. In the United States, the constitutionality of virtual child pornography remains a critical issue. In 2002, a majority of the Supreme Court struck down portions of the Child Pornography Prevention Act of 1996, stating that the category of virtual child pornography created without real or identifiable minors was unconstitutionally overbroad. It might be thought that these pseudo-photographs complicate our understanding of the problem and challenge our understanding of harm. Harm, however, need not always be harm of a specific child. In the United Kingdom, a government task force has been considering the issues raised by computer-generated images in drawings and cartoons that show graphic depictions of sexual abuse of children or childlike characters, and it plans to bring forward legislation with regard to this new offense. Researchers such as David Oswell have argued that the crime of possession, making, or distribution of child pornography (whether virtual or not) is a crime not only against a particular child, but against all children.

Exploitation Through Child Pornography

While it has been suggested that very few children appear to be exploited through child pornography, this is an underresearched area. Children are rarely asked whether a camera was used as part of any sexual abuse, and while police records routinely cite the number of images seized in the conviction of the offender, they do not indicate the number of children abused or provide an adequate understanding of how child pornography is part of a cycle of sexual exploitation. In 2005, ECPAT International (End Child Prostitution, Child Pornography and Trafficking of Children for Sexual Purposes) produced a contribution to the United Nations Study on Violence Against Children that, for the first time, documented evidence that all children were potentially vulnerable to harm through the new technologies, not only those who had access to the Internet. The publication detailed studies of children from Mexico, Nepal, the Czech Republic, the Philippines, India, and Moldova, all of whom had been implicated in a range of sexually abusive activities that included the production of child pornography. What is apparent from these studies is that little is known as to what factors leave these children vulnerable, what resources are available to them, and what happens to the images that are produced. Factors identified as playing a part in the production and distribution of child pornography include poverty, social disruption, corruption, an acceptance of abusive practices, and a willingness of

others to exploit. In addition, the increasing exposure of children to pornography and to media that can facilitate harmful behavior might cause harm to a child. This may include young people's having the opportunity to create harmful or illegal content, particularly through webcams and camera phones, as well as to engage in sexually problematic behavior toward other children.

The lack of knowledge about children being abused through photography is reflected in the relatively small numbers of such children who have been identified. Where identification has taken place, there is little consistent empirical data, although the National Center for Missing and Exploited Children suggested that as of September 2008, 1,660 children (73% female and 27% male) had been identified through distributed and nondistributed images. It is unclear whether the differences between the number of female and male children identified reflects the actual distribution of images currently circulating on the Internet. A Dutch study in 1992 analyzed the content of 1,065 published child pornography magazines that had been in circulation prior to the change of law across a number of European countries. They calculated that a conservative estimate would be that 6,000 children were associated with child pornography in the magazines. The division of photographs in the sample suggested that 42% were pictures of boys, with more girls appearing in extreme images. In 2008 an Australian police report describing the gender, ethnicity, and age of the victims portrayed in child pornography images examined by investigators suggested that they were mostly White, Westernized females between 8 and 12 years old. Asian children were the next most common ethnic group, and there was a comparative absence of indigenous Australian children.

Consequences of Exploitation Through Child Pornography

At present there is very little information about what happens to children therapeutically when they have been identified as being subjected to abuse through the production of child pornography, and the information that is available concerns specific countries (such as Germany and Sweden). Psychosocial approaches to treatment and recovery of children tend to be dominated by therapy that may be thought of as culture bound and disregarding the importance of differing developmental needs and systemic contexts. There are four substantial studies (all but one of which predate the Internet) that have sought to examine the impact of child pornography. The studies examined children's involvement in pornography and sex rings, child pornography production in the context of child prostitution, children exposed to both the production of pornography and intra- and extrafamilial abuse, and in the context of ritual abuse.

All of these studies are broadly similar in the accounts that they give of the symptoms the children produced during the abuse (e.g., physical symptoms such as urinary infections and genital soreness, as well as behavioral symptoms such as sexualized behaviors). However, it is difficult to disentangle the consequences of abuse from the consequences of being photographed. Carl-Gören Svedin and Christina Back provided responses from their sample of children that included restlessness, depression, hunger, exhaustion, concentration difficulties, and aggressive behaviors. Earlier studies also suggested that children who were exposed to longer periods of abuse suffered more intense emotional reactions, such as feelings of isolation, fear, anxiety, and emotional withdrawal. The studies cited above do not specifically deal with the affect that the production of child pornography has on sexually abused children. Nor are there more than anecdotal accounts of how children perceive the fact that images of their abuse are distributed through the Internet.

Bengt Söderström, a psychologist working with children who have had images of their abuse distributed via the new technologies, notes that the disclosure of being abused and photographed has different facets to it. The child's cognitive perception of the abuse is made especially difficult because the child constantly needs to defend himself or herself from facing the fact that photographs were taken. Söderström suggested that the picture taking in itself is an issue almost separate from the abuse experience. That photographs have been taken of the abuse makes it difficult for the child to control how the information is disclosed or to limit what is disclosed. Adults who have contact with the child will often assume that the photographs portraying the most abusive activities will be the ones that will affect the child most. However, it is often the case that images that are not illegal, which portray the child with clothes on but that were taken by the abuser, are equally or even more disturbing, since these images are part of the entire experience of abuse and may remind the child of how the perpetrator has violated his or her trust. This makes discussion about the abuse and related photographs difficult.

What is clear from these studies is that the abused children exhibit a pattern of enforced silence. Children appear reluctant to disclose the abuse, and it appears that the recording of the abuse exacerbates, and in some cases prevents, disclosure. Even when confronted with the visual evidence of the abuse, children continue to limit disclosure, telling people only what they already knew. In 2003 the Swedish authorities were faced with an investigation of a number of children whose images had been traced elsewhere in the world and were eventually identified as coming from Sweden. When interviewing the children, the same resistance to acknowledging that they were the subjects of the images was found. Mimi Silbert had earlier coined the phrase *silent conspiracy* to describe this. It is unclear as to whether the sense of shame and humiliation, often reported in these studies, relates to the photography itself or the fact of disclosing it to others. It may also be that children fear being thought to be complicit in the abuse or photography through the evidence of, for example, their smiling faces in the images. Tink Palmer has suggested that probably the greatest inhibitors to disclosing what has occurred is the humiliation that children feel regarding who may have seen their images and their fear of being recognized. They feel they have been caught in the act.

In her study of children abused through prostitution, Silbert noted that the long-term effects of being photographed are being more debilitating than short- or medium-term effects, and that these effects are compounded when children are involved in more than one form of sexual exploitation. The effects may also be exacerbated by the knowledge that others may see or distribute the films. Such feelings have been described as psychological paralysis. This is also accompanied by the knowledge that such photographs may be used to exploit other children and that, in the context of the Internet, they will never go away.

Intervention

After the famous case in Sweden was uncovered, Svedin and Back from the youth psychiatric clinic at the University Hospital in Linköping reached an agreement whereby the police would inform the clinic when they were able to identify any child via the seizure of images. This provided unique possibilities for investigating how children are recruited and what children remember of their participation in relation to the actual course of events depicted in pictures and/or videos. It also sheds light on the psychiatric health of children. The report in 2003 included 30 children. The study highlighted the shame of the children, and that this shame also contributed to the continuation of the relationship with the perpetrator. The children actively sought contact with this adult, with whom they had an emotionally significant relationship in which they were invested. Of the interviewed children, only two of them began to talk spontaneously, and there were five others who eventually gave a fairly complete account without being shown the pictures and without the investigators saying that they knew what had happened (from the seized material). Five children denied that anything had occurred. All the children's accounts were fragmentary, and the children showed great difficulty in talking about their contact with the suspected perpetrator. They often said that they did not remember what had happened. Nevertheless, it became apparent that what the children least wanted to remember had to do with the photography. It was shown that the more interviews in which the children took part, the more they were able to put into words what had happened.

This research has implications for the recovery of children sexually exploited through their involvement in the production of pornographic images and for those professionals wishing to assist them. As noted above, there is a general lack of expertise and experience among professionals wishing to meet the needs of children abused and exploited in this way. A recent German study suggested that many professionals feel helpless about their ability to understand the needs of such children, yet at times these professionals become part of a conspiracy of silence in their unwillingness to ask questions. It is necessary for police officers, social welfare workers, and child professionals to reevaluate their working practices in the light of what has been learned. Palmer has suggested that there are three key areas that need to be addressed: managing the discovery/disclosure process and the investigative interview of the child, assessing the recovery needs for the child, and determining the nature and content of the ensuing intervention programs.

Response and Prevention

Efforts to deter the production and distribution of child pornography have tended to focus on educating children in safe Internet use by providing safety tools online and help lines and education packages for school settings and on targeting offenders by disrupting activities, criminalizing behaviors, and, in some contexts, offering therapeutic intervention. It is unclear what impact these have had on the use and distribution of child pornography. Within a criminological framework, Max Taylor and Ethel Quayle have explored ways in which the Internet itself might be thought to contribute to the commission of criminal behavior such as the trade in pornographic images of children. In doing so they identified a number of characteristics or qualities of the Internet that might be thought to facilitate the commission of criminal acts. Their discussion is framed within a conceptual framework informed by the rational choice perspective on offending, focusing on the environmental constraints and qualities of the Internet. It identifies in particular search activities as being a central rate-limiting activity in Internet crime, and how such an analysis might aid the development of preventive strategies. However, probably the greatest challenge to the prevention of the production and distribution of child pornography is our willingness to see images of abuse as simply pictures, distanced from the reality of the child's experience.

Ethel Quayle

See also Child Abuse, Neglect, and Maltreatment: Theories of; Cyber and Internet Offenses; Cybercrime, Prevention of; Pedophilia; Situational Crime Prevention

Further Readings

Oswell, D. (2006). When images matter: Internet child pornography, forms of observation and an ethics of the virtual. *Information, Communication and Society*, 9(2), 244–265.

Palmer, T. (2004). *Just one click*. London: Barnardos.

Quayle, E. (2008). Internet offending. In D. R. Laws & W. O'Donohue (Eds.), *Sexual deviance* (pp. 439–458). New York: Guilford.

Quayle, E., Lööf, L., & Palmer, T. (2008). *Child pornography and sexual exploitation of children online*. Bangkok, Thailand: ECPAT International.

Renold, E., & Creighton, S. J. (2003). *Images of abuse: A review of the evidence on child pornography*. London: NSPCC.

Silbert, M. H. (1989). The effects on juveniles of being used for pornography and prostitution. In D. Zillman & C. Bryant (Eds.), *Pornography: Research advances and policy considerations*. Hillside, NJ: Lawrence Erlbaum.

Söderström, B. (2006). *Experiences from and questions raised in clinical practice*. Report from the experts' meeting, Children and Young Persons With Abusive and Violent Experiences Connected to Cyberspace. Satra Brük, Sweden: Swedish Children's Welfare Foundation.

Svedin, C. G., & Back, K. (2003). *Why didn't they tell us?* Stockholm: Swedish Save the Children.

Taylor, M., & Quayle, E. (2003). *Child pornography: An Internet crime*. Brighton, UK: Routledge.

Taylor, M., & Quayle, E. (2006). The Internet and abuse images of children: Search, precriminal situations and opportunity. In R. Wortley & S. Smallbone (Eds.), *Situational prevention of child sexual abuse*. Crime Prevention Studies, Vol. 19. Monsey, NY: Criminal Justice Press/Willan.

CHILD PROTECTIVE SERVICES

Child Protective Services (CPS) is a governmental agency under the jurisdiction of the Juvenile Court that is responsible for investigating allegations of abuse and/or neglect for children under 18 years old. This entry provides a brief history, governing laws, the investigative process, and the goals of CPS.

History and Governing Laws

The statutory basis for governmental intervention stems from the legal principle of *parens patriae*, which gives the court the right to act as a parent of a child when the parent is unable or unwilling to do so. As an affiliate of the court, CPS is responsible for ensuring a child's safety and well-being. CPS is governed by U.S. federal and state laws, which outline definitions of child abuse and neglect and organizational operating procedures (e.g., response time to alleged allegations, case management and follow-up, confidentiality restrictions, conflicts of interest, and court and appeal processes). The differences in state laws contribute to organizational variations across state lines. Despite these differences, there are four main steps to the investigative process.

Investigative Process

The first step is the Intake, which involves receiving a report or allegation that a child has been harmed in some way. In some cases, a mandated reporter (e.g., school and day care personnel, social workers, medical and mental health practitioners, law enforcement and fire fighters, clergy, to name a few) will call CPS. In other cases, a concerned family member, friend, or neighbor will report the alleged abuse. During the Intake, CPS will gather as much information as possible regarding the alleged abuse, the abuser, and the alleged victim. Although the call is anonymous, the reporter is asked to identify how he or she learned about the alleged abuse, why there is a suspicion of abuse, and any information pertaining to the child, including where he or she lives and goes to school, family dynamics, and if the child has siblings.

The next step involves determining if the reported allegations meet the legal definitions for child abuse and/or neglect as specified by state law. Once CPS determines that the reported case meets these statutory requirements, then a case is opened. At this point, CPS will assess and investigate the case. The investigative process involves substantiating whether or not the allegations are true by talking with the child, family members, and those who are associated with the child (e.g., school or day care personnel, neighbors, and others). In most states, this includes a home visit to assess the child's living situation. During the home visit, CPS will look at the conditions of the home to see if the child has adequate food, clothing, and shelter. The CPS worker will also observe interactions between the parent or guardian and the alleged child victim and others within the home. After the investigation is completed, CPS must determine whether the alleged abuse is substantiated (true) or unsubstantiated (not true). If the allegations are unsubstantiated, the case is closed. Once a case is substantiated, a report is made to Juvenile Court indicating recommended actions on behalf of the child. The goal of the recommendations is to establish an action plan to ensure the child's safety and well-being. Some possible actions taken for the child and/or his or her siblings include emergency removal from the home and placement in a safe environment, medical and mental health care, and referrals to other social service agencies. If the abuser is a parent or guardian, this individual may be required to attend anger management classes, a behavioral modification program, substance abuse treatment, parenting classes, job training, and/or any other program deemed appropriate by CPS. The Juvenile Court will make findings of jurisdiction (who has authority over the child) and disposition (the decision of the court). If the court determines that emergency removal is necessary, the child is adjudicated and becomes a ward of the court. CPS is then responsible for the care and custody of the child until he or she can be placed with another family member. If there are no family members and/or the family is unable or unwilling to care for the child, the child is placed within the foster care system. If there are multiple siblings, the preference is to keep all of the children together. The child will remain under the court's custody until there is sufficient proof that the child can safely return to the parent or guardian. Once a child is removed, CPS will create a reunification plan to help the family reunite. If the case does not require emergency removal, CPS will work with the family to determine appropriate referrals and programs to prevent future acts of child maltreatment.

The third stage involves case management, evaluating the situation, and updating the court. CPS is required to review the case periodically. The frequency of the follow-up is determined by the court. During the evaluation period, the CPS worker may alter the action plan based upon the needs of the child and family. During the entire process (removal, reunification, and family maintenance), the CPS worker will evaluate the situation and update the court regarding the status of the case.

The final stage involves closing the case, which occurs after CPS conducts a final evaluation, often including a home visit to ensure that the child is no longer in danger. During the evaluation, the CPS worker assesses the situation based on several criteria, including family functioning, household stability, and the child's access to nutrition, health care, education, and shelter. Upon completion of the evaluation, when CPS determines that the family no longer needs follow-up services, as the action plan has been successfully completed, the case can be closed. Case closure also happens when the family's rights to the child are terminated through adoption by another adult who is then responsible for the permanent care and custody of the child. A case will remain closed unless another report is made and the process begins again. Throughout the entire process, the overarching goals of CPS are to protect and ensure the safety and well-being of the child and improve family functioning in a nonpunitive and rehabilitative manner.

Bernadette T. Muscat

See also Child Abuse, Identification of; Child Abuse, Neglect, and Maltreatment; Child Abuse, Neglect, and Maltreatment: Interventions for; Child Abuse, Neglect, and Maltreatment: Mandatory Reporting; Child Abuse, Neglect, and Maltreatment, Measurement of

Further Readings

Holder, W., & Morton, T. D. (1999, February). *Designing a comprehensive approach to child safety.* Duluth, GA: National Resource Center on Child Maltreatment, Child Welfare Institute, and ACTION for Child Protection.

Morton, T. D., & Holder, W. (1997). *Decision making in children's protective services: Advancing the state of the art.* National Resource Center on Child Maltreatment. Retrieved December 10, 2008, from http://www.nrccps.org/documents/1997/pdf/DecisionMakinginCPS.pdf

Morton, T. D., & Salovitz, B. (2001). *The CPS response to child neglect: An administrator's guide to theory, policy, program design, and case practice.* National Resource Center on Child Maltreatment. Retrieved December 10, 2008, from http://www.nrccps.org/documents/2001/pdf/CPSResponsetoChildNeglect.pdf

CITIZEN PATROLS

Citizens patrolling their neighborhood have been a staple of police efforts to enhance crime prevention and community cohesion. Citizen patrols serve as the "eyes and ears" of the police, and provide a visible sign of a defended community to deter potential lawbreakers. They are a component of grassroots and top-down efforts to stimulate or preserve community efficacy, often sponsored by or coordinated with other crime prevention activities, such as Neighborhood Watch.

Citizen patrols are voluntary activities, unpaid, usually conducted during the hours when street activity is at its peak and police patrol capacities are stretched thin. Most involve some visible symbol, like the Orange Hats of Washington, D.C., that provide a token of legitimacy and distinguish the patrols from other persons abroad in public space.

Historical Precedents

Though citizen patrols have deep historical roots in the English system of obligatory service in the watch and ward, the advent of professional policing in the early and mid-20th century diminished their importance severely. American history had slave patrols and committees of vigilance that performed similar duties under limited circumstances. A combination of social changes, including the end of slavery and the settling of the West, led to their demise, although the lynch mobs that punished alleged violations of the Jim Crow race laws represented a more sinister permutation for many years.

Modern Revival

The concept was revived in the wake of the rising crime rate and general dissatisfaction with police performance in the 1960s. The professional policing movement had staked its claim to crime control on the basis of three things: the deterrent effect of police patrol, the rapid response to reports of crime to catch criminals in the act, and relentless investigation of completed crime. Scientific investigation of these activities during the 1970s undercut each of the claims. The Kansas City Preventive Patrol Experiment cast doubt upon the deterrent effect of patrol. A four-city study of response time found that citizen delays undercut the effectiveness of police response to most calls. The Rand Corporation's study of detective work in California police departments revealed that most investigators' time was spend on routine case preparation tasks; less than 5% of criminal apprehensions resulted from "detective work" as portrayed in the popular media.

In response, Herman Goldstein proposed to move police response beyond its incident-driven tactical mind-set into a more problem-oriented strategic approach. Under financial duress, the police department in Flint, Michigan, experimented with a renewal of foot patrols to supplement rapid motorized response policing. The community policing movement arose from those two main thrusts, and a host of less publicized local initiatives. Two assumptions distinguished community policing from the professional policing model. The first was that the community's views were an important element in prioritizing police operations, which effectively led to greater attention to minor problems of disorder and incivility.

The second foundation of community policing was a renewal of the proposition that citizens have an important role to play in the defense and maintenance of their own communities. Drawing upon crime prevention concepts, particularly Oscar Newman's "defensible space" propositions, the police began to work in concert with community residents to articulate viable roles for citizens to play.

Neighborhood Watch provided the framework for police–community cooperation, and Newman's concept of natural surveillance was inherent in its mission. Citizen patrols were a natural outgrowth of the new partnership, creating a mechanism of visible, assertive surveillance to supplement the more passive watching envisioned by Newman.

For newly created community policing efforts in socially unorganized areas, the citizen patrols had a secondary benefit. They provided a vehicle for greater interaction between and among residents who shared common concerns of safety and community viability. As Neighborhood Watch meetings broke down the veils of anonymity, citizen patrols allowed neighbors to have more frequent interactions, learn more about the other "good guys," and solidify social bonds. They also served as a recruiting device for neighborhood groups, informally spreading the word and thus creating renewed hope that citizens could do something to take back control of their neighborhood.

For their part, the police had a long history of urging the community to be the eyes and ears of the police by reporting crimes and suspicious conditions. The creation of citizen patrols was a logical, organized extension of that general exhortation.

The police were not universally in favor of citizen patrols, however, and some of the early efforts were ad hoc campaigns mounted by citizen groups without police assistance, sometimes in the face of active police discouragement. Some police agencies did tolerate the initiatives, however, and encouraged them without offering overt sponsorship or logistical support. A few jurisdictions took ownership of the concept, organizing and coordinating the patrol efforts, providing training and official liaison as a way of bolstering their larger community policing initiatives.

Concerns

Potential negative consequences attend citizen patrols in crime-ridden neighborhoods, and accounted for part of the police reluctance to promote patrols. The most serious is the potential for violence directed against patrol members by the criminal element, particularly the street-level drug dealers whose business is a primary target of patrol activity. Police were also concerned about a resurgence of vigilantism, citizens unaware of the requirements and limits of the law taking unwarranted actions based on moral viewpoints but fundamentally at odds with the requirements of law. Both retaliatory violence and lawsuits were possible consequences of ill-considered citizen actions, and police sponsorship would open the city to financial responsibility for volunteers' errors.

Police were also concerned that citizen patrols would flood the police with reports of minor behaviors, drawing scarce resources away from the serious problems that demanded police presence. These concerns were addressed by training programs conducted by police liaisons that covered police operations as well as legal requirements. Police-sponsored patrols are almost always predicated upon a "no intervention" rule: the patrols' responsibility is to show the flag and to call for the police when their presence alone is insufficient to deter unwanted behaviors. (Citizens' academies,

with their more expansive exposure to the police role and areas of community support, were often an outgrowth of the early training efforts.)

On the street, some of the initial concerns about confrontation were assuaged over time. Residents proved to have a good sense of who "the players" were in their neighborhood, and often a better sense of how to approach them than did the police—especially if the players lived in the neighborhood themselves. Often police threats were less persuasive than the patrols' quiet dialogues centering on respect for the neighborhood, which forged mutually tolerable accommodations. While citizen patrols might not eliminate activity like drug sales and prostitution, they could go a long way to mitigating the more abrasive public behaviors that attended the illicit markets.

Over the long term, citizen patrols came to share the concerns that attend most crime prevention activities: maintaining interest past the group's initial formation, recruiting and orienting new members, and sustaining members by spreading the burden of donated time and effort equitably. The hours when the patrols are needed tend to be during the evening, after the residents return home from work, and on weekends.

Not every organized citizen group works in concert with the police. Some have been openly antagonistic to the police. During the 1980s, the American Indian Movement used citizen patrols to shadow the police patrolling Native American neighborhoods, with the intent to capture any police brutality on videotape. In Chicago and other cities, parents in inner-city neighborhoods have formed convoys to walk their children safely through the gauntlet of drug sellers who line the streets near schools.

Impact

It is difficult to measure the impact of citizen patrols on crime, as their activities are often part of an extensive menu of intensive police–community endeavors. The visible presence of neighborhood guardians should serve as a deterrent, lowering reported crime. The possibility exists that they will report more suspicious incidents to police, elevating the call load and the initial reports of crime. The greatest contribution that citizen patrols make to crime prevention may be to empower residents. Their efforts are seen not only by potential offenders, but also by other residents who may have been too fearful to join the initial community organizing efforts. The enhancement of feelings of community efficacy cannot be measured by direct analysis of crime rates, but they have long-lasting positive effects for communities.

Michael E. Buerger

See also Crime Prevention; Neighborhood Watch Programs

Further Readings

Newman, O. (1972). *Defensible space: Crime prevention through urban design.* New York: Macmillan.

Pennell, S., Curtis, C., Henderson, J., & Tayman, J. (1989). Guardian angels: A unique approach to crime prevention. *Crime & Delinquency, 35*(3), 378–400.

Yin, R. K., Vogel, M. E., Chaiken, J. M., & Both, D. R. (1976). *Citizen patrol projects: National Evaluation Program Phase 1 summary* (NCJ-036435). Washington, DC: U.S. Department of Justice.

CIVIL ABATEMENT

Civil abatement constitutes a purposive application of civil regulatory law to crime prevention goals. It encompasses a wide range of tactics, from code enforcement to licensing, and from boarding up (or demolishing) derelict properties to issuing injunctions against gang members. Though it is an enforcement action, it does not target criminal law breakers, but nominally respectable citizens. Ultimately, civil abatement strives for a type of general deterrence, extending informal social control through nongovernmental entities who nevertheless exert a localized influence over the conduct of potential criminal offenders.

Philosophically, civil abatement measures belong to the routine activities wing of criminology. The expanded understanding of crime as an event involving offenders, victims (or targets), and guardians illuminated new possibilities to disrupt opportunities for crime to occur. Civil abatement places responsibility upon the owners and managers of places, whether commercial or residential in nature, to maintain strict standards for their premises. Such a climate is believed to have a shaping influence on the environment, and both direct and indirect influences upon the behavior of their clients and patrons.

Unlike the "broken windows" hypothesis of James Wilson and George Kelling, civil abatement does not depend upon the actions of the public police acting on the lawbreaking and the marginally disruptive. Instead, it focuses on respectable intermediaries whose sphere of influence over the behavior of potential lawbreakers is more immediate than is the attenuated deterrent impact of the criminal sanction.

The movement to civil abatement as an intervention technique also represents a shift in philosophy regarding the distinction between private enterprise and public responsibility. Landlords long maintained that their responsibilities were limited to the private contractual relationship between themselves and their renters. Business owners claimed that their responsibility for client behavior ended at the door of their establishment. Both asserted that crime prevention was the responsibility of the tax-funded public police, not private persons.

Civil abatement refutes those "not my responsibility" claims. It reflects a growing trend in regulation of conduct that has serious, if unintended, consequences for the public. It creates new responsibilities for business owners and managers to promulgate and enforce rules of conduct for their clientele, whether renters, patrons, or visitors.

Civil abatement is most effective when it is an organized, coordinated campaign instituted by civic government, such as the Beat Health program of the Oakland Police Department in California. When police target a drug location for civil abatement, it coordinates police actions with the city's SMART (Specialized Multi-Agency Response Team), whose members are inspectors for the various civil code enforcement agencies. Civil abatement can also be implemented on an as-needed basis by individual police officers and small units, as was done in Minneapolis, Minnesota, by the RECAP unit. Invocation of the process by individual officers often is more difficult, since it creates additional work for the regulatory agencies and runs the risk of bringing political pressures against the agencies and their employees.

Origins

Until the 1980s, civil regulatory law and criminal law rarely intersected. The one area where the two strains of law intersected was alcohol and beverage control, because the impact of alcohol upon criminality and uncivil behavior was well documented. Liquor law inspectors (by whatever title they were known) had a specific responsibility for enforcing laws regulating the business practices of any establishment with a liquor license. Included in their mandate were the standards for selling and serving (particularly for not selling to minors, intoxicated persons, and persons whose past behavior under the influence led to their being banned). In this, their inspection duties overlapped with those of the municipal police, who would routinely walk through bars and check in on liquor stores to monitor behaviors there. The purpose was to discourage disruptive behavior by patrons (who would carry those behaviors out into the public streets at closing time), and also discourage bartenders from "bending the rules" in favor of intoxicated patrons.

Nominally, the two spheres were separate. Liquor inspectors had the power to suspend an establishment's license, but generally could do so only for egregious behavior. Although they often had police authority, liquor inspectors were responsible for covering a wide territory, and would concern themselves with the conduct of patrons only in extreme circumstances. By contrast, the police lacked the ability to close a bar except in extreme circumstances (and then only temporarily), and referred liquor law violations to the liquor inspectors when stronger action was needed. In practice, the two sides often developed a close working relationship: The liquor inspectors wielded the legal clout, and the local police had strength of numbers to back up the inspectors in difficult situations.

Modern Evolutions

In the 1980s, the development of computer technology coincided with new philosophical strains in the policing community. Computers gave the police the ability to move beyond paper records and rudimentary pin maps, and to examine their activity patterns more closely and link calls for police services to other municipal data. At the same time, Herman Goldstein's call for problem-oriented policing merged with the community policing reform movement, bringing the police out of their law-enforcement isolation, broadening their vision, and increasing the demands upon them.

Police had long known that demands for their services were greatest in a limited number of areas: those with poverty, transient populations, persons with multiple social problems (mental illness, drug abuse, alcoholism), a concentration of persons released from prison or under controls as sex offenders, and other social ills. Computer technology allowed the police to link their 9-1-1 calls to individual properties, to ownership and land use patterns, and eventually to complaints to other regulatory bodies.

In community meetings, police found that neighborhood concerns extended far beyond the robbers and drug dealers the police considered important. The police came to understand that drug-dealing was linked to lax management practices, substandard housing, the sporadic nature of municipal services in low-income areas, and many other conditions outside the purview of the criminal law. At the same time, police officers came in contact with their counterparts in the agencies with the power to take action in the other areas. Local partnerships evolved, and the foundations for civil abatement were laid.

The Obstacle of Routinization

Because the perceived need for regulation arose at different times for specific conditions, the regulatory functions of municipal government tend to be isolated, working in "stovepipes" of their own making. The normal course of their duties is routinized, and their work is organized around a schedule of processing new applications for licensing, conducting routine (usually annual) inspections of their licensees, and investigating complaints and allegations of noncompliance.

Routinization included a regular schedule of inspections (to manage the workload by spreading it across the calendar) and notices of impending inspections sent to the licensees (a bureaucratic courtesy that facilitates the discharge of the inspection on the first scheduled attempt). A grace period is usually granted to correct any deficiencies found during the annual inspection. The majority of licensees conduct their businesses in accord with the requirements of their licenses: Violations tend to be minor and easily corrected, so routine checks by the regulatory agencies are all that are necessary.

A pernicious minority of owners of problem properties routinely ignored standard business practices, allowing the properties to decline, oblivious to the activities going on there. Absentee landlords—whether individuals living in the suburbs or a conglomerate headquartered 1,000 miles away—invested little in the physical condition of their properties and less in their operations. Upon receiving notice of the coming annual inspection, they would make minimal, often cosmetic repairs to the physical property in order to meet the minimal requirements of the inspection. Any violations found during the inspection would be corrected in perfunctory fashion or appealed, effectively putting off any need for improvement for another year.

Civil abatement provisions coalesced when the police and other civic authorities recognized the relationship between substandard business practices and crime and disorder. When the police identified a problem property based upon the activities of the residents (most likely drug activity), they also found that the problems were highly resistant to the traditional interdiction of search warrants and arrest. Developing the basis for search warrants and conducting raids was labor intensive and time consuming. Offenders released on bail would immediately resume their activities, prolonging their court appearances, and the corrective influence of the raid upon conditions in the neighborhoods was negligible. The police could not maintain a crime-suppressive presence at every property; a more consistent influence was needed to obtain different results.

Building asset seizure and forfeiture into the drug laws created a stronger tool for enforcement. Because it constituted a deprivation of property, it fell under the Fourth Amendment and was regarded by many prosecutors as a last resort. The specter of eventually losing one's property for tolerating certain activities of residents created a new dimension for regulation, however, and provided room for the police and civil authorities to take lesser actions.

A considerable gap exists between the "private contract" defense of landlords and others, and the reality of business as practiced by slumlords. Legitimate landlords require some sort of credit check and background check for their prospective tenants, and require certain behaviors as part of the contract (the lease). Slumlords tend to accept anyone with the deposit and first month's rent in hand or a Section 8 voucher that guarantees the slumlord a hassle-free income stream without ever coming in contact with the tenants. The first type of tenant is likely to be a drug dealer; the second may not be a problem individual, but the probability is increased that the tenant will have additional social problems and no social capital. Neither type of tenant is likely to make demands for better conditions, and any requests these tenants make can be safely ignored. Civil abatement changes that assumption of no-work income.

Targeting a property for civil abatement is usually a police-initiated activity, but not always. Local neighborhood groups have used the civil process to sue landlords for unsightly or unsafe conditions, in order to force the landlords to rehabilitate properties or change tenant standards. Drug sales, which have an inordinate negative impact on the surrounding neighborhood, have been a prime source of selection, but other conditions have similar potential.

When a property comes under the aegis of civil abatement, it is visited without prior notice by a team of inspectors from multiple regulatory agencies—Housing, Code Inspection (electrical and plumbing), the Health Department, among others—accompanied by police officers. The resulting inspection usually turns up a raft of violations, ranging from occupancy by persons not on the lease to substandard maintenance that constitutes both health and safety risks for the occupants. In the case of serious violations, the property may be condemned immediately and the residents removed. The usual outcome, however, tends to be a ream of violations—each bearing either a civil penalty or a documented requirement for expensive repairs (with a monetary penalty for noncompliance).

For their part, the police will document the people found at the residence during the inspection, and check for criminal records and outstanding warrants. Their presence signals to the residents, the owners (and managers, if any), and the neighborhood the enhanced power behind police requests for corrective measures at other properties.

Some property owners will take steps to correct the deficiencies, including hiring managers and instituting the lease and background check measures requested by the police (or demanded by local ordinance). Others find it easier to sell the property: If they sell to another slumlord, the cycle begins again, but if they sell to a more responsible owner, the police have an opportunity to help create another crime-free establishment.

Although civil abatement is largely a police-initiated endeavor, other avenues of redress are available. In the past, neighborhood groups have filed lawsuits against landowners in order to close crack houses, shooting galleries, and other dens of iniquity. Banning orders have been levied against street prostitutes and others engaged in criminal acts. Los Angeles created an ordinance that permits authorities to ban gang members from certain areas based on the gang's unlawful activities, not the individual's. Perhaps the most widespread civil abatement provision applied to individuals in America today is the ordinances that ban sex offenders from living within a certain radius of schools, child care centers, bus stops, playgrounds, and other places where their potential victims gather.

Michael E. Buerger

See also Community Policing; Crime Prevention

Further Readings

Buerger, M. E., & Mazerolle, L. G. (1998). Third party policing: A theoretical analysis of an emerging trend. *Justice Quarterly, 15*(2), 301–328.

Mazerolle, L. G., & Ransley, J. (2005). *Third party policing.* New York: Cambridge University Press.

Mazerolle, L. G., & Roehl, J. (Eds.). (1998). *Civil remedies and crime prevention.* Monsey, NY: Criminal Justice Press.

CIVIL LITIGATION

When someone is a victim of a crime, it is considered a crime against society, in the form of violating the laws of the state or federal government. Thus the government, represented by the prosecutor's office, may file charges against an offender for violating society's laws. The victim's role in a prosecution can vary from minimal, in which the victim cannot or will not cooperate with the prosecution, to heavily involved, in which the victim seeks to press charges and is present and participates throughout the adjudication process. Once the prosecution is over and the offender is either convicted or acquitted, the criminal justice process is generally over for the victim. However, victims are able to seek other avenues of relief in the form of civil lawsuits against the offender.

A civil lawsuit can be filed by the victim (or, if the victim is dead, by the victim's family) to recover some of the losses that were incurred as a result of the crime. Victims also may pursue civil lawsuits if they feel that justice was not served by the criminal justice system; for instance, if the offender was never charged or was acquitted of the crime, or if the offender's sentence seemed too lenient. However, victims are able to file civil lawsuits regardless of whether or not "justice was served" by the criminal prosecution. Thus a victim may file a lawsuit on the basis of personal injury incurred during a crime. For example, someone who was assaulted may incur large medical costs as a result of the assault, and suing the offender in civil court may compensate him or her for those costs. In addition, the family of someone killed during a crime may file a lawsuit on the basis of wrongful death.

Differences Between Civil Lawsuits and Criminal Prosecution

Civil lawsuits differ from criminal prosecutions in a number of ways. First, as mentioned above, criminal prosecutions are brought by state or federal governments for violations of their respective laws. Civil lawsuits are filed by private citizens for injury inflicted during the course of a crime. Whereas the prosecutor acts on behalf of the victim in a criminal prosecution, it is the victim's responsibility to file a civil lawsuit if he or she so chooses. The victim takes a more active role in a civil lawsuit than he or she does in a criminal prosecution. A criminal prosecution and a civil lawsuit are mutually exclusive, meaning that either one can occur in the absence of the other. For example, a victim may be satisfied with a criminal prosecution or may not want to spend time and money on a civil lawsuit; thus, a civil lawsuit will not be initiated. If the victim wishes to pursue a civil lawsuit, courts have ruled that these lawsuits in addition to criminal prosecutions do not violate an offender's double jeopardy rights, which only apply to successive criminal prosecutions.

A second difference between civil punishments and criminal prosecutions is the terminology used. In criminal prosecutions, the government, represented by the prosecutor, is labeled "the state" and the offender is labeled the "defendant." When criminal charges are filed against the defendant, the case name reflects both parties in the case (e.g., *State v. Smith*), but does not include the victim's name. In civil lawsuits, the victim's name appears in the case name, since the victim is filing the civil action against the offender. In these cases, the victim is labeled a "plaintiff" and the offender is labeled a "respondent" or "defendant"; however, this is not the same as a criminal defendant, but rather, is someone who is defending himself or herself in the lawsuit. Thus the case name reflects both parties in the lawsuit (e.g., *Jones v. Smith*). In addition, if an offender is convicted in a criminal prosecution, he or she is found "guilty" of the charge and will be subject to "punishment" (e.g., prison, jail, probation). In a civil lawsuit, if an offender is held "liable" for the injuries caused by the crime, he or she will be subject to a "penalty" in the form of monetary compensation that must be paid to the victim or victim's family.

Another difference between civil lawsuits and criminal prosecutions is found in the due process provisions that apply. Criminal prosecutions are considered more punitive than civil lawsuits, in that offenders may be subject to deprivation of life, liberty, or property. With civil lawsuits, offenders are only subject to deprivations of property. As such, there are more due process requirements found in criminal prosecutions. One such requirement is the burden of proof. In criminal prosecutions, the burden of proof is "beyond a reasonable doubt." This means that a prosecutor must provide evidence of the offender's guilt, and that evidence must show beyond a reasonable doubt that the offender is guilty. This is usually defined as a "moral certainty" or 95% certainty. In civil lawsuits, victims must provide evidence of the offender's liability only by "a preponderance of the evidence." This is usually defined as "more likely than not" or 51% certainty.

Other due process rights are limited in civil lawsuits. The offender has the right not to take the stand and testify during a criminal trial, but the offender may be forced to testify in a civil case. In addition, an attorney can be provided for the offender in a criminal trial if he or she cannot afford one, but the offender has no constitutional right to appointed counsel in a civil trial. Finally, evidence that is illegally seized by law enforcement may be excluded at a criminal trial, but may be brought out in a civil case.

Damages

As mentioned earlier, if an offender is found liable in a civil case, he or she may be required to pay monetary compensation for injuries sustained by the victim during the crime. This compensation is called "damages" and takes two forms: compensatory damages and punitive damages. Compensatory damages can encompass an actual dollar amount that represents the losses suffered by the victim. If a victim is injured in the crime and seeks medical attention, compensatory damages will be awarded to the victim to pay for the medical bills. Compensatory damages may also be awarded if the victim was forced to miss work due to the crime; thus, the damages will compensate the victim for lost wages. In some cases, however, compensatory damages are an estimated value of the "pain and suffering" or "mental distress" felt by the victim. It is said that compensatory damages are used "to make the victim whole again." Punitive damages are usually much higher than compensatory damages and serve to "punish" the offender for the harm done. Although not a criminal punishment, like fines, punitive damages may be awarded to teach the offender a lesson or to warn others that crime does not pay.

Punitive damages have been the subject of lawsuit reform in recent years, with juries awarding punitive damages in the millions of dollars to some victims of crime. It is argued that, whereas compensatory damages put an actual dollar amount on injury, punitive damages are subject to the whims of juries. For instance, juries in jurisdictions with higher crime rates have been shown to be antioffender, awarding millions of dollars in punitive damages to the victim. Victims of similar crimes in other jurisdictions may not receive the same amount of punitive damages. Further, research has shown that there are what is perceived as "worthy" and "unworthy" victims, and this can influence a jury's willingness to award damages. For example, a suburban mother of two who is a victim of a robbery may be awarded more in punitive damages than a robbery victim who is homeless and living in the inner city. Thus, the awarding of punitive damages—and the amount awarded—is a subjective determination on the part of the jury.

Problems Associated With Civil Litigation

One problem regarding damages—both compensatory and punitive—is that many offenders cannot or will not pay the amount specified. If offenders cannot afford to pay damages, a compromise may be reached in which the offender and the victim agree on payment or other settlement. If an offender simply refuses to pay damages, the court can institute garnishment actions (in which the court will impose a lien on the offender's wages and will collect the damages on a weekly or monthly basis), or the offender's real and personal property may be seized and sold at auction to pay the damages. Another alternative is to hold the defendant in contempt of court until the damages are paid. Thus if the defendant still withholds payment, he or she can be held criminally responsible for failure to pay. Despite this, a number of assets are not subject to collection by the courts. An example of this is found in the O. J. Simpson case. Although Simpson was acquitted in a criminal trial of murdering his ex-wife and her friend in 1995, he was found liable for those murders in a civil trial that was instituted by the victims' families. The jury awarded the victims' families more than $8 million in compensatory damages and $25 million in punitive damages. However, most of Simpson's assets were in pension and retirement accounts, which cannot be seized for use in paying civil damages.

Another problem associated with civil lawsuits is their cost—for victims, the court system, and society. Lawsuits are costly for the victim because victims must hire lawyers to assist them; this does not occur with criminal prosecutions, where the prosecutor acts on behalf of the victim. Lawsuits are also costly for the court system, as it has seen an increase in civil litigation over the past decade. Society also pays for civil lawsuits. An example of this would be when lawsuits filed by victims of drunk drivers result in an increase in auto insurance premiums.

Usefulness

Despite the problems associated with civil lawsuits, they serve many useful purposes. Thus, if the offender does pay damages, it helps the victim recover some of the financial costs of the crime. For many victims, civil lawsuits also provide a sense of vindication and personal justice, especially if a criminal prosecution was not undertaken or did not have the outcome the victim wanted. In fact, some researchers argue that vindication is the primary motivation for victims' filing civil lawsuits. Related to this is the issue of accountability, in that a judgment against an offender indicates that he or she is the responsible party in the action, even if no punishment results. Civil lawsuits can also bring about meaningful change in policy. For example, a number of lawsuits have been filed in recent years by those who were victims of police use of excessive force. Judgments in favor of plaintiffs in these cases have led police departments to review their use of force policies and to institute better training to ensure that incidents such as these do not happen again.

Marian R. Williams

See also Punitive and Compensatory Damages; Restitution; Third-Party Lawsuits; Victim Compensation

Further Readings

Goldberg, J., Sebok, A., & Zipursky, B. (2008). *Tort law: Responsibilities and redress.* New York: Aspen.

Ross, D. (2006). *Civil liability in criminal justice.* Newark, NJ: Lexis-Nexis/Matthew Bender.

Sarnoff, S. K. (1996). *Paying for crime: The policies and possibilities of crime victim reimbursement.* Westport, CT: Praeger.

Smith, R. (2008). *Seventh Amendment: The right to a trial by jury.* Edina, MN: ABDO.

CLOSED-CIRCUIT TELEVISION

Closed-circuit television (CCTV) cameras are one of the most high-profile and indeed controversial security measures available to help prevent victimization. Locating cameras in areas that then transmit images to a central base enables operators to keep watch over different places at the same time. The logic is that offenders, knowing they are being watched, will refrain from committing an offense. Meanwhile, law enforcement, including private security, is able to assess situations to decide if, when, and how to intervene, and the images can also help with postincident investigation. The problem is that although CCTV appears to be a practical security measure, the evidence on its effectiveness in reducing victimization is mixed. This entry examines some of the research findings and explains key factors that determine what makes CCTV effective.

Overview

CCTV has been responsible for catching some high-profile offenders (and some less high-profile ones, too). Some are caught on camera as they commit the offense, and the image of them doing so is used to identify them and to help support the prosecution case. Sometimes the cameras capture evidence left by an offender at the scene, such as a fingerprint, that can be followed up and subsequently provide evidence against a suspect. Sometimes the cameras pick up a license plate, placing that vehicle in the area at the time of the offense, and this can help to connect suspects to scenes. Similarly, images can be used to eliminate people from suspicion by showing that they were elsewhere or did not fit the characteristics of the person that the police know committed the crime.

From this very simple synopsis it is not difficult to see why CCTV appeals to law enforcement. It can be a very useful tool in the fight against crime. It has other uses, too. For example, retailers can check whether customers who say they were injured when they slipped in a store really did slip; it helps protect them against malicious liability claims. This can help business owners to obtain lower insurance premiums. Beyond these, CCTV has other potential uses, sometimes controversial ones, such as monitoring the behavior of employees to ensure they comply with company policies and expected levels of conduct. Indeed, the whole issue of CCTV presenting a challenge to individuals' right to privacy is a major one. In some countries, such as the United Kingdom, this has been comparatively circumspect, but in many others it

has been a major reason for the restricted use of CCTV in public space. Important though this issue is, and it really is a major factor, the focus in this entry is on the role of CCTV in preventing victimization, or at least in attempting to do so.

It is important when discussing CCTV to clarify what is being discussed. Often researchers do not do this, implying that CCTV systems are similar, but they are not. They vary greatly in terms of coverage, density of cameras, and type and quality of transmission and recording methods; therefore, they vary in the number and quality of the images—as well as in the competency of operators, and their supervision and management, the relationships of these people with those who act on the images, and so on. Some cameras and some systems are intelligent but badly used and managed; some rudimentary systems provide good images that are used effectively. There are plenty of reasons for systems to be different (quite independent of the type of area or context they operate in), and understanding these sorts of details about CCTV is important.

Effectiveness

The research evidence paints a somewhat mixed picture. Even those studies with a minimum level of rigor have reached different conclusions. Indeed, a summary of the research findings would suggest that sometimes CCTV works, sometimes it does not, and sometimes the effects are neutral. The usual measure of effect is upon crime rates, but this is problematic with regard to CCTV. While it may seem logical that cameras will deter offenders and therefore reduce crime, this is not the only possibility. Cameras can also be responsible for noticing more offenses than previously were noticed. Or they can give the public the confidence and/or incentive to report more offenses. This, logically, will bring more offenses into the public gaze and to police attention, resulting in more offenses being recorded by the police and consequently an increase in the crime figures. Put simply, the crime rates going up could be an indication that cameras are successful in focusing attention on more of the "dark figure of crime" (unreported crime). Of course, there are always problems in whatever measures are used, but it is important to bear this limitation of CCTV in mind.

Looking at what types of offenses are affected by CCTV can be informative, although clearly this needs to be viewed in context. For example, where images from cameras located in car parks are being measured, the main impact is usually on offenses involving cars. In schemes focused on town and city centers, more varied types of offenses may be targeted. Generally though, crimes of violence are less likely to be reduced by the presence of cameras than are crimes of financial gain. One reason for this is that violent crimes are more likely to be fueled by alcohol and high emotions, which affect people's ability to think about the consequences of their actions.

But crime figures are not the only measure, as public perceptions also are important. Interestingly, recent U.K. national evaluation results show that across all areas surveyed there was a reduction in the perceived effectiveness of CCTV just after installation, compared to earlier results. Support was still high (from 69% to 96% across areas), but not as high as it had been. The national evaluation findings in the United Kingdom enable the effectiveness of CCTV to be put into perspective. Of the 14 schemes, 6 showed a reduction in crime, although in only 2 of these were the differences with the control area statistically significant. However, in one of these there were confounding factors that could also explain the reduction, so in only 1 area out of 14 was there evidence of a CCTV success story, and this was in a car park scheme. There were 2 schemes that used redeployable cameras, which can be moved about the area to meet changing requirements, but these were focused on very short-term needs and did not have an impact on crime levels.

But does CCTV make people feel safer? Here, too, the findings are mixed. When asked about CCTV before its introduction into an area, the public generally believe that CCTV will make them feel safer. After the event, research has suggested that the results are not as good as the public thought they would be. One Scottish study argued that all CCTV did there was make the people who already feel safe feel even safer, and it had little impact on those who felt unsafe. The U.K. national evaluation found that while feelings of safety increased after CCTV was installed, in only 3 of 12 areas was the increase greater than in control areas, and in none was this statistically significant.

So what will make people feel safe? Noticing the cameras in the first place is one thing; however, they are often unobtrusive. And believing that there will be some sort of response (especially from the police) is another. But the national evaluation results suggested that the biggest determinant of whether people feel safer had much less to do with CCTV—not least because there was little difference between experimental and control areas—than with the level of crime that people experienced. In short, if you want to make people feel safer, then the best way is to cut crime, and if CCTV or for that matter any other measure does not do that, then it is unlikely to be successful at making people feel safer let alone be safer.

It has often been said that using CCTV merely displaces crime elsewhere (spatial displacement), but the results on this are mixed. Its presence seems to displace crime more in some areas with some types of crime than in other areas, although there are no easily discernible patterns across studies. Sometimes crime is displaced to areas not covered by CCTV, as offender accounts confirm, or the presence of CCTV results in less serious offenses, a good outcome rather than a bad one.

There is one other group to consider in the context of whether CCTV reduces victimization, and this is the offenders. There is no doubt that CCTV is a risk that has to be managed, but many offenders have not found it a major one. Some were put off by CCTV or proceeded more cautiously, but many said that they are able to get around CCTV by wearing a disguise or by ensuring that they do not look at the cameras directly. Some noted that they have been caught on camera before, but the images were not good enough to support a prosecution, and subsequently the cameras were much less of a deterrent. Shoplifters pointed to the lack of total coverage of stores and the availability of blind spots. Some thieves noted that when they are stealing they have to worry about anyone seeing them—especially those close by, after all they could intervene—and CCTV did not change things much. Unsurprisingly, the offenders most likely to point to the success of CCTV as a real threat were those who had been caught on camera and the image was good enough to force them to plead guilty or be found guilty.

Overall it has to be said that there are problems in interpreting the research on the effectiveness of

CCTV. It has already been noted that often research does not make clear what types of systems are in place. What is known is that there is often implementation failure, which means schemes are not working as effectively as they could be (and in the worst cases, not working at all). But often research does not specify what other interventions existed at the same time, and there is rarely a focus on CCTV where it is not the main intervention but merely a supporting one. Clearly, it would be good to know the effects in these cases. Further, evaluations involving comparisons of what is happening in different areas are never easy. Isolating the effects of any one measure at a point in time is complicated because what goes on in areas is rarely static.

Key Factors

For CCTV to be effective it needs to be introduced in response to a specific problem and to be the right solution to that problem. CCTV needs to be a part of a strategy and be coordinated with other measures that are being used. Most often what is required is an effective response to suspicious circumstances generated by images, and this means that there needs to be effective communication with responders, often the police or private security. But research suggests that sometimes the police don't trust CCTV operators and are too busy with work generated from other sources. Making CCTV intelligent involves not just creating technically advanced cameras, but also providing operators with information to help them target the right places and suspects. Various types of watch schemes can be helpful here. The CCTV operation itself needs to be guided by a strategy and objectives. It also requires people trained in the requisite skills—and there are definite skill sets associated with being an effective operator that are frequently underestimated—who are properly managed and focused on delivering a quality service to meet meaningful outputs. There is quite a lot involved in making CCTV work effectively at reducing victimization, and much of the evidence suggests that we have not got it right yet.

Martin Gill

See also Crime Prevention; Crime Prevention, Domains of; Crime Prevention Through Environmental Design; Lighting

Further Readings

Ditton, J. (2000). Crime and the city: Public attitudes toward open-street CCTV in Glasgow. *British Journal of Criminology, 40*(4), 692–709.

Gill, M. (2006). Closed circuit television. In M. Gill (Ed.), *The handbook of security*. London: Palgrave.

Gill, M., & Spriggs, A. (2005). *Assessing the Impact of CCTV* (Home Office Research Study No. 292). Retrieved from http://www.homeoffice.gov.uk/rds/pdfs05/hors292.pdf

McCahill, M., & Norris, C. (2003). *Four CCTV systems in London* (UrbanEye Working Paper No 10). Retrieved from http://www.urbaneye.net/results/ue_wp10.pdf

Welsh, B., & Farrington, D. (2003). *Effects of closed circuit television surveillance on crime: Protocol for a systematic review* (3rd ed.). Campbell Collaboration Crime and Justice Group. Retrieved from http://www.aic.gov.au/campbellcj/reviews/2003-11-CCTV.pdf

Cognitive–Behavioral Therapy

Cognitive–behavioral therapy (or CBT) is a psychotherapeutic approach that attempts to change the *cognitions* (i.e., thoughts, beliefs, attitudes, or self-talk) that are influencing problem behaviors. CBT is based on the premise that our thoughts (and not situations, events, or people) cause our feelings and behaviors. As such, the goal of CBT is to employ strategies to identify and monitor the cognitions that maintain problem behavior, and to replace these maladaptive thoughts with more adaptive (i.e., realistic and useful) ones. The historical roots of CBT include the development of behavioral theories at the beginning of the 20th century (i.e., early experimental work on classical and operant conditioning), as well as the emergence of social learning theories and cognitive therapies in the 1960s.

The term *cognitive–behavioral therapy* is used to refer to a collection of specific strategies that share a number of defining themes and common characteristics. CBT interventions are now commonplace in corrections, and the empirical evidence clearly supports the effectiveness of CBT with offender populations.

Common Themes and Characteristics

Cognitive–behavioral therapy is generally considered to be an umbrella term for a number of diverse techniques that merge concepts from behavior therapy and cognitive psychology. Nevertheless, Michael Spiegler and David Guevremont have noted that CBT interventions share four defining themes. First, CBT is committed to the scientific approach, in that it requires precision in specifying target behaviors as well as empirical evaluation in monitoring client progress. This reliance on data is perhaps one of the primary reasons that CBT is considered to be an evidence-based approach to the treatment of many conditions. Second, CBT is considered to be active, in that clients are required to engage in planned interventions in order to change behaviors. For example, clients will often be asked to examine and record their thoughts, feelings, and behaviors during daily activities or specific situations. Clients are also taught new coping skills, and they have the opportunity to actively practice these skills through role-play (rehearsal). Moreover, clients often receive and complete homework assignments. Third, CBT focuses on the present maintaining conditions of problem behaviors. In other words, this psychotherapeutic approach focuses on the "here and now" by employing techniques and strategies to change current factors influencing problem behaviors. Fourth, CBT is based on theories of learning. In essence, this model contends that the emergence and continuation of most problem behaviors occurs primarily through learning. Thus, to change problem behaviors, an individual must learn new behaviors. While the important role of heredity and genetics is recognized, CBT interventions focus on creating learning experiences for clients that replace old (maladaptive) cognitions and behaviors with new (adaptive) ones.

Spiegler and Guevremont also have noted that CBT interventions share several characteristics. First, treatments are often delivered in vivo, or in the client's natural environment. This is an important component of CBT in that it encourages the generalization of new learning outside of the treatment setting. For example, therapists often train "support therapists" (or influential individuals in the client's life) to assist with monitoring problem behaviors and implementing intervention strategies.

In addition, clients are often encouraged to take responsibility for the change process by practicing procedures under the guidance of the therapist. This is often referred to as the self-control approach. Moreover, CBT treatments are often individualized or tailored to the unique characteristics of the client and to the maintaining conditions of his or her problem behavior.

Second, CBT interventions are typically delivered in a stepwise progression—they begin with simple, minimally threatening tasks and progress to harder tasks. To illustrate, many structured curricula teach basic social skills (e.g., active listening) before instructing clients on more challenging or complex social skills with multiple steps or components (e.g., conflict resolution or problem solving). Similarly, clients might be asked to practice a new coping skill in less threatening or "easier" situations before applying the skill to more difficult ones. This is also referred to as graduated rehearsal.

Another common characteristic of CBT interventions is that treatment is designed to be brief and time limited. In fact, CBT generally involves fewer therapy sessions and less overall time in comparison with other psychotherapies. It should be noted, however, that the length of treatment often varies with the problem being treated; it is not uncommon for more complex or severe problems to require additional time and sessions. To illustrate, Samuel Turner, Deborah Beidel, and Rolf Jacob reported that the average number of hours required to treat specific phobias (considered to be a less complex condition) was 13.4, compared with 46.4 for obsessive-compulsive disorder (considered to be a more complex condition). In the field of corrections, research on the appropriate "dosage" of treatment is still underdeveloped. The results of meta-analyses (or quantitative syntheses of the literature) have suggested that the intensity of treatment should be varied by the risk and need level of the offender, and should last between 3 and 9 months. This makes CBT a practical approach to the treatment of offenders, given the constraints associated with delivering interventions within the context of the criminal justice system. A more recent study conducted by Guy Bourgon and Barbara Armstrong suggested that 100 hours of treatment is sufficient for offenders who are assessed as moderate risk or possess few criminogenic needs, whereas 200 hours of treatment is required for offenders who are assessed as high risk or possess multiple criminogenic needs. For offenders who are both high risk and possess multiple needs, more than 300 hours is likely needed.

It is also worth noting that CBT approaches stress the importance of developing a therapist–client relationship that is based upon openness, warmth, and empathy, with a firm but fair application of reinforcement contingencies. Ongoing research in the area of corrections also underscores the importance of the quality of the therapeutic relationship between the offender and the agent of change. For example, Jennifer Skeem and her colleagues surveyed probationers mandated to psychiatric treatment and found that the quality of the therapist–client relationship predicted future compliance with rules (i.e., fewer probation violations and revocations).

The advantages of a good therapist–client relationship are numerous. For example, it enhances clients' positive expectations about treatment, increases homework and treatment compliance, and improves the reinforcement value of the therapist's praise and approval. Spiegler and Guevremont describe the therapist–client relationship as a "necessary but not sufficient condition of treatment," meaning that, while the therapist should foster a collaborative effort with the client, it is not the focus; the therapist must also possess the requisite knowledge and skills to implement competent intervention strategies consistent with the CBT approach.

Application to Offender Population

There are three general classes of CBT commonly applied to offender populations. While these general classes of intervention strategies are briefly introduced in what follows, it should not be considered an exhaustive list. It is also important to note that these techniques overlap, and specific strategies are often combined into *treatment packages* in order to address the individual needs of offenders.

1. *Operant conditioning.* Most behavioral treatments with offenders are based on the principle of operant conditioning, whereby prosocial behavior is immediately reinforced and antisocial behavior is punished or ignored. This is often referred to as *contingency management.* For example, many correctional settings employ token economies in which offenders earn points for engaging in prosocial behaviors. Points can then be exchanged for back-up reinforcers. Classical conditioning is also used in correctional settings, as in the treatment of deviant sexual behaviors or substance abuse, but these applications are more limited and less common.

2. *Social learning.* Social learning programs rely extensively on modeling appropriate behaviors so that offenders can learn through observation and practice. Planned modeling activities often involve defining the behavior, demonstrating the behavior, and then having the offender engage in behavioral rehearsal to develop a sense of self-efficacy.

3. *Cognitive therapy.* Cognitive therapists employ a variety of techniques, such as cognitive restructuring, problem solving, and moral reasoning, to target offenders' antisocial attitudes and values.

Empirical Support for Use With Offenders

The use of CBT has proliferated over the past 25 years, and it continues to evolve as a set of techniques. The continued growth and expansion of CBT is attributable, at least in part, to the fact that this approach has received considerable empirical support in the treatment of a variety of clinical and nonclinical problems, including psychotic disorders, mood disorders, anxiety disorders, personality disorders, parenting skills, substance abuse, and criminal behavior, to name only a few. Within correctional settings, CBT has been most successful when it has been used to target the criminogenic needs (i.e., attitudes, behaviors, personality factors, and life circumstances that contribute to criminality) of higher-risk offenders. In other words, CBT programs are designed to teach offenders prosocial skills that will reduce criminal behaviors. It has become commonplace for CBT program strategies to be used in prisons and community-based correctional facilities, although program integrity is a concern in these settings. It should also be noted that CBT is used in individual therapy as well as group settings.

One of the first meta-analyses on the effectiveness of CBT with offender populations was conducted by D. A. Andrews, Ivan Zinger, Robert Hoge, James Bonta, Paul Gendreau, and Francis Cullen. This research group reviewed a total of 124 treatment comparisons and found that behavioral treatments produced a substantially greater average effect on recidivism in comparison with nonbehavioral treatments ($r = .29$, $k = 41$ vs. $r = .04$, $k = 113$). More than 20 subsequent meta-analyses have compared the effectiveness of various treatment modalities with offender populations, and the results have *consistently* favored cognitive–behavioral interventions over other treatment modalities. For example, Paula Smith, Paul Gendreau, and Kristin Swartz recently summarized the results of meta-analyses in the area of corrections and found that approximately 73% (or 16/22) of meta-analytical studies on the effectiveness of CBT produced estimates greater than $r = .15$. Using the binomial effect size display (BESD) statistic, an $r = .15$ can be interpreted as a 15% reduction in recidivism for the treatment condition over the control condition. In contrast, "other" (i.e., nonbehavioral) treatment modalities were associated with much smaller reductions in recidivism (mean r values ranging from .01 to .19). In fact, Smith and her colleagues determined that 88% (or 7/8) of these estimates were less than $r = .15$.

Paula Smith

See also Offender-Based Programs; Treating Violent Offenders

Further Readings

Andrews, D. A., & Bonta, J. (2006). *The psychology of criminal conduct* (4th ed.). Newark, NJ: LexisNexis.

Andrews, D. A., Zinger, I., Hoge, R. D., Bonta, J., Gendreau, P., & Cullen F. T. (1990). Does correctional treatment work? A clinically relevant and psychologically informed meta-analysis. *Criminology, 28*, 369–404.

Bourgon, G., & Armstrong, B. (2005). Transferring the principles of effective intervention into a "real world" prison setting. *Criminal Justice and Behavior, 32*, 3–25.

Gendreau, P., French, S. A., & Gionet, A. (2004). What works (what doesn't work): The principles of effective correctional treatment. *Journal of Community Corrections, 13*, 4–6, 27–30.

Skeem, J. L., Louden, J. E., Polaschek, D., & Camp, J. (2007). Assessing relationship quality in mandated community treatment: Blending care with control. *Psychological Assessment, 19*, 397–410.

Smith, P., Gendreau, P., & Swartz, K. (2009). Validating the principles of effective intervention: A systematic review of the contributions of meta-analysis in the field of corrections. *Victims and Offenders, 4*, 148–169.

Spiegler, M. D., & Guevremont, D. C. (2003). *Contemporary behavior therapy* (4th ed.). Belmont, CA: Wadsworth/Thomson Learning.

Turner, S. M., Beidel, D. C., & Jacob, R. G. (1994). Social phobia: A comparison of behavior therapy and atenolol. *Journal of Consulting and Clinical Psychology, 62*, 350–358.

COGNITIVE MAPPING

Cognitive mapping, also referred to as mental mapping, is an activity undertaken by all species. This activity may be thought of as a coping mechanism that is used to help us decide where we need to go within our environment and how we should get there. Though the first study of cognitive mapping was published in 1913 by C. C. Trowbridge, the roots of academic exploration of cognitive mapping are commonly placed in cognitive psychology. In studies of the cognitive abilities of rats, Edward Tolman found the time the rats took to get to the food source in a maze decreased rather sharply and quickly, indicating that the rats learned the layout of the maze. In other words, they formed a cognitive, or mental, map of maze to facilitate their finding subsistence. Though geographers often claim that cognitive mapping is a subfield of geography, contained within behavioral geography, cognitive mapping is best understood as a component of the field of ecology.

Ecology is the study of how organisms, such as humans, adapt to an ever-changing and sometimes hostile environment. Because of our social, biological, and cultural needs, we have routine activities that we perform within our environment. Our environment, however, is very complex, and we must have a method of organizing all of this environmental information. Therefore, environmental cognition (cognitive mapping) is as old as life itself because we must perceive our environment in order to survive within it. This entry defines the process of cognitive mapping, the output of cognitive mapping (the cognitive map), and how cognitive mapping may be used to understand crime and victimization.

The Process of Cognitive Mapping

Cognitive mapping begins with the acquisition of spatial knowledge. Kevin Lynch has outlined the three fundamental components of our spatial knowledge: landmarks, activity nodes, and pathways. Landmarks are discrete locations within our environment, such as an intersection, a building, or some other identifiable object within our environment; activity nodes may be thought of as areas in which we spend our time, such as shopping malls or markets, entertainment districts, or industrial districts; and pathways are the ways in which we move from activity node to activity node and landmark to landmark. Because the information we gather for the landmarks, activity nodes, and pathways is spatial, we are subsequently able to form the topographical relationships of these components to create cognitive maps.

The Cognitive Map

The cognitive map, also referred to as the mental map, is a representation of our environment used to guide the ways in which we move through that environment. Thus in order to get to work we must move from one activity node to another activity node, and the best method of such a movement is along a particular pathway. Consequently, cognitive maps simultaneously define and limit our actions.

Stephen Kaplan lists the four elements that are the minimum requirement for our cognitive maps to be functional. First, we need to be able to recognize where we are and identify "common" objects within the environment; such common objects would be particular types of buildings, roads, and other pathways. Second, we need to know what leads to what and where; in other words, how should we travel from one place to another—we need to understand locations, direction, and distance. Third, we need to be able to learn and modify our cognitive maps as necessary, because a static cognitive map quickly becomes nonfunctional, particularly because of changes in our experiences within the environment. Fourth, based on any new information, we need to be willing to take new or alternative courses of action; in other words, we need to be willing to use our new updated cognitive map, not sticking to our old ways despite new spatial information.

As outlined by Roger Downs and David Stea, cognitive maps acquire, code, store, recall, and decode information regarding the relative locations or places within our environment. Because cognitive mapping is a process, cognitive maps are in a constant state of flux. However, particularly because many aspects of our environment change slowly, cognitive maps are relatively fixed for extended periods of time. Cognitive maps are subject to change, but only when new spatial information we deem essential for our survival is obtained. Our current cognitive maps are also necessarily incomplete because they only contain information relevant to each individual. As such, cognitive maps are a distorted view of reality (our perceptions) that are altered through new primary information (direct experience) as well as new secondary information (spatial knowledge obtained from others or data such as maps and the media). Cognitive mapping involves gathering information about not only the location and items within our environment but also the events and experiences that occur within that environment, and the latter may distort our perception of reality.

The Cognitive Map as a Cartogram

A cartogram is a form of spatial visualization that purposefully distorts standard planimetric maps of our environment. This distortion, however, is performed to convey the importance of particular spatial information. For example, a relatively small geographic area that contains a very large number of people (an urban center with many high-rise buildings) can be expanded to represent the volume of people in the area rather than the geographic area, and there will be a corresponding reduction in the size of areas that contain very few people. A cognitive map operates on a similar principle: an individual's spatial knowledge. Those places for which an individual has a lot of spatial knowledge are represented in that individual's cognitive map as being rather large, whereas those places for which an individual has very little spatial knowledge are represented in the cognitive map as being small.

This analogy is instructive for understanding why our cognitive maps are always incomplete, and why cognitive maps are relatively unique to each individual. Not all people have the same degree of spatial knowledge for all places. Therefore, different areas of individuals' cognitive maps are disproportionately large and small. Moreover, even if two (or more) individuals have similar spatial knowledge regarding a particular location (the actual physical environment, such as buildings and roads), their experiences within that same place have been (and are) different such that no two individuals can have the same distorted view of that environment.

Because we have different degrees of spatial knowledge of the locations within our environment, we do not frequent all locations within our environment. This is why our cognitive map both defines and limits our movements; whenever possible, we go to and move through places we know. This characteristic of our behavior has implications for crime and victimization.

Cognitive Mapping and Crime

The behavior resulting from cognitive maps affects both victimization and offending patterns. Once we leave the relatively protective environment of the home, we are much more vulnerable to criminal victimization. Therefore, because our cognitive maps define where we spend most of our time, they also define where we are most likely to become victims of crime. With regard to offending, once the decision to offend has been made, potential offenders will search out and evaluate targets using their cognitive maps. Just like any other activity, the search for criminal targets occurs within the portions of the environment that are most familiar to the offender. Only if suitable targets are not found or exhausted will a potential offender expand his or her horizons.

Paul and Patricia Brantingham formulated their geometric theory of crime using concepts very similar to those of the cognitive map. Invoking the concepts of activity nodes and pathways, they theorized about our awareness and activity spaces; awareness space consists of the places for we have spatial knowledge and activity space consists of the places we move through and spend our time. As such, awareness and activity spaces would be the areas on our cognitive map that are disproportionately large. Though this is an oversimplification of the geometric theory of crime, when the activity spaces of a potential offender and potential victim intersect, there is great potential for criminal victimization. In other words, if the disproportionately large areas of a potential offender's cognitive map intersect to a significant degree with the disproportionately large areas of a potential victim's cognitive map, the probability of criminal victimization is greater. This greater probability is present because the offender and victim spend significant portions of their time in close proximity to each other, operating within the same area. It is important to note that spatial knowledge is not necessarily positive; rather, spatial knowledge may very well be negative, meaning that an individual does not feel comfortable at a particular location.

Cognitive Mapping and the Fear of Crime

If an individual does not feel comfortable in a particular place, it is often stated that the individual has a fear of place. When that fear is related to crime, it is a fear of crime. This fear of crime is part of our cognitive maps and is related both to the objective aspects (physical environment) and our individual experiences (prior victimization, for example).

As outlined by Patricia Gilmartin, perceived and actual distances depend on people's perception of the safety of a neighborhood. This holds for most people. There are also meaningful differences in the cognitive maps of men and women, young and old. These differences manifest themselves through differential levels of fear and perceptions of risk. Generally speaking, women and the elderly limit and/or alter their routine activities more than do men and the young, respectively. Women and men, young and old, feel safe and unsafe in different places at different times of the day. These different fears of crime, as all components of the cognitive map, are based on both primary and secondary information. The end result is a vastly different cognitive map of the fear of crime for different groups of individuals. Consequently, cognitive maps are at once unique to individuals and shared by different groups of individuals.

Martin A. Andresen

See also Cognitive–Behavioral Therapy; Crime Mapping; Fear of Crime; Fear of Crime, Individual- and Community-Level Effects; Fear of Crime, Measurement of; Hot Spots of Fear; Prospective Crime Mapping

Further Readings

Brantingham, P. L., & Brantingham, P. J. (1981). Notes of the geometry of crime. In P. J. Brantingham & P. L. Brantingham (Eds.), *Environmental criminology* (pp. 27–53). Beverly Hills, CA: Sage.

Canter, D., & Hodge, S. (2000). Criminals' mental maps. In L. S. Turnbull, E. H. Hendrix, & B. D. Dent (Eds.), *Atlas of crime: Mapping the criminal landscape* (pp. 186–191). Phoenix, AZ: Oryx.

Downs, R. M., & Stea, D. (1973). Cognitive maps and spatial behavior: Process and products. In R. M. Downs & D. Stea (Eds.), *Image and environment: Cognitive mapping and spatial behavior* (pp. 8–26). Chicago: Aldine.

Gilmartin, P. (2000). Cognitive maps and the fear of crime. In L. S. Turnbull, E. H. Hendrix, & B. D. Dent (Eds.), *Atlas of crime: Mapping the criminal landscape* (pp. 192–198). Phoenix, AZ: Oryx.

Helstrup, T., & Magnussen, S. (2001). The mental representation of familiar, long-distance, journeys. *Journal of Environmental Psychology, 21,* 411–421.

Kaplan, S. (1973). Cognitive maps in perception and thought. In R. M. Downs & D. Stea (Eds.), *Image and environment: Cognitive mapping and spatial behavior* (pp. 63–78). Chicago: Aldine.

Nichols, W. W., Jr. (1980). Mental maps, social characteristics, and criminal mobility. In D. E. Georges-Abeyie & K. D. Harries (Eds.), *Crime: A spatial perspective* (pp. 156–166). New York: Columbia University Press.

Rengert, G. F., & Pelfrey, W. V., Jr. (1998). Cognitive mapping of the city center: Comparative perceptions of dangerous places. *Crime Prevention Studies, 8,* 193–217.

Smith, C. J., & Patterson, G. E. (1980). Cognitive mapping and the subjective geography of crime. In D. E. Georges-Abeyie & K. D. Harries (Eds.), *Crime:*
A spatial perspective (pp. 205–218). New York: Columbia University Press.

Tolman, E. C. (1948). Cognitive maps in rats and men. *Psychological Review, 55,* 189–208.

COLLEGE AND UNIVERSITY CAMPUS LEGISLATION, FEDERAL

The involvement of the federal government in how institutions of postsecondary education, including trade schools, colleges, and universities, deal with crime on their campuses has expanded greatly since the early 1990s in response to high-profile incidents of violence involving campus communities. The general focus of this activity has been to provide for the greater disclosure of security information so that campus community members can make informed decisions about avoiding and preventing criminal victimization.

Since 1990, the federal government has adopted laws requiring institutions to disclose information about crimes occurring on their campuses and about their security policies, and to afford certain rights to the victims of sex crimes. The government has also permitted institutions to disclose more crime-related information from educational records and expanded sex offender registration guidelines to capture information about campus enrollment and vocational status.

The Jeanne Clery Disclosure of Campus Security Policy and Campus Crime Statistics Act (Clery Act), first enacted as the Crime Awareness and Campus Security Act of 1990 and amended in 1992, 1998, 2000, and 2008, has been the primary means of federal involvement in campus crime issues. It requires institutions to report crime statistics, alert the campus community to ongoing threats, disclose security policies through an annual security report, and, if they maintain either a police or security department, keep a public crime log. Both public and private institutions must comply with the Clery Act's requirements in order to be eligible to participate in the student financial aid programs authorized by the Higher Education Act of 1965. As of 2008 this included more than 6,000 individual institutions with 9,638 campuses.

Crime Reporting

Statistics

The Clery Act requires institutions to annually report statistics for certain serious crimes occurring on campus, on public property within and adjacent to campus, and on certain noncampus properties, including remote classrooms and student organization housing. The reporting protocols are based on those found in the Federal Bureau of Investigation's Uniform Crime Reporting (UCR) Program, but they include several major differences. Most notably, institutions are obligated to collect and report crime data not only from campus and local police but also campus security and other campus officials, such as a dean of students. In addition, the act requires institutions to report the broader categories of forcible and nonforcible sex offenses that are drawn from the National Incident-Based Reporting System (NIBRS), as opposed to the narrower category of rape used by UCR Program. Institutions must also report criminal homicide, robbery, aggravated assault, burglary, motor vehicle theft, and arson as well as arrests or disciplinary referrals for liquor law violations, drug law violations, and illegal weapons possession. Three years' worth of statistics for these crimes, as well as hate crimes, are disclosed to current and prospective students and employees in an annual security report. Statistics are also submitted to the U.S. Department of Education each year and publicly disclosed on a searchable Web site.

Ongoing Disclosures

In addition to crime statistics, the Clery Act also requires institutions to make disclosures to the campus community on an ongoing basis. Every institution is required to issue timely warnings when a crime that must be reported in the statistics is considered to present an ongoing threat. Institutions that maintain a police or security department are also required to maintain a public crime log recording every crime reported to the police or security department, not just those reportable in the annual statistics. The public crime log is required to be updated within 2 business days and must be open for inspection by any member of the public during regular business hours.

Policy Disclosures

Victims' Rights

In response to the wide scope of acquaintance rape and other forms of sexual assault in campus communities, the Clery Act was amended in 1992 to require institutions to adopt a sexual assault policy that addresses educational programming and affords victims certain basic rights. The "Campus Sexual Assault Victims' Bill of Rights" provisions require institutions to change a victim's academic and living arrangements after a sex crime if such accommodations are requested and reasonably available, among other things. If an institutional disciplinary proceeding is held in a sexual assault case, the accused and accuser are entitled to the same opportunity to have others, such as an attorney, present and to be unconditionally notified of the final results.

Security Procedures

The Clery Act also requires institutions to disclose statements of campus security policy in seven other areas in addition to sexual assault. Institutions must disclose summaries of their policies concerning crime reporting; the security of and access to campus facilities, including residence halls; the status of campus law enforcement; security awareness programming; crime prevention programming; drug and alcohol policies; and where information about registered sex offenders enrolled or working at the institution may be found such as a state Web site. Each of the required disclosures is included in an annual security report that must automatically be made available either on paper or online to current students and employees by October 1 of each year, as well as to prospective students and employees upon request.

Privacy of Educational Records

When the Campus Security Act was first adopted by Congress, it was found that approximately 80% of campus violence was student-on-student;

in response, Congress amended the federal law, the Family Educational Rights and Privacy Act (FERPA), that governs the confidentiality of educational records so that there could be greater public disclosure of campus crime information. Congress initially permitted the disclosure of institutional disciplinary results to the victims of violent crimes but in 1992 restructured FERPA so that it would no longer restrict the disclosure of campus law enforcement records. In 1998 Congress further amended FERPA to permit the public disclosure of disciplinary results in cases of alleged violent crimes where there was a finding of responsibility.

S. Daniel Carter

See also Campus Crime, College and University; Campus Policing and Security; College and University Campus Legislation, State; Intimate Partner Violence; Megan's Law; National Incident-Based Reporting System (NIBRS); National Victimization Against College Women Surveys; Rape, Acquaintance and Date; Uniform Crime Reporting (UCR) Program

Further Readings

Fisher, B. S., & Sloan, J. J. (Eds.). (2007). *Campus crime: Legal, social and policy perspectives* (2nd ed.). Springfield, IL: Charles C Thomas.

Karjane, H., Fisher, B. S., & Cullen, F. (2005). *Sexual assault on campus: What colleges and universities are doing about it*. NIJ Research for Practice Series. Washington, DC: U.S. Department of Justice.

U.S. Department of Education, Office of Postsecondary Education. (2005). *The handbook for campus crime reporting*. Washington, DC: U.S. Department of Education.

COLLEGE AND UNIVERSITY CAMPUS LEGISLATION, STATE

With passage of the Student Right to Know and Campus Security Act of 1990 (20 USC 1092[f]; now known as the Jeanne Clery Disclosure of Campus Security Policy and Campus Crime Statistics Act), Congress set federal policy concerning how postsecondary institutions should respond to campus crime and security. The Clery Act requires that all postsecondary institutions eligible to receive federal financial aid prepare and make publicly available each year a security report containing information such as crime statistics for the campus, institutional policies for addressing on-campus sexual assaults, a description of the jurisdiction and authority of the campus police/security department, and other information. Given that states often follow the lead of Congress by passing statutes designed to address the same policy issue, be it public school education, immigration, or the "war on drugs," it would seem reasonable to assume that states would pass their own campus crime legislation.

In the case of campus crime and security, Michael C. Griffaton argued the states are uniquely situated to address the problem. Griffaton noted that while Congress could mandate *general* policies relating to campus crime, a *state* could pass legislation calling for specific policies, such as mandating that all colleges and universities compel incoming freshmen to complete an "orientation" about campus crime. Further, the states could bring additional sanctions against institutions who failed to comply, such as revoking their state-level accreditation or withholding state financial aid from them.

Because little systematic analysis of state-level campus legislation has been published, not much is known about these statutes. Griffaton found that a few states had passed such statutes and their provisions strongly paralleled those found in the Clery Act. More recently, Security On Campus, Inc. classified state-level statutes and identified which states' statutes fit into one or more the categories:

- Campus Crime Statistics Reporting Laws— Pennsylvania, Florida, Tennessee, Louisiana, California, New York, Massachusetts, Delaware, Wisconsin, Washington, Virginia, Connecticut, Texas and Kentucky
- Campus Crime Log Laws—Massachusetts, West Virginia, Oklahoma, Tennessee, California, Minnesota, Pennsylvania, and Kentucky
- Off-Campus Crime Reporting Laws—Tennessee and Georgia
- Campus Sex Offender Registration Requirements—California and Tennessee
- Campus Courts Disclosure Requirement— Tennessee

- Joint Investigation of Campus Murders and Rapes—Tennessee, South Carolina

As can be seen from the above scheme, there is wide variation in the substantive content of state-level campus crime legislation. Tennessee's statute, for example, contains provisions addressing multiple aspects of campus crime and security, while West Virginia's statute apparently addresses only the issue of campus crime "logs"—publicly available records of reported crimes occurring on campus.

In a recent comprehensive study of state-level campus crime legislation, John J. Sloan and Jessica Shoemaker not only identified states that had passed such legislation, but also assessed how closely the statutes adopted both the language and key provisions found in Clery. Specifically, Sloan and Shoemaker were interested in whether the state statutes required postsecondary institutions to (1) disseminate a multifaceted annual report on crime and security at the school, (2) annually report their campus crime statistics, (3) keep publicly accessible daily crime logs, (4) provide "timely warnings" to the campus community of crimes occurring on campus, (5) report the power and authority of campus police/security officials, and (6) report policies relating to on-campus sexual assaults. Finally, they also examined whether state legislation included sanctions for institutional noncompliance, and if so, what form they took.

Sloan and Shoemaker determined that, as of late 2006, 31 states (60%) had passed what appeared to be Clery-type legislation that could be divided into two categories: "true" Clery-type statutes that were relatively comprehensive in their provisions and "enabling legislation" that states passed and that made it possible for colleges and universities to create campus police/security departments and define their powers. Sloan and Shoemaker identified 19 states as having "true" Clery-type legislation (California, Connecticut, Delaware, Florida, Illinois, Iowa, Kentucky, Louisiana, Massachusetts, Minnesota, New Jersey, New York, Oregon, Pennsylvania, Tennessee, Virginia, Washington, West Virginia, and Wisconsin), and 12 states that had passed the less comprehensive "enabling legislation" (Alabama, Georgia, Indiana, Kansas, Maryland, Montana,

North Carolina, Ohio, Oklahoma, Rhode Island, South Carolina, and Texas).

Further analysis by Sloan and Shoemaker revealed that among the 19 states with "true" Clery-style legislation, two states' statutes (those of California and Pennsylvania) contained at least five of the seven key Clery provisions, eight states' statutes contained at least three provisions, and four states' statutes contained two Clery provisions. None of the states included provisions for sanctions for institutional noncompliance. Thus, of the 31 states Sloan and Shoemaker initially identified as having passed Clery-type legislation, very few states' statutes could be considered comprehensive in scope, and 12 states had statutes that provided the legal framework necessary to create campus police/security agencies on college campuses.

Sloan and Shoemaker ultimately concluded that because so few states had actually passed even halfway comprehensive statutes, along with the fact none included sanctions for institutional violators, state-level campus crime legislation represented little more than "symbolic public policy" and would likely have little substantive effect on how postsecondary institutions addressed issues of crime and security on their campuses.

John J. Sloan

See also College and University Campus Legislation, Federal; School Violence

Further Readings

Edelman, M. (1964). *The symbolic uses of politics.* Urbana: University of Illinois Press.

Griffaton, M. C. (1995). State-level initiatives and campus crime. In B. S. Fisher & J. J. Sloan (Eds.), *Campus crime: Legal, social, and policy perspectives* (pp. 53–73). Springfield, IL: Charles C Thomas.

Sloan, J. J., & Shoemaker, J. (2007). State-level Clery Act initiatives: Symbolic politics or substantive policy? In B. S. Fisher & J. J. Sloan (Eds.), *Campus crime: Legal, social and policy perspectives* (2nd ed., pp. 102–121). Springfield, IL: Charles C Thomas.

Web Sites

Security On Campus, Inc.: http://www.securityon campusinc.org

COMMUNITY ANTIDRUG PROGRAMS

Community antidrug programs are efforts by citizens to thwart drug activity in their neighborhoods, usually in response to the inability of the government and law enforcement to control crime and illegal drug sales in their neighborhoods. This entry begins with an overview of illegal drug selling, then focuses on the issue of outdoor drug sales, and concludes with a discussion of citizen-based strategies for combating such drug sales, including some examples of successful programs.

Illegal Drug Selling

Illegal Drug Use and Its Consequences

Illegal drug use in the United States poses a serious threat to public health and safety, and has a wide range of pernicious effects on individuals, families, and communities. From 1985 to 2001, national surveys found consistently that Americans list "drugs" among the top 10 problems facing the country. Illegal drug use can lead to life-altering and frequently fatal consequences, including overdoses, infectious diseases (e.g., HIV disease, hepatitis, and tuberculosis), premature aging, accidents, and crippling addictions. Illegal drug use also places a tremendous strain on the nation's health care system and increases the cost of health care for all Americans. Rampant illegal drug use and sales further accelerate the spiral of decline in inner-city neighborhoods that are already isolated and impoverished.

Demand Reduction

For nearly a century, the federal government has engaged in an array of enforcement activities to stem the production, distribution, and sale of illicit substances. Overall, these efforts have failed to reduce the demand or supply of drugs. Moreover, they have led to deleterious collateral consequences. Still, these efforts have persisted despite the lack of evidence supporting their effectiveness. Most antidrug strategies are implemented at the street level; they are usually conducted by special units of police officers and involve the arrest of low-level drug sellers and people in possession of small quantities of illicit substances.

Since the 1980s, an overwhelming emphasis on law enforcement strategies to combat illegal drug use and sales has resulted in dramatic increases in the nation's arrest and incarceration rates. The enforcement of drug laws has been highly rigorous, extremely punitive, and exceedingly expensive, both in criminal justice and in social costs. During the first half of 2006 alone, the war on drugs cost federal and state governments more than $30 billion. In addition, drug law enforcement activities have contributed substantially to the costs of building and maintaining prisons, the number of which has increased fourfold in the past 20 years.

Outdoor Drug Sales

Drug Profits

The sale of illegal drugs in the United States is extremely profitable, earning an estimated $60 billion, and catering to at least 16 million customers annually. In underclass communities with scant economic and employment opportunities, the drug trade offers one of the few options for a steady income. Drug sales in poor neighborhoods are more likely to occur in open-air drug markets—on streets and in parks—whereas drug sales in suburban neighborhoods are more likely to take place indoors, in private settings.

Neighborhood Disorder

Street corner drug selling and its corollaries are highly disruptive to neighborhood safety and stability. Outdoor drug markets, characterized by a steady stream of pedestrian and car traffic, are frequented by nonresident and indigenous drug users, who transit the neighborhood for minor purchases. The people who live near these drug markets view drug buyers as unwelcome interlopers who make it extremely difficult for them to leave home or park on own their property without experiencing inconvenience or risking potential conflicts with drug buyers or sellers. Open-air drug sales may force residents to remain locked in their homes as prisoners of fear.

Flagrant drug markets depend heavily on the ability of customers to patronize a well-known, consistent, and safe location to complete their drug transactions. Drug sellers are careful to choose spots that are easily accessible to customers and have several escape routes that help protect them and their customers from law enforcement authorities or rival drug dealers. Open-air drug markets are commonly found on littered streets with empty lots, abandoned buildings, liquor stores, and take-out food establishments. They thrive on poorly lit streets and in dark alleys, and are often situated near public housing developments where drug sellers can hide from the police or their drug-selling competitors.

Local drug buyers sometimes loiter on the streets, using their drugs before they leave or haggling with sellers about the cost and quality of the substances. These disputes can turn violent and affect innocent bystanders who are unwillingly and unwittingly caught in the conflict. Those who want to earn money to purchase drugs might perform sexual acts near the site of drug selling. They might also engage in sex acts with drug sellers in exchange for the substance. Thus, outdoor prostitution becomes another disruptive criminal activity that reduces the quality of life in neighborhoods plagued by flagrant drug markets.

One of the most threatening aspects of drug sales to community safety is the systemic violence that occurs among drug sellers who are fighting with one another to control the local drug market. This violence is most likely to erupt into pitched battles when sales are controlled by rival street gangs, which is common in large urban areas and when a new drug is introduced into the market.

Police Tactics to Combat Outdoor Sales

Open-air drug sales are easier for police officers to investigate and target for sting or reverse-sting operations than are private, indoor drug sales. In sting operations, the police pose as drug sellers in established sales locations; customers are arrested shortly after the purchase. In reverse-sting operations, police officers pose as customers; following the transaction, officers arrest the sellers and confiscate their cache of drugs and money as evidence. Undercover operations

are more likely to be conducted in unstable and loosely knit lower-class neighborhoods rather than in more stable and close-knit middle- or working-class neighborhoods, where the undercover officers would be more conspicuous.

As noted above, public drug sales are highly disruptive to the social order in poor neighborhoods; hence, they elicit a plethora of calls for police services. Arrests are a gauge of police performance and effectiveness at both the individual officer and department levels. Neighborhood sweeps of drug sellers, in which police saturate the streets and arrest several people complicit in the drug trade, and sting operations that net numerous arrests of buyers and sellers, bring public and media accolades to the police. Therefore, the concentration of drug enforcement efforts in poor neighborhoods makes tactical sense and signifies greater police responsiveness and sensitivity to residents' concerns about safety and public order.

Despite these massive efforts and expenditures, little evidence supports the conclusion that the passage and street-level enforcement of stringent drug laws through sweeps and buy-and-bust operations have reduced illegal drug use and sales or any other types of crime. The effects of these strategies are generally short-lived and result simply in the displacement of drug selling from one street corner to the next. Frustrated by police inability to control crime and drug sales in their neighborhoods, citizens have taken the lead in launching community antidrug programs based on generic community crime prevention models.

Citizen-Based Antidrug Strategies

Community Crime Prevention

Community crime prevention programs built their foundations during the Johnson Administration. Thus crime reduction became one of the top priorities of community organizations. The popularity of the community programs stemmed from the public's realization that the police alone are unable to control crime and must depend on citizens to supply them with the information necessary to solve crimes. In fact, research showed that simply putting more police on the streets and improving crime-solving technology was not enough to lower crime, which grew at unprecedented rates from the 1960s through the early 1990s.

Community crime prevention programs were implemented in the 1970s to prevent street crime and residential burglary. These programs were based on the principle of informal social control, which suggests that crime reduction is a by-product of social processes, such as the rigorous enforcement of social norms, the inculcation of a stronger sense of community, and the empowerment of citizens to solve their own problems (collective efficacy). They were also based on the opportunity reduction approach to crime prevention, which encourages residents to adopt deterrent measures to reduce their vulnerability to criminal victimization. Determined citizen activities to combat crime and disorder embodied widespread sentiments, such as "citizens have to be the eyes and ears of the police," "by themselves, the police are losing the war against crime," and "it's time we fought back to regain control of our neighborhoods from the criminals and the dope dealers." Community crime prevention programs assumed various forms that included resident patrols, block watch programs, property-marking projects, home security surveys, and police–community councils.

Program Theory and Practice

With the emergence of flagrant drug markets in the mid-1980s and early 1990s, community crime prevention programs began to focus on the eradication of street corner drug sales. The direct involvement of community residents in antidrug initiatives can be an effective strategy for combating outdoor drug selling. Community antidrug programs encourage residents to regain a sense of informal social control and collective efficacy, both of which lower crime and increase residents' feelings of safety and belonging. By joining community antidrug programs, residents are expressing their duty to protect themselves, their families, and their neighbors from criminal activities and other disruptive and deviant behaviors that decrease residents' well-being and freedom.

Citizen-based antidrug initiatives employ an assortment of tactics to interfere with drug sales; these vary in terms of their aggressiveness and dependence on law enforcement. For example,

citizens who belong to traditional Neighborhood Watch Programs call the police or anonymous tip lines whenever they witness drug sales. Others provide police with more detailed reports about drug transactions, which can be delivered during beat meetings—a component of community policing programs. Such programs encourage citizens and police officers to work in problem-solving partnerships to combat drug sales. Beat meetings also allow civilians to hold the police accountable for their actions (or inactions) in thwarting drug sales in the community.

A few citizens have engaged in independent activities to interrupt drug transactions. These include slowly driving past outdoor drug markets and calling attention to the drug dealing by broadcasting a running commentary of the activities through a megaphone. This public harassment steers both customers and sellers away from the site, the success of which depends, in part, on preserving the surreptitious nature of the business enterprise. Such noisy disruptions can also compel the police to take action.

Another proactive and potentially dangerous antidrug approach is for residents to record the license plate numbers and descriptions of the vehicles of drug buyers, calling the information into the police immediately so that they can arrest the buyers with the drugs still in their possession. Other citizen-initiated antidrug efforts consist of less conspicuous but highly coordinated neighborhood patrols. In these programs, civilians identify hot spots of criminal activity and drug selling, and communicate the locations of the troublesome areas on police-band radios.

Successful Programs

Implemented in diverse communities during the 1980s, four extraordinary citizen-based antidrug programs showed that they can be an effective mechanism for increasing the willingness of residents to report drug transactions and join the police in cooperative efforts for controlling crime and drug dealing at the street level. These programs produced significant, positive changes in citizens' perceptions of crime, social cohesion and control, and signs of physical decay in the neighborhood. Notable among these are Operation Push-Out-the-Pusher in Miami, which encouraged citizens to call the police to report drug-related information and to forge partnerships with police officers working in narcotics units; Operation Results in Seattle, which used mobile citizen patrols in areas of drug selling; Let's Clean It Up in Philadelphia, which established a phone tree for reporting drug activity; and Citizens on Patrol in Baltimore, which used CB radios to inform police about suspected drug sales.

Program Limitations

Already besieged by many other social and economic challenges, low-income, high-crime communities, where visible drug use, drug sales, and signs of disorder are most prevalent, typically struggle with launching and sustaining antidrug projects. In general, community anticrime programs are most successful in affluent, stable, residential communities with less severe crime problems. In most poor neighborhoods, only about 10% of community residents actually participate in such activities. Many people do not become involved in antidrug programs because of apathy, distrust of the police, denial of the drug problem, tolerance for drug use, or fear of retaliation from drug sellers and gang members. Nonetheless, proactive citizen attempts to take back the streets from drug dealers can exert a favorable influence on the quality of life in urban communities even when undertaken by a small number of residents.

Arthur J. Lurigio and Justyna Lenik

See also Citizen Patrols; Crime Prevention; Drug Use Forecasting/Arrestee Drug Abuse Monitoring; Neighborhood Watch Programs; Substance Abuse, Prevention of; Substance Abuse, Treatment of

Further Readings

Davis, R. C., & Lurigio, A. J. (1996). *Fighting back; Neighborhood antidrug strategies*. Thousand Oaks, CA: Sage.

Davis, R. C., Lurigio, A. J., & Rosenbaum, D. P. (Eds.). (1993). *Drugs and the community: Involving community residents in combating the sale of illegal drugs*. Springfield, IL: Charles C Thomas.

Lurigio, A. J., & Davis, R. C. (1992). Taking the war on drugs to the streets. *Crime and Delinquency, 38,* 522–538.

Rengert, G. F., Ratcliffe, J. H., & Chakravorty, S. (2005). *Policing illegal drug markets: Geographic approaches to crime prevention*. Monsey, NY: Willow Tree.

Roehl, J. A., Wong, H., Huitt, R., & Capowich, G. E. (1995). *A national assessment of community-based antidrug initiatives: Final report*. Pacific Grove, CA: Institute for Social Analysis.

Rosenbaum, D. P. (1998). Community crime prevention: A review and synthesis of the literature. *Justice Quarterly, 5,* 323–395.

Weingart, S. N. (1993). A typology of community responses to drugs. In R. C. Davis, A. J. Lurigio, & D. P. Rosenbaum (Eds.), *Drugs and the community: Involving community residents in combating the sale of illegal drugs* (pp. 85–105). Springfield, IL: Charles C Thomas.

COMMUNITY POLICING

Community policing "reforms" have sought to provide the police with greater public acceptance and political grounding. These reforms were created over time and came together in the 1990s under the umbrella of "community policing" (which is also called community-oriented policing). At that time, it had become clear that other 20th-century police efforts—the "wars" waged by the police on crime, drugs, and youth participation in violence—were not working as intended. Herman Goldstein, arguably the architect of modern community and problem-oriented policing, suggested that the police often emphasized means over ends—that is, arrest over community safety, or the number of calls for service responded to as opposed to the underlying problems that produced the need for those responses. This means–ends inversion resulted in the police and the public talking past one another, with the police concentrating on effort and the public on effect.

Moreover, Goldstein emphasized that the police acting alone rarely had sustainable results. That is to say, the police rarely touched the "root" problems of crime and social disorder, responding instead to "branch problems," visible crime, and social disorder in public settings. Without attachments to other institutions of social control (e.g., the community, civic groups, other government agencies, and the like), the police were often relegated to the role of "picking up the pieces" after events had already occurred. Reactive policing was shaped more by the public's willingness to call the police than by police-derived interventions. And, when the police sought to become more "proactive" in their crime prevention and suppression activities, they invariably confronted a level of public resistance to what was perceived as "police overzealousness."

Goldstein's ideas shaped a generation of reform that emphasized a broader communal role for the police, and particularly the use of partnerships and problem solving. The idea of community policing emerged from Goldstein's critique—it represented a sharp detour from conventional police crime-attack approaches, and it set the stage for decades of experimentation on police practices.

Thinking About Policing History

Throughout modern history, policing in democratic societies has observed a palpable tension between police extension of formal social control into communal life and the level of acceptance that the general public accords the police in making such extensions. Generally speaking, the community wants visible, civil, and unobtrusive policing, wherever possible. The police, however, are asked to intervene often in the civic life of individuals, and sometimes in that of groups. The attempt to balance proactive police action and civic legitimacy was discernable throughout the 20th century, which was the period when policing became more formal. This was the case in the United States as well as much of the Western world.

At differing intervals throughout the 19th and 20th centuries, the overextension of police interventions has resulted in large-scale civic protest. In the period preceding the Civil War, the police often served as slave patrols. In big cities the police were also most responsible for dealing with large waves of immigrants in the late 19th and early 20th centuries. Here the police had an important role in providing order and safety in immigrant tenements in large U.S. cities like New York, Philadelphia, Baltimore, and Boston. At the beginning of the 20th century the police were used to break union organized strikes and enforce management and property laws. From this period into the 1950s, the police were also used to enforce racial segregation and Jim Crow Laws. In each of these periods, the police in the United States were often distant from those policed, and were often pitted against the disenfranchised and newly arrived immigrants.

In the 1960s and 1970s the police were confronted by a powerful youth culture, the civil rights movement, and antiwar protests whose participants' goal was "taking it to the streets." This resulted in an era of unprecedented civil disobedience. In the 1970s and 1980s the police "war on drugs" witnessed an era of the most aggressive police interventions, often in the poorest neighborhoods. The "war" rhetoric has been part of the domestic scene in the United States for many generations, having gained prominence in the Johnson administration as the "war on poverty." This was then extended to a "war on drugs" that continues today. Since the 1980s, the war metaphor has been extended to gang activity and violence as well. Thus the latter half of the 20th century witnessed a growing gulf between the police and those policed, most especially when those policed were persons of color.

In the late 20th century and moving into the 21st century, policing in Western democracies has had to more fully confront the incongruities of past policing practices, namely those that seemed to further alienate the public from the institution of policing. Beginning in the 1950s and continuing to the present, the police as a social and formal institution have been the target of ongoing reforms and change. These reforms came together in the 1990s under the umbrella of community policing.

Roots of Community Policing

The roots of community policing can be found in the late 1940s and into the 1950s, when police leaders and academics began to focus on police race relations. Gordon Allport and Louis Radelet argued that improvements in race relations, especially with the police, required a closer examination of prejudice itself, as well as thinking more broadly about police and community relations. Racial communities had been long segregated in American society, and by 1960 these communities often became the places in which urban riots erupted, typically following some overt police action.

Radelet and his successors argued that the police needed to build bridges with communities, especially communities that were racially and economically segregated from mainstream American society. This conception of police and community interaction, and indeed the overlapping social control roles of these groups, comported well with ideas introduced by Sir Robert Peel a century earlier during the formation of the Metropolitan Police of London in 1827. These included the statement that "the police are the public and the public the police," meaning that the police in Britain were rooted in a rather homogeneous society where the police and public accepted the legitimacy of law and government policing in practice.

From their inception in the mid-1800s in cities such as Philadelphia, New York, and Boston, among others, the police struggled with public acceptance. The role of the U.S. police in enforcing slavery and property rights, and in dealing with the waves of migration that occurred from the late 19th century into the 20th century, as well as police ties to the emerging political machines forming in major cities across the United States, left the public quite wary of the local police.

In the 1950s, 1960s, and 1970s, race relations, particularly in the United States, were quite difficult. Crime in urban communities was often associated with the poorest and non-White sections of cities, and police actions taken in these communities often precipitated massive social disorder. The National Commission on Civil Disorders of 1968 attributed much of the urban strife that cities witnessed to actions taken by the police, which ignited large-scale riots and social disorder. However, the commission was careful to state that the police actions alone did not account for massive rioting, but rather, that it was deep frustration with racism that was often enflamed in these communities by police actions. The tensions between White and Black America were pronounced, and the divisions deep.

Between the 1970s and the 1990s, the police and academics searched for ways to make the police more effective and the community more sensitive. Studies of police patrol practices and criminal investigations showed that the police were less effective than previously thought, and assessments of police and community interactions often portrayed the police as socially distant and more often than not disdainful of minorities. Increasing drug crime and violent crime in the

mid-1980s called attention to thinking about new ways of policing. Experiments in "team policing" in the 1970s and 1980s spawned a wave of research on alternative policing modes, such as foot patrol and community policing.

Since the late 1980s, community policing and problem solving have grown rather exponentially, with significant federal investment in both. That investment included a commitment by the Clinton Administration to put 100,000 community police officers in America's cities and towns, and the creation of an office for community-oriented policing (COPS) that has invested more that $9 billion in community policing programs.

Elements of Community Policing

At its base, community policing is focused on three things. First, it seeks to move the police from a reactive approach to addressing crime and community disorder to one that emphasizes prevention. Much of 20th-century policing was rooted in notions of deterrence and apprehension. Under this orientation the police often reacted to crime situations after they had occurred, and applied a limited range of interventions, such as saturation patrol or aggressive street tactics, to address visible crime problems occurring in public places.

Second, in moving to a preventive approach, community policing seeks to better understand and then address discrete community crime and social order problems. Historically, the police were rather unanalytical about their approach to dealing with these issues. Ideas about the effects of random patrolling suggested that the police were not deployed for prevention, or for deterrence, for that matter. Random patrolling was simply that— random. However, targeted patrolling, on foot or in vehicles, with community partners could see the connection between what crime was occurring (any why) and what the police and others could do about it.

Third, under the community policing philosophy and practice the police are expected to develop a range of partnerships between the police and civic groups, other government agencies, and, where appropriate, the private sector. Such partnerships are meant to broaden the information coming to the police and the range of interventions that may be available to address discrete problems.

Moreover, such partnerships may also suggest that institutions other than the police actually may be more effective in preventing or addressing specific kinds of crime and social order problems.

Thus community policing seeks to better align the police with their community, the government, and organizations in order to prevent crime and to ensure that communities feel and are safe. This is done through a more open process of communication, and the development of strategies and programs that mobilize and leverage community participation in the crime and social order discourse.

Community policing is an umbrella concept, which has also spawned several allied policing strategies, including problem-oriented policing and intelligence-led policing. Each seeks to make the police more analytical in what they do to address crime and social order problems, and each seeks a broader array of partners with whom the police can work to address these issues.

Effectiveness of Community Policing

This question has proved difficult to answer. During the 1980s and 1990s and into the 21st century, when there was considerable investment in community policing strategies, programs, and tactics, there was not a corresponding rigor in the assessment of these efforts. In some ways the advocacy for community policing approaches outstripped thorough analysis of the consequences and impacts of such a strategy shift for the police.

Nonetheless, in evaluating the effectiveness of police strategies and tactics, the National Research Council had this to say about community policing:

> It is particularly instructive that community policing strategies may be effective . . . the research available suggests that when the police partner more generally with the public, levels of citizen fear will decline. Moreover, when the police are able to gain wider legitimacy among citizens and offenders, non-experimental evidence suggests that the likelihood of offending will be reduced. . . . There is greater and more consistent evidence, although it is based on non-experimental studies, that focused strategies drawing on an array of non law enforcement tactics can also be effective in reducing crime and disorder. (pp. 250–251)

Interestingly, while it is difficult to measure and demonstrate the crime control capacities of community policing remain problematic, the "community building" and "fear reduction" impacts of such efforts are clear. And these are the areas on which community policing was originally conceived to have the greatest effect. That is to say, the crime control functions of community policing are difficult to establish independent from a renewed civic attachment to the legitimacy of the police. If the police are to be effective, they must first be accepted and seen as legitimate by those being policed.

Perhaps what can be said about community policing in contrast to more conventional police strategies is that it performs about as well as the "crime attack" model, while incurring few of its negative ramifications. Research on community policing suggests several things.

First, community policing has been difficult to implement fully in police agencies, as the structures and cultures of the police have been difficult to substantially alter. For nearly a century, policing in the United States embraced a crime-control and crime-attack posture. Communities were not seen as a central partner to policing; rather, communities—particularly racial and poor communities—were the targets of police interventions. The mind-set of crime attack and the police organizational structures that have grown up around that idea have been difficult to reshape. While police departments across the United States preach the philosophy of community policing, their structures and cultures are not entirely supportive of such fundamental changes in policing.

Second, since many of the anticipated outcomes of community policing interventions involve the perceptions and feelings of the community, the measurement of these effects has been difficult to understand. In some important ways, community policing has been about social affect—the way communities feel about themselves and "community quality of life." How communities become more self-reliant and engaged through community policing and other social interventions is not particularly clear, yet we do know that, generally speaking, socially disorganized communities lack the capacity to resist crime.

Third, the history of assessment of community policing includes studies with little scientific rigor, making the findings achieved less compelling. As previously indicated, the advocacy for community policing often outstripped rigorous analysis of how such efforts were conceptualized and implemented and the effects of such implementation. Today, police research has moved more toward evidence-based arguments and the need to clearly evaluate policing strategies consistent with scientific method.

Finally, community policing was implemented in late 1980s and beyond, in an environment in which crime was already declining, which has made assessing whether the decline in crime is associated with community policing or other larger social trends more difficult. There is an old adage that when crime goes down it has many parents, but when it goes up it is an orphan. Such is the case with the advent of community policing as a major strategy for the police across America. Disentangling the effects of the economy, social shifts in population, the decline in those between the ages of 14 and 24, and the like from what the police do in social communities is a difficult process. Nonetheless, improvements in community assessments of social capital and community levels of organization provide opportunities to link such changes to the interventions of the police, and hence the contributions that community policing can make to increasing community orderliness and safety.

Future of Community Policing

Early in its development, community policing was criticized as being more rhetoric than reality. As community policing was first promulgated as a "philosophy" rather than a coherent set of practices, shifts in rhetoric associated with a changing policing world substantially preceded intended and actual changes. In the early stages of its development, and indeed continuing well into the 21st century, community policing was seen as an "umbrella concept" incorporating concerns for community engagement, proactive policing, and problem solving.

Over the past several years, community policing has been shown to have important effects on public perceptions of neighborhood safety, as well as to increase public acceptance and even support of local police. Community policing's impact on crime and its allied program of problem solving have been less clearly demonstrated, but when the

police do concentrate on specific crime or social disorder problems in a restricted area of the community, they do have a modest impact on these concerns, albeit often for a limited time. This said, it is clear that community policing does have an impact on improving community assessment and a "voice" in defining crime and social problems most affecting the communities it serves, and that assessment of improvements in community quality of life and police practice generally improve under community policing.

As the United States and other Western democracies have indeed shifted the police role to include matters of internal security, the connections between the police and those policed are likely to once again be strained. The partnerships and other connections that the police have made in the community via community policing are likely important hedges in how those tensions play out in the coming years. In that sense, community policing may indeed be an important mediating factor in such relationships.

Jack R. Greene

See also Problem-Oriented Policing

Further Readings

Allport, G. W. (1954). *The nature of prejudice*. New York: Addison-Wesley.

Black, D. (1980). *The manners and customs of the police*. New York: Academic Press.

Center for Research on Criminal Justice. (1977). *The iron fist and the velvet glove: An analysis of the U.S. police* (expanded and rev. ed.). Berkeley, CA: Author.

Fogelson, R. (1977). *Big city police*. Cambridge, MA: Harvard University Press.

Goldstein, H. (1977). *Policing a free society*. Cambridge, MA: Ballinger.

Goldstein, H. (1990). *Problem-oriented policing*. New York: McGraw-Hill.

Greene, J. R., & Mastrofski, S. D. (Eds.). (1988). *Community policing: Rhetoric and reality*. New York: Praeger.

Greene, J. R., & Mastrofski, S. D. (2000). Community policing in America: Changing the nature, structure and function of the police. In J. Horney (Ed.), *Criminal justice 2000: Vol. 3. Policies, processes, and the decisions of the criminal justice system* (pp. 299–370). Washington, DC: U.S. Department of Justice, National Institute of Justice.

Kelling, G., & Moore, M. (1988). From political to reform to community: The evolving strategy of the police. In J. R. Greene and S. D. Mastrofski (Eds.), *Community-policing: Rhetoric re reality*. New York: Praeger.

Miller, W. R. (1975). Cops and bobbies, 1830–1870. *Journal of Social History, 8*, 81–101.

Miller, W. R. (1979). London's police tradition in a changing society. In S. Holdaway (Ed.), *The British police* (pp. 14–23). London: Edward Arnold.

National Advisory Commission on Civil Disorders. (1968). *Report of the National Advisory Commission on Civil Disorder*. Washington, DC: U.S. Government Printing Office.

National Research Council. (2004). *Fairness and effectiveness in policing: The evidence*. Washington, DC: National Academies Press.

Radelet, L. A. (1968). The idea of community. In A. F. Brandstater & L. A. Radelet (Eds.), *Police and community relations: A sourcebook* (pp. 80–84). Beverly Hills, CA: Glencoe.

Schwartz, A. I., & Clarren, S. N. (1977). *The Cincinnati Team Policing Experiment: A summary report*. Washington, DC: Police Foundation.

Skogan, W. G. (1990). *Disorder and decline: Crime and the spiral of decay in American cities*. New York: The Free Press.

Walker, S. (1977). *A critical history of police reform*. Lexington, MA: D.C. Heath.

COMPARATIVE VICTIMOLOGY

The term *comparative victimology* means the analysis of victimological subthemes like victim behaviors, victimizations, victim rights, and victim services, which are the same or unique in different cultures, societies, and nations. This perspective helps victimologists understand to what extent the victim behaviors of individuals or groups are universal and common to all humans and to what extent they are by-products of different physical and social environments.

This entry discusses the concept's two terms, *comparative* and *victimology;* the origins of the comparative approach; and how comparative victimology has been applied. It concludes by describing how the concept affects victimology today and will likely affect it in the future.

Definition

The words *comparative* and *victimology* require clarification separately and then as a complete concept. In academia, "comparative" concepts become better regulated through disciplined analysis. Through the process of induction and deduction, abstract information is collected and analyzed and allows scientists to learn unique forms of pioneering knowledge and speculative inquiry. In the social sciences, the word *comparative* usually refers to an evaluation between and among social forces, individual behaviors, groups of persons, research methods, public policies, theories, cultures, and so on. Perhaps the most common application of the word *comparative* in the social sciences is to research, especially to explain the similarities and differences in cross-cultural, cross-societal, and cross-national findings. These forms of information processing allow social scientists to discover facts about human social life that can be generalized to all people. The power to discriminate is greatly enhanced by the disciplined collection and synthesis of information expanding understanding and resulting in knowledge.

Historical Perspectives

Criminological Roots

The word *comparative* in criminology involves the analysis of how criminal behaviors, criminal laws, and justice practices are unique or the same in different cultures and societies. One of the earliest calls for a comparative criminology was made at the International Congress on Criminology of 1960 in The Hague, by Sheldon Glueck. He asked for more than just comparing different countries; he wanted research that could be replicated and intended to expose causal universals irrespective of cultural differences between countries. One of the early manifestations of Glueck's call was the major work produced by Herman Mannheim in 1965 that drew together criminological research, theories, and practices from countries such as the United States, Britain, Germany, France and Italy; it also included works from other countries, especially in Europe. The value of this comparative work has become legend and has created a rich resource of information within the field of criminology. Thus the "comparative criminology" tradition can be seen in such publications as the *Journal of Offender Rehabilitation and Comparative Criminology* and the book *Different Responses to Violence in Japan and America* by John P. J. Dussich, Paul C. Friday, Akira Yamagami, and Richard D. Knudten.

Victimological Roots

The term *victimology* is understood by most laypersons as having to do with victims. Sometimes they erroneously use it to mean victimization or victim services. Since the term *victimology* in the English language is only about 50 years old, it has not permeated all educational institutions adequately. The origin of the word *victimology* comes from its two parts, *victim* and *logy*. *Victim* comes from the Latin word *victima,* which refers living creatures sacrificed for religious purposes. *Logy,* from the Greek word *logos* (which was derived from the verb "to speak"), is often associated with divine wisdom, study, or science. Today, among international victimologists, the term *victimology* is defined mostly from the victim's perspective. Some limit this definition to *crime victimology;* others refer to victimizations caused by humans— *human victimology;* and still others have embraced Mendelsohn's concept of *general victimology.* This victimology, not so concerned with the victimizing force, studies all types of victims, theories and research used to explain victimizations, victim behaviors, analysis of laws, policies, and interventions and programs for helping victims recover. It includes victims of crime, traffic accidents, abuse of power, human rights violations, wars, and natural phenomena. Within the field of scientific victimology, these three perspectives exist side by side and are understood by their respective proponents not as confusions in logic, but rather, as decisions to embrace a wider or lesser range of victims and violent forces.

Pioneer Works

One early comparative victimological study was presented by Vahakn N. Dadrian at the First Symposium on Victimology, which compared the common features of the genocides of the Armenian and Jewish people. Another comparative study was the cross-national victimization research conducted

by Jan van Dijk of the Dutch Ministry of Justice, with Pat Mayhew of the British Home Office and Martin Killias of Laussane University in Switzerland. These victimologists created the International Crime Victimization Surveys (ICVSs). The surveys, which began as a project of the Dutch Ministry of Justice, were limited to developed nations; however, later the United Nations Interregional Crime and Justice Research Institute (UNICRI), led by van Dijk, greatly expand the ICVSs to also measure victimization in developing countries and in Eastern Europe. Unique research methods were created to account for the challenges of different languages, national practices, cultures, and laws. The aforementioned victimologists, plus Anna Alvazzi del Frate, John van Kesteren, and Ugi Svekic, measured frequency of victimizations, details of the victim's experiences, and perceptions of safety, policing, and prevention across the globe. One of the recent major follow-up studies using the results of these surveys was published by Paul Nieuwbeerta, who edited a comprehensive book, *Crime Victimization in Comparative Perspective,* which provides a rich source of findings from across the world. Another comparative victimological work, by Marion Brienen and Ernestine Hoegen, compared 22 European criminal justice systems to evaluate victims within the framework of criminal law and procedures. An important contribution to this literature was the extensive synthesis by Hans Joachim Schneider of victimological developments in the world during the three decades since the First International Symposium. A more recent comparative survey is the European Survey on Crime and Safety (EU ICS) by van Dijk and his colleagues, which in large part used the methods and instruments for comparative surveys from the ICVS's work.

Applications

Examples of comparative victimology can be found in the extensive cross-cultural studies that have been conducted over the 50 years since Beniamin Mendelsohn's seminal article introduced his concept as the science of victimology in a Swiss journal in 1956; and, especially since the First Symposium on Victimology held in Jerusalem in 1973. In the short existence of this new discipline, victimology has been greatly enriched by the hundreds of books, newsletters, research notes, and articles that have used the comparative approach to study the wide range of victimological phenomena. Some examples of journals that reflect the comparative victimological approach are *Victimology: An International Journal,* started in the United States by Emilio Viano; *Victimología,* begun in Argentina by Hilda Marchiori; *The International Review of Victimology* founded in England by John Freeman; and *The International Perspectives in Victimology,* started recently in Japan by John Dussich. Some examples of books that reflect the comparative victimological approach are the German volume *Viktimologie: Wissenschaft vom Verbrechensopter* (Victimology: Science From Crime Victims) by Hans J. Schneider; *Victims and Society,* edited by Emilio Viano; *Critical Victimology: International Perspectives* by Rob Mawby and Sandra Walklate; *Support for Crime Victims in a Comparative Perspective,* edited by Ezzat Fattah and Tony Peters; and the Spanish work *Victimología: Estudio de la Víctima* (Victimology: The Study of Victims) by Luis Rodríguez Manzanera. Because of comparative research, the field of victimology has learned much about the behaviors surrounding victimization and its key associated themes, such as victims' rights, vulnerabilities of persons, prevention strategies, victim services, victim advocacy, victimization recovery, and so on. The World Society of Victimology is the international organization that personifies the comparative victimological approach in its mission, newsletters, symposia, symposia proceedings, committees, and structure. This society was proposed by Mendelsohn in his early writings and became a reality at the Third International Symposium of Victimology held in Münster, Germany, in 1979. Its members come from a wide range of nations, which is reflected in its executive committee and its subcommittees, especially its United Nations Liaison Committee and its International Courses Committee.

Future Directions

The field of victimology is continuing to mature, and it requires the extension of the disciplined inquiry that comparative victimology provides. Thus researchers are compelled to further study victims—prior to, during, and after victimization. A major text dedicated to comparative victimology is needed to synthesize the growing number of findings that have evolved over the past 30 years. Comparative victimology needs more refinements of the instruments and greater applicability in gathering data from countries that have not been accessible to previous surveys and by countries that have had success with promising programs. More international evaluations of services and interventions from different countries also are needed. These types of research are now being conducted at the National Crime Victim Research and Treatment Center, in Charleston, South Carolina; Tokiwa International Victimology Institute in Mito, Japan; and the International Victimology Institute in Tilburg, the Netherlands. Victimological theories based on comparative victimology, rather than borrowed from comparative criminology or other disciplines, may result from research conducted in the near future and play a significant role in helping solve the victimological problems facing humanity today. In addition, wider adoption of principles based on the 1985 United Nations' Declaration of Basic Principles of Justice for Victims of Crime and Abuse of Power may give rise to new laws, new policies, and new programs on behalf of victims. Finally, new standards likely will be embraced by all nations to support international legal instruments like the one currently being proposed by the World Society of Victimology that is known as the Convention on Justice and Support for Victims of Crime and Abuse of Power.

John P. J. Dussich

See also International Crime Victimization Survey (ICVS); Public Perceptions of Victims; Victimization Surveys; Victimology; Victims' Rights Movement, International

Further Readings

Brienen, M. E. I., & Hoegen, E. H. (2000). *Victims of crime in 22 European criminal justice systems.* Nijmegen, the Netherlands: Wolf Legal Productions.

Dussich, J., Underwood, T., & Petersen, D. (2003). New definitions for victimology and victim services: A theoretical note. *The Victimologist, 7*(2), 1.

Fattah, E., & Peters, T. (Eds.). (1998). *Support for crime victims in a comparative perspective.* Leuven, Belgium: Leuven University Press.

Manzanera, L. R. (2003). *Victimología: Estudio de la víctima*, Octava Edición. México D. F.: Editorial Porrúa.

Mawby, R. I., & Walklate, S. (1994). *Critical victimology: International perspectives*. London: Sage.

Mendelsohn, B. (1974). A new branch of bio-psycho-social science: Victimology (included in The origin of the doctrine of victimology). In I. Drapkin & E. Viano (Eds.), *Victimology*. Lexington, MA: D.C. Heath. (Original work published 1956)

Nieuwbeerta, P. (2008). *Crime victimization in comparative perspective*. Annandale, Australia: Federation.

Schneider, H. J. (1975). *Viktimologie: Wissenschaft vom verbrechensopter* (Victimology: Science from crime victims). Tübingen, Germany: J. C. B. Mohr.

van Dijk, J. J. M. (1999). Criminal victimization and victim empowerment in an international perspective. In J. J. M. van Dijk, R. G. H. van Kaam, & J. Wemmers (Eds.), *Caring for crime victims: Selected proceedings of the 9th international symposium on victimology*. Monsey, NY: Criminal Justice Press.

Viano, E. (Ed.). (1976). *Victims and society*. Washington, DC: Visage.

COMPASSION FATIGUE

Crime victims suffer psychologically from their traumatic experiences and their consequent increase in vigilance. But rarely is there attention to the psychological trauma of those who care for and care about these victims of crime. These caregivers are not only family members and dear friends who provide personal support on a regular basis; caregivers of crime victims also include the police, 9-1-1 operators, victim advocates and others in the criminal justice system, emergency medical technicians, nurses, and other medical professionals who care for crime victims. They often suffer from a special form of psychological trauma: compassion fatigue (CF).

Definitions

Compassion fatigue is the fatigue that results from compassionate caregiving to help relieve the distress of others. This type of fatigue is caused by the built-up stress (compassion stress) from the memories and emotions of responding to suffering without having fully relieved the suffering. Compassion fatigue is synonymous with secondary traumatic stress and similar to the traumatic stress experienced by those who survive violent crimes; it is the stress that results from helping a traumatized or suffering person; it is the natural and consequent behaviors and emotions resulting from knowing about a traumatizing event experienced by a significant other.

Professionals who work with crime victims who have experienced trauma may themselves become indirect victims of the trauma. More specifically, the negative effects of secondary exposure to traumatic events are the same as those of primary exposure, including intrusive imagery, avoidance of reminders and cues, hyperarousal, distressing emotions, and functional impairment. In addition, compassion fatigue may result in significant disruptions in an individual's sense of meaning, connection, identity, and worldview, as well as affect tolerance, psychological needs, beliefs about self and other, interpersonal relationships, and sensory memory.

Theory

In order to facilitate the healing process, caregivers working with traumatized populations, including but not limited to crime victims, often share the emotional burden of the trauma, bear witness to damaging and cruel events, and come face-to-face with the reality of terrible and traumatic acts in the world. Compassion fatigue results from the demand placed on the professional to understand the traumatized person in order to help him or her. The transmission of trauma from helped to helper is believed to occur through the gateway of empathic response. This fundamental element of helping is a function of the helper's empathic ability as well as direct exposure to the traumatized and a motivation to help them. The resolution of traumatic stress often requires that the traumatized person engage in a process in which they slowly, vividly, and repeatedly relive the event. Through this process, the professional is repeatedly exposed to vivid trauma imagery, and thereby secondarily exposed to the traumas experienced by the crime victim.

Prevalence and Risk and Protective Factors

CF has been empirically documented in professionals who work with crime victims in fields such as law enforcement, domestic violence, sexual assault, and child welfare. Exposure to traumatized individuals is the primary risk factor for CF. For professionals, level of exposure to traumatized clients is more important than length of exposure, in that higher proportions of traumatized clients in caseloads and higher proportions of time spent in trauma-related clinical activities are more predictive of CF. In addition, younger professionals and those with less experience are at increased risk for CF, and professionals' own trauma history, particularly in childhood, also is a significant risk factor. Professionals who use social support and positive coping strategies experience fewer symptoms of CF. More specifically, active coping, seeking emotional and instrumental support, planning, and humor are associated with lower levels of CF. Conversely, negative coping strategies, such as drug or alcohol use, aggression, and withdrawing from others are associated with higher levels of CF.

Minimizing the Effects of Compassion Fatigue

The first step in preventing or ameliorating compassion fatigue is to recognize the signs and symptoms of its emergence. By learning about the potential effects of CF and continually monitoring for the presence of symptoms, professionals may be able to prevent the more negative aspects of CF. In addition, there are a number of self-care strategies that professionals can implement to reduce the impact of CF, such as engaging in leisure activities, exercise, meditation, spending time with loved ones, and seeking personal psychotherapy as needed. Prevention of CF also requires that organizations implement proactive strategies. A supportive organizational culture in which caregivers are able to validate feelings and readily have access to support teams is essential. Professionals must feel safe to openly talk about the impact of their work with traumatized individuals. Further, the organization must recognize CF as a natural consequence of serving crime victims, rather than as a deficiency of the professional.

Brian Bride and Charles R. Figley

See also Posttraumatic Stress Disorder (PTSD); Survivor Patterns; Victimology

Further Readings

Bride, B. E. (2004). The impact of providing psychosocial services to traumatized populations. *Stress, Trauma, and Crisis: An International Journal, 7,* 1–18.

Figley, C. R. (1995). *Compassion fatigue: Coping with secondary traumatic stress disorder in those who treat the traumatized.* New York: Brunner/Mazel.

Pearlmann, L. A., & Saakvitne, K. W. (1995). *Trauma and the therapist: Countertransference and vicarious traumatization in psychotherapy with incest survivors.* New York: Norton.

Radey, M., & Figley, C. R. (2007). The social psychology of compassion. *Clinical Social Work Journal, 35,* 207–214.

Stamm, B. H. (Ed.). (1999). *Secondary traumatic stress: Self-care issues for clinicians, researchers, and educators* (2nd ed.). Lutherville, MD: Sidran.

COMPSTAT

From its genesis on a napkin at Elaine's in New York, Compstat (or "Comstat," as it is sometimes pronounced) has revolutionized policing. Developed for New York City Police Commissioner William Bratton by Jack Maple and John Miller, Compstat was the end result of what Maple believed to be simply what police agencies needed to do to fight crime.

Compstat as originally conceived and used today focuses on four principles:

1. Accurate, timely intelligence

2. Rapid deployment

3. Effective tactics

4. Relentless follow-up and assessment

The first principle—accurate, timely intelligence—refers to gathering the data, that is, the numbers for every place in the city on a daily basis. It also refers to mapping the crimes. Both approaches allow police agencies to use analysis, intelligence, and information to determine what's happening, where, when, and who might be involved.

For Maple, the second principle—rapid deployment—was to be "concentrated, synchronized and focused" (Maple & Mitchell, 1999, p. 32), requiring the various components of a police agency to talk with each other, to share information, to talk about the hot spots, patterns, trends, and so on, that come from accurate, timely intelligence.

The third principle—effective tactics—is whatever is needed to "reduce crime or improve the quality of life" (Maple & Mitchell, 1999, p. 32). This principle, coupled with the first two, encourages innovation on the part of "the boots, the bosses, and the suits." It allows for decentralized decision making and for each precinct to do what works for its crime situation and set of officers. Relentless follow-up and assessment is the glue that holds everything else together. It requires precinct commanders to be competent and to know what is happening in their sphere of influence and control, why it is happening, and what their game plan is for attacking it. This gave rise to the Compstat meetings that have been depicted in a number of movie and television shows. Perhaps the most negative depiction was in *The Wire*, in which precinct commanders were grilled incessantly about any and everything happening in their precinct, the stress causing many to upchuck both before and after a meeting.

In New York City, in just 2 years of using Compstat, crimes in all categories were reduced significantly and morale in the organization greatly improved. Cops were allowed to return to the practice of their profession, to do what they were trained to do, only this time armed with the information needed to make a significant and serious dent in all manner of crime.

Compstat provides a framework for accountability up and down the command chain. It also allows police to transfer of information horizontally and vertically, which they do routinely during every day at every level.

More important, Compstat makes a dent in crime. When it is applied properly, crime decreases. But its effect is not only on crime. Compstat is based on the idea that if serious crime is dealt with quickly and efficiently, the police are then better able to deal with the bulk of their tasks, such as order maintenance and other community problems that might be related to public safety. Compstat, then, not only deals with crime, but in dealing with crime also deals with a wide variety of other social disorders, many of which might lead to crime if left unchecked.

In addition, Compstat allows officers to return to being proactive rather than reactive. With the four principles feeding into each other, policing takes a more assertive and proactive approach, holding all of the parties accountable for results. Law enforcement leaders, armed with accurate and timely intelligence, are expected to develop and implement a plan of action. Like decision makers in other fields, they sometimes need to make decisions without having complete information. This is accomplished by allowing the patrol officers not only to have input into how to attack the problem but also to have the freedom to try new things. Patrol officers are empowered to solve problems. Using the Compstat approach, all officers in the department also are allowed and even encouraged to take risks and even to fail. As Thomas Edison said, "Every wrong attempt discarded is another step forward." Compstat allows for these steps forward.

When Compstat is implemented properly, there should also be an increase in morale, as everyone in the organization is given the right information to solve problems. When Compstat was implemented in the New York Police Department (NYPD), no one ever got in trouble for crime rates going up; what got them in trouble was when they (the commanders) either did not know the rates were up or did not have a plan to address the problem. Compstat is a huge morale builder, as the officers at every level know that they are being given the tools to solve problems while at the same time being supported in their mistakes and rewarded for their successes. Compstat allows for integration to occur across and within police agencies.

Compstat is not just for the NYPD, however—it's for policing everywhere. It addresses all types of crime in all types of cities, and has been successful wherever it has been tried. Compstat allows police officers to engage in doing policing, and when that happens we know that police *can* and *do* make a difference. Compstat is part of that difference.

Jeffrey P. Rush and Thomas J. O'Connor

See also Community Policing; Crime Mapping; Crime Prevention; Problem-Oriented Policing; Prospective Crime Mapping

Further Readings

Maple, J., & Mitchell, C. (1999). *The crime fighter*. New York: Random House.

McDonald, P. P. (2002). *Managing police operations: Implementing the New York crime control model— Compstat*. Belmont, CA: Wadsworth.

Shane, J. (2004). Compstat process. *FBI Law Enforcement Bulletin, 73*(4), 122–124.

COMPULSORY HIV TESTING

The HIV pandemic in the United States is widespread, and it poses an unprecedented threat to the general public as well as to the incarcerated. Many preventive measures have been enacted to restrict the spread of this infectious disease. Major HIV/AIDS awareness campaigns have placed emphasis on the benefits of HIV testing of all citizens, with the topic of compulsory HIV testing being widely discussed. This entry provides definitions of HIV, describes HIV testing methods used in the general population and in prisons, and examines the potential ethical impact of compulsory HIV testing.

Definitions

The human immunodeficiency virus, widely known as HIV, infects and destroys vital cells in the immune system and often progresses to AIDS (the more serious acquired immunodeficiency syndrome) within 10 to 15 years of infection. With the introduction of antiretroviral treatment methods, patients diagnosed with AIDS can be expected to live 5 years or even longer—if they have access to adequate health care. However, the only guaranteed defense against HIV/AIDS is prevention.

HIV testing is one of the main components in the campaign for HIV prevention. Testing centers are located across the United States in clinics, hospitals, schools, and correctional facilities. Free testing is available at most locations; however, some health insurance policies will cover the cost in the event of an emergency. These testing centers have varying policies on patient confidentiality, depending on national, state, and regional regulations. Different locations may also offer different methods of testing. The *ELISA test* and the *EIA test* are standard antibody blood tests that are given to patients and are also used to screen the blood supply used for medial transfusions. *Rapid testing* is also a blood test conducted in a single batch, yielding results in

less than 10 minutes. *Home test kits* can be purchased that use a finger-pricking device mailed to testing centers for analysis. *Urine-based tests* and *oral tests* can also be ordered and conducted by a physician upon request. When these tests show positive results, the blood is further analyzed using the *Western blot test* for HIV confirmation.

Upon receiving a positive diagnosis of HIV, patients are encouraged to seek counseling. Through a process known as Partner Counseling and Referral Service (PCRS), most health care providers offer assistance in tracking down patients' previous partners who may have been exposed to or infected by the patient. Despite all of these available and relatively inexpensive testing methods, it is believed that at least 25% of the U.S. population who have contracted HIV are unaware of their infections.

HIV Testing in the General Population

According to the *HIV/AIDS Surveillance Report* published by the Centers for Disease Control and Prevention (CDC), 31,217 people were diagnosed with HIV in 2006. The Kaiser Family Foundation conducted the *Survey of Americans With HIV/AIDS* in 2006 and reported that 48% of United States adults have been tested for HIV at some point in their life. This same study revealed that 17% of the people tested in 2006 did not receive their test results or refused them. In response to the HIV pandemic, the CDC has proposed routine HIV screening offered in all health care settings on multiple occasions, with emphasis on universal screening of pregnant women. This screening was recommended to void any opt-out policy, making the testing mandatory for all pregnant women. The Kaiser Family Foundation reported that in 2004, four states required HIV testing of pregnant women unless they refused to be tested, and another thirteen states were required by law to offer testing.

As testing becomes less controlled (e.g., no pretest counseling and without specific written consent), human rights activists argue that compulsory testing would be an infringement of individual rights, especially when counseling and written consent are absent. Due to the controversy surrounding this prevention method, policies supporting compulsory testing include opt-out standards.

HIV Testing in Prisons

The threat of HIV is higher among incarcerated populations than other populations due to their high-risk lifestyles. According to the U.S. Bureau of Justice Statistics, the overall estimated rate of AIDS in the prison population in 2006 was .46%—more than 2½ times the rate of the general population of the United States. Florida was first in fatalities, with 26 AIDS-related deaths in 2006. The high reported rates of prison rape pose one of the greatest risks to the spread of the virus. Measures have been taken to help hinder the spread of the virus, including condom dispensing, provision of clean injecting equipment, and methadone maintenance treatment. Each of these measures is controversial. For example, sex in prison is generally against prison rules, so it seems contradictory for the prison administration to provide condoms for illicit activity. Furthermore, these methods have not proven to have great success, and some state legislators have consequently urged heightened measures of precaution. In 2007, the Texas attorney general ruled that the Texas Board of Criminal Justice can now mandate HIV testing among new inmates upon prison entry. Advocates for compulsory HIV testing of prison inmates assert that the HIV-positive inmates would receive proper care, and that more accurate data on the spread of the disease could help researchers estimate the population being infected in prison.

Future Prevention

Compulsory HIV testing is a preventive measure being explored to help bring an end to the pandemic caused by HIV. One of the greatest methods used to capture public awareness has been celebrity endorsement. CNN reported in 2006 that former president Bill Clinton was lending support to compulsory HIV testing of people in high-risk areas of infection. The Clinton Foundation has worked to lower the costs of instant tests for HIV and for antiretroviral drugs. As Clinton said, "This is a public health problem; it's not about rich and poor. AIDS affects the social stability of a country and it is inconceivable that you can drastically lower rates of infection with testing."

Human rights activists fear the stigmata and discrimination brought about by the AIDS culture, despite the existence of antidiscrimination statutes.

Discrimination and ostracism may be particularly severe in closed societies such as prisons and jails. With an estimated 40,000 people diagnosed with new infections each year in the United States, the risk of infection is great for many people, and especially for those who become incarcerated.

Mark M. Lanier and Courtney Juergens

See also Rape; Rape, Prison; Rape Law Reform

Further Readings

Centers for Disease Control and Prevention. (2008). *HIV/AIDS Surveillance Report, 2006* (Vol. 18, pp. 11–13). Retrieved from http://www.cdc.gov/hiv/topics/surveillance/resources/reports

de Boer, B. (2008). *HIV and AIDS in America.* Retrieved April 17, 2008, from http://www.avert.org/hiv-testing-usa.htm

Frieden, T. R., Das-Douglas, M., Kellerman, S. E., & Henning, K. J. (2005). Applying public health principles to the HIV epidemic. *New England Journal of Medicine, 353*(22), 2397–2401.

Kaiser Family Foundation. (2006). *The public's experiences with and attitudes about HIV testing.* Retrieved May 19, 2008, from http://www.kff.org/hivaids/index.cfm

Maruschak, L. M. (2008). *HIV in prisons, 2006.* Retrieved April 24, 2008, from http://www.ojp.usdoj.gov/bjs/pub/html/hivp/2006/hivp06.htm

Spooner, M. H. (2003, March 4). HIV testing now compulsory for new NHS staff. *Canadian Medical Association Journal.* Retrieved April 17, 2008, from http://www.cmaj.ca/cgi/content/full/168/5/600-a

Wilkinson, P. (2006, March 29). *Clinton supports wider AIDS testing.* Retrieved April 17, 2008, from http://www.cnn.com/2006/HEALTH/conditions/03/28/clinton.aids/index.html

CONFLICT TACTICS SCALE (CTS/CTS2)

The Conflict Tactics Scales (CTS) and Revised Conflict Tactics Scales (CTS2) are quantitative measures that were developed to study violence and conflict between family members. The CTS was an important research development because it was the first quantitative scale developed and used for measuring violence against intimates.

Development

The CTS was developed throughout the 1970s by sociologist Murray A. Straus and his colleagues at the University of New Hampshire (UNH). Richard J. Gelles was an important early collaborator. Straus and Gelles had done qualitative research on family violence prior to developing the CTS, and this informed the development of the quantitative measures for use in large, statistically representative samples. The use of large representative samples to study violence within the family was an innovation in the social sciences at that time. Earlier research had overwhelmingly utilized smaller nonrepresentative clinical, shelter, or criminal samples.

Straus and Gelles were interested in measuring the prevalence and incidence of family violence, which they hypothesized was more pervasive than commonly believed; was triggered by dynamics inherent in the family but exacerbated by other stresses; and was engendered by interpersonal interaction within relationships. This research orientation is frequently referred to as the family violence or family conflict approach.

The CTS was used in the 1970s in the first federally funded representative sample study of family violence in the United States. Since then, the full CTS, CTS2, and their subscales have been widely used in research in the United States and many other countries. The CTS is the most widely used tool in large representative samples of violence within the family or against intimates. The CTS owes its influence in part to the early federal funding for research on violence within families that supported its development and continues to support its application today. According to the Department of Health and Human Services' Computer Retrieval of Information on Scientific Projects database, since 1975, Straus's Family Research Laboratory at UNH has continuously received National Institutes of Health (NIH) National Research Service Award Institutional Research Training Grants (T32 grants) to support graduate students and postdoctoral fellows. No other scholar of, or research approach to, violence against intimates or family members has received such consistent funding from the United States government.

Variations

In addition to the CTS and CTS2, there is the Conflict Tactics Scales: Parent-Child Version, which is used for quantifying conflict tactics used by parents and children. That tool includes scales for the following: nonviolent discipline, psychological aggression, physical assault, weekly discipline, neglect, and sexual abuse. This entry focuses on the CTS and CTS2, although some of its content may apply to other versions of the scales.

Specifications

The CTS measures violence by counting conflict tactics. Conflict tactics, as conceptualized by the authors of the CTS, are methods of managing or responding to conflicts or anger between family members or intimate partners. The CTS is theoretically rooted in conflict theory, which sees conflict as inevitable because people have differing personal interests and agendas. Because conflict theory sees conflict as engendered by the interaction of two people, the CTS is designed to count tactics used by both parties. However, both parties are not surveyed. Instead, the questions are asked in pairs, with twinned items asking about conflict tactics the respondent has used and tactics a partner has used against him or her. This method of assessing partners' behavior is practical because it increases the safety of respondents, cuts down on research costs, and facilitates CTS administration in other ways—such as saving time and allowing greater response rates. The standard time frame covered by the CTS is the previous year, but the authors present other time limits as possibilities, including a lifetime, the past 6 months, and since the beginning of a program or intervention.

The original CTS included 38 multiple choice questions representing 19 conflict tactics divided into three categories: reasoning, verbal aggression, and violence. The CTS measured nine violence tactics, six verbal aggression tactics, and three reasoning tactics as well as the item "cried," which was not intended to be scored. The CTS may be self-administered as a written survey or administered in an interview format facilitated by research staff or clinicians. Although the results can be scored by the presence or absence of each tactic, the standard scoring provides an 8-point scale that divides responses by frequency, ranging from never to more than 20 times. The conflict tactics within each category are designated as either more severe or less severe based on the authors' presumptions about the harmfulness of the tactic.

The revised CTS, or CTS2, was developed by Straus, Sherry L. Hamby, Susan Boney-McCoy, and David B. Sugarman. The CTS2 is comprised of 78 questions, including 39 tactics in twinned pairs addressing victimization and perpetration. The items include revised versions of the original scales, slightly adjusted and organized into the categories renamed negotiation, psychological aggression, and physical assault. The CTS2 includes 6 items about negotiation, 8 items about psychological aggression, and 12 items about physical assault. CTS2 also added two new scales. Six new items are about injury and seven are about sexual coercion. Like the original CTS, scoring is based on eight response options divided by frequency and the items are designated as more severe or less severe. The estimated time to administer the full CTS2 is 10 to 15 minutes. When shortening the CTS2 to save time, Straus recommends omitting the injury and sexual assault scales rather than asking only about victimization or perpetration. Omitting these scales leaves the original scales, which Straus refers to as the core scales, on negotiation, psychological aggression, and physical assault. Alternatively, a shortened version of the CTS2 is available which includes all the scales but fewer items on each. The short version can be administered in 3 minutes. Straus cautions that using shortened versions results in reporting decreased by about half.

Context

Knowledge of the context in which the CTS is used is important to understanding its significance. Family studies research using the CTS is frequently contrasted with what is loosely termed feminist research, which places relatively more emphasis on power relations, gender, and social inequality. Both family conflict and feminist approaches acknowledge that gender differences persist. However, there are significant differences between these research, theoretical, and epistemological orientations. While Straus and his colleagues acknowledge gendered inequalities between women and men in places, critics note that these inequalities are not considered at

measurement nor, increasingly, in the conclusions drawn by family studies scholars using the CTS. Family studies research is also contrasted with crime research, which consistently finds marked sex differences between women's and men's violence perpetration and victimization and much lower rates of violence. Crime surveys such as National Crime Victimization Survey and the National Violence Against Women Survey are the other major representative quantitative studies on violence against intimates. These and other crime studies have been extensively assessed elsewhere, but are generally regarded as limited by their emphasis on the most severe forms of violence. These are the three major approaches to research on violence between intimates. All of these approaches to the study of human violence find greater harm to women from male intimates than the reverse. All scholars of violence state that their goal is the elimination or reduction of violence.

Critiques

The CTS and CTS2 have been widely criticized as well as widely utilized. Straus has repeatedly noted the limitations of the CTS as covering only a limited set of acts; using unrealistic response categories; underreporting; covering only the current intact relationship; and not linking injuries directly to assaults. He has repeatedly rejected several other critiques of the CTS as ideological or erroneous. Critics have noted that unlike the many other tools and methods for measuring and studying violence, the CTS consistently finds equivalent rates of violence for women and men. Straus and his colleagues claim the consistent findings of the CTS are due to the superiority of the tool and their theoretical approach. However, critics argue that results that are so divergent from shelter, medical, crime, homicide, and other research—including quantitative research with items on the context, meaning, and motives of violence, as well as the qualitative literature—must indicate a serious measurement problem. While no one advises against using the CTS items, many scholars advise that in order for the CTS to yield meaningful or comprehensible results, other items must be used alongside it.

Critiques of the CTS cluster around issues with reporting, sampling, context, meaning, motive, and outcomes of violence. While Straus has commented on underreporting, and has remarked that men underreport their violence relative to women, he addresses this problem by asking women about women and men's behavior. However, critics contend that this does not solve the problem, because women and men underreport men's violence and overreport women's violence, especially in the intact couples included in CTS-based studies. Sampling issues include the failure of large random survey studies to capture the kind of violence that most people think of when they hear the terms *domestic violence, spouse abuse, wife beating,* and *intimate partner violence.* Scholars have noted the disparities in the average number of violent incidents reported by CTS studies using large random samples versus shelter samples. Context concerns include the failure of the CTS to include information about the context of the conflict tactics in a particular relationship as well as in the larger cultural context in which dramatic differences between men's and women's violence are extensively documented. The historical context of the legitimization of men's proprietary violence against spouses and children is not captured by the CTS. The cultural context in which women and men normalize and legitimate men's violence against women is also omitted. Meaning concerns stem from other research that finds that credible threats of violence are just as effective as individual violent acts at controlling a partner, as well as research that documents that conflict tactics have very different meanings for women and men. Concerns about motives include the failure of the CTS to discern between offensive and defensive violence. Such a distinction is a courtesy that scholars extend to victims of all other forms of violence, and many argue that it is essential to meaningful understanding of what has transpired. Finally, many scholars argue that the outcomes of violence matter in terms of human experience, well-being, and survival. Outcomes are especially important given scarce resources allocated to prevention, education, and services. The CTS can yield important and meaningful results with the addition of measures of context, meaning, and outcomes.

Molly Dragiewicz

See also Abuse, Spouse; Calculating Extent of Victimization: Incidence, Prevalence, and Rates; Domestic Violence; Family and Domestic Violence, Theories of; Family Violence; Intimate Partner Violence

Further Readings

Bograd, M. (1984). Family systems approaches to wife battering: A feminist critique. *American Journal of Orthopsychiatry, 54*(4), 558–568.

DeKeseredy, W. S. (2000). Current controversies on defining nonlethal violence against women in intimate heterosexual relationships: Empirical implications. *Violence Against Women, 6,* 728–746.

DeKeseredy, W. S., & Schwartz, M. (1998). *Measuring the extent of woman abuse in intimate heterosexual relationships: A critique of the Conflict Tactics Scales.* Retrieved from http://new.vawnet.org/Assoc_Files_VAWnet/AR_ctscrit.pdf

Desai, S., & Saltzman, L. E. (2001). Measurement issues for violence against women. In C. M. Renzetti, J. L. Edleson, & R. K. Bergen (Eds.), *Sourcebook on violence against women* (pp. 35–52). Thousand Oaks, CA: Sage.

Dobash, R. P., Dobash, R. E., Wilson, M., & Daly, M. (1992). The myth of sexual symmetry in marital violence. *Social Problems, 39,* 71–91.

Kimmel, M. S. (2002). Gender symmetry. *Violence Against Women, 8*(11), 1332–1363.

Straus, M. A. (1979). Measuring family conflict and violence: The Conflict Tactics (CT) Scales. *Journal of Marriage and Family, 4,* 75–88.

Straus, M. A., Gelles, R. J., & Steinmetz, S. K. (1980). *Behind closed doors: violence in the American family.* Garden City, NY: Doubleday.

Straus, M. A., Hamby, S. L., Boney-McCoy, S., & Sugarman, D. B. (1996). The revised Conflict Tactics Scales (CTS2). *Journal of Family Issues, 17,* 283–316.

White, J. W., Smith, P. H., Koss, M. P., & Figueredo, A. J. (2000). Intimate partner aggression: What have we learned? Comment on Archer (2000). *Psychological Bulletin, 126*(5), 690–696.

CONJUNCTION OF CRIMINAL OPPORTUNITY THEORY

The conjunction of criminal opportunity (CCO) theory is a framework designed to draw together the major, immediate causes of criminal events, and in parallel, the major "families" of intervention principles deployable to block, weaken, or divert those causes, thereby preventing crime. It serves theoretical, academic purposes; the development and management of practice knowledge; and practitioner education. This entry first explains the origins of the CCO framework and describes it, then examines alternatives to it, the varieties of crime covered by the theory, and future developments as CCO continues to evolve.

Origins

In the 1990s an attempt was made to classify several thousand crime prevention projects implemented through the U.K.'s Safer Cities Programme. One purpose was to put "like with like" when evaluating project impacts. The diversity of those projects was challenging. They covered a range of institutional settings and preventive methods, and no single existing framework could handle their complexity or breadth. Likewise, even using detailed entries from the program's management information system, determining exactly what the individual projects were endeavoring to do proved difficult. There was no universal, rigorous, and consistent schema or language that could be used to describe the preventive interventions—and no systematic map of preventive possibilities. Terminology for causation and prevention was confused, unclear, and overlapping, with spurious contrasts such as "situational versus social." This not only inhibited retrieval and replication of success stories, it also constrained the realization and monitoring of each original project as it unfolded.

Exacerbating the confusion was the fragmentation of the field of crime prevention into situational and offender-oriented territories, with their own languages and theories, as well as into institutional settings such as "enforcement and judicial-based" and "civil" prevention (i.e., changes made in everyday life, such as the ethos of schools or the layout of parks). This generated spurious contrasts such as "prevention versus deterrence." Even within situational prevention, the main theories were (and remain) poorly integrated, so each novice practitioner must assemble them afresh.

Therefore, it was decided to design a new framework: one that was inclusive of types and theories of crime, and types and contexts of prevention, and

based on a suite of clear and consistent definitions. The focus was to be on the immediate, or proximal, causes of criminal events, whether originating in offenders or crime situations. Distal, or remote, causes (e.g., children's early upbringing, aspects of social structure such as inequality, or market forces such as those that made copper piping expensive and therefore worth stealing) were important. But they were too varied and complex, and often too hard to measure and define, to supply the basis of a theoretical and conceptual framework.

Contemporaneously, Nick Tilley was introducing a scientific realist perspective to the crime prevention domain. This emphasized the importance of understanding, and manipulating, the causal mechanisms that underlie preventive interventions. According to this perspective, the key question is not simply what works, but what works in what context and how—using what causal mechanisms. So, closed-circuit television in car parks might work simply by scaring offenders off, or by facilitating detection and arrest. Only the second mechanism is potentially durable (the offenders soon ignore the cameras if nobody catches them), so it is important for practitioners to know which is operating. They must also tune the intervention to their context, because mechanisms are quite delicate, in that only the right combination of circumstances triggers them. This means that understanding and reproducing mechanisms is vital for replication of "success story" projects. In effect, the CCO framework offers a universal mechanism map of the causal preconditions that must come together for a crime to occur. The mechanism perspective has enabled CCO theory to center on analytic causal and contextual factors rather than simply being a superficial listing of causes and a "natural history" of preventive methods.

The framework was assembled from familiar theories of crime causation, including rational choice theory, crime pattern theory, and routine activities theory. The last was in effect from the start, with the questions posed including "*How* is the target suitable?" and "*Why* is the offender likely?" Since these "situational" theories intentionally contained only minimalist reference to offenders, psychological and interpersonal aspects of criminals were taken from theoretical writings such as those of David Farrington. Seeking an exhaustive map of causes led to identification and filling of gaps, out of which came such concepts as "crime promoters" and "offender resources."

From these beginnings, what became the CCO framework evolved iteratively while it was applied to classify descriptions of several thousand Safer Cities projects, and progressively extended or refined as new kinds of cause or intervention were encountered. Eventually the framework stabilized at 11 generic causes and equivalent intervention principles, as described below. Moreover, what began as classification produced a framework with much wider potential, as interest was growing in the education and training of a new cadre of crime prevention and community safety practitioners in the police and beyond, and in equipping them with tools for a demanding job. To reflect this wider applicability, the original 1998 proximal circumstances framework was rebranded the "conjunction of criminal opportunity" theory. By 2003, the development of the CCO theory within this practitioner and program delivery context had led to an accretion of "preventive process" elements that were eventually "hived off" to a separate (and equally deliberately designed) process model, the 5Is framework, which is equivalent to SARA of problem-oriented policing but contains more detail.

Definition

CCO theory, like routine activities theory, is an ecological model of the immediate causes of criminal events centering on human agents acting out particular roles in a particular setting.

Agents

The *offender* is the one agent without whom a crime by definition cannot occur. Offenders are covered in more detail below. The other agents about to be described, and the physical setting, are the situation *for the offender*. These agents can play one of two roles in the causation of crime.

Crime preventers are people who make criminal events less likely by their mere presence or actions, such as surveillance of strangers, supervision and (more distally) socialization of their children, or using window locks. Preventer roles can be undertaken in various institutional or noninstitutional settings; examples include police patrols, vigilant employees, neighbors chastising neighbor's children,

or "good citizens" reporting hazards. Preventers can act before the criminal event (securing their car), during it (repelling assailants), or afterward. Regarding the last, the prevention will strictly speaking not affect the current crime, but it may involve action to fix a vulnerability before the next offense, arrest of the current offender, and perhaps deterring other offenders. However, offenders' *anticipation* of such responses to their crimes also may serve to prevent the current instance.

Crime promoters are people who, by contrast, play roles that actively increase the risk of criminal events, with varying degrees of intentionality and responsibility. They include someone accidentally provoking the (potential) offender; a "friend" encouraging the offender to avenge an insult; a fence buying stolen goods or supplying weapons; or simply someone leaving his or her laptop visible when parking the car. The aim of much prevention is to change the careless promoter into the careful preventer.

Note that *victims* do not directly feature here, although unsuccessful preventers may become victims. Victims are not only enacting active *roles* in which they seek to limit, repair, and recover from the harms of the criminal event (and participate in investigatory and justice processes), but may also be the *targets* of violent crime.

Entities

Entities are the "things" in crime situations. The *target* of crime may be a person or object that is inherently criminogenic, that is, vulnerable, valuable, or provocative. (The person as target is considered in passive terms; active human provocation is covered under the promoter role.)

The target may be located in a *target enclosure* such as a safe, locked rooms, or gated compound. Enclosures are characterized by structural features such as periphery, boundary fence, access doors/gates, and interior. Each of these may have criminogenic properties (or criminocclusive ones—reducing the probability of crime).

Enclosures are situated in turn in a *wider environment*. This could be a shopping mall, park, transport interchange, or housing estate. The environment (whether wide or the interior environment of an enclosure) can be characterized by two distinct sets of properties. The *instrumental* environment relates to the goals of offender and preventer. The extent to which the physical layout (like sightlines and barriers), lighting, and so on affect the balance of tactical advantage between, for example, stealth and surveillance, ambush and awareness, pursuit and escape, respectively favoring one or other party. The *motivating* environment covers how many attractive targets the environment contains. As noted by Richard Wortley in his description of situational "precipitators," the environment may also supply physical conditions that directly prompt, pressure, or provoke aggressive actions (such as "collision points" at busy commuter stations), or that routinely contain crime promoters such as a ready audience for youth racing stolen cars, who may prompt, pressure, or permit the action.

The Offender

As noted, CCO theory adds greater psychological depth to the offender concept than do situational approaches, but it does so in as generic a way as possible rather than by adhering to specific psychological theories.

The offender side of crime causation starts with *predisposition to offend*—aggressive tendencies, antisocial attitudes, and so on which comprise a permanent potential for criminal behavior that is present, but not necessarily expressed, in all situations the (potential) offender encounters.

The next element is *resources to avoid offending*, which include both inhibitory capacities such as self-control and skills to make an honest living (and hence to make honest choices when confronted with tempting criminal opportunities).

Remaining offender elements move gradually away from omnipresent potential toward factors activated in particular situations. *Readiness to offend* comprises emotional or motivational states induced by current life circumstances (like unemployment, poor housing, and/or long-standing conflict) or recent experiences (like a stressful commuter journey, intoxication, or the desperate need for money for a drug fix).

Resources for offending empower offenders to tackle the risks and exploit the possibilities for instrumental crime and to realize expressive crimes such as revenge attacks. They range from facilitators like tools or weapons to skills and predispositions such as courage and strength, perpetrator techniques, knowledge of opportunities, and social

contacts accessing trusted resources as offered by fences or co-offenders. Offenders may also be aided by their ability to neutralize guilt or psych themselves up for an attack. Notably, whereas in much of the situational prevention literature, "opportunity" is considered a situational/environmental concept, the notion of resources makes it an ecological one. For example, an open window several floors up is only an opportunity to someone with strength, agility, courage, and maybe a ladder.

Decision to commit offense captures the offender's immediate perception and anticipation of and response to the "rational choice" agenda of risk, effort, and reward, as well as reaction to situational prompts and provocations. The immediate decision (with familiar qualifications on rationality) will be influenced by the offender's predisposition, resources to avoid and commit offenses, and readiness. Habits and more strategic career choices (to be a burglar, to be a criminal, and so forth) may also come into play and be influenced in turn by outcomes of individual attempts. *Perceived* risks, effort, and the like operate parallel causal mechanisms to their objective counterparts: The robust *appearance* of a bus shelter may discourage vandalism, or its robust *construction* physically resist attack.

Finally, *presence of offender in situation* is of course necessary, although that presence could be a telepresence, as in obscene phone calls, or "sending the boys 'round."

Two Perspectives on the Offender

CCO theory incorporates two perspectives on the offender. On the one hand, offenders are seen as *agents*, with goals, decisions, and actions intended to realize them. On the other, they are themselves as much *caused* as causing, as a result of their early experiences and current experiences, as well as the operation of their cognitive processes, such as perception, motivation, and emotion. Recent formulations of CCO theory therefore refer to offenders as *caused agents*; likewise with preventers and promoters. CCO causes are illustrated in Figure 1.

Dynamics

CCO theory is a static, analytic picture of elements with the immediate potential to cause criminal

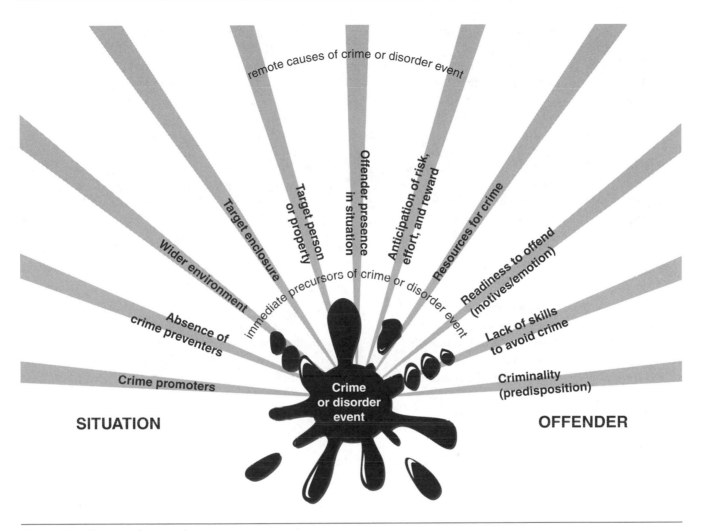

Figure I   Causes of criminal events

Source: Copyright © Paul John Ekblom.

events. This is useful for many purposes, but it is also necessary, when focusing on causal mechanisms, to consider the dynamic, interactive nature of the conjunction. At one level this relates to offenders perceiving, being provoked perhaps, choosing, reacting and acting, applying skills and capacities to exploit the opportunity and overcome the risks of crime; to the preventers and promoters making equivalent contributions; and to the several players anticipating and adapting to one another's perceived actions. At another level, dynamics covers the processes whereby the elements of the conjunction come together: for example, the lifestyle routines of the players, market processes, people-flows on foot or in public transportation

(the "nodes and paths" of pattern theory)—all of which may count as crime generators. Of course, some offenders deliberately seek favorable places (defined as crime attractors); they may even actively plan to bring the elements of the conjunction together, as in a "professional" robbery or fraud.

Prevention

Crime prevention is about intervening in the causes of criminal events to reduce their probability of occurrence and any ensuing harm. The map of causes that is the CCO theory can therefore be overlaid by an equivalent map of intervention principles aimed at blocking, weakening, or diverting those causes. This relationship is shown in brief in Table 1, and illustrated in Figure 2.

CCO theory can thus be used to articulate interventions in some theoretical depth. A practical intervention *method* may act via more than one mechanism—for example, creating an enclosure around an industrial estate may physically block the offender, deter through perceived risk, and aid preventers, who now only have to guard the access point, not the entire perimeter. The CCO approach encourages precision; for example, target hardening often relates to hardening the target enclosure, such as by making a house resistant to burglary.

Alternatives

A few alternative integrating theoretical frameworks exist within crime and crime prevention. The most familiar is probably the minimalist crime triangle—victim/target, location, offender—that originated within the problem-oriented policing movement. This has been extended in recent years to allow crime preventer roles to influence each node; thus targets have guardians, locations have place managers, and offenders have handlers.

The "general theory of crime" of Michael Gottfredson and Travis Hirschi combines propensity and opportunity in an equally minimalist way. A more complex newcomer is the situational action theory of P.-O. Wikström. This focuses on causal mechanisms, and offenders as agents perceiving and acting in particular ecological settings, but in addition explains how the environment influences the development of people's crime propensities.

Varieties

CCO theory has been extended to cover various specific kinds of crime and criminal context. These include complex organized crime, cybercrime (CCO can be rewritten in cyberspace terms where the target is information, the enclosure is firewalled

Table 1   Basic causes and intervention principles

Immediate Causes of Criminal Event	Possible Interventions in Cause
Predisposition to offend	Reducing criminality through developmental/remedial intervention
Lack of resources to avoid crime	Supplying cognitive, social, work skills to avoid crime
Readiness to offend	Reducing this by aiding in control of disinhibitors (e.g., alcohol or stressors and provocations), legitimate satisfaction of psychological and social needs
Resources for committing crime	Restricting resources—tools, weapons, knowledge
Decision to commit offense	Deterrence (influencing perceived risk) and discouragement (influencing perceived effort in relation to reward)
Offender presence in situation	Excluding offenders from crime situation
Target property or person	Reducing target vulnerability, attraction, provocativeness
Target enclosure	Perimeter/access security
Wider environment	Environmental design and management to reduce motivating and instrumental properties
Crime preventers	Boosting preventers' presence, competence, motivation, responsibility
Crime promoters	Discouraging and deterring promoters, converting them to preventers

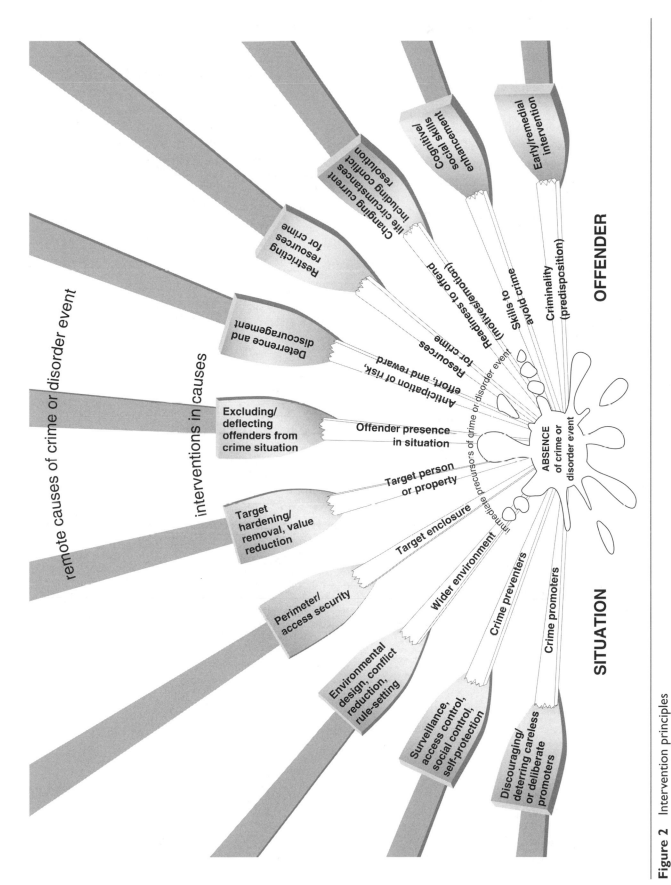

Figure 2 Intervention principles

Source: Copyright © Paul John Ekblom.

computer system, and so on), drug dealing, and terrorism.

Future Developments

Current work on the CCO framework centers on developing its dynamic aspect principally through use of scripts and "script clashes" (surveillance versus stealth, pursuit versus escape, etc.) and adapting the theory for use by designers of products and places. Exploration of its use as a basis for computerized crime simulation and crime impact assessment is also under way.

CCO is undoubtedly more complex than individual equivalents such as the crime triangle, although it offers compensatory simplification because it integrates all major theories of crime and its prevention in a single 11-factor framework. The key issues are whether that greater complexity adds greater value to practice and theory, and whether it is, or can be made, sufficiently user-friendly for practitioners to be prepared to use it.

Paul John Ekblom

See also Crime Pattern Theory; Offender-Based Programs; Problem-Oriented Policing; Rational Choice Theory; Routine Activities Theory; Safer Cities Program; Situational Action Theory; Situational Crime Prevention

Further Readings

Ekblom, P. (2000). The conjunction of criminal opportunity—a tool for clear, "joined-up" thinking about community safety and crime reduction. In S. Ballintyne, K. Pease, & V. McLaren (Eds.), *Secure foundations: Key issues in crime prevention, crime reduction and community safety*. London: Institute for Public Policy Research.

Ekblom, P. (2002). From the source to the mainstream is uphill: The challenge of transferring knowledge of crime prevention through replication, innovation and anticipation. In N. Tilley (Ed.), *Analysis for crime prevention* (pp. 131–203). Monsey, NY: Criminal Justice Press; Cullompton, UK: Willan.

Ekblom, P. (2003). Organised crime and the conjunction of criminal opportunity framework. In A. Edwards & P. Gill (Eds.), *Transnational organised crime: Perspectives on global security* (pp. 241–263). London: Routledge.

Ekblom, P. (2005). How to police the future: Scanning for scientific and technological innovations which generate potential threats and opportunities in crime, policing and crime reduction. In M. Smith & N. Tilley (Eds.), *Crime science: New approaches to preventing and detecting crime*. Cullompton, UK: Willan.

Ekblom, P., & Tilley, N. (2000). Going equipped: Criminology, situational crime prevention and the resourceful offender. *British Journal of Criminology, 40,* 376–398.

Roach, J., Ekblom, P., & Flynn, R. (2005). The conjunction of terrorist opportunity: A framework for diagnosing and preventing acts of terrorism. *Security Journal, 18*(3), 7–25.

Web Sites

Design Against Crime Research Centre: http://www .designagainstcrime.com

CONTEXTUAL EFFECTS ON VICTIMIZATION

Criminal victimization is a widespread social problem that has long been the subject of public interest and scholarly work. Discussions concerning victimization typically focus on the likelihood of being victimized. Specifically, what increases the odds that an individual will be the victim of a crime? While research shows there are certain characteristics of individuals (i.e., age, gender) that increase their chances of being victimized, it also shows that victimization is more likely to occur in certain types of neighborhoods. It is these social and physical neighborhood characteristics or contextual effects on victimization that are the focus of this entry.

Neighborhoods

A neighborhood can be simply defined as a physical area where individuals reside. However, it can be defined by more than just its physical boundaries, as it is also a community consisting of friendships, social networks, and collective life. This is referred to as a systemic approach to neighborhood organization. The belief is that both physical space and community dynamics significantly contribute to identifying and labeling neighborhoods. If a neighborhood is a sociophysical area, then both social and physical characteristics of the neighborhood influence its environment.

Adopting the sociophysical definition of a neighborhood is important in understanding how certain neighborhood characteristics affect the neighborhood environment, and subsequently, victimization. Neighborhoods that are comprised of both formal and informal social networks are more likely than other neighborhoods to possess a sense of community. The belief is that residents of a community are going to share ideas of acceptable social behavior and general community standards. One such standard is to live in a safe, crime-free neighborhood.

The expectation is that residents who live in a neighborhood with a strong sense of community are able to act collectively and exercise informal social control, which provides them with a mechanism by which they can regulate the neighborhood environment. They are able to control the activities that occur in the area and the physical appearance of the neighborhood. It is important to recognize that both social and physical aspects of a neighborhood affect its environment, and it is the environment of a neighborhood that arguably influences victimization.

Social Environment of Neighborhoods

Researchers have argued that the social environment of a neighborhood is an important factor in victimization because crime is a result of a neighborhood being unable to regulate itself. This social environment is largely determined by relationships—relationships among residents and relationships between the residents and local institutions. These are the informal and formal networks that enable residents to act collectively and exercise informal social control. Neighborhoods that lack these networks are considered socially disorganized.

Socially disorganized neighborhoods often lack a sense of community, are comprised of weak institutions, have residents who do not know their neighbors, and include residents who do not know how or want to act collectively to solve problems. Socially disorganized neighborhoods are often characterized by ethnic heterogeneity, population turnover, lack of

social integration, and poverty. It is these four social characteristics of a neighborhood that have a significant influence on its environment.

Ethnic Heterogeneity

Ethnic heterogeneity refers to the ethnic composition of residents in a neighborhood. The degree of ethnic heterogeneity is important to consider, as it is argued that heterogeneous neighborhoods have higher victimization than do homogeneous neighborhoods. Because increased heterogeneity may lead to isolated groups within the neighborhood, heterogeneity potentially weakens the ability of a neighborhood to act collectively. In addition, ethnically heterogeneous neighborhoods may face language barriers and moral and value differences. These differences not only increase the likelihood of isolated groups of residents, but also hinder the ability to solve problems across ethnicities. The multiplicity of ethnicities leads to groups being unable or unwilling to identify common goals and rules for the neighborhood; therefore, neighborhoods with more heterogeneity are also more likely to have more victimization.

Population Turnover

Population turnover is also referred to as residential mobility. The average number of years residents live in the neighborhood is important, as over time, residents of a neighborhood are more likely to build friendships, foster ties to local organizations, and develop a strong sense of community. Essentially, residents become invested in their neighborhood over the years. On the contrary, neighborhoods that are characterized by high population turnover are comprised of residents who do not necessarily have an interest in their neighbors or the local community. Transient populations are typically unwilling and uninterested in investing time or energy in a neighborhood that they do not intend to inhabit for very long. Thus, neighborhoods with high population turnover are less likely to have the informal and formal networks that allow residents to exercise informal social control in the area in an attempt to minimize criminal activity. Increased residential mobility, then, affects the social environment of a neighborhood in such a way that risk of victimization increases.

Neighborhood Integration

Neighborhood integration (cohesion) is a social characteristic of a neighborhood that focuses on the social interaction of neighbors and the involvement of residents in the local community. Integration can refer to interactions such as having dinner with the neighbors or simply agreeing to watch a neighbor's house while he or she is away. These types of interactions among neighborhood residents serve as social ties to the neighborhood and the local community; they also establish a foundation of communication. If residents are communicating or at least open to communicating, then they are in a position conducive to expressing and upholding community-oriented goals and norms. Neighborhood integration or even just an increase in social ties within a neighborhood contributes to the development of informal and formal networks within the neighborhood, and therefore, increases the likelihood of residents banding together in an attempt to control the neighborhood's environment.

Poverty

Poverty level can be assessed as a socioeconomic measure of a neighborhood's status. Specifically, poverty level is actually a household classification that is based on annual income. In 2008, the Department of Health and Human Services declared that a family of four whose household income is less than $21,400 is classified as living below poverty level. Poverty affects neighborhood environments, in that neighborhoods that are characterized as impoverished are typically socially disorganized and exhibit visible signs of physical deterioration. Impoverished neighborhoods, then, arguably lack the basic mechanisms necessary for exercising informal social control—extensive formal and informal networks. In addition, these neighborhoods lack the visible signs of community standards because physical deterioration is evident and seemingly acceptable or tolerated by the residents. In sum, neighborhoods that are considered to be impoverished are often seen as lacking a general sense of community.

It should be noted that assessment of poverty level is arguably considered an overarching or umbrella measure that actually captures numerous other social characteristics of neighborhood life.

Physical Environment of Neighborhoods

Studying the physical characteristics of a neighborhood is important when considering its environment. The physical appearance of neighborhood buildings and streets and the public social activity evident in that space contribute to public perceptions of the neighborhood. Characteristics such as litter on the streets or loud, boisterous teenagers are often considered signs of physical and social deterioration of the community. These visible signs of deterioration are referred to as disorder or neighborhood incivility.

Incivility in a neighborhood indirectly affects victimization in that it influences both residents' and outsiders' attitudes toward the neighborhood. How the neighborhood is perceived is important because visible signs of deterioration, physical or social, are often equated to a breakdown of community standards on acceptable behavior. The neighborhood could be viewed as being out of control. Neighborhood incivility may also lead to diminished neighborhood cohesion as residents lose a sense of efficacy. If residents assume a direct relationship between physical and social deterioration and an increase in victimization, then they are less likely to feel empowered to act collectively.

Physical Disorder

Physical signs of disorder include litter, abandoned buildings, vandalism, graffiti, and poor street lighting. People often associate these physical characteristics in a neighborhood with the occurrence of crime. Littering and vandalism are in fact classified as misdemeanor crimes, and therefore, evidence of these substantiates that the neighborhood has been unable to regulate even the most minor criminal activity. If neighborhood residents are unable to collectively act to reduce or stop vandalism and littering, then they are also unlikely to act collectively to deter more serious crimes.

Social Disorder

Social signs of disorder include fighting, visible drug use, and unsupervised teenagers. Fighting and visible signs of drug use are viewed as signs of social deterioration, in that individuals who engage in these activities do not respect social norms. Both of these activities can also be classified as criminal.

The argument follows that individuals who engage in this type of behavior do not observe general social norms of acceptable behavior, and therefore, may be more likely to engage in additional, more serious forms of criminal activity.

The argument that unsupervised teenagers are a sign of social deterioration is similar. Statistics support the commonly held belief that youth are more likely than adults to engage in delinquent behavior. When supervision is lacking, teenagers are provided with an opportunity to engage in criminal or delinquent behavior. And unsupervised teenagers are associated with increased victimization.

Research Findings

Numerous studies have been conducted in an attempt to identify contextual effects on victimization. Many of these studies include both disorganization and disorder measures. These studies include different combinations of variables, depending upon the theoretical premise of the study, and the variables are not always measured or defined identically across studies. The findings generally indicate that neighborhood environments do affect victimization.

When generalizing discussion on the empirical support for contextual effects on victimization, it is important to remember that variables may be defined and measured differently across studies. One important example is disorder. Many studies find that disorder is a strong predictor of victimization. Disorder is an index measure, which means that it is comprised of different component variables. Thus, disorder may be defined as an index including poor street lighting, litter, vandalism, and visible drug use in one study; but in another study the disorder index may only include poor street lighting, litter, and vandalism.

Overall, there is empirical support for evaluating contextual effects on victimization. When what affects the chances of being victimized is assessed, individual characteristics are often the first consideration. Sociological theory and empirical research, however, suggest that individual-level characteristics alone do not fully explain victimization. Neighborhood environments do, in fact, affect victimization. Regardless of the biological makeup of individuals, contextual factors are going to influence victimization because individuals are social beings. Thus it is critical to consider the environment in which they live.

Kristina J. Hawkins

See also Correlates of Victimization; Fear of Crime, Individual- and Community-Level Effects; Incivilities/ Social Disorder; Social Control and Self-Control Theory; Victimization, Theories of

Further Readings

Berry, B., & Kasarda, J. (1977). *Contemporary urban ecology*. New York: Macmillan.

Bursik, R. J., & Grasmick, H. G. (1993). *Neighborhoods and crime: The dimensions of effective community control*. New York: Lexington Books.

Hipp, J. R. (2007). Block, tract and levels of aggregation: neighborhood structure and crime and disorder as a case in point. *American Sociological Review, 72*(5), 659–680.

Miethe, T., & McDowall, D. (1993). Contextual effects in models of criminal victimization. *Social Forces, 71*, 741–759.

Sampson, R. J., Morenoff, J. D., & Gannon-Rowley, T. (2002). Assessing "neighborhood effects": Social processes and new directions in research. *Annual Review of Sociology, 28*, 443–478.

Shaw, C., & McKay, H. (1969). *Juvenile delinquency and urban areas* (Rev. ed.). Chicago: University of Chicago Press.

Skogan, W., & Maxfield, M. (1981). *Coping with crime: Individual and neighborhood reactions*. Beverly Hills, CA: Sage.

CO-OCCURRENCE OF VICTIMIZATION

Co-occurrence of victimization is a fairly broad term describing an individual's experience of multiple types of victimization. Although advances in research and practice in criminology largely address separate types of victimization (e.g., sexual assault, domestic violence, child abuse), there is considerable evidence that persons who experience one type of victimization are at risk for other types. Due to its association with severe psychological distress and posttraumatic stress disorder

(PTSD), co-occurrence of victimization is important to study; it is relevant for understanding all victimization experiences and for treating victims. Etiologically, it is important to recognize how and under what circumstances one type of victimization increases the likelihood of another type. Co-victimization is a consideration in treatment development, particularly when treatments targeting one type of victimization are less effective with co-victimized persons. Identifying the mechanisms underlying co-victimization can also inform prevention efforts, particularly with the goal of developing effective strategies to mitigate the risk of future victimizations.

Definitions and Explanations

Co-victimization generally is defined as multiple types of harm perpetrated by one or more outside sources. Self-harm, such as substance abuse and suicidal behaviors, frequently accompanies victimization and contributes to aversive consequences, but typically is not included in the definition of co-victimization. Childhood co-victimization, similar to childhood victimization more generally, can refer to the experiences of both boys and girls. Adulthood co-victimization, in contrast, frequently refers to some combination of women's experiences of intimate partner violence, sexual assault by a known assailant or stranger, and conventional crimes (e.g., robbery). Children who experience physical abuse may also experience neglect as well as exposure to interparental aggression. Similarly, adult female victims of sexual assault are at risk for intimate partner aggression. Co-victimization is particularly insidious when it occurs across the life span, with victimized children have a higher likelihood of being revictimized during adolescence and adulthood.

There are several theories for how one type of victimization increases the risk of other such experiences. Environmental explanations attribute co-victimization to characteristics of the perpetrator, or of the home and community contexts. Childhood co-victimization is likely if a parent perpetrates violence on the child and on the other parent. Or, there may be a contagion of violence in which one parent victimizes the other parent or older sibling who, in turn, victimizes the child. Environmental explanations also attribute co-victimization to external factors, or "third variables," such as poverty, unemployment, and homelessness, which are associated with both family and community violence. For example, a large percentage of homeless youth are abused children who then turn to high-risk behaviors (e.g., exchanging sex for money) that put them at risk for revictimization. Alternatively, intrapersonal explanations suggest ways that victimization severely compromises the ability to function adaptively and thus increase vulnerability to other victimization experiences. PTSD symptoms of dissociation and avoidance following victimization may impair judgment regarding future danger and result in additional victimization. Engaging in aggressive and delinquent behaviors subsequent to child physical abuse may increase the likelihood of revictimization through gang membership, bullying, or crime.

Rates of Co-Occurrence

Data on rates of co-occurrence are highly variable, due to widely different measurement techniques, sample characteristics, and definitions of victimization. Based on a random sample from across the United States in 1995 and 1996, the National Institute of Justice (NIJ) National Violence Against Women Survey (NVAWS) indicated that, for women first raped as minors, 18.3% were raped as adults; this rate is twice as high as the 8.7% who reported being raped as adults but not as children. Other NIJ studies suggest that experiencing multiple types of victimization in childhood or adolescence (e.g., the combination of sexual and physical abuse) is related to sexual abuse in young adulthood. In 2005, Smith Slep and O'Leary reported on patterns of co-occurring violence in representatively sampled families, and 22% of the families reported co-occurring patterns of physical aggression between the adult partners along with both parents aggressing against the child. Studies that use very broad definitions of victimization, including peer and sibling assaults, corporal punishment, witnessing of nonweapon assaults, and emotional bullying show much higher rates of co-occurring victimization.. Studies that use very broad definitions of victimization, including peer and sibling assaults, corporal punishment, witnessing of nonweapon assaults, and emotional bullying show much higher rates of co-occurring victimization.

Consequences

Research has generally shown that the greater the amount of victimization, the more the distress suffered by the victim. In studies of recurrent and co-occurring violent victimization, problems such as depression, anxiety, dissociative symptoms, health problems, underutilization of health care, and drug and alcohol abuse were worsened by increased victimization. Individuals who have experienced repeated or multiple types of violence are incrementally more likely than others to suffer psychological and physical distress and to require more time for recovery.

In children, the multiplicity of victimization types is related to greater trauma symptoms, which are sometimes more severe than the effects of multiple exposures to a single type. Children who witness domestic violence in addition to suffering physical abuse tend to suffer worse consequences than children who experience one of these alone. For adult female victims, the co-occurrence of sexual abuse, whether in the past or present, intensifies the difficulties caused by physical assault alone. Similarly, women who have been repeatedly sexually assaulted have worse mental and physical health outcomes than those who were raped once.

One concern for repeat victims is PTSD, which is often viewed as a link between co-occurring victimization and severe, adverse mental and physical health consequences. PTSD is traditionally defined as a reaction to a specific life-threatening event, so further research is needed to understand the experience of trauma in response to multiple and repetitive victimization experiences.

Treatment

Trauma-focused treatments, which are available for children and adults, offer relevant interventions for the co-occurrence of violence. These treatments typically address safety planning, psychoeducation, and coping skills for reducing stress. Nonetheless, little is known about what treatments are optimally suited to persons experiencing co-occurring victimizations, as treatments are often developed for one specific type of victimization (e.g., rape or domestic violence). Greater attention needs to be directed to assessing all victimization experiences, to developing strategies to avoid revictimization, and to understanding the compounding and complicating nature of co-occurring victimizations.

Gayla Margolin, Lauren A. Spies, and Esti Iturralde

See also Child Abuse, Neglect, and Maltreatment; Contextual Effects on Victimization; Domestic Violence; Family Violence; Intimate Partner Violence; Psychological and Behavioral Consequences of Victimization; Rape; Repeat Victimization

Further Readings

Appel, A. E., & Holden, G. W. (1998). The co-occurrence of spouse and physical child abuse: A review and appraisal. *Journal of Family Psychology, 12,* 578–599.

Finkelhor, D., Ormrod, R. K., & Turner, H. A. (2007). Poly-victimization: A neglected component in child victimization. *Child Abuse & Neglect, 31,* 7–26.

Noll, J. G. (2005). Does childhood sexual abuse set in motion a cycle of violence against women? What we know and what we need to learn. *Journal of Interpersonal Violence, 20,* 455–462.

Rossman, B. B. R., & Rosenberg, M. S. (Eds.). (1998). *Multiple victimization of children: Conceptual, developmental, research and treatment issues.* Binghamton, NY: Haworth.

Smith Slep, A. M., & O'Leary, S. G. (2005). Parent and partner violence in families with young children: Rates, patterns, and connections. *Journal of Consulting and Clinical Psychology, 73,* 435–444.

CORPORAL PUNISHMENT

Although there is no one definition of corporal punishment, it is generally described as the use of physical force with the intention of causing a person pain, but not injury, for the purpose of either correction or control of behavior. The term *corporal punishment* can refer to the act of striking another's body (e.g., spanking, slapping, caning, whipping), pulling or yanking a part of another's body, or throwing objects at another individual. However, the types of socially accepted corporal punishment, the prevalence of corporal punishment, and the population subjected to corporal punishment are continually influenced by changing cultural norms and public attitudes.

Historically, corporal punishment has been utilized for cases of adults by penal institutions and the military, as well as cases of children through juvenile courts, reformatories, schools, and parents. Today, however, the United States limits the use of corporal punishment to the disciplining of children, while most other Western countries have outlawed corporal punishment outright.

History

Corporal punishment is considered the oldest form of punishment known to humankind. Numerous acts of whipping and flogging can be found in the Old Testament, and the Laws of Moses reference the use of "up to forty strokes of the rod" as a punishment for a variety of offenses. In addition, King Solomon promised that parents who spared the rod would spoil their children.

In 1530, Henry the Eighth added the Whipping Act to English law as a punishment for vagrancy, whereby offenders would be tied naked to a cart and whipped in the marketplace until bloody. Whippings were administered for offenses such as peddling, being drunk on a Sunday, giving birth to a bastard child, and participating in or suspicion of witchcraft. In America, whipping was used as punishment for crimes of slander, theft, idleness, rioting, and prostitution and was used unmercifully as a punishment for slaves. It was not until the mid-1900s that the use of corporal punishment was deemed inhumane and thus terminated in the United States prison system.

Contemporary Use

Currently in the United States, corporal punishment is permitted solely in cases regarding children and may only be administered by parents or those acting in place of a parent such as a guardian or school administrator. Although the use of corporal punishment has been waning over the last several hundred years and has been outlawed in most of the Western world, corporal punishment is still used as a means of discipline for children in the United States.

Prevalence in the Home

According to Murray Straus and his colleagues, a large study by the National Family Violence Council found that a large percentage of American children have been hit at some point by at least one parent, with males being hit more often than females. Parents' use of corporal punishment often begins in a child's infancy, reaches a peak when the child is around age 3 or 4, and then declines. However, about one in four American children are still subjected to some form of corporal punishment through their teen years (ages 15–17). Parental attitudes about acceptable types of corporal punishment seem to be changing, as more severe punishments such as throwing objects are on the decline.

Prevalence in the Schools

In 1977, in *Ingraham v. Wright*, the U.S. Supreme Court heard arguments on corporal punishment violating children's Eighth Amendment rights, but on a 5–4 decision declared that schoolroom corporal punishment did not constitute cruel and unusual punishment. However, since the Supreme Court decision, 29 states have banned corporal punishment in U.S. schools, and states without corporal punishment bans have seen a continual decline in the use of corporal punishment in their school systems. As noted by Human Rights Watch, however, three states, Mississippi, Arkansas, and Alabama, still consistently use corporal punishment at the highest rates.

Corporal punishment in U.S. schools is almost invariably applied with a wooden paddle to the student's clothed posterior. A typical punishment constitutes two or three strokes, typically referred to as "swats" or "licks." For decades, it was routine for corporal punishment to be administered in the classroom or directly outside the classroom in the adjoining hallway. It is now customary for corporal punishment to be delivered privately in an office, often by the principal or deputy principal or at least in his or her presence. It is very unlikely today for a student to be subjected to paddling on the spur of the moment and more likely to require bureaucratic protocol such as formal documentation and informing parents.

Opposition

Although corporal punishment continues to be accepted and supported by some American parents, there is a growing opposition movement working to stop its use both privately in the home and publicly by state actors. Opponents of corporal punishment cite psychological and medical evidence linking the use of corporal punishment to harmful side effects such as hyperaggression and the acceptance of violence in interpersonal relationships. In addition, opponents point out disparities in the use of corporal punishment and claim that the public school system targets male and minority students.

Ultimately, corporal punishment is still an accepted part of child rearing that some American parents endorse as necessary to raising children. However, scholars and social service providers acknowledge that the very fine line between legal corporal punishment and physical abuse sometimes creates a barrier to protecting children. In addition, future exploration of the potential link between corporal punishment and interpersonal violence is paramount.

Tara N. Richards

See also Child Abuse, Identification of; Family Violence; Juvenile Offending and Victimization

Further Readings

Human Rights Watch. (2008). *A violent education.* Retrieved from http://www.hrw.org/en/reports/ 2008/08/19/violent-education

Scott, G. R. (2005). *The history of corporal punishment: A survey of flagellation in its historical, anthropological, and sociological aspects.* London: Kegan Paul.

Straus, M. (1994). *Beating the devil out of them: Corporal punishment in American families.* New York: Lexington Books.

Straus, M. A., Gelles, R., & Smith, C. (1999). *Physical violence in American families: Risk factors and adaptations to violence in 8,145 families.* Edison, NJ: Transaction.

Turner, S. M. (2002). *Something to cry about: An argument against corporal punishment of children in Canada.* Waterloo, ON, Canada: Wilfrid Laurier University Press.

Van Yeler, R. G. (1952). *The whip and the rod.* London: Gerald G. Swan.

Corporate Crime

Corporations are rarely seen as offenders; rather, corporations tend to be held in high esteem in the United States. After all, corporations embody the entrepreneurial initiative, creativity, and free market capitalism that American society embraces. Furthermore, corporations are a major factor in the nation's high standard of living, which is created through the production of numerous products for consumers. Yet these positive aspects of corporations are accompanied by negative aspects. Corporations have enormous resources that can be used to influence politicians and public policy to their benefit (e.g., monetary contributions, lobbyists). They are often controlled by their investors, which may lead to a culture of pursuing monetary success at all costs in order to please stockholders. As recently seen with the economic crisis of 2008, some corporations staunchly fight governmental regulations yet may call on the government for help when all else has failed.

Corporations are in a unique position that allows for unethical and illegal actions that can lead to victimizations at numerous levels. Corporate crimes are hard to investigate and prosecute because a single crime may be very complicated, involve several actors, and produce numerous victims. The victims of corporate crime may include the employees, consumers, competitors, and society in general. The FBI has estimated the costs of white-collar crime in general to be between $300 billion and $600 billion annually. Yet research on victims of corporate crime is limited. In fact, research on the victimization of white-collar crime in general is only now starting to receive attention in the mainstream victimology literature.

Distinguishing Characteristics

Corporate crime includes both violent and nonviolent forms. Corporate violence includes environmental crimes affecting society, unsafe products that harm consumers, and unsafe working conditions that harm employees. It differs from other types of violence in five basic ways. First, corporate violence typically consists of indirect harm. The corporation does not intentionally hurt others; rather, harm comes indirectly from the unintended consequences of improper policies and actions. Second, the motivation for corporate crime differs from that of conventional crimes. Corporate violence is motivated by the desire to maximize profits and minimize costs; the violence is a consequence of the crime rather than an intended outcome. Third, in corporate crime, causal relationships are hard to establish. Typically, the effects of the policy or action are separated in time from the harm, thus making it difficult to directly pin the policy or action on the harm caused. A fourth factor is that there usually are a large number of individuals collectively involved in corporate violence, whereas in other types of violence only one or a few individuals are responsible for the action. Corporate violence is not the result of one individual's decisions; rather, it is a collaboration involving decisions made throughout the process by numerous people in different departments, with their collective actions leading to the situation that results in the later harm. Finally, corporate violence does not receive the same response from the criminal justice system as other types of violence. For example, corporate violence is hard to prosecute for many of the reasons listed above (e.g., it may be hard to prove causation, involve numerous actors, involve lack of intent). Nonviolent corporate crime, however, generally involves vast political and economic consequences as opposed to physical harm. This is the type of crime that Edwin Sutherland focused on when he introduced the study of white-collar crime in 1939. Nonviolent crime typically involves corporate abuse of power, fraud, and economic exploitation. The following sections identify the toll of corporate crime on the various victims.

Corporate Crimes Against Society

Corporations can victimize society in numerous ways. Perhaps one of the most common forms of corporate violence against society is unsafe environmental practices such as the release of toxic chemicals and air pollution. It has been estimated that approximately 90% of hazardous waste is improperly handled and/or disposed of. Furthermore, pollution has been cited as the cause of the increase in the number of cancer cases in the 20th century. Pollution has also been linked to heart disease, genetic disorders, sterility, birth disorders, and other ailments. While companies that handle toxic chemicals are allowed to release a certain amount of the chemicals into the environment through various methods, there have been extreme cases in which companies have knowingly

or accidentally released amounts that exceeded acceptable limits. One such infamous example is that of the Love Canal and Hooker Chemical Corporation in Niagara County, New York, which is described below.

Hooker Chemical Corporation bought the Love Canal in 1940, drained it, and dumped 22,000 tons of highly toxic chemical waste into the canal, then buried it all under clay. The site was then sold to the Niagara School Board for a dollar. Concerned about future repercussions from the toxic waste, Hooker disclosed the contents of the landfill and inserted a clause in the deed that released the company of any liability and cautioned the buyer against any excavations on the property. Despite warnings, a community and a school were built on and around the property. Over a period of decades, schoolchildren and residents were exposed to noxious fumes and surfacing chemicals. Residents were experiencing adverse medical effects including rashes, burns, miscarriages, birth defects, liver ailments, emotional disorders, and cancer. However, a causal link between the medical ailments and the chemicals was never clearly established. The Department of Justice and the state of New York filed lawsuits against Hooker Chemical, and in 1994, the court found no cause to hold the company liable. In the end, several hundred families were evacuated from the area and Hooker paid $20 million to the former residents. It is important to note that at the time (in the 1940s), Hooker's method of hazardous waste disposal was not illegal; while morally irresponsible, it was in line with disposal methods of the time.

In response to the Love Canal incident, Congress passed the Comprehensive Environmental Response, Compensation, and Liability Act (CERCLA) of 1980. CERCLA taxes all oil- and chemical-based companies and places the money into a fund to clean up hazardous waste sites. CERCLA identifies Superfund sites and requires the companies responsible for the pollution to aid in the funding of cleanup efforts. As of 2008, there were 1,650 federally identified Superfund sites in the United States, but CERCLA funds are running low and taxpayers may soon have to start paying for these cleanup efforts.

Society is also victimized when corporations fail to pay taxes or when a corporation defrauds the government. In such instances, the taxpayers pick up the tab. For example, in 1998, 24 Fortune 500 companies did not pay taxes, which resulted in several billions of dollars of losses to the government. Furthermore, the U.S. government has been repeatedly defrauded by defense contractors who overcharge for products and supplies. In one noteworthy example, a defense contractor charged the government $9,606 for an Allen wrench worth 12 cents. Taxpayers make up for these losses through the increase of taxes or the reallocation of tax money to other departments.

Corporate Crimes Against Consumers

Perhaps the most infamous case of corporate violence against consumers was the case of the Ford Pinto in the 1970s. The Ford Motor Company was the first company to ever be charged with murder. The Ford Pinto was built in response to competition from foreign markets in the late 1960s. In order to increase profits, Ford president Lee Iacocca ordered the production of a car weighing less than 2,000 pounds and costing less than $2,000 to manufacture (the "Rule of 2000"). Because of the poor design of the Pinto, namely the location of the gas tank, rear-end collisions could cause the gas tank to explode while the body of the car shifted, jamming the doors and trapping occupants inside. Investigations found that Ford knew about this problem and made a calculated decision that it would be cheaper to pay civil damages (death suits) than to recall all of the cars and fix them. In the end, Ford paid millions of dollars in civil lawsuits, recalled and fixed all Pintos, and was acquitted on the criminal charges due to inadmissible evidence.

A more recent example of corporate violence against consumers in the form of unsafe products can be seen in products manufactured in China that have been tainted with melamine, a chemical used to make plastic and fertilizer. The Food and Drug Administration reported approximately 12,000 reports of animal illnesses related to the melamine contamination of popular pet foods. One year later, melamine-tainted baby formula from China resulted in six infant deaths and more than 300,000 illnesses.

Price fixing is a common form of nonviolent corporate crime against consumers that involves the artificial inflation of prices for goods and services. Price fixing has been done on various products from shoes to video games, and even college educations. In 2000, Nine West paid $34 million for illegally inflating the price of its shoes since 1988. Nintendo was fined $197 million in 2002 for fixing prices on video games. In 1992, MIT (the Massachusetts Institute of Technology) and eight other Ivy League schools were charged with price fixing of tuition. Frequently, price fixing is not a result of a conspiracy, but rather a result of parallel pricing in which an industry leader sets an inflated price and competitors adjust their prices accordingly; the former is illegal, the latter may be unethical yet not necessarily illegal. Price fixing is an interesting crime because victims generally do not know they are being victimized. Consumers unknowingly pay inflated prices, to the economic benefit of the corporation; individual losses may be small, but overall losses can amount to millions of dollars.

Consumers can also be victimized when companies engage in fraud and false advertising through the use of lies, deceit, and/or misrepresentation in efforts to entice consumers to purchase their goods or services. For example, Campbell's Soup was charged with false advertising when it was discovered that they placed marbles at the bottom of their bowls of soup during commercial shoots to make it appear that the soup was loaded with chicken and noodles. In another case, it was found that Beech-Nut Nutrition Corporation had earned an estimated $60 million through the sale of "100% apple juice" that contained absolutely no apples.

Corporate Crimes Against Employees

Crimes against employees can occur in many forms, such as economic exploitation, unfair labor practices, creating dangerous working conditions, discrimination, and outright stealing from the employees. When Enron declared bankruptcy in December 2001 due to misrepresentation of profits and overwhelming debt, employees lost $1.3 billion in retirement savings, as retirement accounts were largely invested in Enron stock. In the year leading up to bankruptcy, Enron stock values continued to decline, yet employees were not allowed to withdraw their retirement funds, when all the while Enron's CEO, Ken Lay, and other top executives earned hundreds of millions of dollars in salaries, stock options, and bonuses. In another case, Wal-Mart was accused of cheating employees out of hundreds of millions of dollars by requiring them to work after clocking out with no additional pay while managers received bonuses for keeping labor costs down.

Not only are employees victimized through outright theft and economic exploitation, but employees may also be subjected to unsafe working conditions. In efforts to cut costs companies may cut corners when it comes to the safety and well-being of their employees. According to a press release by the U.S. Bureau of Labor Statistics in 2008, there were 5,488 fatal work-related injuries recorded in the United States in 2007. While these numbers are down from previous years, it still represents 3.7 fatal work injuries per 100,000 workers. The construction business incurred the most fatalities of any industry in the private sector due to the nature of the business and the safety issues involved on the job. It was also found that nonfatal workplace injuries and illnesses in private industries declined from previous years. The nonfatal injury and illness rate in 2007 was 4.2 cases per 100 full-time workers. These numbers suggest that work fatalities and nonfatal injuries nationwide are down in almost all industries, which may signify safer working conditions overall, among other things.

Consequences

Corporate crimes not only have financial and physical consequences, but they also have heavy social consequences. These violations of trust hinder people's quality of life and perpetuate further feelings of victimization. Corporations are in a unique position to victimize people and society on numerous levels. Unfortunately, many reprehensible behaviors of corporations are unethical as opposed to illegal, which makes policing corporate crime a difficult task. Due to the nature of the offense, the number of people often involved, and the complexities of the actions, corporate crimes may be punished rather leniently if they are punished at all. In addition, many victims do not even know they have been victimized. Much of what is known about corporate crime victimization comes from case studies of incidents after the fact. What researchers have determined is that unlike conventional crime, corporate crime does not discriminate; everyone is at risk for corporate victimization.

Andrea Schoepfer

See also Exploitation by Scams; Future of Victimology; Internet Fraud; Methodological Issues in Counting Victims; Occupational Violence; Public Opinion and Crime Prevention, United States

Further Readings

BBC News Online. (2002, October). *Nintendo fined for price fixing*. Retrieved September 2008 from http://news.bbc.co.uk/1/hi/business/2375967.stm

Depalam, A. (1992, June). Price-fixing or charity? Trial of M.I.T. begins. *The New York Times*. Retrieved September 2008 from http://query.nytimes.com/gst/fullpage.html?res=9E0CE0DE1E38F935A15755C0A964958260

Federal Trade Commission (FTC). (2000, March). *Nine West settles state and federal price fixing charges*. Retrieved September 2008 from http://www.ftc.gov/opa/2000/03/ninewest.shtm

Food and Drug Administration (FDA). (2007). *FDA update and synopsis on the pet food outbreak*. U.S. Department of Health and Human Services. Retrieved September 2008 from http://www.fda.gov

Friedrichs, D. (2004). *Trusted criminals* (2nd ed.). Belmont, CA: Thomson Wadsworth.

Greenhouse, S. (2002, June 25). Suits say Wal-Mart forces workers to toil off the clock. *New York Times*. Retrieved September 2008 from http://www.nytimes.com/2002/06/25/us/suits-say-wal-mart-forces-workers-to-toil-off-the-clock.html

Rosoff, S., Pontell, H., & Tillman, R. (2006). *Profit without honor: White collar crime and the looting of America* (4th ed.). Upper Saddle River, NJ: Prentice Hall.

U.S. Bureau of Labor Statistics. (2008). *Census of Fatal Occupational Injuries summary, 2007*. Retrieved December 2008 from http://www.bls.gov/iif/oshcfoil.htm

Wade McCormick, L. (2008, December 2). *Chinese infant death toll from tainted formula rises*. Retrieved December 2008 from http://www.consumeraffairs.com/news04/2008/12/chinese_formula15.html

CORRECTION OFFICIALS AND VICTIMS

Victims have become an important focal point within correctional programs throughout recent decades. It is important to note, however, that this has not always been the case. Correction officials have now instituted programs such as restorative justice and victim notification programs in order to increase the roles that victims play within correctional settings. This entry examines how these programs have increased the victim's role in correctional proceedings.

Restorative Justice

While restorative justice programs have been common throughout different countries for some time, they did not come into popularity in the United States until the 1990s. Until then the dominant philosophies within corrections had been rehabilitation, retribution, deterrence, and incapacitation. With the advent of restorative justice, correction officials have been given an alternative to the traditional forms of justice. The key concepts of restorative justice are to "restore" victims and have a more victim-centered criminal justice system. The process of restoring the victim includes (1) restoring the property lost or injury, (2) reinstating their sense of security, dignity, and sense of empowerment, (3) restoring deliberative democracy, (4) reestablishing harmony based on feelings of obtained justice, and (5) restoring social support from family and friends. While these programs boast wonderful ideals, research has shown that they have limited success with regard to offender recidivism. However, this does not mean that these programs are of little to no value.

Restorative justice puts its primary focus is on the victim, and it is seen by some as an extension of the victims' rights movement. Research has shown that victims express greater satisfaction with cases sent to restorative justice conferences than with cases sent to traditional court proceedings. Studies also have shown that the increased satisfaction with restorative justice proceedings is often due to the symbolic compensation given in the form of an apology. In addition, the majority of the victims surveyed experienced a reduction in fear and an increase in emotional restoration after participating in the restorative justice program.

Restorative justice proceedings are often held through mediation conferences, and are actually quite simple in the way they work. Typically, after an offender admits his or her wrongdoing, he or she will be asked to participate in the conference. The offender is also asked to bring his or her loved ones as supporters to the conference. Once the victims agree to participate in the conferences, they are also asked to bring supporters with them. The conference proceedings are typically held in the community, as this is an essential part of the philosophy. Typically, the conference is mediated by a local judge or legal professional. At the beginning of the conference, there is a discussion of the crime that was committed and how it affected everyone in the room. This will typically focus on the victim's suffering as well as the stress that has been felt by the offender's family. Once everyone has reached a point of understanding, there is then a discussion of what needs to be done in order to "repair" the harm that has been caused. An agreement is signed that specifies what the offender has agreed to do to repair the harm and suffering that has been caused to the victim. Once this contract is fulfilled, both the victim and offender have been restored to their prior standing within the community.

Programs such as restorative justice have become increasingly popular with juvenile offenders; however, they are also used with some adult offenders. These programs have helped increase awareness within the correctional field of the needs of victims as well as their important role within correctional programs. While restorative justice is becoming an important way for correction officials to work with victims, other victim-centered programs have also emerged. For example, as a result of the victims' rights movement, notification programs are becoming a staple within corrections.

Victim Notification Programs

Currently, 43 states are involved, in at least some capacity, in a nationwide victim notification program. The most comprehensive nationwide program is the Victim Information and Notification Everyday (VINE), which provides victims with current, reliable information as to the custody status of offenders at any time. Using a database, victims can select a state and then search for an offender via offender ID number or name. When the offender is found, the offender's date of birth, current age, custody status, and location are provided. Once the offender is located in the database, the victim can register to be notified via phone or email when the offender's custody status changes.

Programs such as VINE have become increasingly available to victims due to technological advancements. Of the 43 states with some form of program, 35 states include complete state records, while the other 8 include records from multiple counties. Historically, these programs were only available to victims of violent or sexual crimes; however, due to technological advances and the victims' rights movement, now the victim of any crime can secure the peace of mind of knowing the current custody status of the offender, as well as being notified when his or her release occurs.

Role of Victims and Correction Officials

The role of the victim has changed dramatically in the past several decades. Through the development of programs such as restorative justice, which seeks to help restore the emotional and financial losses of the victim, the importance of the role of the victim has increased exponentially. While correction officials have increased the role of victims through programs such as restorative justice, they have also increased their responsibility to victims. Programs such as victim notification have allowed victims to have an increased security with regard to potentially dangerous offenders. While victims were once not a central part of the criminal justice process, their roles have been forever changed due to a variety of circumstances. Correction officials now have a duty to respond and respect the role of victims within criminal justice proceedings. Programs such as restorative justice and victim notification are only two areas of many where correction officials are now fulfilling their new roles.

Catherine M. Arnold

See also Restorative Justice; Victims' Rights Movement, International; Victims' Rights Movement, United States

Further Readings

Beatty, D., & Gregorie, T. (2003). Implementing victims' rights: Why corrections professionals should care. *Corrections Today, 65*(5), 78–82.

Braithwaite, J. (1999). Restorative justice: Assessing optimistic and pessimistic accounts. *Crime and Justice: A Review of Research, 25*, 1–127.

Trone, J. (1999). *When victims have a right to know: Automating notification with VINE®*. New York: Vera Institute of Justice.

CORRELATES OF VICTIMIZATION

Correlates of victimization refer to either the characteristics of victims—such as their age, race, and sex—or the contexts that are predictive or statistically associated with higher risk of victimization. Scientifically locating such correlates enables policy makers to target prevention efforts toward those persons or situations likely to be targets of crime. Victimization researchers are interested in these correlates as well, as they help with organizing into a conceptual framework those processes that might lead some individuals to have a higher risk of victimization than others.

If no correlates of victimization existed, that is, if victimization was essentially a random event, then there would be no need for victimization policy or theory. Everyone would have the same probability of becoming a victim, with chance determining which individuals in fact fall prey to offenders. In this case, no action or omission by a person, or personal or situational characteristics, would influence the likelihood or level of victimization one way or the other. The data reveal that this perception about victimization is simply not true. The first systematic look at who is likely to become a crime victim began in the early 1970s with the National Crime Survey (or NCS, and its successor, the National Crime Victimization Survey, or NCVS). These data sources, and many others that have emerged since the 1970s, have provided an increasingly clear picture of factors that are predictive of victimization. We know that individual victims of crime tend to be disproportionately young, male, and African American. Research over the past several decades has also uncovered many other personal and situational factors that elevate the risk of victimization. Note that these correlates do not mean that everyone who possesses these risk factors will definitely become a victim. Official statistics indicate that victimization, and particularly violent victimization, is a statistically rare event even among those at high risk. Thus, these characteristics only signify that for the average person with these traits, there is a higher probability of victimization occurring.

This entry outlines the variables that research has indicated affect an individual's likelihood of becoming the victim of a crime. Correlates are useful in creating profiles of the "typical" victim, or establishing patterns of victimization. The most basic correlates are demographic in nature, such as age, race, and sex. Recent work, driven by victimization theory, has uncovered additional factors that appear to elevate the risk of victimization.

Demographic Correlates of Violent Crime

The NCS was the first to provide national-level systematic data on the basic predictors of victimization. Before the NCS, official crime statistics—namely, those provided by the Uniform Crime Reporting Program—contained no data about victim characteristics for any crime besides homicide, thus precluding the ability to create a statistical portrait of victimization in the United States. Additional similar sources of victimization data have also emerged in other countries, from such sources as the United Kingdom's British Crime Survey, or BCS. The most recent detailed summary report for the successor to the NCS, the NCVS, is based on 2006 data. The patterns identified in these data sets have generally been impressively consistent.

Gender, for many years, has been one of the most striking correlates of personal victimization. In 1973, for instance, the rate of violent victimization among males of all ages was approximately 73 per 1,000 respondents, whereas the rate for females was less than half the male rate (about 30 per 1,000 respondents). The BCS shows similar patterns, where males generally experience more victimization than do females. One interesting trend that has become apparent over the past several years in the United States has been the narrowing of violent victimization rates of males and females. In 2006, for example, males were victims of violence at a rate of 27 per 1,000; however, females had only marginally lower rates (23 per 1,000). While this narrowing appears to have begun during the early 1980s, it has become more

marked since 1993. In England and Wales, in contrast, males in 2007 were still twice as likely to experience violence than were females. Rape or sexual assault is the only type of violent victimization where females have consistently had a higher risk of becoming a victim, although the risk itself is not especially great for the average female. In 2006, 1.8 women (out of each 1,000) reported rape or sexual assault, in comparison to 0.2 males per 1,000.

Clear patterns have emerged as well with respect to the age of victims of personal crime. The major national-level victimization data sources in the United States show that violent victimization risk is greatest among those 12 to 24 years old, with the rate of victimization decreasing precipitously throughout the remainder of life. In 1994, 16- to 19-year-olds had a rate of violent victimization of 125 per 1,000 (12- to 15-year-olds and 20- to 24-year-olds had slightly lower rates), whereas 25- to 34-year-olds had a substantially lower rate (55 per 1,000) and those 65 and older experienced hardly any violence (4 per 1,000). By 2006, although these rates had declined substantially from their 1994 peak (down to a rate of 53 per 1,000 for the 16- to 19-year-olds), the basic pattern in which young people are at the highest risk still held.

The factors of age and gender combine to affect individuals' risk of victimization. For instance, although females have the greater risk of sexual violence, this risk is concentrated among younger females, as the 12- to 15-year-olds had a rate of 6.4 per 1,000 in 2006, whereas females 65 or older had a rate approaching zero. This same pattern carries for all personal crimes. Put differently, regardless of gender, younger people are more likely to experience personal victimization than are older people.

While BCS data do not report the distribution of victimization across race or ethnicity, NCVS data do. Since the inception of the collection of victimization data at the national level, it has been found that Blacks have the highest risk of victimization. As with gender, however, the rates of Blacks and Whites have narrowed somewhat since 1973. In 1973, for example, Blacks had a rate of violent victimization that was approximately 37 per 1,000, while Whites that year had a rate of only 20 per 1,000. By 2005, the rate for Blacks had declined to under 14 per 1,000. The comparable rate for

Whites was about 7 per 1,000. Although the rate of violent victimization of Blacks has declined substantially since it peaked at 40 per 1,000 in 1981, the rate remains at about twice the level for Blacks as for Whites.

Combining the effects of age, race, and gender for 2006, the NCVS shows that the most typical victim of violence is a young male who is Black (with a rate of 35 per 1,000). Black females, as a group, had the next highest rate (about 30 per 1,000). White males had the third highest rate (26 per 1,000) and white females were statistically the safest (21 per 1,000). Rates of personal victimizations were also much greater for Hispanics than for Whites. The notion of correlates does obscure one fact: Whites substantially outnumber Blacks as a proportion of the population. That is, the estimated raw number of White victims greatly exceeds the number of Black victims (4.7 million vs. 1 million incidents in 2006). What these correlates show is that person for person, Black males have a disproportionately greater risk of violence than any other group.

The NCVS also reports several other correlates worth noting. A person's marital status, for instance, appears relevant for predicting violent victimization risk. In 2006, individuals who were never married had a rate of 43 per 1,000, and those who were either divorced or separated had a rate of about 47 per 1,000. In marked contrast, those individuals who were married (12 per 1,000) or widowed (4 per 1,000) had a substantially lower risk. This differential holds no matter what crime type; that is, single or divorced/separated people have a significantly higher risk for any of the types of violent crime the NCVS measures. This same pattern holds whether the individual is male or female.

Personal income, too, appears connected with the risk of violence. Those persons making $7,500 or less in 2006 had a rate of 65 per 1,000 for violent crimes. The rate generally declines as income levels increase. Those persons making $75,000 or more per year reported a rate of only 15 violent victimizations per 1,000 people. Even in robberies, where money is quite often the motive for the crime, offenders are more likely to target persons making less than $35,000 per year. Interestingly, income might well have a substantial connection with the violent victimization of

Blacks. With few exceptions, Blacks in 2006 had only nominally higher rates of violent victimization than their White counterparts making the same income (e.g., for those making less than $7,500 per year, a rate of 68 per 1,000 for Blacks and 65 per 1,000 for Whites).

Correlates of Household Victimization

The NCVS also records information about crimes that do not target a specific person, but rather, target a household. Such crimes include burglary, motor vehicle theft, and household theft. Some of the patterns of personal victimization persist in household data. For instance, Black households (185.6 per 1,000) had somewhat higher rates of household victimization than did White households (156.7 per 1,000). The racial differences were most apparent in household burglary rates (28.6 per 1,000 for Whites vs. 42.4 for Blacks) and motor vehicle theft (7.3 vs. 14.8); however, the difference in rates for theft, the most likely form of property victimization, was only nominal (120.8 vs. 128.4).

Beyond race, the age of the head of household, whether the subject owned his or her home, and the location of the residence also are correlated with property crime. Overall, property crime is more likely for homes headed by younger individuals. In this respect, age is correlated with property victimization as well as violence. In 2006, homes headed by teenagers experienced property victimization at a rate of 366.5 per 1,000 households. Where the head of the household was aged 65 or more, the rate diminished to 70.2 per 1,000 households. The age differential is most noticeable for general theft, but is still present for burglary and motor vehicle theft as well.

The income of the household, to some degree, predicts property victimizations, but not to the same level that it predicts violent victimization. The poorest households, those making $7,500 or less in 2006, experienced property crime at a rate of 217.3 per 1,000 households. The rate for those households making $75,000 or more was lower— 162.0 per 1,000—but not substantially so. Whereas burglary rates tended to decrease as household income increased, the same was not necessarily true for motor vehicle theft or theft. The highest rate of theft was for those households making

$15,000 to $24,999 at 15.9 per 1,000. Only above this income level did the motor vehicle theft rate begin to decline as income increased. With respect to theft, the poorest households had the highest rate at 150.3 per 1,000 households; however, the next highest rate was for those making incomes of $25,000 to $34,999 (136.2). The third highest was for the highest income category (those making $75,000 or more, at 133.2 per 1,000 households). In sum, household income is a very inconsistent correlate of property victimization.

The number of individuals in the household might correlate to some degree with the amount of property crime experienced. The 2006 NCVS shows this to be the case for overall property crime. Households with one member only had a rate of 101.4 per 1,000 households. The rate increased to as much as 347.8 per 1,000 for those households with six or more people. The correlation holds generally true no matter what property crime—whether burglary, motor vehicle theft, or theft. In short, the greater the number of residents in a household, the higher the risk that the household will experience property crime.

The BCS provides additional information about households most likely to experience burglary victimization. In a recent BCS report, the percentage of burglary for all households was only 2.4%. This percentage doubled when there were high levels of physical disorder in the area. This base percentage tripled (to 6.4%) in households headed by a single adult with children or where the households were headed by those who were unemployed or between the ages of 16 and 24. When the home had no security measures, the percentage of households experiencing burglary increased to a remarkable 25%.

The NCVS and BCS report similar patterns for motor vehicle theft. As with violence, for both the United States and the United Kingdom, households headed by with younger people are more likely to experience motor vehicle theft crime than are households headed by older people. Heads of household who were teenagers reported a rate of 20.1 per 1,000, versus a rate of only 3.1 for heads aged 65 or more (in the United Kingdom, 9.4% of heads of household ages 16–34 suffered a motor vehicle theft, but only 1.9% of those ages 75 or older did). Also, those heads of household living in rented properties reported higher rates of motor vehicle theft (13.2 per 1,000) than those who owned

or were paying mortgages for their homes (6.3 per 1,000). With respect to location, urban residences had the highest risk (12.8 per 1,000), with risk diminishing substantially as residences were located further from an urban core (8.0 per 1,000 for suburban homes vs. 3.6 for rural residences). The BCS looked at additional measures, finding that wealthier families and those living in areas with less disorder had a lower prevalence of motor vehicle theft.

Substantive Correlates

The term *substantive correlates* refers to risk factors for victimization that are derived from victimization theory, which is the systematic explanation developed by social scientists to account for why some people experience victimization and others do not. Researchers began to consistently use theory to develop new predictors for victimization and to guide research during the 1970s, most notably with the work of Lawrence Cohen and Marcus Felson on routine activity theory, as well as Michael Hindelang, Michael Gottfredson, and James Garofalo on lifestyle theory. During the 1980s and 1990s, the two aforementioned theories dominated victimization research; however, the work of scholars Richard Felson and Simon Singer pointed toward such new directions as research into social–psychological or cultural risk factors. Starting in the late 1990s, building from the studies showing that offenders and victims shared almost every meaningful predictor, researchers turned increasingly to applying criminological theories to account for victimization risk. Contemporary victimization research has thus produced a considerable array of new correlates of victimization, far beyond those recorded or even anticipated in the NCVS and BCS. This section focuses on these substantive predictors. It must be noted, however, that much of the research examining these correlates does not usually come from national-level data.

Lifestyle Theory and Routine Activities Theory

The perspective taken by lifestyle theory and routine activities theory (also known as routine activity theory) is perhaps the first to garner sustained and widespread scientific attention. This approach focuses on the role of situations and ecological context as factors responsible for victimization. Routine activities theory argues that for victimization to occur, a given situation or context must have a combination of (1) a likely offender, (2) a worthwhile target, and (3) ineffective guardianship. Circumstances where these three factors are present will have the highest incidence of victimization. Other, relatively more recent, scholarship has identified the qualities of routine activities or lifestyle that ought to be predictive of victimization. It specifies that those who engage in unsupervised and unstructured social activity with peers will have a higher risk. Such activities would include hanging out with friends and going to parties.

The earliest tests of these theories focused only on explaining the demographic patterns mentioned earlier, as found in the NCVS. Through the 1980s and into the 1990s, research turned toward specific situations and activities that enhanced the probability of victimization. For instance, starting in the mid-1980s, researchers noted that self-reported offending was highly correlated with victimization. That is, people who said they committed more crimes were also more likely to report being victimized. The basic idea was that those with a deviant lifestyle are more likely to spend time with those who commit crime and who would not scruple at victimizing their peers (thus implying proximity to motivated offenders). Note that this correlation does not mean that all victims commit crime or else have done something to deserve to experience victimization. Rather, it means that offending behavior appears to have a strong connection with victimization risk. Indeed, some researchers, for instance, Schreck, Stewart, and Osgood, have found that a few individuals consistently played the role of victim or offender, but not both roles; however, in general the experience of both criminal offending and victimization was typical of those who reported multiple encounters with violence.

Researchers have also attempted to identify situational correlates of victimization beyond demographic variables and self-reported deviance. The BCS, for instance, asks subjects about drinking activity, including going out to pubs. According to the BCS, those who went out drinking were more than twice as likely to experience violence as those who did so less frequently or not at all. Researchers, for example, have identified a number of activities that college students engaged in that elevated their risk of violent victimization, such as partying at night and using drugs. Others using the same theoretical approach have further explored specific daily routines that increased risk of major and minor forms of theft victimization. This body of work in fact studied the relationship of dozens of predictors of theft victimization, noting that some of these (e.g., owning a dog, going out of the home to study) were indeed connected with having a greater likelihood of experiencing a theft. In recent years, researchers have used the lifestyle and routine activities theories to make predictions about how a teenager's peer network structure affects his or her risk of violent victimization, as well as the specific qualities of lifestyles that influence risk. Christopher Schreck and his colleagues, Bonnie Fisher and Mitchell Miller, found that teenagers who were central and popular members of dense conventional friendship networks were less subject to violence than those who were similarly situated in deviant peer networks. They theorized that in deviant peer networks, friends provide information to each other on targets that others might find worth taking or attacking, as well as provide ineffective guardianship and proximity to motivated offenders.

Self-Control Theory

Michael Gottfredson and Travis Hirschi's self-control theory specifies that low self-control, which is a person's unwillingness to act as if long-term negative consequences mattered in decision making, relates not only to crime but also to such adverse outcomes as failure at work and school as well as broken relationships. Self-control theory was one of the first criminological theories to be extended to account for victimization. Self-control, according to the theory, is not something that can be directly observed. However, Hirschi and Gottfredson offered many strategies for measuring self-control, preferring measures that focused on low self-control, such as those involving crime and failure in work and relationships. The most commonly used index of low self-control in criminological as well as victimization research is the Grasmick personality/attitudinal scale or some variant of this scale. This index measures respondents' tendency to become angry, take risks, be impulsive, think only of the short term, and so forth. Victimization research using self-control theory has tended to use the latter approach, finding that low self-control does in fact predict victimization.

Social Interactionist Theory

Richard Felson described the relevance of what he termed the social interactionist (SI) theory to violent victimization. The basic argument of the theory presents the onset of victimization as the product of emotional distress, which directs human interaction toward aggression. The basic process begins with a person who has experienced a negative event, such as getting fired or going through a divorce, and who is feeling emotionally down as a consequence. Almost perversely, emotional distress, far from eliciting pity in those persons nearby, actually irritates and angers them. This aversive reaction emerges because the distressed person is more likely to perform at an offensively unsatisfactory level at work or school. He or she is also more likely to be rude or inconsiderate toward others and violate social rules and expectations. As a consequence, the other person in the interaction will have a grievance, which may provoke physical attack if the distressed person is unable or unwilling to make satisfaction (e.g., apologize). The initial attack may then result in a cycle of retaliation and counter-retaliation.

Social interactionist theory, at least with respect to victimization, has not received extensive testing in the scientific literature to date. Richard Felson examined the role of negative events as predictors of victimization, finding that they indeed made victimization more likely to occur. However, he was not able to explore whether negative affect or emotions explained away the effect of these negative events (as in his theory). Other researchers later added early pubertal development as a potential negative event, finding that it, too, made victimization more likely to occur. This later research directly measured indicators of depression, finding (1) that those individuals who reported more symptoms of depression had a higher risk of victimization, and (2) that for the girls in the sample, depression was the reason that those who matured earlier had higher odds of being attacked.

Subcultures of Violence Theories

Simon Singer was one of the first to link subcultural norms of violence with victimization. His basic idea is that the subculture is infused with values that promote violence. Quite often, a consequence of this violence is retaliation on the part of those victimized, creating a cycle where individuals alternate roles as offenders and victims.

Until recently, research did not examine whether norms of violence affected victimization risk. However, research has now begun to directly test the influence of subcultural norms. For example, Elijah Anderson, in his ethnographic study of Blacks in severely disadvantaged neighborhoods in Philadelphia, reported the existence of what he termed the "Code of the Street." The street code is essentially a system of rules governing the use of violence to informally address grievances. The individual, in effect, has beliefs that allow him or her to become physically violent toward others in situations where social control is perceived as necessary. These beliefs also translate into a distinctive personal style: a belligerent persona that exists simply to build a reputation ("rep") and thus intimidate would-be victimizers. Outside of disadvantaged neighborhoods, in the event of violence, individuals have recourse to the courts or the police; however, norms of violence exist for a functional reason in disadvantaged neighborhoods. Here, the legal and courts system has become so ineffective as to have lost legitimacy in the eyes of many residents, thus making it necessary for neighborhood residents to be willing to take the law into their own hands and use the threat of or actual violence to terrify would-be offenders. Put another way, having a reputation for violence enhances "respect," which in turn deters would-be offenders (who would thus risk their lives by trying a person who has "respect"). A collaborative project of Eric Stewart, Christopher Schreck, and Ronald Simons, however, found that Blacks who reported having attitudes that favored the use of violence in fact had a greater risk of experiencing violent victimization. A belligerent set of beliefs, rather than being protective, is in fact correlated with more violent victimization.

Victim Profiles

This entry examined some of the major correlates of victimization, based on those reported in major national surveys as well as those identified in the scientific research literature on victimization. The profile of the typical victim of violent crime, according to the national data, is a person who is young, male, Black, single, and poor. Households most likely to have property stolen are disproportionately likely to be those headed by young people, those who do not own their place of residence, and those with a large number of people. The substantive research goes further, finding that victims of crime exhibit many lifestyle, cultural, and social–psychological markers. Persons who become victims are unusually likely to be deviants. They spend more time away from the home and in the presence of their same-age peers (and away from supervision by responsible authorities). They are more likely than others to have friends who are criminal. They are more likely to have attitudes that are markedly belligerent, which puts them at significantly greater risk for violent victimization. Those who become victims are also more likely to have low self-control and to exhibit signs of emotional depression.

In short, victimization is not a random event. Those with a high risk of victimization consistently reveal the same traits. This fact, in turn, identifies the people and households that might benefit most from crime prevention policies targeted specifically for them.

Christopher J. Schreck

See also Age and Victimization; British Crime Survey (BCS); National Crime Victimization Survey (NCVS); Race/Ethnicity and Victimization; Sex and Victimization; Victimization, Theories of; Victimization Surveys

Further Readings

Anderson, E. (1999). *Code of the street: Decency, violence, and the moral life of the inner city.* New York: Norton.

Bureau of Justice Statistics. (2008). *Criminal victimization in the United States, 2006 Statistical Tables.* Washington, DC: Department of Justice.

Cohen L. E., & Felson, M. (1979). Social change and crime rate trends: A routine activity approach. *American Sociological Review, 44,* 588–608.

Felson, R. B. (1992). Kick 'em when they're down: Explanations of the relationship between stress and interpersonal aggression and violence. *Sociological Quarterly, 33,* 1–16.

Gottfredson, M. R., & Hirschi, T. (1990). *A general theory of crime.* Stanford, CA: Stanford University Press.

Grasmick, H. G., Tittle, C. R., Bursik, R. J., & Arneklev, B. J. (1993). Testing the core implications of Gottfredson and Hirschi's general theory of crime. *Journal of Research in Crime and Delinquency, 30,* 5–29.

Hindelang, M. J., Gottfredson, M. R., & Garofalo, J. (1978). *Victims of personal crime: An empirical foundation for a theory of personal victimization.* Cambridge, MA: Ballinger.

Hirschi, T., & Gottfredson, M. (1993). Commentary: Testing the general theory of crime. *Journal of Research in Crime and Delinquency, 30,* 52–53.

Kershaw, C., Nicholas, S., & Walker, A. (2008). *Crime in England and Wales 2007/2008: Findings from the British Crime Survey and police recorded crime.* London: Home Office.

Lauritsen, J. L., & Laub, J. H. (2007). Understanding the link between victimization and offending: New reflections on an old idea. *Crime Prevention Studies, 22,* 55–75.

Sampson, R. J., & Lauritsen, J. L. (1990). Deviant lifestyles, proximity to crime, and the offender-victim link in personal violence. *Journal of Research in Crime and Delinquency, 27,* 110–139.

Schreck, C. J. (1999). Criminal victimization and low self-control: An extension and test of a general theory of crime. *Justice Quarterly, 16,* 633–654.

Schreck, C. J., Burek, M. W., Stewart, E. A., & Miller, J. M. (2007). Distress and violent victimization among young adolescents: Early puberty and the social interactionist explanation. *Journal of Research in Crime and Delinquency, 44,* 381–405.

Schreck, C. J., Fisher, B. S., & Miller, J. M. (2004). The social context of violent victimization: A study of the delinquent peer effect. *Justice Quarterly, 21,* 23–48.

Schreck, C. J., Stewart, E. A., & Osgood, D. W. (2008). A reappraisal of the overlap of violent offenders and victims. *Criminology, 46,* 871–906.

Singer, S. (1981). Homogeneous victim-offender populations: A review and some research implications. *Journal of Criminal Law and Criminology, 72,* 779–788.

Stewart, E. A., Schreck, C. J., & Simons, R. L. (2006). I ain't gonna let no one disrespect me: Does the code of the streets increase or reduce violent victimization? *Journal of Research in Crime and Delinquency, 43,* 427–458.

COST-BENEFIT ANALYSIS AND CRIME PREVENTION

Everyday decisions invoke cost-benefit analysis (CBA). Yet everyday decisions are so easy and mundane that we barely notice. Choosing to make scrambled egg for breakfast, we know the anticipated costs—price of eggs, time and effort of cooking, cholesterol risk—and the anticipated benefits—some protein, a full belly, the tasty pleasure when a little pepper is added. So we make everyday decisions seemingly without pause for thought because we have almost perfect knowledge and because the consequences of a wrong decision are usually fairly trivial. But when we pause for thought, this comes closer to a formal cost-benefit analysis. We come closer still with major personal decisions such as buying a car or property, when we list and weigh costs and benefits that are both immediate (my neighbors will be jealous) and long term (will I still have the emergency fund for a rainy day?). Generally speaking, the more complete the accounting, the closer we get to formal CBA, which, in the present context, is an evaluative framework used to assess the effectiveness of policy and programs.

While the overall concept of a CBA is simple (compare costs to benefits and see which is greater), the methodological specifics and practice can be less so. As the focus here is crime prevention and victimology rather than generic CBA issues, the key area of interest is the intricacies of defining and estimating benefits, particularly the enumeration of the harms from victimization. And here be methodological dragons.

The Costs of Crime

While a relative newcomer to victimology and crime prevention, CBA has an established pedigree. Decades of use informing engineering and health projects—dam building, airport location, vaccination efforts—mean key aspects of the methodology are well established, including discounting (estimating future costs and benefits) and the use of sensitivity analysis (seeing how costs vary with uncertainty). The use of CBA in environmental impact statements and estimation of nonmonetary and knock-on costs are increasingly common in major engineering works.

In crime prevention and victimology, the estimation of project or program costs is usually relatively straightforward. It is the estimate of benefits, specifically the cost of a crime, where difficulties lie (and although costs are "monetized," technically money is only used as a proxy for utility). In order to know the value of a prevented crime, an estimate must be made of what it would have cost a victim had the crime been committed. That requires putting a dollar value on the harms suffered by a victim. While the direct losses from crimes (medical bills, lost wages, value of stolen property) are easy to value, the indirect harms from crime—pain, suffering, and fear—are more difficult to estimate, and a number of different methods have been used to date. The issue is important because such estimates can inform how crime control, victim-related services, and other resources are allocated.

The first credible estimates of the value of indirect harms were developed from jury awards. The goal of jury compensation is to make victims "whole" again. In the 1980s, Vanderbilt University economist Mark Cohen used civil jury awards to estimate the average value society placed on different crime types, including the intangible costs of these crimes. From this foundation, his 1996 work with Ted Miller and Brian Wiersema produced the first credible U.S. national-level estimates of the cost of crime. Their work, which was sponsored by the U.S. Department of Justice, remains a landmark because of its sophistication and the magnitude of its estimates—at $450 billion for the United States (of which $350 was the emotional and psychological cost), it was far higher than previous estimates. Far from just an academic exercise, enumerating the total cost of crime shines a spotlight on the scope of damage to victims of crime, and these estimates produced considerable ripples in crime-related policy circles.

Following this lead, the U.K. government sponsored research to produce its own national estimates. The significance of that work, done first by Sam Brand and Richard Price but more recently by Richard Dubourg and his colleagues, lies in its methodology. The researchers drew on studies by Paul Dolan and his colleagues that estimated crime cost based on quality-adjusted life years (QALYs).

QALYs, a concept that evolved in health studies, estimate quality of life for a person between a value of 1 (good or normal health) and 0 (death) in any given year. Crime reduces the value to below 1 to an extent determined by the nature and seriousness of the crime. Thus, if the monetary value of a year's life is known (and it is admittedly estimated in a rather arbitrary fashion), then the cost due to crime can be derived.

In parallel to this use of QALYs, Cohen produced a further set of U.S. estimates by asking people their willingness to pay (WTP) for reductions in crime. If the amount a person will pay to reduce a type of crime by, say, 10% is known, then the implicit value that the person places on that type of crime can be derived. Each of the approaches has merit. The WTP methodology has been fairly widely used in fields unrelated to crime. However, WTP survey-based estimates (stated preferences) are often a lot higher than those based on observation of what people actually do (revealed preferences), such as how much they pay for security. The Cohen team's estimates of the value of crime were, depending on crime type, between 1.5 and 10 times higher than those produced elsewhere. There are substantial potential repercussions for policy on crime and victims if these higher estimates become widely accepted. It would suggest, *ceteris paribus*, that public resources allocated to crime control should be far greater. But at present, such wide discrepancies between estimates reduce the credibility of CBA in the sphere of crime prevention and victimology, particularly among those academics, practitioners, and policy makers who interpret the situation as meaning that the disparities show that little, if anything, of use can be derived from such estimates. Whatever the methodological issues that remain to be resolved, however, the basic fact remains that recent cost estimates, by drawing attention to the relatively huge intangible costs of pain and suffering (particularly for violent crimes), have made a major contribution to the policy debate.

The Value Added by Cost-Benefit Analysis

CBA allows different programs and policies to be compared on a level playing field, with effect compared pound for pound, regardless of whether the investment was large or small. This is important because a CBA can have different implications for an impact evaluation. Consider the situation where an impact evaluation (typically the count of the percentage drop in crime or something similar) shows that a lot of crime was prevented. If the types of crime prevented had a high social cost, the project is more likely to be replicable than if the types of crime had a relatively low social cost. Hence the impact evaluation does not provide all of the information needed for resource-allocation decisions and the development of policy. It is therefore interesting to note all the instances of policy that have been developed based on guesswork about cost effectiveness, and especially how immense some of those decisions have been. With the multimillion dollar investments in criminal justice, CBA could make a major contribution even if its contribution is marginal, and some researchers suspect it has the potential to go further than that.

The Budgeting Game Winners and Losers

CBA details who wins and who loses when a cost-effective program is employed. From a victim's perspective, this is a critical issue. Drug courts have proven to be quite a cost-effective intervention in both the United States and the United Kingdom, but they have failed to grow beyond modest, localized initiatives. The reason that they have failed to grow appears to involve who wins and who loses in the budgeting game. Drug courts tend to be a substantial burden on courts, costing $4,000 per participant per year, several times more than a typical case. Corrections does not pay for these programs, but experiences some benefit, since fewer beds have to be set aside for this population. But the big winner is the public, whose risk of victimization is reduced by effective programs. However, because victims are not a line item in any budget, their gains are considered tangential, and so growth of these programs is slow.

Externalities and Crime "Pollution"

Externalities are a critical concept in other disciplines, such as in climate control. The idea is straightforward—if someone who is not part of a transaction pays a cost because of that transaction, that person's cost should be considered in order to create a fair market. Suppose a manufacturer pumps out pollution as a cost of making a product. If the cost from that pollution is not included in the cost of the product, the market is not fair and efficient, and far more pollution will be created than if this cost was added, or "internalized," into the product cost. As in climate control, it is most often the victims of crimes, their families, and their communities who have an external cost that is not considered. For years, car manufacturers made products that were highly attractive targets and implicitly caused a lot of car crime. We now know that in-built security devices (central locking, immobilizers) cost little compared to the saving from reduced crime. There may be significant potential in promoting corporate social responsibility based on CBA that promotes crime prevention via better design of products, systems, and environments.

Criticisms

One basic objection to CBA rears its head often. How on earth, critics ask, can society put a monetary price on something like a rape? Surely that is not just cold and heartless but entirely impractical? Proponents argue that the opposite is true, and that it is far more heartless to fail to estimate the (statistical average) cost of rape. Absent such an estimate, including the huge intangible (emotional, psychological) cost, the financial cost of rape would appear to be lower than the cost of the average burglary. This, some propose, is an untenable and far more heartless position. Technically, the answer is that a monetary price is not put on anything—money is used only as a proxy metric for utility—and individual instances of crime are not being considered, only statistical averages.

Other aspects of CBA are quite frequently criticized in the field of crime prevention and victimology, and some of this criticism is considered valid and useful. The bulk of the useful criticism relates to the fact that CBA is still in its infancy in this field. There is little agreement on cost of crime estimates, and nothing close to methodological standardization. There is still little definitional standardization, which can lead to confusion (although the Crime Reduction Programme of the U.K. Home Office, the biggest crime-related CBA undertaken to date, sought to standardize terms and methods via a series of guidebooks). It is certainly the case that variations in definitions and cost-estimation methods can lead to significant variation in results, and it is here that it is hoped CBA will make forward strides in the future.

Final Note

Cost-benefit analysis for victimology and crime prevention is in its infancy. There is an emerging literature on estimating intangible costs of crime to victims, including the fear of crime. There are important insights from this literature, most notably that the crime prevention programs that appear effective may not necessarily be appealing to policy makers. That is, programs that tend to cost governmental agencies money but return benefits to the public and not that agency tend to be underfunded. And policies that might most benefit the public, and reduce victimization by reducing externalities, may prove tricky from a political standpoint. Overall, while it would be fair to say that the contribution of CBA to policy and practice is limited at present, the corollary is that it has significant potential.

Graham Farrell and John K. Roman

See also Crime Prevention; Economic Costs of
  Victimization; Fear of Crime; Victimology

Further Readings

Bowles, R., & Pradiptyo, R. (2004). *Reducing burglary initiative: An analysis of costs, benefits and cost effectiveness.* Retrieved from http://www.homeoffice.gov.uk/rds/pdfs04/rdsolr4304.pdf

Cohen, M. (2005). *Cost of crime.* London: Routledge.

Dolan, P., Loomes, G., Peasgood, T., & Tsuchiya, A. (2005). Estimating the intangible victim costs of crime. *British Journal of Criminology, 45*(9), 958–976.

Dubourg, R., Hamed, J., & Thorns, J. (2005). *The economic and social costs of crime against individuals and households 2003/4.* Online Report 30/05. Retrieved from http://www.homeoffice.gov.uk/rds/pdfs05/rdsolr3005.pdf

Farrell, G., Bowers, K., & Johnson, S. D. (2005). Cost-benefit analysis for crime science: Making cost-benefit analysis useful via a portfolio of outcomes. In M. Smith & N. Tilley (Eds.), *Crime science: New approaches to preventing and detecting crime* (pp. 56–81). Cullompton, UK: Willan.

Farrington, D. P., & Painter, K. A. (2001). The financial benefits of improved street lighting, based on crime reduction. *Lighting Research and Technology*, *33*(1), 3–12.

Flyvberg, B., Holm, M. S., & Buhl, S. (2002). Underestimating costs in public works projects: Error or lie? *APA Journal*, *68*(3), 279–295.

Roman, J. (2004). Can cost-benefit analysis answer criminal justice policy questions, and if so, how? *Journal of Contemporary Criminal Justice*, *20*(3), 257–275.

Roman, J., & Harrell, A. (2001). Assessing the costs and benefits accruing to the public from a graduated sanctions program for drug-using defendants. *Law and Policy*, *23*(2), 237–268.

Viscusi, W. K., & Zeckhauser, R. J. (2003). *Sacrificing civil liberties to reduce terrorism risks* (Discussion Paper No. 41). John M. Olin Center for Law, Economics and Business. Cambridge, MA: Harvard Law School.

COUPLES THERAPY

Couples therapy addresses any number of issues that may cause discordance between two individuals in a relationship. The challenges to a relationship may come from society, family, emotional or physical health, culture, religion, and/or economics. The relationship is usually defined by intimacy and the partners' past or current commitment to each other. Couples therapy might also be referred to as marriage counseling or family therapy. Given the modernization of society, "couple" reflects those in a marriage, partnership, or civil union. This entry provides a definition of couples therapy, discusses conflicts this therapy helps to resolve, and examines the role of therapy in reunifying couples.

Definition

Couples therapy is engaged in by two individuals (of the same sex or different genders) attempting to enhance their relationship, work on problems that have arisen in their relationship, or address the termination of their relationship. Couples therapy is an approach to helping couples improve their communication in order to address problems, adjust to new situations, and seek solutions. It is a process that may be used throughout the life of a relationship to address a specific issue or to sustain a positive bond. Licensed marriage and family therapists, psychologists, psychiatrists, social workers, counselors, and physicians may practice couples therapy.

Conflicts Benefiting From Couples Therapy

Negotiating a prenuptial agreement may be the initial experience with couples therapy for those with significant wealth or successful professional careers. Prenuptial agreements involve careful delineation of ownership of financial holdings, disbursement in case of death to one member's family, or property to be excluded from consideration in case of the termination of the relationship or marriage. Most often such an agreement focuses on the financial determination of wealth that was earned or inherited prior to the marriage or initiation of the relationship. In states where community property is a policy, a couple may file a prenuptial agreement when they intend to get married. However, in states where a couple can prove cohabitation (i.e., 8 years of living together), then the cohabitation itself proves that the couple jointly own property and share responsibilities as well as all privileges associated with the relationship. The prenuptial agreement is a contract where both individuals comprehend the issues, as evidenced by their signatures. Both states and courts often define the rights and duties of partners associated with cohabitation. At that time, all assets are considered "community property" within that state, irrespective of the agreement. In this circumstance, it is common for parties to find a legal firm that includes the practice of mediation to assist in making the final determination for the agreement. The prenuptial agreement is typically settled prior to the actual marriage or purchase of property in both names.

Infidelity often brings couples to therapy either to terminate the relationship or to make an effort to save it. While the act of infidelity may be considered the sole issue, research indicates that marital discord may have been evident prior to the adulterous act. Support groups can help couples deal with not only the infidelity but the antecedent issues. For instance, couples addressing addictive behaviors, along with infidelity, may need to augment their therapy with support groups such as Alcoholics Anonymous (AA), Al-Anon, Sex Addicts Anonymous (SAA), Narcotics Anonymous (NA), or Gamblers Anonymous (GA). These self-help groups, based on the 12-step program of AA, offer 24-hour support in the community at little or no cost. They also address the problem of codependency, in which the nonaddicted partner has acquired behaviors that serve the addiction rather than the healthy behaviors needed to improve the situation. Research indicates that group therapy away from the partner may offer the nonaddicted partner additional support for making behavioral changes.

Sexual incompatibilities usually stem from unmet needs in terms of frequency, particular types of sexual acts, sexual roles, or the unsatisfactory execution of the sexual act. Such incompatibility may arise from emotional issues that one or both may have brought to the relationship. Sometimes experiences from childhood sexual abuse or sexual assault may need to be addressed before the sexual issues in the partnership can respond to couples therapy.

Issues arising from health conditions, physical appearance, medication, or the lack of communication may add to the complexities of couples therapy. Medicine continues to move forward in terms of its ability to treat erectile dysfunction and infertility, which may result in couples' experiencing communication difficulties about the choices and costs of treatment. In vitro fertilization is costly in many ways. These costs may be incurred as a result of stress, mood changes from hormones, medications, testing, determination of fault, and failure or success. Not all types of insurance pay for infertility treatment, and some couples accruing substantial financial hardships in their desire to have a child. Other medical treatments may require surgical interventions, pharmacological alternatives, and lengthy treatments that often complicate and obscure the original goal of benefiting the relationship. In some circumstances, couples involved in therapy and medical treatment will need to recognize the limitations of the treatment and when to end their attempts. Those considering adoption may also benefit from couples therapy, which can help them communicate about choices such as the gender, age, and race of the child.

Divorce, custody arrangements, remarriage, and blended families benefit from couples therapy. Therapy creates an environment that allows two individuals to discuss solutions, express anger, and make decisions under guidance. There are also "retreats" where couples go to work on their relationship away from their home, their routine, and their habitual communication. The sheltered environment may change the couple's decision to terminate the relationship. It may be that open communication about long held resentments may lead to remediation and reconciliation. Research discusses the changed circumstances that may result from couples therapy and the potential for a positive outcome for the couple in therapy.

If the dissolution of the relationship is the final decision, resolving problems that involve custody issues, disbursement of the assets, and the future of the relationship may be aided by therapy. There are some states where a divorce may not be granted to the couple with children unless the couple undergoes therapy for a period of time. These courts may be referred to as family court or courts of reconciliation and are statutorily required.

Remarriage and blended families present significant challenges to some couples. Couples therapy can prepare couples for presenting the change to the children and other family members, as well as for the possibility of biological children resulting from the new marriage. Couples therapy helps to prepare individuals for possible challenges to their decision, their authority, and their lifestyles. It is possible that family therapy may also be beneficial for those whose union creates a blended family and who need to learn to cope with change as a family.

Child rearing poses its own challenges to relationships, as conflicts reflect beliefs about gender disparities, discipline, education, curfews, peers, and generational differences. There are times when generational differences might merge with cultural differences and turmoil appears insurmountable. Questions arise about the differences between raising boys and girls, which then may become exacerbated by conformity to culture or custom. Couples therapy may help address such conflicts before the turmoil requires family therapy. In such circumstances, a couple's therapist should be well versed in the culture and the expectations held by a particular community.

Couples therapy may also be required in cases of domestic violence. Some couples may seek it out in an attempt to find ways to address conflict in the relationship without resorting to violence. This violence may be physical, mental, or sexual. An abusive partner may resort to economic intimidation, threats to pets or children, and/or coercive statements. If couples seek the therapy independently of the courts and are truthful in the therapy sessions, then there may be a positive outcome for them. This outcome may mean the termination of the relationship or the basis on which to work toward a more positive one. However, if the couples therapy is repeatedly court ordered and the victim of the violence does not feel safe, couples therapy is not appropriate. Couples therapy is not meant to place or keep one partner in a dangerous situation. Both members of the relationship need to be in a situation that is safe from violence and from the opportunity to commit violence. Domestic violence is a social issue that remains intractable to treatment and uncomplicated solutions.

Financial trouble and unemployment cause significant strife in a relationship. When economic burdens result in the loss of housing, health care, and basic necessities, a family is in serious jeopardy. The members of a couple may blame each other for the inability to support the family, resulting in the diminished role of the former breadwinner. It is common for both partners to seek employment in order to meet their financial obligations. This may result in conflict about child care, financial decisions, and the freedom of either partner to leave a contemptible job. This stress is then taken back to the home, and the relationship may be seriously strained. In this case, couples therapy along with a referral for debt counseling may be appropriate. As with other counseling situations, couples therapy may be augmented with other community services or group therapy.

Life presents changes that may require couples therapy. The catastrophic illness of one partner may alter who makes financial decisions and make the other partner into a caretaker. Decisions about health care, do not resuscitate orders (DNRs), and assisted-living communities can be made easier with the aid of couples therapy. Geriatric clinics and philanthropic organizations often have numerous community resources available to assist couples. A couple's decision to retire, relocate for health issues, move from the family home to a retirement community, or allow an adult child to return home may benefit from couples therapy.

Those in same-sex relationships may experience the problems discussed above as well as constraints imposed by statutes, politics, customs, and religious dogma. While two individuals may see themselves as in a committed marriage, they may not be seen that way by others, and may come into conflict with legal policies, family traditions, and community mores. Couples in same-sex relationships may need therapy in order to overcome the prejudice and shunning they may experience from friends and family. A therapist may be recommended from within the gay or lesbian community, with the goal of enhancing communication between the partners. Depending on where the couple resides, legal contracts may have to determine financial issues, estate planning, guardianship issues in case of illness, and burial requests. Whether to adopt children or use surrogate mothers, sperm donors, or artificial insemination is an important decision for same-sex couples, and couples therapy can help them with such a decision.

Reunification of Couples

In today's society, separation may result from a number of issues, and reunification poses significant challenges to couples. Some couples reunite after years of separation, and couples therapy may be beneficial to ensure that past mistakes will not be repeated. Military deployment and tours of duty often leave one partner with the responsibility for the family. This may include financial responsibility as well as child-rearing decisions. A particular challenge is the deployed family member's reassimilation into the family and community upon his or her return; this is especially difficult when an individual's repeated tours to war-torn areas have resulted in posttraumatic stress disorder. It is not unusual for the returning family member to experience periods of depression and behavioral changes requiring medication. The reunification of the family following these challenges often comes with difficulties as the couple learns to communicate and become a partnership once again. Couples therapy and support from their community may ease the transition for this couple.

Likewise, the burgeoning prison population also presents the challenge of reunification to couples whose members have had disparate experiences, often for a significant period of time, as a result of one member's incarceration. Couples therapy, along with family therapy, may be very important to the success of the relationship, as well as to secure a successful transition from incarceration to freedom. Support from the community and support groups associated with addictive behaviors also may help to secure the relationship.

Couples therapy appears to primarily be required for problems with communication. As previously noted, the surrounding community may offer couples a number of supportive services that can augment couples therapy and its efficacy.

Toni DuPont-Morales

See also Domestic Violence; Family Therapy

Further Readings

Brimhall, A., Wampler, K., & Kimball, T. (2008). Learning from the past, altering the future: A tentative theory of the effect of past relationships on couples who remarry. *Family Process, 47*(3), 373–387.

Hellmuth, J., Follansbee, K., Moore, T., & Stuart, G. (2008). Reduction of intimate partner violence in a gay couple following alcohol treatment. *Journal of Homosexuality, 54*(4), 439–448.

Heyman, R. (2001). Observation of couple conflicts: Clinical assessment applications, stubborn truths, and shaky foundations. *Psychological Assessment, 13*(1), 5–35.

Katz, A. (2008). Postcombat sexual problems. *American Journal of Nursing, 108*(10), 35–39.

Schermer, V. (2009). On the vicissitudes of combining individual and group psychotherapy. *International Journal of Group Psychotherapy, 59*(1), 149–162.

COURT ADVOCATES

Court advocates, also commonly referred to as victim advocates, victim witness liaisons, or victim witness coordinators, are professionals employed within the criminal justice system to provide a variety of services to crime victims, including the assurance of their legal rights to provisions, protection, and information pertaining to their criminal case. These services begin when the crime has been committed and often extend beyond the disposition of the case. The profession of court advocate has existed for about three decades, beginning at the grassroots level during the victims' rights movement in the 1970s. This entry discusses the emergence of court advocacy as a profession within the criminal justice system, the role of court advocates, and the professional challenges faced by advocates.

The victims' rights movement in the 1970s marked the beginning of a large-scale movement to bring attention to the needs of crime victims. With the development of crime victim compensation programs in the late 1960s and the first funded victim assistance programs in the mid-1970s, the need for professionals designated to assist victims of crime became clear. Although funding sources for advocacy programs have historically waxed and waned, the Federal Victim and Witness Protection Act of 1982 and the Victims of Crime Act (VOCA) of 1984 offered the first federal legislation to address the needs of crime victims, and they have led to the development of advocacy programs within numerous criminal justice and community agencies. Since then, there have been additional federal policies and every state has enacted victims' rights statutes. Most employ advocates within the criminal justice system to ensure that crime victims receive the rights, protections, and services to which they are legally entitled.

Court advocates typically hold a bachelor's degree, though many have graduate degrees, and come from a variety of disciplines, including criminal justice, sociology, psychology, public health, social work, and mental health counseling. The level of education and training required differs from agency to agency, and the level of specialization varies according to the size of the jurisdiction. The number of advocates employed in a jurisdiction can range from one to dozens. Advocates are employed by prosecutor's offices, within the court system, and within a number of law enforcement and other social services agencies.

Advocates work on cases involving a variety of crimes. The most common are domestic violence, stalking, sexual assaults, and other felony cases, such as armed robbery and homicide. Some advocates are highly educated and trained in one area, and the majority of their caseload consists of those types of cases. For example, advocates who work exclusively with survivors of homicide victims and those who work with children who have been sexually assaulted typically are more experienced in these areas than are other advocates and have additional crisis intervention training. In smaller jurisdictions, however, one advocate may work on behalf of victims of several different types of crimes, due to smaller caseloads or fewer resources to employ more advocates.

The responsibilities of court advocates typically begin when a victim or witness reports a crime. The court advocate notifies the victim or witness of his or her legal rights and explains the criminal justice process. Regular contact is then made to inform this person of upcoming hearings, depositions, trial dates, and so on.

In addition to the logistics of the case, advocates continually assess the needs of the victims and maintain relationships within other community service organizations in order to provide referrals and, in some cases, emergency shelter. Advocates also assist victims with the process of applying for victim compensation, enrolling in address confidentiality and other protection programs, and obtaining orders of protection (i.e., restraining orders, injunctions). They accompany victims to all court proceedings and, in addition to educating them about the nature of the proceedings and explaining the outcome, advocates provide continual emotional support. They help prepare victims emotionally for what can be a daunting process through a variety of hearings, depositions, and trial; they assist with the preparation of victim impact statements, continually offer social services referrals, and work to minimize potential revictimization by the criminal justice system process. In addition, advocates relay input and concerns from the crime victims to prosecutors and other court personnel, acting as an important source of guidance to other personnel.

The work of victim advocates can be physically and emotionally demanding due to the heavy caseloads, lack of adequate resources, frustrations associated with victims who are sometimes resistant to services, and continuous threats to funding that jeopardize valuable resources for victims and advocacy positions. Advocates have historically struggled for professional recognition, but with the implementation of advanced education programs and extensive training, advocates are now widely regarded as an integral part of the criminal justice system. Currently, advocates are being sought for input in academic research, as expert witnesses, and in the media for commentary on the plight of crime victims and for their perspective on specific cases.

Many victims of crime encounter the criminal justice system for the first time upon their victimization and are thrust into what is commonly perceived to be a confusing, intimidating process of navigating through the system. The advocate acts as an important liaison between the victim and the system and strives to empower people who are likely to have suffered emotionally, physically, and financially from their victimization.

Rae Taylor

See also Court Appointed Special Advocates for Children; Homicide, Victim Advocacy Groups; Victim Assistance Programs, United States; Victims' Rights Legislation, Federal, United States; Victims' Rights Movement, United States; Witness Assistance Programs

Further Readings

Davies, J., Lyon, E., & Monti-Catania, D. (1998). *Safety planning with battered women: Complex lives/difficult choices.* Thousand Oaks, CA: Sage.

Dunn, J. L., & Powell-Williams, M. (2007). Everybody makes choices: Victim advocates and the social construction of battered women's victimization and agency. *Violence Against Women, 13*(10), 977–1001.

Wasco, S. M., Campbell, R., & Clark, M. (2002). A multiple case study of rape victim advocates' self-care routines: The influence of organizational context. *American Journal of Community Psychology, 30,* 731–760.

COURT APPOINTED SPECIAL ADVOCATES FOR CHILDREN

Every year approximately a half million victims of child abuse and neglect come to the attention of child protective service agencies across the United Stares and are placed into protective custody.

More than half of these child victims have the benefit of a court appointed special advocate (CASA). A CASA is a volunteer who is appointed by a judge to represent the best interest of abused and neglected children in cases that come before the court. These community volunteers work under the supervision of local CASA programs to ensure the rights of children who have been removed from their homes by the state child protective service agency in their jurisdiction. Unlike other professionals with high caseloads, CASAs have the luxury of concentrating their efforts on one child or one family of children. Every day advocates face the devastation caused by child abuse and neglect and are confronted with the family dynamics that lead to child maltreatment. Volunteers are challenged by issues of parental poverty, violence, and isolation. They are trained to respond to an overburdened and complex child welfare system as they advocate for the right of every child to a safe and permanent home. Advocates often find themselves maneuvering their way through a maze of laws, mandates, administrative policies, procedures, and philosophies. CASA programs exist so that children in out-of-home placement do not slip through the cracks of an overburdened social service and judicial system.

Program History

In 1975 Judge David Soukup of Seattle, Washington, questioned whether he was getting all the facts about each juvenile case that came before him, and if the welfare of each child was being represented. He obtained funding to recruit and train community volunteers to act on behalf of children. These volunteers were called court appointed special advocates. In 1977 a pilot program was implemented in Seattle. In 1982 the National Court Appointed Special Advocate Association was formed; it has since developed national standards and a national training curriculum for CASA programs. The National CASA Association promotes the growth of existing state and local agencies and startup agencies through technical assistance, training, funding, and public awareness services. According to the National CASA Association, there are 930 CASA affiliated programs and 73,000 volunteers nationwide. CASA programs have a presence in 49 states, the District of Columbia, and the Virgin Islands. Community volunteers in partnership with the judiciary serve approximately 290,000 children every year. Advocates improve outcomes for children and assist juvenile courts in meeting their responsibility to provide dependent children with a safe, stable, and permanent home.

Program Models

The National Court Appointed Special Advocate Association recognizes two program models. Under the Guardian Ad Litem (GAL) model, trained CASA volunteers are appointed to act as a party to the case in child abuse and neglect proceedings. The GAL is responsible for investigating the issues that led to the out-of-home placement and for presenting a written report and recommendations to the judge. The GAL is entitled to review all relevant materials and interview all relevant parties. The GAL works under close supervision of the staff and has access to an attorney who provides information and legal advice. The Friend of the Court model utilizes CASA volunteers to serve as witnesses and impartial observers to case activities. These volunteers are not a party to the litigation. They act as information gatherers and are free to interview birth parents, the child, therapists, social workers, foster parents, school personnel, and any other interested parties. Volunteers investigate case activity and submit written reports to the court. They are present at all legal proceedings as observers. The Friend of the Court model is used when an attorney has been assigned by the court to serve as a GAL. Attorneys acting in this capacity represent a child's wishes to the court even when they do not agree with the child's judgment. Often these volunteers and GALs will work cooperatively to ensure a positive outcome for the child. CASA volunteers are effective when they have the backing of a structured CASA program and the support of the court, the child protective service workers, the mental health professionals, and other community representatives and agencies involved in a case.

Role and Responsibilities

CASA volunteers are not required to have specialized degrees or experience in the mental health field, social services, or the law. They are required to be mature and responsible adults committed to the needs of children. They must be willing to undergo a rigorous screening process in accordance with the standards of the national CASA association. A judicial appointment to a case provides a volunteer access to all confidential records relevant to his or her assigned case. CASA/GAL volunteers must conduct a thorough investigation of all issues that led to the removal of the child from his or her home before making responsible recommendations to the court. These volunteers begin the process by reviewing all case documents and case files. They interview all professionals, family members, foster parents, and community representatives, including school personnel and day care providers who are involved in the case. They may act as liaisons and mediators between interested parties, appear at hearings as observers, and at times provide testimony to the court. CASA/GAL volunteers spend time getting to know the children to whom they are assigned while building a trusting relationship. They are responsible for assessing a child's developmental stage, cultural background, and sense of self. Armed with the facts they have gathered, CASAs make recommendations to the court for services for the child and family with the goal of facilitating permanency. CASA/GAL volunteers are also charged with monitoring case plans to ensure that court-ordered services are provided in a timely fashion and the case plan is moving forward. Children who have been removed from their homes have no other advocate whose sole agenda is the best interest of the child.

Francine C. Raguso

See also Child Abuse, Identification of; Child Abuse, Neglect, and Maltreatment; Child Abuse, Neglect, and Maltreatment: Interventions for; Child Abuse, Neglect, and Maltreatment: Mandatory Reporting; Child Abuse, Neglect, and Maltreatment: Measurement of; Child Abuse, Neglect, and Maltreatment: Statutory Responses; Child Abuse, Neglect, and Maltreatment: Theories of

Further Readings

Duquette, D. N. (1990). *Advocating for the child in protection proceedings: A handbook for lawyers and court appointed special advocates.* Lexington, MA: Lexington Books.

National CASA Association. (2002). *CASA: A guide to program development.* Retrieved November 22, 2008, from http://www.casanet.org/program-services/guides/guide-program-development/index.htm
National CASA Association. (2004). *Judges guide to CASA/GAL program development.* Retrieved August 6, 2008, from http://www.casanet.org/download/guides-manuals/0709_judges_guide_0119.pdf

Web Sites

National CASA Association: http://www.nationalcasa.org

CRIME AND DISORDER ACT

The U.K. Crime and Disorder Act 1998 is legislation that was passed by both Houses (Commons and Lords) of the U.K. Parliament in December 1997 and subsequently received Royal Assent in July 1998. It has been of great interest to criminal justice academics and practitioners because it changed U.K. law and criminal justice strategy in relation to a number of key areas. These include the introduction of antisocial behavior orders and parenting orders, sex offender orders, the introduction of a law specific to "racially aggravated" offenses, the abolition of the rebuttable presumption that a child is "doli incapax" (i.e., incapable of committing an offense because he or she is under the age of 10), and the abolition of treason (the crime of "disloyalty to the Sovereign," which can include plotting murder, planning war, assisting enemies of the State, or undermining the lawfully established line of succession). Finally, possibly the most widely discussed innovation was the extension of local authority responsibilities for crime reduction. While it is not possible to discuss the entirety of the act here, it is pertinent to discuss the background of the act in terms of its social and political context and also to highlight the key areas of interest, namely youth justice and community safety.

Context of the Act

It is important to understand the social and political context of any legislation. In relation to the U.K. Crime and Disorder Act (hereinafter referred to as CDA), there are three key issues. First, the competition for political power in the United Kingdom rests, as it does in many democracies, on the law and order platform and the wish to present a political party to the British electorate as being tough on crime. Legislation is therefore surrounded by politics, which is usually driven by a responsiveness to populist public demand. In this sense, the CDA represents part of a wider response to the perceived need for the British government to respond to rising crime rates. Unlike many acts, however—which are often knee-jerk responses to situations—the CDA was planned over a period of time. The Labour Party had announced in their 1997 general election manifesto that crime reduction and community safety were central to their criminal justice strategy, should they be elected, but the source of this focus actually lay in a previous report, which explored the second of the key issues referred to here. The Home Office's 1991 Morgan Report, *Safer Communities: The Local Delivery of Crime Prevention Through the Partnership Approach*, had reflected a change in thinking about who should be responsible for preventing crime. This report suggested that the responsibility for crime reduction, which was traditionally thought of as being the sole remit of the police, should be allocated to local authorities. This was later reflected in the Home Office consultation document *Getting to Grips With Crime: A New Framework for Local Intervention* (1997, p. 1), which stated that the purpose of the strategy was to "give the vital work of preventing crime a new focus across a very wide range of local services. . . . It is a matter of putting crime and disorder at the heart of decision making." The third and final key influence on the enactment of the CDA was the Audit Commission's report on youth justice that was published in 1996 and titled *Misspent Youth: Young People and Crime*. This report indicated that the youth justice system was both inefficient and expensive and suggested that the British criminal justice system was failing to address offending by young people; there was a lack of programs directed at offending behavior; the system needed to be speeded up; and there needed to be much closer working relationships between the main agencies involved in youth justice. The CDA can also be seen as an integral part of the rebranding and modernization of the old into "New" Labour Party, in which the manifesto on public services and public policy changed dramatically.

Overall the CDA is a substantial piece of legislation covering a multitude of criminal justice issues. However, the main focus of debate about this act has revolved around two of the main substantive areas it covers: youth justice and community safety. While these will provide the main focus of this entry, Table 1 usefully outlines the main provisions of the act.

Youth Justice

In terms of youth justice, the CDA made a number of significant changes. The existing formal and informal cautions were replaced with a reprimand or (for more serious offenses) a final warning. It also introduced the recommendation that all young offenders receiving a final warning should be referred to a youth offending team (YOT) and take part in rehabilitation programs that would normally include some form of reparation. However, what the CDA is probably most famous for, in terms of its youth justice approach, is the antisocial behavior measures that it introduced—in particular, the Anti-Social Behaviour Order (popularly referred to as the ASBO).

Anti-Social Behaviour Order

The U.K. Home Office describes antisocial behavior as any activity that impacts people in a negative way. The type of behavior that is normally thought of as being antisocial for the purposes of Part I of the Crime and Disorder Act 1998 is rowdy, nuisance, yobbish, or intimidating behavior that takes place in public areas, but it can also be extended to include vandalism, graffiti, flyposting, dealing and buying drugs on the street, dumping trash, abandoning cars, begging, and antisocial drinking. In an effort to tackle what the government viewed as unacceptable activity that was impacting the quality of community life, the Crime and Disorder Act introduced a civil remedy called the Anti-Social Behaviour Order (ASBO). This order can be issued by a Magistrates Court (or the Sheriff's Court in Scotland) against people who have

Table I   Crime and Disorder Act 1998: Main provisions, England and Wales

Section	
1.	Anti-social behaviour order
2-3	Sex offender orders
4	Appeals against orders
Crime and Disorder Strategies	
5	Authorities responsible for strategies
6 -7	Formulation and implementation of strategies (& supplemental)
Youth crime and disorder	
8-10	Parenting orders
11-13	Child safety orders
14-15	Local child curfew schemes
16	Removal of truants to designated premises etc
Miscellaneous	
17	Duty to consider crime and disorder implications
25	Powers to require removal of masks etc
26-27	Retention and disposal of things seized/failure to comply
Racially-aggravated offences & miscellaneous criminal law provisions	
28-32	Racially-aggravated offences: assaults; criminal damage; public order; harassment
34	Abolition of doli incapax
35	Effects of child's silence at trial
36	Abolition of the death penalty for treason and piracy
Youth justice	
37	Aims of the youth justice system
38-40	Local provisions: Youth Offending Teams, youth justice plans
41-2	Youth Justice Board
43-6	Time limits
47	Powers of youth courts
48-52	Other court provision
Miscellaneous criminal justice	
53	CPS: powers of non-legal staff
54-56	Bail
57	Use of television links

Dealing with offenders

58-60	Extended sentences for sexual or violent offenders
61-4	Drug treatment and testing orders
65-66	Reprimands and warnings
67-8	Reparation orders
69-70	Action plan orders
71-2	Supervision orders
73-79	Detention and training orders
80-1	Sentencing guidelines and the Sentencing Advisory Panel
82	Increase in sentences for racial aggravation
115	Disclosure of information to reduce crime

Source: This table has been reproduced with the kind permission of Professor Tim Newburn from his paper, *New Labour, Modernisation and the Crime and Disorder Act 1998,* which was given at Leeds University Centre for Criminal Justice Studies 21st Anniversary Conference "Crime and Disorder Act: 10 years," May 7–8, 2008.

engaged in antisocial behavior that—in the United Kingdom and according to section 1 (1) of the Crime and Disorder Act 1998—is defined as "conduct which caused or was likely to cause alarm, harassment or distress to one or more persons not of the same household as himself or herself and where an ASBO is seen as necessary to protect relevant persons from further anti-social acts by the defendant." Each ASBO and what it prohibits must be individualized to the person regarding whom it is issued. For example, it can include a prohibition from entering a particular area or speaking to certain people. Breach of an ASBO is a criminal offense and conviction may result in imprisonment from a minimum of 2 years to a maximum of 5 years. Although most ASBOs are issued regarding the types of behavior indicated earlier, there have been instances where they have been issued in more unusual circumstances, and this has led to criticism. For example, in February 2003, a 16-year-old boy was banned from showing his tattoos, wearing a single golf glove, or wearing a balaclava in public anywhere in the country. The oldest recipient of an order has been an 87-year-old man who among other things was

forbidden, in July 2003, from being sarcastic to his neighbors. In December 2004, a man from Norfolk became the first farmer to be the subject of an ASBO when he was ordered to keep his pigs and geese under control after people living near his farm complained that they had escaped and caused damage.

Since the introduction of the ASBO, controversy has surrounded it for a number of reasons. Some critics of the ASBO argue that it criminalizes behavior that would otherwise be lawful, and others have voiced concerns about the open-ended nature of ASBO penalties, as there is little restriction on what a court may impose as the terms of the ASBO, and little restriction on what can be designated as antisocial behavior. More recently concerns have been expressed about the implementation and effect of ASBOs on youth. Specifically, in some cases it has been suggested that ASBOs were granted without lower-tier measures (such as home visits and warnings letters) being tried. It has also been suggested that the ASBO has resulted in some young people being taken into custody who would not previously have found themselves there.

Parenting Orders

A further measure introduced by the CDA is the parenting order that can be made against the parent/s of a child who has been given an Anti-Social Behaviour Order or has been convicted of an offense. The parenting order imposes certain requirements upon the parent/s to ensure that the child does not perpetrate behavior similar to that for which the ASBO was given, and any breach of this order results in a fine.

Community Safety

Local Authority Responsibilities

One of the most radical aspects of the CDA was its emphasis on enabling a sharing of the responsibility for crime reduction. Specifically, under section 17 of the CDA, each local authority in England and Wales was given the responsibility to formulate a strategy to reduce crime and disorder in their area and to work with appropriate agencies, such as the police authority, probation authority, and the health authority, in order to achieve this. To enable this it was necessary to develop 376 new localized partnership bodies, which were called Crime and Disorder Reduction Partnerships (CDRPs). These partnerships were tasked with carrying out a 3-year crime and disorder strategy within each local area, and relatedly, to regularly audit local crime and disorder. The origins of this reorganization of the responsibilities for crime reduction and community safety can also be traced to the 1991 Morgan Report, as it represented a substantial change in thinking about what Tim Newburn calls "the local nature and governance of crime control." The Crime and Disorder Act 1998 contained many radical innovations, but section 17 has been perceived as among the most radical because it highlighted the notion of shared responsibility for crime reduction across a wide range of local authority services. It should also be acknowledged that section 17 was primarily conceived by the U.K. Home Office as an "enabling device" for the promotion of effective crime reductive activities within the police and local authorities. In the decade since its enactment, however, section 17 has remained somewhat poorly articulated and implemented for a number of reasons. First, its

feasibility as a crime reductive tool has been somewhat impaired because central government departments have not themselves been bound by the same statutory criteria, and this has led to some inconsistencies of approach to crime reduction, particularly in areas such as development and planning law. Second, no Home Office Guidance was issued at the time of the legislation, and this created problems of interpretation. The result of this is that section 17 has not had the impact it could have had as a radical and innovative crime reductive tool.

Information Sharing

The second way in which the CDA 1998 sought to emphasize the crime reductive responsibilities of local authorities was through its section 115. This section permits the disclosure of personal information to the police, local authorities, probation committees, and health authorities, as long as that disclosure is connected with the legitimate prevention of crime. It has been suggested that this section of the act provides a "statutory gateway" for the flow of information, since it gives the local crime reduction partnerships described previously the legal authority to exchange data or information as long as any exchange conforms with other legal restraints and does not breach either human rights or administrative law. What is perhaps particularly interesting about this legislation is that it signaled a radical repositioning of the responsibility for crime and made it very clear that the government's view was that the exchange of information, within certain legal constraints, was a mechanism by which more crime could be prevented or reduced. This approach subsequently became more important after it was highlighted that poor information-sharing mechanisms may have contributed to the Soham murders in which Ian Huntley's appointment as a school caretaker in Cambridge, England, enabled the murders of two young girls, Holly Wells and Jessica Chapman. It is worth pointing out that the subsequent government inquiry into the case by Sir Michael Bichard in 2004 found the police in Humberside (the area from which Huntley had relocated to Cambridge) wanting regarding their record keeping, and advised the creation of a national police intelligence database that would be capable of exchanging information with social services. However, the problem here—which has been referred to by P. A. J. Waddington in his article in *Jane's Police Review*—is that that Huntley had never been convicted, so any information held by Humberside Police and Hull Social Services could arguably have not been relied upon. This illustrates clearly that the statutory capacity to share information will only be of use if the information exists.

Problems and Commendations

There is little doubt among either practitioners or academics that the Crime and Disorder Act 1998 was a radical, innovative, and in some ways controversial piece of legislation that has changed the way that approaches to crime reduction and community safety in the United Kingdom are perceived. It is relevant, however, to conclude by mentioning some of the problems that have been associated with its implementation.

First, it has proved somewhat difficult for the 376 CDRPs mentioned previously to develop and implement the strategies that the act required of them. For some this has resulted in a lack of focus about crime reduction strategies, while for others it has simply come down to a lack of expertise or the capacity to undertake this type of work effectively. It has been particularly difficult in some cases to implement community safety strategies where the police have no longer been the dominant partner. Some agencies have been unwilling to share information—most notably health services—and have consequently not sought to involve themselves in these activities. Second, there has been some tension between local and national imperatives, as referred to by Daniel Gilling, who suggests that the structure of managerial control is hierarchical, with the Treasury and Home Office at the top and neighborhoods at the bottom. This, he says, has resulted in them being at the end of "the chain of command," and consequently their function is merely to perform as directed by those higher up the chain. It has thus been difficult for local community safety and crime reduction initiatives to flourish in some cases because there exists a conflict between delegating responsibility to local authorities under the terms of the CDA and abrogating the desire for central government control.

It should be noted that there is much to commend the approach that this piece of legislation took. Indeed, there have been substantial declines in crime in the United Kingdom during the last decade. However, the British government has been somewhat reluctant to acknowledge that these declines are in any way indicators of the success of a crime reductive approach.

Kate Moss

See also Crime Prevention Partnerships, International; Crime Prevention Partnerships, United States; Project Safe Neighborhoods; Safer Cities Program

Further Readings

Byrne, S., & Pease, K. (2008). Crime reduction and community safety. In T. Newburn (Ed.), *Handbook of policing* (2nd ed.). Cullompton, UK: Willan.

Crawford, A. (2007). Crime prevention and community safety. In M. Maguire, R. Morgan, & R. Reiner (Eds.), *Oxford handbook of criminology*. Oxford, UK: Oxford University Press.

Garland, D. (2001). *The culture of control.* Oxford, UK: Oxford University Press.

Gilling, D. (2007). *Crime reduction and community safety: Labour and the politics of local crime control.* Cullompton, UK: Willan.

Home Office (U.K.). (n.d.). *Anti-social behavior.* Retrieved from http://www.homeoffice.gov.uk/anti social-behavior

Home Office (U.K.). (1997). *Getting to grips with crime.* London: Author.

Home Office (U.K.). (2005). *National Community Safety Plan 2006–2009.* London: Author.

Jones, T., & Newburn, T. (2007). *Policy transfer and criminal justice: Exploring US influence over British crime control policy.* Maidenhead, UK: Open University Press.

Moss, K., & Stephens, M. (Eds.). (2006). *Crime reduction and the law.* London: Routledge.

Newburn, T. (2002). Community safety and policing: Some implications of the Crime and Disorder Act 1998. In G. Hughes, E. McLaughlin, & J. Muncie

(Eds.), *Crime prevention and community safety: New directions*. London: Sage.

U.K. Parliament, Select Committee on Home Affairs. (n.d.). *Anti-social behavior orders—analysis of the first six years*. Retrieved from http://www.publications.parliament.uk/pa/cm200405/cmselect/cmhaff/80/80we20.htm

Waddington, J. (2007, March 23). Someone's got their eye on you. *Jane's Police Review*. Available at http//:www.pr.janes.com

CRIME MAPPING

Crime mapping is the direct application of considering two particular qualities of crime—that there is an inherent geography to crime and that crime does not happen randomly. This inherent geography is seen in many theoretical forms. For example, Paul Brantingham and Patricia Brantingham's four dimensions of crime state that for a crime to occur it must have a legal dimension (a law must be broken), a victim dimension (someone or something has to be targeted), an offender dimension (someone has to do the crime), and a spatial dimension (it has to happen somewhere). It is also known that crime does not happen at random. The role of geography in this sense can be seen theoretically, for example, in Brantingham and Brantingham's crime pattern theory and Lawrence Cohen and Marcus Felson's routine activity theory and principles of least effort (i.e., that more activities take place closer to home than those further away). This nonrandom nature of crime can also be observed empirically from mapping crime, most typically performed using a geographical information system (GIS), by showing that there are patterns in the spatial distribution of criminal activity. Crime mapping therefore draws from geographical and environmental criminology concepts to help explain why crime occurs, and makes use of geospatial tools (such as GIS) to capture, analyze, and visually interpret these geographical qualities.

This entry provides a short history of GIS and crime mapping before describing, with examples, applications of crime mapping in policing used for crime prevention and understanding geographic patterns of victimization. It concludes by describing future advances in crime mapping.

History

In the 1960s GIS began to emerge as a discipline. Its origins can be traced to the development of land use applications in Canada, and it then grew through applications that included the automation of the cartographic drafting process used by mapping agencies such as the British Ordnance Survey, and by acting as a platform to aid military intelligence gathering, display, and analysis from satellite and other remote sensing imagery (e.g., aerial photography and radar). The use of GIS in policing did not begin until the 1980s, in large part due to computer hardware prices being too prohibitively expensive before this time, the lack of suitable GIS software that could be used to support policing requirements, and the lack of electronic recording of police records. Even then, it was not until the late 1990s that the use of GIS in policing took hold, mainly due to its being held back by organizational and management problems, issues with sharing information, technical problems, and geocoding issues, as noted by Spencer Chainey and Jerry Ratcliffe. Many of these problems are still apparent today, but through developments in the practical use of GIS, several innovators have identified how these can be overcome and have shared this knowledge across a network of users who engage via forums, conferences, training courses, and publications that since 1998 have begun to capture evidence of how crime mapping can be effectively used to support policing and crime prevention.

Innovators in crime mapping include the National Institute of Justice's Mapping and Analysis for Public Safety (MAPS) program in the United States and the Association for Geographic Information (AGI) in the United Kingdom. The MAPS program has raised awareness of crime mapping (not just in the United States but also internationally) through arranging seminars, conferences, and producing publications, as well as by developing crime mapping software tools. In the United Kingdom, the AGI, through its Special Interest Group on Crime and Disorder that was formed in 2000, has helped to raise the profile of crime mapping across senior levels in government and policing and acted as an information exchange forum for practitioners. Other leading innovators include academics at Temple University (Philadelphia), Simon Fraser University (Vancouver, Canada), and The Jill

Dando Institute of Crime Science (JDI) at University College London (England), who all operationalize new techniques and theories by working directly with policing agencies. The JDI also hosts the United Kingdom's annual National Crime Mapping Conference and has begun an edited series of crime mapping case studies that draws from material that is presented at this event.

Examples

Crime mapping contributes to policing and crime prevention by helping to generate a real understanding of criminal activity and a direction in tackling it. It is used in the following situations:

- Responding to and directing calls for service;
- Supporting the briefing of operational police officers;
- Identifying and interpreting crime hot spots for targeting, allocating, and deploying suitable policing and crime reduction responses;
- Through pattern analysis using other local data, helping to explain why crime may occur at certain places;
- Catching serial crime offenders (geographic profiling); and
- Monitoring the impact and performance of targeted policing and crime prevention initiatives.

Mapping the location of a crime naturally references the spatial distribution of the area where victimization has occurred. This could be a street location if the offense was perpetrated against a person (such as robbery), or it could be the location of a property, a building (such as a person's home or a premise a person owns), or a vehicle.

Figure 1 is an example of a crime hot spot map. It shows precise locations in an area in central London where thefts of vehicles have occurred. Crime maps such as these can then be used to help identify those areas where problems are most apparent and focus efforts toward understanding why crime is most concentrated at these locations. Each of the three hot spots in this example was due to high numbers of motorbikes, mopeds, and scooters being stolen, with the locations coinciding with where there were large motorbike parking bays. This then helped the police and their municipal government partners to consider what improvements

could be made in each of these areas that could prevent motorbike owners being victimized in the future. The option they decided on was to install anchor points in the curbside of the parking bays to allow vehicle owners to improve the security of their unattended vehicles by locking them down (using a padlock and chain that they could run through the back wheel of their vehicle and through the anchor point). In this sense, crime mapping helped to identify the specific locations where vehicle crime was a problem and to explain why it was a problem and direct an effective situational crime prevention initiative.

Exploring the spatial distribution of criminal activity can also extend to considering where people of a certain age, gender, ethnicity, or occupation are most victimized. An example of this type of approach is illustrated in Figure 2, identifying separately where 12- to 17-year-olds, 18- to 23-year-olds, 24- to 29-year-olds and 35- to 44-year-olds have been victims of crime in the district of Middlesbrough, England. Mapping crime in this way can help better explain the spatial characteristics of victimization experienced by different age groups, why there are differences, and the types of initiatives that can be implemented to help prevent crime against certain groups of vulnerable people. For example, analysis supported by the generation of these maps highlighted the high levels of victimization experienced by all age groups in Middlesbrough town center. However, the levels were highest for 18- to 23-year-olds and 24- to 29-year-olds, reflecting their activities and vulnerability to crime, which are associated with the nighttime economy in the town center (i.e., pubs, bars, and nightclubs). Victimization of 12- to 17-year-olds in the town center was more related to their daytime and early evening activities in this area, such as passing through the main transport hubs or visiting shops. However, a number of other areas across the district were hot spots for this group of young people, coinciding with the locations of several of the main schools. Mapping helped identify particular areas where young people were vulnerable to offenses such as street robbery and theft. Thus, mapping crime in this manner by considering the differences in the spatial distribution of victimization by age helped the police and their crime reduction partners consider specific crime prevention strategies for different age groups.

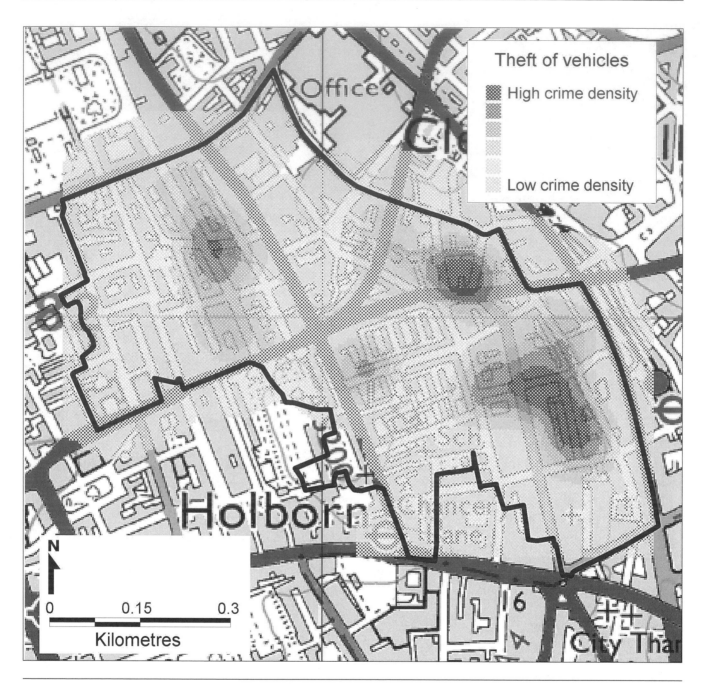

Figure I   Vehicle crime hot spots in Holborn, central London. The three hot spots were due to the high number of motorbike, moped, and scooter thefts. Mapping crime in this manner helped the police and the local municipal government implement a crime prevention initiative that helped prevent future victimization.

Source: Chainey, S. P., & Ratcliffe, J. H. (2005). *GIS and crime mapping.* London: Wiley.

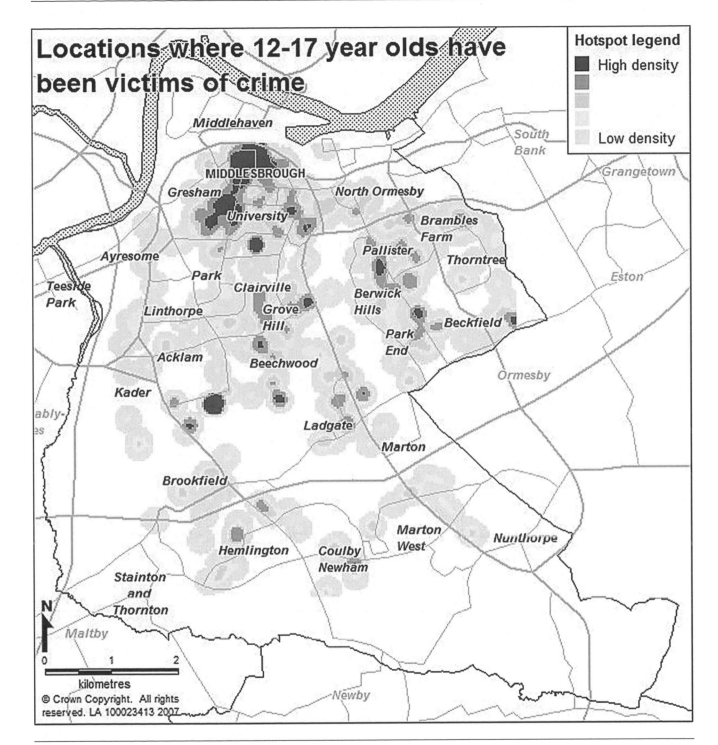

Figure 2a   Mapping victimization of crime by age in Middlesbrough, England, for 12- to 17-year-olds

Source: Safer Middlesbrough Partnership. (2007). *Safer Middlesbrough Partnership strategic assessment.* Middlesbrough, UK: AIM Unit.

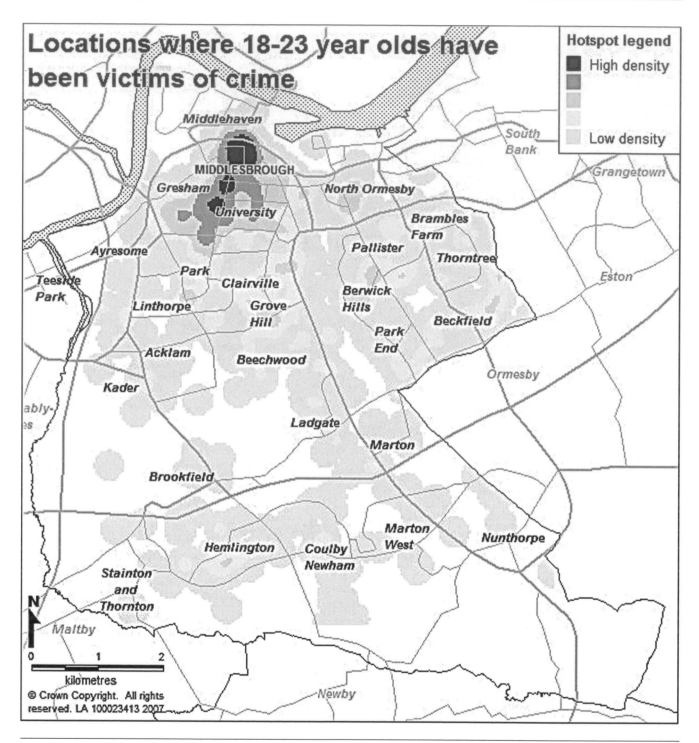

Figure 2b   Mapping victimization of crime by age in Middlesbrough, England, for 18- to 23-year-olds

Source: Safer Middlesbrough Partnership. (2007). *Safer Middlesbrough Partnership strategic assessment.* Middlesbrough, UK: AIM Unit.

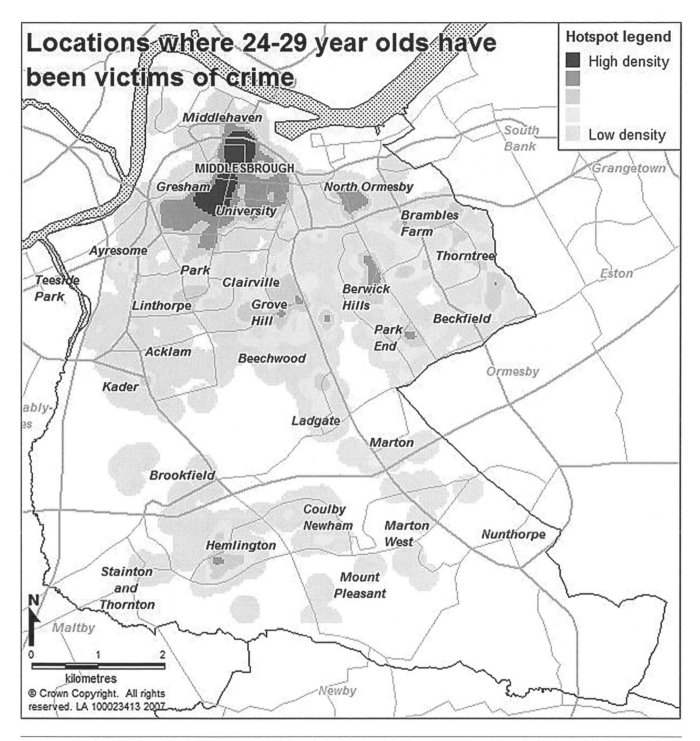

Figure 2c   Mapping victimization of crime by age in Middlesbrough, England, for 24- to 29-year-olds

Source: Safer Middlesbrough Partnership. (2007). *Safer Middlesbrough Partnership strategic assessment.* Middlesbrough, UK: AIM Unit.

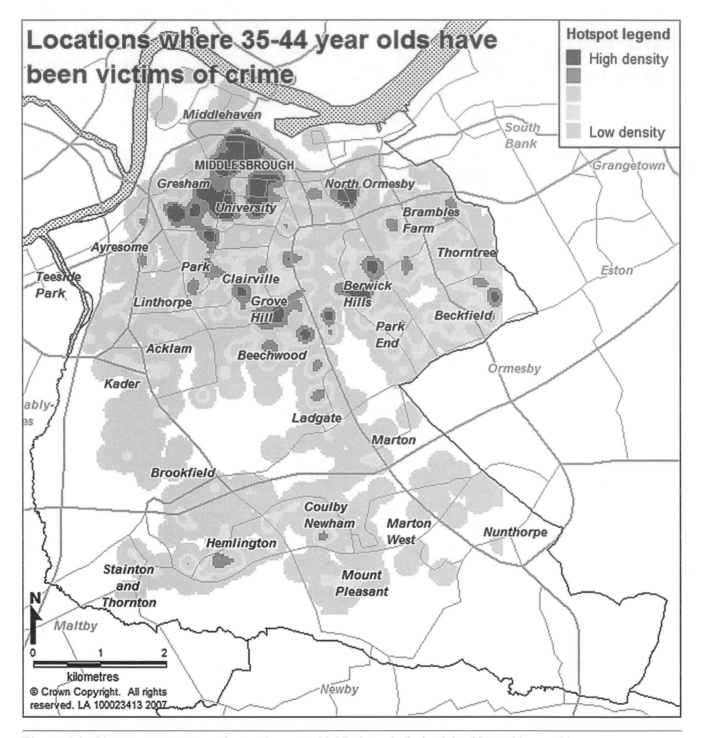

Figure 2d   Mapping victimization of crime by age in Middlesbrough, England, for 35- to 44-year-olds

Source: Safer Middlesbrough Partnership. (2007). *Safer Middlesbrough Partnership strategic assessment.* Middlesbrough, UK: AIM Unit.

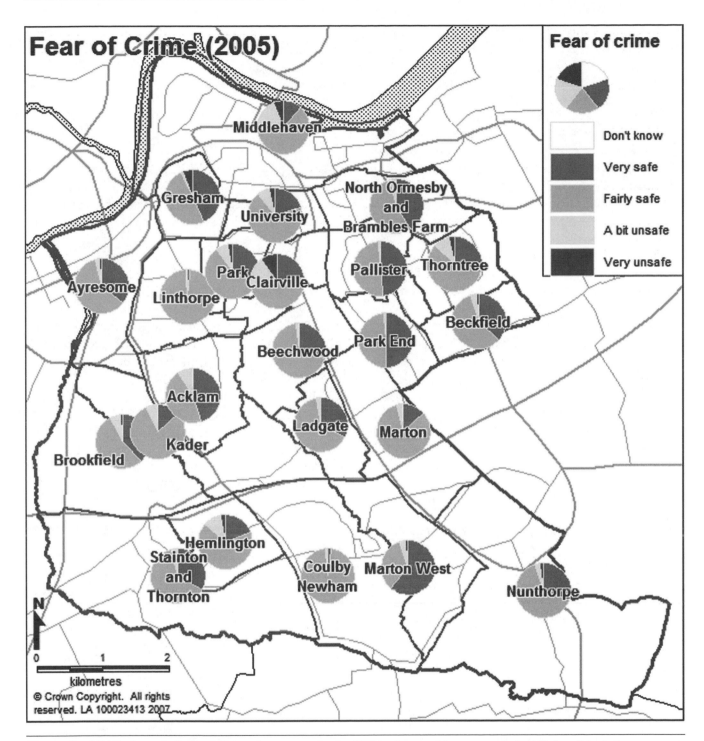

Figure 3 Middlesbrough Fear of Crime Survey results for 2005, when residents were asked if they felt their neighborhood was safe

Source: Safer Middlesbrough Partnership. (2007). *Safer Middlesbrough Partnership strategic assessment.* Middlesbrough, UK: AIM Unit.

Crime mapping can also be used to help explore the spatial patterns of the fear of crime and the perceptions and concerns that communities have about crime and antisocial behavior. Figure 3 shows an example of this, again illustrated for Middlesbrough in England by using the results from the district's 2005 Fear of Crime Survey. This revealed that residents from Clairville and Middlehaven felt most unsafe about the area in which they lived and that Marton West and Park End were perceived as the safest areas.

Another method for assessing perceptions and concerns of residents that is increasingly being used in the United Kingdom is exploration of the British Crime Survey (BCS) results, which have been linked to lifestyle geodemographic data (the BCS is a large-scale victimization survey that is repeated annually). An example of this is illustrated for the district of Middlesbrough. The main lifestyle groups in Middlesbrough are shown in Figure 4 (left) alongside a comparison of the neighborhood problems asked about in the BCS (right) as expressed by residents with these lifestyles. Burdened Singles, Struggling Families, and Blue Collar Roots are the lifestyle groups that dominate in Middlesbrough—representing approximately a half of the district's residents. These groups expressed high levels of concern about teenagers hanging around on the street and noisy neighbors. This concern appeared to be most pronounced for the two largest groups—Burdened Singles and Struggling Families.

Those categorized as Flourishing Families expressed a particular concern with noisy neighbors, but did not express concerns in their neighborhood with people using or dealing drugs, teenagers hanging around, or vandalism, graffiti, and deliberate property damage. Those described as Settled Surburbia expressed no particular problems about their neighborhood.

These lifestyle geodemographic data are also geographically referenced, allowing for these data to be mapped to identify those areas where it is likely that residents' consider their neighborhood to experience certain crime and community safety problems. This is illustrated in Figure 5 for the district of Middlesbrough, showing differences between the perceptions and concerns of different communities in terms of whether they consider their neighborhood to experience problems associated with drug use and drug dealing. Exploring patterns in this manner can then help police and crime reduction agencies target resources that address the problems that are evident in these areas and offer positive messages of reassurance that help alleviate the concerns of residents.

Future Advances

Advances in computing technology create opportunities to apply more sophisticated analysis of geographical patterns and apply new technology that supports improvements in reducing victimization and crime prevention. For example, greater use of Internet-based crime mapping tools can help support publication of neighborhood-level crime statistics, creating public awareness. It also may help to provide positive messages of reassurance or alert residents to spates of crime in their neighborhood that may place them at a heightened risk of being victimized, as well as the precautions they can take to minimize this risk.

To date, geographical analysis of crime patterns in policing has focused on the generation of descriptive material that helps identify geographical patterns of crime (such as crime hot spots), but it has yet to fully embrace more sophisticated forms of geographical information analysis. New developments that are expected in crime mapping include:

- Analysis of the *significance* of geographical patterns—spatial significance testing identifies geographical patterns that are considered to be particularly unusual by applying the principles of significance testing;
- A harmonization of the geographical and temporal exploration of crime, so that areas are explored together and as a continuum rather than in isolation;
- The development of local spatial regression techniques to help examine relationships between crime patterns and other variables—to explain why crime occurs at certain places;
- The development of techniques that predict where and when crime will occur in the future; and
- Spatial modeling processes that test what-if scenarios, such as examining the impact that a crime prevention initiative may have on crime levels.

Spencer Chainey

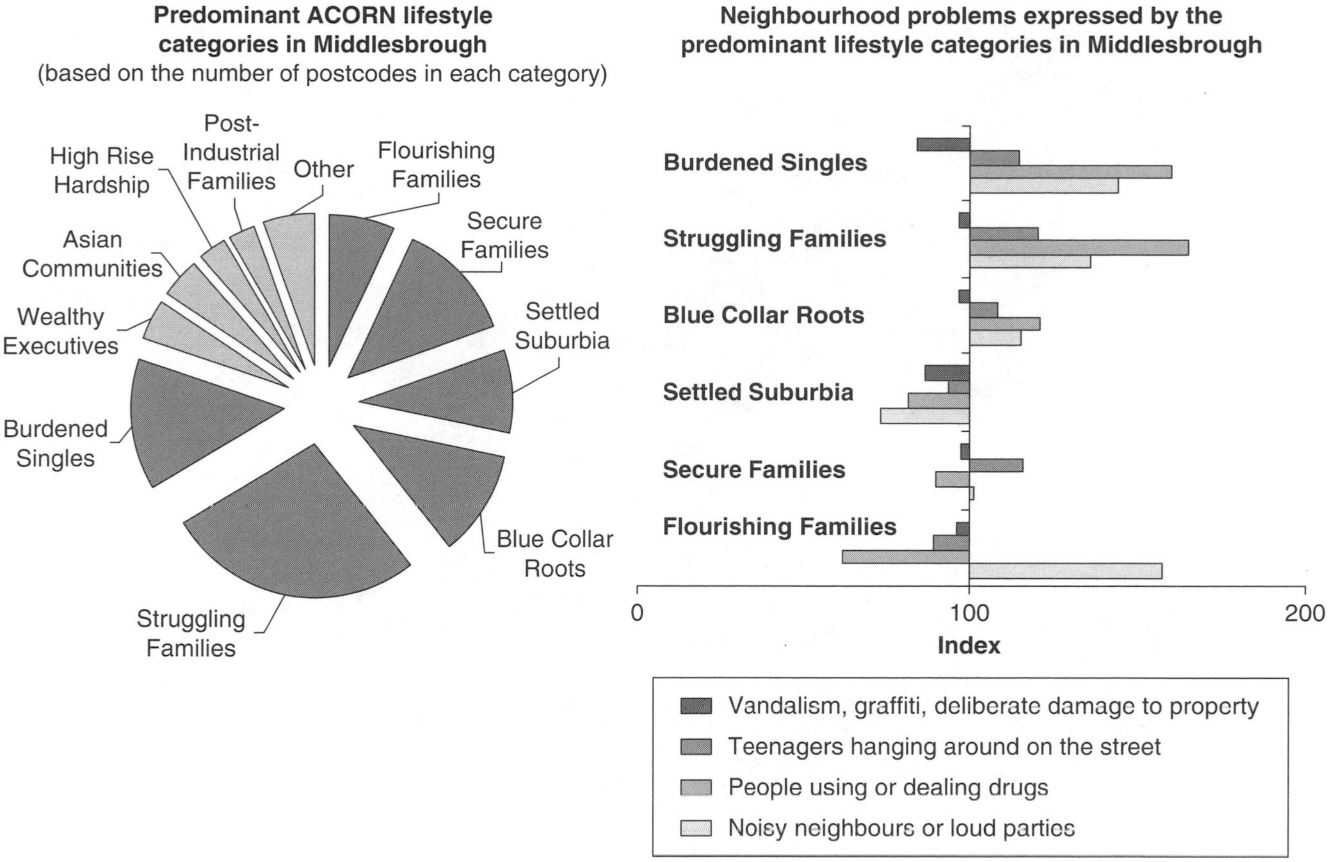

Predominant ACORN lifestyle categories in Middlesbrough
(based on the number of postcodes in each category)

Neighbourhood problems expressed by the predominant lifestyle categories in Middlesbrough

Figure 4 The predominant ACORN geodemographic lifestyle categories in Middlesbrough, England (left), expressed in relation to neighborhood problems (right). The groups shown in dark grey on the pie chart are illustrated in the bar chart. An index value greater than 100 signifies that the issue listed is a problem in the group's neighborhood. The higher the value, the greater the problem. Values less than 100 signify that the issue is not a problem for this lifestyle group in their neighborhood.

Source: Safer Middlesbrough Partnership. (2007). *Safer Middlesbrough Partnership strategic assessment.* Middlesbrough, UK: AIM Unit.

See also Crime Pattern Theory; Fear of Crime; Reassurance Policing; Routine Activities Theory; Situational Crime Prevention; Victimization Surveys

Further Readings

Brantingham, P. J., & Brantingham, P. L. (1981). *Environmental criminology.* Prospect Heights, IL: Waveland.

Brantingham, P. J., & Brantingham, P. L. (1984). *Patterns in crime.* New York: Macmillan.

Chainey, S. P., & Ratcliffe, J. H. (2005). *GIS and crime mapping.* London: John Wiley.

Chainey, S. P., & Tompson, L. (2008). *Crime mapping case studies: Practice and research.* London: John Wiley.

Cohen, L. E., & Felson, M. (1979). Social change and crime rate trends: A routine activity approach. *American Sociological Review, 44,* 588–608.

Home Office (U.K.). (2005). *Crime mapping: Improving performance.* Retrieved from http://www .jdi.ucl.ac.uk/crime_mapping/crime_mapping_guide/ index.php

Johnson, D. (2008). The near repeat burglary phenomenon. In S. P. Chainey & L. Tompson (Eds.), *Crime mapping case studies: Practice and research.* London: John Wiley.

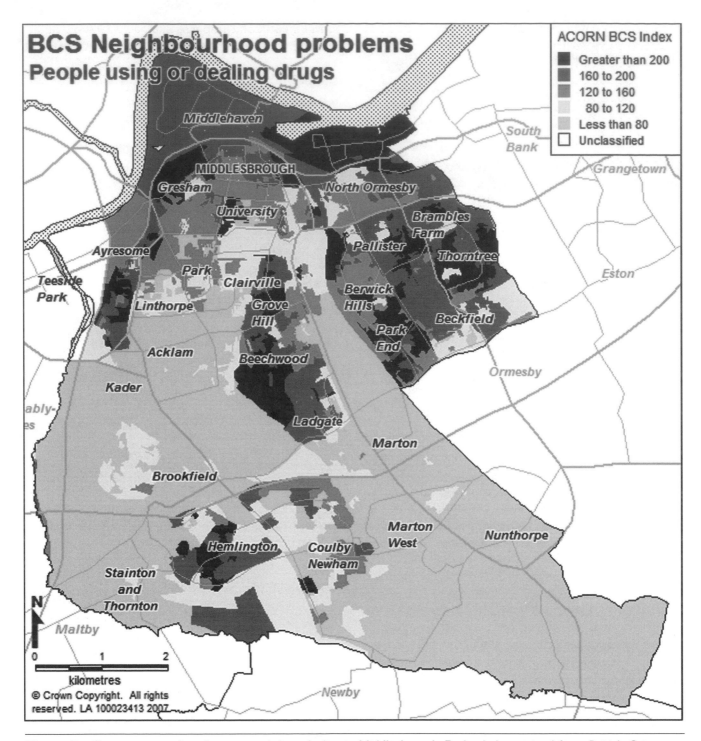

Figure 5   Concerns regarding drug use and drug dealing in Middlesbrough, England, determined from British Crime
Survey results modeled to geodemographic lifestyle classifications

Source: Safer Middlesbrough Partnership. (2007). *Safer Middlesbrough Partnership strategic assessment.* Middlesbrough, UK:
AIM Unit.

LaVigne, N., & Wartell, J. (Eds.). (1998). *Crime mapping case studies: Successes in the field* (Vol. 1). Washington, DC: Police Executive Research Forum.

LaVigne, N., & Wartell, J. (Eds.). (2000). *Crime mapping case studies: Successes in the field* (Vol. 2). Washington, DC: Police Executive Research Forum.

Safer Middlesbrough Partnership. (2007). *Safer Middlesbrough Partnership strategic assessment*. Middlesbrough, UK: AIM Unit.

CRIME NEWSLETTERS

Crime newsletters seek to provide relevant information to concerned citizens to improve crime prevention knowledge and reduce victimization. The most informative newsletters match the message to the audience. Before a crime prevention newsletter can be devised, the targeted crime problem must be carefully analyzed. For instance, if the analysis of a burglary problem indicates that victims would benefit the most from prevention information, a newsletter is more likely to succeed if it focuses on educating victims. However, antigraffiti efforts should be targeted at the offending population to educate them about the possible legal penalties for graffiti. Newsletters cannot be relied on as a generic response to crime problems, and agencies need to make every effort to highlight ongoing police initiatives or other programs designed to affect specific social problems. It also is best for agencies to consider using newsletters only in the context of a broader response to a problem.

Crime prevention newsletters can advertise:

- Self-protection techniques
- New ways to report criminal activity
- Locations of police facilities or resources
- Dangerous areas
- Offenders living in an area (sex offenders)
- Crime problems in neighborhoods

Crime newsletters can take one of two forms. On the one hand, they can attempt to provide general information to residents concerning crime and its prevention or they can advertise a specific program occurring in the community. General campaigns attempt to raise awareness in the hopes that some members of the public will avoid victimization. The second type of campaign focuses on a particular crime and offers victims concrete steps to avoid victimization or reduce their fear of crime. These campaigns often promote home security surveys, obtaining steering wheel locks, or classes in various security-enhancing behaviors. Flyers and newsletters demonstrating techniques to make cars and houses "burglar-proof" are common in these target hardening–type campaigns.

Efforts to educate people in order to reduce victimization rates have been met with mixed results. A 4-month campaign tried to educate people about the importance of locking their parked cars, but it failed to change people's behaviors. Another campaign used posters and television spots to remind people to lock their car doors, but it was also ineffective. These studies demonstrate that people often pay little attention to crime prevention messages. A common reason given for this behavior is that potential victims do not feel that it concerns them. For instance, domestic violence awareness campaigns have to compete with the possibility that women do not want to see themselves as victims. Some other explanations include boredom, not seeing the message, choosing to ignore the message, or even defiance from adopting the "it won't happen to me" mentality. However, crime newsletters that are focused on specific crimes and carried out in small geographic regions seem to be more effective. These seem to have more success because people feel the message is more relevant to their immediate situation than are generic warnings about crime. Thus agencies must determine how best to reach their target audience. For example, to reach the intended audience, newsletters warning the elderly of repair and construction scams should be aimed at retirement facilities. Conversely, a newsletter designed to reduce car break-ins through mass residential mailings is not appropriate if the majority of the victims are commuters from out of town.

Design Elements

Content

The content of the message is the central component of any campaign. The message needs to be relevant to the target audience by being salient and timely. If victims are the target audience the message should avoid blame, as most individuals will not pay attention to a campaign reminding them of their shortcomings. Research shows that messages directed at offenders that advertise an increased threat of apprehension are more successful than campaigns that focus on the legal consequences if they are caught.

Sensitivity

When deciding on the content of a campaign, attempting to scare people is not recommended. Publicity should be about education, not threatening people or producing emotionally disturbing images. Newsletters thus need to avoid messages that may upset the intended audience, such as that in a campaign designed to educate women about rape prevention which questioned women about their attire and offered "loud praying" as a method of scaring off potential attackers.

Specificity

Newsletters need to be relevant and offer specifics to the target audiences. Antidrinking efforts that state, "Know when to stop" tend not to be effective because different audiences may interpret the message differently. Quantifying the point at which to stop drinking (e.g., two drinks per hour) is less vague and more likely to result in audiences changing their behavior. Newsletters should also provide the target audience with as much practical information as possible.

Logo

A well-designed logo can help to increase the impact of a crime newsletter. This notion comes directly from commercial advertisements that are highly laden with pictures, cartoon characters, and other appealing visuals to attract customer attention. A good example of an effective logo accompanying a crime prevention campaign is the renowned McGruff crime dog. The cartoon figure portrays an imposing yet friendly dog dressed as a detective. While it is hard to measure the exact impact of the McGruff campaign on crime reduction, an evaluation of the "Take a Bite Out of Crime" campaign found that one in four people

exposed to the campaign adopted some crime prevention techniques.

Emmanuel Barthe

See also Community Policing; Crime Prevention; Crime Stoppers; Neighborhood Watch Programs

Further Readings

Bowers, K., & Johnson, S. (2003). *The role of publicity in crime prevention: Findings from the reducing burglary initiative* (Home Office Research Study No. 272). London: Home Office.

Decker, S. (2003). Advertising against crime: The potential impact of publicity in crime prevention. *Criminology & Public Policy, 2*(3), 525–530.

Lavrakas, P., Rosenbaum, D., & Kaminski, F. (1983). Transmitting information about crime and crime prevention to citizens: The Evanston newsletter quasi-experiment. *Journal of Police Science and Administration, 11*(4), 463–473.

O'Keefe, G., Rosenbaum, D., Lavrakas, P., Reid, K., & Botta, R. (1996). *Taking a Bite Out Of Crime: The impact of the National Citizens' Crime Prevention media campaign.* Thousand Oaks, CA: Sage.

Web Sites

National Crime Prevention Council: http://www.ncpc.org

CRIME PATTERN THEORY

Crime pattern theory focuses on crime as a complex event that requires many different elements for its occurrence. This places it in sharp contrast with traditional criminology, which is focused on the development of criminal propensity in offenders.

Fundamental Assumptions

Criminal Events Require Specific Elements

At a minimum, a crime requires the confluence in space and time of an offender and a target or victim in a social and physical context that includes a preexisting criminal law, target access, and the absence of conditions and other persons who might interfere with current action or facilitate subsequent criminal prosecution.

Crime pattern theory assumes the existence of motivated offenders and seeks to understand their decision processes and actions within the context of the other elements of the criminal event. These other elements form the basis of criminal opportunities.

Crime Is Not Random

Crime pattern theory observes that neither motivated offenders nor opportunities for crime are either randomly or uniformly distributed in space and time. Probably the strongest physical characteristic of crime is that the sites where crimes occur are concentrated. Regardless of whether the crime under consideration is murder or rape, assault or theft, burglary or vandalism, a limited number of sites, times, and situations constitute the space-time loci for the vast majority of offenses.

Crime pattern theory places special emphasis on the geography and temporal patterning of crime in order to understand how the physical and social environment structure criminal events.

Offenders and Victims Make Normal Use of Time and Space

While much traditional criminology searches for some pathology that would explain criminal behavior, crime pattern theory assumes that people who commit crimes have normal perceptions and make normal use of time and space. Offenders and victims exhibit movement patterns tied to personal activity and awareness spaces that are similar to those of everyone else. The likely location for a crime is near this normal activity and awareness space.

Structure of Criminal Opportunities and Criminal Events

Routine Activities

Daily life plays out through a series of routine activities following common activity clocks such as the morning commute to work or the rhythm of the school year. Routine activities are anchored to persistent personal activity nodes and travel paths. Routines vary from weekday to weekend and from normal days to holidays, but are generally structured around home, work, school, shopping, entertainment, and recreation points. People develop routine pathways between their anchor points. Over time, people develop strong awareness spaces along these pathways and around their activity nodes.

Although awareness spaces are personal, they are limited and structured by the built environment so that many people share the same activity nodes and paths. As a consequence, there are general flows of people and activities toward some parts of a city and away from others along predictable paths at predictable times.

Criminal activity is primarily a by-product of routine activity patterns. Routine activities of potential offenders generally define both the areas where and the times when they are likely to commit a crime. The routine activities of potential victims also shape the patterns of crimes.

The Frictions of Time and Distance

People typically use the least time and effort necessary to accomplish some specific activity or goal. This saves time and energy for additional activities and purposes. It also predicts that most of any person's activities will concentrate around a few routine activity nodes in a few small areas or neighborhoods.

Activity Spaces and Awareness Spaces

Routine activities shape a person's normal activity space. From that activity space, the person develops an awareness space. The awareness space shapes the time and location of future activities.

The awareness space is limited, both physically and temporally. Residents do not know their entire city or town. Workers are typically aware of only a limited area around their work place. People know activity spaces for discrete times, and may not understand the dynamics of the same space at different times of the day, week, month, or year.

Routine activity space places people in situations, both physically and temporally, where crime-triggering events are more or less likely to occur. If a criminal event is triggered, the awareness space shapes the search area in which targets or victims are sought.

The routine activity and awareness spaces of repeat offenders change as a result of their prior crimes. They also change as modes and means of transit change. Suburbanization, mass transit, and new highways alter movement patterns, routine activities, and awareness spaces.

Social Networks

When individuals are making their decisions independently, individual decision processes and crime templates can be treated in a summative fashion, that is, average or typical patterns can be determined by combining the patterns of individuals.

Most people do not function as social isolates, but have a network of family, friends, and acquaintances. These linkages have varying attributes and influence the activity and awareness spaces and the action decisions of others in the network. Social networks influence criminal activity patterns of the people who belong to them.

Urban Structure

Urban form and structure shape the activity patterns of everyone, including criminals and victims. Key aspects of urban structure considered in crime pattern theory include nodes, paths, edges, and backcloth.

Nodes

At the aggregate level, activity nodes are gathering places where large numbers of people concentrate for specific purposes: business districts and office buildings, sports stadiums, schools, shopping malls, recreation centers, train stations and airports, religious institutions such as churches, and theater districts.

At the individual level, activity nodes are the places to which people repeatedly go and at which they spend substantial time: home, work, school, a favorite shopping center, a favorite recreation center, a favorite bar or cinema.

Paths

Paths between nodes—transit systems, road networks, walking paths—collect and constrain human activity. The pathways between high activity nodes are also the sites of many offenses. Violent offenses tend to occur at the nodal "endpoints" of paths. Property crimes occur near high activity nodes, but also occur with some intensity along the paths between nodes.

Viewed in the aggregate, it is clear that many property crimes—notably vehicle theft, robbery, and thefts from vehicles—occur on or *near* main roads and *near* major public transit stops. The physical structure of the road network itself seems to influence how far crime spreads from major pathways. Limited access highways seem to concentrate crimes near highway exits. Complicated road networks tend to keep the offender closer to the main roads.

When a person lives in an area, more of the road and pedestrian pathways become well known as a result normal daily activities area. When an area is well known to offenders, "nearness" covers a much broader area away from the main road and the offender crimes cover a wider area.

Edges

The urban setting is full of perceptual edges, places where there is so much characteristic difference from one part to another that the change is noticeable. Some edges between areas are physical, some are social, some are economic. At an extreme, the house bordering on a river or sitting on a beach is on an edge; the houses behind a commercial strip development and the businesses on the strip form a perceptual edge. Parks have edges. Residential areas have edges. Commercial areas have edges.

Land use zoning and transportation planning frequently work in tandem, with the result that major roads follow perceptual edges between different types of areas. The major roads themselves can produce an edge between areas or neighborhoods.

Edges can be characterized in variety of ways. They can be considered in terms of physical barriers or of the strong cognitive images of paths with diverse land uses on either side of a road. Edges describe the limits of perceptual comfort on the part of outsiders or the spatial limits of mutual territorial functioning among a group of people. Edges mark areas of potential territorial conflict between different groups or land uses.

Areas that experience high crime rates often fall on edges between distinctly different neighborhoods. Sometimes edges create areas where strangers are more easily accepted because they are frequently and legitimately present, exposing local criminal opportunities to a wider array of potential offenders. In addition, edges sometimes contain mixtures of land uses and physical features that concentrate criminal opportunities.

Backcloth

The environmental backcloth is an ever changing set of sociocultural, economic, legal, structural, and physical surroundings upon which the other elements of crime pattern theory are arrayed. It includes, among other things, the activities of individuals, of groups, and of organizations. Elements of the backcloth are interconnected and never static. Change is a constant condition of the backcloth, but the types of changes, degrees of change, and rate of change among the elements vary.

Insiders and Outsiders

Insiders

Insiders are people who know an area well because they have legitimate access as residents or workers, for instance, and who belong to the area in a social and cultural sense. Insiders have a better awareness of the area, of the routine daily activities of individuals and families, of workers and visitors than outsiders are ever likely to develop.

Insiders commit their within-neighborhood offenses across a much wider area than do outsiders. Insiders are likely to commit offenses that are keyed to specific timings and locations unique to local individual activities.

Outsiders

Outsiders are people who neither live in nor work in a neighborhood. They are unlikely to know the area beyond its edges and most of their crimes are likely to be committed on or near neighborhood edges.

Outsiders may or may not match the visible physical, social, or economic characteristics of neighborhood insiders. Those who do not match neighborhood insiders' characteristics may feel uncomfortable wandering very far into the neighborhood from its edges. Such outsiders may also be subject to extra scrutiny on the part of neighborhood insiders because they do not "fit in." Crimes by such outsiders are likely to be even more concentrated on neighborhood edges.

Crime Generators and Crime Attractors

Crime generators and crime attractors are places that become crime hot spots for different reasons.

Crime Generators

Crime generators are particular nodal areas to which large numbers of people are attracted for reasons unrelated to any particular level of criminal motivation they might have or the particular crime they might end up committing. Crime generators are a result of the summative combination of awareness and activity spaces of large numbers of people acting in the course of daily routines.

Crime Attractors

Crime attractors are particular places, areas, neighborhoods, or districts that create well-known opportunities for particular types of crime to which intending criminal offenders are attracted because of those known opportunities. They become activity nodes for repeat offenders. Crime attractors are a result of the cumulative impact of criminal experience and network communication.

Crime Neutral Areas

Crime neutral areas neither attract offenders who expect to do a particular crime in the area nor produce crimes by creating criminal opportunities that are too tempting to resist. Instead, they experience occasional crimes by local insiders.

Very simple distance decay and pathway models can describe the geography of crime in such locations. The offense mix is different from the offense mix at either crime attractor or crime generator locations.

Hot Spot Formation

Hot spots can be predicted at specific locations by taking into account the convergence of key elements discussed in crime pattern theory: the residential and activity locations for predisposed offender populations, the residential and activity locations of vulnerable populations, the spatial and temporal distribution of other types of crime targets, the spatial and temporal distribution of different forms of security and guardianship, the broader residential and activity structures of the city, the mix of activity types and land uses, and the modes of transport and the structure of the transport network as well as the actual transportation flows of people through the city's landscape and timescape.

Criminal Decisions and Patterns in Criminal Events

Offender Readiness and Motivation

The commission of any particular crime requires someone who is in a state of readiness for crime. Particular criminal motivation levels or states of readiness to commit crime come from diverse, but quite understandable sources. Motivation or readiness may be seen as tied to goals. Whether a potential offender's general state of readiness is reflected in criminal acts depends in part on his or her psychological, social, and cultural background state; on the economic environment; on the individual's history of past activities; and, to a large extent, on the opportunities available. Criminal readiness levels are not constant in any individual but vary over time and place given both the individual's background behavior and site-specific situations.

Journey to Crime

Normal Travel: The Confinement of Routine Activities and Normally Patterned Crime

Any particular offender's pattern of offending will be tied to areas around his or her key personal activity nodes, including home, work or school, shopping, recreation, and the homes of friends, family, and acquaintances, as well as the paths between them. Crimes will typically occur in places where these nodes and paths intersect with criminal targets at times and in situations matching the offender's criminal opportunity template.

Nonroutine Travel and Crime

Long distance travel for work or for holiday making may cause a temporary relocation of a persistent offender's journey to crime. A local pattern explicable in terms of normal journey to crime patterns may develop in the new location.

Rare and unusual events may influence actions and, consequently, impact on crime. Natural disasters such as hurricanes, earthquakes, or floods or administrative disasters such as police strikes or electric power blackouts may open areas to looting. Large crowds at special events such as soccer matches, rock concerts, movie openings, and civic festivals may push people from boisterousness into riot. In most of these situations, the nonroutine event has no long lasting impact on crime patterns, but it does have a strong influence on criminal behavior in the short run.

Decision Processes

Crime Template

Criminal events can be viewed as the endpoints in a decision process or as a sequence of decision steps taken by a potential offender. The number and sequence of decision points in the process that leads to a criminal event vary with the type and quality of crime.

Individuals develop "images" of what surrounds them. These images, representing a process-based perception of objects within a complex environment structured by all the elements discussed above, are called mental templates. They are used to make rapid decisions about the existence and exploitability of criminal opportunities.

Templates vary by specific crime type and the general context for the crime. They contain images of both the ideal target and the ideal setting and situation comprising the ideal criminal opportunity. Target suitability is tied both to the characteristics of the target and to the characteristics of the target's surroundings. The identification of suitable target is itself a multistage decision process contained within some general environment.

Offenders do not always wait until they locate ideal targets and situations before acting. They often engage in satisficing rather than maximizing searches, acting on criminal opportunities comprised of partially ideal targets found in partially ideal situations.

Safe Place Template

People in general develop mental maps of familiar places that are keyed to comfort zones and perceptions of "safe" places. They also develop mental templates of "safe place" indicators. Most people believe that activities in unusual places can create dangers and become more cautious when they must engage in such activities. Errors and mistakes framing "safe place" templates can create real but unappreciated dangers because potential victims run risks of crime whenever their activity spaces and immediate locations intersect with the activity and awareness spaces of potential offenders.

Triggers

There are triggers that actually touch off individual criminal events. These triggers and the consequences of criminal acts are sometimes, though not always, predictable, but they generally can be understood retrospectively.

A particular criminal event depends on an individual's criminality potential being triggered. The triggers are generated or experienced during an activity, an action process. The triggers occur in nonstatic, though mostly routine, situations. They are shaped by the surrounding environment, past experience, and the crime template.

The Event Process

Potential targets and victims have passive or active locations or activity spaces that intersect the activity spaces of potential offenders. The potential targets and victims become actual targets or victims when the potential offender's willingness to commit a crime has been triggered and when the potential target or victim fits the offender's crime template.

Crime Displacement

Displacement depends on the type of crime hot spot at which the intervention takes place. Intervention at crime generator hot spots is unlikely to result in crime displacement because the crimes that occur there are opportunistic. Displacements from crime attractor hot spots are much more likely and can be encapsulated in three limited statements: First, criminal activity at a crime attractor is likely to be displaced into the neighborhood surrounding it if there are nearby attractive targets or victims. Second, criminal activity that cannot be displaced to the neighborhood surrounding the original attractor is likely to be displaced to other important attractor nodes. Third, criminal activity that cannot be displaced to the

neighborhood surrounding the original attractor, and is not displaced to some other important crime attractor, is likely to be displaced back into the offender's home neighborhood rather than to neighborhoods nearby and similar to the crime attractor neighborhood. This is a function of the interplay of awareness spaces with urban form. The result is most likely some abatement and some displacement to a variety of locations.

Additional Considerations

Crime is not randomly distributed in time and space. It is clustered, but the shape of the clustering is greatly influenced by where people live within a city, how and why they travel or move about a city, and how networks of people who know each other spend their time. There will be concentrations of overlapping activity nodes and within those nodes some situations that become crime generators and some that are crime attractors.

When looking at the representation of crime locations, researchers need to consider individual offenders and their routine activity spaces, networks of friends who engage in some crimes and their joint activity spaces, the location of stationary targets and the activity spaces of mobile victims and mobile targets, and the catchment areas of fixed targets. The patterns are dynamic. Keeping that in mind will make it possible for researchers to understand crime patterns so that crime reduction interventions that produce minimum levels of displacement can be designed.

Patricia L. Brantingham

See also Conjunction of Criminal Opportunity Theory; Lifestyle Theory; Routine Activities Theory; Situational Crime Prevention; Structural Choice Theory

Further Readings

Brantingham, P. J., & Brantingham, P. L. (1997). Understanding and controlling crime and fear of crime: Conflicts and trade-offs in crime prevention planning. In S. P. Lab (Ed.), *Crime prevention at a crossroad*s (pp. 43–60). Cincinnati, OH: Anderson.

Brantingham, P. J., & Brantingham, P. L. (2003). Anticipating the displacement of crime using the principles of environmental criminology. *Crime Prevention Studies, 16,* 119–148.

Brantingham, P. J., & Brantingham, P. L. (2008). Crime pattern theory. In R. Wortley & L. Mazerolle (Eds.), *Environmental criminology and crime analysis* (pp. 78–93). Cullompton, UK: Willan.

Brantingham, P. L., & Brantingham, P. J. (1993). Environment, routine and situation: Toward a pattern theory of crime. *Advances in Criminological Theory 5,* 259–294.

Brantingham, P. L., & Brantingham, P. J. (1993). Nodes, paths and edges: Considerations on the complexity of crime and the physical environment. *Journal of Environmental Psychology, 13,* 3–28.

Brantingham, P. L., & Brantingham, P. J. (1995). Criminality of place: Crime generators and crime attractors. *European Journal on Criminal Policy and Research, 3,* 5–26.

Brantingham, P. L., & Brantingham, P. J. (1999). A theoretical model of crime hot spot generation. *Studies on Crime and Crime Prevention, 8,* 7–26.

CRIME PREVENTION

There is no single definition for crime prevention. Different authors and studies offer varying definitions. Many early definitions actually used the term *crime control* either in place of *crime prevention* or within the definition. However, crime control alludes to maintenance of a given or existing level of crime and the management of that amount of crime behavior. True crime prevention looks to do more than just maintain a certain level of crime or to manage offenders and crime. Paul Ekblom offers a definition that revolves around interventions that reduce the risk of crime and its consequences. Such a definition addresses both crime and its impact on individuals and society. One of the very important consequences of crime that should be addressed in prevention initiatives is the fear of crime. While most definitions of crime prevention incorporate the ideas of lessening the actual levels of crime or limiting further increases in crime, few specifically deal with the problem of fear of crime and perceived crime and victimization. Steven P. Lab offers a definition that explicitly addresses crime and the fear of crime: Crime prevention entails any action designed to reduce the actual level of crime and/or the perceived fear of crime.

Crime prevention actions are not restricted to the efforts of the criminal justice system. They include activities by individuals and groups, both public and private. Just as there are many causes of crime, there are many potentially valuable approaches to crime prevention. This entry examines crime prevention from a very broad perspective. Included here is a discussion of the history of crime prevention, different crime prevention models, and major crime prevention approaches, as well as insight into the effectiveness of prevention activities.

History

Crime prevention is not a new idea. Indeed, for as long as people have been victimized there have been attempts to protect one's self and one's family. The term *crime prevention,* however, has only recently come to signify a set of ideas for combating crime. Many people suggest that crime prevention today is new and unique, particularly in terms of citizen participation. In reality, many recent activities classified as crime prevention can be seen throughout history. "New" crime prevention ideas and techniques are often little more than reincarnations of past practices or extensions of basic approaches in the (distant) past. It is only in the relatively recent past that the general citizenry has *not* been the primary line of defense against crime and victimization.

The earliest responses to crime were left to the individual and his family. Retribution, revenge, and vengeance were the driving forces throughout early history. While such actions would serve to make the victim whole again, it also would eliminate the benefit gained by the offender. It was assumed that potential offenders would see little gain in an offense, thereby deterring the individual from taking action. The Code of Hammurabi (approximately 1900 BCE) outlined retribution by victims and/or their families as the accepted response to injurious behavior. *Lex talionis,* the principle of an eye for an eye, was specifically set forth as a driving principle in the Hammurabic law. Such laws and practices provided legitimacy to individual citizen action.

The existence of formal systems of social control is relatively new. Early "policing," such as in the Roman Empire and in France, was concentrated in the cities, was conducted by the military, and dealt with issues of the central state and the nobility (i.e., king). The general public was left to continue self-help methods. After the Norman conquest of England in 1066, male citizens were required to band together into groups for the purpose of policing each other. If one individual in the group caused harm (to a group or nongroup member), the other members were responsible for apprehending and sanctioning the offender. *Watch and ward* rotated the responsibility for keeping watch over the town or area, particularly at night, among the male citizens. Identified threats would cause the watcher to raise the alarm and call for help (*hue and cry*). It was then up to the general citizenry to apprehend and (possibly) punish the offender. The "watch and ward" and "hue and cry" ideas were codified in 1285 in the Statutes of Winchester, which also required men to have weapons available for use when called, and outlined the role of a constable, which was an unpaid position responsible for coordinating the watch and ward system and overseeing other aspects of the law. It is apparent throughout these actions that crime prevention was a major responsibility of the citizenry. In the New World colonies and the early United States, the vigilante movement, which mirrored early ideas of hue and cry, was a major component of enforcing law and order in the growing frontier of the young country. Posses of citizens were formed when an offender needed to be apprehended and punished.

The individual, often voluntary, responsibility for crime prevention in England generally persisted until the establishment of the Metropolitan Police in 1829. A key to the Metropolitan Police organization was the idea of crime prevention. Sir Robert Peel, who was the driving force behind the Metropolitan Police Act, and Charles Roman, the commissioner of the new organization, both saw crime prevention as the basic principle underlying police work. Even earlier attempts at formal policing, such as that in 17th-century Paris, emphasized crime prevention through methods such as preventive patrol, increased lighting, and street cleaning.

While much of this discussion has emphasized individual action and self-help, it should not be construed as indicative that protective actions were solely a matter of retribution and revenge. There are numerous examples of alternative approaches that would be considered preventive in nature. Easy examples were the use of walls, moats, drawbridges, and other physical design features around cities that protected the community from external invasion. Surveillance, as provided by watch and ward, allowed the identification of problems before they got out of hand. Yet another early prevention approach was the restriction of weapon ownership as a means of eliminating violent behavior.

The advent of the 20th century witnessed a great deal of change in societal response to deviant behavior. The growth of sociological and psychological studies of crime and criminal behavior offered new responses to deviant behavior. Researchers were starting to note patterns in where and when offenses occurred and who was involved in the offenses, and to relate these facts to changing social structure and personal relationships. The logical result of this growing study was a movement away from simple responses involving repression, vengeance, retribution, and the like to actions that would attack the assumed causes of deviant behavior. The emerging criminal and juvenile justice systems, therefore, responded by incorporating more prevention-oriented functions into their activity.

One prime example of an early crime prevention approach was the development of the juvenile court and its efforts to combat the problems of poverty, lack of education, and poor parenting among the lower classes. The preventive nature of the juvenile system can be seen in the *parens patriae* philosophy, which argued that youth needed help and that processing in adult court was geared to punishment rather than prevention. Yet another example of early crime preventive action was the Chicago Area Project in 1931. The Chicago Area Project sought to work with the residents to build a sense of pride and community, thereby prompting people to stay and exert control over the actions of people in the area. Recreation for youth, vigilance and community self-renewal, and mediation were the major components of the project. In essence, the project sought to build ongoing, thriving communities that could control the behavior of both its residents and those who visited the area.

Crime prevention is an idea that has been around for as long as there has been crime. While the form has changed and the term *crime prevention* is relatively new, the concern over safety is age old. Since the late 1960s there has been a growing movement toward bringing the citizenry back as active participants in crime prevention. While many see this type of community action as new, in reality it is more a movement back to age-old traditions of individual responsibility than it is a revolutionary step forward in crime control. Crime prevention must utilize the wide range of ideas and abilities found throughout society. Community planning, architecture, neighborhood action, juvenile advocacy, security planning, education, and technical training, among many other system and nonsystem activities, all have a potential impact on the levels of crime and fear of crime. The realm of crime prevention is vast and open for expansion.

The Crime Prevention Model

Crime prevention encompasses a wide range of actions and activities, all geared toward reducing crime and/or the fear of crime. One way to organize the many approaches is to look at models of crime prevention. Perhaps the most recognized model is borrowed from the approaches found in the public health models of disease prevention. Three areas of prevention appear in this model—primary, secondary, and tertiary—and each attacks the problem at different stages of development. From the public health viewpoint, primary prevention refers to actions taken to avoid the initial development of the disease or problem. This would include vaccinations and sanitary cleanups by public health officials. Secondary prevention moves beyond the point of general societal concerns and focuses on individuals and situations that exhibit early signs of disease. Included at this stage are screening tests such as those for tuberculosis or systematically providing examinations to workers who handle toxic materials. Tertiary prevention rests at the point where the disease or problem has already manifested itself. Activities at this stage entail the elimination of the immediate problem and taking steps designed to inhibit a reoccurrence in the future. Paul Brantingham and Frederic Faust took this public health model and outlined an analogous crime prevention model.

Brantingham and Faust note that primary prevention within the realm of criminal justice "identifies conditions of the physical and social environment that provide opportunities for or precipitate criminal acts" (1976, p. 288). The types of prevention approaches subsumed here included environmental design, Neighborhood Watch, general deterrence, private security, and education about crime and crime prevention. Environmental design includes a wide range of crime prevention techniques aimed at making crime more difficult for the offender, surveillance easier for residents, and feelings of safety more widespread. The use of building plans conducive to visibility, the addition of lights and locks, and the marking of property for ease of identification fall within the realm of environmental design. Neighborhood watches and citizen patrols increase the ability of residents to exert control over their neighborhood and add risk of observation for potential offenders.

Activities of the criminal justice system also fall within the realm of primary prevention. The presence of the police may affect the attractiveness of an area for crime as well as lower the fear of crime. The courts and corrections may influence primary prevention by increasing perceived risk of crime for offenders. Public education concerning the actual levels of crime and the interaction of the criminal justice system and the public may also affect perceptions of crime. In a related way, private security can add to the deterrent efforts of the formal justice agencies.

Primary prevention also includes broader social issues related to crime and deviance. Sometimes referred to as *social prevention*, activities aimed at alleviating unemployment, poor education, poverty, and similar social ills may reduce crime and fear by attending to the root causes underlying deviant behavior. These and many other primary prevention behaviors are implemented with the intent of avoiding initial, as well as continued, crime and victimization and may be instrumental in lowering the fear of crime.

For Brantingham and Faust, secondary prevention "engages in early identification of potential offenders and seeks to intervene" (1976, p. 288) prior to commission of illegal activity. Implicit in secondary prevention is the ability to correctly identify and predict problem people and situations. Perhaps the most recognizable form of secondary prevention is situational crime prevention. Situational prevention seeks to identify existing problems at the micro level and institute interventions that are developed specifically for the given problem. These solutions may involve physical design changes, altering social behaviors, improving surveillance, or any number of other activities. Closely allied to situational prevention is community policing, which relies heavily on citizen involvement in a problem-solving approach to neighborhood concerns.

Many secondary prevention efforts resemble activities listed under primary prevention. The distinction rests on whether the programs are aimed more at keeping problems which lead to criminal activity from arising (primary prevention) or focused on factors which already exist and are fostering deviant behavior (secondary prevention). Secondary prevention may deal with predelinquents or deviant behavior that leads to injurious criminal activity. For example, alcohol and drug use are highly related to other forms of deviance. Targeting drug use as an indicator of criminal propensity is a secondary prevention approach. Schools can play an important role in secondary prevention both in terms of identifying problem youth and in providing a forum for interventions. Clearly, much secondary prevention may rest in the hands of parents, educators, and neighborhood leaders who have daily contact with the individuals and conditions leading to deviance and fear.

According to Brantingham and Faust, tertiary prevention "deals with actual offenders and involves intervention . . . in such a fashion that they will not commit further offenses" (1976, p. 288). The majority of tertiary prevention rests within the workings of the criminal justice system. The activities of arrest, prosecution, incarceration, treatment, and rehabilitation all fall within the realm of tertiary prevention. Non–justice system input into this process includes private enterprise correctional programs, diversionary justice within the community, and some community corrections. Tertiary prevention is often ignored in discussions of crime prevention due to its traditional place in other texts and the great volume of writing on these topics that already exists.

While the primary/secondary/tertiary model to organize the discussion of crime prevention is very common, other models exist. Jan van Dijk and Jaap de Waard offer one variation on this tripartite view. Their model adds a second dimension of victim-oriented, community/neighborhood-oriented, and offender-oriented approaches. For example,

primary prevention techniques can be divided into actions that target victims, the community, or potential offenders. The authors attempt to refine the public health-based classification system. Adam Crawford offers another two-dimensional typology that again uses the primary/secondary/tertiary view as a starting point, and adds a distinction between social and situational approaches within each category. Both of these models offer alternative views of crime prevention and ways of conceptualizing crime prevention interventions.

An emerging area within the realm of crime prevention is that of crime science. Gloria Laycock suggests that crime science is a new discipline, or at the very least a new paradigm, for addressing crime by coupling efforts to prevent crime with the detection of and intervention with offenders. This is in contrast to the existing paradigm within criminal justice where the focus is on offenders rather than situations. The emphasis on offenders means that responses to crime primarily involve the criminal justice system in the apprehension, adjudication, and punishment/treatment of offenders. Little or no concern is paid to prevention crime. Conversely, crime science attempts to apply various scientific methods and disciplines in the fight against crime.

In essence, crime science attacks crime from a wide range of disciplines using a broad array of tools. Among the disciplines included are those traditionally found in discussions of crime and criminality—sociology, psychology, criminology, and criminal justice. Also included, however, are the fields of engineering, biology, physics, architecture, genetics, communications, computer science, education, and many others. Each of these disciplines offers insight into the behavior of individuals, how to control or manipulate the physical and social environment, the development of safety and security devices, or others among the myriad factors that play a role in crime and crime control. A primary goal of crime science is to bring these divergent disciplines together into a functional, coordinated response to crime.

In many ways, crime science fits nicely with the public health model of crime prevention. Crime prevention requires a wide array of actions and interventions that rest on knowledge and expertise from disciplines beyond those typically involved in the criminal justice system. At the same time, the criminal justice system is intimately involved in the detection of, apprehension of, and intervention with offenders, as well as the implementation of new prevention initiatives.

The Physical Environment and Crime

One of the more well-known approaches in primary prevention entails modifying the physical environment. Changing the physical design of a home, business, or neighborhood has the potential of effecting crime in a variety of ways. It is also possible to change the design of different items. Such changes may make it more difficult to carry out a crime. This difficulty can result in lower payoff in relationship to the effort. Another potential impact is that the risk of being seen and caught while committing an offense may be enhanced. Finally, the physical design changes may prompt local residents to alter their behavior in ways that make crime more difficult to commit. Efforts to alter the physical design to impact crime are generally referred to as crime prevention through environmental design (CPTED). Included in this approach are architectural designs that enhance territoriality and surveillance, target hardening, and the recognition of legitimate users of an area.

The basic ideas of CPTED grew out of Oscar Newman's concept of defensible space. Newman's defensible space proposes "a model which inhibits crime by creating a physical expression of a social fabric which defends itself" (1972, p. 53). The idea is that the physical characteristics of an area can influence the behavior of both residents and potential offenders. For residents, the appearance and design of the area can engender a more caring attitude, draw them into contact with one another, lead to further improvements and use of the area, and build their stake in the control and elimination of crime. For potential offenders, an area's appearance can suggest that residents use and care for their surroundings, pay attention to what occurs, and will intervene if they see an offense.

The ideas of defensible space/physical design include a wide range of potential interventions for combating crime. Increasing street lighting; reducing concealment; adding locks; installing unbreakable glass; using closed-circuit television (CCTV), cameras, and/or alarms; marking property for

identification; and changing street layouts are only a few of the available means of prevention. Most crime prevention programs rely on a range of activities and not just a single approach. Almost without exception, most evaluations look at the direct impact of physical design on crime and/or fear of crime.

Examination of the existing evidence on physical design shows some promising results along with a number of instances where the impact of the techniques is inconsistent. The literature reveals that there are a number of instances where physical design techniques have been found to be effective at reducing crime and fear of crime. Evaluations of lighting, CCTV, street layout, reduced concealment, alarms, and alterations to communities that use multiple approaches have all revealed positive results. Interestingly, there are also numerous examples where the evidence is still uncertain, with the results varying across places and situations, and there are several examples where techniques have been found to have no impact.

Physical design for prevention has also been applied to product design. Ronald Clarke and Graeme Newman point out that the targets of crime are everyday objects. It is possible to alter the design of objects to make them lass amenable to crime. Many products lend themselves to crime. These so-called hot products that are highly targeted by thieves may be characterized by being CRAVED—concealable, removable, available, valuable, enjoyable, and disposable. In essence, these are products desired by people that, because of their construction or make-up, are easily targeted by offenders. While the idea of product design for prevention purposes has been gaining attention, relatively few initiatives have been subjected to evaluation. Evaluations that have been completed typically suggest that the design changes are effective at bringing about significant reductions in crime.

Neighborhood and Community Organizing

An alternative prevention approach that grew out of evaluations of physical design is neighborhood/community organizing. In essence, this involves techniques that prompt the retention, retrieval, and/or enhancement of the community. Neighborhood/block watch, citizen patrols, community-oriented policing, and similar reactions reflect community-oriented responses to crime and fear. These efforts should reduce crime and fear over time as the community reasserts itself and takes control of the behavior and actions of persons within the community. Rather than assume that alterations in a sense of community, neighborhood cohesion, and similar factors follow physical design changes, a community-oriented model suggests that interventions specifically directed at increasing social interaction, social cohesion, feelings of ownership, and territoriality and reducing fear will be more effective at combating crime and victimization.

A wide variety of neighborhood crime prevention strategies have been proposed and implemented over the years. Included in this category are neighborhood/block watch, community anti-drug programs, citizen patrols, and community-oriented policing. The past 35 years have seen a great proliferation of programs in the United States and Great Britain. While many programs in both countries have been instigated and aided by various government agencies or policies, other programs emerged from the simple realization by citizens that the formal criminal justice system was incapable of solving the crime problem on its own. Regardless of the source of stimulation, neighborhood crime prevention has become a major form of crime prevention.

Evaluation of neighborhood crime prevention shows that preventive actions can have an impact on the level of crime and fear in the community. This assessment holds true whether the crime is measured by either official police records or victimization surveys. The level of the change, however, is not equal in all studies, and a few studies suggest that crime can become worse in some targeted neighborhoods. The key to successful crime prevention activities appears to lie in the level of program implementation and citizen involvement. Different background characteristics of the target communities, varying types of available data, and varying evaluation designs also impact on the results.

Mass Media and Crime Prevention

Crime prevention through the mass media can take a variety of forms and has the potential to impact crime in different ways. Kate Bowers and Shane Johnson show that the media (publicity) can be used for several purposes: increasing the risk to offenders, increasing the perceived risk to offenders, encouraging safety practices by the public, and reassuring the public. Successful use of the media may result in reduced crime and fear of crime. Examples of the use of media in crime prevention are the Take a Bite Out of Crime campaign, crime newsletters, information lines such as Crime Stoppers, and the recent growth of reality television shows. These efforts attempt to provide varying amounts of crime education, fear reduction, and crime prevention activity that, hopefully, will translate into lower levels of actual crime.

The use of the media is a relatively new approach in crime prevention. Analysis of media crime prevention campaigns shows that media presentations can affect fear of crime, feelings of self-confidence in avoiding victimization, and the adoption of crime prevention precautions. Unfortunately, the level and extent of these changes is not uniform across evaluations. It appears that the choice of presentation format and the modes of evaluation are key elements in uncovering positive effects. Any modification in actual crime is extremely hard to uncover. This is primarily due to the focus on perceptions of fear and crime and not on crime itself. Changes in the level of actual crime must rely on the successful modification of these other factors. Once the fear of crime and the level of crime prevention efforts are changed, then the ultimate goal of reduced crime can start to appear.

Situational Crime Prevention

Many proponents of crime prevention argue that interventions need to be targeted in order to have an impact. Nowhere is this more evident than under the rubric of situational crime prevention. Instead of attempting to make sweeping changes in an entire community or neighborhood, situational prevention is aimed at specific problems, places, persons, or times. The situational approach assumes that a greater degree of problem identification and planning will take place prior to program implementation, and that the impact will be more focused and, perhaps, identifiable. The identification of places and individuals at risk of victimization, especially focusing on repeat victimization, is central to a great deal of situational prevention.

Situational crime prevention is most easily understood from Derek Cornish and Ronald Clarke's typology of situational interventions. The typology includes five general categories of prevention actions, each with five subgroups. The five categories are Increasing the Effort, Increasing the Risk, Reducing the Rewards, Reducing Provocations, and Removing Excuses. This classification system addresses the opportunity factors related to crime, as well as different levels of motivation to commit crime.

Several observations can be drawn from studies of situational prevention. First, there is an emphasis on property crimes, which is to be expected given the theoretical bases underlying the approach. Second, a wide array of interventions appears in the literature, and this diversity is evident both across different crime problems and within the same offenses. What this suggests is that the prevention initiatives truly are "situational" in nature and cannot be simply applied to the same crime that appears in different places at different times. Third, research successfully demonstrates the effectiveness of programs that target effort, risk, and reward. Fourth, in many analyses there is evidence of either displacement or diffusion, despite the fact that many of the research designs do not specifically test for them. Finally, the focused nature of situational prevention efforts may help maximize the success of the programs. Programs that attempt to make modest changes in specific problems at specific times and places should be more successful than multifaceted programs aiming for large-scale changes.

Deterrence and Incapacitation

Deterrence and incapacitation are two potential crime prevention methods that are used by the criminal justice system. Deterrence can be broken down into two distinct types—general and specific. *General deterrence* aims to impact more than the single offender. The apprehension and punishment of a single individual hopefully serves as an example to other offenders and potential law violators. *Specific deterrence* seeks to prevent the offender from further deviant actions through the imposition of punishments that will negate any pleasure or advantage gained by participation in criminal activity. *Incapacitation* also seeks to prevent future crime on the part of the offender. The method by

which this occurs is the simple control of the individual that prohibits the physical possibility of future criminal activity. Both deterrence and incapacitation are major forms of crime prevention and have served as cornerstones of the criminal justice system.

First and foremost, the research presents contradictory results on the deterrent effect of sentences, particularly the death penalty. There is little or no evidence that severity has an individual deterrent effect. Conversely, certainty of apprehension and punishment seems to have some impact on the level of offending. One problem with this latter statement is the fact that many of the studies that look at certainty also are dealing with crimes which have a fairly severe penalty attached. Clearly, increasing the certainty of apprehension and punishment for homicide is accompanied by either the death penalty or a substantial length of imprisonment. The occurrence of one factor results in the second. Why then do studies that look at both severity and certainty only find an effect related to certainty?

The deterrence literature fails to find any strong compelling arguments that the law and sanctions have any major impact on the level of offending. The most clear-cut finding seems to indicate that increased certainty of apprehension and punishment results in reduced offending. Meanwhile, the severity of punishment appears to have little influence on behavior. Studies of specific deterrence present findings contradicting a deterrent effect of harsh punishment. These studies find that recidivism increases as the length of time served in prison or the harshness of the sanction increases. Other studies, however, show that punishment does deter future behavior or reveals inconsistent results. While society calls for stronger sanctions, it may be that these interventions play an aggravating role in deviant behavior. The offender may view harsh punishment as a breaking point with conventional society and an opportunity to turn to further deviant activity. The act of putting an individual behind bars may be more criminogenic than deterrent.

Incapacitation has great intuitive appeal for society. The idea of punishing an individual for the harm he caused is an accepted method for dealing with deviant behavior. Extending that period of punishment in order to keep an individual from committing another offense is an easily acceptable modification. The costs of such a policy, however, may be high. The number of persons who must be housed to achieve even a small decrease in crime is staggering even using the most conservative figures. Translating these bodies into dollars leads to budgets that the public has not been willing to accept. As with deterrence, the research literature holds little promise for an acceptable incapacitation strategy at this time.

One possible incapacitative approach is controlling offenders in the community through the use of electronic monitoring (EM). EM offers a cost-effective means for releasing offenders into the community while providing a degree of control over them. The evaluation research suggests that the level of both technical violations and new offending is relatively low. Despite problems and concerns with EM programs, they appear to be a viable alternative to incapacitation through incarceration.

Conclusion

Crime prevention encompasses a wide diversity of ideas and approaches. Indeed, no two individuals will necessarily see or define crime prevention in exactly the same way. There should be no doubt that crime prevention works. Effective interventions using a wide array of approaches are evident in the literature. The extent of crime prevention's impact, however, varies across time and place, as well as from one approach to another. Indeed, not every program has the same impact in every situation. Crime may be reduced in one place while there is no impact on the fear of crime. Transplanting that same program to another location may result in the opposite outcome—crime stays the same but fear is reduced. No single approach to crime prevention has proven to be applicable in all situations. Indeed, most interventions appear to work in limited settings with different types of offenders and problems. The greatest challenge, therefore, is to identify the causal mechanisms at work so that effective programs can be replicated in other places and other times.

Steven P. Lab

See also Crime Prevention, Domains of; Crime Prevention Through Environmental Design; Crime Science; Defensible Space; Deterrence; Future of Crime Prevention; Neighborhood Watch Programs; Product Design: Concealable, Removable, Available, Valuable, Enjoyable, and Disposable (CRAVED), and Value, Inertia, Visibility and Access (VIVA); Situational Crime Prevention; Take A Bite Out Of Crime

Further Readings

Bowers, K. J., & Johnson, S. D. (2005). Using publicity for preventive purposes. In N. Tilley (Ed.), *Handbook of crime prevention and community safety*. Portland, OR: Willan.

Brantingham, P. J., & Faust, F. L. (1976). A conceptual model of crime prevention. *Crime and Delinquency, 22*, 284–296.

Clarke, R. V., & Newman, G. R. (2005). Introduction. In R. V. Clarke & G. R. Newman (Eds.), *Designing out crime from products and systems*. Monsey, NY: Criminal Justice Press.

Cornish, D. B., & Clarke, R. V. (2003). Opportunities, precipitators and criminal decisions: A reply to Wortley's critique of situational crime prevention. In M. J. Smith & D. B. Cornish (Eds.), *Theory for practice in situational crime prevention*. Monsey, NY: Criminal Justice Press.

Crawford, A. (1998). Crime prevention and community safety: Politics, policies and practices. London: Longman.

Ekblom, P. (2005). Designing products against crime. In N. Tilley (Ed.), *Handbook of crime prevention and community safety*. Portland, OR: Willan.

Lab, S. P. (2007). *Crime prevention: Approaches, practices and evaluations*. Cincinnati, OH: LexisNexis.

Laycock, G. (2005). Defining crime science. In M. J. Smith & N. Tilley (Eds.), *Crime science: New approaches to preventing and detecting crime*. Portland, OR: Willan.

Newman, O. (1972). *Defensible space*. New York: Macmillan.

Tilley, N. (2005). *Handbook of crime prevention and community safety*. Portland, OR: Willan.

van Dijk, J. M., & de Waard, J. (1991). A two-dimensional typology of crime prevention projects. *Criminal Justice Abstracts, 23*, 483–503.

CRIME PREVENTION, DOMAINS OF

Crime prevention is broad term that carries many different meanings. It is claimed as a principal goal or objective by every criminal justice agency. Lawmakers, schools, social agencies, medical services, and community groups see their activities as fundamental to the prevention of crime. Businesses and homeowners spend large sums and engage in many different activities intended to effect crime prevention. Crime prevention claims are made for electronic merchandise tags, prenatal interventions in expectant mothers' consumption habits, burglar alarms, remedial reading programs, street lighting, high school vocational training courses, prison counseling programs, Little League sports, police street checks, neighborhood organizing activities, control of sightlines in new construction, particular management styles in bars pubs, subsidized day care programs, and many other actions and activities.

Dimensions of Domains

The domains of crime prevention can be analyzed along multiple dimensions flowing from this understanding of the criminal event.

Criminality and Crime

The field of crime prevention is divided into the domains of criminality and of crime.

The Domain of Criminality

This domain is focused on changing the individual's propensity to commit crimes. Crime prevention efforts are intended to change an individual's fundamental character so that he or she will not want to commit a criminal act (or will at least be able to resist the temptation to do so) when a provocation or temptation is encountered.

This domain is grounded on the assumption that criminals (persons with high levels of criminality) are somehow pathologically different from the vast majority of people who are fundamentally noncriminal (that is, are highly resistant to both provocations and temptations).

Most traditional crime prevention strategies fall within the domain of criminality, drawing on a variety of biological, psychological, and social assumptions about the development of personality and sociality as well as assumptions about the capacity of home neighborhood residents (communities) to exercise effective informal control over the criminal impulses of individuals. These traditional strategies tend to prescribe interventions aimed at changing individual propensity and community control capacity in the long run.

Criminal justice operations aimed at producing general or specific deterrence also fall within the domain of criminality. They aim to prevent crime on the part of the general public by illustrating the punishments inflicted upon offenders, modifying the balance of benefits and costs associated with doing the crime in such a way that most people will choose to resist most temptations and provocations. They also aim to prevent repeat offenses on the part of offenders by imposing actual punishments and illustrating the specific costs of criminal action to those who do not understand or do not believe the general deterrence message.

The Domain of Crime: The Criminal Event

This domain is focused on understanding all of the elements of a criminal event. While a legalist conception of "crime" can be restricted to the idea of "an act in violation of a criminal law," an actual criminal action requires convergence of at least four elements in space and time: law, offender, target, and situation. Convergence creates the criminal event. The domain of crime tends to assume the existence of a set of people who will readily give in to any provocation or temptation to crime. It looks at the *other* elements of the criminal event in search of interventions that will prevent the provocation or temptation from occurring, or that will separate potential offenders, in space and time, from those provocations and temptations that cannot be prevented.

Law. A valid criminal law prohibiting and providing some specific punishment for some specific action is a necessary precondition for the occurrence of a crime. This is a fundamental presumption of the modern political world that sets *crime* apart from deviance, recklessness, immorality, negligence, rudeness, selfishness, foolishness, and a variety of other undesirable types of behavior, even though a particular crime might encompass some or all of them.

Offender. An offender, some person who takes action in violation of a criminal law, is central to the criminal event. Such a person exhibits *criminality*, a propensity to engage in criminal actions.

Target. An offender's action in violation of the law must have some target, a person or place, an institution or object, a process or community upon which the crime has some concrete effect. Some targets are highly exposed by their own actions; some targets are hidden and well protected and must be sought out with considerable effort.

Situation. The intersection of offender and target in space and time must also occur in a social and physical context that makes the criminal act possible.

> *Facilitators and inhibitors.* Every space–time context includes some characteristics that could facilitate the criminal action and some that could inhibit it. People, institutions, social expectations, and physical conditions can all serve as facilitators or inhibitors.

> *Guardians, managers, and handlers.* Key inhibitors include guardians, place managers, and personal handlers. Key facilitators include the absence of guardians, place managers, and personal handlers.

Public and Private

The domains of crime prevention can be classified as public and private. The *public domain* encompasses the activities of governments and their agencies, including the various agencies of the criminal justice system. It involves the making and reform of law as well as law enforcement. It also involves activities by agencies as diverse as municipal planning departments, provincial departments of transportation and hospitals, social housing agencies, and welfare organizations. The *private domain* encompasses families and communities, businesses and the labor market, nongovernmental organizations (NGOs), and various religious organizations and congregations. Crime prevention programs originating in the public domain can sometimes impinge on private rights, while private actions can have major impacts on the volume and character of crime and criminality in a society.

Temporal

The temporal domains of crime prevention sort activities into near-term, medium-term and long-term categories based on how long the intervention must be continued before a prevention effect can be anticipated to occur. Introduction of exit attendants and security cameras in a parking facility has been shown to have immediate preventive effects. Introduction of a national day care

Table 1 A table of criminality domain crime prevention actions at primary, secondary, and tertiary levels

Domain	Primary	Secondary	Tertiary
Public Sector			
Police	Citizen education programs, Antidrug education	Social service operations Intervention and diversion	Arrest and charge Prolific offender management
Courts	General deterrence through exemplary sentences	Pre-adjudication diversion Civil alternatives (e.g., drug courts)	Sentences aimed at special deterrence, reform, rehabilitation Prolific offender management
Corrections	General deterrence through existence	Diversion program operations	Incapacitation Reform Restorative justice programs Psychological counseling Rehabilitation Vocational education Prolific offender management

(Continued)

(Continued)

Domain	Primary	Secondary	Tertiary
Schools	General education Educational day care programs Antibullying education Life skills education Parenting skills education Vocational education	Educational intervention programs for at-risk children Antibullying intervention Remedial education for school dropouts Predelinquent screening	Prosecution of truants and delinquents Correctional institution educational programs
Urban planners	Crime prevention through environmental design (CPTED) Routine activity management through social, temporal, and physical planning		Institutional design
Health agencies	General health programs Antidrug education	High-risk persons, identification and intervention Detoxification programs	Harm reduction programs Drug abuse rehabilitation Prolific offender management
Social services agencies	Community development Provision of social safety net	Social services for high-risk individuals and groups: • Domestic abuse interventions • Social housing • Job placement • Income supplements	Social interventions in established cases of: • Endemic poverty • Domestic abuse • Prolific offender management
Private Sector			
Businesses	Developing robust economy High employment levels	Efficient, humane personnel policies	Hiring and management of ex-offenders
Churches and other faith-based organizations	Moral training General social work	Programs for the disadvantaged Crisis intervention	Aftercare services
Other non-governmental organizations (NGOs)	Recreation programs General social work		12-step programs
Families	Good parenting: Moral training		
Individual private citizens	General charity	Volunteer work with at-risk populations	Correctional volunteers

program for 2-year-old children would be unlikely to provide any substantial crime prevention effect in the near term or even the medium term. Crime prevention programs situated in different temporal domains require very different levels of political support, both at the outset and over time.

Primary, Secondary, and Tertiary Prevention

Crime prevention activities can, borrowing from the public health approach to problem prevention, be usefully viewed in terms of where, along the course of crime problem development, interventions are made.

Primary Prevention

Primary crime prevention identifies conditions in the social and physical environment that facilitate the development of criminality or provide opportunities for or precipitate criminal events. Primary preventive interventions aim to change these general conditions, reducing their criminogenic potential, without focusing on specific at-risk groups, individuals, or places.

Secondary Prevention

Secondary crime prevention identifies specific at-risk situations and places, groups, and individuals before they develop persistent crime problems or engage in criminal activity. It also provides physical and social interventions aimed at modifying those at-risk places and situations so that they present minimal criminal opportunities or provocations. It provides physical and social interventions aimed at ameliorating criminogenic social conditions so that at-risk groups and individuals develop minimized criminal propensities.

Tertiary Prevention

Tertiary crime prevention deals with places with established crime problems and with actual offenders. It provides interventions aimed at changing the physical site and social situations found at crime generators, crime attractors, and other crime hot spots in ways that minimize the criminal opportunities found at them. It provides interventions aimed at incapacitating, reforming, and rehabilitating actual offenders so that they commit no further offenses.

The Primary, Secondary, and Tertiary Prevention in Public and Private Domains

Tables 1 and 2 depict the primary, secondary, and tertiary crime prevention activities undertaken with respect to criminality and criminal events in the public and private sector domains. These are further broken into their most prominent crime prevention subdomains. In the public sector these include: police, courts, corrections, schools, urban planning agencies, health agencies, and social service agencies. In the private sector these include: businesses, churches and other faith-based organizations, other nongovernmental organizations, communities, families, and individual private citizens.

Paul J. Brantingham

See also Crime Prevention; Crime Prevention: Micro, Meso, and Macro Levels

Further Readings

Brantingham, P. J., & Brantingham, P. L. (1995). Environmental criminology and crime prevention. In P.-O. H. Wikstrom, R. V. Clarke, & J. McCord (Eds.), *Integrating crime prevention strategies: Propensity and opportunity* (pp. 207–240). Stockholm: Brä.

Brantingham, P. J., & Brantingham, P. L. (2001). The implications of the criminal event model for crime prevention. *Advances in Criminological Theory, 9*, 277–303.

Brantingham, P. J., Frederic, L., & Faust, F. L. (1976). A conceptual model of crime prevention. *Crime and Delinquency, 22*, 284–296.

Graycar, A. (2002). *Domains of crime prevention*. Paper presented at the Australian Crime Prevention Conference, Sydney, Australia.

Hope, T., & Lab, S. P. (1998). Variation in crime prevention participation: Evidence from the British Crime Survey. *Crime Prevention and Community Safety: An International Journal, 3*, 7–22.

Lab, S. P. (1990). Citizen crime prevention: Domains and participation. *Justice Quarterly, 7*, 467–492.

Sherman, L. W., Gottfredson, D. C., MacKenzie, D. L., & Eck, J. (1998). *Preventing crime: What works, what doesn't, what's promising* (NCJ 171676). Washington, DC: National Institute of Justice.

Table 2 A table of criminal event domain crime prevention actions at primary, secondary, and tertiary levels

Domain	Primary	Secondary	Tertiary
Public Sector			
Police	General deterrence through presence and patrol Community policing Citizen education programs Advice on situational prevention strategies	Crime and intelligence analysis Emergent hot spot policing Problem-oriented policing programs (POP)	Established hot spot policing Arrest and charge Prolific offender management
Courts	General deterrence through exemplary sentences		Sentences aimed at incapacitation Prolific offender management
Corrections	General deterrence through existence		Incapacitation Prolific offender management
Schools	School time frame management School access control After-school programs such as sports and drama	Situational prevention programs on school grounds	
Urban planners	Crime prevention through environmental design (CPTED) Routine activity management through social, temporal, and physical planning	Hot spot redesign Traffic flow control	Institutional design
Health agencies	General health programs Antidrug education	High-risk persons, identification and intervention	Drug abuse rehabilitation Prolific offender management
Social agencies	Community development	Social services for high-risk individuals and groups: • Social housing • Job placement • Domestic abuse interventions	Social interventions in established cases of: Domestic abuse Prolific offender management
Private Sector			
Businesses	Crime prevention through environmental design (CPTED) Security and loss prevention General situational prevention	Employee screening Security focus on hot spots Hot spot focus for situational prevention Participation in POP	Prosecution of offenders Hiring and management of ex-offenders Environmental modifications aimed at situational prevention

Domain	Primary	Secondary	Tertiary
Private Sector			
Churches and other faith-based organizations	Moral training General social work	Programs for the disadvantaged Crisis intervention Participation in POP	Aftercare services
Other non-governmental organizations (NGOs)	Recreation programs General social work	Participation in POP	
Communities	Neighborhood Watch and similar programs Neighborhood-based sports program (e.g., Little League, Minor Hockey)	Neighborhood cleanup projects designed to "fix broken windows" Participation in POP	Cocooning and other community-supported repeat victimization interdiction programs
Families	Good parenting: • Supervision • Temptation reduction • Rule setting and consistent enforcement		
Individual private citizens	Household and business security precautions General charity	Participation in Neighborhood Watch, POP, and similar programs	Crime site modifications

CRIME PREVENTION: MICRO, MESO, AND MACRO LEVELS

For every type of crime there are competing (and often contradictory) explanations for offender motivations and victim involvement. Individual, social, and legal responses to crime and victimization are likewise impacted by the myriad theories that exist. The design and application of crime prevention and victimization avoidance strategies are no less complex. This entry explores the effects of different areal strategies (levels) in regard to successful crime prevention planning and implementation. In this context, *level* refers to a potential area, crime site, or victim's location, not just as a geographical or physical space at which crime may occur, but as a site or individual's position within social orders and/or political entities. Potential crime locales are divided into three levels: *micro*—specific individuals, groups, businesses, and similar neighborhood sites; *meso*—individuals, groups, and sites in larger communities, small cities, rural counties, and remote areas; and, *macro*—collectives of individuals, groups, and sites within large cities, populous counties, states, nations, and international settings. The level at which an individual or site is located directly impacts the crime prevention techniques utilized, as well as their success.

The Micro Level of Crime Prevention

The design and application of crime prevention and victimization avoidance strategies at the micro level often utilize victim-oriented, community/neighborhood-oriented, and offender-oriented as well as situational approaches. The types of prevention used (education, target hardening, environmental design, access control, enhanced surveillance, neighborhood cohesiveness, etc.) are specifically designed to address individual or specific site vulnerabilities.

Crime prevention strategies may be broken down into three categories: *primary prevention*—reducing a site or individual or small group's vulnerability or a motivated offender's perceptions of opportunity in order to keep crimes from occurring; *secondary prevention*—reducing an obvious vulnerability on the part of potential victims or crime sites, or addressing community or area issues that might encourage at-risk individuals or groups to engage in criminal activities; and *tertiary prevention*—dealing with individuals or sites that have been victimized, or apprehending and dealing with those individuals or groups who have committed crimes within a community or local area.

Victim-based primary prevention techniques at the micro level seek to prevent crimes from occurring by reducing vulnerability or target attractiveness. Examples include: residential/small business security, self-defense training, target hardening, crime awareness programs, and similar strategies for reducing or deterring vulnerability of a specific person or potential crime site.

Offender-based primary prevention techniques at the micro level emphasize reducing potential offenders' perceptions of success. Any activities that make a target less attractive or reduce the opportunity to successfully engage in a crime would be relevant. Examples include: the presence of additional people, security personnel, aggressive police patrols, as well as the strategies mentioned above.

Secondary prevention techniques at the micro level seek to address identified or obvious vulnerabilities by first promoting awareness of the victim, group, or site users in regard to their potential for victimization. Training programs such as rape awareness, self-defense techniques, promoting good cash handling, home security surveys, parent/teacher instruction, after-school programs, and other stratagems designed to correct known deficiencies would fall within this category.

Techniques may also be geared to reduce the likelihood of individuals or groups within an area

or community of being drawn into criminal behaviors. These could be recreational or educational programs designed to provide alternative activities for at-risk youth, policies designed to reduce the impacts of poverty within a designated area, vocational and job training, neighborhood crime watches, as well as other community enhancement initiatives.

Victim-based tertiary prevention techniques at the micro level seek to reduce the trauma of victimization for individuals and to reduce the potential for further victimization. Domestic violence programs, victim support programs, victim restitution/compensation programs, child protection/guardian programs, crime mediation, environmental design, neighborhood crime watches, financial aid for security enhancements, and increased police activities are examples.

Offender-based tertiary prevention techniques at the micro level include restorative justice programs, restitution programs, education and training programs, mandatory prosecutions, counseling, incarceration, probation treatment, community corrections, or any of the myriad correctional methodologies that attempt to keep individual offenders from becoming involved in further criminal activity.

The Meso Level of Crime Prevention

Meso-level crime prevention addresses its efforts to potential crime targets and victims within larger communities, small cities, suburbs, rural counties, and remote areas such as parks and tourist attractions that draw larger numbers of visitors. Convention facilities, sports arenas, shopping centers, and public housing are exemplars of areas that require prevention programs beyond the micro level. Prevention programs for small towns, suburban counties, and rural areas also are included in this level.

Programs such as Neighborhood Watch, community development, civic awareness, and police–community initiatives are especially relevant. The complexities of dealing with larger facilities, expanded geographical areas, reaching across political subdivisions, and larger numbers of people require extensive planning for greater coordination of efforts and utilization of resources.

Secondary prevention at the meso level differs from that at the micro level in that it involves greater coordination of programs designed to address issues that impact identified communities, institutions, and categories of people in order to eliminate or reduce the potential for criminal behaviors to develop and victimization to occur.

Tertiary techniques at the meso level are the same as at the micro level, except that greater demands on limited resources are placed upon the justice system and victim support organizations due to greater numbers of offenses and the complexities of coordinating efforts within larger jurisdictions and diverse populations.

The Macro Level of Crime Prevention

The macro level of crime prevention addresses collectives of individuals, groups, and sites within large cities, populous counties, states, nations, and international settings. While crime prevention is mainly addressed by community and local entities, densely populated metropolises, global business interests, transnational travel, and international relations require increasingly greater resources and coordination of crime prevention efforts.

Macro-level strategies are those efforts on the part of large cities, states, nations, and international organizations to prevent or reduce the occurrence of crime and victimization. Due to the impact of global communications and travel within modern societies and the increased potential for organized crime and international terrorism, the coordination of crime prevention efforts requires increasingly greater involvement on the part of states, nations, and international organizations.

The chief function of states and nations in crime prevention and control is through legislation. In addition to crime legislation to provide for general deterrence, states and nations also develop policies and programs designed to eliminate social ills that serve as catalysts for crime.

Macro-level secondary prevention includes those efforts discussed previously. In the United States the requirements, policies, and funding for the majority of secondary prevention programs are the products of state and federal initiatives.

Tertiary prevention at the macro level has been the predominant and arguably the least effective strategy utilized. While progress has been made in the areas of treatment, restorative justice, and victim–offender mediation, the focus of tertiary prevention

at all levels has been specific deterrence through the punishment of offenders.

Ronald D. Hunter

See also Crime Prevention, Domains of; Crime Prevention Through Environmental Design; Defensible Space; Situational Crime Prevention

Further Readings

Brantingham, P. J., & Faust, F. L. (1976). A conceptual model of crime prevention. *Crime and Delinquency, 22*, 284–296.

Clarke, R. V. (Ed.). (2002). *Situational crime prevention: Successful case studies.* Albany, NY: Harrow & Heston.

Jeffrey, C. R. (1971). *Crime prevention through environmental design.* Beverly Hills, CA: Sage.

Lab, S. P. (2007). *Crime prevention: Approaches, practices and evaluations* (6th ed.). Cincinnati, OH: LexisNexis Anderson.

Web Sites

National Crime Prevention Council: http://www.ncpc.org

CRIME PREVENTION INITIATIVES, INTERNATIONAL

While crime prevention strategies have a long history of success and have been an integral part of the criminal justice system in the United States, Canada, and Europe, they are not common in developing countries. However, these strategies have been gaining acceptance in many developing nations. While the United Nations (UN) can be credited with many of the most successful initiatives and programs, it is by no means the only international player. Some of the credit for the paradigm shift in international crime prevention can be attributed to contributions from nongovernmental organizations and local governments. Both have played a critical role in bringing about the change.

International Standards

Over the last 20 years, the UN has played a pivotal role in the realm of crime prevention. The UN follows a balanced approach, paying attention to both justice and prevention modalities. On the global scale, government instability and a lack of security make this balanced approach at best complicated and at worst unworkable. In an effort to create norms and standards that could prove useful internationally, the UN promulgated *Guidelines for Cooperation and Technical Assistance in the Field of Urban Crime Prevention* in 1995. The 1995 guidelines were updated and revised in 2002 when the UN adopted *Guidelines for the Prevention of Crime*. Both documents signify a movement to a best practices approach to crime prevention utilizing strategic and comprehensive approaches to crime prevention.

Recently, the United Nations Office on Drugs and Crime (UNODC) has articulated the goal of creating community-centered prevention as a response to crime, violence, drugs, and victimization. The UNODC's strategy for 2008–2011 was shaped, in part, by increasing pressure from the UN Commission on Crime Prevention and Criminal Justice and the UN Economic and Social Council (ECOSOC). In 2005, ECOSOC passed two resolutions that encouraged the UNODC to give attention to crime prevention with a view to achieving a balanced approach between crime prevention and criminal justice responses.

The function of the United Nations Crime Prevention and Criminal Justice Program Network (PNI) is to sustain the effort of UNODC and support global collaboration in the fields of crime prevention and criminal justice. The members of PNI are the United Nations Asia and Far East Institute for the Prevention of Crime and the Treatment of Offenders; the United Nations Interregional Crime & Justice Research Institute in Turin, Italy; the National Institute of Justice in Washington, D.C.; the International Institute of Higher Studies in Criminal Sciences in Siracusa, Italy; the Australian Institute of Criminology in Canberra; El Instituto Latinoamericano de las Naciones Unidas para la Prevención del Delito y el Tratamiento del Delincuente in San José, Costa Rica; the Naif Arab Academy for Security Sciences in Riyadh, Saudi Arabia; the European Institute for Crime Prevention and Control in Helsinki, Finland; the Raoul Wallenberg Institute of Human Rights and Humanitarian Law in Lund, Sweden;

the Korean Institute of Criminal Justice Policy in Seoul; the United Nations African Institute for the Prevention of Crime and the Treatment of Offenders in Kampala, Uganda; the International Centre for Criminal Law Reform and Criminal Justice Policy in Vancouver, Canada; the International Scientific and Professional Advisory Council of the United Nations Crime Prevention and Criminal Justice program in Milan, Italy; the Institute for Security Studies in Cape Town, South Africa; and finally, the International Centre for the Prevention of Crime in Montreal, Canada.

The United Nations Human Settlements Program (UN-HABITAT) is the UN agency for human settlements. In 1996, at the request of a set of urban African mayors, UN-HABITAT created strategic responses to urban crime and violence. The main goal of the Safer Cities initiative is capacity building at the local level to effectuate an effective crime prevention strategy. Moreover, the hope is that initiative will foster a culture of crime prevention. The Safer Cities initiative has expanded and now boasts 16 local projects spread over five continents. The hallmarks of all the Safer Cities initiatives are (1) encouraging good government through transparency and accountability, (2) capacity building, and (3) free exchange of experiences between cities and residents including previously marginalized populations.

Like other crime prevention initiatives, Safer Cities systematically identifies potential stakeholders to create a local safety coalition along with elected officials guided by an initiative coordinator. A detailed analysis of local problems is performed with the goal of identifying attainable short- and long-term goals. Typically, modalities include urban and environmental design, community-based policing, prosocial activities, and programs for youth.

Nongovernmental Organizations

Besides the UN, many nongovernmental organizations (NGOs) have attempted to address issues of public safety and crime prevention. For example, the Instituto Latinoamericano de Seguridad y Democracia based in Buenos Aires, Argentina, helps build a system of both public and private mechanisms for crime prevention and protection of the rights and interests of individuals while paying special attention to community organizations that are already working in the field.

The International CPTED (Crime Prevention Through Environmental Design) Association based in Alberta, Canada, is concerned with the creation of a safer environment that improves the quality of life through the use of CPTED principles and strategies. The organization accomplishes this through the use of e-learning modules and conferences that can lead to certification.

Created in 2006, the Fórum Brasileiro de Segurança Pública (Brazilian Forum for Public Safety) is an NGO that disseminates ideas, news, and knowledge for the improvement of public security in Brazil. It also provides technical assistance to police, researchers, practitioners, and journalists. The organization publishes the *Brazilian Journal of Public Safety,* a journal dedicated to providing relevant information on crime and crime prevention in Brazil.

In Cape Town, South Africa, the Center for Justice and Crime Prevention (CJCP) works to develop and promote evidence-based crime prevention based practices in South Africa and other developing countries. The organization conducts research and reports findings to governments, police, and practitioners. CJCP also provides customized training modules in crime prevention.

Local Governments

Local authorities across the globe have worked to strengthen relations and promote interactions between municipalities and other echelons of government on the issues of crime prevention and safety. For example, European Forum for Urban Safety (EFUS) works with local governments in more than 300 cities across Europe to provide training, technical assistance, conferences, and seminars to aid with the implementation of crime prevention programs aimed to reduce crime and violence. Perhaps the most salient contribution from the EFUS happened during the Security, Democracy, and Cities convention in Zaragoza Spain with the promulgation of the *Zaragoza Manifesto on Urban Security and Democracy.* The *Zaragoza Manifesto* mandates exchanges between local governments and pledges mutual assistance

to prevent crime, victimization of women and immigrants, and terrorism.

The stated purpose of the United Cities and Local Governments (UCLG) is to represent and defend the interests of local governments on the world stage. While the UCLG lists many concerns, one primary concern is security. The organization advocates before international organizations like the United Nations on behalf of its members. Although there is an increasing willingness to implement crime prevention, resources and tools are often lacking.

Current Status

Major advancements have been made internationally in the past few years in the adoption of crime prevention strategies. Because of groups like the UN, nongovernmental organizations, and local governments, the goal of dissemination of sound crime prevention principles, recommendations, and innovative practices to policy makers and practitioners is now a reality.

Roger Enriquez

See also Crime Prevention; Crime Prevention Initiatives, International; Crime Prevention Through Environmental Design

Further Readings

Chawla, S. (2004). How to develop more effective policies against crime: Some reflections on drugs and crime research in an international context. *European Journal on Criminal Policy and Research, 10,* 85–98.

Ferreira, B. R. (1995). The prevention of international economic crime: Make it unprofitable for criminals and cohorts. *International Journal of Comparative and Applied Criminal Justice, 19,* 313–320.

International Center for the Prevention of Crime. (2008). *International compendium of crime prevention strategies.* Retrieved from http://www.crime-prevention-intl.org

International Center for the Prevention of Crime. (2008). *International report on crime prevention and community safety: Trends and perspectives.* Retrieved from http://www.crime-prevention-intl.org

Junger, M., Feder, L., Clay, J., Côté, S. M., Farrington, D. P., Freiberg, K., et al. (2007). Preventing violence in seven countries: Global convergence in policies. *European Journal on Criminal Policy and Research*, 13, 327–356.

Shaw, M., & Andrew, C. (2005). Engendering crime prevention: International developments and the Canadian experience. *Canadian Journal of Criminology and Criminal Justice*, 47, 293–316.

Zvekic, U. (1996). The international crime (victim) survey: Issues of comparative advantages and disadvantages. *International Criminal Justice Review*, 6, 1–21.

CRIME PREVENTION PARTNERSHIPS, INTERNATIONAL

Crime prevention partnerships are a way to reduce crime by mobilizing and coordinating the work of schools, social and youth services, law enforcement, public health, housing, families, and so on. The partnerships endeavor to mobilize those agencies and individuals most able to tackle the social and developmental risk factors that are known to predispose individuals to engage in crime.

The partnerships are recommended by organizations such as the World Health Organization (WHO), the United Nations (UN), and Habitat as a key to reducing crime. The governments in countries such as Belgium, France, and Sweden contract with municipalities to be the hub for such partnerships at the local level.

A key component of these partnerships is a planning process that is recommended by WHO, UN, and Habitat and is required by law for municipalities in England and Wales. The first step is a process to diagnose where and for whom additional services are needed to reduce crime. The diagnosis leads to a plan to implement increased services by the different agencies followed by actions to implement the services. In principle, implementation is followed by monitoring and evaluation. The core of the partnership is a secretariat that coordinates the four-step process (see Figure 1).

Longitudinal studies of the personal experiences of young men confirm that those most likely to offend had more frequently experienced risk factors such as inconsistent and uncaring parenting, teachers who identified them as trouble makers in primary school, and dropping out of secondary school. Efforts tackling these risk factors through visits by public health nurses, enriched preschool, and initiatives to stop kids dropping out of school have been shown to reduce offending. The partnerships are based on strong evidence about how risk factors contribute to crime and how interventions tackling risk factors are likely to reduce crime.

Further, the local partnerships at the city level are able to focus on the concentrations of crime found in cities. It is well known that

- 5% of offending is committed by 50% of the persons born each year, and
- 4% of addresses account for 44% of victimizations.

The offenders and victims tend to be concentrated geographically in areas that have disproportionate numbers of persons in relative poverty, who do not stay at the same address, and who experience other disadvantages. So the partnerships often concentrate new services in those areas.

In 2008, the Province of Alberta in Canada established a community safety secretariat to coordinate the partnership between departments responsible for health, schools, youth services, policing, and courts. The objective of the partnership was to reduce crime and enhance community safety. The secretariat is implementing 30 recommendations from a provincial task force as well as developing a province wide strategic plan. It controls $500 million in new funds allocated for the next 3 years in a three-pronged approach that balances prevention, treatment, and enforcement.

Similar partnerships are commonplace at the local government level in Western European countries. For instance, the government of England and Wales passed the Crime and Disorder Act in 1998, requiring every local government to establish a community safety and crime reduction partnership. These partnerships include a range of local agencies and must develop a plan based on a common diagnosis of the local crime problems, a plan to solve the problems, ways to implement the actions, and steps to monitor and evaluate the outcomes from the actions.

Crime prevention partnerships are a key ingredient in the "new" crime policy that focuses on outcome such as reduction of victimization rather than debates about punishment of offenders. The

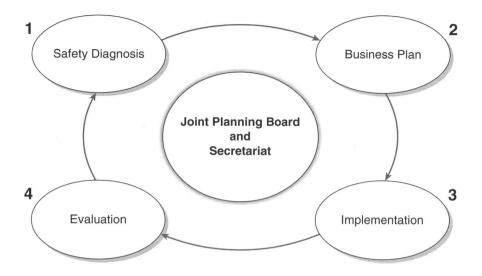

Figure 1   City crime prevention planning office

Source: Waller, Irvin. (2006). *Less Law, More Order: The Truth About Reducing Crime.* Westport, CT: Praeger, p. 116. Copyright © Irvin Waller.

new policy and its basis in science are articulated by Irvin Waller in *Less Law, More Order: The Truth About Reducing Crime*, a book written for the makers of criminal policy and the taxpayers. This book brings together the research on the limits of more police, more lawyers, and more prisoners. It gives examples of proven ways of preventing crime by tackling its causes, along with examples of crime prevention partnerships, and uses knowledge endorsed by agencies such as the U.S. National Academy of Sciences and the British Home Office and Treasury.

There is considerable experimental and scientific research to show that tackling the causes of crime is more effective and efficient in reducing crime than the dominant reactive and retributive policy. Nevertheless, U.K. and U.S. research on the effectiveness of partnerships is not able to conclude that citywide strategies are the major reason for crime reductions in a city. Strategies that apply universally across a city by definition cannot be tested through random control trials. However, correlation studies generally support the logic that they would be effective. There are impressive examples of achievements by crime prevention partnerships, such as the 50% reduction in rates of homicide in Bogotá, Colombia, over a 10-year period.

The main impediment to successful crime prevention partnerships is the dominance of the standard reactive approach to crime, in which increases in the budgets of the police, the courts, and corrections make it difficult for new funding to go to the partnerships. In addition, the advocates of reducing crime through environmental design and problem-oriented policing argue for funds for their approaches, which may appear to politicians to be more short term. In England and Wales, the local government partnerships moved away from crime prevention through social development and into crime prevention through environmental design (CPTED) and policing approaches, involving widespread use of closed-circuit television and strategies to arrest prolific offenders.

Advocates believe that crime prevention partnerships will significantly reduce crime if funding for their operation and implementation of the targeted social programs is tied to increases in funding for the standard approaches. The Canadian Big City Mayors have recently endorsed a framework specifying that all increases in funding for law enforcement should be accompanied by similar increases for services that tackle the social risk factors associated with crime.

After reviewing the results from reviews by the U.S. National Research Council and other leading agencies, such as WHO, Waller concluded that government strategies based on crime prevention partnerships at all levels of government could achieve large and sustainable reductions in rates of victimization. Thus Waller recommends an additional investment of about 10% of what is currently spent on reactive and retributive crime policy to achieve a 50% reduction in rates of crime and violence within a 10-year period. This investment would have to go to the programs that have been shown to work by tackling known risk factors and to crime prevention partnerships to implement them.

Irvin Waller

See also Crime Prevention Initiatives, International; Crime Prevention Partnerships, United States

Further Readings

International Centre for the Prevention of Crime. (2008). *International report on crime prevention and community safety: Trends and perspectives*. Montreal: Author.

United Nations Economic and Social Council. (2002). *Guidelines for the prevention of crime*. Eleventh Commission on the Prevention of Crime and Criminal Justice. Retrieved from http://www.unodc.org/unodc/en/commissions/crime-congresses.html

Waller, I. (2008). *Less law, more order: The truth about reducing crime*. Toronto: Manor House.

World Health Organization. (2004). *Preventing violence: A guide to implementing the recommendations for the World Report on Violence and Health*. Geneva: Author.

CRIME PREVENTION PARTNERSHIPS, UNITED STATES

This entry provides information regarding crime prevention partnerships in the United States, including what these partnerships are and why they exist. It also presents selected examples of such partnerships.

Definition and Purpose of Crime Prevention Partnerships

Crime is multifaceted and complex. In consists of a variety of behaviors and stems from many causes.

It is therefore not surprising that crime is often intractable and difficult to prevent. Crime problems are also not solved by one segment of society. Often, a focused, sustained effort including multiple partners is necessary to solve particular crime problems. Many systems can be involved in crime prevention, including the justice, health, education, local government, community and neighborhood organizations, business, and both family and faith-based systems. Forming partnerships to prevent crime allows all of these different but related groups to come together for the community. Partnerships acknowledge the fact that crime affects communities in multiple ways, and preventing it thus requires a team that comprises the many stakeholders of the community representing a wide and broad community voice.

In this entry, *crime prevention partnerships* is defined as "a linkage between community organizations and government agencies formed for the purpose of reducing a community's defined social problem or improving the conditions of the community" (Roman, Moore, & Jenkins, 2002, p. 18). Many types of crime prevention partnerships exist today in the United States. They can include any number of government, business, nonprofit, and faith-based organizations. Two that stand out are community policing partnerships and comprehensive community partnerships.

An effort has been made in the United States to provide research-based guidance on forming effective crime prevention partnerships. Much has been learned and some insights have been made about this multilayered process. It has been found that there are four basic stages of partnership (formation, implementation, maintenance, and outcomes) that every crime prevention partnership will go through. When attempting to form a crime prevention partnership, one should first assess the community's readiness for such a partnership. Is there partnership saturation? Are there any turf wars? Are there any stakeholders that want to partner? These are just a few of the questions that should be asked. Groups must be willing to deal with issues of distrust and any disputes that may have occurred in the past in an effort to come together in a collaborative effort. Once it has been established that a partnership is needed, that the community is ready for it, and that there are stakeholders ready to partner, partnership goals and objectives need to be clearly defined. The group should study different leadership types to identify the style that is best suited for the organizations and groups involved in the partnership. The partnership also needs to remember to keep the community engaged in its activities. It is important to always be attentive to the needs of the different members of the partnerships. Combining resources (including human, capital, time, and space resources) can be difficult and can take time.

Examples

Comprehensive Community Initiatives Supported in Part by the U.S. Department of Justice

Weed and Seed Program

The Weed and Seed program is a comprehensive, multiagency approach to law enforcement, crime prevention, and community revitalization that has been supported by the U.S. Department of Justice since 1991. It is characterized as a strategy that aims to prevent, control, and reduce violent crime, drug abuse, and gang-related crime in high crime neighborhoods in the United States. Each local Weed and Seed program is managed by a steering committee, organized by the relevant U.S. Attorney's Office, which includes local officials, community representatives, and other key stakeholders.

Strategic Approaches to Community Safety Initiatives

Strategic Approaches to Community Safety Initiatives (SACSI) was initiated by the U.S. Department of Justice in the late 1990s to see whether the dramatic results of Operation Ceasefire, launched in Boston, Massachusetts, in the early 1990s could be replicated. SACSI was a problem-solving effort designed to reduce and prevent serious gun violence in 10 U.S. cities. Led by the local U.S. Attorney's office in each location, each site included multidisciplinary, multiagency core groups to plan and oversee problem-solving efforts. As in project Ceasefire, local researchers were incorporated into the core groups. The partnerships then engaged in their problem-solving activities using an enhanced SARA (scan, analysis, response, assessment) model as the basis for their efforts.

Project Safe Neighborhoods

Project Safe Neighborhoods (PSN) was launched in 2001 as a commitment at the federal level to reduce gun crime in the United States by networking existing local programs that target gun crime and providing these programs with the additional tools necessary to be successful. PSN has provided support to hire new federal and state prosecutors, support investigators, and promote community outreach efforts as well as to support other gun violence reduction strategies. PSN has used an action research and problem-solving process to better target and reduce gun crime. This has been done using lessons learned from Operation Ceasefire and SACSI as well as other efforts. PSN groups have been convened by the U.S. Attorney's Offices in each of the 94 districts in the United States. Each office has convened a multidisciplinary, multiagency group with a research partner to address local gun crime.

Community Policing Partnerships

The federal Office of Community Oriented Policing Services (COPS) notes on its Web site that "community policing is a philosophy that promotes organization strategies, which support the systematic use of partnerships and problem-solving techniques, to proactively address the immediate conditions that give rise to public safety issues such as crime, social disorder, and fear of crime." Partnerships are thus a defining part of community policing and can include multiple entities, such as other government agencies, community members/groups, nonprofits/service providers, private businesses, and media. Often community policing partnerships are engaged in crime prevention activities.

Chicago's Alternative Policing Strategy

Chicago's Alternative Policing Strategy (CAPS) is one of the community policing programs in the United States that has engaged extensively in developing partnerships. In Chicago, police and citizens have been expected to work together to solve neighborhood problems at least since the mid-1990s when CAPS was implemented citywide in Chicago. The CAPS program has also been the focus of research to help understand its implementation and outcomes. Because of this effort, it is starting to become clear how to better involve the community in community policing. According to Jill Dubois and Susan Hartnett, the first lesson resulting from this research is that community buy-in must be obtained. This is often a difficult task, but it is one that must be accomplished and maintained. Second, an organized community (e.g., a community that has formal and/or informal community organization) requires more effective involvement in community policing. Third, training is as essential for the community as it is for the police. Community members need guidance to be effective partners in community policing. Finally, there is a danger of unequal outcomes; that is, some members of the community will find it easier than others to be involved in community policing, and those who really need to partner with the police may be the last to get involved if they become involved at all.

National Organization of Black Law Enforcement Executives

National Organization of Black Law Enforcement Executives (NOBLE) provides another example of a community policing–based partnership. In a recent effort, NOBLE led town hall meetings in five different cities in response to juvenile crime incidents among minority youth. In these meetings NOBLE pulled together community members, local law enforcement officers, public and private officials, academics, and most important, youth to have an open discussion of juvenile crime in their respective communities. In the second phase of the project, each local NOBLE chapter will hold a "community engagement" workshop for all key community stakeholders to have an opportunity to further develop crime prevention strategies for their community.

Winifred L. Reed and Deshonna Collier Goubil

See also Crime Prevention Partnerships, International; Operation Ceasefire/Pulling Levers; Project Safe Neighborhoods

Further Readings

Coldren, J. R., Jr., Costello, S. K., Forde, D. R., Roehl, J., & Rosenbaum, D. P. (2002). *Partnership, problem-solving, and research integration: Key elements of success in SACSI: Phase I findings from the National Assessment of the Strategic Approaches to Community Safety Initiative.* Washington, DC: U.S. Department of Justice.

DuBois, J., & Hartnett, S. M. (2000). Making the community side of community policing work: What needs to be done. In D. J. Stevens (Ed.), *Policing and community partnerships* (pp. 1–16). Upper Saddle River, NJ: Prentice Hall.

Graycar, A. (2000). Local government's effective community responses. In A. Graycar (Ed.), *Reducing criminality: Partnerships and best practices* (pp. 1–11). Symposium conducted at the meeting of the Australian Government Australian Institute of Criminology Conference, Novotel Langley, Perth. Retrieved September 11, 2009, from http://www.aic.gov.au/en/events/aic%20upcoming%20events/2000/~/media/conferences/criminality/graycar.ashx

Miller, L., & Hess, K. (2005). *Community policing: Partnerships for problem solving.* Belmont, CA: Wadsworth/Thomson Learning.

O'Shea, T. C. (2007). Getting the deterrence message out: The Project Safe Neighborhoods Public-Private Partnership. *Police Quarterly, 10*(3), 288–306.

Reuland, M., Morabito, M. S., Preston, C., & Cheney, J. (2006). *Police-community partnerships to address domestic violence.* Washington, DC: U.S. Department of Justice.

Roman, C. G., Moore, G. E., & Jenkins, S. (2002). *Understanding community justice partnerships: Assessing the capacity to partner.* Retrieved from http://www.urban.org/UploadedPDF/410789_Community_Justice_Partnerships.pdf

Web Sites

National Organization of Black Law Enforcement Executives: http://www.noblenatl.org

Office of Community Oriented Policing Services (COPS): http://www.cops.usdoj.gov

Project Safe Neighborhoods: http://www.psn.gov

Strategic Approaches to Community Safety Initiatives (SACSI): http://www.ncjrs.org/pdffiles1/nij/grants/212866.pdf

Weed and Seed, Community Capacity Development Office (CCDO): http://www.ojp.usdoj.gov/ccdo

CRIME PREVENTION THROUGH ENVIRONMENTAL DESIGN

Crime prevention through environmental design, also known as CPTED, is an approach aimed at preventing criminal victimizations, offending, and the fear of crime at places by using environmental design as a tool for discouraging crime. Rooted in the principle that the design of the built environment plays a central role in the selection of a crime site and the crime event itself, the CPTED approach relies heavily on the principles set out by Oscar Newman's defensible space theory. The CPTED strategies and the course of their development mirror that of the defensible space concepts, and as such, involve the strategic manipulation of various environmental design–related features in order to encourage increased surveillance, control, and protection of potential victims, targets, and target areas.

Like defensible space, the CPTED approach falls squarely under the purview of environmental criminology and, as such, is consistent with the opportunity theories of crime. This entry highlights the interdisciplinary foundations of the CPTED strategies aimed at reducing the risk of criminal victimization at places, and in doing so, reveals how CPTED emerges at the intersection of victimology and crime prevention. It discusses how the CPTED approach specifies why criminal victimizations are likely to occur in certain places, and how to proactively prevent them through the manipulation of environmental design. The entry goes on to chart the development of the CPTED approach, revealing some of its strengths and highlighting some areas of weakness that warrant empirical attention.

Description and Development

Empirical research in environmental criminology has demonstrated that crime tends to be concentrated in time and space, and according to CPTED, environmental design explains why crime occurs disproportionately at certain locations and not at others. The CPTED approach to preventing crime is based on six overarching principles that highlight strategies for designing physical and spatial characteristics of a potential crime target or crime location/place in ways that make them resistant, rather than vulnerable, to criminal victimizations. Thus the CPTED principles are designed to be implemented at the neighborhood level, the street level, and the property level. These strategies are based on an integration of knowledge from the

fields of architecture/planning, cognitive and behavioral psychology, and criminology.

The six main principles that drive the CPTED approach have been designed to block opportunities for crime generated by the environment, while simultaneously discouraging potential offenders by increasing the risk and effort involved in committing crime at a specific location. In this way, the CPTED strategies are based on the assumption of a rational offender whose decision to commit crime is based on assessment of the risks, effort, and reward of the crime event. The aim of the CPTED approach, therefore, is to manipulate the offender's perception of these factors so that the offender is deterred from committing crime because the risks and effort required are too high. The six CPTED strategies that are discussed include *natural surveillance*, *territorial reinforcement*, *natural access control* and *target hardening*, *activity support*, and *image/space management*.

Natural Surveillance

The natural surveillance principle of CPTED, which is based on the defensible space concept, was devised to discourage potential offenders by maximizing the visibility of space and its users, thereby increasing the probability that offenders will be detected by inhabitants and other legitimate users. Natural surveillance is enhanced through the use of techniques that ensure that space is easily observable. These include the use of lighting, closed-circuit television (CCTV), the orientation of doors and windows toward public space and other surrounding units, and the use of physical barriers (e.g., walls, gates, fences) and symbolic barriers (e.g., garden landscaping) in moderation so that lines of sight between private and public space remain clear of obstructions.

In this way, the interventions that help enhance natural surveillance can be structural or mechanical. The structural interventions—such as the use of street/property lighting and the orientation of windows—involve the implementation or manipulation of environmental design/layout features in order to facilitate surveillance by available guardians in the form of inhabitants or other legitimate users of space. Mechanical interventions, such as the use of CCTV, are designed for periods or situations in which guardians are not available to carry out surveillance. In these cases, guardians are replaced by electronic surveillance devices that are designed to have the same deterrent effect on offenders as guardians.

The CPTED principle of natural surveillance, therefore, is based on the notion that while surveillance works as a protective mechanism that reduces the fear of crime for legitimate users of space, it simultaneously discourages potential offenders by increasing the risk that they will be detected. Several empirical studies have demonstrated how the use of design features to maximize the visibility of space and its users—including not only residential spaces but also commercial spaces such as car parks and markets—works to control the amount of crime that occurs at places.

Territorial Reinforcement

The CPTED approach suggests that the effectiveness of natural surveillance as a crime deterrent is enhanced when the surveillance is complemented by design features that reinforce territoriality. The second core CPTED principle, territorial reinforcement, mirrors the defensible space concept of territoriality, and as such, calls for the clear demarcation of manageable zones that are visibly controlled and influenced by inhabitants of the surrounding space. The territorial reinforcement strategies are designed so that the inhabitants' level of territorial control is perceived to be high, consequently serving to discourage potential offenders in search of opportunities for crime.

In the first instance, territorial reinforcement requires that public and private spaces are clearly delineated; this is achieved by ensuring that property lines are well defined through the use of physical and symbolic barriers such as walls, gates, fences, landscaping, or the inclusion of porches in property design. It also suggests that extensions of private property, such as parking bays, are included in these zones of control by ensuring that they are attached to or within view of private properties. The barriers serve to restrict entry to the zones, and to communicate that the properties therein are private and capably managed and controlled by their owners.

Like defensible space theory, the CPTED approach highlights the interdependence of natural surveillance and territorial reinforcement. It warns against the danger of overusing physical and symbolic barriers to the extent that surveillance opportunities are obstructed. In this case, territorial reinforcement ceases to be a protective factor, and instead turns into fortressing of properties, which encourages more opportunities for crime due to the restricted visibility and increased concealment it provides for offenders.

Natural Access Control and Target Hardening

Going hand in hand with territorial reinforcement is the next CPTED principle: natural access control. Similar to territoriality, this principle focuses on the strategy of blocking off access to crime targets and target areas by using structural interventions. These structural elements involve the use of physical barriers—such as lockable gates, fences, and traffic barriers—to limit access to target areas and targets themselves. Natural access control may also involve minimizing the number of entrances into and exits from to a building, street, or neighborhood, and making these entry and exit points secure (by requiring keys or electronic passes) and accessible only to private owners and legitimate users.

Subsumed under the natural access control umbrella is the dimension of target hardening. Target hardening can be viewed as the micro-level version of natural access control, as it functions as the mechanism through which entry to individual property targets can be restricted to all but legitimate owners and users. This is achieved, for example, through the installation of door and window locks, the use of antirobbery screens, designing doors and windows to withstand forced entry, and the installation of burglar-proofing. These access control strategies are designed to deter potential offenders by increasing the effort required to gain access to the target. Several evaluations of crime prevention strategies that employ natural access control and target hardening techniques report that these function as effective crime control strategies.

Activity Support

One of the more recent additions to the CPTED strategies is activity support, defined as using physical design as well as signage to encourage the use of public space as it was intended. Activity support, therefore, is focused on communal areas of residential spaces, such as parks, playgrounds, and so on. It encourages legitimate users to communal spaces to ensure that they are used for safe activities. A park in a neighborhood, for example, may be used to host a sports day or other social events designed to bring members of the community together and encourage the legitimate use of a neighborhood park. Encouraging legitimate use of these types of communal areas is meant to discourage illegitimate use, such as drug dealing and vandalism. Because communal areas of a residential space do not necessarily fall under the control and influence of any particular resident, activity support is designed to ensure that these areas are used predominantly by legitimate users and for legitimate activity.

The implementation of legitimate activity generators is also an important part of the activity support strategy. The types of facilities and land uses in an area help determine the type of local activity that is encouraged at a place. The activity support strategy, therefore, is acutely context specific, as it encourages the inclusion of activity generators that discourage crime rather than those that create opportunities for crime. Such activities vary depending on very specific situational factors.

Image/Space Management

The other most recent addition to the CPTED strategies is that of image/space management. Even though this is one of the original concepts from defensible space theory, image/space management has only recently been explicitly included as part of CPTED as developments in environmental psychology and environmental criminology have revealed it to be an important factor determining the fear of crime and the risk of victimization at places. The image/space management strategy is aimed at the consistent maintenance and upkeep of the physical environment in order to foster a positive place image and maintain good place management practices. This strategy aims to discourage potential offenders by creating the perception of increased risks of detection through the communication of high levels of care and control by inhabitants.

This is achieved by ensuring that the exterior of buildings, common areas, gardens, and plantings are all maintained consistently, and to a high standard. Compatible with broken windows theory, image/space management involves preventing the physical deterioration of the environment by ensuring that there are no abandoned buildings or other physical evidence of a breakdown in control and management, such as broken lights or windows. Effective and consistent maintenance not only creates a positive image for the users of space, it also serves to reinforce positive territorial attitudes and enhance natural surveillance by ensuring well-maintained lines of sight.

CPTED, therefore, hinges on the idea that the risk of criminal victimization at places can be significantly minimized when environments are designed using a combination of the guidelines provided by the six aforementioned principles. The outcome of the implementation of these principles is the regulation of crime through enhanced territorial control, increased opportunities for natural surveillance, and consistent management and maintenance of the physical environment over time.

Second-Generation CPTED and the Social Context

Just as defensible space theory underwent development and emerged with a new dimension to its approach by incorporating social factors into its model of crime prevention, CPTED developed along a similar path. Having been criticized for neglecting the social dimensions of crime prevention that are at the root of community dynamics, second-generation CPTED has moved beyond the six strategies described above, and it has been refined to reflect the ways in which the social characteristics of inhabitants interact with the physical features of the environment to affect crime. Thus, second-generation CPTED has emerged in response to the critique that environmental design manipulations alone are not as effective in preventing crime as they are in conjunction with social interventions.

Against the backdrop of physical construction or reconstruction, second-generation CPTED aims to simultaneously attend to the community dynamics that are vital to people's interaction with their physical environment. As original CPTED strategies were criticized for applying "quick-fix," "band-aid" solutions to crime while ignoring the real "root causes," second-generation CPTED aims to reduce what has been referred to as the "motivations" for crime by employing four strategies designed to foster positive social and cultural dynamics. These include *social cohesion*, *connectivity*, *community culture*, and *threshold capacity*. In this way, second-generation CPTED develops the social dimensions of the territoriality concept. Rather than assuming the existence of fully engaged residents as defensible space as the original CPTED strategies did, second-generation CPTED attempts to devise strategies that ensure that residents are fully engaged in their community and committed to shared ideas about its security and overall positive development.

The *social cohesion* and *community culture* strategies are aimed at encouraging community participation by organizing social events and other activities that promote the establishment of a network of relationships among residents and a vibrant sense of community culture. *Connectivity*, on the other hand, focuses on building up a positive network of relationships between neighborhoods and external public support agencies, such as the media or governmental agencies. Finally, *threshold capacity* refers to the natural capacity of a neighborhood to serve particular functions or host specific activities. This principle is based on the premise that physical deterioration of the environment causes neighborhoods to reach their threshold capacity, and can result in increasing deterioration and abandonment, thereby increasing the outflow of residents and disrupting the social and economic stability that communities are dependent on. CPTED encourages balanced land use and increased social stability within neighborhoods as a mechanism to curtail opportunities for crime that may be generated when neighborhoods exceed their threshold capacity.

Implementation and Effectiveness

In spite of these developments, CPTED is still viewed primarily as a set of strategies that represent a functional approach to crime prevention, aimed principally at using environmental design techniques to eliminate the immediate, situational opportunities for crime. It is this practical approach and the highly visible techniques of environmental manipulation offered by CPTED that have made it

a politically popular approach with policy makers across the world—including the United States, Canada, Europe, Australia, and New Zealand—using the CPTED principles as quality control criteria for planning and construction. In fact, CPTED has enjoyed such widespread appeal that it has been adapted in many countries to suit the local environmental terrain. These adaptations of CPTED can be seen in the Netherlands as Politiekeurmerk Velilig Wonen (PKVW), in Australia and Europe as Designing Out Crime, and in the United Kingdom as Secured by Design. CPTED also recently has been adapted for application to products (smaller targets) to discourage theft by making them "crime proof" using an offshoot scheme called Design Against Crime.

The growing international support for CPTED by policy makers has been fueled by the mounting evidence from evaluations of CPTED interventions that demonstrate the effectiveness of various combinations of CPTED design strategies in substantially reducing crime. The success of CPTED interventions has been documented in different international contexts, and in different types of local settings. In the United Kingdom, for example, CPTED strategies have been successfully implemented to secure car parks, markets, alleyways, housing projects, and buses. In the United States, they have been applied to shopping centers, schools, and prisons; and in Australia, CPTED principles were incorporated into the design and layout of venues for the Sydney 2000 Olympics.

Limitations and Critiques

In spite of these successes in implementation, the CPTED approach faces two major challenges to its long-term effectiveness, namely the adaptability and durability of its strategies. British researcher Paul Ekblom has drawn attention to one of the major shortcomings of CPTED-based initiatives, pointing to the failure of designers to adapt to adaptable criminals. It has been argued that many of the offenders can learn, over time, how to circumvent or navigate around CPTED interventions so that they cease to function as an obstruction to the crime event. Ekblom argues that, as a result of this, design interventions run the risk of becoming obsolete over time. Furthermore, the approach assumes that the offender will be rational and therefore does not apply to offenders who are, for example, under the influence of drugs or alcohol, and who may not perceive environmental cues in the way the CPTED strategies predict.

The durability of the CPTED design initiatives is also limited as a result of the inadequate understanding of the specific processes that underlie their functioning. The range of interventions and the processes they affect are so broad under the CPTED umbrella that it is difficult to isolate the specific mechanisms that work, and to develop systematic knowledge about why they work and under what conditions they work most effectively. The continued development and improvement of CPTED, therefore, requires specific focus on the empirical exploration of the microprocesses at work behind the design–crime relationship.

Danielle M. Reynald

See also Defensible Space; Rational Choice Theory; Routine Activities Theory; Situational Crime Prevention; Situational Crime Prevention, Critiques of

Further Readings

Atlas, R. I. (2008). *Twenty-first century security and CPTED: Designing for critical infrastructure protection and crime prevention.* London: CRC.

Cozens, P. (2008). Crime prevention through environmental design. In R. Wortley & L. Mazerolle (Eds.), *Environmental criminology and crime analysis.* Portland, OR: Willan.

Cozens, P., Hillier, D., & Prescott, G. (2001). Crime and the design of residential property: Exploring the theoretical background (Part 1). *Property Management, 19*(2), 136–164.

Ekblom, P. (1997). Gearing up against crime: A dynamic framework to help designers keep up with the active criminal in a changing world. *International Journal of Risk, Security and Crime Prevention, 2*(4), 249–265.

Jeffery, C. R. (1971). *Crime prevention through environmental design.* Beverly Hills, CA: Sage.

Newman, O. (1972). *Defensible space: Crime prevention through urban design.* New York: Macmillan.

Poyner, B. (1998). The case for design. In M. Felson & R. B. Peiser (Eds.), *Reducing crime through real estate development and management.* Washington, DC: Urban Land Institute.

Poyner, B., & Webb, B. (1991). *Crime free housing.* Oxford, UK: Butterworth Architecture.

Sherman, L., Farrington, D., Welsh, B., & Mackenzie, D. (2002). *Evidence-based crime prevention.* London: Routledge.

Saville, G., & Cleveland, G. (2003). An introduction to second-generation CPTED: Part 1. *CPTED Perspectives, 6*(1), 4–8.

Saville, G., & Cleveland, G. (2003). An introduction to second-generation CPTED: Part 2. *CPTED Perspectives, 6*(2), 7–9.

Wagers, M., Sousa, W., & Kelling, G. (2008). Broken windows. In R. Wortley & L. Mazerolle (Eds.), *Environmental criminology and crime analysis.* Portland, OR: Willan.

CRIME SCIENCE

Crime science is the application of scientific method to the reduction of crime. Here, *crime* means volume crime such as theft and burglary, violent crime such as homicide and assault (including terrorism), antisocial behavior such as vandalism and graffiti, and that collection of behaviors falling under the often poorly defined category of organized crime. *Science* means the use of data, logic, rational argument, experimentation, theory development, and the accumulation of knowledge and understanding about the behavior under consideration. Crime science aims at the prevention and detection of offending that leads to the reduction of crime and, therefore, fewer victims.

At this stage, those who promote crime science are not addressing such issues as the function of the courts or the effect of prison treatment programs. Although these issues might well benefit from the application of scientific principles in their investigation (as is done by some criminologists and others), for now they are regarded as too far "downstream" of the offending behavior to attract the immediate interest of crime scientists concerned with stemming the potential growth in crime and the attendant growth in imprisonment here and now. Similarly, although some of the early intervention programs intended to prevent crime are discussed, developed, and evaluated by social scientists (some of whom are crime scientists), these approaches are generally considered too far "upstream" of the offending behavior to be of critical interest to those concerned with the immediate reduction of crime.

These are the general characteristics of crime science. It does not follow that all those investigating or researching the prevention and detection of crime are crime scientists. Some may feel science is not for them and adopt what might be seen as "unscientific" methods in their work. Others, while using scientific techniques and approaches fully compatible with the notions of crime science, may identify themselves as belonging to another discipline entirely, such as sociology, psychology, criminology, or some other field. This is as much a matter of personal choice as rocket scientists choosing to call themselves that or describing themselves as astrophysicists or simply as scientists. Crime scientists, whatever their "home" discipline, are primarily interested in reducing crime, while paying due attention to issues of human rights, socially responsible design, and ethical principles.

The extent to which crime science can claim to be a new academic discipline has been questioned by some academics, who ask that if anything done in the name of crime science could as easily have been accommodated under the heading of criminology, why invent something else? This question has been addressed directly by Ronald Clarke, who compares the characteristics of environmental criminology (which is an established part of mainstream criminology) with crime science and concludes that they have much in common. They are both concerned with the prevention of crime, with experimentation, with the analysis of crime data rather than data about offender characteristics, and both employ action research methods. They do, however, differ in a number of respects, including the specific interest of crime science in increasing the probability of detection following an offense, and the emphasis of crime science on the importance of testing hypotheses about crime and methods to reduce it. Clarke's own conclusion that there is a case to be made for the new discipline is based on his view that environmental criminology has long been poorly taught and somewhat marginalized by mainstream criminologists.

The first institute of crime science, the Jill Dando Institute, was established at University College London in 2001 as a center for research, teaching, and consultancy. Since then a number of other academic establishments have developed courses in crime science and more are expected.

Four Elements of Crime Science

It has been suggested that science and the technologies that it spawns can contribute to crime control in four ways. First, it can assist us in understanding the notion of crime itself. Much of this work falls under the general heading of social science and of criminology in particular. Second, science and the associated technologies can help in the prevention of crime. Deadlocks and immobilizers on cars are an example here, as might be the satellite technology upon which some surveillance systems work. Third, it can help with the detection of crime. This general area falls under the heading of forensic science—fingerprint technologies have been around for many years and have been brought up to date with the advent of recent computer technology that now allows the rapid searching of fingerprint databases. More recently, DNA has contributed to the detection of a number of offenses, including cold case reviews of serious crimes such as rape and murder.

The final element in the application of science to crime control is the use of the scientific method. This is the crux of crime science—the application of the scientific principles of investigation to the phenomenon of crime itself. It is crime in general as well as individual criminal offenses that are the interest of the crime scientist. Thus how to prevent or detect large categories of offending is a focus of interest, just as the application of scientific principles to the detection of a specific offense or series of offenses.

So crime science is the scientific study of crime. When it comes to the challenge of actually preventing or detecting crime, then, one may look to the application of already existing sciences and technologies. Forensic science, for example, draws heavily on the expertise of chemists, entomologists, and biologists, whereas the technologies of prevention draw on electrical or electronic engineering, optics, and so on. Thinking like a scientist and applying a systematic approach to studying the problem of crime and socially acceptable methods for its reduction is really what crime science is about.

Drawing on Theories of Crime

As with any science, crime science is concerned with the identification and further development of useful theories. One such set of theories (which purists would argue are perspectives on or approaches to crime rather than formal theories) has become known as the *criminologies of everyday life,* reflecting their day-to-day usefulness to practitioners. There are three—crime pattern theory, developed by Paul Brantingham and Patricia Brantingham; routine activity theory, originally described by Lawrence Cohen and Marcus Felson; and the rational choice perspective in the work of Derek Cornish and Clarke. These scholars have been working in their respective areas for about 40 years and have recently contributed to the book *Environmental Criminology and Crime Analysis,* edited by Richard Wortley and Lorraine Mazerolle, in which they set out the background and current state of development of their ideas.

Crime pattern theory draws on the observation that crimes cluster spatially (and as it happens, temporally too), and it forms a basis for understanding the mechanisms that determine the nature of that clustering. It has been observed that people (both offenders and potential victims) move about during the course of their daily lives in fairly routine ways and as a consequence become familiar with various spaces—those around their homes, their place of work or school, their shopping areas, and the places they go to for leisure activities. These places (or nodes, as they are called) are joined by pathways with which people are also routinely familiar. It is around nodes, and the pathways that connect them, that offending typically takes places. So when there is a crime pattern displaying incidents of burglary on a map, it is the accumulation of the offending of perhaps a number of offenders who have carried out their crimes in those areas with which they are familiar. Understanding the ways in which these patterns are developed is the work of the crime scientist.

Routine activity theory (which is also called routine activities theory) has similarly evolved since it was first articulated by Cohen and Felson. It began with an apparently simple notion, displayed in the form of a triangle, that when a vulnerable victim and a motivated offender come together in the absence of a capable guardian, an offense will happen. The vulnerable victim is now described as a vulnerable target, reflecting the fact that, for example, a home can be the "victim" of burglary in the absence of the homeowner (the "real" victim). It also reflects the focus on the perspective of the offender rather than the victim (i.e., from the property offender's point of view it is your property that is of interest, not you). The "absence of a capable guardian" concept has been expanded, as it is now acknowledged that a *capable* guardian may be absent even where a person, closed-circuit television camera, or guard dog is present, as mere presence does not of itself guarantee capability; a capable guardian is one prepared and able to intervene in a crime. In addition, the concept of the "crime triangle" has been developed, the three sides of which are offender, victim, and place, with the offender having a "handler," the victim a "capable guardian," and the place a "manager." These distinctions enable the elaboration of the underlying principles and pointing more clearly to what might be done by way of prevention. So, for example, in the United Kingdom, many place managers were removed from transportation systems, public parks, shopping malls, and apartment blocks as budgetary pressures led to staff reductions during the 1980s. An unplanned consequence of this was an increase in specific forms of crime.

The rational choice perspective has also changed considerably since its first articulation by Cornish and Clarke. The approach is based upon the view that offenders make more or less rational decision when deciding whether or not to commit an offense. In the process, they take into account the possible rewards, the effort required to commit the offense, and the perceived risk of capture or some other adverse consequence. They also consider the extent to which they feel provoked and the ease with which they can excuse their offending behavior. By way of example, "reducing rewards" might be achieved through regularly cleaning off graffiti, and if it was possible to make it clear to burglars that many of their victims are not insured, this would remove the potential excuse that it is okay to commit a burglary because the victim is covered by insurance. The range of options for preventive action within this framework is vast and goes well beyond simply putting locks and bolts on doors, as situational crime prevention is sometimes characterized to be doing.

All three theoretical approaches described above are associated with the here and now, with the delivery of more immediate reductions in crime that rely, in the main, on first understanding the crime opportunity structure (through careful data collection, analysis, and observation), and then changing it to reduce those opportunities and thereby reduce crime. These aproaches have developed significantly since their first expression, and this is a characteristic of the development of science through experimentation, further research, and academic discourse.

In addition, these approaches provide a theoretical context within which hypotheses about crime can be developed and understood, but they are not of course the only resource available to those wishing to speculate about crime and its causes and to develop preventive options. As in other sciences, researchers can draw on a range of other theoretical perspectives as well as their experience, common sense, the views of their colleagues, and in the case of crime, the community itself in formulating ideas about the nature of crime at the local, regional, or national level. An important point is that these ideas are then tested against reality.

Engagement With Other Sciences

As crime science is developing, so is its engagement with other relevant sciences. There is a small but growing number of U.K. universities offering courses in crime science or talking about security science, which is similarly concerned with the engagement of science with the security of communities, regions, and States. This engagement will assist scientists in seeing new applications for their work, but it should also offer a context within which they can be exposed to the social consequences of the application of technologies to crime control. Overly mechanistic or technological control mechanisms can be seen as offering a quick and simple solution to the security threat, at the expense of human interactions or more socially sensitive solutions. It is sensible, therefore, to ensure that scientists, engineers, and technologists are sensitive to the application of their work and to the need to take account of ethical and related concerns.

Methodological Issues

Each science has its preferred methodology. Thus chemists and experimental physicists can be described as typically working in laboratories and carrying out carefully controlled experiments predicting the outcome of various experiments and testing theories, although it is important to note that this is an oversimplification. These scientists do not use randomized controlled trials (RCTs), for example, which is the preferred methodology for the medical scientist concerned to evaluate the effect of a new drug or treatment program. RCTs are the gold standard for medical research, but they are not the gold standard for chemists and physicists. Similarly, in the area of crime science, it is the use of scientific method that is encouraged rather than the adoption of any particular experimental design or form of statistical analysis. The preferred experimental design is that judged most appropriate to address the hypothesis under investigation.

The important methodological issues of science apply also to crime science—how to control for bias, how to facilitate replication, how to test theories and thus to establish knowledge. At present it is probably fair to say that, unlike scientists in the well-established physical sciences, crime scientists are still developing their preferred experimental methods. This is to some extent because any experimentation is being carried out in a social context rather than a controlled laboratory setting, and as such is not amenable to the levels of control that might be achieved in a laboratory. This lack of control also has implications for the ease of replication that is itself an important element of scientific exploration.

As crime science is developing, it is becoming clear that there are two key questions that need to be addressed when approaching the prevention of crime. The first is the exact nature of the problem—this needs to be highly specific and detailed and is often the subject of considerable experimental effort. The second concerns how to reduce the crime, once it is properly defined, and this requires a specification of the proposed mechanism through which the reduction will be achieved. It is the efficacy of this mechanism that is determined during the evaluation of a crime prevention program.

Future Directions

Crime evolves as new opportunities arise. So, for example, there has been a massive increase in crime opportunities with the growth in Internet use. These are not new crimes: We are still talking about theft, child abuse, fraud, and so on, but the Internet has provided a whole set of new opportunities to commit these well-established offenses. If crimes such as these are to be reduced, then detailed analysis of the associated opportunity structures need to be carried out. Interestingly, in the case of Internet crime in particular, it is extremely difficult to arrest the offenders in many cases: The global reach of the system means that offenders can be based in any country and operate with relative impunity. Interestingly, in the case of Internet crime in particular, it is extremely difficult to arrest the offenders in many cases: The global reach of the system means that offenders can be based in any country and often operate with impunity. The relatively recent disclosure by the FBI of the banking details of people downloading child pornography from the Internet is an illuminating departure from this and showed, among other things, the extent to which child pornography had apparently been downloaded by individuals not normally associated with serious crime. Of course, it is not the perpetrators of the child abuse that are caught here; it is the customers for it (without which it would be less lucrative). If the concern is about reducing child pornography on the Internet more generally, then the system's design may need to be modified it in such a way as to make the offending less easy to commit.

Analyzing opportunity structures in this way is not common practice among many police crime analysts, although they are the ones who might be expected to do such analysis. If crime analysts are to be encouraged in this direction, which is essentially the same as encouraging what is usually called problem-oriented policing (POP), then they will need more training. Much of the material to support this effort is now available online at the Center for Problem-Oriented Policing's Web site. Although it is presented as a POP Web site, its approach is essentially drawing on scientific method and as such is promoting crime science. There remains, however, much to be done.

Gloria Laycock

See also Crime Mapping; Crime Pattern Theory; Crime Prevention; Hot Spots; Journey to Crime; Methodological Issues in Evaluating Effectiveness of Crime Prevention; Rational Choice Theory; Routine Activities Theory; Situational Crime Prevention

Further Readings

Clarke, R. V., & Eck, J. (2003). *Become a problem-solving crime analyst*. Cullompton, UK: Willan.

Cohen, L. E., & Felson, M. (1979). Social change and crime rate trends: A routine activity approach. *American Sociological Review, 44*, 588–608.

Cornish, D. B., & Clarke, R. V. (Eds.). (1986). *The reasoning criminal: Rational choice perspectives on offending*. Retrieved December 1, 2008, from http://www.popcentre.org

Laycock, G. (Ed.). (2008). *Policing: A Journal of Policy and Practice, 2* (Special edition on crime science).

Smith, M. J., & Tilley, N. (Eds.). (2005). *Crime science: New approaches to preventing and detecting crime*. Cullompton, UK: Willan.

Wortley, R., & Mazerolle, L. (Eds.). (2008). *Environmental criminology and crime analysis: Situating the theory, analytic approach and application*. Cullompton, UK: Willan.

Web Sites

Center for Problem-Oriented Policing: http://www.popcenter.org

CRIME STOPPERS

There are a variety of organizations that utilize media coverage in their crime prevention campaigns. The National Crime Prevention Council's "Take A Bite Out Of Crime" (starring McGruff the Crime Dog) is one of the oldest and best-known public information campaigns. John Walsh's long-running television show *America's Most Wanted* is perhaps the best known of the programs calling for public support in apprehending fugitives. *Cops* is one of several "crime time programs" promoting the efforts of law enforcement agencies in combating crime. The National Association of Town Watch utilizes media resources to promote crime and drug prevention programs such as America's Night Out. Numerous other programs throughout the world use a variety of media and Web formats to encourage opposition to criminal activities, provide for citizen awareness of crime, promote public cooperation with law enforcement agencies in suppressing crime, and endorse crime prevention strategies. One organization that has consistently performed all of the above for more than 30 years is Crime Stoppers.

Crime Stoppers is viewed by its membership as being a partnership of the community, law enforcement, and the media. Citizens within the community provide organizational and financial support for program activities and the funding of reward payments for crime information. Local law enforcement agencies act on tips received through phone and Web hotlines to solve crimes and apprehend fugitives. The media (print, broadcast, and Web based) provide free information on criminal events, unsolved crimes, wanted fugitives, and crime prevention activities. Each partner is seen as essential to the success of Crime Stoppers.

History

Crime Stoppers traces its origins back to 1976 when an Albuquerque, New Mexico, police detective ran a television reenactment soliciting information in regard to the unsolved murder of a college student. Detective Greg MacAleese offered a reward for anonymous tips that would lead to the arrest of those responsible for the murder. The success of this strategy in solving the case and arresting the murderers led to further collaborations among the Albuquerque Police Department, local media, and concerned citizens. Similar outcomes in other cases resulted in the creation of the first Crime Stoppers chapter.

The achievements of Crime Stoppers in Albuquerque were quickly noted by other communities. Soon other cities were developing local chapters that televised crime reenactments, posting crime details in newspapers, and offering rewards for anonymous tips. Within a few years, local and state chapters could be found across the United States and Canada. Now local Crime Stoppers programs are located around the world. National/regional programs (such as Crime Stoppers USA) can be found in the United States, Canada, the Caribbean, Bermuda, Latin America, Europe, the United Kingdom, Australia, and the Western Pacific region. Crime Stoppers International, headquartered in Austin, Texas, serves as the umbrella organization for programs worldwide.

Structure and Funding

Currently, more than 1,200 Crime Stoppers programs exist in all 50 U.S. states and more than 25 nations. All Crime Stoppers programs (whether at the local, state, national/regional, or international level) are organized as nonpolitical, not-for-profit associations. Each local chapter is run by a board of directors made up of private citizens from within the community that directs the financial and promotional activities of their program. Organizational costs and the payment of reward monies by every Crime Stoppers program are funded by membership dues, private donations, and fund raising. No tax dollars are involved. These boards meet monthly to evaluate arrests and to decide on the size of rewards to be paid (up to $1,000).

State and/or area associations comprise boards of directors that are selected by their membership. They provide training, assistance, and support to programs within their state or area. The national and/or regional organizations provide additional support and training for members, including annual conferences, Web sites, and newsletters. Crime Stoppers International is comprised of a board elected from member regions/nations. It provides additional support and coordination for members as well as maintaining an international Web site, conducting an annual international conference, publishing international reports and newsletters, and coordinating efforts with national and international law enforcement organizations.

Purpose

The primary goal of local Crime Stoppers is to provide citizens with an anonymous means to assist law enforcement in apprehending criminals and in helping to make their communities safer places to live. Crime Stoppers seeks to eliminate the fear of reprisals against those who provide information by stressing anonymity. They strive to reduce citizen apathy by promoting community awareness and shared responsibility for public safety. And, they attempt to overcome reluctance to get involved by offering cash rewards. Through these efforts Crime Stoppers view themselves as being the connection between community residents who want to fight against crime (without having their identity revealed) and law enforcement, which needs community cooperation to effectively prosecute criminals and stop crime.

The state, regional, national, and international organizations serve to support existing Crime Stoppers programs, to encourage and assist in the growth of additional programs, and to enhance communications and coordination of efforts among members, law enforcement, the media, and the general public. Whether at the local, state, national, or international level, the mission of Crime Stoppers may be seen as promoting the partnership of communities, the media, and law enforcement in order to solve crimes and promote public safety.

Crime Reporting Programs

Crime Stoppers is best known for publicized crime reenactments and offers of rewards for information that may lead to the arrests of criminals. Individuals who wish to contact Crime Stoppers may do so through a designated telephone line or secure Web connection. No police reports are required and the caller is not asked for personal or identifying information. During the initial conversation the tipster is provided with a code number to insure his or her anonymity. This code number is the only means that Crime Stoppers has of identifying the tipster. The caller is asked to contact Crime Stoppers later using this code number for identification.

During the initial conversation, Crime Stoppers will ask tipsters to provide as much detail as possible regarding the crime or offender. These questions may include: the type of crime committed, when the crime was committed, when and where a crime is expected to be committed, any personal or identifying information available on those involved in the crime, what a fugitive is wanted for, where and when a fugitive will be at a specific location, as well as any other details that might help law enforcement solve the case or capture the fugitive.

The information received through the tips is passed on to the appropriate local law enforcement agency for investigation. If the tipster's information led to solving a crime, preventing a crime, or the arrest of a criminal, the tipster will be approved to receive a reward up to $1,000. The person who provided the tip meets with a Crime Stoppers volunteer in a public place. Despite the amount, rewards are always paid out in cash.

The following programs are examples of the types of information programs offered.

Crime of the Week

The Crime of the Week is the oldest and best known of the Crime Stoppers programs. Reenactments of serious crimes that law enforcement agencies need assistance in solving are publicized by media partners (television stations, radio stations, newspapers, and their Web sites). Viewers/ readers are encouraged to provide any information they may have to Crime Stoppers. The possibility of a cash reward and the guarantee of anonymity are included in the broadcast or article.

Unsolved Crimes

In addition to publication of the Crime of the Week, Crime Stoppers also posts information on other unsolved crimes. These additional crimes may be broadcast but usually are of shorter duration and do not include reenactments. They are also posted on Web sites and included in media notices. As in the Crime of the Week, citizen assistance is requested with the offer of potential rewards for relevant information.

Wanted Suspects

Crime Stoppers often also posts information on fugitives from justice whom the police have been unable to apprehend. Photographs, personal descriptions, the nature of the crimes for which fugitives are wanted, law enforcement and/or Crime Stoppers tip lines, as well as other relevant information is provided through the media and is usually available for review on the local chapter's Web site.

Potential Crimes

It is customary for one to think of Crime Stoppers only as being involved in apprehending fugitives and solving crimes that have previously been reported to law enforcement agencies. However, it is frequently involved in providing information to the police about crimes that are being planned, are in progress, or have occurred but have not been reported. While knowledge from tipsters in regard to potential crimes must be treated with even greater care to protect innocent persons, numerous crimes have been prevented thanks to Crime Stoppers.

Missing Persons

While the circumstances in cases involving a person's disappearance may not be crime related, these cases may warrant presentation by the media and are often found on the Web sites of local chapters of Crime Stoppers. The nature of the circumstances regarding the person's disappearance determines whether or not information regarding a missing person warrants the consideration for a reward.

Informational Programs

In addition to programs calling for information and offering rewards regarding crimes, criminal offenders, and missing persons, Crime Stoppers also offers information designed to inform the public regarding criminal activities and/or perceived threats to the communities. They also seek to enhance community relations with local law enforcement agencies. The following are some of the programs that may be made available through the media and chapter Web sites.

Advice on Crime Prevention

Many chapters provide advice about how to prevent crimes and reduce the potential of becoming a victim of crime. Crime prevention advice includes tips on Crime Stoppers Web sites and in their publications as well as referrals to other agencies and crime prevention organizations for information. Crime Stoppers has actively advised and collaborated with other organizations in crime prevention initiatives, although this is less common in the United States than in other nations, such as the United Kingdom.

Registered Sex Offenders

Another service often found on Crime Stoppers Web sites in the United States is the identification of registered sex offenders residing within an area. While some may find this controversial or even inappropriate, the identification is generated from available public information and usually refers the viewer to official sites for additional information. The logic for this inclusion is to enhance public awareness among those who may not be aware of other sources to learn about sex offenders in the community.

Good Cops

Yet another informational program is Good Cops. This is a program used by some local Crime Stoppers to recognize the accomplishments of meritorious law enforcement officers. These accolades are consistent with the promotion of the police community partnership in dealing with crime.

School Programs

A program currently receiving a great deal of emphasis from Crime Stoppers is the development of student/campus programs. Concern for the safety of children and the potential for crime within school environments led to the creation of the first school program in Boulder, Colorado in 1986. Crime Stoppers claims more than 2,000 such programs at middle schools, high schools, community colleges, and colleges across the United States. In some ways Crime Stoppers programs are similar to the previously discussed crime reporting programs. Students are encouraged to report crimes and potential crimes through anonymous tip lines. Rewards for tips may include cash awards, passes to school activities, gift certificates, and free school items. Crime Stoppers emphasizes that the student/campus programs are much more than just crime hotlines. The programs are proactive means of promoting school safety. In addition, the involvement of students in the structure and organization of these programs is seen as encouraging responsibility, supporting school spirit and pride, and creating a positive campus image for students.

Effectiveness

It is not easy to determine the impact of Crime Stoppers in the prevention of crime and victimization. By their very nature such programs are extremely difficult to evaluate. The fact that in a little more than 30 years, they have grown from the appeal of a detective trying to solve a frustrating case into a worldwide organization, with thousands of local chapters, speaks to the appeal of the methods. Certainly one can make an argument that the millions of cases cleared, and billions of dollars of property recovered, and even more billions of dollars of drugs seized, are justification enough for its existence. In addition, the argument can be made that the positive effects of promoting community, media, and law enforcement partnerships are invaluable assets that reach beyond the realm of crime control.

Criticisms

Crime Stoppers does have its detractors. Some have argued that the media efforts may actually increase the public's fear of crime. Other critics express concern that the inducement of rewards may result in entrapment of innocent people by those seeking monetary gain. Still others stress that the emphasis on anonymity enables "snitches" to retaliate against those they do not like and may actually be abused by criminals seeking to eliminate competition. Crime Stoppers advocates respond by pointing out that all accusations still have to be investigated by the police and that many tipsters do not seek rewards. Finally, they assert that it is better to provide a safe mechanism for crimes to be reported than to allow crimes to go unsolved.

Ronald D. Hunter

See also Community Antidrug Programs; Crime Newsletters; Crime Time Television Shows; Media Coverage of Victims; Take A Bite Out Of Crime; Vigilantism

Further Readings

Lab, S. P. (2007). *Crime prevention: Approaches, practices and evaluations* (6th ed.). Cincinnati, OH: LexisNexis Anderson.

Web Sites

Canadian Crime Stoppers Association: http://www.canadiancrimestoppers.org
Crime Stoppers in Australia: http://www.crimestoppers.com.au
Crime Stoppers International: http://www.c-s-i.org
Crime Stoppers UK: http://www.crimestoppers-uk.org
Crime Stoppers USA: http://www.crimestopusa.com
"Good Cops" at Big Bend Crime Stoppers: http://www.bbcsi.org/localnews.aspx

CRIME TIME TELEVISION SHOWS

Crime time television shows have been a staple of programming since the popularization of television in the 1950s. This entry opens with a description of the types and themes of crime television shows. Next, the entry outlines debates surrounding television's influence on criminal behavior and violence. A historical timeline of efforts to regulate television programming is also highlighted in this section. The entry concludes with a discussion of television's influence on public fear of crime and on the activities of the criminal justice system.

Types and Themes of Crime Shows

There are two types of television crime shows: fictional and reality based. Fictional crime shows have a longer history on television, with the first crime shows airing in the 1950s. Themes in fictional crime television include depictions of police work (e.g., *Dragnet, The Closer*), legal processes (e.g., *Perry Mason, Law & Order*), specialized criminal investigations (e.g., *Man Against Crime, Magnum, P.I.*), and the lives of criminals (e.g., *The Sopranos*). Violent crimes, though rare events in real life, are overemphasized in fictional television crime shows. Crime victims in these shows are most often White. While young males are the most likely victims of crime in real life, crimes with female victims are more often depicted on television; the majority of female victims on television are victims of violent crimes such as sexual assault. In fictional crime shows, Blacks are underrepresented as perpetrators of crimes in comparison to their rates in official crime statistics.

The first reality-based crime television show, *Aktenzeichen XY*, was aired in Germany in 1967. Since then, reality crime shows have appeared in the Netherlands (*Opsporing Verzocht*), Britain (*Crimewatch UK*), and France (*Témoin No. 1*). Reality-based crime programming first appeared in the United States in the mid-1980s. Themes in reality-based crime shows include engaging the public in solving crimes, reconstructions of real crimes or criminal investigations, and the use of footage of crimes or criminal investigations caught on film by the public or by closed-circuit television (CCTV) cameras. In reality-based crime shows, Whites are most often depicted as victims, and Blacks are overrepresented as perpetrators in comparison to their rates in official crime statistics.

America's Most Wanted and *Cops* were the longest running reality-based crime shows in the United States, airing for 20 seasons and 19 seasons, respectively. *Cops* was the first American crime show to utilize actual crime or criminal investigation footage. CCTV footage is appealing because it costs less to produce than traditional television programming and because it lends an air of authenticity to its depictions. Critics of CCTV footage question its authenticity, pointing out the significant editing and processing of the footage before it is aired.

Both types of shows highlight the predatory personalities of offenders to explain the causes of crime. Rarely is crime linked to larger social problems or structural conditions conducive to crime.

Crime Television's Influence on Violence

The ability of television to reach large numbers of people and its consistent depiction of crime and violence has left a number of scholars and politicians concerned with the negative influence of television programming on criminal and violent behavior. Scholars from a broad range of disciplines, including sociology, psychology, political science, and communications, are interested in the media effects of violence on television. Media effects refer to television's influences on the behavior, beliefs, and attitudes of its viewers. Media effects research has focused on answering two primary questions: Does watching crime on television encourage people to commit more crime? And, does watching violence on television lead people to be more violent or aggressive?

Research supporting the claim that television promotes crime among its viewers is largely anecdotal. Examples do exist of people committing "copycat crimes" (i.e., criminal endeavors modeled after crimes shown in the media); however, the current consensus is that watching crime on television may influence the way people commit crimes but does not influence whether or not individuals will commit crime.

Research shows that television affects different viewers in different ways and that not all violence or criminal depictions on television are likely to have the same effects. There is a lack of empirical support for the argument that viewing violence on television has a strong, direct effect on violent behavior. Current research suggests that increases in violent behavior after watching violence on television may be explained by individuals who are predisposed to violence and aggression actively seeking out violent television programming.

Some have argued that watching violence on television may have a cathartic effect and that it provides a safe venue for releasing pent-up aggression or hostility. This argument has garnered little empirical support.

A Timeline of the Regulation of Violence on Television

In 1955, the U.S. Senate commissioned the first subcommittee to investigate the impact of violence on television on children. Though children were exposed to violence in other forms of popular media, such as comic books, radio programs, and motion pictures, television was thought to be the most threatening form of media. This report was the first of many that urged the Federal Communications Commission (FCC) to set standards for television programming.

Concerns over violence on television reemerged as a federal concern in the 1960s when President John F. Kennedy appointed Newton Minnow to chair the FCC. Though Minnow never drafted formal regulations of television programming, he was a vocal critic of television, calling it a "vast wasteland." Minnow's criticisms, the assassinations of President Kennedy, Robert Kennedy, and Martin Luther King Jr., and violent riots occurring across the United States inspired television writers, actors, producers, and directors to take a "pledge of conscience" to reduce the contribution of television to the "climate of murder."

In the late 1960s and early 1970s, President Lyndon B. Johnson maintained a federal focus on violence on television and appointed a National Commission on the Causes and Prevention of

Violence. The commission's report, released in 1969, found that television did encourage aggressive behavior and violence. These findings were mirrored in the 1972 report of the Surgeon General's Scientific Advisory Committee on Television and Social Behavior. Also in the 1970s, national and local branches of the Parent–Teacher Association organized a series of nationwide hearings on television violence and passed several resolutions to reduce the amount of violence in television.

Federal interest in violence on television waned in the 1980s in part due to President Ronald Reagan's hands-off approach to regulation by the federal government and to the introduction of cable television. Cable television channels do not use public airwaves for broadcasting and are not subject to the same constraints as mainstream television programming.

In 1990, Illinois Senator Paul Simmons successfully passed a bill that protected television and cable networks from charges of violating antitrust agreements if they agreed to work together to come up with standards regarding violence in television.

Since the 1990s, emphasis on parental control as a strategy to reduce children's exposure to violence on television has remained the primary strategy advocated by television networks and political officials. In 1993, the major television networks agreed to broadcast parental advisory warnings about the content of television programs. In the 1996 Telecommunications Act, President Bill Clinton mandated the inclusion of v-chip technology in new television sets. V-chips allow parents to block programs considered too violent or sexually explicit. Critics of the v-chip argue that the technology is confusing for parents and that technologically savvy children are easily able to bypass its restrictions. Though a 2007 FCC report encouraged Congress to implement more stringent regulation of violence on television, including violence on cable and satellite networks, no formal regulation of television content have yet been attempted.

Crime Television's Influences on Fear of Crime

Recent scholarship on television and crime considers the influence of television crime shows on public fear of crime. There are six theories of media effects on the fear of crime. Substitution theory argues that people who lack access to alternative and reliable sources of information on crime substitute the information on crime that they receive from the media. As violent crime is overrepresented in the media, those using media sources as a substitute will be more fearful of crime than those who have access to more reliable information. Resonance theory argues that persons with prior experiences of victimization are more fearful of crime because their experiences of victimization are reflected and reinforced by images they are exposed to in the media. Vulnerability theory suggests that persons who are most vulnerable to victimization are made more fearful by media depictions of crime. Affinity theory suggests that those who share demographic characteristics with those victimized in the media are more fearful. Ceiling effects theory argues that the media does not increase fear of crime, as the public's fear of crime is present prior to watching television. Finally, there is the argument that crime shows may reduce fear of crime because they reassure viewers that they will not be crime victims or that, if they are victimized, their perpetrators will be apprehended and punished.

Crime Television's Influence on the Criminal Justice System

Three areas of new research consider television's effects on the treatment of suspects by criminal justice personnel, on public support for "law and order" crime policies, and on jury reactions to scientific evidence during criminal trials (popularly known as the "CSI effect"). Scholars interested in the "echo effect" of media on the behavior of law enforcement and court personnel argue that police officers and court officials treat suspects in unpublicized cases poorly based on prior ill treatment of a similar suspect by the media in a well-publicized case. Researchers are also interested in television's effects on public support for "law and order" approaches to crime reduction. "Law and order" approaches emphasize increased police presence and stricter policing and punishment of offenders as the most effective crime reduction strategies. Television depicts our world as one filled with violence, where possible victimization is an ever-present threat. Increased popular support for law and order approaches is linked to images of unabated violence perpetuated by the media. A third area of research is on the "*CSI* effect" on criminal juries. *CSI*, an acronym for crime scene investigation, refers to a popular fictional crime drama that features a police crime laboratory and investigators that use science and scientific evidence (e.g., DNA) to solve crimes. There are two kinds of CSI effects: (1) pressure members of criminal juries exert on prosecutors to provide scientific evidence supporting the accused's culpability and (2) pressure on defense attorneys to overcome jury members' convictions of the infallibility of science and scientific evidence. While the CSI effect on juries has not been verified empirically, there is some evidence to suggest that criminal lawyers are responding to it as if it is a real phenomenon.

Elyshia D. Aseltine

See also Closed-Circuit Television; Correlates of Victimization; Crime Newsletters; Fear of Crime; Media Coverage of Victims; Public Opinion and Crime Prevention, United States

Further Readings

Barak, G. (Ed.). (1994). *Media, process and the social construction of crime: Studies in newsmaking criminology*. New York: Garland.

Doyle, A. (2003). *Arresting images: Crime and policing in the front of the television camera*. Toronto: University of Toronto Press.

Fishman, M., & Cavendar, G. (Eds.). (1998). *Entertaining crime: Television reality programs*. Hawthorne, NY: Aldine de Gruyter.

Kidd-Hewitt, D., & Osborne, R. (Eds.). (1995). *Crime and the media: The post-modern spectacle*. London: Pluto.

Postman N. (1986). *Amusing ourselves to death*. London: Heinemann.

Surette, R. (2007). *Media, crime and criminal justice: Images, realities and policies* (3rd ed.). Belmont, CA: Thomson/Wadsworth.

Watson, M. A. (2008). *Defining visions: Television and the American experience in the 20th century* (2nd ed.). Oxford, UK: Blackwell.

CRIME TRIANGLES

The causes of crime are the subject of criminology, but most criminological theories seek to explain why some people become criminals rather than how crimes are committed. Explaining the willingness of people to commit crimes does not explain crime events. True theories of crime account for the behaviors of offenders and targets, the settings of target–offender interactions, and behaviors of people who control these settings and the people in them.

Routine activities theory (also called routine activity theory) is a true theory of crime and, with its sister theories within the field of environmental criminology, it provides a foundation for crime prevention. This theory has been expanded since it was first described by Lawrence Cohen and Marcus Felson in 1979. A relatively recent formulation of routine activities theory has been widely used by police and others to reduce crime. This new formulation is often depicted as a pair of "crime triangles." This entry describes the crime triangles, why they are important, and how they have been used to prevent crime, as well as new research programs on the crime triangles.

Elements of the Crime Triangles

There are two triangles, as shown in Figure 1. The inner triangle names the *necessary conditions* for crime. Without any one of these three conditions, crime cannot occur. The outer triangle names the *controllers* of these necessary conditions. When all necessary conditions have been met and all three controllers are absent, or are present but ineffective, then crime is highly likely. When one or more of these controllers are present and effective, crime is highly unlikely, even if all necessary conditions for crime have been met. Felson originally referred to these six elements as "Eck's Triplets" because they were first proposed by John E. Eck. Since the most common way of portraying these six elements is by way of the double triangle motif, they are typically referred to as elements of the crime triangles.

Offenders and Their Handlers

"Offenders" are people who commit crimes. Research indicates that a relatively small proportion of all offenders are responsible for the majority of crimes. Offenders choose their targets and the places to commit crimes. The label "offender"

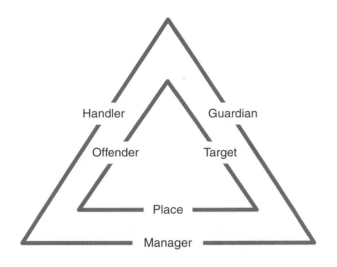

Figure I   The crime triangles

Source: Adapted from Eck, John. (2003). "Police Problems: The Complexity of Problem Theory, Research and Evaluation." In Johannes Knutsson, ed. *Problem-Oriented Policing: From Innovation to Mainstream*. Crime Prevention Studies, volume 15. pp. 67–102. Monsey, NY: Criminal Justice Press.

is specific to a particular circumstance. Thus in the case of a robbery, for example, the person threatening harm if another person does not provide money is the offender. But if the offender who committed the robbery is later attacked in a bar, the offender is the victim in the assault. In some circumstances it is not clear who is the offender. In illicit drug, sex, or stolen property sales both the seller and the buyer are offenders. Similarly, in many fights, it is not clear who started the altercation; both participants may be offenders. The crime triangles have been applied to noncrime events, such as pedestrian–vehicle crashes in which none of the parties are offenders.

"Handlers" are people who are emotionally connected to potential offenders and have an interest in keeping them out of trouble. Typical handlers include parents, spouses, clergy, coaches, and even children. Offenders seek to hide their illicit behavior from handlers, and often will refrain from offending if a handler is present. Offenders with few or no handlers commit more crimes than those with handlers. The desistance from offending often associated with marriage is an example of the influence of handlers.

Targets and Their Guardians

"Targets" are people, animals, or things that offenders attack, steal, or destroy. Victims are human targets. Research shows that some victims suffer repeated victimization, though most victims do not. Who is a victim is specific to the circumstance being examined. In the robbery example above, the victim was the person whose money was taken. If the robbery victim later shoots the robber in retaliation, then the original victim and offender have switched roles. So as was the case with offenders, "target" or "victim" is not a permanent label.

People who protect targets are "guardians." In the simplest cases, we are guardians of our belongings. We are also guardians of each other when we engage in any of the many activities we use to prevent our friends and relatives from being harmed. In some circumstances we employ guardians, as in the case were a jewelry store hires a security guard. And we often view police as guardians—public employees who protect us and our possessions from harm. Nevertheless, most guardianship comes from the routine protection we offer to our material possessions, relatives, friends, and associates.

Places and Their Managers

"Places" are small areas or locations that are far smaller than neighborhoods or communities, such as addresses or street corners. Considerable research shows that most places have little or no crime, but a few places have many crimes. This is not just a matter of place size or type. Whether large or small, and regardless of type, a few places are responsible for most crime, just as a few offenders and a few victims are involved in most crimes.

There are several important features of places. First, from the center of a place, one should be able to detect activity at most parts of it. Second, places often have a single owner who can exercise control over the location. Third, places have functions. Stores sell goods. Public swimming pools are for recreation and exercise. Classrooms are for education. And third, the characteristics of the place influence the decisions of potential offenders and victims at the location.

"Managers" are people who either own places or are employed to keep the place functioning. Common types of managers include store clerks, lifeguards, flight attendants, school custodians, teachers, and bartenders. Managers have both direct and indirect effects on crime. Tamara Madensen identified four management processes that influence crime: *organizing the physical space* (including selecting and designing the site, repair, and upkeep), *regulating conduct* (promoting and restricting different activities), *controlling access* (setting the times and conditions for people to enter the place), and perhaps most critically, *acquiring resources* (through sales, user fees, donations, or other means). So, for example, a person seeking to own a bar wants to make a profit (acquire resources). To do this she must select a location, design the layout and have it constructed, and make repairs and modifications as needed (organizing physical space). Through advertising she encourages the types of patrons she wants (controlling access). Drink serving policies, promotions, games, entertainment, rules, and enforcement (regulating conduct) structure how people behave within the bar. If the manager's choices are good, she will make a profit and crime will be low or absent. If her choices are bad, the bar may become unprofitable, or profitable but crime ridden.

The three controllers just discussed—handlers, guardians, and managers—are roles that are also dependent on the situation. A parent, for example, can have all three roles, as a handler of his child to keep him from creating mischief, a guardian of his child to protect him from harm, and a manager of his home so that it serves his family well. A store clerk is simultaneously a manager of the store (or part of it) and a guardian of the materials on display.

Importance of the Crime Triangles

There are three reasons the crime triangles are important. First, they organize three basic factors: repeat offending, repeat victimization, and repeat places. Though these factors were originally considered separately, with the crime triangles it is clear that each repeat involves the breakdown of controls along different sides of the outer triangle.

The crime triangles also are important because they reveal that there are multiple forms of controls that different types of people can apply. Originally crime was seen as the outcome of the lack of guardianship when offenders and targets came together.

However, the outer crime triangle shows that there are others—handlers and managers—who also can influence crime. This is important because some forms of crime are unlikely to be prevented by focusing on guardianship. Drug dealing, prostitution, and other forms of consensual crimes involve willing participants, none of whom desire guardians. The presence of managers is more critical for preventing these forms of crime. Changing the handling orientation of street groups can curb shootings stemming from intergroup conflicts.

The third reason the triangles are important is that they point directly at six classes of crime prevention. Focusing on the inner triangle of the figure, it is apparent that removing any one of the inner elements prevents crime; most obviously, keeping the offender from targets. However, keeping tempting targets away from places with offenders is another effective approach. This is exemplified by shelters for battered women that remove the target from the offender. And places—their function, not their geographic location—also can be removed. The relocation of an ATM from an outside street location to inside a store or bank is an example of this.

On the outer triangle, there are other classes of prevention: add handlers, guardians, or managers. Providing greater guardianship where it has not been present, or improving guardianship where it has been ineffective, has long been widely advocated. The outer triangle points to two other possibilities. Some malls, for example, to prevent juvenile misbehavior, require that people under a specific age must be accompanied by parent, thus increasing handling. Finally, improving the way place managers regulate conduct has proven effective in controlling drug dealing in apartment complexes and in reducing drink related violence in and around bars.

Use of the Crime Triangles to Prevent Crime

Crime triangles are widely used in problem-oriented policing to show police how to analyze crime problems, and the double triangle has become the symbol for the Center for Problem-oriented Policing. In this context, they are referred to as the "problem triangles." A police problem is a recurring set of events that causes harms within a community and that leads to the expectation that the police will address it. While the idea of crime triangles describes how a *single* crime event occurs, the idea of problem triangles suggests that these circumstances *repeat*, involving the same places, victims, or offenders. So a crime occurs when the necessary conditions are met in the absence of effective controllers. But if this happens repeatedly, then there is a problem. Police are guided to look for the particular repeat and identify elements of the triangles that need to be altered. Along with situational crime prevention, the problem triangles are tools of problem-oriented policing and have been built into much of the training materials used within problem-oriented policing.

Future of the Crime Triangles

In addition to improving the way police prevent crime, the crime triangles have spurred several research programs. Among the most recent are the following.

Examining Management Practices

The management practices of stores, banks, parks, homeless shelters, and other places have received little scrutiny from criminology and are often overlooked in designing crime prevention programs. This is changing as more research is examining how routine business and other organizational practices prevent crime or encourage it.

Improving Understanding of Handling

Handling has received even less attention, but very recent research suggests that it may have important roles in preventing not only minor infractions by young people but also serious crimes by adults.

Managing Systems Crimes

Routine activities theory describes how crimes occur when the victim and the offender need to occupy the physical space. However, there are some crimes where the offender is not physically close to the target. Mail bombings, phone fraud, and Internet crimes are examples. These are "systems" crimes because a network connects the target and offender: the mail system, the telephone, and the Internet. If "place" is replaced with "network," then it becomes apparent that systems crimes and normal crimes have very similar characteristics. Networks connect people just as they connect places, and they are managed by organizations that can alter network operations to make crimes more difficult. Large reductions in obscene phone calls, for example, were realized by the introduction of caller ID by phone companies.

Creating Computer Simulations of Crime Patterns

It is impossible to study all of routine activities theory at the same time because there is no way to collect data on all six elements and crime. Further, the data that are available contain many errors and omissions. So researchers have recently turned to computers to simulate crime patterns. Programmed virtual offender agents move around a virtual street network and encounter virtual target agents. Agents can make rudimentary decisions based on their circumstances at a particular moment. Depending on the simulation, characteristics of offenders, targets, and managers can be altered to create patterns of different types of crime. A number of street crime and white-collar crime patterns have been simulated in this way. The results have shown that complex patterns can arise from very simple decisions of individual agents.

John E. Eck

See also Crime Pattern Theory; Crime Prevention; Rational Choice Theory; Routine Activities Theory; Situational Crime Prevention

Further Readings

Clarke, R. V. (1997). Deterring obscene phone callers: The New Jersey experience. In R. V. Clarke (Ed.), *Situational crime prevention: Successful case studies* (pp. 90–97). Albany, NY: Harrow & Heston.

Cohen, L. E., & Felson, M. (1979). Social change and crime rate trends: A routine activity approach. *American Sociological Review, 44,* 588–605.

Eck, J. (1994). *Drug markets and drug places: A case-control study of the spatial structure of illicit drug dealing.* Doctoral dissertation, Department of Criminology and Criminal Justice, University of Maryland, College Park.

Eck, J. (2003). Police problems: The complexity of problem theory, research and evaluation. In J. Knutsson (Ed.), *Problem-oriented policing: From innovation to mainstream* (pp. 67–102). Monsey, NY: Criminal Justice Press.

Eck, J., & Clarke, R. V. (2003). Classifying common police problems: A routine activity approach. In M. J. Smith & D. B. Cornish (Eds.), *Theory for practice in situational crime prevention* (pp. 7–40). Monsey, NY: Criminal Justice Press.

Felson, M. (1986). Linking criminal choices, routine activities, informal control, and criminal outcomes. In D. Cornish & R. V. Clarke (Eds.), *The reasoning criminal: Rational choice perspectives on offending* (pp. 119–128). New York: Springer-Verlag.

Felson, M. (1995). Those who discourage crime. In J. E. Eck & D. Weisburd (Eds.), *Crime and place* (pp. 53–66). Monsey, NY: Criminal Justice Press.

Heinonen, J., & Eck, J. E. (2007). *Pedestrian injuries and fatalities*. Problem-Specific Guides Series. Washington, DC: U.S. Department of Justice, Office of Community Oriented Policing Services.

Hirschi, T. (1969). *Causes of delinquency*. Berkeley: University of California Press.

Liu, L., & Eck, J. E. (2008). *Artificial crime analysis systems: Using computer simulations and geographic information systems*. Hershey, PA: IGI Global.

Madensen, T. (2007). *Bar management and crime: Toward a dynamic theory of place management and crime hotspots*. Doctoral dissertation, Division of Criminal Justice, University of Cincinnati.

Tillyer, M. S., & Kennedy, D. M. (2008). Locating focused deterrence approaches within a situational crime prevention framework. *Crime Prevention and Community Safety*, 10(2), 75–84.

Web Sites

Center for Problem-Oriented Policing: http://www.popcenter.org

CRIME VICTIMS FUND

In 1984, with the passing of the Victims of Crime Act (VOCA), the Crime Victims Fund was established by the federal government to protect the rights of victims. The Crime Victims Fund was created in order to provide federal assistance to victims of criminal activity with medical expenses, funeral and burial costs, mental health counseling, and lost wages or financial support related to their specific victimization. In addition to remuneration mandated by VOCA, victims may be compensated for the following expenditures as well: costs related to transporting the bodies of homicide victims from another country or state, building modifications and equipment required as a result of a compensable crime, financial counseling for victims facing fiscal difficulty as a result of a crime, and pain and suffering. The Crime Victims Fund does not cover costs related to property damage or property loss.

Distribution

The statute allocates money levied as fines, penalties, bond forfeitures, and special assessments from convicted federal offenders as the monetary source for the Crime Victims Fund. The deposits from the fund are apportioned in the following manner: (1) child abuse prevention and treatment grants receive the first $20 million, with 85% going to the U.S. Department of Health and Human Services and 15% assisting Native American tribes; (2) the federal criminal justice system receives an undetermined amount for crime victims in that system; and (3) the Antiterrorism Emergency Reserve receives an allocation of up to $50 million, which was initially authorized from the Crime Victims Fund in response to the attacks of September 11, 2001.

The remaining funds are redistributed to the states to aid victims of criminal acts: Forty-seven and a half percent of the remaining funds are available to eligible state programs that provide compensation for crime victims; forty-seven and a half percent are also available to crime victims in the form of victim assistance grants; five percent of the funds are allocated for discretionary grants in the form of demonstration projects, training and technical assistance, and support for victims of federal crime. Each of the 50 states, the District of Columbia, the U.S. Virgin Islands, Puerto Rico, and several other United States' territories receive funding from the Crime Victims Fund through VOCA grants. These grants are awarded based upon certain criteria being met by the state receiving the grant. Criteria for receiving a grant include but are not limited to the following: (1) the compensation program must be administered by the state and currently operational; (2) the program must offer compensation to victims of crime and survivors of victims of crime, giving priority to violent crime victims but not excluding nonviolent crime victims; (3) the program must promote the cooperation of crime victims with law enforcement; (4) residents victimized outside of their own state must receive compensation on the same basis as in-state residents; and (5) victims of federal crimes within the program's state must be compensated on the same basis as the victims of state crimes.

Recent History

The Crime Victims Fund is based on the concepts of restorative justice. Restorative justice advocates the idea that offenders should pay for their criminal actions. In the 1960s, President John F. Kennedy's and President Lyndon Johnson's administrations were responsible for laying the groundwork for the federal government's concern for crime, crime victims, and restoration. The 1970s saw an increased federal interest in the idea of victims' rights and compensation. In 1976, Congress passed a bill that compensated the survivors of public servants who died in the line of duty, including police officers, firefighters, and other law enforcement officials. As a precursor to VOCA, in 1982, Congress passed the Federal Victim and Witness Protection Act. The recompensatory component of this act allowed judges to order restitution to the victims for medical costs, funeral and burial costs, and costs due to property loss. In 1982, President Ronald Reagan's administration assembled the Presidential Task Force on Victims of Crime. The task force concluded that the determination to insure the rights of offenders had inadvertently resulted in neglected victims' rights. As a direct result of the task force's findings, Congress passed VOCA, in turn establishing the Crime Victims Fund, which fostered the concept that convicted offenders should be held financially responsible for their crimes.

Joshua Lawrance Balay

See also President's Crime Commission Report, 1967; President's Task Force on Victims of Crime, 1982; Restitution; Restorative Justice; Victim Compensation

Further Readings

Davis, R. C., & Mulford, C. (2008). Victim rights and new remedies: Finally getting victims their due. *Journal of Contemporary Criminal Justice, 2,* 198–208.

Marion, N. E. (1995). The federal response to crime victims, 1960–1992. *Journal of Interpersonal Violence, 4,* 419–436.

Newmark, L. C. (2004). *Crime victims' needs and VOCA-funded services: Findings and recommendations from two national studies.* Report to the National Institute of Justice. Retrieved September 27, 2008, from http://www.ncjrs.gov/pdffiles1/nij/grants/214263.pdf

Office for Victims of Crime. (2005). *OVC fact sheet: Victims of crime act victims fund.* Retrieved September 16, 2008, from http://www.ojp.usdoj.gov/ovc/publications/factshts/vocacvf/fs000310.pdf

CRISIS REACTION REPAIR CYCLE

Not all survivors of a life crisis suffer from stress reactions. However, when individuals survive a catastrophic event, they may very well experience such reactions for several years. These are natural responses of people who have survived a traumatic occurrence that posed a serious threat to their physical well-being or sense of self. This threat may range from the obvious result of physical harm incurred as a victim of a violent crime, tragic accident, or natural disaster to a less apparent but potentially devastating threat, such as the loss of financial security during an economic downturn.

While the intensity and frequency of crisis reactions usually decreases over time, victims may never fully recover from the effects of a life crisis occurrence. Even victims who have successfully reconstructed their lives (and achieved relative levels of normalcy) find that new life events may trigger memories and reactions to their previous victimization. *Crisis reaction repair cycle* is the term introduced in 1979 by police psychologist Morton Bard to describe the sequence of healing phases that those who have experienced such a major life crisis pass through as they seek to recover from the event (or events) that caused them to suffer physical and/or emotional harm.

The crisis reaction repair cycle is also referred to as the *crisis response and recovery cycle* and the *grief process,* as well as by other similar terms. Regardless of the terminology utilized (which tends to vary slightly depending on the backgrounds of those attempting to assist victims), victims pass through three distinct stages within the crisis reaction repair process. These stages are most commonly referred to as: the *impact stage,* the *recoil stage,* and the *reorganization stage.* The time required for a victim to work through the stages of the crisis reaction repair cycle depends on the nature and severity of the crisis, the individual's emotional makeup, the potential for recovery from the harm incurred, how quickly intervention efforts are begun, and the types of support available to victims.

The Crisis Experience

During a crisis, human behaviors are often based on animal instincts and physiological responses. Physical reactions include the following: *frozen fright*—in which shock, nausea, numbness, and/or inability to control bodily activities may occur; *flight or fight*—an adrenaline rush resulting in physical arousals such as increased heart rate, hyperventilation, and sweating; and *tunnel vision*—disorientation in which a particular sense may appear to be heightened while others seemingly shut down. Emotional responses often include disbelief that the event is occurring, followed by extreme fear. Victims initially may be panic stricken but eventually tend to enter into a less excited (or even a seemingly emotionless) state in which survival takes precedence. The combination of physical and emotional reactions will ultimately result in physical exhaustion.

The traumas from these crisis experiences are often so severe that victims are unable afterward to function as they could previously. A considerable amount of time may be required before they are able to recover enough to regain control of their lives, or they may never recover. While the nature of the crisis may vary considerably, victims are initially unable to cope with the situation by themselves. Their reactions may involve posttraumatic stress disorder (PTSD), phobias, and anxiety attacks. The intensity and duration of the event, along with the victim's personal factors (education, maturity, emotional stability, etc.), cultural influences, religious beliefs, and support from significant others, all influence the extent of the victim's recovery and how long it takes. A victim's progress within the crisis reaction repair cycle is influenced by the following:

1. *Crisis severity*—the extent to which the person is threatened or actually harmed. Quite logically, the greater the harm that has been imposed on a victim, the more severe the emotional trauma.

2. *Victim's abilities*—the victim's intellectual capacity to comprehend what has occurred and emotional stability at the time the crisis occurred. These impact the victim's abilities to cope with a problem of such personal magnitude.

3. *Primary intervention*—the kind of intervention, or help, that a person receives immediately after the crisis. The responses of emergency workers, police officers, and/or medical personnel in reducing the initial trauma may significantly affect how long it takes the victim to regain control of his or her life.

4. *Supportive environment*—the extent of emotional support provided by friends, family, colleagues, social groups, and others within the victim's community.

5. *Validation of experience*—the concern and support demonstrated by the government/legal officials and medical/mental health professionals charged with helping the victim to cope with the harm experienced.

6. *Potential for recovery*—the likelihood of the victim being able to regain a satisfactory equivalent to the quality of life enjoyed prior to the crisis. If the victim has little chance of overcoming the harm done, his or her emotional recovery will most certainly be more difficult.

Depending on the length of time involved, some victims may actually begin entry into the first stage of the crisis reaction repair cycle while the crisis is still occurring. Others will not do so until well after the event has ended.

Stage One: Impact

During a crisis, it is normal for victims to produce automatic physiological responses as well as emotional coping mechanisms; the coping mechanisms continue as victims enter into the initial phase of the reaction repair cycle. These emotional responses include a shocked disbelief that the event actually took place followed by the denial of harm incurred during (or because of) the crisis. As victims move further along in the impact stage, these reactions eventually give way to the realization that the event did indeed occur and acknowledgment that they were actually harmed.

As indicated in the prior section, the actions of first responders immediately after the crisis occurrence are extremely important. The practice of what some refer to as "psychological first aid" by first responders may be crucial to the victims' later recovery. A variation of this would consists of three components: *assuring victims* that the threat to them is over and that they are safe; *encouraging victims* to talk about what has occurred and empathizing with how they feel; and then *preparing victims* for what is going to happen next.

When victims accept the reality of their having been victimized, they move from the impact stage into the recoil stage of the crisis reaction repair cycle.

Stage Two: Recoil

Even though entry into the recoil stage is a significant step in the healing process, victims often experience great pain as these acknowledgements are followed by a roller coaster of feelings, including alternating periods of horror, anger, guilt, anxiety, depression, social withdrawal, emotional numbness, memory loss, flashbacks to the event, and feelings of helplessness. Physical responses that victims frequently incur during this period include headaches, stress-related illnesses, lowered immunity to diseases, sleep disturbances, nightmares, forgetfulness, inability to concentrate, irritability, mood swings, hyperactivity, hypoactivity, gastrointestinal problems, and eating disorders. While these reactions may have begun in the impact stage, they intensify during the recoil stage and often continue to occur throughout the crisis reaction repair cycle.

The emotional and physical responses described above persist as victims begin working through their grief and sense of loss. It is within this stage that victims contend with feelings of injustice, lack of control, loss of faith, vulnerability, loss of self-respect, and hopelessness. Physical maladies and emotional turmoil during this period can result in lifestyle aberrations, addictive behaviors, and substance abuse that cause greater difficulties. Posttraumatic stress disorder (PTSD) is also a common condition experienced by victims. It should be noted that even if they do not serve as catalysts for PTSD, that "triggering events" that remind the victim of the crisis can lead to setbacks in the recovery process. These events vary with different survivors, but may include identification of the assailants; sensing something similar to something that one was acutely aware of during the trauma; anniversaries of the event; the proximity of holidays or significant life events; hearings, trials, appeals, or other critical phases of the criminal justice process; and news reports about a similar event. These episodes can bring back emotions that occurred with the original trauma. For victims who have lost loved ones or suffered severe harm, the recoil stage may last for many months.

Stage Three: Reorganization

It is typical for the frequency of memory occurrences and the intensity of the emotions associated with them tend to become more moderate over time. Therefore, it is normal for the effects of the trauma suffered during a crisis to diminish with the passage of time. As victims become more able to cope with their feelings, they are more capable of placing the crisis event in its proper perspective within their lives. This begins the reorganization stage of the crisis reaction repair cycle. During this stage an environment of support from friends, family, and community members greatly enhance the potential for a quicker recovery.

The issues that victims must work through in reconstructing their lives include getting control of the crisis event intellectually, working out an understanding of what transpired, reestablishing a new personal equilibrium, reestablishing trust, and reestablishing meaning and a sense of self within their lives. It is extremely important during this process that crisis reactions are not made worse by the actions of others. Lack of concern by others, insensitive remarks, being blamed for what occurred, condemnation for cooperating or not cooperating with the prosecution of an offender, and continued subjection to fear and shame are examples of *secondary victimization*. It is also important during this phase that victims achieve some degree of vindication (acknowledgment by others that they were actually harmed and that they did not deserve what happened to them).

The final phase within the reorganization stage is one of emotional resilience. During this time mood swings, depression, and anger gradually give way to philosophical reflection.

What transpired is absorbed into the victims' overall view of themselves as a significant occurrence but not the defining event in their lives. While the victims may never be completely "healed," this emotional reassembly of their lives enables them to emerge from the shadow of the crisis that dominated their existence.

Importance of the Cycle

As indicated previously, the ability of victims to progress through the stages of the crisis reaction repair cycle is greatly influenced by those with whom they interact. Indeed, the importance of the crisis reaction repair cycle is not grasping the terminology of this healing process but understanding the importance of others in achieving recovery. The goal of caregivers should be to assist victims in completing their transition through this healing cycle. Otherwise, victims may merely move from their initial reaction of "This can't be happening to me!" to a continuously frustrating repetition of "Why me?"

Ronald D. Hunter

See also Bereavement Process; Peacemaking: Alternative Court Remedies; Psychological and Behavioral Consequences of Victimization; Rape Trauma Syndrome; Restorative Justice; Stockholm Syndrome; Victim Assistance Programs, United States; Victim Compensation; Victim Support Groups

Further Readings

Bard, M., & D. Sangrey, D. (1979). *The crime victim's book*. New York: Brunner/Mazel.

Davis, R. C., Lurigio, A. J., & Herman, S. (Eds.). (2007). *Victims of crime* (3rd ed.). Thousand Oaks, CA: Sage.

Karmen, A. (2010). *Crime victims: An introduction to victimology* (7th ed.). Belmont, CA: Wadsworth.

Lab, S. P. (2007). *Crime prevention: Approaches, practices and evaluations* (6th ed.). Cincinnati, OH: LexisNexis Anderson.

Miller, L. (2008). *Counseling crime victims*. New York: Springer.

Montgomery, B., & Morris, L. (2000). *Surviving: Coping with a life crisis*. Tucson, AZ: Fisher Books.

Web Sites

National Center for Victims of Crime: http://www.ncvc .org

National Crime Victims Research & Treatment Center: http://www.colleges.musc.edu/ncvc

National Institute of Mental Health: http://www.nimh .nih.gov

Office for Victims of Crime: http://www.ovc.gov

CRITICAL VICTIMOLOGY

Not everyone is at equal risk of being the victim of crime, and some victims get more attention than do others. For example, ironically, at a time when North American crime discussion is dominated by calls for more prisons, more executions, and victims' rights, some female crime victims are belittled. Some fathers' rights groups, academics, and politicians fervently challenge research showing high rates of wife beating, sexual assaults committed by male acquaintances and dating partners, and other types of woman abuse that occur behind closed doors. Moreover, while some politicians based in Western nations repeatedly point out human rights violations in totalitarian countries, they simultaneously hide or ignore the victimization of women in their own so-called democratic societies. Similarly, many mainstream or positivist victimologists ignore the plight of women and girls abused by male acquaintances and intimate partners. However, when they do focus on this harm, they typically examine victims' culpability instead of the broader structural and cultural forces that motivate men to engage in the abuse of women and female adolescents.

Critical victimologists, however, carefully examine the myriad ways in which women and girls are victimized by males they know and/or with whom they are romantically involved. They also emphasize the political nature of crime and victimization and, like labeling theorists, are sharply opposed to only using legal definitions of crime. Another key element of their work is studying the many harms experienced by those who are socially and economically excluded, such as gay men and lesbians, who are subjected to harassment and bias crime.

If the term *crime victim* comes up in the course of an individual's daily conversations with friends, relatives, co-workers, or even university peers and professors, it generally is in reference to a person harmed by an act of interpersonal violence on the street. Still, critical victimologists sensitize us to the fact that, knowingly or unknowingly, everyone has been, or will be, victimized by one or more highly injurious experiences that commonly escape the purview of criminal law. They also want to broaden definitions of crime to include serious damage done to workers, consumers, and to the environment by corporations, as well as other harms done by economic and political elites that are not typically considered illegitimate (e.g., false advertising). Furthermore, critical victimologists call for studying and criminalizing the following: violations of human rights, poverty, unemployment caused by moving corporations to developing countries, inadequate social services (e.g., substandard housing, day care, education, and medical care), pornographic and racist media, terrorism, the creating of weapons of mass destruction, and so on.

Critical victimologists remind us that sometimes entire categories of people (and often women) are not "allowed" to be crime victims. Certainly street sex workers, panhandlers, runaway youth, and others are seen as responsible for their pain and suffering by scores of political and business leaders, agents of social control, and the general public. Also noteworthy is that studies conducted by critical victimologists reveal that, contrary to popular belief, many workers are safer on the streets than they are on the job. Some scholars estimate the corporate death rate at more than 6 times greater than the street crime death rate, and the rate of nonlethal assault in the workplace at more than 30 times greater than the rate of predatory street crime. Although close to 75% of North American women in the paid workforce are in so-called pink ghettos (i.e., clerical jobs, nursing, and retail sales), they are not immune to safety hazards. Critical victimologists found that these workers are at great risk than are others of experiencing the ill effects of exposure to toxic substances, stress, repetitive strain injury, and other work-related dangers. Indeed, a back injury suffered by a female nurse who was not provided help lifting a patient is just as debilitating as the same injury suffered by a male construction worker at an unsafe heavy construction site.

Critical victimologists do not dismiss or reject all the empirical and theoretical work done by their positivist counterparts. For example, critical researchers frequently use mainstream methods, such as representative sample surveys. However, such surveys include quantitative and qualitative questions that generate data on social problems generally considered irrelevant by some, such as woman abuse; sexual harassment and the verbal harassment of gay men, lesbians, and people of color in public places; and corporate crime. Even when government agencies decide to gather data on one or more of these topics, critical victimologists generally uncover higher incidence and prevalence rates because they define criminal harms more broadly.

Certainly, there are social scientists who find critical victimologists' broad definitions to be problematic. Some critical criminologists, for instance, suggest that sweeping accounts may be too broad or vague. Others have even gone so far as to state that they encompass "everything but the kitchen sink." Then there are others who assert that broad critical definitions are simply political agendas rather than scientific contributions. Critical victimologists respond to this claim by stating that no scientific method, theory, or policy proposal is value free and that mainstream scholars are also trying to advance a political agenda that guides their own work. They also respond to the previous criticism by stating that regardless of whether they are officially defined as crimes, economically, socially, environmentally, and physically injurious acts committed by political and economic elites are just as, if not more, important as those committed by powerless people.

Walter S. DeKeseredy

See also Corporate Crime; Feminist Victimology; Hate and Bias Crime; Homeless, Violence Against

Further Readings

DeKeseredy, W. S., Alvi, S., & Schwartz, M. D. (2006). Left realism revisited. In W. S. DeKeseredy & B. Perry (Eds.), *Advancing critical criminology: Theory and application* (pp. 19–42). Lanham, MD: Lexington Books.

Elias, R. (1986). *The politics of victimization: Victims, victimology and human rights.* New York: Oxford University Press.

Elias, R. (1993). *Victims still: The political manipulations of crime victims.* Newbury Park, CA: Sage.

Lowman, J., & MacLean, B. D. (Eds.). (1992). *Realist criminology: Crime control and policing in the 1990s.* Toronto: University of Toronto Press.

Mawby, R. I., & Walklate, S. (1994). *Critical victimology.* London: Sage.

CYBER AND INTERNET OFFENSES

Victimization in society results from many types of harmful behaviors committed by individuals or groups against other people. Behaviors considered negligent or abusive, or that otherwise are considered criminal in a particular place, often depends on the amount of harm inflicted, the technological means employed, and existing laws that forbid specific activities. Technological means used to commit cyber offenses refers to a combination of networked systems, hardware devices, software tools, and methods that people use on the Internet. Modern information technology (IT) hardware like computers, personal digital assistants (PDAs), cellular phones, and gaming devices can be used offline (in standalone mode), online, or wirelessly, from private or public places, in ways that are not easily recognized as illegal and that transcend more the one geopolitical or legal jurisdiction. In addition, illicit use of computing devices can facilitate many forms of traditional in-person crimes.

To fully understand cyber and Internet offenses, it is necessary to consider (1) the ways in which computerized devices and telecommunications systems came to be increasingly used for illicit purposes, (2) the myriad forms of online abuse and crime now taking place in our interconnected world, (3) the categories of people and organizations likely to fall prey to online forms of abuse and crime, (4) the social and economic impact of cyber and Internet offenses, and (5) what is being done to help prevent cyber offenses and provide services to victims of cybercrime.

Internet Crime History

Online crime began in the early 1960s when universities and certain government agencies and banking institutions began using networked computers to send text messages, for research, financial transactions, and record keeping. The earliest abusers of computer systems were college students who experimented with using them to play games and solve problems. Early abuse involved relatively harmless pranks and computer hacking (i.e., breaking into computer systems) to view files and sometimes manipulate or steal data. By the 1970s, as computer use in society increased, so too did the amount and variety of online abuse. Offending evolved beyond pranks and hacking into high-tech forms of embezzlement and fraud that were increasingly difficult to detect, investigate, and prosecute. In response, U.S. government and many states began creating computer crime laws during the 1980s. Even so, the real onset of modern cyber offenses began in the 1990s as more sectors, organizations, and individuals in computerized countries like the United States increasingly purchased more affordable, powerful, and interconnected personal computers (PCs), and later, portable devices such as mini- and laptop computers, PDAs, and cellular phones. This trend, which is continuing into the 21st century, along with the millions of broadband (high-speed) Internet connections made available via thousands of Internet service providers located around the world, makes it possible for billions of Internet users to become victims of cyber offenses.

Forms of Online Abuse and Crime

Every form of online abuse and crime may have from one to many victims, and hundreds, thousands, or even millions of people may be victimized. According to Samual McQuade, categories of cybercrime offending now include illegal or abusive online activities such as the following:

Cyber negligence by users of information systems who violate recommended or required security policies or sound online practices, thereby exposing their systems, devices, or data to cyber attacks

Traditional in-person crimes by users of computers or other IT devices for illicit communications and/or record keeping

Fraud and theft by people who illegally phish, spoof, spim, spam, or otherwise socially engineer people to commit identity theft or gain financially

Computer hacking and password cracking by individuals or groups who crack computer account passwords and unlawfully access information systems or exceed their online system permissions

Writing and releasing malware (i.e., malicious software), including disruptive or destructive viruses, Trojans, worms, and adware/spyware programs as well as illegal massive distributions of email known as spam

Pirating of music, movies, or software using computers and other IT devices to violate criminal or civil copyright laws to replicate, distribute, download, sell, or possess software applications, data files, or code

Online harassment and extortion to threaten, intimidate, intentionally embarrass, annoy, coerce or some combination of these which when involving youth is commonly referred to as "cyberbullying"

Cyber stalking, pedophilia, and other cyber sex offenses by online offenders who acquire illegal sexual pleasure by exerting power or control over their victims, including cases of human trafficking for sexual purposes and so-called sex tourism (traveling to have sexual relations with minors)

Academic cheating, as when students use portable IT devices to plagiarize or cheat on assignments or exams, or when researchers fake study methods or findings for profit or fame

Organized crime, including the online activities of ethnic-based gangs who use computers, cell phones, or other kinds of computers and telecommunications devices in the course of their legal and illegal business enterprise

Corporate, government, and freelance spying that relies on cyber-enabled tools and methods of espionage, including spyware and key logger applications to snoop for personal or professional purposes

Cyber terrorism, as when a group advances its social, religious, or political goals by instilling widespread fear online or by damaging or disrupting critical information infrastructure

The categories of cyber offenses listed above may overlap depending on many circumstances and a combination of skills, knowledge, resources, access to information systems, and intensity of motives possessed by individual and groups of perpetrators involved. For example, a group of computer hackers may consist of expert malware code writers who release remotely controlled and/or self-morphing programs onto the Internet where they can be downloaded by unsuspecting users. Results from such an "attack" vary considerably depending on the intent and skill of perpetrators and the potential value of a victim's data. Online theft or destruction of data belonging to a large corporation may be worth millions of dollars, and losses of personal, personnel, or client data can be very traumatic to individual victims, as in cases of identity theft.

Social and Economic Impact of Online Offenses

Firms that lose computerized data due to system user neglect or abuse, to cybercrimes committed by insider employees or external attackers, or to a natural or human-made disaster may never fully recover from their losses. Firms that do not have data saved on their information systems automatically backed up to an offsite location along with business continuity plans ready to implement on a moment's notice risk much. Losses of data, money, or other property, along with emotional and psychological harm and even physical injury or death as the indirect result of cyber offenses, are experienced every day by thousands of individuals, families, and groups of people.

Cybercrimes such as those previously listed are normally considered nonviolent property crimes, and many also qualify as financial crimes. This is especially true if the primary goal of offenders is to illegally acquire funds or control electronic banking or credit card accounts. Identity theft, for example, is a financial crime and often also constitutes bank fraud.

Despite frequent occurrences of identity theft and many other forms of online crime, the amount of financial loss and other social and economic harm caused by or associated with cyber and Internet offenses is not truly known, and the accuracy of any estimate depends on how offenses are defined; however, specific forms of online crime are periodically estimated for specific forms of crime, and annual economic losses from cybercrime have been estimated to be in the tens of billions of dollars worldwide. A single release onto the Internet of a malicious virus, Trojan, or worm program has on more than one occasion affected millions of users and cost billions in damages to information systems and loss of data (e.g., the "I Love You" virus released in May 2000 was estimated to have cost between $1 billion and $10 billion worldwide).

The wide variety and apparent increases in many forms of online offenses make it very difficult to determine or even estimate the social and economic costs of primary, secondary, or tertiary victimization that result from cyber abuse and crime in society. Part of the problem is that America's national crime reporting systems, such as the National Incident Based Crime Reporting System and the Uniform Crime Report Program managed by the Federal Bureau of Investigation (FBI) in cooperation with thousands of U.S. law enforcement agencies, do not specifically identify or distinguish between many forms of online offenses. Nor do they effectively distinguish between traditional in-person forms of crime that are substantially facilitated by online activities of offenders.

Victimization surveys also generally do not ask questions about specific computing and telecommunication technologies involved in crimes that have been committed, though this is beginning to change. Since 2001, the U.S. Department of Justice has conducted specific studies of cybercrime against business and identity theft. Results of this research suggest that millions of businesses and households are affected by online offenses each year. For example, of 7,818 businesses surveyed in National Computer Security Survey by the Bureau of Justice

Statistics, 67% identified one or more cybercrimes in 2005, nearly 60% detected one or more attacks against their information systems, 11% discovered a cyber theft of data, and 24% experienced other types of information security events.

The Computer Security Institute based in San Francisco and New York City, in partnership with the FBI, issues annual reports of cyber offenses and information security issues of concern to security professionals employed in large firms, academic and health institutions, and government agencies. The National White Collar Crime Center, also in partnership with the FBI, provides the annual *Internet Fraud and Crime Report* based on complaints received by consumers through the Internet Crime Complaint Center. Studies consistently reveal that cyber and Internet offenses threaten many organizations, families, and individual users of computers and other types of IT devices and information systems.

Likely Victims of Cyber and Internet Offending

Cyber offenses can directly or indirectly harm anyone. Indeed, everyone who connects to the Internet via unprotected information systems or IT devices. The great variety of online offending methods also means that thousands, even millions of victims, can be harmed anywhere they happen to be connected to the Web while browsing, chatting via instant or text messaging, emailing, blogging and uploading or downloading any form of content (e.g., text, pictures, video, or audio recordings). The greatest potential danger rests on using unprotected systems and IT devices, along with having confidential information discovered and used or manipulated for illicit purposes.

Four primary types of victims likely to be targeted by cyber offenders include youth, elderly people, financial institutions, and government, health care, and academic organizations.

Youth

Millions of youth now use computers and IT devices to game online, for other social computing purposes, for schoolwork, and to shop. In the process, many "friend" other youth online via personal profiles on Web sites like MySpace and

Facebook. They exchange personal information about themselves and their friends and family. If they are not extremely careful, they may be "socially engineered" by online offenders who pretend to be someone they know or betray them later, as when cyberbullies create and spread rumors that cause embarrassment. Youth who are never taught about Internet safety, information security practices, *and* cyber ethics are especially vulnerable. Many youth do not regularly patch up their operating systems and software applications or backup their valuable data. Combined mobile and social computing abilities along with willingness to share personal information make youth extremely vulnerable to being manipulated and victimized online.

In a major study of more than 40,000 K–12 students in 14 New York State school districts, researchers discovered important facts about cyber offending and victimization experiences of youth, including:

- Cyberbullying begins in the second grade when children first report "being mean" to each other online.
- Of students surveyed in second and third grades, 35% reported having been exposed within the prior year to online content that made them feel uncomfortable, 13% reported they used the Internet to talk to people they do not know, 11% reported having been asked to describe private things about their body, and 10% reported being exposed to private things about someone else's body.
- In fourth through sixth grade, the overall number of youth cyber abuse and crime offenders exceeded the number of youth cyber abuse and cybercrime victims.

Researchers also discovered online promiscuity among seventh- through twelfth-grade students, some of whom reported taking nude photos of themselves or each other and distributing them via the Internet. Youth also reported that they send and receive from each other unwanted pornography and solicitations for sex, and also chat online about things of a sexual nature. By middle school, students are exposed to all known forms of online offending and abuse and begin to specialize in the types of offending they commit. This trend continues into high school and college and has serious implications for the policing of high-tech crimes by adults.

Elderly People

People who grew up prior to the widespread use of the Internet (beginning in about 1993) often do not understand the risks being online. Many, though not all, elderly people have limited savvy when it comes to using computers or other types of IT devices. As a group, elderly people tend to be very trusting and consequently may be susceptible to being manipulated online. Many older people also have a limited or fixed income, are worried about their health and financial futures, and therefore are more vulnerable to being conned into "get rich" schemes. Conversely, many elderly people are proportionately quite wealthy. In fact, they naturally possess or control most of the most money in society. This combination of factors makes them attractive victims to cyber criminals.

Financial Institutions

Banks, credit unions, insurance companies, and other types of financial institutions that manage large amounts of money online are also often targeted for online and Internet crimes. This happens despite the fact that financial institutions employ the best policies, practices, and technology for keeping money safe. Special laws and government regulations specify the kinds of protections they need to have in place. Yet the vast sums of electronic currency and volume of financial transactions processed by banks and similar institutions is so large, in the trillions of dollars each day, that they remain very attractive targets for cyber thieves.

Government, Health Care, and Academic Organizations

These kinds of organizations are responsible for protecting massive amounts of sensitive and personal data. Cyber offenders recognize the value of such data for committing crimes like identity theft. Some offenders will go to great lengths to steal an identity. Until the late 1980s and early 1990s, most government, health care, and academic organizations were unregulated with regard to the provisions for data protection they afforded citizens, patients, and students. Much has changed, with new laws and regulations now requiring organizations to ensure more protections. Mishaps continue to occur with alarming frequency, however, resulting in the personal data of thousands of people being used in various kinds of online offenses.

Prevention and Victim Services

Primary strategies that people can use to prevent becoming a victim of cyber and Internet offenses include buying computer and telecommunications products and services from reputable firms; regularly patching up operating systems, software applications, and drivers like those that enable printing functions with security updates; and backing up data on storage devices not always connected to a primary computer or other IT device as well as automatically to off-site locations. Users should also interact online only with people and organizations they trust and be wary of sharing personal or confidential information. Shredding documents containing personal information, using strong nonalphanumeric passwords (that do not spell a name or word in a dictionary in any language), and not sharing passwords along with changing passwords regularly can also help to prevent cybercrimes.

Many government and nonprofit organizations now provide Internet safety and information security tips for consumers. The OnGuard Online Web site of the U.S. Department of Commerce Federal Trade Commission is a great example. This resource provides cybercrime prevention content for consumers of all ages and for businesses that perform various kinds of online services. In addition, the National White Collar Crime Center maintains the Internet Crime Complaint Center, which works to report allegations of Internet offenses to appropriate state and federal authorities. Notable organizations that provide sound advice for educators, parents, and youth in how to prevent cyber and Internet offenses include the Family Online Safety Institute, Internet Keep Safe (I Keep Safe) Coalition, the National Center for Missing and Exploited Children, and the Cyber Safety and Ethics Initiative.

The latest and most ambitious efforts in the United States to prevent cyber and Internet offenses and provide victims with counseling, legal, and referral services are now being piloted by the government and within certain state and local government agencies. For example, beginning in 2001 the Office of Victims of Crime (OVC), a Bureau of the Office of Justice Programs, solicited grant applications for demonstration programs to service victims of cybercrime. The Maryland Crime Victims' Resource to Center with OVC funding received in 2007 now provides counseling and referral services victims of identity theft and fraud, among other types of crime and abuse.

Samual C. McQuade III

See also Bullying; Child Pornography and Sexual Exploitation; Cybercrime, Prevention of; Human Trafficking; Identity Theft; Internet Fraud; National Incident-Based Reporting System (NIBRS); Offending and Victimization; Stalking Laws; Uniform Crime Reporting (UCR) Program

Further Readings

McQuade, S. C. (2006). *Understanding and managing cybercrime*. Boston: Allyn & Bacon.

McQuade, S. C. (2009). *The encyclopedia of cybercrime*. Westport, CT: Greenwood Press.

McQuade, S. C., & Sampat, N. M. (2008). *RIT survey of internet and at-risk behaviors*. Rochester, NY: Rochester Institute of Technology.

Rantala, R. R. (2005). *Cybercrime against businesses* (NCJ 221943). Washington, DC: U.S. Department of Justice.

Wall, D. S. (2007). *Cybercrime: The transformation of crime in the information age*. Cambridge, UK: Polity.

Web Sites

Cyber Safety and Ethics Initiative: http://www.bcybersafe.org

Family Online Safety Institute: http://www.fosi.org/cms

Federal Trade Commission OnGuard Online: http://www.onguardonline.gov

Internet Crime Complaint Center: http://www.ic3.gov/default.aspx

Internet Keep Safe (I Keep Safe) Coalition: http://www.ikeepsafe.org

National Center for Missing and Exploited Children: http://www.missingkids.com

National White Collar Crime Center: http://www.nw3c.org

Office of Victims of Crime: http://www.ovc.gov

CYBERCRIME, PREVENTION OF

Cybercrime is crime that occurs when computers or computer networks are involved as tools, locations, or targets of crime. This means that cybercrime may include a wide variety of traditional types of crime, such as theft or even extortion, but that these may take on novel forms because of the opportunities provided by the cyber environment.

Scope of Cybercrime

Since computers and networks now pervade almost every corner of our lives, from making a telephone call to driving on the freeway, the crimes that occur in the cyber environment are many. Some of these crimes may or may not be crimes, depending on the jurisdiction, especially as the Internet transcends international borders. Gambling, for example, or even trading in child pornography, may not be crimes in some countries. Some of these crimes are old crimes with a new face. For example, a thief may purchase an item from an online store using a false identity or credit card; a robber may force a victim to divulge his PIN number at an ATM; an embezzler may siphon off money from online bank accounts.

New crimes inherent to the cyber environment are shown in Table 1.

Apart from the cyber enhancement of traditional crimes described above, we are probably all victims of some aspect of cybercrime, since the costs (both economic and social) of maintaining secure networks is in the long run passed on to consumers. This is reflected not only in the necessity of purchasing antivirus software to protect our personal computers, but also in the high risk we take when we give out personal information to the many organizations with which we deal in our everyday lives. The opportunities available for the theft of our personal information are legion. The challenge for prevention, therefore, is to identify these opportunities and reduce them.

Cybercrime Prevention

Identifying Opportunity

The cyber environment enhances the attractiveness of targets, the effectiveness of tools, and the viability of locations for carrying out cybercrime.

Computers and Networks as Targets

Generally, in the cyber environment, information is *the* target, and a very attractive one. Its features are almost identical to those Ronald Clarke delineated as characterizing a "hot product" coveted by thieves; that is, CRAVED—concealable, removable, available, valuable, enjoyable, and durable. Examples of these features of information are described as follows.

Table 1 Types of cybercrime

Hacking	Offender uses existing security flaws in computer and network operating systems to break into private or corporate computer networks
Privacy violation	Offender uses keystroke detectors, spyware, and other advanced technologies to spy on computer use
Release of viruses	Offender releases viruses that exploit weaknesses in existing computer systems
Identity theft	Offender uses the cyber environment to obtain the personal information of others and assume their identities
Pfishing	Offender uses trick Web sites and emails to con individuals into giving up their private information and/or money
Denial of service	Offender uses software techniques to take over hundreds of individuals' computers to mount an attack on a commercial or government Web site and cause its collapse
Information theft	Employee steals computer disks or files and sells them on the street

Concealable	Information can be easily hidden in untraceable computer files
Removable	Information does not have to be removed, simply copied
Available	Information is everywhere and readily available
Valuable	Credit card and bank account files are information
Enjoyable	Users enjoy the movies and songs they download illegally
Durable	Stolen identities can be used for months if not years before they are discovered

Cyber Tools

The cyber environment provides considerable tools, often at little cost to the offender. These include the ready availability of new techniques and technologies such as the following:

- A fake identity can enable a child predator to enter a chat room pretending he is a 15-year-old and find potential victims.
- Hacker software makes it possible to crack passwords, find security holes in networks, and much more.
- Hacker hardware such as keystroke recorders enable hackers to collect passwords and PINS, modify chips for use in mobile phones, and counterfeit documents of identification.
- Available Web site technology makes it easier to counterfeit the Web sites of respectable businesses and agencies.

Cyber Locations

These may be physical or "virtual" sometimes both. Offenders will use physical locations such as Internet cafés or public libraries in an effort to avoid identification through the computer they use to access the network. They may also enter virtual locations such as teen chat rooms, or online gaming places such as Second Life, where they may play at and even commit actual crimes.

Techniques for Cybercrime Prevention

Ronald Clarke, in his book *Situational Crime Prevention: Successful Case Studies,* has outlined a range of prevention techniques that can easily be adapted to cybercrime. These techniques are arranged according to four aspects of offending as shown in Table 2 with some cybercrime prevention examples.

Implementing the Techniques

These techniques of prevention must be applied to the specific situations in which they occur. This means that the guardians of the targets, tools, and locations of cyberspace must be employed to implement them. These will range from private individuals who must install firewalls on their own computers to large corporations that are responsible for designing operating systems that contain security flaws. Between these two extremes are organizations such as Internet service providers, including corporate and university computing services, that must take

Table 2   Prevention techniques and examples

Increase the effort	Use firewalls, ban hacker Web sites
Increase the risks	Conduct background checks of employees with access to ID databases, require a traceable ID for online chat rooms
Reduce rewards	Specify no social security numbers on official documents, institute severe penalties for hacking
Reduce provocation and excuses	Maintain positive management–employee relations, do not boast of security features in software, display responsible use policy in colleges, libraries, chat rooms

steps to protect information that is valuable to hackers and others.

Most of the techniques to prevent cybercrime do not involve complex computing skills. This is because the majority of major cybercrimes on record were achieved not through the brilliance of a computer wizard, but through human weaknesses where guardians of valuable information became offenders themselves, or were either duped or coerced into giving up passwords or other access information to offenders. Training and education in security procedures of those who are the guardians of information is therefore crucial. Technological innovations that transfer security procedures from humans to computers are the ultimate but difficult solution to the problem of cybercrime (such as, for example, "smart credit cards"), but even here offenders have demonstrated their ability to adapt to and overcome new technologies.

Graeme R. Newman

See also Cyber and Internet Offenses; Cyberstalking; Exploitation by Scams; Exploitation by Scams, Interventions for; Identity Theft; Internet Fraud; Situational Crime Prevention

Further Readings

McNally, M., & Newman, G. R. (Eds.). (2008). *Perspectives on identity theft: Research and prevention.* New York: Criminal Justice; Cullompton, UK: Willan.

Newman, G. R., & Clarke, R. V. (2003). *Superhighway robbery: Crime prevention in the ecommerce environment.* Cullompton, UK: Willan.

Wall, D. S. (2007). *Cybercrime: The transformation of crime in the information age.* Cambridge, UK: Polity.

CYBERSTALKING

Cyberstalking is a relatively new phenomenon. So new in fact that many in the general public do not know what it entails. Though researchers and law enforcement professionals have adopted a wide array of definitions, cyberstalking is most generally defined as any course of conduct that utilizes electronic communication devices to knowingly and willingly commit any of the following acts on two or more occasions, with no legitimate purpose:

contact or attempt to contact someone after being requested by that person to desist from contacting them;

persistently harass, torment, or terrorize someone;

steal or attempt to steal someone's identity or information about that person, harming that person;

make unwanted and unwarranted sexual advances toward someone; and/or

communicate violent intentions or threaten to cause physical injury to someone.

In this context, electronic communication devices include all devices that can electronically transmit text, images, or sound from one location to another through wires or via electromagnetic waves. This includes but is not limited to computers, cellular phones, and personal digital assistants (PDAs).

History of Cyberstalking

The birth and continued development of cyberstalking has closely coincided with advancements in technology. Many electronic devices, such as cellular phones, PDAs, and computers, have become staples in everyday life. Their speed, ease of use, and capabilities—in addition to their increasing affordability—have made them both widely popular and frequently used. Unfortunately, those same features, along with the relative anonymity of the Internet, have made many of these devices key tools for cyberstalkers. Though it is impossible to pinpoint the exact date cyberstalking became an actual phenomenon, both the Internet and mobile communication devices, such as cell phones, were adapted for widespread public use in the early 1990s. Conservatively, the birth of cyberstalking can be traced to that era.

Throughout the mid- and late 1990s, the number of cyberstalking incidents is believed to have increased dramatically, with cyberstalking developing into a large-scale problem by the turn of the 21st century. Research indicates that the numbers of reported and nonreported cyberstalking incidents have steadily increased since the beginning of the

21st century. Though cyberstalking has become an ever-increasing problem, there is still relatively little public knowledge regarding the extent or even the existence of cyberstalking. In fact, the bulk of the public's perception of cyberstalking actually stems from very specific subcategories of cybercrime that are often associated with cyberstalking, such as cyberbullying and identity theft. Further, there has been only a minimal amount of legislative and law enforcement progress in attempting to control cyberstalking.

Cyberstalking Versus Traditional Stalking

There has been a growing debate between members of the academic, law enforcement, and political communities as to the true nature of cyberstalking. On one side of the debate, cyberstalking is considered merely a component of the larger phenomenon of traditional stalking (also referred to as physical or offline stalking). According to this argument, the Internet, computers, and/or mobile communication devices are simply additional tools utilized by stalkers. On the other side of the debate, it is argued that cyberstalking is an independent phenomenon, which should be considered separate from traditional stalking. According to this argument, cyberstalking is a new and unique type of victimization that has been created and expanded with the development of the Internet, computers, and mobile communication devices.

The cyberstalking debate is further exacerbated by the limitations of stalking research. Very few research studies examine the occurrence of both traditional stalking and cyberstalking. Further, the methodology and measurement techniques utilized in many traditional stalking and cyberstalking research studies vary significantly, making it problematic to attempt to compare the findings of different studies. Many victimization researchers are of the opinion that the typical stalker may likely switch between traditional stalking and cyberstalking. What begins as traditional stalking may later involve the use of electronic communication devices, and what begins as cyberstalking may later evolve into traditional stalking. However, there has yet to be any substantial evidence to support this position.

No matter which side of the debate one takes, however, there are several clear differences between traditional stalking and cyberstalking. First, one of the key components of traditional stalking is close physical proximity between the offender and victim. Traditional stalking frequently involves voyeurism, pursuant behavior, and direct physical communication. Conversely, cyberstalking does not require close physical proximity. With the use of the Internet and/or electronic communication devices, cyberstalkers could be long distances away from their victims.

Similarly, the majority of traditional stalking incidents involve a short time frame, meaning that offenders are typically at locations at relatively the same time as the victim. Actions such as pursuant behavior or voyeurism necessarily require the offender and victim to be in the same place at the same time. With cyberstalking, however, actions do not require a short time frame. For example, a cyberstalker could send harassing emails that the victim may not receive for days or even weeks.

Finally, there is a distinct difference in the type of guardianship most often utilized in order to protect potential stalking victims. For traditional stalking victims, guardianship often comes in physical forms. Friends and family, home security systems, and even restraining orders are often utilized to protect victims from offenders. However, guardianship from cyberstalking often comes in cyber forms. Improved Internet security, stronger firewalls, and privacy settings for email and social network accounts are the most common forms of guardianship against cyberstalking.

Extent of Victimization

Though it is generally agreed upon that the number of cyberstalking incidents has continued to grow each year, this is largely based on comparisons of results from cyberstalking research studies and law enforcement estimates. In actuality, the true prevalence of cyberstalking is unknown. Though this is typically the case for every category of victimization, as a large number of victimization incidents go unreported, it is especially true for cyberstalking. None of the major U.S. crime-victimization databases directly include cyberstalking as a measured category. The Uniform Crime Reporting (UCR) Program and National Crime Victimization Survey (NCVS) do not include categories of cybercrime. The National Incident-Based

Reporting System (NIBRS) and National Computer Security Survey do include cybercrime categories; however, neither specifically measures cyberstalking. As a result, the best estimate of the number of incidents of cyberstalking comes from large-scale research studies. The number of cyberstalking research studies has increased considerably since the beginning of the 21st century; however, the rate of technological advancements has increased exponentially, making it difficult for research to remain up-to-date with the newest technological developments.

While the actual number of cyberstalking incidents is unknown, the characteristics of the typical cyberstalking incident are known. Much like traditional stalking, cyberstalking victims are typically female. Also, cyberstalking victims are often relatively young (under the age of 30) and unmarried or divorced. Cyberstalking perpetrators, however, are typically male. As with cyberstalking victims, perpetrators are often relatively young (under the age of 30) and unmarried or divorced. In the majority of reported cyberstalking incidents, the perpetrator is known to the victim. In many cases, the perpetrator is a former spouse or boyfriend. Finally, very few incidents of cyberstalking are reported to the police or other agencies. This is especially true if the victim knows the perpetrator.

Legislation and Law Enforcement

Cyberstalking has proven very difficult for law enforcement to combat. Often, many of the actions taken by cyberstalkers are not technically illegal. Looking up information about others, communicating with others through email, chat rooms, or instant messengers programs, and/or sending or copying pictures are routine activities performed on the Internet. It is only when these normal activities pose a legitimate threat that legal measures can be taken. As previously stated, unlike traditional stalking, which most often involves the offender and victim being in the same spatial vicinity, a cyberstalker can be in a completely different city, state, or country than the victim. The potentially problematic effect of offender and victim being in different locations not only makes it difficult to determine what agency has jurisdiction, but also compounds the process of performing typical investigative techniques.

In the United States, stalking statutes became part of state and federal legislation in the early 1990s. However, neither state nor federal stalking laws originally included acts falling into the category of cyberstalking. The first state law recognizing cyberstalking went into effect in California in 1999. Several other states soon followed suit. As of 2008, 47 states had some form of cyberstalking legislation. The majority of states simply amended their previous stalking and/or harassment statutes to include acts involving the Internet and electronic communication devices, while a few created completely new cyberstalking statutes. Three states—Idaho, Nebraska, and Utah—and the District of Columbia have no cyberstalking legislation.

Cyberstalking was first recognized as a wide-scale issue by the federal government in 1999. In February of 1999, Vice President Al Gore assigned Attorney General Janet Reno the task of investigating the nature of cyberstalking—including the extent of occurrence, victim groups, and law enforcement techniques. At that time, several laws already in place could be applied to certain aspects of cyberstalking, such as 18 U.S.C. 875(c), which prohibits interstate threatening communication, and 47 U.S.C. 223, which prohibits the use of telecommunication devices to annoy, abuse, harass, or threaten someone without identifying oneself.

The Violence Against Women Act of 1994 was amended in 2000, and reauthorized in 2005, to include previsions prohibiting and providing increased protection against electronic stalking. However, these laws require very specific actions to occur before they can go into effect. To date, there are no federal laws that are specifically aimed at cyberstalking. In 2000, Senator Spencer Abraham (R-MI) proposed the Federal CyberStalking Bill (S2991), also referred to as the Just Punishment for Cyberstalkers Act of 2000, which would amend U.S.C. 18 to extend antistalking legislation to include cyberstalking. In 2000, Senator Spencer Abraham (R-MI) proposed the Federal Cyberstalking Bill (S2991), also referred to as the Just Punishment for Cyberstalkers Act of 2000, which would have amended U.S.C. 18 to extend antistalking legislation to include cyberstalking. The bill was placed on hold in 2000, however, because Senator Abraham was appointed Secretary of Energy by President George W. Bush. He is no longer in office and no other legislator adopted the position of arguing for the bill. As a result, the bill never passed.

Cyberstalking: An Example

Soon after California passed the first state law recognizing cyberstalking, the first case was successfully prosecuted. In 1999, a 50-year-old security guard pleaded guilty to attempting to use the Internet to solicit the rape of a 28-year-old woman. After being repeatedly rejected by the young woman in a chat room, the security guard assumed her identity and placed personal ads stating she fantasized about being raped. The ads also provided her name, physical description, and contact information. He even gave information about how to bypass the woman's home security alarm. Eventually, six men came to the woman's home, offering to rape her. After extensive investigation, law enforcement agents were able to trace the ads back to the security guard. He was sentenced to 6 years in California state prison.

Future Developments

With advances in technology and electronic communication, in addition to the slow progress of legislation and the problematic nature of effectively policing incidents of cyberstalking, it is unlikely that the rate of cyberstalking victimization will significantly decrease in the near future. In fact, as a result of many new developments, such as online social networking and photograph-/video-sharing sites, the rates of cyberstalking victimization will most likely show continued growth. Worldwide, millions of new online social network accounts have been created every year since 2000. Many of these account profiles include personal information—such as demographic, contact, and employment information, as well as addresses, daily schedules, and photographs. Much of this information is available to anyone who creates an account. Further, there has been a dramatic increase in the number and size of photograph- and video-sharing Web sites that allow individuals to post images and/or streaming video of their daily lives, viewable by anyone who logs on. Though extremely popular with users, these and other new developments in online communication directly increase the likelihood of exposure of potential targets to potential offenders. It will take time to see if research and law enforcement can keep up with technology.

Billy Henson

See also Cyber and Internet Offenses; Cybercrime, Prevention of; National Victimization Against College Women Surveys; Stalkers, Types of; Stalking; Stalking, Measurement of; Stalking Laws; Violence Against Women Act of 1994 and Subsequent Revisions

Further Readings

Bocij, P. (2004). *Cyberstalking: Harassment in the Internet age and how to protect your family.* Westport, CT: Praeger.

D'Ovidio, R., & Doyle, J. (2003). A study on cyberstalking: Understanding investigative hurdles. *FBI Law Enforcement Bulletin, 72*(3), 10.

Ogilvie, E. (2000). *Cyberstalking* (Trends and issues in crime and criminal justice series, no. 166). Canberra: Australian Institute of Criminology.

Reno, J. (1999). *1999 report on cyberstalking: A new challenge for law enforcement and industry.* Retrieved June 1, 2007, from http://www.justice.gov/criminal/cybercrime/cyberstalking.htm

Web Sites

National Center for Victims of Crime (NCVC): http://www.ncvc.org

Working to Halt Online Abuse (WHOA): http://www.haltabuse.org

CYCLE OF VIOLENCE, THEORY OF

Intimate partner violence has become a national and global public health and welfare problem. Much research has been conducted on the myriad issues related to intimate partner violence, including but not limited to the incidence and prevalence of violence and victimization, theories of battering behavior by the abuser, and theories explaining the behavior of the victim, which attempt to answer the long-standing question: Why doesn't she (or he) leave? This entry attempts to provide an answer to that question with a thorough discussion of the cycle of violence theory, which was originally developed by Lenore Walker in 1979. In addition, the entry provides critiques of the theory, information about the implications of the cycle of violence theory, including battered woman syndrome and learned helplessness, the historical context of theory in the battered women's movement and the legal and social changes resulting from the movement, and prevention and intervention efforts that address the victim's behaviors in this cycle of abuse.

The Cycle of Violence: A Theory of Battering

The question of why women (or men) would stay in abusive relationships has been posed by researchers, professionals who work with victims, and the public. To stay with an abusive partner seems illogical at best, but some explanations for this behavior have been offered over the years. Psychological theories, for example, suggest that a number of factors may be responsible for victims' behavior: self-blame, denial, loyalty to the institution and sanctity of marriage, feeling responsible to the batterer and/or children. One of the first theories developed to explain this seemingly illogical response to a terrifying situation is the cycle of theory of violence, which was the theoretical brainchild of Lenore Walker. In 1979, Walker interviewed 1,500 battered women and found that each of them described a similar pattern of spousal abuse. In her research, Walker identified this pattern as the "cycle of violence," which contains three distinct phases. It begins with a period of positive or close relations in which tension builds over a period of time (the "tension-building" phase). This time frame will vary from couple to couple; it could be 6 weeks, 6 months, or 1 year or longer. During this phase, the abuser may behave in a charming, caring, gentle, and affectionate way with the victim. The abuser may even present her or him with gifts, go out of the way to do nice things, and make the victim feel accepted and loved. Over time though, according to Walker, tension develops. Tension can be generated by anything from a tough day at work, a personal crisis, to anything in between.

According to Walker, periods of stress and tension within the relationship occur prior to an act, or acts, of violence. Over time, with increasing jealousy, paranoia, and shorter tempers among abusers, victims dance around their abusers, placating them and protecting them. For example, victims sometimes claim that the reasons for the appearance of physical injuries have nothing to do with abuse. Unfortunately, and typically, abusers' anger cannot be rationally calmed or quelled, leaving victims with few options for avoiding upsetting the batterer.

The battering incident occurs in the second stage of the cycle. This phase is sometimes called the "acting out phase" or "acute battering phase," which may or may not include physical contact; it may involve verbal, emotional, and/or psychological abuse. In this stage of the cycle, the abuser tries to gain power and control. When physical injuries do occur, they usually happen in this second phase. This phase typically ends when the batterer stops and the physiological tension between the two people markedly declines. Walker maintains that this decrease in tension is, in itself, reinforcing. In other words, violence wins because it works and the abuser gets what he wants in the relationship.

The third and final stage of this triangular cycle is the "honeymoon phase," when the batterer tries to reunite with his partner. The batterer may feel guilt but will minimize the event by claiming that it was the victim's fault that she was hit. Typically, both partners deny the severity of the abuse, often pretending as if nothing happened, and the cycle continues. The members of the couple convince each other that each abusive episode is an isolated event, claiming that the incidents are unrelated to each other, which ultimately provides the positive reinforcement necessary for the victim to remain in the relationship. Walker's results showed that the behavior exhibited by the abuser in this phase reinforces the relationship because it often has no tension or violence, yet offers no loving behavior on the part of the abuser. Sadly, the violence becomes more serious as time moves on, and eventually the possibility of a third stage that involves apology and denial no longer exists.

Walker's theory asserts that eventually, over a period of time that can range from a day to 6 months to a year or more, the acting out phase will circle around again into the honeymoon phase. Despite the fact that batterers can be very charming at times, victims often feel manipulated and chained to an emotional roller coaster from which there is no escape. Walker argues that each phase becomes shorter and shorter in duration and distance from the previous incident and phase, until the victim either escapes or is killed.

Critiques

Since its inception, Walker's theory has endured criticism. Some researchers have argued that her sample size was too small and not representative enough to provide an accurate picture of violent relationships in the United States. Based on their own research, others have questioned the high level of predictability of violence in relationships that Walker claims in her study, as studies have shown vast differences in abuser behavior, motivation, level of manipulation, and method of abuse. For example, some abusers employ verbal and emotional tactics of abuse, while others resort mostly to physical harm. Additional critiques demonstrate that not all abusers cycle through all of the phases of abuse that Walker outlines in her research. Instead, some abusers vacillate between extreme violence and peace. Nonetheless, despite the fact that Walker's cycle of violence may not accurately predict or portray every instance of intimate partner violence, it remains an important volume of research.

Most of the battered women in Walker's sample did not perceive their abusers as being in control of their lives, despite the fact that their reality suggested otherwise. Walker concluded that one of the reasons that these victims, who were all women, did not terminate their marriages and leave the relationships is due to the fact that that they did not realize that their batterers were in control of every facet of their lives.

In the years following Walker's contribution of the cycle of violence theory to intimate partner violence literature, additional related theories of battering, including learned helplessness and battered woman syndrome, emerged to explain the dynamics in abusive relationships.

Learned Helplessness

Learned helplessness explains the victim's psychological frame of mind over the course over the course of the abusive relationship. Though often described as a condition, it may be better described

as an effect of the cycle of violence on a battered woman. This theory was originally based on psychologist Martin Seligman's research on dogs. Seligman placed dogs in cages and administered random shocks to them. As in most intimate partner violence situations, the shocks were not administered in response to, or based on, the dogs' behavior. The dogs tried to escape but couldn't, so they stopped fighting and became helpless; they could no longer help themselves. It wasn't until the researchers intervened—and dragged the dogs to their rescue—that they escaped. Learned helplessness kicked in when they perceived their efforts to be pointless. That is why the battered woman's perception of her own situation is important in terms of her ability to escape—if she believes she cannot leave or cannot survive on her own, she will not leave.

Since the late 1990s, there has been some debate among researchers as to whether victims of intimate partner violence are actually helpless, since some battered women do make calls to friends and family for help, contact the police, and/or file a restraining order. However, numerous researchers have concluded that these women's feelings of helplessness may be better described as a reflection of their reality than as a response that has been learned. Given the cyclical nature of the violence, however, the helpless behavior indicates a pattern that gives the appearance of being learned. This learned helplessness, or feeling of helplessness, emerges during the course of the cycle of violence that has been ongoing over a period of time (at least 6 months or more). Early in the abuse cycle, perhaps in the honeymoon phase, battered women may feel that they can fix the relationship. However, over a longer period of time, the cycle of violence wears these battered women down mentally to the point where they perceive they can no longer help themselves or even conceive of thoughts of escape. In other words, when these women see the futility of their efforts to repair the relationship, escape, or survive, learned helplessness, or rather, a feeling of helplessness, emerges.

Battered Woman Syndrome

Battered woman syndrome is a psychological condition that develops over a long period of time, as a result of the cycle of violence, and it is related to the cycle of violence theory and learned helplessness. Walker theorized that some women remain in physically, emotionally, and sexually abusive relationships due to extreme fear and the belief that there is no escape and that they have no choice but to stay in the abusive relationship. This is the effect of learned helplessness. Battered woman syndrome is a condition that, like learned helplessness or the feeling of helplessness, is formed over the course of many cycles of abuse, over a long period of time. In addition, with battered woman syndrome and the cycle of violence, the severity of the abuse also increases over time. However, both partners usually deny the increase in severity and have convinced themselves that each instance of violence is a distinct, unique event. Ultimately, the connection between battered woman syndrome and the cycle of violence that shapes the condition is that, with every passing cycle, the psyche of the battered woman is worn down to the point where she loses hope and cannot deal effectively with her situation.

Historical Perspectives on Battering and Intimate Partner Violence

Intimate partner violence and battering can only be fully appreciated and understood within a sociopolitical and sociohistorical context that examines women's status in the social and economic hierarchy and slow acquisition of rights over time. In the United States, there was historically an acceptance of abuse against women. In fact, women were regarded as property until the latter half of the 19th century. Until then, the "rule of thumb" and "stick rule" were applied to domestic relations; these rules specified that a husband could discipline his wife in any manner he saw fit as long as the implement involved was no thicker than the width of his thumb or a particular stick.

The turn of 20th century marked the establishment of family and domestic relations courts across the country. They were created to deal with incidents of family violence. Although they seemed to be a positive development at the time, they actually encouraged female subservience and economic dependence, thus rendering family and domestic violence a private, not criminal, problem to be dealt with in the private sphere. In the late 1960s, activists began to politicize the plight of the battered woman. At that time, the police usually would not assist victims of domestic violence, despite the fact that such violence was against the law. Like many others within and outside the criminal justice system, the police viewed domestic violence as a private matter, or if it was to be dealt with publicly, as a social services concern.

It was not until the feminist movement of the 1960s and 1970s that battered women were recognized by the legal system. Following research done by Walker and others in the 1970s, testimony about battered woman syndrome was introduced in criminal trials. Prior to the 1970s, the battering and murder of women took place in a social context that considered wives to be property of their husbands. In fact, the topic of "marital rape" had never been considered and, therefore, was not considered a crime. One reason that domestic violence/intimate partner violence, marital rape, and incest have been handled so poorly socially and legally is due to the walls that have been erected around the place where these things typically occur—the home. Our society has placed a high premium on privacy rights, and, as a society, we are very reluctant to change. Why? Society does not want the government interfering with its private business; laissez-faire ideology has prevailed for a long time in U.S. social and legal history.

In order to truly understand the context in which the cycle of intimate partner violence occurs, it is important to examine U.S. political ideology and predisposition toward the separation of the public and private spheres. In general, as a society, the United States has been very reluctant to interfere with private behavior that occurs behind the walls of citizens' homes. Many legal decisions on child abuse and domestic violence cases rest on the notion that justice dictates that human rights considerations not be forsaken for the right of privacy. In other words, a home may be a castle for a "man," but it may be a torture chamber for victims. Battered women have had very few resources when violence occurs. Women have been driven to kill, and some been sentenced to life in prison for it.

Legal and Social Changes Resulting From the Battered Women's Movement

Between 1975 and 1980, 44 U.S. states passed some kind of domestic violence legislation. Presently, all 50 states and Washington, D.C., have domestic violence laws on their books. This legislation focuses on the prevention of and protection from partner abuse and assistance for victims and prosecution of abusive partners. The criminal justice system also responded with changes with respect to arrest policies. Following the infamous 1982 Minneapolis Experiment, researchers and law enforcement personnel contended that the mandatory arrest of batterers in a domestic violence situation results in lower recidivism rates than other types of responses, such as mandated counseling or sending the batterer away for a night. Essentially, mandatory policies direct the police to a specific action ("shall arrest") and limit police discretion, while pro-arrest policies might say that arrest shall be the "preferred" or "presumptive" response in a case of domestic violence.

Ultimately, this legislation provides protection orders for victims, establishes shelters and services for victims, and encourages the police and courts to adhere to the criminal code by asserting that violence between people involved in intimate relationships is still violence and should be treated as such under the law. *Thurman v. City of Torrington* (1984) forever changed the landscape of domestic violence legislation. In that case, the judge held the city's police department civilly liable for the abuse sustained by the victim, Tracy Thurman. Thurman had been repeatedly abused by her husband, and though she called the police for help numerous times, they did not do much of anything to offer her assistance. In the wake of this case, police departments throughout the country began implementing pro-arrest policies and increasing training on domestic violence. Since the mid-1980s, states have passed laws expanding the police's arrest powers in cases of domestic assault, although many police departments utilize alternatives to arrest, including mediation.

In the 1990s, Congress passed the Violence Against Women Act; this law was reauthorized in 2000. This law mandates that that various professions form partnerships and work together to respond to all forms of violence against women. The U.S. Attorney General is required to make a report to Congress annually on the grants that are awarded under the act and ensure that research examining violence against women is encouraged. In addition, the act provides funding for a variety of research-based studies, and it also requires that federal agencies, such as the National Institute of Justice, engage in research regarding violence against women.

The battered women's movement ultimately brought to light many acts and situations that were ignored by the law. First, the movement identified the dilemma of the victims who remained bonded to their intimate partners who beat them. The research on the cycle of violence, learned helplessness, and battered woman syndrome helped to define and give credence to the predicaments in which battered women found themselves. Second, the movement defined and recognized the types of violence and the heightened probability of repeated abuse that is reflected in the cycles of violence particular to partner abuse. Third, the movement challenged the law's reluctance to treat this violence with the same concern that other violence received under the criminal law, and this reluctance has been partially overcome through legislative action. For example, in 1976, civil protection orders marked the commencement of modern domestic violence law in which victims could seek protection by the court on an emergency basis. The protection order typically prohibits further abuse and contact with the victims, including telephone contact.

Other grassroots efforts were aimed at developing shelters and providing services for domestic violence victims. In the 1980s, programs were developed and services offered that also recognized that wife beating is a crime. Shelters create a "safety net" for women escaping abusive domestic situations, and shelters and/or battery hotlines are the first sources to which most victims turn for assistance. Finally, the battered women's movement, along with the feminist movement, focused its efforts on educating the public about domestic violence and changing society's perceptions about victims of battering.

Finding a Way Out: Prevention and Intervention Efforts

As Walker's cycle of violence theory illustrates, intimate partner violence is a problem that will continue to exist unless it is recognized and additional efforts are made to eradicate it. In her most important work, *The Battered Woman,* Walker described her theory of battering and prescribed various options for helping victims out of violent situations. She provided two intervention prescriptions: primary and secondary intervention. Primary intervention involves mostly public education in which consultation with agencies, institutions, and other support groups is done to ensure that services are in place and efforts are being made to assist victims of intimate partner violence. Walker specifically identified four things that should be done: eliminate sex-role stereotypes during childhood, reduce violence in our society, reduce harshness in child discipline, and understand the victimization process of battered women and other victims. In terms of secondary intervention, Walker noted that shelters, or safe houses, need to provide immediate, temporary housing to victims. In addition, mental health services could also assist victims in dealing with the effects of battering, which can include posttraumatic stress disorder, self-esteem problems, depression, and other emotional and physical problems. At the moment, it is critical to address the immediate effects of battering on individuals, but on a larger scale, what is necessary is a societal and cultural transformation that recognizes that battering, in any form, is not acceptable. Only then will the cycle of violence be broken.

Sue Cote Escobar

See also Battered Woman Syndrome; Intimate Partner Violence

Further Readings

Barnett, O., Miller-Perrin, C. L., & Perrin, R. D. (Eds.). (2005). *Family violence across the lifespan: An introduction* (2nd ed.). Thousand Oaks, CA: Sage.

Buzawa, E. S., & Buzawa, C. G. (1996). *Domestic violence: The criminal justice response* (2nd ed.). Thousand Oaks, CA: Sage.

Dutton, D. G. (1988). *The domestic assault of women: Psychological and criminal justice perspectives.* Boston: Allyn & Bacon.

Roberts, A. R. (Ed.). (2002). *Handbook of domestic violence intervention strategies: Policies, programs, and legal remedies.* Oxford, UK: Oxford University Press.

Walker, L. E. (1979). *The battered woman.* New York: Harper & Row.

Walker, L. E. (1989). *Terrifying love: Why battered women kill and how society responds.* New York: HarperCollins.

D

DATING VIOLENCE

Victims of intimate partner violence can be found within all cultures, ethnicities, and socioeconomic backgrounds. The term *intimate partner violence* often draws forth an image of a husband battering his wife. However, violence in relationships is not exclusive to married couples. The term *dating violence* is used when discussing violence that occurs among dating couples, and most often refers to young adults' and adolescents' experiences with intimate partner violence. This entry gives the definition of dating violence and examines theories regarding its causes. It then describes the prevalence, potential risk factors, and consequences of dating violence. The entry concludes with a discussion of prevention and intervention methods.

Definition

As with intimate partner violence, dating violence is comprised of several components: (1) physical acts of aggression or force, which range from minor acts of violence such as pushing and shoving to severe acts of violence such as punching, kicking, choking, or the use of a weapon; (2) sexual violence, which includes forceful sexual acts ranging from the use of physical force to verbal coercion; (3) emotional abuse, which includes calling a partner degrading names to eliciting feelings of worthlessness, isolation, and disempowerment; and (4) coercion and isolation, which include controlling the partner's mobility, finances, and social networks. All of these components contribute to dating violence and can be examined independently or in conjunction with one another. However, dating violence research has focused primarily on physical violence.

The perpetration of dating violence is not exclusive to males or females and both can be victims of dating violence. Furthermore, dating violence can been found within heterosexual relationships and same-sex relationships. Although differences can be found among the type of violence used, rates of violence, and motivation with regard to gender, race/ethnicity, sexual orientation, and culture, no one group is immune to the victimization or perpetration of dating violence.

Theories

Many theories of the etiology of dating violence have been proposed, of which the most commonly discussed are social learning theory, attachment theory, feminist theory, gender symmetry, and coercive control. These are presented below.

Social Learning Theory

The social learning theory of dating violence is derived from Albert Bandura's theory of social learning, which states that individual patterns of behavior are developed by observing the behavior of others. Children model their behaviors predominately after their primary caregiver and important figures in their lives. When applied to dating violence, social learning theory hypothesizes that individuals who commit acts of violence against their intimate partner learned this behavior by observing a primary caregiver in a violent relationship. Regardless of whether their primary caregiver was the perpetrator of violence or the victim of the violence, the child internalizes this behavior as a way of interacting with an intimate partner.

In 1989, David Riggs and K. Daniel O'Leary developed a model based upon social learning theory of dating violence, which postulates that both contextual and situational factors contribute to dating violence. Their model stresses the importance of both having observed partner violence at an early age and physical victimization by a parent or caregiver. If the child accepts violence as an appropriate reaction to conflict, he or she may act out violently to solve conflicts in a variety of contexts, including intimate relationships. Situational factors that include alcohol and/or drug use, problem-solving skills, the partner's level of aggression, and the length of the relationship are further postulated to increase risk of violence within a relationship.

Attachment Theory

Similar to social learning theory, attachment theory emphasizes the importance of early childhood relationships with caregivers. Developed by John Bowlby in 1969, attachment theory differs from social learning theory in that it is not the observation of the caregivers' intimate relationship that develops inappropriate perceptions of conflict resolution, but rather the actual relationship between the caregiver and child that forms a child's image of intimate relationships. Therefore, if a child and caregiver have a relationship that includes violence, the child will later reenact this dynamic with an intimate partner in a dating relationship.

While many dating violence researchers assume a social learning or attachment theory perspective, few have directly tested models based on theory. Moreover, both social learning and attachment theory are criticized for not taking into account power disparities between partners and people's ability to modulate their own behaviors separate from their history of abuse.

Feminist Theory

Feminist theories of dating violence argue that men hold greater power than do women in most areas of life, that this patriarchal power is socially sanctioned, and that relationship violence is used to ensure male–female domination. Crime statistics, which indicate higher levels of male-to-female dating violence than female-to-male dating violence support traditional feminist theories. However data from community and college populations challenge this theory: These data find that young men and women are equally likely to use relational violence. The debates on whether men use violence to control women unidirectionally or whether both men and women use violence to exert mutual control has stimulated two different schools of thought, the gender symmetry school and the coercive control school, which uses fundamental principles of feminist theory.

Gender Symmetry

Proponents of gender symmetry theory question the assumption that men are socially privileged over women and instead argue that individual differences in power sharing exist that are not rooted in culturally sanctioned gender difference. Gender symmetrists argue that the perpetration of dating violence is equally likely to be initiated by men and women for the same reasons and that both parties should be held accountable. Most gender symmetrists agree that although both male and female partners may commit violence, males tend to cause greater injury. The strongest support for gender symmetry comes from young dating couples where data suggest that men and women use equal, albeit mild levels of violence. The strongest critique of gender symmetry comes from cases where there is extreme violence and or battering, sexual abuse and femicide research. In all of these more severe instances, most women do not use reciprocal violence. When they do retaliate in self-defense rather than initiate, they rarely acquire power through violence and are either severely injured or killed by male partners. Taken together, this body of research suggests that men continue to dominate over women and that relational violence is a form of control. In response, gender symmetry proponents argue that battered women populations and other victim populations represent the extreme end of violence and are not representative of dating violence.

Coercive Control

This theory argues that the definition of relational violence has a misplaced focus on physical acts of violence and should instead measure who has greater coercive power in the relationship. Proponents further argue that men typically have greater coercive power because of traditional gender roles and societal validation of such roles. Further, while physical and sexual abuse are correlated with coercive control, abuse can happen in the absence of coercion and successful coercion may preclude the need to use violence to control. Because this theory has only recently received attention, research in this area is new. Existing data support the notion of coercive control in older cohabiting couples, but the presence of coercive control has not yet been tested in younger dating couples.

Prevalence

Estimates of the occurrence of dating violence differ substantially across studies and range from 12% to 87%. When assessing the prevalence of intimate partner violence as a whole, numerous studies have found women use physical violence at similar rates as men and in some studies even higher rates. However, data drawn from crime statistics indicate that males are almost the sole perpetrators of partner violence. Research focused on the prevalence of dating violence finds rates among college students to be as high as 20% to 50%. In 2005, the Bureau of Justice Statistics reported that 43 per 1,000 females between the ages of 18 and 24 who are enrolled in college fall victim to violent crime annually.

Most research has focused on heterosexual dating college samples, and a lesser number focusing on the prevalence of dating violence in community samples of same-sex relationships. Their findings indicate that those in same-sex relationships experience dating violence at similar or even higher rates. These findings have increased awareness for the need to expand inquiry on the nature, type, and dynamic of violence within same-sex dating relationships.

Risk Factors

Risk factors for dating violence can be conceptualized as family-level risks, individual-level risks, community-level risks, and larger, societal-level risks. At the family level, the most commonly noted risk factor is prior exposure to either witnessing partner violence between caretakers or experiencing child abuse. At the individual level, both past history of dating violence and an individual's personality or propensity toward the use of aggression is a risk factor for dating violence. At the community level, residents in neighborhoods with higher levels of crime and poverty experience higher levels of dating violence. Finally, at a societal level, risk factors include patriarchal values, inequities of power among gender, and normative beliefs surrounding violence. Few studies examine the intersectionalities across the levels, which closely correlate to researchers disciplinary loyalties, and debates remain about the degree to which each of these factors impact dating violence.

Consequences

As with partner violence, dating violence can result in severe physical and psychological injury. Victims of dating violence often report lowered self-esteem, disempowerment, and feelings of isolation. All of these factors may result in more severe forms of depression. The cycle of ill effects may be intensified because dating violence may impede a person in taking steps to end the violence or leave the abuser and may isolate that person from outside support systems due to feelings of shame.

Prevention and Intervention

Most prevention programs focus on educating young couples to communicate effectively without violence, as well as in effective conflict resolution and relationship equality. Other programs seek to teach appropriate perceptions of dating violence. Interventions with individuals currently experiencing dating violence typically involve individual and/or couples counseling. To date, it is not clear which strategies will lead to higher prevention. Efforts to intervene once violence has occurred can take many forms and depends on the therapist's training. As such, strategies may address the power imbalance in the relationship, as well as focusing on anger control for the perpetrator and trauma healing and supportive resources for the victim.

Dating violence remains a widespread problem, affecting numerous young adults and adolescents. Through continued research and increased awareness, dating violence may be understood in greater depth and lead toward the prevention of this epidemic.

Abbie Tuller and Chitra Raghavan

See also Battered Woman Syndrome; Conflict Tactics Scale (CTS/CTS2); Domestic Violence; Femicide; Intimate Partner Violence; Male Victims of Partner Violence; National Victimization Against College Women Surveys

Further Readings

Archer, J. (2000). Sex differences in aggression between heterosexual partners: A meta-analytic review. *Psychological Bulletin, 126,* 651–680.

Dutton, M., & Goodman, L. (2005). Coercion in intimate partner violence: Toward a new conceptualization. *Sex Roles, 52,* 743–756.

Ismail, F., Berman, H., & Ward-Griffin, C. (2007). Dating violence and the health of young women: A feminist narrative study. *Health Care for Women International, 28,* 453–477.

Johnson, M. (2006). Conflict and control: Gender symmetry and asymmetry in domestic violence. *Violence Against Women, 12,* 1003–1018.

Luthra, R., & Gidycz, C. (2006). Dating violence among college men and women: Evaluation of a theoretical model. *Journal of Interpersonal Violence, 21,* 717–731.

O'Leary, K. D., Woodin, E., & Fritz, P. (2006). Can we prevent hitting? Recommendations for preventing intimate partner violence between young adults. *Journal of Aggression, Maltreatment & Trauma, 13,* 121–178.

Straus, M. (2008). Dominance and symmetry in partner violence by male and female university students in 32 nations. *Children and Youth Services Review, 30,* 252–275.

Turrell, S. (2000). A descriptive analysis of same-sex relationship violence for a diverse sample. *Journal of Family Violence, 15,* 281–293.

DEATH NOTIFICATION

The death notification task is one of the most difficult and dreaded within criminal justice. The death notification is the process undertaken to share with a surviving family member or members that a loved one has died. Whether the death was expected or unexpected, the task is a difficult one and carries with it a host of emotions for both the receiver of the information and the notifier.

Typically, death notifications are carried out by coroners, medical examiner office staff, or police officers. Few of these individuals receive adequate training concerning the best and most effective approaches to carrying out a death notification. Rather, death notification techniques tend to be developed through practice. While trial and error can be an effective means of developing best practices, in this case it may lead to deleterious consequences for notifiers without the benefit of sufficient training as well as for survivors.

While effective training can produce a more competent and confident notifier capable of addressing the myriad survivor needs, no level of training can truly prepare a criminal justice professional for the unpleasant task of death notification. However, the following discussion is intended to inform the reader of some practices that might ease the difficulties found within this role. It is not intended as a substitution for professional training within this area.

Death Notification Literature

It has only been in the past 30 years that most death notification literature has been published, and the literature on this topic has tended to focus on three areas. First, there have been practical pieces provided in law enforcement trade journals, and training keys published by the International Association of Chiefs of Police (IACP) are available. Second, there are publications dealing with a variety of criminal justice personnel who deliver "bad news," including Deputy U.S. Marshals who serve arrest warrants. Third, scholarly articles and book chapters addressing the psychological nature of crises and effective notification techniques based on a clear understanding of crisis theory are also available. Some training videos have also been made on this topic, one of which is by Mothers Against Drunk Driving (MADD).

Preparation for Death Notification

Most of the literature on death notification directs the reader to the importance of understanding the nature of personal crises. Since the death of a loved one is one of the most traumatic experiences that might befall a person, professionals' grasp of crisis responses to a death notification is essential. While death notifications can follow either expected deaths (e.g., attended deaths in hospitals and other health care facilities) or unexpected deaths (e.g., accidents, suicides, homicides, and natural causes), death notifications by criminal justice professionals tend to be conducted after deaths from accidents and natural deaths that are not expected. This adds to the difficulty of death notifications, as the notifier is bringing crisis-producing news to the receiver of the information.

It is advisable for a professional to do the notification in person. If this is not possible due to the involvement of different jurisdictions, it is usually possible for a professional to find a trustworthy and experienced person in another jurisdiction who is willing to give a notification. This is sometimes necessary when a person dies far from where the surviving family members are located. In this case as in other cases, it is essential for the notifier or investigator to have all the necessary information about the incident and the circumstances surrounding the death.

Once all information about the case is assembled, the notifier should take time to prepare to deliver the notification. There are two key reasons that time and attention should be given to preparation. First, while the notification may be one of many a professional has delivered or will deliver, individual notifications have a lasting impression on the receivers of the news. A second reason is less obvious. The death notification may perhaps be the only crisis situation criminal justice practitioners encounter that involves bringing the crisis-producing news. In most if not all other crisis situations, the practitioner is responding to a crisis already in process. For these reasons, the death notification provides the notifier with a unique opportunity to fully prepare and to try to anticipate possible responses.

Delivering the News

While a number of authors and trainers have provided specific steps or phases to the death notification, most experts agree that it is best to provide the news of a death in "doses." In a dosing procedure,

the notifier provides information in smaller pieces in an effort to allow the receiver of the information time to incorporate its reality. The first steps of a notification must always be to identify oneself, gain entry to the location where the notification will take place, request that the receiver to be seated, and confirm that the correct party is being notified. Concerning confirmation, a simple statement such as "Are you Mr. Smith, the father of Virginia Smith who lives at [address]" can be sufficient to determine that the correct party is being addressed. Once this is established, the notification can proceed.

While there is little one can do to ease the shock of the receiving the information that a loved one has died, giving the information in doses can assist the receiver. One can begin with a statement such as, "Your daughter was involved in an accident this evening," "Your husband was involved in an accident at work," or "The police and EMTs were called to your brother's home." Once there is acknowledgment from the receiver that he or she has understood the statement, one can proceed by giving the receiver slightly more information, until it is appropriate to share the news of the death. Ideally, the notifier wishes for the receiver to be ready to receive this message. If the receiver asks if the person has died, this can then be confirmed. The purpose of this dosing procedure is to allow the receiver an opportunity to incorporate the news of tragedy and to adjust to the information provided. The sample dialogue below illustrates the process that follows the initiation of the conversation:

Notifier: I have some bad news for you.

Receiver: Yes, what is it?

Notifier: Your son John was involved in a traffic accident.

Receiver: What happened?!

Notifier: John was driving down Highway 2 and his car went off the road and hit a tree.

Receiver: Is he okay?

Notifier: No, he is not. He suffered very serious injuries.

Receiver: How serious?

Notifier: I am sorry to inform you that John died of his injuries.

As can be seen from this sample dialogue, several techniques are incorporated into the notification process. First, the notifier sets the stage at the very beginning with the phrase "bad news." This sets the tone for the conversation, making it clear that the visit deals with a serious matter. Second, the notifier uses the name of the deceased several times. This is important because it maintains the focus on the fate of the deceased. Third, the information is provided to the receiver in doses that allow the individual time to digest each conversational exchange.

Bryan D. Byers and James E. Hendricks

See also Bereavement Process; Victim Support Groups

Further Readings

Byers, B. D. (2006). Death notification: The theory and practice and delivering bad news. In J. E. Hendricks & B. D. Byers (Eds.), *Crisis intervention in criminal justice/social service* (4th ed., pp. 341–373). Springfield, IL: Charles C Thomas.

Hendricks, J. E. (1984). Death notification: The theory and practice of informing survivors. *Journal of Police Science and Administration, 12,* 109–116.

Hendricks, J. E., & Byers, B. D. (1992). "When the time comes . . ." *Police, 16*(9), 49–51.

Iserson, K. V. (1999). *Grave words: Notifying survivors about sudden, unexpected deaths.* Tucson, AZ: Galen.

Iserson, K. V. (1999). *Pocket protocols for notifying survivors about sudden, unexpected deaths.* Tucson, AZ: Galen.

Leash, R. M. (1994). *Death notification: A practical guide to the process.* Hinesberg, VT: Upper Access.

DEFENDANTS' RIGHTS VERSUS VICTIMS' RIGHTS

The ability of the criminal justice system to simultaneously deliver defendants' and victims' rights has been a concern throughout history. In the United States, defendants' rights are upheld by the Constitution; victims' rights have more recently been entered into the system through state statutes and constitutions as well as legislation of the federal government. A brief history of the development of victims' rights is provided in this entry, as well as a more in-depth examination of defendants' and victims' rights that includes arguments for and against formal inclusion of victims' rights in the criminal justice system, specifically the court process.

History

The United States built its penal institution on English common law traditions, including the belief that the criminal court process is one that puts the federal or state government's interests above the interests of the individual. Consequently, the criminal court is designed for the collective "we" of society, not the specific victim against whom the crime was committed. Historically, victims were not of great concern or importance unless they were needed to act as witnesses and provide testimony. Traditionally, victims' needs were not addressed through the criminal court process because the rights of victims were not as highly regarded as defendant rights. Subsequently, the civil court process was created to aid individuals in addressing personal wrongs perpetrated against them, including the ability to gain restitution from criminal perpetrators. Hence, the United States constructed its criminal proceedings not to honor victims but to shield society.

Due to the possibility of government and court officials misusing the power bestowed upon them during the criminal court process, checks had to be placed on officials' use of power to protect defendants who could easily become subject to abuse. This situation contributed to the development of the Bill of Rights to ensure that the federal government could not remove rights from citizens while they were engaged in the court process as defendants.

Although concerns existed about the importance of the victim's role in the criminal court process and about the victim's rights, these were not deemed important issues until the mid-1900s. The concern for victims' rights and rise of the victims' rights movement correspond with the civil rights movements in the 1980s and 1990s. The push for victims' rights also was in response to the 1982 Presidential Task Force on Crime, which asserted that victims were being mistreated by the criminal justice system and made recommendations for balancing the rights of defendants and victims.

Currently, all 50 states have adopted legislation either by statute or constitutional amendment that provides victims' rights during the criminal court process. In 2004 the federal government passed the Crime Victims' Rights Act, or what has been termed the Justice for All Act; however, the ability and intention of the state and federal courts to implement victims' rights has been questioned. It is therefore important to understand the controversy and arguments for and against victims' rights being placed in the criminal court process, as well as why opinions exist as to the inability of defendants' and victims' rights being simultaneously honored without the erosion of defendants' rights.

Defendants' Rights

Federal and state due process rights are afforded to defendants by the Fifth and Fourteenth Amendments, but they are also based on a lengthy history of English common law. These traditions support the separation of private and public matters between the civil and criminal courts in order to ensure that defendants and society are protected. Further, the criminal court process must honor several protections and rights of defendants as outlined in constitutional amendments. Specifically, defendants are granted the following due process rights during criminal investigations and court functions:

- Fourth Amendment—protection against all unreasonable searches and seizures,
- Sixth Amendment—right to a speedy trial and to be tried by an impartial judge and/or jury,
- Eighth Amendment—excessive bail shall not be imposed nor cruel and unusual punishment inflicted.

Further, these rights are ensured under due process clauses of the Fifth Amendment (federal) and Fourteenth Amendment (state). These rights guarantee that defendants are not taken advantage of or persecuted by the government, criminal justice system, or criminal court process.

The crux of the arguments against placing victims' rights in the criminal court process is that this will erode and diminish the courts' capacity for ensuring the above due process rights and protecting society as it fights for the collective "we." The specific concerns with respect to the erosion of defendants' rights are as follows:

- The Fourth Amendment can be eroded if emotional or contextual information is allowed into the court process. This passes undue information to the judge and/or jury that the defendant was not aware of at the time of the offense and is similar to letting unreasonable evidence into the legal process.
- The Sixth Amendment is of concern in that it affects the court's ability to provide a speedy trial. If victims must be notified of proceedings and have a right to be heard at crucial decision points of the process, the progress will be slowed and proceedings will take more time as more information will be provided. In addition, allowing the victims to present their emotions and concerns during trial and sentencing may unduly bias the jury and/or judge and impact the ability to remain impartial and concentrate and the legal facts of the case.
- The Eighth Amendment is of concern because if impartiality is compromised, bias may be added to the system, which ultimately alters the type and length of sentences received. Thus, if a judge or jury is swayed by the emotion of the victim, it may result in harsher and disparate sentences.

Victims' Rights

Historically, victims' rights were ignored, but recently they have been placed into the criminal court process as legitimate rights to be upheld at the federal and state level. States first provided victims' rights in the latter part of the 20th century. Wisconsin led the movement in 1979 by creating a statute offering victims' rights, and California passed the first state constitutional amendment in 1982. Currently, all 50 states offer victims' rights protections in criminal courts. Although states vary as what they protect, the following general rights are afforded to victims in all states: the right to compensation, the right to notification of court appearances, and the right to submission of a victim impact statement before sentencing.

This state response urged the federal government to place victims on their agenda and the Presidential Task Force of 1982 launched the federal concern over victims by declaring that victims were being subjugated by an uncaring and unsympathetic system and defined an agenda for restoring a balance between the rights of defendants and victims. It called for increased participation by victims throughout criminal justice processes and for restitution in all cases where victims suffered a financial loss. Federal legislation has since addressed victims' rights through the Victims' Rights and Restitution Act of 1990, the Violent Crime Control and Law Enforcement Act of 1994, and the Crime Victims' Rights Act of 2004.

The Victims' Rights and Restitution Act of 1990 gave crime victims in federal cases the right to notification of court proceedings and the right to attend them, the right to notice of changes in a defendant's detention status, the right to consult with prosecutors, and the right of protection against offender aggression. The omnibus Violent Crime Control and Law Enforcement Act of 1994 gave victims in federal cases the right to speak at sentencing hearings, made restitution mandatory in sexual assault cases, and expanded funding for local victim services. The Crime Victims' Rights Act of 2004 provides the most comprehensive protection to victims, including the right to be heard during critical states of the process, the right to attend court proceedings except if it may alter personal witness testimony, the right to be notified of all court dates within a reasonable time frame, and the right to be treated with fairness, dignity, and respect at all times.

Concerns and Controversies

Although the victims' rights now protected by state and federal criminal courts do not appear overly taxing, many concerns and controversies exist as to why criminal courts need to afford rights to victims. The overarching question is whether victims' rights and defendants' rights are compatible and if both can be protected without the erosion of defendant due process rights. This section addresses the arguments against and for providing victims' rights in the criminal court process.

Arguments Against Victims' Rights

In addition to the due process arguments addressed above, several other arguments have been made against victims' rights. Some argue in favor of purposively separating the victim from the process, in line with the historical roots of the court and common law traditions. They believe that victims' rights simply do not have a place in criminal court proceedings, and that as long as the facts of the case are presented and societal concerns are addressed, the victim has been served. Further, the argument has been made that since the purpose of the civil court is to address private wrongs, functions such as restitution should be a civil not a criminal matter. In addition, some argue that since the criminal court is already clogged with cases and defendants who must be protected, there is no time or resources for victim concerns. Finally, one last concern is the inability to properly define who is and is not a victim when taking into account all direct and indirect harm caused by the offense. This has the potential of making the list of potential victims limitless. To illustrate, if someone has been found guilty of murder, it is necessary to ask if the direct victim who was killed was the only victim. Indirect victims could include the victim's family, friends, employer, co-workers, and anyone attached to the individual in anyway. If these are all victims, do they all have rights to be heard and involved in the criminal court process, and if not, where should the line be drawn?

Arguments for Victims' Rights

The strongest argument for victims' rights rests with the belief that victims should be engaged in and allowed to participate in the criminal court process because they were the individuals who were wronged. To leave victims out of the process increases feelings of victimization and beliefs that the system is uncaring. Further, victims should not be forgotten, and allowed a chance to heal and have their voice heard by the judge and/or jury instead of making crime nothing more than the facts. It is argued that crime is a psychologically draining event that diminishes individuals' trust in society; however, when individuals are allowed to take part in the criminal trial process, they can gain closure for the traumatic event and gain satisfaction and confidence with the societal function and process of court. In addition, if the victim remains intertwined with the process, restorative functions and mediation can benefit not only the victim but also the defendant. Finally, victims will be more understanding of the criminal court process and have less questions and concerns about what happened and why.

Implementation

Although rights have been afforded to victims at federal and state levels, scholars, academics, politicians, judges, victims' rights groups, and others still debate over the necessity and compatibility of defendants' and victims' rights in the criminal court process. It can be simply stated that whether one is for or against victims' rights, implementation of these rights is the main concern for both groups. The argument can be boiled down to whether defendants' and victims' rights are compatible and if criminal courts have the ability, safeguards, and construction to afford to provide the victim rights without sacrificing those of the defendant. Ultimately, implementation is of urgent concern, as it is now the duty of all state and federal courts to provide and protect rights of the defendant and victim.

Jennifer L. Huck

See also Civil Litigation; Court Appointed Special Advocates for Children; Double Victimization; President's Task Force on Victims of Crime, 1982; Victim–Offender Mediation

Further Readings

Crime Victims' Rights Act, 18 U.S.C. § 3771.

Davis, R. C., & Mulford, C. (2008). Victim rights and new remedies: Finally getting victims their due. *Journal of Contemporary Criminal Justice, 24*(2), 198–208.

Faherty, S. (1999). *Victims and victims' rights*. Philadelphia: Chelsea House.

Marion, N. E. (1995). Federal response to crime victims, 1960–1992. *Journal of Interpersonal Violence, 10*(4), 419–436.

Moriarty, L. J. (Ed.). (2003). *Controversies in victimology*. Cincinnati, OH: Anderson.

Shichor, D., & Tibbetts, S. G. (Eds.). (2002). *Victims and victimization*. Prospect Heights, IL: Waveland.

DEFENSIBLE SPACE

Defensible space is the term introduced into criminological literature by North American architect Oscar Newman to describe residential environments that are designed and utilized in ways that maximize their security and protection against crime. Defensible spaces are created when the design and layout of the physical environment is manipulated in such a way that it facilitates the supervision, maintenance, and overall control of residential spaces by residents themselves. In this way, defensible space is aimed at using physical design and layout characteristics of the environment to obstruct opportunities for crime, disorder, and other related outcomes by generating opportunities for residents to defend their residential space. Thus, Newman's defensible space theory was put forward as the first comprehensive theoretical framework of its kind to clarify the ways in which environmental characteristics of a place can help explain crime and victimization patterns.

The components of defensible space include *territoriality, natural surveillance,* and *image and milieu,* all of which explain the various ways in which people's behavior and interaction with space are determined by their responses to environmental cues. These components offer explicit strategies for minimizing the risk of victimization in residential environments by manipulating people's perception of environmental cues and determining their behavioral response to those cues. The concept of defensible space, therefore, naturally fuses together the areas of victimization and crime prevention as it explains how the design of residential spaces either increases or decreases the risk of victimization, while simultaneously offering explicit techniques for preventing various types of crime that occur in residential areas. This entry explains the tenets of defensible space theory in greater detail, engaging in a critical discussion about how the theory has developed, exploring what it reveals about crime victimization patterns, and discussing how it has formed the foundation for internationally applied crime prevention initiatives.

Dimensions of Defensible Space

The creation of defensible space is dependent on the confluence of four critical dimensions, all of which can be activated through the implementation of specific environmental design/layout interventions.

Territoriality

The first component central to the creation of defensible space is *territoriality*. Territoriality refers to the use of the physical environment to create clearly defined zones of territorial control and influence. These zones are created primarily through the use of physical and symbolic barriers and are intended to be easily perceived by local inhabitants and outsiders. Physical barriers include walls, fences, and gateways, while symbolic barriers include hedges, shrubs, and other forms of plantings or landscaping, as well as property signs and nameplates. These physical and symbolic barriers are used as territorial markings that serve three important functions: (1) to make marked distinctions between public, semipublic, and private space by using barriers that clearly delineate where public space ends and private space begins, and in doing so, (2) to psychologically convey the message of restricted access to private spaces by using barriers to direct the flow of movement along public spaces and away from private spaces, and finally, (3) to communicate to outsiders that residential space is well managed, cared for, and controlled by its inhabitants.

Territoriality, therefore, is central to the creation of defensible space, as the physical and symbolic barriers that it employs are vital to the subdivision of space into smaller zones of control and influence. Smaller, more identifiable zones of control enhance place management capabilities by residents, as they determine what behavior is or is not acceptable in that delimited space. As a consequence, this makes it easier to detect crime or related behavior that is not part of the established norm. The restriction of accessibility encouraged by territoriality mechanisms also reduces the flow of movement within defensible spaces, making it easier to identify the users of space and detect potential offenders. Furthermore, expressions of territoriality have the potential to affect other residents' perceptions of their residential space by reinforcing a sense of community and a desire to work collectively in defense of their residential space.

Territoriality, however, can easily result in *fortressing* if physical and symbolic barriers are used excessively to encourage privacy, as this can compromise the visibility between private and public space and therefore undermine the defensibility of an area.

Natural Surveillance

The second essential component of defensible space is *natural surveillance*, or the opportunities provided by the design and layout of the physical environment that enable residents to carry out surveillance over residential space. This concept is hinged on bringing the residential environment under the control of its residents by maximizing their potential to supervise residential space during the course of regular daily activities within the home. This can be achieved, in the first instance, by ensuring that residences are designed to face each other and overlook public space, so that doors and windows are oriented toward the street. This creates the opportunity for residents to clearly and easily monitor the activities occurring in the space immediately surrounding their homes.

In the second instance, natural surveillance is achieved by ensuring that the lines of sight between private residences and the public street are clear and unobstructed by trees, plants, or walls. In light of the mechanisms it relies on for effective functioning, natural surveillance can easily be compromised if physical and symbolic barriers are used in excess as a means of barricading properties for privacy. The natural surveillance techniques are designed to help maximize the visibility of an area by ensuring that residents are likely to have a clear view unto their own property, the properties of others, and the wider residential area when they look out of their windows or open their doors. This increased visibility of private residences and the semipublic and public space around them contributes to the creation of defensible space by (1) increasing the likelihood of detecting potential offenders or potentially deviant behavior within a residential space, and (2) reducing the fear of crime and increasing the sense of security among users because they are under the constant supervision of other residents. In this way, natural surveillance also helps to encourage the mechanisms that foster territoriality, as it boosts the ability to exercise territorial control and the desire to act in defense of residential space.

Image and Milieu

The final components of defensible space are *image and milieu*, or the capacity of the layout, management, and geographical location of the physical environment to create a perception of the aesthetic image and reputation of a place. This dimension of defensible space suggests that the image of a place provides a symbol of the lifestyle and degree of control of its inhabitants, and this image is reinforced by the milieu or the types of areas and facilities that surround it. As a result of the aforementioned factors, image and milieu are mechanisms that are dependent on the outward appearance of a place, its location, its layout, the ways in which it is utilized, and the type of activity that is encouraged therein.

Defensible space theory suggests, for example, that if a residential place has the appearance of being abandoned, run-down, and badly maintained (indicated by environmental cues, such as graffiti, broken windows, or general disrepair) it runs the risk of being negatively differentiated from adjacent areas, and therefore, more susceptible to criminal victimization. Not only does it communicate low levels of resident care and control over their space to outsiders, it also reinforces negative territorial attitudes by increasing fear of crime and resulting in residents' withdrawal from caring for and maintaining their surrounding space. On the other hand, if a residential area is clean and well managed and maintained, it creates the perception that residents are invested in the care and control of their space, and serves to reinforce community pride and the desire to utilize communal spaces and to participate in the continued maintenance and defense of space. Adjacent areas are said to benefit from this image of safety simply because of their proximity and association with nearby areas.

Analysis

The preceding explanation of the dimensions of defensible space highlights the ways in which the concept represents a fusion of psychological, planning/architectural, and criminological perspectives that aid in illuminating some of the ways in which the physical environment can be used to provide mechanisms that reduce the chance of criminal victimizations at places. These defensible space mechanisms have a dual function that serves to (1) empower the resident to become a capable guardian over potential targets and target areas, and (2) remove opportunities for crime as they are perceived by the potential offender through a series of cues that are provided by the physical environment.

In this way, defensible space can be viewed as a framework that suggests ways of reducing opportunities for crime by increasing opportunities for informal guardianship, as it draws attention to the importance of citizen participation in crime prevention and control. This highlights the natural connection that exists between defensible space and the opportunity perspectives on crime, specifically the *routine activity* (or *routine activities*) and *rational choice* approaches. Defensible space considers residents in the same way that guardians are conceived in routine activity theory, as informal control agents against crime. Much of the explanation in this entry thus far has focused on the how residential guardians or informal control agents can exploit the physical environment to enhance their ability to defend their space.

Defensible space also provides the alternative perspective of the offender, explaining potential offenders' perceptions of crime opportunities in terms of risk, effort, and reward, along lines similar to rational choice and routine activity theories. Defensible space suggests that crime can be prevented in residential spaces by manipulating offenders' perception of the risk that they will be detected. This is achieved by using territoriality, natural surveillance, and image cues to increase the offender's perception that the residents are in control of the area, and that he or she is, therefore, more likely to be caught in the act and apprehended in that area. Thus, defensible space emerges as a system that offers residents the potential to gain control over their residential environment, while outsiders and potential offenders are provided diminished opportunities to misbehave.

Perhaps one of the most vital contributions of defensible space is the clarification it provides in explaining *where* people are likely to become crime victims. Defensible space essentially shifts the focus from *who* is being victimized, and *by whom*, to *where* the victimization takes place, as it draws attention to the fact that physical place characteristics play a significant role in determining vulnerability to victimization; it may also help explain spatial patterns in offending.

Development and Details

Defensible Space as a Sociospatial Concept

Notwithstanding its contribution to our understanding about crime prevention at places, defensible space theory has weathered criticisms about its vague definition of concepts and the absence of systematic explanation of how defensible space is perceived at the macro level following its implementation at singular units. The most forceful critiques came from those who argued that the concept of defensible space promoted ideas of physical determinism that assumed fully committed residents and neglected the importance of residents' social characteristics in creating defensible space.

Testing of the theory and subsequent developments in its conceptualization have since revealed that there are indeed dimensions of defensible space that go beyond the physical dimensions previously highlighted. Tests of territoriality in particular revealed socioeconomic factors—including the homogeneity of residents and the extent of social ties among residents—to be key variables that interact with physical defensible space factors to affect the extent of residents control over their space and the amount of crime experienced there. Several other empirical studies have shown that the extent to which residents in an area know each other and the degree of their social cohesion can function as a protective factor against criminal victimization at places. Social psychologists have theorized that the development of these types of social bonds can also be promoted by the physical design of the environment by including communal areas that encourage residents to use public space more readily, and therefore create increased opportunities for social interaction.

The concepts of image and milieu have also been developed further by research that examines the extent to which the image of a place and its land-use patterns affect residents' ability to exercise control over their space. There is much debate about whether the defensibility of an area is negatively affected by a high volume of daily users. Defensible space is based on the assumption that

insiders or residents act as guardians or crime controllers, while outsiders represent the potential threat to defensibility. In line with this assumption, defensible space suggests that one of the main ways in which an area can be made more defensible is by controlling its accessibility. Restricting accessibility results in limiting the volume of users of space, thereby restricting the opportunities available for offending and making it easier to carry out natural surveillance of space.

This perspective is in direct conflict with that expressed by Jane Jacobs regarding safe urban planning. Jacobs argued in favor of mixed and diverse land use in order to encourage a steady and consistent flow of users, whom she characterized as extra "eyes on the street," to provide a secondary source of natural surveillance and contribute to the control of crime. There is, however, a growing body of literature from the field of environmental criminology that demonstrates that increased accessibility and nonresidential land uses serve, under certain conditions, to create a negative effect on resident control over those places, resulting in higher levels of crime as well as physical and social incivilities.

Defensible space has thus evolved into a sociospatial concept that draws on the interaction of several different but interrelated dimensions of space that include physical/spatial and social/demographic components. In so doing, it has highlighted a network of manipulable environmental factors that provide a promising avenue for place-specific crime prevention initiatives.

Practical Application and Policy Implications

Defensible space highlights the roles of two critical actors in the crime event—the capable guardian and the potential offender. In doing so, it suggests the importance of (1) the role of the capable guardian in contributing to the creation of defensible space by blocking opportunities for crime that are available in a residential space, and (2) the ways in which the behavior of capable guardians may be used to manipulate the potential offender's perception of the risks and effort required to commit a crime in that space. This structure intuitively lends itself to the situational crime prevention framework, as it highlights specific strategies that can be employed in residential contexts to thwart crime opportunities. These strategies involve elevating the offender's perception of the risk and effort involved in committing crime and thus ultimately lead to deterrence.

Consequently, defensible space has been used as the justification for the proliferation of the gated community and cul-de-sac configurations, both of which are viewed as residential designs that implement many of the design and layout principles highlighted by defensible space. The most noticeable of these is the limitation of accessibility to outsiders through the use of single entry and exit points, and the layout of residences so that they face each other and facilitate natural surveillance that maximizes coverage over the residential area.

Perhaps even more significantly, over the course of the last 30 years defensible space has been adopted as the cornerstone for crime prevention initiatives and housing design and planning policies all over the world, including crime prevention through environmental design in North America, New Zealand, South Africa, and parts of Australia and Europe, and its adaptations, such as Designing Out Crime in Western Australia and Europe, Secured by Design in the United Kingdom, and Politiekeurmerk Velilig Wonen in the Netherlands. These initiatives systematically employ defensible space guidelines in new constructions as well as the redesign of housing and housing developments, commercial establishments and shopping centers, and institutions such as schools and prisons. These defensible space–based initiatives have also been adopted at large-scale social events and ceremonies as mechanisms through which crime can be controlled.

However, little is known about what specific types of victimization, beyond property victimizations, are effectively controlled by defensible space. While its effectiveness in deterring property crime is to be expected, it is unclear whether its effectiveness extends to other types of crime, such as street violence or domestic abuse. In this way, the limits of the preventive capabilities of defensible space have yet to be explored. On the whole, empirical studies evaluating these defensible space–based initiatives suggest that they do demonstrate some level of success in controlling crime, although very little is understood about why these initiatives are successful, and what specific features of defensible space result in lower crime levels. The environmental interventions and the mechanisms that stimulate them as outlined by defensible space are so fluid, and closely interconnected, that it creates challenges for isolating discrete variables and their direct effect on crime and related outcomes. For many years, the academic community has been concerned with testing defensible space theory, and investigating whether or not it works to control crime. Now that the relationship between environmental design and crime has been demonstrated empirically, and some consensus has been established in terms of its effectiveness as an avenue for crime prevention, the future of defensible space rests on developing our understanding of why it works.

Danielle M. Reynald

See also Crime Prevention Through Environmental Design; Rational Choice Theory; Routine Activities Theory; Situational Crime Prevention; Situational Crime Prevention, Critiques of

Further Readings

Cozens, P., Hillier, D., & Prescott, G. (2001). Crime and the design of residential property—exploring the theoretical background: Part 1. *Property Management, 19*(2), 136–164.

Cozens, P. M., Pascoe, T., & Hillier, D. (2004). Critically reviewing the theory and practice of Secured by Design (SBD) for residential new-build in Britain. *Crime Prevention and Community Safety: An International Journal, 6*(1), 13–29.

Eck, J. E., & Weisburd, D. L. (1995). Crime places in crime theory. In J. E. Eck & D. L. Weisburd (Eds.), *Crime and place* (pp. 1–33). Monsey, NY: Willow Tree.

Jacobs, J. (1961). *The death and life of great American cities.* New York: Random House.

Mawby, R. I. (1977). Defensible space: A theoretical and empirical appraisal. *Urban Studies, 14,* 169–179.

Mayhew, P. (1979). Defensible space: The current status of a crime prevention theory. *The Howard Journal, 18,* 150–159.

Merry, S. E. (1981). Defensible space undefended: Social factors in crime control through environmental design. *Urban Affairs Quarterly, 16,* 397–422.

Newman, O. (1972). *Defensible space: Crime prevention through urban design.* New York: Macmillan.

Newman, O., & Franck, K. A. (1980). *Factors influencing crime and stability in urban housing development*. Washington, DC: U.S. Department of Justice, National Institute of Justice.

Reynald, D. M., & Elffers, H. (2009). The future of Newman's defensible space theory: Linking defensible space and the routine activities of place. *European Journal of Criminology, 6*(1), 25–46.

Taylor, R. B., Gottfredson, S. D., & Brower, S. N. (1981). *Informal control in the urban residential environment: Final report*. Washington, DC: U.S. Department of Justice, National Institute of Justice, Community Crime Prevention Division.

DETACHED YOUTH WORK INITIATIVES

Detached youth work is a unique approach to connecting with disadvantaged, at-risk youth in the community. Targeted youth include those who are not reached by typical youth initiatives. Youth workers meet with adolescents and young adults in areas where youth typically congregate, such as on the street, in parks, and outside stores and shopping malls. This entry provides an overview of detached youth work initiatives, a brief discussion of the evolution of these programs, and a comment on the current research on these programs.

Overview

Detached youth work initiatives, also called youth outreach initiatives, encompass a broad array of programs and services designed to facilitate the personal, emotional, and social development of young people. These can include informal conversations, drama productions, workshops, service agencies referrals, advocacy, transportation, and residential programs. Often times these services focus on issues pertinent to young people, such as racism, drugs and alcohol, sexuality, education, employment, homelessness, bullying, abuse, and delinquency. Many programs aim to empower teens to make better decisions by giving them tools to make informed decisions.

History and Evolution

Detached youth work initiatives began to take place in the United States in the latter part of the

1800s. Individuals, often religious groups and child advocates, who were concerned with the welfare of street youth began creating clubs or groups for these children to join as well as providing residential settings for these children to live. While youth clubs were the most common form of youth work, other individuals found themselves being approached by youth and asked for help. One such encounter resulted in the creation of the now well-known Boy Scouts of America.

Throughout the early 1900s, more and more groups began forming and expanding. Most of these groups were highly organized, requiring youth to be present during specified hours for predetermined activities. The Federated Boys Clubs was one such club that developed in Boston during this time period. It is now known as the Boys and Girls Club of America. It was also at this time that the Girls Scouts of America was formed.

Following World War II, these types of arrangements began to change to reflect the shifting social climate. Youth were allowed to "drop-in" when they desired and clubs began allowing mixed-sex membership. Despite concern among policy makers, it was decided that participation among youth in these programs should remain voluntary for fear that some form of premilitary training would result if mandatory participation was instated. In later years, some youth even created their own clubs, such as the Salinas Warlords Youth Outreach Project. This project was created by former juvenile delinquents in order to help other similarly situated youth. They provided peer counselors at their youth-run service center to assist with employment, educational, and social problems. While the program received mixed reviews from the community, official agencies such as the California Youth Authority and the Office of Economic Opportunity have provided continued support.

It was not until the late 1950s and early 1960s that the idea of youth work initiatives took hold in the United Kingdom, where they remain most popular. Individuals had heard about these programs developing in the United States and were interested in utilizing them in their own country. This was a particularly attractive idea to the British public, as the increasing news coverage of delinquent youth and street gangs terrorizing the streets of the United States caused them to fear problems with youth in the United Kingdom. Funding became available for experimental programs in this area as the fear of these youth and their prospective futures increased. Unfortunately, this initial support and funding did not continue long term. Instead, youth workers began having to focus limited resources on what they believed were the worst neighborhoods with the teenagers who needed services the most.

With the increased popularity of the Internet, some youth workers are also turning to social networking Web pages to contact youth and create awareness for community groups. Youth workers are also networking on the Internet in order to share ideas and sparse resources with other youth workers across the globe. This type of contact can reduce travel expenses and can reach an entirely different group of untapped youth and colleagues. This is leading to a much different picture of how detached youth workers interact with the juveniles in their areas.

While the programs that target at-risk youth have changed over the past century, the underlying principles of youth work initiatives have also changed. Now, detached youth work initiatives have evolved into more of a case management approach. Rather than focusing on long-term support of groups of youth, youth workers spend their time providing short-term interventions to individual high-risk children or specific groups of high-risk children to meet their individual needs. While these youth work programs have declined, resources such as Alan Rogers's book, *Starting Out in Detached Work*, still exist to guide youth workers in the skills of the past.

Research to Date

At the current time, research on the topic of detached youth work initiatives remains limited. Few studies have been conducted to evaluate their effectiveness, with most publications consisting solely of program reviews. Common problems reported by youth in these programs include mental health issues, drug and alcohol abuse, and criminal activity, suggesting a great need for services in these areas. Also of concern is that most programs tend to service considerably more boys than girls. Reviews of programs also report high staff turnover, with a great reliance on volunteer workers due to the unstable nature of employment

positions that fluctuate with the programs offered. Many programs also report problems with an increasing lack of funding.

Ashley Bauman

See also Bullying; Juvenile Offending and Victimization; Youth Centers; Youth Crime Prevention Initiatives, International; Youth Crime Prevention Initiatives, United States

Further Readings

Pitts, J., Pugh, C., & Turner, P. (2002). Community safety and detached and outreach youth work. *Community Safety Journal, 1,* 9–18.

Rogers, A. (1981). *Starting out in detached work.* Leicester, UK: National Association of Youth Clubs.

Smith, M. K. (2005). Detached, street-based and project work with young people. In *The encyclopaedia of informal education.* Retrieved July 2, 2009, from http://www.infed.org/youthwork/b-detyw.htm

Web Sites

Sandwell Metropolitan Borough Council—Detached youth work: http://www.laws.sandwell.gov.uk/ccm/navigation/education-and-learning/youth/youth-service/youth-provision/detached-youth-work

DETERRENCE

Deterrence can be understood as the prevention of criminal behavior through fear of punishment. Deterrence theory posits that criminal behavior can be prevented by threatening would-be offenders with punishment that produces pain or loss that outweighs any pleasure, reward, or gain associated with criminality.

Types

There are two types of deterrence, special or specific deterrence and general deterrence. Special or specific deterrence means punishing an offender with the specific intent of instilling fear in that offender so that he or she will not commit crimes in the future. Typically, special or specific deterrence is aimed at people who have already broken the law in order to deter them from breaking the law again. General deterrence involves punishing offenders to instill fear in society generally so that others will not want to commit crimes. Special or specific deterrence is aimed at stopping a known criminal offender from committing future crimes, whereas general deterrence is aimed at teaching others a lesson about what might happen if they were to commit crimes.

Deterrence is evident throughout the fight against crime. For example, the most common punishment in the United States—probation—leads to the application of many rules to offenders who are allowed to live in the community. Offenders should be deterred from committing future crimes for fear that they might have to check in with a probation officer, abide by travel restrictions, and so forth. Similarly, individuals should be deterred by the thought of being incarcerated in prisons or jails, given that they are violent and repressive places. Any criminal who goes to prison ought to be afraid to go back. In addition, all of society should fear suffering the pains of imprisonment, which include loss of freedom, loss of autonomy, loss of privacy, loss of goods and services, and so on. Thus, crime will be specially and generally deterred. Capital punishment is built around the assumption that executions deter would-be murderers.

Deterrence is based on the logical notion that being punished for criminal activity will create fear in people so that they will not want to commit crime. Deterrence as a justification for punishment is based on several assumptions:

- Offenders are hedonistic or pleasure seeking (and criminal behavior provides pleasure or reward);
- Offenders seek to minimize costs or pains associated with crimes (i.e., they do not want to get caught and be punished); and
- Offenders are rational (i.e., they choose to commit crime after weighing the potential costs or punishments and benefits or rewards).

Many criminologists believe human beings are rational and motivated by the desire for personal pleasure and the desire to avoid pain. If these assumptions are accurate, it is perfectly logical to assume that punishment should deter would-be law-breaking behaviors. However, for punishment to deter criminality, it must be certain, swift, and severe.

Elements of Punishment

These three elements of punishment—certainty, celerity or swiftness, and severity—are important to the effectiveness of deterrence. Certainty of punishment refers to the likelihood that punishment will follow a criminal behavior. Celerity or swiftness of punishment refers to the amount of time that passes between the crime and the punishment. When the duration is short, it can be said that punishment is swift; when the duration is long, the punishment is not swift and thus celerity is absent. Finally, severity of punishment refers to the amount of pain produced by the punishment. When the punishment is more painful than the pleasure or reward produced by the crime, one can say the punishment is severe; if the pleasure or reward of the crime outweighs the pain of the punishment, then severity of punishment is lacking.

To deter would-be offenders effectively, punishment must be certain (or at least likely), swift (or at least not delayed by months or years), and severe enough to outweigh the pleasures associated with crimes. Of these requirements, the most important is the certainty of punishment, although this varies based on the type of offense being studied, the level of sophistication of the offending population, would-be offenders associations with deviant peers, and other social influences.

The more likely that punishment is to follow a criminal act, the less likely the criminal act will occur. Here is an example: If a lightning bolt were guaranteed to strike an offender who stole property, how many thefts would there be each year? Probably not many. If it was absolutely certain that some higher being would strike a person dead upon stealing someone else's property, then everyone would know this and would refrain from committing theft in order to remain alive.

Such punishment would be certain, swift, and severe. But this example is misleading. For deterrence to be effective, it must be certain and somewhat swift, but it has to be only severe enough to outweigh the pleasure gained by committing the offense. For most crimes, certain death by lightning strike is not required.

The noted Italian criminologist Cesare Beccaria wrote, in his 1764 *An Essay on Crime and Punishments,* that certainty of punishment is much more important than severity since the inevitability of the punishment is paramount to most people. Most contemporary research supports Beccaria's original statement. For example, criminologist Alfred Blumstein has noted that research routinely shows that certainty has a greater impact than the severity of the punishment. However, this does not mean severity of punishment does not matter. In fact, each component of deterrence is significant as to whether punishment works to reduce future crimes. For example, getting caught will mean little to an offender in terms of deterrence unless a significant punishment follows.

Probability of Punishment

When scholars assess the effectiveness of American punishment to deter crime, they begin by establishing the likelihood of punishment following a crime. The key question is: Is punishment a certainty in the United States?

Comparisons of data from the Uniform Crime Reporting Program and National Crime Victimization Survey demonstrate that for every 100 serious street crimes, only about 40 are known to the police. Of these 40 crimes, only about 10 will lead to an arrest. Of those arrested, some will not be prosecuted, and some will be prosecuted but not convicted. Finally, only about three of the original 100 crimes will lead to an incarceration in prison or jail. Thus, only 10% of serious crimes in the United States lead to an arrest, and only 3% lead to a serious punishment like prison or jail. Studies show that the largest effect of incarceration on the crime rate is a reduction due to incapacitation rather than deterrence. These data show that punishment is anything but certain in the United States. Not surprisingly, experienced offenders know this.

Why is punishment so unlikely? There are two main reasons. First, studies confirm that there are not enough police in the United States to deter crime sufficiently. For example, Matt Robinson recently demonstrated that there are only about 3 police officers for every 1,000 people in any given city. Of every 1,000 people, roughly 50 to 80 regularly commit crimes, meaning there are only about 3 police officers for every 50 to 80 serious criminals, not to mention the remaining hundreds who occasionally commit crimes and/or disturb the peace. Second, a large portion of crimes are never reported to the police in the first place, as there are various reasons people choose not to report their victimizations. When police do not learn of crimes, they cannot make arrests, thereby eliminating the possibility of deterrence through official government action.

Problems With the Deterrence Argument

There are at least four major problems with the deterrence argument. First, the main problem with deterrence as a justification for punishment is that it is impossible to demonstrate empirically that deterrence works. How can researchers prove the absence of criminal activity as a result of some criminal justice policy or program? This is one reason why many criminal justice scholars argue that there is no empirical evidence supporting deterrence.

Second, many criminal justice scholars posit that deterrence of criminal behavior through deterrence is a myth because numerous human behaviors seem quite irrational. Many forms of criminality are impulsive, shortsighted, stupid, and risky behaviors—the types of behaviors that are not likely to be deterred by future punishment.

Third, many types of crimes are committed with only short-term gain in mind and with little or no thought of likely outcomes. This is not consistent with the view of the rational criminal underlying deterrence theory.

Fourth and finally, the great bulk of evidence suggests that what is important in terms of preventing criminal and antisocial behavior is informal sources of control such as parents, teachers, and religious figures. That is, if deterrence occurs, it is likely due to threats of punishment carried out against children by their parents, although positive reinforcement of prosocial behavior is much more effective.

Deterrence and Capital Punishment

Much of the research on deterrence has been conducted with regard to whether capital punishment deters murder. Although it is certainly logical that the thought of execution ought to create fear in would-be murderers—thereby producing a general deterrent effect—the vast majority of the available scientific evidence suggests that the death penalty is not a deterrent to murder. The primary reason why executions are not thought to be a deterrent by capital punishment scholars is that the most important element of punishment—certainty—is missing.

National data show that there were 592,580 murders and nonnegligent homicides from 1977 to 2006, an average of 19,752 killings per year. During this time, there were only 7,225 death sentences, an average of 241 death sentences per year, and only 1,099 executions for an average of 37 executions per year. Thus, only 1.2% of killings nationally lead to death sentences and only 0.185% of killers have thus far been executed.

These numbers include non–death penalty states; in death penalty states, only 2.2% of killers are sentenced to death. Even Texas—which has executed 37% of all death row inmates in the United States since 1977—sentences only 1.6% of its killers to death and thus far has executed only 0.63% of its murderers. In other words, more than 98% of killers in Texas will not die for their crimes. The rare use of capital punishment is precisely why it is so ineffective at providing a deterrent effect.

Studies from dozens of states have shown that executions do not serve as a greater deterrent to murder than alternative punishments such as life imprisonment. Deterrence studies tend to compare states with the death penalty and without, nations with the death penalty and without, changes in crime rates in jurisdictions before and after having death penalty, the effects of highly publicized executions, and relationships between executions and the murder rate, controlling for other factors. All of these studies lead to conclusions inconsistent with the deterrence hypothesis.

According to the evidence, murder rates are lower in states without the death penalty than those with it, and these rates are lower in nations without the death penalty than with it. In addition, according to Robert Bohm, when states and nations abolish capital punishment or simply stop carrying out executions, the murder rate generally falls. Highly publicized executions tend not to have any effect on murder rates. And empirical studies, properly conducted, rarely find a deterrent effect of executions on murder rates. Given the findings of such studies, it is not surprising that top experts in the nation—including criminologists, death penalty scholars, and even law enforcement chiefs—report that the death penalty does not deter murder.

The largest, most sophisticated study of murder rates from 1935 to 1969, conducted by Isaac Ehrlich, did find evidence of deterrence and concluded that for each execution, eight murders would be prevented. However, this study was replicated numerous times and no effect was found. The study was plagued by numerous flaws that rendered the results almost meaningless. Although there are not many studies of the modern execution period, most of these studies have found no evidence consistent with the deterrence hypothesis.

A bit of controversy recently emerged over the deterrence argument when some of the most recent studies did support a general deterrent effect of executions. These studies, using various methodologies and data sets, found that each execution was associated with between 3 and 150 fewer murders. This research, some of which has not been published in peer-reviewed journals or replicated, offers findings that are inconsistent with the great breadth and depth of knowledge on this topic. The studies are thus viewed with great skepticism by capital punishment experts. Because of numerous flaws in the studies, the findings have been highly disputed.

For example, John Donohue and Justin Wolfers, who examined recent studies finding deterrent effects of the death penalty, point out several very significant problems with the studies. The many problems with the prodeterrence studies include failing to control key (and also unknown) variables, leading to spurious findings; confounding the effects of capital punishment with broader trends in society; failing to use rates of executions to control for population size in states; failing to consider the effects of imprisonment on crime rates; presenting results that are inconsistent with the regression models actually run; relying on measures of key variables generated by scholars with clear ideological biases; using invalid instruments; reporting faulty confidence intervals; and reporting biases caused by inappropriate treatment of standard errors.

Final Thoughts

The great bulk of evidence with regard to criminal punishment suggests that it is generally not a deterrent to future criminality. While some forms of punishment can be effective, this is only possible when the likelihood of punishment is high, that is, when punishment is certain.

What many offenders do tell us, and what is evident from their offending patterns, is that the great bulk of criminal behavior seems to be motivated by the desire to obtain short-term, immediate pleasures and gains. Long-term concern about potential punishment seems not to enter the minds of most offenders. If they thought there was a good chance of getting caught, after all, offenders would not likely engage in their criminal behaviors, especially if they are as rational as criminologists tell us. Further, there are numerous risk factors that increase the likelihood that individuals will choose crime. This suggests rationality is not something possessed equally by all.

Finally, it appears that informal sources of social control, particularly parents, are the most effective sources of deterrence. This suggests that parental influences on prosocial and criminal behavior are much more significant than effects of formal sources of social control such as government-imposed punishment.

Matthew Robinson

See also Corporal Punishment; Crime Prevention; Electronic Monitoring; Offender Based Programs; Restorative Justice

Further Readings

Beccaria, C. (1819). *An essay on crime and punishments* (E. D. Ingraham, Trans.). Philadelphia: H. Nicklin. (Original work published 1764)

Bhati, A., & Piquero, A. (2007). Estimating the impact of incarceration on subsequent offending trajectories: Deterrent, criminogenic, or null effect? *Journal of Criminal Law & Criminology, 98*(1), 207–253.

Blumstein, A. (1995). Prisons. In J. Wilson & J. Petersilia (Eds.), *Crime* (pp. 387–419). San Francisco: San Francisco Institute for Contemporary Studies.

Bohm, R. (2007). *DeathQuest III* (3rd ed.). Cincinnati, OH: Anderson.

Donohue, J., & Wolfers, J. (2005). Uses and abuses of empirical evidence in the death penalty debate. *Stanford Law Review, 58,* 791–845.

Ehrlich, I. (1975). The deterrent effect of capital punishment: A question of life and death. *American Economic Review, 65,* 397–417.

Robinson, M. (2004). *Why crime? An integrated systems theory of antisocial behavior.* Upper Saddle River, NJ: Prentice Hall.

Robinson, M. (2008). *Death nation: The experts explain American capital punishment.* Upper Saddle River, NJ: Prentice Hall.

Robinson, M. (2009). *Justice blind? Ideals and realities of American criminal justice* (3rd ed.). Upper Saddle River, NJ: Prentice Hall.

DEVELOPMENTAL AND SOCIAL CRIME PREVENTION

Developmental and social crime prevention seeks to address a variety of conditions that affect the likelihood of future crime. The argument for such efforts is based on the growing body of research identifying the individual, familial, community, and social structural factors that place individuals and communities at risk for future crime and disorder. A variety of terms are found in the literature to describe social and developmental crime prevention interventions. In this entry, however, *social crime prevention* refers to interventions targeting macro-level problems and structural processes that may engender crime. Efforts to reduce unemployment and improve employment opportunities, develop the quality of educational services, and increase access to social services can be considered social crime prevention. *Developmental crime prevention* attempts to reduce early childhood risk factors for future delinquency and crime and strengthen those factors that appear to protect individuals from future persistent criminal behavioral patterns. This entry begins with a discussion of the developmental crime prevention. Next, risk factors for serious delinquency and adult criminality are reviewed. This is followed by an examination of interventions consistent with a developmental perspective. Finally, the social crime prevention model is reviewed and examples of interventions consistent with this approach are described.

Developmental Criminology and Crime Prevention

Most generally, developmental models of crime examine how social and psychological processes at different stages of the life course affect the likelihood of the development of negative behavioral outcomes, and how life experiences and transitions can alter individual pathways away from or toward criminal behavioral patterns. From this perspective, it is most fruitful to engage individuals, families, and communities at the earliest stage possible, before such pathways become negatively "embedded." Developmental interventions aim to improve the likelihood that individual paths will lead away from crime and other antisocial behaviors prior to becoming a behavioral pattern. Thus, many interventions from a developmental perspective target risk factors for future criminal behavior rather than crime itself. The goal of such interventions is to create healthy, happy, and prosocial children and individuals. Crime reduction is thus a by-product of successful interventions at a much earlier life stage.

The Scholarly Debate

There is some debate between the advocates of a life course approach to studying crime, and desistance from crime, and those who emphasize targeting early developmental protective and risk factors. While some of the debate concerns methodological and statistical questions, there are some important differences between these perspectives for purposes of crime prevention. For example, *life course criminology,* which studies behavioral patterns over the individual life, places considerable emphasis on turning points in later life associated with desistance from crime. Many who examine crime from a developmental criminology perspective, however, focus on the relationship between infant and early childhood experiences and circumstances and the extent to which these are associated with future violent or deviant behavior.

Although these differences may appear insignificant, and they are certainly not mutually exclusive views on crime, they do have significance for crime prevention policy. A life course approach would allocate crime prevention resources across the life span, such as job and life skills training, drug treatment, marriage/family counseling, and targeted programs for offenders that may lead to significant "turning points" (such as marriage, employment, etc.) that encourage desistance. While developmental criminology would likely value such efforts, its emphasis on early life experiences *prior* to criminal behavior would focus resources

on interventions targeted at the very earliest stages of child development, such as parent–child bonding and proper behavioral reinforcement. Given the limited funds for crime prevention efforts, the debate is one of resource allocation. Although many of the interventions discussed in this entry are consistent with life course and developmental perspectives, the following focuses on early child, family, and larger social interventions that are touted for their ability to prevent the onset of crime, rather than its desistance.

Risk Factors for Criminal Behavior

Rather than speaking in terms of "causes" of delinquency and criminal behavior, developmental and social crime prevention efforts target risk and protective factors. *Risk factors* are individual or environmental conditions that have been found to be associated with an increased likelihood of antisocial behavior such as crime or substance abuse. *Protective factors* are those individual or environmental factors that tend to increase resistance to or inhibit the development of problematic behaviors or outcomes, even when risk factors may be present. While there are exceptions, protective factors are often positive indicators on measures of known risk. Thus, while poor parent–child bonding is an important risk factor, evidence of emotionally warm and caring relationships between children and parents has been found to be an important protective factor, even in the face of multiple risk factors. Children exposed to multiple risk factors have a substantially greater likelihood of future delinquency, though the presence of protective factors may exert sufficient influence to counterbalance such factors. The following discussion focuses on risk factors for serious and/or persistent offending, rather than risk factors in general. This highlights characteristics related to offending patterns identified as most problematic and avoids the repetitiveness of reviewing frequently related protective factors.

Risk factors at the individual and familial level are among those that receive the greatest attention. While the strongest and most consistent predictor of future crime and violence is a prior history of such acts, developmental crime prevention efforts are most interested in those risk factors that may be altered prior to the onset of offending and problematic behaviors. For example, the early presence of conduct disorders has been one of the most consistently identified risk factors other than prior criminal acts. In particular, behavioral patterns that have identifiable attributes, such as conduct disorder, attention deficit hyperactivity disorder, and oppositional defiant disorder, are considered significant risk factors for juvenile and adult antisocial behavior. Other individual risk factors include aggressive and antisocial behavior, having antisocial peers, negative attitudes toward school, and poor school performance.

It should be no surprise that familial conditions and behaviors are associated with individual behavior. In particular, having criminal or antisocial parents or siblings is consistently found to be a risk factor for future criminality. Other family risk factors include child abuse and neglect, parental conflict in the home, a lack of familial support, and poor child-rearing practices. Particular parenting strategies and actions such as a lack of adequate supervision or monitoring of children, insufficient or excessive discipline, and a lack of child–parent bonding have also been found to be risk factors for future offending.

Research has also found a number of nonfamilial risk factors for future offending. The relationship between having delinquent peers and delinquency and future criminality is central to several important criminological theories and continues to be found as an important risk factor. Several characteristics related to school and educational activities, such as negative attitudes toward school, truancy, and negative school environments, have also been found to put a child at risk. Finally, there are several social and environmental risk factors, such as low socioeconomic status and income inequality, that increase the likelihood that a particular individual or group will have higher levels of involvement in serious or persistent offending.

Developmental Crime Prevention Interventions

There is often skepticism about the ability of social programs to make significant improvements in individual behavior, especially among at-risk populations. However, studies report that recent interventions have met with considerable success in improving important protective factors and reducing risk factors, resulting in reduced levels of antisocial behavior among participants. The use of improved quasi-experimental and true experimental designs in the implementation and evaluation of these programs offers even greater confidence in these results.

Individual-Focused Interventions

Many early childhood interventions address low intelligence, poor academic performance, and cognitive deficiencies and are often provided in preschool settings in conjunction with home visits. Programs such as Head Start, the Yale Child Welfare Project, and the Syracuse Family Development Program attempt to intervene in the earliest stages of a child's development to improve intellectual and cognitive skills and success in later educational contexts. A number of these programs have shown considerable success, including better school performance, fewer behavioral problems, and lower levels of crime and antisocial behavior among participants. In particular, when early educational interventions are combined with prenatal and parent training services, significant improvements in child, family, and parent outcomes are reported.

Other individual-focused interventions provide children with problem-solving techniques, teach negotiation and interpersonal skills, and help children to develop self-control. Such programs may involve prosocial behavioral messages and reinforcements, academic enhancement strategies, and social competency training and skills development. Programs such as Promoting Alternative THinking Strategies (PATHS) have demonstrated success at reducing the number of behavioral problems among participants. Research has found, however, that the intensity and duration of the program, as well as the quality of programmatic components and instruction, can significantly affect outcomes.

Family-Focused Interventions

There are also developmental interventions designed to improve the family environment, parenting skills, and parent–child relations. Various prenatal and infant nursing programs target parent knowledge about child care, nutrition, and social bonding techniques, and provide important medical and nutrition services to pregnant women and their infants. The first 3 years of a child's life appear to be particularly important for physical and cognitive development, and these programs target risk and protective factors considered essential to healthy social development. A number of health-related factors have been associated with intelligence, aggression, and hyperactivity, and these have been linked with antisocial and delinquent behavior. Prenatal care and perinatal follow-ups can reduce the frequency and seriousness of health problems among infants and reduce the likelihood of child maltreatment and neglect, both of which are risk factors for later antisocial behavior and delinquency.

Family interventions designed to improve parent management skills teach parenting skills that emphasize identifying problematic behaviors, communicating clear and consistent expectations for conduct, and providing appropriate positive and negative consequences for prosocial and antisocial behavior, respectively. Increasing the level of communication between parent and child and the use of token economies have been found to be effective at improving family relations and reducing antisocial behaviors. Given that parental rejection and excessively harsh and inconsistent punishments are strong risk factors for delinquency, a primary target of these interventions is to improve parent–child relations.

Prenatal care visits, parent education combined with preschool programs, and school-based child and parent training programs have demonstrated significant improvements in a variety of risk and protective factors and reducing antisocial behavior. It is clear that dysfunctional family environments are not conducive to providing proper supervision, positive role modeling, or behavioral reinforcements, or developing children's cognitive and behavioral skills. However, the context and mechanisms required to successfully alter those factors is not yet completely understood.

Multimodal Interventions

Problems such as poor school performance and attachment, emotional and mental health problems, and problems in the family environment are likely overlapping and interactive rather than independent. As a result, several programs have been created to simultaneously address problems on multiple dimensions and utilize a systematic approach to crime prevention. For example, the multi-systemic therapy (MST) program involves the provision of parental and family interventions, social–cognitive strategies, and academic skills services to address a range of related risk factors and behavioral problems. Despite the fact that MST deals with a traditionally difficult population, studies have found MST to significantly reduce a number of important target outcomes, including recidivism.

Another example of a comprehensive crime prevention strategy is the Seattle Social Development Project, which created the "Communities That Care" program. This program targets known risk factors at different stages of child development (e.g., preschool, elementary, middle, and high school) and builds upon available protective factors. Evaluations indicate that the project has been successful at reducing a number of negative behavioral outcomes, including violence and drug and alcohol use. This intervention is commonly cited as an example of the importance of a community-led, multifaceted crime prevention strategy utilizing a social and developmental approach.

The Seattle Social Development Program and other comprehensive interventions have provided insight into the programmatic elements essential to successful developmental interventions. First, children must be provided meaningful opportunities to make responsible contributions to the people and institutions that define their social lives. Children and families must also possess the skills necessary to capitalize on opportunities. Interventions such as antibullying programs, early education programs, parenting skills training, and cognitive skills–building programs target improving individuals' decision making and self-esteem, as well as children's intellectual development and academic performance and parenting management practices. The possession of these skills and protective factors can provide children and parents the tools to improve their behavioral choices and the ability to take advantage of positive opportunities. Finally, children must receive recognition and positive reinforcement for their efforts, be provided with clear explanations about why certain behaviors are inappropriate, and receive consistent consequences for such actions.

Social Crime Prevention

Social crime prevention efforts seek to improve structural processes such as economic and political opportunities that directly affect the environment in which children, families, and schools exist. Since its inception, social science research has noted the relationship between poverty and community disorganization and crime and antisocial behavior. Political and public support for large-scale changes necessary to improve such conditions, however, has often been lacking. The remainder of this entry discusses how community and poverty are thought to affect the nature and frequency of crime and provides examples of interventions designed to alter criminogenic social conditions.

Community Crime Prevention

The idea that changes in the organization and social processes of a community can have a direct effect on crime and disorder has a long history in social science research. For example, influenced by research in the Chicago School of sociology, crime prevention programs such as the Chicago Areas Project sought to alter the larger social environment thought to affect levels of crime and disorder in that community. Community mobilization, structural improvements, and increased resident participation in the political and social life of the community are often undertaken to strengthen residents' commitment to their community. The degree of involvement in community affairs, the extent and quality of social networks, and the nature of internal social processes and relationships significantly influence the quality of life within a community. These are also important for their influence on how well residents can exert informal social controls, the everyday norms and expectations that tend to inhibit disagreeable or deviant conduct. Zoning laws and the use of tax expenditures for social services and physical infrastructure influence where residents live, whether they remain in a community, and the types of activities in which they engage. While community improvement programs have improved various areas of community life, they have not all resulted in unqualified success. A major problem is that residents' commitment to and participation in community life is often affected by larger and underlying conditions and factors that require interventions of a more complex and controversial nature.

Poverty and Income Inequality

Although the issues of poverty and income inequality are not the only social crime prevention concerns, the manner in which economic forces shape social life cannot be overestimated. Research has demonstrated that extreme poverty and inequality reduce the social supports necessary to control antisocial behavior, such as crime and drug use. Furthermore, poverty reduces the ability of families, social institutions, and communities to exercise informal social controls over its youth and residents. In particular, isolated and concentrated areas of extreme poverty reduce the amount of social, human, and cultural capital available to individuals and families in these areas. Communities with relatively few individual, family, institutional, or community resources provide few positive opportunities for residents while placing numerous constraints on individual choices. Life in these communities is characterized by a number of barriers and distractions, such as heightened family stress, violence, and high levels of substance abuse, which weaken attachment to school activities and increase the difficulties for academic achievement. Many scholars argue for an approach to crime prevention that utilizes developmental strategies to address individual and family risk factors and combining these with policies designed to address some of the social and economic conditions that put individuals and families at risk in the first place. Policies directed at creating a "living" minimum wage and improving access to physical and mental health care could reduce important risk factors while strengthening protective factors for individuals, families, and communities. Social policies that allow parents to spend more time with their family can increase parents' ability to exercise formal and informal controls over their children. Ultimately, social crime prevention seeks to create conditions that facilitate the development of healthy and prosocial individuals, families, and communities that, in turn, protect against the onset and/or persistence of serious offending and unhealthy behaviors. Even healthy families and communities, however, can benefit from developmental efforts to minimize the likelihood that observed risk factors develop into embedded negative behavioral patterns.

Jefferson E. Holcomb

See also Cost-Benefit Analysis and Crime Prevention;
   Early Education Programming; Offender-Based
   Programs; Perry Preschool Project; Risk and Protective
   Factors and Resiliency; Seattle Social Development
   Project; Substance Abuse, Prevention of; Substance
   Abuse, Treatment of

Further Readings

Bernazzani, O., Côté, C., & Tremblay, R. E. (2001).
   Early parent training to prevent disruptive behavior
   problems and delinquency in children. *Annals of the
   American Academy of Political and Social Science,
   578,* 90–103.

Currie, E. (1989). Confronting crime: Looking toward
   the twenty-first century. *Justice, 6,* 5–25.

Farrington, D. P. (1995). The development of offending
   and antisocial behaviour from childhood: Key findings
   from the Cambridge study in delinquent development.
   Journal of Child Psychology and Psychiatry, 360,
   929–964.

Hawkins, J. D., & Catalano, R. F. (1992). *Communities
   that care.* San Francisco: Jossey-Bass.

Kramer, R. C. (2000). Poverty, inequality, and youth
   violence. *Annals of the American Academy of Political
   and Social Science, 567,* 123–139.

Kury, H., & Obergfell-Fuchs, J. (2003). *Crime
   prevention: New approaches.* Mainz, Germany:
   Weisser Ring.

Loeber, R., & Farrington, D. P. (1998). *Serious and
   violent juvenile offenders: Risk factors and successful
   interventions.* Thousand Oaks, CA: Sage.

Nagin, D. S., & Tremblay, R. E. (2005). Developmental
   trajectory groups: Fact or fiction. *Criminology, 43,*
   873–904.

Sampson, R. J., & Laub, J. L. (Eds.). (2005).
   Developmental criminology and its discontents:
   Trajectories of crime from childhood to old age.
   *Annals of the American Academy of Political and
   Social Science, 602,* 12–45.

DEVELOPMENTAL AND SOCIAL VICTIMIZATION

Developmental and social theories of victimization are a subset of the larger body of literature related to the assessment of risk factors. These theories recognize that children are more susceptible than adults to certain types of victimization as a consequence of their lack of maturational development. Instrumental to developmental theories is an understanding of the degree of autonomy and independence children have at various stages of development. Developmental and social theories are also concerned with the impact of victimization on the individual, and they include analysis of the short-term maladies associated with victimization as well as their impact on the future trajectory of the individual. The theories emphasize how those consequences manifest themselves at various stages of development, which is related to a notion derived from social theories that posits that where a child envisions himself or herself in relation to the social status of his or her peers impacts his or her likelihood of victimization. This entry outlines some of the theoretical issues surrounding developmental theories of victimization, identifies some of the risk factors associated with the victimization of youth, and discusses the impact of victimization on the developmental process of individuals.

Theoretical Issues

David Finkelhor, sociologist and director of the Crimes against Children Research Center, proposed the concept of "developmental victimology" in 1995. He articulated that the study of childhood victimization is important for a variety of reasons. First, children are "in the process" of maturational development, and victimization can have serious ramifications for the normal progression of this development. Developmental theories of crime causation concerned with the correlates of delinquent and criminal behavior have found that victimization in childhood (particularly with respect to physical or psychological abuse) is highly correlated with the early onset of subsequent deviant behavior on the part of the victim. Second, children may be more susceptible to certain types of victimization, which is conjectured to be related to their dependent status. For example, neglect is typically an offense charged to those who care for dependents, be they children or animals, and is taken seriously given that both are dependent upon others for essential care. There is no adult analogue, given the relative ease with which we are capable of living among the ostensibly neglected homeless populations of adults. Third, criminology (as a discipline) is typically only concerned with children insofar as they are the perpetrators of delinquent and criminal acts, a focus that is not without merit given the long-standing empirical validity of the relationship between age and crime, which some criminologists contend is invariant.

Finkelhor noted that the key to a developmental theory of victimization resides in the limited amount of autonomy young people possess. As they mature, children become more autonomous, and the nature of their victimization changes. Consequently, he proposed that the victimization of children can be thought of as occurring along a continuum representing degrees of dependency. In general, very young children spend most of their time at home with their parents or guardians, and thus victimization of these children usually occurs in the home; they are rarely the victim of stranger-perpetrated homicide. In contrast, adolescents have been viewed as making choices that increase their risk of being victimized (like staying out on the streets late at night), and as a consequence are seen as contributing to their own victimization, a variation of the "blaming the victim" mentality. The focus on adolescents as perpetrators by mainstream criminology has been implicated in an ideology that sees them as complicitous in their own victimization. Exacerbating this is the empirical evidence indicating that children who have been victimized are more likely to have affiliations with delinquent youth, which differential association research shows is correlated with delinquent behavioral outcomes.

Risk Factors

Developmental and social theories of victimization account for the risk factors associated with the victimization of children as well as the impact victimization has on a child's prospective development and psychological well-being. The risk factors associated with the victimization of children include their suitability as targets, their ability to protect themselves, and environmental factors that may contribute or mitigate their susceptibility to victimization. Thus, the theory accounts for factors that are similar to those included in several existing theories and perspectives related to the positive causes of criminal and delinquent behavior. The concepts of children's "self-protection ability" and

"level of suitability as targets" are functionally similar to Lawrence Cohen and Marcus Felson's routine activity theory (also called routine activities theory), which states that crime is more likely where there is a motivated offender and a suitable target in the absence of capable guardians, a theory driven by the philosophical underpinnings of rational choice theory. The inclusion of environmental factors like neighbors' ability to monitor the activity of potential offenders against children is epistemically related to the structural components of social disorganization theory.

Several risk factors have been identified as salient to the victimization of children, although researchers are quick to note that the most frequently used official sources of data on crime and delinquency (i.e., those from the Uniform Crime Reporting (UCR) Program and National Crime Victimization Survey) do not include data on the victimization of children at all ages. This is limiting in testing the verisimilitude of developmental hypotheses, since they are contingent upon examining victimization at the very earliest stages of childhood development for comparative purposes. Unfortunately, this is where most data sources fall short due to the anonymity typically granted young victims of crime. Consequently, some researchers have suggested using data retrieved from child protective services, although its validity has been the subject of debate among researchers.

Developmental and social theories of victimization presume that children are susceptible to victimization at rates that vary, depending upon their stage of development. For example, very young children (under age 5) are less likely to become the targets of robbery than are their adolescent counterparts, who are more likely to carry money in public places, making them significantly more attractive targets to potential robbers. Also, empirical research indicates that young women are more likely to become the targets of sexual abuse after they have reached sexual maturity, pedophilia aside. Another example resides in the fact that as children age, they become more capable of fleeing, as well as defending themselves against, attacks from potential offenders. Empirical evidence shows that parental physical abuse is more prevalent when children who are the subject of such abuse are very young.

There is empirical evidence linking children's self-perception of social status with victimization in the school setting. Of particular relevance is their perception of self-worth within their peer group. Where children place themselves in a position of lower social value, they are at greater risk for victimization. This has been hypothesized to occur for several reasons. First, feelings of inadequacy and social failure in children have been linked to increased rates of victimization. Second, where children are more confident of their social standing among their peers, it can serve as a bulwark against victimization. As a result, researchers have suggested assertiveness training may have some impact on preventing future victimization from peers in social settings.

Aside from the developmental and social characteristics of children themselves, there are environmental factors that vary with maturational development that impact their susceptibility to different types of victimization. These factors are functionally similar to those invoked in the name of routine activities theory, namely that children are more likely to be victimized where they are in close proximity to a motivated offender, or where there is the absence of capable or willing guardians. However, the traditional interpretation of both of these constructs is challenged when one considers that children are frequently victimized by their intimates and family members. In these cases, an abusive parent may serve as a motivated offender to a dependent child who is incapable of distancing himself or herself because of his or her dependent status. Furthermore, it is often the case that the neighborhood itself (and not parents) serves as a capable guardian in instances of parental abuse and neglect. Where neighbors are unwilling or incapable of intervening, the child is often left without suitable protection, increasing the likelihood of victimization. Exacerbating this situation is the fact that, as much empirical research indicates, victimization is not evenly spread throughout society. Those most likely to be victimized are young, minority males who come from socioeconomically disadvantaged communities, a finding compatible with the empirical findings related to social disorganization theories of crime causation.

Impact

The impact of victimization on the future development of individual children is also within the domain of developmental and social victimology. Unfortunately, most of the literature related to victim experiences tends to be framed in terms of posttraumatic stress disorder (PTSD), which has traditionally been applied to either adults or children suffering the consequences of having experienced gross traumatic experiences like natural disasters. PTSD typically manifests itself in individuals' reexperiencing the stressing event, avoiding the circumstances that brought about the event, and experiencing hypersensitivity to analogous events. It has been noted in the literature that children may manifest the effects of PTSD differently than do adults. For example, they may assume a more limited view of their future prospects, altering the trajectory of their development.

It has been proposed that children experience two distinct types of effects as a consequence of victimization—developmental and localized effects. *Localized effects* are described as those that typically do not have long-term consequences for an individual's development. Examples of localized effects are insomnia, experiencing nightmares, and feelings of anxiety around grown persons.

Developmental effects refer to those effects that broadly inhibit or impact a child's prospective development, often with significant ramifications. Some examples of developmental effects are exhibiting age-inappropriate signs of hypersexuality, developing eating disorders, becoming withdrawn from interactions with adults, and engaging in unusually aggressive behavior. Developmental effects are more likely to occur for a variety of reasons related to the nature of the victimization. First, when the victimization occurs over a protracted period, it is more likely to impact the developmental process. Second, the victimization is more likely to result in developmental effects when a child or adolescent experiences it in conjunction with some other type of serious stressor. Examples of additional stressors are suffering from the loss of a parent or family member and experiencing racial discrimination. Third, when the victimization involves those who are part of the child's primary system of support, it is more likely to have long-term consequences; this is likely to impede normal development, which presumes the existence of such a support system. Fourth, developmental effects are more likely to be experienced when the victimization occurs in the midst of some critical stage of personal development. For example, developmental effects may become manifest if a youth were to become the victim of a robbery while working the very first day on his or her first job.

The consequences of victimization also vary depending upon the stage of development of the individual. For example, victimization can interfere with the formation of attachments with other individuals. This restriction on attachments can carry through to other stages of development throughout the life course. As hypothesized in social control theories of crime causation, preclusion of attachment to prosocial individuals may be associated with delinquent and criminal behavior.

Victimization can also lead to chronic dissociation with others, as well as other psychological abnormalities. There is strong empirical evidence indicating that adults who suffer from multiple personality disorders tend to have suffered from physical or psychological abuse at a young age. Research also shows that children who have been victimized are at increased risk of showing physiological signs of the experience, in the form of impaired endocrine and neurological functioning as well as a delayed onset of puberty. Some researchers implicate impaired cognitive development to victimization in young children, although the results of that research have been the subject of considerable debate. For example, some researchers have found that children were impacted more by how their parents reacted to their victimization than they were by the victimization experience itself. Empirical evidence also does not support the suggestion that younger children are more traumatized as a consequence of victimization; it stands to reason that they may be incapable of recognizing the full gravity of the victimization when it occurs.

Stephen Shirk noted that the symptoms associated with victimization manifest themselves in accordance with the individual victims' stage of development and are a product of victims' use of the age-specific "vocabularies" available to them. He provides the example of very young girls tending to display "hypersexualized" behavior subsequent to sexual abuse. In contrast, older teens and adolescents tend not to exhibit such behavior, instead displaying symptoms of withdrawal, self-injurious behavior, and/or substance abuse.

Victimization has also been implicated in impacting subsequent delinquent and criminal behavior

on the part of the victim, perhaps exacerbating the difficulties in interpreting the relationship between age and crime. Empirical evidence indicates that youth are more likely to be victims of violent offenses than are adults, and violent victimization has been implicated in the early onset of delinquent behavior, perpetuating what has been termed the *cycle of violence*. According to empirical research related to developmental theories of crime causation, the early onset of delinquent behavior is associated with criminal "careers" characterized as both long in duration and active in terms of the frequency of offenses committed over the life course. Some scholars suggest this is related to the acquisition of what Edwin Sutherland termed *definitions* favorable to the commission of crime. Others suggest it may lead to the adoption of a subculture of violence favorable to the subsequent commission of criminal and delinquent acts.

The physical abuse of children has been implicated as a precursor to theft, prostitution, and illicit drug use. A limitation of research in this area is that researchers typically do not specify the stage of development in which the victimization occurred, obfuscating the relationship between development and subsequent antisocial behavior. Preliminary findings from studies that control for stage of development have found that childhood-only victimization is not related to delinquency while adolescent and that persistent victimization is positively related to an increased risk of delinquent behavior on the part of victims.

The effect of victimization on the development of the individual transcends its impact on prospects for subsequent delinquent and criminal behavior. Victimization can also have consequences for educational and occupational attainment. Empirical evidence indicates that abused children tended to perform more poorly in school, in the form of increased rates of truancy, lower grade point averages, and lower graduation rates. Compatible research has found that victims of abuse in childhood also suffered significant consequences upon entering the workplace. One study found that those who were subject to violent victimization at a young age earned 14% less per hour in young adulthood than did nonvictims.

It has been reasoned that these consequences result because victimization undermines two fundamental sets of beliefs within the individual: perceptions of self-efficacy/self-agency, and perceptions about the intentions of others. Perceptions of self-agency and self-efficacy are hypothesized to be related to the loss of control experienced as a result of victimization, and they are associated with enhanced perceptions of vulnerability concerning the potential for future victimization. They are also related to negative self-images in the form of feelings of helplessness or the perceptions of being weak in relation to others. In a related vein, research has found that some victims blame or see themselves as deserving or contributing to their own victimization. Victimization has also been found to impact the way victims view the intentions of others in society. This is troublesome because victims often unwarrantedly view potential systems of support as potential threats.

Developmental and social theories of victimization account for the risk factors associated with the various stages of development, as well as the ramifications of victimization on individual development. In doing so, they bring together theoretical constructs form a variety of theories of victimization as well as theories related to the positive causes of crime and delinquency.

Douglas J. Dallier

See also Age and Victimization; Child Abuse, Neglect, and Maltreatment; Correlates of Victimization; Juvenile Offending and Victimization; Posttraumatic Stress Disorder (PTSD); Psychological and Behavioral Consequences of Victimization; Risk and Protective Factors and Resiliency

Further Readings

Boney-McCoy, S., & Finkelhor, D. (1995). Psychological sequelae of violent victimization in a national youth sample. *Journal of Consulting and Clinical Psychology, 63,* 726–736.

Cohen, L. E., & Felson, M. (1979). Social change and crime rate trends: A routine activity approach. *American Sociological Review, 44,* 588–608.

Egan, S. K., & Perry, D. G. (1998). Does low self-regard invite victimization? *Developmental Psychology, 34,* 299–309.

Finkelhor, D. (1995). The victimization of children: A developmental perspective. *American Journal of Orthopsychiatry, 65,* 177–193.

Hagan, J., & McCarthy, B. (1997). *Mean streets: Youth crime and homelessness.* New York: Cambridge University Press.

Ireland T. O., Smith C. A., & Thornberry, T. P. (2002). Developmental issues in the impact of child maltreatment on later delinquency and drug use. *Criminology, 40,* 359–399.

Karmen, A. (1990). *Crime victims: An introduction to victimology.* Pacific Grove, CA: Brooks/Cole.

Koenen, K. C. (2006). Developmental epidemiology of PTSD. *Annals of the New York Academy of Sciences, 1071,* 255–266.

Macmillan, R. (2000). Adolescent victimization and income deficits in adulthood: Rethinking the costs of criminal violence from a life course perspective. *Criminology, 38,* 553–588.

Macmillan, R. (2001). Violence and the life course: The consequences of victimization for personal and social development. *Annual Review of Sociology, 27,* 1–22.

Shirk, S. R. (1988). The interpersonal legacy of physical abuse of children. In M. B. Straus (Ed.), *Abuse and victimization across the lifespan.* Baltimore: Johns Hopkins University Press.

Widom, C. (1989). The cycle of violence. *Science, 244,* 160–166.

DEVELOPMENTAL VICTIMOLOGY

Developmental victimology focuses on the victimization of children. Its attention is expansive and includes abuse and neglect and physical and sexual abuse as well as other kinds of victimization, such as peer and sibling assaults. It looks at the ways children are victimized throughout their developmental period, the categories of victimizations, and the possible reasons that this phenomenon is underreported. An important aspect of developmental victimology is that it addresses the need for more serious study by sociologists, criminologists, developmental psychologists, child behavioral specialists, and educators.

Definitions

Victimization by definition is the act of exploiting or victimizing another, typically through an act of force or power over another. Child victimization is the exploitation of a child between 0 and 17 years of age. This form of victimization is especially serious because children's dependence upon others makes them particularly vulnerable to harm. Other terms that are used to refer to child victimization are *child maltreatment, child abuse and neglect, child sexual abuse,* and *child physical abuse.*

Children are the most victimized group within the larger society, yet there is less understanding about child victimization than about adult victimization due to the lack of data on the extent of the problem. According to David Finkelhor, a widely published author on this topic, the lack of information is due to a number of factors, including how current data are collected. For example, in the United States, the National Crime Victimization Survey and Bureau of Justice Statistics both report on victims ages 12 and above; hence, data on crimes against children younger than age 12 are excluded. Also, much of public policy concerning younger children is driven by information about child abuse and neglect and child abduction, but these items are not part of the collected data. The absence of such information has created a paucity of theoretical guidelines for the field. Developmental victimology recognizes the theoretical gaps surrounding child victimizations as a result of this theoretical scarcity and seeks to provide a means of getting new information through more inclusive survey instruments and broader definitions of victimizations to capture the attention of criminologists, developmental psychologists, and justice studies.

This effort requires a new understanding of childhood victimizations. Finkelhor has categorized it in three ways: pandemic victimizations that are prevalent throughout the development of the child, acute victimizations, and extraordinary victimizations. The pandemic victimizations include peer assaults, assaults by siblings, theft, vandalism, and robbery. These can be described as common occurrences of childhood, which may be the reason they are not seen as problematic. An example of a pandemic victimization is peer assault. This issue is typically attended to by a caregiver, so the matter never comes to the attention of the police or a child protective agency as it might with older children.

The second category is that of acute victimizations. These may occur less frequently and in a smaller number of children, but they are more severe. These kinds of victimizations include physical and sexual abuse and abandonment, neglect, and abduction by family. This category has received the most research and public policy attention.

The final category is extraordinary victimizations, which include homicide, child abuse homicide, and abduction by a stranger. There are fewer occurrences of these victimizations, but they demand more attention and are easier for criminologists to fit into their paradigm.

The lack of attention to the first category is noteworthy because of its prevalence. This category tends to be more difficult for criminologists to fit into their paradigm for action. The pandemic victimizations are viewed as less serious to the development of the child, yet the child's view of these events is unknown because it is unsolicited. Younger children are viewed as incapable emotionally and cognitively of providing accurate and plausible descriptions of their experiences, so their perspectives are often overlooked. Another part of this lack of communication from the child's perspective is the fact that a child who has been victimized early in development learns from his or her environment the code of silence. This child is less likely to want to talk to authorities, for fear of further harm from his or her environment. A child who has experienced such victimizations is more likely to have personality disorders, emotional and mental health problems, and academic difficulties.

Historical Overview of Child Victimization

Childhood victimization is a part of the history of the United States. Up until the late 1800s, immigrants from many European countries who came to the United States with their children faced great economic challenges and often dealt with their children as if they were property, selling them into apprenticeships or involuntary servitude as a means of alleviating the financial burden of caring for a child. Children were required to work like other members of the family without any regard for their unique developmental needs. Young children were made to grow up quickly and infant mortality rates were very high. Until the Settlement House Movement started by Jane Addams and others in the late 19th century, there was little regard for the overall well-being of children. Public policy began to change with the enactment of child labor laws, and there began a wide social movement to ensure the protection of children. In 1912, the Children's Bureau was created to oversee the welfare of the country's children. Three years later the Children's Welfare League was established, and in 1930 the Social Security Act was amended to include child welfare and protective services.

By the late 1950s and early 1960s, the topic of child physical abuse was brought to the nation's attention, and by 1974 Congress enacted the Child Abuse Prevention and Treatment Act. There was a growing national awareness of the reality of child victimization and the need to address it. There are now federal, state, and local agencies and laws in place to focus on children's rights to be protected and safe within their environments.

Incidence of Victimization of Children

Neglect and physical abuse are the two most commonly reported forms of child victimization. In 2006, about 905,000 children were reported to be victims of child abuse or neglect. The maltreatment rate was 12.1 per 1,000 during the federal fiscal year 2006. In 1998 there were 903,000 children who were victims of abuse or neglect. During this same time, children under the age of three accounted for 75% of the annual deaths. The data consistently show that children who died as a result of maltreatment from one or both parents. During 2005, about 1,300 children died as a result of abuse or neglect. Children under the age of 3 are more likely to be victimized at rates of 16.5 per 1,000, compared to 6.2 per 1,000 of children ages 16 to 17.

Recent research has enabled us to better understand the victimization of children younger than 2 years of age. For example, researchers Robin Karr-Morse and Meredith S. Wiley have documented that a child experiences indirect victimization in utero, and that this trauma can create serious changes to the brain's functioning that impacts the release of certain hormones which regulate responses to stress and danger. These children have more incidents of aggression, hostility, and other violence than their counterparts as they move into early childhood and adolescence. The predominant research about domestic violence supports this fact: Young boys who have witnessed violence in their homes are more likely to become adult men who abuse their partners. The notion that this victimization begins before birth (i.e., during gestation) is what is noteworthy.

Effects of Childhood Victimization

Children who have been victimized are often at great risk of being revictimized. The notion of polyvictimization has been documented by Finkelhor and others. Polyvictimizations are serial victimizations, and the literature is showing increasing relationships between witnessing domestic violence and child abuse or sexual victimizations in childhood and adolescence. The Developmental Victimization Survey provides statistical confirmation of the notion that younger children who experience an initial trauma during their development are more likely to be a target for future victimizations. The revictimizations are different and occur over a developmental time period.

One of the reasons for this stems from the nature of the child himself or herself. The child is the most vulnerable member of the family, the child's primary social group, and is the least likely to be able to protect himself or herself from this environment. Younger children are more likely to be victimized by a caretaker, as the data show that the likelihood of their reexperiencing a subsequent victimization is very high.

An example of how indirect victimization from family violence can result in polyvictimization is evidenced by the story of a 4-year-old Black male child. He was the youngest boy and the middle child with an older brother and a younger sister. At the age of 2, he had witnessed violence against his mother; he also experienced sexual assault at age 3 by his older male sibling. He then went on to be sexually aggressive with his younger sister, as he had witnessed his older brother sexually act out against her. This child suffered great remorse and guilt and expressed suicidal ideation. He had a suicide plan, although he did not act it out. At the age of 4, he was targeted as child with behavioral problems often showing anger and using profanity against his teachers. His family no longer experienced physical violence within the home, but he witnessed his mother's substance abuse and his brother's sexual assault of their younger sister. This child's situation is an example of what the study regarding polyvictimization uncovered.

The Juvenile Victimization Questionnaire (JVQ), a complete questionnaire that gathers information from young children and their caregivers, provided the data regarding polyvictimization. The data reflected the number of victimizations occurring within a single year. The results showed that the average victim was Black and male, with a lower socioeconomic level who was living in an urban setting in a single-parent home. These findings are important in understanding certain traumatic symptomatology. They might also help predict patterns of victimizations but the question that remains is the reason for the polyvictimizations.

Implications for Further Study

The JVQ can be a useful tool for future studies to establish the validity of the polyvictimization argument. The findings certainly point to the need to determine the need for improved assessments to gain a more holistic approach to understanding child victimization that can lead to more effective public policy and research. Focusing on those types of child victimizations that are pandemic but not currently getting attention warrant more research and expanded child welfare public policies can benefit from the polyvictimization studies. This new focus can help those within the criminal justice community, child welfare specialists, and sociologists intervene earlier and ultimately put in place methods of prevention for children at earlier points in their development.

Valerie D. Wise

See also Bullying; Child Abuse, Neglect, and Maltreatment; Child Protective Services

Further Readings

Child maltreatment. (n.d.). Retrieved from http://www.childtrendsdatabank.org/pdf/40_PDF.pdf

Davidson, H. (n.d.). *Mandating multidisciplinary review of serious child maltreatment cases: An overview of law and policy issues.* Retrieved from http://www.icann-ncfr.org/documents/Howard_Davidson_Article.pdf

Finkelhor, D. (2007). Developmental victimology: The comprehensive study of childhood victimizations. In R. C. Davis, A. J. Luirigio, & S. Herman (Eds.), *Victims of crime* (3rd ed., pp. 9–34). Thousand Oaks, CA: Sage.

Finkelhor, D., Ormrod, R. K., & Turner, H. A. (2007). Poly-victimization: A neglected component in child victimization. *Child Abuse and Neglect, 31,* 7–26.

Gil, E. (1996). *Systemic treatment of families who abuse.* San Francisco: Jossey-Bass.

Karr-Morse, R., & Wiley, M. S. (1997). *Ghosts from the nursery.* New York: Atlantic Monthly.

Malley-Morrison, K., & Hines, D. A. (2004). *Family violence in a cultural perspective: Defining, understanding and combating abuse.* Thousand Oaks, CA: Sage.

National Child Abuse and Neglect Data System. (2006). National and state statistics. *Child maltreatment, 2006.* Retrieved from http://www.childwelfare.gov/can/prevalence/stats.cfm

2002 National Victim Assistance Academy. (2002). *Chapter 11: Child victimization.* Retrieved from http://www.ojp.usdoj.gov/ovc/assist/nvaa2002/chapter11.html

Web Sites

Children's Defense Fund: http://www.childrensdefense.org

Child Trends DataBank: http://www.childtrendsdatabank.org

Child Welfare Information Gateway: http://www.childwelfare.gov

UNH Crimes Against Children Research Center: http://www.unh.edu/ccrc

DIFFUSION OF BENEFITS

Outcome evaluations of crime prevention efforts focus on changes in the level of the targeted crime, fear of crime, and/or citizen behavior. The fact that most prevention programs are place specific means that evaluations typically focus only on changes within the target neighborhood or community. At the same time, crime prevention programs could have an impact beyond that which is intended. The other changes could be either positive or negative. The crime prevention techniques in one area may unintentionally result in increased crime in another area, on other targets, or at different times. In essence, the level of crime or fear may have simply shifted in response to the prevention efforts. This shift in crime is referred to as crime displacement. The opposite may also occur. Crime prevention efforts targeted at a specific problem in one location may have a positive impact on other locations or crimes. That is, there may be a diffusion of benefits. This entry examines the idea of the diffusion of benefits and presents evidence on the extent to which such diffusion occurs.

Defining Diffusion

After Thomas Reppetto delineated different forms of displacement in 1976, research began to consider the degree of displacement in evaluations, particularly in terms of the movement of crime from one location to another. The tenor of most discussions of displacement was clearly one of disappointment or dismay at the thought that crime is simply being moved rather than eliminated. Robert Barr and Ken Pease, however, suggested that displacement may be a positive result of prevention actions. This *benign displacement* would benefit society by spreading crime around the community rather than concentrating it in one location, or by substituting less harmful offending in place of more serious criminal behavior. Barr and Pease proposed that the main question should be how displacement can "be used to achieve a spread of crime that can be regarded as equitable" (p. 284). One possible equitable outcome of crime prevention would be the displacement/shift of the crime prevention impact. Essentially, this would diffuse the positive effects of the intervention.

Ronald Clarke and David Weisburd define diffusion of benefits as "the spread of the beneficial influence of an intervention" (p. 169) to other people, places, times, or things that were not the specific focus of the intervention. This means that two things have probably occurred. First, there has been a positive impact on crime as expected in the planning of the intervention. Second, the prevention efforts have benefited people and places besides those specifically targeted. Diffusion has been discussed under a variety of names, including "halo effect" and "free bonus effect."

What accounts for diffusion? Clarke and Weisburd offer two potential sources for diffusion—deterrence and discouragement. Deterrence can have an impact in various ways. While many prevention efforts are short-lived, the impact on crime often outlasts the period of intervention. Similarly, targeting one location or certain merchandise may result in protecting other targets. In each case, there is an assumption that the chances of being apprehended are heightened and potential offenders are deterred by the risk of being caught. Discouragement works by reducing the payoff and increasing the effort needed to commit a crime.

Interestingly, displacement and diffusion have traditionally received little attention in the crime prevention literature. It is only in recent years that evaluations have begun to make claims about apparent displacement or diffusion. The difficulties inherent in assessing displacement and diffusion mean that these issues are not central to many evaluations. In every case, the degree to which displacement or diffusion occurs is related to the degree to which offenders can and do make judgments about offending.

Uncovering Diffusion

Diffusion of benefits means that areas, items, or individuals not targeted by a crime prevention program also benefit from the intervention. For example, if half of the homes in a neighborhood join block watch, mark their property, and take part in surveillance activities, and everyone in the neighborhood experiences reduced victimization and fear, it is probable that the crime prevention of the participants had an impact on the nonparticipants. This would be a diffusion of benefits. However, measuring diffusion is very difficult.

Attempts to assess diffusion need to consider a couple of factors. First, diffusion is not necessarily limited to movement from one place to another. As with displacement, prevention techniques can diffuse across several dimensions. It is possible that prevention efforts will diffuse to different places (territorial/spatial), times (temporal), victims or items (target), methods of committing an offense (tactical), and/or other offenses (functional). All of these possibilities of diffusion should be considered. Most analyses only consider territorial diffusion and ignore the other forms.

A second concern in investigating diffusion is that each crime/problem being targeted by the prevention initiative should be examined in detail. Several key questions should be answered. Who are the likely offenders? When are the offenses taking place? How are the crimes being committed? Where are they occurring? What purpose does the crime serve (i.e., why does it happen)? The answers to these questions will provide insight to what types of diffusion could be expected. It may not be necessary to investigate for diffusion across all possible dimensions if what is known about the crime and potential offenders suggest only one or two possibilities. Interestingly, while most crime prevention programs answer these questions when developing the intervention, they are typically ignored when discussions of diffusion (or displacement) occur (if they are discussed at all).

A typical approach to measuring diffusion is to examine the change in crime and fear in areas contiguous to the target area. Reductions in the contiguous areas could be due to diffusion effects. At the same time, however, the reductions in both the target and control areas could be a result of general decreases in society. Rather than a diffusion effect, the crime prevention intervention has no impact. Determining whether there is no change or if the changes are due to diffusion would require study of additional comparison areas (or targets) that would not be expected to experience diffusion due to distance or other circumstances.

Another problem with identifying a diffusion effect would appear when both the displacement of crime and diffusion of benefits occur at the same time, resulting in no apparent change in the nontreatment area. In this case, the crime prevention program is successful at reducing crime and/or fear in the target area. At the same time, some of the reduction is the result of displacing offenses to another area, which would normally mean that crime and/or fear in the other area increases. A simultaneous diffusion effect of equal magnitude, however, would offset the increase and show no net change in crime and/or fear in the other areas.

Evidence of Diffusion

Despite these concerns with identifying diffusion effects, evaluations are beginning to pay more attention to the possibilities of diffusion in their designs and analyses. Efforts to address drug problems in neighborhoods have reported a diffusion impact in areas surrounding the targeted sites. Evaluations of Neighborhood Watch in various communities also have found evidence that the watch efforts diffuse to nonparticipating targets in the same area. Street lighting has been tried as a prevention tool in many areas. The expectation is that nighttime offending should diminish after the installation of lights or the improvement in existing lighting. Interestingly, research has found that daytime offending in areas that have had lighting improvements has also been reduced. This clearly suggests temporal diffusion. Diffusion also is apparent in the U.K. Safer Cities program, particularly in areas where the prevention efforts are intensively implemented.

In one interesting study, Marcus Felson and his colleagues reported that diffusion may actually occur in the opposite direction from what would be expected. That is, changes occurring outside the target area may impact on the target, leading to the appearance of program effectiveness. In their study of the New York City bus terminal, Felson and his colleagues found that reductions in crime outside the terminal, dating from prior to the terminal improvements, may have contributed to crime reductions inside the terminal. In essence, reductions in robbery and assault occurring outside the terminal may have diffused into the terminal. The fact that the reductions inside the terminal were greater that outside suggested that the targeted prevention efforts were effective beyond any possible diffusion that took place.

A final interesting finding in relation to diffusion involves the idea of *anticipatory benefits*. Anticipatory benefits refers to changes in crime which predate the actual implementation of a crime prevention program. That is, the impact may actually occur prior to or separate from the actual prevention initiative. Publicity about the prevention program (or as a part of the program) may reduce crime in and of itself. In one sense, this could be a form of diffusion of benefits that arises most probably from the fact that offenders, victims, and others know about a forthcoming prevention activity and begin to respond prior to the activation of the intervention. Publicity about an impending intervention may be the impetus for the anticipatory benefits. Several studies reveal evidence of anticipatory benefits stemming from publicity. These analyses range from efforts to address theft of and from autos in parking lots to the use of closed-circuit television (CCTV) in town centers to burglary intervention programs. The publicity that precedes the actual intervention prompts crime reductions before any preventive activity has occurred. This is a diffusion of benefits in anticipation of an action.

Summary

While concerns over displacement have existed for some time in the literature, diffusion is a more recent topic. Diffusion should be considered as a counterbalancing force to displacement. Given the fact that both forces could be at work in a project, it is important to design projects that can uncover each of these possible factors. The inability to identify displacement and diffusion would result in an incomplete analysis of program effectiveness.

Steven P. Lab

See also Crime Prevention; Displacement

Further Readings

Armitage, R., Smythe, G., & Pease, K. (1999). Burnley CCTV evaluation. In K. Painter & N. Tilley (Eds.), *Surveillance of public space: CCTV, street lighting and crime prevention* (pp. 225–250). Monsey, NY: Criminal Justice Press.

Barr, R., & Pease, K. (1990). Crime placement, displacement, and deflection. In M. Tonry & N. Morris (Eds.), *Crime and justice: A review of research* (Vol. 12, pp. 277–318). Chicago: University of Chicago Press.

Clarke, R. V., & Weisburd, D. (1994). Diffusion of crime control benefits: Observations on the reverse of displacement. In R. V. Clarke (Ed.), *Crime prevention studies* (Vol. 2, pp. 165–184). Monsey, NY: Criminal Justice Press.

Felson, M., Belanger, M. E., Bichler, G. M., Bruzinskie, C. D., Campbell, G. S., Fried, C. L., et al. (1996). Redesigning hell: Preventing crime and disorder at the port authority bus terminal. In R. V. Clarke (Ed.), *Preventing mass transit crime* (Vol. 6, pp. 5–92). Monsey, NY: Criminal Justice Press.

Green, L. (1995). Cleaning up drug hot spots in Oakland, California: The displacement and diffusion effect. *Justice Quarterly, 12,* 737–754.

Johnson, S. D., & Bowers, K. J. (2003). Opportunity is in the eye of the beholder: The role of publicity in crime prevention. *Criminology and Public Policy, 2,* 497–524.

Reppetto, T. A. (1976). Crime prevention and the displacement phenomenon. *Crime and Delinquency, 22,* 166–177.

Smith, M. J., Clarke, R. V., & Pease, K. (2002). Anticipatory benefits in crime prevention. In N. Tilley (Ed.), *Analysis for crime prevention* (pp. 71–88). Monsey, NY: Criminal Justice Press.

DISABILITIES, VICTIMIZATION OF INDIVIDUALS WITH

Disability is an impairment that limits one or more basic functions such as seeing, hearing, walking, communicating, processing information, or caring for oneself. Disability can also be seen as the barrier individuals face in architectural designs, practices, or attitudes that were based on a conception of human functioning that excludes those with disabilities. The high rates of victimization of these individuals in some categories of crime and significant barriers to effective intervention and prevention outcomes related to disability make studying victimization of those with disabilities particularly important.

Incidence

More than 51 million individuals with disabilities are living in the United States, according to recent U.S. Census Bureau data. The data on rates of victimization of individuals with disabilities are generally acknowledged to be problematic. Disability information is rarely included in crime data collection. When disability data are collected, they are frequently related to certain types of crime and sample only a subcategory of disability, such as developmental disability. The incidence of victimization of individuals with disabilities as a general category including all crimes and all disabilities is unknown.

There is evidence linking certain categories of disability to high rates of victimization in certain categories of crime. Women with disabilities have been found to be the victims of sexual assault or intimate partner/domestic violence at rates four or more times greater than the rates for women in the general population. The incidence is even higher for women with developmental disabilities, which are defined as cognitive, physical or both types of disabilities that appear before the age of 22 and are likely to be lifelong. Individuals with severe mental illness are victims of violent crime at rates significantly higher than those of the general population. Children with disabilities may have higher than average rates of maltreatment such as neglect, physical abuse, or sexual abuse, although this has been debated.

Incidence data may be improved as a result of the Crime Victims with Disabilities Awareness Act of 1998, Public Law 105-301, which resulted in new National Crime Victimization Survey instruments to measure the nature of crimes against individuals with developmental disabilities and specific characteristics of the victims of those crimes.

Intervention

Individuals with disabilities who are victimized rely on the same sources for assistance and intervention as any other citizen in a community, although there are disability-specific services available. Intervention efforts for individuals with disabilities have a number of aspects relevant to disability. Successful intervention faces a fundamental barrier in the low reporting rate of crimes against individuals with disabilities. Several factors contribute to this low reporting rate. Crimes may not be reported due to the fear of losing critical services from agencies that might be implicated or inconvenienced. Individuals with disabilities may not report crimes if they have not been educated as to what their rights are or how to identify victimization. Individuals with disabilities may also choose not to report a crime because of past experiences in which their ability to understand or communicate was discounted.

When individuals with a disability choose to report a crime, the reporting process must be accessible to them. The process is defined as accessible if it is able to be used as effectively by people with disabilities as by those without. An individual who is deaf may require an interpreter or video conferencing. An individual with an intellectual disability who expresses himself or herself differently may not be taken seriously, or be misunderstood, unless intervention professionals have been trained to be aware that there is a broad range in the way people think and communicate. Obtaining intervention services also requires that affordable and accessible transportation be available to the victim with disabilities.

Intervention may also be hampered by resistance from service providers who feel unprepared or otherwise unable to adequately serve an individual with a disability. Even subconscious beliefs can affect services, including the belief that an individual with a disability is not likely to be the victim of a crime. In the criminal justice system, there is evidence of low rates of prosecution when the victim has a disability, especially if it is an intellectual disability. Individuals with disabilities who have reported a crime may be discouraged from proceeding with prosecution based on the belief that prosecution will not be successful. Another factor contributing to the low rate of prosecution is the concern that individuals with disabilities, in particular intellectual disabilities, may not be competent to testify on their own behalf or able to handle the stress of court proceedings. An assumption of incompetence of individuals with intellectual disabilities may still exist in some legal systems.

Prevention

Prevention efforts are primarily concerned with educating and empowering individuals with disabilities, the professionals that work with them, and the community at large. The involvement of individuals with disabilities in all aspects of community life is a relatively new development. Several factors associated with this development have hampered prevention efforts. The late 20th century saw the release of many individuals with disabilities from residential institutions that did not prepare these individuals to protect themselves from victimization. The historical isolation of individuals with disabilities, in institutions and other segregated settings, has also contributed to the idea that these individuals are not subject to the risks of victimization that come with participation in community life.

The belief that individuals with disabilities are not capable of contributing to their own safety is in decline but still affects prevention efforts that rely on empowerment of the individual. The concept that individuals with disabilities are childlike or incapable of making decisions on their own behalf has also contributed to the encouragement of habits of compliance at the expense of assertiveness and the ability to protect oneself.

As is the case with intervention, prevention efforts for victims with disabilities succeed when they are accessible (i.e., they enable individuals with disabilities to maneuver in the setting where services are provided, communicate, and be welcomed). Successful prevention is also connected to skill building and increased awareness that recognizes the challenges and dynamics described above. The Crime Victims with Disabilities Awareness Act of 1998 and the Violence Against Women Act of 2000 contain provisions designed to reduce the victimization of individuals with disabilities along these lines.

Robert Bonney

See also Domestic Violence; Elder Abuse, Neglect, and Maltreatment: Institutional; Intimate Partner Violence; Mental Illness and Victimization; Rape; Sexual Victimization

Further Readings

Martin, S. L., Ray, N., Sotres-Alvarez, D., Kupper, L. L., Moracco, K. E., Dickens, P. A., et al. (2006). Physical and sexual assault of women with disabilities. *Violence Against Women, 12,* 823–837.

Powers, L. E., Curry, M. A., Oschwald, M., Maley, S., Saxton, M., & Eckels, K. (2002). Barriers and strategies in addressing abuse: A survey of disabled women's experiences. *Journal of Rehabilitation, 68,* 4–13.

Steinmetz, E. (2006, May). *Americans with disabilities: 2002.* Retrieved February 27, 2009, from http://www .census.gov/prod/2006pubs/p70-107.pdf

Teplin, L., McClelland, G., Abram, K., & Weiner, D. (2005). Crime victimization in adults with severe mental illness: Comparison with the National Crime Victimization Survey. *Archives of General Psychology, 62,* 911–921.

DISPLACEMENT

Displacement, or more specifically crime displacement, is the phenomenon of criminal activities shifting in some form as a response to crime prevention initiatives such as increased policing, Neighborhood Watch, and target hardening. Displacement is an important phenomenon to consider when designing crime prevention initiatives because if crime is simply displaced to other locations, times, methods, crime types, or victims, crime prevention is a zero-sum game for society. Moreover, if displacement of some form and degree does occur the societal benefits to crime prevention are not as great. This forces us to ask whether crime prevention initiatives should be undertaken or not, as well as what crime prevention initiatives should be undertaken given that we expect some form of displacement to occur. This entry discusses the context of displacement in terms of theoretical expectations, the forms of displacement, methodological issues with measuring displacement, and evidence for the existence of displacement.

The Displacement Model of Crime

The fact that researchers and practitioners discuss the possibility of displacement means that there is some underlying belief in the structure of crime that would lead to such a phenomenon. Consequently, there is a model of displacement in the criminological literature that is referred to sometimes explicitly and sometimes implicitly. Steven Lab outlines the four primary assumptions of such a model, a useful starting point for considering the impact of crime prevention initiatives.

The first assumption is that offenders have a need to commit a certain number of offenses. The place, time, crime classification, method, and target are not particularly important, as crime must simply be performed. Such a view almost necessarily implies some form of pathology or antisocial characteristic within offenders that forces them to satisfy this need. Lab uses the term *inelastic* to describe this need for committing crime. It is a term used in choice theory (most commonly in microeconomics) to describe a product that must be consumed at a certain level. The best example of an inelastic good is insulin. Regardless of the price, a diabetic must consume a certain quantity of insulin to avoid health complications. In the context of the offender, regardless of the "price" of offending (risks, payoffs, etc.), crime must be committed.

The second assumption is that offenders are willing to be mobile. This simply means that offenders are willing to operate in different locations, at different times, use different tactics, select different targets, and perform different types of crime. Consequently, if a crime prevention initiative is undertaken, then offenders must be flexible and able to adapt to the changes it brings.

The third assumption is critical and become very important when questioning the displacement model of crime: Offenders act rationally. Though a contentious statement at times, the rational offender is the only type of offender that is displaced. Otherwise, the offender will continue to undertake crime in the manner before any crime prevention initiative began. Derek Cornish and Ronald Clarke point this out through the use of the term *choice-structuring properties*. Choice-structuring properties of crimes involve the assessment, by offenders, of the potential payoffs of a crime and its corresponding risks. It is because of any changes in payoffs and risks that offenders *choose* to displace their criminal activities.

The fourth, and last, assumption is that alternative places, times, methods, crimes, and targets are *available* to the offender. If the second assumption of willing to be mobile is satisfied, then this fourth assumption must also be satisfied for crime to be displaced.

Questioning the Displacement Model of Crime

The purpose of questioning the displacement model of crime is not to deny that displacement exists, or that some offenders are always willing to commit crime no matter how it comes about. Rather, the purpose of questioning this model is to show that displacement is not absolute.

The assumption of the inelastic commission of crime assumes that the root of all crime is within the offenders. As mentioned above, this could be some pathological condition or other antisocial characteristic. Both Marcus Felson and Ronald Clarke challenge this view. They state that it is opportunity that is at the root of crime. In his book *Crime and Everyday Life*, Felson goes into great detail to show how this is the case. These theorists do not deny that motivation for committing crime exists, but they do stress that motivation means nothing without the presence of suitable targets. If criminal activities are at least partially opportunistic and/or unplanned, the assumption of the inelastic commission of crime is violated.

The assumption of mobility is also easily challenged. Though the methods used to commit a crime, the crime type chosen, and the victims of crime have some degree of substitutability, location and time are not always flexible. Patricia Brantingham and Paul Brantingham have outlined the importance of geography to criminal offenses, describing the geometry of crime. Offenders do not commit crime randomly in their environment. Rather, crimes are committed in the places they frequent most often as well as the pathways between them. In the context of time, there are certain commitments that people have. Consider a young offender in school; if the criminal opportunities between 3 p.m. and 6 p.m. are removed, the young offender has few options to commit other crimes.

The assumption of the rational offender is particularly instructive here. If offenders change their criminal activities because of the perception of increased risks or decreased rewards, then it must follow that risks can be made high enough and reward low enough to prompt some (or most) offenders desist from criminal activities. As such, the displacement model of crime contains an assumption that does not have to be shown to be violated. The mere presence of the assumption states that displacement is not inevitable.

Finally, the assumption of (available) alternative targets for crime is probably the easiest to accept. As discussed below, there is evidence of displacement, so there must be alternative targets available. However, not all targets are equally attractive to all offenders. This may be the simple reason why crime concentrates in particular areas of urban (and other) environments. The easy and most attractive targets are chosen first. Once these targets are removed, less attractive and more difficult targets are selected, and so on. However, this process can only go so long before the payoffs are simply not worth the risks.

Forms of Displacement

Regardless of whether one subscribes to a displacement model of crime or not, displacement comes in a number of forms. More than 30 years ago, Thomas Reppetto listed five different forms of displacement: territorial, temporal, tactical, target, and functional. Each is discussed, in turn.

Territorial, or geographical, displacement is the most common form of displacement that is expected to occur. To paraphrase David Weisburd and his colleagues, crime simply moves around the corner. For example, if there is some form of crime prevention activity in one neighborhood (Neighborhood Watch, increased police presence, target hardening, etc.), criminals simply move to another neighborhood without such crime prevention activities. Most often, territorial displacement is assumed to occur in neighborhoods, or areas, close to the original crime area, but this is not necessarily the case. Rather, crime moves to the next best location for committing the relevant offense that *may* be in close proximity.

Temporal displacement occurs when offenders commit their offenses at different times of the day, days of the week, and so on. This form of displacement will only occur in response to certain forms of crime prevention activities. These are the type of activities, defined by the presence of a citizen or police patrol, that only occur at certain times of the day or week. Depending on the nature of the offenders, who may also be constrained by time, temporal displacement may be expected. A crime prevention activity such as target hardening is not expected to result in temporal displacement because such an activity is always present. In addition, if temporally based crime prevention activities are targeted at youth who are enrolled in school (extra police patrols between 3 p.m. and 6 p.m., for example), temporal displacement is not expected to occur.

Tactical displacement is a change in methods used by offenders to commit crime. This form of displacement is most likely a response to target hardening crime prevention initiatives. Changes in the technology to prevent automotive theft has shown this to be the case quite clearly with the advent of steering column locks, steering wheel locks, alarms, and electronic disabling devices. Automobiles are still stolen, just through different means.

Target displacement occurs when there is a change in victims, but no change in the area where offenders search for opportunities. A prime example would be a target hardening initiative that only some proportion of homes undertakes within a neighborhood. If that crime prevention initiative is identifiable by the offenders (burglar alarm signage, for example), the remaining homes in that same neighborhood would become the victims of crime. Though the distinction between target and territorial displacement is an important one, target displacement may be thought of as micro-territorial displacement: Crime still occurs; it just occurs next door rather than in another neighborhood.

Functional displacement occurs when an offender actually stops committing one type of crime and switches to another type of crime. In this situation, the crime prevention initiative removes all criminal opportunity, or makes the commission

of crime so difficult that it is easier for offenders to switch their activities, albeit to other criminal activities. Functional displacement may also be subdivided into two different forms: benign and malign. Robert Barr and Ken Pease point out that even if displacement occurs, perfectly, it may actually benefit society. Though this may initially be thought of an odd statement, most people, if asked about their "preferences" for victimization would prefer one crime over another; the cost of a simple assault to the individual and society is far less than the cost of a sexual assault. Of course, functional displacement may go the other way: Rather than committing automotive thefts, offenders may switch to committing armed robberies.

Finally, Barr and Pease also have contributed to the measurement of different types of displacement through the addition of a sixth form of displacement: perpetrator displacement. In this form of displacement, one offender stops criminal activity (incarceration, ages out of crime, begins to view criminal activities as too risky, etc.), but another offender takes his or her place. Alternatively, though a crime prevention initiative may make crime unattractive (too risky or too few rewards), it may allow another offender to see opportunity.

It should be clear from this brief discussion that it is possible to predict, to some degree, the form of displacement that will occur. Consequently, holding the view that displacement is not always perfect, or 100%, enables those involved in crime prevention activities to take them in stages to minimize overall displacement.

Methodological Issues for Measuring Displacement

Being able to classify and, potentially, predict the form of displacement is a powerful tool for those involved in crime prevention. However, actually measuring displacement can be problematic. Though there are other difficulties, as outlined in some of the Further Readings at the end of the entry, one methodological issue is particularly problematic: measuring significant change. The most obvious example of this problem involves the use of territorial displacement, but similar difficulties exist with other forms of displacement.

Consider an urban environment that is divided into a set of equally sized neighborhoods, representing a grid. Suppose there are nine of these neighborhoods organized in a square, and a crime prevention initiative is undertaken in the center neighborhoods. The crime prevention initiative is undertaken in the middle neighborhood because it has the greatest volume of crime (an average of ten per some unit of time), whereas the other neighborhoods have much lower volumes of crime (an average of five per the same unit of time). Now suppose the crime prevention initiative is a success with a 50% reduction in crimes: now five per unit of time. However, there is perfect displacement. The five crimes that are reduced now occur in five of the adjacent eight neighborhoods. Here is the problem: Because crime will vary over time, an increase of one crime in five of the other neighborhoods will likely not lead to any statistically significant changes being measured. Based on averages, those assessing the crime prevention initiative may think that territorial displacement has occurred, but they cannot make any meaningful statements. This problem only becomes more difficult when the number of neighborhoods to which crime may move increases.

This measurement problem, however, is not confined to territorial displacement, as indicated above. If an assessment of increased police presence after school hours is being undertaken, then temporal displacement must be considered a possibility. Again, suppose crime falls between 3 p.m. and 6 p.m., but there is a corresponding increase in crime at other times of the day. If the comparison period is the rest of the day, then displaced crimes that were committed 3 hours of the day will be counted with crimes that occur in the other 21 hours of the day. Measuring any statistically significant change will likely be very difficult even if perfect displacement occurs. Tactical, target, functional, and perpetrator displacement may also be difficult to measure for similar reasons; it takes time for some of these forms of displacement to occur, so are they due to actual displacement or the variability of crime over time?

(A Lack of) Evidence for Displacement

This methodological difficulty, and others not discussed here, has not stopped researchers from attempting to assess the presence of displacement from crime prevention initiatives. Though there has not been a comprehensive review for over a decade, the 1990s saw three such reviews of the empirical assessments of displacement undertaken by Barr and Pease, John Eck, and René Hesseling, all of which are listed in the Further Readings at the end of this entry.

Because it is easiest to measure, it should come as no surprise that territorial displacement is the most common form of displacement investigated. This is followed by target displacement and offense displacement—temporal and tactical displacement are studied the least of all forms. All three of the reviews come to the same conclusion: Displacement is not inevitable, and if present, is not significant enough to have cause for concern. These rather strong statements are made by these authors because more often than not there is evidence of some, but not perfect, displacement. In fact, both Eck and Hesseling suggest that different types of crime prevention initiatives and different crimes will have different degrees of displacement. Given the methodological problem discussed above and the fact that these authors can identify differential degrees of displacement for different crime prevention initiatives and crimes, displacement should be taken seriously. Because of the methodological problem outlined above, however, the measurement of displacement is likely to be biased downwards.

An additional problem for assessing the evidence for displacement, as pointed out by Weisburd and his colleagues, is that most evaluators of crime prevention initiatives do not employ methodologically sound research designs for detecting displacement. This lack of methodologically sound research designs is because of a number of constraints (time, money, and other resources), but it is very real and has not been dealt with until very recently in the context of territorial displacement.

Weisburd and his colleagues set out to assess territorial displacement in the context of drug crimes and prostitution. They assumed that if territorial displacement was to occur, it would occur within these crime classifications because of the explicitly economic nature of these crimes. In their study, many of the methodological problems are dealt with at the outset of the research or dismissed based on their results. They find no evidence of territorial displacement, but do find evidence for the diffusion of benefits. The diffusion of benefits occurs when crime is reduced in areas close to, but not included in, the targeted crime prevention area. Thus the methodological concern outlined above is not relevant in this particular case.

However, there are some limitations in their analysis. Weisburd and his colleagues only asked whether or not crime moves around the corner. This assumes that the second best locations for crime are geographically close to the targeted area. This is not necessarily the case. It may be that the second best area for crime is across town and easily accessible by public transit—a parking lot at another shopping mall 3 miles away, for example. Given the limitations of the displacement model of crime discussed above, it is unlikely that perfect displacement will occur, and only measuring crime in immediately adjacent areas is limited, at best. Also, Weisburd and his colleagues have found evidence for tactical displacement. Though the quantification of this form of displacement is difficult, the fact that it can be observed or measured indicates that its presence is significant.

Consequently, the current state of research evaluating displacement indicates that displacement is not a significant concern for those implementing crime prevention initiatives. Or, alternatively, displacement is not significant enough to discourage the implementation of crime prevention initiatives. However, as with most social science, very few definitive statements can be made.

Martin A. Andresen

See also Burglary, Prevention of; Crime Prevention; Crime Prevention, Domains of; Crime Prevention Through Environmental Design; Diffusion of Benefits; Methodological Issues in Evaluating Effectiveness of Crime Prevention; Situational Crime Prevention

Further Readings

Barr, R., & Pease, K. (1990). Crime placement, displacement, and deflection. *Crime and Justice: A Review of Research, 12,* 277–318.

Brantingham, P. L., & Brantingham, P. J. (1981). Notes of the geometry of crime. In P. J. Brantingham & P. L. Brantingham (Eds.), *Environmental criminology* (pp. 27–53). Beverly Hills, CA: Sage.

Cornish, D. B., & Clarke, R. V. (1987). Understanding crime displacement: An application of rational choice theory. *Criminology, 25,* 933–947.

Eck, J. E. (1993). The threat of crime displacement. *Criminal Justice Abstracts, 25,* 527–546.

Felson, M. (2002). *Crime and everyday life* (3rd ed.). Thousand Oaks, CA: Sage.

Felson, M., & Clarke, R. V. (1998). *Opportunity makes the thief: Practical theory for crime prevention.* London: Home Office.

Hesseling, R. B. P. (1994). Displacement: A review of the empirical literature. *Crime Prevention Studies, 3,* 197–230.

Lab, S. P. (2007). *Crime prevention: Approaches, practices and evaluations* (6th ed.). Cincinnati, OH: Anderson.

Reppetto, T. (1976). Crime prevention and the displacement phenomenon. *Crime and Delinquency, 22,* 166–177.

Weisburd, D., & Green, L. (1995). Measuring immediate spatial displacement: Methodological issues and problems. *Crime Prevention Studies, 4,* 349–361.

Weisburd, D., Wyckoff, L. A., Ready, J., Eck, J. E., Hinkle, J. C., & Gajewski, F. (2006). Does crime just move around the corner? A controlled study of spatial displacement and diffusion of crime control benefits. *Criminology, 44,* 549–591.

DISPUTE RESOLUTION

The field of dispute resolution developed as an alternative to formal court processes. As such, it typically refers to a process of alternative dispute resolution (ADR) or informal dispute resolution. Rather than going through formal court proceeding, the dispute is negotiated or facilitated by a third party, often through mediation or arbitration, out of court. Through this less formal and rigid process, the facilitator assists people in dispute (the parties) by listening to their concerns and helping them negotiate an agreement. This process often results in a more consensual outcome, compared to adversarial court proceedings. While the most common forms of ADR are negotiation, mediation, collaborative law, and arbitration, there are many other forms: judicial settlement conferences, neutral fact-finding, ombudsmen, restorative justice, and so on. Though often voluntary, ADR is sometimes mandated by the courts, which require that disputants try mediation before the case is heard by the court.

Although informal dispute resolution goes back hundreds of years, across many cultures, alternative dispute resolution has grown rapidly in contemporary society since the political and civil conflicts of the 1960s. During this time, new laws protecting individual rights, as well as less tolerance for discrimination and injustice (particularly in the areas of race, sex, or national origin) led more people to file lawsuits in order to settle conflicts (e.g., Civil Rights Act of 1964). These new laws gave people new grounds for seeking compensation for injustice. Other social (e.g., women) and environmental movements further highlighted a range of issues, which led to further court cases. The result was a significant increase in the number of lawsuits being filed in courts. This increased demand led to long delays in cases being brought forward, overburdened court professionals, and procedural errors within a stretched system. Hence, informal alternative dispute resolution soon became a popular way to deal with a variety of conflicts, as the process helped relieve pressure on the overburdened court system.

Informal dispute resolution processes are now used to settle a variety of disputes across a range of institutions, including the family, religious institutions such as churches, schools, the workplace, government agencies, and the courts. As already noted, the most common forms of ADR are negotiation, mediation, collaborative law, and arbitration. Negotiation is a voluntary process where there is no third party who facilitates the resolution process or imposes a resolution (although the parties involved may be coached behind the scene by a professional or support person). Mediation is a process where there is a third party, a mediator, who facilitates the resolution process (and may even suggest a resolution, typically known as a "mediator's proposal") but does not impose a resolution on the parties. Collaborative law is a process where each party has an attorney who facilitates the resolution process within specifically contracted terms. The parties reach agreement with support of the attorneys (who are trained in the process) and mutually agreed upon experts. Unlike formal legal proceedings, no one imposes a resolution on the parties. Arbitration is a process where a third party acts as a private judge and imposes a resolution. Arbitrations often occur in the context of contractual agreements, wherein it

is agreed that disputes will be resolved by arbitration. Arbitrators are also brought in when a stalemate has developed within a form of dispute resolution where a resolution is not imposed.

Informal dispute resolution is argued to be a better option to lawsuits and litigation for a range of reasons: It is generally faster and less expensive than formal adversarial proceedings; stalemates can be avoided; it is based on more direct participation by the disputants, rather than being run by lawyers, judges, and the state; and disputants can outline the process they will use and define the substance of the agreements. This degree of participation by the disputants has been shown to increase people's satisfaction with the outcomes, as well as their compliance with the agreements reached. The integrative approach of most ADR processes is more cooperative and less competitive than adversarial court-based methods like litigation, and consequently can curb the escalation of conflict and ill will between parties. In fact, some research has found that the participatory process of ADR can potentially strengthen the relationship between the disputing parties rather than weaken it. This is a key advantage in situations where the parties must continue to interact after settlement is reached, such as in child custody or labor management cases.

There are potential drawbacks and criticisms of alternatives to court based adjudication. For some, ADR is seen as a less legitimate form of justice, as it aims to be a more "informal" justice process, with less rigorous procedural safeguards in place. As such, ADR has been referred to as "second-class justice," particularly as people who cannot afford to go to court are those most likely to use ADR procedures, and less likely to "win" their case due to the cooperative, and potentially compromising, nature of ADR.

The confidential and private nature of ADR has also been criticized, as the settlements are not in the public record and exposed to public scrutiny. For example, private disputes with companies and organizations can result in an agreeable settlement between the parties, but not resolve the issue for other potential disputants. For example, consumers may be affected differently by a defective product. While one disputant could find an agreeable settlement, others may not be aware of the defective product or reach an agreeable settlement. A court ruling, on the other hand, could force the company to fix all problems associated with the product or remove it from the market.

While the arguments for and against the development of alternative (informal) dispute resolution remain, the field continues to grow and develop, with hundreds of different models and forms now available, including the delivery of ADR services through the Internet.

Brenda Elizabeth Morrison

See also Peer Mediation; Restorative Justice

Further Readings

Moffitt, M. L., & Bordone, R. C. (Eds.). (2005). *The handbook of dispute resolution*. San Francisco: Jossey-Bass.

DOMESTIC VIOLENCE

Since the late 1970s, attention paid to domestic violence has increased exponentially. It is now one of the types of victimization garnering the most policy and research attention. Initially, domestic violence was defined narrowly as physical violence perpetrated by husbands against their wives. This definition has evolved in the last 30 years as people have come to realize that violence exists in all kinds of romantic relationships. Here *domestic violence* is defined broadly as abuse perpetrated by one romantic partner (or ex-partner) against another. Other terms used to characterize abuse in romantic relationship are *intimate partner violence, spouse abuse, battering*, and *dating violence*. This entry details how common domestic violence is, the kinds of abuse victims experience, risk factors for abuse, and how abuse impacts victims, their children, and the community.

Prevalence and Incidence

There are two ways to measure how common domestic violence is: incidence and prevalence. In the case of domestic violence, incidence is best thought of as the number of acts of domestic violence during a given time in a given population.

Prevalence is best thought of as the proportion of a population that has experienced domestic violence in a specified time period. If every victim experienced only one act of domestic violence in a year, incidence and prevalence numbers would be the same for that year. However, typically incidence figures are higher than prevalence figures when based on the same data. These are typically calculated on an annual and lifetime basis, so both are presented here.

Yearly national estimates of domestic violence are taken from the National Crime Victimization Survey (NCVS), an annual national survey conducted by the U.S. Census Bureau. In 2008, the NCVS estimated that there were 593,100 incidents (69,100 against men and 504,980 against women) of violent victimization by an intimate partner in the United States, which translates to an annual incidence rate of less than 1 victimization per 1,000 men age 12 and older and 4 victimizations per 1,000 women age 12 and older. The National Violence Against Women Survey (NVAWS) was a one-time national survey focused on physical violence, sexual assault, stalking, and threats of violence. The NVAWS (conducted from 1994 to 1996) estimated there were 2.3 million domestic violence victims (counting physical assault and sexual assault) in the United States, which translated to an annual prevalence of 1.2% of the population age 18 and older (a rate of 12.1 per 1,000 people)—1.5% of women and .9% of men. The NVAWS also provided estimates of how many adults in the United States had experienced domestic violence over the course of their lives. The lifetime prevalence estimate was 16.5% of the population age 18 and older (a rate of 165 per 1,000 people)—24.8% of women and 7.6% of men. Homicide is the most extreme form of domestic violence, and it is tracked by the FBI through its Uniform Crime Reporting Program's Supplementary Homicide Reports (UCR-SHR). In 2008, there were 1,333 intimate homicides in the United States. According to the NCVS and UCR-SHR, domestic violence has declined considerably over the last few decades. Between 1993 and 2008, the annual rate of domestic violence victimization reported by the NCVS has dropped 60% for women, from 9.8 to 3.9 per 1,000 women age 12 or older, and more than 50% for men, from 1.6 to 0.7 per 1,000 men age 12 or older. During the same time, domestic violence homicides tracked by the UCR-SHR have dropped from 2,201 in 1993 to 1,333, even as the U.S. population increased.

The weakness of all of the estimates in this section is that they measure only physical acts of violence and thus underestimate the true extent of domestic violence. The more severe an act of domestic violence, the less common it is. So, for example, screaming at, swearing at, or threatening a partner are much more common forms of abuse than hitting or beating up a partner.

Abuse Experiences

Initial conceptions of patterns of abuse focused on abuse of women by men and were based on work by Lenore Walker in the late 1970s and the "power and control wheel" created by Domestic Abuse Intervention Programs. Walker outlined the concept of a "cycle of violence" with three stages. In the initial stage, abuse and tension build, leading to the second stage, which is the explosion of abuse. Following the explosion is stage three, the "honeymoon" period, in which perpetrators attempt to make up for their abuse and the relationship is often characterized positively by victims. Inevitably, the honeymoon fades and tension builds again, according to the theory, and the cycle repeats itself. Since psychological and related types of abuse typically onset in a relationship before physical abuse, the initial passes through the cycle may not even include physical abuse. However, over time, it is believed that the cycle accelerates, abuse increases in intensity and frequency, and in some cases the honeymoon disappears altogether. This can lead to severe physical abuse, to which the term *battering* is often applied.

Domestic violence encompasses far more than acts of physical abuse. It involves a perpetrator attempting to exert power and control over his or her partner, and a variety of types of abuse can be used as tools to achieve that goal. These can include physical abuse (e.g., hitting the victim, physically restraining the victim, breaking objects, physical acts against others); sexual abuse (e.g., rape, unwanted touching); verbal, psychological, and emotional abuse (e.g., swearing, ethnic slurs, insults, playing "mind games," isolating victim from friends and family); financial abuse (e.g., running up debt in the victim's name, barring victim

access from money, not allowing a victim to work); and threatening acts against victims and others, most notably the children, family members, and pets. It is impossible to create an exhaustive listing of actions that can be abusive, but perpetrators are creative, taking advantage of their intimate knowledge of their partners. Understanding aspects of a partner such as his or her religious or cultural context or immigration status allows a perpetrator to profit from that knowledge. For example, in Orthodox Jewish communities, a perpetrator can refuse to grant a "get" (Jewish religious divorce), which means that his wife cannot remarry or date in the eyes of the community.

The above conceptualization of domestic violence is what some victims experience, but is not the case for other victims. For example, while some victims experience a very high frequency of abuse, others do not. According to the NVAW, victims averaged 6.9 physical assaults for women and 4.4 physical assaults for men by the same partner over the course of a relationship. There is now a theory, advanced originally by Michael Johnson, that there is more than one type of domestic violence. The type already described, in which physical abuse is used as part of a larger pattern of power and control, with abuse that is more likely to be severe, frequent, and escalate over time, is referred to as "intimate terrorism." This is also the type of domestic violence more likely to been seen by criminal justice and shelter/social service agencies, and the type that has been the subject of most research and policy attention. The other major type of domestic violence, "situational couple violence," is not embedded in an attempt at power and control. It is best described as conflict that spins out of control and escalates to physical violence. It is less severe, less frequent, less likely to escalate, and less likely to be encountered by the criminal justice and shelter/social service systems than is intimate terrorism. The different types of domestic violence have different impact on victims and likely require different prevention and intervention approaches.

Risk Factors

Victims of domestic violence are men and women, of all races and ethnicities, rich and poor, young and old. However, domestic violence is more common in certain populations, which helps identify risk factors. There is ongoing debate regarding gender and domestic violence—are men victims of domestic violence as often as women (gender symmetry) or are women predominantly the victims of domestic violence (gender asymmetry)? It is commonly understood that women are victims of domestic violence more often than men. National victimization surveys (NCVS and NVAW) find much higher domestic violence victimization for women. Female victims also dominate arrest statistics and are more than 90% of the clients seeking help at domestic violence service agencies. For less severe forms of domestic violence, the ratio of victims between men and women is roughly equal. Most of these comparisons are based only on measures of physical violence. If sexual violence is included, domestic violence victimization is more frequent for women. Domestic violence is a subcategory of general violence, and shares some risk factors, including age, substance abuse, and socioeconomic factors. Domestic violence decreases with age— older adults are less likely to be victims of domestic violence than are younger adults. Being victimized by domestic violence is more common for those with substance abuse problems. Finally, domestic violence knows no cultural boundaries, but it is more common among the poor and immigrants.

Risk factors for domestic violence also include characteristics of couples. Couples who are "just living together" or cohabiting are more likely to experience domestic violence than are married couples. Some risk factors for couples are a function of combinations of characteristics of partners. For example, an imbalance of power in a relationship, when a woman's occupation yields higher income or occupational prestige, creates a higher risk for male perpetration of domestic violence. Similarly, a mismatch of attitudes about gender roles can increase risk of male perpetration of domestic violence. It appears that if a man believes in traditional gender roles, but his female partner does not, that increases the risk of his perpetrating domestic violence, although that may only be the case if the economic situation of the couple dictates that traditional gender roles cannot be maintained.

Impact and Reactions

Domestic violence is a social issue that has attracted hundreds of millions of federal dollars for prevention and intervention. This is because the impacts of domestic violence are considerable for victims, their children, and other people in their lives, including family, neighbors, co-workers, and members of the general community. This is especially the case for victims who have experienced intimate terrorism, although victims of situational couple violence experience many of the same impacts and reactions, just at a lower level.

Physical

Physical injury is the most obvious impact of domestic violence for victims, especially if that injury is visible. Victims sustain physical injuries ranging in severity from soreness, cuts, and bruises to burns, broken bones, and internal injuries to, in rare cases, permanent disabilities and death. For women, there is the additional possibility of miscarriage, complications with pregnancies, and harm to an unborn child. Women are more likely to sustain a physical injury from domestic violence than are men, and women are seen in emergency rooms more often for domestic violence–related injuries. For example, the NVAW found that in the most recent domestic violence incident involving physical assault, women were injured more than 40% of the time, and men 20% of the time. Experiencing domestic violence over an extended period of time lowers the overall physical health of victims. This is likely a result of injuries from physical abuse as well as decreased physical health from the stress of the situation and from psychosomatic illnesses.

Psychological

Physical impacts of domestic violence are often focused on by outsiders, but many domestic violence shelter clients report that the nonphysical abuse and psychological impact were much more difficult for them to handle. Research has found that domestic violence negatively impacts psychological functioning across a host of measures. Those who are victims of intimate terrorism may exhibit especially high levels of fear, to the point that it drastically modifies their behavior. Domestic violence victims, compared to the general population, have lower overall mental health, and higher levels of depression, suicidal ideation, and post-traumatic stress disorder (PTSD), along with all of its underlying symptoms, including anxiety, difficulty sleeping, inability to concentrate, hypervigilance, angry outbursts, detachment, and a limited range of affect. Battered woman syndrome (BWS) is a specific form of PTSD exhibited by domestic violence victims, and it is raised as an issue more in court cases than elsewhere. In BWS, a woman's ability to see outside her current situation is severely compromised, to the point that she may see very limited alternatives to her situation.

Behavioral and Lifestyle

Domestic violence victimization has considerable impact on victims' behavior and lifestyle choices in ways that affect the victims, their marriage or partnership, and any children they may have. For instance, domestic violence victims have higher levels of use and abuse of alcohol and drugs than the general population. For some, this may be because they are using these substances to escape their situation or self-medicate for their physical and psychological injuries. Their use of drugs and alcohol may exacerbate the abusive situation and escalate the violence.

One of the most common questions asked of domestic violence victims is why they did not leave. In fact, most women do ultimately leave abusive relationships—on their own, using private resources, or utilizing outside services. While in domestic violence relationships, victims often actively try to manage the abuse. In some of these relationships, victims are successful in managing or eliminating the abuse, although very little is known about such relationships. For those who do leave, leaving is a process, often a long one. The process entails managing the abuse and considering a number of things, including how they feel about the relationships and how leaving would impact their lifestyle, their safety, and any children they have. Although the relationship includes domestic violence, victims' desire is often for the abuse to stop, but for the relationship to continue. Like other intimate relationships, these relationships typically did or still do include love, companionship, coparenting, and fun times together. Victims may not want to lose that, and often feel the pressure to keep the family together. In terms of the relationship, marriages with domestic violence are of lower quality than marriages without violence and are more likely to lead to divorce.

Divorce or otherwise leaving the relationship introduces a number of negative possibilities, including decreased standard of living, perhaps even poverty, residential instability, and homelessness. Some of this is complicated by how domestic violence may have impacted victims before they left the relationship, such as how the victimization negatively impacted their employment. For some, it kept them out of the workforce, while for others, it limited what jobs they could take or compromised their ability to do a job because they were not very productive, were harassed by their partner at work, and had high use of sick days to cover their injuries. Things like this lead to an uneven work history or poor references, which limits victims' ability to financially support themselves should they leave. Leaving the relationship and/or divorce does not guarantee that the domestic violence will cease. In many cases, victims continue to suffer abuse after leaving the relationship, and abuse may even increase as victims try to leave or after they have left.

Children

Victims of domestic violence evidence considerable concern about the effects of the violence on their children. In spite of that conscious concern, domestic violence victimization can decrease victims' quality of parenting. These parents are more likely to neglect or abuse their children, as is the perpetrator. Therefore, in addition to witnessing violence, children in homes with domestic violence are at higher risk of other forms of child maltreatment. For example, it is difficult for domestic violence victims suffering from PTSD to marshal the energy and focus to parent consistently. All their energy for parenting may be exhausted by attempting to manage the abuse and keep the children isolated from it. The reduced quality of the parenting children receive, as well as exposure to separation and divorce, are difficult for children. In addition, exposure to domestic violence has been linked to a number of problematic outcomes for children, the severity of which may in part depend on the age and gender of the child. Children who witness domestic violence exhibit increased externalizing behaviors (e.g., physical aggression, criminal behavior) and internalizing behaviors (e.g., withdrawal), impaired mental health, and lower self-esteem. Externalizing behaviors are more likely for boys and internalizing behaviors are more likely for girls, although increased levels of both are found for girls and boys who live in households with domestic violence. The greatest concern has been a particular externalizing behavior—that of becoming involved in domestic violence as an adult, which is often referred to as the intergenerational transmission of violence or as a cycle of violence. Children who were raised in a home with domestic violence are more likely to be involved in domestic violence as an adult, as either a perpetrator or a victim, but most children do not repeat the "cycle."

Community

Costs of domestic violence are also borne by the community. It is estimated that billions of dollars are spent annually in medical expenses, lost wages, and reduced work productivity. For example, one study estimated that female victims of intimate partner violence cost health care plans an additional $1,700 annually. This is a figure that does not include the increased out-of-pocket costs for those victims in terms of copayments or costs not covered. Millions of taxpayer dollars are spent annually on the costs of policing domestic violence, processing and enforcing restraining orders, prosecuting domestic violence cases, treating and monitoring convicted domestic violence offenders, and providing services to domestic violence victims and their children.

Alison C. Cares

See also Battered Woman Syndrome; Dating Violence; Domestic Violence, Same-Sex; Domestic Violence and Arrest Policy; Family and Domestic Violence, Theories of; Intimate Partner Violence; Women's Shelters/Help Lines

Further Readings

Campbell, J., Rose, L., Kub, J., & Nedd, D. (1998). Voices of strength and resistance: A contextual and longitudinal analysis of women's responses to battering. *Journal of Interpersonal Violence, 13*(6), 743–762.

Johnson, M. P. (2006). Conflict and control: Gender symmetry and asymmetry in domestic violence. *Violence Against Women, 12*(11), 1003–1018.

Kirkwood, C. (1993). *Leaving abusive partners.* Newbury Park, CA: Sage.

Tjaden, P., & Thoennes, N. (2000). *Extent, nature, and consequences of intimate partner violence: Findings from the National Violence Against Women Survey* (NCJ181867). Washington, DC: National Institute of Justice and Centers for Disease Control and Prevention.

Domestic Violence, Committed by Police and Military Personnel

Concerns about incidents of domestic violence committed by police and military personnel arise from the special nature of their occupations. Both occupations involve training in use of force and general deference to their authority. In addition, uniformed personnel often receive the benefit of the doubt when their accounts of events are in conflict with others', even if the other is their spouse. Though police and military personnel share superficial similarities (uniformed service and firearms), the primary link between them lies in the risk factor of exposure of service personnel to highly stressful situations. The two groups are distinct in important other ways.

Military

The link between military service and domestic violence has been brought into high relief by a series of domestic homicides on military bases. These incidents made headlines during a relatively short period of time, and were unrelated except for a single common thread. All the homicides were committed by servicemen who had recently returned from overseas deployment in the Middle East, in either Iraq or Afghanistan.

The homicides opened the door for inquiry into nonlethal forms of domestic violence among military personnel. Incidents of violence that occur in private housing off the grounds of military bases fall under local police jurisdiction, and are reflected in the statistics of those agencies. On-base offenses fall under the U.S. Military Code of Justice rather than the state's criminal code, and are not necessarily reflected in the official data collected by the criminal justice system.

It is possible to argue that an unhappy coincidence of rare events created a media-driven moral panic. However, domestic violence by soldiers falls under a larger umbrella of concerns about the long-term impact on soldiers of exposure to asynchronous warfare. Concurrent studies of the impact of deployment, and particularly combat, on military personnel stem from high numbers of diagnosed cases of posttraumatic stress disorder, suicides, and brain injuries suffered during the Long War conflicts.

It is logical to infer that increased levels of domestic violence may reflect the frustrations and other trauma resulting from combat and combat-theater assignment. Domestic violence may be one of many difficulties associated with making the transition from combat environments back to stateside and civilian life.

Definitive data are not yet available, and it is not possible to make conclusive determinations as to whether the cluster of homicides is a statistical anomaly or the leading edge of a systemic problem. The armed services are treating the issue seriously, however, providing both predeployment counseling and postreturn support. Command-level attention to the problem may not be equal across bases, or even within them. Numerous advocacy Web sites contain victims' assertions that their spouse's superiors failed to treat their complaints seriously, though others report positive responses from the base's chain of command. Minimizing of the offense is commonly cited, as is active discouragement of pursuing the matter because it might jeopardize the spouse's career.

The role of one potential protective factor has been publicized in the mainstream media: the establishment of mutual support systems among the spouses of deployed personnel. Whether these support networks function as a protective factor against domestic violence, or are undercut by the traditional reflex to keep interpersonal troubles private, it not yet known.

Police

Domestic violence by police officers charged with enforcing the law has long been one of policing's dirty little secrets. As with intimate partner violence among military personnel, reliable data are difficult to come by, though for different reasons.

Domestic violence by police officers is often explained as a symptom resulting from the stresses of police work. While generally insulated from the dangers of improvised explosive devices and ambush attacks by insurgents to which military personnel may be subjected, police officers encounter a wide range of stressors in the course of their duties. Rotting corpses, horrible injuries inflicted on children, mutilations in automobile and industrial accidents, and many other events can create trauma. Though police officers have access to mental health services and other forms of relief, they have been reluctant to make use of them. A major reason for this avoidance is a lack of trust in the confidentiality of employer-sponsored services, and the belief that seeking assistance for mental health issues will be injurious to their career.

Police culture has traditionally been based on a "suck it up" reaction to traumatic events. A systemic ethos of "don't take the job home" prevails: officers are reluctant to discuss the most powerful events they encounter with family members, thinking that they are protecting their loved ones from the horror. Keeping those horrors bottled up can lead to psychological changes, of which angry outbursts and even violence are one result.

An older hypothesis asserts that the predominately male police are heavily invested in male superiority. In this view, domestic violence is utilitarian in nature, maintaining male officers' dominance in the household. This theory of police behavior has also been used to explain police officers' reluctance to take seriously the domestic violence episodes that they respond to in the course of their duties.

Both hypotheses are anchored in studies and surveys of earlier generations of police, and their validity in the absence of reliable contemporary data is suspect. Officers entering police service now come of age in a more gender-balanced world than their fathers and grandfathers. Two-officer marriages are not uncommon. Organizationally and culturally, the police have a more nuanced understanding of the impact of job stress. Postshooting teams of officers (who have been shot or had to shoot suspects) are assembled to assist other officers through the steps in the process that follows such events. While the approach is not comprehensive, it is considered far superior to the old "suck it up" attitude, and it has at least opened the door for peer-to-peer discussion of the psychological impact of other traumatic events.

High-profile cases such as the April 2003 shooting death of Crystal Brame by her estranged husband, the chief of police of Tacoma, Washington, keep the issue alive. The Web page of the National Center for Women and Policing cites studies from the early 1990s indicating that 40% of police families suffer domestic violence, compared to 10% of American families overall. The studies were based on answers to questionnaires distributed to relatively small groups of police officers in single locations. Whether those results can be generalized to the occupation as a whole, or whether they represent only a geographically or time-bound cohort, is unknown.

Of greater concern is whether or not police officers actively close ranks, "protecting their own" by failing to respond to domestic violence committed by officers as the law requires. Anecdotal and testimonial evidence offered by police spouses suggests that in at least some departments, this is or has been the case. Whether it is a pervasive condition anchored in the police culture, or simply an episodic aberration, has not been determined.

For victims' advocates, the issue of gatekeeping by the police is a critical one. Police hold the power to define an event as legitimate or "unfounded," and access to police records is often limited. Verification of the phenomenon through official records is correspondingly difficult if the police refuse to acknowledge or record complaints by officers' spouses.

The police do acknowledge in generic fashion that the problem exists: "We recruit from the human race" is a true statement, and domestic violence is found in almost all strata and groupings of humanity. The salient issue remains whether or not the police pursue their sworn duty, or avoid it, when faced with allegations and evidence that a crime has been committed by one of their own.

One plausible reason to suspect police officers' greater reluctance to investigate domestic violence complaints against their fellow officers is found in the 1996 Domestic Violence Offender Gun Ban, which amended the U.S. Code established by the

1968 Gun Control Act (which barred felons from possessing firearms). The U.S.C. Chapter 18 §922(g)(9) prohibits persons convicted of crimes of violence (including misdemeanor domestic violence offenses) from possessing firearms, and the firearm is an essential tool of police work. Challenges to the law have failed in several jurisdictions (*Emerson v. United States*; *Gillespie v. City of Indianapolis*; *FOP v. United States*).

Police agencies have a variety of mechanisms for retaining officers who are temporarily relieved of their duty weapons or otherwise rendered incapable of street work. Light duty assignments allow injured or pregnant officers to contribute (and draw a salary) despite not being fully street certified. Officers involved in shooting incidents are often relieved of their firearms and placed on paid administrative leave: The action allows the officers a relief from the continued stress and affords the agency the opportunity to investigate the incident. Many large police departments have some form of "rubber gun" or "bow and arrow" squad for officers who demonstrate mental health problems.

All of those mechanisms are temporary, however, preserving the officer's paycheck and status within the agency in the face of adverse or limiting circumstances. Postconviction removal of the right to carry a firearm is a permanent condition, one that renders the officer unfit for his or her position. To many officers, that penalty is disproportionate to the offense. Depriving officers of their livelihood is a heavier penalty than that imposed upon other citizens for the same offense. And police officers are far more likely to consider the act within a larger context of the offending officer's service with the department, minimizing rather than accentuating its harm.

Victims' advocates counter that police work demands a greater fealty to observing the law than is expected of the average citizen. Police misconduct constitutes an inherent betrayal of the public trust in addition to the betrayal of marital vows or nonmarital commitment. The act itself calls into question the officer's willingness and capacity to respond to other cases of domestic violence fairly. Advocates also note the various ways that police officers and their agencies get around the law's provisions, from plea bargaining to lesser offenses that do not trigger the law's provision to agencies' outright failure to implement the law.

Domestic violence committed by police officers and by military personnel tarnishes the carefully crafted image of those occupations as defenders of the weak. Developing conclusive evidence of a link to stress of the job or to personality types drawn to police work remains to be done. Establishing the true dimensions in each setting is difficult, and lack of evidence often gives rise to groundless speculation. The offense is a serious one regardless of the offender's occupation, but distrust of the investigative process in both services accentuates public concerns.

Michael E. Buerger

See also Domestic Violence; Family Violence; Intimate Partner Violence; Minneapolis Domestic Violence Experiment and Replication; Victimology; Violence, Theories of

Further Readings

FOP v. United States, 173 F.3d 898 (D.C. Cir. 1999).

Gillespie v. City of Indianapolis, Indiana, 185 F.3d 693 (7th 1999).

Johnson, L. B. (1991). *On the front lines: Police stress and family well-being.* Hearing before the Select Committee on Children, Youth, and Families House of Representatives: 102 Congress First Session May 20 (pp. 32–48). Washington, DC: U.S. Government Printing Office.

Neidig, P. H., Russell, H. E., & Seng, A. F. (1992). Interspousal aggression in law enforcement families: A preliminary investigation. *Police Studies, 15*(1), 30–38.

United States v. Emerson (No. 99-10331) (5th Cir. 2001).

Web Sites

National Center for Women and Policing: http://www .womenandpolicing.org

DOMESTIC VIOLENCE, SAME-SEX

Although scholars have studied intimate partner violence for decades, when it comes to same-sex domestic violence there is a considerable gap in the research, even though the issue has gradually received more attention.

Undeniably, family violence and intimate partner violence historically applied only to traditional, heterosexual couples. So when scholars started studying same-sex domestic violence, attitudes from the public as well as social scientists ran from widespread ignorance to denial; either people believed that same-sex intimate abuse did simply not exist or they clung to stereotypical, sometimes homophobic, beliefs. However, over the years, the recognition of lesbian battering and violent gay male partnerships has continuously been challenging the view of domestic violence as unique to heterosexual intimate relationships. Although violence in gay male and lesbian relationships is in many ways similar to violence in heterosexual relationships, there are important differences. Some consider that gay male and lesbian batterers usually use the same coercive and abusive conducts as heterosexual male batterers, with identical motives and comparable consequences. This might be true to some extent; however, as described in this entry, there are unique features to same-sex domestic violence. This is apparent in the definition of domestic violence in this context and the behaviors that are labeled as violent, but it also shows in the way the phenomenon is somehow still invisible and in the way that many victims do not have anyone to tell.

Lesbian Battering and Violent Gay Male Partnerships

In *Naming the Violence: Speaking Out About Lesbian Battering,* a 1986 book edited by Kerry Lobel, Barbara Hart provided a definition of lesbian battering that could serve as a reference for many. Her definition situates the motives of violence in the victim's resistance to the perpetrator's control. Building on this idea, a decade later, David Island and Patrick Letellier presented in their work a definition of gay men's domestic violence. According to these texts, the forms that domestic violence may take in same-sex relationships include physical violence, sexual violence, isolation, psychological and emotional abuse, threats and intimidation, economic violence, and property destruction. This definition stems in essence from the classical definitions of domestic and intimate partner violence, with one notable exception: the appearance of the threat of "outing." When the abused partner is not out to his or her family, friends, or colleagues, or within the community, the abusive partner may use this secret as a way of control. If controlling behaviors are common in intimate partner abuse, such homophobic control, as named by Hart, is by definition unique to same-sex domestic violence.

Prevalence of Violence in Same-Sex Relationships

For several methodological reasons—nonrandom sampling procedures and self-selection factors, among others—it is not possible to assess the extent of same-sex domestic violence. Studies on abuse between gay male or lesbian partners usually rely on small convenience samples such as lesbian or gay male members of an association. For example, many studies on lesbian battering have surveyed young, White, middle-class, educated women who were members of lesbians' rights associations or attending large social events for activists. These women are probably not representative of all lesbians and their experiences should not be generalized. Until researchers are able to draw a probability sample from the homosexual community, they will not be able to accurately determine the extent of same-sex domestic violence.

Yet many researchers have discussed the prevalence of gay men's domestic violence and lesbian battering. A common assumption is that lesbian battering occurs at a rate similar to that of domestic violence in heterosexual couples. In their pioneer study on lesbian battering, Claire Renzetti and Charles Harvey Miley estimated that between 22% and 46% of lesbians had been in an abusive relationship. As far as gay men's domestic violence is concerned, researchers have been more cautious and few figures have been published. Often-cited works include annual reports done by the National Coalition of Anti-Violence Programs estimating the prevalence of domestic violence among gay male partners to around 25% of couples.

Theories, Risk Factors, and Explanations

Research on same-sex domestic violence is recent. Given that feminism in the late 1960s and early 1970s put quite a lot of effort into developing a feminist analysis of domestic violence, the fear that same-sex domestic violence could be used to deny the central role of sexism in domestic violence partially explained the reluctance of social scientists to address this issue. In a pinch, people could contemplate violence between male partners, but the image of the lesbian batterer broke traditionally established roles built upon the dyad violent husband/abused wife. For some theorists, male violence was considered intrinsic; hence, abuse between male partners appeared somehow logical, whereas domestic violence in lesbian partnerships was unthinkable. Indeed, according to some radical feminists, removing the man from the equation would amount to stopping the violence.

Mainstream gender-based feminist theories have attributed domestic violence to patriarchal values and traditional sex roles stereotypes. However, the idea that sexism and male dominance contribute to the prevalence of domestic violence seems of little help for explaining abuse within same-sex couples. Still, explanatory models specific to lesbian battering or gay men's violence are scarce. Most risk factors that appear to play a role in the occurrence of same-sex domestic violence have been shown to be predictors of violence in heterosexual couples as well. Unsurprisingly, scholars most of the time rely on explanations of heterosexual domestic violence to explain violence in same-sex couples. However, this leads to common misconceptions linking domestic violence in same-sex relationships to partners' role-play.

Domestic violence studies often focus on the existence of two roles within a relationship, those of perpetrator and victim. As pointed out by Renzetti and Miley, within the context of heterosexual intimate partnerships, these two roles become gender specific. Drawing upon studies presenting masculinity as often associated with aggression and control in intimate relationships, some researchers may wrongly conclude that, in homosexual partnerships, the abuser will be a more masculine character, whereas the victim will be more feminine. Following from this is the idea that violence is more likely to be reciprocal in homosexual couples than in heterosexual ones, because same-sex relationships are mistakenly believed not to reflect traditional power and control dynamics.

Beliefs and attitudes are changing, and studies that are more reliable have recently shown that there is as much diversity of roles in gay or lesbian couples as in heterosexual couples. Knowing that mainstream theories may be heterosexist enables scholars to apprehend domestic violence not as an issue of gender but as an issue of power and control, and thus to understand same-sex domestic violence. In any intimate relationship, a partner of either sex might try to control the other partner. According to this perspective, male dominance in the history of the heterosexual family becomes one—although probably the most common—manifestation of the use of violence to control an intimate partner. The key element might then not be gender itself, but the opportunities created by the structure of society and social roles. Sexism creates an opportunity for abusive men to be violent toward their partners, and homophobia creates the same opportunity for abusive gay men and lesbians to exercise control over theirs.

Services Provided to Lesbian and Gay Male Victims of Partner Violence

For decades, battered women have received advocacy and support, mostly at the initiative of the battered women's movement and other feminist organizations. Services have been built on the idea that all batterers are men and all victims are women. In this context, same-sex domestic violence appears to be confusing for many, including social and mental health professionals and criminal justice authorities. Mistakes and misunderstandings are common. Abusive lesbians may be wrongly referred to a women's shelter or sent to mandatory treatment for violent husbands; abused gay men may be sent home with their abuser after the police considered the case as "fair fight" between two men.

It is commonly assumed by both the public and professionals that because lesbians are women, they can simply seek help at battered women's crisis centers or shelters. Most centers do have nondiscrimination clauses in their statutes, yet using gender-neutral wording is not equivalent to explicitly recognizing the existence of domestic violence between female partners and the need for the abused partner to find support. Research has shown that most battered lesbians do not seek help from conventional crisis centers. Either they truly believe that these services are for heterosexual women only or they simply feel uncomfortable going to the centers. Agency services for abused gay men are sparse, and victims are reluctant to

seek assistance from formal sources. Although battered gay men may seek support from individual counselors in diverse settings, these professionals by and large have not been trained to address the specific needs of victims of same-sex domestic violence.

At this point, some scholars have suggested that it may be more efficient to develop services and counseling within the gay male and lesbian communities rather than through the system. Whatever the model, alternative services need to be developed. Programs are rarely conceptualized to fit the specific needs of the homosexual community. Even when specifically designed to help gay men or lesbians, they are mainly oriented toward responding to hate crimes and not to domestic violence.

Victims' Rights and Reporting

Homosexuality is still stigmatized today. Homophobia in the police and criminal justice system has often been documented by researchers as one reason for gay male and lesbian victims not to report domestic abuse. Traumatic experiences of gay men and lesbians run from not being believed to being demeaned or insulted by officials. Real, and perceived, homophobia prevents victims from seeking help, as many fear they will be denied such support. Seeking help becomes even more delicate when victims have not told their friends or family about their homosexuality.

Gay male and lesbian victims of domestic violence often do not have the same rights as battered heterosexual individuals. In many U.S. states, it is not possible to prosecute such incidents as domestic violence because legal statutes require the partners be of opposite sex, legally married or civilly united. Even though, worldwide, more domestic violence laws now explicitly grant the same rights to same-sex and heterosexual partners, there is still a long way to go.

The Role of the Gay Male and Lesbian Community

Ironically, even though lesbian activists were working hand in hand with battered women for the recognition of domestic violence, the awareness of lesbian battering came much later. For their part, gay men were not particularly involved in the movement and have had even more difficulty acknowledging that domestic violence also occurs between gay intimate partners. Traditionally, the homosexual community has been reluctant to address this issue for fear of homophobic reactions or conservative backlash. Alternatively, the concern was that it could be used as evidence of the inherently dysfunctional nature of same-sex relationships. Because of their history of rejection and discriminations, those in same-sex relationships wanted to protect the fragile credibility they have earned. Hence, fighting for civil rights, such as nondiscrimination and the right to get married and to raise children, ranked higher on activists' agenda. Yet, the problem of same-sex domestic violence is compounded when the homosexual community itself refuses to accept the seriousness of the problem.

Véronique Jaquier

See also Domestic Violence; Family and Domestic Violence, Theories of; Hate and Bias Crime; Intimate Partner Violence; Intimate Partner Violence, Theories of

Further Readings

Bernhard, L. A. (2000). Physical and sexual violence experienced by lesbian and heterosexual women. *Violence Against Women, 6*(1), 68–79.

Girshick, L. B. (2002). *Woman-to-woman sexual violence. Does she call it rape?* Boston: Northeastern University.

Greenwood, G. L., Relf, M. V., Huang, B., Pollack, L. M., Canchola, J. A., & Catania, J. A. (2002). Battering victimization among a probability-based sample of men who have sex with men. *American Journal of Public Health, 92*(12), 1964–1969.

Island, D., & Letellier, P. (1991). *Men who beat the men who love them: Battered gay men and domestic violence.* New York: Harrington Park.

Lobel, K. (Ed.). (1986). *Naming the violence: Speaking out about lesbian battering.* Seattle, WA: Seal.

Pattavina, A., Hirschel, D., Buzawa, E., Faggiani, D., & Bentley, H. (2007). A comparison of the police response to heterosexual versus same-sex intimate partner violence. *Violence Against Women, 13*(4), 374–394.

Renzetti, C. M., & Miley, C. H. (Eds.). (1996). *Violence in gay and lesbian domestic partnerships.* Binghamton, NY: Harrington Park.

Domestic Violence and Arrest Policy

As all states and the federal government have addressed domestic violence crimes through their criminal statutes, they have also consistently determined that arrest is the preferred law enforcement response in domestic violence cases. The process of the arrest has been widely studied by criminal justice researchers, especially the use of arrest in domestic violence cases. In the last 30 years, states have moved from treating domestic violence as a private family matter toward treating it as a criminal act against society. This movement, promoted widely by women's rights advocates, has led to dramatic changes in state and federal criminal law.

In the early 1980s, pioneering studies found that when law enforcement officers made an arrest in a domestic violence case (instead of merely separating the parties or trying to mediate the conflict), the arrest had a deterrent effect, and it was far less likely that the defendant would recidivate. Other researchers found similar results, and states began mandating or encouraging arrest in all domestic violence cases. By the 1990s, all states and the federal government had enacted statutes that guide the arrest decision in domestic violence cases.

Mandatory Versus Pro-Arrest Policies

There is a difference between the types of arrest policies that exist in state laws. There are two broad categories of arrest policies for domestic violence cases: mandatory arrest and pro-arrest. In mandatory arrest jurisdictions, a law enforcement officer must make an arrest when he or she has probable cause to believe that an act of domestic violence has been committed. This means that if, based on the evidence, it is more likely than not that a crime of domestic violence was committed the officer must arrest the perpetrator. In these jurisdictions, the victim cannot make a decision about the arrest. This means that even if the victim asks the officer not to make an arrest, the offer must do so anyway, as long as he or she has probable cause that a crime has occurred.

In pro-arrest jurisdictions, law enforcement officers are encouraged, but not required, to make an arrest in a domestic violence case. This means that arrest is the preferred response. In these jurisdictions, officers have some limited discretion in deciding whether or not to make an arrest, even if the officer has probable cause. In some states where the statewide policy calls for pro-arrest, many local law enforcement agencies have individual policies that mandate arrest response. Some agencies state that they want to make the arrest decision easier by removing the officer's discretion once he or she has reached probable cause.

Determining Probable Cause

The determination of probable cause to make an arrest in a domestic violence case can be based on a number of factors known to the officer at the time of an arrest. Determining whether or not probable cause exists is one of the most important decisions an officer can make at the scene of a domestic violence call. Language varies from state to state as to what the officer should believe to establish probable cause. Most combine wording that there is probable cause to believe that an act of domestic violence was committed or, that continued violence is likely. The act typically is one of physical violence and consists of the officer's belief that is more likely than not that the act occurred. This standard is more than mere suspicion but less than proof beyond a reasonable doubt.

Statutory language often directs the officer to investigate to determine the "primary aggressor" in domestic violence complaints. Visible injury, bruising, or red marks are often, but not always, apparent. Interviewing available witnesses, including children in the home, is an important method of gaining information upon which probable cause may be based. The condition of the dwelling or location where the alleged act took place may provide further physical evidence. This may take the form of whether there is disarray at the location such as broken items or indications of a recent struggle.

The demeanor of all parties involved or present can provide further information about what occurred. The victim and offender may be excited, calm, or appear fearful. Officers must question each person to construct as accurate a picture as possible into what happened. There is not always the need to observe a physical injury to document the physical act. The victim's account alone, if believed by the investigating officer, is sufficient to establish probable cause.

If the domestic violence involves stalking or harassment, there may be evidence in the form of recorded messages or caller ID readouts. The existence of a protective order or injunction should be determined as well as any previous reports of assault by the alleged offender. Officers can easily determine whether an active protective order exists by checking law enforcement databases. An offender can violate a protective order by simply going to the victim's residence or place of employment. In most states, the officer's probable cause obviates the need for a warrant normally required for arrest in a misdemeanor crime case. State laws have specified that officers can make an arrest in a domestic violence when probable cause exists. The victim's consent or cooperation is not needed for an arrest to be made or to establish probable cause.

Dual Arrests

Most state laws address the issue of dual arrests. Dual arrests occur when a law enforcement officer arrests both parties at the domestic violence crime scene. In many instances where dual arrests have occurred, officers claim that both parties committed crimes during the altercation. Yet many studies on domestic violence have shown that when there is a domestic violence incident, a victim may try to defend himself or herself during the altercation. Such defense may involve the use of some physical force for self-protection. An officer may find, for instance, that both parties have injuries consistent with the use of force by both. A defendant may have scratch marks or bite marks, while the victim may have facial bruises or contusions. State laws discourage the use of dual arrests, and instead give guidance to law enforcement officers in trying to determine the primary aggressor. If an officer can determine primary aggressor, state laws require that the officer arrest only the primary aggressor, and not both parties. In order to determine primary aggressor, an officer needs to investigate the scene closely and determine the following:

- Who called the police?
- Does the physical evidence show that one party was attempting to defend oneself?
- What is the demeanor of each party?

- What are the relative sizes and physical capabilities of the parties?
- Is there a history of domestic violence between the parties?
- Does one person seem afraid of the other person?

The answers to these questions should guide the officer in determining whether arresting both parties is necessary. Since state laws are clear on discouraging dual arrest, officers need to carefully attempt to determine primary aggressor.

The Use of Victim Advocates at the Scene

State laws on domestic violence also frequently suggest that law enforcement officers utilize victim advocates at the crime scene whenever possible. Victim advocates can assist victims and their children by providing emotional support. Victims may prefer to talk to victim advocates instead of law enforcement officers, and may be more willing to speak to civilians than to uniformed officers. Victim advocates employed by either a law enforcement agency or a prosecutor's office can assist in preparing a victim for what he or she may potentially face in deposition or court. The victim advocate can assist in the filing of a protective order or injunction and in filing for victim crime compensation funds where available. Victim advocates also serve the important function of following up with the victim days or weeks after the incident occurred.

Implications of Arrest

When there is an arrest in a domestic violence case, most state laws require specific conditions. One of the most common conditions is that the perpetrator cannot be released on bond until after a first appearance in front of a judge. Most first appearances do not happen until the day following the arrest. This means that most offenders will be required to spend some time in jail, and must wait to have their cases evaluated by a judge before release. This condition is a way to protect victims of domestic violence from the difficult situation of having an offender arrested and then quickly released to return home. When a judge conducts a first appearance hearing, the judge can review the defendant's prior history, can allow the victim to give input on whether the

offender should be released, and can determine whether any other special conditions should be placed on the defendant's release from jail pending the next court appearance.

When a law enforcement officer makes an arrest in a domestic violence case, state laws require the officer or agency to send a copy of the arrest report to the local domestic violence shelter. This process serves as a check within the system and assists the shelters in making contact with victims to provide follow-up services and support. The provision of the arrest report is typically mandated within 24 hours.

Model Law Enforcement Policies

Since state statutes have become so specific on the use of arrest in domestic violence cases, it is imperative that law enforcement agencies continue to provide training to their officers on handling domestic violence calls. These cases require special investigation, and officers need training on understanding the dynamics of domestic violence. Based upon the ongoing research into what works in domestic violence enforcement, many states have adopted model law enforcement policies. States have encouraged law enforcement agencies across the state to adopt these polices to gain consistency and compliance with state law.

Kimberly M. Tatum

See also Minneapolis Domestic Violence Experiment and Replication

Further Readings

Dugan, L. (2003). Domestic violence legislation: Exploring its impact on the likelihood of domestic violence, police intervention, and arrest. *Criminology and Public Policy, 2*(2), 283–312.

Eitle, D. (2005). The influence of mandatory arrest policies, police organizational characteristics and situational variables on the probability of arrest in domestic violence cases. *Crime & Delinquency, 51*(4), 573–597.

Felson, R. B., Ackerman, J. M., & Gallagher, C. A. (2005). Police intervention and the repeat of domestic assault. *Criminology, 3*(3), 563–588.

Jones, D., & Belknap, J. (1999). Police response to battering in a progressive pro-arrest jurisdiction. *Justice Quarterly, 16*(2), 249–273.

Maxwell, C., Garner, J., & Fagan, J. (2002). The preventive effects of arrest on intimate partner violence: Research, policy, and theory. *Criminology and Public Policy, 2*(1), 51–80.

Miller, N. (2004). *Domestic violence: A review of state legislation defining police and prosecution duties and powers.* Alexandria, VA: Institute for Law and Justice.

Rizer, A. L. (2005). Mandatory arrest: Do we need to take a closer look? *University of West Los Angeles Law Review, 36,* 1–26.

Tatum, K. M., & Clement, K. (2007). An exploratory analysis of Florida law enforcement domestic violence policies. *American Journal of Criminal Justice, 32*(1–2), 45–56.

DOMESTIC VIOLENCE/ FAMILY VIOLENCE COURTS

Family courts and domestic violence courts are nontraditional courts intended to handle cases that deal with social and legal issues. Both types of courts process domestic violence cases. If a jurisdiction docs not have a specialized domestic violence court, these cases would most likely be processed in a family court. Due to weaknesses of family courts in handling domestic violence cases, advocates have encouraged the establishment of specialized domestic violence courts. This entry first discusses the legal history of domestic violence, and then covers the history, philosophy, and structural programming of family courts, in addition to their handling of domestic violence cases. Following the family courts section, the entry describes the history, philosophy, and structural programming of domestic violence courts, as well as a study evaluating the effectiveness of a domestic violence court in Lexington County, South Carolina. The entry concludes with a discussion of the two courts' management of domestic violence.

Domestic Violence Legal History

As a result of the civil rights and women's rights movements of the late 1960s, advocates within the battered women's movement and domestic violence movement organized a grassroots campaign to bring public attention to the issue of domestic violence. In 1966 the California Governor's Commission on the Family recommended the implementation of no-fault divorce proceedings and family courts. Following California's example, family courts were implemented in jurisdictions all over the nation to handle legal proceedings regarding family matters, such as divorce, child custody and visitation, child support, and juvenile delinquency.

In the progressive culture of the 1970s, the domestic violence movement spread the message that domestic violence had damaging consequences for victims, families, and communities. Coinciding with this movement, Lawrence Sherman and Richard Berk published findings from a landmark study about the deterrent benefits of arresting domestic violence offenders. Their study suggested that arresting offenders for domestic violence served as a deterrent to future violence. As a result of the findings from this study, mandatory arrest laws for domestic violence offenders were implemented in jurisdictions throughout the United States. Regrettably, research attempting to replicate Sherman and Berk's study found inconsistent results for recidivism.

Advocates and other practitioners in the criminal justice system began to realize that mandatory arrest laws wcrc not rcsulting in consistent legal outcomes due to the unique social and legal complexities associated with domestic violence cases. Despite prosecutors' offices being inundated with domcstic violencc indictments, only a small proportion of offenders were actually arraigned in court. Many prosecutors felt they were wasting time on domestic violence cases because they produccd vcry low prosccution ratcs. Instcad, thcy discouraged women from taking legal action and pushed them toward counseling as an intervention. In response to the hasty policy actions instituted in the 1980s, the Violence Against Women Act (VAWA) was passed in 1994 to broaden assistance for victims of domestic violence and to increase accountability of offenders. Consequently, funding became available through federal grant programs for the implementation of specialized domestic violence courts. The development of these courts involved the acknowledgement that incidents of domestic violence encompassed distinct phenomena that made these cases inherently different from other legal matters. Because of these differences, many scholars and practitioners argued that these cases should be handled separately, similar to cases that are heard in specialized drug courts or mental health courts. Overall, specialized domestic violence courts attempt to address the underlying source of conflict between the concerned parties, and make victim safety, offender accountability, and offender treatment priorities.

Family Courts

Family courts were established in the United States to deal with legal issues surrounding families in order to protect victims of abuse and neglect, and optimally, rebuild healthy family relations. The focus of family courts includes issues such as divorce, juvenile delinquency, paternity, child custody, and adoption.

During the 1990s, the family court system underwent a series of reforms. Although the family court was originally based on a medical model, with the judge acting as a doctor prescribing a remedy, reforms were made paralleling theoretical advances in the social sciences. The court came to view the family as a system of interactions among family members, and a family's problems as requiring to be assessed and treated through the examination of these interactions, as opposed to by focusing on one family member's behavior. These court reforms were based on the notion that state intervention could prevent social problems by addressing the root of the problem—abusive and negligent families, rather than the punishment of individual behavior.

Family court reforms during the 1990s were also motivated by multiple-case families. A multiple-case family is one that has legal issues that are being dealt with at the same time by more than one court. Family courts were frequently not equipped to handle multiple-case families, and these families would face time-consuming barriers by having to familiarize multiple judges with their specific family issues.

A group of advocates and the American Bar Association proposed a Unified Family Court (UFC) system, under the assumption that for multiple-case families, compartmentalized hearings further damaged their already fractured families. The UFC enables families to have one court that handles all of their family legal problems.

Philosophy

Unified Family Courts (UFCs) are based on a model of therapeutic jurisprudence. This model is rooted in the premise that the law can be a therapeutic agent, one that results in therapeutic or nontherapeutic outcomes for those who come in contact with the legal system. This philosophy encourages the monitoring of the judicial system, so that it is always beneficial to those it serves and reformed when it is not. Because of the private nature of the family and the interventionist quality of the courts, advocates of UFCs demand that when intervention becomes necessary, it must be done well so that harm is minimized. The underlying goal of UFCs is to preserve the family while addressing the legal and psychological issues.

Structural Programming

Under the UFC model, one judge is responsible for case management, and he or she directs a team that includes a case manager, court clerks, advocates, and representatives from social service agencies. If possible, this judge handles a family's case from intake to postdisposition review. Having one judge allows the family to have consistency throughout their legal process, and permits the judge to become familiar with each family and their individual dynamics. It also prevents multiple judges from making conflicting orders due to a lack of shared information, and prevents families from having to make recurring trips to the court. In addition, UFC judges partner with child welfare services and other social service agencies in order to achieve the best therapeutic outcome for the family.

There are, however, some weaknesses to the procedural model utilized by UFCs. Often times the courts' therapeutic approach can interfere with the interests and rights of individuals in the family. Another complication occurs when familiarity with each family leads to judges being lax about procedural details and punitive measures. Family courts can also push cases to be handled through dispute resolution rather than judicial means in order to clear their dockets, which are usually overloaded with cases. Dispute resolution is an especially controversial intervention for child protection and domestic violence cases, both of which involve power dynamics. All of these weaknesses of the family court model can particularly impact domestic violence cases.

Family Courts and Domestic Violence Cases

Domestic violence cases that are heard in family courts provide an example of concurrent legal problems that interfere with proper legal case processing. Critics of the family court system's handling of domestic violence cases purport that custody of children is too frequently given to the offender, or abusive parent. The legal system may be ill equipped to recognize the power dynamics of abuse, and often judges view domestic violence as entirely separate from the ability to parent. Those who support the use of the family court system for domestic violence claim that the parents' relationships with one another should not be a factor when evaluating parental relationships with children. However it is important to note that abuse between parents negatively impacts children, and that partner abusers frequently offend against children as well.

Another criticism of using the family court system for domestic violence is that mediation, a tool employed to reduce conflict between parents, is frequently ineffective in domestic violence cases. The goal of mediation is to reach a resolution more quickly and inexpensively than would be possible in court. Mediation employs a neutral third party to reach a peaceful settlement among parties. Abusers often have the ability and power to manipulate mediation, which leaves victims' feeling powerless, intimidated, and unable to speak openly. Victims of abuse often report dissatisfaction with mediation and feel that participation in the process leads to feelings of disempowerment. If power dynamics prevent victims from speaking openly during mediation, the mediator may inaccurately perceive that their relationship is peaceful and grant joint custody. In addition, mediation, which requires a base level of cooperation between parties, is likely most effective in cases with low levels of conflict.

Despite these problems, mediation is frequently used in child custody cases. A majority of states require mandatory mediation for cases involving custody and visitation. This requirement plays into the power dynamics in cases that involve violence, as abusers may seek custody of children as an additional source of control over their victims. Research has shown that abusers seek sole custody of their children at higher rates than do nonabusers. Battered women frequently report less personal decision-making power in custody agreements than do nonabused women. Victims of domestic violence often describe low satisfaction with family courts, and often feel revictimized by those managing the system.

One final issue is that in many cases family court judges are appointed for life without participating in a meaningful and continuous review processes. In jurisdictions with these appointing procedures, there may be few effective and accessible complaint procedures, which discourage abuse victims from having to face unsympathetic judges or undergo costly and time-consuming complaint procedures.

Family Court Conclusions

UFCs have been established throughout the nation, in a progressive attempt to improve problems facing multicase families in the family court system. Unfortunately, domestic violence advocates feel these courts are not sufficient to handle the unique power dynamics facing families with violence. Many legal professionals acknowledge this problem, and as a result, discourage the use of mediation and acknowledge the problem of judges persistently preferring joint custody despite the presence of violence. The domestic violence community proposes domestic violence courts as another resolution to problems experienced by UFCs.

Domestic Violence Courts

Philosophy

Although domestic violence is categorized as a crime, it comprises unique elements that necessitate these cases being handled outside the traditional court system. Domestic violence cases routinely involve extenuating concerns relating to children, property, finance, and victim safety. As advocates and legal insiders recognize these unique needs, specialized courts have emerged so that these cases are processed differently than other types of crime. Like UFCs, the theoretical basis of domestic violence courts is therapeutic jurisprudence. These courts favor a problem-solving approach over a punitive one, in order to achieve the best outcome for the offender, the victim, and the community.

According to the philosophy of therapeutic jurisprudence, the law is a powerful tool that can have mental health consequences for individuals involved in the case. Domestic violence courts can apply therapeutic jurisprudence in the courtroom by emphasizing the goals of victim safety, offender accountability, and offender treatment. To most effectively achieve these goals, domestic violence courts operate in collaboration with other agencies. Focusing on the need for treatment in legal matters is another important component of therapeutic jurisprudence.

Structural Programming

There are enough differences in specialized domestic violence courts so as to exclude one model that represents every court. Jurisdiction size dictates the number of cases that are processed in courts, and therefore larger jurisdictions require more resources to operate the courts. Similarly, components of specialized processing vary according to the availability of resources. Several common procedural features in domestic violence courts include specialized judges, case screening and subsequent monitoring, intake units, and the provision of treatment services. Case assignment involves selecting judges who have specific knowledge or specialize in domestic violence issues. After becoming more familiar with the dynamics of domestic violence and developing relationships with the domestic violence advocacy community, specialized judges may be at risk of becoming biased over time. However, this risk of bias exists among all judges who work with specialized courts and dockets. Cases are screened to determine if families are involved in other open cases and whether they have a history with the domestic violence court. Due to inadequate technology and/or insufficient information exchange, it is especially important for current court models to have open information channels for the transfer of documents relevant to specific victims and families. With domestic violence cases, effective service referral and provision requires collaborative relationships between the court and other state, county, and community organizations in order to provide all the needed services to victims and offenders. Case monitoring requires coordination of the criminal justice system, service providers, and victim advocates,

involving frequent meetings to discuss case specific information and progress. Other important features of domestic violence courts that enhance their effectiveness are judicial monitoring and victim involvement. In fact, continual judicial monitoring is often reported to be the most effective method for reducing recidivism. Liberty Aldrich and Robyn Mazur outline six key components of judicial monitoring, including domestic violence training for judges, offender supervision, specialized dockets, the creative use of resources, strong relationships with programs and agencies that provide direct services, and the continual exploration of effective methods for judicial monitoring. Offender monitoring is a key component of domestic violence courts. In many courts staff meetings are held on a regular basis to discuss case files and monitoring strategies. Despite various differences in the structure of domestic violence courts, the overall common goals of these courts include keeping victims safe and holding offenders accountable.

Domestic Violence Court Evaluation

One study evaluating a domestic violence court was conducted on the Lexington County Criminal Domestic Violence Court (CDVC) by Angela Gover, John MacDonald, and Geoffrey Alpert. Compared to traditional courts, there were several unique aspects of this court. For example, all domestic violence cases were assigned a dedicated domestic violence investigator who would collect evidence, testify as witnesses, offer "expert" testimony, and serve warrants for arrest. The CDVC also emphasized offender treatment by providing first-time offenders the option to bypass jail time by successfully participating in and completing a 26-week group-based cognitive therapy program. Deputies had digital cameras for evidence collection and were trained on the importance of obtaining thorough reports from victims when responding to emergency calls. The CDVC also used no-contact orders (NCO) for domestic violence offenders as a condition of bond, which prohibits offenders from having any contact with the victims between bond hearings and case dispositions. In theory, NCOs are similar to other civil orders of protection, but they do not require the victim to request that they be in place. In addition, the CDVC had a dedicated victim's advocate who provided general information about courtroom procedures and their specific legal rights, attended court with the victim, provided emergency crisis counseling, and prepared victims to testify.

The results of the Lexington County Court evaluation were positive. Court staff and law enforcement both reported that they perceived domestic violence cases differently after being involved with the court. Case processing was viewed as fair and just by nearly 70% of victims and defendants interviewed. In terms of criminal justice impact, the odds of being re-arrested for a domestic violence offense decreased by 40% for offenders processed in the domestic violence court compared with offenders who had been processed in traditional magistrate courts.

No-Drop Policies

One controversial issue in the domestic violence community is prosecution no-drop policies. These prosecution policies are commonly found in domestic violence courts. No-drop policies are intended to decrease the number of domestic violence re-offenses by prosecuting offenders regardless of whether victims participate in the process or supports the prosecution. These policies provide stronger incentives for police to take accurate statements and to carefully collect evidence. Further, these policies are designed to protect the victim from being held accountable by the offender for his or her prosecution. A criticism of these policies, however, is that they disempower the victims by ignoring their opinion as to whether or not the prosecution should move forward. This may create a lack of trust between victims and the criminal justice system, which could decrease the likelihood that they will utilize the system in the future.

Domestic Violence Court Conclusions

The implementation of domestic violence courts is a progressive movement focused on keeping victims safe, holding offenders accountable, and providing treatment for offenders. These specialized courts are equipped to handle many of the unique social aspects of domestic violence cases more proficiently than traditional courts. In addition, many are based on the unique therapeutic jurisprudence model, which emphasizes the psychological outcomes of the victim and offender rather than merely resorting to punitive measures.

Domestic Violence Legal Conclusions

Using unified family courts to handle domestic violence cases was a progressive response to the overlooked legal issue of domestic violence. However, many aspects of UFC procedures are considered limited in handling all the distinct challenges facing domestic violence cases. Thanks to the response of domestic violence advocates and experienced legal personnel, domestic violence courts have been implemented to address the limitations of family courts. While components of these specialized courts tend to differ, some common procedural aspects are case assignment, specialized judges, screening for related cases, intake units and case processing, service provision, and case monitoring. Regardless of programming differences, domestic violence courts prioritize the safety of the victim, offender treatment, and offender accountability. With the capability of these applied, specialized courts, research has demonstrated their effectiveness in victims' feelings of empowerment and reducing offender recidivism.

Angela R. Gover and Elizabeth A. Tomsich

See also Abuse, Spouse; Domestic Violence; Domestic Violence and Arrest Policy; Intimate Partner Violence; Intimate Partner Violence, Theories of; Minneapolis Domestic Violence Experiment and Replication; National Violence Against Women Survey (NVAWS)

Further Readings

Aldrich, L., & Mazur, R. (2005). *Applying key principles of domestic violence courts in smaller jurisdictions* (Center for Court Innovation Report No. 1–8). Washington, DC: Bureau of Justice Assistance.

Comment. (2003). Developments in the law. The law of marriage and family. *Harvard Law Review, 116,* 1996–2122.

Gover, A. R., MacDonald, J. M., & Alpert, G. A. (2003). Combating domestic violence: Findings from an evaluation of a local domestic violence court. *Criminology and Public Policy, 3,* 109–132.

Sherman, L. W., & Berk, R. A. (1984). The specific deterrent effect of arrest for domestic assault. *American Sociological Review, 41,* 261–272.

Wexler, D. B., & Winick, B. J. (1996). *Law in a therapeutic key: Developments in therapeutic jurisprudence.* Durham, NC: Carolina Academic Press.

Winick, B. J. (1997). The jurisprudence of therapeutic jurisprudence. *Psychology Public Policy & Law, 3,* 184–206.

DOMESTIC VIOLENCE FATALITY REVIEW TEAM

A domestic violence fatality is a fatality where a relative or a current or former intimate partner is believed to have played a role in the death. The majority of these deaths are of women who are killed by their intimate partners. Intimate partner abuse and homicide is a leading cause of injury and death to young women in the United States. A *domestic violence fatality review team* (also called *intimate partner violence fatality review* and *female fatality review board*) is a multidisciplinary team of medical examiners, law enforcement, social service providers, and others. Domestic violence fatality review teams review the events leading up to and including the deaths to identify "red flags" of escalating lethality preceding the deaths and points where prevention and intervention might have been possible. Some teams study a subset of these deaths, such as deaths of women, or deaths by intimate partners, and others include homicide by all intimate partners and other family members. As of 2008, review boards operated in 35 U.S. states with several states having multiple review boards; in Ontario, Canada; and in all four branches of the U.S. military.

The boards work to strengthen communication and develop partnership between agencies providing services to victims of domestic violence. Typically review teams release reports with aggregate data and specific recommendations to prevent future domestic violence and improve the community response to victims.

Specifics of Fatality Review

The frameworks used to establish review boards vary. All are confidential and most have each member sign a confidentiality agreement. Some are established at the state level by legislation (20 states) or executive order (2 states), and some have provisions so that members cannot be subpoenaed and proceedings cannot be used in court or for disciplinary actions. Other review boards are inter-agency and are at the county or city level. Many boards only review closed cases (the perpetrator was found guilty, and appeals have been exhausted) or homicide–suicides. Other boards with protection from subpoena and civil lawsuit might review closed and open cases. Some boards run by domestic violence coalitions or nongovernmental groups might rely on public records.

Fatality review boards determine the scope of fatalities they will review. Some review all female fatalities of all causes in a geographic area, some review all intimate partner homicides (male and female), some include all family homicides and all intimate partner homicides, some include homicides by "sexual competitors," and some are considering including female suicides where abuse was decided to be a contributing factor to the death, or some deaths due to HIV, deaths of sex workers, or deaths during sexual assaults or kidnappings. Some teams review a small number of cases and delve into sociological, cultural, economic, and psychological detail, while others may review many cases and review less data per case. A new trend is to review "near misses" where a victim survived a nearly lethal assault. Deaths are identified from many sources, including police and prosecutor databases, newspapers, and the medical examiners' files.

Review boards typically have members from the medical examiner's office or coroners, a district attorney or prosecutor, a legal aid lawyer, a law enforcement officer, a court administrator, a private business member, emergency room representative, victim advocate, public defender, public health agency person, a child protective services officer, animal control officer, mental health/social worker, school representative, media person or expert, public or other housing specialist, researcher or statistician and a batterer intervention worker. Other members can include clerical support staff, a civil and criminal judge, a domestic violence service provider, clergy, probation/parole officer, someone from the office of the court administration, citizens at large, or state-level representatives.

Often review board members donate their time and are granted time off from regular duties. Some boards have funding at the state level or from a domestic violence initiative, or grants to pay for costs relating to preparation of reports.

The type of data that are reviewed varies depending on whether the review board uses only public records, has access to some private records, or has the ability to subpoena. Some boards interview witnesses and some boards have the authority to subpoena agencies and records. Records that might be reviewed include court transcripts; police homicide files and investigator reports; police call transcripts and prior calls to 911; medical examiner files, including autopsies; crime scene data and investigations; newspaper reports; details of prior protection orders and related court hearings; civil and family court records regarding divorce, custody, and parental rights; criminal, parole, and probation histories of victims and perpetrators; child and family services records; psychological evaluations from police, court, or other public providers; records from workplace such security logs; domestic violence shelters or agencies the victim was in contact with prior to death; information on weapons used, purchased, or confiscated; school records; and substance abuse and treatment records.

Fatality review boards generally release a report with aggregate data and/or recommendations. Typical data collected includes age, sex, race, and ethnicity of victim and perpetrator and location of the assault and death (urban or rural, home or work). Also reported are risk factors for homicide such as prior abuse, recent divorce/separation, possessiveness/jealousy by abuser, suicidality of abuser, threat to kill victim, substance or alcohol abuse, criminal history of the perpetrator, perpetrator history of violence and firearms, weapon used, presence of gun in home, presence of children during assault. Also, information is collected about services used by the victim prior to the fatality, such as police calls, hospital visits, restraining orders, or court visits. Some boards interview friends and family members of victims to learn about events preceding the death. The aggregate data are used to refine risk factors for homicide in relationships with domestic violence. Several risk assessment and lethality assessment tools are in use in medical, social service, and other settings for women to use to evaluate their relationships.

Recommendations by review teams have already been implemented in several jurisdictions. The multidisciplinary nature of teams brings together psychologists, police officers, physicians, pathologists, and sociologists. This helps each agency improve its delivery of services. For example, in Washington State the review process illustrated the dangers of family killings by suicidal abusers. Now a state-level police chief recommendation has been made that has law enforcement responders ask about homicidal and suicidal threats or tendencies. If such dangers exist, there are procedures in place to deal with the now recognized risk. The sociological and cultural viewpoint used by many teams has unveiled some challenges specific to groups such as immigrants, gay men and lesbians, and urban African Americans. Multiple teams found that often one family member, at times even a young child, is used to interpret for police officers. As a result, many review boards have recommended and set up local networks for law enforcement to obtain trained interpreters with domestic violence experience.

Also, greater use of electronic and other methods of communication between agencies have closed some gaps so that police, courts, and social service agencies have access to all the available information when working with victims and families facing abuse and violence.

Heather E. Finlay-Morreale

See also Domestic Violence; Homicide, Victim Advocacy Groups

Further Readings

McHardy, L. W., & Hofford, M. (1999). *Domestic violence fatality reviews: Recommendations from a national summit*. Washington, DC: U.S. Department of Justice, Office of Justice Programs, Office for Victims of Crime.

National Domestic Violence Fatality Review Initiative. (2008). *Guiding principles and themes: FAQs*. Retrieved July 20, 2008, from http://www.baylor.edu/ndvri

Websdale, N. (2003). Reviewing domestic violence deaths. *National Institute of Justice Journal Special Research Bulletin on Intimate Partner Homicide, 250,* 26–31.

Websdale, N., Town, M., & Johnson, B. (1999, May). Domestic violence fatality reviews: From a culture of blame to a culture of safety. *Juvenile and Family Court Journal, 50,* 61–74.

Wilson, J. S., & Websdale, N. (2006). Domestic violence fatality review teams: An interprofessional model to reduce deaths. *Journal of Interprofessional Care, 20*(5), 535–544.

Double Victimization

There is a growing recognition that crime victims are twice victimized or suffer double victimization. Double victimization implies that victims incur costs during two distinct periods. First, they sustain a variety of losses directly from the criminal incident. Afterwards, when victims turn to the criminal justice system seeking redress, they encounter even more obstacles and must absorb additional costs. In other words, cooperating with the authorities and venturing into the halls of justice exacerbates, rather than ameliorates, the situation. Thus, double victimization refers to the immediate suffering from the criminal episode and the later negative experiences stemming from exposure to an errant criminal justice system.

These experiences carry serious ramifications. Citizens may feel alienated, instead of protected, by the criminal justice system. Results from the annual National Crime Victimization Survey (NCVS) have uncovered the persistent existence of a substantial "dark figure of crime" (i.e., number of unreported crimes). More than half the violent victimization incidents and 4 out of every 10 property crimes in the United States go unreported to the police. In addition, public opinion surveys reveal that a considerable portion of the citizenry worries about becoming victimized. It appears that the court and the correctional systems do not cultivate confidence. Convicted offenders seldom serve their entire sentences, and high recidivism rates, especially among early releases, remain the norm. Essentially, the system is failing to safeguard its constituency and public confidence is eroding.

This essay inventories crime-related losses and elaborates on system-related costs. These expenditures culminate in a very significant impact. In general, victims recognize that one way to reduce or minimize these intrusions is to avoid any future involvement with the criminal justice system. Seen in this light, disenchantment, as opposed to apathy, compels people not to get involved with the police, the prosecution, and the courts.

Meanwhile, officials have come to the realization that they need to address victim concerns to keep the system functioning. Prosecutors have established victim-witness programs in an effort to encourage victims to participate. These initiatives aim to make the criminal justice system appear more "friendly" and to lower the perceived costs of participation. While the program personnel may have good intentions, critics remain wary. They label these court-supported programs "prosecutory assembly lines." Dissenters note that prosecutors marginally invest no more than what is necessary to induce witnesses to cooperate and aid in convictions.

Double victimization has a dire impact. The ongoing study of victims and the costs of crimes needs to focus on creating the appropriate incentives to encourage victim participation in the justice system. To appreciate the plight of victim-witnesses, the remainder of this entry explores the different stages of victimization, the incurrent costs, and the established social service programs available throughout the process.

The First Insult

The criminal incident marks the first time that the victim suffers losses. Direct costs can include physical injury, medical expenses, property loss or damage, time missed from work, loss of income, and decreased productivity from sustained injuries. Being a crime victim also affects the victim's surrounding network of family members and friends (*derivative victims*) as the victim continues to suffer from pain and emotional damages.

When a person is victimized, there is immediate harm to the professional and personal aspects of his or her life. Costs are not simply pecuniary; they can also involve a victim's future interactions with other people and society. There are two types of costs: explicit and implicit. *Explicit costs* are sufferings that one can quantify easily. Property losses, medical or mental health care, victim services, and death expenses would be some examples of explicit costs. *Implicit costs* involve what a victim would have done or would have been able to do had the crime not taken place. While these items are more difficult to estimate, implicit costs may include lost wages due to missed work hours and decreased productivity, absences from school, permanent pain and suffering, diminished levels of affection, worsened quality of life, fear of future crimes, and generation effects that carry over to children, family, or co-workers. The combination of explicit and implicit costs makes it extremely difficult, if not impossible, to pinpoint correctly a victim's appropriate compensation.

The 2005 NCVS documented losses exceeding $17 billion for selected personal and property crimes. Earlier NCVS estimates for 10 common crimes pegged crime-related damage at $1,800 per capita. This figure ignores monetary losses due to such things as statutory violations, tax evasion, white-collar crime, corporate malfeasance, and other criminal matters. Placed in a different context, violent crime is responsible for 3% of all health care spending, 14% of injury-related medical expenditures, and a loss equal to 1% of domestic wage earnings.

While implicit costs are harder to assess, fear of crime affects many citizens. Ongoing Gallup polls and other surveys show that a substantial portion of the public is fearful of crime. Many Americans avoid going out alone or being in certain places, have altered their routines in response to crime, and have adopted precautionary measures such as installing home security devices or purchasing weapons for self-protection. Such ripple effects further detract from people's quality of life.

The Second Insult

The impact of a crime does not cease once the physical wounds heal or when missing property is recovered. People turn to the legal system for justice. As victims fight for their rights, they encounter additional costs that may be beyond their control. Rarely are victims reimbursed. Even when they do receive reparation, the amounts are often nominal in comparison to the actual suffering. Navigating the halls of justice can turn into an obstacle course that quickly deteriorates into an ordeal.

Most victims and witnesses will be served with a subpoena once the criminal trial is scheduled or placed on the docket. A *subpoena* is a legal document commanding the recipient to appear at the courthouse or other location at a specified time for the

purpose of giving testimony. Failure to comply with a subpoena can result in a contempt of court citation and other penalties. The usual practice is to require all the witnesses to appear at the start of the proceeding, even though it is impossible for each of them to testify at the same time. In some instances, the lawyers may have prepared motions to file or wish to bring other matters to the court's attention before any witness testimony can begin. If the judge grants a request for a continuance, then the witnesses will be instructed that their service is not needed at this moment. Instead, they will have to return at a later date.

The legal procedures, case delays, long times waiting to testify, and impersonal interactions with justice system representatives can be frustrating and bewildering. Witnesses may lose time from work, which may translate into lost wages and lower productivity. Waiting conditions might be uncomfortable. In addition, witnesses have to provide their own transportation to the courthouse and also pay for parking after they arrive. Persons with infants or young children must make arrangements for child care and after-school activities. At the same time, trials are seldom swift; punishments never occur as quickly as a victim experienced the original crime. As a result, discontent is common when victims and witnesses experience this second stage of incurred costs.

Implications

Victims and witnesses may believe that the system does not have their best interests at heart. Cooperating with the authorities and getting involved in the prosecution may further increase their losses. While a victim may not be able to avoid the first insult, the choice to call the police and get involved with the rest of the criminal justice system is completely voluntary and controllable. If these secondary costs become excessive, victims may elect to treat the crime as a *sunk cost*. In other words, although the crime-related losses have already occurred and are not recoverable, there is no need to run up additional costs. Victims and witnesses can minimize the remaining secondary losses by refusing to participate further.

There are some indications that such a wave is taking place already. The NCVS reveals that half the violent crimes and 40% of property victimizations are not reported to the police. Data from the *Sourcebook of Criminal Justice Statistics* indicate there is no "truth in sentencing." Convicted felons are typically released after serving approximately half their prison sentences. Annual Gallop polls show that public confidence in the criminal justice system continues to ebb. Slowly, but surely, Americans are losing their enthusiasm for this institution.

While some system representatives denounce victims as being apathetic and uncaring, it can be argued that such a portrayal is self-serving. If a case progresses too slowly, emotional and personal costs continue to grow. If the justice system appears unfriendly, it runs the risk that victims will feel disregarded. As the costs multiply and the benefits to participation remain fixed, the victim confronts a complex decision. Hence, there is an intense need for an efficient, visible, and trustworthy mechanism that can address victim needs.

Victim-Witness Management Projects

System personnel are generally aware of this eroding base of support. Prosecutors realize they need to take corrective action to address the problems that compromise victim and witness participation in the system. One avenue is to deal with issues surrounding the second insult. If the goal is to preserve the testimonial value of victims and witnesses, then officials need to make the courthouse experience more user-friendly.

Early studies found that many people were unaware of what went on inside the halls of justice. The federal government began promoting victim-witness management programs by providing seed money to local prosecutors during the 1970s. The original thrust concentrated mainly on court-related services. Informative brochures designed to demystify the system accompanied subpoena deliveries. Instead of merely receiving a subpoena that commanded their appearance, witnesses were handed additional materials that contained directions to the courthouse, parking information, contact telephone numbers, an explanation of what transpires in court cases, tips on how to dress and behave on the stand, reminders about securing their witness fees, and the like. Structural improvements were also made at the courthouse. Information booths were placed in the vestibules where victims and witnesses could check-in upon arrival and be

directed to waiting areas. Making televisions, newspapers, and other reading materials available in waiting rooms made the passage of time more tolerable. Escorting witnesses through the maze of hallways to their destinations when it came time to testify made the courthouse seem less formidable.

As time went by and experience mounted, many victim-witness projects expanded into allied areas. Notification services informed witnesses of cancellations or continuances so they would not make an unnecessary trip to the courthouse. Personnel helped victims get their property returned after a case was disposed. In short, an effort was made to provide more comprehensive services to victims and witnesses as their cases threaded their way through the system. More than 250 witness management programs were in place by 1980.

The federal government did not intend to underwrite these ventures permanently. Gradually, financial responsibility shifted to state and local governments. Because of strained budgets, funding for these peripheral programs was often cut back. As quickly as they had begun, it looked as if victim-witness programs would disappear from the legal landscape.

Around the same time that victim-witness programs saw their monies dwindling, President Ronald Reagan formed the Task Force on Victims of Crime. Its mandate was to analyze the criminal justice system. The task force held public hearings at various locations throughout the United States. Citizens provided disturbing accounts of how the system mistreated victims and witnesses in their quest for justice. In the end, the task force crafted a series of recommendations urging prosecutors to take remedial steps to alleviate the plight of victims and witnesses once they entered the local courthouse.

The Department of Justice issued a follow-up report in 1986, titled *Four Years Later*, which monitored compliance with the 1982 task force's recommendations. It seemed as if the system was improving tremendously. In 1998, another report (*New Directions From the Field*) took stock of the field. While progress was evident, there was still room for improvement.

Dissenting Voices

As mentioned above, critics have labeled court-based programs as nothing more than "prosecutory assembly lines." They also accuse bureaucrats of placing the needs of their organizations before the best interests of the clients. In other words, opponents claim that victim-witness programs are not sufficiently sensitive to what it is that ails victims. Little is done to address injuries that stem from the "first insult," and the costs of the "second insult" are handled in a very superficial manner. The solution, according to some observers, is to either craft a more genuine approach to victim-witness programs or eliminate these services entirely.

As victims look to minimize their costs, dissenters note that prosecutors marginally invest no more than what is necessary to gain witness cooperation and acquire convictions. Sensitive cases should require more slowly developed rapport, children necessitate specialized treatment and methods, and advocates should include opportunities for postadjudication meetings with victims. If service delivery were improved, victims would emerge more satisfied. In turn, the likelihood of their participating again in the justice system, should it be necessary, would increase.

Moreover, current victim-witness services employ a fix-it-up, rather than a preemptive, strategy. Victim programs need to treat all victims. Instead, suitable clients are culled from a preselected group of criminal victims. Only those persons who report the episode to the authorities and subsequently cooperate with the investigation are accepted. The attrition at this point may be large if victims perceive the justice system as a dysfunctional institution. Of those cases that do continue, participation is limited to incidents where the police have identified and captured a suspect. In the end, services are rendered to a small subset of the victims who enter the halls of justice, which itself is a mere sliver of all afflicted people. Few give a second thought to the citizens who rationally choose to avoid the system.

Final Thoughts

Initially, victims are not in a strategic position where they can anticipate the full array of costs that will be foisted upon them. At best, they may anticipate the costs from the first insult. But few people are able to fathom, let alone predict, the second battery of expenses that awaits them. As victims are funneled through the system, there are numerous opportunities for them to revolt and withdraw. Given the myriad costs and the escalating price that continued participation extracts, a person may choose not to testify or pursue the accused. In these situations, the victim is not apathetic—he or she is an active protestor. In a sense, the system's inadequacies have bred its own opposition.

Those parties who persist through adjudication may be too exhausted and dismayed to ever get involved again with the criminal justice system. There are programs designed to help ease some of those incurred costs, but the data are sparse as to whether these initiatives achieve the desired goals. Victims and witnesses are crucial to our justice system. Those designing policies need to avoid creating economic and other hardships that discourage them from participating in the criminal justice process.

William M. Doerner and William G. Doerner

See also Critical Victimology; Economic Costs of Victimization; Fear of Crime; National Crime Victimization Survey (NCVS); Nonreporting/Failure to Report Victimization; President's Task Force on Victims of Crime, 1982; Victim Assistance Programs, United States; Victim-Witness Projects; Witness Assistance Programs

Further Readings

Ash, M. (1972). On witnesses: A radical critique of criminal court procedures. *Notre Dame Lawyer, 48,* 386–425.

Cassell, P. G. (1997). *Statement before the Committee on the Judiciary, United States Senate, concerning a constitutional amendment protecting the rights of crime victims on April 16, 1997.* Retrieved from http://www.law.utah.edu/faculty/bios/cassellp/website/test97.htm

Davis, R. C. (1983). Victim/witness noncooperation: A second look at a persistent phenomenon. *Journal of Criminal Justice, 11,* 287–299.

DeFrances, C. J., Smith, S. K., & Does, L. V. D. (1996). *Prosecutors in state courts, 1994.* Washington, DC: U.S. Department of Justice.

Miller, T. R., Cohen, M. A., & Wiersema, B. (1996). *Victim costs and consequences: A new look.* Washington, DC: National Institute of Justice.

Office for Victims of Crime. (1998). *New directions from the field: Victims' rights and services for the 21st century.* Washington, DC: U.S. Department of Justice.

The President's Task Force on Victims of Crime. (1982). *Final report*. Washington, DC: U.S. Government Printing Office.

Tomz, J. E., & McGillis, D. (1997). *Serving crime victims and witnesses* (2nd ed.). Washington, DC: U.S. Department of Justice.

U.S. Attorney General. (2005). *Attorney General guidelines for victim and witness assistance*. Washington, DC: U.S. Department of Justice, Office for Victims of Crime.

U.S. Department of Justice. (1986). *Four years later: A report on the President's Task Force on Victims of Crime*. Washington, DC: U.S. Government Printing Office.

Web Sites

City of Jacksonville Victim Services: http://www.coj.net

Clark County Victim/Witness Services: http://www .clarkprosecutor.org/html/victim/victim.htm

National District Attorneys Association: http://www .ndaa.org

U.S. Department of Justice, Office for Victims of Crime: http://www.ojp.usdoj.gov/ovc

DRUG ABUSE RESISTANCE EDUCATION (D.A.R.E.)

Drug Abuse Resistance Education (D.A.R.E.) is a set of school-based programs designed to prevent drug use among students of different age groups. Substance abuse, including excessive alcohol use, drug abuse, and smoking, accounts for approximately one quarter of all deaths in the United States every year. Thus, society has a vested interest in developing programs that are effective in preventing substance abuse. A focus on school-age children is a reasonable strategy for preventing drug abuse, and schools, with their captive audience of students, would seem to be an ideal environment in which to introduce new programs.

The D.A.R.E. Program

The D.A.R.E. program was introduced in Los Angeles, California, in 1983 as a partnership between the Los Angeles Police Department and the local school district. The program has expanded dramatically over the years to become the largest school-based drug prevention in the nation and is now used in more than 50 countries.

In practice, D.A.R.E. is administered by sworn law enforcement officers from state, county, and local agencies who typically receive 80 hours of formal training prior to entering the classroom. Uniformed officers deliver a standardized curriculum in diverse urban, suburban, and rural school districts. Typically, students receive D.A.R.E. instruction once a week for 45 minutes.

There are several distinct curricula across 13 grade levels that comprise the D.A.R.E. package. Schools can elect to participate in one or more program focusing on the following target audiences: early elementary school (grades K–4), elementary school (grades 5–6), middle school (grades 7–8), and high school (grades 9–12). The number of lessons or classroom visits by a D.A.R.E. officer varies by type of program: K–4 program (1–5 lessons), grades 5–6 (17 lessons), middle school, and high school (10 lessons). D.A.R.E. began as the core curriculum for grades 5 and 6 and it has expanded over the years. Because the core elementary school curriculum is the only program to be widely implemented and widely evaluated by researchers, the public's knowledge of D.A.R.E. is largely limited to this component.

The Theory Behind D.A.R.E.

The core D.A.R.E. curriculum was based on several theoretical approaches to the prevention of adolescent health problems, and it emerged from successful smoking program programs in the 1970s and 1980s. Three social psychological approaches to prevention served as the foundation for D.A.R.E.: psychological inoculation, resistance skills training, and personal/social skills training. *Psychological inoculation*, which uses the analogy of medical vaccines and antibodies, is a strategy of exposing students to small amounts of the "disease" (in this case, temptations or pressures to use drugs) in the hope that they will learn to resist or reject them. The *resistance skills* approach directly teaches students the skills needed to resist negative peer pressure and media influences to use drugs. The *personal/social skills* approach does not focus on resisting drugs per se, but instead, gives attention to strengthening the basic interpersonal skills needed for healthy social development. Finally, D.A.R.E. utilizes two additional prevention strategies—*increased knowledge* and *affective education*. By increasing students' knowledge about drugs and the negative consequences of drug use, the hope is that students will be "scared straight" and avoid harmful substances. Also, by providing affective education (e.g., techniques to build self-esteem and manage stress), the assumption is that students will have less interest in using drugs and alcohol to cope with the difficulties and stresses that emerge in their lives.

The Effectiveness of D.A.R.E.

Does the D.A.R.E. program prevent drug use or have other beneficial outcomes? For many prevention programs, there is insufficient evidence to draw solid conclusions, but D.A.R.E. is an exception. It has been studied extensively by researchers, many using the most rigorous scientific methods, including longitudinal randomized experiments. Although the D.A.R.E. program is viewed as effective by most teachers, school administrators, police officers, and parents associated with the program, the research on its actual effectiveness is much less encouraging. Reviews of the best evaluations lead to some consistent conclusions. First, the core D.A.R.E. curriculum has short-term beneficial effects on student's knowledge of drugs and attitudes about drugs, but these effects disappear within a year or two. Second, and most importantly, D.A.R.E. usually has no impact on drug use behavior, and when it does show positive results, the effects are small and short lived. Finally, the potential for adverse effects is noteworthy. One longitudinal study by the University of Illinois at Chicago found that suburban students exposed to D.A.R.E. reported significantly more drug use than students in the control group. Overall, the most sensible conclusion is that the D.A.R.E. core curriculum for fifth and sixth graders does not prevent drug use, either immediately or over time. The drug use of students exposed to D.A.R.E. is virtually identical to that of students who do not participate in the program.

When Science and Advocacy Collide

What happens when scientific evidence runs counter to popular opinion? Beginning in the mid-1990s, the research evidence of D.A.R.E.'s ineffectiveness collided with the views of parents, school officials, D.A.R.E officers, and others who felt that the program was beneficial to their communities. A heated debate erupted between researchers and program advocates that lasted for many years and played out in the media. As a consequence of this widely publicized debate, communities across the United States were under pressure to choose sides—to either reject their local D.A.R.E. program or reject the scientific evidence.

In the heat of this crisis, meetings were called by the federal government in 1998 to mediate the conflict between researchers and D.A.R.E. One of the consequences of this debate is that academic attention shifted away from the (ineffective) core curriculum toward the development of a new middle school D.A.R.E. curriculum in 2001. A 5-year longitudinal experiment was conducted by the University of Akron in Ohio, involving more than 15,000 students in six cities, but it has produced mixed results at best. Students' decision-making skills and normative beliefs (about the prevalence of drug use by peers) were improved in the short run, but drug use was not affected by the program (reports on this study have yet to be published, so it is not possible to see the total picture).

Policy Implications

There are several lessons from the D.A.R.E. experience. First, when a program's popularity is in conflict with knowledge of its effectiveness, decisions to modify or discontinue a program can be slow and painful.

Second, while change can be slow, knowledge can make a difference in policy and practice. Since learning of these D.A.R.E. studies, several federal agencies and many local communities have sought the truth about drug education for the benefit of all school-age children.

Clearly, more research and development is needed to construct school-based programs that work in tandem to prevent drug use for an extended period. Research can tell us whether there are cumulative effects of multiple prevention programs over several years and whether some program components are more effective than others.

Dennis P. Rosenbaum

See also Drug Use Forecasting/Arrestee Drug Abuse Monitoring; Gang Resistance Education and Training (G.R.E.A.T.); Risk and Protective Factors and Resiliency; School-Based Violence Programs, United States; Substance Abuse, Prevention of; Substance Use and Victimization

Further Readings

Carnevale Associates. (2003). *The University of Akron Adolescent Substance Abuse Prevention Study: Progress report for "year two."* Retrieved from http://www.cj.msu.edu/~outreach/dare/newdare_2ndyear_eval.pdf

Gottfredson, D. C. (1997). School-based crime prevention. In L. W. Sherman, D. Gottfredson, D. L. MacKenzie, J. Eck, P. Reuter, & S. D. Bushway (Eds.), *Preventing crime: What works, what doesn't, what's promising.* A report to the United States Congress. College Park: University of Maryland Press.

Perry, C. L., Komro, K., A., & Veblen-Mortenson, S. (2003). A randomized controlled trial of the middle and junior high school D.A.R.E. and D.A.R.E. Plus programs. *Archives of Pediatrics & Adolescent Medicine, 157,* 178–184.

Rosenbaum, D. P. (2007). Just say no to D.A.R.E. *Criminology and Public Policy, 6,* 1701–1711.

Rosenbaum, D. P., & Hanson, G. S. (1998). Assessing the effects of school-based drug education: A six-year multilevel analysis of project D.A.R.E. *Journal of Research in Crime and Delinquency, 35,* 381–412.

West, S. L., & O'Neal, K. K. (2004). Project D.A.R.E. Outcome effectiveness revisited. *American Journal of Public Health, 94,* 1027–1029.

DRUG USE FORECASTING/ ARRESTEE DRUG ABUSE MONITORING

In 1987 the National Institute of Justice initiated the Drug Use Forecasting (DUF) program to complement other drug use monitoring systems in the United States, studies such as the National Survey on Drug Use and Health (NSDUH, formerly called the National Household Survey on Drug Abuse), Monitoring the Future (MTF), and the Drug Abuse Warning Network (DAWN). NSDUH, MTF, and DAWN each examine drug use trends among different populations: NHSDU targets the civilian, noninstitutionalized population age 12 or older; MTF collects data from nationally representative samples of 8th graders, 10th graders, and 12th graders enrolled in public and private schools each year; and DAWN collects data on drug-related visits to hospital emergency departments and drug-related deaths investigated by medical examiners and coroners. None of them collect data from members of the military, transient, or institutionalized populations—those in jails, prisons, and mental hospitals. As a result, these studies underestimate the level of drug use in the United States.

The intent of the DUF program was to gather drug use information from those booked into local jails. By focusing on arrestees, a group known to be at particularly high risk for illicit drug use, DUF provided a more comprehensive picture of local drug use patterns and trends than was previously possible by establishing local prevalence estimates of illicit drug use by arrestees and identifying changes in these rates over time. A secondary goal of DUF was to contribute to the growing literature on the nexus between illicit drugs and crime. Because the population sampled was comprised of people suspected of committing at least one criminal offense, DUF was well positioned to collect data helpful for advancing scientific knowledge and understanding on this topic. Finally, as implied by its name, the program was also intended to serve as an early warning system for community drug epidemics. Because of their high rate of drug use, arrestees could serve to warn the community of impending danger.

To measure the prevalence of illicit drug use among arrestees, DUF differed markedly from the other major drug use monitoring systems, which relied solely on respondent self-reports. DUF included a truly objective measure of drug use—urinalysis—in addition to extensive self-report data. There were two reasons the National Institute of Justice included urinalysis in the DUF data collection protocol. First, urinalysis results would provide a measure of illicit drug use not subject to intentional deception on the part of arrestees. Urinalysis was seen as a way to avoid the problem of arrestee underreporting by obtaining a "true" estimate of arrestee drug use.

In addition to the benefit of having an objective measure with which to calculate drug use rates, the inclusion of urinalysis results in the DUF protocol was an important methodological innovation because it provided a means to cross-validate arrestees' self-reports of drug use. Prior research had established that although people were generally truthful when asked questions about drug use when their confidentiality was assured and they were interviewed in a nonthreatening environment, their willingness to disclose illegal drug use was diminished when interviews occurred in criminal justice settings. If DUF was going to have an impact, scientists and policy makers had to have confidence in the accuracy of the self-report data collected. Including urinalysis in the study protocol permitted researchers to directly assess the validity of self-reported measures of drug use, and from there make inferences about the accuracy of other self-report information.

From Drug Use Forecasting to Arrestee Drug Abuse Monitoring

Was DUF successful in accomplishing its stated goals? The results are somewhat mixed. Incorporation of urinalysis into the DUF data collection protocol undoubtedly was a success. For the first time ever, researchers and policy makers had ready access to drug use data from tens of thousands of respondents that was free from the validity and reliability problems that had plagued previous studies relying on respondent self-reports.

Researchers have made extensive use of DUF urinalysis results to develop empirical measures of the veracity of arrestees' self-reports of recent drug use. This research has consistently documented that most arrestees (though certainly not all) accurately reported their recent use of illicit drugs, with reported disclosure rates as high as 92% for marijuana users, 80% for heroin users, and 62% for cocaine users. It remains an open question as to whether these findings provided researchers and policy makers with confidence in the other self-report data collected by DUF.

In addition, comparisons of drug use in the general population and arrestees confirmed what many had expected: Arrestees were much heavier users of illicit drugs than members of the general population, and were thus influential participants in local drug markets. This reinforced the belief that monitoring drug use among arrestees is critical

for understanding local drug markets more generally. Due to a dearth of research comparing DUF results with measures of drug use among the general population (e.g., substance abuse treatment enrollments and drug-related emergency room admissions), it is less clear whether or not DUF was successful in detecting new drug use trends.

Despite these successes, the DUF program suffered from some serious methodological problems. The most significant issue was the DUF sampling procedure. Instead of using a probability-based sampling methodology, each DUF site employed a convenience sampling procedure. As a result, the data collected had poor external validity—that is, they were not generalizable. A second set of difficulties facing DUF was a lack of standardized data collection procedures, which negatively impacted the reliability of the data collected across sites. There was significant variation across sites with respect to defining the geographic unit ("catchment area") for booking facilities, inclusion/exclusion criteria for respondent participation, and privacy of interview areas. Ultimately, the inability of the program to provide scientifically *valid* and *reliable* drug use data to local policy makers and treatment providers led to its redesign in 1998, when DUF was transformed into ADAM (Arrestee Drug Abuse Monitoring).

On the surface ADAM closely resembled DUF. Just as in DUF, ADAM data collection took place in jails, and the information collected still originated in face-to-face interviews and voluntary urine specimens. But there were dramatic differences, particularly with respect to the procedures for selecting arrestees and collecting the data. The most significant changes were the development of data collection procedures that would be common to all sites, and the adoption of probability-based sampling plans for each research site designed to account for variations in the size and structure of local criminal justice systems, the flow of arrestees through booking facilities, and the types of offenses for which people were arrested. In addition to these methodological changes, ADAM included considerable substantive changes as well. Most notably, the questionnaire was expanded to cover not only arrestees' recent drug use behaviors but also their prior criminal justice experiences, their exposure to various forms of substance abuse and mental health treatment, an assessment of substance abuse and dependence risk, and the dynamics of local drug markets. Finally, although the program was not designed to provide nationally representative estimates of arrestee drug use, the number of ADAM sites was increased to 35 from 24 under DUF to provide a more comprehensive assessment for the United States. As initially proposed, the ADAM program was to include a total of 75 research sites across the United States. In 2003 when the ADAM program was suspended, there were 39 sites participating.

ADAM was fully implemented in 38 sites across the United States in 2000. The National Institute of Justice published data for the first two quarters of the 2000 ADAM data collection from 27 sites in December 2001. These results confirmed findings previously reported for DUF: Arrestees demonstrated high rates of problem drinking and illicit drug use, with marijuana being the most common drug of use in all but four jurisdictions. Cocaine was the second most common drug used by arrestees in every jurisdiction but one. In general, methamphetamine was the drug least likely to be used by arrestees. ADAM results also showed that the extent of drug use varied widely across jurisdictions, lending support to the conclusion that attempting to calculate "national" estimates of arrestee drug use would be not only misleading but also counterproductive. Rather than a "national" drug use picture, ADAM showed that drug use in the United States is a mosaic of local and regional drug use patterns. Finally, ADAM confirmed that self-reports provide conservative estimates of drug use due to arrestee underreporting.

But, ADAM did much more than simply recapitulate the findings of DUF. Because of the extensive instrumentation redesign, ADAM was able to provide much more information about arrestees, their drug use behaviors, and local drug markets. One of the more unique features of the ADAM redesign was the adoption of a "calendaring" methodology. Calendaring is a technique used to aid with the accurate recall of events of an extended period of time. It accomplishes this by dividing a recall period (for ADAM the recall period was 1 year) into "conceptually manageable units" (1-month segments), and then "anchoring" memory around interconnected real-life events occurring within each of these units. Examples of the sort of significant life events used as memory anchors are birthdays, deaths, marriages, separations/divorces, secular and religious holidays, and other miscellaneous events such as the purchase of a new car or starting a new job. Using this methodology, ADAM collected month-by-month data on housing, inpatient and outpatient substance abuse treatment, mental health hospitalization, arrests, incarceration, and the level of alcohol and drug use of arrestees in the 12-month period preceding their arrest.

ADAM also collected extensive information on the characteristics and dynamics of illicit drug markets. Arrestees who had obtained illicit drugs within 30 days of their arrest were asked a series of questions about whether or not drugs were obtained via a cash transaction, some form of noncash transaction, or both; the goods and services exchanged in noncash drug transactions; the manufacture of illicit drugs; drug prices; the quantities of drugs obtained for purchase; the location of drug transactions; the frequency of drug purchases; and unsuccessful purchase attempts and the reasons for them.

The Future of ADAM

The National Institute of Justice terminated ADAM at the end of 2003, citing budget cuts by Congress. In the final year of the program, the ADAM budget was approximately $8 million, but NIJ's discretionary research budget, which was the source of ADAM funding, had been reduced to only $6 million. NIJ's discretionary research budget had been $20 million the preceding year.

In 2006 the White House Office of National Drug Control Policy commissioned Abt Associates, a for-profit policy research institute headquartered in Cambridge, Massachusetts, to lead the development of ADAM II, which continues to utilize urinalysis results to monitor drug use among arrestees in 10 former ADAM sites. Unlike the DUF and ADAM programs that preceded it, each of which adopted a broad view of illicit drug use, ADAM II focuses particular attention on a single drug—methamphetamine—rather than many. Data collection efforts for ADAM II delve deeply into patterns of methamphetamine use and the dynamics of methamphetamine markets.

Brad A. Myrstol and Robert H. Langworthy

See also Gangs and Victimization; Guns and Victimization; Substance Use and Victimization

Further Readings

Golub, A., Johnson, B. D., Taylor, A., & Liberty, H. J. (2002). The validity of arrestees' self-reports: Variations across questions and persons. *Justice Quarterly, 19,* 477–502.

Golub, A., Liberty, H. J., & Johnson, B. D. (2005). The variation in arrestees' disclosure of recent drug use across locations, drugs, and demographic characteristics. *The Journal of Drug Issues, 35,* 917–940.

Katz, C. M., Webb, V. J., & Decker, S. H. (2005). Using the Arrestee Drug Abuse Monitoring (ADAM) program to further understand the relationship between drug use and gang membership. *Justice Quarterly, 22,* 58–87.

Rosay, A. B., Najaka, S. S., & Herz, D. C. (2007). Differences in the validity of self-reported drug use across five factors: Gender, race, age, type of drug, and offense seriousness. *Journal of Quantitative Criminology, 23,* 41–58.

U.S. Department of Justice, Bureau of Justice Programs, National Institute of Justice. (2001, December). *ADAM preliminary 2000 findings on drug use & drug markets: Adult male arrestees* (NCJ 189101). Washington, DC: Author.

U.S. General Accounting Office. (1993). *Drug use measurement: Strengths, limitations, and recommendations for improvement* (GAO/PEMD-93-18). Washington, DC: Author.

Webb, V. J., Katz, C. M., & Decker, S. H. (2006). Assessing the validity of self-reports by gang members: Results from the Arrestee Drug Abuse Monitoring Program. *Crime & Delinquency, 52,* 232–252.

Wish, E. D. (1995). Drug Use Forecasting program. In J. H. Jaffe (Ed.), *Encyclopedia of drugs and alcohol* (pp. 321–391). New York: Simon & Schuster Macmillan.

E

EARLY EDUCATION PROGRAMMING

High-profile shooting incidents in schools over the past decade, and public concern about juvenile gangs and drug offenses in schools, have contributed to the general perception that schools are unsafe environments and delinquency is rising. There is also concern about the number of offenders younger than age 13, as these younger children have a much greater risk than older children of becoming serious, violent, and chronic offenders.

Recognition of risk in early childhood has prompted a number of studies and initiatives aimed at contributing to the prevention of very young offending in the early grade levels. This has led to the development and implementation of numerous programs within educational institutions to address a variety of deviant behaviors, such as substance abuse, antisocial behavior, theft, violent crime, and gang membership. Early education programming can target different categories, such as the individual, the family, the school, the peer group, and the community, and some programs specifically target children in low socioeconomic families.

Many early education programs attempt to change the school environment by creating guidelines, norms, and expectations for student behavior. This is known as *normative education*. Other programs focus on instructional strategies that target students, known as *educational interventions*. This entry explores some of the early education programs implemented in elementary and middle schools that address the various behavior problems in the educational environment by using normative education and educational interventions. While it is nearly impossible to provide an exhaustive overview of early education programs, this entry describes the different types of strategies they employ and provides relevant examples of programs. It is important for those considering implementation of any early education program to examine evaluation studies of the program's effectiveness.

Normative Programming in Early Education

Normative education programming focuses on many behavioral problems, such as bullying, substance abuse, and violence. These programs set behavioral guidelines for children by providing them with fact-based information and attempt to teach them about law-abiding behavior.

Normative Program Examples

Start Taking Alcohol Seriously Program

One example of a normative educational program is the Start Taking Alcohol Seriously (STARS) program. This program has been implemented in school and after-school settings, and aims to prevent or reduce alcohol use among middle school children between the ages of 11 and 14. Youth participating in the program receive brief individual consultations in school or in after-school programs about why and how to avoid using alcohol, and they are provided with a follow-up consultation.

The sessions are standardized and provided by trained adults. A series of eight postcards are mailed to the children's parents or guardians, which provide facts about how to talk to their children about avoiding alcohol. The family program includes take-home lessons designed to enhance communication between the parent and child about prevention.

Too Good for Violence Program

Too Good for Violence (TGFV) is a school-based violence prevention and character education program that includes developmentally appropriate curriculum for each grade level from kindergarten through eighth grade. It is designed to enhance prosocial behaviors and skills and address factors related to conflict and violence. Trained teachers, counselors, and prevention specialists deliver the program, which utilizes between seven and nine weekly 30- to 60-minute lessons. The program also has a similar program that addresses drug use (Too Good for Drugs), which provides information about the negative consequences of drug use and the benefits of a nonviolent, drug-free lifestyle.

Incredible Years

The Incredible Years program targets children between the ages of 2 and 8 who exhibit or are at risk for conduct problems. Aggressive behavior in young children is increasing and occurring at earlier ages, and it may become fixed in a child at an early age and continue into middle school. This program consists of three components that include the child, the parent, and the teacher. The focus is on strengthening children's social and emotional abilities by teaching them how to communicate feelings, solve problems, manage anger, develop friendship skills, and behave appropriately in the classroom. Trained facilitators use videos, interactive presentations, and role-playing techniques to solve problems and share ideas.

School Transitional Environmental Program

The School Transitional Environmental Program (STEP) aims to ease the transition of high-risk youth from elementary school to middle school. This program acknowledges that stressful life events, such as making transitions between schools, can place children at risk for behavioral disorders.

Changing schools can lead to increased anxiety, truancy, poor academic performance, and classroom behavioral problems. The STEP program provides students with guidance, counseling, and specialized instruction to address violence-related behaviors, social competency, and life skills.

Educational Interventions in Early Childhood

Gilbert Botvin has identified five common types of educational approaches, and he relates them specifically to drug use/abuse. The first is *informational dissemination*, which Botvin identifies as the most widely used approach to substance-abuse prevention. Information dissemination views students as passive recipients of fact-based information. Within the schools, factual information often includes school assembly programs with guest speakers, films, antidrug plays, skits, and/or poster projects. Other programs include using older student leaders to address younger pupils about the dangers of substance use.

The second method, *fear-arousal*, emphasizes the risks associated with substance use. This approach assumes that fear is a more effective deterrent than fact-based information. One recent example that uses a fear-arousal approach is a display of a mangled automobile with a sign informing passersby that the vehicle was involved in a drunk-driving accident. Perhaps the most famous fear-arousal approach was the Partnership for a Drug Free America's commercial depicting a frying egg with the narrator warning that "this is your brain on drugs."

Moral appeal is the third instructional method, and it is frequently combined with information dissemination by "preaching" to students about the evils of substance use. This strategy often relies on religious values and appealing to the students' belief in right and wrong.

Affective education is the fourth method, and it focuses on self-esteem building and the development of interpersonal skills. Several programs were developed that are based upon this method and target children in primary grades. One example is the Here's Looking at You 2000 program. This program attempts to prevent substance abuse by focusing on skill development, the forming of healthy relationships with peers and adults, and bonding with family, peers, and the community as an effective mechanism for coping with stress.

Finally, *alternative* approaches provide older children with positive experiences. Botvin acknowledges that while some of these approaches may be effective at decreasing substance abuse, some may, in fact, encourage it. Original programs based upon alternative approaches include youth centers, tutoring, or community service activities. The assumption underlying this strategy is that older children's involvement in constructive activities will take the place of substance use. One example of this method is the Outward Bound program. Outward Bound is a wilderness-based program that emphasizes challenging mental tasks through outdoor adventures and nature trips.

Traditional Instructional Methods in Early Education Programming

Some instructional methods are less interactional and rely upon a more traditional teaching and lecturing approach. Two of the most popular and well-known examples of classic, broad-based prevention strategies are the Drug Abuse Resistance Education (D.A.R.E.) program and the Gang Resistance Education and Training (G.R.E.A.T.) program.

Drug Abuse Resistance Education

Early education programming that addresses drug use prevention has been part of a broad range of antidrug strategies adopted by American public school administrators. Perhaps the most well-known initiative is Project D.A.R.E., which was created in 1983 by the Los Angeles Police Department and the Los Angeles Unified School District, and currently operates in all 50 U.S. states. The program is taught to pupils in fifth or sixth grade, and variations of the program now are being offered in kindergarten and other grades. The core curriculum consists of 17 lessons, usually offered once a week for 45 to 60 minutes, and focuses on increasing students' skills in recognizing and avoiding peer pressure to use drugs. In addition, the program teaches information about drugs, decision-making skills, self-esteem building, and healthy alternatives to drug use. Teaching techniques include question-and-answer sessions, group discussions, role-playing, and workbook

exercises. The kindergarten through fourth-grade curriculum introduces pupils to some of the traditional D.A.R.E. concepts, along with topics that include obeying laws, personal safety, and the legal and illegal uses of medicines and drugs.

Police officers who teach the D.A.R.E. program must first undergo extensive training, which involves 80 training hours in classroom management, teaching strategies, communication skills, adolescent development, drug information, and curriculum instruction. Experienced D.A.R.E. officers who want to qualify as instructors must undergo additional training.

Despite the program's popularity, endurance, and widespread use, almost all evaluations of the D.A.R.E. program show that it has little to no effect on reducing or preventing drug use. Even the program's short-term effectiveness for reducing or preventing drug use is small and shown to not be as effective as programs with more interactive methods.

Gang Resistance Education and Training

In 1991, police officers from the Phoenix, Mesa, Glendale, and Tempe, Arizona, Police Departments, along with special agents from the Bureau of Alcohol Tobacco and Firearms, developed the G.R.E.A.T. program with the purpose of reducing adolescent involvement in gang activity. Similar to the development of D.A.R.E., the G.R.E.A.T. program evolved into a nationwide, school-based program that uses uniformed police officers who teach a 13-week curriculum to pupils at the middle school level, primarily seventh grade. In addition, there are shorter programs available for fifth and sixth graders, as well as for pupils in the third and fourth grades, which can be used in conjunction with and as reinforcement of other prevention programs, and as a precursor to the G.R.E.A.T. middle school program.

The objectives of the G.R.E.A.T. program are to reduce gang activity and to teach students about the negative consequences of gang involvement. Officers who teach the program undergo specialized training similar to that of D.A.R.E. officers. The G.R.E.A.T. instructors use detailed lesson plans that contain clearly stated purposes and objectives with the purpose of reducing gang activity and teaching students about the consequences of belonging to a gang. The program is intended to provide life skills that give youth the ability to resist peer pressure to join gangs. The program attempts to produce positive attitudinal and behavioral change through instruction, discussion, and role playing.

Evaluations of the G.R.E.A.T. program have suggested that it is slightly more promising than D.A.R.E. The few studies that have been conducted of G.R.E.A.T. reported more positive prosocial changes in the attitudes of G.R.E.A.T. participants than nonparticipants as a result of exposure to the program.

Jonathan M. Kremser

See also Bullying; Drug Abuse Resistance Education (D.A.R.E.); Gang Resistance Education and Training (G.R.E.A.T.); Gangs and Victimization; Perry Preschool Project; School-Based Bullying Prevention; School-Based Theories of Delinquency; School-Based Violence Programs, International; School-Based Violence Programs, United States; School Crimes, Elementary Through High School; School Shootings; School Violence

Further Readings

Botvin, G. (1990). Substance abuse prevention: Theory, practice, and effectiveness. In M. Tonry & J. Q. Wilson (Eds.), *Drugs and crime* (pp. 461–519). Chicago: University of Chicago Press.

Bry, B. (1982). Reducing the incidents of adolescent problems through preventive intervention: One- and five-year follow-up. *American Journal of Community Psychology, 10,* 265–276.

Ennett, S., Tobler, N., Ringwalt, C., & Flewelling, R. (1994). How effective is Drug Abuse Resistance Education? A meta-analysis of Project D.A.R.E. outcome evaluations. *American Journal of Public Health, 84,* 1394–1401.

Esbensen, F., Osgood, D., Taylor, T., Peterson, D., & Freng, A. (2001). How great is G.R.E.A.T.? Results from a longitudinal quasi-experimental design. *Criminology and Public Police, 1,* 87–118.

Felner, R., Ginter, M., & Primavera, J. (1982). Primary prevention during school transitions: Social support and environmental structure. *American Journal of Community Psychology, 10,* 277–290.

Greenwood, P. (1999). *Costs and benefits of early childhood intervention* (OJJDP Fact Sheet No. 94). Washington, DC: Office for Juvenile Justice and Delinquency Prevention, U.S. Department of Justice.

Loeber, R., Farrington, D., & Petechuk, D. (2003, May). *Child delinquency: Early intervention and prevention* (Child Delinquency Bulletin). Washington, DC: Office of Juvenile Justice and Delinquency Prevention, U.S. Department of Justice.

Moffitt, T. (1993). "Life-course-persistent" and "adolescence-limited" antisocial behavior: A developmental taxonomy. *Psychological Review, 100,* 674–701.

Winfree, L., Lynskey, D., & Maupin, J. (1999). Developing a local police and federal law enforcement partnership: The sometime tortuous journey from a great idea to implementation of G.R.E.A.T. *Criminal Justice Review, 24,* 145–168.

EARLY VICTIMIZATION THEORIES

Most work in criminology focuses on developing and testing theoretical models of crime that are centered on explicating offender behavior. In developing these perspectives, criminologists often disregard or underestimate the role of crime victims in understanding crime. This is despite long-standing recognition that a comprehensive approach to explaining crime requires an emphasis on offenders, victims, and situations/contexts. The theories that come closest to recognizing all of these elements are those that focus on victimization, particularly lifestyle-exposure and routine activities theories. This entry reviews these early victimization theories with an emphasis on their origins, key concepts, and ability to organize the facts of victimization. It discusses work on victim precipitation and the advent of national crime victimization surveys, which provided the bases for the development of lifestyle-exposure and routine activities theories, and articulates the main arguments of the theories, providing a discussion of their key concepts.

Victim Precipitation

The idea that attention should be focused on the contribution of victims to crime is one with a long tradition, originating in the field of victimology. Hans von Hentig was among the first to articulate this stance, positing in the 1940s that victims often contribute to their own victimization. While recognizing that the provocative behaviors of individuals can contribute to their victimization, his classification of victims also emphasizes that the contribution of victims can result from characteristics or social positions beyond their control. Some of the victim types in his classification scheme include the female, the old, the mentally defective, the immigrant, and the acquisitive. Many of these categories represent the inability of potential victims to resist perpetrators due to social, physical, or psychological disadvantages. The importance of von Hentig's classification scheme is in suggesting that victim characteristics or social positions can contribute passively to victimization.

Beniamin Mendelsohn expanded on the concept of victim precipitation by emphasizing degrees of victim precipitation. His classification scheme focused principally on active precipitation, or the behaviors and actions of victims that contribute to their victimization. Based on his observations as a practicing attorney, he delineated a classification scheme of victims based on legal considerations of the degree of victim culpability. The scheme ranges from completely innocent victims to victims who are completely responsible. In an additional effort, Stephen Schafer provided a typology that combined von Hentig's discussion of social characteristics or social positions of individuals—passive precipitation—with Mendelsohn's discussion of victim behaviors and the degree of victim culpability—active precipitation. This typology includes victims with no responsibility (biologically weak, socially weak, political, and unrelated victims), victims with some responsibility (provocative and precipitative victims), and victims with total responsibility (self-victimizing).

The commonality in these classification schemes is that they emphasize victim precipitation, or the possibility that victims either passively or actively contribute to their victimization. In other words, victim contribution is implicated as a causal factor in crime. Marvin Wolfgang's analysis of U.S. police homicide records marked the first attempt to systematically explore victim precipitation. Defining victim-precipitated homicides as instances in which the ultimate victim was the first in the homicide event to use physical force against the subsequent offender, this study reported that 26% of homicides that occurred from 1948 to 1952 in Philadelphia resulted from active victim precipitation. After

Wolfgang's pioneering study, others assessed the role of victim precipitation in aggravated assault, armed robbery, homicide, and forcible rape. These studies indicated that victim precipitation contributes to a variety of crimes, although estimates of its contribution vary across crime type. Specifically, studies suggest that 22% to 26% of homicides, 14% to 21% of aggravated assaults, 4% to 19% of forcible rapes, and 11% of armed robberies involve victim precipitation.

The primary contribution of these studies to criminology, and particularly to victimization theories, is in suggesting that a comprehensive analysis of crime should incorporate a discussion of the role victims may play in the evolution of crime. However, these studies also served a secondary function in paving the way for victimization theories through the controversy and debate surrounding them. The controversy was sparked in the 1970s, largely by Menachem Amir's study of forcible rape in which the operationalization of victim precipitation included using indecent language or gestures, possessing a "bad" reputation, and consuming alcohol. After this study, the concept of victim precipitation came under attack for blaming the victims of crime for their victimization.

Although the controversy over victim blaming marked a blow for victimization studies and for the appreciation that victims are an important element in many crime scenarios, it also marked an important turning point for victimization research. Specifically, the debate made it clear that victimization research would have to be broadened considerably before it would be able to attain prominence in criminology. The victim precipitation studies focused almost exclusively on the actions of victims, affording little attention to offenders and/or contexts. As such, critics noted that the studies failed to realize that many factors identified as precipitous—for example, drinking alcohol—are present in situations where individuals are not victimized. A clear implication here is that precipitative acts are not sufficient causes of criminal events. Rather, a compelling explanation of victimization must focus on additional factors, including offenders and contexts. In a related vein, some critics suggested that the singular focus on victim behaviors as contributors to victimization diverted necessary attention from the social institutions and cultural values that shape the lives and behaviors of both offenders and victims.

The development of victimization theories in criminology benefited from the lessons learned through the debates over victim precipitation and victim blaming. However, victimization theories were not developed in the immediate aftermath of these debates. Instead, they emerged in the late 1970s, nearly half a decade after some of the controversial precipitation studies. It is at this time that data from the newly developed National Victimization Survey revealed demographic and temporal patterns in victimization in the United States that required explanation.

National Crime Victimization Surveys

Prior to the development of national victimization surveys, criminologists seeking to understand patterns in victimization and crime had to rely on official reports of offending (e.g., arrest statistics). The first national surveys of victimization began in the late 1960s, following the recommendations of a presidential commission on urban crime and unrest. The early victimization surveys provided both national and supplemental city-level estimates of victimization. Due to budget restrictions, only the national estimates of victimization portion of the surveys remained by 1973. The U.S. Bureau of Justice Statistics sponsors these surveys, which are carried out by the U.S. Census Bureau.

The National Victimization Survey (NVS), later called the National Crime Victimization Survey (NCVS), obtains data twice yearly on personal and household victimizations using a nationally representative sample of approximately 80,000 persons in 43,000 households (reduced from 72,000 households in the original NVS). The survey collects incident-based data on victimization episodes (e.g., time, location, use of weapons, offender use of drugs and alcohol, number of offenders, and actions of the victim), victim–offender relationships, consequences of victimization (e.g., extent of injury and property loss), and victims' demographic information. These data are particularly vital for revealing temporal and social distributions of property and violent victimizations.

The demographic patterns in personal victimization revealed in early victimization surveys included the finding that people under the age of 24 are more likely to be victimized than those over this age. Other groups that were shown to have relatively high victimization rates included males, the unmarried, low-income persons, and racial minorities. These demographic patterns have remained constant over time, with the same groups consistently reporting relatively high levels of victimization. However, the time trend data indicated significant variations over time in violent and property victimizations that required explanation. For instance, both property and violent victimization rates increased from the 1960s to the 1970s. Whereas violent victimizations remained relatively stable between 1973 and 1977 and then began fluctuating until the beginning of the crime drop in 1994, property victimizations started a trend of steady decline in 1974 that continued during the crime drop of the past decade.

Explaining these patterns was among the core impetuses for the development of Michael Hindelang and his colleagues' lifestyle-exposure theory and Lawrence Cohen and Marcus Felson's routine activities theory of victimization. The lifestyle-exposure perspective was developed to explain the demographic patterns of victimization revealed in the NCVS, and the routine activities perspective intended to explicate the temporal changes in victimization rates revealed in these data.

Lifestyle-Exposure and Routine Activities Theories of Victimization

Although aimed originally at addressing different questions, the lifestyle-exposure and routine activities perspectives are nearly indistinguishable. Indeed, each theory has been used over the past few decades to answer the questions initially addressed by the other. In addition, both theories focus on explicating victimizations from direct-contact predatory crimes, including robbery, forcible rape, homicide, aggravated assault, larceny, and theft. As such, most scholars discuss the fundamental difference between the perspectives as one of terminology rather than substance.

The lifestyle-exposure and routine activities explanations for victimization reflect the theme that individuals contribute to their own victimization. Rather than emphasizing the active provocation in early studies of victim precipitation, however, these theories link the lifestyles or routine activities of individuals/groups to their rates of predatory victimization. The routine activities of individuals/groups are posited to be shaped, in turn, by structural opportunities/constraints and cultural expectations. Although the lifestyle-exposure and routine activities perspectives are often used and discussed interchangeably, this entry discusses each in turn.

The lifestyle-exposure perspective posits that status characteristics—including age, race, marital status, gender, and income—shape rates of victimization through their effects on lifestyles. Hindelang and his colleagues define lifestyles as the patterns of daily activities individuals engage in during the course of work and leisure. The lifestyles of individuals are deemed important for understanding victimization risk because they influence the amount of exposure individuals and/or their property have to crime-prone areas or persons. That is, individuals who spend their leisure time in bars or other public spaces are more likely to come into contact with offenders than are individuals who spend their leisure time watching television at home. Similarly, individuals whose employment requires work with the public (e.g., sales) are more likely to come into contact with criminals than are individuals who work alone in their offices.

The lifestyle-exposure perspective rightfully notes that where and how individuals spend their leisure and work time is influenced by the very status characteristics—age, race, income, gender, and so on—that pattern criminal victimization. This is because these status characteristics are associated with varying cultural expectations and opportunity structures that shape behaviors and lifestyles. According to this perspective, then, understanding why males are more likely than females to be victims of crime simply requires the recognition that cultural expectations and social-structural arrangements encourage males more than females to spend their work and leisure time outside the home, where they may come into contact with offenders.

Routine activities theory is similar to lifestyle-exposure theory in focusing on daily activities and the social institutions and cultural expectations that shape them. The initial focus of this perspective, however, was on elucidating trends in victimization. The theory posits that changes in victimization trends can be accounted for largely by shifts in social institutions and cultural expectations that shape daily activities. Cohen and Felson note that changes in the culture and social structure that improve the quality of life for groups of individuals ironically may also increase victimization rates. For instance, the women's movement produced changes in cultural expectations and social opportunities for females that altered their daily activities in fundamental ways. That is, more women were working outside the home, attending college, remaining single, and engaging in leisure activities away from the home and family members. These changes in activities increased the chances that women and/or their property, in the absence capable guardians, would come into direct contact with motivated offenders.

This discussion highlights the components identified as necessary for victimization in routine activities theory. These components include the following: (a) a motivated offender, (b) a suitable target/victim, and (c) the absence of capable guardians that may prevent the crime. When these three components converge in space and time, criminal events are likely to ensue. Therefore, the risk of victimization is greatest for persons or groups, in the absence of guardians, whose daily activities bring them and/or their property into contact with motivated offenders.

Motivated offenders are defined by the routine activities perspective as any persons who might commit illegal offenses for any reason. This definition is rather ambiguous because the routine activities approach deals with motivated offenders as given and makes no explicit statement about their motivations for crime. However, the approach implicitly offers that offenders are rational actors who try to maximize profit and minimize pain. The assumption is that the victim-selection process involves a rational decision to prey upon suitable targets who lack guardianship. In holding motivation constant, the perspective focuses primary attention on suitable targets and guardianship.

Target suitability consists of the proximity of potential targets to motivated offenders and the material or symbolic attractiveness of a person or property target. Proximity of potential targets to offenders refers to the physical proximity of potential victims to populations of motivated offenders. Thus, where individuals reside and where they spend their work and leisure time affects their victimization risk. Those who reside in socially disorganized neighborhoods and spend their time in risky environments—for example, nightclubs or bars—are at increased risk of victimization because they often are in close proximity to motivated offenders.

Attractiveness of objects is also a component of target suitability. For instrumental crimes, it is relatively simple to define the attractiveness of objects—small, expensive objects that are not properly secured are most attractive. However, for crimes that are more expressive in nature, including most violent crimes, the precise definition of an attractive target is likely to vary depending on the motivations of the offender. This suggests that a target that is defined as suitable or attractive for theft may not be suitable for a crime such as aggravated assault, vandalism, or homicide. As such, many theorists advocate crime-specific tests of routine activities theory.

The final element identified in routine activities theory is a lack of guardianship, which takes into consideration situation/context. Guardianship refers to the ability of persons or objects to prevent crime, suggesting that the concept has both social and physical dimensions. Social guardianship refers to the availability of people—friends, neighbors, family members, police—who may prevent crime simply through their presence in the situation or through offering assistance to defend against victimization. Physical guardianship includes such things as burglar alarms, guard dogs, firearms, and streetlights that help prevent crime.

Overall, routine activities and lifestyle-exposure theories propose that static and changing social structures and cultural expectations influence the daily activities of individuals/groups in ways that influence victimization risks. These theories take into consideration the fact that motivated offenders must come into contact with suitable targets/victims under situations that are conducive to crime, thereby addressing all of the core elements of criminal events. These perspectives admittedly pay less attention to offenders than they do to victims and situations, which has led some theorists to call for integrations of offender theories and these early victimization theories.

Although the lifestyle-exposure and routine activities perspectives focus on the contribution of victims to their victimization, they effectively eschew the victim-blaming characteristic of early victim precipitation studies. This is because the theories are sensitive to the ways in which the everyday behaviors of individuals are constrained or facilitated by social institutions and cultural expectations. Furthermore, the theories posit a symbiotic relationship between conventional activities and crime, positing that criminal victimization arises from the regular activities of ordinary citizens. Felson notes that by failing to adopt the "pestilence fallacy"—that bad things, such as crime, arise from other bad things—the theories attend to victim contribution without suggesting the victim did something "bad."

Stacy De Coster and Rena Cornell

See also Crime Triangles; Lifestyle Theory; Rational Choice Theory; Routine Activities Theory

Further Readings

Amir, M. (1967). Victim-precipitated forcible rape. *Journal of Criminal Law, Criminology, and Police Science, 58*, 493–502.

Cohen, L. E., & Felson, M. (1979). Social change and crime rate trends: A routine activity approach. *American Sociological Review, 44*, 588–608.

Collins, J. J., Cox, B. G., & Langan, P. A. (1987). Job activities and personal crime victimization: Implications for theory. *Social Science Research, 16*, 345–360.

Curtis, L. (1974). Victim-precipitation and violent crimes. *Social Problems, 21*, 594–605.

Felson, M. (1994). *Crime and everyday life: Insights and implications for society.* Thousand Oaks, CA: Pine Forge.

Hindelang, M. S., Gottfredson, M., & Garofalo, J. (1978). *Victims of personal crime.* Cambridge, MA: Ballinger.

Luckenbill, D. F. (1977). Criminal homicide as situated transaction. *Social Problems, 25*, 176–186.

Messner, S. F., & Blau, J. R. (1987). Routine leisure activities and rates of crime: A macro-level analysis. *Social Forces, 65*, 1035–1052.

Schafer, S. (1968). *The victim and his criminal: A study in functional responsibility.* New York: Random House.

Timmer, D. G., & Norman, W. H. (1984). The ideology of victim precipitation. *Crime and Justice Review, 9*, 63–68.

von Hentig, H. (1948). *The criminal and his victim.* New Haven, CT: Yale University Press.

Wolfgang, M. (1958). *Patterns of criminal homicide.* Philadelphia: University of Pennsylvania Press.

ECONOMIC COSTS OF VICTIMIZATION

The costs of victimization are substantial. Victims, third-party individuals, relatives, witnesses, employers, the criminal justice system, and society in general are affected by victimization. There are economic and noneconomic costs of victimization. Noneconomic costs of victimization often include "intangible" losses such as physical and mental trauma, pain, suffering, fear, and the loss of quality of life that victims often endure. Economic costs of victimization focus on the "tangible" losses incurred as a result of victimization, such as property damage or loss, medical care, police and victim services, and loss or reduction of workers' productivity. This entry describes how estimates of victimization and the economic costs of victimization are derived. It then discusses what constitutes these economic, or tangible, costs of victimization, and provides estimates for the costs of murder, assault, rape and sexual assault, robbery, drunk driving, larceny/theft, and property damage.

Estimates of Victimization: Police Reports and Victim Surveys

Generally, police reports and victimization surveys are used to calculate estimates of the prevalence of crime and victimization throughout the United States. It is important to note that although these reports are informative, they likely undercount the number of crimes, especially crimes relating to domestic violence, rape, and assaults with a gun or knife. Nonetheless, police reports and victimization surveys are vital to understanding the breadth of victimization, as well as the nature of victimization, across the United States.

The largest and most widely used measure of crime comes from the Uniform Crime Reporting (UCR) Program of the Federal Bureau of Investigation. The UCR Program collects annual data regarding the index crimes of personal offenses (e.g., murder, rape, robbery, aggravated assault) and property offenses (e.g., burglary, larceny/theft,

motor vehicle theft, arson) from police departments throughout the United States. While the UCR Program collects a large amount of data regarding these crimes within multiple jurisdictions across the country, it does not include much information regarding characteristics of the victims or account for the "dark figure of crime." That is, the UCR Program data only reflect the crimes that are known to the police, and therefore the program has been criticized for underreporting much of the crime that occurs in the United States.

Because of these concerns, the reports of the UCR Program have been changed over the years to include the Supplementary Homicide Reports (SHR) and the National Incident-Based Reporting System (NIBRS). The SHRs center on homicides and provide additional data on victim and offender characteristics, such as the relationship between the victim and offender as well as the circumstances surrounding the homicide. The NIBRS also supplements information provided by the UCR Program. This system provides information on more types of crimes than does the UCR Program and collects information regarding the injuries and losses incurred by victimization events. Although designed to provide more data on victims than the UCR Program, the police reports detailed here continue to undercount the total amount of victimization throughout the United States and provide limited information regarding victims' characteristics.

Victimization surveys were derived to address some of these concerns. Victimization surveys more accurately uncover the details of circumstances surrounding crime events, as well as the nature of victimization and the characteristics of victims. These types of surveys are useful for estimates of crime and victimization because they measure the crimes that are both known and unknown to the police. The most often cited victimization survey is the National Crime Victimization Survey (NCVS). Although it is a very important measurement of crime and victimization because it provides valuable information on victims of rape, robbery, assault, larceny, burglary, and motor vehicle theft, the NCVS also excludes many types of crimes, such as murder, arson, drunk driving, and child abuse. Supplementing data acquired by the UCR Program with data acquired by the NCVS provides a more complete picture of the "total" crimes and subsequent victimizations committed each year in the United States.

Tangible Costs of Victimization

Victimization is a serious health problem resulting in billions of dollars in costs as well as intangible consequences for both victims of crime and society at large. Research on victimization has attempted to place an accurate monetary value on the physical, sexual, and psychological consequences of these offenses. Victims typically suffer three types of losses: (1) out-of-pocket expenses resulting from medical costs or property damage, (2) reduced productivity in various settings such as work or school, and (3) nonmonetary losses such as those associated with pain or suffering and loss of quality of life. The economic costs of out-of-pocket expenses and reduced productivity are known as "tangible" costs of victimization because they are more easily quantified and estimated than are the "intangible" or nonmonetary losses associated with pain and suffering or reduced quality of life.

It is estimated that victimization costs approximately $450 billion per year in the United States. Of that, about $105 billion is considered to be tangible costs of crime, while $345 billion is due to the intangible losses due to crime. This estimate does not include the costs involved in operating the criminal justice system, such as lawyers' fees and court costs. Only the quantified costs of crime incurred directly by or on behalf of the victim are detailed.

Costs related to medical care, mental health care, police and fire services, victim services, property loss or damage, and reductions in work productivity combine to produce the $105 billion per year estimate of the tangible costs of victimization. The expenses of medical care and mental health care provided to victims of crime comprise a large portion of yearly economic costs of crime. Economic costs of medical care include payments for hospital and physician care, emergency medical transportation, rehabilitation efforts, and medication. Insurance administrative expenditures, such as claim processing and reimbursement payments, as well as funeral and coroner expenses, are considered to be medical costs of victimization. These medical costs of victimization are more easily estimated than

the tangible losses associated with mental health care; in fact, the economic costs related to mental health care following victimization is one of the least researched, documented, and understood consequences of crime and victimization. However, it is estimated that between 10% and 20% of all United States mental health care spending is provided to victims of crimes for services from psychiatrists, psychologists, and social workers. This translates to between $6 million and $7 million per year spent on mental health care services for victims of recent crimes or for victims of crimes inflicted during childhood. Together, medical and mental health care costs due to crime and victimization are estimated to total approximately $18 billion per year. This estimate includes medical and mental health care expenses incurred from fatal crimes, child abuse, rape and sexual assault, robbery, arson, drunk driving, larceny, burglary, and motor vehicle theft. The expenditures that are not reimbursed by insurance companies are felt directly by the victim and family, while costs that are covered by insurance are borne by society in general.

Aside from the medical and mental health care costs of victimization, approximately $87 billion per year is spent on or lost to property damage, loss of productivity, police and fire services, and victim services. The largest tangible expense of victimization each year is due to property damage or loss and costs related to insurance claim processing and resulting high insurance rates. Crimes most typically resulting in property loss or damage are burglary, larceny, arson, and motor vehicle theft; victims pay the direct costs of these crimes, while society shoulders the reimbursement costs dispensed by insurance companies.

The second most costly tangible consequence of victimization each year is due to the loss of or reduction in productivity at work, at school, or within the household. These expenses include lost wages and fringe benefits, missed school, and reduced housework suffered by victims and their families. Further, loss of or reduced productivity includes expenditures associated with worker's compensation or worker's disability, processing insurance claims, and the legal expenses involved in securing reimbursement from offenders. Lost wages for missed work are clearly felt by the victim, while decreased job productivity is a concern for the employer and for society.

Police and fire services needed in response to victimization cost approximately $4 billion per year, most of which is shouldered directly by society and may be most detrimental to county or municipal budgets. Police and fire services provide the initial response to victimization and also provide the time, money, and effort involved in follow-up investigations. Importantly, police and fire services are needed in almost all arson and murder cases as well as in many drunk driving crashes. Finally, victim service agencies such a Child Protective Services and foster care agencies also provide costly but necessary services to victims each year. These agencies provide care for maltreated children as well as programs and services for reintegrating families of maltreated children. Much of the expenses for such services are charged to and assumed by the victim, while any expenses paid by the agency are endured by society.

Pain and suffering and loss of quality of life are clearly consequences of victimization. It is important to note that pain and suffering and loss of quality of life are felt as costs of crime by victims. Estimates of reduced quality of life, pain, and suffering are difficult to derive, but often include the experience of physical and psychological pain, emotional suffering, reduced feelings of safety, security, privacy, and increased fear. An estimated $345 billion is spent on or lost each year to these intangible costs of victimization.

Economic Costs of Specific Crimes

The economic costs of victimization are difficult to estimate. This is due to many factors. First, it is difficult to estimate the value of the "intangible" costs of crime, such as the trauma, pain, suffering, fear, and loss of quality of life that often result from victimization. Further, the shortcomings of police reports and victimization surveys discussed above suggest that the true level of crime in the United States is often undercounted, resulting in underestimates of the annual costs of crime. The occurrence of and subsequent costs of repeat victimizations are also difficult to measure. Finally, the pain and suffering that is inflicted upon victims often translates into economic costs in the form of hospital visits, mental health care, and other services provided to victims. The figures presented below attempt to take such factors into account;

still, these estimates may continue to undercount the economic costs of victimization.

It is estimated that each year, victims lose approximately $450 billion due to the crimes committed against them; this includes both tangible and intangible losses. To derive more precise estimates of the costs of crime to victims as well as the aggregated costs of crime to society, research has been conducted on the costs of certain crimes, such as fatal crimes, assault, rape and sexual assault, robbery, drunk driving, and property crimes related to arson, larceny, burglary, and motor vehicle theft. Tangible losses, such as medical costs, mental health care costs, police, fire, and victims services, and property loss or damage have been estimated, both with and without estimates of intangible losses such as reduced quality of life for the victim.

While victims of fatal crimes pay the ultimate price of the crime (i.e., death), society also suffers losses. Rape, robbery, abuse, assault, arson, and drunk driving crimes causing victims' deaths costs families and society more than $33 billion per year. Of the tangible expenses, fatal rape, robbery, abuse, and assault account for more than $24 billion, while fatal arson crimes comprise more than $600 million. Drunken driving deaths result in more than $7 billion lost each year. Intangible costs associated with pain, suffering, and reduced quality of life total approximately $60 billion per year for all fatal crimes. Fatal rape, robbery, abuse, and assault account for $46 billion of the total $60 billion in intangible costs. Arson deaths comprise $1.7 billion annually, while drunk driving deaths constitute more than $12 billion. When combined, economic and noneconomic costs associated with fatal victimizations in the United States each year total about $93 billion.

Generally, victimization surveys disaggregate assaults into three categories—child abuse and assault, rape and sexual assault, and other types of assaults. Child abuse may take the forms of rape, sexual abuse, physical abuse, and emotional abuse. Tangible losses for these crimes cost more than $7 billion per year, with medical and mental health care costs comprising more than $3.6 billion of that. The costs associated with child abuse victims' reduced quality of life approach a staggering $48 billion per year. In all, it is estimated that child abuse accounts for $56 billion in tangible and intangible costs each year.

Rape and sexual assault are said to be the most costly types of crime in terms of monetary and non-monetary expenditures of victimization each year. Accounting for tangible and intangible losses, rape and sexual assault is estimated to cost $127 billion per year; more than $7 billion is accounted for by tangible losses associated with medical expenses, mental health care, and police services, while $119 billion is due to costs associated with victims' reduced quality of life.

Other types of assault or attempted assault, including stranger and domestic assaults, are also very costly. Approximately $15 billion per year is lost or spent on these crimes due to medical expenses, police services, and loss of productivity at work or at home. An additional $77 billion dollars is accounted for by pain, suffering, and reduced quality of life. Taken together, it is estimated that approximately $93 billion each year is lost to victimization from these types of assaults. Domestic abuse against adults is estimated at $67 billion per year, which accounts for nearly 15% of the total crime costs. Of that total, $8.8 billion is associated with tangible costs such as medical expenses, while $58 billion is accounted for by costs associated with reductions in quality of life.

Robbery and attempted robbery may result in injury inflicted on the victim or no injury to the victim. Regardless of whether the victim was wounded, tangible costs associated with robbery exceed $3 billion each year. The majority ($2.5 billion) of that is attributable to lost or damaged property, police and fire services, and victim services. It is estimated that an additional $8 billion is due to intangible losses, resulting in $11 billion in total costs of robbery or attempted robbery victimization.

Drunk driving, like robbery, can result in injury to the victim. Drunk driving victimization resulting in death is accounted for under the costs associated with fatal crimes; however, it is noteworthy that drunk driving deaths result in an estimated $7 billion in tangible costs, $12.3 billion in intangible costs, and $20 billion in total costs each year. Nonfatal drunken driving crimes result in more than $13 billion in tangible losses and $27 billion in intangible losses each year. In all, drunk driving accidents that are not fatal cost about $41 billion in the United States each year.

Property crimes include nonfatal arson and successful or attempted larceny, burglary, and motor vehicle theft. Taken together, the annual tangible costs of these crimes exceed $25 billion per year. The bulk of this is due to the expenses associated with lost or damaged property. The intangible losses associated with arson, larceny, burglary, and motor vehicle theft approximates $4.7 billion per year. In all, the tangible and intangible costs of these crimes are estimated to be $30 billion each year. Nonfatal arson accounts for $5 billion of the estimated $30 billion, costing about $2.6 billion and $2.4 billion in tangible and intangible losses, respectively. Larceny accounts for $9 billion each year, with all $9 billion attributed to monetary losses; in other words, it is believed that larceny does not result in reduced quality of life or pain and suffering on the part of the victim. Of the $30 billion attributed to property victimization each year, burglary also accounts for about $9 billion. More than $7 billion and about $1.8 billion are due to tangible and intangible losses, respectively, each year. Finally, motor vehicle theft costs about $7 billion each year. The majority of this cost is due to tangible losses associated with the loss of or damage to vehicles, expenditures of police services, and related insurance costs. Approximately $500 million is attributed to intangible losses resulting from motor vehicle theft.

Emily M. Wright and Melanie J. Vicneire

See also National Crime Victimization Survey (NCVS); Victim Compensation; Victimization, Theories of; Victimization Surveys; Victimology

Further Readings

Arias, I., & Corso, P. (2005). Average costs per person victimized by an intimate partner of the opposite gender: A comparison of men and women. *Violence and Victims, 20*(4), 379–391.

Miller, T. R., Cohen, M. A., & Wiersema, B. (1996). *Victim costs and consequences: A new look.* Washington, DC: U.S. Department of Justice, National Institute of Justice.

U.S. Department of Justice, Bureau of Justice Statistics. (2006). *Percentage of victimizations resulting in economic loss, by type of crime and type of loss.* Washington, DC: Author.

U.S. Department of Justice, Bureau of Justice Statistics. (2006). *Total economic loss to victims of crime.* Washington, DC: Author.

ELDER ABUSE, NEGLECT, AND MALTREATMENT

Ideally, families provide all members with mutual love, respect, and support. An alternate disturbing reality is that the majority of elder abuse takes place within the context of family. This entry examines elder abuse that occurs within the context of a family, including intimate partner violence (IPV) and abuse perpetrated by adult children and grandchildren against parents and older relatives.

Definitions

According to the National Center on Elder Abuse, elder abuse is any knowing, intended, or careless act that causes harm or serious risk of harm to an individual age 60 or above. This broad term encompasses many types of mistreatment:

Physical abuse is the use of force to threaten or physically injure a vulnerable elder.

Emotional abuse encompasses verbal attacks, harassment, threats to evict or institutionalize, rejection, isolation from friends or family, destroying possessions, or belittling that could cause mental anguish, pain, or distress to an elder.

Sexual abuse occurs when sexual contact is forced, tricked, threatened, or otherwise coerced upon another person, including anyone who is unable to grant consent. This is one type of intimate partner violence.

Exploitation consists of theft, fraud, misuse or neglect of authority, and use of "undue influence" to gain control over an older person's money or property.

Abandonment is desertion of a frail or vulnerable elder for extended periods of time by anyone with a duty of care.

Neglect is a caregiver's failure or refusal to provide for a vulnerable elder's safety, physical, or emotional needs.

Self-neglect is the inability to understand the consequences of one's own actions or inaction, which leads to, or may lead to, harm or endangerment.

Prevalence

Few estimates of elder mistreatment in the United States exist. State- and community-specific studies offer varying estimates. A wide range of prevalence rates in itself indicates how much we have yet to learn about elder abuse. The most widely cited elder abuse study is a 1986 survey of Boston residents by Karl Pillemer and David Finkelhor. Their findings indicated that the most common perpetrators of elder abuse were spouses (59%), followed by children (24%).

Ten years later, the National Elder Abuse Incidence Study used data reported to and substantiated by Adult Protective Service agencies. They found that 25.6% of people age 60 and older experienced physical abuse. Of those, 71.4% were women.

Another 10 years later, in 2006, Therese Zink and Bonnie Sue Fisher estimated that elder mistreatment affects at least 3% to 5% of the population. Conservative estimates by the National Center on Elder Abuse put the number of elders who have been injured, exploited, or otherwise mistreated at 1 million to 2 million, and the number of elder abuse cases is expected to rise along with the aging population.

However, most studies of intrafamilial abuse focus on child abuse or domestic violence rather than elder abuse. These types of abuse also have been studied longer than elder abuse. Clearly, additional current and broad-based studies are needed to determine reliable elder abuse prevalence figures.

Underreported Abuse

Underreporting adds to the already difficult task of tabulating prevalence. Only one out of fourteen domestic elder abuse incidents, excluding self-neglect, come to the attention of authorities, according to Pillemer and Finkelhor.

Victims may be too intimidated, afraid, or ashamed to implicate family members. Denial, shame, and feelings of inadequacy about raising children or grandchildren who would abuse their elders may silence parents or grandparents experiencing abuse. The elders' physical or mental state may render them unable to tell, and they may be dependent on the offending family members. Elders may be overwhelmed by the betrayal at the hands of "their own." It may be psychologically easier to report abuse by an unrelated scam artist than family. Their belief system may dictate that families should handle problems privately.

Underreporting is also complicated by unclear definitions of what constitutes abuse. Many women in a 2006 study by Zink and Fisher reported that family members were "too busy" to take them to the doctor or assist in other ways. It is difficult to discern when family members reasonably need to attend to their own priorities, and when their actions constitute caregiver neglect. Similarly, when adult children or neighbors accompany older adults into the doctor's exam room against the wishes of the elder, is it classified as concern, ageism, or abuse?

Risk Factors

While there is no acceptable rationalization for intrafamilial elder abuse, the following risk factors might contribute to this form of abuse.

Issues Within the Abuser

The perpetrator may be mentally unstable or alcohol or drug dependent, or may have anger management issues or previous criminal history. Long-standing personality traits like having a bad temper, being hypercritical, and having a tendency to blame others are also risk factors. Severe personal stress and personal and financial crises can contribute. Some individuals see violence as an acceptable way to solve problems, or they have limited nonviolent techniques to solve problems.

Abuse can be understood as a quest for power and control, as explored in 2006 by Lisa Manuel and by others. The abusive person exerts controls by creating barriers to the outside world through social isolation. Cutting off access to the telephone and assistive technology like hearing aids, walkers, and so on is a common tactic in this scenario. In 2006, Zink and her colleagues noted cases of older women involved with homosexual or bisexual partners they labeled "women haters." Perpetrators of elder abuse may project their frustration and anger over their own problems onto their intimate partners or family members.

Retaliation and Cycle of Violence

Elder abuse can be the continuation of long-standing domestic violence or abusive family dynamics. When family members have always related to each other in abusive ways and older adults can no longer hold their own, the playing field becomes uneven. Other family members continue to play their dysfunctional parts, and elder abuse results. A cycle of violence can be perpetuated by abusers trying to get back at their elders for actual or imagined past mistreatment.

Caregiving Resentment

Abuse can begin in later years. Most people receive the majority of their long-term care from informal, unpaid family caregivers. The Family Caregiver Alliance estimates 34 million adults (16% of the population) provide care to adults aged 50 and older. Declines in mental and physical status of the elder create overwhelming caregiving stresses that, especially when combined with other risk factors, can lead to abuse.

Lack of Services

Without needed health and social services in the community, caregivers may be unable to handle the stress and responsibility of caring for a parent.

Isolation

Isolation can lead families to become very confused about acceptable treatment. Small changes over time can slowly escalate into abuse without family members noticing the evolution and the new abusive "normal."

Longer Life Spans

According to the Administration on Aging, individuals 85 and over are the fastest growing segment of the population. This group of the oldest old is expected to rise from 5.3 million in 2006 to 8.9 million in 2030. Higher prevalence of elder abuse may correspond to expanded longevity, as increased stresses and pressures within families can lead to abuse.

Ageism

Financial exploitation may stem from an extreme sense of entitlement by adult children. They may consider their parents' resources already theirs or under their jurisdiction. Financial abuse can be an expression of ageism, based on the idea that needs of older people are less important than needs of younger people.

Financial Dependence

Financial dependence is common in the current generation of older women who were generally discouraged from earning significant incomes. Elders may rely on family members for financial support. Or relative caregivers may depend on the older adult for money. Both situations may lead to abuse.

Emotional or Physical Dependence

Many elders depend on spouses or other family members for help with driving; with activities of daily living like getting dressed, eating, and personal care; and with instrumental activities of daily living like cleaning, laundry, grocery shopping, and managing medications. Older adults in declining health can become more vulnerable to abuse because of increasing dependence.

Social Problems

Unemployment, poor or crowded housing, and other poor living conditions can put elders at high risk of abuse.

What Keeps Elders From Escaping Intrafamilial Abuse?

Studies by Zink and her colleagues in 2003 and 2004 found that the majority of older women are likely to remain in their abusive relationship. In 2006, these researchers found that over time women developed a philosophy of life to make sense of the demeaning treatment in their intimate partnerships. They used a variety of internal and external coping strategies. First, they reappraised their abusers, themselves, and their situations. For instance, they labeled their spouse a "hotheaded Italian" or a "hardheaded German" or a "Jekyll & Hyde" in order to make sense of the mistreatment and maintain self-respect. Second, women focused on their culturally prescribed roles of wife, mother, and homemaker to find meaning beyond the abuse and despite the abuse. Third, they looked outside of the relationship to their friends, extended family, job, and volunteer work for emotional support. Nearly half of the women noted escalations in abuse when the perpetrator was under the influence of alcohol or drugs. All of the women who remained in their abusive relationships made efforts to maintain the appearance of a conjugal connection or unity to the outside world.

Older women with physical or mental illness must overcome significant obstacles to stop abuse. They may not have the requisite knowledge regarding health care providers. In addition, community services, such as temporary shelters, respite care facilities, and other protective services for older people, may be lacking. Finally, abusers may not be aware of the services and professional agencies available to help them learn to express their feelings in proper ways, and victims may not be aware of those who could help them to set boundaries and keep themselves safe.

Legal Protection

No federal law currently protects older adults from elder abuse. However, state laws offer some protection. Mandated reporters vary widely by states. Toll-free hotline numbers exist in most states, and the Web site of the National Center on Elder Abuse has a page called "Where to Report Abuse." Most states accept anonymous reports; however, it is preferable if the caller provides contact information in case the investigator has follow-up questions.

Safety Planning

According to Zink and her colleagues in 2006, intimate partner violence of both a physical and sexual nature decreases as perpetrators age. Over time, women develop coping strategies that enable them to live with the abuser. Since older women are likely to remain in an abusive relationship, the main task of service providers becomes safety planning, or helping older women to be as safe as possible within their abusive relationship.

Health care professionals are often the ones with the most opportunities to see elders alone and ask specific questions about abuse. Lack of awareness of the potential for abuse by health care professionals, including medical providers, dentists, older adult services workers, police, postal workers, and bank employees make it easy for abuse to go undetected.

In 2006, Zink and her colleagues recommended that providers identify treatable mental health problems that may be undiagnosed in the abuser and victim in intimate partnerships. When leaving appears not to be an option, appropriate management of diagnoses such as depression, anxiety, or oppositional behaviors may improve the safety and quality of life for the couple.

Protective Factors

Encouraging older adults to remain busy and engaged in life protects these adults against elder abuse. Also protective is helping to older adults to cultivate multiple sources of positive social support and linking them with spiritual resources, social services, and aging network community-based services. This normalizes their day-to-day functioning and protects them against isolation.

The older person can be advised to protect himself or herself against financial exploitation by keeping family members from adding their names to his or her bank accounts unless they have clear consent; never making financial decisions under pressure; and not signing over money or property to anyone, even family, without getting independent legal advice.

Providing community education about all forms of elder abuse will help people understand that they do not have to live with abuse and it is not their fault. Offering phone numbers and hotlines for social service agencies like elderly protective services, public health agencies, and the police can help raise older people's awareness of community resources available to help them and encourage them to ask for help when they need it.

Donna B. Fedus

See also Elder Abuse, Neglect, and Maltreatment: Institutions; Elder Abuse, Neglect, and Maltreatment: Interventions for; Elder Abuse, Neglect, and Maltreatment: Measurement of; Elder Abuse, Neglect, and Maltreatment: Statutory Responses; Elder Abuse, Neglect, and Maltreatment: Theories of

Further Readings

Family Caregiver Alliance. (2005). *Selected caregiver statistics*. San Francisco: Author.

Manuel, L. (2004). Does caregiving lead to abuse? *Education Wife Assault Newsletter, 13*(1), 14–15.

National Center on Elder Abuse. (2005). *Fifteen questions & answers about elder abuse*. Washington, DC: National Center on Elder Abuse, National Association of the State Units on Aging.

U.S. Administration on Aging. (2008). *A statistical profile of older Americans aged 65+*. Washington, DC: U.S. Department of Health and Human Services.

Zink, T., & Fisher, B. (2006). The prevalence and incidence of intimate partner and interpersonal mistreatment of older women in primary care offices. *Journal of Elder Abuse & Neglect, 18*(1), 83–105.

Zink, T. M., Jacobson, J. C. J., Pabst, S., Regan, S., & Fisher, B. (2006). A lifetime of intimate partner violence: Coping strategies of older women. *Journal of Interpersonal Violence, 21*(5), 634–651.

Zink, T. M., Jacobson, J. C. J., Regan, S., Fisher, B., & Pabst, S. (2006). Older women's descriptions and understandings of their abusers. *Violence Against Women, 12*(9), 851–865.

Zink, T. M., Jacobson, J. C. J., Regan, S., & Pabst, S. (2004). Hidden victims: The health care needs and experiences of older women in abusive relationships. *Journal of Women's Health, 13*, 898–908.

Zink, T., Regan, S., Jacobson, J., & Pabst, S. (2003). Cohort, period, and aging effects: A qualitative study of older women's reasons for remaining in abusive relationships. *Violence Against Women, 9*, 1429–1441.

Web Sites

National Center on Elder Abuse: http://www .elderabusecenter.org

ELDER ABUSE, NEGLECT, AND MALTREATMENT: INSTITUTIONAL

The maltreatment of people over the age of 60 is commonly referred to as elder abuse. The National Association of Adult Protective Services delineates three basic categories of elder abuse: (1) domestic elder abuse, (2) institutional elder abuse, and (3) self-neglect or self-abuse. State statutes addressing elder abuse provide their own specific definitions of these three categories and generally exclude self-neglect or self-abuse, instead focusing on "types" of domestic and institutional elder abuse. These types include physical abuse, sexual abuse, emotional or psychological abuse, neglect, and exploitation.

This entry focuses on institutional abuse whereby individuals within institutions are victims of maltreatment and neglect. This is distinguished from institutionalized abuse, whereby the administration or milieu of the institution is determined to be abusive or negligent (i.e., use of physical/chemical restraints, lack of attention to bedsores, inadequate nutrition). However, in most situations of maltreatment in institutions, it is difficult to verify whether the abuse or neglect was caused by an individual act or through some failing on the part of the institution. Most experts believe that institutional abuse is an invisible problem because residents within long-term care facilities represent the most isolated, dependent, and voiceless population within society. Elder abuse is a public health and criminal justice concern that requires worldwide attention. This entry discusses the different types of institutions that provide long-term care for older adults, provides information on the prevalence of elder abuse within these institutions, explores the theories of such abuse within institutions, and ends with a brief discussion on responding and preventing elder abuse within institutions.

Long-Term Care Institutions

Generally, an institution is a facility that provides long-term care (i.e., nursing care and related medical or psychosocial services) for individuals who cannot obtain this care within their own homes. The most common type of long-term care institution is the nursing home, but assisted living is now the fastest growing segment of long-term care within the United States. Nursing homes can be for-profit, nonprofit, or government facilities. All three ownership groups provide skilled and basic nursing care and assistance with activities of daily living (ADLs) for individuals who are having difficulty performing tasks such as bathing, toileting, transferring from bed to chair, and eating. Currently, slightly more than 5% of the U.S. population aged 65 and older resides in nursing homes and assisted living facilities. However, the percentage of institutionalized

elders increases to 24.5% for those over the age of 85 and approximately 50% of those 95 and older. Because residents within nursing homes are considered to be the most physically and emotionally vulnerable group of elders, they are especially in jeopardy of being victimized.

Prevalence of Elder Abuse Within Institutions

Because elder abuse in general has gone unrecognized, the rates of elder abuse within institutions have not been adequately documented, and there is little empirical data on the actual prevalence of abuse, neglect, and exploitation of nursing home residents. The accurate identification of elder abuse within nursing homes is especially problematic because often the deaths of residents within institutions have been attributed to natural, accidental, or undetermined causes when in fact they may have been due to abuse and/or neglect. In addition, because mistreatment within institutions occurs outside the view of family and friends, the likelihood of abuse being reported is low. Although the exact magnitude of maltreatment against residents within institutions is not known, according to information gathered by the National Center on Elder Abuse (NCEA), the mistreatment of residents in nursing homes is not uncommon. In 2005, the Long-Term Care Ombudsman Program (LTCOP) received more than 20,000 complaints of abuse, neglect, and exploitation, and another 92,000 complaints related to resident care. Among the different types of abuse categories, physical abuse was the most common type reported. Although the incidence of sexual abuse within institutions is estimated to be low (with less than 1% of Adult Protective Services' investigations), this is also considered to be the most hidden and unreported forms of abuse.

Theories of Elder Abuse Within Institutions

There are a variety of theories that have been proposed to explain elder abuse, neglect, and maltreatment among csommunity-dwelling older adults. This section describes the unique dynamics of elder abuse within institutions. The maltreatment of elders within institutional settings occurs in both covert and overt forms. Three covert forms of elder abuse within nursing homes were first identified by Dorothy Meddaugh in the early 1990s. The first form is the resident's loss of personal choice concerning basic daily activities. Residents are forced to bathe, eat, and sleep on the institution's schedule rather than their own schedule. The second form is isolation. Residents who are considered to be aggressive, combative, or disruptive are often banished from group activities and social functions, and they are often forced to stay in their beds and/or rooms for extended periods of time. The third covert form of elder abuse is labeling. Residents are labeled by staff as "the good resident," "the bad resident," "the mean resident," and so on. These labels usually result in differential treatment by the staff. Although it can be argued that these situations do not meet the generally accepted criteria for abuse and/or mistreatment, from the residents' and/or their family's perspective, this may be considered abusive.

Overt forms of elder abuse include physical abuse, sexual abuse, psychological/emotional abuse, and neglect. Within institutions, the risk of these cases of elder maltreatment occurring can be categorized into three areas: facility staff risk factors, resident risk factors, and relationship risk factors.

Facility Staff Risk Factors

Abuse by staff within institutions can occur due to the stressful working conditions. These stressful working conditions include long shift hours, low staff-to-patient ratios, a heavy workload, being underpaid, and receiving minimal or no benefits. Providing hands-on care for older adults who are physically and/or cognitively impaired is highly demanding and requires sufficient training and supervision. Nurses aids (who provide the majority of hands-on care) often receive minimal training and/or supervision, which frequently results in nurses aids not having the necessary skills, information, resources, and or disposition to handle potentially aggressive and/or rebellious behaviors of residents. In addition to the demands of the institution, nurses aids are often attempting to deal with external stressors such as juggling home responsibilities (e.g., raising children), personal financial concerns, and/or relational problems. Nursing home staff may become abusive with residents in retaliation for being underpaid and overworked, or

staff with their own history of abuse may bring this learned aggressiveness with them to the workplace. Facility staff risk factors can also include the lack of adequate training initiatives and policies to prevent elder abuse and neglect.

Resident Risk Factors

Institutionalization itself is viewed as a risk factor for elder abuse and neglect. Nursing home residents are the most vulnerable of populations, and subsequently are at greatest risk for abuse and neglect. Nearly half of all nursing home residents are experiencing severe cognitive deficits, and 50% are confined to a bed or wheelchair. These cognitive and ambulatory limitations increase the vulnerability of nursing home residents. The likelihood of being victimized is especially evident when one considers that the "typical" nursing home resident is female, Caucasian, over the age of 79, and widowed. Because the majority of nursing home residents are widows, they do not have the support or guardianship of a spouse or partner.

Relationship Risk Factors

Although nursing home residents who do not have frequent visitors or familial support are at a particular risk for abuse and/or neglect due to social isolation, perpetrators of institutional abuse can also be family members. Abuse by family members is often a continuation of maltreatment that occurred prior to the placement within the institution. For example, a son may continue to be verbally abusive to his mother at the nursing home whenever he calls and/or visits. However, the most frequent cases involve residents striking out at other residents because of a lack of impulse control due to mental health problems (i.e., psychosis, dementia, delirium) or lack of adequate supervision. In addition, convicted felons who are transferred to nursing homes from correctional facilities can pose safety risks for both residents and staff. Finally, visitors to nursing homes can also inflict abuse upon unsuspecting residents.

The National Association of State Units on Aging (NASUA) for the National Center on Elder Abuse (NCEA) developed the Nursing Home Abuse Risk Prevention Profile and Checklist in 2005. This resource was specifically designed to assist nursing home administrators in assessing the facility, resident, and relationship risk factors of abuse and neglect within their particular facility.

Reporting Elder Abuse in Institutions

Since the enactment of Medicare and Medicaid in 1965, there have been federal regulations established to protect the well-being of older adults residing in institutions in the United States. The enforcement of these regulations has been the responsibility of the Health Care Finance Administration through the Department of Health and Human Services. Congress authorized the most ambitious nursing home regulations under the Omnibus Budget Reconciliation Act of 1987 (OBRA '87). OBRA '87 mandated that each nursing home must provide individualized resident care that ensures physical, mental, and psychosocial well-being. OBRA '87 also gave states the authority to establish and maintain investigatory units and Long Term Care Ombudsman Programs (LTCOP). As a condition of receiving federal funds under the Older Americans Act, each state is mandated to have a LTCOP, which advocates on behalf of residents within long-term care facilities who have experienced maltreatment, violations of their rights, and/or any other problems. If the LTCOP discovers an abusive situation when responding to complaints within a facility, a referral is made to an appropriate agency (i.e., APS program, law enforcement agency, or agency responsible for licensing/certifying such facility).

Prevention of Elder Abuse Within Institutions

Although there are numerous strategies that institutions can use to reduce the vulnerability of residents and prevent institutional abuse (i.e., facility-based prevention measures, education, community outreach, and building security), the most promising ways are reflected in current and proposed federal policies. Recent amendments to Title II and Title VII of the Older Americans Act mandate the development of multidisciplinary and collaborative programs to address the incidence of elder maltreatment within institutions. The Elder Justice Act, which was reintroduced in both the U.S. Senate and House in 2009 is intended to

(1) elevate elder justice issues to national attention, (2) promote accountability through a new federal law to prosecute abuse and neglect within nursing homes, (3) improve ombudsman capacity, (4) provide incentives for the training and retention of nursing home staff, (5) provide and improve training of nursing home surveyors with respect to investigation of abuse, and (6) require criminal background checks for all employees within long-term care facilities. Addressing elder abuse, neglect, and maltreatment within institutions requires collective action across governmental agencies and professional disciplines.

Nancy A. Orel

See also Adult Protective Services; Elder Abuse, Neglect, and Maltreatment; Elder Abuse, Neglect, and Maltreatment: Interventions for; Elder Abuse, Neglect, and Maltreatment: Statutory Responses; Elder Abuse, Neglect, and Maltreatment: Theories of

Further Readings

Daly, J., & Jogerst, G. (2007). Nursing home abuse report and investigation legislation. *Journal of Elder Abuse & Neglect, 19*(3/4), 119–131.

Gibbs, L. M., & Mosqueda, L. (2004). Confronting elder mistreatment in long-term care. *Annals of Long-Term Care, 12*(4), 30–35. Retrieved from http://www .annalsoflongtermcare.com/altc/attachments/ 1083074443-Elder%20

Harris, D., & Benson, M. (2006). *Maltreatment of patients in nursing homes: There is no safe place.* Binghamton, NY: Haworth Pastoral.

Meddaugh, D. (1993). Covert elder abuse in nursing homes. *Journal of Elder Abuse and Neglect, 5*(3), 21–38.

National Association of State Units on Aging (NASUA) for the National Center on Elder Abuse (NCEA). (2005). *Nursing home abuse risk prevention profile and checklist.* Retrieved from http://www .elderabusecenter.org/pdf/publications/Nursing HomeRisk.pdf

Payne, B., & Fletcher, L. (2005). Elder abuse in nursing homes: Prevention and resolution strategies and barriers. *Journal of Criminal Justice, 33*, 119–125.

Teaster, P. B., Oto, J. M., Dugar, T. D., Mendiondo, M. S., Abner, E. L., & Cecil, K. A. (2006). *The 2004 survey of state Adult Protective Services: Abuse of adults 60 years of age and older.* Retrieved from http://www.ncea.aoa.gov/ncearoot/Main_Site/pdf/2–14–06%20FINAL%2060+REPORT.pdf

Web Sites

The National Center on Elder Abuse (NCEA): http://www.elderabusecenter.org

National Long Term Care Ombudsman Resource Center: http://www.ltcombudsman.org

ELDER ABUSE, NEGLECT, AND MALTREATMENT: INTERVENTIONS FOR

Elder abuse and *elder maltreatment* (also referred to as *mistreatment*) are broad terms referring to different forms of abusive actions taken against an older person. *Elder neglect* is typically categorized as one type of elder abuse and is the most common form of elder abuse reported to Adult Protective Services (APS), the state agency responsible for investigating elder abuse. This entry briefly describes elder abuse and its occurrence in the community, then discusses interventions that may prevent elders from becoming victims of abuse and neglect.

Types and Occurrence

Elder abuse, maltreatment, and *neglect* can be either intentional acts by a person trusted for the elder's care or unintentional acts by a caregiver who is improperly trained or overwhelmed with the stress of caring for an older person. This abuse includes physical, psychological, sexual, and financial abuse and neglect. The 1998 National Elder Abuse Incidence Study (NEAIS) estimated that approximately 450,000 elders age 60 and over experienced an incidence of abuse by another person and that for every case of abuse reported, five cases went unreported. The National Center on Elder Abuse (NCEA) reports that between 1 million and 2 million elders age 65 and over experience an occurrence of abuse.

Several issues make determination of elder abuse, maltreatment, and neglect complex. One such issue is that there are federal laws against domestic violence and child abuse, but not against elder abuse, maltreatment, and neglect. Therefore all 50 U.S. States, the District of Columbia, U.S. territories, and Native American tribal organizations have their own elder abuse statutes, which may differ in their definition of the age a person is considered an elder, what constitutes a vulnerable person, who is entitled to protection, what constitutes abuse, what has to be investigated, and who is mandated to report, as well as their guidelines for substantiating a report and criminal or civil penalties for conviction. The 1965 Older Americans Act (OAA) was amended in 1992 to include programs for prevention of elder abuse, neglect, and exploitation; in 2000 to encourage social service agencies to work with law enforcement and the justice system when dealing with elder abuse; and in 2006 to encourage multidisciplinary efforts and to allow states to use part of their OAA funding to pay for coordinating strategies and interventions for elder abuse.

Interventions

Interventions are developed and implemented for screening, identification, prevention, and treatment of elder abuse. As a result, interventions can be targeted to various groups and individuals, including the justice system, law enforcement, health care providers, social service personnel, financial providers, caregivers, and older people. There is no simple rule for developing an intervention. Every case is different, and every state defines and enforces elder abuse statutes differently. However, one similarity among statutes is the requirement that the older person be vulnerable, which usually means that he or she is unable to make decisions because of physical or mental impairment. APS investigates and substantiates elder abuse cases, but does not have the authority to remove a competent elderly person from his or her situation. Thus, if an older person refuses help or makes the decision to stay in an abusive or neglectful environment, the person has that right.

The criterion of vulnerability affects the type of intervention developed, as there are several types of interventions. The first type is educational interventions, which assist in defining elder abuse. Defining elder abuse is complicated, and so one intervention is to train providers to use validated screening tools that help distinguish elder abuse from advancing age and chronic health conditions, and to inform those in the state obligated to investigate. Successful interventions create multidisciplinary teams of law enforcement, district attorneys, health care providers, social service providers, financial advisors, educators, researchers and elder abuse advocates to review cases to determine substantiated abuse of a vulnerable elder and a coordinated plan of action.

A second category is prevention. Prevention interventions have primarily raised awareness in communities about elder abuse. These interventions involve public service announcements for media and billboards describing abuse with a toll-free number to encourage reports. Also included is programming for civic and religious groups to raise awareness and foster a commitment to respect and care for elders in the community.

Other prevention interventions involve those implemented for caregivers of older people and for the older people themselves. Caregiving in a family can be a complex undertaking. There are many issues that can arise when a person must care for an ill, older spouse, parent, or relative. Prevention interventions try identifying and dealing with issues that increase the risk of abuse, such as a history of abuse, substance abuse, mental health issues, and financial dependency. Issues that have been suppressed can be exacerbated by the stress of caregiving or becoming dependent. Many interventions educate caregivers about self-care and providing elder care. This includes information about community resources such as respite care, adult day care, sharing care, and support groups. Other programs instruct caregivers to recognize that changes in cognitive, physical, or financial status can lead to abuse.

Finally, if there is abuse, treatment interventions target the abusive caregiver or elder. These programs intervene to attempt to change the abusive behavior through counseling, education, or treatment of mental health conditions. If these interventions fail, vulnerable elders may be removed from the home and placed in another facility or institution, the outcome that everyone involved was attempting to avoid.

The issues of elder abuse, maltreatment, and neglect are extremely complex. But gains have

been made to increase awareness of the problem and identify and implement solutions. Federal law and funding would support the creation of consistent and cohesive definitions of the elder and elder abuse, in addition to mandating reports and developing and evaluating interventions for this abuse.

Saundra Regan

See also Adult Protective Services; Elder Abuse, Neglect, and Maltreatment; Elder Abuse, Neglect, and Maltreatment: Measurement of; Elder Abuse, Neglect, and Maltreatment: Statutory Responses; Elder Abuse, Neglect, and Maltreatment: Theories of

Further Readings

Anetzberger, G. (Ed.). (2005). *The clinical management of elder abuse.* New York: Haworth.

Bonnie, R. J., & Wallace, R. B. (2003). *Elder mistreatment: Abuse, neglect, and exploitation in an aging America.* Panel to review risk and prevalence of elder abuse and neglect. Washington, DC: National Academies Press.

Brandl, B., Bitondo Dyer, C., Heisler, C., Marlat Otto, J., Stiegel, L. A., & Thomas, R. W. (2007). *Elder abuse detection and intervention: a collaborative approach.* New York: Springer.

Web Sites

National Center on Elder Abuse: http://www.ncea.aoa.gov

ELDER ABUSE, NEGLECT, AND MALTREATMENT: MEASUREMENT OF

The field of elder mistreatment has been plagued by problems with how to measure the extent of the phenomenon. Prevalence estimates range from 10 to 32 per 1,000 elders, with overall national estimates between 500,000 and 1 million elders existing at any point in time. The only two peer-reviewed prevalence estimates, published 20 years apart, do not estimate prevalence of mistreatment in facility settings.

Agreement on Definitions

The first of the measurement issues is agreement on definitions, which are typically driven by statutes and regulations and vary from state to state. Though various entities have tried to establish definitions, the most commonly held are those by Margaret Hudson, a researcher; the National Center on Elder Abuse; and the National Research Council (NRC) efforts, a text edited by Richard Bonnie and Robert Wallace.

The NRC panel defined elder mistreatment as being intentional and unintentional acts of harm committed by a trusted other. The NRC definition excludes self-neglect. Conundrums presented by the NRC definition are at what point a trust relationship is established and who constitutes a trusted other. Problems with establishing a commonly held definition are also frustrated by an inability to understand the scope of the problem. Before meaningful action can be taken, it is critical to know how much mistreatment actually exists.

Studies Counting the Problem of Elder Abuse

The second measurement issue concerns how best to count the problem to accurately represent it. At this time, incidence and prevalence of the problem in facility and community settings remain virtually unknown, although more researchers than ever are now addressing the problem, primarily due to increased funding by the National Institute of Justice and the National Institute on Aging. The most familiar and referent study of prevalence of elder abuse is that of Carl Pillemer and David Finkelhor. Theirs was a large-scale random sample survey in which interviews were conducted with 2,020 community-dwelling elders in the Boston, Massachusetts, metropolitan area regarding their experiences with physical violence, verbal aggression, and neglect. The prevalence rate was found to be 32 maltreated elders per 1,000. Physical violence was the predominant form of maltreatment, and living with another person heightened an elder's likelihood of experiencing abuse. Neither age nor economic circumstance was predictive of abuse. Study results indicated high rates of spouse abuse and of the abuse of men, findings that diverged from those of previous studies. Based on a calculation of an incidence rate (26 per 1,000), the authors

suggested that 1 in 14 cases were reported. The study did not include financial elder abuse.

A second and also widely used number is based on a national survey that gathered information on elder abuse based on report from Adult Protective Services (APS) in each state. In a year's time APS received a total of 253,426 reports on persons age 60 and over, according to Pamela Teaster and her colleagues. With a statistically inferred number used for nonresponding states, the reports of elder abuse in one year totaled 381,430. Toshio Tatara reported that 10 years earlier, and also in one year's time, APS received 293,000 domestic reports of elder abuse. Comparing the numbers of reports from these two studies and spanning a 10-year period, reports of elder abuse and neglect have risen by 30%.

In the APS study by Pamela Teaster and her colleagues, physical abuse constituted 10.7% of all substantiated abuse, sexual abuse constituted 1.0%, emotional/psychological abuse constituted 14.8%, 20.4% concerned caregiver neglect/abandonment, exploitation constituted 14.7%, and self-neglect was involved in 37.2% of substantiated reports. Findings with 15 states reporting revealed that 65.7% of victims were female and that 52.7% of alleged perpetrators were female. The major limitations of this study are that it is based only on reports of abuse to one agency and that it encompasses definitions of the problem that vary by state.

In 2008, Edwin Laumann, Sara Leitsch, and Linda Waite attempted to calculate elder mistreatment using the already established National Social Life, Health, and Aging Project, a nationally representative sample of community-dwelling elders ages 57 to 85. The study drew heavily upon recommendations from the NRC panel and included 3,005 participants who were asked if, in the past year, they had experienced verbal, financial, or physical mistreatment. For those who reported mistreatment, additional questions were asked about their relationship with the perpetrator.

Findings revealed a prevalence rate of 10 per 1,000 elders. Specifically, 9% of elders reported experiencing verbal mistreatment, 3.5% experienced financial mistreatment, and .02% reported experiencing physical mistreatment by a family member. Verbal mistreatment was more often reported by women and by those with physical vulnerabilities. The odds of experiencing financial mistreatment were higher for African Americans and lower for Latinos/as than for Whites. Most mistreatment was perpetrated by someone outside the respondent's immediate family. Information collected for this estimate may have been affected by an attempt by the researchers to focus contextually on negative, non-life-threatening social behaviors rather than those more typically associated with legalistic definitions of elder abuse.

The Common Goal

These three studies represent the most comprehensive information currently available. Clearly, it is critical that researchers and practitioners alike understand the scope of the problem so that they can help effect change to prevent and address the problem of elder mistreatment. Only then can what is learned be realistically and systematically applied to the mistreatment of older adults.

Pamela B. Teaster

See also Adult Protective Services; Elder Abuse, Neglect, and Maltreatment; Elder Abuse, Neglect, and Maltreatment: Institutional; Elder Abuse, Neglect, and Maltreatment: Interventions for; Elder Abuse, Neglect, and Maltreatment: Statutory Responses; Elder Abuse, Neglect, and Maltreatment: Theories of

Further Readings

Bonnie, R. J., & Wallace, R. B. (2003). *Elder mistreatment: Abuse, neglect, and exploitation in an aging America*. Washington, DC: National Academies Press.

Hudson, M. (1989). Analysis of the concepts of elder mistreatment: abuse and neglect. *Journal of Elder Abuse and Neglect, 6*(1), 5–25.

Hudson, M. (1994). Elder abuse: Its meaning to middle-aged and older adults: Part II. Pilot results. *Journal of Elder Abuse and Neglect, 6*(1), 55–81.

Laumann, E. O., Leitsch, S. A., & Waite, L. J. (2008). Elder mistreatment in the United States: Prevalence estimates from a nationally representative study. *Journal of Gerontology, Series B: Psychological Sciences and Social Sciences, 63*(4), S248–S254.

National Center on Elder Abuse. (2007). *Major types of elder abuse.* Retrieved April 3, 2008, from http://www.ncea.aoa.gov

Pillemer, K.A., & Finkelhor, D. (1988). The prevalence of elder abuse: A random sample survey. *The Gerontologist, 28*(1), 51–57.

Tatara, T., & Kuzmeskas, L. (1997). *Elder abuse in domestic settings.* Elder Abuse Information Series. Washington, DC: National Center on Elder Abuse.

Teaster, P. B., Otto, J. M., Dugar, T. D., Mendiondo, M. S., Abner, E. L., & Cecil, K. A. (2006). *The 2004 survey of state Adult Protective Services: Abuse of adults 60 years of age and older.* Report to the National Center on Elder Abuse, Administration on Aging. Washington, DC: National Center on Elder Abuse.

ELDER ABUSE, NEGLECT, AND MALTREATMENT: STATUTORY RESPONSES

Although *abuse, neglect,* and *maltreatment* of individuals over the age of 60 (i.e., elders) have taken place throughout history, the precise definitions of these terms continue to evolve. The National Association of Adult Protective Services delineates three basic categories of elder abuse/elder maltreatment: (1) domestic, (2) institutional, and (3) self-neglect. State statutes regarding elder abuse provide their own definitions of these three categories. Generally, state statutes exclude self-neglect and focus on "types" of domestic and institutional elder abuse. These types include physical abuse, sexual abuse, emotional/psychological abuse, neglect, and exploitation. This entry provides information about state criminal statutes, federal statutes, and adult protective laws as they apply to elder abuse, neglect, and maltreatment. The majority of elder abuse cases require a response from the criminal justice system. Statistics show that of all age groups, older adults (i.e., those over the age of 65) have the highest reporting rate of personal crimes to the police. In order to adequately address the increasing rates of elder maltreatment, the criminal justice system and society as a whole must view elder abuse as not just a social problem but also a legal problem.

State Law on Elder Maltreatment

The laws and definitions of terms related to elder maltreatment vary tremendously from state to state. These variations are evident in the definition of abuse; types of abuse, neglect, and exploitation that are covered; classification of the abuse as criminal or civil; reporting (mandatory or voluntary); investigation responsibility and procedures; and remedies for abuse. Generally, most physical, sexual, and financial/material abuse are considered crimes in all U.S. states as long as these acts violate statutes prohibiting crimes such as assault, battery, rape, theft, and so on. In addition, certain emotional abuse and neglect cases are subject to criminal prosecution, depending on the conduct and intent of the perpetrator and the consequences for the victim. There are some states that have enacted special elder abuse statutes (i.e., Arizona, California, Illinois, and Washington), and many states have established laws pertaining to guardianship, conservatorship, general or durable powers of attorney, and family violence prevention that may be applicable in cases involving elder abuse.

All 50 states, the District of Columbia, Guam, Puerto Rico, and the Virgin Islands have systems in place for reporting and investigating allegations of abuse, neglect, and exploitation of the elderly as well as some form of elder abuse prevention laws. The investigation and substantiation of elder abuse and neglect is the primary focus of Adult Protective Services (APS) agencies. All states have designated either an APS agency or a subunit of the state aging unit to receive and investigate reports of suspected elder maltreatment and for the provision of victim services. However, these procedures vary from state to state. Further, some state APS laws are applicable only to individuals who reside in the community (domestic abuse cases) and exclude individuals who reside in long-term care facilities (institutional abuse cases).

Federal Law on Elder Maltreatment

Although there are federal laws on child abuse and neglect that provide minimum definitions that states must incorporate in their statutory definitions to receive federal funds, there is no comparable federal law on elder abuse. However, the federal Older Americans Act (OAA) authorizes the use of federal funds for the National Center on Elder Abuse (NCEA) and provides grants to promote comprehensive state elder justice systems. New language in Title II and Title VII of the Older

Americans Act (42 U.S.C. § 3001 et seq., as amended in 2007) emphasizes multidisciplinary and collaborative approaches to addressing elder maltreatment and the establishment of elder abuse shelters and safe havens.

In addition to the OAA, other federal statutes that relate to elder maltreatment are the Social Security Act, the Violence Against Women Act, the Victims of Crime Act, and the Family Violence Prevention and Services Act. The Nursing Home Quality Protection Act and the Omnibus Budget Reconciliation Act both provide guidelines on the quality of care for nursing home residents and the enforcement of state licensing and federal standards for care.

Current Developments

In the past 5 years significant state legislation has expanded mandatory reporting statutes, enactment of civil remedies, and the creation of new criminal statutes and penalties. Currently, there is pending legislation that, if passed, could raise attention to the issues of elder abuse in the same way as federal action raised attention to the issues of domestic violence and child abuse. The Elder Justice Act (S. 795/H.R. 2006), which was reintroduced in April 2009 in both the Senate and House, is intended to provide federal resources to support state and community efforts in the prevention of elder abuse as well as provide assistance to victims.

Although there has been some increase in the number of elder abuse, neglect, and maltreatment cases being prosecuted, efforts are still needed to improve the criminal justice system's response to elder abuse. This system has embarked upon a variety of state and local initiatives to better respond to suspected cases of elder abuse. These include fatality (forensic) review teams, multidisciplinary teams (MDTs), fiduciary abuse specialist teams (FASTs), and specialized elder abuse investigation and prosecution units. Each of these initiatives reflects the collaborative efforts of professionals from law enforcement, Adult Protective Services, aging service providers, and the state attorney general offices.

Nancy A. Orel

See also Adult Protective Services; Elder Abuse, Neglect, and Maltreatment; Mandatory Reporting Statutes

Further Readings

American Bar Association Commission on Law and Aging. (2005). *Statutory provision: Types of abuse defined in adult protective services statutes.* Retrieved from http://www.ncea.aoa.gov/NCEAroot/Main_Site/Find_Help/APS/Analysis_State_Laws.aspx

Breaux, J. B., & Hatch, O. G. (2003). Confronting elder abuse, neglect, and exploitation: The need for elder justice legislation. *Elder Law Journal, 11,* 207–271.

Morgan, E., Johnson, I., & Sigler, R. (2006). Public definitions and endorsements of the criminalization of elder abuse. *Journal of Criminal Justice, 34,* 275–283.

Stiegel, L. (2000). *The changing role of the courts in elder abuse cases.* Retrieved July 2, 2009, from http://www.utahbar.org/sites/noecomm/html/the_changing_role_of_the_court.html

Web Sites

National Adult Protective Services Association: http://www.apsnetwork.org

National Center on Elder Abuse: http://www.ncea.aoa.gov/

ELDER ABUSE, NEGLECT, AND MALTREATMENT: THEORIES OF

Theories, or explanations, for the causes of elder abuse, neglect, and maltreatment can be found in literature from the fields of criminal justice, gerontology, psychology, sociology, medicine, and social work. This entry discusses the most prevalent of these theories, as well as factors that increase the probability of elders being victimized. An understanding of these theories and contributory factors is necessary in order to provide direction to the development of prevention and intervention strategies. For the purposes of this entry, elder abuse/maltreatment includes physical abuse, sexual abuse, emotional/psychological abuse, neglect, abandonment, and financial or material exploitation. Self-neglect by elders is not discussed.

The theoretical perspectives most frequently cited in the literature suggest that the incidence of elder maltreatment can be attributed to societal/cultural factors and/or individual characteristics of the abuser and victim. The most commonly proposed theories are social learning theory, social exchange theory, psychopathology of the perpetrator/abuser, overwhelmed and stressed caregiver, and impairment/dependency of the elder.

Social learning theory suggests that elder maltreatment is a learned problem-solving behavior that is transmitted from one generation to another. Adults exposed to violence and/or abuse as children are less likely to develop norms that prohibit physical aggression. As adults, they may retaliate against their aging parents (or grandparents) and, out of revenge, become abusive. Therefore, intergenerational transmission of violence is seen as a learned behavior that reflects the impact of cultural values and norms on family members' likelihood of mistreating their elders.

According to social exchange theory, individuals are prone to maximize their rewards and minimize punishments. Applying this theory to elder maltreatment, the perpetrator who is providing care to a nonreciprocating elder believes he or she is entitled to use control and violence to impose punishment on the victim. A variation of social exchange theory is dependency theory, which suggests that impaired elders' constant need for assistance and care causes severe stress for caregivers, who may then react to the stress through aggressive and/or neglectful behavior. The dependency hypothesis also suggests that as the dependency of the elder increases, the likelihood for abuse escalates because the perpetrator can take advantage of the vulnerability and dependency of the victim.

Research has determined that focusing on the psychopathology of the perpetrator/abuser can provide greater clarity regarding the dynamics of elder maltreatment. Common traits among perpetrators of elder abuse include financial or emotional dependence on their victims, lack of social supports, personal/economic problems, and alcoholism, substance abuse, mental illness, and/or cognitive deficits.

Providing care for an older adult can be stressful, overwhelming, and burdensome. According to the overwhelmed and stressed caregiver theory, if the caregiver is ill equipped and ill prepared to perform the caregiving tasks, this can create a significant risk factor for elder maltreatment. Additional risk factors for elder abuse among caregivers are inability to cope with stress, depression, lack of support from other potential caregivers, and social isolation. Further, caregivers who perceive the caregiving role as burdensome and without psychological reward are at significant risk of resorting to maltreatment of the elder needing care.

Researchers have found specific characteristics or behaviors of elders that may increase elders' risk of being victimized. The impairment/dependency of the elder theory proposes that maltreatment occurs in caregiving situations where the stress/burden is intensified as a result of the elder's increased impairment and/or dependency on the caregiver. Elders are at greater risk of abuse if they have poor health, poor social skills, display disruptive behaviors, and suffer from personality disorders, depression, or dementia. Additional risk factors include impairments in activities of daily living (e.g., eating, bathing, toileting) and instrumental activities of daily living (i.e., light housework, taking medication, managing finances). It is important to note that some research has concluded that abuser characteristics are better predictors of elder abuse than victim characteristics.

In addition to the aforementioned theories, researchers have also attributed elder maltreatment to structural inequalities within society that create an imbalance of power within relationships (feminist theory) and the marginalization of elders (political economy theory). Brian Payne suggests that elder abuse be explained from an integrated perspective, whereby existing theories on elder abuse are combined with current explanations of crime. One crime theory, called routine activities theory, proposes that elder abuse occurs when there is a suitable target, the absence of a capable guardian, and a motivated offender. According to the routine activities theory, older adults are often viewed as being frail, powerless, incompetent, and "easy targets" for victimization, especially if they are socially isolated (without a capable guardian). In addition, the characteristics of the motivated offender help account for elder abuse (e.g., stress, dependency on the elder, substance abuse problems, a history of violence, irrational belief system, and psychopathology).

No one theory can explain the etiology of elder abuse, neglect, and maltreatment, and there is currently insufficient empirical evidence supporting the theories described above. To understand and prevent elder abuse, one must take into consideration the myriad interactions between multiple systems (e.g., individual, relationship, community, and society). It is also important to note that contributory factors rarely operate in isolation; rather, they interact in unique ways depending on the victim, the perpetrator, the environment, and the situation.

Nancy A. Orel

See also Elder Abuse, Neglect, and Maltreatment; Elder Abuse, Neglect, and Maltreatment: Interventions for; Family Violence; Psychological/Emotional Abuse; Violence, Theories of

Further Readings

Brandl, B., Bitondo Dyer, C., Heisler, C. J., Otto, J. M., Stiegel, L. A., & Thomas, R. W. (2007). *Elder abuse detection and intervention: A collaborative approach.* New York: Springer.

Payne, B. K. (2002). An integrated understanding of elder abuse and neglect. *Journal of Criminal Justice, 30,* 535–547.

Quinn, M., & Tomita, S. (1997). *Elder abuse and neglect: Causes, diagnosis, and intervention strategies.* New York: Springer.

Richard, B. J., & Wallace, R. B. (Eds.). (2002). *Elder mistreatment: Abuse, neglect, and exploitation in an aging America.* Washington, DC: National Academies Press.

Web Sites

National Center on Elder Abuse: http://www.ncea.aoa.gov

ELECTRONIC MONITORING

The term *electronic monitoring* (EM) mainly refers to a range of technologies that can be used to achieve remote oversight of the locations and schedules of offenders *under supervision in the community.* The concept, and basic patents for the technology, were developed by behavioral psychologists Ralph and Robert Schwitzgebel at Harvard University in the 1960s, and entailed the monitoring of movement rather than of specific locations, although this was also possible. Convinced Skinnerians, the Schwitzgebels (who subsequently changed their surname to Gable, and remain engaged with debates on EM) envisaged it as an adjunct to rehabilitation, not as the punitive and controlling measure it subsequently became, but at the time neither correctional applications nor commercial sponsorship could be found for it. Practical applications were not triggered until the early 1980s, after Judge Jack Love of Albuquerque, New Mexico, persuaded an electronics engineer, Michael Goss, to develop the available technology as a means of enforcing house arrest (rather than tracking movement). By this time, the components for making portable signaling devices (ankle bracelets) were smaller, lighter, and cheaper, and the *controlling* potential of EM becoming more readily appreciated by commercial and correctional interests alike. Love's original intention had been to find ways of supervising prisoners' on home leave from the local penitentiary, but EM initially gained ground in the United States as a mainstay of the "intermediate sanctions" movement.

For local political reasons, EM was not sustained in Love's jurisdiction, but experimental schemes were established elsewhere, notably Kenton County, Kentucky, and Palm Beach, Florida. Florida rapidly became the main site of innovation in EM and remains so to this day. EM spread patchily but rapidly across the United States in the 1990s and also began to spread abroad—initially to Canada, Australia, and Singapore. The first European jurisdiction to experiment with EM was England and Wales (which referred to it as "tagging"), while Sweden was the first to develop a fully national scheme. At the present time, approximately 30 countries make use of EM, at least experimentally—South Africa and Norway are among the latest adopters. Supervisory schemes involving EM have developed at the pretrial, community sentence, and release from prison stages of the criminal justice process—some countries utilize all three, some focus more on one than the others.

Forms of Electronic Monitoring

The manufacture of EM technology, and quite often the delivery of monitoring services themselves, resides with commercial organizations contracted to state agencies rather than with state agencies themselves. These organizations are part of an international "commercial corrections complex" and, alongside governments seeking both to increase the onerousness of community supervision and to reduce the high costs of imprisonment,

they have played a significant part in the global expansion of EM by creating innovative products for the emerging "crime control" market. EM now encompasses voice verification (confirming presence at a particular location using telephony and a person's unique biometric voice print) and remote alcohol monitoring (checking alcohol intake at home via a digitized breathalyzer linked to the phone), as well as the original radio frequency (rf) technology that had turned house arrest into a viable intermediate sanction. Worldwide, however, in comparison to solely rf-based systems, these are used relatively little. The advent of satellite tracking using the global positioning system (GPS) in the late 1990s vastly increased the potential of EM, enabling the monitoring of movement, either in real time or through retrospective route tracing, as well as the creation of exclusion zones from which offenders could be prohibited. Satellite tracking has expanded significantly as a postrelease program in the United States, sometimes displacing rf-based systems, and has been piloted in England and Wales, France, and the Netherlands.

Electronic Monitoring and Crime Reduction

While the merely ideological and commercial drivers of EM's global expansion cannot be underestimated, criminal justice practitioners and policy makers have to a greater or lesser degree always justified its use to the public in terms of crime reduction and public protection. It has been persistently claimed by EM's champions that offenders' wearing an electronic anklet while confined for a set period in their own homes, or having their movements monitored in real time by satellites, will reduce the propensity of offenders to reoffend, at least for the duration of the court order. It is true that remote electronic monitoring exerts more moment-by-moment control over an offender than does periodic personal contact with a probation officer or social worker, and most research indicates that rates of compliance are high while the anklet is being worn. Compliance is largely a product of the inherently surveillant aspects of EM—compared to monitoring by people, it significantly increases the likelihood of violations being detected—and the fear of more punitive consequences (usually prison sentences) if the initial order or sentence is breached. One major advantage of EM is that it enables offenders to remain in daytime employment while undergoing nighttime curfews (or vice versa). Some jurisdictions, however, permit 23- or 24-hour periods of home confinement for some offenders and demand relatively rapid follow-up action if a violation is recorded in the monitoring center, and while this is arguably tantamount to turning the home into a "virtual prison," it is still misleading to consider EM an incapacitative measure. Tagged offenders can always remove or disregard the bracelet and choose to reoffend in the community (or the home), something that the locks, bolts, and bars of a real prison preclude.

The capacity of EM to reduce criminal behavior is limited, however, because EM contains no inherent mechanism for changing offenders' attitudes or giving them positive incentives to be law abiding. Some—mostly anecdotal—evidence exists that periods of home confinement can in themselves create windows of opportunity for offenders, prompting them to review the direction in which their lives are going and perhaps exposing them to beneficial influences from the family members into whose proximity such confinement draws them. This is a slender basis on which to claim a significant crime reductive role for EM, and no evidence exists to show that EM reduces reconvictions *after* the duration of an order or sentence. However, some evidence from Canadian research shows that EM house arrest combined with participation in rehabilitative programs increases the likelihood of offenders with unstable lifestyles completing those programs and thereby benefiting from them, although in respect to juvenile offenders, evidence from research conducted in Scotland implies the opposite—tagged youngsters on an intensive supervision program fared less well than those on the program who were not tagged. A large-scale survey of EM use in Florida purports to show that there is a significant crime-suppression effect among offenders while they are subject to EM. This may be true, but the study fails to distinguish between EM home confinement and GPS tracking (which are distinctly different forms of surveillance), and also fails to indicate which offenders also had probation support and which did not, implying, implausibly, that this was irrelevant to the outcome. The study also extrapolates from the seemingly high rates of compliance with EM over

relatively short periods of time the idea that compliance and crime suppression will be sustained over much longer periods, perhaps even over the remaining life span of released sex offenders (and this surveillance program is one to which a number of American states are now committed).

Electronic Monitoring and Victim Protection

While the public protection aim of tagging offenders implicitly encompasses the general prevention of victimization, the use of EM technology to protect specific victims from specific offenders is a much smaller-scale development in use in the United States, Scotland, and Spain. Protecting children from sexual predators has been a potent feature of debate in the United States about satellite tracking of released sex offenders, and some offenders, depending on where they resettle, have been given exclusion zones around the homes of former victims. Exclusion zones around particular neighborhoods can also be imposed on drug-using burglars who have habitually targeted these neighborhoods—this was a significant rationale of satellite tracking in the England and Wales pilots. The use of "bilateral electronic monitoring" in a domestic violence context can use either rf or GPS technology to protect specific victims. The victim's home is equipped with a receiver sensitive to the signal from an offender's ankle bracelet; if the offender goes near the home, both the victim and the police are alerted. Small-scale research in the United States suggests that such interventions have value for victims, while recognizing that they are a short-term solution to a long-term problem, and may create false expectations of security. Swedish research into crime victims' attitudes regarding the desirability and legitimacy of EM as a penalty for offenders found victims to be moderately supportive of EM, skeptical of EM being used too much as a substitute for custody, and insistent that particular victims should be informed if "their" offender was given EM. In general, far too little is known about the attitudes of crime victims toward EM. These attitudes probably vary on a country-by-country basis, but victim advocacy groups such as Mothers Against Drunk Driving have been known to campaign against EM when it is used as an alternative to custody of DUI offenders.

In recent years, the term *electronic monitoring* has ceased to be associated solely with supervising offenders in the community and providing alternatives to prison; it is now possible to create *electronically monitored prisons* by tagging inmates (and possibly staff and visitors too) and placing a network of sensors high on the building walls and (in the case of open prisons) around the perimeter. All can be monitored on a single screen in a small room, making individual prisoner locations and "online headcounts" of the entire institutional population available whenever needed, instantaneously if required. The technology was pioneered in the United States, but has not yet become widespread, possibly because it has implications for custodial staffing levels. In Europe it was pioneered in the Netherlands, followed by Sweden, both of which use it in several prisons. As with all forms of prison security, the rationale behind the introduction of this technology is a mix of institutional efficiency and public protection, but insofar as the systems can be programmed to alert staff when inmates who might harm each other (e.g., rival gang members) are coming into close proximity, it can also be used to reduce victimizations in prisons.

The Future of Electronic Monitoring

The ethical questions at the heart of all debates about EM technologies relate to the extent to which they could or should displace or augment more humanistic practices in the management of offenders, which respect their personhood and mobilize community resources to encourage positive changes in their behavior. "Technical fixes" alone usually have their limits, but even where they are effective they may be unethical, something easily overlooked when dealing with publicly despised malefactors. The prospect of purely automated systems of surveillance and management of offenders, in prison or out, devoid of social approaches to effecting behavioral change, is surely unappealing to many. EM sometimes does play a part in crime reduction during the periods offenders are subject to it, but only a small one, and it can easily be oversold. Former crime victims might well opt for electronic early warning systems in order to protect themselves, and it may well be preferable for female victims of domestic abuse and their children to remain in their own homes rather than going into shelters, but the creation of safe and just communities requires far more than merely technical interventions.

Insofar as the availability of a global information and communication technology infrastructure nowadays now makes possible unprecedented means of pinpointing an offender's location in social space, modern government agencies will always be pressed to consider how customizing such technology might advance their crime control agendas, particularly if cost and efficiency savings in offender management might accrue. The precise forms of EM technology will change, and its application will be shaped by the perceived penal needs and traditions of different countries, but the concern with monitoring offenders' schedules and locations will henceforth remain an integral part of what it means to supervise offenders and to protect society.

Mike Nellis and J Robert Lilly

See also Closed-Circuit Television; Drug Use Forecasting/Arrestee Drug Abuse Monitoring

Further Readings

Erez, E., & Ibarra, P. I. (2007). Electronic monitoring and victim-re-entry in domestic violence cases. *British Journal of Criminology, 47*(2), 100–120.

Mair, G. (2005). Electronic monitoring in England and Wales: Evidence-based or not . . . ? *Criminology and Criminal Justice, 5*(3), 257–277.

Nellis, M. (2004). Electronic monitoring and the community supervision of offenders. In A. E. Bottoms, S. Rex, & G. Robinson (Eds.), *Alternatives to prison* (pp. 224–247). Cullompton, UK: Willan.

Renzema, M., & Mayo-Wilson, E. (2005). Can electronic monitoring reduce crime for medium to high risk offenders? *Journal of Experimental Criminology, 1*(2), 215–237.

EXPERT TESTIMONY AND FORENSIC EVIDENCE

The success of any court case rests on the quality of the evidence presented. That quality can be greatly affected by the use of expert witnesses and forensic evidence. Each of these is addressed in this entry.

Expert Testimony

An expert witness is an advocate for the truth who works for neither the prosecution nor the defense. Expert testimony is used in criminal and civil cases, where an expert in a particular field assists the trier of facts in comprehending evidence that the trier otherwise would not understand. For example, an expert witness may testify to appropriate standards of care and explains various medical terms and/or procedures. This person has specialized education, experience, and/or training and thus possesses knowledge about a subject that exceeds that of the layperson. The job of an expert witness includes educating the trier. It is necessary for the expert to be objective and willing to limit his or her discourse to the relevant facts. Expert witnesses are called upon to provide two types of evidence—information on the facts in issue and inferences drawn about facts—by testifying as to their professional opinion. Such witnesses play a vital role in cases requiring scientific evaluation and interpretation of facts beyond the capabilities of the layperson.

Expert testimony in the consideration of a forensic exam usually describes the narrative history, which is the verbal history of the crime, and a physical examination of the victim. This includes the evidence collected (such as photos and swabs) and documentation of the evidence. Other documentation includes findings consistent with the victim's history, findings consistent with the ingestion of various types of medications and alcohol, and any reactions the victims demonstrate. Medical expert witnesses can appropriately conclude whether there is evidence of sexual contact and/or recent trauma. They can testify to the consistency between the physical findings and the narrative history. The medical expert must have specialized education and experience, including extensive experience with normal exams. The expert's understanding of the research literature and its limitations can support impartial statements about evidence observed or collected. In addition, an expert witness is able to describe standards or review work done by professionals from the same discipline.

An expert witness is a justice advocate looking and working for justice for both the victim and the defendant. The witness is familiar with courtroom procedures and conduct. Expert witnesses come from many disciplines, such as law enforcement, the medical profession (including nursing), advocacy, toxicology, and forensic science. The expert witness needs to maintain a current curriculum vitae (CV) and a log for each case that contains dates of deposition or testimony as well as the names of the court, judge, and defendant. It is extremely important for the expert witness to stay current in his or her area of expertise.

Experts are qualified by court based on extensive experience and training. They explain the process of collecting and analyzing evidence. Most states have adopted the federal rules of evidence that give a definition of how a person is qualified. A witness qualified by knowledge, skill, experience, training, and/or education may testify thereto in the form of an opinion. In regards to the federal rules of evidence, hearsay exceptions include statements for the purposes of medical diagnosis and treatment. These can describe medical history or past and present symptoms, including pain.

For expert testimony to be admitted it must be consistent with the federal standards outlined in *Daubert v. Merrell Dow Pharmaceuticals* (1993), which clarified standards for admissibility and emphasizing reliable scientific evidence. Trial judges have discretion in deciding whether to admit expert testimony. Generally it will be allowed when it is scientifically valid, beyond the common understanding of jurors, and will clarify issues.

Forensic Evidence

Forensic evidence helps establish the truth that the witnesses can supply. There are many types of evidence admissible, including circumstantial evidence, documentary evidence, and real evidence. Circumstantial evidence is usually a collection of facts maintained by a considerable quantity of verifying evidence. It is circumstantial, however, because it was not directly witnessed. Documentary evidence is that which is recorded on evidentiary and chain-of-custody forms. Documentation of evidence is one of the first steps in correct evidence collection. Real or direct evidence is observed and/or witnessed evidence.

Physical evidence is any substance, solid, liquid, or gas, used to determine facts in a given situation showing that a crime has occurred or establishing a link between the victim and perpetrator. This evidence can be tangible evidence, which means touchable; trace evidence, which is not always seen by the naked eye; or transient evidence, which can be washed away, destroyed, lost, or damaged.

It is critical in medicolegal cases that any and all evidence is handled, documented, and disposed of properly. Accurate and objective documentation of the location, size, type, number, and appearance/character of injuries/defects is critical. A photograph is needed with a scale or ruler to assist with size determination, while diagrams are helpful in documenting evidence. The terminology used to describe evidence needs to be specific and accurate.

Forensic packages are sealed and labeled with the date, time, patient's name, description and source of material, name of health care provider, and names and initials of all who handled or transferred the material. The documentation on evidence needs to be detailed to ensure the chain of custody. The labeling assists in the identification of the evidence and its hand-off to the appropriate authority. This follows state and federal requirements for the systematic process of forensic evidence.

The chain of custody is a legal process referring to the paper trail that ensures the integrity and security of the evidence. The chain of custody forms and labels document possession from the moment of collection until the evidence is introduced into court. This links each person who handles the evidence. It is important to have detailed protocols for the collection of forensic evidence in cases, including meticulous documentation guidelines. Evidence from the body of the victim represents a critical thread in the legal proceedings. Personnel are specifically trained in maintaining the proper chain of evidence. The injured party needs to be completely undressed and all body surfaces inspected for the best collection of evidence. For best evidence collection practice, the crime scene needs to be secured; thus, each piece of evidence is placed in separate paper bags to avoid cross-contamination, and then each bag is labeled.

Carol Buschur

See also In-Camera Proceedings; Medical Examiner Response Team (MERT); Sexual Assault Nurse Examiner (SANE)

Further Readings

Assid, P. A. (2005). Evidence collection and documentation: Are you prepared to be a detective? *Topics in Emergency Medicine, 27*(1), 15–26.

Lonsway, K. A. (2005). *The use of expert witnesses in cases involving sexual assault.* Minneapolis, MN: Violence Against Women Online Resources.

Lynch, V. A. (2006). *Forensic nursing.* St. Louis, MO: Elsevier Mosby.

Rutz-Contreras, A. (2005). The nurses as an expert witness. *Topics in Emergency Medicine, 27*(1), 27–35.

Stokowski, L. A. (n.d.). *Forensic nursing: Part 1. Evidence collection for nurses.* Retrieved March 30, 2008, from http//:www.cme.medscape.com/view article/571057

Zadunayski, A. C. (2006). *Directed research: Expert medical evidence in the criminal justice system: The case for sexual assault nurse examiners.* Submitted to Alberta Association of Sexual Assault Centres.

Web Sites

Medscape: http://www.medscape.com

EXPLOITATION BY SCAMS

A scam is a fraud involving trickery to obtain a financial or other benefit. The term *scam* can be used broadly to refer to most types of fraud, but it usually implies a deliberate and planned hoax, often one that can be repeated on different victims and involves a false offer or "bait." Scams appear to be at least as old as recorded history. For example, in *Swindled: The Dark History of Food Fraud, From Poisoned Candy to Counterfeit Coffee,* Bee Wilson chronicles the extraordinary range of ways in which imitation food products have been manufactured or additives used to enhance degraded foods, often resulting in illness and death from poisoning. Fake medicines have been a traditional favorite of fraudsters, including the infamous snake oil remedies sold at traveling fairs. Counterfeiting, including of artworks and antiquities, has been another favorite of scammers.

Numerous scams can be categorized as *consumer frauds,* but these are also highly diverse. Relatively simple consumer frauds involve selling faulty products with false specifications or worthless warranties.

More sophisticated consumer scams deploy tactics such as bait and switch, where customers are lured by discounts, told the discounted product is sold out, and redirected to a more expensive product. Scams can also occur within the workplace. An employee might embezzle funds from his or her employer through an elaborate scheme for siphoning company monies. Conversely, an employer might perpetrate a scam against employees, such as through a fraudulent pension plan. Scams can also be perpetrated in professional settings. Doctors have defrauded medical welfare services by techniques such as *upgrading* (charging for phantom services or exaggerated injuries) and *ping-ponging* (unnecessarily referring patients among their colleagues).

Offenders and Victims

Various terms have been coined to describe the perpetrators of scams, including *confidence trickster, conman, swindler, fraudster, shyster,* and *grifter.* Accomplices are sometimes called *shills.* Although it appears that people in all walks of life are capable of inventing and carrying out scams, studies have identified a fraudster-type personality—typically an older male with sociopathic tendencies who obtains gratification from tricking victims and serially offends despite repeat criminal convictions. Fraudsters of this type are often itinerant—targeting an area and then moving on before being exposed. Lone fraudsters also often specialize—in marriage scams, for example, or maintenance scams.

Victims of scams are sometimes referred to as marks or targets. Fraudsters often "prey on the weak," such as the elderly, pensioners, sick and handicapped persons, or travelers. At the same time, the victims of many frauds include intelligent, well-educated, and wealthy persons. Greed, or simply a desire for a better lifestyle, blinds otherwise rational people to the improbabilities inherent in most scams.

Types of Scams

While trickery is at the heart of any scam, there is enormous variation in scams and constant innovation in the types of scams perpetrated. The following is a brief list of contemporary scams, many of which have been prominent in media reports and law enforcement crackdowns in recent years.

- Investment scams work by sales pitches promising high returns, often on glamour projects such as ostrich farms or diamond mines. Instead of properly developing the project, the investment manager siphons the monies into personal accounts (often in a financial safe haven).
- Ponzi-type investment scams use new borrowings to pay dividends on earlier borrowings and attract more investors until the fraudster shuts down the operation.
- In "pump and dump" schemes company directors artificially boost stock prices by false advertising and "leaks." They sell their stocks when the price peaks.
- In a pyramid scheme money is shared up a pyramid of members, with fresh input from new members sustaining it until lack of recruits leads to its collapse.
- Invoice fraud involves billing businesses for services they have not requested.
- Lottery scams work by notifying people they have won a prize but need to send a small amount of money for administrative purposes.
- In maintenance scams offenders provide a quote for repair work. They then disappear with the deposit or their poor workmanship comes to light after they have moved on.
- In agency scams the victim pays for an agent to find him or her an acting role or a publisher for a manuscript, and no genuine efforts are made.
- Portfolio shoots involve charging the victim fees for photographic sessions linked to false promises of work as a model.
- Introduction agencies take fees while making few or no efforts to provide matches.
- "Passing off" refers to the false identity of someone posing as a door-to-door charity worker or government agent. The caller presents false identification, takes the donation or fee, and issues a false receipt.
- With phone fee scams, callers are kept on the line while being billed by the minute.

Current Trends

Many scams work by cold calling large numbers of persons in order to obtain a percentage payoff. The spread of the Internet has vastly enlarged the means by which offenders can access targets.

Direct mail and telemarketing have been overtaken by broadcast emails—a component of "spam." Electronic funds transfer facilitates access to victims' bank accounts from remote locations. The most notorious contemporary Internet scams are "Nigerian advance fee" schemes, which offer a share in a fortune if the target provides a transfer fee or their bank account as a repository. In the latter case the offenders are able to withdraw money from the victim's account. ("The Spanish prisoner" is a generic term for an offer to share in a fortune as a reward for assisting a wealthy person who is in a difficult situation.) The Internet, electronic banking, and the spread of credit cards have been major facilitators of scams involving identity theft to obtain services or loans under another person's name. The growth of the welfare state has also enlarged opportunities for fraudsters to claim welfare payments with multiple false identities or sham disabilities.

Tim Prenzler

See also Exploitation by Scams, Interventions for; White-Collar Crime

Further Readings

Wilson, B. (2008). *Swindled: The dark history of food fraud, from poisoned candy to counterfeit coffee.* Princeton, NJ: Princeton University Press.

Zukhoff, M. (2005). *Ponzi's scheme.* New York: Random House.

Web Sites

SCAMwatch: http://www.scamwatch.gov.au

EXPLOITATION BY SCAMS, INTERVENTIONS FOR

As part of a drive against white collar crime, governments in the last few decades have increasingly engaged in prohibition and enforcement of scams. The results have been mixed. Outlawing pyramid schemes can be fairly effective, as they normally involve personal contact and are easily reported and prosecuted. Investment scams, on the other hand, are much more difficult to stop because they are easily disguised as legitimate business ventures and the law in many jurisdictions is designed to support free enterprise. Internet-based scams also appear to be flourishing, in part because of the versatility of the technology and in part because of the difficulties of policing crime across jurisdictions. Impoverished countries with weak or indifferent law enforcement provide safe havens for Internet scammers.

Historical Background

In the past, the prosecution of scams was highly selective. Extreme punishments could be applied to fraudsters who breached monopolies or royal prerogatives. At the same time, there was little or no protection from the State for ordinary victims. Those with means were obliged to pursue private investigations and prosecutions to attempt to recover losses. In many jurisdictions it was not until after World War II that adequate laws were introduced against medical quackery, the adulteration of foods, or consumer hoaxes. Even then, enforcement usually lagged well behind the scale of the problem. For much of the capitalist period the philosophy of caveat emptor—or buyer beware—governed State responses to scams. The laissez faire approach placed responsibility on the purchaser to judge the quality of a product and take action in the civil courts to obtain compensation for breach of contract. Critics of this approach, such as consumer watchdog groups, have argued that the technical complexity of products and the power of companies to deflect dissatisfied customers means that a large regulatory infrastructure is needed to protect consumers and investors, and that this is a fundamental function of government.

Smart Regulation

The success of consumer watchdog groups in exposing scams and embarrassing governments into action has led to the contemporary adoption, at least in theory, of "smart regulation" intended to prevent or preempt the development of scams. Smart regulation involves a mix of strategies designed to minimize crime as effectively and efficiently as possible. A feature of modern policing has been the proliferation of specialist law enforcement agencies, including those targeting fraud. Larger police departments now have specialist fraud units that include staff with qualifications in accounting and information technology. There are many other government agencies that have a significant role in combating fraud. In relation to scams, the two main types of agencies are consumer protection (or fair trading) agencies and financial regulatory agencies.

Prohibitions on false and misleading advertising have been a cornerstone of the criminalization of scams. Closely allied with this are regulatory requirements for product information disclosure statements, and the production of receipts and warranties with all purchases. Licensing of investment advisers and the application of enforceable codes of conduct have been important means by which governments underwrite the integrity of financial service providers. Identity theft has been countered in part by tighter cross-referencing procedures, with points systems for combinations of documents, and the introduction, in some countries, of national identity cards with high security features. Reforms in contract law have also supported consumers, with more information required on contracts (such as agents' fees and dispute resolution options) and cooling off periods that allow a purchaser to withdraw from a contract. The following additional strategies have been adopted in various locations as model "smart" strategies:

- Publicizing prosecutions to deter offending
- Issuing warning notices
- Banning convicted persons from owning or managing companies
- Providing legal and technical advice to companies to aid compliance
- Confiscating the proceeds of fraud and illegally obtained assets
- Using confiscated proceeds to compensate victims
- Proactively conducting sweeps of advertising outlets and Web sites to identify and investigate suspect advertisements
- Setting email traps to attract spam and assist in the targeting of investigations
- Making it easier for people to make complaints through free call services and email access

- Creating consumer education campaigns, especially to target groups such as the elderly and retirees
- Introducing scam alerts through the media and agency Web sites

Some regulatory agencies have tried novel ideas such as annual campaigns in which they advertise scams and then alert respondents to their gullibility. Independent consumer groups also play a key role in protection against scams by publicizing scientific evaluations of products, presenting sham awards to expose and shame offenders, and lobbying governments for reform. There have also been improvements in institutional in-house defenses for blocking spam, and in private–public partnership agencies that monitor the Internet for scams such as theft of intellectual property.

The Regulatory Gap

Despite enlarged efforts to get tough on fraudsters, a major feature of regulatory systems is the high "attrition of complaints." Most complaints are never investigated nor dealt with in any substantive fashion. Agencies will claim they do not have the resources, or there is insufficient preliminary evidence, to investigate most complaints. They argue they need to focus their efforts on major cases and exemplary prosecutions of serious and high-profile offenders. While their annual reports usually reveal significant activity, they are vulnerable to the accusation that they deflect complainants, lack investigative zeal, and are prosecution averse. Many victims remain obliged to resort to the uncertainties of civil action as a remedy. Regulatory agencies also tend to have underdeveloped capacity in primary prevention or early detection and intervention. Internationally, there is an urgent need for all countries to agree to protocols to halt the proliferation of Internet-based scams. Action in this area could in part be facilitated by wealthy countries—where the main targets reside—supporting law enforcement interventions in nations that host scammers.

Tim Prenzler

See also Crime Prevention; Exploitation by Scams

Further Readings

Friedrichs, D. (2007). *Trusted criminals: White collar crime in contemporary society.* Belmont, CA: Thomson Wadsworth.

Web Sites

Home Office, Internet Crime: http://www .homeoffice.gov.uk/crime-victims/reducing-crime/ internet-crime

FAMILY AND DOMESTIC VIOLENCE, THEORIES OF

Domestic violence is one of the most common forms of criminal victimization, particularly of women and children. Research on family and domestic violence is guided by theories from four disciplines: feminist/gender studies, sociology, psychology, and criminology. Within each of these disciplines there are multiple, often competing theoretical explanations for the causes of violence between intimate partners and family members. This entry describes the most prominent theories of domestic violence developed within each discipline.

Feminist/Gender Theories

Feminist theories of domestic violence contend that the most common form of adult domestic violence is men's violence against their heterosexual female partners. Although feminist theorists acknowledge that domestic violence is perpetrated by women against men and by partners in gay and lesbian relationships, feminist theories contend that the structure of gender inequality makes women in heterosexual relationships particularly vulnerable to control and coercion by their husbands or boyfriends. Moreover, feminist theories of domestic violence propose that the cultural connection between masculinity and violence facilitates men's violence against their wives or intimate partners and men's abuse of children. Feminist theories of domestic violence differ in their explanations of the specific mechanisms that facilitate women's victimization and men's perpetration of domestic violence. Theorists in the radical feminist tradition propose that domestic violence is a tool used by men to maintain women's subordinate position within the family and within society. Radical feminist theorists argue that violence against women that is perpetrated by husbands or boyfriends is similar to the violence against women that is perpetrated outside of intimate relationships, such as sexual harassment and stranger-perpetrated sexual assault. Liberal feminist theorists emphasize that women are vulnerable to domestic violence because of their consignment to domesticity and economic dependency on men, which is due to occupational sex-segregation and wage discrimination by sex. In addition, liberal feminist theorists suggest that gender role ideologies encourage men's domestic violence against their wives and girlfriends. By defining masculinity using characteristics such as leadership, aggression, and independence and defining femininity using characteristics such as passivity and nurturance, these ideologies legitimize men's dominance over women and male authority within families.

Recent feminist scholarship on domestic violence emphasizes that gender is a multilevel construct that affects human behavior at the levels of identity, social interaction, and social structure. At the level of identity, gender refers to individuals' inner sense of themselves and others as masculine or feminine. Feminist scholars argue that gender socialization facilitates domestic violence by encouraging women to believe that they can heal an abusive partner through feminine love and nurturance. At the level of interaction, gender is a performance enacted for the benefit of an observer. Drawing on sociologist Erving Goffman's theory of gender as ritualized performance, feminist theorists have argued that domestic violence is a way for men to perform or demonstrate their masculinity to others when they feel a threat or challenge to their masculine status. At the level of social structure, gender organizes the assignment of people into social roles and positions and distributes resources unequally to women and men. From the gender as structure theoretical perspective, men's violence against women is facilitated by the fact that men receive more training and instruction in violence within society than do women.

Sociological Theories

Sociologists study the structural forces that influence violence in families, including economic forces such as poverty and unemployment and social inequalities of gender, race/ethnicity, and sexual orientation. In addition, sociologists study cultural forces that influence domestic violence, including normative beliefs about the legitimacy of violence in families, gender stereotypes, and violence in the media. Sociologist Murray Straus has proposed a cultural spillover theory of domestic violence, suggesting that when society legitimizes violence in one sphere, such as corporal punishment, people are more likely to perpetrate illegitimate violence. Sociologists have also theorized that the structure of families and cultural norms of family privacy lead to high rates of violence between family members.

Sociological theories can be categorized according to the level of analysis. Macro-sociological theories focus on the ways in which the organization of society and distribution of resources influence domestic violence. For example, the resource theory of domestic violence postulates that domestic violence may be a response to the stress and frustration of poverty, unemployment, and/or an absence of educational and occupational prospects. Studies find higher rates of domestic violence, including domestic homicide, among people who are economically and educationally disadvantaged. Social disorganization theory proposes that

domestic violence is influenced by characteristics of the social environment such as the presence of community and neighborhood amenities, residential stability and overcrowding, and the level of neighborhood street violence. Economically unstable, crowded, and high-crime neighborhoods discourage residents from forming close social bonds with neighbors and discourage reporting or intervention in cases of domestic violence.

Micro-sociological theories of domestic violence examine the ways in which violence emerges from face-to-face encounters in which individual actors interpret the situation that confronts them. In his micro-sociological theory of violence, Randall Collins has proposed that violence is rare in human interaction. In order to perpetrate violence, people must be encouraged or trained to overcome their fear and hesitation. Collins has argued that one way for humans to overcome this "confrontational tension/fear" of violence is by finding a weak and defenseless victim. According to Collins, domestic violence occurs because men perceive that female partners are weak and unable to defend themselves against attack.

Psychological Theories

Psychologists propose that domestic violence results from specific characteristics of personality and interaction that lead some individuals to perpetrate violence in family relationships. One psychological theory, that of the intergenerational transmission of violence, presents the idea that those who experience domestic violence are more likely to become abusers themselves. One of the ways to explain this association is with social learning theory, which asserts that individuals learn behavior through observation and modeling. In this way, a victim of abuse may determine that violence provides the abuser with some positive outcome and is therefore an appropriate response to conflict or environmental pressures. The relationship between victimization and perpetration is not assumed to be direct or unavoidable, but is instead seen as a facet of a much more complex constellation of potentially causal factors. Another way in which social learning may lead to the intergenerational transmission of violence is by contributing to a learned helplessness reaction in the victim. This response is characterized by feeling a lack of control over abusive situations, which results in feelings of helplessness that inhibit the victim's agency. Therefore, through social learning, children may sometimes adopt a learned helplessness response to violence that can carry over into adult relationships.

Attachment theorists propose that domestic violence in adult relationships stems from patterns of insecure attachment to others that are learned in childhood. Psychologist John Bowlby has theorized that people have an innate need for close relationships to others in order to survive. Thus, infants and children seek out secure attachments to caregivers to meet that need. If a child's need is not met, the child develops an insecure attachment to the caregiver. Insecure adult attachment styles are characterized by chronic anxiety about dependency on and fear of abandonment by intimate others. Theorists of adult attachment propose that the internal working models of attachment developed in childhood carry over into adult relationships. According to the adult attachment theory of domestic violence, individuals who developed insecure attachment styles during childhood are at higher risk for perpetrating domestic violence as adults.

Other psychological theories propose that domestic violence is linked to specific types of personality disorders such as borderline personality disorder or antisocial personality disorder. Psychologist Donald Dutton has suggested that there are two types of abusive personalities. The first type, the abuser with "borderline personality organization," experiences feelings of emptiness, fears of being alone, and insecure attachment to others. People who perpetrate domestic violence as a result of borderline personality disorder tend to use violence in an expressive and impulsive fashion. The second type of abusive personality is characterized by psychopathic traits such as shallow affect and frequent manipulation of others. People who possess psychopathic personality traits are more likely than others to engage in serious violence both within and outside of the family, and their violence is instrumental, designed to gain control over others.

Theories of Crime

Theories developed in criminology have been utilized less often in domestic violence research than have theories developed in feminist/gender studies, psychology, and sociology. Prior to the 1970s, domestic violence was generally viewed as a private family matter rather than a crime against society. People who perpetrated domestic violence were rarely arrested and prosecuted. Legal reforms since the 1970s have increased rates of arrest and prosecution for domestic violence, and the culture has gradually accepted the notion that domestic violence is criminal behavior. Following this trend, researchers have applied general theories of crime and violence developed in criminology to the study of violence in family relationships. Michael Gottfredson and Travis Hirschi's general theory of crime proposes that violence and other crime are caused by ineffective parenting that inhibits children's development of self-control. This theory posits that individuals who lack self-control use violence when they are frustrated or desire to gain control over a situation.

Strain theory offers a structural account of crime, suggesting that structural forces such as inequality and poverty can create incentives for crime. Strain theory posits that individuals engage in crime and violence when they are frustrated or blocked in their attempts to achieve their goals using legitimate methods. Robert Agnew has proposed that certain types of strains are more likely to lead to violence than others. According to Agnew, strains that result in illegitimate coping responses such as violence are those that are perceived as unjust, occur frequently, and are linked to low self-control. These types of strains are particularly likely to result in crime and violence because they encourage negative feelings such as anger, fear, and jealousy.

Comparing Theories

The theories of domestic violence developed in feminist/gender studies, sociology, psychology, and criminology emerged from different methodological traditions. Feminist theories propose that, due to gender inequality, women's voices are silenced and domestic violence is hidden from public view. Thus, feminist theories of domestic violence are based on studies of female survivors' narrative accounts of violence they experienced at the hands of their husbands and male partners. Sociological theories of domestic violence come primarily from large-scale survey studies that identify the individual and structural predictors of violent behavior. Micro-sociological studies, which focus on the interactive situations and contexts that encourage violence, are comparatively rare. Psychological theories of domestic violence are informed by clinical studies of people who are identified as having pathological or psychopathological characteristics. Research in criminology employs large-scale survey methods and pseudoexperimental research design.

Recent calls for integrating these theories propose that domestic violence is caused by a combination of psychological, cultural, and structural factors and is linked to systems of gender, racial/ethnic, and social class stratification. In addition, ecological theories of domestic violence posit that violence is rooted in a combination of individual, interactive, contextual, sociocultural, and social structural factors. However, efforts to develop and test integrated theories of domestic violence using multiple research methods are rare.

Kristin Anderson and Amanda Turner

See also Dating Violence; Domestic Violence; Intimate Partner Violence; Intimate Partner Violence, Theories of

Further Readings

Anderson, K. L. (2005). Theorizing gender in intimate partner violence research. *Sex Roles, 52,* 853–865.

Collins, R. (2008). *Violence: A micro-sociological theory.* Princeton, NJ: Princeton University Press.

Dobash, R. E., & Dobash, R. R. (1979). *Violence against wives: A case against the patriarchy.* New York: The Free Press.

Dutton, D. G. (2007). *The abusive personality: Violence and control in intimate relationships* (2nd ed.). New York: Guilford.

Dutton, D. G., Saunders, K., Starzomski, A., & Bartholomew, K. (1995). Intimacy-anger and insecure attachment as precursors of abuse in intimate relationships. *Journal of Applied Social Psychology, 24,* 1367–1386.

Heise, L. L. (1998). Violence against women: An integrated, ecological framework. *Violence Against Women, 4,* 262–290.

Sellers, C. S. (1999). Self-control and intimate violence: An examination of the scope and specification of the general theory of crime. *Criminology, 37,* 375–404.

Straus, M. A. (1990). *Beating the devil out of them: Corporal punishment in American families.* New York: Lexington Books.

FAMILY GROUP CONFERENCING

The *family group conference* (FGC) is a vehicle through which family members (and sometimes other involved parties) come together, in partnership with professionals, to resolve matters of child care and protection and youth offending. Although originally developed in Aotearoa, New Zealand, in 1989, the family group conference has since been adopted in a number of countries as a way of operationalizing notions of partnership and empowerment. In the area of child care and protection within the United States, family group conferencing has been incorporated into the process called *family group decision making.* In the United Kingdom, FGCs have been introduced in the context of partnership with families and the strengthening of voluntary and cooperative relationships between social service departments and the people they serve. In the context of youth justice, family group conferencing has also influenced service delivery as countries have explored ways of resolving youth offending issues through processes of restorative justice. Declan Roche has identified several dimensions of restorative justice, including bringing victims, offenders, and their families and friends together in an attempt to repair the harm done in the deviant act.

Restorative values have been influential in the development of youth justice practice internationally, and the conferencing process is now seen as both a progressive and socially acceptable means of responding to youth crime.

The Family Group Conference

In the context of the care and protection of children, an important aim of the FGC is to bring the family together to find safe solutions for children at risk. In the context of youth justice, the conference is a mechanism for holding young people accountable for their offending, making amends to victims, and providing support for both young people and their families. While the nature of the issues involved in care and protection and youth justice may differ, the process of family group conferencing follows a reasonably straightforward formula across the two domains: people are brought together to talk through the issues, information is provided to participants, the family is given the opportunity to discuss the issues privately and to develop a plan about what should happen next, and agreement is then reached on the plan. It is, however, family group conferencing in the area of youth offending that is of particular relevance to this discussion. Youth justice FGCs represent one of the earliest legislated examples of involving victims in a restorative process.

Bringing People Together

Consultation begins the FGC process, with the coordinator contacting participants and preparing them for the meeting. Wide family participation in the FGC is encouraged, and it is the coordinator's role to create a welcoming environment for participants by being responsive to cultural practices and preferences with respect to when and where the meeting may be held. The coordinator also ensures that victims to the crime are consulted and invited to attend the FGC. The coordinator uses the consultation process to explain to participants the purpose and process of the FGC and to identify any additional information or resources that may be useful in supporting a successful outcome. This may include any assessments that need to be undertaken prior to the meeting.

Information Phase

The meeting typically begins with a welcome that is responsive to the cultural needs of participants. After confirming the purpose of the FGC, the meeting moves into the information-sharing phase. This begins with a review of the charge against the young person and the opportunity for the young person to admit guilt or deny the charge. In situations where the young person denies the charge, the matter is returned to the enforcement professionals and the FGC cannot continue. However, where the youth admits guilt, FGC facilitates a process in which those involved are provided with the opportunity to express their views in the conference. The victim's report can be

particularly powerful, as the youthful offender hears directly the impact the crime has had on those involved.

The information-sharing phase of the meeting provides the opportunity for participants to ask questions and to clarify any issues they may have, as well as to ensure that the FGC in general has all the relevant information and advice necessary to reach good decisions.

Private Family Deliberations

Once the information-sharing phase of the meeting is complete, the coordinator asks those who are not family members to withdraw from the meeting to allow the family to consider the issues in private and to develop a plan or reach an agreed outcome. While FGCs share many features with other restorative justice processes of mediation, it is this private family time that distinguishes the FGC as originally developed in Aotearoa, New Zealand. The principle of private family time is strongly reinforced in practice, as it provides a greater opportunity for honest exchange between family members, provides a greater sense of family ownership of the process, and, arguably, provides a greater family support for the plan and commitment to the outcome than does the more public conference.

Reaching Agreement on the Plan

After the family has completed their private deliberations, the coordinator brings all participants back together to consider proposed decisions and plans. The plan typically includes a number of elements: the young person's ideas about how he or she may make amends and address the needs of the victim; attention to the future well-being of the young person, in particular, his or her rehabilitative needs; building on the strengths of the young person and reducing the likelihood of his or her reoffending; harnessing the strengths of the family; and the support or resources that may be required to achieve good outcomes. It is expected that young people are held accountable for their offending, while at the same time they are provided opportunities to develop nonoffending paths. Outcomes do not necessarily need to be complicated. It is nevertheless important that they are appropriate and relevant to the offending. A simple solution, such as a letter of apology, may be sufficient in some situations, while in other situations a more comprehensive plan will be required in which the young person may expect to perform services to the victim or to the wider community.

Strengths and Challenges

From a broader philosophical perspective, family group conferences and other such restorative conferencing models have the potential to support the democratization of state systems by increasing the participation of a broader group of citizens in matters of youth justice and the care and protection of children. Gale Burford and Sally Holland and their colleagues have argued that family group conferencing supports a more inclusive civil society by providing liberating processes for those exposed to state service intervention. Restorative justice conferencing has also featured in rights-based discourses with respect to both service-users right to involvement in matters that concern them and the accountability and agency rights of young people.

Resolving issues of youth offending through restorative means and keeping young people out of the court systems for as along as possible are aims that often have the potential to respond to the developmental needs of young people. From a developmental perspective, keeping young people out of the court system provides them with the time they need to move through transient phases of offending behavior. Jeffrey Butts, Susan Mayer, and Gretchen Ruth have argued that many young people move through difficult developmental transitions and over time acquire adult capacities for reasoning, taking responsibility and making enduring commitments. Restorative justice conferencing thus responds to the developmental needs of young people. In addition, in keeping young people out of the criminal justice legal system, it can have the additional benefit of disassociating them from criminal peer groups—an association that has the potential to worsen behavior rather than providing conditions for improvement.

Perhaps not surprisingly, restorative justice processes have been identified as responding well to the needs of victims. Heather Strang and her colleagues have noted that victims value the ability to participate in their cases, to confront the offender, and to be kept informed of the process. Research also indicates that restorative justice processes can significantly reduce the victim's feelings of fear and anger toward the offender. This provides a degree of confidence that restorative justice processes offer safe interventions for victims.

While family group conferencing has grown in strength across a variety of practice domains, practice challenges inevitably occur as restorative processes attempt to respond to the needs and interests of both victims and offenders. Voluntary participation has been identified as an important component of restorative justice interventions; however, offenders who reject the restorative justice process may face severe penalties that inherently compromise the voluntary nature of their response. The emphasis on accountability and the need for the young person to make amends for the crime also have the potential for focusing conferences more strongly on the victim's rights than on the well-being of the offender. Young people who offend, by virtue of their relative immaturity, have special needs that must be considered. They are likely to have problems such as poor mental health, drug and alcohol misuse, underdeveloped interpersonal skills, and poor educational outcomes, all of which require that they receive rehabilitative services to support their future well-being.

While interventions inevitably present challenges in practice, it is nevertheless possible to ensure that both participatory rights and the reconciliation of welfare and justice concerns regarding youth offending are professionally managed and receive support. Maintaining a rights focus while also responding to the young offender's needs can help to protect the interests of everyone involved in the process.

Final Thoughts

In recent years, family group conferencing and other restorative justice processes have had an undeniable impact on the delivery of youth justice services across international jurisdictions. Yet while they clearly offer a promising way forward, they remain in the margins of practice. Importantly, however, they are representative of a wider social movement that acknowledges both the importance of human agency and self-determination in the context of human service delivery and the need to explore less punitive alternatives to criminal justice.

Marie Connolly

See also Peacemaking: Alternative Court Remedies; Restorative Justice; Victim–Offender Mediation

Further Readings

Braithwaite, J. (2002). *Restorative justice and responsive regulation*. New York: Oxford University Press.

Burford, G. (2005). Families: Their role as architects of civil society and social inclusion. *Practice, 17*(2), 79–88.

Doolan, M. (2009). Social work and youth justice. In M. Connolly & L. Harms (Eds.), *Social work: Contexts and practice* (pp. 304–318). Melbourne: Oxford University Press.

Lo, T. W., Wong, D., & Maxwell, G. (2005). *Alternatives to prosecution: Rehabilitative and restorative models of youth justice*. Singapore: Marshall Cavendish Academic.

Maxwell, G., & Lou, J. H. (2007). *Restorative justice and practices in New Zealand: Toward a restorative society*. Wellington, New Zealand: Institute of Policy Studies.

Maxwell, G., Morris, A., & Vos, B. (2006). Conferencing and restorative justice. In D. Sullivan & L. Tifft (Eds.), *Handbook of restorative justice*. London: Routledge.

Morrison, B., & Ahmed, E. (Eds.). (2006). Restorative justice and civil society [Special issue]. *Journal of Social Issues, 62*(2).

Ward, T., & Langlands, R. (2009). Repairing the rupture: Restorative justice and the rehabilitation of offenders. *Aggression and Violent Behavior, 14*(3), 205–214.

FAMILY NURTURING PROGRAMS

Rates of family violence, conflict, and child maltreatment are high nationally and internationally, and the cost of such violence to society is very great. Family violence and child maltreatment are associated with multiple negative consequences for all family members and include physical injury, child neglect, separation and divorce, incarceration, psychological problems, child removal from the home, multigenerational substance, and youth delinquency, perpetration of violence, and death. This entry discusses the incidence and prevalence of child maltreatment and the relationship between child maltreatment and parental substance abuse; the need for prevention services focusing on family interventions, which are called nurturing and family-strengthening interventions; the definition of different types of family preventive interventions; and the most effective family interventions. The entry ends with a call for research on the critical core components of child abuse prevention programs with a family focus, the theories behind the evidence-based programs (EBPs), and the need for the widespread dissemination of such programs.

According to the Child Welfare League of America (CWLA), nationally, substance abuse is a factor in about 40% to 80% of substantiated cases of child maltreatment. Over 80% of state child protection agencies report that parental alcohol and drug abuse and poverty are the two major factors associated with child maltreatment. Parental substance abuse increases child abuse by about 300% and child neglect by about 400%. In addition, research showed that youth who had ever been in foster care had higher rates of illicit drug use than youth who had never been in foster care (33.6% vs. 21.7%). A greater percentage of youth who had been in foster care also were in need of treatment for both alcohol and drug abuse (17%) than youth who had never been in foster care (9%).

Need for Prevention Services

Despite significant need, many families and children involved in child welfare are not getting the prevention and treatment services they need. In 1997, the CWLA estimated that 43% of children and adolescents in care needed substance abuse services, while agencies obtained treatment for only around a third of these youth. In addition, it was estimated that 67% of the parents whose children were involved in child welfare needed such services, while agencies had capacity to serve around 31%. Beyond basic substance abuse treatment, it is unknown how many families learn skills and receive support to raise healthy children. A study by Teresa Ostler and her colleagues of children involved with child protective services due to parental methamphetamine abuse found that the children had few social resources for coping with emotions, problem solving, or talking about the experience.

Further, a multitude of developmental theories support the critical role of families in child raising. The National Longitudinal Study of Adolescent Health (also known as the Add Health study), published by Michael Resnick and his colleagues in 1997, suggests that parents have a larger impact on their children's development and health than previously thought. Although peer influence is the major reason adolescents initiate negative behaviors, a positive family environment (i.e., one with family bonding, parental supervision, and communication of prosocial family values) is the major reason youth do not engage in unhealthy behaviors such as substance abuse, delinquency, and early or unprotected sex. These protective family factors have been found to exert an even stronger influence on girls than on boys.

These statistics support the need for development of and research on EBPs for child welfare and substance abuse, as well as their implementation in community settings. Unfortunately, research in this area is scarce due to a lack of funding for child abuse prevention research that tests evidence-based family nurturing programs. In addition, family intervention researchers lack access to the cross-systems service delivery databases that would clearly prove that their interventions work to reduce child abuse. New grants to states and tribes by the Administration for Children and Families should enable researchers to show that family-strengthening interventions that improve parenting skills, family communication, problem solving, and stress management will result in reductions in family violence and child abuse.

Family Nurturing Interventions: Definitions of Types

Through national expert reviews of research, a number of family interventions have been found to be effective in strengthening family systems and reducing family violence. As these are recent interventions, there is not yet agreement among researchers about definitions and components of the different types of family-focused approaches. The Center for Substance Abuse Prevention (CSAP) reviewed family-strengthening approaches in 1997

and defined eight approaches; however, at that time only four approaches had sufficient research evidence to be considered evidence-based approaches to improving parenting skills and family relations: (1) *behavioral parent training* (primarily cognitive/behavioral parent training); (2) *family skills training* (parent training, children's skills training, and family practice); (3) *family therapy* (structural, functional, or behavioral), and (4) *in-home family support*. Since the CSAP review in 1998, two promising low-cost approaches have emerged: *mailed-out parenting homework assignments* like those used successfully by Karl Bauman and his colleagues in 2001 with parents of 12- to 14-year-old (Caucasian) children, and the *CD-ROM technology or learning videos* that several effective family interventions have utilized.

The last national review of family-strengthening approaches, conducted by Karol Kumpfer and Rose Alvarado in 2003, found 35 evidence-based practices. However, only 14 of these have been tested in randomized control trials and 7 independently replicated, thus meeting the criteria for programs with the highest level of evidence of effectiveness, or Exemplary I programs. The Exemplary I family programs for children from birth to age 5 include Helping the Noncompliant Child and The Incredible Years. The only Exemplary I rated program for families with 6- to 12-year-old children is the Strengthening Families Program. The preteen and adolescent programs are Functional Family Therapy, Multisystemic Family Therapy, Preparing for the Drug Free Years (now called Guiding Good Choices), and Treatment Foster Care. According to a meta-analysis of all school-based universal alcohol prevention programs, which was conducted by David Foxcroft and his colleagues in 2003 for the Cochrane Collaboration Reviews in Medicine and Public Health at Oxford University, the Strengthening Families Program for 10- to 14-year-olds is the most effective program and is twice as effective as the next best program, Preparing for the Drug Free Years. (For additional reviews of these effective family-strengthening approaches, see Kumpfer and Alvarado's 2003 *American Psychologist* article, "Family Strengthening Approaches for the Prevention of Youth Problem Behaviors," and the NIJ/OJJDP Strengthening America's Families Web site developed at the University of Utah, both of which are listed in the Further Readings at the end of this entry.)

In 2008, a systematic review by Kumpfer for the United Nations of all the most effective parenting and family programs in the world identified several additional EBP parenting programs, including Triple-P from Australia, which has evidence of reduction in child maltreatment in families participating a CDC-funded randomized control trial in South Carolina. There are currently no research results on this program being tested with high-risk families; however, a study is now under way. Adapting EBPs to local families was found by Kumpfer in 2002 to improve family recruitment and retention by 40%. A useful compendium for the UN project is a manual on how to locally or culturally adapt EBP family interventions to maximize family recruitment, retention, and outcomes. A summary of these steps to cultural adaptation of family programs was published in 2008 by Kumpfer and her colleagues.

Core Components of Child Maltreatment Prevention Programs

Jennifer Kaminski and her colleagues in 2008 analyzed the critical core components of EBP family-strengthening interventions from 77 studies of programs for child maltreatment prevention in children from birth to age 7. These core components include the following:

1. The format should include practice time for parents (with both children and group leaders in the sessions).

2. During family session, parents should be taught to interact positively with children (e.g., showing enthusiasm and attention for good behavior, letting the child take the lead in play activities).

3. Content for parents should include increasing attention to and praise for positive children's behaviors, understanding normal development, and developing positive family communication skills and effective discipline.

4. Content for children should include teaching children social skills.

5. Generalization of new behaviors should be facilitated through assignments involving practice at home or in other social settings.

Intervention Theories

Attention to mechanisms of change has been identified as a crucial component for advancing theory in family-based treatment, and ultimately for developing more effective prevention programs. The psychological theories underlying most family EBPs come from cognitive-behavioral psychology, social learning theory, and/or family systems theory, according to Howard Liddle and his colleagues. A key concept incorporated into many of the EBPs is to reduce coercive parent–child interactions that give rise to child abuse and family violence—a process well documented by Gerald Patterson at the Oregon Social Learning Center. The family systems approach uses reframing and cognitive restructuring methods to foster behavior change. Evidence-based family prevention interventions involve the whole family (rather than just the parents or children) in interactive change processes, rather than in didactic educational lessons. These EBPs stress the importance of the engagement process and reducing barriers to attendance, often through relationship-building services, such as personal invitations, meals, child care, transportation, and other incentives. Most begin with sessions designed to improve positive feelings through positive reframing or skills exercises stressing family strengths.

Dissemination

Web site lists by state and national organizations as well as regional clearinghouses have helped local practitioners to locate EBPs in parenting and family interventions. However, learning how to effectively disseminate EBPs has only come with experience for the university researchers who were not adept at marketing and dissemination 20 years ago. Today, evidence-based family interventions are highly structured programs with rigorous training programs to assure adherence or fidelity to the model. Most EBP family interventions require initial training workshops with some type of ongoing quality assurance system via outcome evaluations that include standardized measures.

Final Thoughts

Increased research on, dissemination of, and training in effective parenting and family intervention approaches will be important tools in helping societies address the problems associated with family violence and child maltreatment. Practitioners in the field should seek training in identifying effective parenting programs, as well as addressing how to adapt these models to create localized culture-, gender-, and situation-appropriate interventions.

Karol L. Kumpfer and Jody Brook

See also Child Abuse, Neglect, and Maltreatment; Cycle of Violence, Theory of

Further Readings

Alvarado, R., & Kumpfer, K. L. (2000). Strengthening America's families. *Juvenile Justice, 7*(2), 8–18.

Bauman, K. E., Foshee, V. A., Ennett, S. T., Pemberton, M., Hicks, K., King, T., et al. (2001). The influence of a family program on adolescent tobacco and alcohol use. *American Journal of Public Health, 91*, 604–610.

Child Welfare League of America. (2003). State child welfare agency survey. Washington, DC: Author.

Holleran Steiker, L. K., Castro, F. G., Kumpfer, K. L., Marsiglia, F. F., Coard, S., & Hopson, L. M. (2008). A dialogue regarding cultural adaptation of interventions. *Journal of Social Work Practice in the Addictions, 8*(1), 154–162.

Kaminski, J. W., Valle, L. A., Filene, J. H., & Boyle, C. L. (2008). A meta-analytic review of components associated with parent training program effectiveness. *Journal of Abnormal Psychology, 36*, 567–589.

Kumpfer, K. L. (2008). Why are there no effective child abuse prevention parenting interventions? *Substance Use and Misuse, 43*(9), 1262–1265.

Kumpfer, K. L., & Alvarado, R. (2003). Family strengthening approaches for the prevention of youth problem behaviors. *American Psychologist, 58*(6/7), 457–465.

Kumpfer, K. L., Alvarado, R., Smith, P., & Bellamy, N. (2002). Cultural sensitivity in universal family-based prevention interventions. *Prevention Science, 3*(3), 241–244.

Kumpfer, K. L., Pinyuchon, M., de Melo, A., & Whiteside, H. (2008). Cultural adaptation process for international dissemination of the Strengthening Families Program (SFP). *Evaluation and Health Professions, 33*(2), 226–239.

Kumpfer, K. L., Smith, P., & Franklin Summerhays, J. (2008). A wake-up call to the prevention field: Are prevention programs for substance use effective for girls? *Substance Use and Misuse, 43*(8), 978–1001.

Liddle, H. A., Santisteban, D., Levant, R., & Bray, J. (2002). *Family psychology: Science-based interventions*. Washington, DC: American Psychological Association Press.

National Clearinghouse on Child Abuse and Neglect. (2003). *Prevention pays: The costs of not preventing child abuse and neglect*. Retrieved February 2, 2004, from http://nccanch.acf.hhs.gov/pubs/prevenres/pays.cfm

National Research Council. (1993). *Understanding child abuse and neglect*. Washington, DC: National Academy Press.

Resnick, M., et al. (1997). Protecting adolescents from harm. Findings from the National Longitudinal Study on Adolescent Health. *Journal of the American Medical Association, 278*(10), 823–832.

Web Sites

NIJ/OJJDP Strengthening America's Families: http://www.strengtheningfamilies.org

FAMILY THERAPY

Family therapy is a therapeutic approach in which a family is under treatment as a unit, usually with a licensed therapist. The therapist may be a licensed counselor, a family and marriage counselor, or a psychologist or psychiatrist, or for short-term therapy, a pediatrician or general practitioner. Often the choice of therapist depends on the nature of the family's problem.

Definition

Family therapy is a process used to address behavioral problems, school problems, chronic or acute illnesses, critical transitional periods, cultural adaptation, and/or communication difficulties. Social problems such as poverty, addiction or imprisonment, and/or separation and divorce that may be found within the family unit may benefit from family therapy. When physical or congenital conditions occur, family therapy may work to alleviate the placing of blame and instill positive alternatives of treatment. A counseling environment may include individual sessions followed by congregated family sessions in an effort to identify ineffective forms of communication and reactions to problematic issues. This type of therapy addresses family problems within context. Unlike other forms of counseling, family therapy includes all members living in the home.

Multidimensional Challenges

In some cultures, parents, children, grandparents, cousins, aunts, and/or uncles may live in the same household. Family therapy requires cultural awareness, as a family's language, rituals, customs, and religious expectations may clash with those of the dominant culture. The environment that the children, in particular the females, find in the community may lead to significant problems within the home. Family therapists work to build on family members' inner resiliencies to help them develop positive forms of communication and behavioral changes within family relationships. This therapy may be short term (6 months) or long term, reflecting the presence of more complex issues that require sustained assistance.

Single parenting, poverty, and the financial stresses associated with being young parents often include referrals for welfare assistance, supportive mentoring, and periods of reflection on the significant changes associated with parenthood. Therapy may include development of coping techniques, healthy stress releases, and an awareness of when outside support may be wise. Some examples of stressful situations might include the colic of infants and sleeping problems of children, toilet training, separation anxiety, and illness.

Mental illness such as bipolar disorder, schizophrenia, and depression, or developmental disorders such as autism often causes numerous challenges to the family. In these cases there are often pharmacological interventions requiring consistent monitoring and evaluation. Family therapy includes numerous professionals working with the family to address ongoing physical challenges and behavioral changes. The family environment may require therapeutic specializations to address specific challenges.

Educational associated issues, including attention deficit/hyperactivity disorder (AD/HD), oppositional defiant disorder (ODD), learning disabilities, bullying, or being victimized by bullies may be addressed using therapies combining educational psychology and relationship issues. Family therapy may initiate supportive techniques and alternative

manners of resolution to prevent the transfer of the negativity to the home environment.

The difficulties posed by juvenile behaviors, including delinquency, running away, substance abuse, and the onset of puberty, may be addressed through family therapy in collaboration with court or school-related professionals. Very often the multistressors of puberty and social issues find their way into the therapy milieu. The economy, unemployment, employment that required transfer, unpaid child support, and/or significant economic stresses related to illnesses may be mitigated by family therapy. In some instances, the family therapist will work closely with community resources to alleviate some of the problems.

Relevant Family Therapy

Particular traumas such as divorce, blending of families, natural disasters, catastrophic illnesses, victimization, death, and bereavement often respond to family therapy, as it helps define behavioral boundaries and initiate the healing process. Periods of war cause difficulty for families left to fend for themselves, with one or, in some cases, both parents deployed. Grandparents and other family members become guardians of children who live under stress and fear. The reunification of the family often poses difficulties that respond well to family therapy. Family therapy offers members of the family the opportunity to share their perspectives on the changes, express their anger in a constructive manner, and share their fears and concerns for the future.

Family therapy addresses situations in which chronic mental illness or special needs must be balanced with general family welfare. Given the current demographics, older family members may no longer live independently and may move in with their family. This may prove a challenge to everyone in the household as autonomy is redefined. The new family environment may call for working within the context of the family and addressing periods of crisis through long-term collaboration or support groups. Generally health insurance pays for limited visits per year, and ongoing therapy may pose an economic hardship. In this instance it is likely that the family will find a therapist associated with a larger clinic or a philanthropic association.

Family Therapies and Policy

There is mixed research on the effectiveness of family therapies for those in situations involving physical and sexual child abuse and domestic violence. The literature includes challenges to court-mandated family therapy, where the violence includes repetitive interactions with the criminal justice system. However, therapists recognize that they often have little control over the court's programming mandates for dysfunctional or violent families.

Public policy has used the status of the family for political gain, setting moral standards, and research. Social science research promotes a position that the United States is not as concerned about the welfare of families as the rhetoric might indicate. Indicators such as family leave, adequate health care and child care, family therapy, and quality education are routinely noted as lacking in the United States compared to countries such as Europe, Great Britain, Australia, and Japan.

Toni DuPont-Morales

See also Cognitive–Behavioral Therapy; Couples Therapy; Multisystemic Therapy; Parents Anonymous

Further Readings

Bodden, D., Dirksen, C., & Bogels, S. (2008). Societal burden of clinically anxious youth referred for treatment: A cost-of-illness study. *Journal of Abnormal Psychology, 36*(4), 487–497.

Chang, Y., & Fine, M. (2007). Modeling parenting stress trajectories among low-income young mothers across the child's second and third years: Factors accounting for stability and change. *Journal of Family Psychology, 21*(14), 584–594.

Hoffman, L. (2002). *Family therapy: An intimate history.* New York: Norton.

Santisteban, D., Suarez-Morales, L., Robbins, M., & Szapocznik, J. (2006). Brief strategic family therapy: Lessons learned in efficacy research and challenges to blending research and practice. *Family Process, 45*(2), 259–271.

Web Sites

American Family Therapy Academy: http://www.afta.org

FAMILY VIOLENCE

Family violence is defined as the many types of violent behaviors committed by an offender who is related to the victim. Offenses such as domestic violence, intimate partner violence, elder abuse, and child abuse are all encompassed by the broad term *family violence*. It also includes verbal assaults, physical assaults, sexual assaults (including rape), intimate partner stalking, child abuse and/or neglect, emotional abuse and, at the extreme end, homicide. Family violence can happen to anyone and is not limited to those of any gender, race, ethnicity, socioeconomic background, or educational level.

Family violence is the most common violent crime in the United States today. Although as a proportion of the total number of violent victimizations, family violence has not really increased over the past 10 years, the rate of family violence (per 1,000 persons age 12 and older) has been decreasing over the last decade.

Prevalence and Frequency

It is important to note that any estimate of either the prevalence or frequency of family violence is probably incorrect. These statistics are notoriously hard to gather. Estimates are frequently gathered in one of two main ways. First, researchers will examine official statistics of those who came to the attention of the criminal justice system (through police, homicide, and court statistics), the public health system, or social service agencies. However, these statistics vastly underestimate the true nature of this offense, as it has been estimated that over half of these types of offenses do not come to the attention of public agencies. The second, more common, and more valid way to gather data is through the use of victimization surveys in which individuals are asked about their personal experiences with violence. These surveys also have problems with definitional issues since different surveys can define the problem differently due to the reluctance of some victims to admit their victimization.

In 2005, the Bureau of Justice Statistics, which collects family violence statistics, estimated that family violence accounted for 11% of all reported and unreported violence during the years 1998 to 2002.

Almost half were crimes against spouses, 11% were crimes against children, and 41% were against other family members. Only 60% of these offenses were actually reported to the police, and only 49% of those crimes resulted in an arrest. The average offender arrested for some type of family violence was a White male who was 30 years old or older. The average victim was reported to be a female, either White or Black, and was approximately 34 years old.

The National Violence Against Women Survey conducted in 1995 to 1996 found that almost 25% of the women and 8% of the men reported that they had been raped and/or physically assaulted during their lifetime. Extrapolating from these results, it was estimated that 1.5 million women and 834,732 men per year experience this type of family violence. The actual number of victimizations exceeds these estimates, as many individuals are victimized multiple times.

Recent statistics from the National Child Abuse and Neglect Data System indicate that approximately 905,000 children were found to be victims of child abuse or neglect in the year 2006. The statistics show that this is a widespread problem affecting millions of people each year and should be treated as a significant social problem. Moreover, it is important to remember that most of the statistics gathered to estimate the extent of these problems are thought to underestimate the problem.

Historical View

Evidence of family violence has been found as far back historically as we have records. It cuts across various cultures and civilization. Yet family violence encompasses a set of offenses that did not even exist as crimes historically. This is for a variety of reasons. Perhaps the most prominent reason is that both wives and children were considered property. As far back as ancient Roman law, men were granted the right to use violence to keep their wives in line. English common law provided that husbands were allowed to beat their wives as long as they used a stick no wider than their thumbs.

Historically children were not considered to have equal rights with adults and were believed to be the property of their parents. The societies were patriarchal; therefore, men were in charge and women and children were seen as essentially inferior.

Physical abuse was often used for discipline and punishment, and even the religious traditions of early America supported the notion of harsh discipline for children.

Thus family violence has a long historical tradition. In certain societies, such as that of ancient Rome, fathers were given the absolute right to sell their children, or mutilate or kill them; husbands were given similar rights with regards to their wives.

Many of these beliefs were brought over to America when the country was first formed. In addition, there was a long-standing tradition that family matters, including acts of violence, were private. As a result, in the early 1800s there were very few laws on the books dealing with this type of violence. In the late 1800s states had laws criminalizing wife beating, although these laws were rarely if ever enforced.

The modern child protective movement is thought to have started in 1874 with the case of Mary Ellen Wilson. Mary Ellen was an 8-year-old girl in New York City. Her mother, unable to care for her after her father's death, turned her over to the Department of Charities. This department placed her with a couple who beat her quite regularly and also neglected her. Her abuse was reported by a neighbor. However, since this was prior to the establishment of such things as the Department of Family Services or even juvenile courts, there was no clear way to deal with her case.

As a result of Mary Ellen's case, the New York Society for the Prevention of Cruelty to Children was founded in 1874. This was the first organization that focused on children's rights. The society helped to pass laws to prevent and punish wrongs that occurred to children in the home. In 1899 the first juvenile court was created in Illinois. The creation of a specialized court just for juveniles allowed for the handling of neglect and dependency cases as well as delinquency cases.

In 1962, C. Henry Kempe wrote an article that coined the term *battered-child syndrome* and was the first to draw public attention to this issue. In 1974 the Child Abuse Prevention and Treatment Act was passed. This act provided federal financing to support state protection agencies.

Although states criminalized domestic violence in the late 1800s, these laws were rarely if ever enforced. It was not really until the 1970s in the United States that domestic violence began to get any serious attention. In part because of the women's movement, issues of domestic violence were often brought into public view. In response to this grassroots movement, efforts were made to start addressing the issues. Researchers started collecting statistics to examine the extent of the problem, theories were developed to attempt to explain the problem, and interventions were created. For example, it was during this time period that battered woman shelters were created and developed. The medical profession also started to get involved in these issues. Legislation was passed to assist in the prosecution of such offenses. Although familial violence has existed throughout all of history, it is has really been only in the last couple of decades that we as a society have really attempted to address the issue.

Theories of Family Violence

There have been several models and theories advanced to attempt to explain family violence. In general these theories fall into several broad categories. Below is a sample of some of the more prominent perspectives in the field that illustrates the various ways in which researchers have attempted to explain family violence.

The Medical Model

This model focuses on explaining family violence as a result of individual psychiatric or psychopathological problems. It assumes that the perpetrator is suffering from some type of mental illness or mental problem that caused him or her to be abusive. Theories based on this model have attempted to identify specific personality traits or characteristics associated with family violence. They hypothesize that persons with such problems as depression, substance abuse, anger issues, mental illness, and so on are at an increased risk of perpetrating family violence. In particular, they have identified a number of risk factors with men who use violence against women. In general batterers tend to objectify women, have low self-esteem and low social-economic status, and have often witnessed violence in their own lives. Theories based on the medical model have also focused on explaining the victim's behavior and attempted to identify personal characteristics (such as dependency) that are sometimes associated with being a victim of family violence.

Sociopsychological Models

Several proposed theories fall under the broad category of sociopsychological models. These theories attempt to explain family violence in terms of the interaction between the family members.

Resource Theory

This theory focuses on the amount of resources individuals within the family possess. These include a variety of different types of resources such as personal, social, economic, and other resources. Some theorists believe that the more resources a person has, the more power he or she has in the family, and that this therefore places the individual in a position to make and enforce decisions in the family context, and, in some situations, to use abuse in this enforcement. Conversely, other theorists see those who have limited resources as being the ones most likely to be abusive, as these individuals use violence to establish their dominance.

Power-Control Theory

This theory examines the disparities in power between various family members, which are in part due to gender and age differences. In traditional families the men typically have the most power. According to this theory, the purpose of violence is to control and maintain power over the victim. This theory is supported by evidence of patterns of abuse, which shows that it is typically the person with the most power who abuses the person or persons with the least power.

Exchange Theory

This theory looks at the family dynamics in terms of costs and benefits. If individuals invest their resources (costs) in the family, then they expect certain benefits from that situation. The idea is that family members use violence to obtain the desired benefits.

Social Learning Theory

This theory describes what researchers have definitely ascertained: Violence is learned. Children who are either abused or who witness abuse in the home are at a higher risk than others of becoming abusive. The family is considered to be the primary socialization agent in which children learn their roles as future spouses and/or parents. In addition, they learn how to cope with stressful situations. Parents model violent coping strategies that are then modeled and reinforced.

Sociobiological Theory

This theory explains child abuse. Its main premise is that vulnerable children are abused because of natural selection and the family's desire to ensure that its genes survive for the next generation. Therefore, children who are physically or developmentally handicapped or chronically ill are the most likely to suffer abuse. It is also believed that parents who are more invested and/or attached to their children are less like to abuse them.

Sociocultural Models

These models examine the structure of the culture in which the violence is occurring. They explore the influence of norms and values that contribute to the acceptance of violence in our society.

The Cultural Theory of Violence

This theory postulates that violence is generally accepted in society as a whole. Therefore, if violence is acknowledged as a legitimate means of conflict resolution or as a method of achieving goals in the society, then it is logical that this would also be the case within the familial context. Further, it is suggested that a subculture of violence exists within the greater society. In other words, there are certain cultures that value the use of violence as a tool, and therefore these groups will resort to violence to help them accomplish their desired goals.

Feminist Theories

In these theories, the social structure of our society is examined. Traditionally, men have played a dominant role in our society. They have been the ones with access to the resources—the employment, education, property, and so on. This patriarchal structure is changing, but men still play powerful roles in most of the major establishments

responsible for dealing with incidents of abuse, such as the criminal justice system. Therefore, they are the individuals with control over the situation—both in terms of being the abusers and in terms of controlling how society responds to the abuse.

The reality is that family violence is a very complex problem that is not well explained by any one theory. The current trend is to incorporate a multidisciplinary approach to explaining this type of violence.

Risk Factors

The typical domestic violence offender is male, and the typical victim is female. In terms of age, research on spouse abuse has found that the typical batterer is usually under the age of 40, while the majority of victims are between the ages of 20 and 29. However, the National Crime Victimization Survey found that when intimate partner violence (i.e., violence in nonmarital as well as marital relationships) is included in the survey, the rates of violence are highest for women ages 16 to 24. Data from the NCVS indicate that the race and ethnicity of both the offender and the victim do not appear to affect rates of domestic violence. In terms of socioeconomic status, there is some evidence that rates of domestic violence are inversely related to income level and that blue-collar workers are more likely to be involved in domestic violence than are white-collar workers. Similarly, unemployment has been found to be a significant predictor of domestic violence.

In terms of child abuse, research has found that mothers are more likely than fathers to abuse their children. The majority of persons who abuse children are between the ages of 20 and 40. Similar to the research into domestic violence, research consistently shows that race and ethnicity have little impact on an individual's likelihood to engage in child abuse. Like spouse abuse, there is evidence that child abuse is more prevalent in populations with lower socioeconomic statuses.

In addition to the influence of demographic characteristics, a number of other factors have been found to increase the risk of becoming either a perpetrator or a victim. For example, domestic violence itself puts children at significant risk for child abuse. Further, having witnessed such violence as a child and/or experienced child abuse puts an individual at a higher risk of potentially becoming an abuser as an adult. In fact, this propensity has been referred to by researchers as the intergenerational theory of child abuse.

A relationship between alcohol and drugs and family violence has also been established. Substance use and abuse has been related to domestic violence, intimate partner violence, and child abuse. Social isolation is another factor that seems to be common among abusive families. Social isolation refers to situations where family members are cut off from extended family members, neighbors, and other sources of social support within their communities.

Consequences

In addition to the obvious physical damage sometimes inflicted by abuse, which can range from bruises to death, the psychological consequences are considerable. The Bureau of Justice Statistics reports that 9.2 million victims between 1998 and 2002 sustained injuries during an incident of family violence, although only 16.5% of these individuals received medical care for their injuries. Nevertheless, millions of medical personnel treat injuries from family violence annually. Victims of family violence are also at an increased risk for mental health problems, including such issues as depression, anxiety, posttraumatic stress disorder, low self-esteem, and so on. Domestic violence can also interfere with a woman's economic potential.

Children who witness abuse in the family suffer from stress, depression, and low self-esteem as well as feelings of powerlessness. They also are at an increased risk for other problematic behaviors, such as substance abuse, running away, and sexual behaviors. As mentioned previously, they have an increased risk of becoming abusers themselves. In fact, research has found that boys who witnessed abuse in the home are seven times more likely to become abusers than those who did not witness domestic violence. Girls exposed to violence in the home are significantly more likely to become victims of dating and/or domestic violence.

Society also pays a high price for the cost of family violence. Aside from the obvious physical injuries that are suffered by women and children in abusive situations, the cost of family violence includes other less obvious repercussions. For example, children who are exposed to family violence are also at risk for poor development—emotionally, physically, and mentally. This can lead to mental health and educational problems, and even future involvement with the criminal justice system.

Both the Centers for Disease Control and Prevention and the World Health Organization recognize family violence as a public health issue. The health-related costs of family violence in the United States are thought to exceed 5.8 billion each year.

Why People Stay in Abusive Relationships

A number of explanations have been put forth to explain why people stay in abusive relationships. Perhaps one of the best known explanations was developed by Lenore Walker, who coined the term *battered woman syndrome* in 1979. Walker also proposed the cycle of violence theory, which describes domestic violence as cyclical in nature and following a general pattern. She identified three distinct phases of the battering cycle. Although each of these cycles or phases can vary in length, the total cycle can occur many, many times in a particular relationship. The three phases she identified are (1) the tension-building phase, (2) the serious battering phase, and (3) the honeymoon phase. The tension-building phase involves a gradual escalation of stress and tension and is characterized by verbal abuse and often minor physical abuse. The next stage is the acute or serious battering phase. This is the phase where the woman is abused both verbally and physically. After the battering comes the third stage, which is characterized as loving contrition. The batterer apologizes, tries to assist the victim, and often displays remorse. This is the point at which the abuser often promises never to repeat his actions and is on his best behavior. These behaviors can provide the woman with positive reinforcements for remaining in the relationship. The victim must complete two cycles to be considered a battered woman. (This cycle may also be experienced by battered men.)

The cycle is important as it can both reinforce a woman's belief that things will get better and lead to a situation known as learned helplessness. *Learned helplessness* is the conditioned response of a woman whose ability to control her situation is weakened when she realizes that the abuse she receives is not contingent on her behaviors or actions. Women and children in these situations will often try to minimize and control the abuse only to discover that the results of their efforts are not predictable. They begin to believe that they are essentially helpless over their situation. When this happens, victims will not utilize their abilities to escape the situation even when such escape is possible. When the abused woman develops the belief that she is totally helpless, this often results in depression, a sense of powerlessness, self-blame, and feelings of helplessness. This mind-set influences a woman's perceptions of her options in the situation, including her ability to leave.

In addition to these impediments, battered women often face difficulties such as economic dependency, the responsibility for children, and other such challenges when they contemplate leaving their abusers. Because of the isolation many of these women face, they have little access to outside resources that could help them.

Furthermore, it is important to remember that many of these victims grew up in homes where violence was normative. As a result, they do not necessarily view violence in the same way as individuals who have not had this exposure.

Finally, some of these women still love their abusers and are reluctant to give up on the relationship. Again, this affection can be fed by the cycle of violence when the partner enters the loving contrition phase.

Society's Responses

The criminalization of domestic violence did not really occur until the 1970s. Recall that traditionally family violence was viewed as a private family matter. From the 1970s to the present, a number of different approaches have been taken to combat the problem. In general, the problem of family violence has been addressed by the medical profession, the criminal justice system, social service agencies, and state legislatures, as well as by a variety of other public and private agencies.

Criminal Justice System

The criminal justice system has addressed the issue of family violence in a variety of ways. Until 1984, the typical police responded to issues of domestic violence either by ignoring them entirely or by viewing them as a private matter to be handled by calming the situation down and/or offering informal counseling to the couple. A major research study conducted by Lawrence Sherman and Richard Berk in 1984 examined the effectiveness of these strategies compared to arresting the suspects. They found the lowest recidivism rates among those who were arrested. As a result, police departments around the country started to adopt mandatory arrest policies to deal with domestic violence. However, further evaluation of these policies found that while they worked for some (married and employed spouses), they increased the risk of violence for others (unmarried and unemployed persons). Nevertheless, mandatory arrest policies have been found to help the police in situations where victims are reluctant to prosecute. Victim reluctance is much more common in situations of family violence than in other situations.

Police departments have been sued for failing to provide equal protection of the law to victims of domestic violence, and the claim has been made that the police would have handled the case differently if it had been nonfamilial violence. These cases have been won and have in some jurisdictions required officers to make an arrest when there is probable cause to believe familial violence is occurring. As a result of these cases, police departments are now taking these offenses seriously and addressing them similarly to violent offenses that occur outside of the home.

Police also are responsible for enforcing protective orders or restraining orders granted to victims by courts in some situations. These orders may, for example, prohibit the abuser from contacting the victim or specify that the abuser stay a specified distance away from the victim. An emergency protective order can be obtained at any time, but it is only good for a short period of time. A temporary restraining order can be requested by a victim without the offender present. The order is in effect when it is served on the offender, and a hearing is scheduled shortly thereafter. At that point, with both parties participating, a permanent protection order can be issued. These orders can also include further restrictions, such as ordering the abuser to leave the home, get counseling, or pay child support. The orders also make it easier for the police to arrest an offender; if the order is violated the offender can be arrested for either a misdemeanor or a felony, depending on the offender's original offense.

In child abuse cases, strides have been made to make it easier to prosecute offenders. Prosecuting such cases presents unique challenges to the courts. Children often have been retraumatized by testifying in court. This is particularly significant, as there are frequently no witnesses and little evidence in these cases. Courts have allowed technology such as closed-circuit televisions to be used to enable children to testify without having to confront the offender directly. The Supreme Court has held that as long as the defendant has the opportunity to cross-examine and observe the demeanor of the witness, these technologies do not violate the Sixth Amendment right to confrontation.

Since 1996, when the first domestic violence court was started in New York, the criminal justice system has seen the development of a variety of specialized courts. These specialized courts allow the handling of family violence in several ways. For example, the courts allow for better interaction between civil and criminal courts and for persons who have experience with these types of cases to be involved in each case. The courts also stress accountability by offenders and focus on victim advocacy. Cases are centralized and the same judge will preside over all aspects of the case, adding continuity to each case.

Social Services and Community Agencies

Community agencies have been involved in a variety of both preventive and intervention programs. Of course, prevention is the ultimate goal of any intervention designed to address society's problems. Prevention programs in this context include educating children about violence in the family and providing assistance such as counseling and interventions to children who have been exposed to such violence to prevent the transmission of violence to future generations. Richard Gelles, a leading researcher in the field, has suggested several policies that could help prevent family violence. These include doing away with the traditions that legitimize violence in our society, reducing violence-provoking stress, reducing social isolation, changing sexual inequality, and breaking the cycle of violence in families.

Safe havens for women and children have been created with the advent of battered women's shelters. They give persons who want to leave abusive relationships or who are in immediate danger a place to go. These shelters were developed to help women and/or children in violent relationships and have become an important tool in combating the problem. Today there are a variety of different types of shelters. Some offer temporary safe houses for women to escape abusive relationships, while others are more long term and offer services such as counseling, job training services, and education.

In addition, we have in the last three decades seen the growth of a number of treatment programs aimed toward the batterers. Although these programs vary in nature, the vast majority of them are court mandated and involve group treatment plans. These programs work with the men on such issues as anger management and power and control issues. However, such programs have been criticized for such things as attrition (dropout rates). Studies examining the effectiveness of such programs are somewhat mixed, basically demonstrating a modest improvement in recidivism rates.

For children who are experiencing violence in the home, the primary responsibility for dealing with these cases lies in each jurisdiction's child protective services agency. The agency investigates and responds to allegations of child neglect and abuse. If the allegations are supported, the agency will decide whether the child needs to be removed from the family, whether the offender needs to be removed, and what other interventions are necessary. Children removed from their homes are placed in foster care.

Medical Profession

The medical community has become very involved in the diagnosis and reporting of family violence incidents. The medical community is in an excellent position to be able to recognize abuse in patients. Health care professionals are receiving additional training to help them recognize and respond more effectively to family violence. Physicians and medical personnel are now being trained to use their unique position to offer treatment, advice, information, and referrals to victims.

Legislative Initiatives

In the wake of the focus on family violence, many states began to pass a number of legislative acts designed to help prosecute offenders and protect victims. One of the first types of laws to be passed was the mandatory reporting law. At this point, all 50 states have mandatory child-abuse reporting requirements. Legally, professionals who work with children are required to report any suspicions of abuse and/or neglect. In general, these statutes require that individuals who have frequent contact with children (professionals such as teachers, doctors, day care providers) report their suspicions to the appropriate law enforcement agency or child welfare agency (typically child protective services). Persons generally responsible for reporting include teachers, doctors, child care providers, and social workers. Those who fail to report suspected abuse can be held civilly liable.

In response to family violence, Congress passed the Violence Against Women Act of 1994 and reauthorized it in 2000 and 2005. This is a comprehensive act designed to end violence against women by offering both technical and financial assistance to communities to help create programs and policies designed to end domestic violence, sexual assault, dating violence, and stalking. It helps improve the services offered to victims of these crimes and subsidizes grant programs to investigate causes of and ways to deal with violence against women. The act funds violence prevention programs, trains physicians and other medical personnel, and helps to fund transitional housing for women and children.

Some jurisdictions, such as South Carolina, recently began to prosecute women who abuse drugs during their pregnancy. These women had been tested under a policy at the Medical University of South Carolina. A woman sued claiming that this violated her right to privacy and her right to be free from unreasonable searches and seizures, and the Supreme Court eventually agreed, stating that such drug tests (searches) were unlawful without a warrant or the patient's consent. However, some jurisdictions have successfully prosecuted such cases by charging these women under other statutes, such as child abuse or child endangerment statutes. Some states have also defined exposing a child to domestic violence as child abuse. In addition, there have been laws passed to restrict access to weapons by convicted offenders and to mandate that courts consider histories of family violence in custody decisions.

Hidden Victims

Teen Dating Violence

Recently, there has been a focus on the topic of dating violence among teens and young adults. Although in the strict sense of the definition, dating violence does not fall under the umbrella of family violence, it is considered an aspect of intimate partner violence. The Centers for Disease Control and Prevention reports that 1 out of 11 American adolescents has been a victim of physical dating violence. The Bureau of Justice Statistics states that females between the ages of 16 and 24 are the most frequent victims of intimate partner violence. In fact, their rate of violence is triple that of the national average.

Elder Abuse

Elder abuse includes such things as physical abuse, psychological abuse, neglect, and exploitation (illegally or improperly using a person and/or his or her resources for one's own or another's advantage). Although there are few estimates of the extent of this offense in the United States, the National Center on Elder Abuse estimates that thousands of older persons each year are victimized. National estimates also reveal that between 1 million and 2 million persons have been victims of elder abuse, and that adult children are the most frequent perpetrators and neglect the most common form of abuse.

Sibling Violence

This type of intimate violence is one of the most frequent and the most overlooked. It is assumed that siblings will hit each other. Sibling rivalry is considered normal. Parents, in part, will often contribute to the situation by allowing their children to work it out among themselves and to learn to handle these situations on their own. Research has found that boys and younger children tend to be more violent toward siblings than are girls and older children.

Gay and Lesbian Couples

While the term *family violence* is often used to refer to violence that takes place in traditional heterosexual families, the term *intimate partner violence* also encompasses violence in the context of dating and nontraditional relationships. Although research in the area of violence in homosexual relationships has been quite limited, the findings from the existing studies suggest that overall violence in these relationships is similar to violence in heterosexual relationships. However, studies have found that lesbian couples experience less violence and gay male couples experience more violence than do heterosexual couples.

Battered Husbands

Getting a figure on the exact amount of husband abuse that occurs each year is extremely difficult, as parties are reluctant to admit that the abuse occurred and sometimes fail to categorize their situations as abusive. However, estimates from the National Family Violence Survey conducted in 1995–1996 indicate that 12% of the husbands reported some level of physical assault by their spouses in the preceding year. Importantly, research has shown that men are much less likely than women to report their abuse.

Immigrant Women

This is a population that faces unique challenges in this area. Domestic violence is often thought to be more prevalent among this population. Often the cultures that these women come from implicitly or explicitly approve of violence in the family. In addition, these individuals do not necessarily have the same access to the legal system and often face serious economic problems, language problems, and problems with their immigration status. This population also is more likely to believe that family violence is a private matter and is less likely to report such abuse.

Future Outlook

Family violence has been documented throughout history in all types of families. In the past few decades the pervasive view of this problem as a private family matter has changed, and we now recognize it as a serious societal problem. As resources in the United States continue to be focused on addressing all the complex facets of this problem, from recognizing abuse to developing successful intervention programs, it is hoped that U.S. society will be able to successfully tackle the issue and give victims the help they need.

Beth Bjerregaard

See also Battered-Child Syndrome; Battered Woman Syndrome; Child Abuse, Neglect, and Maltreatment; Domestic Violence; Family and Domestic Violence, Theories of; Intimate Partner Violence; National Violence Against Woman Survey (NVAWS); Violence Against Women Act of 1994 and Subsequent Revisions

Further Readings

Durrose, M. R., Harlow, C. W., Langan, P. A., Motivans, M., Rantala, R. R., Smith, E. L., et al. (2005). *Family violence statistics: Including statistics on strangers and acquaintances.* Washington, DC: U.S. Department of Justice, Bureau of Justice Statistics.

Gelles, R. J. (1997). *Intimate violence in families* (3rd ed.). Thousand Oaks, CA: Sage.

Hampton, R. L. (Ed.). (1999). *Family violence: Prevention and treatment* (2nd ed.). Thousand Oaks, CA: Sage.

Hines, D. A., & Malley-Morrison, K. (2005). *Family violence in the United States: Defining, understanding, and combating abuse.* Thousand Oaks, CA: Sage.

Kempe, C. H., Silverman, F. N., Steele, B. F., Droegemueller, W., & Silver, H. K. (1962). The battered-child syndrome. *Journal of the American Medical Association, 181,* 17–24.

Sherman, L. W., & Berk, R. A. (1984). *The Minneapolis Domestic Violence Experiment.* Washington, DC: Police Foundation Reports.

Tjaden, P., & Thoennes, N. (2000). *Extent, nature and consequences of intimate partner violence: Findings from the National Violence Against Women Survey.* Washington, DC: U.S. Department of Justice, National Institute of Justice.

Walker, L. E. (1979). *The battered woman.* New York: Harper & Row.

Web Sites

National Center on Elder Abuse: http://www.ncea.aoa.gov

U.S. Department of Health and Human Services, Administration for Children and Families: http://www.acf.hhs.gov/programs/cb/systems

U.S. Department of Justice, Bureau of Justice Statistics: http://www.ojp.usdoj.gov/bjs

U.S. Department of Justice—Violence Against Women Act: http://www.ovw.usdoj.gov/regulations.htm

FEAR OF CRIME

Fear is a response that allows individuals to avoid danger, and many individuals who are fearful of criminal victimization, and the danger associated with it, may limit their activities or take other actions designed to avoid this danger, and thus reduce their fear. Individuals who are fearful of crime may not travel at night, may avoid certain areas that they consider dangerous, and may engage in myriad avoidance behaviors and adaptive strategies.

Fear is a natural, often beneficial emotion under many circumstances. Under the wrong circumstances, however, fear can restrict individual freedom, constrain behaviors, and negatively influence the quality of life of a fearful individual. Fear of crime differs from most hazards of life because it is often based on limited or inaccurate information about crime risk and crime realities. Because crime victimization has the potential to be catastrophic, many individuals often err on the side of caution, fearing crime far more than is necessary. As such, it is imperative that reliable information about crime and the potential for criminal victimization, as well as the personal and social characteristics that reduce the risk of criminal victimization, be provided to individuals, particularly those most fearful of crime. Reducing the gap between factual information on the potential for crime and the often distorted information available from media and anecdotal sources will go a long way toward reducing fear of crime and upgrading the quality of life for many fearful individuals.

Definitions

One of the most controversial issues in recent studies that examine the psychological consequences of crime is that of defining fear of crime; this debate regarding definitions of fear of crime has raged over three decades. Although a number of researchers have defined and conceptualized fear in a variety of ways, the most well-accepted definition is generally traced to Kenneth Ferraro's seminal work, *Fear of Crime: Interpreting Victimization Risk*. In this book, Ferraro argued that many investigators apparently assume that the definition of fear of crime is obvious, and thus they refrain from clearly delineating exactly what fear is. Ferraro attempted to remedy this problem by clearly defining fear of crime as an emotional response of anxiety or dread to crime victimization or symbols associated with crime. Although there are many different definitions of fear of crime, Ferraro's definition captures its essence: Fear of crime comes as an emotional response to what an individual perceives to be a crime situation. Fear of crime can also be categorized into two global categories: personal fear (fear for one's own personal safety) and altruistic fear (fear for others, including spouses, children, etc.). Only recently have researchers begun to consider altruistic fear.

In the United States particularly, many people argue that fear of crime may be a greater problem than crime itself. From its inception, the General Social Survey (GSS), a national survey conducted by the National Opinion Research Center, has asked respondents, "Is there any area right around here—that is, within a mile—where you would be afraid to walk alone at night?" In 2008, 37% of respondents answered "Yes," a percentage that has remained relatively unchanged for 15 years, despite decreasing crime rates over that time. Even though there is some controversy over whether this question is a valid measure of fear, it is apparent that whatever the question is measuring, a substantial minority of Americans experience this phenomenon, and their number appears to remain relatively stable regardless of what is happening with the actual crime rate.

Nevertheless, despite the plethora of researchers who have considered fear of crime over the past four decades, fear of crime research is a relatively recent phenomenon. Based on the attention it received from criminologists throughout the 19th century and first half of the 20th century, most criminologists apparently considered it unworthy of study or assumed that the fear of crime and its consequences were directly proportional to the risk of criminal victimization, and any efforts to reduce crime would necessarily reduce fear of crime as well.

Whether coincidentally or by design, fear of crime research began to appear on the scene soon after the President's Commission on Law Enforcement and Administration of Justice released a report that argued that fear of crime was a detrimental impact of violent crime. The report informed its readers that consequences of crime brought about not only physical harm but emotional and psychological harm as well. Beginning in the early 1970s, then, researchers begin to consider fear as a consequence of crime and criminality.

Methods of Measuring

For the first two decades of fear of crime research, fear of crime was measured most often with a single item indicator; in fact, almost half of all studies about fear of crime that were reviewed in the late 1980s used a single item indicator of fear of crime. One measure commonly used in early fear of crime research was the National Crime Victimization Survey (NCVS) question, "How safe do you feel or would you feel being out alone in your neighborhood at night?" A number of researchers found that measure problematic because it does not mention the word *crime*, and the respondents are asked to think about their safety in a hypothetical situation they rarely encounter (when they are alone at night in their neighborhood), among other reasons. Other studies have used a slightly different measure by asking, "Is there any area right around here—that is, within a mile—where you would be afraid to walk alone at night?" This is the most frequently employed single-item indicator in the fear of crime literature and is the measure used by the GSS as an indicator of fear of crime. This indicator had some advantages over the previous one, such as defining what the neighborhood is, but it still has some of the same problems. The question is still a single item indicator, it does not specify "fear of what," and the likelihood of being out alone at night in the neighborhood is relatively remote, even for the most active people.

Because of these and other criticisms, researchers began to use multiple-item indices to assess fear. Mark Warr was one of the first researchers to measure fear of crime by asking questions about individuals' fear of specific crimes. Warr used indices measuring fear of specific crimes in his analysis of data collected via mail survey from residents in Seattle in 1981, and Ferraro and others determined

that his scales were some of the best available, recommending that all fear of crime researchers use these types of questions to measure fear of crime. As such, by the end of the 20th century, most fear of crime researchers began to use multiple items that used the words *fear* or *afraid* and asked respondents about their fear regarding a number of different types of crime. This method has yielded a number of reliable measures of fear of criminal victimization that are commonly accepted as the most reliable survey measures available.

Who Is Fearful of Crime?

Gender

The vast majority of studies examining fear of crime have determined that females are more fearful of crime than are males. In addition, this difference seems to hold true regardless of the measure used for fear. Several explanations have been offered for women's higher levels of fear of crime. One explanation centers on both the social and physical vulnerability of women, arguing that women are socialized to perceive themselves as weaker than men and thus feel a powerlessness to resist attack that causes heightened levels of fear. Socialization experiences also provide another explanation for gender differences. Because the vast majority of those who research fear of crime use self-report questionnaires to determine levels of fear, and women are socialized to be more open about their fears, women are more likely to report their fear than are men, who are socialized not to show signs of weakness such as expressions of fear. Another well-accepted explanation for the differential fear by gender is the suggestion that women have an inordinate fear of sexual assault, especially rape, and that this fear pervades all aspects of their lives, causing them to express greater overall fear levels. This explanation suggests that women associate rape with myriad forms of crime (burglary, robbery, etc.) because they realize that, if they become victims of any of these crimes, there is the possibility that they also will be raped. This explanation has been labeled as the shadow of sexual assault hypothesis. Numerous studies have found support for this argument.

Race/Ethnicity

Although there are some exceptions, in those studies where race has been found to have a significant association with fear, Blacks are more fearful than Whites. The most well-accepted explanation for this phenomenon seems to be the social vulnerability explanation (discussed in detail below) that suggests that certain groups (e.g., the poor, Blacks) realize that they are at a higher risk of crime victimization by crime and thus are more fearful of crime.

Age

A large number of studies have determined that older people are significantly more fearful than younger people, although a number of researchers have pointed out that the positive relationship between age and fear of crime is found to be much stronger when researchers use single-item measures of fear such as those used in the GSS that were discussed earlier. In fact, most recent studies suggest that if the researcher controls for perceived risk of criminal victimization, and uses questions that gauge respondents' fears of specific crimes (e.g., robbery, assault, murder), the relationship between age and fear of crime is much weaker and, in many studies, nonexistent. This research has noted that it is likely that young people realize that they are at greater risk of victimization and thus have higher levels of perceived risk, which leads to higher levels of fear.

Socioeconomic Status

The relationship between socioeconomic status and fear of crime is mixed as well. Although the majority of studies have found that individuals with lower levels of income and education have greater levels of fear, there are a number of studies that have found no relationship between socioeconomic status and fear of crime or a positive relationship between the two. Some researchers suggest that the limited exposure of the higher socioeconomic groups to criminal conditions, their ability to secure private security devices, and their generally greater confidence in the police to protect them from crime may cause them to have lower levels of fear. Nevertheless, because these variables are rarely controlled for, the relationship between socioeconomic status and fear of crime appears to vary by sample and measure of fear of crime.

Theoretical Explanations

Many of the early studies that examined fear of crime were conducted without a priori theoretical expectations. Most of the initial efforts tested bivariate relationships (e.g., gender and fear of crime, age and fear of crime) or used national data such as the GSS or NCVS to determine the prevalence of fear of crime and the demographic predictors of fear of crime. The accumulation of evidence regarding fear of crime, however, has led most researchers to accept that there are at least three important theoretical perspectives that can be used to understand fear of crime and its causes and consequences. Each of these three perspectives is discussed in detail below.

The Vulnerability Perspective

As a theoretical perspective, vulnerability refers to the interaction of three factors: (1) probability of victimization, (2) seriousness of anticipated consequences of crime victimization, and (3) powerlessness to control the previous two factors. According to this perspective, the most fearful people are those who rate their probability of victimization as high; realize that crime victimization would have serious personal, emotional, and financial consequences; and realize they have little control over either their probability of victimization or the detrimental consequences it has for their lives. As mentioned earlier, this perspective has been used to explain racial and socioeconomic differences in fear of crime and is also regularly used to explain gender and age differences in fear of crime. Assuming this perspective, some researchers have suggested that the discrepancy between females' higher levels of fear of crime and lower levels of victimization (when compared to males) is not an irrational fear, but a fear due to their very real physical and social vulnerabilities when compared to males. The aforementioned shadow of sexual assault hypothesis also fits well in this perspective, as girls' and women's vulnerability to sexual assault also may foreshadow their fear of other crimes. This explanation, that perceived physical vulnerability leads to higher levels of fear of crime, has also been used to explain higher levels of fear of crime among the elderly. Additional evidence supporting the vulnerability perspective is also found in the interaction between age and gender, as women tend to report higher levels of fear regardless of age, while fear of crime increases with age for men, and gender differences regarding fear of crime lessen as people age.

Despite the relevance of vulnerability to fear of crime, race, class, gender, and age, a number of critics have questioned the relevance of the vulnerability perspective for explaining fear of crime and argue that level of fear of crime can be predicted by controlling for either the real or perceived risk of criminal victimization. As most research indicates that the best predictor of fear of crime is often an individual's perceived risk of crime, and this relationship is often far stronger than any other predictor variable included in models to explain this fear, it is obvious that risk of victimization is an important correlate of fear of crime. Where that relationship fits in the vulnerability perspective is a question that researchers will continue to explore in the future.

Direct and Indirect Experience With Crime

A second theoretical explanation of fear of crime involves experience (both direct and indirect) with criminal victimization. According to this perspective, individuals' fear of crime is caused by their personal encounters with crime (direct experience) and/or what they hear about crime (indirect experience). Intuitively, one would reason that those who have been victimized by crime would be most fearful of crime (and this appears to be one explanation for the dearth of research on fear of crime in the early years of criminology). Interestingly, however, this is not necessarily the case. Although several researchers have found that those who have been victimized by crime (particularly violent crime) are more fearful than those who have not been victimized, almost as many studies have found a weak or nonexistent relationship between fear of crime and prior victimization experiences. A number of explanations have been offered for this counterintuitive finding, but the most relevant seem to center around the measurement issues discussed earlier, and the fact that few studies consider the number of victimizations an individual has experienced or the seriousness of the victimization. In addition, some studies argue that the impact of previous victimization may be affected by people's beliefs regarding the reason for the victimization experience (e.g., I did something stupid and brought it on myself, I was in the wrong place at the wrong time) or the use of psychological and coping techniques (e.g., neutralization strategies).

Indirect experience with crime refers to all the methods, besides direct experience, by which a person develops attitudes and perceptions about crime. These methods may include situations where an individual hears about crime from family or friends or reads about crime in the newspaper or a magazine; in addition, practically everyone is regularly exposed to crime through television and the Internet. As with direct victimization, the research findings on the relationship between indirect victimization and fear of crime are mixed, with some studies having found that those who read or watch stories about crime (particularly in their local area) are more fearful than those who do not, and other studies not having found a relationship between indirect victimization and fear of crime. However, knowing someone who has been victimized by crime, especially locally, or learning of victimization in one's own neighborhood does appear to increase levels of fear of criminal victimization. Some researchers have suggested that psychological proximity is more important to engendering fear of crime than is geographical proximity; in other words, the more similar individuals believe they are to a victim, the more likely they are to be fearful of crime.

Ecological Explanations

The research that discovered that individuals' victimization experiences did not have a strong association with their fear of crime led researchers to explore a third perspective as an explanation for fear of crime. This explanation, often entitled the ecological perspective, suggests that individuals' fear of crime is affected by a number of contextual variables related to their place in society. These variables include their place of residence (urban residents often have higher levels of fear of crime than do rural residents) and, among urban residents, the characteristics of their neighborhood (people living in inner-city areas often have higher levels of fear of crime than those living in other parts of the same city).

Within this perspective, there are a number of explanations for these findings. One explanation suggests that fear of crime is a rational response to the higher victimization rates of urban and inner-city residents, although a number of studies have found no relationship between the actual crime rate of an area and the fear of crime of the residents of that area. A second explanation focuses on the demographic heterogeneity of a neighborhood, or its lack of social capital and social climate. This explanation follows the tenets of the Chicago School of Sociology's ideas of social disorganization and suggests that inner-city and urban neighborhoods have much higher transition among residents, much more anonymity and apathy, and thus much less social capital than neighborhoods with less heterogeneity. Following this explanation, then, residents from areas with these characteristics should have higher levels of fear of crime. As with the previous explanations, some researchers have found support for this argument, while others have been unable to find sufficient evidence to support the argument.

In addition to the explanations focusing on differential rates of victimization and social capital found in inner-city and urban areas, there is a third ecological explanation, which focuses on the design and appearance of an area when examining the relationship between location and fear of crime. Researchers following this explanation argue that individuals who live in areas with higher visibility and surveillance opportunities (in other words, areas where crimes are easily seen because of the built design or human surveillance in an area) are less fearful of crime. Some (although certainly not all) researchers have found support for this hypothesis, finding that increasing levels of lighting and/or social surveillance in an area decreases fear of crime in that area. Finally, a number of researchers have focused on a fourth ecological explanation, that of incivilities. According to the neighborhood incivility explanation, individuals who live in neighborhoods characterized by certain criteria have higher levels of incivility in their neighborhoods and thus are more fearful of crime. These criteria include incivilities such as noisy neighbors, graffiti, loitering teenagers, garbage and litter in the streets, and abandoned houses and cars, among others. A large body of research has supported this argument that people living in neighborhoods with high levels of incivility are more fearful of crime.

Reactions

As a result of fear of crime, many individuals take actions that have an impact on their daily lives. The actions people take as a result of this fear are commonly grouped into two categories: defensive behaviors (e.g., installing security systems, buying a guard dog, purchasing a gun) and avoidance behaviors (e.g., limiting activity, avoiding unsafe areas at night). Polls that ask individuals if/how they change their activities due to their fear of crime suggest that a number of these actions occur regularly, with as many as half of the respondents in some polls saying they have avoided certain places because of their concern about crime. In addition, about one in four Americans keep a dog or a gun for protection and have a burglar alarm installed in their home.

Much of the research on the relationship between fear of crime and behavior indicates that fear has a positive effect on both avoidance behaviors and defensive behaviors. Fear of crime limits social behavior by leading people who are fearful of crime to avoid seemingly dangerous situations, a decision that often intensifies that fear. Some research suggests that defensive and avoidance behaviors do not necessarily differ by age, but do differ by income, gender, and race. Thus women appear to be more likely to engage in avoidance behaviors (e.g., avoiding places at night or when they are alone), whereas men are more likely to engage in some defensive behaviors (e.g., purchasing a gun). In addition, fearful people of color appear to be less likely to engage in both defensive and constrained behaviors than are Whites.

Strategies to Reduce Fear of Crime

Because of the detrimental effects of fear of crime, a number of strategies have been considered to help alleviate fear of crime among the public. Some of these policies are discussed below.

One strategy to help alleviate people's fear of crime is to educate the public about criminal activity, its causes and correlates, and methods to prevent crime from occurring. This strategy is based on the previously discussed impact of indirect victimization on fear of crime, and the realization that even those who do not have direct experience with crime victimization often have increased levels of fear of crime because of their knowledge of criminal activities in their community or among those they know. As such, educating people about their generally low likelihood of victimization by crime, and the steps they can take to protect themselves and to reduce personal fear, could lower fear of crime among those with that knowledge. This strategy not only may help reduce fear of crime but also may help people have a better understanding of their risk and what measures do actually increase public safety.

A second strategy is designed to involve communities both in crime prevention through social development and in community-based justice programs. The premise behind this strategy is that citizens who are directly involved in the justice system are generally better informed about their risk of crime victimization and their understanding of what affects crime and how criminal activity can be reduced.

A third strategy by which fear of crime may be reduced involves community corrections agencies handling of offenders supervised in the community. This strategy focuses community supervision and treatment resources on individuals with the greatest need for those resources and individuals who pose the greatest risk to society. This strategy, coupled with those mentioned above, could inform the public about how criminal justice resources are being used, and the fact that those most at risk of committing crime in the community are also those most closely supervised, thus reducing fear of crime among those potentially targeted by those offenders.

Given the detrimental impact of incivilities on fear of crime among residents of those neighborhoods where incivilities are found, a fourth strategy in reducing fear of crime involves supporting (or leading) organized community efforts to reduce disorder in communities. Strategies as simple as having public works agencies paint over graffiti on public buildings immediately after it is found could reduce perceptions of neighborhood incivility and thus reduce fear of crime in those neighborhoods as well. Condemning and destroying abandoned buildings, towing abandoned cars, and replacing broken windows in public buildings soon after these are discovered also could reduce perceptions of incivility and decrease fear of crime.

A final strategy for reducing fear of crime involves a policing strategy that began in the United States in the early 1970s, was very popular for one or two decades, and then lost popularity at the end of the 20th century. That strategy is community policing. Community policing is a police agency organizational strategy and philosophy that promotes a partnership between police officers and the public that they serve. Community policing is based on the idea that the police and citizens should work together as partners to identify crime problems in their community and then work together to solve those problems. Each of the strategies mentioned above involves community residents taking a more active role in reducing crime and fear of crime in their community. The goal of community policing is not just to prevent and/or respond to crime in an area. The primary goal of community policing is to improve the overall quality of life in an area; one method of doing so is to reduce residents' fear of crime in their neighborhood. By actively working with the community, police gain the trust of the community. This increased trust often leads to an increased awareness of criminal activity and allows police to both uncover and prevent crime that traditional policing methods may not uncover. A number of studies have suggested that when police officers follow the tenets of community policing, neighborhood residents have more confidence in the police and feel safer from crime in their community.

Despite the evidence that has accumulated over four decades of research into fear of crime, there are a number of methodological weaknesses that have limited the impact of this research. As mentioned earlier, there is still some debate regarding the definition and conceptualization of fear of crime. Future research could seek to clarify both the definition and conceptualization of this fear; this would prevent researchers in the future from having to justify their understanding of fear of crime.

In addition, only recently have fear of crime researchers begun using theoretical models to attempt to explain fear of crime, and none of the current models do a satisfactory job in explaining fear of crime in every location among every sample of respondents. As such, more work is needed to continue to develop these theories of why fear of crime occurs.

Further, most of the research on fear of crime has been primarily quantitative research, and researchers have only recently begun to use qualitative strategies to attempt to understand the causes and consequences of fear of crime. Additional qualitative research efforts could help advance the limited theoretical perspectives currently available and yield more well-defined theories.

Finally, despite the admitted methodological shortcomings of self-report measures of fear of crime, few (if any) researchers have used either physiological or observational methods to better understand the impact of fear of crime in a person's life. As such, these methods have the potential to dramatically influence fear of crime research in the future.

David C. May

See also Age and Victimization; Community Policing; Contextual Effects on Victimization; Correlates of Victimization; Fear of Crime, Individual- and Community-Level Effects; Fear of Crime, Measurement of; Hot Spots of Fear; Incivilities/Social Disorder; Shadow of Sexual Assault Hypothesis

Further Readings

Ferraro, K. F. (1995). *Fear of crime: Interpreting victimization risk*. Albany: State University of New York Press.

Ferraro, K. F. (1996). Women's fear of victimization: Shadow of sexual assault. *Social Forces, 75*(2), 667–690.

Hale, C. (1996). Fear of crime: A review of the literature. *International Review of Victimology, 4*, 79–150.

Lagrange, R., & Ferraro, K. F. (1989). Assessing age and gender differences in perceived risk and fear of crime. *Criminology, 27*(4), 697–719.

Rader, N. E. (2004). The threat of victimization: A theoretical reconceptualization of fear of crime. *Sociological Spectrum, 24*(6), 689–704.

Warr, M. (2000). *Fear of crime in the United States: Avenues for research and policy* (NCJ 185545). Rockville, MD: National Institute of Justice.

Wilcox Rountree, P. (1998). A reexamination of the crime-fear linkage. *Journal of Research in Crime and Delinquency, 35*(3), 341–372.

FEAR OF CRIME, INDIVIDUAL- AND COMMUNITY-LEVEL EFFECTS

Fear of crime has been defined as an emotional response, or anxiety, caused by crime or environmental cues that a person associates with crime. Fear of crime is important to study because fear levels do not always directly coincide with the amount of crime in the community or one's own particular experience with or risk of being victimized by crime. Individual personal characteristics and perceptions of environmental features other than crime often are better at predicting one's amount of fear.

There have been two key trends in fear of crime research over the last three decades—the first related to improving measurement of fear, and the second related to better understanding seemingly illogical findings in some studies. Because these trends are connected and together have led to important advances in the understanding of individual and community effects on fear, both are discussed in this entry.

Improving Measurement to Better Understand Individual Predictors

Early studies on fear of crime found that women and the elderly were most afraid of crime, even though young males were most likely to be victimized by crime. The scholarly assumption was that those who were most at risk of being victimized or had been victimized would be most afraid. The unusual findings led researchers to look for other factors that might cause people to be afraid. One line of research focused on the quality of the measures that were being used to operationalize fear of crime. Most studies in the 1970s used a variation of two questions. The one used in the National Crime Victimization Survey (NCVS) read, "How safe do you feel or would you feel being out alone in your neighborhood at night (or during the day)?" The General Social Survey (GSS) question generally read, "Is there any area around here—that is, within a mile—where you would be afraid to walk alone at night (or during the day)?" Scholars noted that these questions were limited in their ability to gauge fear because they were too general, did not mention the word *crime*, and did not capture the likelihood that people do not fear all crimes in the same way. Some researchers argued that these questions better measured "perceived risk," or thoughts (rather than emotions) about individuals' likelihood of being victimized by crime.

Consequently, researchers began to design different questions to measure fear, focusing on using the concept "afraid" and indicating the type of crime in the question (e.g., burglary, homicide, or rape). In studies using these revised questions, researchers continued to find that women were more afraid, but they now often found that older people were not as afraid as younger people.

The age findings then became more logical, but the strong and continued finding that women were more afraid than men led some scholars, such as Mark Warr and Ken Ferraro, to argue that it was because fear of rape "shadowed" women's fear of other crimes. Specifically, they argued that women were afraid of other crimes, like burglary and harassment, because they were afraid that these offenses could lead to rape. Warr called these "perceptually contemporaneous offenses," because they were coupled in women's minds, and Ferraro called it the "shadow of sexual assault." A number of studies since have found that for women (and sometimes for men), fear of rape is strongly related to fear of other crimes, and that accounting for it sometimes lessens or reverses the effect of gender on fear (i.e., men and women show more similar levels of fear). One study by Jodi Lane and James Meeker attempted to separate the harm (assault) aspect of rape from the sexual part. They found that while fear of rape was still related to fear of other crimes, it was less important when they also measured fear of assault. In other words, the physical harm component of rape contributes to fear, but there is something unique about the sexual intrusion that matters. Elizabeth Stanko has argued that women are appropriately more afraid because their "ordinary experiences" with men's unruly behavior (such as crimes that occur in private, like incest and rape, and less serious behaviors like harassment) lead women to believe that they might be victimized at any time. More recent studies have attempted to further refine the measurement of fear of crime by specifying the perpetrator in their questions (e.g., gangs or terrorists) and asking about crimes that are typically specific

to these types of offenders. The idea is that like some offenses, some types of offenders might invoke more fear than others.

Environmental Cues and Community Networks

As the measurement of fear was being refined, many scholars studied other factors that might predict fear of crime in those who were less likely to be victimized. Researchers developed four theoretical models to predict individual fear of crime. The first perspective involves *indirect victimization,* that is, the possibility that people are afraid because they hear about crime through the media or others in their community. Local social ties, such as knowing neighbors or participating in community groups, are thought to increase fear because people hear about things that happen to other people in the area or elsewhere. The *disorder* or *incivilities* perspective argues that when people see evidence of social and physical disorder (or incivilities), they become more afraid because they associate those problems with crime. Social incivilities are problems such as prostitution, drug use, homelessness, and gangs. Physical incivilities are problems such as graffiti, trash, unkempt yards, and rundown buildings. The *community concern* or *community decline* model points to the probability that some people are afraid because they believe their community is not the way it "used to be." For example, parents might say that their children used to be able to play alone in the park but now they can't because gangs hang out there. *Racial heterogeneity* or *subcultural diversity* is the fourth model predicting individuals' fear of crime, and it focuses on the possibility that in communities without strong friendship networks, people are afraid because they encounter people who are racially, ethnically, or culturally different. Sally Merry has argued that fear of crime is prompted by residents' inability to interpret the mannerisms and behaviors of people who look and act differently. In other words, people do not understand people who are different, and it makes them afraid.

Some studies have examined these models of fear of crime independently, under the assumption that people are thinking about only one of these issues when they are afraid (e.g., worrying about diversity *or* disorder, but maybe not both), and found that each issue can explain fear of crime. Other studies have examined connections between the theoretical models and found that people do not necessarily think about these things independently. In addition, researchers have examined the possibility that worry about disorder causes worry about community decline and have found that it does. For example, people might see homeless people or lawns that are not well maintained and worry that the community is going "downhill," which may cause them to become more afraid of crime. People might also be worried about community decline for other reasons, however, such as increasing diversity or population density, and so the disorder and decline arguments remain distinct.

In her qualitative study of fear of gang crime in neighborhoods in Santa Ana, California, Lane found that people indicated very specific connections among all of these issues. Her respondents noted that they believed that an increase in diversity (and especially in the number of undocumented immigrants) led to more disorder in their neighborhoods, which led to community decline, which led residents to feel more perceived risk and fear of gang crime. Respondents also noted that they learned of crimes and other problems through their neighbors. Other researchers have examined some specific issues that might cause fear at certain times, such as dark places, tunnels, or walkways, because women, especially, worry that there might be hiding places for potential offenders or that they will be unable to get away from an attacker.

Other Individual Characteristics and Fear

Although much of the focus on individual factors has been on gender and age, and much of the research on community factors originated to explain women's and older people's seemingly illogical fear, research has shown that other personal characteristics can be related to fear of crime. Most studies have found that minorities (e.g., African Americans and Hispanics) are more afraid of crime than are Whites, probably because, as a group, they experience more of the environmental factors that lead to fear. Probably for similar reasons, lower-income people and those in urban areas are generally more afraid of crime than are upper-income people and those who live in rural areas. Personal experience with victimization is sometimes related to more fear, but sometimes not. Some scholars have speculated that those who are less afraid may have taken more precautions to protect themselves after the victimization and therefore feel safer.

Fear of crime does not always correspond directly to the level of crime in one's community or one's own personal risk of being victimized. Sometimes personal characteristics are important (e.g., gender, age, race, and income) in explaining fear, and sometimes increased fear can result from other problems in the community (such as unseemly people hanging out or people not taking care of their homes and yards). Consequently, those who hope to lessen fear must fight more than crime. They must also work to improve communities more generally and share information and strategies to avoid crime with those who are most afraid.

Jodi Lane

See also Fear of Crime; Fear of Crime, Measurement of; Shadow of Sexual Assault Hypothesis; Victimology

Further Readings

Ferraro, K. F. (1995). *Fear of crime: Interpreting victimization risk*. Albany: State University of New York Press.

Ferraro, K. F. (1996). Women's fear of victimization: Shadow of sexual assault? *Social Forces, 75,* 667–690.

Fisher, B., & Nasar, J. L. (1995). Fear spots in relation to microlevel physical cues: Exploring the overlooked. *Journal of Research in Crime and Delinquency, 32,* 214–239.

Lane, J. (2003). Fear of gang crime: A qualitative examination of the four perspectives. *Journal of Research in Crime and Delinquency, 39,* 437–471.

Lane, J., & Meeker, J. W. (2003). Fear of gang crime: A look at three theoretical models. *Law & Society Review, 37,* 425–456.

Lane, J., & Meeker, J. W. (2003). Women's and men's fear of gang crimes: Sexual and nonsexual assault as perceptually contemporaneous offenses. *Justice Quarterly, 20,* 337–371.

Merry, S. E. (1981). *Urban danger: Life in a neighborhood of strangers*. Philadelphia: Temple University Press.

Skogan, W. G. (1990). *Disorder and decline: Crime and the spiral decay in American neighborhoods*. Berkeley: University of California Press.

Stanko, E. A. (1985). *Intimate intrusions: Women's experience of male violence*. London: Routledge & Kegan Paul.

Warr, M. (1984). Fear of victimization: Why are women and the elderly more afraid? *Social Science Quarterly, 65*, 681–702.

Warr, M. (1985). Fear of rape among urban women. *Social Problems, 32*, 238–250.

Fear of Crime, Measurement of

The development of any meaningful measure of "fear of crime" requires a conceptual understanding of the construct. This understanding can then drive the measurement of fear of crime. From a psychological perspective, fear is an emotion. Fear of crime, therefore, is the emotion that is associated with, as Kenneth Ferraro and Randy LaGrange put it, "crime or symbols associated with crime." A measurement of the fear of crime therefore is an attempt to measure this emotion in the context of crime. Instruments that measure fear of crime focus on the measurement of danger, safety, and threat, and much research emphasizes and measures safety.

Fear of crime first emerged as a political construct from studies commissioned by the President's Crime Commission on Law and Enforcement and the Administration of Justice in the United States in 1967. These studies made the first attempt at a measure of fear of crime by asking questions on anxiety, a proxy measure of fear. From these studies came one of the now standard National Crime Victimization Survey (NCVS) questions "How safe do you feel walking alone in your neighborhood after dark?" Other questions were "How concerned are you about having your home broken into?" and "How likely is it a person walking around here at night would be held up or attacked?" These questions were intended to gauge people's attitudes rather than consciously measure a coherent and cogent fear of crime; they both significantly influenced the genesis of measures of this fear.

Researchers such as Mark Warr and Mark Stafford, over a quarter of a century ago, expressed their concerns on proximate causes of fear asking such questions as "Does risk enter into the cognitive equation of fear?" Their study was one of the first in the literature that attempted to move away from the aggregated measures of crimes to measures of more specific fear of different kinds of crimes. Their measures were later elaborated in the literature.

In offering his measurement of fear of crime, Ferraro, a major contributor to fear of crime measures, cautioned that measures of fear of crime need to capture the emotional states of the respondents; an assessment of events in respondents' lives as related to fear of crime; and fear of specific crimes rather than just a generic measure of fear, with risk of being a victim and fear of crime treated as distinct constructs.

A deficiency in the fear of crime literature is the absence of identifiable different dimensions of fear. Differentiation between feelings of "unsafety" from fear of crime is important. According to Ferraro, feelings of unsafety are determined by a risk assessment (probability of victimization), while "fear of crime is an emotional response of dread or anxiety to crime or symbols that a person associates with crime" (1995, p. 24).

However, dozens of studies on fear of crime have used safety questions from the General Social Survey (GSS) or the National Crime Survey (NCS) to measure fear. The problem with these questions is their inability to distinguish fear from perceived risk and fear from general concerns about crime. Steve Farrell, Elizabeth Gilchrist, and Jason Ditton referred to these measures as standard "formless" questions, and they include questions such as "Is there any area right around here—that is, within a mile—where you would be afraid to walk alone at night?" and "How safe do you feel or would you feel being out alone in your neighborhood at night?" Similar questions sometimes are asked about feelings of safety while out alone during the day and when at home. A criticism of these measures is that a person may have a high sense of safety but yet still feel afraid.

In assessing fear of crime, researchers should be cognizant of its cognitive (i.e., risk perception) and emotional (i.e., being afraid) dimensions. There may be a validity problem with many of the measurements of fear of crime because of the inadequacy of their definitions, as many such measurements carry the implicit definition of the probability of being victimized.

The concepts of "formless" and "concrete" fears are important. Measurements of formless fears try to articulate information on a general assessment of fear (e.g., safety questions), while measures of concrete fears try to acquire information on particular offenses (e.g., murder). The phrasing of safety/risk questions gives geographical and temporal (but not criminal) specificity; for example, "How safe would you feel to walk alone in your neighborhood during the night?" Given the time and space parameters set by safety questions, responses are governed by information on the immediate environment (e.g., the neighborhood). In other words, safety questions are specifically asking respondents to consider internal happenings in their community. The questions about fear of crime used by some researchers do not have time and space parameters. This lack of parameters can create cognitive ambiguity in respondents and, therefore, may provoke stereotypes, especially those related to crime. This is not necessarily a weakness of the measure but, in fact, assists researchers to acquire a gestalt level of fear of crime from respondents. There are no explicit theoretical articulations that can be used to integrate the concepts of perceived risk (which is cognitive) and fear of crime (which is affective).

A classic study on measurement of fear of crime, undertaken by Ferraro and LaGrange in 1987, evaluated important measurements of fear of crime in the literature and identified the problems of the duplication of risk and fear in these measurements. They further noted two important dimensions into which many questions about fear of crime often fall. The first dimension is the level of crime perception, and it ranges from general (community-oriented) to personal (self-oriented) measurements. The second dimension is the type of crime perception, and it ranges from the cognitive level to the affective level.

The gender paradox, that is, that females are more likely to be fearful of crime than are males, yet males are more likely to be victims of crimes aggregately, needs to be methodologically revisited. Often this paradox is explained as the result of a shadow effect of sexual assault. However, the paradox may be the result of the persistent use of quantitative measures of fear of crime that are correlated with gender. Such structured measures may prevent males, who are socialized to show toughness, from articulating their true cognitions and emotions about the issue of crime. More qualitative measures may be considered by researchers when undertaking research on gender and fear of crime.

Measures of fear of crime have generally emerged from a data-driven approach. To move away from the current modus operandi, more researchers in this field could be driven by theory, rather than quickly absorbing scales from the literature into their research. On a final note, the more diverse the application of a measure across groups, the greater should be the sensitivity of the measuring instrument, so that nuances with explanatory power would be picked up by the measure. In other words, any attempt at a universal fear-of-crime scale allowing for standardizing of research findings must consider the multifaceted cultural reality of societies as well as the relevance and reliability of scale items. Therefore, the issue of transferability of scale, which has been a norm in research on fear of crime, needs to be seriously revisited—not only across cultures but within cultures.

Derek Chadee

See also Fear of Crime; Fear of Crime, Individual- and Community Level Effects; Hot Spots of Fear

Further Readings

Chadee, D., & Ditton, J. (2003). Are older people most afraid of crime? Revisiting Ferraro and LaGrange in Trinidad. *British Journal of Criminology, 43*(2), 417–433.

Chadee, D., Ditton, J., & Austen, L. (2007). The relationship between likelihood and fear of criminal victimization: Evaluating risk sensitivity as a mediating factor. *British Journal of Criminology, 17*(1), 133–153.

Ditton, J., & Chadee, D. (2006). People's perceptions of their likely future risk of criminal victimization. *British Journal of Criminology, 46*, 505–518.

Ennis, P. (1967). *Criminal victimization in the United States: A report of a national study.* President's Commission on Law Enforcement and Administration of Justice Field Surveys II. Washington, DC: U.S. Government Printing Office.

Farrall, S., Bannister, J., Ditton, J., & Gilchrist, E. (1997). Questioning the measurement of fear of crime. *British Journal of Criminology, 37*(4), 658–679.

Ferraro, K. (1995). *Fear of crime: Interpreting victimization risk.* Albany: State University of New York Press.

LaGrange, R., & Ferraro, K. (1987). The elderly's fear of crime: A critical examination of the research. *Research on Ageing, 9*(30), 372–391.

LaGrange, R., & Ferraro, K. (1989). Assessing age and gender differences in perceived risk and fear of crime. *Criminology, 27*(4), 697–719.

Rountree, P. W., & Land, K. (1996). Perceived risk versus fear of crime: Empirical evidence of conceptually distinct reactions in survey data. *Social Forces, 74*(4), 1353–1377.

Vanderveen, G. (2006). *Interpreting fear, crime, risk and unsafety.* The Hague, the Netherlands: Boom Juridische Uitgevers.

Warr, M., & Stafford, M. (1983). Fear of victimization: A look at the proximate causes. *Social Forces, 61,* 1033–1043.

Yin, P. (1980). Fear of crime among the elderly: Some issues and suggestions. *Social Problems, 27,* 492–504.

FEMICIDE

Femicide, the murder of women, is a leading cause of premature death in the United States for women. Women in the United States are murdered by intimate partners (husband, boyfriend) or former partners approximately nine times more often than by strangers. Between 40% and 50% of women killed by a known perpetrator are killed by an intimate partner, compared to 5.5% of men killed by an intimate partner. Femicide rates are highest among women 20 to 49 years old. Also important to consider are intimate partner attempted femicides, as at least eight such near-fatal incidents occur for every actual intimate partner femicide.

From 1981 to 1998, intimate partner homicides decreased by almost 50% in the United States, with rates decreasing far more for male victims (67.8%) than for female victims (30.1%). The rates have since stabilized, with three to four female partners killed for every male partner. The decreases in intimate partner homicides occurred during the same time period as national social programs and legal interventions to reduce intimate partner (domestic) violence; in states where the laws and resources (shelters and crisis hotlines) were the most available, there were the greatest decreases in women killing male intimate partners. Increases in women's resources, decreases in marriage rates, domestic

violence policies such as proarrest mandates, as well as decreases in gun accessibility, are all associated with the decreases in intimate partner homicides. Recently, rural intimate partner femicides have increased, while urban intimate partner femicides have stayed stable or decreased.

The vast majority (67%–80%) of intimate partner homicides involve physical abuse of the female by the male partner or ex-partner before the murder, no matter which partner is killed; therefore, prior domestic violence against the female partner is the number one risk factor for intimate partner homicide. A national case control study completed in 2001 found the following factors most strongly associated with increased intimate partner femicide risks over and above prior domestic violence:

- Perpetrator access to a gun
- Estrangement
- Perpetrator unemployment
- Perpetrator highly controlling
- Perpetrator threatens to kill partners
- Prior threats or use of weapons by perpetrators against their partners
- Biological child of female partner not the perpetrator's
- Forced sex

Protective factors include the victim and perpetrator never having lived together and the perpetrator's prior arrest for domestic violence. Another risk factor that is only now completely understood is attempted strangulation, or in the vernacular most often used by abused women, "choking." This is not only a risk factor for intimate partner femicide but also a serious health problem that can result in death by stroke or pneumonia following aspiration in the days following the attempted strangulation. Due to the seriousness of this event, many states have passed laws to make these attempted strangulations a felony.

Femicide–Suicide

Jane Koziol-McLain and her colleagues in 2006 reported that in about a third of the cases of intimate partner femicide, or about 400 to 500 cases per year, the male partner kills himself (and sometimes his children) after killing his partner. (Only about one case of intimate partner homicide–suicide per year involves a female killing a male partner.) The major risk factors, including prior domestic violence, are the same as for intimate partner femicide cases without suicide, with an additional factor present of the perpetrator's prior threats of or attempted suicide. This type of perpetrator was also more likely to have been seen in the mental health care system in the year before he killed his partner. Suicidal perpetrators are more likely to be married, employed, and report less illicit drug use and abuse during the woman's pregnancy than those who did not kill themselves. These differences suggest that men who kill their partners and then kill themselves may have a larger "stake in conformity" than those who kill their female intimate partners and do not commit suicide. In other words, they may appear at first assessment, or by risk of domestic violence re-assault assessment, to be somewhat less dangerous perpetrators than others who are seen in the domestic violence systems. Even so, Koziol-McLain and her colleagues have shown that femicide–suicide perpetrators and femicide-only perpetrators have a similar background in terms of prior arrest for violent crimes (18% and 23%, respectively), and that they engender a similar amount of fear in their partners (who think their partner is capable of killing them, 53% and 49%, respectively).

One of the recent explanations for femicide–suicide relates to male proprietariness—"a pathological possessiveness" connected to issues of power and control in intimate relationships. Femicide–suicides often occur following estrangement and are planned acts by the perpetrator, supporting the explanation of male proprietariness. However, this explanation is also incomplete; combining male proprietariness and perpetrator mental health issues with a history of intimate partner violence may more comprehensively account for high stakes placed on the relationship with the partner. Interestingly, the constant across the literature is the perpetrator statement echoing, "If I can't have you, nobody can." Yet this statement and the estrangement and controlling behavior are also significant risk factors for femicide without suicide. Again, these dynamics are the extreme end of the continuum of other forms of domestic violence.

Same-Sex Intimate Partner Homicide

According to the Centers for Disease Control and Prevention in 2008, the proportion of intimate partner homicides committed by same-sex partners is greater for gay men than for lesbians. Nationally, among male victims of homicide, 6.2% were murdered by a same-sex partner, and among female victims, less than 1% (0.5%) were murdered by a same-sex partner.

Using the data from the large multicity study on femicide conducted by Jacquelyn Campbell and her colleagues, a case study of the five (1.6%) female-perpetrated intimate partner femicides was conducted. Among the five cases, prior physical violence, controlling behaviors, jealousy, alcohol and drugs, and ending the relationship were consistently reported antecedents to the murder. These preliminary findings support that power and control are central to models of intimate partner femicide, whether it is perpetrated by a man or a woman.

Maternal Mortality and Intimate Partner Femicide

The national homicide database does not indicate if a woman was pregnant or had recently given birth when she was killed. Even so, detailed record reviews in some urban areas and a review of the national mortality surveillance system data by the Centers for Disease Control and Prevention have demonstrated that homicide is the second leading cause of injury-related maternal mortality, or pregnancy-associated death (death during pregnancy or in the year after pregnancy termination by delivery or other means) in the United States, causing 2 maternal deaths for every 100,000 live births. In at least three major urban areas in the United States (New York City, Chicago, Washington, D.C.) and the entire state of Maryland, homicide is the leading cause of maternal morality, causing as many as 20% of maternal deaths. The increased proportion related to homicide is attributed to decreases in other causes of maternal mortality such as medical complications of pregnancy and delivery.

Although current limitations in the data do not allow the identification of the perpetrator in these maternal mortality homicides, we can assume that the majority were by an intimate partner, as in cases when women were not pregnant. We can also deduce that the majority of cases that were intimate partner homicide were preceded by domestic violence against the woman.

Abuse during pregnancy was associated with a threefold increase in risk of intimate partner completed or attempted femicide in the multicity femicide study. Violent victimization during pregnancy has also been associated with outcomes such as prenatal and postpartum depression, substance use, smoking, anemia, first- and second-trimester bleeding, poor weight gain, and maternal death. These findings lend support to medical and nursing organizations' insistence on the need for health care settings, including prenatal care settings, to assess for and intervene in domestic violence.

Ethnic-Specific Issues

Among African American women between the ages of 15 and 44 years, femicide is the leading cause of premature death. Recent national data from the Centers for Disease Control and Prevention reveal that African American women are murdered by men at a rate (2.70 per 100,000) nearly three times higher than that of White women (1.00 per 100,000). African American women are also disproportionately affected by pregnancy-associated homicide.

American Indian and Alaska Native women also had higher rates of murder by a male (1.33 per 100,000) than did Caucasian women, while Asian and Pacific Islander women were the least likely (0.52 per 100,000) women of any race to be murdered. Among the five states that report ethnic/racial background (Arizona, California, Nebraska, Oregon, Texas), Hispanic women have the second highest rate compared to Caucasian women in 2003, but in 2006 there were insufficient states reporting Hispanic/Latina femicides to make comparisons. In New York City, immigrant women have been found to be more at risk for intimate partner femicide than those born in the United States. Near-fatal femicide of African American and other ethnic minority women also contributes to long-term disabling injuries and conditions. In the majority of these fatal and near-fatal femicides, the men who kill or abuse these women are intimate partners (husbands, boyfriends, ex-husbands, or ex-boyfriends).

Several multiyear studies of femicide (homicide) trends have also reported ethnic-specific data. The majority of African American women killed (84%) are between the ages of 18 and 64, with the mean age being 32. African American women, similar to other women in the United States, are more likely to be murdered by a man they know, such as a spouse (59%) or intimate acquaintance, than by a stranger. In cases when the male perpetrator is known, 94% of the homicides of African American women were intraracial.

Hispanic women have the second highest rate of femicide victimization. The data for Hispanic women are very similar to those of African American women, except for age data. The mean age of Hispanic women killed is 28 years, younger than both Caucasian and African American women, with the overwhelming majority being killed between the ages of 18 and 64 (86%). Similar to African American women, they are most likely to be killed by a spouse (69%) or intimate acquaintance, and the majority of the perpetrators are of the same race, although the percentage was slightly lower (84%) than that for African American women.

Risk Factors

In general, studies have shown that poverty, low educational level, partner unemployment, and young age are associated with a group's increased intimate partner homicide experiences. Among the few intragroup studies examining these risk factors and intimate partner homicide rates among African American women, low socioeconomic status, lack of employment of the partner, and the establishment of limited social networks within a community have been found to be significant risk factors for intimate partner violence. Similarly, Hispanic women often find that the context of their lives is characterized by poverty, lower levels of education, discrimination, and an environment with high use of alcohol and drugs, often by their male intimate partners. Often both African American and Hispanic women live in communities where there is a high level of violence, and there are limited resources in general, and even fewer resources to protect women and children from intimate partner violence and ultimately intimate partner homicide. In the multicity intimate partner femicide study, unemployment was found to be a stronger risk factor than ethnicity or race, suggesting that it is the context of lack of resources that drives the increased risk associated with minority status rather than any culturally or racially specific characteristics.

Research Conclusions

Intimate violence continues to be a major public health issue for all women, and even though it has decreased, it ends with an intimate partner homicide all too frequently. Many studies have identified characteristics of intimate partner homicide that distinguish it from other forms of homicide. Despite these findings that enhance our understanding of intimate partner homicide, there is still a lack of systematic research studies on several issues, especially ethnic-specific issues related to intimate partner homicide. Research on Hispanic, Native American, and Asian American women, among others, is very limited, and in studies that include ethnic/racial minority groups, most comparisons are made to Caucasian women. Thus more studies are needed to examine within ethnic group comparison across socioeconomic groups. The research to date suggests that disproportionate risk related to ethnic/racial minority status may be less a reflection of race than of poverty, discrimination, and unemployment and its negative consequences, which result in a lack of access to resources that could help women escape from abusive relationships or make the violence end, thereby preventing intimate partner homicide. In addition, more studies are needed that clearly define and identify ethnic/racial minority groups rather than grouping all Black women (i.e., American, African, and Caribbean women), all Hispanic women (i.e., Puerto Rican, Mexican, and Cuban women) or all Asian women (i.e., Korean, Chinese, Japanese women) together as if they are homogenous groups.

Interventions

Demonstration projects are needed that test and evaluate evidence-based interventions aimed at reducing intimate partner violence and ultimately intimate partner homicide. Such interventions must reflect what is known about gender issues and cultural influences as well as intimate partner violence, and also incorporate mental health (depression, posttraumatic stress disorder), substance use/abuse issues, and parenting.

Advocates, health care providers, law enforcement, lawyers, and community activists must also continue to support coordinated community responses to reduce risks for intimate partner homicide. In a health care, legal, law enforcement, or community setting, a woman identified as abused should be assessed for risk factors for lethal violence in the abusive relationship. This assessment can be done using an instrument such as the Danger Assessment or the brief assessments for lethality used by criminal justice first responders. In particular, it is important to assess the perpetrator's access to guns and warn the woman of the risk he presents. This is especially true in the case of women who are estranged from their partners and/or who have been threatened with a gun or another weapon. Under federal law, individuals who have been convicted of domestic violence or who are subject to a restraining order are barred from purchasing or possessing firearms, although there are some variations in state laws. Judges issuing orders of protection in cases of intimate partner violence should consider the heightened risk of lethal violence associated with the abuser's access to firearms and order removal of such guns whenever possible.

An excellent resource for referral, shelter, and information is the National Domestic Violence Hotline (1-800-799-SAFE). If a woman confides that she is planning to leave her abuser, it is critical to warn her not to tell him face-to-face that she is leaving. It is also clear that extremely controlling abusers are particularly dangerous under conditions of estrangement. A question such as "Does your partner try to control *all* of your daily activities?" can quickly assess this extreme need for control. Professionals can also expeditiously assess whether the perpetrator is unemployed, whether stepchildren are present in the home, and whether the perpetrator has threatened to kill the victim. Under these conditions of extreme danger, it is incumbent on professionals to be extremely assertive with abused women about their risk of homicide and their need for shelter, as this has been shown to be effective in preventing severe re-assault in domestic violence cases.

Evidence suggests that where there are shelters, legal advocates, health care professionals, and police trained to intervene collaboratively in cases of intimate partner violence, and where communities are consistently made aware of the issues related to intimate partner violence and intimate partner homicide, women and children are more likely to survive the violence in their lives.

Jacquelyn C. Campbell, Phyllis Sharps, and Nancy Glass

See also Intimate Partner Violence; Intimate Partner Violence, Risk Assessment

Further Readings

Campbell, J. C. (2007). *Assessing dangerousness: Violence by batterers and child abusers.* New York: Springer.

Campbell, J. C., Glass, N. E., Sharps, P. W., Laughon, K., & Bloom, T. (2007). Intimate partner homicide: Review and implications for research and policy. *Violence, Trauma & Abuse, 8*(3), 246–269.

Campbell, J. C., O'Sullivan, C., Roehl, J., & Webster, D. W. (2005). Intimate Partner Violence Risk Assessment Validation Study: The RAVE Study. Final Report to the National Institute of Justice (NCJ 209731–209732). Retrieved from http://www.ncjrs.org/pdffiles1/nij/grants/209731.pdf

Campbell, J. C., Webster, D., & Glass, N. E. (2008). The Danger Assessment: Validation of a lethality risk assessment instrument for intimate partner femicide. *Journal of Interpersonal Violence, 23*(4), 454–473.

Campbell, J. C., Webster, D., Koziol-McLain, J., Block, C., Campbell, D., Curry, M. A., et al. (2003). Risk factors for femicide in abusive relationships: Results from a multi-site case control study. *American Journal of Public Health, 93*(7), 1089–1097.

Dobash, R. E., Dobash, R. P., Cavanagh, K., & Lewis, R. (2004). Not an ordinary killer—just an ordinary guy: When men murder an intimate woman partner. *Violence Against Women, 10,* 577–605.

Dugan, L., Nagin, D., & Rosenfeld, R. (2003). Do domestic violence services save lives? *National Institute of Justice Journal, 250,* 20–25.

Fox, J. A., & Zawitz, M. W. (2004). *Homicide trends in the U.S.* Washington, DC: Bureau of Justice Statistics, U.S. Department of Justice. Retrieved from http://www.ojp.usdoj.gov/bjs/homicide/homtrnd.htm

Frye, V., Hosein, V., Waltermaurer, E., Blaney, S., & Wilt, S. (2005). Femicide in New York City, 1990 to 1999. *Homicide Studies, 9,* 204–228.

Glass, N., Laughon, K., Campbell, J. C., Block, C. R., Hanson, G., Sharps, P. W., et al. (2008). Non-fatal strangulation is an important risk factor for homicide of women. *Journal of Emergency Medicine, 35,* 329–335.

Karch, D. L., Lubell, K. M., Friday, J., Patel, N., & Williams, D. D. (2008). Surveillance for violent deaths—National Violent Death Reporting System, 16 States, 2005. *Surveillance Summaries, 57*(SS03), 1–43, 45.

Koziol-McLain, J., Webster, D., McFarlane, J., Block, C. R., Curry, M. A., Ulrich, Y., et al. (2006). Risk factors for femicide-suicide in abusive relationships: Results from a multi-site case control study. *Violence and Victims, 21,* 3–21.

Vigdor, E. R., & Mercy, J. A. (2006). Do laws restricting access to firearms by domestic violence offenders prevent intimate partner homicide? *Evaluation Review, 30,* 313–346.

Violence Policy Center. (2008). *When men murder women: An analysis of 2006 homicide data.* Washington, DC: Author. Retrieved from http://www.vpc.org/studies/wmmw2008.pdf

Websdale, N. (1999). *Understanding domestic homicide.* Boston: Northeastern University Press.

FEMINIST VICTIMOLOGY

Feminist victimology is a victimological perspective that informs research, policy, and practice. It is a lens through which to view how to define, research, and intervene with both male and female victims and offenders, and it is concerned with combating sexism, achieving gender equality, and struggling for women's rights. Feminist victimology is the application of various feminist approaches from a variety of disciplines to victimology and crime prevention.

Given that there are many feminist approaches, there are also many feminist victimological perspectives. Most of these approaches involve uncovering the gendered nature of victimization, recognizing victimization as the product of power relations, combating sexism and other types of prejudice in law and criminal justice, and working toward the empowerment of women. Feminist approaches to victimology are likely to emphasize activism and advocacy for social change.

Among feminist victimological perspectives, the most radical versions are those that reject the terms *victimology* and *victim.* From such a perspective, Sandra Walklate has argued that *feminist victimology* is a contradiction in terms. Since victimology is a scientific approach that stresses differentiation and has endeavored to differentiate victims from nonvictims, its efforts have led to theories of victim precipitation and lifestyle. These theories, which imply that victims either provoke or contribute to offending, through their own lifestyle or decision making, cannot be applied to situations that are the product of power relations. Most feminist approaches acknowledge that gendered victimization reflects a power imbalance. Thus, Walklate has argued that victimology cannot "see" gender. For feminists, there is no excuse for the victimization of women, and women and their differential patterns of behavior are not responsible for their victimization.

Victimology, say some feminists, is a male-dominated discipline that typically ignores women's victimization as the product of patriarchy, that is, the ubiquitous and timeless domination of women by men, justified by a belief system that can be perpetuated by both men and women. This belief system minimizes the harm done to female victims and sees them as either invisible or blameworthy. It is not surprising, then, that while women's rights organizations from the 1970s to the present have made great strides in recognizing such gendered crimes as rape and domestic violence as serious crimes, and in redefining states' neglecting to intervene and prevent and punish these crimes as major human rights violations, this movement has occurred outside of or parallel to developments in victimology.

For different reasons, some feminists as well as antifeminists have also taken issue with the term *victim*. There is a revisionist stance that attempts to counter the impression created by early feminist activists—those who fought for the recognition of rape and battering as serious crimes—that the only victims of crime are women. According to this stance, the word *victim* has become feminized, implying passivity (a stereotypical quality of women), and thus labeling women "victims" sends the message that women tolerate being victimized or that their fate is to be victimized. Some feminists, particularly those who work in victims' services, feel that the label "victim" serves as a self-fulfilling prophecy to prevent women from recovering from victimization and leading normal lives. Therefore, some feminists prefer the term *survivor* for those who survive rape and battering, which emphasizes positive, postvictimization adjustment. Other feminists simply seek to refute the stereotype that all women are currently or

potentially "helpless victims." From the 1990s onward, participants in the antifeminist "backlash" have argued that women are not really so poorly off and that reports of rape and domestic violence are exaggerated, and that feminists who confer "victim" status on a population of women use it to manipulate society and services to their advantage.

Feminists are particularly concerned with women's victimization and holding perpetrators accountable for their acts. They are also conscious that the victimization of women, while never precipitated, is not a random event but a response to the sexual stratification of society. Most recently, some feminists also have considered that poor women and women of color have specific risk factors for victimization besides their gender. Feminists have partnered with public health advocates to redefine many gender-based crimes as part of a continuum of gender-based violence that occurs throughout the life course. Article 1 of the United Nations Declaration on the Elimination of Violence Against Women states that violence against women is to be understood as "Any act of gender-based violence that results in, or is likely to result in, physical, sexual or psychological harm or suffering to women, including threats of such acts, coercion or arbitrary deprivations of liberty, whether occurring in public or private life." It encompasses a wide range of acts, including son preference, female infanticide, child marriage, female genital mutilation, sexual harassment, rape, forced sterilization, dowry deaths, domestic violence, trafficking for sexual exploitation, and widow abuse. It is through this kind of internationalization of the conceptualization of violence against women that a feminist approach to victimology gains ground.

For feminists, much of the crime prevention advice that is given to women to prevent their victimization is ideologically tainted. For example, using a trusted man to ward off possible perpetrators, never going out alone or late at night, and dressing conservatively are all mechanisms that serve to restrict women's movement and undermine their rights. Instead of using these kinds of mechanisms, feminists could advocate for attitude change among men and women, better provision of public services such as improved lighting and public transportation, holding perpetrators accountable, and women-centered networks of support and safety.

Many feminists are critical of the institutional sexism of the criminal justice system, as it results in minimizing, dismissing, or even blaming female victims. Feminists are responsible for a number of criminal justice mechanisms that are respectful of and responsive to women victims, such as restraining orders, rape shield laws, changes in laws so that the victim no longer needs to prove forceful resistance to rape, video witness testimony, mandated treatment programs for male batterers, stalking laws, recognition of marital rape, and comprehensive violence against women legislation like the United States Violence Against Women Act.

Rosemary Barberet

See also Critical Victimology; Domestic Violence; Intimate Partner Violence; Rape; Sex and Victimization; Victimology; Victim Precipitation; Violence Against Women Act of 1994 and Subsequent Revisions; Women's Shelters/Help Lines

Further Readings

Cole, A. M. (2007). *The cult of true victimhood: From the war on welfare to the war on terror*. Stanford, CA: Stanford University Press.

Cole, A. M. (2007). Victims on a pedestal: Anti–"victim feminism" and women's oppression. In *The cult of true victimhood: From the war on welfare to the war on terror* (pp. 47–78). Stanford, CA: Stanford University Press.

Shaw, M. (n.d.). *Gender and crime prevention*. Retrieved from http://www.crime-prevention-intl.org/publications/pub_22_1.pdf

United Nations General Assembly. (1993). *Declaration on the Elimination of Violence against Women*. Retrieved from http://www.unhchr.ch/huridocda/huridoca.nsf/(symbol)/a.res.48.104.en

Walklate, S. (1996). Can there be a feminist victimology? In P. Davies, P. Francis, & V. Jupp (Eds.), *Understanding victimisation* (pp. 14–29). Northumbria, UK: Social Science Press.

Football Hooliganism

Football hooliganism has no legal definition; neither is it a social scientific nor social psychological concept. Instead, it is a socially constructed generic term that is popularly used—especially by the police, politicians, and the media—to describe the disorderly behavior of football (soccer) supporters. This behavior ranges from verbal abuse and aggressive posturing, to vandalism and the throwing of missiles, to more violent actions (with more severe consequences), such as fighting, rioting, assaults, and even murder. However, as well as being a populist political and media label, the term is also used as a self-referent by those involved, as evidenced by numerous "hooligan" Web sites and autobiographies.

While the term can encompass a range of behaviors, there are two broad forms of public disorder that are labeled *hooliganism*. One form is spontaneous and usually low-level disorder caused by fans at or around football games prompted by, for example, results or officials' decisions, provocation by stewarding or policing strategies, incitement by opposition supporters, or inebriation. The other form is highly organized disorder and involves intentional, often prearranged violence (via the Internet or cell phones) by organized gangs (or "firms") who attach themselves to football clubs and fight hooligans from other clubs. Hooligan groups tend to have strong spatial and locational attachments (not just to their football club but also to their neighborhood, town, region, nation, etc.). These attachments are activated on the basis of the nature and level of external challenges. Some hooligan groups may also have religious or political allegiances. This is particularly the case in southern and eastern European countries where some firms are linked with far-right politics and racism while others have leftist associations.

Organized football hooliganism tends to be targeted at other hooligans and so "victims" are rarely innocent bystanders, and instead are more usually rival firm members or police officers and security personnel. Spontaneous acts of "hooliganism" may inadvertently embroil more innocent victims due to their indiscriminate nature. Also of relevance to students of criminology and victimology are the debates surrounding civil liberties that have arisen following the introduction of legislation and policing strategies to combat hooliganism in some countries, as well as some miscarriages of justice involving those wrongly charged for football-related offenses.

Football hooliganism is a complex, heterogeneous, and dynamic phenomenon that should be studied in its different social and historical contexts. What follows is a brief history of football hooliganism and a consideration of the scale and nature of the phenomenon across the world. An outline of some of the pioneering British responses and strategies to combat the problem will then be presented, followed by some supranational preventive measures.

A Brief Historical Overview

Britain—or, more specifically, England—is commonly perceived as having had the earliest and most severe problems with football hooliganism. Such is the nation's reputation that football hooliganism has been frequently labeled the "English disease." Certainly, England is the only nation to have been excluded from all European football competitions—a ban that lasted 5 years following the 1985 Heysel Stadium tragedy in Brussels, Belgium, in which 39 Italian Juventus FC (Football Club) fans died when a wall collapsed under the pressure of the crowd after attacks from English hooligans from Liverpool FC.

Public disorder has been documented as a feature of football in Britain since the 19th century. Despite these historical origins, and English hooligans' well-deserved reputation in more recent times, the disorderly behavior of football supporters is a worldwide phenomenon that occurs in almost every country in which the game is played, as will be discussed below. However, an increase in levels of football-related disorder in England since the 1960s, alongside a much more sensationalist style of media reporting of the phenomenon, has helped cause a "moral panic" and brought hooliganism to the forefront of the national political agenda in Britain. This was never more pronounced than from the late 1970s on through the 1980s under the Thatcher government—compounded by the nadir of the Heysel Stadium tragedy, which remains Europe's worst hooligan-related disaster in terms of fatalities. This also explains the abundance of British research published on the phenomenon during this period.

The study of football-related disorder has been a focus of British academic investigation for nearly four decades. This research has been at times acrimonious and antagonistic, involving a sociological debate between conflicting schools of thought concerning the socioeconomic or sociopolitical causes of such disorder and the integrity of the ethnographic research into the phenomenon. Despite this debate most sociologists, anthropologists, and psychologists agree that football hooliganism is underpinned by aggressive masculinity, the psychosocial pleasures of football violence that are experienced by the (predominantly) male perpetrators, territorial identification, and a sense of solidarity and belonging. While incidents of football hooliganism may appear to share many features, their nature, causes, and dynamics can differ greatly according to the cultural and historical context in which they occur—fueled and contoured by numerous social, political, and economic factors—and their motives may be rooted in national specificities, which Eric Dunning has suggested reflect the major "fault lines" of respective countries across the world.

Football Hooliganism as a Global Phenomenon

The disorderly behavior of football supporters has been a worldwide phenomenon since the late 19th century. By the start of the 20th century, football-related disorder was commonplace in stadiums throughout Europe, and by the 1980s the phenomenon was perceived as an acute social problem in many European countries. Such disorder was also a staple feature of South American football during this same period, notably in Argentina, Peru, Uruguay, Brazil, El Salvador, and Honduras. The latter two nations infamously fought *La Guerra del Fútbol* ("The Football War")—a 5-day conflict—after existing political tensions between them were inflated by rioting during an FIFA World Cup qualifying fixture.

Arguably the most serious contemporary football-related disorder still takes place in South America, where mass rioting, often inside stadiums, is a frequent occurrence (as it is in sub-Saharan Africa as well). The scale and severity of this violence is such that fatalities are a regular consequence due to the widespread use of guns and knives. In Argentinean football, violence is endemic. The number of fatalities as a result of this violence, since the advent of the country's professional football league in 1931, is estimated by officials to be approaching 200, though others put the figure above this. The Argentine government has introduced various emergency security measures in an attempt to halt the increasing football violence. For example, up to 1,000 security personnel can be appointed to "high-risk" fixtures. While the government has stopped short of suspending the whole football league program, it has suspended some fixtures and imposed stiffer penalties on offenders. In 2007, visiting supporters were banned from attending games.

Anastassia Tsoukala has provided a comprehensive outline of the strategies and methods used to regulate and police football hooliganism in Europe. Some countries have made the decision to suspend all competitions for a period of time. In April 2007, the Greek government decreed that all sports stadiums and all sport should cease for a fortnight following the death of a football fan in a prearranged fight between followers of rivals Panathinakos and Olympiakos in Athens. Just a couple of months previously, the Italian government had also imposed a fixtures break after a police officer died from injuries sustained when he was struck by an explosive while attempting to deal with fighting at the Sicilian derby between Catania and Palermo. Later that year, there was nationwide rioting when a similar break was not observed after a Lazio fan was shot dead by a police officer who was attempting to control fighting between Lazio and Juventus supporters.

Football-related violence is very much in evidence in Eastern Europe (notably Poland and Russia) and the Balkans. It is particularly acute in the former federal states of the Yugoslavia (i.e., Croatia, Bosnia-Herzegovina, Slovenia, Macedonia, Serbia, and Montenegro). Since the break-up of the old Yugoslav multiethnic federation in 1991, the violence has been underpinned by ethnic hostilities between Serbs and Croatians, compounded further by religious rivalries between Orthodox Christians, Catholics, and Muslims. There are echoes of these interethnic resentments in Australian football-related disorder, since most clubs in their National Soccer League were founded by respective ethnic migrant communities, such as Croatians and Serbs, as well as Greeks.

Western European countries—notably France, Germany, Holland, and Belgium—also have problems with hooliganism. Indeed, the label "English disease" is now somewhat misplaced, as disorder in and around English stadiums is now relatively very rare. Incidents of football-related violence over the last decade would suggest that English football fans are more likely to be targeted on their travels around Europe because of their reputation in the past. For example, in 2000, two Leeds United fans were fatally stabbed in Istanbul, Turkey, by Galatasaray supporters. Supporters of Manchester United, Liverpool FC, and Middlesbrough FC also were attacked and stabbed in Rome, Italy, on different occasions during the 2000s. Fans of the English national team have also been the victims of hostile confrontations in Slovakia, Macedonia, Liechtenstein, Estonia, Croatia, and Russia in recent years, as hooligan groups have sought to challenge English notoriety.

British Responses and Strategies

As a result of Britain's unenviable record for football hooliganism, the country has taken the lead in the development of control measures to prevent and combat hooliganism. These measures include deterrent sentencing, the legislative responses of successive British governments, the establishment in 1988 of a Football Intelligence Unit as part of the National Criminal Intelligence Service—replaced in 2005 by the UK Football Policing Unit—and various innovative methods adopted by the British police. The various strategies and responses have been primarily reactive and, increasingly, have been influenced (some would claim, entirely led) by technological developments, such as the use of closed-circuit television (CCTV) and electronic databases. These advances have also helped facilitate supranational cooperation, for example, between the Member States of the European Union.

Legislation

Successive British governments have introduced legislation to combat hooliganism over the past three decades. During the 1970s and 1980s, the government implemented a series of reactionary policies that led to an increasingly confrontational attitude between football supporters and the police, and only really succeeded in moving violent disorder away from the immediate environment of the football stadium. The current legislative framework of enforcement action against football-related violence and disorder is contained in the Football Spectators Act

1989, amended by the Football (Offenses and Disorder) Act 1999; the Football (Disorder) Act 2000, coupled with the Football (Disorder) (Amendment) Act 2002; and football-related provision within the Violent Crime Reduction Act 2006, which underpin the powers available to the police and the courts in this area. Many of these statutes have sought to refine and tighten the "football banning orders" legislation.

The main features of this legislation are that the police can arrest and prevent persons identified as potential troublemakers from attending regulated football games (at home or abroad) by means of a "banning order" granted by a magistrate's court. Even if there is no criminal prosecution, the police may make a civil application for a football banning order against an individual they suspect is involved in organizing or participating in football-related violence or disorder. A person made the subject of a football banning order has to comply with directions given by the Football Banning Orders Authority—most notably to report to a police station and/or surrender a passport at specified times.

Some football supporter groups and civil rights campaigners have complained that these laws breach civil liberties and invest the police with too much power in limiting the activities of supporters—especially in relation to foreign travel, as upon receipt of a football banning order the subject is required to surrender his passport. According to statistics from the British government, 3,172 known hooligans were subject to football banning orders in 2007 to 2008.

Policing Strategies

A number of different approaches have been used by the British police in order to combat football hooliganism. In addition to the new legislation outlined above, these include more rigorous policing of football fans and sophisticated surveillance techniques and intelligence measures. One of the key approaches has been the use of undercover operations. The use of plainclothes officers to infiltrate hooligan firms has been used in Britain since the 1960s. This has become a particularly useful tool since the 1980s, when hooligan groups started to become more organized. One of the main ways in which the police monitor hooliganism today is

through the use of the "spotter system." This involves "spotters" (police liaison officers attached to respective football clubs) identifying and categorizing known hooligans according to the risk they pose; monitoring their presence and movement; and informing other police forces both in the United Kingdom and abroad when appropriate. Clifford Stott and Geoff Pearson provide a comprehensive critical review of the policing of English football hooliganism in their 2005 book, *Policing Football: Social Interaction and Negotiated Disorder*.

Technological Developments

Technology has been an important part of policing football hooliganism since the 1980s when, for example, CCTV cameras were introduced both inside and outside stadiums to monitor the crowd. Today CCTV is used in and around every stadium in Britain. Larger stadiums have police control rooms from which they can monitor the surrounding area for potential public disorder. To supplement this, police officers also use hand-held video cameras to film supporters entering and exiting stadiums, primarily in a bid to deter acts of affray or violence, gather intelligence (which can be used as evidence in prosecutions), and monitor the effectiveness of crowd safety and control measures. Images from this surveillance can be shared with police forces in other countries if appropriate. Developments in information technology further facilitate the swift exchange of police intelligence between countries.

Supranational Preventive Measures

The European Union has a number of policies and measures to prevent and control football hooliganism. Many of these initiatives were pioneered in Britain. The impact of the Heysel Stadium tragedy in 1985 prompted a more concerted effort to establish cross-border cooperation in Europe between the main football authorities of FIFA and UEFA, together with the Member States of the Council of Europe to ensure safety and orderly conduct at sporting events. Since then there has been greater coordination of police forces, governments, and public agencies throughout Europe to prevent and punish violent behavior at football games and sports competitions more broadly. This has included the prompt exchange of police intelligence information, the safer design of stadiums, and the training of stadium stewards and security personnel in crowd safety and control techniques.

Emma Poulton

See also Assault: Simple and Aggravated; Closed-Circuit Television; Homicide and Murder; Sports Violence; Vandalism

Further Readings

Armstrong, G. (1998). *Football hooligans: Knowing the score.* Oxford, UK: Berg.

Armstrong, G., & Giulianotti, R. (Eds.). (2001). *Fear and loathing in world football.* London: Berg.

Dunning, E., Murphy, P., Waddington, I., & Astrinakis, A. E. (2002). *Fighting fans: Football hooliganism as a world phenomenon.* Dublin: University College Dublin Press.

Dunning, E., Murphy, P., & Williams, J. (1988). *The roots of football hooliganism: An historical and sociological study.* London: Routledge & Keegan Paul.

Giulianotti, R. (1999). *Football: A sociology of the global game.* Cambridge, UK: Polity.

O'Neill, M. (2005). *Policing football: Social interaction and negotiated disorder.* New York: Palgrave Macmillan.

Stott, C., & Pearson, G. (2007). *Football "hooliganism," policing and the war on the "English disease."* London: Pennant Books.

Tsoukala, A. (2009). *Football hooliganism in Europe: Security and civil liberties in the balance.* New York: Palgrave Macmillan.

FUTURE OF CRIME PREVENTION

All crime prevention is aimed toward the future, but most criminology is about the past. Looking at criminology databases using the keyword "future" shows that the body of that work concerns the prediction not of crime but of offender careers, specifically, the frequency and timing of reconviction. In fact, an important book by David Farrington and Roger Tarling, titled *Prediction in Criminology,* is exclusively about the prediction of crime careers. The keyword "future" also may turn up the occasional paper or book about the future of agencies of criminal justice, such as imprisonment and policing. Thus a search of the U.S. National Institute of Justice Web site will demonstrate that many of the documents using the word "future" are concerned with the prospects for specific cutting-edge technologies, DNA testing, and the like, rather than developments in crime and its prevention.

It might be supposed that the future of crime prevention will track the future of crime, with prevention efforts responding to emerging threats and criminal opportunities, along with a changing balance of enforcement (for example, ecocrimes may feature more prominently in the future). Certainly, new types of crimes will demand some sort of preventive (and/or punitive) response, but the specifics of crime trends and of attempts to reverse them will be as difficult to predict in the future as they have been in the past. For example, during World War I, many soldiers were taught to drive, and in the years following the war, there was an increase in the theft of cars. While only a few people could drive, the opportunity presented by an unlocked car was insignificant; however, with many people having acquired the new skill came the opportunity for crime. Another example is that of poisoning. Control of poisons and the capacity of forensic pharmacology to identify poisons in a body in ever smaller quantities led to poisoning becoming a very rare means of murder, according to Dermot Walsh.

The pressures that shape the crime reduction landscape have historically been subtle and complex, and are likely to remain so. For example, seed adulteration was a huge and well-organized Victorian business in the United Kingdom. The Adulteration of Seeds Act made this criminal, but the business continued unabated until the Testing of Seeds Order 1917 established testing arrangements that gave rise to meaningful enforcement possibilities. The order took effect during World War I to point out to the people the national importance of growing one's own food, that it was in the national interest to ensure that patriotic vegetable gardening was not hobbled by seed adulteration.

Attempts to characterize crime and crime control sequences for predictive purposes have been meager. The nearest to a generalization has been the observation by Ken Pease that there are always three stages linking new products and emergent crime trends:

1. Innovation of a product or service without considering the crime consequences

2. Reaping the crime harvest

3. Retrofitting a solution, which is usually partial

This sequence has been well-nigh universal. In the United Kingdom, the Penny Black postage stamp was introduced in 1840 and withdrawn in 1841 because it was cancelled by red franking ink, which in 1840 was water soluble, leading people to wash off the franking ink and reuse the stamp. The Penny Black was replaced by the Penny Red, which was cancelled by black ink that could not be washed off. Similar sequences are evident for cars, cell phones, and laptop computers. The manufacture of small, anonymous, valuable items, and the complexities surrounding numbers used for their identification, means that such items have become a target for robbers and in thefts from cars. The magnetic stripe on credit cards was secure until thieves discovered techniques for "skimming," where data from the stripe on one card is copied without the cardholder's knowledge and placed on another card. The widespread use of electronic wallets will almost certainly follow the same sequence. Clearly the sequence applies to software as well as physical products. David Mann and Mike Sutton supplied an early example in their demonstration of how satellite TV services could be obtained by compromising the cards authorizing access.

The two factors selected for attention in this entry—the migration of human interactions to cyberspace and the technological means of locating people and things—are likely to change the profile of the crime reduction enterprise.

Migration of Human Interactions to Cyberspace

Human interaction before written text was invariably direct and physical. Real-time one-way human interaction had to await the telegraph, two-way interaction the telephone. One-to-many and many-to-one real-time communication is now commonplace, by a variety of electronic means. *Meatspace* is the term for the physical world of interaction. The change outlined above is, in brief, the migration of the bulk of human interaction from meatspace to cyberspace. Some forms of crime (like murder and rape) cannot make the transition. Others do so easily. For example, threats to harm are facilitated by the relative anonymity of cyberspace, and criminal damage has its sophisticated doppelgänger in malicious software, or malware. Fraud is facilitated by the one-to-many possibilities of communication in cyberspace, since through the ease of one-to-many communication, fraudsters can cast their net more widely to capture the most gullible potential victims. Among the best-known of these is the advance fee fraud, whereby potential victims, contacted by email, are enticed by the promise of huge wealth. However, for the money to be released, a smaller sum upfront or bank account information is needed. Lawrence Kestenbaum has documented examples of such fraud. For instance, an alleged bank employee wrote in relation to a deceased customer,

Based on the reason that nobody has come forward to claim the deposit as next of kin, I hereby ask for your cooperation in using your name as the next of kin to the deceased to send these funds out to a foreign offshore bank a/c for mutual sharing between myself and you. At this point I am the only one with the information because I have removed the deposit file from the safe. By so doing, what is required is to send an application laying claims of the deposit on your name as next of kin to the late Engineer. I will need your full name and address telephone/fax number, company or residential, also your bank name and account, where the money will be transferred into.

By harvesting addresses from Web sites, or undertaking dictionary attacks, the fraudster is availed of a plentiful supply of email addresses.

Conventional law enforcement is primarily territorially based (as is reflected in the names and functions of police forces) and does not map comfortably onto cybercrime. What agency is primarily motivated to prevent cybercrime? The BBC News has noted that in the case of "advance fee fraud," its more common name, "Nigerian letter fraud," means that Nigeria has a national interest in avoiding its national commerce becoming equated with fraud and corruption. Of greater scale than advance fee fraud is crime associated with Internet commerce. According to the ACAPS

(Automated Credit Application Processing System), in the United Kingdom, one index of this is "card not present fraud," which rose in value from £140 million to £190 million annually between 2004 and 2006 and by a further 37% in 2007. Gill Montia has suggested that in fact the sums defrauded are much greater, by dint of lack of victim awareness of offenses committed, being estimated at £700 million in 2007. There are other scams, and some of those perpetrated in the eBay marketplace have been detailed, which is helpful to law enforcement efforts.

The major implication of the movement to cyberspace for the future of crime prevention is that it will increasingly be seen as the function of central governments and international agencies, and of banks, vendors, and Internet service providers whose profitability depends upon trust in e-commerce. In the commercial context, loss prevention rather than crime reduction will be the focus in that, for business purposes, the money lost rather than the number of victims is the unit measured, up to the point at which trust in the system is compromised. The enhanced role of central government, in contrast, may involve an overreach of prevention, since what is deemed necessary is the prevention of *every* catastrophic crime rather than loss minimization. Terrorism, the protection of critical national infrastructure, and the thwarting of denial of service attacks provide a backcloth to this overreach, which will itself invite reaction in the name of civil liberties. In the wake of the Brighton bombing of the Conservative government on October 12, 1984, a Provisional IRA spokesperson admitting responsibility regretted that the attack had failed to kill Margaret Thatcher and her senior ministers.

Locating People and Things

The second major change to be considered is the locatability and identifiability of people and things. If one conceives of crime as the interaction between degree of criminal inclination and *perceived* ease of commission without an ensuing penalty, reducing the latter raises the threshold at which criminal inclination is sufficient to carry through with a criminal act. Locatability may be anticipatory, real-time, or retrospective. Work on local offense sequencing has recently provided more powerfully predictive software

enabling patrolling police to be in places where crime is most likely to occur. The next four examples involve real-time location finding.

Bar coding is one simple means of identifying things. Shaun Whitehead has noted that the radio frequency identification (RFID) tag is slightly more sophisticated. RFID is an automatic identification technology whereby digital data are encoded in a tag or "smart label" available for subsequent capture by a reader terminal using radio waves. RFID is comparable to bar coding, but it does not require the tag or label to be visible for its stored data to be read. The primary use of RFID in commerce has been in stock control, constituting an efficient way of keeping track of merchandise in transit, in warehouses, and in retail outlets. RFID technology has been around since the Second World War. In recent years the use of RFID technology has gathered momentum, particularly due to the following:

- the emergence of global standards;
- advances in manufacturing technology allowing costs of RFID manufacture to fall rapidly;
- infrastructure improvements to meet the requirement to move huge amounts of data so that the location of correspondingly huge amounts of product are known; and
- major buyers' increasing recognition that the technology offers a large return on investment, leading them to demand that all suppliers should apply RFID tags to all bulk orders, and even to some individual items.

Matthew Sparkes has noted that while RFID still allows some crime opportunities, it represents a step change in the technology of location. Real-time position location using mobile telephony is well documented. A recent paper by Whitehead and Pease outlines a "real magic bullet" doctored so that when the firing pin impacts it, it doesn't fire—it sends a quick, high power burst of information by radio wave that identifies it to nearby cell phone base stations, giving away its location.

Retrospective locatability (finding where someone or something was at a point in the past) will be crime reductive via changes in offender perceptions. Forensic analysis of satellite navigation devices is a powerful means of identifying recent travel patterns and home locations. Beverley Nutter has shown how to analyze TomTom records (a GPS navigation system) to retrieve not only locations (and home) entered as destinations, but also other places the TomTom has been located.

Perhaps the most contentious anticipation of retrospective locatability involves DNA analysis, particularly given the technical advances that (through the "low copy number" technique) allow minute DNA traces to be analyzed. Because it is a potentially powerful means of retrospective location of people at crime scenes and will occasion much controversy, it will be dealt with at some length in this entry.

A universal national DNA database seems inevitable, and it is probably justified more in terms of identification of the victims of terrorism and genocide than of crime. However, such a database could save the potential victims of serial killers. The objection that such a database could make everyone a suspect is contested by proponents of a national database. The first forensic use of DNA analysis served to exonerate the prime suspect of two brutal murders; only later was it used to identify the real murderer. This is especially remarkable because the impressionable 17-year-old who had been the suspect confessed to one of the murders. He was saved by DNA evidence from a terrible injustice. Far from turning people into suspects, the database could serve to reduce suspicion of all those whose DNA is not found at a crime scene. Most important, however, is that many accused have been exonerated since DNA evidence became available. For example, in the United States, the Innocence Projects, by bringing DNA evidence to bear, have led to over 200 murder convictions being quashed, and 13 of those exonerated had spent time on Death Row.

The second criticism is that people with a grudge will plant the evidence of others at crime scenes, as a means of revenge. This is likely to happen much more frequently with DNA than it did with fingerprints, since all that is needed is a hair, a drop of blood, or a cigarette stub. The police already emphasize that DNA analysis must be considered along with traditional police work in order to identify the perpetrator. The danger of framing someone previously arrested already exists, and the police are well aware of this.

The third criticism of a national database is that the government's record of keeping sensitive data safe is poor, and we could not trust the government with our DNA. But advocates counter by asking, "Is this criticism relevant?" With your bank account details lost, you are vulnerable to identity theft. But with your DNA information on computer disk, what is the problem? The technology of DNA profiling does not allow the examination of every single difference between people's DNA. However, techniques used by the Forensic Science Service in the United Kingdom look at specific areas of nuclear DNA that are known to vary widely between people. These areas of different people's DNA vary in length. DNA profiling analyzes and measures these differences in length. So someone in possession of your DNA profile cannot access money with it. The DNA information as recorded only concerns selected genetic markers, so you cannot be cloned using this information. If someone wanted to frame you, there is insufficient information to synthesize your blood or saliva, even if the technical capacity to do so existed. In short, there is no key to your privacy that would be unlocked by posting this DNA material on the Internet. Moreover, the particular segments analyzed are of "junk DNA" (i.e., sequences that do not code for proteins with health implications), so the insurance value of such information is zero. An offender's criminal career is often well advanced before his or her DNA sample finds its way into the database. Aspirations to have all active criminals on the database, frequently voiced in official documents, are not feasible because of this time lag between the onset of a criminal career and the criminal's first contact with the police that enables DNA sampling.

Final Thoughts

Crime prevention will be driven in part by crime, in part by the threat of terrorism, in part by commercial interests in loss prevention and protection of the credibility of e-commerce, all interacting in subtle ways requiring close monitoring. Crime will increasingly migrate to cyberspace. The technologies of location (anticipatory, real-time, and retrospective) will advance and change the threshold at which criminal inclination is translated into action.

Ken Pease

See also Closed-Circuit Television; Crime Prevention; Electronic Monitoring; Innocence Projects

Further Readings

Association for Payment Clearing Services. (2008). *Latest figures show UK card fraud losses continue to decline in first six months of 2006*. Retrieved November 11, 2009, from http://www.cardwatch.org.uk/images/uploads/national%20release%20fraud%20figs%20final.doc?Title=PressReleases

Edwards, G., & Jayne, R. (2005). Location tracking using differential range measurements. *International Journal of Computers and Applications, 27,* 199–205.

Farrington, D. P., & Tarling, R. (1986). *Prediction in criminology.* London: HMSO.

Flood, R. (1998). Seed quality and seeds legislation—the story so far. *Seed News* (Ryton Organic Gardens), pp. 3–8.

Mann, D., & Sutton, M. (1998). NETCRIME: More change in the organisation of thieving. *British Journal of Criminology, 38,* 201–229.

Moore, D. (1999). *The evolution of car crime and car security.* Unpublished criminology dissertation. Nottingham, UK: Nottingham Trent University.

Morgan, R., & Newburn, T. (1997). *The future of policing.* Oxford, UK: Clarendon.

Nutter, B. (2008). Pinpointing TomTom location records: A forensic analysis. *Digital Investigation, 12,* 1–27.

Pease, K. (1997). Predicting the future: The roles of routine activity and rational choice theory. In G. Newman, R. V. Clarke, & S. G. Shoham (Eds.), *Rational choice and situational crime prevention.* Aldershot, UK: Avebury.

Pease, K. (2003). Crime prevention. In M. Maguire, R. Morgan, & R. Reiner (Eds.), *Oxford handbook of criminology* (3rd ed.). Oxford, UK: Clarendon.

Sparkes, M. (2006). Is RFID automating crime? *Computing and Control Engineering Journal, 17,* 12–13.

Whitehead, S. (2008). Physical security of RFID devices subject to electromagnetic attacks. In G. Farrell (Ed.), *Technological approaches to crime reduction.* Cullompton, UK: Willan.

FUTURE OF VICTIMOLOGY

The field of victimology is certain to expand in the future. The exact direction of victimology cannot be predicted perfectly; however, several factors will likely shape the field for years to come. These include (1) the broadening of victim status in the research community and society as a whole; (2) the consideration of the victim's social position by examining the intersections of race, class, and gender; (3) the relationship between the victim and the legal system; (4) advances in the way victimization is measured; and (5) the attention that society and social movements give to victims. The directions that the relatively new field of victimology will take can in part be predicted by the evolution of the field and recent trends within the discipline.

Broadening the Use of the Term *Victim*

One fundamental way in which the field of victimology will likely continue to grow in the future is in recognition and classification of more individuals as victims of crime by both researchers and the general public. Specifically, victim status has been and will continue to be broadened, because there are victims of crimes that did not exist before and certain groups were not previously recognized as victims. Simply stated, victimologists will have more to study.

Certain groups of victims have only emerged recently. Thus victims of cybercrimes did not exist until the Internet became accessible to the general public. These victims are often minors, so the focus of many recent research studies considers the extent and nature of online victimization of young people. Society in general is becoming more aware of victimization of minors and other persons through the Internet and is calling for more safety and security measures for children and other vulnerable populations. The recent information gathered about illegal online activity will provide rich sources of data and subsequent scholarly analysis in the future.

Another factor contributing to the broadening of the use of the term *victim* is that there are groups of individuals who have just recently been given the designation of "victim." This category includes criminal offenders who have been victimized. For example, prostitutes often experience abuse and other criminal victimization in their work. They can be victims of rape, and many have histories of physical and sexual abuse and neglect as children. Instead of focusing on prostitutes' "offending," victimologists, most often writing through a feminist lens, have brought to light the victimization of these men and women. Another group whose victimization has recently received national attention are prisoners victimized during their incarceration.

Examining the Intersections
of Race, Class, and Gender

Amanda Burgess-Proctor has highlighted the importance of considering the intersections of race, class, and gender in feminist criminology. Her approach has obvious relevance to the study of victimology in the future. Categories of victims, such as "rape survivors" and "spouse assault victims," are not homogeneous groups. The characteristics of persons who have survived the same crime may vary in many ways, including social class, race, and gender. In the future, victimologists will likely consider these intersections in more thorough studies of crime victims.

Rape victims, for example, may experience their victimizations differently based in part on their social location. When describing a rape, women of color may have to deal with the skepticism of the police, whereas White women may be more likely to be believed. Differential treatment of rape victims by criminal justice officials based on race may affect these victims throughout case processing—from the time they report a rape until the case is closed by a conviction, plea bargain, or dismissal. Likewise, the social class of a victim may affect the responses of criminal justice actors. Poorer women may not be given as much sympathy after a rape as wealthier women. The implication of this is that poorer women may be less likely than wealthier women to report rape to authorities.

Gender can also play a considerable role in the way a rape victim experiences his or her victimization. Some states have yet to recognize male rape victims, thus undermining the perception of these individuals as legitimate victims. The healing process may be different for male and female rape victims due to the effects of gender role socialization and prejudices in our society. Alan McEvoy has studied the differences in rape recovery for males and females and documents important differences in the impact of rape on men and women and the role others can play in their recovery.

Understanding how the intersections of race, class, and gender affect the crime victim needs to be emphasized in the future. Simply doing research on any category of "victim" is incomplete without an understanding of the victim's social position. Future studies of the nature of victimization and victims' involvement with the criminal justice system and recovery process will need to assess these intersections to be complete.

How the Legal System
Defines and Acknowledges Victims

Over the past three decades, the role and relevance of the "victim" in the American legal system has undergone a dramatic transformation. The victims' rights movement's recent accomplishments include the drafting of victims' bills of rights, several international victims' rights conferences, and the development of numerous victim assistance programs.

Victims' Rights

The participation of the victim in legal proceedings has increased in the United States in the last 30 years, although the proceedings do vary somewhat from state to state. Victims now have myriad rights, including the following: the right to attend criminal proceedings and parole hearings, the right to victim compensation, the right to be heard at sentencing and parole hearings, the right to be notified by the court system of important dates in the criminal case, the right to be protected from intimidation and violence by the defendant, the right to restitution from the offender, and the right to have property returned to the victim after it has been used as evidence. Presently, every state allows victims to give a written or oral statement before sentencing, which may include a description of the physical, psychological, and financial harm that they endured as a result of their criminal victimization. Some jurisdictions even allow victims to state their opinion on what they feel is an appropriate sentence. In 1991, the Supreme Court ruled in *Payne v. Tennessee* that victim impact statements would be permitted in capital murder trials. These statements, given prior to the pronouncement of a sentence by the victim's family, serve to contrast the victim's worth and innocence with the convicted offender's guilt.

Role of the Victim in the Legal System

Throughout American history the purpose and role of the victim in the legal system has varied. In recent years, states have begun to implement means of being more responsive and sensitive to the needs of victims. This trend is likely to continue in the future. Presently, all state legislatures have passed laws granting victims increased rights within the criminal justice process. A major goal of these reforms is victim empowerment. As the parameters of the victim's place and role within the legal system continue to evolve, victims will feel less disconnected from the judicial system. Future evaluations of whether victims have taken advantage of or benefited from these reforms will enhance the field of victimology.

Moreover, in the future, the U.S. legal system and the legislatures are likely to incorporate and balance the victim's interest with more ease. It is important to note that in the vast majority of jurisdictions, the role of the victim in initial charging decisions (e.g., specific charges, counts) and the decision to agree to a plea bargain still rest exclusively with the prosecutor, often to the victim's dismay. Thus, victims may often feel disconnected from the early phases of the prosecutorial process and the interests of the state. Some jurisdictions provide victim advocates to accompany the victim to the various criminal justice proceedings and educate the victim about what to expect in the proceedings and offer emotional support. These advocates are usually from the prosecutor's office. The interests of the victim become most relevant in the sentencing phase of the prosecutorial process. In the future, courts and legislatures will likely continue working to identify the appropriate role of victim within the legal system.

The fact remains that criminal adjudication in the American legal system is dominated by the public prosecution model. This dominance is enhanced by the system's explicit focus on defendants' rights (and thus exclusion of victims' rights). More precisely, neither the United States Constitution nor the Bill of Rights includes any reference to the rights of the crime victim, while several amendments are devoted to the rights of criminal defendants. Generally, the public prosecution model removes from consideration of the judge and jurors the direct and specific harm suffered by the victim as a result of the perpetrator's actions. Damages suffered by the victim, whether they are physical, emotional, economic, and/or psychological, tend to be viewed as incidental and inferior to the state's primary objective of deterring and punishing criminal behavior. The role of

victims will likely change along with changes in the public prosecution model, including those resulting from the influence of restorative justice, which seeks to restore the victim to his or her pre-crime status. Restorative justice programs began in the 1970s and have produced alternative methods and venues for settling conflicts.

One of the main impediments to the victims' rights movement is the concern that the rights of victims might conflict with and circumvent defendants' rights. The rights of victims may continue to gain significance in the balancing of interests as the definition of victim and the victim's role in the legal system become more dimensional and expansive. Rather than simply theorizing what victims may desire or need, the field of victimology offers a vehicle for actually examining victims' needs and concerns in relation to the crime and the offender. Extending the criminal justice system to include programs and services that can restore victims and move beyond punishment and guilt may open new pathways for the crime victim's journey to recovery. In sum, victimology is evolving as a major field of study with profound importance to the legal profession.

In criminal law, punishment serves as the enforcement mechanism. However, punishment is not the singular goal of criminal law. Rather, the goal of criminal law has been viewed by scholars as both an assenting expression of a community's norms and values, the violation of which warrants punishment, and a mechanism to prevent criminal behavior by creating law-abiding citizens. In some states, such as North Carolina, victim attributes have been included in a formal list of aggravating factors that can affect the minimum sentence a judge can hand down to the offender. For example, if the victim is very young or very old or if he or she suffered debilitating injury, these factors are recognized aggravating factors that can affect sentence length, within the confines of North Carolina structured sentencing. This highlights the increasingly relevant role of the victim in the judicial process.

International Law and Victims

During the 20th century, the world community experienced wars fought with new weapons that resulted in devastating human victimization and massive destruction. As a result, the United Nations adopted several General Assembly resolutions dealing with the rights of victims. These resolutions include the 1985 Declaration of Basic Principles of Justice for Victims of Crime and Abuse of Power and the 2006 Basic Principles and Guidelines on the Right to a Remedy and Reparation for Victims of Gross Violations of International Human Rights Law and Serious Violations of International Humanitarian Law. In addition, customary international law has recognized a limited group of universal norms allowing victims to pursue justice. This body of law, also known as the law of nations, has never remained stagnant. However, in recent years, there has been a dramatic expansion in its significance and prevalence in domestic courts. As a result of the development of certain areas of international law, including international human rights law, customary international law has expanded to cover many areas of the law that in the past it did not. As a result, international law now allows for more broadly recognized classes of victims. In the future, the field of victimology will consider these laws, which serve as fertile ground for research and evaluation.

Advances in Measuring Victimization

Victimology is a social science. The quality and nature of future research in the field depends on the availability of data that measure the incidence and characteristics of victimization. More data on crime victims and other data sources are being developed to understand specific victim populations. The future seems promising in these areas.

The two major sources of data which estimate crime on a national level are the Uniform Crime Reporting (UCR) Program and the National Crime Victimization Survey (NCVS). The UCR Program has provided and continues to provide consistency in the measurement of crime known to the police and reported to the FBI. The addition of the National Incident-Based Reporting System (NIBRS), which is used in conjunction with the UCR Program, adds valuable information about victim characteristics that are absent from the traditional UCR. Law enforcement agencies only participate in the NIBRS if they have the resources to do so, therefore the NIBRS data do not provide a representative sample of crimes in the United

States. These data are maintained by the Inter-university Consortium for Political and Social Research and contain several files that capture various elements of a criminal incident that can be linked by key variables. Most notable to the field of victimology are the Victim Segment, in which victim age, sex, race, ethnicity, and injuries are recorded, and the Property Segment, which includes types and value of property stolen and recovered. This reporting contrasts with that of the traditional UCR, which is deficient in providing such victim characteristics. The number of police agencies using the NIBRS will likely grow in the future.

The NCVS is the second major source of data that provide estimates of criminal victimization on a national level. It is rich in data that measure victim characteristics. The NCVS data originate from victimization surveys given to a representative sample of residents in the United States. They include the victim–offender relationship (if known), the victim's perception of substance abuse of the offender, and whether the victim contacted police. Data on background characteristics, such as ethnicity, age, race, gender, annual household income, and marital status are also collected. The NCVS will continue to provide data rich in victim information that can be analyzed by victimologists.

Recent additions to the NCVS questionnaire include questions about identify theft and hate crime victimization. In addition, nonfatal intimate partner violence can be identified via the NCVS for cases of assault and/or rape when the victim identifies the offender as an intimate, and fatal intimate partner violence can be identified through the Supplementary Homicide Reports, which are a part of the UCR. Another data source that incorporates the NCVS data measures violence at and on the way to school. As the subject of school violence has captured the attention of the general public, this data source will continue to be analyzed in the future to help understand and prevent the victimization of youth.

Clearly, not all victimization data can be collected on the national level. Many studies rely on smaller samples and measures antecedent to and concomitant with various forms of victimization and the criminal justice system's response to crime victims. Such studies include analyses of the effects of domestic violence policies, the efficacy of victim protection orders, risk factors for intimate partner violence, and understanding the precursors of child abuse. These studies are conducted in various jurisdictions on state and local levels. They are often focused on a particular type of victimization and can measure much more in-depth information on a particular subject than can general studies. An overview of grant solicitations and independent research that is being published in the field of victimology points to an ever-increasing body of knowledge of social science data that can be used for future victimology research.

The Attention That Society and Social Movements Give to Victims

Since victimology was first recognized as a discipline, the focus in society as well as the research community has gone from what Andrew Karmen labeled "victim blaming" to "victim defending" and "victim empowering." Many social groups have made great strides in increasing social awareness of various types of victims. They have also sought to educate society about the nature of specific types of criminal victimization and dispel myths about the responsibility of the victim for his or her victimization. In the case of rape, the women's movement and victims' rights movement have uncovered myths of victim precipitation. These groups attempt to understand the sociocultural influences on violence against women and to empower, not blame, the rape victim. Social groups that support victims' rights will continue to bring the plight of the crime victim to the attention of the public.

A variety of organizations have also provided victims with information on their rights, advocacy, and offers of various social support resources. The field of knowledge about victims' rights and protections has become richer through the recent establishment of the VictimLaw.Info Web site. This Web site is devoted to educating the public about victims' rights and providing crime victims with resources to help them through the criminal justice system and promote their overall well-being.

VictimLaw.Info lists 50 general Web sites of organizations (including some government agencies) devoted to providing various groups of crime victims with information and resources. VictimLaw also lists for each state any victim assistance, advocacy, and/or compensation services that it provides.

This centralized resource offers great potential for researchers to understand the growth of social movements and organizations. It also will serve as fertile ground for research that can evaluate the efficacy of governmental and nongovernmental resources for victims. The collection of victim resource data is an important part of the future of the field of victimology.

Liz Marie Marciniak and Neil Guzy

See also Cyber and Internet Offenses; Defendants' Rights Versus Victims' Rights; National Crime Victimization Survey (NCVS); National Incident-Based Reporting System (NIBRS); Rape, Prison; Victim Impact Statements; Victimology; Victims' Rights Legislation, Federal, United States; Victims' Rights Legislation, International; Victims' Rights Movement, International; Victims' Rights Movement, United States

Further Readings

Burgess-Proctor, A. (2006). Intersections of race, class, gender, and crime: Future directions for feminist criminology. *Feminist Criminology*, 1, 27–47.

Karmen, A. (2007). *Crime victims: An introduction to victimology* (6th ed.). Belmont, CA: Thomson Higher Education.

McEvoy, A. W., & Brookings, J. B. (2001). *If she is raped: A guidebook for husbands, fathers and male friends* (3rd ed.). Holmes Beach, FL: Learning Publications.

McEvoy, A. W., Brookings, J. B., & Rollo, D. (1999). *If he is raped: A guidebook for partners, spouses, parents, and friends*. Holmes Beach, FL: Learning Publications.

National Center for Victims of Crime. (2007). *VictimLaw: Your source for crime victim rights and protections*. Retrieved November 29, 2008, from http://www.victimlaw.info/victimlaw

U.S. Department of Justice, Federal Bureau of Investigation. (2007, June 8). *National incident-based reporting system, 2005*. Retrieved November 20, 2008, from http://dx.doi.org/10.3886/ICPSR04720

U.S. Department of Justice, Office of Justice Programs, Bureau of Justice Statistics (2007). *Indicators of school crime and safety: 2007*. Retrieved November

23, 2008, from http://www.ojp.usdoj.gov/bjs/abstract/iscs07.htm

U.S. Department of Justice, Office of Justice Programs, Bureau of Justice Statistics (2008). *Crime and victim statistics*. Retrieved November 28, 2008, from http://www.ojp.usdoj.gov/bjs/cvict.htm

Wallace, H. (2007) *Victimology: Legal, psychological, and social perspectives* (2nd ed.). Boston: Pearson Education.

Web Sites

VictimLaw: http://www.victimlaw.info

G

GANG RESISTANCE EDUCATION AND TRAINING (G.R.E.A.T.)

Gang Resistance Education and Training (G.R.E.A.T.) is a school-based prevention program, taught by law enforcement officers, that is designed to help prevent not only gangs but youth violence and delinquency generally. Like Drug Abuse Resistance Education (D.A.R.E.), it is designed for elementary and middle school youth and includes a summer program and a family training component. G.R.E.A.T. has established various partnerships nationally with agencies and organizations to increase the positive relationships between and across community organizations, schools, youth, families, and the police. The program provides enough flexibility for schools and police at the local level to develop similar appropriate partnerships with local agencies and programs.

In 13 lessons, G.R.E.A.T. uses various methodologies, including traditional instruction, role-playing, and discussion, to provide youth with the skills necessary to make good decisions. The program also seeks to foster more positive relationships between the youth and the police. The 13 lessons are as follows:

1. Welcome to G.R.E.A.T.
   a. Program Introduction
   b. Relationship Between Gangs, Violence, Drugs, and Crime

2. What's the Real Deal?
   a. Message Analysis
   b. Facts and Fiction About Gangs and Violence

3. It's About Us
   a. Community
   b. Roles and Responsibilities
   c. What You Can Do About Gangs

4. Where Do We Go From Here?
   a. Setting Realistic and Achievable Goals

5. Decisions, Decisions, Decisions
   a. G.R.E.A.T. Decision-Making Model
   b. Impact of Decisions on Goals
   c. Decision-Making Practice

6. Do You Hear What I Am Saying?
   a. Effective Communication
   b. Verbal Versus Nonverbal

7. Walk In Someone Else's Shoes
   a. Active Listening
   b. Identification of Different Emotions
   c. Empathy for Others

8. Say It Like You Mean It
   a. Body Language
   b. Tone of Voice
   c. Refusal-Skills Practice

9. Getting Along Without Going Along
   a. Influences and Peer Pressure
   b. Refusal-Skills Practice

10. Keeping Your Cool
    a. G.R.E.A.T. Anger Management Tips
    b. Practice Cooling Off

11. Keeping It Together
    a. Recognizing Anger in Others
    b. Tips for Calming Others

12. Working It Out
    a. Consequences for Fighting
    b. G.R.E.A.T. Tips for Conflict Resolution
    c. Conflict Resolution Practice
    d. Where to Go for Help

13. Looking Back
    a. Program Review
    b. "Making My School a G.R.E.A.T. Place"
       Project Review

Through these lessons students are taught conflict resolution, cultural sensitivity, and the negative effects of gang banging. The program is designed to give students the tools and skills necessary to resist the many types of antisocial and deviant pressures they may face.

Evaluations of G.R.E.A.T. have revealed mixed results. Students tend to exhibit more prosocial attitudes after completing the program than do students who did not participate. In addition, evaluations seem to suggest that the program results in less gang activity and more knowledge and education about gangs and gang activity.

However, apparently delinquency has not been eliminated in students as a result of their having been involved in G.R.E.A.T. This was found in both the short- and long-term follow-up evaluations. It would appear that students develop and maintain prosocial attitudes as a result of participation in the program, but their participation in delinquency (including gang banging) does not end.

Educators who are familiar with G.R.E.A.T. seem to favor it for the attitudinal change it appears to make in students, but they do not see any behavioral change. Researchers found that whether educators were in schools with gangs affected their perceptions of the G.R.E.A.T. program. In addition, education evaluations also showed differences in the responses of administrators and teachers, with the former generally favoring G.R.E.A.T. and the latter not. Further, teachers expressed reluctance to incorporate G.R.E.A.T. and related programs into their classrooms, viewing them as disruptions of teaching.

In times of personnel shortages and other financial concerns, the question for law enforcement administrators is whether they want to invest in officers to teach G.R.E.A.T. (or similar programs). There is no question that law enforcement officers are effective in teaching this program, but from a police agency perspective, does it make good sense to do it? The most productive aspect of G.R.E.A.T. appears to be its improvement in students' attitudes.

In a time where many believe it is better to feel good than to be (or do) good, perhaps G.R.E.A.T. is a worthwhile endeavor. But if the goal is to change behavior, G.R.E.A.T., like D.A.R.E., is a failure. Ultimately it is up to the police administrator and school personnel to decide what the goal for their community is going to be.

Jeffrey P. Rush and Gregory P. Orvis

See also Drug Abuse Resistance Education (D.A.R.E.); Gangs and Victimization; School-Based Violence Programs, United States

Further Readings

Development Services Group. (n.d.). *Gang Resistance Education and Training (G.R.E.A.T.).* Retrieved November 5, 2008, from http://www.dsgonline.com/mpg2.5/TitleV_MPG_Table_Ind_Rec_prt.asp?ID=331

Esbensen, F.-A., & Osgood, D. W. (1999). Gang Resistance Education and Training (G.R.E.A.T.): Results from the national evaluation. *Journal of Research in Crime and Delinquency, 36*(2), 194–225.

Esbensen, F.-A., Osgood, D. W., Taylor, T. J., Peterson, D., & Freng, T. (2001). How great is G.R.E.A.T.? Results from a longitudinal quasi-experimental design. *Criminology and Public Policy, 1*(1), 87–118.

Peterson, D., & Esbensen, F.-A. (2004). The outlook is G.R.E.A.T. *Evaluation Review, 28*(3), 218–245.

Ramsey, A. L., Rust, J. O., & Sobel, S. M. (n.d.). Evaluation of the Gang Resistance Education and Training Program: A school-based prevention program. *Education, 124*(2), 297–309.

GANGS AND VICTIMIZATION

Youth gangs have received substantial public and academic attention. Media depictions of the activities of gangs and gang members have evoked considerable public concern, with people in general fearing that they may become the victims of a violent gang crime. While this fear is real, it may be misguided.

Recent research has illustrated the increased victimization risk experienced by gang members relative to their nongang peers, even when other risk factors are taken into account. This may be viewed as somewhat surprising, as it is at odds with the popular commonsense notion that there is strength in numbers and with the accounts of the many gang members who say they joined gangs for protection.

Terrence J. Taylor, Dana Peterson, and Finn-Aage Esbensen, and Adrienne Freng discuss a 1995 cross-sectional study of eighth-grade public school students in 11 U.S. cities that highlights the relationships between gang membership and victimization. Gang members were found to be significantly more likely to be violently victimized during the preceding year and to have experienced significantly more annual victimizations than nongang youth, and this was the case for several types of violence. Substantively, the differences were found to be quite large. For example, 70% of gang youth reported being the victim of general violence (assault, aggravated assault, and/or robbery), compared with 46% of nongang youth. While most of the general violent victimization consisted of assaults (60% of gang members, 43% of nongang youth), differences in serious violent victimization (e.g., aggravated assault and/or robbery) were even more pronounced. Thus 44% of gang youth reported being a victim of serious violence during the preceding year, with 38% of gang members reporting one or more aggravated assaults and 21% reporting one or more robberies during this time. Corresponding figures for nongang youth were 12% for any type of serious violent victimization, 8% for aggravated assault, and 7% for robbery. Gang members who were victims also experienced significantly more violent victimization incidents (4.9 assaults, 3.8 aggravated assautls, 4.1 robberies) than did nongang youth who were victims (3.4 assaults, 2.7 aggravated assaults, 2.4 robberies) during the preceding year.

Gang members are also at increased risk of homicide victimization. This, according to William Sanders, may be due to an informal code among gang members, according to which drive-by shootings of other gang members were generally condoned, but shooting at "innocents" (i.e., those not involved with gangs) was generally prohibited.

While surprising at first, these patterns do make sense. Research has consistently illustrated the "victim–offender overlap" that makes the risk of victimization greater for those involved in offending than for those who are not. Findings have consistently revealed that gang members are involved in a substantial amount of crime relative to nongang members. In fact, longitudinal panel studies of youth have found that while gang members comprise a relatively small proportion of the adolescent population, they account for a majority of offending—particularly serious, violent offending. Given the high levels of offending by gang members, it may be no surprise that gang members are also at higher risk of victimization.

Does Timing Matter?

Several studies have found that girls join gangs to escape violently abusive home environments. For example, Jody Miller's interviews with gang and nongang girls (in Columbus, Ohio, and St. Louis, Missouri) found that gang girls were significantly more likely to have witnessed and personally experienced physical and sexual violence in their homes. Many of the gang girls stated that they began associating with gang members in their own neighborhoods—and eventually became gang members themselves—after spending more time away from home to escape the violence.

Joining a gang seems to enhance the risk of victimization. Youth are typically more likely to be violently victimized *after* they join their gang. Dana Peterson and her colleagues examined this issue by comparing the self-reported victimization of youth prior to joining a gang, when they reported that they were in gangs, and after they exited their gangs. Violent victimization was highest for gang youth, both males and females, in the year following their entry into the gang. Such victimization was more likely to occur and occurred more frequently after youth joined their gang than prior to their gang membership.

Ethnographic studies have detailed the victimization experiences of gang members. Findings from these studies suggest that gang members may be at greatest risk of violence from members of their own gang. Thus members may be required to participate in violent initiation rituals when entering a gang. For example, approximately two thirds of the gang members in Scott Decker and Barrik Van Winkle's ethnographic study of St. Louis gang members reported being "beat in" as part of their initiation process. While the process varied from gang to gang, interviewees often recounted a process whereby prospective members were expected to fight against several current gang members, who were arranged in a line or a circle. Gang members may also be subjected to harsh discipline from members of their own gangs for violating gang rules. Felix Padilla's research on a gang organized around drug sales uncovered the use of violence by the gang to sanction members for violations of collective rules, referred to as "Vs." The process Padilla outlined is similar to the one Decker and Van Winkle described, under which violators are expected to walk through a line of other gang members who take turns beating on them. Gang members may not perceive these experiences as violent victimization. Gang members' accounts of these processes, however, leave little doubt that they may be classified as such. Gang members also may become the victims of predatory offending by others. Previous research has found, for example, that gang members are more likely than nongang youth to be involved in drug-selling activities and possession of weapons, which may make them potential targets of robbers due to their reluctance to report victimizations to authorities.

From the perspective of lifestyle theory and routine activities theory, the enhanced risk of victimization for gang members relative to their nongang peers also makes sense. Gang members may be viewed as suitable targets for serious violent victimization, as they lack capable guardianship and often have extensive interactions with motivated offenders. Exposure and proximity to high risk situations abound. Involvement in delinquency and violence is more common among gang members than among their nongang peers. Recent findings from a study by Taylor, Freng, Peterson, and Esbensen illustrate that the increased risk of serious violent victimization found for gang members relative to their nongang peers was due primarily to gang members being more likely than other youth to engage in unsupervised hanging out with peers, to hang out where drugs and/or alcohol are available, and to engage in a substantially greater amount of delinquent behavior.

From a broader perspective, violence shapes the gang context and the lives of gang members. The belief that potential conflicts with outside forces will occur, such as with the police or other gangs, often creates a sense of group cohesion among gang members. The social cohesion of members within individual gangs is strengthened by living in a situation where violence is viewed as omnipresent, coupled with an "us against them" orientation. Such an approach also adds context for the spread (or contagion) of intergang violence. In addition, violent initiation rituals or enforcement of rule violations may be deemed "acceptable" by gang members, as this violence is viewed as enhancing group solidarity. Indeed, the girls in Miller's study often highlighted the potential "trade-offs" of victimization: Victimization related to their gangs was viewed as more tolerable than violence unrelated to their gangs.

Are Gang Members Lost Causes?

Given the increased victimization risk of gang members, one may ask whether gang members are lost causes. That is, are gang members destined for a life filled with violent victimization?

While there is no definitive answer to this question, it is important to point out that gang membership is a transitory state. The old adage that "once you're in a gang, you're in for life" is typically untrue. For example, findings from longitudinal panel studies of adolescents in high-risk neighborhoods, such as the Denver Youth Survey, Rochester Youth Development Study, Seattle Social Development Study, and of public school students, such as the National Evaluation of G.R.E.A.T., have found that the duration of gang membership typically lasts a year or less for both boys and girls. At that point, the victimization risk of these youth appears to drop from the highs experienced during the period of gang membership.

In some cases, however, violent victimization is synonymous with gang exit. The most striking examples are homicide victimizations. More commonly, however, are instances where youth willingly exit gangs through a process of "aging out" or "fading out" by withdrawing from gang activities over a period of time once ties with other social institutions, such as jobs and family, are established. Perhaps the most striking finding related to gangs and victimization was reported by Scott Decker and Janet Lauritsen: Violent victimization of gang members themselves or of friends and/or family members was found to be the primary reason that St. Louis gang members exited their gangs.

Terrance J. Taylor

See also Correlates of Victimization; Juvenile Offending and Victimization; Victimization, Theories of; Victimology

Further Readings

Decker, S. H., & Lauritsen, J. L. (2002). Leaving the gang. In C. R. Huff (Ed.), *Gangs in America III* (pp. 51–67). Thousand Oaks, CA: Sage.

Decker, S. H., & Van Winkle, B. (1996). *Life in the gang: Family, friends, & violence*. New York: Cambridge University Press.

Howell, J. C. (1999). Youth gang homicides: A literature review. *Crime and Delinquency, 45*, 208–241.

Klein, M. W. (1995). *The American street gang: Its nature, prevalence, and control*. New York: Oxford University Press.

Lauritsen, J. L., Sampson, R. J., & Laub, J. H. (1991). The link between offending and victimization among adolescents. *Criminology, 29*, 265–292.

Maxson, C. L., Curry, G. D., & Howell, J. C. (2002). Youth gang homicides in the 1990s. In W. L. Reed & S. H. Decker (Eds.), *Responding to gangs: Evaluation and research* (pp. 107–137). Washington, DC: U.S. Department of Justice, National Institute of Justice.

Miller, J. (2001). *One of the guys: Girls, gangs & gender*. New York: Oxford University Press.

Padilla, F. (1995). The working gang. In M. W. Klein, C. L. Maxson, & J. Miller (Eds.), *The modern gang reader* (pp. 53–61). Los Angeles: Roxbury.

Peterson, D., Taylor, T. J., & Esbensen, F.-A. (2004). Gang membership and violent victimization. *Justice Quarterly, 21*, 793–815.

Sanders, W. B. (1994). *Gangbangs & drive-bys: Grounded culture & juvenile gang violence*. New York: Aldine de Gruyter.

Taylor, T. J., Freng, A., Esbensen, F.-A., & Peterson, D. (2008). Youth gang membership and serious violent victimization: The importance of lifestyles/routine activities. *Journal of Interpersonal Violence, 23*, 1441–1464.

Taylor, T. J., Peterson, D., Esbensen, F.-A., & Freng, A. (2007). Gang membership as a risk factor for adolescent violent victimization. *Journal of Research in Crime & Delinquency, 44*, 351–380.

Thornberry, T. P., Krohn, M. D., Lizotte, A. J., Smith, C. A., & Tobin, K. (2003). *Gangs and delinquency in developmental perspective*. New York: Cambridge University Press.

GAY, LESBIAN, BISEXUAL, AND TRANSGENDER INDIVIDUALS, VICTIMIZATION OF

Victimization of gay, lesbian, bisexual, and transgender (GLBT) individuals (and especially of bisexual and transgender persons) is a common yet understudied problem. This entry describes some common types of such victimization (including intimate partner violence, sexual assault, hate crimes, and discrimination and institutionalized victimization), noting each type's prevalence, risk factors, and outcomes. It concludes with some recommendations for future research and intervention development.

Intimate Partner Violence

There is a dearth of research focused on intimate partner violence (IPV) among bisexual and transgender persons. IPV among gay and lesbian (same-sex) couples is similar in many ways to IPV among heterosexual (opposite-sex) couples. Like opposite-sex IPV, same-sex IPV consists of emotional/psychological, physical, and/or sexual abuse occurring between current or former spouses or dating/intimate partners. One unique form of IPV among same-sex couples is the threat of "outing" an individual, which can cause extreme psychological distress. Prevalence estimates of same-sex IPV vary dramatically depending on the sample studied and the methods used. A nationally representative survey conducted by the U.S. Department of Justice reported that 11.4% of females and 15.4% of males in same-sex cohabiting relationships experienced victimization by a same-sex partner at some point in their lifetime. Same-sex IPV often evidences a pattern similar to that of opposite-sex

IPV, progressing in frequency and severity over time. Similar to opposite-sex IPV victimization, factors that increase the risk of same-sex IPV victimization include younger age, lower income, history of family violence, childhood sexual abuse, low relationship cohesion, depression, and substance use/abuse. Same-sex IPV victims can suffer from the same immediate and long-term effects as opposite-sex IPV victims, including death; physical injuries; physical health problems such as sexually transmitted infections (STIs), gastrointestinal disorders, and so on; mental health problems such as anxiety, depression, posttraumatic stress disorder (PTSD), and so on; and behavioral problems such as substance use/abuse.

Sexual Assault

Sexual assault may be defined as any type of forced sexual contact without consent. Estimates of its prevalence among GLBT individuals vary depending on the study methodology employed; however, most studies estimate that between 15% and 50% of GLBT individuals experience some form of sexual assault as an adult. In most cases, GLBT women (especially bisexual women), are more likely than GLBT men to have been sexually assaulted. Much of the sexual assault of GLBT individuals is perpetrated by strangers or casual acquaintances; however, intimate partners may also commit such violence. The perpetrators of sexual assault are typically males, for both male and female GLBT victims/survivors. Some risk factors associated with sexual assault victimization among GLBT individuals include low education, low income, young age, history of prostitution, substance use/abuse, and ethnic minority status. Similar to sexual assault of heterosexuals, sexual assault of GLBT individuals can result in death, physical injuries, physical health problems (sexually transmitted diseases, etc.), mental health problems (anxiety, depression, PTSD, etc.), and behavioral problems (increased sexual risk taking and increased substance use/abuse, which may enhance individuals' risk for revictimization).

Hate Crimes

Hate crimes, also known as bias-motivated crimes, are a pervasive form of GLBT victimization that include intimidation, destruction of property, assault, stalking, sexual assault, and murder. Multiple studies find that more than half of GLBT individuals report experiencing a hate crime. According to the U.S. Department of Justice, 15% of all hate crimes are motivated by sexual orientation, with social attitudes toward homosexuality often underlying the perpetration of these crimes. Perpetrators of GLBT hate crimes, who are usually men, have reported committing the offense because of negative beliefs about sexual minorities, or because they perceive themselves as the target of sexual aggression. GLBT hate crimes may result in death, physical injuries, physical health problems, mental health problems, and financial damage. Survivors of GLBT hate crimes often report persistent feelings of stress and anger, and may link feelings of powerlessness and vulnerability with their sexual orientation, which may create long-term harm to their self-identity. Hate crimes also can reverberate throughout the GLBT community, increasing anxiety and fear of attack.

Discrimination and Institutionalized Victimization

GLBT individuals are vulnerable to discrimination and institutionalized victimization because of their sexual minority status. Discrimination includes unfair treatment in areas such as employment, housing, and law enforcement, while institutionalized victimization occurs when laws and social practices result in prejudicial acts against sexual minorities. Nationwide surveys have shown that up to 34% of GLBT individuals have experienced housing discrimination, while 20% to 44% have experienced discriminatory practices in the workplace. Some law enforcement officials also may discriminate against GLBT individuals, viewing same-sex IPV and other crimes against GLBT individuals as being less serious than other bias-motivated crimes. Laws that discriminate against GLBT individuals (such as same-sex marriage bans, prejudicial child custody laws, and criminal statutes prohibiting same-sex relations) promote institutionalized victimization. In the case of housing and employment, no federal laws prohibit discrimination on the basis of sexual orientation, and only a handful of states have enacted specific antidiscrimination laws. The repercussions of such victimization, while less obvious than those of physical or sexual violence, can have lasting negative psychological and financial effects on GLBT individuals.

Future Research and Intervention Recommendations

Given the prevalence of victimization of GLBT individuals, the serious outcomes associated with such violence, and the relative dearth of rigorous empirical information on such victimization, further research of this topic is warranted, with special attention paid to bisexuals and transgender individuals (who have received the least amount of consideration in the scientific literature). Future research should aspire to obtain representative samples of GLBT individuals, and to employ psychometrically sound assessment instruments and sophisticated analytic procedures. Professionals in contact with victimized GLBT individuals, including health care personnel, law enforcement, and social workers, could be better trained to understand and address the specific needs of GLBT populations. Furthermore, increased public awareness of GLBT victimization issues and promotion of community-based prevention programs would help to counteract negative or discriminatory attitudes toward GLBT communities. Finally, legal and political advocacy for GLBT rights would help to dismantle deep-rooted inequitable practices.

Ghazaleh Samandari and Sandra L. Martin

See also Domestic Violence, Same-Sex; Hate and Bias Crime; Intimate Partner Violence; Sexual Orientation and Victimization

Further Readings

Balsam, K. F., Rothblum, E. D., & Beauchaine, T. P. (2005). Victimization over the life span: A comparison of lesbian, gay, bisexual, and heterosexual siblings. *Journal of Consulting and Clinical Psychology*, 73(3), 477–487.

Comstock, G. D. (1991). *Violence against lesbians and gay men.* New York: Columbia University Press.

McClennen. J. C. (2005). Domestic violence between same-gender partners—recent findings and future research. *Journal of Interpersonal Violence*, 20(2), 149–154.

GENERALIZED ANXIETY DISORDER (GAD)

Generalized anxiety disorder (GAD) is characterized by excessive anxiety and worry, often without a discernible source, and can increase a person's risk of victimization. According to Internet Mental Health, approximately 3% of all U.S. adults experience GAD at any given time, with a lifetime prevalence rate of 5%. In addition, GAD will vary in degree throughout a person's lifetime, and two out of every three people with GAD are female.

There are two intertwined paths by which GAD can lead to victimization: (1) the person with GAD is fearful of ending a relationship that is abusive, and (2) the person with GAD is afraid of contacting agencies (e.g., the police, social services) that could stop their victimization.

The abused person with GAD may believe that the abuser is solving other problems in his or her life, and may come to rely on the abuser (e.g., for money and for help in completing daily tasks). It is important to remember that, at times, people with GAD may be socially incapacitated because of the disorder. The abused person may also experience an increase in anxiety at the thought of leaving the abuser. This is not an irrational fear, as many domestic violence victims are murdered while attempting to leave an abusive situation.

Many victims of domestic violence who do leave their abusive situations are helped by various agencies, such as victim services and the police. Although many abused people may have trouble gaining access to these agencies, the victim with GAD would have an especially difficult time doing so. The anxiety caused by calling, visiting, or even thinking about contacting these agencies could be enough to stop the individual from contacting anybody outside of his or her household or present social network.

A practical example may better illustrate this process: Erica is a 23-year-old woman who has GAD. She started experiencing symptoms of anxiety for no particular reason when she was 14 years old. She is similar to two thirds of those with GAD in that she is female, and similar to half of those with GAD in that she began experiencing symptoms as a child. Erica's anxiety has increased and decreased in severity over time, and sometimes it has been so disabling that she has been unable to go to work or school. Erica never thought that her anxiety was unusual, as her mother seemed to experience symptoms of anxiety for no particular reason throughout her life.

Erica never dated much throughout high school. When she was 21 years old she met John. John seemed to be a great guy at first. Erica felt that she could depend on John, and he took care of things for Erica when her fears and physical symptoms flared up and at times disabled her. John would reassure her that she was physically safe when she felt frightened. He would handle things for Erica, like taking her car to get it fixed. While there is nothing wrong with one person helping another, Erica began to become overly dependent on John to provide a sense of security when her fears took over. John was available in the middle of the night and would answer her calls at any other time as well. In fact, Erica had become involved with John to the almost complete exclusion of others. John moved in with Erica and encouraged her to stop working (to calm her nerves), which she did. John also suggested that Erica relax her nerves by severing communication with her family, who he believed did nothing but upset her.

John had focused on Erica's anxiety to completely work his way into her life; he used her anxiety to move into a position where he became her sole economic supply as well as emotional support. This is when the abuse began. John had always been overly concerned with Erica's comings and goings. She appreciated this at first, but later John would become violent when Erica left the house without his permission or didn't answer his phone call by the third ring. Sometimes he would berate her, but at other times he would hit her. He told her that if she left him, he would hurt her and members of her family. Despite the danger she was in, she felt that leaving would be even more dangerous for her and for her family.

Eventually, Erica's sister suggested that together they contact the police and victim services; however, Erica was even afraid to deal with the people at these agencies, not knowing how she would speak to them or explain her situation. Thus Erica continues to live in this cycle of violence today. Although many women have similar stories, Erica was initially trapped in this victimization cycle because her GAD produced fears that were temporarily relieved by an individual who seemed to care about her. Although at first John seemed to relieve Erica's exaggerated fears, later he abused Erica and cut her off from financial and family resources, further increasing her anxiety and dependence on him. GAD made it much more difficult for Erica than for most women in domestic violence situations to make contact with agencies that could help her leave her situation (e.g., police, victim services).

Although most women experiencing domestic violence do not have GAD, when women do, as in Erica's case, GAD makes it more difficult for them to leave the cycle of violence. For someone like Erica, treating her GAD will most likely be an important part of her leaving the abusive relationship in which she is trapped.

For those with GAD, treatment can alleviate symptoms. Various forms of treatment exist for GAD: psychotherapy, antidepressants, and benzodiazepines. According to a *Journal of Clinical Psychiatry* article by Jack Gorman, those with GAD benefit from psychotherapy because it helps them develop cognitive and behavioral strategies to deal with thoughts and somatic complaints. Antidepressants (specifically venlafaxine and paroxetine) also have been shown to be efficacious, and benzodiazepines are appropriate when these approaches do not work and in acute situations.

Daniel W. Phillips III and Jeremiah Diebler

See also Domestic Violence; Posttraumatic Stress Disorder (PTSD)

Further Readings

Gorman, J. (2003). Treating general anxiety disorder. *Journal of Clinical Psychiatry, 64*(Supplement 2), 24–29.

Silver, E., Arseneault, L., Langley, J., Avashalom, C., & Moffitt, T. (2005). Mental disorder and violent victimization in a total birth cohort. *American Journal of Public Health, 95*(11), 2015–2011.

Stanley, M., Wilson, N., Novy, D., Rhoades, H., Wagener, P., Greisinger, A., et al. (2009). Cognitive therapy for generalized anxiety disorder among older adults in primary care. *Journal of the American Medical Association, 301*(14), 1460–1467.

Web Sites

Internet Mental Health: http://www.mentalhealth.com

GUNS AND VICTIMIZATION

Guns are ubiquitous within our society. In fact, over 40% of households within the United States report owning a firearm. Although the Second Amendment guarantees "the right of the people to keep and bear arms," the question as to whether gun ownership is a right or a privilege remains controversial. The controversy lies in part in the large number of fatal and nonfatal crimes that are committed with the use of a firearm. Research has repeatedly found that the availability of firearms has been linked to death and injury. In addition, crimes committed with the use of a firearm are more likely to result in the death of an individual than are crimes committed with any other weapon. This entry discusses the incidents of gun-related victimization in the United States, what groups are most likely to be victims, and the attempts to prevent victimization through firearm regulation in the United States.

Gun Victimization in the United States

Between 1985 and 1993, violent crimes committed with firearms increased at an astronomical rate. In 1992 alone, the Bureau of Justice Statistics reported that crimes committed with handguns reached a record high of approximately 930,000. The vast majority of these crimes were nonfatal, including such crimes as robbery and sexual assault; however, over 13,000 fatalities were a result of gun-related homicide. Although the homicide rate in the United States had systematically increased and decreased over a 35-year period, the sudden increase in gun violence over this relatively short time period can be directly attributed to the emergence of crack cocaine, as has consistently been noted in the literature. The rise in gun violence, which was mainly perpetrated by juveniles and young adults, increased at an inordinately rapid rate; nevertheless, it declined in the same manner. Although the rise in gun violence and gun-related homicides was only temporary and has since stabilized to rates prior to 1985, gun victimization continues to be a problem in American society.

In 2005, over 470,000 individuals reported they had been a victim of a crime in which a firearm was used. In addition, a Federal Bureau of Investigation (FBI) report found that, on average, approximately 60% of all homicides in the United States involved a firearm. Notably, the second leading cause of injury-related deaths results from firearm use. Although much attention is paid to fatal victimizations, there are approximately six nonfatal injuries for each gun-related homicide. An estimated 25% of nonfatal violent crime survivors, including victims of sexual assault and robbery, reported the crime was committed with a handgun; handgun use accounts for approximately 13% of all violent crimes. It is not surprising that the United States leads developed nations not only in gun ownership but in homicide rates as well.

Victims of Gun Violence

Gun victimization crosses all socioeconomic, cultural, and geographic boundaries; however, certain populations are disproportionately involved in the gun-related crimes that occur within the United States. Hence, some groups are more vulnerable to the risk of gun victimization. Age is a determining factor in whether an individual will be a victim of gun violence. The likelihood that an individual will be a victim of a gun crime decreases with age. For instance, approximately 38% of all gun-related homicide victims are between the ages of 15 and 24. Statistics show that risk of gun victimization increases to the age of 17 or 18 and then begins to steadily decline. Ironically, prior to 1985, those between the ages of 24 and 35 had the highest homicide rates; however, after 1985, those between the ages of 18 and 24 had the highest rates of homicide. The likely culprit in the change in homicide rates is most likely the crack-cocaine trade that emerged during that time. Thus, gun-related homicide became the second leading cause of death for the younger group.

Males are disproportionately more likely than females to be a victim of a gun crime. According to the National Crime Victimization Survey, one in three males, compared to one in five females, reported being victimized by a gun-wielding assailant. In homicide cases, males are over three times more likely than females to be murdered with a firearm. Firearm availability in the home, however, has an inordinate impact on the female homicide rate, as women are more likely than men to be killed by an intimate partner or family member.

Race also plays a critical role in risk of victimization from gun violence. African Americans and Native Americans are more likely to be victimized than are Whites and Hispanics. In fact, over half of the victims in gun-related homicides are African American, even though African Americans make up only 13% of the total U.S. population. Further, race coupled with low socioeconomic status further increases the risk of violent victimization. One study found that those in households with an annual income less than $75,000 were more likely to be victims of a firearm-related crime. Since there is an overrepresentation of African Americans living in low socioeconomic areas, the intersection between race and socioeconomic status places these individuals at a greater vulnerability to gun violence. Coupled with factors such as age and gender, the risk of victimization continues to increase.

Geographic location is also a factor in a person's vulnerability to gun victimization. Individuals residing in urban areas are more likely to be a victim of a firearm-related violence than those living in rural areas. A disproportionate number of young minority males are victims in urban areas. Much of the gun violence in urban areas has been associated with gangs and the drug market. In 2004, approximately 94% of gang-related homicides were due to gun violence.

Those living in the Southern United States also have a greater susceptibility to gun victimization than those in other parts of the country. Some theorists have attempted to link this higher risk of victimization to "Southern culture," an approach that is controversial. Most research, however, has found that poverty, an income-related problem, is more likely than culture to be responsible for this higher risk of victimization. The factors listed above can all contribute to gun-related victimization, especially when they intersect with one another. Nevertheless, the vulnerability to gun victimization is not endemic to one group; anyone can be a victim of gun violence, regardless of demographic, cultural, or geographic situation.

Firearms Legislation

Although the past 25 years have seen a wave of gun legislation in the United States, attempts to regulate the sale and manufacture of firearms are neither new nor innovative. During the early part of the 20th century, Congress passed laws to help regulate the sale of handguns through the mail, and even attempted to curtail the use of certain types of firearms. In 1938, the federal government attempted to prevent the "criminal class" from obtaining firearms with the passing of the Federal Firearms Act. This act made it a crime to transfer a firearm to people who were under indictment or had been convicted of a violent crime.

The Gun Control Act of 1968 (GCA), however, is the most significant piece of firearms legislation passed in recent history. The intent of this congressional act was to prohibit interstate firearms sales, the sale of firearms to dangerous individuals, and the importation of inexpensive handguns ("Saturday night specials") and surplus military weapons. It also added certain destructive devices to the list of prohibited weapons. In addition, the GCA placed the monitoring of these provisions under the Bureau of Alcohol, Tobacco, and Firearms (ATF). Nevertheless, with the passing of the Firearms Owners' Protection Act of 1986 (FOPA), the provisions created in the passing of the GCA were curtailed. The FOPA permitted out-of-state sales of long guns, eliminated or reduced recordkeeping requirements, limited the power of the ATF, and made it possible for licensure of temporary events (e.g., gun shows) that had an organizational sponsor. Conversely, it did offer some new antigun legislation, including the prohibition of private ownership of machine guns and expansion of the list of ineligible persons (e.g., illegal aliens and dishonorably discharged military personnel). Although this piece of legislation granted a number of firearms rights to owners in the 1980s, the decade also saw a wave of antigun legislation. Mandatory minimums and sentence enhancements were placed on offenders who were in possession of a firearm during the commission of the crime. In addition, armor-piercing bullets and firearms not detectable by metal detectors and/or X-ray devices were banned. In 1990, the Gun Free School Zones Act was passed making it a federal crime to possess a firearm in a school or school zone; however, in U.S. v. Lopez (1995), the Supreme Court ruled the law unconstitutional. Nonetheless, this ruling does not mean that state and local governments cannot pass such ordinances.

In 1993, the Brady Handgun Violence Prevention Act (Brady bill) was signed into law by President Bill Clinton. This legislation required a mandatory criminal background check on anyone applying to purchase a firearm from a federally licensed firearm dealer. Thus anyone purchasing a firearm must wait 5 days before receiving it so that a background check can be completed. The intent of this legislation was to prevent dangerous individuals from being able to obtain a handgun. Since its inception, the Brady bill has prevented over a million dangerous individuals from obtaining a gun. It must be noted that this law does not apply to gun shows due to the restrictions established under FOPA; therefore, anyone wanting to legally purchase a handgun can do so without violating the law.

Soon after the passing of the Brady bill, the Assault Weapons Ban (AWB) was passed. This law prohibited the importation, manufacture, sale, and possession of assault weapons. The law, however, only applied to weapons sold after 1994. In addition, assault weapons were defined not only as semiautomatic rifles but as weapons that possessed two characteristics in established criteria and included but were not limited to bayonet mounts and protruding pistol grips. The AWB also banned large capacity magazine clips that held more than 10 bullets. This legislation had little, if any, impact on gun victimization rates since these types of weapons are rarely used in the commission of crimes. The ban expired in 2004. Another controversial piece of legislation during the 1990s was the Lautenberg Amendment of 1996. This expansion of the Gun Control Act of 1968 extended the ban of gun ownership to anyone ever convicted of a misdemeanor domestic violence charge, including police officers. This federal attempt to curb gun violence in interpersonal relationships prompted states to change their statutes to protect victims from interpersonal violence.

As noted, gun legislation is implemented not only at the federal level but at the state and local levels as well. Although state legislation cannot be contradictory to federal firearms law, states have different regulations regarding the sale, possession, and licensure of firearms. Similar to the federal system, 44 states have a provision in their state constitutions allowing people the right to bear arms. Most states, however, do not allow municipalities to enact firearm regulations more restrictive than the state's prevailing firearms legislation (e.g., California, Texas, and Vermont); not all states abide by this policy. Although Illinois has extremely restrictive gun policies, it still provides licensure for both long guns and handguns; nevertheless, Chicago prohibits the sale and possession of handguns. Similar to Chicago, the District of Columbia prohibits the sale, manufacture, and possession of firearms; however, in *District of Columbia v. Heller* (2008), the Supreme Court struck down its ban on handgun possession in the home, stating that the provision violates the Second Amendment. In essence, this decision by the Supreme Court recognizes that in the United States, individuals' constitutional right to bear arms supersedes their protection from the "criminal class." Nevertheless, gun control legislation continues to be a crucial factor in reducing the number of gun-related victimizations.

Tammy S. Garland

See also Brady Bill; Homicide and Murder; Lautenberg Amendment

Further Readings

Alvarez, A., & Bachman, R. (2008). *Violence: The enduring problem*. Thousand Oaks, CA: Sage.

Banderman, J. (2001). *Working with victims of gun violence* (OVC Bulletin). Washington, DC: U.S. Department of Justice.

Cukier, W. (2002). More guns, more deaths. *Medicine, Conflict and Survival, 18,* 367–379.

Jacobs, J. B. (2002). *Can gun control work?* New York: Oxford University Press.

Perkins, C. (2003). *Weapon use and violent crime*. Washington, DC: Bureau of Justice Statistics.

H

HATE AND BIAS CRIME

Over the past several decades, advocacy groups and lawmakers have begun to recognize the form of victimization known as hate crime. Hate crime consists of crimes motivated by bias against an individual's real or perceived race, ethnicity, religion, or sexual orientation, and these crimes are addressed through various forms of state and federal legislation. Although such violence had been perpetrated throughout history, it was not until inroads were made by victim advocacy groups that these crimes began to be known collectively as hate or bias crime.

During the 1980s, various states adopted hate crime legislation, and in 1990 the Hate Crimes Statistics Act (HCSA) was passed by Congress and signed into law. This act mandated the collection and dissemination of hate crime data by the Federal Bureau of Investigation (FBI). Nearly every state has some form of hate crime legislation, and currently federal legislation is pending in Congress that would expand the status provisions of crimes "motivated by prejudice based on the actual or perceived race, color, religion, national origin" to include "gender, sexual orientation, gender identity, or disability of the victim." Further, the bill offers additional federal funding for prevention and law enforcement response to hate crimes.

Proponents of hate crime legislation argue that hate crimes cause more harm than non-hate-motivated crimes, and that as a result punishment should be more severe for hate crime offenders. Scholars have made the argument that hate crimes harm not only the victim, but the victim's entire group, as well as the larger community. On its Web site, the National Gay and Lesbian Task Force states that "hate crimes send a message of terror to an entire group and are therefore unlike a random act of violence." An attack or property crime directed toward one individual ultimately impacts all those who identify with the victim. Proponents contend that the implementation of hate crime legislation reinforces society's moral values by promoting tolerance and sending a message that hate-motivated violence is unacceptable.

The extent of hate crime victimization is relatively difficult to gauge because hate crimes are believed to be underreported. According to the FBI's Uniform Crime Reporting (UCR) Program, in 2007 there were 7,160 hate crime incidents. However, the UCR Program only includes those incidents that were reported to police. In 2000, the National Crime Victimization Survey (NCVS) began incorporating questions regarding hate crime victimizations into its survey. According to a Bureau of Justice Statistics (BJS) Special Report containing NCVS and UCR Program data collected from mid-2000 through December 2003, hate crime incidents reach an annual average of approximately 191,000. Globally, according to a 2008 report released by the Human Rights First organization, hate crimes have increased in several of the 56 countries it surveys, including France, Germany, Ireland, the United Kingdom, Sweden, the Slovak Republic, and the United States.

According to the UCR Program, hate crimes are most frequently crimes against persons as opposed to property crimes. The most frequent personal offenses include intimidation, harassment, and simple assault. Property offenses frequently include property destruction, damage, and vandalism. According to the BJS, 83.7% of hate crime victimizations were considered violent crimes (i.e., rape/sexual assault, robbery, aggravated assault, simple assault), as opposed to 22.9% of non-hate-motivated crimes.

Research on whether hate crimes result in more severe physical injuries for victims is mixed. Early work described hate crimes as "excessively brutal" and found that hate crime victims were more likely to experience physical injury than non-hate-crime victims. One study using National Incident Based Reporting System data compared bias- and non-bias-motivated assaults found that bias crime victims were about three times more likely to suffer an injury than were other victims. Other research suggests the opposite—that hate crime victims are less likely to experience physical injury and less likely to require or accept medical treatment. In fact, the vast majority of hate crimes are low-level offenses, including harassment/intimidation or simple assault. However, most research finds that victims of hate crimes are likely to experience greater psychological harm than do victims of other types of crimes. For example, a study of the victims of aggravated assault found that hate crime victims were more likely to experience psychological symptoms such as depression or sadness, nervousness, and loss of concentration; less likely to feel safe after the incident; and more likely to have intrusive thoughts than are victims of non-hate-motivated aggravated assault. Such findings suggest that there are unique after effects resulting from hate crimes that extend beyond any specific occurrence of physical injury.

Hate Crimes Motivated by Race/Ethnicity

According to both the UCR Program and NCVS, racially motivated crimes, specifically anti-Black crimes, are consistently among the most commonly occurring hate crimes. Racial minorities have long been victims of oppression in the United States. Historically, institutionalized forms of racism included slavery, slave patrols, the Jim Crow era, and numerous lynchings that were often explicitly condoned by law enforcement. Though these particular forms of barbaric behavior have been eliminated, violence motivated by racial animus has not. For example, in 1999 three White men were convicted in the murder of James Byrd in Jasper, Texas. The three men, described as attempting to start their own White supremacist group, offered Byrd a ride, beat him, chained him to the back of their truck, and dragged him to his death. Despite the history of violence directed toward racial minorities, there has been little research specifically on Black victims of hate crimes.

Other forms of racially motivated hate crimes include the waves of church arsons primarily directed toward churches with Black parishioners. According to research, a spate of church arsons were documented following the Civil War, during the early 1900s, as a response to the civil rights movement, and during the late 1980s. According to the Southern Poverty Law Center (SPLC), the recent election of Barack Obama as President of the United States has resulted in a "surge" of racially motivated incidents including burning crosses, hanging effigies, and death threats.

In addition to African Americans, other ethnic minorities experience bias-motivated victimizations. Latinos in particular have experienced a substantial increase in hate crimes in the past few years. SPLC points out that much of the growth in hate crimes directed toward Latinos is due to anti-immigrant sentiment in the United States and is concentrated in states with a high immigrant population. According to SPLC, organized hate movements such as the Imperial Klans of America fuel anti-immigrant sentiment and promote violence. Since 2000, the SPLC has documented a 48% growth in hate groups in the United States. Although the majority of hate crimes are not committed by members of organized hate groups, such groups encourage prejudiced attitudes that may result in violence.

Media stereotypes may also contribute to animosity directed toward Latinos. In the media, immigrants, or those perceived to be immigrants, are increasingly being linked to crime. Such linkage, whose logic runs counter to research studies on crime and immigration, ultimately ratchets up fear of "outsiders" and "foreigners." Further, research suggests that hate crimes directed toward immigrants are underreported. Immigrants may be unlikely to report hate crime victimizations due to fear of deportation, language barriers, poor police–community relations, and cultural norms.

Post-9/11 Hate Crimes

Hate crimes were of continuing concern in the aftermath of the attacks of September, 11, 2001. Many Americans who were perceived to be Arab or Muslim were the victims of bias-motivated violence. In the weeks following September 11, the American Arab Anti-Discrimination Committee confirmed over 700 violent incidents, including four hate-motivated murders and as many as seven other suspected hate-motivated murders. This violence was directed toward individuals who were Arab, or perceived to be Arab or Muslim. In a survey of Arab American community leaders, several symbols were mentioned as "triggering" bias-motivated crimes. For example, clothing such as a hijab, Arabic signs on storefronts, Arabic names or accents, and skin color have been specified as triggers. Due to the lack of knowledge of some Americans about Arab ethnicity and the Islamic religion, many victims of anti-Arab and anti-Islamic hate crimes were neither Arab nor Islamic.

Estimating the prevalence of hate crimes against Arab Americans, or those perceived to be of Middle Eastern descent, is difficult. The FBI's UCR Program collects data on ethnicity, but includes only the categories "anti-Hispanic" or "anti-other." Disaggregated data for anti-Arab hate crimes is not available from the program. The UCR Program does, however, provide data on crime motivated by anti-Islamic religious bias. According to this data, there was a substantial increase in anti-Islamic hate crimes following the terrorist attacks, with persons of Islamic faith becoming the victims of various hate-motivated offenses ranging from vandalism to murder. During 2001, 455 of the 546 anti-Islamic hate crimes occurred after September 11.

Researchers found that anti-Islamic attacks peaked after September 11, and then declined after about a 9-week period. The decline is believed to be due to a number of factors, including efforts by the government to condemn hate crime, law enforcement efforts, and community organizations designed to educate and promote tolerance. Since 2001, according to the FBI, anti-Islamic attacks have averaged about 149 per year.

Hate Crimes Motivated by Religion

According to UCR Program statistics, Jewish persons are consistently among the most frequent targets of religious bias. In 2007, there were 1,010 anti-Jewish offenses, compared to 133 anti-Islamic and 65 anti-Catholic offenses. Historical oppression against persons of the Jewish faith has been widely documented. Jews, and to a lesser extent other minorities, were targeted in one of the most heinous atrocities of the 20th century, the Holocaust, in which over six million Jews were systematically murdered. More recently, conflict in the Middle East has resulted in increased animosity and bias attacks directed toward the Jews worldwide. In 2003, *The New York Times* reported an increase in vandalism and assaults against Jews in Europe "at a frequency not seen since the 1930's when Fascism was on the rise."

According to the Anti-Defamation League's annual *Audit of Anti-Semitic Incidents*, after an initial increase post-9/11, domestic incidents directed against Jews declined. The *Audit* found that since 1992, anti-Jewish bias-motivated incidents, both criminal and noncriminal, most frequently have consisted of harassment, threats, and assaults. Other research has shown that hate crimes motivated by religion are likely to be property crimes, such as swastikas and other graffiti sprayed on cars, homes, and synagogues, as opposed to personal crimes.

Hate Crimes Motivated by Sexual Orientation

As hate crime legislation developed at the state and federal level, legislators debated which status provisions should be included. Race, ethnicity, and religion were fairly easily integrated as status provisions, while sexual orientation, gender, and disability provisions were met with more resistance by lawmakers. Part of the contention surrounding the inclusion of sexual orientation involved the notion that including it along with race, ethnicity, and religion served to extend "special rights" to gay men and lesbians. Ultimately, sexual orientation was acknowledged in the federal HCSA, and 31 states currently have legislation that includes sexual orientation.

According to advocacy groups, violence committed against gay men and lesbians is widespread. Over the past few years, both the FBI and the Anti-Violence Project, a group dedicated to preventing violence against gay men and lesbians, have reported increases in antigay hate crimes. Further, in a study to gauge the prevalence of hate crime victimization directed toward individuals because of their sexual orientation, researchers found that about 25% of adults identified as sexual minorities experienced a crime or attempted crime, and about 50% were verbally harassed because of their actual or perceived sexual orientation.

Antigay hate crimes, like other hate crimes, are believed to be underreported. Moreover, researchers have documented that up to 90% of antigay hate crimes remain unreported. Gay men and lesbians may be unlikely to report their victimizations for various reasons, including fear of being outed, mistrust of the police, and fear of a hostile reaction to their victimization. In fact, in a study examining public support for hate crime victims, researchers found that victims of antigay hate crimes are less likely than victims of other types of hate crimes to receive sympathy from the public.

A study examining antigay hate crimes in Los Angeles County found that victims of antigay hate crimes experienced more severe forms of aggression than did victims of other types of bias crimes. Further, the study found that individuals who were members of multiple minority groups (e.g., race, ethnicity, and sexual orientation) were at higher risk for hate crime victimization and greater severity of hate crime victimization. Research indicates that victims of antigay hate crimes are likely to suffer greater psychological effects than are victims of other types of hate crimes, including higher levels of depression, anxiety, anger, and symptoms related to posttraumatic stress disorder.

Antigay hate crimes are often among the most violent, and antigay murders have been described as extremely brutal. One of the most publicized antigay hate crimes was the 1998 murder of Matthew Shepard in Wyoming. Shepard was bludgeoned, tied to a fence, and left unconscious. He never regained consciousness, and he later died. During the trial, one of the defendants unsuccessfully argued a "gay panic" defense, alleging that a sexual advance by Shepard triggered the murderous attack. Though Wyoming has no hate crime legislation, two defendants were convicted of the murder and received life sentences.

One of the most overlooked areas of victimization is that of violence motivated by bias against transgender people. The extent of this type of hate crime is unknown because most states, along with the FBI, do not collect data on these crimes. Acts of violence against transgender people generally go unrecognized as hate crimes. In fact, the SPLC has documented numerous murders believed to be motivated by transgender bias. These murders almost always involved extreme violence. According to the National Center for Transgender Equality, only seven states and Washington, D.C., have legislation that includes protection based on gender identity or expression. Thus, most of these transgender murders go legally unrecognized as hate crimes.

Hate Crimes Motivated by Gender and Disability

The extent of gender-based hate crimes is unknown, since neither the FBI nor the NCVS collects data on hate crimes motivated by gender. Research documenting the development of hate crime legislation found that adding gender as a status provision in hate crime legislation at both the federal and state level was met with some resistance. Scholars have documented a variety of reasons for the difficulty of "fitting" gender into the hate crime paradigm. For example, should all crimes against women, including rape, sexual assault, and domestic violence, be classified as hate crimes? Since there are already laws protecting women against violence, is hate crime legislation in this area redundant? Despite the lack of agreement surrounding gender, according to the Anti-Defamation League, 27 states have legislation inclusive of gender bias. Due to the relatively small number of hate crimes motivated by gender that are documented in official data, there is a lack of research examining gender-specific hate crime victimization.

Currently, 31 states have legislation that includes hate crimes motivated by disability. Official data are collected on hate crimes motivated by disability, and according to NIBRS data that measure crimes reported to law enforcement, less than 1% of hate crime offenses are motivated by bias against disability. Of those, victims with physical disability were more frequently targeted than those with mental disability. According to a BJS Special Report examining hate crimes from mid-2000 through 2003, disability may comprise as much as 10% of the total hate crime victimizations. Researchers suggest that the disabled may be among the most vulnerable to victimization, because they are often reliant on others for assistance and care. Unfortunately, caregivers, family members, acquaintances, and neighbors—those that disabled individuals may rely on for assistance—are frequently the perpetrators of hate crimes against the disabled.

Hate Crime Prevention Programs

Many programs exist to address hate crimes. These programs include training curriculum for law enforcement and guidelines for prosecutors; however, since many hate crimes are unreported—and of those reported, not all result in hate crime prosecutions—reliance on law enforcement efforts alone to combat hate crimes is insufficient. Other programs focus more specifically on prevention and rehabilitation of hate crime offenders. Unfortunately, few evaluations have been conducted, therefore the efficacy of these programs is unknown.

One particularly unique approach to assist current victims and prevent future hate crimes is that undertaken by attorneys seeking legal remedies through civil lawsuits. For example, the SPLC, led by Morris Dees, has been successful in suing several leaders of hate groups, including Tom Metzger, the leader of the White Aryan Resistance. Such lawsuits are designed to disrupt the leadership of the hate group by seizing their assets and rendering them incapable of functioning. Recently, the SPLC successfully won a $2.5 million lawsuit against the Imperial Klans of America for inciting violence leading to the severe beating of a Kentucky resident Klan members believed was an illegal immigrant.

Other alternatives include programs that incorporate components of restorative justice programs designed to integrate the victim into the justice process. Scholars have documented that the use of community forums and victim–offender mediation in response to hate crimes has had encouraging results. For example, one study explored how mediators worked with family members and held community conferences with students and citizens to encourage dialogue in response to racial conflict in a high school. Ultimately, the use of peer mediation was recommended to deal with future incidents. Though many programs show encouraging results, more research is needed to fully evaluate hate crime prevention and offender-based programs.

Nickie Phillips

See also Disabilities, Victimization of Individuals With; Gay, Lesbian, Bisexual, and Transgender Individuals, Victimization of; Hate and Bias Crime, Statutory Responses; Immigration and Victimization; Race/Ethnicity and Victimization; Sex and Victimization; Sexual Orientation and Victimization; Victimology; Victims' Rights Legislation, Federal, United States

Further Readings

Byers, B., & Jones, J. (2007). The impact of the terrorist attacks of 9/11 on anti-Islamic hate crime. *Journal of Ethnicity in Criminal Justice, 5*(1), 43–56.

Coates, R., Umbreit, M. S., & Vos, B. (2006). Responding to hate crimes through restorative justice dialogue. *Contemporary Justice Review, 9*(1), 7–21.

Gerstenfeld, P. (2004). *Hate crimes: Causes, controls, and controversies.* Thousand Oaks, CA: Sage.

Gerstenfeld, P., & Grant, D. (Eds.). (2004). *Crimes of hate: Selected readings.* Thousand Oaks, CA: Sage.

Harlow, C. (2005). *Hate crime reported by victims and police* (NCJ 209911). Washington, DC: U.S. Department of Justice, Bureau of Justice Statistics.

Hendricks, N., Ortiz, C., Sugie, N., & Miller, J. (2007). Beyond the numbers: Hate crimes and cultural trauma within Arab American immigrant communities. *International Review of Victimology, 14,* 99–113.

Herek, G. (2009). Hate crimes and stigma-related experiences among sexual minority adults in the United States: Prevalence estimates from a national probability sample. *Journal of Interpersonal Violence, 24*(1), 54–74.

Jenness, V., & Grattet, R. (2001). *Making hate a crime: From social movement to law enforcement.* Thousand Oaks, CA: Sage.

Kaplan, J. (2006). Islamophobia in America? September 11 and Islamophobic hate crime. *Terrorism and Political Violence, 18,* 1–33.

Local Law Enforcement Hate Crimes Prevention Act (S966). (2004). Retrieved from http://www.govtrack.us/congress/bill.xpd?bill=h110–1592&tab=summary

Perry, B. (Ed.). (2003). *Hate and bias crime: A reader.* New York: Routledge.

Shively, M. (2005). *Study of literature and legislation on hate crime in America*. Washington, DC: National Institute of Justice.

Smith, C. S. (2003, March 22). French Jews tell of a new and threatening wave of anti-Semitism. *The New York Times*, p. A5. Retrieved from http://www.nytimes .com/2003/03/22/world/french-jews-tell-of-a-new-and-threatening-wave-of-anti-semitism.html

Web Sites

National Gay and Lesbian Task Force: http://www .thetaskforce.org

HATE AND BIAS CRIME, STATUTORY RESPONSES

Violence motivated by hate and personal prejudice has existed for centuries; however, explicit statutory responses to crime resulting from these biases have not. Statutory responses differ distinctly from both judicial case law and governmental agency regulations. A statutory response consists of the enactment or passing of a law by the legislative branch of the government, not the judicial or executive branches of the government. Thus, a statutory response to hate and bias crime is any legislation that has or will be put into law by the U.S. Congress or by a state legislature in an effort to prevent hate- and bias-motivated violence.

Propelled by civil rights movements during the last few decades of the 20th century—such as the women's rights movement, the civil rights movement, the disabilities movement, and the lesbian, gay, bisexual, transgender, and queer rights movement—members of the U.S. Congress and members of some state legislatures began advocating for legislation to combat the issue of hate- and bias-motivated violence. Although legislation at the federal level has a national impact, state-level statutory responses vary extensively by type of legislation and the types of biases covered. The following provides an overview of legislation at both levels of government.

Federal-Level Statutory Responses

Even though hate crime legislation did not explicitly appear until the Hate Crime Statistics Act of 1990, other antidiscriminatory legislation existed prior to 1990 that has subsequently become part of hate and bias crime legislation. The Fifteenth Amendment to the U.S. Constitution outlaws the denial of rights based on race. U.S. Code (U.S.C.) Title 18, Section 241, bans conspiracies to deprive individual rights given by the U.S. Constitution, and Title 18, Section 242, makes it a crime to deprive individual rights given by the Constitution in regard to race or color. In addition, the civil rights acts expanded access and barred discriminatory practices in areas such as, but not limited to, employment, housing, access to public goods and services, and equal application of voting regulations.

Hate Crime Statistics Act of 1990

The Hate Crime Statistics Act was established in 1990 as part of 28 U.S.C. 534. The Hate Crime Statistics section of the legislation required the U.S. attorney general to collect data on crimes that were committed based on prejudices, including race, religion, sexual orientation, and ethnicity. Later, reporting requirements were expanded by the Violent Crime Control and Law Enforcement Act (VCCLEA) of 1994 to include crimes committed based on discrimination due to disability.

Violence Against Women Act of 1994

In an effort to combat gender discrimination, the Violence Against Women Act was also enacted in 1994. According to U.S. Code Title 42, Section 13981, it seeks to provide (1) protection to individuals who are victims of gender-motivated crime and (2) legislation explicitly stating that all individuals have the "right to be free from crimes of violence motivated by gender." In addition, the crime must be both motivated by gender and a felony in order to be classified as a *crime of violence motivated by gender*.

Hate Crimes Sentencing Enhancement Act of 1995

Along with the expansion of reporting requirements, the VCCLEA instituted the Hate Crimes Sentencing Enhancement Act. This act requires the sentence for a hate-motivated crime to be enhanced to at least three offense levels above the standard sentence for the offense that was committed. According to section 280003 of the VCCLEA, this act provides enhancements for prejudiced crimes committed intentionally based on the "actual or perceived race, color, religion, national origin, ethnicity, gender, disability, or sexual orientation" of the victim.

Church Arsons Prevention Act of 1996

This act focuses directly on religion-based hate and bias crimes and indirectly on race-motivated crime. It functions as an amendment to a prior statute that gave jurisdiction to federal law enforcement in cases where vandalism of a religious institution was over $10,000. The 1996 amendment expanded federal jurisdiction beyond the commerce restriction for religious-based crimes against religious institutions, provided for enhanced penalties, and increased resources available to both the victims and the investigation teams. Indirectly, this act focuses on race-motivated crime, because African American churches were the most prevalent victims of arson prior to its enactment.

Local Law Enforcement Hate Crimes Prevention Act

Beginning in 1997, members of Congress sought to pass the Hate Crimes Prevention Act. Various versions of this act have been drafted since that time. The most recent version is the Local Law Enforcement Hate Crimes Prevention Act of 2009, which extends the existing federal jurisdiction for bias-based incidents. Without an extension, federal jurisdiction exists only in incidents involving activities protected by federal law that involve bias based on race, color, religion, and ethnicity. Furthermore, this legislation has also sought to broaden federal jurisdiction to include cases involving bias motivation based on sexual orientation, gender, and disability.

State-Level Statutory Responses

State-level statutory responses vary, but most cover a form of bias motivation. According to the Anti-Defamation League, as of August 2008, 45 of 50 states had enacted legislation providing a criminal sanction for bias-motivated violence or intimidation. The five states that do not provide state-level statutory responses are Arkansas, Georgia, Indiana, South Carolina, and Wyoming; however, all but one

of the five provide criminal penalties for institutional vandalism, and two allow for civil action.

Among the 45 states with bias-motivation statutes, provisional coverage differs. Of the 45, 30 allow for civil action. All but one provide coverage for crimes motivated by race/ethnicity and/or religion. The statutes of 31 states include sexual orientation, and 27 states have provisions for gender-motivated crimes. There is legislation covering disability-based biases in 31 states, and 20 states include protection for at least one of the following bias-motivations: political affiliation, age, and transgender/gender identity. In addition, 38 of the 45 protect against institutional vandalism. Furthermore, 28 states require data collection on hate-motivated crimes; however, only 14 states provide hate- and bias-motivated crime training for law enforcement officials.

Jessica R. Dunham

See also Gay, Lesbian, Bisexual, and Transgender Individuals, Victimization of; Hate and Bias Crime; Race/Ethnicity and Victimization; Same-Sex Intimate Partner Violence; Sex and Victimization; Sexual Orientation and Victimization; Violence Against Women Act of 1994 and Subsequent Revisions; Violent Crime Control and Law Enforcement Act of 1994

Further Readings

Perry, B. (Ed.). (2003). *Hate and bias crime: A reader.* New York: Routledge.
Streissguth, T. (2003). *Hate crimes.* New York: Facts on File.
Violence Against Women Act of 1994, 42 U.S.C. 13981 (2006).
Violent Crime Control and Law Enforcement Act of 1994, H.R. 3355, 103 Cong., 2nd Sess. (1994).

Web Sites

Anti-Defamation League: http://www.adl.org
Southern Poverty Law Center: http://www.splcenter.org
United States Code: http://www.uscode.house.gov

HEALTH CARE FRAUD

Health care fraud is a major issue that has attracted the attention of physicians, hospitals, patients, insurers, policy makers, government agencies, and academics. This entry defines health care fraud and health care abuse, describes the prevalence of health care fraud in the United States, discusses the common fraud victims and perpetrators, and reviews efforts to combat the problem. While fraud occurs throughout the health care system, fraud involving publicly funded federal health care programs has attracted the most attention because of its enormous cost. Expenditures for Medicare, the federal health care program for the aged, reached $431.5 billion in 2007; total outlays for Medicaid, the joint federal and state health care program for the poor, were $335.8 billion.

Definitions

There is no concise definition of *health care fraud*; it is a broad phrase encompassing a spectrum of activities in which money that is intended to pay for health care services is in some way diverted to private use. *Fraud* is a legal term that refers to actions taken with the intent to deceive, such as intentional misrepresentation of information that insurers and government programs rely on in making payment decisions. A physician who intentionally submits a bill for services that were never performed, for example, deceives the payer into making an improper payment.

Health care abuse lacks this intent, and often involves taking advantage of ambiguity in payment rules to bill in ways that are not technically illegal, yet may violate the spirit of the law. A physician who performs two separate medical procedures (and receives two payments) when both could have been performed safely and more economically at the same time, for example, will profit at the expense of the health care system, which will then have fewer resources to expend on services for others.

Estimates

The federal government has estimated that 10% of the federal health care budget is lost to fraud. Although useful for conveying the magnitude of the problem, this figure appears to have been derived more from anecdotal than from empirical evidence. Because successful schemes remain hidden, it is difficult to determine the full extent of fraudulent activities.

Audits can be used to estimate a program's "error rate." In 1996, the U.S. Department of Health and Human Services (HHS) Office of the Inspector General (OIG) found that Medicare had improperly paid out more than $23 billion that year. Since that time, the error rate has dropped each year. The Centers for Medicare & Medicaid Services (CMS), which took over the audits in 2003, found $10.8 billion in improper payments in 2007. However, erroneous payments do not equate to fraud. The audits also found errors in claims processing, inaccurate billing, and simple mistakes by health care providers. In short, these audits are not designed to measure health care fraud, and cannot be taken as an accurate indicator of the scope of the problem.

Victims and Perpetrators of Health Care Fraud

Most health care fraud involves relationships among four groups: (1) patients with some form of health insurance coverage (public or private); (2) entities that sponsor health care benefit programs, particularly employers and government programs; (3) institutions and professionals who provide medical services; and (4) insurance entities that administer benefits and process claims.

The potential for fraud exists whenever these groups interact. For example, patients may defraud government programs by falsely claiming to be entitled to benefits, such as by falsifying enrollment information. An employer who offers health care benefits to its employees may fail to deliver the benefits as promised. An insurer may misrepresent its products to potential purchasers, or fail to process and pay claims promptly. And a health care professional or institution may falsify bills in order to obtain payment for services that were not performed. While the methods may vary, experience demonstrates that there is both motive and opportunity for fraud in virtually any health care arrangement.

Health care fraud is characterized as a white-collar crime, a predominantly nonviolent crime undertaken primarily for financial gain. In the federal health care programs, fraud is subject to a broad array of civil, criminal, and administrative laws, virtually all of which consider the federal government to be the ultimate victim. While it is logical to focus on the government as a defrauded payer, however, it is important nonetheless to remember that health care fraud also causes injury to patients.

Financial injury is the most straightforward type of harm to patients, and often is attributable to cost-sharing obligations. Under Medicare Part B, for example, beneficiaries are responsible for paying 20% of the charge for outpatient services such as physician visits. A fraudulently inflated charge results in additional expense to both Medicare and the patient—a problem particularly for individuals with limited incomes. Fraud also may cause physical injury, such as when unnecessary medical procedures are performed on patients solely for the purposes of obtaining additional payments. Patients also may be injured in less tangible ways, such as when private medical information is misappropriated and used to bill for nonexistent services. Ideally, efforts to prevent and prosecute health care fraud will seek to compensate injured patients as well as recover government funds.

Strategies to Prevent, Detect, and Remedy Health Care Fraud

Congress has responded to the problem of health care fraud both by strengthening federal laws and by appropriating more funds to federal agencies, particularly OIG and the Department of Justice (DOJ). In particular, the Health Insurance Portability and Accountability Act of 1996 (HIPAA) increased funding, established new antifraud laws, and created the Fraud and Abuse Control Program, which was designed to coordinate federal, state, and local enforcement efforts. Subsequent legislation, such as the Balanced Budget Act of 1997 (BBA), the Medicare Modernization Act of 2003 (MMA), and the Deficit Reduction Act of 2005 (DRA), provided additional opportunities and incentives for prosecutors to bring fraud actions.

The federal government has taken a multi-pronged approach to addressing health care fraud. First, the government seeks to prevent fraudulent activities, such as by educating health care providers on proper billing rules and clarifying ambiguous provisions that may invite abuse. For example, the MMA changed the way Medicare Part B pays for drugs, from a system based on ill-defined manufacturer-reported "average wholesale prices" to one that better tracks actual sales prices.

Second, the government has stepped up efforts to audit claims, both to identify common fraud schemes and to catch improper claims before they are paid. These audits are undertaken by a number of different entities within the federal health care programs, including the OIG and private contractors. Audits range from routine claims reviews to investigations based on specific complaints. In addition to investigating specific providers, the government has undertaken national and regional initiatives targeting certain sectors of the health care industry. The prototype was Operation Restore Trust, a joint federal and state effort in the mid-1990s that focused on fraud by home health agencies, nursing homes, hospices, and durable medical equipment suppliers in states with large Medicare populations.

Third, the federal government has been proactive in enforcing the myriad federal and state laws prohibiting health care fraud. Some of these laws target improper health care activities, most notably the Medicare and Medicaid Anti-Kickback Statute (designed to prevent the exchange of kickbacks and other financial benefits for the referral of patients or other business) and the Ethics in Patient Referrals Act of 1989 (or the Stark Law, designed to prevent physicians from profiting by referring patients to health care entities with which they have financial dealings). Other laws, most notably the Civil False Claims Act (FCA), apply more broadly to all entities that do business with the federal government. Health care fraud also may be pursued under general criminal laws such as mail fraud, wire fraud, and conspiracy, and HIPAA created a new Health Care Fraud crime applicable to both private and public health benefit programs. Additional administrative remedies are available, including complete exclusion of the provider from federal health care programs.

The financial nature of health care fraud makes civil sanctions an attractive option. The most powerful civil weapon is the FCA, under which a violator can be required to pay a civil penalty of $5,500 to $11,000 for each false claim, plus three times the government's damages. For providers such as physicians, who tend to submit thousands of relatively small claims per year, the result can be devastating. In one notable case, a psychiatrist was accused of submitting 8,000 false claims, each inflated by approximately $30, for a total of $245,000 in damages; when the per-claim penalties were calculated, however, the total amounted to $81 million. The FCA also contains a unique *qui tam* provision that permits a private person who is aware of fraudulent conduct to file suit, on the government's behalf, in return for a percentage of the proceeds if the suit is successful. Since amendments in 1986 modernized the FCA and made it more lucrative to pursue such private suits, the number of health-related FCA suits has grown; by the late 1990s, nearly two thirds of *qui tam* suits involved allegations of health care fraud.

Not surprisingly, most providers who are threatened with such litigation seek to negotiate. As a result, most health care fraud investigations are resolved through settlements in which the defendant, while not admitting liability, nevertheless agrees to repay the government and institute oversight procedures for the future. Provider groups have objected to this trend, alleging that the government engages in a form of "extortion" by threatening to sue for such astronomical amounts that defendants have no choice but to settle. These objections have had moderate success with regard to specific enforcement initiatives.

Fraudulent health care activities also are actionable at the state level. Many state laws mirror the Anti-Kickback and Stark statutes, some pertain only to Medicaid fraud, while others apply broadly to all health care payers. Moreover, the DRA offered incentives for states to enact their own Medicaid false claims provisions. State attorneys general have become adept at using consumer fraud statutes to pursue health-related activities, particularly in the pharmaceutical context. It is increasingly common for health care fraud allegations to result in global settlements that resolve the allegations against not only the federally funded health care programs but also the 50-plus state Medicaid programs, sometimes accompanied by a multistate consumer protection agreement.

Progress and Future Directions

In fiscal year 2007, the federal government won or negotiated approximately $1.8 billion in health care fraud cases. Federal prosecutors convicted 560 defendants for health care–related crimes, and opened 878 new criminal and 776 new civil health care fraud investigations. Under HIPAA, a portion of the recovered money is available for transfer to the Health Care Fraud and Abuse Control Account, where it can be used to fund future antifraud efforts. In 2007, $249.459 million was appropriated to the account, of which $197.666 million was allotted to HHS and $51.793 million to DOJ. Although such recoveries pale in comparison to the overall estimates of health care fraud, there is little question that the efforts are considered successful and will continue. While schemes may vary, fraud unfortunately has proven to be a constant in the health care system.

Joan H. Krause

See also Civil Litigation; Corporate Crime; Punitive and Compensatory Damages; Victimless Crimes; White-Collar Crime

Further Readings

Davies, S. L., & Jost, T. S. (1997). Managed care: Placebo or wonder drug for health care fraud and abuse? *Georgia Law Review, 31,* 373–417.

Hyman, D. A. (2002). HIPAA and health care fraud: An empirical perspective. *Cato Journal, 22,* 151–178.

Krause, J. H. (2003). A conceptual model of health care fraud enforcement. *Journal of Law and Policy, 12,* 55–147.

Krause, J. H. (2006). A patient-centered approach to health care fraud recovery. *Journal of Criminal Law and Criminology, 96,* 579–619.

Mashaw, J. L., & Marmor, T. R. (1994). Conceptualizing, estimating, and reforming fraud, waste, and abuse in healthcare spending. *Yale Journal on Regulation, 11,* 455–494.

U.S. Department of Health and Human Services & U.S. Department of Justice. (2007). *Health Care Fraud and Abuse Control Program Annual Report For FY 2006.* Retrieved September 1, 2008, from http://www.usdoj.gov/dag/pubdoc/hcfacreport2006.pdf

Web Sites

U.S. Department of Health and Human Services, Office of Inspector General: http://www.oig.hhs.gov

HOMELESS, VIOLENCE AGAINST

During the past decade, advocates and homeless shelter workers from around the country have seen an increase in reports of homeless men, women, and even children being killed, beaten, and harassed. Over the 6-year period from 1999 to 2004, the National Coalition for the Homeless documented 156 murders and 386 violent acts against homeless individuals. The violent attacks occurred in 140 cities in 39 states in the United States. Obviously, violence against homeless people is an increasing social problem.

Risk Factors

Research has highlighted factors that increase the risk of violent victimization for the homeless population. Such risks include alcohol and drug abuse, time spent homeless, frequency of homeless periods, mental illness, and criminal history.

Alcohol and drug abuse is a commonly cited risk factor for violent victimization for homeless persons. It has been suggested that this relationship is two-way: substance abuse increases the risks for violent victimization, and the experience of violent victimization increases the use/abuse of alcohol or other substances. The first part of this relationship is likely due to the increased vulnerability of drunk or high persons when they are in public, the second part to the use of substances as coping mechanisms.

The length, conditions, nature, and severity of homelessness vary from person to person, and these variations also represent risk factors for violence. Some homeless persons have only recently become homeless, while others have been homeless for decades; some experience many episodes of homelessness, while others are homeless rarely. The obvious relationship here is that the more time on the street, the higher the odds of violent victimization.

Some additional risk factors for violence for the homeless include mental illness and a criminal history. Mentally ill homeless persons are more vulnerable than other homeless persons and therefore suffer more violence. Regarding criminal history, about a quarter of homeless people have prior felony convictions. It is likely that those with criminal histories are at higher risk for experiencing violent victimizations, since that is the case in the general population and there is no reason to think it would be different for the homeless population.

Most of the literature seems consistent with what are known as the routine activities theory and lifestyle theory of criminal victimization. According to the perspective taken by these theories, risk for victimization results from the daily routines of individuals. These routines influence exposure to potential offenders, the victim's value or vulnerability as a target, and the presence or absence of capable guardians to afford protection. The key insight of these theories is that social context is central in predicting victimization. It is hard to imagine a social context more conducive to victimization than homelessness. Homeless people often spend their days in run-down areas of cities, areas where potential offenders are numerous and where exposure to the risk of violence is an everyday commonplace. High rates of substance abuse and psychiatric impairment and long stretches of homelessness increase their vulnerability and impair guardianship. Various survival strategies (trading sex, panhandling, drug dealing, etc.) increase their exposure to risk.

Violence Against Homeless Women

While most homeless victims of violence are men, the violence that homeless women experience is tremendous. Researchers have reported that homeless women are over 100 times more likely to be raped, nearly 50% more likely to be robbed, and 15 times more likely to be assaulted than similar housed women. Likewise, according to Jana L. Jasinski, Jennifer K. Wesley, Elizabeth Mustaine, and James D. Wright, homeless women tend to report greater amounts of abuse by spouses and more childhood physical and sexual abuse.

One might assume that these higher rates of violent victimization experienced by homeless women are the result of continuous exposure to risk *due to their homeless situation*. However, the housing circumstances through which episodically homeless women cycle are obviously not stable and may not be particularly functional—indeed, research has found that these households are characterized by high levels of domestic violence, which may explain why homeless women abandon them. This raises the notion that the experience of violence is a factor contributing to the cycle of homelessness among women and not just a result of it.

Strategies for Increasing Tolerance of Homeless Persons

Many homeless persons experience an amount of violence in a single year that most housed people might not expect to experience in their entire lifetimes. This makes calls for increased compassion for homeless persons as well as a resolution and reduction in the amount of homelessness urgent.

One of the most common recommendations for increasing understanding of homeless people is an educational curriculum that begins teaching tolerance in pre-K and continues through high school. These kinds of long-term educational efforts can have a significant impact on society's views of homeless persons. Calls for increased affordable housing, increased employment opportunities, and cooperation between homeless and domestic violence shelters are also high on the list of strategies. Given that many homeless people are episodically homeless, greater access to employment and affordable housing may reduce the number of separate incidents of homelessness homeless people go through, thereby reducing the amount of violence they experience as well.

Elizabeth Ehrhardt Mustaine
and Jana L. Jasinski

See also Mental Illness and Victimization; Sex and Victimization; Substance Use and Victimization

Further Readings

Homes for the Homeless. (1998). *A snapshot of family homelessness across America: Ten cities, 1997–1998.* New York: Institute for Children and Poverty.

Jasinski, J., Wesley, J., Mustaine, E., & Wright, J. (2005). *The experience of violence in the lives of homeless women: A research report.* Washington, DC: National Institute of Justice.

National Coalition for the Homeless. (2008). *Hate, violence, and death on Main Street USA: A report on hate crimes and violence against people experiencing homelessness 2007.* Retrieved from http://www.nationalhomeless.org/getinvolved/projects/hatecrimes/hatecrimes2007.pdf

Wood, D., Valdez, B., Hayashi, T., & Shen, A. (1990). Homeless and housed families in Los Angeles: A study comparing demographic, economic, and family function characteristics. *American Journal of Public Health, 80,* 1049–1052.

Wright, J., Rubin, B., & Devine, J. (1998). *Beside the golden door: Policy, politics and the homeless.* Hawthorne, NY: Aldine de Gruyter.

HOMICIDE, CHILDREN AND YOUTH

Youth homicide in the United States has been the focus of considerable public attention over the past several decades for two reasons: increases in the overall youth homicides, in particular significant increases in the homicides by older youth, and homicide being recognized as a leading cause of death among children and youth all over the country. According to official reports, U.S. youth homicide can be distributed by age. For instance, U.S. youth in the older age group (12 to 17 years old) are more often involved in homicides as offenders than are youth in other age groups, whereas U.S. youth across all age groups are at great risk of homicide by their family, friends, acquaintances, or even strangers. Accordingly, it is worthwhile to see the principles and dynamics of how and why with age youth may become either homicide victims or homicide offenders.

This entry begins by illustrating the general trends in youth homicides in the United States. As understanding age is important in studying youth homicides, youth are broken down by age into three groups: young children, children in middle childhood, and teenagers. Then, the factors contributing to homicides by youth and homicides of youth and theoretical explanations of these homicides are described. Finally, preventive programs and policies to fight against youth homicides are suggested.

Patterns

According to the Uniform Crime Reporting Program of the Federal Bureau of Investigation (FBI), the U.S. youth homicide rate drastically increased in the early 1990s and since then has remained relatively stable. This rate is much higher than that in most other developed countries, and further investigation is needed to explain why and how U.S. youth became involved in homicides.

Youth 12 to 17 years old have the highest rate of homicide offending among all age groups. At the same time, this age group is the most victimized by homicide of all U.S. youth, and the rate of homicide victimization for those in this age group has increased significantly over the last two decades. Those 11 years old or younger have been shown to have the lowest proportion of victimization of the youth population in the United States. Although the rate of homicide victimization for children in this age group has remained unchanged, homicide still is reported to be the number one cause of death for these children.

Thus children 12 to 17 years old appear to be at comparatively increased risk of experiencing both homicide offending and victimization, and children 11 years old or younger seem to be at maximum risk of homicide victimization only. These general trends in U.S. youth homicide suggest that consideration of the age distribution of youth homicides is central to understanding why and how the U.S. children are involved in homicide, and in creating effective programs and policies to prevent and reduce the increased youth homicide.

Categorization of Youth by Age

As mentioned above, categorization of children by age is important for a solid understanding of youth homicide, and thus the youth homicide population has been broken down by age into three subgroups: young children, children in middle childhood, and teenagers. The term *young children* is defined as youth 5 years old and younger, *children in middle childhood* refers to youth who are 6 to 11 years old, and *teenagers* refers to youth 12 to 17 years old.

Each age group tends to have unique physical, social, and emotional characteristics. Children 5 years old or younger generally are under the close care and supervision of parents, relatives, and other family members. These children are physically, socially, and emotionally dependent and are less mobile than are children in other age groups.

Children in middle childhood begin to move toward adolescence—sometimes as early as age 9. Many physical and bodily changes occur during this time. Females tend to begin their sexual maturity before males. Emotionally, the children in this age group feel self-centered, need to feel part of something important, and begin to question authority. Thus, they want less parental control and supervision, while still having guidance.

Socially, these children might initiate intimate relationships with persons outside the family, and may have many friends.

Children 12 to 17 years old go through a variety of developmental changes. Physically, there are many changes as their bodies mature. Socially, these children like to have more time with friends than with parents, tend to search for adult role models, are more likely to have adult leadership roles, and are apt to reject solutions from adults or others in favor of their own decisions. Emotionally, teenagers strive to be autonomous and independent from parents and abandon the view that their parents are all powerful; they tend to have unsettled emotions, accept their own uniqueness but still seek approval from peers, and like to initiate and carry out tasks without supervision.

Factors

In relation to homicide, young children are predominantly victims rather than offenders. In homicides of young children, family members are found to be the most frequent offenders. This is likely because young children depend extensively on their parents and family members for their survival and for protection. Homicide can occur when an adult family member misunderstands a child's behavior and overacts to it with abuse, whether or not the adult intended to abuse the child. Even lack of social support can be a contributing factor, causing a family member to experience stress that can lead to such behavior. Homicides of young children can take many forms, including battering, strangulation, and suffocation.

While children in middle childhood are, like young children, at risk of homicide from family members, they also can become victims of homicide perpetrated by adults outside the family. Because of the decreased familial supervision that occurs at this age, and children's greater interaction with nonfamily members, these children tend to be victimized by adults outside the family. The majority of homicides of children in middle childhood are committed by sexual offenders outside of the family. In addition, a significant number of homicides of children ages 6 to 11 are negligent gun homicides. Homicides of children in middle childhood that occur in the course of a crime, such as a robbery or a carjacking, in which the children were unintended victims; in the course of arson attacks; or in whole-family suicide–homicides also have been reported.

Among all children and youth, teenagers have the highest rates of homicide victimization and homicide offending. Usually, teenager homicides are "male-on-male homicides" committed by individuals outside the family, such as a male victim killed by a male offender, using a firearm, a knife, or other object. In most cases, when youth kill youth, victims and offenders are rival acquaintances such as peers or older males. Individual and societal factors have been considered to explain teenager homicides. For instance, drugs and alcohol abuse, drug trafficking, and the availability of guns have been shown to significantly lead youth into both offending and victimization. Also, if teenagers are exposed to violence in their homes, schools, and neighborhoods, to alcohol and drug use/abuse, and to guns in order to defend themselves from danger, they are more likely to experience homicides.

Theoretical Explanations

Many theories have been offered to explain youth homicides: shaken baby syndrome, dissociative disorders, psychoanalytic interpretation, culture of violence, social disorganization theory, social learning, and strain theory. Shaken baby syndrome and dissociative disorders are attributions often made to explain young children homicides. When a baby is shaken hard or handled roughly, the baby's brain might be seriously damaged, which can result in death. In fact, more than half of children who experience shaken baby syndrome die. This syndrome is considered child abuse when the baby lives, and homicide when the baby dies, and many parents have been convicted of homicide in such instances. Dissociative disorder, an inability to recall important memories, perceive an object, and/or develop a conscious awareness, of adults experiencing mood disorder, depression, and anxiety also has been used to explain youth homicides. For example, a young single mother who is depressed because of financial difficulties may experience a resultant dissociative disorder that might lead to murder. Likewise, a pregnant teenager who is stressed out by the reactions of her parents and others, who is experiencing guilty and shameful feelings, and who fears for her future after delivering a newborn child might suffer from a dissociative disorder that leads to murder.

For children in middle childhood, as for young children, dissociative disorder is offered as an explanation for homicide. Psychoanalytic theory has also been employed to explain the motivation of offenders who commit rape and sexual homicides of children of this age group: They are driven by immediate gratification and uncontrolled inhibition of personal impulses. In addition, some have posited that sex offenders may kill to hide their illegal sexually abusive behaviors.

Most theories explaining teenager homicides—such as subculture of violence theory, social disorganization theory, social learning theory, and strain theory—focus on delinquency and crime among youth. These theories argue that juveniles might be involved in delinquency and crime by being a part of gangs or by using firearms after having been exposed in their daily life to violence as a solution to problems, or when social controls by parents, schools, and communities are lessened due to rapid change in economic status, ethnic heterogeneity, and residential mobility in a city.

Policy Implications

The purpose of programs and policies must be to prevent children and youth from being exposed to life-threatening danger. Thus, a variety of preventive programs and policies should be established to aid all individuals in the family, school, and community who are or might be involved, either directly or indirectly, in youth homicides.

For individuals within the family setting, educative information can be provided about family life, family life planning, and child rearing. These programs should target parents because they play an important role within the family. Throughout educative programs, necessary information should be provided to help parents establish good child-rearing practices with young children and to obtain available knowledgeable information about their children's acquaintances.

For individuals within school settings, the main focus of programs and policies should be on creating safe, gun-free, and drug-free schools. These programs and policies must aid schools in removing deadly weapons from the hands of children, preventing children from using/abusing substances, and removing violent offenders from the school community. School-related programs such as well-supervised, after-school sports, art, music, and science programs, counseling programs, and anger management programs can help students to avoid violent situations and thus prevent homicides in the long run.

For individuals within the community, the main goal of programs and policies should be to create a safe and protective environment. For this to be accomplished, a variety of programs and policies targeting the community can be established, such as community programs that are effective in decreasing the cultural acceptance of violence; programs in medical agencies that are designed to identify, treat, educate, and support abuse victims; improving police and community response; and providing nurse home visitation. In addition, neighborhood safe houses, bus stop adoption programs, school safety routes, and community policing are also worthwhile to consider.

Moonki Hong

See also Child Death Review Team; Family Violence; Missing, Exploited, and Murdered Children; Shaken Baby Syndrome

Further Readings

Ewing, C. P. (1997). *Fatal families: The dynamics of intrafamilial homicide*. Thousand Oaks, CA: Sage.

Finkelhor, D., & Ormrod, R. (2001, October). *Homicides of children and youth*. Washington, DC: U.S. Department of Justice, Office of Juvenile Justice and Delinquency Prevention, Office of Justice Programs.

Goetting, A. (1995). *Homicide in families and other special populations*. New York: Springer.

Heide, K. M. (1999). Youth homicide: An integration of psychological, sociological, and behavioral approaches. In M. D. Smith & M. A. Zahn (Eds.), *Homicide: A sourcebook of social research* (pp. 221–238). Thousand Oaks, CA: Sage.

Holmes, R. M., & Holmes, S. T. (1994). *Murder in America*. Thousand Oaks, CA: Sage.

Lord, W. D., Boudreaux, M. C., Jarvis, J. P., Waldvogel, J., & Weeks, H. (2002). Comparative patterns in life course victimization: Competition, social rivalry, and predatory tactics in child homicide in the United States. *Homicide Studies*, 6(4), 325–347.

McDonald, J. M., & Gover, A. R. (2005). Concentrated disadvantage and youth-on-youth homicide: Assessing the structural covariates over time. *Homicide Studies*, 9(1), 30–54.

Riedel, M., & Welsh, W. (2002). *Criminal violence: Patterns, causes, and prevention*. Los Angeles: Roxbury.

Strom, K. J., & McDonald, J. M. (2007). The influence of social and economic disadvantage on racial patterns in youth homicide over time. *Homicide Studies*, 11(1), 50–69.

HOMICIDE, VICTIM ADVOCACY GROUPS

Homicide victim advocacy groups support the victims' friends and family, as they have been victimized by the homicide of someone close to them. Advocates offer them support during the immediate crisis following discovery of the homicide, as well as over the course of justice processes and the recovery from trauma. Advocacy groups also address the larger community impact of homicide and seek legislative and justice policy reform to improve the rights of crime victims. In this overview of victim advocacy groups, some of the terms associated with homicide victim advocacy are described, followed by a brief history of such advocacy in the United States. Numerous homicide victim advocacy groups and their activities are detailed.

Definitions

Various research studies on the aftermath of homicide suggest that friends and family of homicide victims experience vicarious trauma related to the murder. *Vicarious trauma* refers to the stress reaction experienced by those exposed to the extreme and sudden emotional nature of traumatic events, in which the person experiences enduring cognitive shifts in the manner in which they view self, others, and the world. The term *homicide victim* refers to the person killed, yet the "victims" of homicide include the many others left behind, such as the family and friends of the victim. These individuals typically experience trauma without warning and experience a range of physical, emotional, and financial harms and are left to "survive" the violence. The terms *homicide survivor* and *co-victim* identify the friends and family members most directly suffering from the traumatic event.

Homicide *victim assistance* or *victim advocacy* refers to the range of responses to support homicide co-victims and survivors, including initial death notification, social service referrals, and direct advocacy and implementation of victims' rights related to criminal investigation and court proceedings. Legal advocacy for homicide survivors typically includes supporting survivor participation related to the status of the offender with victim impact statements, notification of justice proceedings, and protesting parole or release from prison or mental health facilities. Homicide co-victims may be left with medical bills and funeral expenses, and advocates assist with securing state victim compensation funds, which reimburse such expenses.

Research reports the dissatisfaction resulting from the lack of advocacy in the experiences of homicide survivors. Thus, homicide victim advocacy often entails political action for changes in justice practices, improved service delivery and assistance for crime victims, and legislative or constitutional reform to expand victims' rights. Homicide victim advocates recently have focused attention on legislation to support investigation into cold cases to address unresolved cases of homicide or missing persons. Victim advocacy groups have worked on legislative efforts related to truth in sentencing, restorative justice (which provides for a more meaningful role for victims and communities), and juvenile justice reform.

Historical Perspective

In the United States, homicide victim advocacy groups emerged in the late 1970s as the victims' rights movement gained momentum. During this period, laws began to change in support of victims' rights at both the state and federal level, grassroots organizations continued to advocate for change in policy and practice, and private self-help organizations emerged in direct response to the real lack of services for victims of violence. One such private advocacy group for homicide survivors is Parents of Murdered Children (POMC), which was founded in 1978. Mothers Against Drunk Driving (MADD), founded in 1980, also became an important advocacy group for homicide victims as the organization successfully redefined the drunk driving "accident" as a crime of violence. In 1981, the abduction and murder of 6-year-old Adam Walsh resulted in widespread public attention to the plight of child victims. American Citizens for Justice, based in Michigan, began in 1983 in response to the probation sentences given to the killers of Chinese American Vincent Chin, who was beaten to death.

Howard and Connie Clery, whose daughter Jeanne was raped and murdered at Lehigh University, formed Security on Campus (SOC) in 1987 to advocate for awareness and policy in support of crime victims on campuses. In 1990, federal legislation established the requirement that higher education institutions report publicly the incidences and prevalence of violent crimes on campuses. Throughout the 1990s, victim advocacy groups effectively lobbied for the implementation of state constitutional provisions typically called the Victims' Bill of Rights. While still advocating for amending the Constitution to include victims' rights, homicide victim advocacy groups contributed to the passage of federal legislation for crime victims with the Crime Victims' Rights Act of 2004, which defines the rights of victims to be heard, notified, and to be treated with dignity and respect for privacy.

Homicide Victim Advocacy

Because homicide victims tend to be young men, co-victims of homicide are often their parents, young wives or girlfriends, children, siblings, and friends. Advocacy groups have furthered understanding of the experiences of each of these types of individuals. A co-victim can be devastated and her or his identity permanently altered, as it is when a mother loses her child or a woman loses her husband. The daily disruption to being a "mother" or "wife" serves as a constant reminder to victims of the violence that killed their loved one. Victim advocacy may involve the legal side of those identity changes, such as custody of the surviving children or property. Advocacy for parents of a murdered child might mean supporting parents who first learn of their son's homosexuality due to his death from a hate crime, or who realize the depth of their daughter's abuse when she is killed by her intimate partner.

Homicide Victim Advocacy Groups

Typical of most homicide victim advocacy groups is the practice of telling the story of the victim's life, both to give voice to the crime victim and those impacted by the crime and to provide a positive memorial that emphasizes the victim's life rather than the violent moment of their death. Most homicide victim advocacy groups have Web sites with local resources, and these Web sites serve as a gathering place of sorts as people share stories and post photos and videos of their loved ones.

One of the earliest homicide victim advocacy groups was Parents of Murdered Children (POMC), founded in 1978 in Cincinnati, Ohio, by Charlotte and Robert Hullinger after the murder of their daughter, Lisa. There are now more than 300 local chapters throughout the United States, each offering emotional support and referrals as well as a network of others who can share experiences and ideas for healing. POMC offers immediate crisis response and advocates during criminal justice proceedings. In addition, POMC trains various professionals to be responsive to the homicide events and the after effects experienced by survivors and co-victims. POMC details guidelines for victim impact statements and other court advocacy; holds a national conference; identifies the different forms of grief experienced by siblings, parents, spouses, and children; and highlights current legislative efforts in need of support. Recent examples of legislative advocacy by POMC include supporting bills calling for continuing tax exemption claims for murdered children and procuring victims time off from work so that they can attend court proceedings. When children are the survivors of homicide, help can be found in an organization such as California's Children of Murdered Parents, which offers support groups for children who have lost their parents to murder.

Some homicide victim advocacy groups are housed in hospitals, such as the Family Advocacy Program at the Washington Hospital Center in Washington, D.C. This program, which is staffed with retired homicide detectives, is a coordinated response to gun violence and offers an important first response to co-victims, often in the very place where the death occurs. This group helps survivors to deal with many immediate issues, such as organ transplant decisions, police investigations, media coverage, and referrals for counseling and spiritual support.

Another group that demonstrates a successful working relationship across agencies is the Grief Assistance Program (GAP) in Philadelphia at the Office of the Medical Examiner. Through a program called Jumpstart, GAP works with various funeral homes to create support groups for family members experiencing trauma as a result of the murder.

Families & Friends of Violent Crime Victims, one of the oldest victim advocacy groups in the United States, was founded in 1975 in Washington. Lola Linstad and Linda Barker created this organization after the abduction and murder of Vonnie Stuth, Linstad's 19-year-old daughter. This typical homicide survivor organization offers legal advocacy, an online memorial of victims, and advice about how to manage holidays and anniversaries that may trigger strong emotional reactions and memories of the loved one.

Homicide Survivors, Inc. is an advocacy group located in Tucson, Arizona. It was founded by Gail Leland, whose 14-year-old son, Richard, was murdered in 1981. Leland recognized the need for support for parents of murdered children. Because crime victim rights advocacy and assistance were not allowed under the POMC charter, members created the separate Homicide Survivors, Inc. to provide services and lobby for legislative reform. This group's efforts contributed to important legal changes in Arizona, including a "guilty except insane" law and the victims' right not to receive inmate mail law.

Memorial projects, such as the Texans for Equal Justice Victim Memorial Wall in Conroe, are public displays that honor the life of homicide victims. The Mothers of Murdered Sons/Daughters (M.O.M.S.) Web site includes a "memory board" with pictures and biographies of murdered children, and a message board for mothers to support each other and share victim impact statements.

Advocacy for Victims of Mass Homicide

Victim advocacy groups highlight the need for quality crisis response, in the form of coordinated community teams, to the victims and co-victims of mass homicides and disasters, including terrorist attacks, workplace violence, school and campus shootings, and international violence such as war crimes. The 2007 Virginia Tech shootings caused countless co-victims and renewed national attention to coordinate community response to such events. Advocacy groups have led efforts for new protocols and policies on college campuses to address issues such as weapons on campus, intervention and mental health, privacy rights, and public safety. Some examples of changes made on campuses include new text alert systems, enhanced mental health screening and support groups, and the creation of coordinated crisis response teams and trainings of campus and community law enforcement personnel, medical and mental health professionals, campus student affairs officers, and victim advocates.

Homicide Victim Advocacy Groups for Alternative Justice Responses

Some homicide victim advocacy groups challenge the conventional policy response to violence in our society by desiring alternative sentencing. Murder Victims' Families for Reconciliation was founded in 1976 to represent murder victims' families who oppose the death penalty. Its members detail examples of how they face additional barriers because of their advocacy for alternative sentencing. In one example, two family members who oppose the death penalty were barred from speaking at a pardon hearing in Nebraska, while the victim's sister who supports the death penalty was allowed to speak (crime victims' right to speak is guaranteed in the state constitution). Murder Victims' Families for Human Rights is an organization with an international human rights focus against the death penalty, comprised of family members of murder victims and those killed in state killings, terrorist killings, and "disappearances." These two organizations often discuss the discrimination they face due to their politically unpopular view of capital punishment and direct challenge to the state. The National Organization of Victims of "Juvenile Lifers" advocates for the rights of co-victims in cases of murderers under age 18 and to oppose legislative efforts to end the juvenile life without parole sentence.

Lynn Jones

See also Death Notification; Homicide, Children and Youth; Homicide and Murder; Secondary Victims of Homicide; Victim Assistance Programs, United States; Victim Support Groups

Further Readings

Acker, J. R., & Karp, D. R. (Eds.). (2006). *Wounds that do not bind: Victim-based perspectives on the death penalty*. Durham, NC: Carolina Academic Press.

Bucholz, J. (2002). *Homicide survivors: Misunderstood grievers*. Amityville, NY: Baywood.

Hickey, E. (1990). Responding to missing and murdered children in America. In A. R. Roberts (Ed.), *Helping crime victims: Research, practice, and policy* (pp. 158–185). Newbury Park, CA: Sage.

Horne, C. (2003). Families of homicide victims: Service utilization patterns of extra- and intrafamilial homicide survivors. *Journal of Family Violence, 18*(2), 75–82.

Kilpatrick, D. G., Amick, A., & Resnick, H. S. (1990). *The impact of homicide on surviving family members*. Charleston: Crime Victims Research and Treatment Center, Medical University of South Carolina.

Rock, P. (1998). *After homicide: Practical and political responses to bereavement*. Oxford, UK: Clarendon.

Spungen, D. (1998). *Homicide—the hidden victims: A guide for professionals*. Thousand Oaks, CA: Sage.

Vollum, S. (2008). *Last words and the death penalty: Voices of the condemned and their co-victims*. New York: LFB Scholarly.

HOMICIDE, VICTIM-PRECIPITATED

According to the common law, murder is the intentional taking of another human life with premeditation or with extreme malice (i.e., in "cold blood"). This is the basis for the scenarios—either real or imagined—that come to mind when people are asked to describe the crime of murder. However, both criminologists and homicide investigators know that this type of murder is only one type of criminal homicide, and is one of the least common at that. In his seminal study of criminal homicide, criminologist Marvin Wolfgang pored over hundreds of Philadelphia homicide cases circa 1950 with the purpose of describing the extent, nature, and correlates of lethal violence. Wolfgang's research was—and remains—influential to how violence and victimization are perceived. Contrary to taking a one-sided view of a predatory offender and an innocent victim, Wolfgang argued that we can neither understand nor ultimately prevent homicide without understanding the relationship between the victim and the offender. Wolfgang was instrumental in bringing the inquiry into "heated" personal interaction to the forefront of theorizing about homicide and leaving in the background the inquiry into much less common "cold-blooded" killings. He found that although in some cases a homicide involved a predatory offender and a victim who, if not "innocent," was powerless, in other cases it would not have been clear at the time who would ultimately be the offender and who the victim. In some incidents the individual parties were involved in an altercation that was in fact initiated by the victim, but ended up with his or her demise at the hands of the person initially attacked. The victim therefore played a direct role in his or her own death. Wolfgang coined the term *victim precipitated* for these types of homicides, and it is a term that remains analyzed and debated today. This entry outlines how victim-precipitated homicide has been defined and classified (along with classification problems), research findings on victim-precipitated homicide, and the special case of "suicide by cop."

Definition and Examples

Victim-precipitated homicides refer to criminal homicides—both murders and manslaughters—involving at least one victim and one offender, but are limited to cases of interpersonal violence. Mass and serial murders would therefore be omitted from this category, as would noncriminal homicides (e.g., homicides that are justifiable, as in cases of self-defense). Some have argued that a homicide is merely an assault (i.e., fight, brawl, attack) in which a death occurs. A victim-precipitated homicide is therefore a case where an assault was initiated by the eventual victim. According to Wolfgang's definition, harsh words or insults hurled by the victim are not enough; in order for the homicide to be classified as victim precipitated, the victim must have physically attacked the offender and therefore initiated the conflict that resulted in his or her death. Based on his classification, Wolfgang defined 150, or 26%, of the 588 homicides he analyzed as victim precipitated. Some of the many examples from the Philadelphia case files provided by Wolfgang include (1) an argument over money in which the victim shot first, and was then fatally wounded when the other

party returned fire; (2) someone started a fight, landing several blows on his victim, but then became the victim when the initial victim landed the fatal blow; and (3) a husband argued with and then began beating his wife, but his wife reached for a knife in the kitchen and fatally stabbed her husband. Since Wolfgang's initial study the essential definition of victim-precipitated homicide has not changed. However, some analysts have argued for a less rigid definition that includes nonphysical precipitates (e.g., insults, dirty looks), and others have argued that such modifications make case classification more difficult.

Classification and Critique

As noted above, based on his own definition of the concept, Wolfgang classified 26% of homicides as victim precipitated. Subsequent studies employing this definition have found prevalence rates between 13% and 38%. Although the concept is relatively straightforward, some of the variation in the prevalence of victim-precipitated homicides no doubt belies the difficulty in measuring the concept (i.e., classification based on actual homicide data). Accurate classification relies on an accurate account of how the homicide transpired. Accurate accounting may be difficult for a number of reasons. First, the analyst seeking to classify homicides in this manner must assume that the narratives associated with homicide cases, which are usually provided by police investigators and rely on confessional and eyewitness accounts (if available), are accurate and reliable. Reliability, or the consistency with which a concept is measured, may be particularly problematic, as it is well known that not all homicide investigations are as rigorous as popular accounts often portray them to be. As such, there may be scant information on the circumstances involved in a homicide, and not enough to determine with confidence whether or not it involved victim precipitation. While it may be known that, for example, a homicide resulted from a fight outside a tavern, the circumstances leading up to the fight may be unknown. Thus, an analyst seeking to determine whether or not the victim was the one who threw the first punch would be stymied by cases such as these. Classification in homicide incidents involving firearms may prove even more difficult, given (1) the brutal efficiency of this weapon in comparison to others and (2) the strong tendency for individuals to leave the scene at the sound of gunfire. Deaths from shootings were not the norm in Wolfgang's data, but firearms are the most common implement in cases of lethal violence today. Second, since by definition the victim-precipitated homicide—or any homicide, for that matter—rules out gathering an accounting of the incident from the victim him- or herself, the accounts that are recorded may be subject to what Australian criminologist Kenneth Polk colorfully described as the "Rashomon effect." The "Rashomon effect" refers to the Japanese film *Rashomon*, in which the central event in the film—a rape–murder—is recounted by several different parties, and as the film proceeds it becomes clear that each account is biased in favor of the person doing the recounting. The determination of whether or not a homicide was victim precipitated may rely solely on the account given by the offender, who implicates the victim in the interest of self-preservation. If narratives about an incident differ and are biased either in favor of or against the offender, whether or not the victim "started" the altercation that led to his or her demise may or may not be sorted out in the case description. Third, although Wolfgang ruled out verbal or gestural actions as sufficient precipitates, some homicide researchers have argued that this excludes too many cases in which the offending action—despite being nonphysical—could be deemed to be just as offensive and provocative as a first blow.

Research

Beyond the initial classification of victim-precipitated homicides, Wolfgang sought in his study to identify correlates, or factors that might differentiate such homicides from those where the precipitation was not an issue. As a social scientist, Wolfgang's purpose was to test statistical hypotheses that might allow for improved understanding and theorizing about the circumstances surrounding the perpetration of criminal homicides. However, he also stressed the possible practical implications of his research for investigators in the business of solving homicides. Given the access he obtained to the Philadelphia homicide files, Wolfgang had at his disposal a wealth of information about the individuals involved in these crimes,

including their age, race/ethnicity, and gender, along with information on the circumstances of the homicide, including the method by which the offender dispatched the victim, the motive for the homicide, the nature of the relationship between the victim and offender, the victim's previous arrest record, and the use of alcohol or drugs by either offender or victim at the time the homicide occurred.

In a comparison of victim-precipitated with non-victim-precipitated homicides, Wolfgang found that significantly more victim-precipitated cases involved victims who were African Americans. Men were more likely to be the victims in victim-precipitated homicides (94% of the victims in victim-precipitated cases vs. 72% of the victims in remaining cases), and women were twice as likely to be offenders in victim-precipitated cases. Wolfgang also found that more victim-precipitated homicides took place at home, and involved domestic violence between intimate partners (e.g., spouses). He found no differences in the two types of cases with regard to age of the victim. Stabbings appeared more frequently in victim-precipitated homicides (probably partially due to the higher proportion of female offenders), but motive did not vary significantly by type of homicide. Finally, Wolfgang found that victims in victim-precipitated cases were more likely to have used alcohol at the time of the homicide, and were more likely to have a prior arrest record, than victims in other types of homicide cases. These results led Wolfgang to conclude that the victim, rather than being a helpless or weak individual, in these cases may have been as much a threat as the offender. The victim could have easily ended up the killer in many of these cases.

Since Wolfgang's initial analysis several studies, using data from other cities, have for the most part replicated the findings regarding correlates of victim-precipitated homicides.

Suicide by Cop

An interesting line of research on victim-precipitated homicides has involved a phenomenon known as "suicide by cop." Essentially, this is a special case of victim precipitation in which the victim has suicidal intent, and brings about his or her own demise, albeit at the hands of another. Although Wolfgang noted that some victims in victim-precipitated homicides are set on dying in the event, the "offender" in this case is a police officer, and one whose actions may be deemed justified and reasonable. This is so because the victim presents him- or herself as a deadly threat, usually by brandishing or perhaps even shooting a firearm at or in the vicinity of a police officer. Therefore, unlike the majority of cases analyzed by Wolfgang, suicide by cop is a type of victim-precipitated homicide that is not a criminal homicide. Since the landmark case of *Tennessee v. Garner* decided by the U.S. Supreme Court in 1985, the prevailing legal rule across the United States is that a police officer is justified in using deadly force against a person if the officer *perceives* that person to pose an immediate, deadly threat to the officer or others nearby. A case where an individual is shot because he or she pointed a fake gun at a police officer, but the officer perceived the gun to be real and therefore a deadly threat, is considered a justifiable homicide. It is a victim-precipitated homicide because the victim initiated the homicide by pointing the fake gun at the police officer, and would be considered suicide by cop if the victim was seeking to end his or her own life through this action. Why suicide by cop? Researchers have argued that many individuals with suicidal intent do not have the fortitude to take their own lives, and thus pursue another avenue (sometimes by calling the police to their homes) to have the police do it for them. Finally, some suicides by cop are the outcome of a horrific ordeal, such as the taking of hostages and/or the murder of one or more individuals by the eventual victim (so-called suicide-homicides).

Michael O. Maume

See also Homicide and Murder; Offending and
  Victimization; Public Perceptions of Victims; Rape,
  Victim Precipitated; Victim Precipitation

Further Readings

Block, C. R., & Block, R. (1991). Beginning with Wolfgang: An agenda for homicide research. *Journal of Crime and Justice, 14,* 31–70.

Felson, R. B., & Messner, S. F. (1998). Disentangling the effects of gender and intimacy on victim precipitation in homicide. *Criminology, 36,* 405–424.

Green, E., & Wakefield, R. P. (1979). Patterns of middle and upper class homicide. *Journal of Criminal Law and Criminology, 70,* 172–181.

Klinger, D. A. (2001). Suicidal intent in victim-precipitated homicide: Insights from the study of "suicide by cop." *Homicide Studies, 5,* 206–226.

Polk, K. (1997). A reexamination of the concept of victim-precipitated homicide. *Homicide Studies, 1,* 141–168.

Wolfgang, M. E. (1958). *Patterns in criminal homicide.* Montclair, NJ: Patterson Smith.

HOMICIDE AND MURDER

Homicide and murder are the most egregious and feared violent crimes. This entry begins by defining the various types of homicide and murder. The prevalence, victim and offender characteristics, and risk factors are also explored. Murders with multiple victims, such as serial, mass, and spree murder are discussed, as well as some of the various criminological explanations for these crimes. The entry includes a section on indirect victims that examines the impact of homicide and murder on the family, friends, and community of the victims. It concludes with discussions of potential homicide and murder prevention strategies, as well as various punishment options.

Definition

Homicide includes a group of actions that result in the death of a human being. Not all acts of homicide are criminal. For example, some forms of noncriminal homicide include acting in the line of duty (as does a police officer), a citizen acting in self-defense, and the state executing an offender who has been found guilty of capital murder.

Murder is the unlawful killing of another person, marked by no legal justification. Murder is further divided into first and second degree murder. First degree murder involves intention and is marked by malice aforethought, which includes the intent to kill or inflict serious bodily harm, as well as a reckless indifference to human life. Second degree murder is separate from first degree murder in that it does not involve any premeditation. Murder also includes the felony-murder doctrine, which transfers the intent of an individual committing a felony (such as robbery or kidnapping) to the murder. The two elements that are generally present to classify a homicide to a murder are the actus reus (guilty act) and the mens rea (guilty mind).

Killings that are not justifiable but which are accidental are generally classified as manslaughter. Some states have statutes that further classify manslaughter as either vehicular or nonvehicular manslaughter, depending on whether or not an automobile is involved. Manslaughter is viewed as a much less severe form of homicide that may or may not involve a criminal sanction.

Prevalence

Homicide rates vary greatly by geographic location. The United States ranks among the nations with the highest rates in the world for all types of homicide. As with all crimes, cross-national comparisons are often difficult, as different countries use different data-gathering and reporting sources. Despite the difficulty in these comparisons, homicide is the crime most commonly used to compare violent crime rates across countries.

The primary source of homicide data in the United States is the report of the Uniform Crime Reporting Program. This report includes data as collected by local law enforcement agencies and compiled by the Federal Bureau of Investigation. Criminal homicides are categorized and counted as (1) murder, (2) nonnegligent manslaughter, or (3) manslaughter by negligence.

Although the United States has higher murder rates than most other countries, murder is still a relatively infrequent occurrence in the nation, representing only a fraction (about .02%) of all violent crimes committed. The 1960s and 1970s experienced a sharp increase in the homicide rate. The rate increased in 1980, and then from the 1980s and early 1990s showed a series of peaks and valleys. However, from 1992 until 2000, the rate began to decrease dramatically, and then it began to level off after 2000.

Violent crime in general has been declining over the past several years. There have been several potential reasons posited for the decline in the homicide rate in particular. In 1998, Alfred Blumstein and Richard Rosenfeld noted that improved economic conditions had led to an increase in the number of legitimate employment opportunities, decreasing the likelihood that people would engage in the criminal activities that might lead to homicide. In conjunction with this, drug markets began to stabilize, leading to less involvement in the illegal substance market. It may also be that the decline is due to the decrease in the age group most likely to perpetrate a homicide, those between the ages of 15 and 24. Increases in gun control, such as with the passage of the Brady bill, have also been credited for the decline in the homicide rate. Finally, an increase in the incarcerated population may have led to some of the decline. From the 1980s into the new millennium, a "get tough" on crime approach, realized through mandatory minimum sentences, three-strikes laws, and truth-in-sentencing laws, has placed more individuals behind bars for longer periods of time, resulting in fewer potential offenders on the streets.

Victim and Offender Characteristics

To understand the dynamics of homicide, it is important to understand the relationship between the victim and the offender. In slightly more than one third of incidents, the relationship between the victim and the offender is undetermined; however, approximately one third of homicides occur among acquaintances, and about 15% involve family members. Slightly less than 14% of homicides occur among strangers.

The age distribution of victims and offenders is also worth noting. Those age 18 to 24 are the most likely to be a perpetrator or a victim. Those who are the least likely to be involved in a homicide as either a victim or an offender are those age 14 and younger.

Gender and race differences have also peaked interest with respect to homicide. Males are disproportionately represented as both victims and offenders. They are four times more likely than females to be a victim, and ten times more likely to perpetrate a homicide. Females are more often the victim of homicide than the offender, and are likely to be victimized by an intimate partner. The methods used also vary according to gender, with males being more likely to use a firearm, and females being more likely to use either poison or arson against their victims.

Homicide ranks as a leading cause of death among Blacks, who are six times more likely to be victimized than are Whites. In terms of offending, Blacks are seven times more likely to perpetrate a homicide than are Whites. Homicide also tends to be an intraracial crime, with White offenders generally killing White victims, and Black offenders generally killing Black victims.

Risk Factors

In addition to the issues described above, other factors may be considered to determine whether an individual will be involved in a homicide, either as a victim or as an offender: drugs and alcohol, geographic location, availability of weapons, and socioeconomic status. Thus drugs and alcohol may play a vital role in whether a homicide will occur; however, the link between substances and the causal order between the substance and the offense are difficult to determine. Nevertheless, it has been found that many violent offenders do use illegal drugs and/or alcohol, and that many offenses are precipitated by the existence of either illegal substances or alcohol consumption.

Homicide rates and risk also vary according to region within the United States. The South and the West have substantially higher homicide rates then the Midwest and the Northeast. Many explanations have been posited for this. The correlation between warm weather and homicide is one explanation, as portions of both the Western and Southern regions enjoy year round warmer climates, leading to more interpersonal interaction and potentially creating more opportunities for homicide. With respect to the South, there may be a subcultural issue where violence is an acceptable means of dispute resolution. The history of strained race relations and the availability of firearms may contribute to some of the high homicide rates in the Southern states.

In the United States, handguns are involved in approximately half of all homicides committed, and some type of firearm is used in approximately 65% of homicides. Other weapons used in homicides include knives, blunt objects, and poison.

Social class also may have an impact on homicide rates. People who live in the households with the lowest incomes typically experience the highest rates of violent crime. This may be due to the effects of living in lower socioeconomic status neighborhoods. Thus individuals who reside in areas where there is high crime, high unemployment, lower education levels, and lower income brackets are more likely to experience violent victimization in part because of their proximity to or involvement in illegal drug and gun markets and gang activities.

Murder With Multiple Victims

Serial Murders

Although many people fear being the victim of a serial killer, serial murders are rare events, representing less than 1% of all homicides. The term *serial murderer* was coined in the 1980s, though murderers whose crimes conform to the definition of a serial killing have always existed. The generally accepted definition of a serial murderer is someone who has committed a murder on at least three separate occasions.

Because serial murders are an extremely rare event, they are difficult to study. Most researchers who study serial murderers state that they are generally ordinary in appearance, blending easily into society, maintaining stable relationships, and holding regular employment. Although most serial killers are White males, there have been several cases in which the killer was female or Black.

Mass and Spree Murders

Mass murder is generally defined as the murder of four or more victims in one place as part of the same incident. This type of murder most frequently occurs in the home, in the workplace, or at schools, likely because these are the locations where people spend the most time and because these locations often have several people congregated in one area. Many mass murders are preceded by the expression of some sort of prior grievance, threat, or warning. After commission of the crime, mass murderers often commit suicide.

It should be understood that mass and serial murder are distinctly different from spree murder. A spree murder is defined as a murder that occurs at two or more separate locations, with no "cooling off" period between the murders. The concept of a "cooling off" period proves to be a difficult one, as the term is defined differently by various people; however, it is an important concept to consider, as it may be used in determining the amount of premeditation involved in the murders, which ultimately affects the punishments that are meted out.

Explanations

Various criminological theories may be used to explain murder and homicide, depending on the circumstances of the crime. Because many murders are situational and involve little to no planning or premeditation, symbolic interaction theories (such as those which state that individuals become criminal once society has labeled them as criminals) may explain many of these incidents. It is particularly noteworthy that many murders begin as some type of confrontation or assault, often in the typical course of daily interactions.

Almost any type of conflict may result in an assault and eventual homicide. In some situations, individuals may feel compelled to retaliate against an insult, accidental physical encounter, or intentional confrontation. In this way, homicides and murders are often situational, with neither the victim nor the offender intending to kill the other. Rather, a situation may escalate as a result of each party's attempting to "save face."

Subcultural theory may also provide some explanations for murder. According to this theory, individuals form their values, norms, beliefs, and expectations based on their surroundings. Ultimately, those who reside in crime-ridden neighborhoods are likely to believe that violence is an acceptable means of problem solving and conflict resolution. This theory is also useful in explaining homicides that are ignited by conflict.

Other criminological explanations are tied to psychological or biological theories. Some of these theories posit that those who commit murder are fundamentally different from those who do not. For example, it has been hypothesized that males may be more likely to commit homicide than females because they have more testosterone than females. Other theories suggest that males who are predisposed to violent behavior may have an extra Y chromosome; rather than having one X and one Y chromosome, these males would have one X and two Y chromosomes. Still others claim that some individuals who commit murder suffer from some type of psychological dysfunction, leading them to not be able to recognize that their actions are wrong, or to not care about the consequences of their violent behavior.

Many theories can be used to explain homicide. Some of these theories focus on the individual offender, while others are more concerned with the environment of the particular offender at the time of the offense. It is important to remember that because a variety of factors are used to explain homicide, multiple theories may be valid explanations, depending on the individual criminal act.

Indirect Victims

The deceased individual is obviously the direct victim of a homicide or murder; however, there are other individuals who are impacted by the offense, such as the family or friends of the offender. Because their loved ones may have died unexpectedly or in a particularly tragic manner, the victims' family and friends often suffer from trauma, stress, anger, and anxiety at the loss of a loved one. Survivors of victims have been called co-victims. Not only do co-victims have to deal with the crime, but they must also contend with legal issues and the criminal justice system after the death of their loved ones.

The death notification process can be especially problematic for co-victims. This notification often comes directly to the surviving family members from homicide detectives or police officers. The U.S. Department of Justice and the Office for Victims of Crime specifically outline the procedures that are to be taken by law enforcement personnel when notifying the family of the victims.

Many states allow certain rights to the surviving family members of a homicide victim, in part as a result of the efforts of victims' rights organizations. These rights are called the Victims' Bill of Rights and often include stipulations such as return of the victim's personal property, the right to attend all court proceedings, potential compensation, and input during the various stages of the trial.

The community also often suffers as a result of a homicide or murder. This can be especially true if there are multiple victims, such as with a serial, mass, or spree murder. Because these incidents are often high profile, the communities in which they occur may be devastated, leaving residents feeling helpless, fearful, and/or angry as a result of the crimes occurring in their community.

Prevention

Because there are numerous factors that can contribute to the commission of a murder, attempting to intervene or prevent murders can be difficult. If the recent decline in the murder rate can be attributed to increases in the prison population, incarcerating violent offenders may provide a potential solution. However, research suggests that most offenders who commit a murder are highly unlikely to recidivate.

In order to address issues with intimate partner homicides, social policies have been passed to address the specific issues surrounding intimate partner violence. An increase in attention to this topic has lead to an increase in the number of shelters and services for battered individuals. Also, though the efficacy of mandatory arrest laws in preventing escalating abuse is controversial, these laws require that law enforcement remove one party from the scene of a domestic violence call.

Other prevention methods may involve increased security or surveillance in areas where violent crime is likely to occur. Increased police patrols and security cameras may be used to prevent violent crime in general from occurring, which may also prevent a crime from escalating into a murder.

These are only a few of the potential prevention strategies. Because murders are committed for a range of reasons and under a variety of circumstances, prevention methods vary according to the motivations of the offender, the relationship between the victim and the offender, and the circumstances surrounding the crime.

Punishment

Punishments for homicides and murders vary depending on several factors. The higher the level of the offense classification, the more likely the offender will receive a harsh sentence. For example, manslaughter is generally punished less severely than second degree murder, and first degree murder more severely than second degree murder. Sentences also vary according to state and federal legislation, with each state within the United States setting its own sanction ranges for specific forms of homicide.

One controversial form of punishment allocated for murder is capital punishment. States using this as a form of punishment reserve this sanction for the forms of murder that are deemed the most severe, termed *capital murder*. Currently, 38 states and the federal government have statutes that allow for the death penalty to be carried out against those found guilty of capital murder, but many of these states do not commonly hand down death sentences. Some common specific statutes for a murder to qualify for capital punishment may include the murder of more than one individual, a young child, during the commission of a felony, or against a police officer acting in the line of duty.

Most forms of murder and homicide rely on prison sentences as the primary sanction. These sentences vary according to the state and the severity of the individual offense. States generally reserve life in prison sentences for the murders that they deem the most severe. Some states retain the life in prison without the possibility of parole; however, life sentences can also equate to approximately 20 years behind bars, with parole possibilities introduced after the offender has served a specified amount of time.

Kristine Levan Miller

See also Guns and Victimization; Homicide, Victim-Precipitated; Serial Murder; Uniform Crime Reporting (UCR) Program; Violence, Theories of

Further Readings

Alvarez, A., & Bachman, R. (2002). *Murder American style*. Belmont, CA: Wadsworth.

Blumstein, A., & Rosenfeld, R. (1998). Explaining recent trends in U.S. homicide rates. *Journal of Criminal Law and Criminology, 88,* 1175–1216.

Fox, J. A., Levin, J., & Quinet, K. (2008). *The will to kill: Making sense of senseless murder* (pp. 7–81). Boston: Pearson.

Hickey, E. W. (2005). *Serial murderers and their victims.* Belmont, CA: Wadsworth.

Luckenbill, D. F. (1977). Criminal homicide as a situated transaction. *Social Problems, 25,* 176–186.

Spungen, D. (1997) *Homicide—the hidden victims: A resource for professionals.* Thousand Oaks, CA: Sage.

Wolfgang, M. E., & Ferracuti, F. (1967). *The subculture of violence: Towards an integrated theory in criminology.* London: Tavistock.

HOT SPOTS

Hot spots of crime are defined in various terms, but are usually understood to be areas containing substantially higher than average levels of crime. The observation that crime is concentrated in particular places is not a new one; it is arguably the oldest in criminology, dating to Adolphe Quetelet and Andre-Michel Guerry in the early 19th century. The significance of hot spots of crime lies in the hope that because a disproportionate amount of crime is located in relatively small areas, effective management of public places can lead to lower levels of crime.

Conventional Explanations

There are two primary theoretical explanations for why crime hot spots form and exist. The first of these can be characterized as *demographic* by virtue of a focus on the underlying social and economic conditions of an area. The most well known of these approaches is social disorganization theory, which predicts that areas with low socioeconomic status (high levels of unemployment, housing density, ethnicity, single-parent households, public housing, household turnover, and low educational attainment) will be associated with high levels of crime. The residents of these types of areas are said to be ill equipped to provide effective social control over potential criminals.

The main criticism of demographic explanations of hot spots is that they are, at best, meso-level explanations and do not provide sufficient explanatory granularity to predict hot spots. There is burgeoning empirical evidence that crime events are highly spatially concentrated; thus even in high crime areas, most locations are crime free. For instance, one of the first hot spot studies showed that 50% of police calls for service originated from a mere 3% of locations (and this distribution has been found in many cities worldwide). As almost all demographic explanatory factors are measured at the neighborhood or community level, it is difficult to see how they are able to account for patterns at the micro level. They cannot explain, for example, why 80% of a suburb's crime might occur at one intersection and the adjoining street segments.

The second major theory of crime hot spots can be found in environmental criminology and is heavily reliant on explanations involving routine activities of both offenders and victims and the factors that facilitate these individuals intersecting in space and time. The specific theories that help explain crime hot spots at a micro level are *routine activity theory* (also called *routine activities theory*) and *crime pattern theory*. Routine activity theory posits that a criminal incident is only possible when a motivated offender comes into contact with a suitable victim in the absence of a capable guardian. Much of the recent development and refinement of this theory has been on how effective *place managers* regulate places that would otherwise be settings for crime events. For instance, while some studies find that the presence of bars greatly increases the chance of crime occurring, there are a number of other studies that show that only a fraction of licensed venues account for the disproportionate volume of police calls for service. At its most abstract, routine activity theory suggests that much of opportunity structures for crime are determined by the routine activities of society and that the majority of offenders' time is spent conducting routine activities such as work or travel.

Crime pattern theory attempts to explain the spatial and temporal configuration of crime events. This is achieved by positing that individuals spend the vast majority of their time at one of several *nodes* (places of particular activities are carried out such of work, study, entertainment, home) or traveling on specific *paths* between them. Combining an individual's nodes and paths produces an *awareness space*. It follows then that the spatial configuration of crime events by a single perpetrator will be strongly determined by the extent of that individual's awareness space. Given that certain nodes feature in many people's awareness space (shopping precincts or public transport interchanges), crime hot spots are the result of overlapping awareness spaces.

Theoretical Model of Hot Spot Generation

The clearest and most complete theoretical description of hot spots has been provided by Patricia and Paul Brantingham in their model of crime hot spot generation. They argued that the generating process relies on three distinct elements, each of which is evidenced by associated theories. First, *criminal residence concentration*, the distribution of likely individuals to commit crime, forms the baseline potential for hot spots. As noted in the social disorganization literature, the types of environments that are associated with high levels of delinquency are those that are characterized by indicators synonymous with deprivation. There are two established literatures that explain why criminal residences may cluster. Ecological theories, the best known being Ernest Burgess's concentric zonal model, predict clusters of criminal residences developing in transitional areas at the periphery of economic centers within a city, be they central or outlying. The rival explanation comes from theories about the relationship between public housing policies and crime and provides more powerful explanations in cities where governments are active in the housing market. The work of Sir Anthony Bottoms has been influential in this area, showing that housing allocation determines, in a nontrivial manner, the distribution of criminal residences.

The second element Brantingham and Brantingham identified is *target concentration*, reflecting the observation that many types of targets are concentrated in space and time. Thus a car thief will seek out car parks attached to public transport services in commuter belt suburbs to locate a wide variety of vehicles easy to steal. Pickpockets, however, seek out places where close personal contact is unavoidable (crowded public transport or nightclubs). These locations are advantageous for those crime opportunities because they provide many targets in a finite location and time with minimal protection from their owners. Predictions of target concentration are provided by routine activities theory and land use theories. The latter describes how the distribution of land uses within a city determines the distribution of crime opportunities, with the greatest number of opportunities concentrated in certain locations and few opportunities in other, larger areas. An elegant example of this was given by George Rengert in his analysis of car theft opportunities in Philadelphia. He showed that distinct hot spots emerge at different times of the day, and he was able to link these to different routine activities and land uses.

The final element identified as critical to hot spot generation is *movement patterns*. This simply reflects the fact that offenders need to locate and travel to crime opportunities if they wish to exploit them. In their theoretical model, Brantingham and Brantingham specify that movement patterns are strongly determined by two interdependent but separate factors: the permeability of the road network and the modes, rhythms, and volume of transport. For example, open air drug markets require that buyers have fast access and egress routes into and out of the market, whereas this is not the case for closed drug markets. On the crime-generating influence of road networks, Daniel Beavon and Brantingham and Brantingham provide compelling evidence that street accessibility and crime are positively associated (cul de sacs host the least crime), as is the relationship between traffic volume and crime (busy roads have more crime). The Brantingham and Brantingham model provides a powerful explanation of the process of hot spot generation by subsuming the demographic explanation within it.

Types

In separate work, Brantingham and Brantingham distinguish two types of hot spots: *crime generators* and *crime attractors*. Crime generators are those places where large numbers of people gravitate to for legitimate purposes (shopping, entertainment, work, etc.). Among these will be potential offenders, who may be traveling without a purposive intent to commit a crime, but nevertheless decide to do so when confronted by the abundance of opportunities. For instance, an offender parking in a large multistory car park may notice a nearby parked car with a purse on the back seat. While there may have been no prior intention of stealing, when confronted with an opportunity, accompanied by suitable accompanying circumstances, the offender may decide to exploit it. It follows that the larger the car park, the more likely the offender will be to come across an opportunity to steal, all things being equal.

Crime attractors are locations that motivated offenders travel to with the intent to commit a certain form of crime, and they choose these locations because of the reputation of the area and the opportunities associated with it. Examples of crime attractors are large transport nodes, night time entertainment areas, large shopping malls, and major tourist locations. It is possible that a single location could be a crime generator and attractor simultaneously.

Thus, what makes hot spots different from other places is the abundance of opportunities they present for committing crime. Hot spots differ among themselves with respect to the reason potential offenders are drawn to each location; offenders travel to crime attractors *because of* the opportunity to commit crime, but travel to crime generators *irrespective of* the supply of opportunities.

Michael Townsley

See also Crime Mapping; Crime Pattern Theory; Prospective Crime Mapping; Repeat Victimization; Routine Activities Theory

Further Readings

Beavon, D. J. K., Brantingham, P. L., & Brantingham, P. J. (1994). The influence of street networks on the patterning of property offenses. In R. V. G. Clarke (Ed.), *Crime Prevention Studies* (Vol. 2). Monsey, NY: Criminal Justice Press.

Brantingham, P. J., & Brantingham, P. L. (2008). Crime pattern theory. In R. Wortley & L. Mazerolle (Eds.), *Environmental criminology and crime analysis* (pp. 78–93). Cullompton, UK: Willan.

Brantingham, P. L., & Brantingham, P. J. (1995). Criminality of place: Crime generators and crime attractors. *European Journal of Criminal Policy and Research*, 3(3), 5–26.

Brantingham, P. L., & Brantingham, P. J. (1999). A theoretical model of crime hot spot generation. *Studies on Crime and Crime Prevention*, 8, 7–26.

Eck, J. E., Clarke, R. V., & Guerette, R. T. (2007). Risky facilities: crime concentration in homogeneous sets of establishments and facilities. In G. Farrell, K. J. Bowers, S. D. Johnson, & M. Townsley (Eds.), *Imagination for crime prevention: Essays in honour of Ken Pease*. Monsey, NY: Criminal Justice Press.

Rengert, G. F. (1997). Auto theft in Central Philadelphia. In R. Homel (Ed.), *Policing for prevention: Reducing crime, public intoxication and injury* (pp. 199–220). Monsey, NY: Criminal Justice Press.

Roncek, D. W., & Maier, P. A. (1991). Bars, blocks, and crimes revisited: Linking the theory of routine activities to the empiricism of hot spots. *Criminology*, 29(4), 725–753.

Sherman, L. W., Gartin, P., & Buerger, M. (1989). Hot spots of predatory crime. *Criminology*, 27(1), 27–56.

Hot Spots of Fear

Hot spots are specific places where a large proportion of crimes are committed, or specific sites within a particular area where a high level of fear of crime is concentrated. A hot spot of fear is defined as a place where users of the space (e.g., those who walk around or through, sit in, play in the space) report high levels of fear due to three distinct site features: prospect, refuge, and escape. Each site feature varies in effect for the would-be offender and the potential victim. When users characterize site features in a specific area as lacking prospects to see a would-be offender, providing few avenues for escape from a would-be offender, and presenting refuge for a would-be offender, they interpret these areas as potentially threatening or dangerous to their personal safety. Users are fearful of being victimized in such areas. Bonnie S. Fisher and Jack L. Nasar labeled an area characterized by low prospect, high refuge, and low escape for a potential victim as a hot spot of fear or a fear spot.

Mental Maps

Physical environmental characteristics aid in the development of mental templates that shape individuals' cognitive assessment and emotions. Individuals develop mental or cognitive maps of their environments based on physical site features and informed by direct experience with their surroundings, as well as indirect experience (e.g., media reports, rumors). Utilizing these mental maps, it is possible to assess one's surroundings, perceive danger, and consider future consequences and courses of action based on physical site features of the proximate physical environment. The presence or absence of these cues serves as a warning to individuals about the dangerousness of places or situations. In terms of victimization, individuals build cognitive maps through observing proximate physical cues in their present environment. Cognitive maps shape individuals' perceived risk for victimization, and provide a basis for determining levels of fear of crime in specific environments that individuals currently inhabit.

Theory of Fear Spots

Jay Appleton's prospect-refuge theory describes why prospect, refuge, and escape are useful in explaining fear of crime in relation to the proximate physical environment. According to this theory, prospect and refuge are evolutionary throwbacks related to survival. Environments offering an open view (prospect) and places to hide (refuge) were those most suited for survival. Individuals could both see what dangers were on the horizon and take shelter for defense or protection if necessary.

Erving Goffman suggested that the people scan the environment for signs of danger. Once individuals see or detect danger, they avoid, if at all possible, the specific place they perceive as dangerous. Researchers have reasoned that certain site features of the proximate physical environment communicate to individuals signs of safety or threat and, as a result, heighten their fear of crime.

Prospect, Refuge, and Escape

Work by both Appleton and Goffman suggests that three site features provide cues to users of an area about the relative safety or danger of the site. *Prospect* is characterized by openness, as in an open view of one's surroundings. An area or site that offers potential victims high levels of prospect would theoretically result in a feeling of safety and security, all else being equal. *Refuge*, on the other hand, implies a place to hide. A site lacking potential places of refuge (e.g., blind alleys) for offenders would be more likely to elicit perceptions of safety. Finally, *escape* refers to one's ability to avoid pursuit or get away from peril. Less confining areas offering many avenues of escape for potential victims would feel the safest.

Different scenarios involving varying levels of prospect, refuge, and escape offer an ideal opportunity for potential offenders to successfully commit a crime against their target. This same ideal set of circumstances is also the most likely to induce fear of crime among other site users. A site characterized by low or blocked prospect would be most likely to instill in site users a feeling of uncertainty and fear of crime. If the line of sight is restricted (e.g., by narrow corridors, many trees, or shrubs obscuring the view), area users are more likely to experience fear. Similarly, areas offering refuge or concealment for potential offenders (e.g., brick walls or large planters to hide behind) would be more likely to elicit a sense of fear in site users. Finally, sites lacking opportunities or avenues for victims to escape (e.g., dead ends) would be most likely to bring out feelings of fear among site users.

The combination of low prospect for the victim, high refuge for the potential offender, and few avenues of escape for the victim are those most likely to elicit fear and result in concentrations of fear at the proximate level.

Levels of Fear Spots

Fear spots exist at three levels of analysis: macro, meso, and micro. The macro-level concentration of fear occurs within nations or cities. For example, a country in a state of war would be perceived as unsafe and a fearful environment in which to find oneself. The meso level represents a narrower scale, such that an entire city may not be perceived as dangerous, but only certain parts or neighborhoods within that city. Finally, micro-level fear spots are site specific. That is, fear is concentrated within a specific site, area within a site, or situation. To date, only micro-level fear spots have been subject to empirical attention, and the research of Fisher and Nasar and others indicates that fear does indeed concentrate at the site level based on elements of prospect, refuge, and escape.

Fisher and Nasar's Hot Spots of Fear Research

Different constellations of aspects of the physical environment are known to generate fear of crime. Fisher and Nasar introduced the idea that fear of crime may be concentrated in sites that are characterized by varying degrees of prospect, refuge, and escape.

Fisher and Nasar designed a study to examine fear of crime in relation to physical site features on a college campus to understand more fully the role of these site features on fear of crime. Based on examinations of site features at and around Ohio State University by graduate students in landscape architecture, planning and design, observations of pedestrian site user (e.g., college student) behaviors, official campus crime data, and self-reported survey responses from site users, the researchers identified specific site features that resulted in concentrations of high levels of fear. The researchers reported that those areas most avoided were characterized by low prospect and high refuge. Areas considered low prospect, but offering only moderate refuge were avoided only after dark. In addition, student surveys indicated that females reported feeling significantly less safe than did males while traveling at night. Pedestrians traveling in groups were more likely than those traveling alone to enter into the areas judged to be unsafe. The consistent findings related to site behavior based upon physical design are that areas that seem unsafe are avoided after dark, and that the combination of low prospect, lack of escape, and high refuge are most likely to affect behavior through feelings of fear.

Research on Site Characteristics as Predictors of Fear of Crime

Research subsequent to Fisher and Nasar's work has examined different types of environments characterized by varying degrees of prospect, refuge, and escape. Many of these studies have been conducted by showing study participants pictures or videos of different environments and asking them about their fear and perceived risk if they were actually in such an environment. Such studies have generally been supportive of the earlier conclusions that elements of prospect, refuge, and escape are important predictors of fear, hot spots of fear, and perceived risk of attack.

Research has also been conducted that considered the role of physical features in different types of environments (e.g., settings in nature, urban spaces such as alleyways). Findings from these studies indicated that feelings of tranquility are most related to settings in nature, and danger is associated with urban settings. Other examinations of urban settings (e.g., alleyways) have extended the site features of prospect, refuge, and escape identified by Fisher and Nasar to also consider the role of additional features such as entrapment, setting care, mystery, shadow, curvature, length, and the width of alleyways in provoking fear. Aspects of setting care are most related to feelings of preference, and shadow is the strongest predictor of feelings of danger. With respect to measurement, prospect and escape have been combined and measured as one single concept, and refuge has been further refined to include measures of dark spots and hiding places. The studies using refined measures of proximity, refuge, and escape have reported statistically significant relationships between these measures and fear of crime that is similar to those reported in earlier studies.

Bradford W. Reyns and Bonnie S. Fisher

See also Crime Mapping; Defensible Space; Fear of Crime; Fear of Crime, Individual- and Community-Level Effects; Fear of Crime, Measurement of; Hot Spots; Situational Crime Prevention

Further Readings

Appleton, J. (1975). *The experience of place.* London: John Wiley.

Blöbaum, A., & Hunecke, M. (2005). Perceived danger in urban public space. *Environment and Behavior, 37,* 465–486.

Doran, B. J., & Lees, B. G. (2005). Investigating the spatiotemporal links between disorder, crime, and fear of crime. *The Professional Geographer, 57,* 1–12.

Fisher, B. S., & Nasar, J. L. (1992). Fear of crime in relation to three exterior site features: Prospect, refuge, and escape. *Environment and Behavior, 24,* 35–65.

Fisher, B., & Nasar, J. L. (1995). Fear spots in relation to microlevel physical cues: Exploring the overlooked. *Journal of Research in Crime and Delinquency, 32,* 214–239.

Goffman, E. (1971). *Relations in public: Micro studies of the public order.* New York: Harper & Row.

Herzog, T. R., & Chernick, K. K. (2000). Tranquility and danger in urban and natural settings. *Journal of Environmental Psychology, 20,* 29–39.

Herzog, T. R., & Flynn-Smith, J. A. (2001). Preference and perceived danger as a function of the perceived curvature, length, and width of urban alleyways. *Environment and Behavior, 33,* 653–666.

Nasar, J. L., & Fisher, B. (1993). "Hot spots" of fear and crime: A multi-method investigation. *Journal of Environmental Psychology, 13,* 187–206.

Nasar, J. L., Fisher, B., & Grannis, M. (1993). Proximate physical cues to fear of crime. *Landscape and Urban Planning, 26,* 161–178.

Nasar, J. L., & Jones, K. M. (1997). Landscapes of fear and stress. *Environment and Behavior, 29,* 291–323.

Wang, K., & Taylor, R. B. (2006). Simulated walks through dangerous alleys: Impacts of features and progress on fear. *Journal of Environmental Psychology, 26,* 269–283.

HUMAN TRAFFICKING

Human trafficking, also known as modern-day slavery or trafficking in persons, is a criminal act and a violation of basic human rights (e.g., right to freedom, right to dignity, right to equal protection of the law) that affects every country in the world. Human trafficking is one of the few crimes that has been pursued from a victim's perspective, with a focus on prevention of trafficking, protection of victims, and prosecution of traffickers. This entry explores the definition of trafficking and related common misunderstandings, and includes an examination of the size, scope, and patterns of trafficking; sample profiles of traffickers and victims; and responses to human trafficking.

Definition

In December of 2000 in Palermo, Italy, the world came together on the issue of trafficking in persons, finalizing the drafting of the Protocol to Prevent, Suppress and Punish Trafficking in Persons, Especially Women and Children, supplementing the United Nations Convention against Transnational Organized Crime, commonly known as the Protocol. The Protocol entered into force in December 2003. It defines the crime of human trafficking using three components: the process of obtaining the victim (e.g., recruiting, transporting, transferring, receiving, harboring), the means (e.g., deceit, coercion, abduction, threat, fraud, deception, abuse of power), and the goal (e.g., violence/sexual abuse, pornography, forced labor, involuntary servitude, debt bondage, prostitution, slavery). It includes human trafficking both for sexual exploitation and for labor.

Since the meeting in Palermo, 117 countries have signed the Protocol, but many of them have not yet modified their legislation to incorporate the crime of human trafficking into their penal code or fully implemented the process. This is not an easy task. It takes time, money, and a political will to change. The Protocol was developed through a process of consensus that then must be modified to operate within the various criminal justice systems throughout the world. For example, the United States legislation mirrors the Protocol, except that the United States does not include trafficking in human organs as a crime of human trafficking. The lack of full implementation within any country poses a problem for prosecution of traffickers within that country, as well as a problem for cooperation between countries that have differing legislation.

While many countries have signed the Protocol, the level of understanding of human trafficking is limited, resulting in several common misunderstandings. It is widely known that at least 75% of the law enforcement officials around the world are unable to accurately define human trafficking, and the ability to define it is even less common among the general population, who serve as the frontline observers of the phenomenon. Trafficking refers to the act of commerce but is often mistaken to mean the individual must be moved or transported. Because commerce can occur without movement, human trafficking can be domestic as well as transnational.

Another common misunderstanding involves the confusion of human trafficking with illegal migration, smuggling, or labor exploitation. Illegal migration occurs when an individual crosses a national border without the appropriate paperwork or visa. Smuggling is the transportation of willing participants by a third party across a national boundary without the appropriate paperwork. Labor exploitation is the act of obtaining labor without the appropriate remuneration.

The crime of trafficking may begin as smuggling. For example, an individual may pay a smuggler for his or her services to gain entry into a country. Once in the country, the smuggler may request additional money. When the smuggled client cannot pay, the smuggler becomes a trafficker if he coerces the client to do something, such as prostitution, to gain the additional money. In the same way, an employer may exploit an individual, such as by expecting him or her to work for less than the standard minimum wage, but it becomes trafficking when the employer houses the employee and will not let him or her leave.

Size, Scope, and Patterns

The size and scope of the human trafficking problem throughout the world is unknown. Similar to other types of abuse, human trafficking remains hidden, thus underreported, as a result of victims' fear and shame. Estimates of the number of victims have ranged from a few thousand to many millions, but none of the estimates are based on reliable data. For example, 14,500 to 17,500 trafficking victims per year entering the United States has been widely used in estimates for several years. However, only approximately 300 to 500 victims per year have been identified through many sources (e.g., newspapers, court cases).

The solution to these unreliable estimates has been to collect data on actual cases, thus undercounting the problem. Although collecting such data is in its relative infancy, there are several known databases. The International Organization for Migration held a meeting of researchers in 2004 that has resulted in development of the most complete global database, with approximately 7,000 victims of trafficking listed as of 2005.

It is accepted that every country is involved in human trafficking as a country of origin, transit, or destination. However, some countries are more likely to be a country of origin (e.g., extreme poverty, war torn), while others are likely to be a transit country due to geographic location (e.g., Mexico, which borders the United States) or a destination country as a result of its relative wealth (e.g., United States, Italy, United Kingdom). Trafficking patterns vary across time and reports are often based on a few known cases. However, generally, trafficking origins often are found in situations of dire poverty, frequently a result of war or economic devastation. For example, in the aftermath of the economic devastation and the fall of the Soviet Union, many of the Balkan states became countries of origin, supplying desirable women for sex trafficking throughout the Mediterranean and European regions.

Profiles of Traffickers and Victims

While the profile of traffickers includes a wide array of actors and organizational types, much of the literature reports small operations consisting of one or two traffickers, often a male and female team. On the other end of the continuum is organized crime, with its structures varying from loose networks to hierarchical organized crime families. Several typologies have been developed in the literature, but one incorporates both the organizational type and structure with the potential economic gains. This typology describes the continuum as moving from a sole proprietor (e.g., one man prostitutes one female, one household has one domestic servant in debt bondage) to a cottage industry (e.g., one native man sends his "girlfriend" back to her country to recruit one or two more friends or family to be prostituted), to a mall (e.g., several cottage industries in close proximity that often share their trafficked victims when the demand is high to

maximize profits), to the corporation (i.e., a highly structured organization with many victims). Women, as willing and/or unwilling partners, are often used in the recruitment phase, adding credibility to the deception involved in the process.

There is no universal profile of victims because of the wide variation in characteristics. For example, a child may be recruited by family members or community elders with the promise that the child will be given to a rich family and provided with an education and a skilled trade, but instead the child is sold into a life of pornography, sex tourism, or harsh labor. On the other hand, a woman may be recruited for prostitution or domestic service. Identification of victims is most effective using indicator characteristics. Indicators of trafficking include lack of freedom of movement, abuse, lack of personal documents, and an exaggerated fear response. For example, victims may be found living in rooms adjacent to massage parlors or under guard in an apartment or home. They are seldom seen in public and are frequently escorted when outside the work environment. In addition, many victims have untreated health needs.

Responses to Human Trafficking

The complexities involved in this covert crime necessitate that responses to human trafficking take a multidisciplinary approach to ensure their effectiveness. From a supply perspective, strategies that interrupt the "push" factors are likely to be effective. For example, extreme poverty without local employment opportunities and the perceived increase in the standard of living in foreign countries, combined with having children and no husband, have pushed young women to seek employment outside their home country. This desperation leaves the women vulnerable to those who come with promises of employment and a better life. Coupled with the fact that traffickers are often women from the home country, often from the same city, the promises are believable. Public awareness programs targeting these women are likely to assist them in making different choices.

From a demand perspective, strategies that interrupt the "pull" factors are likely to be effective. Demands often take the form of a general desire for cheap labor to decrease the prices and increase the profits on goods and services, as well as the desire for sex. Public awareness and public shaming about forced labor (e.g., the Prohibition of Acquisition of Products Produced by Forced or Indentured Child Labor has resulted in a list of products produced using forced labor and the related country) are believed to be effective in reducing the use of this type of labor among major corporations. Other examples of demand reduction activities in the United States include prosecution of those who go abroad for sex tourism and "john" schools that educate males on the harm inflicted when they enlist the services of trafficked prostitutes.

Prevention efforts are focused on those who are most vulnerable (e.g., conflict zones) by increasing general awareness. Protection of the victims comes in many forms. Victims are often threatened by their traffickers, and their families are in danger. The Trafficking Victims Protection Act (TVPA) provides funds for victim assistance, including medical and mental health assistance, as well as T-visas that allow a trafficked victim and his or her family to live in the United States if he or she assists in the prosecution of the trafficker. Prosecution of traffickers has been plagued with problems, including insufficient evidence to prove the act of trafficking, difficulty in identifying the victims, and the general lack of awareness of human trafficking in law enforcement, the courts, and the jury pools.

The United States has responded to human trafficking with vigor since 2000. In October 2000, the TVPA became law, and in 2003 and 2005 its mandates were renewed. The 2000 legislation created the Office to Monitor and Combat Trafficking in Persons within the U.S. State Department. The 2003 legislation included a presidential initiative with $50 million to support the development of multidisciplinary trafficking task forces, external research, and other activities. The 2005 legislation called for a biennial report on the state of human trafficking research.

In 2001, the U.S. State Department began producing the annual *Trafficking in Persons Report,* which ranks each country into three tiers according to compliance with the minimum standards for the elimination of trafficking. Self-assessment of the United States is not included in the *Trafficking in Persons Report,* due to the appearance of bias. Instead, the U.S. Department of Justice issues an annual report on the activities of the United States.

Other countries have responded to the call to action housed in the Protocol. For example, Lebanon has completed its country assessment with the assistance of funding from the United Nations. The findings of the assessment indicate that the current penal code has all of the component laws necessary to prosecute traffickers, but lacks an overarching law labeling the aggregate behavior as human trafficking with the associated severity of penalties.

Cindy J. Smith

See also Child Pornography and Sexual Exploitation; Immigration and Victimization; Innocence Projects; Sex and Victimization; Victim Assistance Programs, International; Victim Assistance Programs, United States; Victim Blaming

Further Readings

Anti-trafficking Unit. (2006, September). *Toolkit to combat trafficking in persons.* United Nations: Vienna. Retrieved December 1, 2008, from http://www.unodc.org/pdf/Trafficking_toolkit_Oct06.pdf

General Assembly of the United Nations. (1948, December). *The Universal Declaration of Human Rights.* Retrieved December 1, 2008, from http://www.un.org/Overview/rights.html

General Assembly of the United Nations. (2000, November). *Protocol to prevent, suppress and punish trafficking in persons, especially women and children, supplementing the United Nations Convention Against Transnational Organized Crime.* Retrieved December 1, 2008, from http://www.uncjin.org/Documents/Conventions/dcatoc/final_documents_2/convention_%20traff_eng.pdf

Public Law 106-386. (2000, October 28). Victims of Trafficking and Violence Protection Act of 2000. Retrieved December 1, 2008, from http://www.state.gov/documents/organization/10492.pdf

Smith, C. J., Nakib, W., Hanna, C., Statistics Lebanon, & UNODC. (2008). *Measures to prevent and combat trafficking in human beings: Lebanon country assessment.* Retrieved December 1, 2008, from http://www.unodc.org/documents/human-trafficking/Lebanon-HTreport-Oct08.pdf

Web Sites

United Nations Office on Drugs and Crime: http://www.unodc.org/unodc/en/human-trafficking/index.html

U.S. Department of State, Office to Monitor and Combat Trafficking in Persons: http://www.state.gov/g/tip

I

Identity Theft

Identity theft—the theft or unauthorized use of personal or credit information—is a relatively new form of crime that can result in its victims having to spend thousands of dollars and years of their lives restoring their good names. Little research has been conducted on this crime, so it is not well understood. This entry discusses the multiple definitions of identity theft, its prevalence and consequences, and legislative responses to it. It also presents findings from the first ongoing data collection of identity theft in the United States, the National Crime Victimization Survey (NCVS). Findings from 2005, the first full calendar year of data collection using the survey revealed that 5.5% of all U.S. households had experienced this crime.

Definitions

In 1998, Congress passed the Identity Theft and Assumption Deterrence Act (U.S. Public Law 105-318). Prior to this act, the victims of identity theft were seen as the businesses that suffered losses (such as bank and credit card companies) rather than the individuals whose identifying information had been used to commit the theft. Although this legislation aided prosecution of cases involving harm caused to individuals, the legislation is so broad that it did not serve to tighten the definition of identity theft for the research community.

There is no one universally accepted definition of *identity theft,* as the term describes a variety of illegal acts involving theft or misuse of personal information. Under the Fair Credit Reporting Act, identity theft is defined as the use or attempted use of an account or identifying information without the owner's permission. Using this guiding legislation, the Bureau of Justice Statistics added identity theft to the household portion of the ongoing National Crime Victimization Survey that collects data from over 40,000 households twice a year. For the NCVS, identity theft was defined as including three behaviors: (1) unauthorized use or attempted use of existing credit cards, (2) unauthorized use or attempted use of other existing accounts such as checking accounts, and (3) misuse of personal information to obtain new accounts or loans.

Prevalence

In 2005, 6.4 million U.S. households discovered that at least one member of the household had been the victim of identity theft during the preceding 6 months. This figure represents 1 in 20 households in the United States. Victimization rates vary depending on the type of an identity theft. Thus almost half (46.2%) of victimized households experienced unauthorized use of an existing credit card, whereas a quarter (24.7%) experienced unauthorized use of other existing accounts. Misuse of personal information, or the form that some argue is "true" identity theft, was experienced by about 1.1 million households, representing one in six victimized households.

Not all households in the United States are equally likely to experience identity theft. The households most likely to experience any form of identity theft are those headed by the youngest members (those 18–24 years old), in urban or suburban areas, in the West, of non-Hispanics, and with the highest incomes ($75,000 or more). Households headed by persons age 65 or older and by those earning less than $50,000 have victimization rates that are at least half those of younger or more affluent households.

Of great importance to the public is how identity theft is detected, as Americans' focus is on preventing such theft or mitigating the extent of damage. The most common way households became aware of the identity theft was by missing money or noticing unfamiliar charges on an account (30.8%). One fifth of victimized households discovered the identity theft when someone was contacted about a late or unpaid bill. For 1 in 20 households, the identity theft was detected by noticing an error in a credit report, noticing a missing credit card or checkbook, or having an account blocked by the issuer.

Consequences

Examples of problems that can arise as a result of identity theft include having banking problems, being contacted by a debt collector, or even paying higher interest rates. Overall, in 2005, one in five households experienced some type of problem as a result of the identity theft. Households with theft of existing credit card accounts were the least likely to experience problems associated with the identity theft (9%), while households that experienced misuse of personal information were more likely to experience problems than households with unauthorized use of other existing accounts (33.7% vs. 18.0%).

When examining time spent resolving all problems associated with the episode of identity theft, households report two extremes of time spent. More than a quarter (28.6%) of victimized households were able to resolve all problems within one day or less. Households that experienced unauthorized use of credit card accounts were more likely than households victimized by other types of identity theft to spend a day or less resolving problems (36.5%). At the other end of the spectrum, 17% of victimized households report having to spend one month or more resolving all problems.

More than two thirds of victimized households reported a financial loss of $1 or more as a result of the identity theft. This figure is limited to only the most recent loss if a household reported discovering more than one episode during the preceding 6 months, and costs or losses to businesses may or may not be included. The remaining households reported not experiencing any loss (18.3%) or did not know the amount of the loss (12.9%). In 40% of the victimized households, the dollar loss was less than $500. About 5% of the victimized households sustained a loss of $5,000 or more.

Policy and Legislation

Identity theft has come to the attention of policy makers and the public over the last decade. In 2004, the Identity Theft Penalty Enhancement Act, which carries a mandatory 2-year prison term, was signed into law. In addition, President George W. Bush established the President's Task Force on Identity Theft on May 10, 2006. This interagency task force examined the problem of identity theft and the federal response to it, and released a list of recommendations. The work of the task force has been compiled in the report *Combating Identity Theft: A Strategic Plan*, released in 2007, which provides guidance for federal agencies involved in preventing, responding to, and investigating the problem of identity theft.

One of the recommendations in the strategic plan is for the Federal Trade Commission and the U.S. Department of Justice to work together to better understand the scope of the problem. With funding from both agencies, a supplement to the NCVS was administered for the first 6 months of 2008. The Identity Theft Supplement collected detailed information about the offender, interaction with credit reporting agencies and financial institutions, emotional response of the victim, financial loss, and risk avoidance. Findings from this supplement are expected to be released in 2010 and represent the culmination of coordinated efforts of several federal agencies to bridge knowledge gaps and better understand the problem of identity theft.

Katrina Baum

Further Readings

Baum, K. (2007). *Identity theft, 2005* (NCJ 219411). Washington, DC: U.S. Department of Justice, Bureau of Justice Statistics.

Fair Credit Reporting Act (FCRA), 15 U.S.C. § 1681 et seq. Retrieved November 11, 2009, from http://www.ftc.gov/os/statutes/031224fcra.pdf

Newman, G., & McNally, M. (2004). *Identity theft literature review* (NCJ 210459). Washington, DC: U.S. Department of Justice, National Institute of Justice.

President's Identity Theft Task Force. (2007). *Combating identity theft: A strategic plan.* Washington, DC: Author. Retrieved from http://www.idtheft.gov/reports/StrategicPlan.pdf

IMMIGRATION AND VICTIMIZATION

Understanding the victimization of immigrants was of great importance to pioneer victimologist Hans von Hentig, who listed "the immigrant" as one of thirteen categories in his 1948 typology of victims. As an immigrant himself, he knew how vulnerable immigrants can be. He described the experience as a temporary reduction to an extreme degree of helplessness in human relations. Despite von Hentig's interest, victimologists did not pursue the topic until recently. The new interest in immigrant victimization is usually billed under more politically compelling rubrics like trafficking of human beings, hate crime, or domestic abuse, or it is recast in terms of studies of race, ethnicity, nationality, or religion. These labels are expedient for research purposes, but they do not address the fact that being a foreigner and a minority member makes an individual a more vulnerable target for victimization than does just being a minority member.

Patterns of Victimization

There is considerable evidence that immigrants suffer higher rates of victimization than autochtons for both violent and certain property crime. They also suffer other types of victimization, including theft of wages, fraud, labor and housing violations, economic exploitation, trafficking in humans, and hate crime. In terms of common crimes of violence and property crimes, immigrants are more likely to be victimized by their own people than by autochtons.

This varies, however, depending on the type of crime and the gender of the victim. The patterns of victimization fit well with opportunity and conflict theories. Immigrants are suitable targets who are accessible and often have no guardians—unless they are living in enclaves. The vulnerability of immigrants who are illegal is even greater. The fact that a person is a foreigner and/or has ethnic characteristics that make him or her seem "foreign" incites some people to hate crime. Immigrants living in close proximity to high-crime-risk areas are more likely to be victimized. In general, the same sociodemographic characteristics associated with being a criminal are associated with being a victim of crime.

Immigrants have been found to be at higher risks than autochtons of being the victims of homicide in Australia and in the United States. Australian homicide victimization rates for various immigrant groups, calculated as age–sex standardized mortality ratios (SMRs) using the Australian-born rate as the standard, show that male SMRs ranged from 0.13 for immigrants from Africa and the Americas to 5.83 for Koreans.

California death certificates show that among residents who died of homicide in the 1990s, foreign-born persons were overrepresented. Risk rates varied by ethnicity and across time. Foreign-born Whites, Hispanics, and Asians were at significantly higher risk, while foreign-born Blacks were at a statistically similar risk of homicide compared with their U.S.-born counterparts.

Using 1999 Italian data, Marzio Barbagli distinguished between immigrants from developed and those from developing countries, and he calculated the risk of victimization for these two groupings compared to the risk for Italians (Italian = 1). Immigrants from developing countries had risks that were higher than both Italians and immigrants from rich countries for six crimes (burglary, purse snatching, robbery, aggravated assault, sexual assault, and homicide). They had lower risk than both immigrants from developed countries and Italians for auto theft and shoplifting. They were more than five times more likely than Italians to be pickpocketed, but half as likely to be pickpocketed as were immigrants from wealthy countries. With regard to homicide, they were 3.32 times as likely as Italians and 10.3 times as likely as immigrants from rich countries to be victims.

Victim surveys for 1990 and 1992 in Sweden found that immigrants had higher rates of victimization than native Swedes for three forms of violent crime (violence causing death, serious violence, and threats of violence), but not for theft and property damage. Certain factors increased victimization rates among both immigrant and indigenous groups—specifically, being young, being single, living in public housing, and living in an urban environment.

Dutch studies from the 1990s showed that ethnic minorities (i.e., immigrants) were twice as likely as the entire city populations to be the victims of threats of violence and one-and-a-half times more likely to be victims of property crimes. Comparing the responses of Turks and Moroccans with those of a "matched" Dutch group who lived in the same neighborhoods, however, the immigrants appeared to be less often the victims of violent and property crime. Another study found no significant differences in general victimization rates of immigrants and natives living in the same neighborhoods.

Many studies have shown that immigrants are more likely to be victimized by their own kind than by autochtons. A simulation estimated that if foreigners were only 3% of those charged with homicide in Italy, the rate of victimization of immigrants would be reduced by 50.8%, while that of Italians would be reduced by only 2.3%. Of immigrant victims of homicide in Australia, 51.3% were killed by their compatriots. This varied from zero for New Zealanders to 100% for immigrants from the Middle East.

The terrorist attacks in the United States and the United Kingdom spawned a surge of retaliatory hate crimes against foreigners. Hate crime against immigrants, however, was commonplace before terrorism. Mary Beth Sheriden has reported that immigrants are regularly cheated by employers and defrauded by labor recruiters.

In major countries of destination, women immigrants from around the world share common characteristics of vulnerability and disproportionately high rates of abuse. Numerous studies document this vulnerability for women in situations involving domestic abuse, "mail order brides," and human trafficking. In Sweden, for example, women with foreign backgrounds were found to have an 80% greater likelihood of being "victims of violence indoors" (an indirect measure of domestic violence) than are native Swedish females. Ironically, immigration policies often make immigrant women suffer their domestic abuse without protest by giving their spouses the power to have them deported.

The trafficking of human beings for sexual or labor exploitation reappeared on the agenda of the international community in the 1990s. Although the official estimates of the number of cases of trafficking appear to be seriously inflated, there is no doubt that the practice is a large and vicious one. Domestic abuse among mail order brides in the world is believed to be increasing. Filipina "mail order brides" in Australia have been found to be at extraordinarily high risk for violence and murder—almost six times more likely than other women to be victims of homicide.

The victimization of many immigrants begins even before they set forth on their journey. Predators of all kinds lie in wait. Labor recruiters lie to them. Bandits, police, immigration officials, shopkeepers, bus drivers, smugglers, and traffickers extort bribes, inflate prices, beat them, leave them to be cooked to death in locked vehicles abandoned in the desert, and exploit them in numerous ways.

William F. McDonald

See also Correlates of Victimization; Domestic Violence; Hate and Bias Crime; Human Trafficking; Race/Ethnicity and Victimization; Victimization, Theories of; Victimology

Further Readings

Barbagli, M., & Colombo, A. (2009). Immigrants as authors and victims of crimes: The italian experience. In W. F. McDonald (Ed.), *Sociology of crime, law, and deviance: Vol. 13. Immigration, crime and justice* (pp. 69–95). Bingley, UK: Emerald/JAI.

Cunneen, C., & Stubbs, J. (2002). Migration, political economy and violence against women: The post immigration experience of Filipino women in Australia. In J. D. Freilich, G. Newman, S. G. Shoham, & M. Addad (Eds.), *Migration, culture conflict and crime* (pp. 159–183). Aldershot, UK; Burlington, VT: Ashgate, Dartmouth.

Haan, W. de. (1997). Minorities, crime, and criminal justice in the Netherlands. In I. H. Marshall (Ed.), *Minorities, migrants and crime* (pp. 198–223). Thousand Oaks, CA: Sage.

Kliewer, E. (1994). Homicide victims among Australian immigrants. *Australian Journal of Public Health, 18,* 304–309.

Maler-Katkin, D. (Ed.). (1995). Immigration, xenophobia and right wing violence in unified Germany [Special issue]. *Crime, Law and Social Change, 24,* 1–75.

Martens, P. L. (1997). Immigrants, crime, and criminal justice in Sweden. In M. Tonry (Ed.), *Ethnicity, crime, and immigration: Comparative and cross-national perspectives* (pp. 183–255). Chicago: University of Chicago Press.

McDonald, W. F. (2009). Adding insult to injury: Unintended consequences for immigrants of hate crime legislation. In W. F. McDonald (Ed.), *Sociology of crime, law, and deviance: Vol. 13. Immigration, crime and justice* (pp. 165–189). Bingley, UK: Emerald/JAI.

Sheridan, M. B. (2005, June 23). Pay abuses common for day laborers, study finds. *The Washington Post*, p. A1.

Smith, D. J. (1997). Ethnic minorities, crime, and criminal justice. In M. Maguire, R. Morgan, & R. Reiner (Eds.), *The Oxford handbook of criminology* (2nd ed., pp. 703–759). Oxford, UK: Clarendon.

Sorenson, S. B., & Shen, H. (1996). Homicide risk among immigrants in California, 1970 through 1992. *American Journal of Public Health, 86*(1), 97–101.

In-Camera Proceedings

A significant characteristic of the criminal justice system in the United States is its openness. There are no "star chambers" that operate out of the public view and behind closed doors. The televised trial of O. J. Simpson for the murders of Nicole Brown Simpson and Ron Goldman is an example of the public nature of such proceedings. Not only were the proceedings reported each day in the press, but the trial was carried live on television. There are also numerous books that have been written as a result of the trial. The private lives of Simpson, Brown Simpson, and Goldman were displayed before the world. However, the question remains as to whether every portion of every trial should be played before the public and/or a jury. In-camera proceedings—where a matter (usually a question of law or discretion) is heard in private, in the judge's chambers—are an alternative approach.

The victims of crimes come to court having already been harmed. The legal system is designed to provide a remedy, not only for the victim, but for the good of society and, it is hoped, the system will not exacerbate an injury or cause another. The remedies available to society are to punish the person who commits the crime, prevent similar crimes from occurring, and attempt to make the victim whole again. Despite these objectives, many victims and their families will forever bear the scars of the crimes that are committed against them.

The issues addressed in in-camera proceedings may be preserved on the record (i.e., recorded as a part of the trial transcript outside of the jury) or off the record, where only the outcome becomes part of the court record. It is important to note that the proceeding is not *ex parte* (i.e., one in which only one side is present), thus counsel for both parties to the dispute are usually present. Matters that are likely to be addressed may involve testimony of a rape victim or child, past sexual activity of the victim, the propriety of crime scene or autopsy photographs, expert testimony, medical information, informant testimony, informant identification, admissibility of evidence, national security information, review of an attorney's work product, motions to sever the trials of defendants, grand jury minutes, and other similar topics. While this may sound like the star-chamber proceedings that operated behind closed doors of 16th-century English courts, it bears little resemblance to those proceedings.

There have been several recent cases in the news involving in-camera proceedings. The first one involves the use in court of testimony of an alleged rape victim's past sexual history and the other involves the use of intelligence (national security and/or source) information in a public trial. The first case involved basketball star Kobe Bryant.

Bryant was accused of the sexual assault and rape of a 19-year-old woman who was an employee of the facility where he was recuperating from knee surgery. There were numerous pretrial hearings that the court held in chambers regarding sensitive private information. Among the matters discussed in-camera were evidence concerning a waiver of the victim's medical and/or mental health privileges and the admissibility of evidence contrary to a Colorado rape shield statute. These hearings were held to determine if otherwise private information regarding the accuser would be released to the defendant and, later, be admissible in court during the trial. The concern here is whether a victim of an alleged sexual assault and rape must suffer additional harm by being opened up to public scrutiny of personal and/or private matters regarding sexual activity and medical treatment. Should the nature of a rape charge automatically result in the waiver of any physician–patient privilege? And how much of the victim's private life should be open for scrutiny as a result of coming forward to the police about the assault?

However, it should be noted that the concern for the privacy of the accuser needs to be balanced with the Sixth Amendment guarantees to an accused of impartiality and due process. In particular, the concern for a crime victim's privacy must be balanced with the defendant's right "to be confronted with the witnesses against him," as set forth in the Confrontation Clause of the U.S. Constitution.

There were similar issues presented in the case involving three Duke lacrosse players and an exotic dancer who was hired to entertain at a party they attended. In order to provide a full defense, there were motions by the defendants to disclose her past sexual activity and medical information, particularly on the night of the alleged crime. As in most cases involving such sensitive information, courts are inclined to examine facts and rule on such evidence in chambers and outside of public view. In chambers, only the judge makes the initial review of the material that the defense requests.

In some matters concerning national security, the court has also seen it appropriate to examine material in-camera. Litigation in cases involving national security information may be the result of criminal charges regarding terrorism or espionage, or simply a government agency's response to a Freedom of Information Act request. The burden of denying the existence of information based on national security is on the agency. In such a case, the agency will ask the court to review in-camera, in private, a "classified" document or an affidavit as the basis for withholding documents pursuant to the request. In the case of *Vaughn v. Rosen*, 157 U.S. App. D.C. 340, 346, 484 F.2d 820 (1973), the court determined that a public record of the justification for withholding the information "would compromise the secret nature of the information." *Hayden v. National Security Agency* (197 U.S. App. D.C. 224, 608 F.2d 1381 [1979]) noted that the submission of in-camera affidavits and a discussion regarding the request are most likely to occur in matters involving national security.

The court system functions to preserve rights and remedy wrongs, and the techniques it uses prioritize pursuit of this goal. The courts effectively use in-camera proceedings to ensure that liberty and justice are maintained and that the rights of the people under the U.S. Constitution have been preserved.

Keith Gregory Logan

See also Double Victimization; Mental Illness and Victimization; Pedophilia; Rape Law Reform; Rape Shield Laws

Further Readings

Allen v. Central Intelligence Agency, 636 F.2d 1287 (D.C. Cir. 1980).

Letelier v. United States Department of Justice, Civil Action No. 79–1984 (D.D.C. June 24, 1980).

Mead Data Central, Inc. v. United States Department of the Air Force, 184 U.S. App. D.C. 350, 369, 566 F.2d 242, 261 (1977).

INCEST

In the 1940s psychoanalysts began looking at cases of incest, especially those of father–daughter incest. However, the first in-depth examination of incest did not occur until 1955, when sociologist Kirson S. Weinburg completed his research on the topic. Even after Weinburg's study, however, cases of incest were believed to be uncommon—until a shift from this belief occurred in the 1970s. Currently incest is viewed as more common than reports show and as a prevalent sexual crime against adolescents and young children.

Definitions

The definitions of incest vary. However, incest is often classified as any sexual contact (e.g., touching, fondling, oral sex, verbal seduction or abuse, and/or intercourse) between closely related persons (often within the immediate family) in which an adult coerces a child or adolescent or an older child coerces a younger child. Under this definition, incest includes father–daughter, stepfather–daughter, mother–son, stepmother–son, sibling–sibling, and extended family–child incest. The majority of reported incidents of incest occur between fathers and daughters and stepfathers and daughters (however, it is believed the true rate of sibling incest is underreported). Based on the majority of the information currently available, the most often discussed incidents of incest are those between a paternal figure (e.g., father or stepfather) and a child, thus this entry sometimes refers to the perpetrator of incest as male.

Prevalence

Determining the number of incidents of incest within the United States is a difficult task. This void in information can be attributed to a number of different factors, the most significant of which is that incest remains highly underreported. Victims of incest are extremely reluctant to reveal the abuse occurring against them because of fear, shame, and blame. Nevertheless, incest has still been cited as the most common form of child abuse. In addition to being severely underreported, accurate rates of incest are also difficult to ascertain due to differences in definitions and methods of data collection and sampling. To the detriment of investigations of the prevalence of incest, research often fails to distinguish between familial child abuse and nonfamilial child abuse. Thus, though there is not an accurate prevalence rate for incidents of child incest, it is recognized that this is a significant crime that needs significant attention.

Occurrence of Incest

Incidents of incest occur when someone uses a position of power, emotional manipulation, and threats to achieve the goal of sexual satisfaction. Incidents of incest often do not include physical force or coercion; however, the perpetrator's use of verbal threats is a common strategy used to coerce the child into committing the desired behaviors. Using verbal threats allows the perpetrator to guarantee the silence and compliance of the child victim. This manipulation may include threats of family division or dissolution and/or termination of the relationship between the child and perpetrator, and it often evokes personal shame or blame in the child. In addition, the perpetrator may threaten to harm himself, the child, or other family members if the acts of incest are revealed or discontinued.

There is no particular length of time that incest lasts. The occurrence of incest may be a single act, or it can span decades. Incidents may be occasional, or may be compulsive in nature and occur numerous times a day. While incest is believed to occur more often in families of lower socioeconomic class, in ethnic minorities, and in rural families, those beliefs have not been adequately supported by research. Rather, a more likely premise is that incest occurs in all types of families regardless of sociodemographic factors (e.g., socioeconomic status, ethnic origin, or geographic location).

Incest remains one of the most underreported and least discussed crimes in the United States. Victims of incest employ a number of coping mechanisms to manage the emotional and psychological consequences of incest (e.g., guilt, shame, and fear). In addition, victims often deny the incidents or dissociate from the incidents in order to minimize or normalize the acts perpetrated against them. These strategies often prevent them from coming forward or reporting the crimes. Finally, victims are often too frightened to report incest. Because the perpetrator is often a person in a position of power over the victim, the coercion and fear tactics used against the victim are often successful (i.e., the victim declines to report the incest, and thus the perpetrator is free to continue his crime).

Effects of Incest

The act of incest leads to a number of short-term and long-term individual and social consequences. For example, girls who experience incest have higher rates of risky behaviors (e.g., running away, suicide attempts, and pregnancy). In addition, anxiety, panic, major depression, and alcohol abuse and dependence are significantly higher in victims of incest than in others. Moreover, posttraumatic stress disorder (PTSD) is common in incest victims. Finally, incest also has severe social consequences because it is considered socially taboo. Fearing the social reprisals enforced by society (e.g., social isolation and name-calling), incest victims often suppress and internalize the anger and shame they feel. This often leads to significant personal turmoil; thus, the need for intervention in the lives of victims of incest is often necessary and prevalent.

Response to Incest

Though incest is illegal in most jurisdictions, the definition and legal consequences of committing incest vary by country and, at times, between different states. In the United States, the states and the District of Columbia have individual specifications and statutes, but they all have some form of incest prohibition.

Currently there are few formal services available to victims of incest or their families. Resources for incest victims include books, self-help groups, therapy programs, and limited legal responses. When cases of incest are reported, treatment often includes individual, family, couple, or group therapy for the offender, the victim, and other family members. All parties also are evaluated for preexisting and coexisting problems such as substance abuse, domestic violence, and psychiatric disorders. This type of intervention is critical because many men who sexually abuse their children often participate in other forms of sexual deviance.

Victims of incest face a long road toward recovery. Regardless of the factors surrounding a case of incest (e.g., the length of time, number of times, relationship between parties involved), the recovery process for the victim is extensive. It is evident that a greater number of services are needed for victims and their families. With increasing awareness of the issues of incest, including the related emotional, psychological, and physical consequences, it is imperative that greater resources be allocated for victims of incest.

Devon G. Thacker

See also Child Abuse, Identification of; Family Violence; Pedophilia; Psychological/Emotional Abuse; Sex and Victimization; Sexual Victimization

Further Readings

Herman, J. L., & Hirschman, L. (2000). *Father–daughter incest*. Cambridge, MA: Harvard University Press.

Myers, J. (1997). *A mother's nightmare—incest: A practical legal guide for parents and professionals*. Thousand Oaks, CA: Sage.

Roesler, T. A., & Weissmann Wind, T. (1994). Telling the secret. *Journal of Interpersonal Violence, 9,* 327–338.

Shaw, J. (1999). *Sexual aggression*. Washington, DC: American Psychiatric Press.

INCIVILITIES/SOCIAL DISORDER

In the late 1970s, many researchers and policy makers interested in community crime prevention held out high hopes for crime prevention through environmental design (CPTED). Popularized by architect Oscar Newman, who borrowed the core of many of his ideas from urban writer and activist Jane Jacobs, the idea was that certain site-level design features would facilitate specific behaviors of residents. These design features would result in the regulars or residents of the setting exercising both enhanced surveillance that would prevent crime and greater willingness to intervene in the event a crime occurred. The designs also would alter the perceptions of potential offenders about how good these locations were for criminal activity. The residents' or users' behavior and attitudes were subsumed under theoretical ideas like territorial functioning and informal social control. When delinquency was discussed, the process referenced was social disorganization. Research did show some of the expected connections between design and behavior in urban residential and public housing contexts, but the connections were not as strong or consistent across settings as had been previously promised.

Attention switched to a different aspect of the physical environment in the early 1980s—a broken window left unfixed. At a time when urban police departments were casting about for proactive roles, James Wilson and George Kelling suggested that unfixed physical deterioration in a neighborhood setting could undercut residents' willingness to intervene in situations and embolden potential offenders. They had police officers on foot, working collaboratively with resident and business constituencies, work to alleviate physical incivilities: graffiti, abandoned cars, litter, and the like. Social incivilities also were viewed as relevant and needing to be ousted; these included drunks, panhandlers, squeegee kids, and homeless people.

At about this same time several researchers were finding strong connections between residents' reports of physical incivilities, disorderly behavior by groups such as unsupervised teens, and reactions to crime like fear or avoidance.

Police and crime prevention specialists and resident improvement groups had a new target: disorderly neighborhood conditions, both social and physical. Their belief was that if they could just clean the place up, scrub out the gang tags, and get the drunks and dealers to hang out somewhere else, things would be fine. The balance of this entry looks at the efficacy of this approach to incivilities and social disorder.

Prospect of a Long-Term Solution

In the late 1980s, Wes Skogan expanded this core idea by suggesting that controlling incivilities would be the key not only to making residents feel safer, but also to driving down neighborhood crime rates and preventing neighborhood decline. Entire areas of cities might be saved from decline and made safe through clean-up campaigns. Big city mayors signed on, including, among others, David Dinkins (New York City), Rudolph Giuliani (New York City), Kurt Schmoke (Baltimore), and Martin O'Malley (Baltimore).

At the time, zero-tolerance policies were considered the means of solving the problem of incivilities. The first zero-tolerance policies emerged from corporate work requirements. Organizations would have a zero-tolerance policy on drug use, for example. Implementing such a policy was relatively straightforward: The organizations would simply employ random drug testing.

However, implementing zero-tolerance *policing* strategies proved far more complicated for many reasons. Police cannot afford to cite or arrest every citizen for every violation or crime committed. They simply do not have the time or the proclivity for the paperwork. For many in the police, it is not their idea of "real" policing. In addition, most communities do not really want zero-tolerance policing. Historical research on what happened in some cities during Prohibition-era crackdowns on alcohol violations amply demonstrated that very few communities really wanted equal justice for all. This is probably still true. Therefore, inevitably, zero-tolerance policing amounts to geographically varying enforcement of different intensities around different neighborhood problems. Zero-tolerance policies, Australian researchers have suggested, when applied to open-air drug markets, can actually significantly elevate public health problems. These policies cause the markets to disperse, making it more difficult for public health workers to contact the addict population and carry out needle exchange programs, and increasing the chances that drug users will be "shooting up" in ways or under conditions that are riskier.

Empirical Work

The most recent solid empirical work has found only extremely modest beneficial impacts of zero-tolerance policing on later crime shifts. The studies have suggested that enormous police effort was required, either through citations or misdemeanor arrests, to generate less than overwhelming crime prevention benefits.

In the mid-1990s, some work began on gauging the longitudinal effects of incivilities at both the street block and neighborhood levels in Baltimore, Maryland, and Salt Lake City, Utah. The analysis of street blocks suggested later changes in reactions to crime and local commitment sometimes were not shaped by earlier perceived incivilities but were contingent on other local features. The analysis of neighborhoods suggested modest and sometimes contingent effects of incivilities. The effects were contingent in that they depended both on the specific outcome and on the specific type of incivility indicator used.

Questions have also been raised about what assessed or perceived incivilities represent. Earlier research suggested they reflected underlying disorder in the residential setting. More recent work, however, has failed to find confirming patterns of convergent validity when multiple incivility indicators were used. A survey-based approach might ask residents to rate the intensity of local physical incivilities, like graffiti, vacant houses, litter, poorly maintained houses, and the like, as well as social incivilities, like unsupervised or rowdy teen groups, neighbors fighting, or public drunkenness or drug sales. Alternatively, trained raters can walk street blocks and count incivilities. They can do so reliably. From a construct validity perspective, the indicators of incivilities from different data sources should converge. However, sometimes they do not converge, especially when changes over time are examined. It is not clear what single or multiple underlying concepts these indicators are capturing, net of underlying socioeconomic and racial variations across contexts.

By the late 1990s, counterreactions to the sociopolitics of incivilities and zero-tolerance emerged. Bernard Harcourt suggested these zero-tolerance policies reflected a collapse of the harm principle, being disproportional responses to the harm occurring. Handing out stiff fines or even jail time to litterers and those urinating in public harkened back disturbingly to an era in the middle of the preceding century when vagrancy laws were widely used by police to remove "undesirable elements" from their locale. Harcourt also suggested these policies widened social divisions. Ralph Taylor has argued that zero-tolerance policing policies represent a return to the harsh policing practices seen in large cities in the early 1960s and are based on fundamentally flawed or at least unsubstantiated program logic models. Martin Innes, returning to a symbolic interactionist argument made 30 years ago by Albert Hunter, has argued that the same incivility can have markedly different meanings for and effects on different groups of people or even different individuals, suggesting it will be difficult figuring out which incivilities to target.

Current Status and Future Outlook

Where does this leave us in solving the issue of incivilities and social disorder? The situation can be examined from the policy side, the prevention side, and the theory side.

In terms of policy, draconian enforcement of laws or regulations targeting disorderly behavior or deteriorating physical conditions will probably continue to be popular, in large part due to the politically asymmetrical consequences surrounding this debate in an era of late modernity, as described by David Garland. To favor less enforcement is to appear soft on crime. Appearing soft on crime can lose elections.

The popularity of these policies will continue despite weak empirical support suggesting that these policies, *in the long term*, are unlikely *on their own* to result in significant crime or victimization prevention. Targeted enforcement, third-party policing, or saturation of places with police can have a dramatic impact for a short period, but it is not feasible to keep up such a dramatic response over time. Most of the work on crackdowns shows short, temporally limited effects. The effects of enforcement against incivilities are probably the same.

Prevention and reduction of incivilities cannot work in the long term for several reasons. First, as intimated above, the agency resources are not there. Police cannot make and keep this a high priority over an extended area for an extended time. Second, if these problems crop up in a location, the occurrence is probably overdetermined. Crime pattern theory, and environmental criminology more generally, have demonstrated over the last three decades that local social, economic, household, land use, site, land, and traffic arrangements strongly shape what crime problems will crop up where. Barring wholesale forced out-migration of

residents, wholesale reconstruction of segments of neighborhoods, or changing large numbers of nonresidential land uses and rerouting traffic, the long-term differentials in crime across areas of a city or of a neighborhood will remain.

In terms of theory, three broad issues remain unresolved. First is the construct validity question around incivilities. Do they reflect underlying disorder? With ecological units of analysis, incivility indicators do not converge as expected across method types. Are perceived incivilities or assessed incivilities separable from low-level misdemeanor rates of a locale? At the individual level, no one has yet demonstrated discriminant validity of perceived incivilities from mental health indicators like anxiety and depression, or from reaction to crime and local attachment to place indicators. Thus, at the psychological, small group (street block), and ecological levels, a successful case has not yet been made that variations in incivilities *primarily* reflect variations in an underlying unitary construct called disorder. Second, continuing confusion surrounds the relevant psychological and behavioral processes that lead incivilities to have the impacts they do. Different labels have been applied to the relevant processes—informal social control, willingness to intervene, collective efficacy, human territorial functioning—but clear longitudinal demonstrations at different levels that these processes are affected by incivilities, *net* of other fundamental sociodemographic and physical site features, are lacking. This is parallel in some ways to the early arguments about defensible space and territorial functioning. Defensible space was theorized to disinhibit residents' territorial cognitions and behaviors. In an opposite way, incivilities are theorized to inhibit some of those same cognitions and behaviors. But data linking these two—changing incivilities and changing territorial indicators or social control indicators—are lacking.

Ralph B. Taylor

See also Crime Prevention Through Environmental Design; Defensible Space; Neighborhood Watch Programs

Further Readings

Brantingham, P. L., & Brantingham, P. J. (1993). Nodes, paths, and edges: Considerations on the complexity of crime and the physical environment. *Journal of Environmental Psychology, 13,* 3–28.

Brown, B. B., Perkins, D. D., & Brown, G. (2004). Crime, new housing, and housing incivilities in a first ring suburb: Multilevel relationships across time. *Housing Policy Debate, 15*(2), 301–345.

Brown, B. B., Perkins, D. D., & Brown, G. (2004). Incivilities, place attachment and crime: Block and individual effects. *Journal of Environmental Psychology, 24*(3), 359–371.

Harcourt, B. E., & Ludwig, J. (2006). Broken windows: New evidence from New York City and a five city social experiment. *University of Chicago Law Review, 73*(1), 271–320.

Innes, M. (2004). Signal crimes and signal disorders: Notes on deviance as communicative action. *British Journal of Sociology, 55*(3), 335–355.

Robinson, J., Lawton, B., Taylor, R. B., & Perkins, D. D. (2003). Longitudinal impacts of incivilities: A multilevel analysis of reactions to crime and block satisfaction. *Journal of Quantitative Criminology, 19,* 237–274.

St. Jean, P. K. B. (2007). *Pockets of crime: Broken windows, collective efficacy, and the criminal point of view.* Chicago: University of Chicago Press.

Taylor, R. B. (1988). *Human territorial functioning.* Cambridge, UK: Cambridge University Press.

Taylor, R. B. (2001). *Breaking away from broken windows: Evidence from Baltimore neighborhoods and the nationwide fight against crime, grime, fear and decline.* New York: Westview.

INFANTICIDE

Infanticide is a serious problem, both in the United States and throughout the world. It is a serious crime that affects not only the victim and offender but society as a whole. This entry explores the definition of infanticide, possible explanations, prevalence and reporting issues, and the unique characteristics of the victims and offenders. It then discusses risk factors, prevention measures, and the particular punishments associated with this crime.

Definition

Infanticide is generally defined as the intentional killing of an infant. Although the precise age of the victim that is required to qualify a murder as infanticide

varies, in the United States it is generally accepted that children under the age of 1 who are murdered are classified as infanticide victims. Other definitions may include murder of a child under the age of 5. Neonaticide, or the killing of a newborn within 24 hours of birth, is a specific type of infanticide. The most common perpetrators of infanticide are the infant's parents, which also classifies the homicide as filicide.

Explanations

Infanticide has been a somewhat common practice throughout history. In ancient times, it often took the form of child sacrifice for religious or supernatural purposes. Infants who were unwanted by their parents were often subjected to abandonment and subsequent death by exposure to the elements. Early cases of infanticide were partially legitimized by the existing societies because of the belief that newborns were not considered human.

Although many documented cases of infanticide are tied to psychological, sociological, or criminological explanations, other explanations are relevant. Residents of some countries may practice infanticide as a means of population control, especially against female infants. In countries where a limitation is placed on the number of children that a family may have, parents, immediate and extended family, and community members often prefer the production of male children, and decide to destroy the female children upon or shortly after birth. The level of social acceptance of this practice varies by country. Feminist scholars have suggested that the regulation of gender demographics through the controlling of births through "reproductive work" plays a pivotal role in shaping women's societal roles. In some countries, the exploitation of women through reproductive work may be used as a sociopolitical means to control the gender demographics, thereby maintaining the male-dominated power structures. The control exerted through formally and informally enforced gender preferences may be connected with rates of infanticide as well.

Prevalence

The rate of homicide of children under the age of 4 in the United States ranks among the highest rates of child homicide in the world. In the United States, between 600 and 700 children under the age of 5 are killed annually, and about 45% of all child murders are classified as neonaticide cases. However, the actual prevalence of infanticide is difficult to determine, as it often resembles other forms of death among infants. For example, sudden infant death syndrome cases include children who stop breathing in their sleep, whereas shaken baby syndrome includes cases in which a child is shaken and suffers internal bleeding or swelling. Because it is difficult for policing agencies to make these determinations, incidents that may be infanticide cases may be officially classified as either accidents or deaths from natural causes. Furthermore, the reliability of system-detected infanticide cases hinges on official government recognition of a child's birth. In countries or specific regions within countries where record keeping is lacking, or childbirth frequently occurs outside of medical facilities, there may be no way of detecting cases of infanticide short of parents' self-reports.

The only major reporting tools that currently exist in the United States to measure infanticide are those of the Uniform Crime Reporting Program and the National Incident Based Reporting System, both of which rely on official reports of infanticide as documented by law enforcement agencies. For the reasons stated above, these numbers are not necessarily reliable. The National Crime Victimization Survey cannot be used to capture unreported infanticide, as the victims cannot be surveyed.

Victims and Offenders

When dealing with any type of family violence, it has been noted that there is a positive correlation between the age of the victim and the social distance between the victim and the offender. For child homicide cases, this means that the youngest victims are likely to be killed by parents, babysitters, or other caregivers. Of all the age groups, children under the age of 5 are the most likely to be killed by a parent or guardian, in part because these young children spend most of their time with their parents and guardians. Once children reach age 5, they spend more time with people outside the family, which means that other individuals, such as teachers and friends, may be inclined to

notice warning signs of abuse that might lead to murder. The second largest group responsible for infanticide are those persons classified as friends or acquaintances; a group largely comprised of boyfriends of the victims' mothers. Similar to many types of violent crime, a very small percentage of infanticides are committed by strangers.

However, infanticide has some unique characteristics not shared by other types of violent crime. Unlike many other forms of murder, females make up a significant portion of the perpetrators, with many acts being committed by the mother of the victim. Also, nearly all cases result from the child being beaten, strangled, shaken, drowned, or suffocated, which is in sharp contrast to other forms of murder, in which firearms and knives are the most prominent weapons. This is in part due to the vulnerability and relative small physical stature of the victim, who is rendered defenseless against the perpetrator.

Risk Factors

One risk factor associated with infanticide is the age of the parent, and more specifically, the age of the mother. Very young mothers may be experiencing denial, or find themselves overwhelmed or unprepared for their new motherhood role, thus cases of neonaticide are often linked to the young age of the mother. In particular, severe cases of postpartum depression may lead a mother to feel unable to care for her child. Several high-profile cases of murder committed at the hands of the child's mother have brought increased attention to this facet of infanticide.

Other factors, such as poverty, unemployment, and divorce may be indirectly linked to infanticide. These issues often create an increased strain in the household, leading to stress among parents. Parents experiencing higher levels of stress as a result of challenging situations may be violent with their young children and even homicidal. This is not to suggest that "broken" families or those living in poverty are more likely to commit infanticide, however, as other stresses may equally cause other types of families to exhibit risk factors.

One commonality often observed among victims is a history of being abused. Many cases are the result of a pattern of abuse in which the parent or other caregiver was reacting violently to a newborn or child. Among children who are abused, the most frequent cause of death is a physical injury to the head.

There may also be a link between the race of the child and the likelihood of being a victim of infanticide. Black children are disproportionately represented and make up a majority of infanticide victims. In contrast, children who are either White or classified as "other" races make up the minority of reported cases. This may be the result of the issues discussed above, however, such as poverty, unemployment rates, and young parents. These statistics also should be considered with caution because the numbers are based on official police reports and subject to reporting errors.

All of these risk factors contribute to the consideration of infanticide as a social issue. More importantly, it should be understood that the media may play a role in conveying information to the public on these risk factors. As with all violent crime, the news media may disproportionately cover particular stories, especially those that are not the typical case. As such, it may be that stories in which the victims and offenders do not fit the profile of the standard infanticide case are actually more likely to receive widespread media coverage, thereby creating a skewed view of the issue.

Prevention

Because a great number of infanticide cases result from physical injuries inflicted on children by parents or caregivers, preventive measures should focus on these individuals as potential offenders. Possible measures include parenting classes (both before and after the birth of a child) and increased involvement of child protective agencies for cases deemed "at risk." However, like all forms of homicide, infanticide is often situational rather than premeditated. Furthermore, the risk factors associated with infanticide are highly complex, making it difficult to adequately predict potential offenders and victims. Risk factors may be multidimensional, meaning that it may not be psychological or sociological factors alone but combinations of these factors that lead to the crime.

A common response to the issue is child death review teams, which are multidisciplinary investigation teams. These teams are becoming more prevalent, especially in the United States and Canada, and fulfill various duties. Their primary function is often to examine death cases, seeking common patterns. They also often serve as a policy analysis and review board, examining the potential role of Child Protective Services in preventing deaths among children, as well as furthering the understanding of risk factors associated with child homicides and deaths.

In an effort to decrease homicides of infants, many states have passed legislation to allow parents to leave unwanted babies in designated safe locations, such as hospitals or fire stations, without a fear of legal action. These measures may help some of the individuals who are at a high risk of committing infanticide, such as those who do not feel they are economically or psychologically prepared to care for their children. Generally, states allow a grace period for either parent to claim the child before parental rights are terminated.

Punishment

Infanticide is a type of homicide, and is therefore subject to an individual state's or jurisdiction's homicide sanctions. These punishments range in severity, but can include the most severe punishments, such as lifelong prison sentences and capital punishment. Capital punishment statutes may be particularly relevant for infanticide cases, as many states that use the death penalty have specific provisions for those who murder very young victims. Trends in punishment indicate greater leniency for maternal offenders, who often are sentenced to probation or receive suspended sentences, while paternal offenders often receive more harsh punishments.

"Failure to protect" laws may also be used against parents as a means of offering protection to the abused child. Parents who did not murder their child, but who also did not prevent abuse by the offender, can be charged under these laws. These laws are viewed as punishing those who did not murder or abuse the victim, including those suffering from battered woman's syndrome who felt unable to prevent or report the abuse of their children. As such, these laws are controversial and receive mixed levels of support.

Kristine Levan Miller

See also Battered-Child Syndrome; Family and Domestic Violence, Theories of; Family Violence; Homicide, Children and Youth

Further Readings

Finkelhor, D., & Ormrod, R. (2001). Homicides of children and youth (*OJJDP Bulletin*, NCJ187239). Washington, DC: Office of Juvenile Justice and Delinquency Prevention.

Fox, J. A., Levin, J., & Quinet, K. (2008). *The will to kill: Making sense of senseless murder* (pp. 7–81). Boston: Pearson.

Kunz, J., & Bahr, S. J. (1996). A profile of parental homicide against children. *Journal of Family Violence, 11*, 347–362.

Overpeck, M. D., Brenner, R. A., Trumble, A. C., Trifiletti, L. B., & Berendes, H. W. (1998). Risk factors for infant homicide in the United States. *New England Journal of Medicine, 339*, 1211–1216.

Thigpen, S. M., & Bonner, B. L. (1994). Child death review teams in action. *The APSAC Advisor, 7*(4), 5–8.

INNOCENCE PROJECTS

A network of innocence projects has emerged in the United States, Canada, Australia, and the United Kingdom to address the problem of wrongful and unlawful conviction. Driven by the belief that *if the wrong person is put in prison, the actual perpetrator of harm is free to commit more violent crimes*, innocence projects exist to correct miscarriages of justice leading to wrongful and unlawful convictions.

When the wrong person is put in prison, we systemically generate two victims—the actual victim of the original crime and the victim of a conviction for a crime he or she did not commit. This entry explores the role of innocence projects as a vehicle for righting the injustice of wrongful and unlawful conviction.

Definitions

Wrongful and Unlawful Conviction

In the United States, when scholars speak of wrongful and unlawful conviction, they are referring to the conviction of a person who is actually innocent of the crime for which he or she has been charged. Simply put, the person didn't do it; someone else did. Asserting that a *wrongful conviction* has occurred impugns no one. It says nothing about the motivations of law enforcement, prosecutors, defense attorneys, or forensic analysts. By way of contrast, to allege that a suspect has been the victim of an *unlawful conviction* is to identify a case where police officers, prosecutors, and forensic analysts knowingly engaged in illicit behavior. At issue is the question of intention. As human beings, despite our best efforts to the contrary we will make mistakes. In those cases where a criminal justice practitioner professionally, but erroneously, proceeds to convict an actually innocent person, it is referred to as a *wrongful conviction*. Errors of judgment or omission can plague the best investigators, prosecutors, defense attorneys, and analysts. Conversely, to knowingly and willfully participate in the *unlawful* conviction of an innocent man or woman is a pernicious abuse of power, a threat to jurisprudential legitimacy, and a violation of human rights. Innocence projects work to correct both wrongful and unlawful convictions, and try to determine the causes of each.

Legal and Actual Innocence

It is important to distinguish between two common legal references to the notion of "innocence." Attorneys and judges may refer to a defendant as either *legally* innocent or *actually* innocent. The accused in a criminal case can be considered *legally* innocent if he or she has been found "not guilty" by a judge or jury. That is, a jury could not determine beyond a reasonable doubt that the defendant was responsible for committing the crime of which he or she was accused. By way of contrast, actual innocence is the absence of guilt; it is the absence of facts that in any way implicates a suspect with having involvement in a criminal event. Plainly speaking, the accused person who is *actually* innocent was not involved in any way with the planning and carrying out of the crime.

What Is an Innocence Project?

Innocence projects are organizations created for the purpose of investigating cases on post-conviction review (PCR) where actual innocence is being alleged. Post-conviction review is provided for under Rule 32 of the *Federal Criminal Code and Rules,* which provides for judicial consideration of constitutional errors that occurred at trial as well as newly discovered evidence. Innocence projects typically do not get involved in cases prior to the exhaustion of state appeals, so in that way they are seen as the last resort for petitioners who believe they have been wrongfully and unlawfully convicted. Thus far, four innocence project models have emerged in the United States: (1) university based and operating within a law school; (2) university based, combined social science and/or humanities department and law school students and faculty; (3) university based but with no law school affiliation; and (4) community based.

With the exception of the fourth model—the community-based innocence project—the majority of innocence projects operate out of higher educational settings, including both undergraduate and graduate programs. The greatest proportion of innocence projects operate as part of law school clinics. One of the oldest and most successful models combines journalism and law school students at Northwestern University to divide the labor. Undergraduate journalism students investigate cases and turn the case material over to the law school to write PCR briefs. For universities with no law school, but where the faculty expertise exists to operate an innocence project, the third model has proven to be a viable option. At Northern Arizona University in Flagstaff, Arizona, the Northern Arizona Justice Project (NAJP) operates out of the Department of Criminology and Criminal Justice. Both undergraduate and graduate students, primarily in criminology and criminal justice, serve as student investigators. The NAJP receives legal advice and representation from volunteer attorneys living in Northern Arizona. Finally, highly successful innocence projects have operated entirely without university affiliations. Centurion Ministries was established in 1983 and is the longest operating and most successful project in the United States. In addition, the Innocence Project New Orleans is a very successful project that operates by combining the resources of a few paid staff and many volunteer investigators and attorneys.

Presently, there are 60 innocence projects located in 43 U.S. states. In addition, there are innocence projects in Australia, Canada, the United Kingdom, New Zealand, and Germany.

How Do Innocence Projects Work?

Innocence projects have adopted different criteria for the kind of cases they will agree to investigate. Some only investigate cases where DNA is available for testing. These are arguably the "easier" cases to work on, because DNA will determine with some certainty whether or not the petitioner was or was not a participant in the crime for which he or she was accused. However, DNA evidence only exists in about 10% of cases nationally. By far most criminal convictions are obtained without the use of physical evidence. To procure a conviction in these cases, prosecutors rely on some combination of eyewitness testimony, suspect confessions, the testimony of a jailhouse informant (snitch), and ineffective indigent representation. For a host of reasons, these cases are terribly difficult to investigate on post-conviction review. Innocence projects choose what kind of cases they will work on, but most will take both DNA and non-DNA cases.

Innocence projects receive hundreds, and sometimes thousands, of requests for assistance each year. To manage the influx of requests for assistance the projects have extensive screening processes that are used to identify cases where a viable claim of actual innocence exists. While there is local variation, most projects follow the process described below.

Inmate referrals usually appear in the form of a letter from another innocence project, a private attorney, or a family member or friend. If the referral comes from an innocence project, it will most likely include the inmate's initial letter requesting support. A private attorney, family member, or friend might include background information about the inmate's case. Regardless of who refers the case, intake personnel with the innocence project read the letter and, if the inmate is claiming actual innocence, will send a detailed questionnaire to the inmate for completion. The questionnaires are quite similar across the United States and typically seek detailed information about the crime for which the petitioner was convicted, his or her reason for claiming actual innocence, the time remaining on the sentence, information regarding all previous legal counsel and all previous appeals, and a waiver that enables the project to procure documents and speak to case-related people on the petitioner's behalf. In addition, projects request all appellate documents. Once the completed questionnaire and appellate documents are returned to the project, the case is assigned to a student investigator to review. Most cases are rejected at this point in the process (a) for failing to demonstrate that there is a viable claim of actual innocence, (b) because the time remaining on the petitioner's sentence is less than the time it would take to investigate and process a PCR, and (c) due to the perception that there is no way to establish actual innocence (e.g., evidence was destroyed or mishandled or there was no physical evidence).

The students' assessment of the merits of the case is presented at a case-staffing meeting before the project staff and other student investigators. If a decision is made to continue with the case, that is, if the staff is convinced that by virtue of a review of the questionnaire and appellate documents that there is enough doubt about the conviction to continue with the investigation, a follow-up letter will be sent to the petitioner requesting the entire case file. This will include the complete trial transcripts, all police reports, and forensic documents. In short, the innocence project students will receive everything known about the case that was included as part of the written record. Once these materials have been received by the innocence project, the case is assigned to a team of innocence project student investigators. These students will proceed to developing a complete case outline that summarizes key timelines, names, locations, and events. This information is presented to project staff and students for deliberation about ways to proceed with the case investigation. Students are responsible for knowing their cases inside and out. They will be the experts on the case. They will be the ones who must speak with police officers, witnesses, attorneys, and forensic analysts to find out as much as possible about what happened with the case, and whether there is any evidence that the petitioner was wrongfully or unlawfully convicted.

If there is physical evidence available to test, or some other kind of newly discovered evidence or constitutional violation that can be identified for presentation to the court on appeal, briefs will be filed on the petitioner's behalf by the attorneys and students associated with the innocence projects.

Remedies for Wrongful and Unlawful Conviction

Innocence projects not only have committed their time and energy to case investigation, but have also pushed for federal and state-level reforms that will minimize the likelihood of wrongful and unlawful conviction. Nationally, the Innocence Network has created the Innocence Policy Network to work on both state and federal reforms. The Innocence Policy Network played a crucial role in the policy introduction and lobbying efforts that led to passage of the 2004 Justice For All Act that provides for the right to petition for DNA testing, evidence preservation, better training and compensation for death penalty attorneys, increased compensation for wrongfully convicted federal inmates, and funding for independent investigations of state police crime labs. Innocence commissions charged with postmortem review of exoneration cases in order to recommend changes to crime scene investigation and due process have been established in North Carolina, Pennsylvania, Virginia, Illinois, California, Connecticut, and Wisconsin. Barry Scheck and Peter Neufeld have noted that all but eight states have laws allowing postconviction DNA testing, and almost half have provisions for preserving evidence for future analysis. Many jurisdictions have altered other policies dealing with eyewitness identifications and the recording of interrogations.

Innocence projects signify manifestation of a new civil rights movement. By virtue of their existence, across the United States nearly 400 innocent men and women have been freed from prison since 1989. The substantial changes to crime scene investigation, witness and suspect interviewing techniques, crime lab procedures, and improved indigent defense policies have been essential to the projects' success. At bottom, innocence projects are the "canary in the coal mine," revealing serious institutional problems associated with the way criminal cases in the United States are prosecuted.

Robert Schehr

See also Court Advocates

Further Readings

Dow, D. (2005). *Executed on a technicality*. Boston: Beacon.

Findlay, K. (2006). The pedagogy of innocence: Reflections on the role of innocence projects in clinical legal education. *Clinical Law Review, 13,* 231–278.

Medwed, D. (2003). Actual innocents: Considerations in selecting cases for a new innocence project. *Nebraska Law Review, 81,* 1097–1151.

Scheck, B., & Neufeld, P. (2008). *The Innocence Project 2007: Annual report.* Benjamin Cardozo School of Law, Yeshiva University.

Scheck, B., Neufeld, P., & Dwyer, P. (2000). *Actual innocence.* New York: Doubleday.

Schehr, R. (2005). The Criminal Cases Review Commission as state strategic selection mechanism. *American Criminal Law Review, 42*(4), 1289–1302.

Stiglitz, J., Brooks, J., & Shulman, T. (2002). The hurricane meets the paper chase: Innocence projects new emerging role in clinical legal education. *California Western Law Review, 38,* 413–430.

INTERNATIONAL CRIME VICTIMIZATION SURVEY (ICVS)

The International Crime Victimization Survey (ICVS) provides worldwide data on crime victimization, allowing for cross-country comparisons. It comprises standardized sample surveys conducted in several countries. The ICVS was first used in 1989, then repeated in 1992, in 1996, in 2000, and in 2005. The number of countries involved has substantially increased over time, with many countries in Europe, Asia, Latin America, and Africa participating (often with face-to-face samples limited to capital cities). Thus, ICVS has grown to become *the* relevant worldwide source on crime victimization, reporting to the police, and attitudes toward the police, courts, and punishment. Since 1996, the questionnaire has regularly included questions on corruption (bribery) of officials, thus providing a valuable alternative source to the well-known Transparency International index. This entry discusses the background of international crime surveys, the obstacles associated with an international survey, the results and controversies associated with the first multicountry survey, and the future directions of the ICVS.

Background

The first crime surveys used outside the United States were conducted in Zurich, Switzerland; in Stuttgart, Germany; and in the Netherlands. All of these early examples of this American "export" were conducted in 1973. Whereas the Zurich and Stuttgart surveys were joint initiatives of Marshall B. Clinard (University of Wisconsin) and Günther Kaiser (Max Planck Institute of International Criminal Law at Freiburg, Germany) and designed to provide figures that were comparable with the pre-National Crime Survey city surveys, the Dutch survey by J. P. S. Fiselier was a national initiative and ultimately became a permanent survey under the responsibility of the Dutch Statistical Office beginning in 1983. Beyond the Netherlands, national surveys were conducted in England and Wales (beginning in 1981) and in Switzerland (beginning in 1984). Sporadically, surveys were conducted in other European countries, sometimes at the national level, but mostly at city level. Outside of Europe, early crime victimization surveys were conducted in Canada and in Australia.

These surveys, with the exception of the 1973 surveys in Stuttgart and Zurich, were not designed for international comparisons. Richard Block tried to assemble data from some of these surveys in order to compare crime rates and other relevant variables across countries. It turned out, however, that this attempt faced considerable shortcomings due to differences in interview methods, offense definitions, reference periods, and other features of survey methodology. As an alternative, Clinard and J. Junger-Tas proposed to use surveys specifically for purposes of international comparisons. Unlike statistics that by necessity will forever be linked to national offense definitions and processing procedures, survey data could be collected, these authors suggested, through strictly standardized interview methods using identical offense definitions and reference periods.

Obstacles to an International Survey

There remained, however, several practical obstacles to such an international survey, including the development of interview methods that made cost-effective as well as tightly standardized interview methods feasible. The chance to create such an endeavor came through the emergence of computer-assisted telephone interviews (CATI). Starting in the early 1980s, this method became available on a larger scale in Switzerland, due to that country's extremely high telephone penetration rate. Thus, the first Swiss crime surveys of 1984 and 1987 were conducted through CATI by Martin Killias and his team at the University of Lausanne. Although one interview lasted, on average, about 30 minutes, the costs were less than 15% of face-to-face interviews. The results of re-interviewing face-to-face a subsample of seriously victimized respondents showed the high validity of CATI, disconfirming several reservations based on early tests of conventional (i.e., pre-CATI) telephone interviews in the United States. Further, CATI allowed the asking of a large number of questions to a small proportion of respondents through unusually complex questionnaires with many filters. Mail surveys that also were used at that time, even in comparative studies, faced far more limitations in this regard, as did face-to-face surveys where even well-trained interviewers reach limits in handling complex filters. Crime victimization surveys collect much "trivial" information (e.g., on lifestyle, leisure-time activities, and the possession of vehicles). Disclosing such details does not require much thinking on the part of the respondent and thus does not justify the investment required for a personal encounter.

There was, in addition, a further difficulty faced by all European crime victimization surveys up to that point: The surveys were vulnerable to "telescoping" (i.e., the reporting of victimizations experienced before the adopted reference period, which was usually one year preceding the interview). Early American pilot studies, such as those summarized in the volume edited by Wesley Skogan, revealed that many incidents are forgotten after a couple of months, a fact that led to the adoption of the "bounding" design. With this design, the same respondents are re-interviewed every 6 months and the interviewer is aware of the victimizations a respondent reported during the preceding interview. In Europe, this extremely cost-intensive method has never been adopted. The Dutch and the Swiss crime surveys adopted a different approach, namely asking the respondent first whether he or she had experienced the victimization during the last 5 years (or *ever*), and, if so, when the incident had happened. This design has the following advantages: (1) respondents regularly

devote a lot of attention to temporal and/or geographic limitations if the "when" and "where" questions are kept out of screening questions with quasi-legal definitions; (2) any respondent who may feel frustrated when learning that his or her victimization, although very serious, is not relevant in the context of the survey because it occurred shortly before the reference period, has an opportunity to tell the interviewer his or her full story; (3) even if the focus is on a shorter period, collecting data on serious offenses over a longer period is helpful because it increases the absolute number of such cases to more reasonable levels—a fact that is particularly important if, as happens mostly outside the United States, samples are not particularly large; (4) having data over a period exceeding 12 months is critical if the way the victim's case was handled by the police, insurance companies, victim support schemes, prosecutors, and courts is being measured.

First Multicountry Survey

The experience with CATI in Switzerland circulated within a Council of Europe committee on the position and rights of victims in the criminal procedure. Jan van Dijk, who directed the Dutch Ministry of Justice Research and Documentation Center, formed a working group in 1988 to discuss the feasibility of an international crime victimization survey. This working group opted for CATI, primarily because it allows a tighter standardization of data collection than any other method—a critical advantage in international surveys. The group further adopted a reference period of 5 years, with a follow-up question asking the respondent to locate the (last) incident more precisely in space and time (with special interest in the last year). There is no doubt, however, that the low costs of CATI interviews were critical when Europe's governments were approached, through the Dutch Ministry of Justice, to join by funding their national samples. For 1,000 or 2,000 interviews (i.e., the standard sample sizes proposed), the budget was affordable for 11 European countries, the United States, Canada, and Australia. For most of these countries, it was the first crime victimization survey ever conducted. The fieldwork was carried out during spring of 1989, and key results were published by van Dijk, Patricia Mayhew, and Martin Killias in 1990.

Controversies

The results of this first truly multicountry crime survey in criminology were controversial from the beginning, particularly in the Netherlands, where crime was higher than in most other European countries. Criticisms centered on the validity of CATI, the 5-year reference period, and a few offense definitions. Over the following years, these criticisms were addressed in several experimental tests. For example, Annette Scherpenzeel found identical victimization rates on two Dutch samples, interviewed through either CATI or "telepanel" (i.e., an early form of electronic questionnaires). Randomized experiments by Helmut Kury in Bochum and Erfurt, Germany, confirmed that victimization rates do not differ across interview method. The conclusion was more mixed, however, with respect to questions on attitudes (toward the police, punishment, etc.), where Kury observed some social desirability bias.

Scherpenzeel's experiment included a test of the two reference periods. The results showed that a straight 12-month reference period (often used in crime surveys) produced, for burglary and robbery, rates 2.5 and 2.2 times those obtained with the ICVS format (where respondents are first asked about incidents experienced over 5 years, before a more precise indication of the time of occurrence is required). More recent experiments regarding surveys on self-reported delinquency (such as in Sonia Lucia and her colleagues' 2007 article, "How Important Are Interview Methods and Questionnaire Designs in Research on Self-Reported Juvenile Delinquency?") confirmed that telescoping former incidents into the 12-month reference period is a severe and largely underestimated threat to the validity of survey estimates, particularly in countries with low crime rates, such as Japan. Some newly developed surveys, such as the national crime victimization surveys in Sweden, ignore this experimental evidence and persist in asking respondents about events experienced "over the last year." Even more surprising, the British Crime Survey has never considered experimentally testing its 12-month reference period, and it has expanded its sample to 40,000 respondents. Clearly, it is more difficult to control this problem in surveys than in face-to-face interviews where interviewers can devote more attention to geographic and temporal mapping.

Another controversy associated with the ICVS is that it has never included questions on the ethnic identity of victims and offenders, nor on certain explanatory variables (e.g., low performance of governmental services as a source of corruption). Despite all these controversies, the basic methodology has been adopted in other major international surveys, such as the first international survey on violence against women, which was coordinated by Holly Johnson, Natalia Ollus, and Sami Nevala.

Future Directions

At present, it is uncertain whether the European Union (through EUROSTAT) is going to conduct an independent survey, and, if so, how that will affect the ICVS. Challenges to CATI will come from the increasing popularity of cell phones and the decreasing number of households with fixed phones. A combined approach that, as the first choice, uses Internet questionnaires and, in a second stage, interviews nonrespondents through CATI, face-to-face, or mail questionnaires might be a suitable solution. After all, several experiments have shown that interview methods are far less important than the way questions are asked. Pragmatic solutions may, therefore, be best for keeping this unique data collection initiative alive.

Martin Killias

See also British Crime Survey (BCS); Calculating Extent of Victimization: Incidence, Prevalence, and Rates; Comparative Victimology; International Violence Against Women Survey (IVAWS); Victimization Surveys

Further Readings

Block, R. (1993). Cross-national comparison of victims of crime: Victim surveys in twelve countries. *International Review of Victimology*, 2(3), 183–207.

Clinard, M. B. (1978). *Cities with little crime: The case of Switzerland*. Cambridge, UK: Cambridge University Press.

Clinard, M. B., & Junger-Tas, J. (1979). Probleme und resultate beim vergleich internationaler victim surveys [Problems and findings in comparing international victim surveys]. In G. F. Kirchhoff & K. Sessar, *Das verbreechensopfer* [The victim of crime] (pp. 159–176). Bochum, Germany: Studienverlag Brockmeyer.

Fiselier, J. P. S. (1978). *Slachtoffers van delicten: Een onderzoek naar verborgen criminaliteit* [Victims of crime: A study on unrecorded offenses]. Utrecht, the Netherlands: Ars Aequi Libri.

Johnson, H., Ollus, N., & Nevala, S. (2008). *Violence against women: An international perspective.* New York: Springer.

Killias, M. (1989). *Les Suisses face au crime* [The Swiss and their experiences with and attitudes toward crime]. Grüsch, Switzerland: Rüegger.

Kury, H. (1994). Zum einfluss der art der datenerhebung auf die ergebnisse von umfragen [On the impact of data collection methods on survey outcomes]. *Monatsschrift für Kriminologie und Strafrechtsreform, 77*(1), 22–33.

Lucia, S., Herrmann, L., & Killias, M. (2007). How important are interview methods and questionnaire designs in research on self-reported juvenile delinquency? An experimental comparison of Internet vs. paper-and-pencil questionnaires and different definitions of the reference period. *Journal of Experimental Criminology, 3*(1), 39–64.

Scherpenzeel, A. (1992). Response effecten in slachtofferenquêtes: Effecten van vraagformulering en dataverzamelingsmethode [Response effects in victim surveys: The impact of formulating items and data collection methods]. *Tijdschrift voor Criminologie, 34*(4), 296–305.

Skogan, W. G. (1981). *Issues in the measurement of victimization.* Washington, DC: U.S. Government Printing Office.

van Dijk, J. J. M., van Kesteren, J., & Smit, P. (2007). *Criminal victimization in international perspective.* Tilburg, the Netherlands: University of Tilburg.

van Dijk, J. J. M., Mayhew, P., & Killias, M. (1990). *Experiences of crime across the world.* Deventer, the Netherlands: Kluwer.

INTERNATIONAL VIOLENCE AGAINST WOMEN SURVEY (IVAWS)

The past two decades have seen rapid growth both in the number of population-based surveys interviewing women about their experiences of male violence and in the sophistication of the methods used. To date, targeted surveys designed to assess the extent and nature of women's experiences of violence have been conducted in at least 70 countries worldwide. Random sample survey data are preferable to police statistics or records of hospitals or other services, because the majority of assaulted women do not use criminal justice or social services and therefore are not counted in official statistics.

There is growing interest among policy makers and researchers in comparing levels of male violence against women, the consequences of this violence for women and their children, and common explanatory factors at the international level. Internationally comparative data have the potential to make several important contributions, including investigating universal or cross-cultural traits associated with male violence against women; assisting with the implementation of international agreements and norms; assisting participating countries in better understanding the dimensions and contexts of the violence in order to better target aid efforts; planning interventions and services; raising public awareness and debate; implementing legislative change; and, developing research skills and technical expertise at the local level. These activities can be the impetus for social change on a broader scale than is possible with national-level surveys.

Building on lessons learned in conducting national-level surveys in a number of countries, there have been three major initiatives to improve the comparability of statistical data on this topic at the international level. Two have as a primary focus the impact of violence on health: the Demographic and Health Surveys (DHS), which is conducted with the support of MACRO International and the U.S. Agency for International Development, and the Multi-country Study on Women's Health and Violence Against Women which is coordinated through the World Health Organization. A third is the International Violence Against Women Survey (IVAWS), which was developed to respond to the need for internationally comparative data on the prevalence and effects of male violence against women and victims' interactions with the criminal justice system. This entry explores the methodology and challenges of the IVAWS and the potential for surveys of this nature to contribute to international efforts to combat violence against women.

Methodology

The IVAWS has so far been fielded in 11 countries and comparative analysis has been conducted with

9 of those countries. Participating countries and the sample sizes in each country are Australia (6,677), Costa Rica (908), Czech Republic (1,980), Denmark (3,589), Greece (interviewing continuing), Hong Kong (1,297), Italy (25,000), Mozambique (2,015), Philippines (2,602), Poland (2,009), and Switzerland (1,973).

Greece and Italy were not included in the international comparative analysis because their surveys were underway at the time of writing. Each participating country was responsible for fundraising, and in most countries funding was obtained from government sources or some other national fund (e.g., in Mozambique, the survey was cofunded by three United Nations agencies). The selection of countries to participate in the IVAWS was thus in large part determined by the success of individual countries' fundraising efforts.

A mix of telephone and face-to-face interviewing was used. In Australia, Denmark, Hong Kong, Italy, and Switzerland, interviews were conducted over the telephone; in the remaining countries, face-to-face interviews were conducted. Decisions about the mode of interviewing were left to project coordinators in each country and depended on practical matters such as telephone coverage, the budget, and the type of sampling frame available in each country (e.g., households versus banks of working telephone numbers).

The key to ensuring comparability among surveys fielded in different countries is to develop and maintain a standardized approach throughout all components of the project. Thus a standardized questionnaire was developed for the IVAWS through collaboration with project coordinators and field tested in 13 countries. The questionnaire was prepared in English and project coordinators arranged for translation, first into the language of their country then back into English as a way of verifying the accuracy of the translation. Training for project coordinators was centralized, and each project coordinator was provided with a data capture system and a comprehensive manual outlining all steps of the survey methodology. Included in the manual are guidelines regarding budgeting, the skill sets required to form a research team, the technical facilities required for capturing and processing data, the recruitment and training of interviewers, sampling procedures to ensure random selection of respondents, and administering the questionnaire in order to minimize errors, as well as instructions on coding, entering, and validating the data.

A range of ethical considerations must be taken into account when interviewing women on sensitive topics such as intimate partner violence and sexual assault. Training for project coordinators for the IVAWS emphasized the importance of following strict ethical guidelines at all stages of the project. These include protecting confidentiality, ensuring the safety of respondents, careful selection and specialized training and support for interviewers, reducing distress to participants and interviewers, responding to distress by referring respondents to available local services and sources of support, and helping to ensure that research findings are properly interpreted and used to advance policy and interventions.

An important end result of the IVAWS is the transfer of technical expertise and research skills to some countries where none might have existed previously. In such countries, where there is little reliable information on the extent of men's violence against women, participation in the IVAWS can also serve as a basis for raising public awareness, debate, and national and local action. In countries where there have been prior prevalence surveys on violence against women, the IVAWS offers the possibility of international comparisons. International comparative research, like the IVAWS, facilitates comparability among countries and cultures and is an essential component to finding international as well as local remedies and responses to violence against women.

Measuring Violence Against Women

Research has shown that surveys that use specific behavioral measures of a range of types of violent acts will produce more reliable and valid estimates than surveys that employ general all-encompassing terms such as *violence* or *assault*. This is because individual respondents can hold different ideas of what constitutes violence or assault and may be reluctant to include assaults by acquaintances, family members, and intimate partners if not questioned about them in particular. The prevalence of physical violence is estimated on the IVAWS through the following items:

1. Threatened to hurt you physically in a way that frightened you

2. Threw something at you or hit you with something that hurt or frightened you

3. Pushed or grabbed you or twisted your arm or pulled your hair in a way that hurt or frightened you

4. Slapped, kicked, bit or hit you with a fist

5. Tried to strangle or suffocate you, burn or scald you on purpose

6. Used or threatened to use a knife or gun on you

7. Physically violent toward you in a way not already mentioned

The prevalence of sexual violence is measured through the following items:

1. Forced you into sexual intercourse by threatening you, holding you down, or hurting you in some way

2. Attempted to force you into sexual intercourse by threatening you, holding you down or hurting you in some way

3. Touched you sexually when you did not want him to in a way that was distressing to you

4. Forced or attempted to force you into sexual activity with someone else, including being forced to have sex for money or in exchange for goods

5. Sexually violent toward you in a way not already mentioned

Results of the IVAWS in nine countries show the following:

- In the majority of countries studied, between 35% and 60% of women experienced physical or sexual violence by a man since age 16.
- In most countries, between 22% and 40% of women have been physically or sexually assaulted by an intimate partner.
- Between 10% and 31% of women have been sexually assaulted by a man other than an intimate partner.

The IVAWS identified certain factors that are correlated with women's victimization. In multivariate analysis, the following were found to be significant predictors of intimate partner violence:

- Male partners used emotionally abusive or controlling behaviors.
- Male partners were heavy drinkers.
- Male partners used violence toward others outside the home.
- Male partners were abused in childhood or witnessed their fathers' violence.
- Women were abused in childhood or witnessed their fathers' violence.

These findings suggest that appropriate policy responses aimed at reducing violence against women should include targeting social norms that equate masculinity with alcohol abuse, with the use of violence inside and outside the home, and with subordination and control of their female partners. Targeted interventions to prevent child abuse may have the effect of reducing violence against women if fewer women and men grow up affected by the long-term damaging effects of child abuse. Reducing intimate partner violence should have intergenerational benefits as well, by reducing the number of children who are witnesses to violence and who learn that violence is an acceptable way to solve problems in intimate relationships. Reducing public violence by men may have spill-over benefits by also reducing violence against their female partners, and vice versa.

Reporting to the Police

In all countries studied, it was found that less than one third of women who were assaulted by an intimate partner report the violence to the police, and in all but one the figure was less than 20%. Even in cases where the violence or threats of violence were so severe the women feared their lives were in danger, 40% or fewer women in all countries called on the criminal justice system for help.

Societal-level attitudes and a culture that views intimate partner violence as acceptable can be major obstacles to ensuring that women receive the help they need to end the violence. A minority of women in all countries considered intimate partner violence to constitute a crime. Victims were more likely to consider the violence to be wrong but not a crime, or just something that happens. But, even among those who considered the violence to be a crime, less than 40% reported such violence to the police in all but one country. This suggests that women tend to take into account a broader range of considerations than their own personal safety and the criminal nature of these acts, and that they do not always see engagement with the criminal justice system as the most effective strategy for ending the violence. It also points to the need for criminal justice agencies to engage abused women and their advocates in a continuous process of reviewing and improving their policies, training, and interventions strategies.

Challenges of Internationally Comparative Survey Research

Internationally comparative survey research poses many challenges for researchers. In addition to the ethical and logistical challenges associated with interviewing on sensitive topics, cross-national research is influenced by other complexities. For example, there will be differences in the extent to which women are familiar and at ease with responding to surveys and describing their experiences to a stranger in the context of an interview. Differences in culture can affect attitudes toward women and violence, norms protecting family privacy, and ideals and practices of masculinity. Norms that prevent women from speaking out about violence may affect their willingness to name their experiences in terms employed by the survey. Norms that endorse the use of physical and sexual violence against women can be affected by the political context, including the presence of war and conflict, displacement of populations, availability of weapons, and widespread use of violence to solve social problems. There also will be variation in the meaning of physical or sexual assault for individual women depending on their past experience and social situation, and this is bound to exist to a greater extent in cross-national comparative studies where societal-level differences are greater. There are additional challenges in ensuring that translation of the questionnaire and other survey materials into a variety of languages does not affect the results, since certain concepts may not translate well or may be misinterpreted.

Although every effort was made to adhere to rigorous scientific principles in designing, testing,

and conducting the IVAWS, it is difficult to anticipate and control for all the complexities that can arise in cross-national research. While survey designers do their best to ensure that the questions are clear and unambiguous and that they are thoroughly tested on a diverse group of women, in the end respondents will perceive their experiences to fit into the survey categories or they will not. They will perceive some benefit in reporting their experiences and disclose them to interviewers, or they will perceive some risk and choose to keep them private. Because of the importance of the survey results for formulating policy and for public awareness of the breadth of the problem, researchers must continue to search for ways to improve cross-national research methodologies.

Holly Johnson and Sami Nevala

See also British Crime Survey (BCS); International Crime Victimization Survey (ICVS); National Crime Victimization Survey (NCVS); National Victimization Against College Women Surveys; National Violence Against Women Survey (NVAWS)

Further Readings

Ellsberg, M., & Heise, L. (2005). *Researching violence against women: A practical guide for researchers and activists*. Washington DC: World Health Organization, PATH.

Garcia-Moreno, C., Jansen, H., Ellsberg, H., Heise, L., & Watts, C. (2005). *WHO multi-country study on women's health and domestic violence against women*. Geneva: World Health Organization.

Johnson, H., Ollus, N., & Nevala, S. (2008). *Violence against women: An international perspective*. New York: Springer.

INTERNET FRAUD

Internet fraud includes a wide range of illegal behaviors in which various facets of the Internet play an integral role in the transmission of intentionally deceptive and/or false representations for personal or organizational gain. Acts of Internet fraud typically involve the transfer of currency, goods and services, or personal and intellectual property across this interconnected set of computers via applications, including the World Wide Web, email, chat rooms, or software (e.g., online gaming). Rather than being perpetrated face-to-face, Internet fraud is usually perpetrated through lines of network communication that serve to spatially separate the offender from the victim. Since the use of computers or computer networks is an important locus of the illegal act, Internet fraud is considered a special subcategory of cybercrime.

The Nature of Internet Fraud

Most acts of Internet fraud involve the use of deception or false claims that serve to make the behaviors illegal under most circumstances. The legality of Internet fraud is also likely to vary across jurisdictions, especially transnationally. For example, Internet conduct or business dealings considered lawful in Barbados may be deemed illicit in the United States. Describing the nature of Internet fraud is largely a subjective endeavor and entirely contingent on both the circumstances of the crime and the jurisdiction under which the act takes place. Some of the most widely cited types of Internet fraud common to the United States include the following:

Advance fee scams. Offenders promise to disburse significant monetary payoffs to unsuspecting consumers who are to receive such funds after making advance payments of smaller sums of money to the offender. While any number of story lines may be used as a backdrop for an advance fee scam, money is essentially transferred or given to perpetrators under the false promise that they will compensate the consumer at a higher rate in the future. Included in these scams are job offers, inheritance offers, money offers, prize, sweepstakes, lottery offers, and sweetheart swindles.

Credit card fraud. Many Web sites often require consumers to share credit card information at a variety of locations on the Internet to obtain access to the sites' restricted content, or for the purchase of various goods and services. Offenders involved with these sites may then use transferred consumer credit card information for purposes other than those intended by the consumer.

Fake check scams. Offenders fraudulently claiming to be legitimate consumers may overpay unsuspecting individuals with counterfeit checks for goods and services purchased. In turn, offenders will ask the seller to send or wire the overage amount back. The counterfeit check will then bounce, and the seller could potentially lose the product, purchase price of the product, and overage amount from the check as well.

Identity theft. Identity theft can be perpetrated in many ways, but it generally occurs when offenders obtain access to an unsuspecting individual's personal information and identification, via the Internet, with the intention of using it for personal or organizational gain.

Investment scams/Ponzi schemes. Consumers are lured by falsely advertised claims of little-to-no risk and large returns on particular investment opportunities. Once consumers pay to invest in these products or services, they may receive less than initially advertised or their funds may not have been used to actually invest in any product or service. Offenders may profit from initial investment dollars or may invest the funds for themselves, resulting in a future gains.

Multilevel marketing/pyramid schemes. Under the guise of a credible business model, consumers pay for the ability to distribute goods or services to the public by paying for distribution access to members of the scheme. Offenders may profit merely from signing unsuspecting consumers up as distributors, while never delivering on the promise of any goods or services.

Phishing scams. Offenders may mimic respectable sources via emails, Web sites, or advertisements asking unsuspecting persons to confirm or transfer personal information to the illegitimate location and then use the information later for fraudulent purposes.

Online sales or auction fraud. Offenders engage in the nondelivery of payment, merchandise, or services through online sales or auction Web sites (e.g., eBay) to consumers who lawfully sold, paid, or bartered for such goods or services. To date, online sales fraud, followed closely by auction fraud, is the most commonly cited type of Internet fraud.

Travel/vacation fraud. Consumers are promised a particular set of amenities or accommodations upon payment, but receive lower-quality services or receive numerous hidden charges at the time of travel or vacation.

Extent and Cost of Internet Fraud

Conservative estimates place the number of Internet users in the United States at well over a hundred million adults, a figure that will likely continue upward. As the number of Internet users across the entire globe continues to rise, the amount of Internet fraud is likely to increase as well. Anyone who sends information across the Internet is susceptible to Internet fraud. Unlike conventional criminal acts that often result because of the convergence of offenders and victims in time and space, Internet crimes involve temporally and spatially separated offenders and the potential for victimization is always present.

Each year, as part of a collective effort of the Federal Bureau of Investigation and National White Collar Crime Center, the Internet Crime Complaint Center releases an annual report detailing the amount and scope of Internet fraud perpetrated against U.S. citizens. According to results from the 2008 report, Internet fraud complaints jumped nearly 30% from 2007 to 2008. Moreover, almost a third of all offenses reported through Internet fraud complaints in 2008 had to do with the nondelivery of merchandise or payment, while nearly a quarter of complaints concerned Internet auction fraud (e.g., eBay). Both crime categories contributed to substantial growth in the number of filed Internet fraud complaints, up from just over 200,000 grievances in 2007 to more than 275,000 for the 2008 calendar year.

Despite mounting rates of Internet fraud complaints, it is likely the full extent of Internet fraud committed each year is vastly underestimated. This may in part be due to underreporting of fraudulent Internet activities. Underreporting is associated with the nature of the Internet itself and with individuals' uncertainty about where to turn concerning charges of Internet fraud.

While the dollar costs associated with Internet fraud were estimated by the Internet Crime Complaint Center report to exceed $260 million for 2008, it is possible the estimated cost figures have also been heavily influenced by the underreporting of fraudulent Internet activities. The actual costs associated with Internet fraud are likely far greater than even the best estimates available.

Prevention of Internet Fraud

Because Internet fraud can take many different forms, prevention strategies are situationally contingent on the operating environment of both the offender and the victim. Unlike the situational environment for conventional crimes, Internet crimes present a particular set of problems, specifically with regard to the location of crimes, namely, cyberspace. Situational crime prevention methods, those that recognize and address opportunities specific to Internet fraud, present users with a viable fraud prevention strategy.

In an effort to prevent and combat Internet fraud, the Internet Crime Complaint Center provides local, state, and federal law enforcement and regulatory agencies in the United States with information contained in Internet criminal complaints to assist their investigations, make the public more aware of the growing Internet crime problem, and reduce victimization through Internet fraud. Beyond existing U.S. laws and regulations, the existence of an organized set of preventive regulatory and enforcement strategies has been elusive where Internet crimes are concerned. Law enforcement and regulatory agencies have not been provided with adequate resources or the technology training required to effectively combat the growing Internet crime problem. Consequently, little collaboration exists among agencies, as agencies are ill equipped to confront Internet fraud and adapt to the changing landscape of cybercrime

From the perspective of the individual, several situational crime prevention strategies may be helpful in reducing, while not altogether eliminating, the risks associated with Internet use. Specifically, strategies that involve increasing the difficulty of perpetrating an Internet crime, decreasing the benefits and rewards of an offender's engaging in an act, and helping individuals make themselves less attractive targets may be considered the only practical solutions. These may be partially accomplished through the use of firewalls and antispyware/antivirus programs, as well as by educating individuals to be extremely cautious with how and with whom they share personal information when using the Internet.

William A. Stadler

See also Cybercrime, Prevention of; Cyber and Internet Offenses; Cyberstalking; Exploitation by Scams; Identity Theft; White-Collar Crime

Further Readings

Burns, R. G., Whitworth, K. H., & Thompson, C. Y. (2004). Assessing law enforcement preparedness to address Internet fraud. *Journal of Criminal Justice, 32*(5), 477–493.

Ehlen, C. C., Holtfreter, R. E., Langione, J., & Green, A. M. (2005). Fraudsters in cyberspace: Growing global Internet menace, part 1. *Fraud Magazine, 19*(4), 32–35, 60–61.

Holtfreter, R. E., & Ehlen, C. C. (2005). Fraudsters in cyberspace: Growing global Internet menace, part 2. *Fraud Magazine, 19*(5). 32–35, 51–53.

McQuade, S. C. (2006). *Understanding and managing cybercrime.* Boston: Allyn & Bacon.

Newman, G. R., & Clarke, R. V. (2003). *Superhighway robbery: Crime prevention in the Ecommerce environment.* Cullompton, UK: Willan.

Wall, D. S. (2007). *Cybercrime: The transformation of crime in the information age.* Cambridge, UK: Polity.

INTIMATE PARTNER VIOLENCE

Generally speaking, intimate partner violence (IPV) occurs when an individual in an intimate relationship intentionally harms the other person in the relationship. In the 1960s and 1970s, intimate partner violence was increasingly recognized as a problem across the world. Attention from researchers first surfaced when domestic violence advocates called attention to the plight of women victimized by their partners or spouses. Advocates pointed out that victims were being treated poorly by criminal justice officials, and few services were available to help victims of partner violence. Victimologists began to focus on domestic violence to help advance the area of study beyond the discipline's traditional victim precipitation orientation. The issue quickly moved from being an issue that no one talked about to being recognized as a social problem warranting significant attention from researchers, policy makers, academics, practitioners, and advocates.

Since that time, many have accepted that intimate partner violence is a problem that needs to be addressed by different disciplines and practitioners. Most agree that the best response to intimate partner violence involves what is called a "multidisciplinary" or "integrated" response. This means that several different agencies are involved in the preventing and responding to intimate partner violence. Indeed, intimate partner violence is no longer viewed as a family problem that should remain hidden within the confines of victims' homes; rather, intimate partner violence is now regarded as a global public health problem. Fully understanding the integrated response required to address intimate partner violence involves knowledge of the following areas: the types of intimate partner violence, the extent of the violence, the dynamics and patterns surrounding such violence, and the causes of intimate partner violence.

Types

Intimate partner violence is typically categorized as one of three varieties: (1) physical assault, (2) sexual assault, or (3) psychological assault. Physical assaults include a range of behaviors (hitting, kicking, biting, stabbing, shooting, pushing, grabbing, shoving, and so on) that have the potential to result in bodily injury to the victim. Sexual assaults include rape and noncontact offenses such as voyeurism and forced exhibitionism. Psychological assault includes a range of behaviors in which offenders use verbal or psychological tactics to harm their partners.

Extent

After a review of studies conducted across the world, reporter Sheila Hotchkin concluded that worldwide one in three women have been victims of violence. Similar estimates have been found in the United States. The National Violence Against Women Survey, jointly funded by the National Institute of Justice and the Centers for Disease Control and Prevention, is among the most comprehensive studies focusing on issues related to intimate partner violence. Led by investigators Patricia Tjaden and Nancy Thoennes, this project involved phone surveys with 8,000 women and 8,000 men. Respondents were asked about their experiences with different forms of violence, including rape, physical assault, and stalking/harassment. The findings of this national survey related the following:

- 7.7% of women reported being raped by an intimate partner
- 22.1% of women were physically assaulted in their lifetime, and 1.3 million reported being physically assaulted in the preceding 12 months.
- 5% of women reported being stalked in their lifetime, and more than 500,000 reported being stalked in the preceding 12 months

Some researchers have argued that intimate partner violence against men is just as pervasive, if not more pervasive, than intimate partner violence against women. Results of a few studies have shown that a high number of men have been abused by their partners. Critics of these studies point to three problems that call into question the utility of the body of research showing males have higher rates of intimate partner violence. First, many of the studies finding higher rates of intimate partner violence victimization among males have used Murray Strauss's Conflict Tactics Scale. This scale has been criticized for failing to consider the context surrounding victimization and measuring acts that are not universally defined as violence. Second, critics have suggested that violence by women against men is often for self-defense in response to violent actions initiated by an aggressive male partner. Third, critics point out that violence by women is typically of a relatively minor form, at least in comparison to violence by men against women. Simply put, sheer physical strength differences mean that men do more physical harm to women than women do to men. This is not to suggest that intimate partner violence against men is not an issue. Certainly a number of men are victimized and they warrant appropriate services; however, the vast majority of serious intimate partner violence cases appear to be instances where men abuse women.

Dynamics and Patterns

Researchers have devoted a great deal of effort to understanding the dynamics and patterns surrounding intimate partner violence. This research has been useful in generating a description of the nature of intimate partner violence. Patterns and dynamics that have been uncovered are listed below and described in the paragraphs that follow. They include the following:

- The chronic nature of intimate partner violence
- The cycle of violence
- The duration of intimate partner violence
- The battered woman syndrome
- The characteristics of batterers

The *chronic nature of intimate partner violence* has been demonstrated by the National Survey of Violence Against Women, which found that more than half of women sexually assaulted by their partners, and two thirds of those physically assaulted by their partners, were victimized by their partners on multiple occasions. Clearly, intimate partner violence is typically not a one-time incident. Further, in *Policing Domestic Violence*, Lawrence Sherman supports these findings. He argued that a vast majority of domestic violence incidents are committed by a small number of offenders.

Another pattern surrounding intimate partner violence is the *cycle of violence*. This concept recognizes that intimate partner violence does not happen every single day of a victim's life. Originally created by Lenore Walker, the cycle of violence explanation suggests that violence is part of a cycle involving a series of stages. First, during the honeymoon phase, the abusers treat their partners as if they are newlyweds. Gifts, promises of a lifetime of commitment, and romantic displays of affection are frequent. Second, during the tension-building phase, the relationship transitions to one in which angst and disagreements become more frequent. Third, the battering episode stage occurs when the abuser acts out aggressively against the victim. This is followed by the honeymoon phase, during which the abuser "makes up" for his harmful actions.

A related pattern has to do with the *duration of intimate partner violence*. Generally, these actions occur over time. Because of the offender's ability to convince victims that the abuse will stop, victims are sometimes reluctant to leave their abuser. Of course, it is not just the abuser's "charm" that keeps victims in violent relationships. Often, others will ask, "Why doesn't she leave?" when they think of intimate partner violence incidents. Four responses to this question are worth nothing. First, rather than asking, "Why doesn't she leave?" one could ask, "Why doesn't *he* leave?" Why is it that the woman should be expected to be the one to leave? After all, the abuser is ultimately responsible for the abuse. Expecting the victim to leave inadvertently places responsibility on the victim rather than the abuser.

Second, in considering the patterns surrounding leaving domestic violence relationships, an oft-quoted saying from domestic violence advocates comes to mind: "Leaving is a process, not an event." Intimate partner violence victims do leave their abusive relationships. It just takes time for them to leave. A commonly cited estimate suggests that women leave abusive relationships for good after being physically abused between seven and eight times.

Third, some researchers have suggested that asking "why" women don't leave violent relationships holds very little utility in terms of broadening our understanding about intimate partner violence. In their 2005 book *Family Violence and Criminal Justice*, criminologists Brian K. Payne and Randy R. Gainey noted that it is more appropriate to ask *how* women stay in abusive relationships than *why* they stay.

Fourth, domestic violence victims stay in violent relationships for a number of reasons that help to explain why leaving these relationships is so difficult. The National Coalition Against Domestic Violence cites barriers such as lack of resources, institutional responses, and traditional ideologies as making it difficult for victims to leave violent relationships. Lack of resources can be an enormous obstacle to leaving an abusive partner, as victimized women typically do not have the resources required to leave and create a new household on their own. Many intimate partner violence victims have at least one dependent child, and obtaining the financial resources they need to take care of their children can be virtually impossible on their own. Because of the dynamics of control in their intimate relationship, many of these women may not hold jobs.

In addition, the responses of institutions designed to protect women from harm may inadvertently contribute to continued violence. Police officers may not be aware of strategies to help victims or services available. They may actually tell victims that they should simply stay in their relationship and make up with their partner. Helping professionals—like social services professionals, clergy, and counselors—may fail to recognize the abuse. Even when they see it, they may be unaware of effective ways to help women in these relationships.

Traditional ideology also keeps women in abusive relationships. Many battered women grew up in families where their fathers abused their mothers. They are socialized to believe in marriage at all costs. Women may rationalize the abuser's actions as part of a typical marriage, or they may convince themselves that the abuse is not that serious.

Cultural factors may also keep women in these relationships. For some individuals from different cultures, intimate partner violence is something that cannot be disclosed to any outside sources. Describing this phenomenon, the Family Violence Prevention Fund noted that battered immigrant women experience many barriers to leaving abusive relationships. Overriding cultural values from the woman's home culture may conflict with American values, creating conflict between adhering to different sets of values.

Related to the fact that intimate partner violence is often chronic, experts recognize that *battered woman syndrome* is a consequence of this violence for some women. The psychological effects of intimate partner violence can be devastating for victims. The combination of the psychological effects, according to domestic violence expert Lenore Walker in her classic work *The Battered Woman Syndrome*, has the capacity to lead to the syndrome, which is a type of posttraumatic stress disorder. According to Walker, the syndrome is produced by trauma due to repeated experiences of different forms of domestic violence. The foundation of the syndrome includes (1) the flight response and (2) cognitive impairments from the abuse. This syndrome, which is also termed *battering and its effects*, is well accepted in the medical field and in disciplines such as psychology, social work, and counseling. It is sometimes used as a legal defense in murder cases in which women explain their homicides against their abusers by suggesting that their years of abuse caused them to fear for their lives and act out violently toward their abusers.

Another pattern or dynamic in intimate partner violence has to do with the characteristics of batterers. Indeed, to fully understand the dynamics surrounding intimate partner violence, it is imperative that one has understanding about batterers. According to the Centers for Disease Control and Prevention, three types of batterers exist. These include the following:

- The *family only batterer,* who may perpetrate less severe violence, use relatively little psychological or sexual abuse, and display few or no symptoms of psychopathology
- The *dysphoric/borderline batterer,* who may perpetrate moderate to severe violence, mostly confined to the family, and may be generally distressed, dysphoric, or emotionally volatile
- The *generally violent/antisocial batterer,* who may engage in moderate to severe intimate partner violence and, of the three types of batterers, the most extrafamilial violence; the batterer also may have the most extensive history of criminal involvement, alcohol, and drug abuse, as well as antisocial personality disorder or psychopathology

National organizations have provided guidance in further understanding the characteristics of batterers. The American Bar Association, for example, has provided the following characteristics of batterers:

- Batterers discourage victims from getting help.
- Batterers frequently insist on accompanying victims everywhere.
- Batterers harass, stalk, and keep tabs on their victims.
- Batterers isolate victims from their friends, family, and acquaintances.
- Batterers keep victims from working.

Note that each of these characteristics makes it more difficult to leave violent relationships. Also providing insight into the characteristics of batterers, the National Coalition Against Domestic Violence noted that batterers (1) objectify women; (2) have low self-esteem, feel powerless and inadequate, and externalize the causes of their behavior; (3) may be pleasant and charming between violent incidents; and (4) exhibit warning signs such as jealousy, possessiveness, bad tempers, unpredictability, cruelty to animals, and verbal abusiveness.

Causes

Researchers have devoted a great deal of effort to identifying the causes of intimate partner violence. In line with victim precipitation research by victimologists, early explanations focused on how victim characteristics and behaviors contributed to IPV. Criminological theory was noticeably absent from many early explanations of this type of violence. Payne and Gainey have argued that to fully explain intimate partner violence, it is necessary to consider the characteristics and behaviors of offenders rather than victims. They further suggest that traditional criminological theories have some utility in explaining intimate partner violence.

In applying criminological theory to IPV, one can see how the source of this violence can be similar to the source of other forms of harmful behavior. Routine activities theory, for example, can be used to explain intimate partner violence. Abusers are the motivated offenders, victims are the vulnerable targets, and the fact that much of the violence occurs behind closed doors is equivalent to the absence of capable guardians. Social disorganization theory can also be applied to intimate partner violence, as living in disadvantaged areas can exacerbate the risk, and consequences, of this type of violence. And conflict theory can be used to explain the woeful response of criminal justice officials to intimate partner violence. The lack of penalties given to offenders for this violence is consistent with the ideas of deterrence theory. In addition, the consistent finding that intimate partner violence is learned from family members is in line with differential association theory. The list could go on and on. The main point is that criminological theory can be used to explain IPV.

Power and control explanations are the most commonly cited explanations of intimate partner violence. The basic assumption underlying power and control explanations is that abusers use violence to control their partners. The power and control wheel has been used to illustrate the ties between power and control. This wheel was developed by the Domestic Abuse Intervention Project, which was created in Duluth, Minnesota, in 1980. After police began arresting all domestic abusers in Duluth, offenders were given the choice of a 6-month treatment program instead of jail. During the program, facilitators recognized that offenders were describing a series of nonphysical behaviors they performed in order to control their partners. Facilitators of the treatment program categorized the kinds of comments offenders made about controlling their victims into the power and control wheel. After describing their wheel with abusers, the facilitators recognized that abusers increased their nonphysical behaviors when they were unable to physically abuse their partners as part of their desire to control them.

The power and control wheel identified several activities that are performed in order to maintain control. First, offenders use intimidation through tactics such as glances, property destruction, and speaking loudly. Second, offenders use emotional abuse through actions such as verbal abuse and emotional neglect. Third, abusers use isolation as a strategy to make their victim more dependent on them (and thus less likely to leave). Fourth, offenders minimize and deny their behaviors by suggesting to their victim that they are really doing nothing wrong in their relationship. Fifth, offenders use their children to maintain power and control by making their victim fear for her children's safety. Sixth, offenders use male privilege by invoking patriarchal rules in the household and making important decisions without their partner's input. Seventh, abusers use economic abuse by controlling the finances and not allowing their partners access to financial resources. Eighth, offenders use coercion and threats to get victims to comply. Offenders might, for example, threaten to kill their partner, their children, or themselves as a strategy to get their victims to do certain things. The similarity between these tactics is simple: offenders, wanting power, do things to control their victims. This is the underlying assumption of power and control theory.

Brian K. Payne

See also Domestic Violence; Domestic Violence/Family Violence Courts; Elder Abuse, Neglect, and Maltreatment; Family Violence; Minneapolis Domestic Violence Experiment and Replication; Rape; Victimization, Theories of; Victimology

Further Readings

Buzawa, E., & Buzawa, C. (1990). *Domestic violence: The criminal justice response.* Newbury Park, CA: Sage.

Centers for Disease Control and Prevention. (2000). *Male batterers.* Atlanta, GA: Author.

Domestic Abuse Intervention Project. (n.d.). *Power and control wheel.* Duluth, MN: Author.

Doerner, W., & Lab, S. (2006). *Victimology* (3rd ed.). Cincinnati, OH: Anderson.

Family Violence Prevention Fund. (2001). *Cultural issues.* San Francisco: Author.

Hotchkin, S. (2001, January 21). Domestic violence is sweeping. *Lexington Herald-Ledger,* p. A3.

National Coalition Against Domestic Violence. (2000). *What is battering?* In D. D. Matthews (Ed.), *Domestic violence sourcebook.* Detroit, MI: Omnigraphics.

Payne, B., & Gainey, R. (2005). *Family violence and criminal justice.* Cincinnati, OH: Anderson.

Sherman, L. (1992). *Policing domestic violence.* New York: The Free Press.

Tjaden, P., & Thoennes, N. (2000). *Extent, nature, and consequences of intimate partner violence.* Washington, DC: U.S. Department of Justice.

Walker, L. (1984). *The battered woman syndrome.* New York: Harper & Row.

INTIMATE PARTNER VIOLENCE, RISK ASSESSMENT

The science of risk assessment in intimate partner violence (IPV) is relatively new. As research has increased in the field generally, so has demand for demonstrated accuracy in predicting risk in domestic violence cases and for the use of IPV risk assessment in criminal justice, advocacy services, and health care settings. As the science of IPV risk assessment has developed over the past decade, so have the identification of risk factors, for both re-assault and intimate partner homicide or near homicide, and the realization that the risk factors for the two outcomes, although overlapping, are not exactly the same and do not operate at the same degree of risk. In this entry, the term *risk assessment* will be used for assessing the risk of IPV re-assault or recidivism, while the term *lethality assessment* will be used for assessing the risk of an intimate partner homicide or near homicide.

The most commonly used methods for assessing both re-assault and lethality that have been validated in prospective studies in peer-review journal publications are described along with a brief summary of the evidence. The entry ends with recommendations for the use of these methods of risk assessment in a systemwide process.

Risk Assessment Instruments

The three most widely used risk of re-assault instruments are the SARA (Spousal Assault Risk Assessment), the ODARA (Ontario Domestic Assault Risk Assessment), and the DVSI-R (the revised Domestic Violence Screening Instrument). The oldest and most validated IPV risk assessment instrument is the Spousal Assault Risk Assessment, or SARA, which was developed in Canada by Randy Kropp and Stephen Hare as a structured professional judgment guideline intended to assist professionals to come to a judgment of the level of risk of re-assault in cases of IPV. It was primarily intended for use in the criminal justice system and is widely used in probation departments, but it is also used in domestic violence advocacy. Its shorter version, the B-Safer (Brief Spousal Assault Form for the Evaluation of Risk), has not been separately validated but was based on extensive data testing the SARA. The ASAP (Aid for Safety Assessment Planning) incorporates both the SARA and the B-Safer to guide in risk evaluation and safety planning with victims.

The Ontario Domestic Assault Risk Assessment, or ODARA, developed in Canada by Zoe Hilton, was designed for frontline police officers, but it can be used by victim services, health care workers, probation, and correctional services personnel. The ODARA was developed based on Ontario domestic violence arrest data. In subsequent testing with a new data set, also from the Ontario domestic violence criminal justice database, the ODARA achieved an area of .77 under the ROC (receiver operator curve). The area under the ROC reflects the percentage of cases captured under a curve that combines the sensitivity (true positives or cases where recidivism was predicted and occurred) and specificity (cases where no re-assault was predicted and none occurred) across the range of risk scores on an instrument. The receiver operator curve area ranges from 0 to 1.0, where 1.0

represents perfect accuracy. ROC analysis is an appropriate strategy to use to assess the predictive accuracy of a risk assessment instrument.

The Domestic Violence Screening Instrument, or DVSI, developed by Kirk Williams, contains 11 items (and thus is almost as short as the ODARA, which contains 13 items), and it is user-friendly for criminal justice systems, with the information needed for all items available from the police incident files. The DVSI was independently tested in a prospective study of victims of IPV in New York City and Los Angeles (known as the Risk Assessment Validation Experiment, or RAVE study) achieving an area under the ROC of .60. Subsequently, it has been revised (and called DVSI-R) and tested prospectively in a large study in Colorado with an area under the ROC of .71. The DVSI-R is used widely in probation departments in Colorado, Connecticut, and other U.S. jurisdictions.

Lethality and Severe Re-Assault Assessment

DV-MOSAIC, developed by Gavin de Becker and his associates in 2001, is a computerized threat assessment system based on intimate partner homicide data. DV-MOSAIC is longer than the DVSI-R and ODARA, and the only assessment instrument that incorporates protective as well as risk factors. It was developed for use in police departments and by domestic violence criminal justice specialists using data gathered from an investigation of the case. Levels of risk are determined through the programmed algorithm easily communicated to victims from a printout of the level of risk and its meaning. DV-MOSAIC was independently tested in the RAVE study, with 65% of the cases of severe re-assault accurately assessed with ROC curve analysis.

The Danger Assessment (DA) was developed based on IPV homicide data from three published studies, and extensive case and group work with women in shelters, in order to help abused victims determine their level of danger of homicide or near lethal attack. It consists of a calendar assessment filled out with victims that helps them see for themselves the actual pattern of IPV, followed by 15 yes/no items formulated in wording that abused women can understand. Data from a recent case control study of homicide were used to formulate a weighting scoring system and levels. They were subsequently tested on a sample of attempted homicide victims with a receiver operator curve of .90. In the RAVE study, the DA achieved a .69 under the ROC for severe re-assault.

Victims' Assessment of Risk

In the RAVE study, victims' perception of risk accurately captured 61% of "any re-assault" and "severe re-assault," adjusting for the protective actions that put the victim out of possible physical contact from the perpetrator (e.g., the victim going to a shelter or the perpetrator being in jail). This was a greater proportion of accurate prediction than that made by the DVSI (not DVSI-R) and DV-MOSAIC, but smaller than the Danger Assessment. Other examinations of the accuracy of victim perception of re-assault have found that abused women are good predictors of re-assault but are more likely to underestimate than overestimate their risk. The D. Alex Heckert and Edward Gondolf prospective study of abusers in batterer intervention programs and their victims found that the combination of the original 15-item DA combined with victims' perception of risk was the most accurate of the instruments used in assessing risk of re-assault.

Use in Systemwide Process

There have been at least three reviews of DV re-assault and lethality risk assessment approaches, several published investigations of predictive validity of specific instruments, one comparison of the SARA and the DA, and an experimental test to comparatively evaluate four of the methods plus victims' perceptions of risk in the same sample (the RAVE study). This demonstrates that there is beginning to be a body of knowledge that allows choice of an instrument or system based on its predictive accuracy as well as on its utility in a setting and intended use.

Thus, there is sufficient evidence of accuracy to use the methods summarized above and to end the usage of lists without validation. In a recent meta-analysis examining clinical judgment against statistical judgments in 92 studies, statistical methods were found to be more accurate than other methods overall. In the case of domestic violence, victims' perceptions of risk also have a place, but

victims often underestimate their risk of re-assault, and especially of lethality. Therefore, validated statistical assessment of potential re-assault and lethality needs to be part of the overall coordinated response to domestic violence, and used as the basis for safety planning for and by abused women and community strategies to keep women safe.

Jacquelyn C. Campbell and Nancy Glass

See also Domestic Violence; Domestic Violence Fatality Review Team; Femicide; Intimate Partner Violence; Intimate Partner Violence, Theories of

Further Readings

Campbell, J. C. (2007). *Assessing dangerousness: Violence by batterers and child abusers.* New York: Springer.

Campbell, J. C., O'Sullivan, C., Roehl, J., & Webster, D. W. (2005). *Intimate Partner Violence Risk Assessment Validation Study: The RAVE Study.* Final Report to the National Institute of Justice (NCJ 209731–209732). Retrieved from http://www.ncjrs .org/pdffiles1/nij/grants/209731.pdf

Campbell, J. C., Webster, D., & Glass, N. E. (2009). The Danger Assessment: Validation of a lethality risk assessment instrument for intimate partner femicide. *Journal of Interpersonal Violence, 23.* Retrieved from http://jiv.sagepub.com/cgi/rapidpdf/ 0886260508317180v1

Campbell, J. C., Webster, D., Koziol-McLain, J., Block, C. R., Campbell, D., Curry, M. A., et al. (2003). Risk factors for femicide in abusive relationships: Results from a multi-site case control study. *American Journal of Public Health 93*(7), 1089–1097.

Dutton, D. G., & Kropp, P. R. (2000). A review of domestic violence risk instruments. *Trauma Violence & Abuse, 1*(2), 171–181.

Ægisdóttir, S., White, M. J., Spengler, P. M., Maugherman, A., Anderson, L. A., Cook, R. A., et al. (2006). The meta-analysis of clinical judgment project: Fifty-six years of accumulated research on clinical versus statistical prediction. *The Counseling Psychologist, 34,* 341–382.

Hanson, R. K., Helmus, L., & Bourgon, G. *The validity of risk assessments for intimate partner violence: A meta-analysis.* Ottawa: Public Safety Canada.

Hilton, N. Z., & Harris, G. T. (2005). The prediction of wife assault: A critical review and implications for policy and practice. *Trauma Violence & Abuse, 6,* 3–23.

Hilton, N. Z., Harris, G. T., Rice, M. E., Lang, C., Cormier, C., & Lines, K. J. (2004). A brief actuarial assessment for the prediction of wife assault recidivism: The Ontario Domestic Assault Risk Assessment. *Psychological Assessment, 16*(3), 267–275.

Kropp, P. R., Hart, S. D., Webster, C. D., & Eaves, D. (2000). The spousal assault risk assessment guide (SARA): Reliability and validity in adult male offenders. *Law and Human Behavior, 24*, 101–118.

Williams, K. R., & Grant, S. R. (2006). Empirically examining the risk of intimate partner violence: The Revised Domestic Violence Screening Instrument (DVSI-R). *Public Health Reports, 121*, 400–408.

INTIMATE PARTNER VIOLENCE, THEORIES OF

Intimate partner violence occurs in an environment of complex, often interrelated issues, including individual, situational, psychological and couple relationship factors, in the context of a social, political, and economic environment. There are many different theories of intimate partner violence, which concentrate on explaining clusters of issues. These theories can be categorized in many different ways; some describe intimate partner violence in terms of intra- or interpersonal factors that affect the couple dynamic, and others use models which include structural or institutional elements that foster the use of violence in the wider society.

Intrapersonal theories are drawn from the discipline of psychology and encompass a range of personal pathologies, including physiological and mental instabilities and related inability to control emotional outbursts. Examples might be the roles of obsessive ideation, paranoia, disassociation from feelings, substance use or an acquired brain injury in the perpetrator that leads to poor impulse control; in addition, a flawed attachment experience during childhood can lead to hypersensitivity in which any feelings of hurt, fear, or jealousy are immediately transformed into anger. Low self-esteem, depression, and anxiety can trigger both perpetration and victimization. This group of theories also includes discussions of reinforcing behaviors that can be associated with intimate partner violence, such as watching violent movies, using pornography, possessing weapons, and a history of criminal activity.

The range of theories categorized as *interpersonal theories* focus on the dynamic between the couple in the relationship. The Duluth Domestic Violence Project made important contributions to theory by illustrating how control is enforced using psychological and emotional means in addition to violence through the processes described by the *power and control* and *cycle of violence* models. In 2000, Michael Johnson and Kathleen Ferraro theorized that there were two distinct types of intimate partner violence. The power and control dynamic plays little part in the *common couple violence* where either partner may lash out, whereas in *intimate terrorism* the violence is motivated by control. *Exchange theory* explains the calculated use of violent behavior in achieving the perpetrator's goals, while *investment theories* look at the level of commitment in the relationship to explain intimate partner violence.

Structural theories show how social and economic inequalities translate into aggression and violence. *Feminist theories* regard intimate partner violence as the result of a patriarchal society where male coercive power and domination over females is promoted and reinforced. For example, a belief in the rights of a male to chastise and punish his partner, along with a general endorsement of the use of aggression and violence by men in the exercise of power and control in the wider social system. In *resource theory*, power within an intimate relationship is based on the command of resources, whether economic, psychological, or social. When resources are scarce or threatened, aggressive behavior and violence are tactics used to increase control. For example, a man who perceives that he has lost control in an intimate relationship is likely to use violence to restore his power.

Social situation/stress and coping theory provides a two-dimensional explanation as to why intimate partner violence may occur in some situations and not others. The first dimension is the position of the dyad in the social structure (e.g., employment and income levels), and the second dimension is the capacity of the dyad to deal with stress and includes the coping strategies that may be used by either partner. One or both partners may resort to violence to deal with episodes of financial strain in a society where the use of violence is seen as an appropriate response to stress.

Social learning theory explains how the use of violent behavior is transmitted between generations. For example, Debra Kalmuss found that repetitive exposure to violence in the emotionally loaded environment of the family predisposed children to use violence, and adult victims of intimate partner violence were six times more likely than others to have been subjected to violence as children. However, the explanation offered by social learning theory is only partial, as research into the pathways to violent behavior has found that not all children exposed to violence become perpetrators or victims.

Murray Straus first applied *general systems theory* to intimate partner violence in 1973, where the system involved individuals, their behaviors and pathologies, and family backgrounds as well as the social spheres, cultural influences, and organization of the society in which they live. General systems theory describes the processes that characterize the use, management, and stabilization of violence in family interactions.

Donald Dutton proposed an *ecological theory* that integrates many of the above theories of abuse and applies to both victims and perpetrators. The ecosystem of a violent relationship has a foundation layer that is based on intrapersonal psychological factors, followed by a family system layer in which the individual experiences such negative actions as abandonment, neglect, and abuse. The next layer contains peer group issues such as education, religious training, alcohol and drug use, and gender role socialization. The final layer describes the influence of wider sociopolitical gender inequalities, media portrayal of subjugation and violence against women, and racial/ethnic/cultural prejudices. *Life path* theories also take into account the changes in personal and environmental effects over time.

The heterogeneous nature of intimate partner violence makes it problematic for a single theory to take into account all the dynamic and static elements that produce violent acts between intimate partners, such as social conditions, social policy, political events, and shifts in social history that are taking place as well as the situational, individual psychological, and couple relationship factors.

Romy Winter

See also Abuse, Spouse; Battered Woman Syndrome; Cycle of Violence, Theory of; Domestic Violence; Feminist Victimology; Intimate Partner Violence; Intimate Partner Violence, Risk Assessment; Male Victims of Partner Violence

Further Readings

Barak, G. (2006). A critical perspective on violence. In W. DeKeseredy & B. Perry (Eds.), *Advancing critical criminology: Theory and application* (pp. 133–154). New York: Lexington.

Dutton, M. A., Goodman, L., Lennig, D., Murphy, J., & Kaltman, S. (2005). *Ecological model of battered women's experience over time*. Washington, DC: National Institute of Justice.

Jasinski, J. L., & Williams, L. M. (1998). *Partner violence: A comprehensive review of 20 years of research*. Thousand Oaks, CA: Sage.

JOURNEY TO CRIME

Journey to crime (JTC) is one of the better-researched aspects of crime in the crime and space literature. Research on JTC attempts to understand how offenders' movements in space factor into the discovery of unintended targets, leading to crimes of opportunity; into offenses planned by serious criminals taking steps toward known targets; and into purposive hunting patterns in areas thought to be target rich. Clearly, understanding the JTC process more completely would provide the police with a set of tools with which to effectively track down active offenders and lead to tremendous benefits for crime prevention and reduction efforts. Three core aspects of this literature deal with determining (1) the point of origin (or anchor) for a particular crime or set of crimes, (2) the directionality of the crime trip, and (3) the actual distance traveled between nodes. Like economic geography research, which has long studied the characteristics of consumers deciding on where to locate retail outlets (catchment areas, for example), JTC research studies the characteristics of offenders deciding on where to journey "to work" (that is, commit crime). Journey to crime research, although similar in many ways to criminal profiling, should not be confused with it. Whereas journey to crime research is applied to the specific journey (and chain of events and decisions) undertaken by an individual offender leading up to a specific crime, criminal profiling seeks to work back from a set of crime event locations that are thought to be linked in some way in an effort to estimate possible nodes of activity that the offenders may use, such as residences.

Point of Origin and Direction of Travel

"Home" is often used as starting point in JTC research, but it is widely understood that crime trips do not have to start from a residence; they can begin in any central node of activity. As JTC research only considers crimes for which travel was needed, "zero-distance" crimes such as domestic assaults or the production of illegal narcotics or substances in an offender's home are usually not part of a formal JTC analysis, as the origin and endpoint are the same.

Once a point of origin is determined (such as through an examination of police records of convicted offenders), the crime trips can be measured for associated crime sites and areas or locations the suspect is known to frequent. Directional bias, or the tendency for trips from anchor points to a given set of destinations to be clustered in something approaching a mean cardinal direction, helps researchers to determine likely travel paths. Specific types of locations have been shown to have attractor and/or generator properties for crime events, and thus knowing offenders' direction (if not literal paths) will assist both active and "cold case" analyses. Directionality also helps investigators look for additional clues, information, suspects, or any potential, as-yet-undiscovered nodes of activity.

Distance Traveled

Opportunity-based crimes tend to involve the least amount of precrime preparation and occur closest to nodes used during routine activities. According to the least energy (or least effort) principle, equally suitable targets that are closer to the potential offender are preferable to those further away. This principle also suggests that at some point, the potential offender would experience a diminishing return for travel and effort expended and expected/ realized reward from the crime.

Research findings on trip distances by crime type show that more spontaneous and affective crime types, such as domestic assault, involve the shortest distances. Data from the mid-1970s, for example, show distances to rape of approximately 1 mile as a modal measure, burglaries at just over one mile, and robberies at approximately 1.5 miles. These findings are not consistent, but nevertheless, all of these distances are relatively short. For example, a 2007 Finnish study reported average travel distances for burglars as being approximately 2.4 miles (or just under 4 kilometers). Thus, affective or emotionally charged crimes involve shorter distances than do instrumental crimes. Presumably the latter involve a specific target, such as a certain store or warehouse that is known to have a particularly lucrative "haul" of goods, and this may be seen as deserving some additional effort, planning, and travel than other, more immediate targets. This is borne out in research on serial arsonists, for whom any suitable target will do, and who therefore have no need to seek out special targets. Australian research, for example, finds that young offenders set most fires with little motive beyond immediate gratification in the form of excitement or entertainment. This is at least partly why distances traveled for this type of crime are typically among the shortest—often less than half of a mile. This changes when fire settings involve instrumental purposes. These more purposive crimes are more likely to include specific targets to which the offender must travel. Keeping with fire setting as an example, arson for revenge (or for fraud) may call on the offender to travel several miles to attack a former boss or place of employment. Here, the crime is a means to an end, rather than the end itself.

Of course, not all targets are equal, so some level of decision making takes place, but the majority of empirical evidence suggests that most crime trips are undertaken by offenders who traveled relatively short distances, and that as much as four fifths (80%) of all crime occurs as a result of opportunities discovered in the course of routine, noncriminal activities. Burglar interviews and analysis of solved offenses using police incident data show that burglars tend to find (and act on) targets closer to their point of origin rather than those further away, and that they avoid targets close to home. This "buffer zone" of reduced offending quickly fades, however, as the offender moves toward his or her destination. The buffer zone effect, which was first described by Paul and Patricia Brantingham in *Patterns in Crime*, is theorized as being primarily a strategic response on the part of offenders to avoid recognition if they are seen in a potentially compromising set of circumstances. However, not all researchers agree on the existence of the buffer zone. Recent work in Chicago involving police incident data from the late 1990s involving violent altercations showed no such buffer around offenders' home locations, although the researchers found that travel distances were, nevertheless, short (and conformed with expectations arising from routine activities theory, which are described in the entry on the theory in this encyclopedia).

Measurement

Several measurement options are available to JTC researchers, but only two basic forms are discussed here. A Euclidian, or straight line, distance between start and end locations is the simplest distance measurement between two points. This "as the crow flies" distance is easy to calculate, but reflects rather poorly the paths of (and distances traveled by) people in the built environment. To capture more realistic estimates of trips between points in an urban setting, researchers often use the "Manhattan" metric, which estimates the likely distance traveled as the sum of the distances needed to move along two lines that form a triangle, assuming the original, straight path distance forms the hypotenuse.

Actual distance traveled is only part of a JTC analysis. Most people consider the time spent in transit at least as, if not more, important. Simple distance measures, then, need to be adapted to include such "costs" as time spent in transit, among other things (e.g., convenience), and of course the actual monetary costs involved. Such considerations are highly subjective and not always accurately estimated, leading to inefficient travel patterns that "make sense" to the traveler because they are the most comfortable, even when more efficient paths are available. Of course, the mode of travel figures prominently in any travel distance–time estimation. Clearly, people are apt to be less concerned about literal distance traveled than the time spent traveling when they are driving to work every day. Most would drive a bit farther than strictly necessary if it enabled them to cut their travel time.

To improve JTC modeling, researchers often modify expected travel distances by including the impact of a range of additional variables, such as mode of travel, traveler demographics, urban infrastructure (areas known for goods and services, road networks, foot/bicycle pathways, etc.), and topographical features (e.g., bodies of water and bridges).

City planning efforts have an obvious impact on people's daily routines, and consequently, opportunities for licit and illicit activities alike. Certain city zones, such as entertainment districts with bars or nightclubs as major services, are known to attract problems. Knowing something of key areas and locations assists in forecasting likely nodes that serve as points of contact during the journey to—and from—crime. Kim Rossmo's *Geographic Profiling* is one of the most accessible introductions to—the specific methods of analytical work on offender movements, including JTC and the prediction of key nodes where complete travel information is not known. Gravity models are used by geographers to predict the movement of people in space based on some supply-and-demand assumptions, such as the availability of a particular class of goods or services. For example, consumers will undertake a certain amount of effort to find suitable goods, but will eventually stop spending energy and take the best deal that they can find. Such estimations provide the "distance decay functions" (i.e., diminishment of actions as distance traveled increases) included in most research on the journey to crime.

Simulation

JTC research involves both retrospective accounts of known offenders and simulation studies. In retrospective studies, actual paths can be more or less accurately reproduced for a set of offenses. Such examples assist greatly in the calibration of techniques to predict missing information when examining incomplete cases. Given the interest in predicting trip distances, and estimating the start points where points of origin are not known, it is not surprising that simulation work is flourishing. A detailed discussion of simulation methods is not possible here, but key work in this area includes joining geographic information systems (GISs) and agent-based systems modeling. Although there is considerable variation in the types of simulation research in this area, generally, such efforts place a hypothetical offender (agent) into a network of travel options, such as a digitally reproduced road network (or "graph"), and then specify potential targets and start and end points. The simulation then allows the agent to make several hundred "trips" to see what paths and targets are "found" by the agent, and of those, which are actually used and acted on. Simulation models provide an arena in which it is possible to test theory about relatively rare events, such as homicide, as well as to assist in crime prevention and reduction efforts of investigators by supplying a more efficient strategy for resource (surveillance, evidence searches, etc.) deployment in the field. This contribution is subtle but vitally important to the growth of offender movement theory, as it provides a new path for empirical findings to feed back into theory. Finally, simulation studies build on the set of computational approaches—along with geographic information systems techniques—to build on what is becoming more widely referred to as "crime science."

J. Bryan Kinney

See also Crime Mapping; Crime Pattern Theory; Crime Prevention; Crime Science; Routine Activities Theory; Situational Crime Prevention

Further Readings

Brantingham, P. J., & Brantingham, P. L. (1984). *Patterns in crime.* New York: Macmillan.

Brantingham, P. L., Glässer, U., Jackson, P., Kinney, B., & Vajihollahi, M. (2008). Mastermind: Computational modeling and simulation of spatiotemporal aspects of crime in urban environments. In L. Liu & J. Eck (Eds.), *Artificial crime analysis systems: Using computer simulations and geographic information systems* (pp. 252–280). Hershey, PA: IGI Global.

Canter, D., & Gregory, A. (1994). Identifying the residential location of rapists. *Journal of Forensic Science Society, 34,* 169–175.

Laukkanen, M., Santtila, P., Jern, P., & Sandnabba, K. (2008). Predicting offender home location in urban burglary series. *Forensic Science International, 176*(2/3), 224–235.

LeBeau, J. L. (1987). Journey to rape: Geographic distance and the rapist's method of approaching the victim. *Journal of Police Science and Administration, 15*(2), 129–136.

Rengert, G. (2004). The journey to crime. In G. Bruinsma, H. Elffers, & J. D. Keijser (Eds.), *Punishment, places and perpetrators: Developments in criminology and criminal justice research* (pp. 169–181). Cullompton, Devon, UK: Willan.

Rossmo, K. (1999). *Geographic profiling.* Boca Raton, FL: CRC.

JUVENILE OFFENDING AND VICTIMIZATION

Substantial research investigating offending and victimization has found that they may be intertwined. High rates of victimization and offending exist among juvenile populations, and studies have made clear that these categories are not mutually exclusive. Most of the research has focused on one or the other of these phenomena, however, rather than the relationship between delinquency and victimization.

The Victim–Offender Connection

The connection between juvenile offending and victimization has been established. What is less clear is *how* victimization and offending are linked. That is, does offending result in victimization, or does victimization lead to offending? And, are these relationships reciprocal, or are there other factors that explain both offending and victimization?

There is strong support for the idea that participation in delinquency is related to an elevated risk of victimization. Many victims of violence have histories of serious delinquency. Victimization

also appears to be a risk factor for offending, especially for committing violent offenses. Thus, there is some evidence that the relationship between offending and victimization is not unidirectional. It appears that violent offending affects victimization, and violent victimization is related to an increased risk of later victimization and violent offending. Since there appears to be some relationship between victimization and offending, it may not be surprising to find that similar factors may account for both juvenile offending and victimization. Factors such as self-control, family and peer influences, gang fights, drug selling, and carrying a weapon are examples.

Theories

In describing the relationship that exists between offending and victimization, several explanations have emerged. One line of thought suggests that offenders are more likely to be in situations that would result in an increased risk of victimization. This contention is supported by findings that those involved in the most serious delinquency had higher rates of violent victimizations. It is also important to note, however, that many offenders are not victims of crime, nor are all victims offenders.

The primary explanation utilized and supported to clarify this relationship is that in lifestyle theory and routine activities theory. Michael Hindelang and his colleagues developed lifestyle theory to explain differences in victimization. The basic premise of this theory is that victimization occurs due to an individual's lifestyle or associations. In this sense, lifestyles that are characterized as deviant and risky can contribute to offending and victimization in similar ways. A situation that is conducive to offending is also characterized by elements related to victimization. Since these two concepts are invariably linked together—offending does not exist without victimization—those surrounded by delinquency based on their lifestyle may be at higher risk of victimization either in the context of offending or as a result of retaliation or retribution.

Lawrence Cohen and Marcus Felson further developed this area of theory by introducing routine activities theory. This proposition states that when three things—(1) motivated offenders, (2) suitable targets, and (3) lack of capable guardians—converge in time and space, victimization will occur. Thus, participating in delinquency increases the risk of victimization by decreasing the number of guardians or by increasing exposure to motivated offenders. Some individuals, for example, may have more contact with offenders due to their environment, while others may have more contact with offenders because of their activities.

According to these theories, increased victimization results from several factors related to delinquency. First, increased exposure to offenders can result in higher rates of victimization. Those involved in delinquency, for example, often have greater exposure to both delinquent situations and individuals that can result in increased victimization. Second, the nature of offending can affect victimization because situations that are conducive to crime are also conducive to victimization. For instance, prostitutes in the process of committing a crime also expose themselves to situations in which they could become a victim. Third, offenders make extremely suitable victims. Offenders are more likely not to report crimes committed against them, as they try to avoid police detection for their own crimes. In addition, offenders may be less likely to report victimization due to the perception that they are less likely to be believed or have their victimization taken seriously by law enforcement and/or their losses are illegal contraband that would bring additional police scrutiny of their own activities.

Related to these explanations are victim precipitation theory and subcultural theory. Victim precipitation theory proposes that victims encourage victimization by their own behavior. The relationship with offending is most often associated with what is classified as active precipitation. For example, in the case of a barroom brawl, one individual begins a fight by insulting another, but miscalculates the ability of the target and comes out on the losing end. Thus, through their actions, offenders become victims. In addition, subcultural theory states that certain groups possess norms that require a reaction to disputes, such as retaliation,

that turn offenders into victims during the course of the response.

Adrienne Freng and Terrance J. Taylor

See also Lifestyle Theory; Offending and Victimization; Routine Activities Theory; Victimization, Theories of; Victimology; Victim Precipitation

Further Readings

Cohen, L., & Felson, M. (1979). Social change and crime rate trends: A routine activities approach. *American Sociological Review, 44,* 588–608.

Esbensen, F.-A., & Huizinga, D. (1991). Juvenile victimization and delinquency. *Youth & Society, 23,* 202–228.

Hindelang, M. J., Gottfredson, M. R., & Garofalo, J. (1978). *Victims of personal crime: An empirical foundation for a theory of personal victimization.* Cambridge, MA: Ballinger.

Howell, J. C. (2003). *Preventing and reducing juvenile delinquency.* Thousand Oaks, CA: Sage.

Huizinga, D., & Jakob-Chien, C. (1999). The contemporaneous co-occurrence of serious and violent juvenile offending and other problem behaviors. In R. Loeber & D. P. Farrington (Eds.), *Serious and violent juvenile offenders* (pp. 47–67). Thousand Oaks, CA: Sage.

Jensen, G., & Brownfield, D. (1986). Gender, lifestyles, and victimization: Beyond routine activity. *Violence and Victims, 1,* 85–99.

Lauritsen, J. L., Sampson, R. J., & Laub, J. H. (1991). The link between offending and victimization among adolescents. *Criminology, 29,* 265–292.

Meadows, R. J. (2007). *Understanding violence and victimization.* Upper Saddle River, NJ: Prentice Hall.

Sampson, R. J., & Lauritsen, J. L. (1990). Deviant lifestyles, proximity to crime, and the offender-victim link in personal violence. *Journal of Research in Crime and Delinquency, 27,* 110–139.

Shaffer, J. N., & Ruback, R. B. (2002). Violent victimization as a risk factor for violent offending among juveniles (*OJJDP Juvenile Justice Bulletin*). Washington, DC: Department of Justice, Office of Juvenile Justice and Delinquency Prevention.

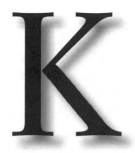

KIDNAPPING

Under the common law, kidnapping was defined as the unlawful confinement and transportation of a person out of the country. Originally it was a misdemeanor, but kidnapping is now statutorily defined in all jurisdictions in America and is considered a serious felony.

Kidnapping, as a crime, was brought to national attention in America when the baby of famous aviator Charles Lindbergh was kidnapped and murdered in 1932. In response to the extensive public outcry, Congress enacted the Federal Kidnapping Act (also known as the Lindbergh Law) in 1934, which provided the death penalty for kidnapping that results in death.

The Law

Although every jurisdiction's criminal laws are different, as a general rule, each one recognizes the crime of kidnapping. Most of the kidnapping laws in America contain the following elements: (1) a person's knowingly or intentionally (2) transporting another person (known as *asportation*) (3) against his or her will, (4) by force or threat of force, and (5) restraining, holding, or confining that person for a certain amount of time. Some kidnapping laws have a requirement of secrecy. Many kidnapping laws include additional elements, such as the purpose of the kidnapping (e.g., ransom, sexual assault, or hostage taking) and whether it was committed in conjunction with another crime (e.g., robbery). The penalty for crimes that include these elements is usually higher. Many jurisdictions have a lesser degree of punishment where the kidnapping involves family members such as children.

Kidnapping differs from false imprisonment, which was recognized under the common law as a crime and is usually defined as having the following basic elements: (1) a person's knowingly or intentionally (2) unlawfully restraining another person, (3) substantially interfering with that person's liberty. The primary difference between the crimes of kidnapping and false imprisonment is the transportation of the victim. Another term often used in place of false imprisonment is *hostage taking*. Hostage taking and kidnapping are similar, but they are often defined in different statutes.

Understanding the Crime

Kidnapping can be divided into several general types. These include (1) political, (2) sexual, (3) financial, (4) domestic, (5) psychological, (6) slavery, and (7) hostage-associated kidnappings. Of course, there is some overlap between the different types. Political kidnappings usually involve the taking of a high-profile person, occasionally a diplomat or government official, to compel a government to take some action such as the release of political prisoners. These kidnappings also are a favorite tool of terrorists, who frequently use them to obtain operating funds. Sexual kidnappings usually involve situations where the perpetrator takes the victim to a remote place for sexual assault. Financial kidnappings are usually done to extort money from a wealthy person or corporation. Executives from large corporations and children of wealthy families are the usual victims in these kidnappings. Domestic kidnappings usually involve the taking of a child where there is an ongoing dispute over custody in a divorce or separation. It should be noted that, as a general rule, if there is no court decree or restraining order in effect, it is generally not considered kidnapping if one parent takes sole possession of the children. Psychologically based kidnappings are usually associated with serial killers, who kidnap their victims and then take them to remote places and kill them. Such kidnappings share some features with sexual kidnappings, but their purpose is not sexual and involves other factors, such as revenge, ritualistic crimes, or a psychological disease. Slavery-related kidnappings involve people, usually women, being taken and held against their will and forced to work, usually in menial occupations or as sex slaves. Finally, hostage-associated kidnappings are usually committed in conjunction with other crimes. For example, if a robbery is interrupted, the perpetrators may take hostages with them to attempt to ensure their escape.

One of the most widespread problems concerning kidnapping is the issue of custody of the children where the parents are separated or divorced and custody is in dispute. Several authorities estimate that more than 300,000 children are kidnapped every year. To prevent domestic kidnapping, a number of laws have been enacted. The Parental Kidnapping Prevention Act of 1980, for example, a federal law that applies to the states, discourages interstate kidnapping of such children by preventing jurisdictional conflicts when children are taken across state lines (Public Law 96-611, 94 Stat. 3568 [1980]). Further, the Uniform Child Custody Jurisdiction Act and its successor, the Uniform Child Custody Jurisdiction and Enforcement Act, one or both of which have been adopted by all the states in various forms, allow for continuing jurisdiction for custody in the home or resident state of the child.

One of the problems with analyzing the prevalence and prevention of kidnapping is that it is not listed as a Part I offense by the FBI's Uniform Crime Reporting Program. This has made it difficult to obtain a complete understanding of the incidence and characteristics of the crime. There have been a number of calls to rectify this problem.

Prevention

Prevention of kidnapping is difficult, given the nature of America as an open society. However, corporations and wealthy people employ security personnel to prevent financial kidnappings, and governments usually have elaborate protection systems for their diplomats and officials to prevent political kidnappings. Domestic kidnappings are extremely difficult to prevent, given that usually both parents are allowed direct access to the children, and court decrees and restraining orders are not always effective tools of prevention. The AMBER Alert system has helped solve and/or terminate these child kidnappings. (For more information on this system, see the entry "AMBER Alert" in this encyclopedia.) Prevention of sexual kidnappings, at least when the victim does not know of a potential perpetrator, are usually best prevented by cautious practices in dating and travel.

Wm. C. Plouffe Jr.

See also AMBER Alert; Domestic Violence; Human Trafficking; Missing, Exploited, and Murdered Children

Further Readings

Alix, E. K. (1978). *Ransom kidnapping in America, 1874–1974: The creation of a capital crime.* Carbondale: Southern University of Illinois Press.

Clutterbuck, R. (1987). *Kidnap, hijack and extortion: The response.* New York: St. Martin's.

De Melis, L. M. (1994). Interstate child custody and the Parental Kidnapping Prevention Act: The continuing search for a national standard. *Hastings Law Journal, 45,* 1329–1378.

Hoff, P. M. (2000). *Parental kidnapping: Prevention and remedies.* Washington, DC: American Bar Association.

KIRKHOLT BURGLARY PREVENTION PROJECT

The Kirkholt area of Rochdale, which is one of the former mill towns common across Lancashire,

England, and is now part of Greater Manchester, is a public housing estate comprising some 2,300 homes. It is historically a challenging area in terms of both reputation and recorded crime. In the early 1980s it was singled out by Greater Manchester Police as the location within their force area with the most acute domestic burglary problem. Funding was put in place to study and reduce the incidence of that offense. A police officer, David Forrester, was assigned to the project, under the supervision of researchers Mike Chatterton and Ken Pease. The report of the first phase of the project was published as *The Kirkholt Burglary Prevention Project, Rochdale.*

Overview

When police records dealing with Kirkholt were scrutinized, it was found that they lacked the detail necessary to inform target hardening (such as clarity about burglars' method of entry), so an ambitious interview program was undertaken. Interviews with local burglars, victims, and other residents confirmed that target hardening should be the police's initial tactic of choice. Lacking funding to target harden over 2,000 dwellings, the police decided that their first step should be to identify the most vulnerable homes for priority attention.

At the time, the police perception of residents of the Kirkholt estate was that they were largely less than upright citizens, but Forrester returned from the interviews infused with a sense of the essential decency of most of the residents—and a burning desire to help those who had been chronically victimized by burglary. Contrary to expectations, it was found that prior burglary victimization was the best indicator of vulnerability to burglary in the future. In fact, the level of repeat burglary in the year before the implementation of the project was such that the majority of crimes were against households that already had been targeted at least once during that calendar year. Thus, putting the possibility of crimes being moved to another location to one side, the prevention of all repeat burglaries would result in the prevention of more than half of all domestic burglaries within a year. The alternatives (such as prioritizing single-parent households and the most victimized part of the estate) would be less efficient and more vulnerable to perceptions of unfairness. For instance, a householder whose

neighbor receives help that she herself does not might well be resentful, and a denizen of one part of Kirkholt who sees resources deployed elsewhere on the estate might be similarly unhappy. By contrast, it is unlikely that citizens would object to burglary victims' receiving help geared toward the prevention of their being burglarized again. In addition, target-hardening burgled and neighboring homes provides a steady (but, it is hoped, declining) workload for those engaged in target hardening the homes, whereas target hardening by demographics or area provides a one-time task for people who are then dismissed or allocated work elsewhere. The steadily declining workload was termed *drip-feeding* and is an often overlooked advantage of target hardening that occurs as a result of criminal events.

At its core, the Kirkholt project involved target hardening both burgled homes and neighboring homes. The inclusion of near neighbors' homes was based on the notion that capable guardianship could be exercised to prevent repeated burglaries, and that target hardening these homes would sensitize their occupants to the situation, causing them to exercise this guardianship. It also was based on the notion that neighbors may have been burglarizing each other, and the manifestation of a serious intent to remedy the burglary problem would be helpful in warning them off. Indeed, the preproject assumption of police in the area was that Kirkholt residents were faking their burglaries. Evidence that emerged in the study made it clear that this was a very minor part of what was happening. The invocation of neighbors to become capable guardians was termed *cocoon watch*, and it extended across Kirkholt to become the more conventional Neighborhood Watch scheme.

Results

The Kirkholt project reduced burglary on the Kirkholt estate immediately and dramatically. The number of domestic burglaries fell from 316 in 1986 to 147 in 1987—a decline that was not reflected in the rest of the police area. Further, repeat victimization showed an especially dramatic decline. Within practical limits, it was shown that crime had not been displaced by place (elsewhere in the area) or crime type. The improvement remained, and the evaluation ended in 1990. A second report on the project by Forrester and his colleagues in 1990 is noteworthy for its early attempt at cost–benefit analysis, and for the observation that it was increasingly householders new to the area who fell victim to burglary. In the year before the project was implemented, 10% of the burglaries in Kirkholt were suffered by those living in the area for less than 2 years. In the third year of implementation, that figure had jumped to 49%. This is in part attributable to the improved reputation of the estate and its consequent increase in the number of occupied homes. Highlighting the vulnerability of newcomers to burglary was an important incidental finding of the study of Kirkholt.

Criticisms

The claimed success of the Kirkholt project came under criticism, no doubt because the success was so dramatic and replications were less successful (at least in part because they were not full replications). It was suggested that the burglary reduction was attributable to general estate improvements rather than target hardening. The Home Office commissioned David Farrington to review the evidence and reanalyze the data. His report (which was never published) indicated that the decline had tracked the target hardening of burglary victims rather than tracking other types of improvements. After more than 20 years, what are we to make of the Kirkholt project? The points worth remembering include the following:

1. Because the burglary rate in Kirkholt was extremely high before the project, one could anticipate a decline in burglary on the basis of the rate simply declining to a more normal level, independent of the intervention.

2. As the project contained a package of measures, it is impossible to tease out the components of its "active ingredient," although some clues can be gathered from the shape of the reduction—for example, there was a greater reduction in burglaries in semidetached homes than in maisonettes (apartments on two floors), where the overall building design and environmental setting provided more crime opportunities.

3. One aspect of target hardening was the removal of the meters, sometimes called "burglars'

piggybanks," into which residents in British public housing up to the 1980s typically inserted coins to prepay for their electricity. These meters, which were in a standard place within the home and easy to break into, often contained a substantial sum. Before the project, 49% of all burglaries involved loss of meter cash, and 27% nothing but meter cash. Thus the meters were the ultimate "low-hanging fruit" for target-hardening crime preventers.

4. In addition to the features that made the project a success beyond the reach of projects that followed it, the Kirkholt project had the distinction of being the first project that used what was known about how victimization is concentrated as the basis for the prioritization of crime reduction efforts.

5. The project "got lucky" in its deployment of cocoon watches, wherein target-hardening help was offered to near neighbors of burglary victims. Later research showed how burglary risk is communicated to near neighbors, but this was not understood at the time. The burglary reductions achieved by the project were greater than the total numbers of preproject repeats, and there were some postproject repeats, so the balance of the reduction came from somewhere else. It is plausible that it came from neighbors of burglary victims, but this was not measured at the time. It is now more productive to think of repeat victimization as a special case of communicated risk.

6. Despite its flaws, the Kirkholt project was an important step forward in placing the prevention of repeat victimization on the crime prevention agenda. And the concepts of drip-feeding and cocoon watch speak to practical crime reduction issues. However, crime concentration at the individual and household levels remains a ubiquitous feature of crime patterns, and an affront to notions of distributive justice. Thus the scope for prevention via the reduction of repeat victimization and other instances of communicated risk remains considerable in scale and worthy in terms of its fairness in spreading the burden of crime around.

Ken Pease

See also Burglary, Prevention of; Neighborhood Watch Programs; Safer Cities Program

Further Readings

Forrester, D., Chatterton, M., & Pease, K. (1988). *The Kirkholt Burglary Prevention Project, Rochdale* (Crime Prevention Unit Paper 13). London: Home Office.

Forrester, D., Frenz, S., O'Connell, M., & Pease, K. (1990). *The Kirkholt Burglary Prevention Project* (Crime Prevention Unit Paper 23). London: Home Office.

Johnson, S. D., Bowers, K., & Pease, K. (2005). Predicting the future or summarising the past? Crime mapping as anticipation. In M. Smith & N. Tilley (Eds.), *Crime science: New approaches to preventing and detecting crime*. Cullompton, UK: Willan.

Tilley, N. (1993) *After Kirkholt: Theory, method and results of replication evaluations* (Crime Prevention Unit Paper 47). London: Home Office.

L

LANDMARK VICTIM-RELATED COURT CASES, FEDERAL, UNITED STATES

The United States Supreme Court and the federal appellate courts have decided many landmark victim-related cases since the 1980s. In the U.S. legal system, laws have little practical meaning without judicial interpretation; therefore, case law is crucial to our understanding of the contours of victims' legal rights and remedies. Landmark victim-related cases are those that establish new legal principles or substantially change existing law and that have great significance to the evolution of the victims' rights movement. Historically, the goals of this movement have been to expand victims' participatory rights in the criminal process, to secure adequate restitution for victims, and to enact better crime control measures. These goals provide a useful framework for this discussion of landmark victim-related cases.

Participation in the Criminal Process

Victim Impact Evidence

The most recognized victim-related cases in the United States are the Supreme Court's decisions involving victim impact evidence (VIE) at sentencing. Although initially disinclined to permit VIE, the Court eventually granted victims the right to participate in capital sentencings. These cases mark the Court's earliest recognition of the victims' rights movement.

In *Booth v. Maryland*, 482 U.S. 496 (1987), the Supreme Court held that consideration of VIE— evidence about victims and their family—at the penalty phase of a capital trial was unconstitutional. Because the jury's focus shifts from the defendant to the victim when presented with VIE, the decision to impose the death penalty could be arbitrary and capricious. Recognizing society's growing concern for victims' rights, the *Booth* dissenters urged deference to state legislatures' decisions to expand victims' role at sentencing.

The Supreme Court extended the holding of *Booth* in *South Carolina v. Gathers*, 490 U.S. 805 (1989), to bar VIE from a prosecutor's argument to the jury. The Court held that the prosecutor's argument, in which he commented extensively on the victim's personal characteristics, impermissibly introduced sentencing factors unrelated to the defendant's blameworthiness. The dissenters in *Gathers* argued that jurors should know the human cost of the crime and called for *Booth* to be overruled.

The reconfigured Supreme Court did just that in *Payne v. Tennessee*, 501 U.S. 808 (1991). The Court held that consideration of VIE at capital sentencings is not unconstitutional. The opinion focused on the direct relationship between the degree of harm suffered by the victim's family and the defendant's punishment. The strong public support for victims' rights influenced the Court's decision. Irrespective of the rationale, *Payne* represented a paradigm shift in the Court's view of victims' rights.

Enforcement of Victims' Rights

Since *Payne*, federal and state legislation has greatly expanded crime victims' rights to participate in criminal cases. Even more significant, however, is the development of mechanisms for victims to enforce these rights.

Enforcement has not always been available to victims. For example, in *United States v. McVeigh*, 106 F.3d 325 (10th Cir. 1997), the district court entered an order prohibiting victim witnesses from attending the trial of Timothy McVeigh, one of the Oklahoma City bombers. The excluded victims appealed. The Tenth Circuit Court of Appeals held that it did not have jurisdiction to overturn the appeal because neither the relevant federal statute nor the Constitution granted the victims a legally protected interest in attending the trial. However, public outcry after the *McVeigh* holding prompted Congress to pass emergency legislation to allow the excluded victims to attend the trial, notwithstanding their intent to give VIE at sentencing.

Recent cases reflect legislative efforts to create enforcement mechanisms for victims and a shift in judicial interpretation of victims' statutory rights. In *Kenna v. United States District Court for the Central District of California*, 435 F.3d 1011 (9th Cir. 2006), the Ninth Circuit Court of Appeals reviewed a provision of the Crime Victims' Rights Act (CVRA). Victims of a multimillion-dollar fraud scheme gave VIE at one defendant's sentencing hearing, but the district court denied them the opportunity to speak again at the other defendant's hearing. On appeal, the *Kenna* Court interpreted the CVRA's right to be reasonably heard to mean the right to speak at every relevant sentencing hearing, not just the right to submit a single written statement. The Court endorsed the CVRA's aim to make victims full participants in the criminal trial process and to give victims equal footing with prosecutors and defendants.

The shift in favor of victims has come so far that, in *United States v. Perry*, 360 F.3d 519 (6th Cir. 2004), the Sixth Circuit Court of Appeals allowed a victim, although not a party to the criminal case, to appeal a restitution order. Until *Perry*, federal courts had found that the Constitution prevented victims from making such challenges.

These cases are significant. They demonstrate that Congress and the courts are responding to public opinion in favor of the expansion of victims' rights. Although the issues of whether a victim has a legal interest in the criminal trial of a defendant and, if so, whether that interest should be enforceable, are still unsettled, the courts appear to be siding with victims.

Victims' Civil Remedies

The questions surrounding victims' legal interests are not limited to the context of criminal trials. Victims also seek civil remedies from defendants and from government entities that have failed to protect them. In contrast to lawsuits against offenders in state courts, victims' federal lawsuits must overcome certain constitutional barriers. Therefore, federal lawsuits have met with limited success.

Lawsuits Against Offenders

For example, when a campus rape victim sued her perpetrators under the Violence Against Women Act of 1994 (VAWA), the statute was struck down. Congress and victims' advocates had intended the VAWA civil rights statute to provide recourse beyond traditional state law remedies to victims of gender-based violence. The Supreme Court held in *United States v. Morrison*, 529 U.S. 598 (2000) that Congress lacked the necessary constitutional authority to enact that particular section of VAWA. Despite this ruling, several states enacted similar legislation, and victims continue to seek civil redress in state courts.

Lawsuits Against the U.S. Government

Victims have secured more rights in the criminal process over the course of the victims' rights movement, yet there has been no corresponding development in victims' lawsuits against governmental entities. The Supreme Court has held that the government generally has no constitutional duty to provide protection against privately inflicted harms or to enforce all laws.

In *DeShaney v. Winnebago County Department of Social Services*, 489 U.S. 189 (1989), the Department of Social Services failed to take action for over 2 years in a suspected child abuse case, which resulted in irreversible brain damage of the 4-year-old victim. The social service officials knew that his father posed a risk of violence but failed to intervene. Nevertheless, because the child's injury occurred at the hands of a private party and the child was not in government custody, there was no constitutional violation.

The Supreme Court recently affirmed the *DeShaney* holding in *Town of Castle Rock, Colorado v. Gonzales*, 545 U.S. 748 (2005). Gonzales reported that her husband had taken their children in violation of a restraining order, but the police repeatedly refused to take action. Later that evening, Gonzales's husband murdered the children and was killed in a shoot-out with the police. The Court found that, despite its mandatory language, the state law did not give Gonzales entitlement to the enforcement of a restraining order because the police and prosecution had some discretion with respect to its enforcement.

In addition to finding that the government has no affirmative duty to protect victims from their offenders, the Supreme Court also has imposed constitutional barriers to federal causes of action. The Court has severely circumscribed crime victims' use of the Constitution as a remedy for the wrongful conduct of government entities and officers.

Crime Control Measures

In addition to imposing limits on victims' ability to secure civil remedies, the Supreme Court has sometimes hindered victims' push for greater crime control. Victims seek the enactment of laws that criminalize more behavior, enhance the severity of criminals' punishment, and provide victims with protections and reparations. The Court has invalidated such laws if they burden criminal defendants' constitutional rights.

Notoriety for Profit

The Supreme Court considered New York's "Son of Sam" law in *Simon & Schuster, Inc. v. Members of the New York State Crime Victims Board*, 502 U.S. 105 (1991). To prevent criminals from profiting from their crimes and to recompense victims, the law required an accused or convicted criminal's income from works depicting his crimes to be collected and distributed to the victims of the crime. The Supreme Court held the law unconstitutional because it imposed a financial burden on speakers solely because of the particular content of the speech. New York and other states subsequently remedied the constitutional deficiencies in their Son of Sam laws.

Hate Crimes

Hate crime legislation seeks to criminalize behavior that is motivated by certain characteristics of the victim. The Supreme Court considered whether expressions of hate against victims, such as cross burning, can be prohibited and punished in *R.A.V. v. City of St. Paul, Minnesota*, 505 U.S. 377 (1992). The Court struck down an ordinance that prohibited hate speech based on race, color, creed, religion, and gender. The Court held that the government may not regulate speech on the basis of the government's hostility or favoritism toward the underlying message expressed.

However, in *Wisconsin v. Mitchell*, 508 U.S. 476 (1993), the Supreme Court upheld a sentencing statute that enhanced the penalty for a defendant convicted of a physical assault who intentionally selected his victim because of the person's race. The Court ruled that the statute did not violate the defendant's free speech rights by punishing his beliefs; the statute punished the bias motivation behind his conduct. The Court affirmed this principle in *Virginia v. Black*, 538 U.S. 343 (2003), in which it upheld a law banning cross burning so long as it required the state to prove that the defendant acted with the intent to intimidate the victim.

These cases epitomize the inherent conflict between victims' rights and defendants' rights. Hate crime legislation attempts to reconcile the two by regulating biased conduct against victims without censoring defendants' speech.

Sex Offender Registration and Notification

Victims' advocates pushed for the enactment of sex offender registration and notification laws to prevent against sexual victimization. Thus the Supreme Court recently considered the constitutionality of state versions of Megan's Law. The Court upheld the state laws in *Connecticut Department of Public Safety v. Doe*, 538 U.S. 1 (2003), and in *Smith v. Doe*, 538 U.S. 84 (2003), finding no constitutional infirmity with regulatory measures adopted for public safety reasons. These cases signal the Court's continued protection of victims; however, they do not end future challenges to these laws.

Future Outlook

Throughout these cases, the Supreme Court has explicitly acknowledged the need to provide victims with more rights and with enforceable remedies. The Court, however, has placed the onus on Congress and state legislatures to create a remedial system within constitutional boundaries. As public sentiment in favor of victims' rights continues to grow, we can expect a legislative and judicial expansion of victims' rights and remedies. Because such rights and remedies will likely conflict with defendants' rights and present constitutional questions, it is inevitable that the Supreme Court will revisit the issues presented in these landmark victim-related cases.

Angela K. Reitler

See also Civil Litigation; Defendants' Rights Versus Victims' Rights; Politics and Victims; Victim Impact Statements; Victims' Rights Legislation, Federal, United States

Further Readings

Beloof, D. E. (2005). The third wave of crime victims' rights: Standing, remedy, and review. *Brigham Young University Law Review, 2,* 255–370.

Blume, J. H. (2003). Ten years of Payne: Victim impact evidence in capital cases. *Cornell Law Review, 88,* 257–281.

Chemerinsky, E. (2006). *Constitutional law: Principles and policies.* New York: Aspen.

Henderson, L. (1999). Revisiting victim's rights. *Utah Law Review, 2,* 383–442.

Tobolowsky, P. M. (2001). *Crime victim rights and remedies.* Durham, NC: Carolina Academic Press.

Wood, J. (2008). *The Crime Victims' Rights Act of 2004 and the federal courts.* Washington, DC: Federal Judicial Center. Retrieved August 26, 2008, from http://www.uscourts.gov/rules/cvra0806.pdf

LANDMARK VICTIM-RELATED COURT CASES, INTERNATIONAL

Starting with the creation of the International Military Tribunals at Nuremberg and Tokyo in the aftermath of World War II, the international community set up various international criminal courts over the course of the 20th century whose goal was to prosecute acts of particular gravity. Victims' rights before international courts, which were completely excluded from the proceedings in the early days of international justice, have considerably evolved in the last decade. After a brief presentation of the existing international criminal jurisdictions, this entry examines their definition of the victim and presents some important cases that have shaped the rights of the victims appearing before them.

International Criminal Tribunals

In 1993 and 1994 respectively, the United Nations established two international criminal tribunals to prosecute very serious violations of international humanitarian law committed in the former Yugoslavia since 1991 and in Rwanda during 1994. Under their rules of proceedings, victims have no autonomous role. They have no legal representatives, have no access to the files of the case, and cannot intervene except as witnesses (and only when asked to do so by the court, the prosecutor, or the defense). They cannot claim any compensation and only have a right to *restitution* (i.e., the return of any property acquired by criminal conduct to their rightful owners). However, a tribunal's guilty verdict can be used by the victim to claim compensation in his or her national jurisdiction. The reason for such a limited role for victims resides in the fact that it was thought at the time of the creation of the tribunals that the prosecution represented the interests of the victims as well as those of the international community. The Rome Statute (1998), however, recognizes that these interests may conflict and thus that victims need their own representatives.

Hybrid Tribunals

In addition to international tribunals, various hybrid criminal tribunals were set up between 2000 and 2007, namely the special courts for Bosnia-Herzegovina, Cambodia, East Timor, Lebanon, and Sierra Leone. Each has its own characteristics, but all are regulated by national as well as international law, are integrated into the national justice systems, and are financially supported by the international community. They all have jurisdiction over massive violations of international criminal law as well as some serious offences of national criminal law, and they employ both international and national magistrates. Being implemented on national territory, where the crimes occurred, the tribunals are culturally and politically close to the victims. Nevertheless, victims' rights in the jurisdictions vary greatly, and though still unclear, the tribunals' provisions seem limited in that respect.

International Criminal Court

The situation is different before the International Criminal Court (ICC), which for the first time in international law grants autonomous rights to the victims. The ICC is an independent and permanent tribunal created and regulated by the Rome Statute, which was joined by 108 state members. It tries individuals prosecuted for crimes against humanity such as genocides and war crimes. The Rome Statute and the Rules of Procedure and Evidence (RPE) both contain provisions that allow the victim to participate in the criminal justice process, which requires that the victim first be defined.

Definition of the Victim

Rule 85 of the ICC RPE defines two types of victims. People are considered victims when they "have suffered harm as a result of the commission of any crime within the jurisdiction of the Court." Organizations and institutions, however, may have the status of victims if they have sustained "direct harm to any of their property which is dedicated to religion, education, art or science or charitable purposes and to their historic monuments, hospitals and other places and objects for humanitarian purposes."

This raises two questions: First, what is *harm*? Second, when does the status of victim take effect?

The definition of *harm* can be problematic: What degree of harm must a person have suffered to qualify as a victim and how direct must it be? As harm is not defined in the Rome Statute or in the RPE, it lies within the court's competence to define it on a case by case basis: physical harm, moral suffering, and material loss all constitute harm. It seems that the court will also consider indirect suffering, In a decision dated June 29, 2006, the court referred to the definition given by

the *United Nations Declaration of Basic Principles of Justice for Victims of Crime and Abuse of Power* in 1985, which includes suffering caused by the loss of a close relative while helping victims or trying to prevent victimization.

Then, as indicated in a decision by the Pre-Trial Chamber I, dated January 17, 2006, there must be a causal link between the harm suffered and a crime falling within the jurisdiction of the Court. This means that the alleged victim must be able to prove that he or she was victimized by the accused; hence the importance that the victim be allowed to participate in the proceedings at an early stage to help establish the identity of his or her aggressor. However, in the *Lubanga* case, the court ruled that, at the early stage of the trial, when a *situation* is investigated, it is sufficient for the victim to establish there are *grounds to believe* that he or she was victimized by the accused. Later, when a *case* is being tried, the victim must show there are reasonable grounds to believe that he or she was victimized by the accused during the crimes for which the accused is being tried by the court.

When does the status of victim take effect? In the decision of January 17, 2006, the court held that the right of the victims to participate starts as early as the investigation on the situation, that is, even before an arrest warrant or a summons to appear is issued.

Rights of Participation

How the provisions of the Rome Statute and the RPE regarding victims should be put into practice precisely is left to the court to determine. Victims have a right to participate at any stage of the proceedings, when *their interests are affected*. This is a flexible criterion, which will depend, among other elements, on the stage of the proceedings.

As stated in the decision of January 17, 2006, the rights of participation of the victims start at pretrial stage, when the court tries to determine whether there is a ground for prosecution. Victims must be informed if the court or the prosecutor decides not to proceed with an investigation. Their rights also include the right to attend the hearing, to present oral and written views and concerns, to present evidence, and to examine and cross-examine witnesses. They have a right to be informed of the requests and conclusions made by the other parties, and of the progress of the proceedings. They also have a right to make observations when the jurisdiction of the court or the admissibility of an action is challenged. However, victims have no right to open an investigation.

Moreover, victims have a right to legal representation: Rule 90 of the RPE states that victims are free to choose a legal representative, which the court shall only limit if it is inappropriate in a specific case.

Victims may benefit from *protective measures*. In the *Lubanga* case, the Pre-Trial Chamber I held that the protection of victims, up to then restricted to victims "appearing before the Court," should be extended to victim applicants, who must be protected from the time the court receives a completed application to participate in the trial. When appearing as witnesses, victims must be protected against reprisals from the offenders, but also from a possible revictimization caused by the trial itself. Their privacy must be protected, and the prosecutor can withhold any evidence that can gravely endanger a witness or a witness's family. The court may derogate to the principle of public hearing and may allow evidence to be presented by electronic means, for example by allowing a witness to testify by video.

But there are limits as to how and when victims may participate: It is the court's competence to decide in what form and when it is appropriate for victims to intervene (i.e., in a manner that is not prejudicial to the rights of the accused). They must apply in writing to the registrar (i.e., the principal administrative officer of the court) before being allowed to address a trial chamber. If there are numerous victims, they may be asked to choose one or more common representatives, unless there is a conflict of interests, in which case separate representation will be allowed. Victims' legal representatives may only examine witnesses, experts, or the defendant once authorized to do so by the trial chamber, and may be requested to do it only in writing.

Rights of Reparation

The ICC is the first international jurisdiction to grant victims a right to reparation. As an individual right, it is independent from the right to participate. But the court can also order collective reparations, which shall benefit all the victims of a crime, including victims not represented during the proceedings. Reparation can be granted to the victims themselves or to their families and dependents.

The ICC statute provides for three forms of reparations, namely, restitution, compensation, and rehabilitation. *Restitution* aims at restoring victims to the situation that was theirs prior to the crime; this includes the restitution of their property and employment as well as their return to their place of residence. *Compensation* is reparation for the damage suffered; it is a substitute for restitution, and can be awarded for medical expenses, loss of earnings, and compensation for physical and mental sufferings. *Rehabilitation* includes psychological and medical care, as well as social and legal assistance. It aims at alleviating the consequences of the crime. However, the list is not exhaustive. For example, the court can request guarantees of nonrepetition or order public apologies, or that a judgment be publicized. The court may ask states to proceed to seizures of property and assets against individuals for the restitution to victims, and states are required to comply with such orders. Yet, the court cannot issue reparation orders against states themselves.

To help the court determine the appropriate compensation, it can appoint experts to help establish loss, injury, and damage. The Rome Statute also establishes a trust fund for victims, which benefits crime victims within the jurisdiction of the court and their families. This serves two goals: providing reparation to the victims when the court makes awards to victims through the fund and managing voluntary contributions to the benefit of larger groups of victims who may not have suffered directly from the crimes within the jurisdiction of the Court.

What is not known yet is at what stage of the trial the victim can apply to obtain them: Must the victim wait until the accused is pronounced guilty, or are reparations due as soon as the victim has proved him- or herself a victim? What about victims who join trial after the guilty verdict? The principles governing reparations are still uncertain and will be established by the court, as prescribed by Article 75 of the Rome Statute.

The Victims and Witnesses Unit

Besides allowing for the participation and reparation of the victims, the court, through the Victims and Witnesses Unit, also provides counseling and protection for the victims, the witnesses, and their families. It supplies them with medical care and psychological support, and it guarantees their protection and right to privacy before, during, and after trial.

Final Thoughts

Many questions relating to victims' rights remain unanswered. However, an international criminal jurisdiction has granted victims the right to participate at any stage of the proceedings. It has been recognized that victims play a unique role in helping to establish the reality of the heinous crimes prosecuted before the International Criminal Court, and thus should be allowed to participate under the best conditions. It also shows the will of the international community to overcome the sole logic of punishment and to establish some sort of restorative justice.

Joelle Vuille

See also Landmark Victim-Related Court Cases, Federal, United States; Restorative Justice; Victims' Rights Legislation, International; Victims' Rights Movement, International; War Crimes

Further Readings

Bassiouni, M. C. (2003). *Introduction to international criminal law*. Ardsley, NY: Transnational.

Calvo-Goller, K. N. (2006). *The trial proceedings of the International Criminal Court, ICTY and ICTR precedents*. Leiden, the Netherlands: Martinus Nijhoff.

Cassese, A. (2003). *International criminal law*. Oxford, UK: Oxford University Press.

Haslam, E. (2004). Victim participation at the International Criminal Court: A triumph of hope over experience? In D. McGoldrick, P. Rowe, & E. Donnelly (Eds.), *The permanent International Criminal Court: Legal and policy issues* (pp. 315–334). Oxford, UK: Hart.

International Criminal Court. (2002). *Rules of procedure and evidence*. Retrieved from http://www.icc-cpi.int/NR/rdonlyres/F1E0AC1C-A3F3-4A3C-B9A7=B3E8B115E886/140164/Rules_of_procedure_and_Evidence_English.pdf

International Federation for Human Rights (FIDH). (2007). *Victims' rights before the International Criminal Court: A guide for victims, their legal representatives and NGOs*. Available at http://www.fidh.org

Scalia, D. (2008). La place des victimes devant la Cour pénale internationale [The place of the victim before the International Criminal Court]. In R. Kolb (Ed.), *Droit international pénal* (pp. 311–340). Basel, Switzerland: Helbing Lichtenhahn/Bruylant.

Schabas, W. (2004). *An introduction to the International Criminal Court* (2nd ed.). Cambridge, UK: Cambridge University Press.

LARCENY/THEFT

The terms *larceny* and *theft* are often used interchangeably, however, *theft* is the more general term and encompasses many different acts of taking property, including larceny. The United States government defines larceny/theft as the unlawful taking and/or possessing of property that belongs to another individual. The majority of statutes require three elements for an act to be considered larceny. The perpetrator must (1) actually take or attempt to take (2) someone else's property, and (3) there must be criminal intent (*mens rea*) to take the property, knowing that it belongs to another. Larceny/theft is one of the four Part I property crimes reported yearly by the the Uniform Crime Reporting (UCR) Program of the Federal Bureau of Investigation (FBI). The FBI distinguishes larceny/theft from motor vehicle theft, as each crime encompasses its own definition within the UCR Program. The other two categories of Part I property crimes are burglary and arson.

Within the UCR Program definition, larceny encompasses many aspects of theft, including shoplifting, pickpocketing, and bicycle theft. Force is not used in cases of larceny-theft. When force is applied when taking property, the crime receives the more severe label of robbery or burglary. Although motor vehicle theft is not considered larceny, the theft of items within the vehicle or on the vehicle (e.g., car parts, stereos) would be considered larceny, as long as force was not applied. Less severe aspects of theft, including embezzlement, writing fraudulent checks, and other forms of forgery are not included within this definition of larceny-theft. Instead they occupy a place within the UCR Program's Part II crime list.

Types

Grand/Petit Larceny

The definitions of grand (big) and petit (little) larceny differ across jurisdictions. Each jurisdiction will set a monetary amount that signifies the point at which a crime's classification changes from petit larceny to grand larceny. Many jurisdictions will use the value of $1,000 to make this determination. Larceny in which the value of what the perpetrator took or attempted to take is $1,000 or more is labeled grand larceny. Thus if the value of the merchandise in question is less than $1,000, the crime is considered petit larceny. The following forms of larceny-theft could be either grand or petit, simply depending on the worth of the goods.

Direct Taking

Shoplifting is the direct taking of merchandise from a retail store without paying for the goods. According to a recent *USA Today* report, occurrences of shoplifting continue to rise as economy struggles. Shoplifting is often one of the first forms of larceny/theft committed by young children. This can include taking penny candy from a grocery store or taking a toy at a garage sale. Other forms of direct taking include bicycle theft, pickpocketing, and taking motor vehicle parts.

Indirect Taking

Indirect taking is defined by the individual's actions immediately after obtaining the merchandise. It is the actions taken by the individual that determine whether the act should be labeled larceny. For example, finding a purse on the subway is not a crime. However, if the individual who finds the purse takes the money and credit cards from the purse, with the intent of using the funds for his or her own purpose, the act becomes larceny. Jurisdictions differ in their responses to indirect-taking crimes. Some choose to follow the common law model, stating that larceny occurs only if the individual intended to commit the crime (*mens rea*) after discovering the property in question. Other jurisdictions use the Model Penal Code, Section 223.5, which defines an act to be larceny if the individual does not attempt to return the merchandise to its rightful owner.

Deceptive Taking

Deceptive taking implies the use of deception to carry out larceny. The perpetrator may pretend to be someone else in order to coerce an individual into turning over his or her property. The perpetrator may also withhold information from the individual to get the property. If an individual willingly turns over or gives his or her property to the perpetrator, but the individual does so based on the deceit or deceptive promises of the perpetrator, larceny has occurred.

Prevalence

Although occurrences of larceny/theft are declining, this crime accounted for the largest percentage of property crimes committed in 2006. Approximately 66.6% of 2006 property crimes were larceny/theft. Furthermore, according to the UCR Program reports, $5.6 billion worth of property was taken in instances of larceny/theft. The UCR Program distinguishes between types of larceny, but not between petit and grand larceny. Except for the "other" category, which encompasses 33% of larceny occurrences, the majority of larceny/theft occurrences were found to be from motor vehicles (26.5%). This does not include the taking of motor vehicle parts and/or accessories. Following theft from motor vehicles were shoplifting (13.2%), theft from buildings (12.6%), theft of motor vehicle accessories (9.7%) and bicycles (3.5%), purse snatching (0.6%), theft from coin-operated machines (0.5%), and pickpocketing (0.4%).

Larceny rates were reported to have declined from 2005 by 3.5%. Furthermore, in the past decade, larceny rates have declined 23.7%. The national average of reported larceny/theft was 2,206.8 per 100,000 people. This rate was found to be highest in cities outside a metropolitan area (2,864.6 per 100,000). The reported rate for both metropolitan statistical areas (2,303.1 per 100,000) and nonmetropolitan areas (992.1 per 100,000) was under the national average.

The prevalence of larceny/theft varies across United States geographical regions. The highest rate of larceny/theft occurs in the South (41.3%). The West is second (22.8%), followed by the Midwest (22.5%), and the Northeast (13.4%). Furthermore, the leading property crime in the South, Midwest, and Northeast is larceny/theft.

Larceny/theft is the lowest reported property crime in the West, however, trailing behind motor vehicle theft (36.8%) and burglary (23.1%).

Clearance/Arrest

In 2006, the UCR Program's reports showed that more cases of larceny/theft were cleared, either by arrest or other exceptional circumstances, than those of any other property crime except arson (18%). Larceny/theft cases were cleared 17.4% of the time. Although this is greater than the burglary (12.6%) and motor vehicle theft (12.6%) rates, it remains exceptionally low compared to the clearance rates of all violent crimes. Violent crime clearance rates in 2006 ranged from 25.2% (robbery) to 60.7% (murder). The Northeast has the highest rate of larceny/theft clearances (20.6%), followed by the South (17.6%), the Midwest (17.1%), and the West (15.7%).

In most jurisdictions, whether a crime is judged grand or petit larceny is what defines the crime as either a felony or a misdemeanor. Grand larceny is usually categorized as a felony and punishable with time in prison. Petit larceny is usually categorized as a misdemeanor, punishable by no more than one year in jail. However, punishments may vary, especially if the jurisdiction utilizes structured sentencing guidelines, which take into account not only the severity of the current offense, but the perpetrator's prior criminal history as well.

Supreme Court Cases

The United States Supreme Court, as well as lower courts, has repeatedly examined the issue of larceny/theft. A 1971 California case examined the idea of indirect taking in *People v Stay* (96 Cal. Rptr 651 [Cal. App. 1971]), in which the defendant was found guilty of grand larceny for collecting shopping carts and demanding that the store give him a "reward" for the return of the carts. The Court held that the carts were not lost and a reward was not justified.

The 2001 case of *People v Rohlfsn* (Illinois Court of Appeals 752 N.E.2d 499) examined the concept of deceitful taking. A prisoner called an elderly woman from the prison phone, claiming to be her relative and asking her to send $1,500 to the jail for him. Correctional officers intercepted the check before it could be cashed, and the court found that the funds had been obtained through deception and charged the individual with larceny.

The United States Supreme Court debated the issue of ownership of property in a 1952 case, *Morissette v. United States* (342 U.S. 246). The defendant claimed that he took scrap metal, believing it to be abandoned property. Abandoned property, or property without an owner, cannot be the victim of larceny/theft. The court held that ownership in this case could not be proven, and the defendant was cleared.

Amanda M. Sharp Parker

See also Burglary; Identity Theft; Motor Vehicle Theft; Robbery; Uniform Crime Reporting (UCR) Program

Further Readings

Dugas, C. (2008, June 18). *More consumers, workers shoplift as economy slows*. Retrieved July 25, 2008, from http://www.usatoday.com/money/industries/retail/2008-06-18-shoplifting_N.htm

Federal Bureau of Investigation. (2006). *Crime in the United States*. Retrieved July 23, 2008, from http://www.fbi.gov

Gardner, T. J., & Anderson, T. M. (2006). *Criminal law* (9th ed.). Belmont, CA: Thomson Wadsworth.

Morissette v. United States (342 U.S. 246).

Pennsylvania Consolidated Statutes. (2000). *Theft by deception*. Retrieved July 23, 2008, from http://members.aol.com/StatutesP3/18PA3922.html

People v. Rohlfsn (Illinois Court of Appeals 752 N.E.2d 499).

People v. Stay (96 Cal. Rptr 651 (Cal. App. 1971)).

LAUTENBERG AMENDMENT

The Lautenberg Amendment is a protective measure for victims of domestic violence. The U.S. Congress enacted it to protect abuse victims, as the possession of a firearm by a chronically abusive partner greatly increases the chance that the victim will receive a fatal injury. In 1996, Congress passed the Omnibus Consolidated Appropriations Act of 1997, enacting the Domestic Violence Offender Gun Act in the process. Because the bill was sponsored by Senator Frank Lautenberg (D) of New Jersey, the Domestic Violence Offender Gun Act became known as the Lautenberg Amendment. The Lautenberg Amendment made possessing, receiving, or shipping a firearm a federal crime for individuals who had been convicted on a misdemeanor domestic violence charge or had been convicted of child abuse. In addition, the Lautenberg Amendment made it illegal to sell or issue a firearm or ammunition to such an individual. It is considered an amendment to the Omnibus Crime Bill and Safe Streets Act of 1968, also known as the Gun Control Act (GCA) of 1968, as it did not provide exceptions that the GCA had included for law enforcement and military personnel, and it expanded the GCA list of persons who were prohibited to possess, receive, or ship firearms. The lack of exceptions for law enforcement and military personnel is the root cause for the extent of the controversy surrounding the Lautenberg Amendment.

Twentieth-Century Gun Control Legislation

During the 20th century, numerous gun control measures were enacted. The National Firearms Act of 1934 called for the registration and taxation of a specific classification of weapons (e.g., machine guns, sawed-off shotguns, silencers). In 1938, the Federal Firearms Act set certain policies for the sale of firearms and introduced the federal firearms license for businesses that sold or repaired firearms. The aforementioned GCA of 1968 provided an extensive set of regulations. The most notable of these regulations dealt with age requirements for purchasing a firearm; the prohibition of certain individuals from possessing firearms, namely felons; the prohibition of shipping firearms and ammunition through the mail system; and specific sentencing guidelines for offenders who used firearms during a crime. When the Brady Handgun Violence Prevention Act was passed in 1994, it was viewed as the next major gun control legislation. The Brady bill instituted the requirements for states to conduct background checks on handgun sales and a 5-day waiting period for the background check. The Violent Crime Control and Law Enforcement Act of 1994 outlawed the manufacturing of numerous types of assault rifles and high-capacity magazines that held more than 10 rounds of ammunition.

The Lautenberg Amendment strengthened the then recently passed Violence Against Women Act (VAWA) of 1994. The VAWA made it against the law for an individual under a restraining order to possess a firearm; however, like its predecessors, it provided exceptions for law enforcement and military personnel. Under the Lautenberg Amendment, individuals under a restraining order for domestic violence are prohibited from possessing a firearm, including those who would normally have the authority to do so under the auspices of law enforcement or military duties.

Arguments Against and For the Lautenberg Amendment

Anti–Lautenberg Amendment

A contingent of law enforcement and military officials opposed the Lautenberg Amendment on the grounds of constitutionality in the following areas: (1) its application to misdemeanor domestic violence and not to other misdemeanor crimes; (2) its lack of application to individuals who are convicted of felony-type domestic violence charges; (3) its unfair singling out of law enforcement. This anti–Lautenberg Amendment contingent complained that the amendment would cause job losses for both law enforcement and military personnel. Another concern for this group is the retroactive nature of the Lautenberg Amendment. The amendment applies to individuals convicted after the date of enactment as well as to individuals with domestic violence convictions dated before the law went into effect.

Pro–Lautenberg Amendment

Advocates of the Lautenberg Amendment, including certain law enforcement organizations, argue that upon receiving a conviction for domestic violence or child abuse, individuals who had been trusted with the duty and corresponding authority to protect society should be seen as having abandoned their posts and be identified as convicted abusers. According to the amendment's supporters, law enforcement or police duties do not afford convicted abusers extra rights or protection from the consequences of their convictions. Those in favor of the Lautenberg Amendment also argue that since so many domestic violence and child abuse incidents are reported to the police every year, the victims reporting the abuse should not have to worry that the officers responding to their calls may be abusers.

Joshua Lawrance Balay

See also Brady Bill; Domestic Violence, Committed by Police and Military Personnel; Guns and Victimization; Violence Against Women Act of 1994 and Subsequent Revisions; Violent Crime Control and Law Enforcement Act of 1994

Further Readings

Adelman, M., & Morgan, P. (2006). Law enforcement versus battered women: The conflict over the Lautenberg Amendment. *Journal of Women and Social Work, 1,* 28–45. Retrieved September 13, 2008, from http://www.jstor.org/stable/1147674

Bellesiles, M. A. (2001). Firearms regulation: A historical overview. *Crime and Justice, 28,* 137–195.

Bridges, S. F., Tatum, K. M., & Kunselman, J. C. (2008). Domestic violence statutes and rates of intimate partner and family homicide: A research note. *Criminal Justice Policy Review, 1,* 117–130.

Spitzer, R. J. (2007). *The politics of gun control* (4th ed.). Washington, DC: CQ Press.

LAW ENFORCEMENT ASSISTANCE ADMINISTRATION (LEAA)

The Law Enforcement Assistance Administration (LEAA) was the first program of significant federal aid for state and local law enforcement and criminal justice efforts. Moreover, the Safe Street Act and LEAA began a new era of federal assistance to state and local governments that continues to this day. Thus the LEAA program, which was initiated in response to the social turbulence of the 1960s and continued through the 1970s, educated and trained thousands of criminal justice personnel.

The 1960s was one of the most tumultuous decades in American history. Serious crimes reported to the police nearly tripled. Robberies doubled. Violent crime rates soared. However, the serious crime conviction rate fell during this period. Crime had reached epidemic proportions, but the criminal justice response to it was seriously flawed. Race relations turned contentious and deadly. Assassinations and random violence increased. In 1962, federal troops were dispatched to the University of Mississippi to enroll the first Black student, James Meredith. The next year federal troops were sent to the University of Alabama. Medgar Evers, an NAACP field secretary, was assassinated by a Ku Klux Klan member in June 1963. Then, in September, four young black girls were murdered in a racially motivated bombing of the Sixteenth Street Baptist Church in Birmingham, Alabama, by Klan members. Two months later, on November 22, 1963, President John F. Kennedy was assassinated in Texas. The 1965 Watts race riot in Los Angeles left 34 dead. Malcolm X, a Black political activist, was assassinated in New York in 1965. In 1966, a sniper at the University of Texas at Austin shot 45 people, killing 14. There were massive race riots in 1967. The first, in Newark, New Jersey, lasted 26 days and left 26 dead. Then in Detroit, Michigan, a riot went on for 8 days and resulted in 43 deaths.

Civil rights leader Martin Luther King Jr. was assassinated on April 4, 1968, in Memphis, Tennessee. Then on June 6, presidential candidate Senator Robert Kennedy was assassinated in Los Angeles. Later that year, the police handling of the protests and resulting riot at the 1968 Democratic National Convention marked the event as a "police riot." In 1969, Charles Manson and his followers killed actress Sharon Tate and three others in Los Angeles. In the waning days of that year, political activist and deputy chairman of the Illinois chapter of the Black Panther Party Fred Hampton was killed under suspicious circumstances by a police tactical unit. Opposition to the war in Vietnam resulted in massive political protests throughout the country, including the killing of four Kent State students at an antiwar demonstration in 1970.

When violence and social protests increased during the 1960s, leading to criminal acts, the need for a federal response became apparent. President Lyndon Johnson prodded Congress into creating the President's Commission on Law Enforcement and Administration of Justice and the passage of the 1965 Law Enforcement Assistance Act. The act created the Office of Law Enforcement Assistance in the Department of Justice to fund demonstration projects to improve the methods of criminal justice administration at state and local levels. This program existed until 1968, when its functions were transferred to the Law Enforcement Assistance Administration.

The 1967 President's Commission's report, *The Challenge of Crime in a Free Society,* recommended that the federal government provide financial assistance to state and local governments for law enforcement purposes, broadly defined as all components of the criminal justice system. Congress responded in 1968 by passing the Omnibus Crime Control and Safe Streets Act. Title I of the act established the Law Enforcement Assistance Administration. The goals of LEAA were (1) to reduce crime and delinquency by encouraging and assisting states in developing comprehensive plans to fight crime, (2) to make block grants to states to provide funding to carry out these plans, (3) to conduct research in law enforcement, and (4) to provide leadership and guidance to state and local governments in their efforts to improve the criminal justice system. The planning assistance, grants, guidance, and leadership were made through state and regional planning agencies. The planning agencies developed comprehensive state plans to improve law enforcement and developed state and local programs and projects. It was a massive centralized federal effort for the decentralized planning, funding, and execution of criminal justice projects at the local level.

The act also established the National Institute of Law Enforcement and Criminal Justice as LEAA's research arm to make grants to public agencies, colleges and universities, and private organizations to conduct studies and research in criminal justice issues. After 1974 the institute also served as a national clearinghouse for the exchange of criminal justice information. In 1979, the functions of the institute were absorbed by the National Institute of Justice.

The program was not without criticism. Congress intended that all criminal justice components would receive grants; however, the law enforcement theme led many to believe it was a "police program." This misunderstanding caused funding problems, with the majority of monies allocated to law enforcement agencies. Block grants to the states were criticized for lax control over the money. There were instances of wasteful use of funds. The program suffered from unrealistic expectations. It was assumed that money was the answer to reducing the crime problem and winning the "war on crime." However, after the expenditure of $7.5 billion, critics pointed out that the program had no real impact on crime. There was one downturn in crime statistics in 1972; however, the reported violent crime rate continued to rise throughout the 1970s. The composition of the planning agencies reduced the transparency of state and local efforts and complicated police–community relations. The planning agencies were composed of only law enforcement agencies and local units of government, which minimized input from community and citizen groups, particularly minorities. The red tape involved was a nightmare for many grant recipients.

Many current criminal justice professors began their education with LEAA grants and loans. And many programs, or variants of these programs, begun with federal seed money are still in place. Thus LEAA demonstrated that the federal government can play a valuable role in helping state and local governments deal with the crime problem. The research emphasis of LEAA is ongoing. Criminal justice planning, analysis, and evaluation became important concepts as a result of LEAA.

Tom Barker

See also President's Crime Commission Report, 1967

Further Readings

Federal crime control efforts. (1994, June–July). *Congressional Digest,* pp. 162–192.

Haynes, P. (1986). Measuring financial support for state courts: Lessons from the LEAA Experience. *The Justice System Journal, 11*(2), 148–167.

Kimberling, W. C., & Fryback, J. T. (1973). Systematic evaluation of criminal justice projects: A state of the art in the United States. *Journal of Criminal Justice, 1,* 145–160.

L.E.A.A., just first step in legal reorganization. (1978). *Lawscope. 64,* 179–180.

President's Commission. (1967). *The challenge of crime in a free society: A report by the President's Commission on Law Enforcement and Administration of Justice.* Washington, DC: U.S. Government Printing Office.

LIFESTYLE THEORY

In 1978, Michael Hindelang, Michael Gottfredson, and James Garofalo published *Victims of Personal Crime: An Empirical Foundation for a Theory of Personal Victimization*. In this book, the authors stated that people play a role in their own victimization by engaging in lifestyles and making certain lifestyle choices that make them more accessible to offenders and easier targets for crime. This assertion started a new line of inquiry in criminological theory by suggesting that the choices victims make either increase or decrease their chances for criminal victimization.

Heretofore, scholars had suggested that crime victims could be held at least partially responsible for their victimization due to characteristics they possessed. In the early years of victimology, these characteristics often were presented as typologies. For example, Beniamin Mendelsohn identified five types of victims: innocent victims, victims with minor guilt, victims as guilty as offenders, victims who were guiltier than offenders, and most guilty victims. Similarly, Hans Von Hentig expanded the idea of the victim typology by naming 12 types of crime victims: young, female, elderly, mentally defective, immigrants, minorities, dull normals, depressed, acquisitive, lonesome and heartbroken, tormentors, and blocked, exempted, and fighting. Finally, Thorsten Sellin and Marvin Wolfgang developed a more generalizable list of victim types: primary victims, secondary victims, tertiary victims, and mutual victims. These typologies were helpful in the early stages of victimological research in that scholars could note and understand that criminal victimization was not an entirely random event, and that crime victims could be identified based on some personality or demographic characteristics they held. One problem with these typologies, though, was that many of the victim types represented individuals who had very low rates of victimization (e.g., youth, females, and elderly people). In addition, these typologies tended to suppose that victims were to blame for their own victimization. The emergence of the lifestyle theory of victimization allowed scholars to move beyond the victim-blaming issues and present a better understanding of the relationships between victims and offenders in the context of lifestyles and locations.

Lifestyle Constraints

The main assertion of lifestyle theory is that various lifestyles of individuals place them in greater proximity to criminal offenders, thus they themselves increase their odds of criminal victimization. Also, individuals with certain lifestyles may make better choices for offenders because of their value as individuals, their valuable possessions, or their unwillingness to protect themselves or their property adequately. Michael Hindelang and his colleagues define lifestyle as daily activities and leisure activities in which individuals participate on a routine basis. The concept of lifestyle includes choices individuals make freely and within imposed constraints, as well as behaviors influenced by societal structures and expectations.

To elaborate, lifestyle includes behavioral expectations of persons occupying various social roles. For example, we do not expect new parents to go out partying and drinking all the time after the birth of their child. We anticipate that they will stay at home and take care of their infant. At the same time, young single men and women are "allowed" more freedom to engage in alcohol-related leisure activities. They are unlikely to have important responsibilities at home and can, therefore, go out and have fun. Another example involves the behavioral expectations associated with employment. Those who are employed are usually expected to go to work in the morning, and then leave work in the early evening. They cannot travel across town to see movies whenever they want. It is only after their working hours that they can choose activities like joining a community theater group, playing on a soccer team, or going to happy hour with friends. These lifestyle impositions are attached to individuals who are parents or employees, for example, simply *because of* the social expectations we hold for the persons occupying these roles. Because much crime is committed on the street, parents staying home would be less likely to come into contact with criminally motivated others than the hypothetical young, single, partying men and women.

Another antecedent of lifestyle includes constraints on behavior by virtue of economic status, education, and familial obligations. An example of this type of limitation may be economic circumstances. An individual who wants to go out to dinner is restricted to restaurants that fall within his or her price range. This individual may not have personal transportation and thus may be restricted to restaurants that are within walking distance of his or her home or can be reached by public transportation. However, the individual who is wealthy and does not have personal transportation may eat at any restaurant he or she wants and can take a cab there. If someone is restricted to eating at restaurants that are close to his or her home, then the amount of crime in that neighborhood and in the area of the restaurant influences the safety of that individual.

A final type of influence over individuals' lifestyles is the individual and subcultural adaptations to behavioral and structural constraints. Here an example could be an individual who, because of a worsening economy, has been laid off and has been unable to find another job. This individual could adapt to this increasingly difficult and depressing situation by drinking and becoming addicted to methamphetamines. Another individual in the same circumstances might take up ultimate fighting and use a punching bag to let out frustrations. Still a third individual might sink down into a deep depression and never get out of bed. Those belonging to various subcultures are likely to handle challenges and opportunities in ways that are similar to other members of the same subculture. To specify, members of highly religious affiliations may turn to prayer in order to get divine guidance on how to get through a difficult economic, jobless time, whereas members of outlaw biker gangs may turn to illegal activity to maintain an income in a tough economy. In these examples, obviously, the persons are more or less likely than each other to encounter criminals and criminal behavior, and, as such, more or less likely to become victims.

Michael Maxfield summarizes these differing lifestyle constraints (or lack thereof) and choices by pointing out that they ensure that criminal victimization is not a random event but a highly patterned and potentially somewhat predictable event. He hammers home his point by noting that middle-aged married women in professional occupations have widely differing and significantly lower risks for criminal victimization than unemployed single males in their early 20s.

Contexts Related to Victimization Risk

Some researchers have noted that lifestyle choices and restrictions shape personal victimization risks in the context of location. Thus there are high-risk locations and low-risk locations for criminal victimization, and the risks associated with these locations may vary, increase, or decrease depending on the type of crime examined. For example, a college student going to the library to study seems to be making a safe lifestyle choice when criminal victimization is considered. And, the library may, indeed, be quite safe when considering the risks for assault or murder. However, the campus library may be relatively risky when other crimes, such as theft, are considered. A library patron who is studying, takes a break to use the restroom, and leaves books and a backpack unattended is at a high risk for larceny. The library stacks may also be dangerous places for victimization by lewd exhibitionists. But, one is quite unlikely to be murdered in a library, particularly by a crazed heroin addict who is looking for money for another fix.

Time, according to Garafalo, is another context in which lifestyle and criminal victimization may intersect. According to this perspective, time of day may be highly significant when examining people's risks for criminal victimization. In this way, the social milieu of any particular location changes depending on the time of day and the regular activities that go on in that location at various times of the day. For example, in a large city, there may be a location where prostitutes solicit during the evening hours. This location may be near shops and restaurants. During the day, the shops are open, the restaurants are serving lunch to businesspeople, and there are no prostitutes. However, at night, the shops close, the restaurants are serving alcoholic drinks, and the prostitutes are soliciting drunken patrons as they leave the establishments. Individuals who frequent that location during the day are presumably relatively safe. But, patrons who hang around that location at night are relatively unsafe, particularly if their normal thinking and functioning is impaired by alcohol.

Additional Considerations

In a further exposition of lifestyle theory, Marcus Felson suggests that while criminal offenders do not need much skill, and criminal opportunities are frequent and everywhere, criminals do try to minimize their risks for getting interrupted, injured, or caught. Some of the elements most offenders will consider are when homes are vacant, the amount of money individuals may be carrying with them, and the times the public transportation system is busy or relatively vacant. Other considerations may include the probability that any particular potential victim may fight back and try to thwart the ensuing robbery. Whether or not the liquor store owner has a gun under the counter and can readily grab it are lifestyle factors that would-be offenders may consider. In this way, individuals' lifestyles influence their chances for criminal victimization when their choices affect offenders' perceptions of their vulnerability or predictability.

Similarly, individuals may or may not consider the safety issues in particular locations and, as such, may or may not take necessary defensive measures. They may be unaware of their personal surroundings or may choose to ignore the factors that make certain locations dangerous. As Richard Sparks has noted, individuals may facilitate predation by routinely failing to take certain precautions. Thus exposure to offenders is not just a lifestyle but involves a certain amount of choice, which is influenced by individuals' perceptions of the likelihood of victimization. People choose to recognize or ignore the threat of crime when structuring their daily activities.

Much of the research on lifestyle theory of criminal victimization includes examinations of demographic characteristics. While demographics are not elements of lifestyle, per se, they are part of the lifestyle model because they tend to be indicators of the structural constraints and role expectations that shape individuals' lifestyle behaviors, activities, and choices. For example, research tends to find that married people do not go out at night for leisure activities as often as single, separated, or divorced people. Here, then, being married can serve as a proxy measure of exposure to offenders. Also relevant is the notion that most offenders victimize people who are like themselves. As such, young, poor, Black males are the most likely perpetrators of crime and they are also the most likely victims of such aggression.

Some scholars of lifestyle theory have delved into examinations of cities and neighborhoods. These scholars have noted that the lifestyles of the

residents in these locations tend to be similar to each other, and the "typical" lifestyle of the neighborhood (or a small town) can influence the amount of crime and victimization that occurs in that location. Here, then, the concept of lifestyle is expanded into a more macro notion. An example of this is a neighborhood where most residents know each other. In a location such as this, stealing would be hard to conceal. Personal items belonging to individuals are known to belong to these individuals, and if someone else took possession of an item, others in the neighborhood would know to whom that item belonged. So, the lifestyle of this type of community is one that involves frequent interaction with neighbors, and the fact that most residents of this type of community engage in that type of lifestyle solidifies the relative safety residents experience. Another example of a location with which specific lifestyles are associated is New York City. Many residents of New York City do not own cars because cars are expensive, there is not enough parking for them and the parking that is available is expensive, and the streets are constantly clogged with traffic. Further, the public transportation system is easy to use, cheap, and sufficient for the needs of most residents. As such, many residents of New York City take the subway or buses to get where they need to go. While this lifestyle is more dangerous than driving a car, most New Yorkers make this choice. Thus the residents of New York City have higher risks for criminal victimization than residents of the aforementioned smaller community, but that increased danger is just one of the characteristics associated with the lifestyle of the larger city.

Time, in the context of history, is also a relevant element in the examination of lifestyle and its relationship to criminal victimization. To elaborate, in the early years of settlement in the United States, walking around was the mode of transportation that most people adopted. Cars and other vehicles had not been invented, and horses were not available to all. Towns were sparsely populated, and residents were spread out across the prairie and farming lands. Walking from home to town was not practical and only happened infrequently when farmers traveled to the county seat to get supplies (or made some such similar trip). With the increase of horse ownership, the trip from home to town or home to home was speedier, thus, the amount of stealing increased, as well as the stealing of horses. With the advent of cars and further increases in the number of horses and buggies, crime became much more of a problem, as getting away from the scene of the crime was easier and faster. In addition, cars, horses, and buggies were increasingly targets of theft. At the same time, with the advent of improved transportation came the industrial revolution, and cities continued to grow, people owned more and more of value, and populations were denser. At this point in history, crime increased due to the increased opportunities and the ability to hide in the crowd as well as the speed of escape. As is clear from this type of historical examination, lifestyle is an element of the historical process of city growth and industrialization.

Role in Understanding Victimization

Lifestyle theory provided an alternative path toward understanding criminal victimization. Previously, victims may have been blamed for the devastating events in their lives, and scholars' understanding of victims was limited to simple characteristics they possessed. The additional consideration of individual lifestyle has allowed scholars to understand that victimization is not a random event, but one that can be assessed and potentially predicted. Risks for victimization can be evaluated by considering the locational exposure of individuals to offenders and any precautions (or lack thereof) such individuals may take because of their perceptions of the safety of the locations they frequent. This theory gave rise to another theory of criminal victimization, routine activities theory, and to analyses of personal safety and effective safety precautions.

Elizabeth Ehrhardt Mustaine

See also Correlates of Victimization; Routine Activities Theory; Victimization, Theories of

Further Readings

Felson, M. (1994). *Crime and everyday life: Insight and implications for society*. Thousand Oaks, CA: Pine Forge.

Garafalo, J. (1987). Reassessing the lifestyle model of criminal victimization. *Journal of Quantitative Criminology, 3*(4), 371–393.

Hindelang, M. J., Gottfredson, M. R., & Garofalo, J. (1978). *Victims of personal crime: An empirical foundation for a theory of personal victimization.* Cambridge, MA: Ballinger.

Maxfield, M. (1987). Lifestyle and routine activity theories of crime: Empirical studies of victimization, delinquency, and offender decision making. *Journal of Quantitative Criminology, 3*(4), 275–282.

Sparks, R. (1981). Multiple victimisation: Evidence, theory and future research. *Journal of Criminal Law and Criminology, 72,* 762–778.

LIGHTING

Improved street lighting serves many purposes, one of them being the prevention of crime in public places. Street lighting improvements are not always implemented with the expressed aim of preventing crime; pedestrian and traffic safety may sometimes be viewed as more important aims. But while the notion of lighting streets to deter lurking criminals may seem too simplistic, it is relevant to the prevention of crime in urban centers, residential areas, and other places frequented by potential criminals and potential victims.

Explanations of the way that street lighting improvements could prevent crime can be grouped into two main perspectives: (1) a situational crime prevention measure that focuses on reducing opportunity and increasing perceived risk through modification of the physical environment, and (2) a method of strengthening informal social control and community cohesion through more effective street use and investment in neighborhood conditions. The first perspective predicts decreases in crime especially during the hours of darkness, while the second perspective predicts decreases in crime during both daytime and nighttime.

Background

Contemporary interest in the effect of improved street lighting on crime began in the United States during the dramatic rise in crime in the 1960s. Richard Wright and his colleagues note that many towns and cities embarked upon major street lighting programs as a means of reducing crime, and initial results were encouraging. This proliferation of projects led to a detailed review of the effects of street lighting on crime by James Tien and his colleagues, funded by the National Evaluation Program of Law Enforcement Assistance Agency funding. Their report described how the 103 street lighting projects originally identified were eventually reduced to a final sample of only 15 that were considered by the review team to contain sufficiently rigorous evaluative information. With regard to the impact of street lighting on crime, Tien and his colleagues found that the results were mixed and generally inconclusive. However, each project was considered to be seriously flawed because of such problems as weak project designs, misuse or complete absence of sound analytic techniques, inadequate measures of street lighting, poor measures of crime (all were based on police records), and insufficient appreciation of the impact of lighting on different types of crime.

In the United Kingdom, very little research was carried out on street lighting and crime until the late 1980s. Kate Painter notes that there was a resurgence of interest between 1988 and 1990, when three small-scale street lighting projects were implemented and evaluated in different areas of London. In each location crime, disorder, and fear of crime declined and pedestrian street use increased dramatically after the lighting improvements. In a recent narrative review, Ken Pease notes that "the capacity of street lighting to influence crime has now been satisfactorily settled." He also recommended that the debate should be moved from the sterile "Does it work or doesn't it?" to the more productive "How can I flexibly and imaginatively incorporate lighting in crime reduction strategy and tactics?" (p. 72).

Evidence of Effectiveness

The best source for evidence of the effectiveness of lighting in preventing crime comes from systematic reviews carried out by Brandon C. Welsh and David P. Farrington. Systematic reviews use rigorous methods for locating, appraising, and synthesizing evidence from prior evaluation studies, and they are reported with the same level of detail that characterizes high-quality reports of original research. They include explicit objectives, explicit criteria for including or excluding studies, extensive searches for eligible evaluation studies from all over the world, careful extraction and coding of key features of studies, and a structured and detailed report of the methods and conclusions of the review.

Studies were included in Welsh and Farrington's systematic review if they met a number of criteria, including if improved lighting was the main intervention, if there was an outcome measure of crime, and if the evaluation design was of high methodological quality. A number of search strategies were employed to locate studies meeting the criteria for inclusion, including searches of electronic bibliographic databases, searches of literature reviews on the effectiveness of improved lighting on crime, and contacts with leading researchers. Thirteen studies met the inclusion criteria, eight from America and five from Britain.

From the 13 evaluations, it was concluded that improved street lighting had a significant desirable effect on crime, with a weighted mean odds ratio of 1.27. This means that crimes decreased by 21% in experimental areas compared with control areas.

Table 1 summarizes the results of all 13 studies. This shows the odds ratio for total crime in each study, plus its 95% confidence interval and statistical significance. It can be seen that only three studies (in Portland, New Orleans, and Indianapolis) had odds ratios less than 1, meaning that improved street lighting was followed by an increase in crime, and in no case was this increase significant. The other 10 studies had odds ratios greater than 1, meaning that improved street lighting was followed by a decrease in crime, and in 6 cases this decrease was significant (or nearly so, in the case of Atlanta). Therefore, the hypothesis that more lighting causes more crime can be firmly rejected.

American Studies

For the most part, residential neighborhoods were the setting for the eight American street lighting evaluations. Improved street lighting was considered to have a desirable effect on crime in four evaluations: those in Atlanta, Milwaukee, Fort Worth, and Kansas City. In all four cases, the odds ratio was 1.24 or greater, which corresponds to a 19% decrease in crimes or better. Improved street lighting was most clearly effective in reducing crimes in the Fort Worth evaluation. Crimes decreased by 22% in the experimental area and

Table 1   Meta-analysis results of improved street lighting evaluations

Study Location	Odds Ratio	Confidence Interval	p-Value
American N Studies			
Portland	0.94	0.75–1.18	n.s.
Kansas City	1.24	0.90–1.71	n.s.
Harrisburg	1.02	0.72–1.46	n.s.
New Orleans	0.99	0.83–1.18	n.s.
American ND Studies			
Atlanta	1.39	0.99–1.94	.055
Milwaukee	1.37	1.01–1.86	.044
Fort Worth	1.38	0.92–2.07	n.s.
Indianapolis	0.75	0.45–1.25	n.s.
British ND Studies			
Dover	1.14	0.58–2.22	n.s.
Bristol	1.35	1.16–1.56	.0001
Birmingham	3.82	2.15–6.80	.0001
Dudley	1.44	1.10–1.87	.008
Stoke-on-Trent	1.71	1.10–2.67	.017
Summary Results			
4 US N Studies	1.01	0.90–1.14	n.s.
4 US ND Studies	1.28	1.06–1.53	.010
5 UK ND Studies	1.62	1.22–2.15	.0008
8 US Studies	1.08	0.98–1.20	n.s.
9 ND Studies	1.43	1.19–1.71	.0001
All 13 Studies	1.27	1.09–1.47	.002

Note: N = only night crimes measured; ND = night and day crimes measured.

increased by 9% in the control area. In the other four evaluations, the improved street lighting was considered to have a null effect on crime (evidence of no effect). For example, in Portland, there was little evidence that improved street lighting had led to any reduction in nighttime crime. The results of the meta-analysis of all eight American studies yielded an odds ratio of 1.08, which was not significant. Overall, crime decreased by 7% in experimental areas compared with control areas.

The key dimension on which the eight effect sizes differed seemed to be whether they were based on data for both night and day (as in the Atlanta, Milwaukee, Fort Worth, and Indianapolis studies) or for night only (as in the other four studies). For the four night–day studies, the average effect size was a significant odds ratio of 1.28, meaning that crime decreased by 22% in experimental areas compared with control areas. For the four night-only studies, the odds ratio was 1.01, indicating no effect on crime. Therefore, the eight American studies could be divided into two blocks of four, one block showing that crime reduced after improved street lighting and the other block showing that it did not. Surprisingly, evidence of a reduction in crime was only obtained when both daytime and nighttime crimes were measured, although this feature may be a proxy for some other aspect of the different evaluation studies.

Unfortunately, all the American evaluations (except that of Indianapolis) are now rather dated, since they were all carried out in the 1970s. More recent American evaluations of the effect of improved street lighting need to be conducted. British evaluations, which were all published in the 1990s, are discussed next.

British Studies

The five British street lighting studies were carried out in a variety of settings, including a parking garage and a market, as well as residential neighborhoods. All studies measured crime at night and during the day. Improved street lighting was considered to be effective in reducing crime in four studies (those in Bristol, Birmingham, Dudley, and Stoke-on-Trent). In the fifth study (done in Dover), the improved lighting was confounded with other improvements, including fencing to restrict access to the parking garage and the construction of an office near the main entrance.

In the Dudley study, crime was measured using before and after victim surveys in experimental and control areas. Large samples were interviewed—431 in the experimental area and 448 in the control area. The response rate was 77% in both areas before and 84% after (of those interviewed before). Substantial crime reduction benefits were achieved after one year of the improved street lighting scheme. In the experimental area, the prevalence of all crime decreased by one quarter (24%), while only a marginal decrease (3%) in the prevalence of all crime occurred in the control area. Also, the incidence (average number of victimizations per 100 households) of all crime decreased in both the experimental and control areas—41% and 15%, respectively. The decrease in the experimental area was found to be significantly greater than the decrease in the control area.

The Stoke study also used large victim surveys, with an 84% response rate before and an 89% response rate after (of those interviewed before). The incidence of crime decreased by 43% in the experimental area, by 45% in the adjacent area, and by only 2% in the control area. When differences in the pretest victimization rates (prevalence and incidence) in the areas were controlled, it was found that the changes in experimental and adjacent areas were significantly greater than in the control area. There was also evidence of diffusion of crime prevention benefits to an adjacent area that did not receive the lighting improvements.

When the odds ratios from the five studies were combined, crimes decreased by 38% in experimental areas compared with control areas (OR = 1.62). These more recent British studies agree in showing that improved lighting reduces crime. They did not find that nighttime crimes decreased more than daytime crimes, suggesting that a "community pride" theory may be more applicable than a "deterrence/surveillance" theory.

Conclusion

It can be concluded that improved street lighting should be included as one element of a situational crime reduction program. It is an inclusive intervention benefiting an entire neighborhood, and it leads to an increase in public perception of safety. Improved street lighting is associated with greater use of public space and neighborhood streets by law-abiding citizens. Especially if well targeted to a high-crime area, improved street lighting can be a feasible, inexpensive, and effective method of reducing crime.

Brandon C. Welsh and David P. Farrington

See also Closed-Circuit Television; Crime Prevention; Crime Prevention Through Environmental Design; Meta-Analysis

Further Readings

Clarke, R. V. (1995). Situational crime prevention. In M. Tonry & D. P. Farrington (Eds.), *Building a safer society: Strategic approaches to crime prevention* (pp. 91–150). Chicago: University of Chicago Press.

Farrington, D. P., & Welsh, B. C. (2002). Improved street lighting and crime prevention. *Justice Quarterly, 19,* 313–342.

Farrington, D. P., & Welsh, B. C. (2007). *Improved street lighting and crime prevention: A systematic review.* Stockholm: National Council for Crime Prevention.

Fleming, R., & Burrows, J. N. (1986). The case for lighting as a means of preventing crime. *Home Office Research Bulletin, 22,* 14–17.

Jacobs, J. (1961). *The death and life of great American cities.* New York: Random House.

Painter, K. (1994). The impact of street lighting on crime, fear, and pedestrian street use. *Security Journal, 5,* 116–124.

Pease, K. (1999). A review of street lighting evaluations: Crime reduction effects. In K. Painter & N. Tilley (Eds.), *Surveillance of public space: CCTV, street lighting and crime prevention* (Vol. 10, pp. 47–76). Monsey, NY: Criminal Justice Press.

Petticrew, M., & Roberts, H. (2006). *Systematic reviews in the social sciences: A practical guide.* Oxford, UK: Blackwell.

Taylor, R. B., & Gottfredson, S. (1986). Environmental design, crime and prevention: An examination of community dynamics. In A. J. Reiss, Jr. & M. Tonry (Eds.), *Communities and crime* (pp. 387–416). Chicago: University of Chicago Press.

Tien, J. M., O'Donnell, V. F., Barnett, A., & Mirchandani, P. B. (1979). *Street lighting projects: National Evaluation Program* (Phase 1 Report). Washington, DC: U.S. Department of Justice, National Institute of Law Enforcement and Criminal Justice.

Welsh, B. C., & Farrington, D. P. (Eds.). (2006). *Preventing crime: What works for children, offenders, victims, and places.* New York: Springer.

Wright, R., Heilweil, M., Pelletier, P., & Dickinson, K. (1974). *The impact of street lighting on crime.* Ann Arbor: University of Michigan.

M

Male Victims of Partner Violence

Male victims of partner violence, which is a major health hazard in the United States, is defined as domestic abuse that is perpetrated by women against men or by men against men. Many people either have never heard of it or do not believe that it is possible for men to be abused. Generally, society defines intimate partner abuse (also known as domestic violence/domestic abuse/intimate partner violence) as women and children being abused—not men. Although males are not abused as frequently as female victims of domestic violence, it happens more frequently than most people realize. Approximately 35% of victims of intimate partner violence are male. However, women who are assaulted are nine times more likely than men to report it to the police and five times more likely to tell a friend or relative.

It is estimated that in the United States a woman is severely assaulted by her male partner every 15 seconds and that a man is severely assaulted by his female partner every 14.6 seconds. About 8%–10% of male-to-female partner violence is reported, whereas only 1% to 2% of female-to-male partner violence is reported. A woman is nearly twice as likely to use an object when she assaults a male partner, which can increase the level of potential injury. According to the Centers for Disease Control and Prevention (CDC), the National Center for Injury Prevention and Control (NCIPC),

and the U.S. Department of Justice, each year women experience about 4.8 million intimate-partner-related physical assaults and rapes and men are the victims of about 2.9 million intimate-partner-related physical assaults. Intimate partner violence resulted in 1,544 deaths in 2004. Of these deaths, 25% were males and 75% were females.

More importantly, before any victim can be helped, one must be willing to believe in the possibility of abuse. Not all abused persons present with black eyes, bloody nose, swollen lips, missing teeth, or a willingness to talk about it. On the contrary, for many abused persons, intimate partner violence is difficult and embarrassing to discuss.

Types of Abuse

Physically abused victims are pushed, kicked, slapped, stabbed, cut, spat on, tripped, knocked down, shot, bitten, raped, stalked, and so on. Economically abused victims are not allowed to have money or to secure jobs. The abuser may give them an allowance, but the victim may have to show receipts for every penny spent. If the victim works, the abuser may control his or her paycheck. The abuser may buy everything the victim needs or may not buy any of the basic requirements of life in order for the victim to sustain life (food, clothing, medical care or assistance, etc.). In psychological abuse, victims are subjected to mental games to keep them confused and/or to make them feel inadequate or even mentally ill (i.e., victims may see or hear something, but the abuser will tell the victim the incident did not happen, when in fact it has happened). After a while, victims may doubt themselves and believe everything they are told by the abuser. Many victims believe their abusers to be omnipotent and omnipresent. Often, intense counseling sessions are needed to assist victims in accepting their abusers as being simply men and women. For the sake of their emotional well-being, it is imperative for victims and survivors to regain their ego.

One of the abuser's most powerful weapons is isolation. Abusers discourage and threaten victims to keep them from associating with anyone without their consent and outside of their control. This includes the victim's family and friends. The cycle of violence comes in three stages. The tension-building stage is when the victim cannot do anything right to please the abuser. The abuser is extremely critical of everything the victim does and creates a lot of tension within his or her surroundings. The victim does everything to calm the abuser, but it is all to no avail. The second stage is the explosive stage when the victim is attacked. Refusing to take ownership of his or her actions, the batter attempts to justify the behavior by telling victims that the abuse is the victim's fault. If the victim had not done this or had not done that, they would not have "had" to hit them. The third stage is the honeymoon stage when the abuser may or may not ask for forgiveness and is very amorous saying he or she will never hurt the victim again. Victims are often nervous, afraid, and in pain but willing to give the abuser another chance. The honeymoon cycle will only last for a little while and then the cycles of abuse begin. It is estimated that the victim will leave his or her abuser between eight and ten times before he or she leaves for good—this is when the victim becomes a survivor.

Sexual abuse can also occur among male victims. According to local police authorities, females are not the only ones being forced into the sex trade. Many young men and boys, especially runaway teens and preteens, may be forced to perform several acts, including prostitution, drug dealing, stealing, and so on, under the threat of bodily harm or harm to their pets, family members, or other loved ones and friends—abusers are very capable of destroying their victims. Those who comply with the wishes of the abuser are readily abused to keep them under control, and many of those who do not are killed.

Characteristics of Abusers

A batter may feel remorse at first, but this can change quickly. Batterers are in control, and they choose the victim, time, place, violent tactics, and the severity of the assault. The batterer presumes to be entitled to control his or her partner and can become more and more violent with each subsequent event. The primary goal of abusers is absolute power and absolute control over their victims by any means necessary, including maiming and murdering. Even today, domestic violence is one of the best-kept personal secrets. It is a nondiscriminatory, albeit not always discrete, personal relationship hazard. It is multifaceted. It crosses all social, economic, and racial boundaries. Many victims will not talk about the abuse in their lives because of embarrassment, and they attempt to keep it a secret. Abusers can be pillars of the community and a great friend to neighbors and co-workers alike, but behind closed doors or in their own home, they can be very violent. One of the most underreported serious public health problems in the United States is still male intimate partner abuse. As stated, only 1% to 2% of female-to-male partner violence is reported.

Abusers are not mentally deranged people who cannot control themselves. One of the most infamous abuses of women was Henry Tudor, better known as King Henry VIII. He forced women to marry him and threw them away when he tired of them (e.g., he had six wives and murdered one of them by using a false charge of treason). Domestic violence is a learned behavior. It is learned through observation, experience, culture, and family. Boys who observe family violence are more likely to be violent toward their family when they become adults if they have remained in the family violence setting until they reach age 6 years or older—girls who observe family violence are more likely to accept violence toward themselves and the family when they become women if they have remained in the family violence setting until they reach age 10 years or older. A mentally ill person may be abusive, but the underlying cause of the mental illness is not the reason for the intimate partner violence. Each behavior must be addressed separately.

In relationships between males and females and males with males, the abuse techniques are basically the same. The primary goal is absolute power and absolute control over the victim. In society, the male is perceived as the dominant force and he is usually in command of his surroundings. He is powerful, fearless, strong, invincible, and protective of the weaker people around him, but when he is afraid, he cannot show his fear. Just as women are afraid and/or embarrassed to let people know about the abuse they are experiencing, male victims of abuse present with these same fears and apprehensions as their female counterparts, with one major exception. Many people do not believe men when they identify—men may be laughed at for being afraid or showing fear. Men, girlfriends, and wives alike are the perpetrators of male partner abuse. The abusers are professionals and nonprofessionals, and absolutely no one is immune to abuse. Male partner abuse is not anything new, but it must be investigated and given credibility to protect the victims. Often men are not afraid of their abusers, but they simply tire of fending off the abuser and leave them in order not to hurt them.

Support for Victims

To provide support and safety for all people, it must be acknowledged that there is domestic violence/intimate partner abuse in various relationships, including in dating and marriage relationships and in the lesbian, gay, bisexual, transgender (LGBT) community.

Not all men who are abused are single men—some of these men are married to abusive women. Women publicly embarrass or humiliate their husbands; withhold affection; threaten to harm themselves, their children, or others; control family finances; and blame men for their behavior. Although the laws available for abused women and children are also available to men, the resources are not in place.

Homosexual men are, and can be, abused by their partner. The Chicago Domestic Violence Help Line reports the aforementioned victims complain about the lack of services (not always feeling comfortable and safe or feeling isolated and "different"), and discrimination is still a problem. Some court personnel and service providers in the domestic violence community still hold negative attitudes toward LGBT clients. Fifty-seven percent of the LGBT community complained about difficulties accessing community-based services and 50% of straight men complained about difficulties accessing community-based services. The Chicago Domestic Violence Help Line, the Mayor's Office on Domestic Violence, and the Center for Urban Research and Learning state that 55 service providers have reported that straight males also complain about the lack of specific services, being taken seriously, and having to "jump through extra hoops" to prove themselves to be victims of abuse.

Regardless of one's race, religion, or lifestyle preference, the Chicago Domestic Violence Help Line is available to help 24 hours a day, 7 days a week, by calling 1-877-863-6338, TTY 1-877-863-6339. The Help Line has access to a language bank for people who do not speak English. Those who are abused are not alone—they must be helped to realize, and accept, that they are not the "only" person in the world being abused. Many domestic violence service providers, volunteers, and survivors are waiting to help them. However, these service providers cannot find abused persons without help. Those abused must make the first step and reach out for help and support. Whether victims choose to leave or to stay with their abuser, service providers must support their autonomy. Counseling and safety planning must be made readily available, and their final decision, whatever it is, must be respected.

Cynthia A. HartKnott

See also Abuse, Spouse; Defendants' Rights Versus Victims' Rights; Developmental Victimology; Hate and Bias Crime, Statutory Response; Intimate Partner Violence, Risk Assessment

Further Readings

Centers for Disease Control and Prevention, National Center for Injury Prevention and Control (NCIPC). (2006). *Intimate partner violence fact sheet: Understanding intimate partner violence 2006.* Retrieved from http://www.cdc.gov/ViolencePrevention/pdf/IPV-FactSheet.pdf

Kelly, L. (2003). Disabusing the definition of domestic abuse: How women batter men and the role of the feminist state. *Florida State Law Review, 30,* 791–855.

Perspective of diverse users: An evaluation of the city of Chicago Domestic Violence Help Line 2006. Retrieved from http://www.batteredwomensnetwork.org/id85.html

Steinmetz, S. K. (1977). The battered husband syndrome. *Victimology, 2,* 499.

Straus, M., & Gelles R. J. (1989). *Physical violence in American families: Risk factors and adaptations to violence in 8,145 families.* Piscataway, NJ: Transaction Publishers.

MANDATORY REPORTING STATUTES

Problems with measuring the extent of child abuse and elder abuse, as well as with addressing the needs of such victims, begin with the need to identify the abusive activity. Unfortunately, statistics on both child and elder abuse are questionable for a variety of reasons. First, the actions involved are most often done out of the eyesight of the public and are easily hidden from agents who can intervene. Second, there has been a historic reluctance to intervene in activity that many view as a family matter. Third, many individuals who potentially see or know about such abuse do not know who to contact and how to proceed with making a claim of abuse. For these and other reasons, the figures on both child and elder abuse are open to question. One major effort to address the problems of reporting and measuring child and elder abuse is the enactment of mandatory reporting statutes that outline who is responsible for making reports, who is to receive the reports, the information that is to be collected, and what is to be done with the information. This entry examines these statutes.

At first glance, it seems reasonable to assume that mandatory reporting is a good first step in dealing with child and elder abuse. Interestingly, however, there has been a great deal of resistance to mandatory reporting and numerous criticisms of these efforts. Most states now have some form of mandatory reporting law for abuse. The Centers for Medicare and Medicaid Services mandates several procedures that facilities receiving federal funds and reimbursement for services must follow, and these regulations require reporting of elder abuse and neglect to state-level agencies.

A couple of important observations can be drawn from existing state statutes. First, mandatory reporting requirements are restricted primarily to public employees or employees of agencies that would most likely have contact with potential victims. Examples of these individuals are social workers, teachers, physicians, mental health professionals, law enforcement personnel, hospitals, and nursing homes. Second, the specificity of who must report suspected abuse varies somewhat from state to state. Some states require attorneys, the clergy, banks, financial advisors, and others who could become aware of abuse to file reports. In Florida, bank employees and inspectors of public lodging establishments must report. In Ohio, the clergy and attorneys are required to report. Persons not included in these categories have no legal obligation to make a report of suspected abuse.

The advent of mandatory reporting statutes resulted in increased numbers of child and elder abuse cases coming to the attention of the authorities. Data on the extent of child abuse and elder abuse reveal generally increasing levels over time. This is at least partly a result of mandatory reporting statutes as well as of changes in the social perception that such abuse is unacceptable and that society has a right to intervene in what some consider a family matter.

The greatest criticism of mandatory reporting efforts has been that they do little more than encourage reporting. Often, these reporting laws fail to define abuse, fail to identify to whom abuse is to be reported, fail to impose penalties for failure to report abuse, and fail to outline what to do with the reports once they are made. Although many states have taken steps to address these gaps in the statutes (such as passing legislation outlining penalties for nondisclosure), many problems still exist in many jurisdictions.

Several other problems also have been identified with mandatory reporting statutes. First, the laws typically deal only with the reporting of abuse and fail to provide resources to follow up on the reports or to do something about the problem. Second, critics claim that these laws intrude into the privacy of the individual. This is particularly problematic in terms of elder abuse where the victim is a legal adult and may be making a choice not to contact the authorities about his or her victimization. Another example of the privacy concern involves laws requiring physicians to report suspected cases of abuse, which critics contend violates client-physician confidentiality. Third, mandatory reporting in relation to elder abuse is perceived by critics as reinforcing ageism by focusing on the victim rather than on the offender. These laws identify the victim of abuse and often prompt reactions that may include removing the victim from the home or blaming the victim for the abuse, rather than focusing on the perpetrator. Similarly, these efforts place the elderly into a category with children, the mentally ill, and others who are incapable of making decisions for themselves. Critics contend that these laws, therefore, fail to treat the elderly as adults and, consequently, degrade the elderly victim.

Despite mandatory reporting laws, many reports are never made or are made after a lengthy delay. When events are not reported in a timely enough fashion, it is not uncommon for the receiving agency to determine that the event was unfounded. This may not be because there was no abuse. Rather it may be because abuse cannot be proven because of the delay in reporting. A prime example involves a General Accounting Office review of the Centers for Medicare and Medicaid Services, the oversight agency for nursing homes. Although the Centers mandate various reporting guidelines for abuse and neglect allegations, most state agencies are not promptly notified in accordance with regulations. Indeed, almost two thirds of the reports are made 2 or more days after the required deadline. This delay is problematic because it makes it difficult, if not impossible, for the investigating agencies to undertake a meaningful investigation. After a delay, it is often difficult to talk to witnesses, the witnesses or victims cannot recall the event clearly, or the evidence is no longer available for the police or other investigators.

Mandatory reporting statutes have been a major change in society's response to elder and child abuse. Despite any shortcomings of the legislation, the goal of identifying and addressing these forms of victimization is important. With the continued growing interest in elder and child abuse, these statutes will probably become stronger and more effective.

Steven P. Lab

See also Adult Protective Services; Child Abuse, Neglect and Maltreatment: Mandatory Reporting; Child Protective Services; Elder Abuse, Neglect and Maltreatment: Interventions for

Further Readings

Child Welfare Information Gateway. (2009). *Mandatory reporters of child abuse and neglect: Summary of state laws*. Retrieved from http://www.childwelfare.gov/systemwide/laws_policies/statutes/manda.cfm

Doerner, W. G., & Lab, S. P. (2008). *Victimology* (5th ed.). Newark, NJ: LexisNexis.

General Accounting Office. (2002). *Nursing homes: More can be done to protect residents from abuse*. Washington, DC: Author.

Kapp, M. B. (1995). Elder mistreatment: Legal interventions and policy uncertainties. *Behavioral Sciences and the Law, 13*, 365–380.

MASS MURDER AND SUICIDES IN CULTS

Although mass murders and mass suicides in new religious movements (popularly known as cults) have attracted media publicity, their occurrence is rare in proportion to the overall numbers of present-day religious organizations—at least 2,000 in the United States alone. This entry discusses some religious movements in which mass murders and/or suicides occurred and then assesses the commonalities among them.

Religious Movements

The Peoples Temple

The Peoples Temple was the first to attract publicity in recent times. Founded by James Warren Jones in California in 1955, it became affiliated with the mainstream Disciples of Christ. Jones was particularly concerned to promote interracial harmony. He also claimed miraculous powers, although most of his "miracles" were faked. Believing in an imminent nuclear holocaust, and facing mounting criticism, Jones and about 1,000 followers moved to Guyana in 1974, where they transformed 300 acres of tropical jungle into a self-sufficient community.

When his critics persisted, Jones came to regard suicide as the alternative to failure. He organized "white nights"—regular rehearsals for mass suicide, which took place at night. Congressman Leo Ryan visited Jonestown to investigate and was shot dead by one of the Jones followers. Jones then ordered the mass suicide, instructing his aides to shoot anyone who tried to escape. In all, 919 people died.

Branch Davidian Waco

David Koresh (born Vernon Wayne Howell) gained control of the Branch Davidian Waco group, an Adventist group, in 1988, and most of the members lived in the compound near Waco, Texas, where he expounded the Bible for long periods, with particular reference to the Book of Revelation.

Koresh claimed exclusive rights to all the group's women and, allegedly, had sexual relationships with minors. He had expertise in firearms and was believed to have modified semiautomatic handguns into fully automatic ones. After four federal agents were killed in an unsuccessful attempt to serve a search warrant, Attorney-General Janet Reno authorized a Federal Bureau of Investigation (FBI) assault on February 28, 1993. The siege lasted until April 19 when fire broke out. It is not known whether the fire was started by the FBI or by Koresh's followers. Seventy-four members were killed in the fire, and five died in the February confrontation.

The Solar Temple

The Ordre du Temple Solaire (OTS—Order of the Solar Temple) was a Templarist group, whose multiple deaths occurred in 1994, 1995, and 1997, in several different locations, the first of which were roughly simultaneous. The deaths seem to have formed part of a ceremony. On October 4, 1994, four adults and a child were found, having been stabbed and burned to death, at Morin Heights, Canada, in the home of OTS co-leader Joseph di Mambro. On October 5, just after midnight, 23 burnt bodies were discovered in Cheiry, Switzerland; the members had been shot and were arranged in a circle. At 03:00, another 25 bodies were discovered at Les Granges sur Salvan, Switzerland. An additional 16 Solar Temple members were found dead in similar circumstances, near Grenoble in France in 1995, and in 1997, five more members were found burned to death at St- Casimir, Quebec.

The organization's interests were eclectic, encompassing Egyptian death rituals, Rosicrucianism, alternative medicine (co-leader Luc Jouret was a medical doctor), reincarnation, and belief in supernatural "Ascended Masters." The group may have regarded fire as the means of transition to the star Sirius, which featured largely in its thinking.

Aum Shinrikyo

In 1985, Aum Shinrikyo, founded by Shoko Asahara, gained notoriety when five followers released sarin gas into trains in the Tokyo subway on March 20, killing 12 people and injuring hundreds more. This incident was one of several violent acts perpetrated by the group. On May 5, 1995, a device was found at another subway station, designed to release hydrogen cyanide, with the potential to claim 20,000 victims. Ashara was arrested and subsequently sentenced to death.

A blend of Buddhism, Indian yogic practices, Japanese folk religion, and apocalyptic ideas derived from the Book of Revelation and Nostradamus, Asahara's teachings predicted an imminent apocalypse. Ashahara's goal was to commission 30,000 *shukkesha*—renunciates who would survive Armageddon—and turn Japan into a paradise. The murders may have been *poa* (salvational murders), aimed at assassinating unbelievers, releasing them from evil *karma*.

Heaven's Gate

Some 39 members of Heaven's Gate were found poisoned in a large house on the outskirts of San Diego, California, in March 1997, apparently as a result of orchestrated suicides. Each member lay on a bunk bed, covered with a purple shroud, and wearing black trousers and Nike trainers. Each had packed a suitcase, as if embarking on a journey. Marshall Herff Applewhite, the leader, taught that extraterrestrials had come to collect them in a spacecraft, docked behind the Hale-Bopp comet, and which could be boarded by undergoing death.

The Movement for the Restoration of the Ten Commandments of God

In 2000, more than 500 members of the Movement for the Restoration of the Ten Commandments of God were found, having been burnt alive in a remote part of Uganda. The doors and windows of the church were barricaded from the outside, preventing the congregation from escaping. Subsequent investigation revealed large numbers of bodies (possibly more than 1,000) buried in mass graves. The group was an African Independent Church, whose members claimed visions of the Virgin Mary and prescribed an austere lifestyle, aiming to heighten the standards of the Ten Commandments, in anticipation of an imminent apocalypse.

The reasons for the deaths are still unknown. The movement is largely undocumented, the local populace speaks little English, and little forensic evidence was collected. Members may have believed that immolation secured entry to heaven; alternatively, leaders may have wished to prevent dissatisfied members from reclaiming forfeited possessions.

Assessment

These organizations are diverse, with different religious antecedents. They are not predominantly "religions of the dispossessed," often attracting well-educated, professional people. They were not principally youth movements; the average age of the Heaven's Gate member was 47 years old. Common to all were apocalyptic expectations, in most cases associated with the turn of the millennium. All groups perceived advantages afforded by death, and their calamitous endings may relate to their worldviews, rather than to authoritarian leadership or "brainwashing."

George D. Chryssides

See also Family Violence; Homicide and Murder; Victimology

Further Readings

Chidester, D. (1991). *Salvation and suicide: An interpretation of Jim Jones, the peoples temple, and Jonestown.* Bloomington: Indiana University Press.

Chryssides, G. D. (1999). *Exploring new religions.* London, UK: Cassell.

Chryssides, G. D. (2006). *The A to Z of new religious movements.* Lanham, MD: Scarecrow Press.

Newport, K. G. C. (2006). *The Branch Davidians of Waco: The history and beliefs of an apocalyptic sect.* Oxford, UK: Oxford University Press.

Perkins, R., & Jackson, F. (1997). *Cosmic suicide: The tragedy and transcendence of Heaven's Gate.* Dallas, TX: Pentaradial Press.

Reader, I. (1996). *A poisonous cocktail? Aum Shinrikyo's path to violence.* Copenhagen, Denmark: Nordic Institute of Asian Studies.

Robbins, T. & Palmer, S. J. (1997). *Millennium, messiahs and mayhem: Contemporary apocalyptic movements.* New York: Routledge.

Wessinger, C. (2000). *How the millennium comes violently: From Jonestown to Heaven's Gate.* New York: Seven Bridges.

MEDIA COVERAGE OF VICTIMS

The focus of this entry is on media coverage of crime victims. Although there is not much research specifically on this topic, there is considerable published work on the media's general coverage of crime. This research highlights the types of crime presented in the media, the processes used to construct these stories, and whether the nature of the coverage affects public perceptions or criminal justice decision making. It is within this body of research that one can begin to understand the key issues related to media coverage of crime victims. Two issues are discussed here. First, the role of the media in highlighting concerns about the treatment of crime victims is discussed. Second, concerns about the quality and the effects of coverage on crime victims are highlighted.

Concerns About Treatment of Victims

There is little doubt that the status of victims in the criminal justice system has changed dramatically during the last 30 years. Policy initiatives, special units, and financial resources have been created or designated to help improve the plight of victims generally. The victims' rights movement strived to address many complaints voiced by crime victims, including that they were being retraumatized by a criminal justice system that was cold, uncaring, and unwilling to recognize the significant harm caused by crime. The media, both news and popular outlets, have played an important role in raising awareness and in creating opportunities for policy makers and advocates to address various grievances voiced by crime victims. For example, the victims' rights movement generally, as well as efforts to help special classes of victims such as child, domestic violence, and hate crime victims, has benefited from media coverage that has highlighted issues related to improving the treatment of these victims.

The media have contributed to significant social change to help victims in multiple ways. The decisions media personnel make about covering certain issues and ignoring other issues can influence agenda priorities. Moreover, how an issue is covered helps to define the contours of the debate about an issue. The unfortunate reality is that there is a limited amount of bureaucratic, financial, and political resources available to address social problems. Priorities need to be set, and often it is the direct or indirect media coverage that determines what issues are given serious consideration. For example, the victimization of child, rape, and domestic violence victims was not considered an important policy issue until the 1970s. Although several factors contributed to recognizing the need to help these victims, media coverage helped to legitimize their concerns.

One way that the media have consistently brought national attention to concerns about victims is by publicizing the facts and circumstances of a specific high-profile case. Such cases then provide a window of opportunity to manufacture new legislative initiatives and strategies to improve the treatment of victims. Consider the creation and widespread adoption of Megan's Law. Megan Kanka was 7 years old when she was raped and murdered by a convicted sex offender. Her parents were outraged when they learned the perpetrator lived across the street, and they thought that they had a right to know that a convicted sex offender lived nearby. National media coverage of this case contributed to the development and adoption of statutes that required convicted sex offenders, when released from prison, to register with the police who then in certain circumstances notify neighbors. The federal government and nearly 20 states have adopted some version of Megan's Law since the case received publicity. The media's role in institutionalizing Megan's Law is only one example of how specific victim cases create opportunities for policy discussions and political change. Other cases include how media publicity of the Francine Hughes case, who

was brutally beaten by her husband for many years before killing him, contributed to policy initiatives to assist domestic violence victims; how the abduction and murder of Adam Walsh increased concerns about missing and exploited children; and how the murder of Matthew Shepard helped create bias-related crime legislation.

Not only did the media help to determine policy agendas by bringing attention to previously ignored harms to crime victims, it also specifically influenced the contours of policy debates about these topics. In his book *Sense and Nonsense About Crime,* Sam Walker discussed that although many policies introduced to support victims' rights would have no effect on crime and might harm the criminal justice system and victims, adopting many of the laws to assist victims were symbolically important. The important point here is that the media emphasized specific legislative initiatives and ignored others. Indeed, the initiatives that were emphasized were those that were much more likely to be consistent with a conservative, crime-control approach. Stuart Scheingold, Toska Olson, and Jana Pershing demonstrated this in their study examining the passage of Washington State's Community Protection Act. This legislation focused on addressing many issues, but the issue that was perhaps the most controversial and generated national media attention was its sexual predator provisions. Specifically, the legislation allowed authorities to bring convicted sex offenders who were being released from the criminal justice system into the civil system to be committed until they are no longer dangerous to the public. Although victim advocates and supporters of the legislation presented both punitive and preventive approaches to respond to sex offenders, it was the punitive measures that resonated in public debates and that were emphasized within the legislation that was passed.

Quality and Effects

Media coverage of specific policy issues have caused policy makers, media executives, and reporters to consider how they could better respond to the needs of crime victims. Numerous symposiums, conferences, and articles have been written that describe the harm caused by reporters when covering victims callously and unsympathetically.

The publication of body bags, bloody scenes, and graphic accounts of a crime may help boost ratings for media organizations but at the same time do considerable harm to crime victims and family members. The public forums that have been conducted on this topic have led to positive reforms in newsrooms and to improved coverage that better balances the public's right to know with an individual's right to privacy. Consider, for example, the Pulitzer Prize–winning story by a *Des Moines Register* reporter about the traumas caused by rape. Although it is media policy to not name a rape victim because of the risk of stigmatization, the victim agreed to be identified for this particular story and the story was a sensitive, gripping account that led to better public understanding about rape trauma. Importantly, the story and the identification of the victim resulted in a healthy debate within newsrooms and by victim advocates about the sensitive coverage of rape and naming rape and other victims in news stories.

During this same period of time, as policy advocates were able to harness media attention to open policy windows that produced significant social change, the media have been criticized for their coverage of crime victims on multiple fronts. The media have been criticized for misrepresenting the presentation of victimization in the news. Specifically, the media distorts the images of victimization presented to the public by emphasizing certain types of victims and ignoring others. Research indicates an inverse relationship between official and constructed realities of crime. For example, crimes that are least likely to occur, such as murder, are most likely to be presented in the news. Similarly, individuals at the greatest risk of becoming a crime victim are often the least likely to be presented in the news. One of the critical variables that influences the salience and prominence of a crime incident in the news is the race of the victim. Murders of African American and other minority victims are significantly less likely to be covered by the media and, if covered, receive much less space compared with crimes with murdered White victims. Specifically, crimes involving White victims may be as much as five times more likely to be covered compared with crimes involving minority victims. Moreover, not only are minorities deemphasized as victims, they tend to be overemphasized as defendants in the news.

Several other victim characteristics either increase or decrease the likelihood that a particular story is covered prominently in the news. First, age is an important variable. Although children and elderly victims are much less likely to be victimized compared with young adults and adults, their victimizations draw considerable media attention. These victims are deemed worthy of protection because of their innocence. Children and elderly victims are ideal victims and are emphasized in the news because it is assumed that they did not contribute to their victimization in any way. Second, the gender of the victim is also an important variable. Female victims are newsworthy, especially when victimized by violent crimes. A third characteristic reflects the status of a victim. Status may be identified in different ways, such as in the occupation of the victim, the community where the victim lives, or in past involvement in the criminal justice system. Crimes with victims from suburban and wealthy communities are much more likely to be covered in the media, and those involving victims with criminal histories are less likely to be covered.

Crime news is produced through a bureaucratic process where reporters develop routines that lead to the efficient production of news about crime. Crime stories are important news stories, and thus, a news organization must devote considerable resources to provide the public with multiple crime stories every day. On average, a newspaper may present ten crime stories. Among the key solutions that increase the efficiency of news production is the media's reliance on easily accessible and cooperative news sources. Specifically, research indicates that most of the sources cited in crime news stories are affiliated with a criminal justice agency. Police officers, especially departmental public information officers, are the most important source used by reporters because most media organizations emphasize the beginning stages of the criminal justice process. Reporters rarely contact crime victims for their perspective about a crime incident, and thus, their views are excluded from crime news coverage. If a story is a potentially important news story, however, reporters will make an effort to contact the victim to discuss the crime. If a victim cooperates, and is able to provide an emotional response to their questions, the story increases in importance.

Role in Understanding Victimization

This entry has highlighted two viewpoints about media coverage of crime victims. On the one hand, the media has, at times, been a champion for the cause of victims, has helped bring attention to previously ignored issues, and has influenced policy makers to consider implementing changes that will better assist victims. On the other hand, there are numerous concerns with the nature of media coverage as some victims are covered extensively, but many victims are ignored. The result is a limited understanding of victimization in society and policies are passed that help some but not all victims.

Steven Chermak

See also Crime Time Television Shows

Further Readings

Berns, N. (2004). *Framing the victim: Domestic violence, media, and social problems.* New York: Aldine de Gruyter.

Chermak, S. (1995). *Victims in the news: Crime and the American news media.* Boulder, CO: Westview Press.

Dixon, T., & Linz, D. (2000). Race and the misrepresentation of victimization on local television news. *Communication Research, 27,* 547–573.

Johnstone, J. W. C., Hawkins, D. F., & Michener, A. (1994). Homicide reporting in Chicago dailies. *Journalism Quarterly, 71,* 860–872.

Martin, R. J. (1996). Pursuing public protection through mandatory community notification of convicted sex offenders: The trials and tribulations of Megan's law. *The Boston University Public Interest Law Journal, 26,* 29–55.

Scheingold, S. A., Olson, T., & Pershing, J. (1994). Sexual violence, victim advocacy, and republication criminology: Washington state's community protection act. *Law & Society Review, 28,* 729–763.

Walker, S. (1989). *Sense and nonsense about crime: A policy guide.* Pacific Grove, CA: Brooks/Cole.

MEDICAL AND MENTAL HEALTH SERVICES

Victims of sexual assault and other bodily crimes have extensive post-assault medical needs, including injury detection and care, medical forensic examination, screening and treatment for sexually transmitted infections (STIs), as well as pregnancy testing and emergency contraception. Because of the traumatic nature of sexual assaults, victims may also develop mental health issues. This entry discusses the services available to victims for their post-assault medical and mental health needs.

Medical Services

Although most victims are not physically injured to the point of needing emergency care, traditionally, police, sexual assault crisis centers, and social service agencies have advised victims to seek treatment in hospital emergency departments for a medical forensic examination. The body of a victim is a crime scene, and because of the invasive nature of sexual assault, a medical professional, rather than a crime scene technician, is needed to collect the evidence. The "sexual assault exam" or "sexual assault kit" usually involves plucking head and pubic hairs; collecting loose hairs by combing the head and pubis; swabbing the vagina, rectum, and/or mouth to collect semen, blood, or saliva; and obtaining fingernail scrapings in the event the victim scratched the assailant. Blood samples may also be collected for DNA, toxicology, and ethanol testing.

Victims often experience long waits in hospital emergency departments because sexual assault is rarely an emergent health threat, and during this wait, victims are not allowed to eat, drink, or urinate so as not to destroy physical evidence of the assault. When victims are finally examined, they may get a cursory explanation of what will occur and it often comes as a shock that they have to have a pelvic examination immediately after such an egregious, invasive violation of their bodies. Many victims describe the medical care they receive as cold, impersonal, and detached. Furthermore, the examinations and evidence collection procedures are often performed incorrectly. Most hospital emergency department personnel lack training in sexual assault forensic examinations, and those trained usually do not perform examinations frequently enough to maintain proficiency.

Forensic evidence collection is often the focus of hospital emergency department care, but sexual assault victims have other medical needs, such as information on the risk of STIs/HIV and prophylaxis (preventive medications to treat any STIs that may have been contracted through the assault). The Centers for Disease Control and Prevention and American Medical Association (AMA) recommend that all sexual assault victims receive STI prophylaxis and HIV prophylaxis on a case-by-case basis after risk assessment. However, Annette Amey and David Bishai point out that analyses of hospital records have shown that only 34% of sexual assault patients are treated for STIs. Yet, data from victims suggest much higher rates of STI prophylaxis: 57% to 69% of sexual assault patients reported that they received antibiotics during their hospital emergency department care. But not all victims are equally likely to receive STI-related medical services. Victims of nonstranger sexual assault are significantly less likely to receive information on STIs/HIV or STI prophylaxis, even though knowing the assailant does not mitigate one's risk. In addition, Rebecca Campbell and associates found that Caucasian women were significantly more likely to get information on HIV than ethnic minority women.

Post-assault pregnancy services are also inconsistently provided to sexual assault victims. Only 40% to 49% of victims receive information about the risk of pregnancy. The AMA and the American College of Obstetricians and Gynecologists recommend emergency contraception for victims at risk for pregnancy, but only 21% to 43% of sexual assault victims who need emergency contraception actually receive it. To date, no studies have found systematic differences in the provision of emergency contraception as a function of victim or assault characteristics, but hospitals affiliated with the Catholic Church are significantly less likely to provide emergency contraception.

In the process of the forensic examination, STI services, and pregnancy-related care, doctors and nurses ask victims many of the same kinds of questions as do legal personnel regarding their prior sexual history, sexual response during the assault, what they were wearing, and what they did to "cause" the assault. Medical professionals may view these questions as necessary and appropriate, but sexual assault victims often find them upsetting. As a result of their contact with emergency department doctors and nurses, most sexual assault victims have stated that they felt bad about themselves (81%), depressed (88%), violated (94%),

distrustful of others (74%), and reluctant to seek further help (80%). Only 5% of victims in S. E. Ullman's study rated physicians as a helpful source of support, and negative responses from formal systems, including medical, significantly exacerbate the posttraumatic stress disorder (PTSD) symptomatology of the victims. Victims who do not receive basic medical services rate their experiences with the medical system as more hurtful, which has been associated with higher PTSD levels.

Mental Health Services

The mental health effects of sexual assault are devastating; many victims experience this trauma as a fundamental betrayal of their sense of self, identity, judgment, and safety. Dean Kilpatrick and associates note that between 31% and 65% of sexual assault victims develop PTSD and 38% to 43% meet diagnostic criteria for major depression. These sequelae are largely from the trauma of the sexual assault itself, but as noted, negative responses from the legal and medical systems exacerbate victims' distress. Clearly, victims may *need* mental health services, but there has been comparatively less research on what services they actually receive and whether that care improved their psychological health. Victims may obtain mental health services in myriad ways (e.g., treatment outcome research, community clinics/private practice, and specialty agencies such as sexual assault crisis centers), and their experiences vary considerably as a function of treatment setting.

First, some victims receive mental health services by participating as research subjects in randomized control trial treatment outcome studies. This option is available only to sexual assault victims who live in communities where such research is being conducted, and who fit eligibility criteria. However, this kind of research is not intended to provide large-scale services; the goal is to establish empirically supported treatments that can then be disseminated for wider scale benefit. Indeed, the results of these trials suggest that cognitive-behavioral therapies, such as cognitive processing therapy and prolonged exposure, are effective in alleviating PTSD symptoms. The victims who participate in these trials receive high-quality treatment and benefit tremendously, but this is not the experience of the typical sexual assault victim seeking post-assault mental health services.

A second, and more typical, way victims receive post-assault mental health services is community-based care provided by psychologists, psychiatrists, or social workers in private or public clinic settings. More victims receive mental health services in these settings relative to treatment outcome studies, but these are still highly underused with serious accessibility limitations. Most victims who seek traditional mental health services, for example, are Caucasian. Ethnic minority women are more likely to turn to informal sources of support (e.g., friends and family) and may not necessarily place the same value on formal psychotherapy. Victims without health insurance are also significantly less likely to obtain mental health services.

When victims do receive community-based mental health services, it is unclear whether practitioners are consistently using empirically supported treatments. Two state-wide random sample studies of practitioners suggest it is unlikely. Most practitioners report using cognitive-behavioral methods with victims of violence (including, but not limited to, sexual assault victims), but almost all practitioners stated they rarely use a single approach and intentionally combine multiple therapeutic orientations and treatments. As a result, it cannot be concluded that most victims receive empirically supported care in traditional, community-based mental health services. As is often the case in the efficacy-effectiveness-dissemination research cycle, it can take quite a while for evidence-based practice to become standard care.

Few studies have examined if and how victims benefit from community-based mental health services. In general, victims tend to rate their experiences with mental health professionals positively and characterize their help as useful and supportive. Whether positive satisfaction results in demonstrable mental health benefits is largely unknown, although Campbell and associates found that community-based mental health services were particularly helpful for victims who had had negative experiences with the legal and/or medical systems. Some mental health practitioners have expressed concern about whether their own profession works effectively with sexual assault victims: 58% of practitioners in a state-wide study felt that mental health providers engage in practices that would be harmful to victims and questioned the degree to which victims benefit from services.

A third setting in which victims may obtain mental health services is specialized violence against women agencies, such as sexual assault crisis centers and domestic violence shelter programs. Sexual assault crisis centers help victims negotiate their contact with the legal and medical systems, and they also provide individual and group counseling. These agencies are perhaps the most visible and accessible source for mental health services for sexual assault victims as they provide counseling free of charge and do not require health insurance. As with traditional mental health services, there is still evidence of racial differences in service utilization as Caucasian women are significantly more likely to use sexual assault crisis center services than ethnic minority women.

Little is known about the therapeutic orientations and treatment approaches used in sexual assault crisis centers, but current data indicate a strong feminist and/or empowerment theoretical orientation (e.g., shared goal setting, focus on gender inequalities, and identification of sexual assault not only as a personal problem but as a social problem too). With respect to counseling outcomes, April Howard and associates compared self-reported PTSD symptoms precounseling and postcounseling among victims receiving sexual assault crisis center counseling services, and they found significant reductions in distress levels and self-blame over time and increases in social support, self efficacy, and sense of control. Because the studies did not examine the content of services or include comparison groups, it is unclear whether these observed improvements are attributable to the services provided.

Rebecca Campbell and Debra Patterson

See also Posttraumatic Stress Disorder (PTSD); Rape Crisis Centers; Sexual Assault Nurse Examiner (SANE); Sexual Assault Response Team (SART)

Further Readings

American College of Obstetricians and Gynecologists. (1998). Sexual assault (ACOG educational bulletin). *International Journal of Gynecology and Obstetrics, 60,* 297–304.

American Medical Association. (1995). *Strategies for the treatment and prevention of sexual assault*. Chicago: Author.

Campbell, R., & Martin, P. Y. (2001). Services for sexual assault survivors: The role of rape crisis centers. In C. Renzetti, J. Edleson, & R. Bergen (Eds.), *Sourcebook on violence against women* (pp. 227–241). Thousand Oaks, CA: Sage.

Campbell, R., & Raja, S. (1999). The secondary victimization of rape victims: Insights from mental health professionals who treat survivors of violence. *Violence & Victims, 14*, 261–275.

Campbell, R., & Raja, S. (2005). The sexual assault and secondary victimization of female veterans: Help-seeking experiences in military and civilian social systems. *Psychology of Women Quarterly, 29*, 97–106.

Campbell, R., Raja, S., & Grining, P. L. (1999). Training mental health professionals on violence against women. *Journal of Interpersonal Violence, 14*, 1003–1013.

Campbell, R., Wasco, S. M., Ahrens, C. E., Sefl, T., & Barnes, H. E. (2001). Preventing the "second rape": Rape survivors' experiences with community service providers. *Journal of Interpersonal Violence, 16*, 1239–1259.

Centers for Disease Control and Prevention. (2002). Sexual assault and STDs—Adults and adolescents. *Morbidity and Mortality Weekly Report, 51*, 69–71.

Howard, A., Riger, S., Campbell, R., & Wasco, S. M. (2003). Counseling services for battered women: A comparison of outcomes for physical and sexual abuse survivors. *Journal of Interpersonal Violence, 18*, 717–734.

Kilpatrick, D. G., Amstadter, A. B., Resnick, H. S., & Ruggiero, K. J. (2007). Rape-related PTSD: Issues and interventions. *Psychiatric Times, 24*, 50–58.

Koss, M. P., Bailey, J. A., Yuan, N. P., Herrera, V. M., & Lichter, E. L. (2003). Depression and PTSD in survivors of male violence: Research and training initiatives to facilitate recovery. *Psychology of Women Quarterly, 27*, 130–142.

Starzynski, L. L., Ullman, S. E., Filipas, H. H., & Townsend, S. M. (2005). Correlates of women's sexual assault disclosure to informal and formal support sources. *Violence & Victims, 20*, 417–432.

Ullman, S. E. (1996). Do social reactions to sexual assault victims vary by support provider? *Violence & Victims, 11*, 143–156.

Wasco, S. M., Campbell, R., Howard, A., Mason, G., Schewe, P., Staggs, S., & Riger, S. (2004). A statewide evaluation of services provided to rape survivors. *Journal of Interpersonal Violence, 19*, 252–263.

Wgliski, A., & Barthel, A. K. (2004). Cultural differences in reporting of sexual assault to sexual assault agencies in the United States. *Sexual Assault Report, 7*, 92–93.

MEDICAL EXAMINER RESPONSE TEAM (MERT)

A Medical Examiner Response Team (MERT) is a group of medical and law enforcement professionals charged with investigating certain fatalities. The goals of a MERT include identifying remains and determining the cause and manner of death. This entry discusses the medical examiner/coroner system in the United States, the death investigation performed by MERTs, the controversies involved with death investigations, and the future of forensic pathology.

Medical Examiner/Coroner System

The medical examiner/coroner system originated in the English crowner system of the 900s. The "crowner" was a public official who collected duties for the king on deaths, hunting, and other events. In 1860, in the United States, Maryland began requiring a physician be present at coroner proceedings. This was the start of a shift in the United States toward the medical examiner system where physicians certified deaths rather than sheriffs and other public officials. In the United States today, fewer than 10 states retain coroner systems with the remaining having medical examiners. A contemporary medical examiner is a physician but not necessarily a specialist in pathology.

The medical examiner/coroner office (ME/C) is responsible for issuing death certificates recording the identity of the deceased, the time of death, the cause of death, and the manner of death. The *cause of death* can be a disease, injury (e.g., firearm), or poison, and there can be primary and contributing causes of death. The mechanism of death is not always listed but is the physiological cause of death such as hemorrhage from a firearm injury. The *manner of death* has limited options: natural, accidental, homicide, suicide, unclassified, or undetermined. A classification of homicide means only one person killed another and does not mean a crime occurred (e.g., self-defense). The determination of murder is made by a court of law.

Local and state law classifies deaths that must be reported to the ME/C. Generally the following deaths are reportable: violent, sudden, or unexpected deaths; fatal injuries; poisonings; fires; and deaths in police custody, after a medical procedure, or involving transportation.

There are multiple goals of the medical examiner investigation. A primary goal is to identify remains to permit family notification. Other goals are determination of cause and manner of death, interval from injury to death, injury documentation, and recovery of evidence. ME findings support prosecution of perpetrators of homicides.

Death Investigation

After a death is reported, the medical examiner begins a death investigation. The procedures after a reported death vary according to the number of deaths at the scene and other circumstances. The investigation might include an on-scene investigation or an autopsy. A death certificate is signed, and in complex cases, a report may be prepared. If there is a legal proceeding, the medical examiner often testifies as an expert witness.

Autopsy

An autopsy performed by an ME/C is a medicolegal autopsy. It is similar to an autopsy performed in a hospital in that it includes both an external and internal examination of the body as well as a microscopic examination of the organs and testing of body and body fluids such as blood, urine, bile, and vitreous (eye fluid). A medicolegal autopsy differs from a hospital autopsy in that a pathologist can collect and interpret physical evidence relating to the manner of death (e.g., metal shavings). As part of an autopsy, a forensic pathologist reviews the deceased's personal history, medical records, toxicology, and laboratory information.

Scene Investigation

A scene investigation is usually completed in suspected homicides and suicides. The size and specialties of a MERT vary depending on the number of reported fatalities, the size and nature of the event, and the condition of the remains.

Scene investigators at a firearm homicide might include a medical examiner, autopsy technician, and forensic photographer/crime scene photographer. Crime scene technicians and/or death investigators collect evidence. These persons might be either law enforcement personnel or medical examiner personnel. Medical examiner and death scene investigators typically handle remains, whereas police investigators handle other physical evidence such as personal possessions.

In contrast, a mass fatality event such as a plane crash or a school shooting would require a larger mass fatality MERT or even aid from the federal Disaster Mortuary System (DMORT system).

Typical members of a mass fatality response team include the following:

- Forensic pathologist
- Forensic odontologist (dentist)
- Police crime scene investigator/death scene investigator—investigate scene; collect and preserve evidence while maintaining chain of custody
- Forensic photographer
- Fingerprint examiner and technician
- DNA analyst
- Radiologist or technician (X-ray)
- Laboratory scientist/toxicologist/microbiologist/ trace evidence technician
- Autopsy technicians/morgue staff
- Forensic anthropologist—examines biological characteristics of the deceased and bones; determines age at death, sex, race, and stature; as well as aids ME in determining circumstances surrounding death. Identify antemortem pathology or abnormalities such as healed fractures or disease and perimortem trauma.

Controversies

The primary goal of a MERT is identification of remains. Medical examiners have a professional guideline to identify remains using scientific standards such as dental records of DNA, which can take days. This can be frustrating for families or public officials who might want quicker identification of remains using nonscientific methods such as visual identification or circumstantial information (pocket contents or seating charts). Unlike a hospital autopsy, permission of next of kin is not required for a medicolegal autopsy. In many jurisdictions, a judge can order an autopsy despite a family's objection.

Future

The availability of DNA technology has brought new questions to the field. Although some states have DNA databases of convicted felons, there is nothing comparable with existing fingerprint databases and there is debate about the legality and constitutionality of a DNA database. In addition, a national backlog of forensic DNA evidence remains.

An emerging international trend is to use the results of forensic pathology in advancing public health. For example, multiple state medical examiner systems are now members of the Violent Crime Reporting System for the Centers for Disease Control and Prevention and report aggregate data on child deaths.

Heather E. Finlay-Morreale

See also Death Notification; Homicide and Murder

Further Readings

Committee for the Workshop on the Medicolegal Death Investigation System, Institute of Medicine. (2003). *Medicolegal death investigation system: Workshop summary*. Washington, DC: National Academies Press.

DiMaio, V. J. M., & Dana, S. E. (2006). *Handbook of forensic pathology* (2nd ed.). Boca Raton, FL: CRC Press.

Fierro, M. F. (2007). Mass murder in a university setting: Analysis of the medical examiner's response. *Disaster Medicine and Public Health Preparedness, 1*(Supplement), S25–S30.

Froede, R. C. (Ed.). (2008). *Handbook of forensic pathology* (2nd ed.). Northfield, IL: College of American Pathologists.

Randall, B. B., Fierro, M. F., & Froede, R. C. (1998). Forensic pathology committee of the college of American pathologists. Practice guideline for forensic pathology. *Archives of Pathology & Laboratory Medicine, 122*, 1056–1064.

Ritter, N. (2007). Identifying remains: Lessons learned from 9/11. *NIJ Journal, 256*.

Spitz, W. U., Spitz, D. J., Clark R., & Fisher, R. S. (Eds.). (2006). *Spitz and Fisher's medicolegal investigation of death: Guidelines for the application of pathology to crime investigation*. Springfield, IL: Charles C Thomas.

Web Sites

National Association of Medical Examiners: http://www.thename.org

MEGAN'S LAW

Washington State was the first to pass a law in 1990 authorizing the authorities to notify the public when sex offenders are released into the community. In 1994, the federal government passed the Jacob Weterling Act, which required all states to develop a registry of sex offenders who had targeted children. The 1996 Megan's Law amendment to this act forced all states not only to register sex offenders but also to notify the community of their presence. Megan's Law was named after 7-year-old Megan Kanka, a New Jersey girl who was raped and murdered by a twice-convicted sex offender who was residing in her neighborhood. Megan's parents argued that had they known their neighbor was a dangerous sex offender who targeted children, they would have taken steps to protect their daughter. Community notification, for better or worse, seems to be with us for the foreseeable future.

It has long been believed that sex offenders, more than other types of criminals, pose a high risk for repetition. In addition, sex offenders often target women and children (who are less able to defend themselves), and their crimes are considered to be particularly offensive. Consequently, the State—which has a duty to protect its citizens—has chosen community notification as one way to discharge this obligation. The government has evidently concluded that the privacy rights of convicted sex offenders are less important than public safety.

The type and method of notification varies widely between and within states, so that not all sex offenders are handled similarly. Distinctions are made between the dangerousness of the offender and the method of notification. For example, New Jersey—which to some extent serves as a model for the rest of the country—uses a three-tier system that differentiates offender risk and guides the method of notification. Here, convicted sex offenders' level of risk is assessed using the Registrant Risk Assessment Scale, developed by a task force of mental health and criminal justice professionals under the auspices of the New Jersey Attorney General's Office.

The New Jersey model uses a graded system of notification, with those offenders found to be at the highest risk receiving the broadest form of community notification. Here, the county prosecutor's office performs door-to-door notification—within a geographic radius of home and work addresses—of all individuals with whom the offender is likely to come into contact. Sex offenders found to pose low risk must only register with the police at least once per year, depending on the jurisdiction. And, for those offenders in the middle third (moderate risk), the local prosecutor's office notifies administrators at facilities dealing with women or children (depending on the offender's historical victims) within a given geographic area. Recently, identifying information for moderate- and high-risk offenders has been placed on the State Police Web site, thus to some extent eliminating the relative benefit (to the offender) of being found moderate as opposed to high risk.

New Jersey's risk assessment scale is an empirically guided instrument that includes both historical, unchangeable risk factors (referred to as static factors) and current, changeable risk factors (referred to as dynamic factors). New Jersey's scale is more heavily weighted toward static risk factors, with the majority of the points derived from items related to offense history; other risk assessment scales focus more on dynamic factors, such as the offender's current and recent adjustment. In assessing a sex offender's risk, both factors need to be included.

Since the introduction of Megan's Law, many concerns have been identified. For example, it is unknown if the notification programs actually work. Some have even suggested that Megan's Law is a "feel good" remedy that may not prevent future crime. In fact, there has been no empirical validation that establishes the preventive value of the programs. There have also been several cases of vigilantism where citizens have taken it upon themselves to use all sorts of (illegal) tactics to get offenders to move; and in several instances, the wrong person was targeted. In addition, the cost of the program and the negative impact on real estate values have been cited as unanticipated consequences of the law, whereas the implications of notification through the Internet have yet to be studied. Moreover, several constitutional issues (e.g., rights of privacy and treating different groups of criminals differently) have been raised, with several cases currently before the U.S. Supreme Court.

Controversy has also developed regarding the handling of several subtypes of sex offenders, specifically juveniles, incest offenders, and cases where the sexual encounter was consensual. Because juveniles are a protected class, releasing their identities to communities seems to undermine the foundation of the juvenile justice system (which generally keeps names of minors sealed). And if the names and addresses of incest offenders are made public, the identities of the victims (who, in many cases, have the same last name and address) also become known. Here, the victims lose their confidentiality, which results in revictimization. In addition to adolescent and incest offenders, some "statutory rape" cases—where a minor has had consensual sex with an adult—have also raised concerns. For instance, should an 18-year-old high-school senior, who had consensual sex with his 14-year-old freshman girlfriend, be subjected to community notification? But despite the many problems associated with several aspects of Megan's Law, the public has been overwhelmingly in favor of this type of program. One can only hope that applied social science researchers begin to determine whether the various community notification laws have the desired effect of lowering recidivism, since at present, the value of these laws has little or no scientific support.

Louis B. Schlesinger and Phillip H. Witt

See also AMBER Alert; Central Registry; Pedophilia

Further Readings

Freeman-Longo, R. E. (1996). Feel good legislation: Prevention of calamity? *Child Abuse & Neglect, 20,* 95–101.

Schlesinger, L. B. (Ed.). (2000). *Serial offenders: Current thought, recent findings.* Boca Raton, FL: CRC Press.

Witt, P. H., DelRusso, J., Oppenheim, J., & Ferguson, G. (1996). Sex offender risk assessment and the law. *Journal of Psychiatry and Law, 24,* 343–377.

MENTAL ILLNESS AND VICTIMIZATION

The victimization of persons with mental illness has both historical significance and contemporary relevance. Because of the nature of mental illness, persons with psychiatric disorders are vulnerable to unfair treatment, including discrimination, stigma, and neglect. This entry situates the complex forms of victimization specific to this population in broader historical perspectives, then critically explores the scope of contemporary forms of mistreatment, and finally turns to the social policies and institutional reforms put in place to protect and to better serve the needs of mentally ill persons.

Historical Perspectives on Victimization

There are three major historical perspectives on the maltreatment of persons with mental illness in American society. First, a major shift in the social management of the mentally ill occurred during the industrial revolution. The shift from family care to institutional care transpired with the decline of rural agricultural communities and the rise of populated urban areas. Many mentally ill people, left adrift without supportive networks, were warehoused in jails and prisons. Championed by Dorothea Dix, the development of mental hospitals was an outgrowth of the modern industrialized society's desire to provide a therapeutic environment for persons in need of psychiatric care. Second, although the number of mental health hospitals grew progressively, they were overcrowded and inadequately staffed. Proponents of patient rehabilitation argued that long-term stays in psychiatric wards had a detrimental effect on the ability of individuals to reintegrate into society. The negative effects of institutionalization were echoed by social labeling theorists who claimed that as a by-product of being labeled "mentally ill," patients suffered depersonalization, a loss of status, and alienation, which exacerbated their symptoms of illness. Patients in mental hospitals were also subjected to various forms of medical experimentation, including electroconductive therapy (shock treatment) and psychosurgery (lobotomies). According to many reports, some patients suffered from the results of unsuccessful surgeries, such as brain damage and other unintended side effects, including, in some cases, death.

A third major development in the mistreatment of the mentally ill occurred as a consequence of the shift from institutionalized care to community-based care, which is referred to as deinstitutionalization. However, despite its positive intentions to improve the lives of persons with mental illness, this public policy failed in many respects. The community mental health movement was underfunded and fragmented. A lack of coordinated care between state hospitals and community agencies meant that former hospital patients were "dumped" into low-income areas without the necessary psychiatric, medical, or social resources to transition successfully back into the community. The systemic failure of deinstitutionalization was particularly harmful for the severely mentally ill. For example, some agencies participate in "creaming" practices whereby they prioritize treatment for people deemed most likely to respond positively to their services rather than those most impaired.

Contemporary Scope of Victimization

Many scholars argue that massive fiscal cutbacks in public mental health services shifted responsibility to law enforcement agencies to manage mentally ill persons. Scholars assert that an apt depiction of this phenomenon is transinstitutionalization. The number of people with mental illnesses in the criminal justice system has increased progressively in recent years; county jails and prisons have become de facto psychiatric institutions at great human cost as well as at public expense. Recent studies report that approximately 16% to 22% of jail and prison inmates suffer from a form of mental illness. Researchers and policy analysts surmise that deinstitutionalization led to the "criminalization of the mentally ill," meaning that individuals with untreated mental illnesses are more prone to police contacts as a result of their disorderly or deviant behaviors. A misguided public perception exists that mentally ill persons are prone to commit violent acts and that police must detain them in the interest of public safety. As a result, those most in need of psychiatric attention, including the homeless, persons with chemical dependency, and those who live in poverty, are more likely to be arrested than to receive care.

Policies, Treatment, and Prevention

Important developments have been aimed at reducing the discriminatory practices against persons with mental disorders. During the community mental health movement, advocacy groups championed the right to treatment by patients as well as their right to refuse treatment. Many states passed legislation to amend the vague and capricious commitment laws. Grassroots organizations, such as the National Alliance for the Mentally Ill, sponsored public education campaigns to increase awareness and fight social stereotypes that portray mentally ill persons as unstable, irrational, and violent. The criminal justice system has also institutionalized reforms to address the needs of mentally ill offenders. Nationwide, jurisdictions are adopting jail alternative programs, including mental health courts, to facilitate in-custody psychiatric assessments and coordinate continued treatment in the community upon release. These trends, however, are not without controversy. Some critical criminologists, for example, argue that these programs widen the net of social control over marginalized populations and raise the specter of coerced treatment.

Ursula Castellano

See also Crime Prevention Partnerships, International; Crime Prevention Partnerships, United States; Homeless, Violence Against; Medical and Mental Health Services; Pathways to Prevention; Substance Use and Victimization

Further Readings

Bureau of Justice Statistics. (2006). *Mental health problems of prisons and jail inmates*. Washington, DC: U.S. Department of Justice.

Cockerham, W. (2006). *The sociology of mental disorder*. Upper Saddle River, NJ: Pearson.

Earley, P. (2006). *Crazy: A father's search through America's mental health madness*. New York: Penguin.

Fuller, T. E. (1988). *Nowhere to go: The tragic odyssey of the homeless mentally ill*. New York: Harper and Row.

Goffman, E. (1961). *Asylums: Essays on the social situation of mental patients and other inmates*. Garden City, NY: Anchor Books.

Hiday, V. (1999). Mental illness and the criminal justice system. In A. Horowitz & T. Scheid (Eds.), *A handbook for the study of mental health: Social context, theories and systems* (pp. 508–525). New York: Cambridge University Press.

Mechanic, D. (2008). *Mental health and social policy: Beyond managed care*. New Brunswick, NJ: Rutgers University Press.

Whitaker, R. (2002). *Mad in America: Bad science, bad medicine and the enduring mistreatment of the mentally ill*. New York: Basic Books.

META-ANALYSIS

Meta-analysis is a systematic literature review technique that uses explicit methods to identify a set of relevant primary studies, followed by objective methods to synthesize results quantitatively from this collection of studies. The approach differs from a traditional narrative literature review, in which findings from multiple studies are discussed and considered qualitatively but are not combined numerically. As an example, a meta-analysis would be a very useful approach to summarize quantitatively evidence on the effects of school-based programs designed to reduce juvenile delinquency, or to synthesize the research on predictors of violent behavior in women. This entry provides a basic overview of the technique of meta-analysis, including its strengths and weaknesses as a form of systematic literature review, as well as provides key steps in the meta-analytic process.

Strengths and Weaknesses

When compared with narrative review, meta-analysis has several advantages. The approach is considerably more objective than a traditional literature review, in part because meta-analysis requires a systematic search for relevant literature and the determination of explicit criteria for study selection into the analysis. A narrative review usually does not implement such criteria and may involve hidden biases because of selecting studies by convenience or through a less systematic search. Furthermore, because a meta-analysis involves explicit, transparent criteria for study identification, selection, and integration, a straightforward replication of the research is possible. It is much less likely that independent narrative reviews will reach identical conclusions.

Meta-analysis also enables greater precision in estimating the outcome or effect in question. This precision is achieved via the specific techniques used to extract results from studies and to convert these results to common metrics, and the explicit manner by which the individual study results are combined into a single pooled effect estimate. In comparison, a narrative literature review might group study results into general themes or use a more basic quantitative approach such as vote-counting the number of studies that report statistically significant versus nil effects. Vote-counting is a preliminary method of summation, because it does not take into account the magnitude of the effects found across studies or any differences in sample sizes. Because sampling error is a function of sample size, because low-power studies with small samples are less likely to find statistically significant effects than are studies with large samples (given the effects of a similar magnitude). Furthermore, because the meta-analysis algorithm assigns greater weight to larger studies when estimating the pooled effect across studies, the meta-analysis estimate has considerably more statistical power than do the individual studies that compose the estimate.

Another advantage of meta-analysis is its ability to summarize large amounts of information across a set of studies, while also allowing for the examination of potential causes of between-study variation in effect magnitude. Narrative reviews face considerable challenges in effectively summarizing large bodies of literature, in particular with consideration to mediator or moderator effects of research design, treatment style, or treatment effectiveness with different populations.

The most frequent criticism of meta-analysis is that analyses may pool together studies that are incommensurate. In other words, it is meaningless to produce a summary effect for studies that are conceptually (or statistically) dissimilar. Another criticism of meta-analysis is the issue of publication bias. This bias occurs when studies with statistically significant findings are selected for publication more frequently than are studies with nonsignificant findings. The extent to which this is true will serve to bias the results of systematic literature searches, because electronic databases and other such sources will fail to identify nonpublished, nonsignificant studies.

General Procedure

1. Specifying the Research Question and Form of Research Findings

A meta-analysis begins with the specification of the research question to be assessed. Because the raw data in a meta-analysis consist of the results from independent studies, it is essential that the collection of studies in the meta-analysis examine the same relationship. More specifically, the individual study outcomes should be comparable with respect to conceptual nature, study design, and statistical form.

2. Determining Study Eligibility Criteria

Next, a protocol is developed that contains specific criteria by which studies will be assessed for inclusion in the analysis. Each potential study is examined along these criteria to determine whether the study is eligible for inclusion. For example, a criterion might require the sample to contain at least 100 subjects or the evaluation to include a control group. Studies might be excluded for reasons such as publication in a non-peer-reviewed source or publication outside a particular date range.

3. Systematic Literature Search and Report Retrieval

A systematic search is undertaken, usually with the goal to uncover the entire pool of eligible studies on a given topic. The search often involves key terms searched in multiple bibliographic databases (e.g., PsycInfo and Criminal Justice Abstracts), hand searches of relevant journals, government databases, and bibliographies of studies that meet inclusion criteria, and queries to experts in the field. From the list of studies identified in the literature search, each potentially eligible study is evaluated based on the inclusion criteria to determine whether it will be included in the meta-analysis.

4. Coding and Extracting Data

For inclusion in a meta-analysis, all study findings are transformed into the same format so that pooling across studies is possible. This format is the "effect size," which is a standardized index that represents both the magnitude and the direction of the outcome. The derivation of each study's effect size based on the particular quantitative outcomes presented in the research report allows for a consistent interpretation of findings over the different types of measures and variables.

5. Computing Effect Size Statistics

Several types of effect size measures exist; most of which have more than one method of computation. Commonly used effect size measures include the standardized mean difference (such as Cohen's *d* or Hedges's *g*), the odds-ratio, the correlation coefficient, the proportion difference, and the relative risk. The choice of effect size measure used in a meta-analysis depends on both the research question of interest as well as on the data reported in the study.

6. Analysis

The meta-analysis algorithm for determining the pooled mean effect size weights the set of effect sizes by their inverse variance weights, as follows:

$$\overline{ES} = \frac{\sum_{i}^{k}(w_i * ES_i)}{\sum_{i}^{k} w_i},$$

in which each study's effect size (ES) is multiplied by its inverse variance weight (w), summed across all studies i through k, and divided by the sum of the inverse variance weights for studies i through k.

The statistical significance of the meta-analysis mean effect size is tested with a Z-test:

$$Z = \frac{\overline{ES}}{SE_{\overline{ES}}},$$

where the standard error is defined by

$$SE_{\overline{ES}} = \sqrt{\frac{1}{\sum_{i}^{k} w_i}},$$

and the upper and lower bound 95% confidence intervals are as follows:

$$95\% \text{ C.I.} = \overline{ES} \pm 1.96(SE_{\overline{ES}}).$$

The confidence intervals indicate the precision of the pooled mean effect size; if the confidence interval does not cross zero, then the null hypothesis of no effect is rejected. In other words, the pooled finding across the set of included studies is determined to be statistically significant.

Meta-analysis is a powerful tool for aggregating the findings across a set of studies in a given body of literature, enabling a systematic, objective estimate of a treatment effect across a set of primary studies with potentially conflicting findings.

Jennifer S. Wong

See also Methodological Issues in Evaluating Effectiveness of Crime Prevention

Further Readings

Cooper, H., & Hedges, L. V. (Eds.). (1994). *Handbook of research synthesis*. Thousand Oaks, CA: Sage.

Egger, M., Smith, G., & Altman, D. G. (Eds.). (2001). *Systematic reviews in health care: Meta-analysis in context* (2nd ed.). London: BMJ Publishing Group.

Lipsey, M. W., & Wilson, D. B. (2001). *Practical meta-analysis*. Applied social research methods series, Volume 49. Thousand Oaks, CA: Sage.

METHODOLOGICAL ISSUES IN COUNTING VICTIMS

Counting victims of crime has methodological difficulties that can result in an inaccurate portrayal of the number of victims that exist. This is caused by various concerns that originate with the nature of victims as well as with data collection and statistical representations of victims. This entry provides an overview of the general methodological concerns of counting victims as guided by the use of crime/victim counting mechanisms in the United States of the Uniform Crime Reporting (UCR) Program and the National Crime Victimization Survey (NCVS). Finally, some recommendations are provided to enhance the ability of calculating a truer number of crime victims in the United States.

General Methodological Concerns

This entry provides the main reasons why victims are difficult to count. It addresses the concerns with determining the absolute number of victims, type of data collection, gaining access to victims, and statistical concerns of counting victims.

Determining the Absolute Number of Victims

The absolute number of crime victims in the United States has never been captured as the true number of victims is impractical and improbable to determine. It would require researchers to survey each and every individual of the United States, and each individual would have to be completely honest in reporting and recalling his or her victimization. Understandably, such efforts would consume much time and resources, which for the most part are unneeded as it is not as important to know an absolute number as it is to obtain the relative number of victimization instances that occur. Relative numbers or approximations still allow for policies, researchers, and scholars to understand general crime patterns. The concern thus rests on how relative numbers can be gathered to not include too much error or inaccuracies. Two means to obtain relative numbers of victimization are the UCR Program and the NCVS.

Type of Data Collection

One major drawback on the ability to collect information on all crime victimization is that researchers or the government are rarely interested in gathering information on all types of illegal behaviors. For instance, the UCR Program collects information from law enforcement on Part I Index crimes of murder and non-negligent manslaughter, forcible rape, robbery, aggravated assault, burglary, larceny-theft, motor vehicle theft, and arson. Similarly, the NCVS gathers information on crimes of rape, sexual assault, robbery, aggravated assault, simple assault, theft, burglary, and motor vehicle theft. Furthermore, single researchers usually only collect information on the specific crime(s) of interest.

A second concern of crime collection is that jurisdictions define crime differently and that no standardized definitions exist from one locale to another. When crime is defined differently, it adds to the confusion and inability to use formal records as a measure of victims. Lastly, data collections methods such as the UCR Program are not difficult to use in counting victims as it focuses on counting crime, not victims.

Gaining Access to Victims

As stated, the task of counting and collecting information on all victims is improbable and more than likely impossible. Thus, no source exists that contains a proper sampling frame or list of all victims. For this reason, samples must be used to determine the relative number of crime victims. When samples are correctly gathered, data can be used to infer or generalize findings to the population providing a relative number of crime victims. The main concern of gaining access to victims is how access can be accomplished to gain the proper amount and type of crime victims without being too limiting or exclusionary. To illustrate this concern, the UCR Program uses formal records of law enforcement and only reports crimes known to police officers. If a victim fails to report an offense, he or she would not be counted as a possible victim and would not be included in the sampling frame.

The NCVS is a more accurate resource than the UCR Program to tabulate the relative number of crime victims since it directly pertains to victims. One concern is that it does not sample individuals and instead samples households. Thus, those who do not live in typical residences (e.g., inmates and the institutionalized) or are homeless will not be in the sample. Additionally, the NCVS completes most of its data collection using telephones, a method that excludes those who do not own telephones. Thus, it is difficult to count victims as it is hard to gain access and appropriate samples that fully represent the population of the United States.

Statistical Concerns of Counting Victims

When there is an inability to gather information on a whole population, such as crime victims, samples are used to build statistical models that allow for inferences to be drawn to the population. The process of inference simply allows for the findings of the sample to be generalized to the population. For instance, if 7% of the sample were victims of auto thefts it could be concluded that roughly

7% of the population were victims of auto theft. Yet, for this conclusion to be accurate, numerous concerns must be accounted for, including coverage error, sampling error, measurement error, and nonresponse error. The *coverage error* suggests that all individuals of the population who were intended to be studied were not in the sample (e.g., a study counting the victims of property crimes fails to include victims of auto thefts). *Sampling error* is unavoidable as it is the natural error that accumulates when using a sample and not the whole population, which is normally set at 5% in the social sciences (e.g., for the auto theft example above, the population could have 2% to 12% of auto thefts because of the 5% of sampling error). The *nonresponse error* occurs when respondents have failed to respond and nonrespondents systematically differ from respondents (e.g., respondents have an average age of 36 years, but nonrespondents have an average age of 20 years). Finally, *measurement error* suggests that data collection is not accurate because of the way the researcher operationally defined the variables of interest (e.g., the definition for victims of rape more accurately describes sexual harassment). Thus, to count victims properly, samples and measurement must be carefully designed to decrease limitations and methodological concerns.

Suggested Improvements and Refinements

Irrelevant of the inability to detect the absolute number of victims in the United States, improvements can be suggested to allow for data to be more representative of victimization. First, more offenses could be regularly counted in the UCR Program and NCVS to include less serious offenses such as vandalism. Second, the NCVS could expand by different collection methods (e.g., mail surveys) or samples (e.g., juveniles, college students, homeless, and prison inmates) to allow previously unexamined individuals to be included into NCVS. Additionally, a mixed-method approach could be used to check the reliability and validity of data collection methods. Finally, more attention could be brought to cultural differences in the population of the United States to ensure that respondents understand all terms being used.

Jennifer L. Huck

See also Calculating Extent of Victimization: Incidence, Prevalence, and Rates; National Crime Victimization Survey (NCVS); Nonreporting/Failure to Report Victimization; Uniform Crime Reporting (UCR) Program; Victimless Crimes

Further Readings

Catalano, S. M. (2006). *The measurement of crime: Victim reporting and police recording.* New York: LFB Scholarly Publishing.

Mosher, C. J., Miethe, T. D., & Phillips, D. M. (2002). *The mismeasure of crime.* Thousand Oaks, CA: Sage.

O'Brien, R. M. (1985). *Crime and victimization data.* Beverly Hills, CA: Sage.

Web Sites

National Crime Victimization Survey: http://www.ojp .usdoj.gov/bjs/cvict.htm

Uniform Crime Reporting Program: http://www.fbi.gov/ ucr/ucr.htm

METHODOLOGICAL ISSUES IN EVALUATING EFFECTIVENESS OF CRIME PREVENTION

Studies evaluating the effectiveness of crime prevention vary in methodological quality, and the most weight should be given to the best studies. It is essential to develop methodological quality standards for evaluation research that can be understood and easily used by scholars, practitioners, policy makers, the mass media, and systematic reviewers.

Discussions about methodological quality standards, and about inclusion and exclusion criteria in systematic reviews, are inevitably contentious because they are perceived as potentially threatening by some evaluation researchers. People whose projects are excluded from systematic reviews correctly interpret this as a criticism of the methodological quality of their work. In systematic reviews of the effectiveness of improved street lighting and closed-circuit television (CCTV) by David Farrington and Brandon Welsh, referees considered that the excluded studies were being "cast into outer darkness."

Methodological quality standards are likely to vary according to the topic being reviewed. For example, because there have been many randomized experiments on family-based crime prevention, it would not be unreasonable to restrict a systematic review of this topic to the gold standard of randomized experiments. However, no randomized experiments have been designed to evaluate the effect of either improved street lighting or CCTV on crime. Therefore, in systematic reviews of these topics by Farrington and Welsh, the minimum methodological standard for inclusion required before and after measures of crime in experimental and comparable control areas.

This standard was also set as the minimum design that was adequate for drawing valid conclusions about "what works" in the book *Evidence-Based Crime Prevention* by Lawrence Sherman and his colleagues, which was based on the Maryland Scientific Methods Scale (SMS). An important issue is to what extent it is desirable or feasible to use a methodological quality scale to assess the quality of evaluation research and as the basis for making decisions about including or excluding studies in systematic reviews. And if a methodological quality scale should be used, which one should be chosen?

Methodological Quality Criteria

According to Thomas Cook and Donald Campbell, methodological quality depends on four criteria: statistical conclusion validity, internal validity, construct validity, and external validity. According to William Shadish and his colleagues, "validity" refers to the correctness of inferences about cause and effect. From the time of John Stuart Mill, the main criteria for establishing a causal relationship have been that (1) the cause precedes the effect, (2) the cause is related to the effect, and (3) other plausible alternative explanations of the effect can be excluded. The main aim of the Campbell validity typology is to identify plausible alternative explanations (threats to valid causal inference) so that researchers can anticipate likely criticisms and design evaluation studies to eliminate them. If threats to valid causal inference cannot be ruled out in the design, they should at least be measured and their importance should be estimated.

Descriptive validity, or the adequacy of reporting, has been added as a fifth criterion of the

methodological quality of crime prevention research. To complete a systematic review, it is important that information about key features of the evaluation be provided in each research report. The CONSORT statement specifies rules for the reporting of randomized trials in medicine, but there is no equivalent specification for crime prevention evaluation research.

Statistical Conclusion Validity

Statistical conclusion validity is concerned with whether the presumed cause (the intervention) and the presumed effect (the outcome, usually crime or offending) are related. Measures of effect size and their associated confidence intervals should be calculated. Statistical significance (the probability of obtaining the observed effect size if the null hypothesis of no relationship were true) should also be calculated, but in many ways, it is less important than the effect size. This is because a statistically significant result could indicate a large effect in a small sample or a small effect in a large sample.

The main threats to statistical conclusion validity are insufficient statistical power to detect the effect (e.g., because of small sample size) and the use of inappropriate statistical techniques (e.g., where the data violate the underlying assumptions of a statistical test). Statistical power refers to the probability of correctly rejecting the null hypothesis when it is false. Other threats to statistical conclusion validity include the use of many statistical tests (in a so-called fishing expedition for significant results) and the heterogeneity of the experimental units (e.g., the people or areas in experimental and control conditions). The more variability there is in the units, the harder it will be to detect any effect of the intervention.

Internal Validity

Internal validity refers to the correctness of the key question about whether the crime prevention method really did cause a change in the outcome, and it has generally been regarded as the most important type of validity. In investigating this question, some kind of control condition is essential to estimate what would have happened to the experimental units (e.g., people or areas) if the intervention had not been applied to them—termed the *counterfactual inference*. Experimental control is usually better than statistical control. One problem is that the control units rarely receive no treatment, but instead, they typically receive the usual treatment or some kind of treatment that is different from the experimental intervention. Therefore, it is important to specify the effect size "compared with what?"

The main threats to internal validity were identified by Cook and Campbell but often do not seem to be uniformly well known:

Selection—the effect reflects preexisting differences between experimental and control conditions.

History—the effect is caused by some event occurring at the same time as the intervention.

Maturation—the effect reflects a continuation of preexisting trends (e.g., in crime rates or in normal human development).

Instrumentation—the effect is caused by a change in the method of measuring the outcome.

Testing—the pretest measurement causes a change in the posttest measure.

Regression to the Mean—where an intervention is implemented on units with unusually high scores (e.g., areas with high crime rates), natural fluctuation will cause a decrease in these scores on the posttest, which may be mistakenly interpreted as an effect of the intervention. The opposite (an increase) happens when interventions are applied to low crime rate areas or low scoring people.

Differential Attrition—the effect is caused by differential loss of units (e.g., people) from experimental compared with control conditions.

Causal Order—it is unclear whether the intervention preceded the outcome.

In addition, there may be interactive effects of threats. For example, a selection-maturation effect may occur if the experimental and control conditions have different preexisting trends, or a selection-history effect may occur if the experimental and control conditions experience different historical events (e.g., where they are located in different settings).

In principle, a randomized experiment has the highest possible internal validity because it can rule out all these threats, although in practice differential attrition may still be problematic. Randomization is the only method of assignment that controls for *unknown* and *unmeasured* confounders as well as those that are known and measured. The conclusion that the intervention really did cause a change in the outcome is not necessarily the final conclusion. It is desirable to go beyond this and to investigate links in the causal chain between the intervention and the outcome, the dose-response relationship between the intervention and the outcome, and the validity of any theory linking the intervention and the outcome.

Construct Validity

Construct validity refers to the adequacy of the operational definition and measurement of the theoretical constructs that underlie the intervention and the outcome. For example, if a project aims to investigate the effect of interpersonal skills training on offending, did the training program really target and change interpersonal skills and were arrests a valid measure of offending? Whereas the operational definition and measurement of physical constructs such as height and weight are not contentious, this is not true of most criminological constructs.

The main threats to construct validity center on the extent to which the intervention succeeded in changing what it was intended to change (e.g., to what extent there was treatment fidelity or implementation failure) and on the validity and reliability of outcome measures (e.g., how adequately police-recorded crime rates reflect true crime rates). Displacement of offending and diffusion of benefits of the intervention should also be investigated. Other threats to construct validity include those originating from a participant's knowledge of the intervention and from problems of contamination of treatment (e.g., where the control group receives elements of the intervention). To counter the Hawthorne effect, it is acknowledged in medicine that double-blind trials are needed, where neither doctors nor patients know about the experiment. It is also desirable to investigate interaction effects between different interventions or different ingredients of an intervention.

External Validity

External validity refers to the generalizability of causal relationships across different persons, places, times, and operational definitions of interventions and outcomes (e.g., from a demonstration project to the routine large-scale application of an intervention). It is difficult to investigate this within one evaluation study, unless it is a large-scale, multisite trial. External validity can be established more convincingly in systematic reviews and meta-analyses of numerous evaluation studies. Shadish and his colleagues distinguished generalizability to similar versus different populations, for example, contrasting the extent to which the effects of an intervention with males might be replicated with other males as opposed to the extent to which these effects might be replicated with females. The first type of generalizability would be increased by carefully choosing random samples from some population as potential (experimental or control) participants in a crime prevention evaluation.

The main threats to external validity listed by Shadish and his colleagues consist of interactions of causal relationships (effect sizes) with types of persons, settings, interventions, and outcomes. For example, an intervention designed to reduce offending may be effective with some types of people and in some types of places but not in others. A key issue is whether the effect size varies according to whether those who carried out the research had some kind of stake in the results; for example, if a project is funded by a government agency, the agency may be embarrassed if the evaluation shows no effect of its highly trumpeted intervention. Boundary conditions may exist within which interventions do or do not work or "moderators" of a causal relationship in the terminology of Reuben Baron and David Kenny. Also, mediators of causal relationships (links in the causal chain) may be effective in some settings but not in others. Ideally, theories should be proposed to explain these kinds of interactions.

Descriptive Validity

Descriptive validity refers to the adequacy of the presentation of key features of an evaluation in a research report. Systematic reviews of the effectiveness of crime prevention methods can only be carried out satisfactorily if the original evaluation reports document key data on issues such as the number of participants and the effect size. A list of minimum elements to be included in an evaluation report would include at least the following:

- Design of the study: How were units allocated to experimental or control conditions?
- Characteristics of units and settings (e.g., age and gender of individuals as well as sociodemographic features of areas).
- Sample sizes and attrition rates.
- Causal hypotheses to be tested, and theories from which they are derived.
- The operational definition and detailed description of the crime prevention method (including its intensity and duration).
- Implementation details and program delivery personnel.
- Description of what treatment the control condition received.
- The operational definition and measurement of the outcome, before and after the intervention.
- The reliability and validity of outcome measures.
- The follow-up period after the intervention.
- Effect size, confidence intervals, statistical significance, and statistical methods used.
- How independent and extraneous variables were controlled so that it was possible to disentangle the impact of the intervention, or how threats to internal validity were ruled out.
- Who knows what about the intervention.
- Conflict of interest issues: Who funded the intervention and how independent were the researchers?

It would be desirable for professional associations, funding agencies, journal editors, and/or the Campbell Collaboration to get together to develop a checklist of items that must be included in all research reports on impact evaluations.

The Maryland Scientific Methods Scale

The most influential methodological quality scale in criminology is the Maryland SMS, which was developed by Sherman and his colleagues for large-scale reviews of what works or does not work in preventing crime. The main aim of the SMS is to communicate to scholars, policy makers, and practitioners in the simplest possible way that studies evaluating the effects of criminological interventions differ in methodological quality. The SMS was largely based on the ideas of Cook and Campbell.

In constructing the SMS, the main aim was to devise a simple scale measuring internal validity that could be communicated easily. Thus, a simple 5-point scale was used rather than a summation of scores (e.g., from 0 to 100) on several specific criteria. It was intended that each point on the scale should be understandable, and the scale is as follows:

Level 1: Correlation between a prevention program and a measure of crime at one point in time (e.g., "areas with CCTV have lower crime rates than areas without CCTV").

This design fails to rule out many threats to internal validity and fails to establish causal order.

Level 2: Measures of crime before and after the program, with no comparable control condition (e.g., "crime decreased after CCTV was installed in an area").

This design establishes causal order but fails to rule out many threats to internal validity. Level 1 and Level 2 designs were considered inadequate and uninterpretable by Cook and Campbell.

Level 3: Measures of crime before and after the program in experimental and comparable control conditions (e.g., "crime decreased after CCTV was installed in an experimental area, but there was no decrease in crime in a comparable control area").

This was considered to be the minimum interpretable design by Cook and Campbell, and it is regarded as the minimum design that is adequate for drawing conclusions about what works in the book *Evidence-Based Crime Prevention* by Sherman and his colleagues. It rules out many threats to internal validity, including history, maturation/trends, instrumentation, testing effects, and differential attrition. The main problems with it center on selection effects and regression to the mean (because of the nonequivalence of the experimental and control conditions).

Level 4: Measures of crime before and after the program in multiple experimental and control units, controlling for other variables that influence crime (e.g., "victimization of premises under CCTV surveillance decreased compared to victimization of control premises, after controlling for features of premises that influenced their victimization").

This design has better statistical control of extraneous influences on the outcome and, hence, deals with selection and regression threats more adequately.

Level 5: Random assignment of program and control conditions to units (e.g., "victimization of premises randomly assigned to have CCTV surveillance decreased compared to victimization of control premises").

Providing that a sufficiently large number of units are randomly assigned, those in the experimental condition will be equivalent (within the limits of statistical fluctuation) to those in the control condition on all possible extraneous variables that influence the outcome. Therefore, this design deals with selection and regression problems and has the highest possible internal validity.

A New Methodological Quality Scale

Although the SMS, like all other methodological quality scales, can be criticized, it has the virtue of simplicity. It can be improved, but at the cost of simplicity. It does seem useful to use some kind of index of methodological quality to communicate to scholars, policy makers, and practitioners that not all research is of the same quality and that more weight should be given to higher quality crime prevention evaluation studies. It also seems highly desirable for funding agencies, journal editors, scholarly associations, and/or the Campbell Collaboration to get together to agree on a measure of methodological quality that should be used in systematic reviews and meta-analyses in criminology. A similar measure should also be used in systematic reviews of studies of the causes of offending (see Murray, Farrington, & Eisner, 2009).

David Farrington's suggestion, put forward tentatively to stimulate discussions, is that a new methodological quality scale might be developed based on five criteria:

1. Internal validity

2. Descriptive validity

3. Statistical conclusion validity

4. Construct validity

5. External validity

Farrington has placed the criteria in order of importance, at least as far as a systematic reviewer of impact evaluations is concerned. Internal validity—demonstrating that the intervention caused an effect on the outcome—is surely the most important feature of any evaluation research report. Descriptive validity is also important; without information about key features of research, it is hard to take account of the results in a systematic review. In contrast, information about the external validity of any single research project is the least important to a systematic reviewer, because the main aims of a systematic review and meta-analysis include establishing the external validity or generalizability of results over different conditions and investigating factors that explain heterogeneity in effect sizes among different evaluation studies.

Conclusion

It is important to develop methodological quality standards for crime prevention evaluation research that can be used by systematic reviewers, scholars, policy makers, the mass media, and the general public in assessing the validity of conclusions about the effectiveness of interventions in reducing crime. Hopefully, the development of these standards will help to upgrade the quality of evaluation research. All research should not be given equal weight, and criminal justice policy should be based on the best possible evidence. The main conclusion is that new methodological quality scales should be developed, based on statistical conclusion validity, internal validity, construct validity, external validity, and descriptive validity.

David P. Farrington

See also Cost-Benefit Analysis and Crime Prevention; Crime Prevention; Crime Prevention Initiatives, International

Further Readings

Altman, D. G. (2005). Endorsement of the CONSORT statement by high impact medical journals: A survey of instructions for authors. *British Medical Journal, 330,* 1056–1057.

Clarke, R. V., & Weisburd, D. (1994). Diffusion of crime control benefits: Observations on the reverse of displacement. In R. V. Clarke (Ed.), *Crime Prevention Studies* (Vol. 2, pp. 165–183). Monsey, NY: Criminal Justice Press.

Cook, T. D., & Campbell, D. T. (1979). *Quasi-experimentation: Design and analysis issues for field settings.* Chicago: Rand McNally.

Farrington, D. P. (2003). Methodological quality standards for evaluation research. *Annals of the American Academy of Political and Social Science, 587,* 49–68.

Farrington, D. P., & Petrosino, A. (2001). The Campbell collaboration crime and justice group. *Annals of the American Academy of Political and Social Science, 578,* 35–49.

Farrington, D. P., & Welsh, B. C. (2007). *Improved street lighting and crime prevention.* Stockholm, Sweden: National Council for Crime Prevention.

Littell, J. H., Corcoran, J., & Pillai, V. (2008). *Systematic reviews and meta-analysis.* Oxford, UK: Oxford University Press.

Morgan, S. L., & Winship, C. (2007). *Counterfactuals and causal inference.* Cambridge, UK: Cambridge University Press.

Murray, J., Farrington, D. P., & Eisner, M. P. (2009). Drawing conclusions about causes from systematic reviews of risk factors: The Cambridge Quality Checklists. *Journal of Experimental Criminology, 5,* 1–23.

Shadish, W. R., Cook, T. D., & Campbell, D. T. (2002). *Experimental and quasi-experimental designs for generalized causal inference.* Boston: Houghton Mifflin.

Sherman, L. W., Farrington, D. P., Welsh, B. C., & MacKenzie, D. L. (Eds.). (2006). *Evidence-based crime prevention* (Rev. ed.). London: Routledge.

Sherman, L. W., Gottfredson, D. C., MacKenzie, D. L., Eck, J., Reuter, P., & Bushway, S. (1998). *Preventing crime: What works, what doesn't, what's promising* (Research in Brief). Washington, DC: U.S. National Institute of Justice.

Welsh, B. C., & Farrington, D. P. (2007). *Closed-circuit television surveillance and crime prevention.* Stockholm, Sweden: National Council for Crime Prevention.

MINNEAPOLIS DOMESTIC VIOLENCE EXPERIMENT AND REPLICATION

Appropriate police response is a critical component of any attempt to control the problem of domestic violence. Historically, however, law enforcement agencies found the determination of what constituted an appropriate response to be somewhat challenging. As a result, clear, consistent policies regarding the handling of domestic violence calls were rare. Most police officers relied on their discretion and handled domestic calls on a case-by-case basis. The *Minneapolis Domestic Violence Experiment*, conducted by Lawrence Sherman and Richard Berk for the Police Foundation, provided evidence that clearly indicated that one approach (i.e., the arrest of the aggressive party) was most effective in reducing future involvement in domestic violence. Consequently, law enforcement agencies across the United States adopted policies mandating arrest in the event of a domestic incident. This entry describes the Minneapolis Domestic Violence Experiment and its results, discusses attempts to replicate the study, and examines its implications for long-term policy regarding law enforcement response to domestic violence.

The Study

Historical Background

In the late 1960s, some evidence was produced that suggested that a nonpunitive law enforcement approach to domestic violence involving the use of psychology might be more effective than traditional approaches in reducing additional violent incidents. However, by the late 1970s, both law enforcement and victim advocates began to question the effectiveness of this approach. Consequently, states began to pass legislation that allowed officers to arrest suspects in domestic violence calls, even when the officers themselves had not witnessed the domestic violence or when no visible evidence was found that a felony had been committed. This movement was largely a response to the need to provide better protection for victims of domestic assault. Evaluation of this stronger approach to determine whether it did, in fact, better serve victims was the next logical step.

In 1980, the Police Foundation received funding from the National Institute of Justice to evaluate the deterrent effect of arrest in cases of domestic violence. Sherman and Berk obtained permission from the Minneapolis Police Department to conduct the study, which commenced in 1981.

Research Design

The study was conducted using classic experimental design. Eligible domestic violence calls occurring during the study period were randomly assigned to one of three police responses: (1) arrest, (2) separation of the parties for a period of 8 hours, or (3) advising in any way deemed appropriate by the officer. Random assignment occurred at the point in time in which the call was determined to be eligible. Eligible calls had the following characteristics: There was probable cause to arrest for misdemeanor domestic assault within the last 4 hours, the victim and offender were clearly defined, no valid order of protection was currently in force, the victim did not insist that the offender be arrested and was not seriously wounded, the officer was not assaulted, and there was no immediate risk of additional violence if an arrest was not made. Each officer was provided with a set of randomly assorted, color-coded report forms that determined the action to be taken in an eligible call. Ineligible calls were handled by officers according to their discretion.

The experiment began on March 17, 1981, and ended on August 1, 1982. During that time period, data were collected on 314 eligible domestic violence calls. The data suggested that the experiment was largely implemented as designed. An arrest was made in nearly all of the cases in which arrest was the assigned response (99%). The percentages were somewhat lower for the calls in which separation or advising was the assigned response, 73% and 78%, respectively.

After the initial encounter with the police, biweekly follow-up interviews were conducted with the victims for a period of 6 months. This portion of the experiment was less successful than the researchers would have liked. The completion rate for the initial interview was only 62%, and only 49% of the victims completed all 12 follow-up interviews. The interviews were supplemented with police reports of repeat domestic violence committed by the suspect during the 6-month follow-up period.

Findings

The results of the experiment were dramatic. Data from both police records and victim interviews indicated that arrest was the most effective option. In fact, arrest reduced the rate of subsequent assaults by nearly 50%. Moreover, arrest was the most effective police action regardless of the suspect's race, employment status, educational level, criminal history, or the length of confinement upon arrest. Furthermore, although there is strong evidence in favor of arrest in most domestic violence cases, the authors were careful to indicate that the evidence does not suggest that a mandatory arrest policy would necessarily be the best approach to the problem.

Results regarding the separation and advisement options were mixed. Official records suggested that separation was the worst option, whereas the interview data indicated that offenders who were advised were the most likely group to reoffend.

Limitations

Like all studies, the Minneapolis Domestic Violence Experiment was limited in ways that may have had an impact on the ability of the researchers to draw valid conclusions. As mentioned, the study was not implemented exactly as designed in that not all of the calls were handled as specified in the color-coded report forms. Although arrest was carried out in nearly all of the cases in which it was required, compliance with the separation and advisement options was not complete. The researchers believed that the lesser compliance in the latter two options was caused by a lack of cooperation from the suspects, which led officers to fall back on arrest as a last resort. They argued that using arrest as a fallback position should have made arrest *less* likely to be the most effective option, because more of the arrested suspects would have been uncooperative. The fact that arrest turned out to be the most effective police action is a testament to the power of this response.

It is also possible that officers did not follow the randomization system. That is, officers may have used their discretion to determine which of the three response options were most appropriate in a particular case and then pulled the report sheet that fit their decision. In such a case, random assignment would not have occurred, thereby undermining the ability of the researchers to compare the data from the three experimental groups. Unfortunately, it is impossible to determine the extent to which officers may have failed to follow the experimental process.

Another issue is the fact that most of the domestic calls in the study were handled by a relatively small number of officers. Three officers produced 28% of the cases, and 200 of the 314 cases were produced by only 12 officers. It is clear that not all officers in the Minneapolis Police Department were willing to participate in the study. However, the researchers believed that the lack of participation on the part of officers did not have a significant effect on the results produced by the study, because each officer's cases were randomly assigned to the treatment conditions. Consequently, lack of participation by any given officer would not have affected the random assignment and thus should not have had a significant impact on the results produced by the study.

The small size of the final sample for which interview data are available (fewer than 100 cases) is also a potential threat to the validity of the study. Often, a small sample size is an indication that the experimental groups are not as comparable as they should be. As a result, the findings may not hold true in the general population. However, the researchers pointed out that this limitation may not be as serious as it first seems. Although many victims either refused to complete the interviews or could not be located to do so, the proportion of victims in each group completing the interview process was approximately the same. This fact rules out the possibility that victims whose aggressors were arrested may have been intimidated by the suspects into reporting less violence.

Replications of the Experiment

It is well known that the results of one study alone are not definitive proof that the hypotheses are correct. Therefore, it is good scientific practice for research to be replicated in other sites in order to determine whether the relationships found in the original research will also be supported in different places and under varying conditions. This is the process by which scientific knowledge is developed.

It is especially important to replicate studies when the results of the research may have a substantial impact on policy, as in the case of the Minneapolis Domestic Violence Experiment. Therefore, it is no surprise that the study was repeated in several sites. This section examines these additional studies, particularly those studies that were part of the Spouse Abuse Replication Project (SARP).

Nonexperimental Replications

The first attempts to replicate the results of the Minneapolis Domestic Violence Experiment involved reanalyzing the original data. As might be expected, these analyses consistently found a deterrent effect caused by arrest. However, the strength and nature of that relationship varied depending on the source of the data (victim vs. official records) and the length of time between arrest and the interview.

Studies also employed statistical analyses of police records in numerous jurisdictions in order to determine whether arrest resulted in a reduction of reported violence. These studies consistently found that arrest had a deterrent effect. However, some of these studies found that the deterrent effect might be more complex than suggested by the findings of the original study.

Spouse Abuse Replication Project

Research Design

SARP replicated the Minneapolis Domestic Violence Experiment in five sites around the country: Charlotte, Dade County, Colorado Springs, Milwaukee, and Omaha. All five studies involved a classic experimental design similar to that employed in the original study. However, the project leaders felt that the original design was flawed in ways that should be corrected in the replications. Consequently, the replications differed from the original study in the following ways:

1. Officers determined whether a case was eligible to be included in the experiment prior to receiving randomized instructions as to how to proceed. In the Minneapolis study, officers carried color-coded report forms that had been randomly mixed prior to their receipt by the officer. The replication researchers believed that completing the random assignment after the officer had determined the eligibility of the case would prevent officers from ignoring experimental protocols.

2. Victim interviews were conducted twice. The first interview occurred within a month of the incident, and the second was conducted at the end of 6 months. The original experiment attempted to interview victims by phone every 2 weeks during the study period. The leaders of the replication believed that the large number of interviews may have resulted in the low number of victims who actually completed the interview process.

3. The measures of repeated aggression on the part of the suspect were more sophisticated. The researchers in the replication recognized that domestic violence may be more complex than simply whether the suspect repeated the behavior. Consequently, several measures of aggression were employed.

4. Arrest was compared with seven different police interventions in recognition of the broad range of alternative actions police officers might take in any given situation.

5. A set of common measures about suspects, victims, treatments, and outcomes was employed to enhance uniformity across the experimental sites.

Across the six replication sites, data were collected on 4,032 incidents of domestic violence. Response rates were high across all sites. Nearly

63% of the victims completed both follow-up interviews.

Findings

Initial analyses of the SARP studies found mixed results. Only Dade County reported a deterrent effect associated with the arrest option, based on analyses of police records. Colorado Springs and Dade County found similar results in the victim interview data, but both sites had lower response rates than the other four locations. It is possible that the result might be a sampling artifact. Omaha, Charlotte, and Milwaukee found that although arrest seemed to deter offenders at first, over time arrest actually resulted in an escalation of the violence committed against the victim.

Three sites (Milwaukee, Colorado Springs, and Omaha) discovered that the effects of arrest may vary with the characteristics of the offender. Data in all three cities indicated that employment status is an important factor. Employed suspects were less likely to repeat the offense, whereas unemployed suspects became more violent. In addition, Milwaukee found similar results for marital status. Arrest was less successful when the suspect was unmarried. In fact, unemployed, unmarried suspects were the most likely group to escalate violence after arrest.

It is unclear why the findings from these studies differed so much from each other and from those reported in the Minneapolis Domestic Violence Experiment. One potential explanation lies in differences in the demographic characteristics of the sites. It is true that the race of the suspects did vary a lot across the sites, although not consistently across the sites that did or did not find a deterrent effect. Other characteristics thought to be important were consistent across the sites, however, limiting the utility of this explanation.

Although the SARP project leaders strove for consistent implementation of the experiment, it is also possible that the protocols were not exactly the same across sites. For instance, only Milwaukee kept precise records regarding how long a suspect was held after arrest. Omaha relied on informal polls of officers to measure this variable. Other sites defined the term differently. Consequently, trying to compare conclusions about the effect of length of time in custody from each of the sites is like trying to compare apples and oranges. This effect may be compounded when comparing the results with the Minneapolis study, which clearly employed different protocols. Some support for this explanation is found in a later analysis of the SARP data across all five sites, which used only those measures that were consistently defined across all locations. The analysis found that victim interviews indicated a reduction in aggression associated with arrest. However, the analysis could not find similar results in the official data. Although a reduction in aggression seemed to occur after arrest in the official data, the relationships were not statistically significant, leaving the question open for additional research.

It is also possible that the effect of specific police actions on future violent incidents is more site specific than generally expected. That is, it is possible that domestic violence is not only a more complex phenomenon than originally expected, but it may also vary across different social contexts. If so, the lack of consistency in the results would reflect true differences across the various locations rather than the limitations of the study designs. That would suggest that a national policy of arrest in domestic violence cases would not be wise.

Policy Implications

The effect of the Minneapolis Domestic Violence Experiment on law enforcement policy is somewhat unclear. Clearly, states were already moving toward the enactment of legislation, giving police more authority to make arrests in domestic violence cases prior to the experiment. Thus, it is impossible to say that the results of the study were the foundation of this movement. However, it is also clear that for many police departments, the experiment provided the evidence they required to adopt a proarrest policy. A 1984 poll of police departments found that more than a third of the respondents indicated that the published results of the study were instrumental in their decision to enact such a policy. Moreover, the 1984 Attorney General's Task Force on Family Violence relied on the experiment in its recommendation that arrest be the preferred policy in these cases. Therefore, it is certain that the experiment played a significant role in the development of this policy across the nation.

Yet, it is also certain that what we learned from the study is not as clear as it originally seemed. The fact that replications of the study were not able to produce consistently the same results as the Minneapolis experiment is problematic. Furthermore, the finding in some sites that arrest might actually result in an escalation of the violence is troubling, particularly given the current situation in which pro-arrest policies have been adopted in virtually all law enforcement agencies around the country. Given the politically sensitive nature of this issue, it would be difficult, if not impossible, at this juncture to modify the policies in such a way as to encourage officers to tailor their approach to the specific situation without leaving victims feeling as if they were abandoned by law enforcement.

Perhaps the best lesson to be learned from the Minneapolis Domestic Violence Experiment and its replications is that a single study should not serve as a primary basis for policy decisions. In this instance, a perfect confluence of events—the right study results combined with the right political and social context—led to policy that may or may not be the best solution to the problem. The wisest course of action would have entailed waiting until the study had been replicated and the findings had been demonstrated to be supported consistently prior to making a policy decision.

AnnMarie Cordner

See also Abuse, Spouse; Deterrence; Domestic Violence and Arrest Policy; Family Violence; Methodological Issues In Evaluating Effectiveness of Crime Prevention; Police and Victims

Further Readings

Binder, A., & Meeker, J. W. (1992). Implications of the failure to replicate the Minneapolis experimental findings. *American Sociological Review, 58,* 886–888.

Buzawa, E., & Buzawa, C. (1991). *Domestic violence: The changing criminal justice response.* Westport, CT: Greenwood.

Dunford, F. W., & Elliott, D. S. (1990). The role of arrest in domestic assault: The Omaha experiment. *Criminology, 28,* 183–206.

Maxwell, C., Garner, J. H., & Fagan, J. A. (2001). The effects of arrest on intimate partner violence: New evidence from the Spouse Assault Replication Program. *National Institute of Justice Research in Brief, July.*

Sherman, L. (1992). *Policing domestic violence: Experiments and dilemmas.* New York: The Free Press.

Sherman, L., & Berk, R. A. (1984). The specific deterrent effects of arrest for domestic assault. *American Sociological Review, 49,* 261–272.

MISSING, EXPLOITED, AND MURDERED CHILDREN

Children are society's weakest and most vulnerable group, and crimes perpetrated against them—such as kidnappings, sexual exploitation, and murder—evoke strong feelings in most of the public. Hence, a study of the serious and multifaceted problem of missing, exploited, and murdered children is vital for law enforcement, society at large, and the victims themselves.

Risk Factors

Victimology has become a large subsection of criminology, and many would say its own discipline. Lawrence Cohen and Marcus Felson, in their famous routine activities theory, stated that all that was needed for victimization to take place (and this is especially germane to many crimes against children) is an available target, a lack of a capable guardian, and the presence of a motivated offender. In many crimes against children, of course, this is the case. Adding to his original routine activities work, Cohen sought to establish a theoretical link between routine activities theory and both lifestyle and proximity theories. Cohen looked at the following five factors that he felt might explain victimization:

1. The exposure of victims to those who may offend against them.

2. The presence of a crime-preventing guardian.

3. The proximity between the residences of the potential victims and the potential offenders.

4. The "attractiveness" of targets.

5. The definitions of any given crime and the difficulty of that level of crime.

When looking at victimology and children, it is important to consider that child molestation is probably the most common crime against the person in the United States today, and 25% of girls and 10% of boys (it is estimated) will experience some kind of sexual abuse during their lifetime; in addition, girls are more likely to be abused from inside the family and boys are more likely to be abused from individuals outside the family.

Recent research has shown that most missing children are not the result of custodial disagreements resulting in kidnapping by parents. Rather, common causes are as follows, in order from most frequent to least frequent:

1. Runaways

2. Family abductions

3. Lost, injured or otherwise missing children

4. Nonfamily abductions (in these cases, the child is at greatest of injury or death)

One study developed a risk factor analysis for victimization in girls and presented the following as potential predictors:

1. Living with a stepfather

2. Living without a biological mother

3. Not close to mother

4. Mother never finished high school

5. Sex-punitive mother

6. No physical affection from (biological) father

7. Family income under U.S.$10,000 (in 1980 dollars; U.S.$26,000 in 2006 dollars)

8. Two friends or fewer in childhood

This study found that if a girl had none of the above predictors, her chance of victimization was virtually zero; if a girl had five of these predictors in her life, then the chance of victimization rose to 66%.

Scale, Nature, and Typology

To study the issue of missing, exploited, and murdered children, it is important to quantify its nature and size. According to the Department of Justice statistics, 797,500 children under the age of 18 years were reported missing in a 1-year period; family members abducted 203,900 of these, nonfamily abductions accounted for 58,200, and 115 children were the victims of *stereotypical kidnapping*. The remaining missing children were due to benign reasons not related to a criminal act. Stereotypical kidnappings are defined as involving someone the child does not know or someone of slight acquaintance, who holds the child overnight, transports the child 50 miles or more, kills the child, demands ransom, or intends to keep the child permanently. One study found that cases of abducted and missing children being murdered were rare; approximately 40 to 150 such incidents occurred each year. This figure represents less than half a percent of all discovered murders carried out each year. A more disturbing finding was that 76.2% of those children not discovered safely within 3 hours of abduction had been murdered within that time.

The 76.2% figure is based on data garnered from nonfamily-abducted children; however, this figure is posited to be much lower in "family abduction" situations where the child is generally taken by another parent in situations of custodial disagreement. Family abduction can be severely psychologically damaging to the child abductee as he or she may be told by the familial kidnapper that the other parent no longer wants or cares for them. In addition, the child may be forced to live life as a fugitive never settling in a residence or school, thereby limiting the normal developmental and social skills to be achieved.

Child pornography, a form of sexual exploitation, is defined by Stephen T. Holmes and Ronald M. Holmes as underage children who have been used in various media to arouse those who chose to view them. Holmes and Holmes also discovered in their extensive research that when pedophiles are arrested and their belongings are inventoried, there is almost always some type of child pornography present. Children can become involved in the production of this material in a variety of ways. Sometimes parents are involved in "sporting clubs," which are groups of like-minded individuals who share indecent photographs or videos of their children among each other. Some of these victims engage in pornographic acts because they are intimidated by authority figures such as a parent, teacher, or relative. LeRoy Schultz discovered another method to involve children in these acts; couples were taking "street kids," some as young as 6 months, into their home, ostensibly to care for them, and then forced these children either into child pornography or prostitution. Furthermore, the Illinois Legislative Investigative Committee in 1980 found a summer camp being used as a front for enticing children into child pornography.

Empirical Analysis

According to some studies, there may well be more than 30,000 children involved in the production of child pornography, and of those 30,000, as many as 10% (under the age of 14 years) were in the greater Los Angeles area. Some question the accuracy of many of these studies and want to approach the problem from a qualitative as opposed to a mainly quantitative issue of the problem. Holmes and Holmes report that many of these studies found some common characteristics in children who had become involved and victimized by the phenomenon of child pornography. These are as follows:

1. Involvement in childhood prostitution

2. Runaway

3. Product of a broken home

4. Typical age between 8 and 17 years

5. Underachiever in school or at home

6. No strong moral or religious affiliation

7. Poor social development

8. Parents physically or psychologically absent

In their more quantitative methodology in Kentucky, interviewing juveniles who had self-reported involvement in child pornography, Holmes and Holmes also discovered that less than 15% of the Kentucky victims had parents who were married and that about 20% reported some form of family discord, lack of a loving environment, and a remoteness from both parents and siblings (if any were present). All the children questioned used alcohol or drugs, and approximately 80% stated that they were runaways.

As repugnant as the loss, kidnapping, or sexual exploitation may be, surely another terror in the hearts of most parents is that of their child being the victim of a kidnap-homicide.

In the empirical analysis of Holmes and Holmes, the victimology involved in kidnap-homicide was broken into groups:

1. Females represented 69% of the victims, whereas males represented 31%.

2. By age, the highest at risk group was 12 to 14 years (38%). Half that figure, 19%, was made up of 0- to 5-year-olds.

3. Whites and blacks were overrepresented in victimization, whereas Hispanics were underrepresented.

4. Seventy-one percent of the perpetrators were strangers as opposed to "slight acquaintances."

5. In 86% of the cases, the perpetrator was male.

6. Only 11% of the identified perpetrators were more than 40 years of age as opposed to 57% being between 20 and 39 years of age.

Katherine Brown and her colleagues discovered females to be greatly overrepresented in child murder than in all murders (38%–74%) and males to be underrepresented in child murders than in all murders (26%–62%). They also found that, contrary to popular belief, children 6 years old and younger represented only 10% of all child murders. The idea of street kids being more vulnerable to such attacks was also debunked by this study as the friends of the victims described more than two thirds of them as "normal," 16.9% as "street-kids," and 13% as "runaways." Females represented 55% of all child murders as opposed to 38% of all murders (an overrepresentation); males represented 45% of all child murders and 62% of all murders.

According to the Department of Justice, many children had the misfortune to encounter a motivated offender randomly (i.e., stranger). In all, 50.5% were abducted in urban areas and 47.2% were incapacitated via direct physical assault. Strangulation was the leading cause of death in 33.2% of the cases; 23.9% were caused by blunt force trauma; and 23.3% by stabbing or cutting.

Initiatives

Among the most successful initiatives is the Child Abduction and Serial Murder Investigative Resource Center, which is run under the auspices of the Violent Criminal Apprehension Program through the Federal Bureau of Investigation. In addition, the number of states that use AMBER (America's Missing: Broadcast Emergency Response) Alerts is increasing. This program recovered 90 children in 2003 alone. In a 2004 Department of Justice press release, John Ashcroft stated, "When a young child is taken by the violent and predatory, we cannot stand idle. We demand accountability. We demand justice. . . . Today is the day to remember those who are gone, but whose imprint on our lives is still felt. It is a day to reflect on our calling as a free people to forge a nation that protects the lives of the most vulnerable."

Gavin Lee

See also Child Death Review Team; Homicide, Children and Youth; Kidnapping; Pedophilia

Further Readings

Department of Justice Office of Justice Programs. (2004). *Attorney General marks National Missing Children's Day; presents awards for efforts in missing & exploited children's cases.* Retrieved from http://www.ojp.usdoj.gov/archives/pressreleases/2004/OJP_05192004.htm

Hickey, E. (2006). *Sex crimes and paraphilia.* Upper Saddle River, NJ: Pearson.

Holmes, S. T., & Holmes, R. M. (2002). *Profiling violent crime: An investigative tool.* Thousand Oaks, CA: Sage.

Holmes, S. T., & Holmes, R. M. (2002). *Sex crimes: Patterns and behaviors.* Thousand Oaks, CA: Sage.

Salter, A. (2003). *Predators: Pedophiles, rapists, and other sex offenders.* New York: Basic Books.

Schultz, L. G. (1980). *Sexual victimology of youth.* Springfield, IL: Charles C Thomas.

Snow, R. L. (2006). *Sex crimes investigation: Catching and prosecuting the perpetrators.* Westport, CT: Praeger.

Walsh, A., & Ellis, L. (2006). *Criminology: An interdisciplinary approach.* Thousand Oaks, CA: Sage.

Web Sites

AMBER Alert: http://www.amberalert.gov
Federal Bureau of Investigation. Investigative Programs Critical Incident Response Groups. National Center for the Analysis of Violent Crime: http://www.fbi.gov/hq/isd/cirg/ncavc.htm
International Centre for Missing & Exploited Children: http://www.icmec.org
National Center for Missing & Exploited Children: http://www.missingkids.com
U.S. Department of Justice. Office of Justice Programs: http://www.ojp.usdoj.gov

MOTOR VEHICLE THEFT

Among the major crime types, auto theft is possibly the most ubiquitous. Motor vehicles are to be found just about anywhere, and as such, they are particularly interesting to crime prevention practitioners and researchers alike. Property crimes—such as those involving vehicles—are often overlooked in planning circles, despite their important impacts on the public perceptions of safety and levels of satisfaction with our respective justice systems.

Definitions

Auto theft is the common term in North America for the taking of a motor vehicle without consent. Subtle, but important, distinctions should be made when attempting to compare auto theft data internationally. Vehicle theft data for both Canada and the United States are similar in counting procedures. Canada, unlike the United States, includes in its motor vehicle theft counts the unauthorized taking of farm and construction equipment; instead, the United States counts these incidents as larcenies. More importantly, each vehicle that is stolen is counted once for both nations, with the exception of thefts from automobile dealerships, which, perhaps curiously, is counted once in the Canadian system. Estimates of the impact of these differences is less than 1%, with the Canadian numbers showing a slight undercounting relative to the U.S. data. England and Wales data are also comparable with their North American counterparts.

Motor vehicle thefts are broken into completed and attempted thefts. Victimization surveys in North America as well as in England and Wales include richer data about household experiences but not about commercial motor vehicle theft. Such surveys also include a potentially larger set of "vehicles" that may not be captured in police data or in all countries. Vehicle-related thefts are counted separately from successful and attempted thefts of the vehicle itself. As a result, concerns regarding counting develop, as it is often hard to distinguish between a "theft from" and a "theft of" situation where the perpetrator was interrupted in the process of stealing the vehicle. In England and Wales, theft of a motor vehicle is broken into five categories under the heading "offences against vehicles." The first is similar with the North American experience; this category includes theft and attempted theft, but it requires that the theft be of a permanent nature. Stealing a vehicle for resale or use of parts would be common examples. These forms of theft are more often linked to more or less organized crime groups. This category is the least likely to be recovered, as the vehicles tend to be modified quickly, "parted-out," and sold. Vehicle theft "rings" often distort or falsify vehicle identification numbers to evade notice or recovery. In some cases, stolen vehicles are moved one or more jurisdictions or even countries to facilitate reuse. The second form involves the unauthorized taking of a vehicle for temporary use or enjoyment (such as "joy riding"). Such vehicles are typically recovered within a short period of time and with few suspects, but those that are known to police tend to be younger males. Aggravated vehicle taking involves dangerous driving or is involved in an accident. The final two forms cover thefts, successful or otherwise, of vehicle contents, and interfering with a motor vehicle, which often includes attempted thefts where intent is not clear regarding permanency.

Trends

National data collected by police and findings from the 2004–2005 International Crime Victimization Survey (ICVS) show declining rates for auto thefts in the United States, England and Wales, Australia, and Canada. These reductions also follow increases of incidents known to the police in the 1960s and 1970s for both North America and England and Wales. Improvements have been made to physical security, such as installation of more sophisticated door and window locks as well as alarm systems. Researchers have noted, however, that despite a doubling of officially recorded offenses, the general consensus is that better counting and record-keeping procedures on behalf of police and increased willingness of citizens to report victimization experiences account for much of the swing in Uniform Crime Reporting Program rates. It should be noted, however, that despite recent discussions of changing/upgrading licensing and registration protocols, it is not yet clear what empirical benefits might be expected—if any—over current practices.

Like burglary, auto theft is trending downward per capita in police statistics and reported victimization, although as several researchers point out, the costs to its victims remain significant, especially as auto thefts have an inherent risk of accidents occurring during the aftermath of the offense. The 2004–2005 ICVS data suggest that for the 30 reporting nations, approximately 1% of respondents experienced auto theft. Researchers cite improved general advancements in protecting the envelope of vehicles and to better electronic immobilization technologies as the main reasons that these offenses are occurring less frequently than in the past, as these improvements have the greatest impact on crimes of opportunity. Nevertheless, it seems that thieves are adapting to less easily exploitable door locks and immobilizers. Some thieves are using keys obtained fraudulently from car dealers, by finding extra copies of keys inside the home or garage, or even in the car itself. Between 1998 and 2001, for example, the use of keys in England and Wales rose from 7% to 12% of all car thefts, showing that even new vehicles and those fortified with immobilization devices and technology remain vulnerable.

Young males are more likely to steal cars than older males or girls or women of any age. Sophisticated and/or highly skilled vehicle thieves still operate and are thought to be more representative of the "professional," for-economic-profit, criminal who sends the vehicle to a "chop-shop" where it will be stripped for parts or modified to avoid discovery. In addition to black market demand, more organized thieves target vehicles to assist in the commission of other offenses such as burglaries.

Spatio-Temporal Clustering

Long-term parking facilities, such as parking lots near major commuter transit stations, for example, serve as attractors for vehicle crime. Targets are plentiful, and car owners are unlikely to return for many hours. Thefts in this setting happen during the day, whereas in residential areas, they tend to occur during the night. Vehicles parked near bars or nightclubs, or at sports venues, are plentiful, easy to assess for target suitability, and often provide enough time to assess likely risks of being caught if an attempt is made.

J. Bryan Kinney

See also British Crime Survey (BCS); Routine Activities Theory; Situational Crime Prevention; Uniform Crime Reporting (UCR) Program; Victimization Surveys

Further Readings

Dhami, M. K. (2008). Youth auto theft: A survey of a general population of Canadian youth. *Canadian Journal of Criminology & Criminal Justice, 50,* 187–209.

Dijk, J. van, Smit, J., Kesteren, J. van, & Smit, P. (2007). *Criminal victimisation in international perspective: Key findings from the 2004–2005 ICVS and EU ICS.* Den Haag, the Netherlands: Boom Juridische uitgevers.

Kershaw, C., Nicholas, S., & Walker, A. (2008). *Crime in England and Wales 2007/08: Findings from the British Crime Survey and police recorded crime.* London: Home Office Statistics, Research Development and Statistics Directorate.

Laycock, G., Burrows T., & Morgan R. (2002). *Crime prevention and the UK vehicle registration and licensing system.* London: Jill Dando Institute of Crime Science, University College London.

Webb, B. (1994). Steering column locks and motor vehicle theft: Evaluations from three countries. In R. V. Clarke (Ed.), *Crime prevention series 2* (pp. 71–89). Monsey, NY: Criminal Justice Press.

Webb, B., Smith, M., & Laycock, G. (2004). Designing out crime through vehicle licensing and registration systems. In R. V. Clarke (Ed.), *Crime prevention series 17* (pp. 67–84). Monsey, NY: Criminal Justice Press.

MULTISYSTEMIC THERAPY

Since the late 1980s, scholars have increasingly documented that becoming a predatory offender is a developmental process. Although exceptions exist, most high-rate juvenile and adult offenders initially manifest conduct problems early in life that are recognized by parents, teachers, and peers. These youngsters experience the early onset of delinquent activities and of serious criminal offenses. They are disproportionately at risk of being incarcerated in a juvenile facility or adult correctional institution.

This recognition that the origins of crime extend to childhood and early adolescence has important policy implications. Until recently, treatment programs have largely targeted older juveniles and adults already in the criminal justice system. Findings revealing the childhood roots of crime, however, challenge this exclusive focus on those who already have embarked on a criminal career. Instead, the logic of life-course criminology suggests that at-risk youths can be identified and reformed starting in childhood and early adolescence, with care extending as the youth ages.

Unfortunately, most serious juvenile offenders do not receive meaningful treatment services until they reach the justice system. This gap in the delivery of services to at-risk youngsters has led to a call for the expansion of early intervention programs. Opinion polls show that the public strongly supports such attempts at "child saving." The more pressing challenge is what programs might be implemented that can intervene with youths who are destined to be entrapped in a life of crime.

Developed in the late 1970s by Scott Henggeler, multisystemic therapy—commonly known by the acronym of MST—is one of the most important early intervention programs that has emerged to address this problem. It is estimated that MST programs serve approximately 10,000 youths annually and can be found in more than 30 states and 11 nations. These programs have been evaluated rigorously, and their effectiveness has been assessed. MST promises to be an important early intervention program aimed at high-risk adolescents for the foreseeable future. The target population includes persistent, violent, or substance-abusing juveniles between the ages 12 and 17 years and their families.

This entry first discusses why MST represented a new paradigm or way of thinking about intervening with at-risk youths. It then explores in more detail what the MST intervention involves. The issues of the effectiveness of MST in reducing wayward behavior and cost-effectiveness as a public policy are also examined. The discussion ends by considering the future of MST.

A New Paradigm

The traditional psychotherapeutic model required troubled youths, and perhaps their parents, to come weekly to an office for an individual session lasting an hour. The length of treatment was open ended and could last months, if not years, on end. Recalcitrant youngsters were candidates for placement in a residential facility. This approach often proved costly, was ineffective in reducing antisocial conduct, and often failed to reach inner-city youths.

Scott Henggeler was part of a community psychology movement that eschewed this individualistic, more psychodynamic approach to counseling wayward adolescents. Instead, he embraced the social-ecological model, which portrays the reciprocal exchange between the individual and familial and community contexts. More concretely, youths not only have individual traits and reside in particular families, but also they are affected by other social systems: peers, schools, and community. In short, they live in multiple systems.

Empirical research has demonstrated that along with individual traits, each of these systems can expose a child or adolescent to criminogenic risk factors that increase the likelihood of law-breaking conduct. For example, a family risk factor might include ineffective parental discipline, a peer risk factor might involve contact with antisocial friends, and a school risk factor might be low achievement. For each troubled youth, the particular set of risk factors underlying his or her misconduct is likely to be unique. The intervention, thus, must be aware of this fact and be flexible enough to address risk factors drawn from different social domains.

Informed by the social-ecological model, MST offered just such an innovative therapeutic paradigm. Again, it is sensitive to the reality that troubled youths are situated in multiple systems that, to a greater or lesser extent, may contribute to their offending. The specifics of this intervention are conveyed in the next section.

The MST Intervention

As Henggeler noted, MST is a holistic intervention that targets the variety of factors that are related to the causes of problem behavior. MST staff members are not office based but deliver services in home or in community settings (e.g., school). Each clinician has a small caseload that is limited to about five families, each of which receives 2 to 15 hours of intervention each week. Recognizing the uncertain timing of crises, clinicians are available 24 hours, 7 days a week. The MST intervention is intended to be intense but also time-limited (about 4 to 6 months), which is a factor that contributes to its cost-effectiveness.

Staff members are given a 5-day orientation regarding MST's treatment model. To ensure quality-of-service delivery thereafter, they receive supervisory visits at least once a week. A special MST expert also consults with the treatment team and provides booster training.

When initiating the intervention, the MST clinician and supervisor take the responsibility to engage or "hook" the youth and family in the treatment. An important task is to diagnose the risk factors or problematic relations that are contributing to the youngster's misbehavior. This might involve persistent conflict with parents, drinking with friends, and truancy. The intervention attempts to build on individual (e.g., high IQ) and system (e.g., a supportive teacher or coach) strengths in a positive way. Services are individualized to meet the unique needs of each troubled youngster. The specific interventions used by clinicians are adapted from empirically supported treatment modalities, such as strategic family therapy, structural family therapy, behavioral parent training, and cognitive behavioral therapies. More broadly, in the *Blueprints for Violence Prevention* series, Henggeler presents the following nine central principles of MST:

1. The primary purpose of assessment is to understand the fit between the identified problems and their broader systemic context.

2. Therapeutic contacts emphasize the positive and use systemic strengths as levers for change.

3. Interventions are designed to promote responsible behavior and to decrease irresponsible behavior among family members.

4. Interventions are present focused and action oriented, targeting specific and well-defined problems.

5. Interventions target sequences of behavior within and between multiple systems that maintain identified problems.

6. Interventions are developmentally appropriate and fit the developmental needs of youth.

7. Interventions are designed to require daily or weekly effort by family members.

8. Intervention effectiveness is evaluated continuously from multiple perspectives, with providers assuming accountability for overcoming barriers to successful outcomes.

9. Interventions are designed to promote treatment generalization and long-term maintenance of therapeutic change by empowering caregivers to address the needs of family members across multiple system contexts.

Effectiveness

Although questions have been raised about the quality of the evidence favorable to MST, a mounting body of evaluation studies exists that suggest that MST may be an effective intervention for a multitude of problem and criminal behaviors. In a meta-analysis of 11 studies conducted by Nicola Curtis, Kevin Rolan, and Charles Borduin, MST was found to reduce criminal behaviors significantly with an average effect size of 0.50. Specifically, MST was associated with a reduction in the number of arrests for all crimes, number of arrests for substance abuse crimes, seriousness of arrests, number of days incarcerated, and self-reported delinquency and drug use.

Studies using randomized experimental designs also provide much support for the effectiveness of MST with serious juvenile offenders. When comparing juvenile offenders placed in MST versus individual therapy, Borduin and his colleagues found that MST was more effective in reducing rearrrests than individual therapy. Specifically, 71.4% of the individual therapy youths were rearrested within 4 years, whereas only 26.1% of the MST youths were rearrested.

Not only is MST an effective intervention with serious juvenile offenders, but it is also effective with juvenile sex offenders. Compared with individual therapy, MST is more effective in reducing rearrests for both nonsexual and sexual offenses. Concerning nonsexual offenses, 25% of the youths treated with MST were rearrested within 3 years, whereas 50% of the youths treated with individual therapy were rearrested. Examining sexual offenses, 12.5% of the MST group was rearrested compared with 75% of the individual therapy group.

Evidence also exists that MST is cost effective. This is an important policy consideration because of the need to show a return of the investment made by the public in an intervention. The cost-effectiveness of MST extends from its demonstrated ability to use a time-limited, community-based intervention to reduce crime among serious offenders who otherwise would have received services for a much longer period or been incarcerated in a residential facility. Henggeler found, for example, that whereas the cost of "usual services" was $17,769, the cost for MST per offender was $3,500. More recent studies have shown similar cost savings.

Future Challenges

MST has emerged as an important early intervention program for adolescents at risk of criminal careers. Much of its credibility derives from its fidelity to evidence-based practices. The intervention targets for change empirically established risk factors for crime; MST clinicians use evidence-based intervention treatments; and from its inception, the programs based on MST principles have been subjected to rigorous evaluation by Henggeler and his colleagues.

The special challenge for MST is whether the program can be disseminated widely and still maintain its effectiveness. Evidence exists that when the principles of MST are adhered to closely, the resulting interventions are successful in reducing serious offending and in improving the lives of children and their families. However, the reverse is true as well: Failure to follow MST principles produces ineffective programs. Still, MST has procedures in place to license interventions and to increase the possibility that program integrity will be sustained. If this strategy proves meaningful, MST could serve as a significant crime prevention resource in communities into the foreseeable future.

Cheryl Lero Jonson and Francis T. Cullen

See also Family Nurturing Programs; Family Therapy; Youth Violence, Interventions for

Further Readings

Borduin, C. M., Henggeler, S. W., Blaske, D. M., & Stein, R. J. (1990). Multisystemic treatment of adolescent sexual offenders. *International Journal of Offender Therapy and Comparative Criminology, 34,* 105–113.

Borduin, C. M., Mann, B. J., Cone, L. T., Henggeler, S. W., Fucci, B. R., Blaske, D. M., et al. (1995). Multisystemic treatment of serious juvenile offenders: Long-term prevention of criminality and violence. *Journal of Consulting and Clinical Psychology, 63,* 569–578.

Cullen, F. T., Vose, B. A., Jonson, C. N. L., & Unnever, J. D. (2007). Public support for early intervention: Is child saving a "habit of the heart"? *Victims and Offenders, 2,* 109–124.

Curtis, N. M., Ronan, K. R., & Borduin, C. M. (2004). Multisystemic treatment: A meta-analysis of outcome studies. *Journal of Family Psychology, 8,* 411–419.

Farrington, D. P., & Welsh, B. C. (2007). *Saving children from a life of crime: Early risk factors and effective interventions.* New York: Oxford University Press.

Henggeler, S. W. (1997). *Treating serious anti-social behavior in youth: The MST approach.* Washington, DC: OJJDP, U.S. Department of Justice.

Henggeler, S. W. (1999). Multisystemic therapy: An overview of clinical procedures, outcomes, and policy implications. *Child Psychology and Psychiatry Review, 4,* 2–10.

Henggeler, S. W., Mihalic, S. F., Rone, L., Thomas, C., & Timmons, Mitchell, J. (1998). *Blueprints for violence prevention: Multisystemic therapy.* Boulder: Institute of Behavioral Science, University of Colorado.

Stouthamer-Loeber, M., Loeber, R., van Kammen, W., & Zhang, Q. (1995). Uninterrupted delinquent careers: The timing of parental help-seeking and juvenile court contact. *Studies in Crime and Crime Prevention, 4,* 236–251.

Web Sites

MST Services: http://mstservices.com

Munchausen Syndrome by Proxy

It is estimated that about 6 million cases of child abuse or neglect occurred in 2006. Although this number is high, many additional incidents of child abuse and neglect go undetected and some forms of abuse are masked by what seem to be common ailments. One such type of child abuse is Munchausen Syndrome by Proxy (MSBP). MSBP is a form of abuse that occurs when a caregiver fabricates or induces an illness in the person being cared for, typically a dependent child. MSBP was first noted in a medical journal, *The Lancet*, in 1977. In this article, Roy Meadow, a pediatrician in the United Kingdom, detailed two case histories of MSBP. The term *Munchausen Syndrome by Proxy* stems from historical accounts of German mercenary officer Baron Karl von Munchausen (1720–1797). He was infamous for telling false stories about his adventures and conquests throughout Europe. Since MSBP is the fabrication of an illness, Munchausen's name was attached to the behavior.

MSBP is not only difficult to detect, it is equally as puzzling to understand. MSBP may be perpetrated by men or women; however, offenders are most often females in a caregiver role, typically the mother. However, she may be an aunt, au pair, babysitter, or foster parent. Victims are usually the child of the offender, but any child for whom the abuser cares for can fall prey to MSBP. Illnesses that are commonly fabricated include sleep apnea, personality changes, vomiting, seizures, diarrhea, and unconsciousness. MSBP manifests itself through the simulation or production of symptoms, or a combination of both. Simulation of symptoms, a quarter of all cases, involves fabrication about the illness by either the caregiver (particularly for young victims who cannot talk or articulate the problem) or the victim (who may have been coerced into lying). The production of symptoms, about half of all cases, involves purposeful infliction of harm to the victim by the offender. The child may be physically beaten, suffocated, orally poisoned, have his or her blood injected with toxins or medications, or have necessary medications withheld to worsen an already existing medical problem. In older children, the production of symptoms may result from somatization (i.e., the psychological onset of an illness or physical disturbance). Victims may be taught by the offender to reproduce ailments on demand. About 25% of all cases involve both simulation and production of symptoms.

In cases of MSBP, the caregiver seeks medical attention for the victim's "illness." Victims are often taken to the hospital, and the offender may tell the physician or attending medical personnel that there is no known cause for the child's symptoms. Ensuing physical examinations may yield no visible signs of sickness, results from medical tests and X-rays may be normal, and patients may not respond to medicines or surgeries. Victims who do not respond to a battery of tests may be hospitalized for continued observation. If the physical abuse and production of symptoms has not occurred before the victim was admitted to the hospital because it was feigned, it will likely begin once the victim is admitted so that medical attention and care will continue and the MSBP offender can maintain control over the situation and victim.

Offenders

Offenders are likely to be seemingly normal and attentive parents. They are often well educated, possibly having attained some medical knowledge either formally through school or being self-taught, and may be fluent in medical terminology. Offenders are often knowledgeable about medical procedures and feel comfortable in a medical setting. They may offer advice or suggestions to the physicians and nurses who are trying to determine the type and cause of the child's illness. They will likely welcome or suggest medical tests that may be painful to the child.

Part of the lure for offenders committing MSBP is the attention and sympathy they receive because their child is sick or the recognition and praise from others, including medical staff, for being an attentive and doting mother who cares for the child. Most MSBP occurs as a result of psychological motivations. They assume the role of a sick person through the dependent child, and this fills a psychological need that varies by offender. Many offenders suffer from psychological problems such as low self-esteem or simply loneliness, and they

may thrive on the "martyr" role and attention they receive from the abuse. Perpetrators may meet a need for dependency or symbiosis by victimizing the dependent child. Other possible reasons for the abuse include the perceived need for control over the victim and an outward manifestation of their inability to care appropriately for the child.

The nonoffending parent, often the father, usually has little involvement in the child or family's life. This lack of attention and care toward the mother and children may allow the abuse to occur and may be causally related in some cases. For instance, the offender may commit MSBP to garner the attention they desire from the noninvolved party.

Psychological Factors

Being an MSBP offender does not by definition constitute mental illness, nor is MSBP caused by mental illness because offenders are not psychotic or dissociative from reality when abusing their victims. However, perpetrators may suffer from psychological disorders such as depression, compulsive lying, and/or borderline, narcissistic, histrionic, or avoidant personality disorders. These disorders may contribute to the abuse because they affect normal coping mechanisms. The term used by the *Diagnostic and Statistical Manual of Mental Disorders, Fourth Edition* (*DSM-IV*) for MSBP is Factitious Disorder by Proxy. *DSM-IV* does not classify MSBP as a mental illness. However, it is listed in the manual's appendix as a category requiring more study. The following *DSM-IV* criteria must be met for a diagnosis of MSBP: intentional production or feigning of physical or psychological distress in an individual under the care of the offender, the motivation of the offender is to assume the sick role by proxy, no external incentives exist, and no other disorder better explains the behavior.

Munchausen syndrome, a disorder related to MSBP, occurs when individuals fabricate or induce an illness affecting not another person but themselves. Similar to MSBP, those presenting with Munchausen syndrome desire the attention and sympathy that accompanies treatment for an illness. Munchausen syndrome is considered a mental illness, whereas MSBP is a medical diagnosis. MSBP occurs "by proxy," and offenders do not typically suffer from Munchausen syndrome. Instead, they project the behavior onto their victims. In doing so, they indirectly assume the role of a sick individual who is purportedly in need of treatment.

Victims and the Effects of MSBP

The victims of MSBP can be either male or female. Age of onset for abuse typically begins shortly after the first birthday, and most victims are younger than 6 years old. Siblings of MSBP victims are at increased risk for abuse because many offenders abuse more than one of their children. As many as 25% of MSBP cases involve more than one victim in the family.

Child victims of MSBP are often prevented by the abuser from engaging in normal contact with people outside the family. Their education may be interrupted because of repeated visits to doctors' offices and hospitals, which can also limit interaction with others. The abuser may often speak for the child or limit the child's relations with peers. Because of the control offenders have over their victims, victims of MSBP may feel more comfortable talking with outsiders (e.g., medical personnel, police, and case workers) when the offender is not around.

Victims of MSBP may suffer physical and psychological damage resulting from the abuse. Psychological manifestations of abuse can appear in the victim such as posttraumatic stress disorder, irritability, aggressiveness, withdrawal, dependency, and depression. Victims may have nightmares, they may be fearful, or their sleep cycles may be disrupted. The victims may learn to accept the illness and symptoms as real, through conditioning, and may learn the art of manipulation themselves. Developmental delays such as immaturity and separation anxiety may also occur. Additionally, children who suffer from any child abuse, not only MSBP, are at increased risk for engaging in violent behavior later in life.

Tragically, victims may even be killed by their abuser. Studies report that the mortality rate for MSBP victims ranges from 9% to about 30%. This wide range shows the difficulty in properly identifying victims of MSBP. The death of a victim may not directly result from homicide, but it may be the result of numerous unnecessary medical procedures having been performed in attempts to pinpoint a cause of the mysterious symptoms. Cases of MSBP may also be misdiagnosed as sudden infant death syndrome (SIDS). In cases of SIDS, children suddenly die without sufficient explanation, even after a thorough investigation and autopsy, as to why the death occurred.

Identification and Prosecution of MSBP

MSBP is not, in and of itself, a violation of the law. However, in the course of MSBP, many offenders commit acts that are consistent with child abuse. Therefore, investigations into MSBP cases must be handled as a criminal investigation. Suspicion should be heightened if any symptoms that the victim presents upon admission to the hospital disappear or lessen once the caregiver has left the child, or if offenders resist separation from the child. Victims are often unresponsive to treatment or may improve drastically once released from the hospital or removed from the care of the offender. The victim may feel better when the offender is not around— what is known as a positive separation test.

MSBP can go undetected simply because it is difficult to imagine that a mother would place her child in danger. Identification and prosecution of MSBP often requires input from various agencies. This input may include medical personnel, law enforcement and attorneys, child protective services, and social services. Physicians may be the most qualified persons to make a diagnosis of MSBP because they have direct access to the medical records of victims and will have interacted with the caregiver directly when trying to determine the cause of illness. However, the field of medicine typically relies on self-report or parental input to assist in determining the cause of the illness and other medical history.

Such a diagnosis is not obligatory before an arrest can be made. However, sufficient evidence must be gathered before the suspect can be formally charged and arrested. Law enforcement officials must make an evidence-based judgment using profiling techniques and taking into account the suspect's personality and history (including any history of having a similar illness as the child), as well as the physical evidence to support an arrest. Investigators should determine whether there is a history of other children having died while under the care of the suspect. Once sufficient evidence is gathered, MSBP offenders may be charged with child endangerment, child abuse, child neglect, or homicide if the victim dies as a result of the abuse.

Treatment for Offenders and Victims

MSBP offenders can be resistant to psychotherapy treatment. They frequently deny that they are responsible for any ill-will or abuse toward their victim. However, it has been documented that some perpetrators who were confronted by medical personnel have stopped the abuse. To treat victims effectively, psychologists need to determine baseline measures of emotional and psychological functioning, cognitive ability, and other developmental abilities. Victims need to learn to develop trust and deal with any emotions stemming from the abuse such as anxiety. Also, the self-image of victims may be fractured. They may continue to see themselves as the "sick" child who is in need of attention and medical care. Play therapy among young victims seems promising. If children are removed from the home and placed either with another family member or in child protective services, such as foster care, any visitation should be strictly supervised to prevent additional abuse by the offender.

Eileen Ahlin

See also Battered-Child Syndrome; Child Abuse, Neglect and Maltreatment; Family Violence; Infanticide

Further Readings

American Psychiatric Association. (1994). *Diagnostic and statistical manual of mental disorders* (4th ed.). Washington, DC: Author.

Artingstall, K. (1999). *Practical aspects of Munchausen by proxy and Munchausen syndrome investigation.* Boca Raton, FL: CRC Press.

Feldman, M. D. (2004). *Playing sick? Untangling the web of Munchausen syndrome, Munchauen by proxy, malingering & factitious disorder.* New York: Routledge.

Meadow, R. (1977). Munchausen by proxy: The hinterland of child abuse. *The Lancet, 2,* 343–345.

Parnell, T. A., & Day, D. O. (1998). *Munchausen by Proxy syndrome: Misunderstood child abuse.* Thousand Oaks, CA: Sage.

Schreier, H. A., & Libow, J. A. (1993). *Hurting for love.* New York: Guilford Press.

MUTUAL BATTERY

Mutual battery is a term that is used to describe intimate partners who both use violence against each other. It is a controversial term that disguises many of the complexities of intimate partner violence. *Mutual* implies two equal individuals who inflict the same level and form of injury for the same reasons. *Battery* is a legal term that describes physical assault. Research on intimate partner violence suggests the limitations of each of these terms and of *mutual battery* for understanding and developing effective interventions for intimate partner violence.

Research Findings and Controversies

Much of our knowledge of intimate partner violence is derived from general social surveys. With some variation, these surveys rely on measurement tools, primarily the Conflict Tactics Scale and Conflict Tactics Scale 2, which ask people to report how often they have been victims or perpetrators of violence in their intimate relationships. Across a range of studies, men and women report about equal levels of violence perpetration in their relationships. However, these surveys do not provide data on the context of, and reasons for, violence. Qualitative studies that rely on interviews with victims and perpetrators drawn from agency and clinical samples suggest that the dynamics of intimate partner violence vary depending on the context and motivation for violence. These studies also find that mutual battery is rare and that men are far more likely to engage in intimate partner violence that is part of a pattern of coercive control. Michael Johnson developed a typology of intimate partner violence that addresses the differences in findings between quantitative general surveys and qualitative, nonrandom studies. Johnson argues that the gender symmetry revealed in general surveys describes "situational couple violence." In this form of intimate partner violence, both members of a couple use violence as a response to a specific conflict. It may be a serious level of violence, but it is not part of a larger pattern of abuse. On the other hand, he describes the primarily male perpetrated violence described in qualitative studies as "intimate terrorism." This violence is motivated by a desire to control a partner coercively and is only one strategy in a pattern of abusive behaviors that also includes emotional, verbal, economic, and sexual abuse. Situational couple violence is often termed "mutual battery." Intimate terrorism may also be mutual, with both partners engaging in violence and coercive control, or what Johnson refers to as "mutual violent control." However, this form of intimate partner violence is unusual and has not been studied in any depth. The term *mutual battery* does not encourage the kind of nuanced understanding of intimate partner violence that has developed in research and scholarship since the 1990s.

Implications for Policy and Treatment

The institution of mandatory and presumptive arrest policies for intimate partner violence has led to increases in dual arrests of both partners. Law enforcement officers who respond to a domestic violence call rarely have access to the history and context of violence. When there is evidence of violence by both parties, it is therefore common for both people to be arrested. Some jurisdictions have instituted primary or principle aggressor language to guide officers in situations where both parties have been violent. These guidelines, however, do not eliminate the difficulties of determining the nature of the abuse and the potential risks to each partner. Criminal law is not designed to regulate the dynamics of intimate relationships but to protect citizens from criminal acts. Most actions that distinguish mutual battery, situational couple violence, and intimate terrorism are not criminal offenses and are not visible to responding officers. These actions include isolating a victim from family and friends, controlling personal decisions and movements, using threatening looks, and denigrating value of a partner, among other techniques of coercive control. The presence of violent actions by both parties may lead to legal decisions that categorize a situation as mutual battery when in fact one partner is perpetrating intimate terrorism and the other is responding with defensive violence.

Most jurisdictions now offer diversion of misdemeanor domestic violence offenses to batterer intervention programs. These programs were developed for male offenders, and many concentrate on issues of power and control. Women who are arrested for engaging in situational couple violence or defensive violence often do not receive appropriate treatment in these groups.

In the civil realm, the presence of domestic violence is one factor that is considered in evaluations of the best interests of children in marital dissolutions. Many states have rebuttable presumption statutes that presume it is not in the best interests of a child to be placed in sole or joint custody with a parent who has perpetrated domestic violence. Claims of mutual battery have become increasingly common in family courts. Judges and family evaluators thus must carefully consider the context of these claims and determine whether violence between parents was truly mutual or was some variation of intimate terrorism, situational couple violence, or violent resistance to abuse. Since nearly half of separating and divorcing couples report abuse in their relationships, determination of the nature and type of abuse and its potential ongoing harm to victims and to children is both complex and essential. The National Council of Juvenile and Family Court Judges, Family Violence Department, sponsors ongoing training and support on evaluating claims of mutual battery in child custody cases.

Continued research on intimate partner violence is needed that attends to the variations that differentiate mutual battery from other forms of violence and abuse in relationships.

Kathleen J. Ferraro

See also Domestic Violence; Domestic Violence and Arrest Policy; Family and Domestic Violence, Theories of; Family Violence; Intimate Partner Violence; Intimate Partner Violence, Risk Assessment; Intimate Partner Violence, Theories of; Male Victims of Partner Violence; Women's Use of Aggression

Further Readings

Johnson, M. P. (2008). *A typology of domestic violence: Intimate terrorism, violence resistance, and situational couple violence*. Boston: Northeastern University Press.

Miller, S. L. (2005). *Victims as offenders: The paradox of women's violence in relationships*. New Brunswick, NJ: Rutgers University Press.

Stark, E. (2007). *Coercive control: How men entrap women in personal life*. New York: Oxford University Press.

Weston, R., Temple, J. R., & Marshall, L. L. (2005). Gender symmetry and asymmetry in violent relationships: Patterns of mutuality among racially diverse women. *Sex Roles, 53,* 553–571.